The California Paralegal

Essential Rules, Documents, and Resources

The California Paralegal

Essential Rules, Documents, and Resources

INCLUDES

- A Comprehensive Legal Dictionary
- Rules of Professional Conduct and the State Bar Act
- Paralegal Ethics
- Employment Resources
- Statutes on Paralegals
- Court Opinions on Paralegals
- CLE for Paralegals
- Employment Law Governing Paralegals
- Timelines
- Sample Documents
- State Research and Citation Guides

By

William P. Statsky

Sharon Sandberg

DELMAR
CENGAGE Learning™

Australia • Brazil • Japan • Korea • Mexico • Singapore • Spain • United Kingdom • United States

DELMAR
CENGAGE Learning™

The California Paralegal: Essential Rules, Documents, and Resources
William P. Statsky, Sharon Sandberg

Career Education Strategic Business Unit:
Vice President: Dawn Gerrain

Director of Learning Solutions: John Fedor

Managing Editor: Robert L. Serenka, Jr.

Acquisitions Editor: Shelley Esposito

Senior Product Manager: Melissa Riveglia

Editorial Assistant: Melissa ZaZa

Director of Production: Wendy A. Troeger

Senior Content Project Manager:
Betty L. Dickson

Art Director: Joy Kocsis

Director of Marketing: Wendy Mapstone

Marketing Manager: Gerard McAvey

Marketing Coordinator: Jonathan Sheehan

For product information and technology assistance, contact us at
Cengage Learning Customer & Sales Support, 1-800-354-9706
For permission to use material from this text or product,
submit all requests online **www.cengage.com/permissions**
Further permissions questions can be emailed to
permissionrequest@cengage.com

Library of Congress Control Number: 2007020396

ISBN-13: 978-1-4180-1294-6

ISBN-10: 1-4180-1294-7

Delmar
Executive Woods
5 Maxwell Drive
Clifton Park, NY 12065
USA

Cengage Learning is a leading provider of customized learning solutions with office locations around the globe, including Singapore, the United Kingdom, Australia, Mexico, Brazil, and Japan. Locate your local office at **www.cengage.com/global**

Cengage Learning products are represented in Canada by Nelson Education, Ltd.

To learn more about Delmar, visit **www.cengage.com/delmar**

Purchase any of our products at your local college store or at our preferred online store **www.cengagebrain.com**

Printed in the United States of America
2 3 4 5 6 15 14 13 12 11

FD239

Dedication

To a great crew: Pat, Jess, Gabe, Randy, Carlie, Hailey, Ava, Myles, and Kaia.

W.S.

To my loving family, Stacy, Brittany, Ryan and Heather. And with special appreciation and many thanks to Eugene I. Pavalon, who has always been there for me professionally as a mentor, teacher, and friend.

S.S.

Preface

What does it take to be an outstanding paralegal in California? Three key ingredients in your success are your paralegal education, native intelligence, and determination. This book seeks to complement all three by bringing together in one volume a vast amount of material that is either essential for all paralegals or useful for many.

Our focus is on the state of California—state resources, state laws, and state associations. Some federal laws and institutions will also be included when they are directly relevant to the state, e.g., federal government jobs for paralegals in federal agencies located in the state.

The book has eight parts:

Part 1. Paralegal Profession
Part 2. Paralegal Employment
Part 3. Ethics, Paralegals, and Attorneys
Part 4. Legal System
Part 5. Legal Research and Records Research
Part 6. Procedure: Some Basics
Part 7. Sample Documents
Part 8. A Comprehensive Legal Dictionary

The last part contains a comprehensive legal dictionary with selected definitions specifically keyed to California law.

Within each of the first seven parts of the book, the sections will often include the following features:

Introduction: an overview of what is in the section and why it is included in the book.

Table of Contents: an alphabetical list of the main topics or areas covered whenever this is helpful because of the lengthy and diverse material included in the section.

Abbreviations Used in the Section

Materials and Resources: the heart of the section.

More Information: leads to further materials, usually on the Internet.

Something to Check: questions that will help you expand and build on the material in the section.

In addition, an online page is planned for the book to provide updates and related material. To use the page, go to www.paralegal.delmar.cengage.com

Contents

PART 7

Sample Documents

PART 8

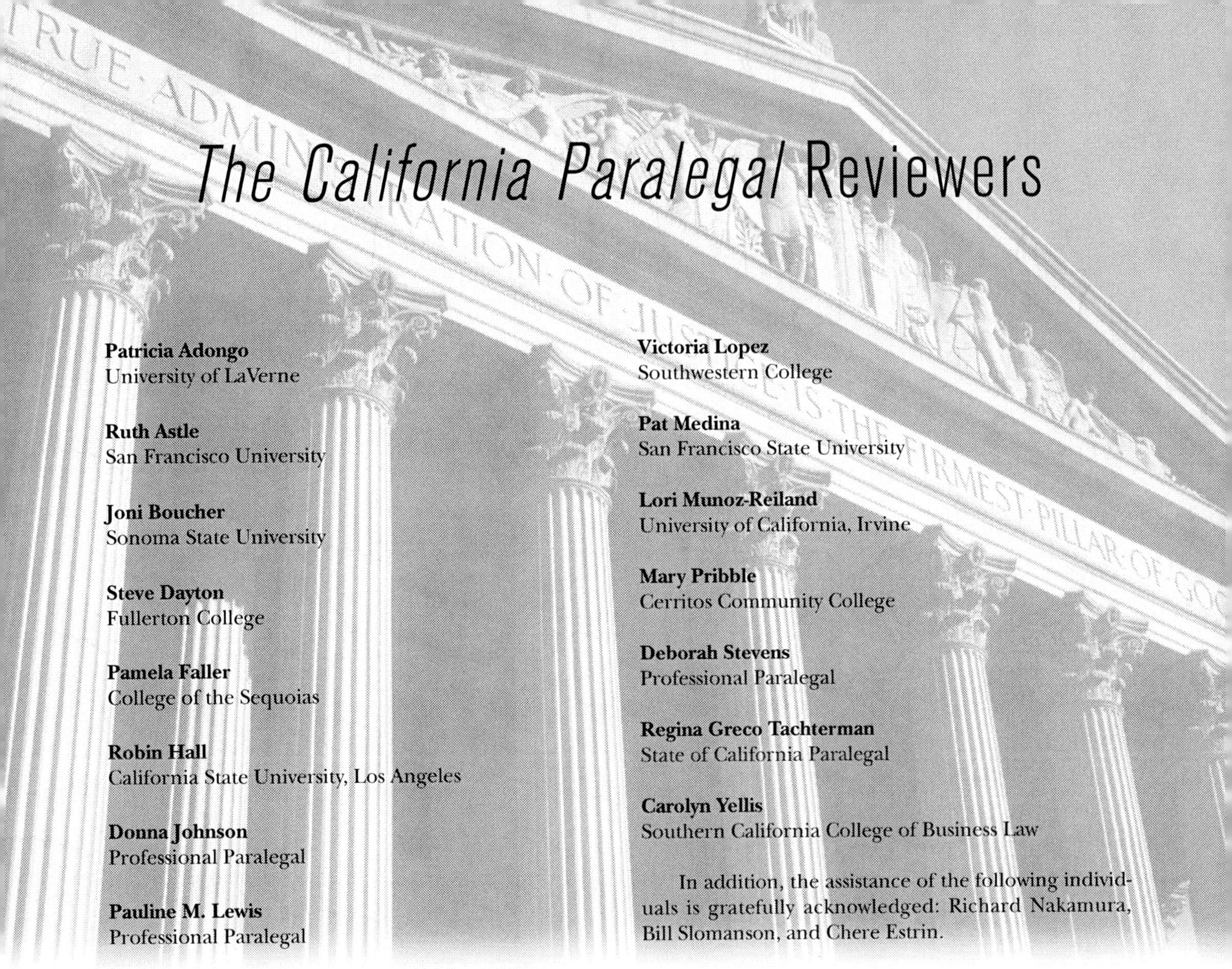

The California Paralegal Reviewers

Patricia Adongo
University of LaVerne

Ruth Astle
San Francisco University

Joni Boucher
Sonoma State University

Steve Dayton
Fullerton College

Pamela Faller
College of the Sequoias

Robin Hall
California State University, Los Angeles

Donna Johnson
Professional Paralegal

Pauline M. Lewis
Professional Paralegal

Victoria Lopez
Southwestern College

Pat Medina
San Francisco State University

Lori Munoz-Reiland
University of California, Irvine

Mary Pribble
Cerritos Community College

Deborah Stevens
Professional Paralegal

Regina Greco Tachterman
State of California Paralegal

Carolyn Yellis
Southern California College of Business Law

In addition, the assistance of the following individuals is gratefully acknowledged: Richard Nakamura, Bill Slomanson, and Chere Estrin.

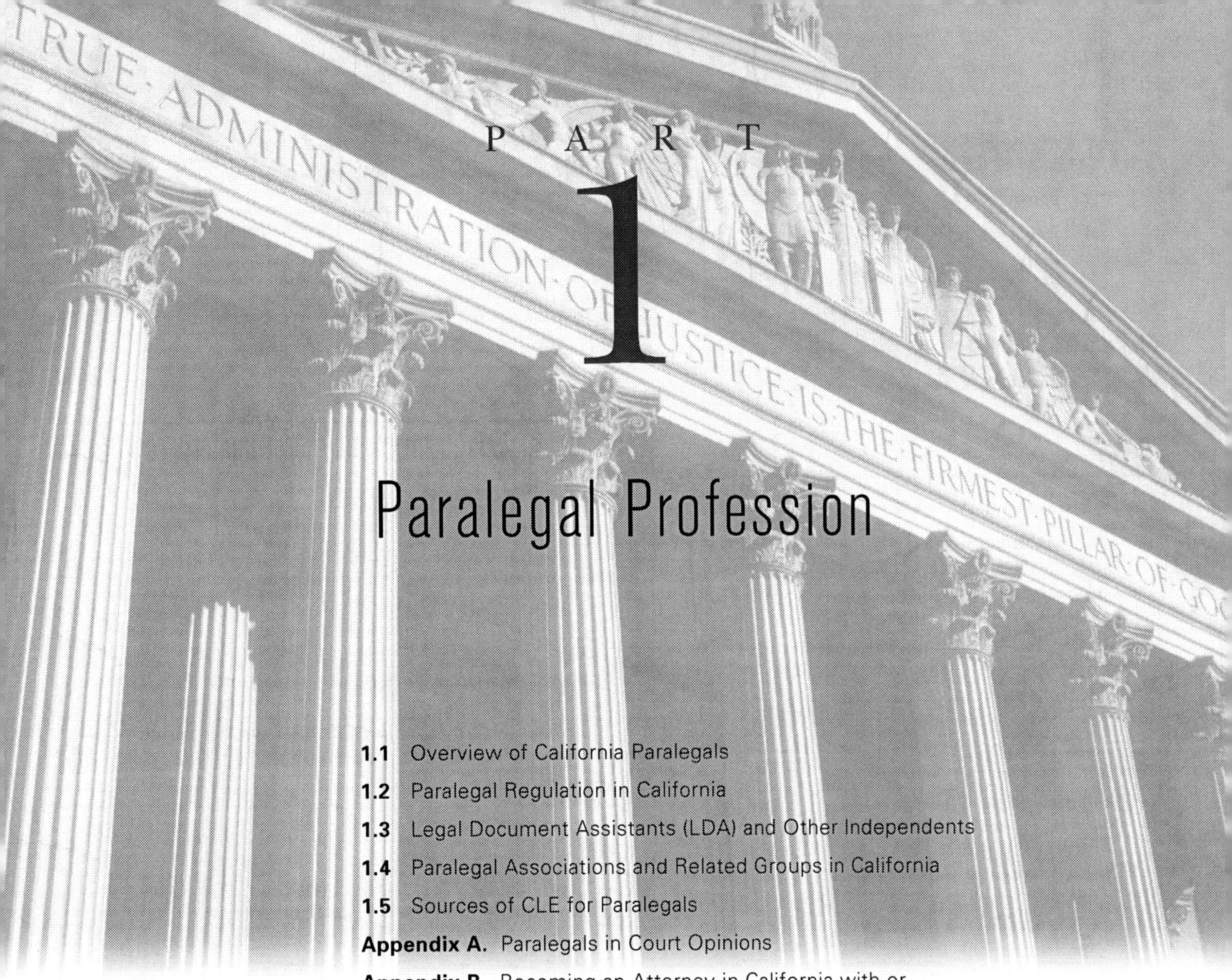

PART 1

Paralegal Profession

A. Introduction

In the United States, a paralegal (sometimes called a legal assistant) is a person with substantive legal skills whose authority to use those skills is based on attorney supervision or special authorization from the government. By substantive skills, we mean skills that (a) are obtained through sophisticated training, and (b) are significantly more advanced than those possessed by clerical personnel in most law offices.

California also has its own definition of a paralegal. Section 6450 of the Business and Professions Code defines a paralegal as follows:

> "Paralegal" means a person who holds himself or herself out to be a paralegal, who is qualified by education, training, or work experience, who either contracts with or is employed by an attorney, law firm, corporation, governmental agency, or other entity, and who performs substantial legal work under the direction and supervision of an active member of the State Bar of California, as defined in Section 6060, or an attorney practicing law in the federal courts of this state, that has been specifically delegated by the attorney to him or her. (Bus. & Prof. Code, § 6450).

This definition also applies to the titles of legal assistant and attorney assistant. We will examine the definition more closely in section 1.2.

This is a fascinating time to be a paralegal in California. Paralegals work in a wide variety of settings and have made major contributions in the delivery of legal services. The state has a rich paralegal history. Our objective in this book is to give you the perspective of this history and to provide resources that will help you:

- find paralegal employment,
- understand the unique features of our state government,
- find the laws that are the foundation of paralegal work,
- examine some of the major documents that paralegals prepare or help prepare on behalf of clients,
- define all or most of the legal terms that give the legal system its unique character,
- abide by the ethics code, and
- participate in organized efforts to continue the growth of the paralegal profession.

B. Paralegals in the Twenty-First Century

Highlights

About 7 out of 10 paralegals in the country work for law firms; others work for corporate legal departments, government agencies, legal aid/legal service offices, and special interest organizations.

Employment is projected to grow much faster than average, as employers try to reduce costs by hiring paralegals to perform tasks that attorneys would otherwise have to perform.

Formally trained paralegals have the best employment opportunities as competition for jobs increases. (*www.bls.gov/oco/ocos114.htm*)

Work Settings

Paralegals are found in all types of organizations, but most are employed by law firms, corporate legal departments, and various government offices. In these organizations, they can work in many different areas of the law, including litigation, personal injury, corporate law, criminal law, employee benefits, intellectual property, labor law, bankruptcy, immigration, family law, and real estate. As the law has become more complex, paralegals have responded by becoming more specialized. Within specialties, functions often are broken down further so that paralegals may deal with a specific area. For example, paralegals specializing in labor law may concentrate exclusively on employee benefits. The United States Department of Labor has estimated that there are 224,000 paralegal jobs in the country. (See Exhibit 1.1A.) Bureau of Labor Statistics, U.S. Department of Labor, *Occupational Outlook Handbook,* 2006–07 Edition (*www.bls.gov/oco/ocos114.htm*).

A small number of paralegals own their own businesses and work as freelance paralegals, contracting their services to attorneys or corporate legal departments. Finally, some paralegals offer limited law-related services directly to the public without attorney supervision. In California (and in a few other states), they are not allowed to call themselves paralegals or legal assistants. As we will see in section 1.3, most are called legal document assistants (LDAs).

Paralegal Work

While attorneys assume ultimate responsibility for legal work, they often delegate tasks to paralegals. In fact, paralegals are continuing to assume a growing range of tasks in the nation's legal offices and perform some of the same tasks as attorneys. Nevertheless, paralegals cannot give legal advice, set fees, represent clients in court, or engage in other categories of activities that constitute the practice of law. (For more on these restrictions, see sections 1.2 and 3.1.)

One of the most important tasks of a paralegal is helping attorneys prepare for hearings, trials, real estate closings, and corporate meetings. Paralegals investigate the facts of cases and help ensure that all relevant information is considered. They also can perform preliminary legal research. After analyzing and organizing the factual and legal information, paralegals may prepare written reports that attorneys use in determining how cases should be handled. If attorneys file lawsuits on behalf of clients, paralegals can help prepare pleadings and motions to be filed in court, perform further factual and legal research, and assist attorneys during trial. Paralegals also organize and track files of case documents so that they can be easily accessible to attorneys.

In addition, paralegals perform a number of other vital functions. For example, they help draft contracts, mortgages, separation agreements, and instruments of trust. They also may assist in preparing tax returns and estate plans. Some paralegals coordinate and supervise the activities of other law office employees. (Many of these paralegal supervisors have joined their own association, the International Paralegal Management Association (*www.paralegalmanagement.org*). The variety and complexity of paralegal tasks depend on the kind of law practiced in the office, the competence and initiative of the paralegal, and the willingness of the attorney to delegate.

Paralegals who work for corporations often assist attorneys with employee contracts, shareholder agreements, stock-option plans, employee benefit plans, and other transactional documents. They may help prepare and file annual financial reports, maintain corporate minutes, record resolutions, and prepare forms to secure loans for the corporation. Paralegals often perform compliance work by monitoring and reviewing government regulations to ensure that the corporation is aware of new requirements and is operating within the law. Increasingly, experienced paralegals are assuming additional supervisory responsibilities such as overseeing team projects and serving as a communications link between the legal team and the corporation. When the corporation retains outside counsel, the corporate paralegal has additional liaison responsibilities.

The duties of paralegals who work in the public sector usually vary within each agency. In general, they analyze legal material for internal use, maintain office files, conduct factual and legal research for attorneys, and collect and analyze evidence for agency hearings. They may prepare informative or explanatory material on laws, agency regulations, and agency policy for general use by the agency and the public. Paralegals employed in legal aid/legal service offices in the community help the poor, the aged, and others in need of legal assistance. They file forms, conduct research, prepare documents, and, when authorized by law, may represent clients at administrative hearings.

Paralegals in small and medium-sized law firms often perform a variety of duties that require a general knowledge of the law. Those employed by large law firms, government agencies, and corporations, however, are more likely to specialize in one area of the law.

Familiarity with computers in the law has become essential to paralegal work. Computer software packages and the Internet are used to search legal literature stored in computer databases and on CD-ROM. In litigation involving many supporting documents, paralegals usually use computer databases to retrieve, organize, and index various materials. Imaging software allows paralegals to scan documents directly into a database, while billing programs help them track hours billed to clients. Computer software packages are also used to perform tax computations and explore the consequences of various tax strategies for clients.

National Job Outlook according to the U.S. Department of Labor

Employment for paralegals and legal assistants is projected to grow much faster than average for all occupations through 2014. Employers are trying to reduce costs and increase the availability and efficiency of legal services by hiring paralegals to perform tasks formerly carried out by attorneys. Besides new jobs created by employment growth, additional job openings will arise as people retire and leave the field. Despite projections of rapid employment growth, competition for jobs should continue as many people seek to go into this profession. Experienced, formally trained paralegals often have the best employment opportunities.

Private law firms will continue to be the largest employers of paralegals, but a growing array of other organizations, such as corporate legal departments, insurance companies, real estate and title insurance firms, and banks hire paralegals. Corporations in particular are boosting their in-house legal departments to cut costs. Demand for paralegals is expected to grow as an expanding population increasingly requires legal services, especially in areas such as intellectual property, health care, elder law issues, criminal law, environmental law, and the global economy. Paralegals who specialize in areas such as real estate, bankruptcy, medical malpractice, and product liability are often in demand. The growth of prepaid legal plans should also contribute to the demand for legal services. (A prepaid plan is like health insurance in which a person pays an ongoing fee or premium for legal service needs that might arise in the future.) A growing number of experienced paralegals are expected to establish their own businesses as independent contractors.

Job opportunities for paralegals will expand in the public sector as well. Community legal aid/legal service programs, which provide assistance to the poor, elderly, minorities, and middle-income families, will employ additional paralegals to minimize expenses and serve the most people. Federal, state, and local government agencies, consumer organizations, and the courts also should continue to hire paralegals in increasing numbers.

To a limited extent, paralegal jobs are affected by the business cycle. During recessions, demand declines for some discretionary legal services, such as estate planning, drafting wills, and handling real estate transactions. Corporations may be less inclined to initiate certain types of litigation when falling sales and profits lead to fiscal belt tightening. As a result, full-time paralegals employed in offices adversely affected by a recession may be laid off or have their work hours reduced. However, during recessions, corporations and individuals are more likely to face other problems that require legal assistance, such as bankruptcies, foreclosures, and divorces. Bureau of Labor Statistics, U.S. Department of Labor, *Occupational Outlook Handbook*, 2006–07 Edition (*www.bls.gov/oco/ocos114.htm*).

Career Videos on Paralegals

To watch a short video that gives an overview of the paralegal career:

- go to *www.acinet.org/acinet*; click video links on this page and type "paralegal" in the search box
- or, go directly to the list of all the career videos at: *www.acinet.org/acinet/videos_by_occupation.asp?id=27*, (scroll down to "paralegals and legal assistants")

EXHIBIT 1.1A **Paralegal and Lawyer Job Openings Nationally and in California**

United States	Employment 2004	Employment 2014	Percent Change	Job Openings*
Lawyers	735,300	845,400	+ 15%	20,460
Paralegals and legal assistants	224,000	290,600	+ 30%	8,460
California	**Employment 2002**	**Employment 2012**	**Percent Change**	**Job Openings***
Lawyers	57,800	71,200	+ 23%	2,000
Paralegals and legal assistants	25,200	30,900	+ 23%	800

* Job Openings refers to the average annual job openings due to growth and net replacement.

Source: Bureau of Labor Statistics, *Occupational Employment Survey*; California Employment Development Department, *Labor Market Information*; America's Career InfoNet, a component of CareerOneStop (*www.acinet.org*).

C. Statistics on Paralegal Employment in California

For employment trends in the state and nationally, see Exhibit 1.1A, which also provides comparable data on lawyers.

Earnings of paralegals vary greatly. Salaries depend on education, training, experience, the type and size of employer, and the geographic location of the job. In general, paralegals who work for large law firms or in large metropolitan areas earn more than those who work for smaller firms or in less populated regions. In addition to earning a salary, many paralegals receive bonuses. In May 2004, full-time wage and salary paralegals had median annual earnings, including bonuses, of just over $40,000. The middle 50 percent earned between $31,000 and $50,000. The top 10 percent earned more than $61,000, while the bottom 10 percent earned just under $26,000. Median annual earnings in government and legal aid offices were as follows:

Federal Government:	$59,370
State Government:	$34,910
Local Government:	$38,260
Legal Aid/Legal Service Offices:	$37,870

Additional Information on Paralegal Salaries

National Federation of Paralegal Associations
www.paralegals.org
(Click "Legal Resources" then "Salary Information")

National Association of Legal Assistants
www.nala.org/Survey_Table.htm
www.nala.org
(Under "General Information" click "The Paralegal Profession" then "Current Survey Info")

Legal Assistant Today
www.legalassistanttoday.com
(Type "salary" in the search box)

Exhibit 1.1B provides an overview of national and California data on compensation.

D. Certification

California paralegals have had a number of options when seeking certification. Keep in mind, however, that no certification program is mandatory. You can be a paralegal in California—or in any other state—without taking and passing a certification examination. Certification is voluntary. Yet some paralegals feel that certification is an extra credential that can enhance their professionalism and commitment to the paralegal career.

Here is an overview of the major certification programs that have been available:

National Certification

- CLA/CP certification of the National Association of Legal Assistants (NALA). Passing an exam and fulfilling the other requirements of NALA entitle you to be called a Certified Legal Assistant (CLA) or a Certified Paralegal (CP) (*www.nala.org*).
- PACE certification of the National Federation of Paralegal Associations (NFPA). Passing an exam and fulfilling the other requirements of NFPA entitle you to be called a Registered Paralegal (RP) or a PACE Registered Paralegal (*www.paralegals.org*)
- PP certification of NALS the Association for Legal Professionals. Passing an exam and fulfilling the other requirements of NALS entitle you to be called a Professional Paralegal (PP) (*www.nals.org*)
- AACP certification of the American Alliance of Paralegals Inc. (AAPI). Fulfilling the requirements of AAPI (which does not include an exam) entitles you to be called an American Alliance Certified Paralegal (AACP) (*www.aapipara.org*).

EXHIBIT 1.1B Paralegal Wages Nationally and in California

Location	Year	Pay Period	10%	25%	Median	75%	90%
United States	2004	Hourly	$12.45	$15.34	$19.45	$24.83	$30.78
		Yearly	$25,900	$31,900	$40,500	$51,600	$64,000
California	2004	Hourly	$14.16	$18.55	$23.87	$30.46	$36.53
		Yearly	$29,500	$38,600	$49,600	$63,400	$76,000
Bakersfield, CA	2004	Hourly	$16.25	$18.18	$20.72	$24.68	$27.85
		Yearly	$33,800	$37,800	$43,100	$51,300	$57,900
Fresno, CA	2004	Hourly	$12.40	$16.52	$19.28	$21.28	$24.91
		Yearly	$25,800	$34,400	$40,100	$44,300	$51,800
Los Angeles–Long Beach, CA	2004	Hourly	$12.15	$16.39	$23.44	$30.90	$39.00
		Yearly	$25,300	$34,100	$48,800	$64,300	$81,100
Modesto, CA	2004	Hourly	$14.00	$16.92	$19.07	$21.17	$24.41
		Yearly	$29,100	$35,200	$39,700	$44,000	$50,800
Oakland, CA	2004	Hourly	$19.25	$23.20	$26.26	$29.96	$35.47
		Yearly	$40,000	$48,300	$54,600	$62,300	$73,800
Orange County, CA	2004	Hourly	$18.57	$24.13	$29.93	$33.92	$36.49
		Yearly	$38,600	$50,200	$62,300	$70,600	$75,900
Sacramento, CA	2004	Hourly	$13.34	$17.12	$22.88	$26.48	$30.22
		Yearly	$27,700	$35,600	$47,600	$55,100	$62,900
San Diego, CA	2004	Hourly	$13.84	$16.58	$21.47	$26.89	$32.71
		Yearly	$28,800	$34,500	$44,700	$55,900	$68,000
San Francisco, CA	2004	Hourly	$18.27	$20.32	$24.17	$30.96	$39.26
		Yearly	$38,000	$42,300	$50,300	$64,400	$81,700
San Jose, CA	2004	Hourly	$17.75	$19.89	$25.47	$33.78	$40.55
		Yearly	$36,900	$41,400	$53,000	$70,300	$84,300

Source: Bureau of Labor Statistics, *Occupational Employment Survey*; California Employment Development Department, *Labor Market Information*; America's Career InfoNet, a component of CareerOneStop (*www.acinet.org*).

California Certification

Until recently, a California paralegal could become a CAS California Advanced Specialist. The CAS program is administered by the Commission for Advanced California Paralegal Specialization (CACPS), an entity of the California Alliance of Paralegal Associations (CAPA). Currently, however, the program has been temporarily suspended while it undergoes revision.

Current Status of the California Certification Program

www.cla-cas.org
www.cla-cas.org/ceo_report_page_1.htm

When California certification resumes, it is expected to continue requiring two steps:

1. Meeting the requirements for becoming a CLA/CP (Certified Legal Assistant/Certified Paralegal) of the National Association of Legal Assistants (*www.nala.org*).
2. Meeting the requirements of becoming a CAS (California Advanced Specialist) of the California Alliance of Paralegal Associations (*www.cla-cas.org*).

The goal of the CAS program is to is "to provide a voluntary, uniform professional credential for those demonstrating an advanced knowledge of California law and procedures and to enhance the quality of services available from California paralegals/legal assistants to the legal community, and to the public which is served." (*www.cla-cas.org*) The details of the CAS program are still being developed. They are expected to include self-directed online education (articulated in "Learning Contracts") and online testing.

E. More Information

Paralegals in the California Labor Market
www.calmis.ca.gov/specialreports/Labor-Market-Economic-Analysis-2007.pdf

California Occupational Guide Number 464
Paralegals
Employment Development Department
Labor Market Information Division
www.calmis.cahwnet.gov/file/occguide/paralegl.pdf

United States Department of Labor, Paralegals
www.bls.gov/oco/ocos114.htm

California Alliance of Paralegal Associations (CAPA)
www.caparalegal.org

National Federation of Paralegal Associations (NFPA)
www.paralegals.org

National Association of Legal Assistants (NALA)
www.nala.org

NALS the Association for Legal Professionals
www.nals.org

American Bar Association Standing Committee on Paralegals (SCOP)
www.abanet.org/legalservices/paralegals

International Paralegal Management Association Survey
www.paralegalmanagement.org
(click "utilization survey results")

Law Firms in California
www.hg.org/northam-firms.html
california.lp.findlaw.com
www.lawresearchservices.com/firms/california-alpha.htm

NALP Directory of Legal Employers
www.nalpdirectory.com

America's Largest Law Firms
www.ilrg.com/nlj250

Law Firm Salaries
www.infirmation.com/shared/insider/payscale.tcl
(click "California")

Paralegal Job Outlook—Stagnant or Full Steam Ahead?
www.buzzle.com/articles/paralegal-job-outlook-stagnant-full-steam-ahead.html

F. Something to Check

1. Pick an area of practice that interests you. Online, find and compare three law firm descriptions of that area. How are the descriptions similar and different? To find law firms online, go to Google (*www.google.com*) or any general search engine, and type "California law firm" and the area of law you are interested in. For example:

   "California law firm" "criminal law"
   "California law firm" "adoption law"
   "California law firm" "estate planning"

2. The definition of a paralegal from § 6450 of the California Business and Professions Code is presented at the beginning of this section. Compare this definition to the definitions of a paralegal found on the Web sites of NFPA, NALA, NALS, and SCOP. (See Section E for their Internet addresses.) List the similarities and differences among the definitions.
3. Pick any three cities not listed in Exhibit 1.1B. What is the median paralegal salary for these cities?

A. Introduction

California has one of the strictest laws in the nation on who can be paralegals, or more precisely, on who can call themselves paralegals. To use this title, you must work under attorney supervision, meet an education requirement, and comply with a mandatory continuing legal education (MCLE) obligation. California's law does not change what paralegals are allowed to do. The scope of what they can do in California continues to be approximately equal to what they can do in other states (e.g., fact gathering, interviewing, file coordination), but the requirements for being able to use the paralegal title in California are much stricter. (Throughout this section, paralegal and legal assistant are used interchangeably; the same rules apply to both titles.) California law also created the new position of legal document assistant (LDA), who can offer services directly to the public without attorney supervision. LDAs will be discussed in section 1.3.

Highlights of Regulation in California

- The title of "paralegal" and "legal assistant" can be used only by individuals who work under the supervision of California attorneys and who meet the education and mandatory continuing legal education (MCLE) requirements of the law.
- Minimum education requirements include attending a paralegal school that meets specified requirements or having a degree plus law-related experience. (An additional option of meeting the education requirement without either expired in 2003.) (See section 6450(c) below.)
- Every two years, paralegals must complete four hours of MCLE in legal ethics. (See section 6450(d) below.)
- Every two years, paralegals must complete four hours of MCLE in either general law or in a specialized area of the law. (See section 6450(d) below.)
- Paralegals must keep their own records of compliance with the education and MCLE requirements. They must "certify" with their supervising attorney that they have met their MCLE requirements. Compliance, however, is not enforced or supervised by any official body or government entity.
- Paralegals do not have to be licensed or to register. Those who sell services directly to the public (legal document assistants) must be registered, but not paralegals. On legal document assistants, see section 1.3.
- Persons who call themselves paralegals without meeting the educational requirements or the MCLE requirements can be convicted of a misdemeanor. (See section 6455(b).)

The original legislation proposing these requirements was found in Assembly Bill 1761 (AB 1761), which was eventually enacted and inserted in the California Business & Professions Code (§§ 6540 et seq.)

B. Statutory Provisions

Table of Contents

(The numbers refer to Sections of Business & Professions Code.)

California Business & Professions Code

§ 6450. Paralegal defined; prohibited activities; qualifications; continuing legal education

(a) "Paralegal" means a person who holds himself or herself out to be a paralegal, who is qualified by education, training, or work experience, who either contracts with or is employed by an attorney, law firm, corporation, governmental agency, or other entity, and who performs substantial legal work under the direction and supervision of an active member of the State Bar of California, as defined in Section 6060, or an attorney practicing law in the federal courts of this state, that has been specifically delegated by the attorney to him or her. Tasks performed by a paralegal include, but are not limited to, case planning, development, and management; legal research; interviewing clients; fact gathering and retrieving information; drafting and analyzing legal documents; collecting, compiling, and utilizing technical information to make an independent decision and recommendation to the supervising attorney; and representing clients before a state or federal administrative agency if that representation is permitted by statute, court rule, or administrative rule or regulation.

Definition of a Paralegal

Tasks Paralegals Perform

(b) Notwithstanding subdivision (a), a paralegal shall not do the following:

Paralegal Prohibitions

(1) Provide legal advice.
(2) Represent a client in court.
(3) Select, explain, draft, or recommend the use of any legal document to or for any person other than the attorney who directs and supervises the paralegal.
(4) Act as a runner or capper, as defined in Sections 6151 and 6152.
(5) Engage in conduct that constitutes the unlawful practice of law.
(6) Contract with, or be employed by, a natural person other than an attorney to perform paralegal services.
(7) In connection with providing paralegal services, induce a person to make an investment, purchase a financial product or service, or enter a transaction from which income or profit, or both, purportedly may be derived.

Paralegal Fees

(8) Establish the fees to charge a client for the services the paralegal performs, which shall be established by the attorney who supervises the paralegal's work. This paragraph does not apply to fees charged by a paralegal in a contract to provide paralegal services to an attorney, law firm, corporation, governmental agency, or other entity as provided in subdivision (a).

(c) A paralegal shall possess at least one of the following:

Legal Education Requirements for Paralegals

(1) A certificate of completion of a paralegal program approved by the American Bar Association.
(2) A certificate of completion of a paralegal program at, or a degree from, a postsecondary institution that requires the successful completion of a minimum of 24 semester, or equivalent, units in law-related courses and that has been accredited by a national or regional accrediting organization or approved by the Bureau for Private Postsecondary and Vocational Education.
(3) A baccalaureate degree or an advanced degree in any subject, a minimum of one year of law-related experience under the supervision of an attorney who has been an active member of the State Bar of California for at least the preceding three years or who has practiced in the federal courts of this state for at least the preceding three years, and a written declaration from this attorney stating that the person is qualified to perform paralegal tasks.
(4) A high school diploma or general equivalency diploma, a minimum of three years of law-related experience under the supervision of an attorney who has been an active member of the State Bar of California for at least the preceding three years or who has practiced in the federal courts of this state for at least the preceding three years, and a written declaration

CLE = continuing legal education

from this attorney stating that the person is qualified to perform paralegal tasks. This experience and training shall be completed no later than December 31, 2003.

(d) Every two years, commencing January 1, 2007, any person that is working as a paralegal shall be required to certify completion of four hours of mandatory continuing legal education in legal ethics and four hours of mandatory continuing legal education in either general law or in an area of specialized law. All continuing legal education courses shall meet the requirements of Section 6070. Certification of these continuing education requirements shall be made with the paralegal's supervising attorney. The paralegal shall be responsible for keeping a record of the paralegal's certifications.

Mandatory CLE in Ethics

Mandatory CLE in General Law or Specialty

(e) A paralegal does not include a nonlawyer who provides legal services directly to members of the public, or a legal document assistant or unlawful detainer assistant as defined in Section 6400, unless the person is a person described in subdivision (a).

(f) This section shall become operative on January 1, 2004.

§ 6451. Paralegal; unlawful practices; services for consumers

It is unlawful for a paralegal to perform any services for a consumer except as performed under the direction and supervision of the attorney, law firm, corporation, government agency, or other entity that employs or contracts with the paralegal. Nothing in this chapter shall prohibit a paralegal who is employed by an attorney, law firm, governmental agency, or other entity from providing services to a consumer served by one of these entities if those services are specifically allowed by statute, case law, court rule, or federal or state administrative rule or regulation. "Consumer" means a natural person, firm, association, organization, partnership, business trust, corporation, or public entity.

Direct Services to the Public

§ 6452. Paralegal; unlawful practices; persons identifying themselves as paralegals

(a) It is unlawful for a person to identify himself or herself as a paralegal on any advertisement, letterhead, business card or sign, or elsewhere unless he or she has met the qualifications of subdivision (c) of Section 6450 and performs all services under the direction and supervision of an attorney who is an active member of the State Bar of California or an attorney practicing law in the federal courts of this state who is responsible for all of the services performed by the paralegal. The business card of a paralegal shall include the name of the law firm where he or she is employed or a statement that he or she is employed by or contracting with a licensed attorney.

Attorney Supervision

(b) An attorney who uses the services of a paralegal is liable for any harm caused as the result of the paralegal's negligence, misconduct, or violation of this chapter.

Paralegal Negligence

§ 6453. Duty of paralegal; confidentiality

A paralegal is subject to the same duty as an attorney specified in subdivision (e) of Section 6068 to maintain inviolate the confidentiality, and at every peril to himself or herself to preserve the attorney-client privilege, of a consumer for whom the paralegal has provided any of the services described in subdivision (a) of Section 6450.

Confidentiality and the Attorney-Client Privilege

§ 6454. Definitions

The terms "paralegal," "legal assistant," "attorney assistant," "freelance paralegal," "independent paralegal," and "contract paralegal" are synonymous for purposes of this chapter.

Freelance Paralegal; Independent Paralegal; Contract Paralegal

§ 6455. Injured consumers; filing of complaints; violations and punishment

(a) Any consumer injured by a violation of this chapter may file a complaint and seek redress in any municipal or superior court for injunctive relief, restitution, and damages. Attorney's fees shall be awarded in this action to the prevailing plaintiff.

Suing a Paralegal

(b) Any person who violates the provisions of Section 6451 or 6452 is guilty of an infraction for the first violation, which is punishable upon conviction by a fine of up to two thousand five hundred dollars ($2,500) as to each consumer with respect to whom a violation occurs, and is guilty of a misdemeanor for the second and each subsequent violation, which is punishable upon conviction by a fine of two thousand five hundred dollars ($2,500) as to each consumer with respect to whom a violation occurs, or imprisonment in a county jail for not more than one year, or by both that fine and imprisonment. Any person convicted of a violation of this section shall be ordered by the court to pay restitution to the victim pursuant to Section 1202.4 of the Penal Code.

A Paralegal Crime

§ 6456. Exemptions from chapter

An individual employed by the state as a paralegal, legal assistant, legal analyst, or similar title, is exempt from the provisions of this chapter.

C. Attorney Attestation on Law-Related Experience

As you can see from § 6450(c), one of the ways to meet the education requirements is by having a baccalaureate degree or an advanced degree in any subject and a minimum of one year of law-related experience under the supervision of an attorney who has been an active member of the State Bar of California for at least three years or who has practiced in the federal courts in California for this length of time. If this route is taken, you must obtain a written declaration or attestation from the attorney that you have one year of law-related experience and that you are "qualified to perform paralegal tasks." Exhibit 1.2A is an example of such a declaration.

D. MCLE Log

The Orange County Paralegal Association has created a log to help paralegals keep track of their compliance with the MCLE education requirements of four hours of ethics every two years and four hours in general or specialized law every two years. The log is presented in Exhibit 1.2B.

EXHIBIT 1.2A

Attorney Attestation of Completion of Law-Related Experience (in Compliance with Business and Professions Code § 6450(c))

ATTORNEY ATTESTATION OF
COMPLETION OF LAW-RELATED EXPERIENCE
(Business and Professions Code Section 6450 et. seq.)

I hereby declare under the penalty of perjury under the laws of the State of California that:

1. I have been a member in good standing of the State Bar of California since ___________ or have been admitted to practice in the Federal Courts in the State of California since ___________.

2. ______________________________ has completed ___ years (commencing ___________ and ending _______________) of law-related experience under my supervision and is therefore qualified to perform paralegal tasks.

___/___/, 20__ Date: __________ Calif. Bar No.   ______________________ Signature

______________________ Printed Name

Pursuant to Business and Professions Code Section 6450(c)(3), individuals with a baccalaureate degree or an advanced degree in any subject must also have completed a minimum of one year of law-related experience under the supervision of an attorney who has been an active member of the State Bar of California for at least the preceding three years or who has practiced in the Federal courts of this state for at least the preceding three years, and obtain a written declaration from this attorney stating that they are qualified to perform paralegal tasks before using the title "Paralegal."

Pursuant to Business and Professions Code Section 6450(c)(4), individuals with a high school diploma or general equivalency diploma must also have completed a minimum of three years of law-related experience under the supervision of an attorney who has been an active member of the State Bar of California for at least the preceding three years or who has practiced in the Federal courts of this state for at least the preceding three years, and obtain a written declaration from this attorney stating that the person is qualified to perform paralegal tasks. This experience and training shall be completed no later than December 31, 2003.

Source: Orange County Paralegal Association, www.ocparalegal.org. (www.caparalegal.org/PDF%20Files/Completion.PDF)

EXHIBIT 1.2B

MCLE: Continuing Legal Education Log

CONTINUING EDUCATION LOG

Name: ______________________

LEGAL ETHICS
(2 YEAR PERIOD – 4 HOURS REQUIRED)

DATE OF ACTIVITY	TITLE OF COURSE	ACTIVITY PROVIDER	SUBJECT MATTER	HOURS EARNED

GENERAL LAW OR SPECIALIZED AREA OF LAW
(2 YEAR PERIOD – 4 HOURS REQUIRED)

DATE OF ACTIVITY	TITLE OF COURSE	ACTIVITY PROVIDER	SUBJECT MATTER	HOURS EARNED

I certify that the information set forth above is true and correct to the best of my knowledge.

Dated:______________________ Signature:______________________

Source: California Alliance of Paralegal Associations (www.caparalegal.org); Orange County Paralegal Association, (www.ocparalegal.org) (www.ocparalegal.org/docs/MCLE%20Compliance%20Log.pdf)

E. Frequently Asked Questions

The major sponsor (or author) of the paralegal legislation was Assemblywoman Marilyn C. Brewer. She was asked many questions about the legislation. Here is a list of the most frequently asked questions with her responses.

What was the intent of the paralegal legislation?
On September 13, 2000, Governor Gray Davis signed AB 1761; a bill which defines the term paralegal/legal assistant as an individual who works under the supervision of an attorney who must meet certain educational criteria and must complete continuing education. The intent of this bill is to differentiate those who work under the supervision of an attorney and those who provide services directly to the public. For those who work under the supervision of an attorney, the only intended change to the profession is a higher standard of education and mandatory continuing education to utilize the title of a paralegal. The duties of those who work under the supervision of an attorney have not changed and the bill codifies existing case law.

Who do I have to be registered with to call myself a paralegal?
AB 1761 does not require paralegals to be registered. Only Legal Document Assistants (LDAs) are required

to register. LDAs are those who work directly for the public and type legal documents and are governed by Business & Professions Code Chapter 5.5.

Who is the governing body?
AB 1761 does not create a governing body for the paralegal profession. However, the bill does create a new crime, and therefore, will be enforced by the courts and the consumer who brings a cause of action against an individual who violated this law. In essence, it is the consumer who will enforce the provisions of AB 1761.

What if I do not possess a paralegal certificate but I have worked for attorneys for over 10 years? Can I call myself a paralegal? Will I be grandfathered in?
The new Business & Professions Code Section 6450(c)(4) specifically grandfathers in paralegals who have been trained by and have been working for an attorney for at least three years by January 1, 2004. A signed declaration by the paralegal's supervising attorney is required under the code. This declaration should be kept with the paralegal and the paralegal's supervising attorney.

To whom should I certify that I have met the initial educational requirements of Business & Professions Code 6450?
AB 1761 does not expressly require a paralegal to certify their education with anyone or a state entity. However, it does require paralegals to keep a record of their certifications.

Practical application of the law dictates that a paralegal would have to certify their education with the supervising attorney since he/she is held liable by the paralegal's actions. In addition, paralegals should be prepared to certify their qualifications to clients, in case the question ever arises.

When is a paralegal certificate from a school acceptable?
Your paralegal certificate is valid under Business & Professions Code Section 6450(c)(1)(2), as long as it meets the following criteria:

1. A certificate of completion of a paralegal program approved by the American Bar Association;
2. A certificate of completion of a paralegal program at, or a degree from a postsecondary institution that requires the successful completion of a minimum of 24 semester, or equivalent, units in law-related courses and that has been accredited by a national or regional accrediting organization or approved by the Bureau for Private Postsecondary and Vocational Education.

What if I come from another state to work in California? Can I qualify under the code?
There would be no problem with a paralegal coming from another state to work in California as long as the educational requirements are met.

What if I work for a national law firm in another state other than California, can my firm send me to California to work on specific cases with them? Will I have to certify continuing education?
It would be acceptable if the paralegal is temporarily working on a case for its law firm which is located out of California. For example, if the firm is in both California and Arizona, and the California firm has a need for additional help on a specified case, the firm may send an Arizona paralegal to work on the case, as long as the paralegal is working for a California attorney who is a member of the State Bar of California and that paralegal qualifies as a paralegal from the state in which they came. It would be acceptable for a law firm to send an "out of state" paralegal to work on specific cases. Continuing education for those working in California temporarily is recommended but is not mandatory.

What happens if the continuing education criteria are not met?
If the educational criteria are not met by the paralegal, the individual is in violation of the Code.

To whom does the paralegal certify his or her continuing education?
AB 1761 requires the paralegal to certify his or her continuing education with his or her supervising attorney. There is no state or local agency or association who will monitor the requirements. Paralegals should keep a record of their certifications.

Who will monitor paralegals to ensure these qualifications are met? What governing body will enforce the code?
No governing body has been created to monitor the continuing education of paralegals. Again, it was not the intent of the author to create a governing body for the paralegal profession. However, the bill does create a new crime, and therefore will be enforced by the courts and the consumer who brings a cause of action against an individual who violated the provisions of Business & Professions Code 6450.

What if I am a certified legal assistant (CLA) with the National Association of Legal Assistants, or a registered paralegal (RP) with the National Federation of Paralegal Associations? Can I use those credits for my continuing education?
The National Association of Legal Assistants has a voluntary certification test (Certified Legal Assistant, or CLA) which requires continuing education to keep the credential. The National Federation of Paralegal Associations also has a voluntary test (PACE) which also requires continuing education. California paralegals must now maintain continuing educational requirements which are approved by the State Bar

of California (MCLE credits). Historically, both the National Association of Legal Assistants and the National Federation of Paralegal Associations have honored MCLE credits. However, it is still ultimately the decision of either association as to what courses will be accepted.

Can I utilize self-study programs if they are MCLE approved by the State Bar of California?
Yes. As long as the courses meet the requirements of Business & Professions Code 6070.

What if I write an article or teach a legal course? Will it meet the criteria as continuing education?
No. The Code is specific in regards to its continuing educational criteria.

What if I come from out of state?
In order to become a paralegal in California, those coming from out of state must meet the qualifications of California paralegals, unless they are working with their law firm on a temporary or loan basis.

If someone graduates from a school with only 21 units, can that student return to school for the 3 additional units to meet the requirement of § 6450(c)(2)?
Yes. The school should then reissue a new certificate to those who have completed the three additional units.

What if someone is in the process of meeting the training requirements but is not totally completed with the training by 2003, as required by AB 1761? For instance, the person has two years and 10 months of training, can they call themselves paralegals?
No. The requirements are clear.

Have the duties a paralegal performed prior to the enactment of the bill changed?
No. The duties a paralegal performs under the supervision of an attorney have not changed, nor has the level of supervision.

What are the duties a paralegal may perform?
A paralegal may still perform the tasks, including but not limited to, case planning, development and management, legal research; interviewing clients; fact gathering and retrieving information; drafting and analyzing legal documents; collecting, compiling, and utilizing technical information to make an independent decision and recommendation to the supervising attorney.

What are the prohibited activities of a paralegal?
A paralegal is governed by the same Code of Ethics and Canons of his or her supervising attorney. The following restrictions have been specifically laid out in the Code:

(b) Notwithstanding subdivision (a), a paralegal shall not do any of the following:
- (1) Provide legal advice;
- (2) Represent a client in court;
- (3) Select, explain, draft, or recommend the use of any legal document to or for any person other than the attorney who directs and supervises the paralegal;
- (4) Act as a runner or capper as defined in Sections 6151 and 6152;
- (5) Engage in conduct that constitutes the unlawful practice of law;
- (6) Contract with, or be employed by, a natural person other than an attorney to perform legal services;
- (7) In connection with providing paralegal services, induce a person to make an investment, purchase financial product or service, or enter a transaction from which income or profit, or both, purportedly may be derived;
- (8) Establish fees to charge a client for the services the paralegal performs, which shall be established by the attorney who supervises the paralegal's work. (This does not apply to fees charged by paralegals in a contract to provide legal services to an attorney, law firm, corporation, governmental agency, etc.)

Are the prohibitions any different than they were prior to the enactment of Business & Professions Code 6450?
No. These activities were prohibited prior to the enactment of AB 1761.

What if I work as a legal document assistant (as defined in Business & Professions Code 6408) (see section 1.3) and I also contract with attorneys? Can I advertise as a paralegal?
A person can only advertise as a paralegal to prospective contracting attorneys. Paralegals do not work directly for members of the public. Under AB 1761, a paralegal does not have clients—his or her supervising attorney does. To advertise as a paralegal directly to members of the public would be confusing to the public and in violation of the Code. In other words, to advertise paralegal services to a prospective client for whom the individual can only type legal forms is misleading and illegal.

An individual can still contract with attorneys and can also perform work as a legal document assistant. When performing paralegal tasks, the individual must meet the criteria of Business and Professions Code 6450. When working directly for the public, the legal document assistant must be registered with the County Clerk/Recorder's Office and post a $25,000 bond. An individual who does both has two different professions, therefore must qualify under both statutes, and keep them separate.

Do I have to have two sets of business cards and, if so, what should they say?
As described above, a person can be both a paralegal and a legal document assistant; however, to avoid

running afoul of either statute, certain precautions should be taken. Namely, a dual-duty professional should have two sets of business cards and letterhead for each activity. The business card for legal document assistants must include their registration number and a statement that they do not work for attorneys. A business card for a paralegal shall include the name of the law firm where that individual is employed and clarification that the person is not an attorney or a statement that he or she is employed by contracting with a California licensed attorney.

What are the penalties for not abiding by Business & Professions Code 6450?
AB 1761 provides for both criminal and civil causes of action for violation of the law. Specifically, any consumer who is injured by a violation of this Code may file a complaint and seek redress in any municipal or superior court for injunction relief, restitution, and damages. Any person who violates this act is guilty of an infraction for the first offense which is punishable upon conviction, for a fine up to $2,500 as to each consumer a violation occurs and a misdemeanor for the second and each subsequent violation which is punishable upon conviction of a fine of up to $2,500 as to each consumer with respect to each violation, or imprisonment in a county jail for not more than one year, or both with respect to each violation that occurs.

As an attorney, do I have to keep a record of my paralegals?
The law does not require you to, but given that the supervising attorney is liable for the actions of the paralegal, it is in your best interest to do so.

Should attorneys check with their malpractice carrier to see if they should increase their malpractice insurance?
No. The paralegal, as defined under AB 1761, is still governed by the same Code of Ethics and same Canons as the supervising attorney. It is not the intent of the author to change the duties of the paralegal, but to elevate the profession with the recognition it so well deserves.

F. Compliance Recommendations to Attorneys

Soon after AB 1761 went into effect, the Orange County Paralegal Association sent a letter to every law firm in its area stating recommendations on how to be in compliance. Here are edited excerpts from those recommendations:

- As attorneys, you are responsible for the negligence and/or misconduct of the paralegals whose services you utilize. As such, attorneys must have a vested interest in making sure that the requirements of B&P Code § 6450 are met. Moreover, law firms should be prepared to prove in court in instances seeking fee recovery that the paralegal performing the invoiced services for which fee recovery is requested is in fact a paralegal as defined in the California statute.
- You may want to consider investigating the education of your current paralegals. While your existing paralegals most likely fall into the qualifying levels of education, you may need to obtain additional information in some instances to ensure compliance with Business & Professions (B&P) Code § 6450. For example, for those relying on § 6450(c)(2), you may need to make sure that the number of units completed to receive the paralegal certificate meet the requirements of 24 semester hours. For those (if any) who do not have a qualifying certificate and are relying on § 6450(c)(3), you should obtain a written declaration from an attorney who has supervised their work for the requisite period of time stating that the person(s) is qualified to perform paralegal tasks.
- You may want to consider establishing a file for each paralegal employed by the firm included within which should be their paralegal certificate, diploma and/or attorney declaration. Paralegal reports regarding their compliance with the continuing education requirements would also be placed in these files.
- When hiring new paralegals, you may want to consider verifying and documenting their compliance with the education requirements, e.g., obtaining copies of diplomas and paralegal certificates. If a paralegal is hired who does not have a qualifying paralegal certificate, law firms should obtain prior to employment a declaration from a qualifying attorney who previously supervised the paralegal for the requisite number of years.
- Some law firms adopt a policy which prohibits those who do not comply with B&P Code § 6450 from holding themselves out as paralegals (and perhaps from holding themselves out in a manner from which others may infer that they are paralegals). At some firms, the most likely instance in which this may occur is with secretaries. Secretaries (as well as persons employed in law libraries, business offices, and other staff) may have billing numbers and are billed as legal assistants on invoices. Unless these employees meet the education requirements *and* are willing to comply with the continuing education requirements, they should not be billed in this manner. If a firm is going to bill a secretary (or other employee) as a legal assistant for paralegal tasks performed, it is recommended that they document their compliance with the

education and MCLE requirements just as for paralegals. Another situation to be considered is the use of the term "assistant to" instead of "secretary" by some law firms' secretaries. Technically, this does not appear to violate B&P Code § 6450. However, clients and others who deal with the firm may incorrectly assume that the person with whom they are dealing is a paralegal.

- You may want to decide to whom within your firm the paralegals report regarding their compliance with the continuing education requirement. For example, will all of the firms' paralegals report to the Human Resources (HR) director or will the paralegals report to a specified attorney? The latter seems to more closely comply with the statute as it speaks to reporting to one's "supervising attorney." If law firms want to handle this on a firm-wide basis, one attorney in the firm could be selected to monitor compliance with the continuing education requirements for all of the paralegals in the firm, regardless of their supervising attorney.
- You may want to consider designing a system to track paralegal compliance with the MCLE requirement. The California Alliance of Paralegal Associations ("CAPA") has developed a Continuing Education Log for paralegals to use in tracking their MCLE compliance. (See Exhibit 1.2B.) The person or persons responsible for tracking compliance with the MCLE requirements should obtain the completed forms by the end of each year.
- This letter is sent for informational purposes only. It is not intended to provide a legal interpretation of B&P 6450 or to constitute legal advice.

G. More Information

Paralegal Statutes Online
www.leginfo.ca.gov/calaw.html
(click "Business and Professions Code" and then type "6450")

Paralegal Regulation in California
www.caparalegal.org/defins.html
www.calda.org/articles.asp
www.calbar.ca.gov/calbar/2cbj/01feb/mclestdy.htm
www.abanet.org/legalservices/paralegals/update/cacannon.html

H. Something to Check

Go to the Web sites of the paralegal associations in California (see section 1.4 for their Internet addresses). Summarize what they say about the regulation of paralegals in California.

1.3 Legal Document Assistants (LDA) and Other Independents

A. Introduction

There are four main categories of non-attorneys in California who can provide law-related services directly to the public without attorney supervision and who can charge fees for such services:

Legal Document Assistants (LDA)
Unlawful Detainer Assistants (UDA)
Immigration Consultants (IC)
Bankruptcy Petition Preparers (BPP)

Our primary focus in this section will be on the LDA and the UDA; to a lesser extent, we will also examine the IC and BPP. At one time all four categories of independents could be called independent paralegals or freelance paralegals. The title of paralegal, however, can no longer be used by anyone in California who does not work under attorney supervision. (See section 1.2 on the regulations governing paralegals.)

B. Legal Document Assistants and Unlawful Detainer Assistants

Legal Document Assistants (LDA)

A Legal Document Assistant (LDA) is a non-attorney authorized to charge fees for providing designated self-help services (without attorney supervision) to members of the public who are representing themselves on legal matters. The primary self-help service an LDA can provide is as follows:

> Complete legal documents that are selected by a person who is representing himself or herself in a legal matter. This assistance must be ministerial, consisting of typing or otherwise completing the

documents at the person's specific direction. The LDA cannot give advice, explanations, opinions, or recommendations about legal rights, remedies, or strategies—including which forms to use. (See § 6400(d) below.)

In addition to helping clients complete their legal documents, the LDA can also file and serve legal documents and provide general published factual information (written or approved by an attorney) on legal procedures, rights, or obligations. LDAs are subject to substantial statutory restrictions that are administered by the California Department of Consumer Affairs (*www.dca.ca.gov*). They must:

- meet educational requirements (the *minimum* of which is a high school or general equivalency diploma and two years of law-related experience under the supervision of a licensed attorney);
- be registered in every county where they offer their services;
- pay a registration fee of $175;
- provide a $25,000 bond to cover claims such as fraud and incompetence that clients might lodge against them;
- display an identification card with their photograph and the following statement, "This person is not a lawyer" (see Exhibits 1.3B and 1.3C);
- state their non-attorney status in advertisements and solicitations;
- state their name and registration number on any documents they prepare; and
- use a state-approved written contract with all their clients (see Exhibit 1.3D)

Unlawful Detainer Assistants (UDA)

Another category of non-attorneys offering services directly to the public is the Unlawful detainer Assistant (UDA). A UDA is a non-attorney authorized to charge fees for providing "assistance and advice" (without attorney supervision) to members of the public involved in unlawful detainer cases such as tenants facing evictions or landlords seeking evictions. (Unlawful detainer refers to a court action against an individual who retains possession of real property unjustifiably even though his or her original possession was lawful.)

As we will see, many of the restrictions governing LDAs also apply to UDAs.

C. Statutes Governing the LDA and UDA

Table of Contents for the LDA and UDA Statutes

All section numbers in the following table of contents are to the Business and Professions Code (B&P) of California.

Business and Professions (B&P) Code of California

§ 6400. Definitions

(a) "Unlawful detainer assistant" means any individual who for compensation renders assistance or advice in the prosecution or defense of an unlawful detainer claim or action, including any bankruptcy petition that may affect the unlawful detainer claim or action.

Definition of Unlawful Detainer Assistant (UDA)

(b) "Unlawful detainer claim" means a proceeding, filing, or action affecting rights or liabilities of any person that arises under Chapter 4 (commencing with Section 1159) of Title 3 of Part 3 of the Code of Civil Procedure and that contemplates an adjudication by a court.

(c) "Legal document assistant" means:

(1) Any person who is not exempted under Section 6401 and who provides, or assists in providing, or offers to provide, or offers to assist in providing, for compensation, any self-help service to a member of the public who is representing himself or herself in a legal matter, or who holds himself or herself out as someone who offers that service or has that authority. This paragraph does not apply to any individual whose assistance consists merely of secretarial or receptionist services.

Definition of Legal Document Assistant (LDA)

(2) A corporation, partnership, association, or other entity that employs or contracts with any person not exempted under Section 6401 who, as part of his or her responsibilities, provides, or assists in providing, or offers to provide, or offers to assist in providing, for compensation, any self-help service to a member of the public who is representing himself or herself in a legal matter or holds himself or herself out as someone who offers that service or has that authority. This paragraph does not apply to an individual whose assistance consists merely of secretarial or receptionist services.

(d) "Self-help service" means all of the following:

(1) Completing legal documents in a ministerial manner, selected by a person who is representing himself or herself in a legal matter, by typing or otherwise completing the documents at the person's specific direction.

Definition of Self-Help Service

(2) Providing general published factual information that has been written or approved by an attorney, pertaining to legal procedures, rights, or obligations to a person who is representing himself or herself in a legal matter, to assist the person in representing himself or herself. This service in and of itself, shall not require registration as a legal document assistant.

(3) Making published legal documents available to a person who is representing himself or herself in a legal matter.

(4) Filing and serving legal forms and documents at the specific direction of a person who is representing himself or herself in a legal matter.

(e) "Compensation" means money, property, or anything else of value.

(f) A legal document assistant, including any legal document assistant employed by a partnership or corporation, may not provide any self-help service for compensation, unless the legal document assistant is registered in the county in which his or her principal place of business is located and in any other county in which he or she performs acts for which registration is required.

LDA Registration Requirement

(g) A legal document assistant may not provide any kind of advice, explanation, opinion, or recommendation to a consumer about possible legal rights, remedies, defenses, options, selection of forms, or strategies. A legal document assistant shall complete documents only in the manner prescribed by paragraph (1) of subdivision (d).

LDAs Giving Advice

§ 6401. Chapter Application; Exceptions

This chapter does not apply to any person engaged in any of the following occupations, provided that the person does not also perform the duties of a legal document assistant in addition to those occupations:

(a) Any government employee who is acting in the course of his or her employment.

(b) A member of the State Bar of California, or his or her employee, paralegal, or agent, or an independent contractor while acting on behalf of a member of the State Bar.

Paralegals not Required to Register as LDAs

(c) Any employee of a nonprofit, tax-exempt corporation who either assists clients free of charge or is supervised by a member of the State Bar of California who has malpractice insurance.

(d) A licensed real estate broker or licensed real estate salesperson, as defined in Chapter 3 (commencing with Section 10130) of Part 1 of Division 4, who acts pursuant to subdivision (b) of Section 10131 on an unlawful detainer claim as defined in subdivision (b) of Section 6400, and who is a party to the unlawful detainer action.

Immigration Consultants not Required to Register as LDAs

(e) An immigration consultant, as defined in Chapter 19.5 (commencing with Section 22441) of Division 8.

(f) A person registered as a process server under Chapter 16 (commencing with Section 22350) or a person registered as a professional photocopier under Chapter 20 (commencing with Section 22450) of Division 8.

(g) A person who provides services relative to the preparation of security instruments or conveyance documents as an integral part of the provision of title or escrow service.

(h) A person who provides services that are regulated by federal law.

(i) A person who is employed by, and provides services to, a supervised financial institution, holding company, subsidiary, or affiliate.

§ 6401.5. Practice of Law by Nonlawyers

The Practice of Law and the Unauthorized Practice of Law

This chapter does not sanction, authorize, or encourage the practice of law by non-lawyers. Registration under this chapter, or an exemption from registration, does not immunize any person from prosecution or liability pursuant to Section 6125, 6126, 6126.5, or 6127. [These sections impose penalties for the unauthorized practice of law.]

§ 6401.6. Legal Document Assistant; Limitation on Service; Services of Attorney

A legal document assistant may not provide service to a client who requires assistance that exceeds the definition of self-help service in subdivision (d) of Section 6400, and shall inform the client that the client requires the services of an attorney.

§ 6402. Registration Requirement; Registration of Disbarred and Suspended Lawyers Prohibited

Registration Requirement

A legal document assistant or unlawful detainer assistant shall be registered pursuant to this chapter by the county clerk in the county in which his or her principal place of business is located (deemed primary registration), and in any other county in which he or she performs acts for which registration is required (deemed secondary registration). Any registration in a county, other than the county of the person's place of business, shall state the person's principal place of business and provide proof that the registrant has satisfied the bonding requirement of Section 6405. No person who has been disbarred or suspended from the practice of law pursuant to Article 6 (commencing with Section 6100) of Chapter 4 may, during the period of any disbarment or suspension, register as a legal document assistant or unlawful detainer assistant. The Department of Consumer Affairs shall develop the application required to be completed by a person for purposes of registration as a legal document assistant. The application shall specify the types of proof that the applicant shall provide to the county clerk in order to demonstrate the qualifications and requirements of Section 6402.1.

Bonding Requirement

Disbarred or Suspended Attorneys Cannot be LDAs

§ 6402.1. Registration Eligibility

Education Requirements for LDAs

To be eligible to apply for registration under this chapter as a legal document assistant, the applicant shall possess at least one of the following:

(a) A high school diploma or general equivalency diploma, and either a minimum of two years of law-related experience under the supervision of a licensed attorney, or a minimum of two years' experience, prior to January 1, 1999, providing self-help service.

(b) A baccalaureate degree in any field and either a minimum of one year of law-related experience under the supervision of a licensed attorney, or a minimum of one year of experience, prior to January 1, 1999, providing self-help service.

(c) A certificate of completion from a paralegal program that is institutionally accredited but not approved by the American Bar Association, that requires successful completion of a minimum of 24 semester units, or the equivalent, in legal specialization courses.

(d) A certificate of completion from a paralegal program approved by the American Bar Association.

§ 6403. Contents of Registration Applications

LDA Registration Application

(a) The application for registration of a natural person shall contain all of the following statements about the applicant:

(1) Name, age, address, and telephone number.

(2) Whether he or she has been convicted of a felony, or of a misdemeanor under Section 6126 or 6127, or found liable under Section 6126.5.

(3) Whether he or she has been held liable in a civil action by final judgment or entry of a stipulated judgment, if the action alleged fraud, the use of an untrue or misleading representation, or the use of an unfair, unlawful, or deceptive business practice.

(4) Whether he or she has ever been convicted of a misdemeanor violation of this chapter.

(5) Whether he or she has had a civil judgment entered against him or her in an action arising out of the applicant's negligent, reckless, or willful failure to properly perform his or her obligation as a legal document assistant or unlawful detainer assistant.

(6) Whether he or she has had a registration revoked pursuant to Section 6413.

(7) Whether this is a primary or secondary registration. If it is a secondary registration, the county in which the primary registration is filed.

(b) The application for registration of a natural person shall be accompanied by the display of personal identification, such as a California driver's license, birth certificate, or other identification acceptable to the county clerk to adequately determine the identity of the applicant.

A Corporation or Partnership as an LDA

(c) The application for registration of a partnership or corporation shall contain all of the following statements about the applicant:

(1) The names, ages, addresses, and telephone numbers of the general partners or officers.

(2) Whether the general partners or officers have ever been convicted of a felony, or a misdemeanor under Section 6126 or 6127 or found liable under Section 6126.5.

(3) Whether the general partners or officers have ever been held liable in a civil action by final judgment or entry of a stipulated judgment, if the action alleged fraud, the use of an untrue or misleading representation, or the use of an unfair, unlawful, or deceptive business practice.

(4) Whether the general partners or officers have ever been convicted of a misdemeanor violation of this chapter.

(5) Whether the general partners or officers have had a civil judgment entered against them in an action arising out of a negligent, reckless, or willful failure to properly perform the obligations of a legal document assistant or unlawful detainer assistant.

(6) Whether the general partners or officers have ever had a registration revoked pursuant to Section 6413.

(7) Whether this is a primary or secondary registration. If it is a secondary registration, the county in which the primary registration is filed.

(d) The applications made under this section shall be made under penalty of perjury.

[For an example of a registration application, see Exhibit 1.3A]

EXHIBIT 1.3A

Example of a Registration Application to become a Legal Document Assistant (in Compliance with Business & Professions Code § 6403)

INDIVIDUAL
REGISTRATION AS LEGAL DOCUMENT ASSISTANT
COUNTY OF VENTURA

Registration number: ____________
If a renewal, same number shall be assigned, provided there is no lapse in the registration.

(This space reserved for County Clerk use.)

☐ **Primary Registration**
☐ **Secondary Registration** (List County of Primary Registration ____________.)

Effective Date: ____________

Expiration Date: ____________
Earliest of: the two-year bond expiration date or two years from effective date of filing.

Filing Fees

Filing registration	$175.00
Filing bond	7.00
Certificate to Attorney-in-fact	5.00
Recording bond, first page	7.00
Total fee	**$194.00**
Recording bond, each additional page	3.00
Each additional ID card	10.00

Completely fill in all personal information requested in Part A. Check each applicable box in Parts B-E and provide information as requested for each box that is checked. Attach legible copies of all documents requested for each box that is checked (attach certified copies and originals as specified). You must sign the completed application under penalty of perjury.

A. Personal Information (type or print legibly)

Applicant's Name: ____________ Date of Birth: ____________

Business Name: ____________

Business Address: ____________

Business Telephone Number: ____________

The following information will be completed by the County Clerk's Office at the time of registration.

Applicant's Identification* (type): ____________

Applicant's Name (as shown on identification): ____________

Identification number: ____________ Expiration Date: ____________
* (Note: The type of identification provided MUST be acceptable to the County Clerk)

Source: recorder.countryofventura.org/Ida.htm.

§ 6404. Fees

An applicant shall pay a fee of one hundred seventy-five dollars ($175) to the county clerk at the time he or she files an application for initial registration, including a primary or secondary registration, or renewal of registration. An additional fee of ten dollars ($10) shall be paid to the county clerk for each additional identification card.

§ 6405. Bonds

$25,000 Bond to Protect Clients

(a) (1) An application for a certificate of registration by an individual shall be accompanied by a bond of twenty-five thousand dollars ($25,000) executed by a corporate surety qualified to do business in this state and conditioned upon compliance with this chapter. The total aggregate liability on the bond shall be limited to twenty-five thousand dollars ($25,000). An application for secondary registration shall meet all of the requirements of this subdivision, except that in place of posting another original bond or cash deposit, the applicant shall include a certified copy of the bond or cash deposit posted in the county in which the applicant filed the primary registration.

(2) An application for a certificate of registration by a partnership or corporation shall be accompanied by a bond executed by a corporate surety qualified to do business in this state and conditioned upon compliance with this chapter in the following amount, based on the total number of legal document assistants and unlawful detainer assistants employed by the partnership or corporation:

(A) Twenty-five thousand dollars ($25,000) for one to four assistants.

(B) Fifty thousand dollars ($50,000) for five to nine assistants.

(C) One hundred thousand dollars ($100,000) for 10 or more assistants. An application for a certificate of registration by a person employed by a partnership or corporation shall be accompanied by a bond of twenty-five thousand dollars ($25,000) only if the partnership or corporation has not posted a bond in the amount required by this subdivision. An application for secondary registration shall meet all of the requirements of this subdivision, except that in place of posting another original bond or cash deposit, the applicant shall include a certified copy of the bond or cash deposit posted in the county in which the applicant filed the primary registration.

(3) If a partnership or corporation increases the number of assistants it employs above the number stated in its application for a certificate of registration, the partnership or corporation shall promptly increase the bond to the applicable amount in subparagraphs (B) or (C) of paragraph (2) based on the actual number of assistants it employs, and shall promptly submit the increased bond to the county clerk. The partnership or corporation shall promptly send a certified copy of the increased bond to the county clerk in any county of secondary registration.

(4) The bond may be terminated pursuant to Section 995.440 of, and Article 13 (commencing with Section 996.310) of Chapter 2 of Title 14 of Part 2 of the Code of Civil Procedure.

(b) The county clerk shall, upon filing of the bond, deliver the bond forthwith to the county recorder for recording. The recording fee specified in Section 27361 of the Government Code shall be paid by the registrant. The fee may be paid to the county clerk who shall transmit it to the recorder.

(c) The fee for filing, canceling, revoking, or withdrawing the bond is seven dollars ($7).

(d) The county recorder shall record the bond and any notice of cancellation, revocation, or withdrawal of the bond, and shall thereafter mail the instrument, unless specified to the contrary, to the person named in the instrument and, if no person is named, to the party leaving it for recording. The recording fee specified in Section 27361 of the Government Code for notice of cancellation, revocation, or withdrawal of the bond shall be paid to the county clerk, who shall transmit it to the county recorder.

Recording the Bond

(e) In lieu of the bond required by subdivision (a), a registrant may deposit the amount required by subdivision (a) in cash with the county clerk.

(f) If the certificate is revoked, the bond or cash deposit shall be returned to the bonding party or depositor subject to subdivision (g) and the right of a person to recover against the bond or cash deposit under Section 6412.

(g) The county clerk may retain a cash deposit until the expiration of three years from the date the registrant has ceased to do business, or three years from the expiration or revocation date of the registration, in order to ensure there are no outstanding claims against the deposit. A judge may order the return of the deposit prior to the expiration of three years upon evidence satisfactory to the judge that there are no outstanding claims against the deposit.

(h) The bond required by this section shall be in favor of the State of California for the benefit of any person who is damaged as a result of the violation of this chapter or by the fraud, dishonesty, or incompetency of an individual, partnership, or corporation registered under this chapter. The bond required by this section shall also indicate the name of the county in which it will be filed.

Claims Based on Fraud, Dishonesty, or Incompetency

§ 6406. Certificates of Registration; Duration; Renewal Denial; Appeal

(a) If granted, a certificate of registration shall be effective for a period of two years, until the date the bond expires, or until the total number of legal document assistants and unlawful detainer assistants employed by a partnership or corporation exceeds the number allowed for the amount of the bond in effect, whichever occurs first. Thereafter, a registrant shall file a new certificate of registration or a renewal of the certificate of registration and pay the fee required by Section 6404, and increase the amount of the bond if required to comply with subdivision (a) of Section

6405. A certificate of registration that is currently effective may be renewed up to 60 days prior to its expiration date and the effective date of the renewal shall be the date the current registration expires. The renewal shall be effective for a period of two years from the effective date or until the expiration date of the bond, or until the total number of legal document assistants and unlawful detainer assistants employed by a partnership or corporation exceeds the number allowed for the dollar amount of the bond in effect, whichever occurs first.

Two-Year Registration Period

Renewal of Registration

(b) Except as provided in subdivisions (d) to (f), inclusive, an applicant shall be denied registration or renewal of registration if the applicant has been any of the following:

(1) Convicted of a felony, or of a misdemeanor under Section 6126 or 6127, or found liable under Section 6126.5.

(2) Held liable in a civil action by final judgment or entry of a stipulated judgment, if the action alleged fraud, or the use of an untrue or misleading representation, or the use of an unfair, unlawful, or deceptive business practice.

(3) Convicted of a misdemeanor violation of this chapter.

(4) Had a civil judgment entered against him or her in an action arising out of the applicant's negligent, reckless, or willful failure to properly perform his or her obligation as a legal document assistant or unlawful detainer assistant.

Denial of Registration or Renewal

(5) Had his or her registration revoked pursuant to Section 6413.

(c) If the county clerk finds that the applicant has failed to demonstrate having met the requisite requirements of Section 6402 or 6402.1, or that any of the paragraphs of subdivision (b) apply, the county clerk, within three business days of submission of the application and fee, shall return the application and fee to the applicant with a notice to the applicant indicating the reason for the denial and the method of appeal.

(d) The denial of an application may be appealed by the applicant by submitting, to the director, the following:

Appealing the Denial

(1) The completed application and notice from the county clerk specifying the reasons for the denial of the application.

(2) A copy of any final judgment or order that resulted from any conviction or civil judgment listed on the application.

(3) Any relevant information the applicant wishes to include for the record.

(e) The director shall order the applicant's certificate of registration to be granted if the director determines that the issuance of a certificate of registration is not likely to expose consumers to a significant risk of harm based on a review of the application and any other information relating to the applicant's unlawful act or unfair practice described in paragraphs (1) to (5), inclusive, of subdivision (b). The director shall order the applicant's certificate of registration to be denied if the director determines that issuance of a certificate of registration is likely to expose consumers to a significant risk of harm based on a review of the application and any other information relating to the applicant's unlawful act or unfair practice described in paragraphs (1) to (5), inclusive, of subdivision (b). The director shall send to the applicant and the county clerk a written decision listing the reasons registration shall be granted or denied within 30 days of the submission of the matter.

(f) If the director orders that the certificate of registration be granted, the applicant may resubmit the application, with the appropriate application fee and the written decision of the director. The county clerk shall grant the certificate of registration to the applicant within three business days of being supplied this information.

§ 6407. Register; Identification Cards

(a) The county clerk shall maintain a register of legal document assistants, and a register of unlawful detainer assistants, assign a unique number to each legal document assistant, or unlawful detainer assistant, and issue an identification card to each one. Additional cards for employees of legal document assistants or unlawful detainer assistants shall be issued upon the payment of ten dollars ($10) for each card. Upon renewal of registration, the same number shall be assigned, provided there is no lapse in the period of registration.

Identification Cards

(b) The identification card shall be a card 3½ by 2¼ inches, and shall contain at the top, the title "Legal Document Assistant" or "Unlawful Detainer Assistant," as appropriate, followed by the registrant's name, address, registration number, date of expiration, and county of registration. It shall also contain a photograph of the registrant in the lower left corner. The front of the card, above the title, shall also contain the following statement in 12-point boldface type:

"This person is not a lawyer."

"THIS PERSON IS NOT A LAWYER"

The front of the card, at the bottom, shall also contain the following statement in 12-point boldface type:

> "The county clerk has not evaluated this person's knowledge, experience, or services."

[Exhibit 1.3B is an example of an identification card of an LDA who works alone. The identification card in Exhibit 1.3B is of an individual who is an employee of an LDA.]

§ 6408. Disclosure of Registration Required

The registrant's name, business address, telephone number, registration number, expiration date of the registration, and county of registration shall appear in any solicitation or advertisement, and on any papers or documents prepared or used by the registrant, including, but not limited to, contracts, letterhead, business cards, correspondence, documents, forms, claims, petitions, checks, receipts, money orders, and pleadings.

EXHIBIT 1.3B

Identification Card of a Legal Document Assistant (in Compliance with Business & Professions Code § 6407)

EXHIBIT 1.3C

Example of an Identification Card of an Employee of a Legal Document Assistant (in Compliance with Business & Professions Code § 6407)

§ 6408.5. Advertisements and Solicitation; Required Disclaimers

Advertisements Solicitations

(a) All advertisements or solicitations published, distributed, or broadcast offering legal document assistant or unlawful detainer assistant services shall include the following statement:

"I AM NOT AN ATTORNEY"

> "I am not an attorney. I can only provide self-help services at your specific direction."

This subdivision does not apply to classified or "yellow pages" listings in a telephone or business directory of three lines or less that state only the name, address, and telephone number of the legal document assistant or unlawful detainer assistant.

(b) If the advertisement or solicitation is in a language other than English, the statement required by subdivision (a) shall be in the same language as the advertisement or solicitation.

§ 6409. Retention of Original Documents

Possession of Client Documents

No legal document assistant or unlawful detainer assistant shall retain in his or her possession original documents of a client. A legal document assistant or an unlawful detainer assistant shall immediately return all of a client's original documents to the client in any one or more of the following circumstances:

(a) If the client so requests at any time.

(b) If the written contract required by Section 6410 is not executed or is rescinded, canceled, or voided for any reason.

(c) If the services described pursuant to paragraph (1) of subdivision (b) of Section 6410 have been completed.

§ 6410. Written Contracts; Contents; Rescinding and Voiding

Client Contract for Services

(a) Every legal document assistant or unlawful detainer assistant who enters into a contract or agreement with a client to provide services shall, prior to providing any services, provide the client with a written contract, the contents of which shall be prescribed by regulations adopted by the Department of Consumer Affairs.

(b) The written contract shall include all of the following provisions:

(1) The services to be performed.

(2) The costs of the services to be performed.

(3) There shall be printed on the face of the contract in 12-point boldface type a statement that

the legal document assistant or unlawful detainer assistant is not an attorney and may not perform the legal services that an attorney performs.

(4) The contract shall contain a statement in 12-point boldface type that the county clerk has not evaluated or approved the registrant's knowledge or experience, or the quality of the registrant's services.

(5) The contract shall contain a statement in 12-point boldface type that the consumer may obtain information regarding free or low-cost representation through a local bar association or legal aid foundation and that the consumer may contact local law enforcement, a district attorney, or a legal aid foundation if the consumer believes that he or she has been a victim of fraud, the unauthorized practice of law, or any other injury.

Fraud Notice

(6) The contract shall contain a statement in 12-point boldface type that a legal document assistant or unlawful detainer assistant is not permitted to engage in the practice of law, including providing any kind of advice, explanation, opinion, or recommendation to a consumer about possible legal rights, remedies, defenses, options, selection of forms, or strategies.

Contract Disclaimer

(c) The contract shall be written both in English and in any other language comprehended by the client and principally used in any oral sales presentation or negotiation leading to execution of the contract. The legal document assistant or the unlawful detainer assistant is responsible for translating the contract into the language principally used in any oral sales presentation or negotiation leading to the execution of the contract.

(d) Failure of a legal document assistant or unlawful detainer assistant to comply with subdivisions (a), (b), and (c) shall make the contract or agreement for services voidable at the option of the client. Upon the voiding of the contract, the legal document assistant or unlawful detainer assistant shall immediately return in full any fees paid by the client.

Forfeiture of Fees

(e) In addition to any other right to rescind, the client shall have the right to rescind the contract within 24 hours of the signing of the contract. The client may cancel the contract by giving the legal document assistant or the unlawful detainer assistant any written statement to the effect that the contract is canceled. If the client gives notice of cancellation by mail addressed to the legal document assistant or unlawful detainer assistant, with first-class postage prepaid, cancellation is effective upon the date indicated on the postmark. Upon the voiding or rescinding of the contract or agreement for services, the legal document assistant or unlawful detainer assistant shall immediately return to the client any fees paid by the client, except fees for services that were actually, necessarily, and reasonably performed on the client's behalf by the legal document assistant or unlawful detainer assistant with the client's knowing and express written consent. The requirements of this subdivision shall be conspicuously set forth in the written contract.

[Exhibit 1.3D contains an example of a contract that complies with these statutory requirements.]

§ 6410.5. First-In-Person or Telephonic Solicitation; Disclaimers and Statements Prior to Conversation

(a) It is unlawful for any legal document assistant or unlawful detainer assistant, in the first in-person or telephonic solicitation of a prospective client of legal document or unlawful detainer assistant services, to enter into a contract or agreement for services or accept any compensation unless the legal document assistant or the unlawful detainer assistant states orally, clearly, affirmatively and expressly all of the following, before making any other statement, except statements required by law in telephonic or home solicitations, and a greeting, or asking the prospective client any questions:

Solicitation

(1) The identity of the person making the solicitation.

(2) The trade name of the person represented by the person making the solicitation, if any.

(3) The kind of services being offered for sale.

(4) The statement: "I am not an attorney" and, if the person offering legal document assistant or unlawful detainer assistant services is a partnership or a corporation, or uses a fictitious business name, "[name] is not a law firm. I/we cannot represent you in court, advise you about your legal rights or the law, or select legal forms for you."

"I AM NOT AN ATTORNEY"

(b) If the first contact between a legal document assistant or an unlawful detainer assistant and a prospective client is initiated by the prospective client, it is unlawful for the legal document assistant or unlawful detainer assistant to enter into a contract or agreement for services or accept any compensation unless the legal document assistant or the unlawful detainer assistant states orally, clearly, affirmatively and expressly, during that first contact, and before offering any contract or agreement for services to the prospective client, the following: "I am not an attorney" and, if the person offering legal document assistant or unlawful detainer assistant services is a partnership or a

EXHIBIT 1.3D

LEGAL DOCUMENT ASSISTANT CONTRACT FOR SELF-HELP SERVICES

This is a contract between me, ________________, and you, ___________________, for the self-help services described in Part I below. I am the "legal document assistant" and you are the "client."

IMPORTANT NOTICES

1. You should read and understand this entire contract before you sign it. You should understand the kinds of services that I can and cannot perform for you (see Part I below).

2. I am not an attorney. I cannot perform the legal services that an attorney performs. I cannot engage in the practice of law.

3. The county clerk has not evaluated or approved my knowledge or experience, or the quality of my work.

4. I cannot keep your original documents if you request that I return them to you. I cannot keep your original documents if you and I do not sign this contract or if this contract terminates (ends) for any reason. I cannot keep your original documents after all of the contract services have been provided (see Part I below). It is a violation of California law if I keep your original documents under any of these circumstances.

5. It is a violation of California law if I make any false or misleading statement to you.

6. I cannot obtain special favors from, and I do not have any special influence with, any court or any state or federal agency.

7. As required by law, I have filed a bond or made a cash deposit and have registered as a legal document assistant in each county where I will perform services on your behalf.

I. SELF-HELP SERVICES

Kinds of services that I can perform for you: I can perform the following self-help services for you in connection with a legal matter in which you are representing yourself: I can type or otherwise complete, as you specifically direct, legal documents that you have selected. I can provide you general published factual legal information that has been written or approved by an attorney, to help you represent yourself. I can provide you published legal documents. I can file and serve legal forms and documents as you specifically direct.

These are the only kinds of services that I can perform for you. I cannot provide you any service if you need additional services. If you need additional services, then you require the services of an attorney.

Kinds of services that I cannot perform for you : I cannot provide you any self-help service unless you are representing yourself in a legal matter and the self-help service relates to that legal matter.

I cannot engage in the practice of law. This means that I cannot give you any kind of advice, explanation, opinion or recommendation about possible legal rights, remedies, defenses, strategies or options that you may have. I cannot give you any advice, explanation, opinion or recommendation regarding selection of forms.

EXHIBIT 1.3D

I will provide you all the following services (list all services for which the client is being charged):

A. ______________________________

B. ______________________________

C. ______________________________

D. ______________________________

You are paying me only for those services listed above and no others. It is unlawful for me to make any guarantee or promise to you unless it is written in this contract and unless I have a factual basis for making the guarantee or promise.

II. FEES AND EXPENSES

You agree to pay me the foling fees, costs and expenses: low

A. A flat fee in the total amount of $____________ for all services, costs and expenses, to be paid as follows (itemize services, costs and expenses and state terms of payment):

____

OR

B. A rate of $________ per hour, not to exceed a total of $___________ for all services, costs and expenses. I will provide you a statement itemizing all services rendered, expenses incurred, and the balance owed, each time a payment is due.

III. CANCELLATION

You may cancel this contract for any reason within 24 hours after we both have signed it.

If you cancel the contract, I must immediately refund any fees which you have paid me. The only fees that I may keep are fees for services which I have actually, necessarily and reasonably performed on your behalf during the 24-hour period. I cannot keep any fees for services performed during the 24-hour period unless you knew that I would perform those services and you agreed in this contract that I would perform them.

To cancel this contract, send me a written notice stating that you are canceling the contract. Mail the notice by first-class mail with the correct postage, and send it to me at my address (see Part V below). Cancellation takes effect on the date of the postmark on the notice. You can also cancel this contract by delivering a written notice of cancellation to my address within the 24-hour period.

You may also cancel this contract at any time if I:

- Fail to give you a copy of this contract before providing any services to you, or
- Fail to specify in the contract the services which I will perform and the costs of those services, or
- Fail to give you a copy of the contract in English and in any other language that you understand and that was principally used in any oral sales presentation or negotiation leading to execution of the contract. If you cancel this contract for any of these reasons, I must immediately refund in full any fees which you have paid me.

You may also cancel this contract at any time if you have legal cause.

IV. ATTORNEY'S FEES AND COSTS

In the event of suit for damages arising from this contract or to enforce any of its provisions, the court may award the prevailing party his or her reasonable attorney's fees and costs.

EXHIBIT 1.3D

LDA Self-Help Services Contract (*cont.*)

V. DESCRIPTION OF THE PARTIES

Legal Document Assistant

Full name: ____________________
Business name (if different): ____________________
Street address of business: ____________________
City, State, ZIP: ____________________
Telephone number: ____________________
Fax number (if any): ____________________
Registration number in county where services will be provided: ____________________
Date of expiration: ____________________
County: ____________________
I have filed a bond or made a cash deposit in the following counties: ____________________

Client

Name of client: ____________________
Name of client: ____________________
Street address: ____________________
City, State, ZIP: ____________________
Telephone number: ____________________
Title or brief description of the legal matter in which the client is representing himself or herself: ____________________

VI. SIGNATURES

Executed at ______________, California.

-- ----------------------
(Signature of Legal Document Assistant (Date)

Notices to Client

You may obtain information from the local bar association or a legal aid or legal services office regarding free or low-cost representation by a lawyer.

You may contact the local police, sheriff, district attorney or legal aid or legal services office if you believe that you are the victim of fraud, unauthorized practice of law or other injury.

-- ----------------------
(Client) (Date)

-- ----------------------
(Client) (Date)

(THIS CONTRACT IS NOT VALID OR BINDING UNTIL THE LEGAL DOCUMENT ASSISTANT HAS GIVEN ALL CLIENT PARTIES A FULLY EXECUTED COPY OF IT, INCLUDING AN ACCURATE TRANSLATION OF IT IN ANY LANGUAGE OTHER THAN ENGLISH THAT THE CLIENT UNDERSTANDS AND THAT WAS PRINCIPALLY USED IN ANY ORAL SALES PRESENTATION OR NEGOTIATION LEADING TO EXECUTION OF THE CONTRACT.)

Source: 16 California Code of Regulations § 3950.

LDA Cannot Give Any Advice, Including Explanations or Selection of Forms

corporation, or uses a fictitious business name,

"[name] is not a law firm." [I/We] cannot (1) represent you in court, (2) advise you about your legal rights or the law, or (3) select legal forms for you."

After making this statement, and before offering the prospective client a contract or agreement for services, a legal document assistant or unlawful detainer assistant who has made the statement in accordance with this subsection may ask the prospective client to read the "Notice to Consumer" set forth [in Figure 1.3E], and after allowing the prospective client time to read the notice, may ask the prospective client to sign and date the notice. The notice shall be set forth in black, bold, 14-point type on a separate, white, 8½ by 11 inch sheet of paper which contains no other print or graphics, and shall be in the following form. The notice shall contain only the appropriate name or other designation from those indicated in brackets below. At the time a prospective client signs the notice and before that prospective client is offered any contract or agreement for signature, the legal document assistant or unlawful detainer assistant shall give the prospective client a clearly legible copy of the signed notice. A legal document assistant or unlawful detainer assistant shall not ask or require a prospective client or a client to sign any other form of acknowledgment regarding this notice.

§ 6411. Unlawful Acts

Misleading Statements, Guarantees, and the Unauthorized Practice of Law

It is unlawful for any person engaged in the business or acting in the capacity of a legal document assistant or unlawful detainer assistant to do any of the following:

(a) Make false or misleading statements to the consumer concerning the subject matter, legal issues, or self-help service being provided by the legal document assistant or unlawful detainer assistant.

(b) Make any guarantee or promise to a client or prospective client, unless the guarantee or promise is in writing and the legal document assistant or unlawful detainer assistant has a reasonable factual basis for making the guarantee or promise.

(c) Make any statement that the legal document assistant or unlawful detainer assistant can or will obtain favors or has special influence with a court, or a state or federal agency.

(d) Provide assistance or advice which constitutes the unlawful practice of law pursuant to Section 6125, 6126, or 6127.

(e) Engage in the unauthorized practice of law, including, but not limited to, giving any kind of advice, explanation, opinion, or recommendation to a consumer about possible legal rights, remedies, defenses, options, selection of forms, or strategies. A legal document assistant shall complete documents only in the manner prescribed by subdivision (d) of Section 6400.

(f) Use in the person's business name or advertising the words "legal aid," "legal services," or any similar term that has the capacity, tendency, or likelihood to mislead members of the public about that person's status as a nonprofit corporation or governmentally supported organization offering legal services without charge to indigent people, or employing members of the State Bar to provide those services.

Using phrases such as "Legal Services" in Advertisements

§ 6412. Recovery of Damages from Bonds; Filing of New Bonds Required

(a) Any owner or manager of residential or commercial rental property, tenant, or other person who is awarded damages in any action or proceeding for

EXHIBIT 1.3E

Notice to Consumer (in Compliance with Business & Professions Code § 6410.5)

NOTICE TO CONSUMER
DO NOT SIGN ANYTHING BEFORE YOU READ THIS PAGE
In the first conversation when you contacted [the unlawful detainer assistant or the legal document assistant] did [he or she] explain . . . . . .

[Name of unlawful detainer assistant or legal document assistant] is not an attorney.
[Name of corporation or partnership, if any, that is offering legal document assistant services or unlawful detainer assistant services] is not a law firm.
[He/she/name of the business] cannot represent you in court.
[He/she/name of the business] cannot advise you about your legal rights or the law.
[He/she/name of the business] cannot select legal forms for you.
Choose one:
Yes, [he/she] explained.
No, [he/she] did not explain.
Date:____________________
Signature:____________________

Notice to Consumer Client of UDA or LDA

Source: § 6410.5(b) Business & Professions Code of California

injuries caused by the acts of a registrant while in the performance of his or her duties as a legal document assistant or unlawful detainer assistant may recover damages from the bond or cash deposit required by Section 6405.

(b) If there has been a recovery against a bond or cash deposit under subdivision (a) and the registration has not been revoked pursuant to Section 6413, the registrant shall file a new bond or deposit an additional amount of cash within 30 days to reinstate the bond or cash deposit to the amount required by Section 6405. If the registrant does not file a bond, or deposit this amount within 30 days, his or her certificate of registration shall be revoked.

Damages or Recovery against a Bond

§ 6412.1. Remedies for Violation; Attorney's Fees

(a) Any person injured by the unlawful act of a legal document assistant or unlawful detainer assistant shall retain all rights and remedies cognizable under law. The penalties, relief, and remedies provided in this chapter are not exclusive, and do not affect any other penalties, relief, and remedies provided by law.

Suing an LDA or UDA

(b) Any person injured by a violation of this chapter by a legal document assistant or unlawful detainer assistant may file a complaint and seek redress in any superior court for injunctive relief, restitution, and damages. Attorney's fees shall be awarded to the prevailing plaintiff. A claim under this chapter may be maintained in small claims court, if the claim and relief sought are within the small claims court's jurisdiction.

§ 6412.5. Waivers from Client

A legal document assistant or an unlawful detainer assistant may neither seek nor obtain a client's waiver of any of the provisions of this chapter. Any waiver of the provisions of this chapter is contrary to public policy, and is void and unenforceable.

§ 6413. Revocation of Registration

Revocation of Registration

The county clerk shall revoke the registration of a legal document assistant or unlawful detainer assistant upon receipt of an official document or record stating that the registrant has been found guilty of the unauthorized practice of law pursuant to Section 6125, 6126, or 6127, has been found guilty of a misdemeanor violation of this chapter, has been found liable under Section 6126.5, or that a civil judgment has been entered against the registrant in an action arising out of the registrant's negligent, reckless, or willful failure to properly perform his or her obligation as a legal document assistant or unlawful detainer assistant. The county clerk shall be given notice of the disposition in any court action by the city attorney, district attorney, or plaintiff, as applicable. A registrant whose registration is revoked pursuant to this section may reapply for registration three years after the revocation.

§ 6414. Appeal of Revocation of Registration

Appeal of Revocation

A registrant whose certificate is revoked shall be entitled to challenge the decision in a court of competent jurisdiction.

§ 6415. Penalties

Criminal Penalties

A failure, by a person who engages in acts of a legal document assistant or unlawful detainer assistant, to comply with any of the requirements of Section 6401.6, 6402, 6408, or 6410, subdivision (a), (b), or (c) of Section 6411, or Section 6412.5 is a misdemeanor punishable by a fine of not less than one thousand dollars ($1,000) or more than two thousand dollars ($2,000), as to each client with respect to whom a violation occurs, or imprisonment for not more than one year, or by both that fine and imprisonment. Payment of restitution to a client shall take precedence over payment of a fine.

§ 6454. Definitions

Contract Paralegal

Freelance Paralegal Independent Paralegal

The terms "paralegal," "legal assistant," "attorney assistant," "freelance paralegal," "independent paralegal," and "contract paralegal" are synonymous for purposes of this chapter.

D. Immigration Consultants and Bankruptcy Petition Preparers

Immigration Consultant

An immigration consultant (IC) is a non-attorney authorized to charge fees for providing "nonlegal assistance or advice on an immigration matter" to members of the public (without attorney supervision).

For example, the IC can complete immigration forms for a client—so long as no advice is provided on what answers should be used on the forms. (Business & Professions Code § 22441). The IC must obtain a $50,000 bond to cover claims by clients who allege fraud or other unlawful act by the IC. Using a standard service contract approved by the Department of Consumer Affairs, ICs must tell a client that they are not attorneys and cannot provide legal services. Civil and criminal penalties can be imposed for violating these regulations.

Bankruptcy Petition Preparers (BPP)

A fourth major independent is the bankruptcy petition preparer (BPP), a position regulated by federal law. A BPP is a non-attorney who is authorized (without attorney supervision) to charge fees for preparing a bankruptcy petition or any other bankruptcy document that a debtor will file in a federal court. Among the restrictions imposed by federal law, BPPs

- cannot use the word "legal" or any similar term in advertisements;
- must print their name, address, and social security number on every document they prepare;
- must give the debtor a copy of each document the debtor signs at the time of signing;
- cannot execute any document for a debtor; and
- must file a disclosure of any fee received from the debtor.

Each violations of these regulations can lead to a fine of $500 and a BPP can be forced to pay the debtor $2,000 or twice the amount the debtor paid for the BPP's services, whichever is greater. (11 U.S.C. § 110)

E. More Information

Agency Regulations in the California Code of Regulations (CCR)
ccr.oal.ca.gov

Application for registration as a legal document assistant
16 CCR § 3900

The procedure before the Department of Consumer Affairs when there has been a denial of an application for registration as a Legal Document Assistant
16 CCR § 3920

Standard legal document assistant contract
16 CCR § 3950

The procedure before the Department of Consumer Affairs when there has been a denial of an application for registration as a Unlawful Detainer Assistant
16 CCR §§ 3860, 3870

Standard unlawful detainer assistant contract
16 CCR § 3890

Obtaining a Bond
pennbrookinsurance.com/forms
(click "Legal Document Assistant Bond")
www.pennbrookinsurance.com/forms/pennbrook_bond_insurance1.pdf

Legal Document Assistant Registration in Selected Counties
recorder.countyofventura.org/lda.htm
www.co.el-dorado.ca.us/countyclerk/legal.html
www.co.solano.ca.us/SubSection/SubSection.asp?NavID=547
www.co.shasta.ca.us
(click "County Clerk" and then "Legal Document Assistant")

California Department of Consumer Affairs
800-952-5210; 916-445-1254
www.dca.ca.gov
www.dca.ca.gov/legal/k-6.pdf

California Association of Legal Document Assistants (CALDA)
www.calda.org

CALDA Code of Ethics
www.calda.org/CodeOfEthics.asp

Unlawful Detainer Assistant Registration in Selected Counties
www.co.el-dorado.ca.us/countyclerk/unlawful.html
www.co.shasta.ca.us
(click "County Clerk" and then "Unlawful Detainer Assistant")

Immigration Consultants
www.ss.ca.gov/business/sf/bond_search.htm
da.co.la.ca.us/immigration.htm

Bankruptcy Petition Preparers
www.canb.uscourts.gov
(click "Guidelines")
www.lawca.com/forms/EC_DISCL.pdf
www.caeb.uscourts.gov/data/formpubs/GL.Prep.pdf

F. Something to Check

1. Go to the Web site of the California Association of Legal Document Assistants (CALDA) (*www.calda.org*). What is CALDA's opinion of California's regulation of legal document assistants?
2. In Google (*www.google.com*), or another general search engine, run the following search "California legal document assistant." Describe the different categories of sites to which you are led by this query.
3. Do an online search for bonds that an LDA can purchase to meet the requirements of California law. What options are available to buy such a bond?
4. Find an online site of a California LDA. What specific sections and subsections of the Business and

Professions Code (§§ 6400–6415) are relevant to statements made on this LDA site? For example, if the site says that the LDA is bonded, one of the relevant B&P sections would be § 6405 on bonds.

1.4 Paralegal Associations and Related Groups in California

A. Introduction

There are many vibrant paralegal associations in the state that have had a major impact on the development of the field. Associations can be very helpful in finding employment and in continuing your legal education while employed. One of the best networking opportunities available to you will be the various meetings regularly held by the associations. The essence of networking is locating other paralegals and exchanging ideas, resources, leads, and business cards with them. Such exchanges can be important even if the subject matter of a particular meeting does not interest you. Furthermore, your involvement in a paralegal association will help strengthen the association and the profession itself.

This section presents an overview of all California associations, including their World Wide Web address and related contact information. When you go to the Web site of an association, find out what services it offers and whether there are special dues for different categories of members. Find out when and where the next meeting will be held. You also want to know if the association has a job bank that lists current paralegal openings.

The following list will also include (a) attorney associations that allow paralegal membership on committees or as associate/affiliate members of the association itself, and (b) other nonattorney associations that have a close relationship to the practice of law.

B. Paralegal Associations in California

Statewide Associations	City and County Associations	
CAPA	Bakersfield	San Jose
CALDA	Central Coast	San Luis Obispo
State Bar, Real Estate	Fresno	Santa Barbara
CAOC	Inland Counties	Santa Clara County
	Kern County	Santa Rosa
	Los Angeles	Sequoia
	Newport Beach	Sonoma County
	Orange County	Tulare County
	Redwood Empire	Ventura County
	Riverside	Visalia
	Sacramento	Other Associations
	San Bernardino County	
	San Diego	
	San Francisco	
	San Joaquin	

Statewide Associations

California Alliance of Paralegal Associations (CAPA)
P.O. Box 1089
San Leandro, CA 94577-0126
caparalegal.org

Background: Founded in 1976, CAPA is an organization of the paralegal associations in California. CAPA also sponsors a state certification program: the California Advanced Specialist (CAS) examination in conjunction with the National Association of Legal Assistants (NALA). The exam is administered by the Commission for Advanced Paralegal Specialization (CAPS) (*www.cla-cas.org*). Note: The exam and CAS program are currently being revised.

Membership: Paralegal associations in California; individual paralegals cannot join CAPA.

National Affiliation: CAPA offers its California Advanced Specialist (CAS) certification in conjunction with the National Association of Legal Assistants (*www.nala.org*).

Newsletter: *RECAP* can be read on CAPA's Web site.

Services Offered: CAPA offers the CAS (California Advanced Specialist) certification. CAPA also publishes a *Handbook on Paralegal Utilization* that contains lists of paralegal duties. CAPA holds an annual organization and education conference to which individual paralegals throughout the state are invited. It also has sponsored continuing legal education (CLE) for paralegals in fulfillment of their mandatory continuing legal education (MCLE) requirements (*www.taecan.com/providers/capa.asp*).

Ethics: CAPA has its own code of ethics (*caparalegal.org/ethics.html*). Here is an example of one if its ethical guidelines: "A paralegal shall avoid conflicts of interest and immediately disclose in writing any potential conflicts."

In recognition of the importance of paralegals, Governor Schwarzenegger has declared June 24th California Paralegal Day. See Exhibit 1.5A.

California Association of Legal Document Assistants (CALDA)
(CALDA does not use a postal mail address)
www.calda.org

Background: CALDA was formerly known as the Association of California Independent Paralegals. The group consists of independent contractors who provide limited law-related services to the public. (See section 1.3.) In 2000, a law was passed restricting the use of the title "paralegal" (and "legal assistant") to individuals who work under the supervision of attorneys. If you do not, you must be called something else, such as legal document assistant (LDA), unlawful detainer assistant (UDA), or bankruptcy petition preparer (BPP). Since most members of the Association of California Independent Paralegals did not work under the supervision of attorneys, the association changed its name to CALDA.

Membership: Regular membership $150 per year ($75 for students).

Newsletter: *Access*

Services Offered: CALDA sells brochures on California law (e.g., Making a Will) and questionnaires to help interview clients (e.g., Filing for Bankruptcy).

Ethics: Members abide by the *CALDA's Code of Ethics* (*www.calda.org/CodeOfEthics.asp*). Example of a code provision: "CALDA members will not financially exploit their customers." (I2C)

State Bar, Real Property Section

California State Bar Association

San Francisco (main office)	Los Angeles office
180 Howard Street	1149 South Hill Street
San Francisco, CA 94105	Los Angeles, CA 90015
415-538-2564	213-765-1000

www.calbar.ca.gov
www.calbar.ca.gov/state/calbar/calbar_generic.jsp?cid=10713

This is what this section of the state bar says about non-attorney membership: "The Real Property Law Section has long offered associate memberships to non-attorneys who wish to participate in Section events, join subsections and receive the Journal. With the recent changes in the regulation of paralegals requiring continuing education hours, we think there may be greater interest in the paralegal community in joining the Section. If there is sufficient interest, we are committed to starting a Paralegal Subsection within the Real Property Law Section to serve the paralegal members and give them a voice in Section activities. Please encourage your paralegal friends and colleagues to become associate members of the Section, and please encourage your law firms to pay their dues ($50 per year)." On the main Web site for the California bar (*www.calbar.ca.gov*), type "associate memberships" in the search box. Also do a search for "paralegal subsection."

Consumer Attorneys of California (CAOC)
770 L. St., Ste 1220
Sacramento, CA 95814
916-442-6902
www.caoc.com

EXHIBIT 1.5A

California Paralegal Day

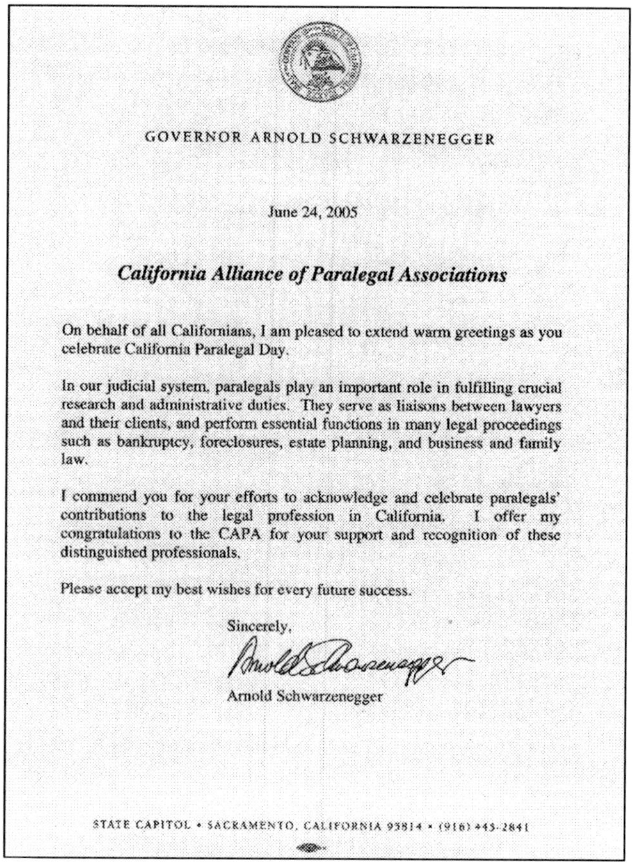

GOVERNOR ARNOLD SCHWARZENEGGER

June 24, 2005

California Alliance of Paralegal Associations

On behalf of all Californians, I am pleased to extend warm greetings as you celebrate California Paralegal Day.

In our judicial system, paralegals play an important role in fulfilling crucial research and administrative duties. They serve as liaisons between lawyers and their clients, and perform essential functions in many legal proceedings such as bankruptcy, foreclosures, estate planning, and business and family law.

I commend you for your efforts to acknowledge and celebrate paralegals' contributions to the legal profession in California. I offer my congratulations to the CAPA for your support and recognition of these distinguished professionals.

Please accept my best wishes for every future success.

Sincerely,

Arnold Schwarzenegger

STATE CAPITOL • SACRAMENTO, CALIFORNIA 95814 • (916) 445-2841

Source: www.sbparalegals.org/pdf/hpsc78.pdf

CAOC offers a law office support membership category to paralegals. "CAOC is an organization of more than 3,000 attorneys who represent plaintiffs/consumers who seek responsibility from wrongdoers." This membership is available to paralegals . . . who work in the office of a CAOC attorney member."

Membership Fee: $90

City and County Associations

Bakersfield
Kern County Paralegal Association (KCPA)
P.O. Box 2673
Bakersfield, CA 93303
www.kcpaonline.org

Background: Founded in 1987, most of KCPA's members are paralegals/legal assistants employed by Kern County law firms, corporations, and administrative agencies. Membership also includes independent contract and freelance legal assistants who provide services to attorneys and law firms, and paralegal students.

Membership: In addition to regular, associate, and sustaining membership categories, students may joint KCPA with limited voting rights.

National Affiliation: KCPA is an affiliate of the National Association of Legal Assistants (*www.nala.org*).

Newsletter: *The Paralegal Post*, a monthly newsletter.

Services Offered: KCPA offers an annual scholarship to member students currently enrolled in a paralegal program. It also has discounts on programs for continuing legal education (CLE). An online job bank of paralegal openings in the county is available to everyone, including those who not members of KCPA (*www.kcpaonline.org/jobbank*).

Central Coast
See San Luis Obispo

Fresno
Fresno Paralegal Association (FPA)
P.O. Box 28515
Fresno, CA 93729-8515
www.fresnoparalegal.org

Background: FPA was founded in 1981. (Its original name was the San Joaquin Association of Legal Assistants.)

Membership: The cost of a regular membership is $40 a year ($20 for students enrolled in a paralegal school).

National Affiliation: FPA is an affiliate of the National Association of Legal Assistants (*www.nala.org*).

Newsletter: *Points and Authorities* (available online at *www.fresnoparalegal.org/newsletter/index.html*).

Services Offered: FPA offers continuing legal education (CLE) programs. An online job bank of paralegal openings in the area is available to everyone, including those who are not members of FPA (*www.fresnoparalegal.org/job_bank/index.html*).

Inland Counties
See Riverside

Kern County
See Bakersfield

Los Angeles
Los Angeles Paralegal Association (LAPA)
P.O. Box 71708
Los Angeles, CA 90071
310-921-3094
www.lapa.org

Background: Formed in 1977, LAPA is the largest local paralegal association in the country with over 1,000 members.

Membership: The annual membership fee is $75 ($60 for students).

National Affiliation: LAPA is an affiliate of the National Association of Legal Assistants (*www.nala.org*). At one time, it was an affiliate of the National Federation of Paralegal Associations (*www.paralegals.org*).

Newsletter: *The Reporter*, a monthly newsletter.

Services Offered: LAPA has several specialty law sections, including bankruptcy, probate & estate planning, litigation, corporate/real estate/securities, and entertainment law. Each offers programs of continuing legal education that offer CLAE/MCLE credits. LAPA awards scholarships for use toward paralegal education. Every two years, LAPA conducts a region-wide survey to bring paralegals the latest developments in employment opportunities and trends affecting salary and benefits. LAPA has a "Career Center" page on its Web site that provides leads to employment opportunities.

Newport Beach

Orange County Paralegal Association (OCPA)
P.O. Box 8512
Newport Beach, CA 92658
714-744-7747
www.ocparalegal.org

Background: Formed in 1977, OCPA was originally a section of the Orange County Bar Association. It became an independent organization in 1986. OCPA has written its own definitions for paralegals and freelance paralegals:

Paralegal: A paralegal is a non-lawyer working under the direction and supervision of a licensed attorney performing substantive legal work that would be performed by an attorney absent the paralegal. A paralegal's work is delegated by and supervised by a licensed attorney and it is the supervisory condition that the client is protected through the confidentiality, work product and attorney-client privilege doctrines.

Freelance Paralegal: A freelance paralegal is a paralegal that contracts only with attorneys or law firms for specific client matters. This individual is not an employee of an attorney or law firm, but simply a contractor for specific projects. The freelance paralegal may or may not work in the attorney's office. The freelance paralegal is an independent contractor whose work product is supervised and reviewed by the contracting attorney. The contracting attorney retains full responsibility for the freelance paralegal's work product.

Membership: The annual membership fee is $60 ($40 for students). OCPA does not allow legal document assistants (LDAs) to become members.

National Affiliation: OCPA is an affiliate of the National Association of Legal Assistants (*www.nala.org*).

Newsletter: *Compendium*, published monthly

Services Offered: OCPA conducts an annual salary survey of its members, provides discounts for continuing legal education (CLE) programs, has had scholarships for paralegal students, and makes mentors available for paralegals recently entering the field. OCPA also has a Career Center to help job seekers (click "Career Center" at *www.ocparalegal.org*). An online job bank of paralegal openings in the area is available to OCPA members (*www.ocparalegal.org/admin/ocpajoblisting.asp*).

Ethics: OCPA members are bound by the code of ethics of California Alliance of Paralegal Associations (*caparalegal.org/ethics.html*) and the National Association of Legal Assistants (*www.nala.org*).

Orange County
See Newport Beach

Redwood Empire
See Santa Rosa

Riverside
Inland Counties Association of Paralegals (ICAP)
P.O. Box 143
Riverside, CA 92502
951-750-1071
www.icaponline.org
info@icaponline.org

Background: Founded in 1985, the association serves San Bernardino and Riverside Counties.

Membership: The annual membership fee is $52 ($38 for students).

National Affiliation: ICPA is an affiliate of the National Association of Legal Assistants (*www.nala.org*).

Newsletter: *ICAPtions*, a bimonthly newsletter.

Services Offered: ICAP conducts an annual salary survey of its members and has a page on its Web site on employment opportunities that is available to members only.

Ethics: ICAP follows the ethics code of the California Alliance of Paralegal Associations (*caparalegal.org/ethics.html*) and of the National Association of Legal Assistants (*www.nala.org*).

Sacramento Valley Paralegal Association (SVPA)
P.O. Box 453
Sacramento, CA 95812
916-763-7851; 916-286-8317
www.svpa.org

Background: Founded in 1978, SVPA was formerly called the Sacramento Association of Legal Assistants.

Membership: The annual membership fee is $65 ($45 for students).

National Affiliation: SVPA is an affiliate of the National Federation of Paralegal Associations (*www.paralegals.org*).

Newsletter: *The Journal*, also available on the Web site to SVPA members only.

Services Offered: SVPA has regular continuing legal education (CLE) programs. It also has a job bank service on paralegal employment in the area. Information on positions will be made available through e-mail announcements.

San Bernardino County
See Riverside

San Diego Paralegal Association (SDPA)
P.O. Box 87449
San Diego, CA 92138-7449
619-685-3488
www.sdparalegals.org
info@sdparalegals.org

Background: SDVA was formed in 1977 when its name was the San Diego Association of Legal Assistants. There are 237 members of SDPA throughout the San Diego metropolitan area.

Membership: The annual membership fee is $75 ($40 for students).

National Affiliation: SDPA is not affiliated with a national association. It recently withdrew its affiliation with the National Federation of Paralegal Associations (*www.paralegals.org*).

Newsletter: *Pre§edents*

Services Offered: SDPA's Web site lists pro bono opportunities for paralegals and résumé tips. It has a job bank on paralegal employment openings in the area. Information on job openings is available on SDPA's employment bank bulletin board and to those who have signed onto the job bank e-mail alert list. A Yahoo group list is available for discussion of topics of interest to paralegals in the county (*groups.yahoo.com/group/SanDiego-Paralegals*). Some of the continuing legal education (CLE) programs of SDPA qualify for MCLE credit.

San Francisco Paralegal Association (SFPA)
975 Darien Way
San Francisco, CA 94127
415-777-2390
www.sfpa.com

Background: SFPA was founded in 1972 as a professional and educational organization for paralegals. One of its goals is to advocate for an "expanded role of the paralegal in the workplace and in the overall delivery of legal services."

Membership: The annual membership fee is $80 ($50 for students).

National Affiliation: SFPA is an affiliate of the National Federation of Paralegal Associations (*www.paralegals.org*).

Newsletter: *At Issue* (available online *www.sfpa.com/ai/ai.htm*).

Services Offered: SFPA has a Career Center that allows you to send your résumé to the SFPA Resume Clearinghouse, which will forward it to employers who have sent in requests for applicants. This service is free to SFPA members; non-members pay $25. SFPA also conducts an annual Career Forum that teaches job-hunting skills and provides tips on getting started in the profession. SFPA offers an annual scholarship to student members of the association.

San Francisco Trial Lawyers Association (SFTLA)
415-956-6401
www.sftla.org

SFTLA has a membership category for non-attorneys ("law office support").

Membership dues: $50

San Joaquin
See Fresno

San Jose
Paralegal Association of Santa Clara County (PASCCO)
P.O. Box 26736
San Jose, CA 95159-6736
408-235-0301
www.sccparalegal.org

Background: Founded in 1978, PASCCO has defined a paralegal as follows:

A paralegal, also known as a legal assistant, is a person who, under the supervision of an attorney, performs legal services traditionally performed by an attorney. A paralegal is qualified to perform such legal services through formal education, training, and/or experience in substantive and procedural law. Paralegals are retained or employed by law firms, corporations, governmental agencies, and other entities. Paralegals may also be authorized to perform services as sanctioned by federal or state authority.

Membership: The annual membership fee is $50 ($40 for students).

National Affiliation: PASCCO is an affiliate of the National Association of Legal Assistants (*www.nala.org*).

Newsletter: *RES IPSA LOQUITUR,* published monthly and available online.

Services Offered: PASCCO sponsors study groups for those planning to take the certification exam of the National Association of Legal Assistants. PASCCO also has a job bank listing of paralegal employment opportunities available in the area. This listing is published in the association's newsletter. PASCCO conducts a salary survey and provides a mentoring program in which "experienced PASCCO members assist students in their transition into our profession."

San Luis Obispo
Central Coast Paralegal Association (CCPA)
P.O. Box 93
San Luis Obispo, CA 93406
805-438-3762
www.ccpaslo.org

Background: CCPA was founded in 1982 to promote the paralegal profession on the Central Coast.

Membership: Regular membership is $50 ($35 for students).

National Affiliation: None

Newsletter: *NewBrief,* a bimonthly newsletter.

Services Offered: CCPA provides discounts on educational programs, scholarships for paralegal students, employment referral services, and online MCLE credit courses.

Santa Barbara Paralegal Association (SBPA)
P.O. Box 2695
Santa Barbara, CA 93120
www.sbparalegals.org

Background: Founded in 1979, the association was originally called the Legal Assistants Association of Santa Barbara. The association was formed to formalize continuing education, to exchange ideas among persons in the paralegal profession, and to encourage newcomers to the field.

Membership: The annual membership fee is $50 ($40 for students).

National Affiliation: SBPA is an affiliate of the National Association of Legal Assistants (*www.nala.org*).

Newsletter: *Law in Motion,* published monthly.

Services Offered: SBPA offers an employment referral service for paralegals and employers, scholarships for paralegal students, and numerous continuing legal education (CLE) programs.

Santa Clara County
See San Jose

Santa Rosa
Redwood Empire Legal Assistants (RELA)
P.O. Box 143
Santa Rosa, CA 95402
redwoodempirelegalassistants.com
redwwodempirela@yahoo.com

Background: RELA was founded in 1981 to serve paralegals in the Sonoma County area.

Membership: The annual membership fee is $40 ($20 for students).

National Affiliation: None

Newsletter: *RELA Newsletter,* published quarterly.

Services Offered: RELA provides educational workshops for continuing education credits; job hotline services on employment opportunities in the area; updates on issues, events, and educational opportunities; and a scholarship award to a qualified student enrolled in an area paralegal program.

Ethics: RELA has adopted its own Code of Ethics, available on its Web site.

Sequoia
See Visalia

Sonoma County
See Santa Rosa

Tulare County
See Visalia

Ventura County Paralegal Association (VCPA)
P.O. Box 24229
Ventura, CA 93002
www.vcparalegal.org

Background: VCPA was formerly called the Ventura County Association of Legal Assistants. It was founded in 1984. According to its Web site, VCPA "is an association comprised of legal para-professionals who, through their association, provide a forum for the exchange of experience, information and opinions."

Membership: The annual membership fee is $35 ($25 for students).

National Affiliation: VCALA is an affiliate of the National Association of Legal Assistants (*www.nala.org*).

Newsletter: *Verdict*, published monthly.

Services Offered: VCALA offers employment referrals, a résumé bank for paralegal employment in the area, scholarships for paralegal students, seminar discounts for continuing legal education (CLE) programs, and a review course for those taking the CLE exam of the National Association of Legal Assistants.

Ethics: VCALA members must abide by the Code of Ethics & Professional Responsibility of the National Association of Legal Assistants.

Visalia

Sequoia Paralegal Association (SPA)
P.O. Box 3884
Visalia, CA 93278
559-737-4422
www.sequoiaparalegals.com
info@sequoiaparalegal.com

Background: SPA was founded in 1986 with the goal of promoting, encouraging, and expanding the paralegal profession.

Membership: The annual membership fee is $40 ($17 for students).

National Affiliation: None

Newsletter: *Brief Encounters*, published monthly.

Services Offered: SPA provides an employment referral service for paralegals and employers and an annual membership directory. An online Job Board is available for members (*www.sequoiaparalegals.com/jobs.asp*).

C. National Paralegal Associations

There are a number of national paralegal associations that California paralegals have joined either directly or through one of their affiliates:

National Association of Legal Assistants (NALA)

National Federation of Paralegal Associations (NFPA)

NALS the Association of Legal Professionals (NALS)

American Alliance of Paralegals (AAPI)

NATIONAL ASSOCIATION OF LEGAL ASSISTANTS (NALA)
www.nala.org
Certification Awarded: Certified Legal Assistant (CLA); Certified Paralegal (CP); Advanced Certified Paralegal (ACP)
Certification Requirements: *www.nala.org/cert.htm*
www.nala.org/apcweb/index.html
Ethics Code: *www.nala.org/benefits-code.htm*
www.nala.org/98model.htm
Newsletter: *Facts and Findings* (*www.nala.org/Facts_Findings.htm*)
Continuing Legal Education: *www.nalacampus.com*
Affiliated Associations: *www.nala.org/Affiliated_Associations_Info.HTM*

NATIONAL FEDERATION OF PARALEGAL ASSOCIATIONS (NFPA)
www.paralegals.org
Certification Awarded: PACE Registered Paralegal (RP)
Certification Requirements: *www.paralegals.org* (click "PACE/RP")
Ethics Code: *www.paralegals.org* (click "Positions & Issues")
Newsletter: *National Paralegal Reporter www.paralegals.org*
Continuing Legal Education: (*www.paralegals.org*) (click "CLE")
Career Center: *www.paralegals.org* (click "NFPA Career Center")
Affiliated Associations: *www.paralegals.org* (click "About NFPA" then "Local Member Associations")

NALS THE ASSOCIATION OF LEGAL PROFESSIONALS (NALS)
www.nals.org
Certification Awarded: Professional Paralegal (PP)
Certification Requirements: *www.nals.org/certification*
Ethics Code: *www.nals.org/aboutnals/Code*
Newsletter: *@Law* (*www.nals.org/newsletters/index.html*)
Continuing Legal Education: *www.nals.org/onlinelearning/index.html*
Career Center: *www.nals.org/careercenter/index.html*
Affiliated Associations:
www.nals.org/membership/states/index.html

AMERICAN ALLIANCE OF PARALEGALS (AAPI)
www.aapipara.org
Certification Awarded: American Alliance Certified Paralegal (AACP)
Certification Requirements: *www.aapipara.org/Certification.htm*
Ethics Code: *www.aapipara.org/Ethicalstandards.htm*
Newsletter: *Alliance Echo* (*www.aapipara.org/Newsletter. htm*)
Job Bank: *www.aapipara.org/Jobbank.htm*

D. Other Law-Related Associations

American Bar Association Associate Membership for Paralegals
www.abanet.org/join

American Association of Legal Nurse Consultants Bay Area Chapter
www.bacnc.org

American Association of Legal Nurse Consultants Greater Sacramento Area Chapter
www.gsac-aalnc.org

American Association of Legal Nurse Consultants Los Angeles Chapter
www.aalncla.org

American Association of Legal Nurse Consultants Orange County Chapter
www.aalnc-orangecounty.org

American Association of Legal Nurse Consultants San Diego Chapter
www.aalncsandiego.org

California Association of Labor Relations Officers
www.calro.org

California Association of Licensed Investigators
www.cali-pi.org

California Association of Photocopiers & Process Servers
www.capps.org

California Background Investigators Association
www.scbia.com

California District Attorney Investigators Association
www.cdaia.org

California Society of Enrolled Agents
www.csea.org

Association of Legal Administrators, East Bay Chapter
www.ebala.org

Association of Legal Administrators, Golden Gate Chapter
www.alasf.org

Association of Legal Administrators, Greater Los Angeles Chapter
www.glaala.org/clubportal/glaala/index.cfm

Association of Legal Administrators, San Diego Chapter
www.alasandiego.org

Defense Investigators Association of California
www.cdia.org

Forensic Expert Witness Association
www.forensic.org

Bay Area Legal Secretaries Forum
www.balsf.org

Beverly Hills/Century City Legal Secretaries Association
www.bhcclsa.org

Capitol City Legal Professionals Association (Sacramento) (a local association of legal secretaries)
www.capitolcitylpa.org

Mt Diablo Legal Secretaries Association (Contra Costa County)
www.angelfire.com/ca6/mdlsa

NALS (Association for Legal Professionals) of Orange County
www.nalsoc.org

Orange Country Legal Secretaries Association
www.oclsa.org

Palo Alto Legal Secretaries Association
www.palsa.net

Sacramento Legal Secretaries Association
www.slsa.org

San Diego Legal Secretaries Association
www.sdlsa.org

San Fernando Valley Legal Secretaries Association
www.sfvlsa.com

San Mateo County Legal Secretaries Association
www.smclsa.com

Santa Clara County Legal Secretaries Association
www.santaclaralegalsecrty.org

Legal Secretaries International
www.lsi.org/localassociations.php

California Lawyers' Assistants Secretaries & Students (Alameda)
www.lawguru.com/users/law/class/class.html

E. Something to Check

1. Examine any two online paralegal newsletters. Find an article or position statement in each that covers the same issue involving the regulation of California paralegals. Compare what each says about the issue.
2. For each of the following three topics, which paralegal association has the most comprehensive links: (a) California law, (b) paralegal employment, and (c) litigation services.

1.5 Sources of CLE for Paralegals

A. Introduction
B. CLE Options
C. Something to Check

A. Introduction

CLE (continuing legal education) is training in the law (often short term) that one receives after completing formal legal training. There are four reasons CLE is important for California paralegals.

First, section 6450(d) of the Business & Professions Code requires four hours of CLE in ethics every two years, and four hours of CLE in general law or specialized law every two years. This requirement is referred to as mandatory continuing legal education (MCLE). (See the text of the statute imposing this requirement and related materials in section 1.2.)

Second, CLE allows paralegals to keep current on changing laws, new developments in law office management, and the dynamics of the practice of law.

Third, CLE programs can be an excellent way to network with paralegals and other professionals in the field of law.

Fourth, if you have received national paralegal certification, you must submit proof of compliance with the CLE requirements for maintaining your certification. For an explanation of these requirements, see:

- National Association of Legal Assistants (*www.nala.org*) for being a Certified Legal Assistant/Certified Paralegal;
- National Federation of Paralegal Associations (*www.paralegals.org*) for being a PACE Registered Paralegal;
- American Alliance of Paralegals (*www.aapipara.org*) for being an American Alliance Certified Paralegal;
- NALS—the Association for Legal Professionals (*www.nals.org*) for being a Professional Paralegal

Not every CLE course will meet the mandatory continuing legal education requirements of section 6459(d) for California paralegals. The course must be approved by the State Bar of California as a "Minimum Continuing Legal Education" course (MCLE). (This abbreviation sometimes also refers to mandatory continuing legal education.)

Paralegals must keep records of the courses they take and certify to their supervising lawyers that they have been taken. (For an example of such a form, see Exhibit 1.2B in section 1.2.) Furthermore, keeping careful records of your attendance at CLE courses and events helps demonstrate your expertise and can be a marketing tool when seeking a raise or other employment.

On the tax deductibility of CLE, see Appendix A of Part 2.

B. CLE Options

Your Local Paralegal Association

Go to the Web site of your paralegal association (see section 1.4). Click on "Education," "Continuing Legal Education," "CLE," or "MCLE" to find out if the association sponsors or links to MCLE-qualified programs. If there is a search box on the site, type in these terms. If there is an e-mail link to the association, send a message inquiring about CLE opportunities.

Other Paralegal Associations in the State

Also check the Web sites of other paralegal associations in the state. They may offer online CLE that you can take from any location. For example, LAPA, the Los Angeles Paralegal Association, announces on its Web site that "LAPA is an MCLE-approved provider of continuing legal education. In addition to our many local face-to-face seminars, LAPA now offers online continuing education." (*www.lapa.org*)

Taecan and California Alliance of Paralegal Associations
www.taecan.com/providers/capa.asp
www.taecan.com

Legal Administrator and Other Non-attorney Legal Organizations

Check the Web sites of related associations in California such as chapters of the Association of Legal Administrators (see the links at the end of section 1.4). They may lead you to additional CLE options you should consider.

National Paralegal Associations

Check the availability of online CLE from the national paralegal associations:

National Association of Legal Assistants
www.nalacampus.com

National Federation of Paralegal Associations
www.paralegals.org
(Click "CLE")

American Alliance of Paralegals
www.aapipara.org/Calendar.htm

NALS—the Association for Legal Professionals
www.nals.org
www.nals.org/onlinelearning/index.html

Continuing Education of the Bar (CEB)
www.ceb.com/capa
(This site is anxious to obtain the business of paralegals who are members of associations affiliated with the California Alliance of Paralegal Associations (CAPA): "Welcome CAPA members! CEB Makes It Easier to Meet Your CLE Requirements and Buy Practice Tools." Of course, this site would also be delighted to sell CLE courses and other materials to paralegals who are not connected with CAPA or any paralegal association.)

State Bar of California
www.calbar.ca.gov
(Type "paralegal MCLE" in search box.)

Approved CLE Providers for Attorneys
www.calbar.ca.gov/state/calbar/calbar_generic.jsp?cid=10962&id=4986
(This site will lead you to an extensive list of CLE providers for attorneys in California. Go to the Web sites of any of these providers to inquire what might be available for paralegals.)

Legal Ethics (Internet for Lawyers)
www.netforlawyers.com/index.htm
www.netforlawyers.com/online_mcle_ethics_special.htm
("California . . . paralegals can satisfy all of their required MCLE credits by completing the . . . MCLE quizzes" on this site.)

Estrin LegalEd
www.estrinlegaled.com
www.careercoachesinternational.com
("A four-hour workshop designed specifically for paralegals by Estrin Professional." "Estrin Professional Careers certifies that this activity has been approved for 4 hours legal ethics MCLE credit by the State Bar of California.")

Center for Continuing Legal Education
www.cce-mcle.com/index.html

Your Local Bar Association
Go to the Web site of your local bar association (see section 3.4). Click "Education," "Continuing Legal Education," or "MCLE" to find out if the association sponsors MCLE-qualified programs that can be taken by paralegals.

West Legal Education Center
westlegaledcenter.com
(In the search boxes or pull-down menus, find California programs. Then type in or click "Paralegal" to find options.)

LexisNexis (Zimmermann's Guide to CLE)
www.lexisnexis.com/infopro/zimmerman/disp.aspx?z=1337

California Association of Legal Document Assistants
www.calda.org
("On April 15, 2003, the California Association of Legal Document Assistants was approved by the State Bar of California for mandatory continuing legal education (MCLE").)

International Paralegal Management Association
www.paralegalmanagement.org
(Click "Events" then "Webinar")

American Bar Association CLE
www.abanet.org/cle/clenow

Washburn (CLE Guide)
www.washlaw.edu/postlaw/seminars.html
www.washlaw.edu/subject/continuing.ed.html

Practicing Law Institute
www.pli.edu/public/mcle/default.asp

General Search Engines
Type "california CLE" in
www.google.com
search.msn.com
metasearch.com

Yahoo CLE Directory
dir.yahoo.com/Government/Law/Continuing_Legal_Education

MCLE Compliance Logs for Paralegals
www.ocparalegal.org/docs/MCLELog.pdf
www.caparalegal.org/compliancelog.doc

C. Something to Check

Pick an area of the law and find five different CLE courses on that area that would qualify for California MCLE credit. Describe and compare the five courses.

APPENDIX A

Paralegals in Court Opinions

A. Introduction

One sign of the prominence of paralegals is the extent to which paralegal issues have been discussed in court opinions. This section demonstrates this prominence by presenting excerpts and summaries from a wide range of these opinions. Some of the opinions raise ethical issues, although most of the opinions cover broader themes such as the award of paralegal fees, paralegals as jurors, litigation brought by paralegals, the consequences of paralegal mistakes, and inmates as paralegals. Of course, even these themes have ethical implications, but a more comprehensive treatment of ethics will come later in sections 3.2 and 3.3.

To compile the material for this section, we did a search on Westlaw (WL) that asked for every case that mentions paralegals, legal assistants, legal document assistants, unlawful detainer assistants, or bankruptcy petition preparers.

Westlaw Query:

paralegal "legal assistant" "legal document assistant" "unlawful detainer assistant" "bankruptcy petition preparer"

This query finds every case that mentions the word paralegal or any of the phrases in quotation marks. The database in Westlaw selected to run this query was CA-CS-ALL. It contains all published and unpublished cases from the following courts:

Supreme Court of California
California Court of Appeal
California Superior Court
State Bar Court of California
United States Court of Appeals (9th Circuit)
United States District Courts in California
United States Bankruptcy Courts in California
United States Supreme Court (when the issue involves California)

The query produced over a thousand "hits" from which excerpts have been selected for this section. We have included opinions that will be (or have been) published in traditional reporters such as California Reporter (CalRptr), Pacific Reporter (P.2d), Bankruptcy Reporter (B.C.), etc. We have also included unpublished opinions (or opinions that have not been certified for publication) whenever they say anything of interest to the paralegal community. If you wish further information about any of the opinions, e.g., whether any have been reversed or otherwise modified on appeal, check the citations in citators such as KeyCite and Shepard's.

B. Abbreviations

BankryCDCal: US Bankruptcy Court, Central District, California
BankryNDCal: US Bankruptcy Court, Northern District, California
BAP9: US Bankruptcy Appellate Panel of the Ninth Circuit
BkrtcyCDCal: US Bankruptcy Court, Central District, California
BkrtcySDCal: US Bankruptcy Court, Southern District, California
B.R. Bankruptcy Reporter
Cal: California Supreme Court
CalApp: California Court of Appeals
CalBarCt: State Bar Court of California
CalRptr: California Reporter
CalSuperior: California Superior Court
CA9: United States Court of Appeals (9th Circuit)
CDCal: United States District Court, Central District, California
EDCal: United States District Court, Eastern District
NDCal: United States District Court, Northern District, California
NOP: Not officially published
NSP: Not selected for publication in the Federal Reporter
SDCal: United States District Court, Southern District, California
SCt: Supreme Court Reporter
US: United States Supreme Court
WL: Westlaw

Westlaw citations are provided by year and document number. For example, 2003 WL 365353 refers to document number 365353 for the year 2002 in the Westlaw system.

C. Case summaries

Here are the major categories of issues covered by these courts when they mentioned paralegals, legal assistants, or other nonattorneys involved in the delivery of legal services:

Categories of Issues Raised
Paralegal fees
Overstaffing with paralegals
Record keeping and billing
Attorneys performing paralegal tasks
Paralegals performing clerical tasks
Paralegal supervision
Miscellaneous violations
Attorney-client privilege
Work-product rule
Paralegal mistakes
Crimes and fraud
Paralegal assistance to inmates
Legal document assistants
Bankruptcy petition preparers
Unlawful detainer assistants

Paralegal Fees: Introduction

The Value of Paralegals

- A competent staff to assist an attorney is a necessary element of the attorney's fee. Paralegals and other assistants can free attorneys to spend their more costly time for greater productivity in more important areas. In the instant case, allowing an attorney's paralegal assistant to be included as "reasonable attorney fees" not only saves the attorney time, but would save the employer [in this workers' compensation case] costs as well. Paralegals can do some of the work that the attorney would have to do anyway and can do it at substantially less cost per hour, resulting in less total cost billed to the employer. Therefore, paralegal time at paralegal rates can reasonably be counted along with the attorney's time as "attorney fees." *Todd Shipyards Corp. v. Director, Office of Workers' Compensation Programs*, 545 F.2d 1176, 1182 (CA9 1976).
- The Court is particularly impressed by counsel's efforts to keep litigation costs low in this case. The Court also notes that counsel made extensive use of paralegals, to the extent that several depositions were conducted with an attorney and a paralegal rather than two attorneys. *Lubliner v. Maxtor Corp.*, 1990 WL 41409 (NDCal 1990).
- Counsel's delegation of work to paralegals demonstrates a form of billing judgment. Legal assistants prepared materials including binders and exhibits for use in trial and communicated with court personnel regarding the organization of evidence. Two of the legal assistants have over a decade of legal experience each. The expertise possessed by the paralegal staff justifies the rates charged. The court finds the requested rates reasonable. *Oberfelder v. City of Petaluma, 2002 WL 4723086 (NDCal 2002).*
- The court demonstrated considerable knowledge of the contributions made by legal assistants to the attorneys, noting "As a matter of practice, most attorneys engaged in the antitrust practice use such legal assistants, particularly in digesting and indexing discovery and trial materials, much of the work heretofore performed by relatively inexperienced lawyers. . . . As a matter of policy, the use of paralegal help in this fashion greatly reduces the cost of legal services to the public and is thus a practice to be encouraged." The court then approved the award of fees for such paralegal help after adjusting it slightly downward. *Pacific Coast Agr. Export Ass'n v. Sunkist Growers*, 526 F.2d 1196, 1210 (CA9 1975).
- A declaration from the landlord's attorney represented that Ms. Silva was a certified paralegal and her work was billed separately, apart from attorney time, to the client. Many statutory provisions in California have been interpreted to include paralegal fees in "attorney's fees." (See, Annot., Attorney's Fees: Cost of Services Provided by Paralegals or the Like as Compensable Element of Award in State Court. (1989) 73 A.L.R.4th 938, 949 [collecting California cases].) We view the objective meaning of "attorney's fees" as used in the Farm Lease to allow the inclusion of reasonable paralegal fees, which were billed separately and were not part of overhead included in the hourly rate charged by the landlord's attorneys. *Gunter v. Perrett*, 2002 WL 337526 (CalApp 2002) (NOP).

Paralegal Fees: Attorneys Performing Paralegal Tasks

- Paralegal tasks should not be undertaken by senior partners who seek compensation for their time at premium rates. *In re Equity Funding Corp.*, 438 F.Supp. 1303, 1330 (DCCal 1977).
- The defendant argues that Horner's billing of 77.8 hours to prepare a chronology of documents in this case should be billed at the paralegal rate rather than an attorney rate. Attorney Horner describes the preparation of the chronology as "reviewing of the documents and selecting the pertinent facts and information." The Court agrees that this is a paralegal task. "[W]hen a lawyer spends time on tasks that are easily delegable to non-professional assistance, legal service rates are not applicable." [citing a 10th Circuit case] *Mogck v. Unum Life Ins. Co. of America*, 289 F. Supp. 2d 1181, 1193 (SDCal 2003).
- Time spent on work that could have been performed by paralegals has been reduced. An attorney spent 7.75 hours summarizing the deposition

of Taylor. The activity could have been performed by a paralegal. *Rothfarb v. Hambrecht*, 649 F.Supp. 183 (NDCal 1986).

- The City points to entries in the time sheets as constituting clear examples of billing abuse. Many of these entries have to do with time billed for clerical matters such as the filing of pleadings and the travel time associated therewith. Appellees' counsel are not entitled, the City argues, to attorneys' fees for the performance of such tasks. We agree with the City. In *Missouri v. Jenkins*, 109 S.Ct. 2463 (1989), the Supreme Court noted that "purely clerical or secretarial tasks should not be billed at a paralegal [or lawyer's] rate, regardless of who performs them . . . '[The] dollar value [of such nonlegal work] is not enhanced just because a lawyer does it.'" It simply is not reasonable for a lawyer to bill, at her regular hourly rate, for tasks that a nonattorney employed by her could perform at a much lower cost. *Davis v. City and County of San Francisco*, 976 F.2d 1536, 1543 (CA9 1992).
- Appropriate billing judgment should have been exercised by the attorney. Her tasks were ones which could have been accomplished by paralegals—for example, .4 hours, preparing change of attorney forms; .4 hours, preparing and filing automatic stay notice. The Court reduces her time to that of a paralegal. *In re Maruko Inc.*, 160 B.R. 633, 642 (BkrtcySDCal 1993).
- Malpass argues that the trial court erred when it deducted fees based upon Malpass's failure "to properly utilize junior associates or paralegals for less sophisticated legal tasks." Malpass claims that his firm's paralegals were not sophisticated litigation paralegals and were unable to perform the services he performed. Malpass argued below that he should not be penalized because he is a sole practitioner. He also states that the trial court did not point to a specific instance in which a paralegal was available to perform particular services. Malpass misperceives the trial court's ruling. Although the trial court reasoned that certain tasks could have been performed by a paralegal, it also stated: "Even if he did not have any other staff members capable of performing less sophisticated legal tasks, Malpass is still not entitled to bill at a partner's rate for such work." *In re Music Merchants*, 208 B.R. 944, 948 (BAP9 1997).

Paralegal Fees: Paralegals Performing Clerical Tasks

- Thirteen hours spent xeroxing are hereby deducted as not properly compensable paralegal time. *U.S. v. City and County of San Francisco*, 748 F.Supp. 1416, 1426 (NDCal 1990).
- Fees incurred for administrative tasks is not compensable. This maxim applies without regard to whether an attorney or a paralegal performs the tasks. The time entries for services that are primarily clerical or ministerial in nature total $51,225.45 and are disallowed. *In re Sonicblue*, 2004 WL 856624 (BkrtcyNDCal 2004)
- Purely clerical or secretarial tasks should not be billed at a paralegal rate, regardless of who performs them. In this case, the detailed billing summaries indicate that paralegals performed, and billed for, such tasks as inputting or typing data into a computer; bates stamping; preparing mailings; and copying and faxing. This Court believes that such tasks could have been performed by a person without any legal training at a much lower rate. Accordingly, the number of paralegal hours must be reduced by 30% from 3,014.3 to 2,110.01. *Howard v. Shay*, 1998 WL 566648 (CDCal 1998).

Paralegal Fees: Inadequate Recordkeeping/Timesheets/Documentation

- This court was not provided with any explanation of the complexity of the tasks for which billing is sought. The organization of the trustee's files appeared to be routine secretarial work, for which the attorneys could not be compensated at the hourly rate of a paralegal providing this service. *In re Garcia*, 317 B.R. 810 (BkrtcySDCal 2004).
- Plaintiffs make no attempt to distinguish between the skill or experience of the paralegals. Indeed, Plaintiffs attribute some 244 hours to various paralegals without any indication of their identity, much less their experience. *Howard v. Shay*, 1998 WL 566648 (CDCal 1998).
- In awarding attorney fees to the prevailing plaintiff in this case, the United States Census Bureau and Bureau of Labor Statistics (BLS) data established that a reasonable hourly rate for attorneys in San Francisco area was $190, and a reasonable hourly rate for legal assistants was $70. The court concedes that the census and BLS data are not likely the "best data available." Nor does the court contend that its simple methodology could not be refined. The court uses this data because the parties have provided nothing better. *Yahoo!, Inc. v. Net Games, Inc.*, 329 F. Supp. 2d 1179 (NDCal 2004).
- Appellant has not explained why it was necessary to spend so many paralegal hours on this case. Nor has it justified a paralegal hourly rate of $150. It "presented no evidence that $150 per hour was the 'fair market rate for similar services' in Los Angeles County, or that it was the rate counsel billed clients for paralegal time. In the absence of evidence to the contrary, we cannot say that the trial court abused its discretion in awarding an hourly paralegal rate of $40." *West Century v. City Of Inglewood*, 2004 WL 886384 (CalApp 2004) (NOP).

- In this case an objection is raised to some of the hours billed by the paralegal, Ms. Camp, because they constitute clerical work. Non-billable hours involving saving documents as PDF files were "block billed" with hours including billable document preparation tasks. Courts generally frown on block billing where discrete and unrelated tasks are lumped into one entry, as the practice can make it impossible to determine the reasonableness of the hours spent on each task. In block billing, billable tasks are very difficult to separate from the non-billable tasks. Ms. Camp spent around 60 hours assisting with preparation of many of the court documents in this case and saving them as PDF files. Without more information, it is almost impossible to ascertain if she spent more time preparing or saving these documents. This Court's best estimate is that a 50 percent reduction for these block-billed entries is appropriate. *Navarro v. General Nutrition Corp.*, 2004 WL 2648373 (NDCal 2004).
- 49.1 hours billed by legal assistant Pickett for work described as "Review and analysis of newly received case materials and update file the same" is unreasonably vague. Accordingly, the total fee award is reduced by $3,682. *Oberfelder v. City of Petaluma*, 2002 WL 4723086 (NDCal 2002).
- Review of the timesheets also reveals 195.75 hours of work performed by paralegals at hourly rates ranging from $105 per hour to $135 per hour. Counsel fails to address the reasonableness of the time expended for these charges and the reasonableness of the hourly rates charged. The timesheets reveal paralegals performing "filing" at a rate of $105 per hour, more than twenty-six hours of "document organization" at a rate of $105 to $110 per hour, and "misc. projects" at a rate of $105 per hour. In addition, the timesheets note two hours spent on "delivery" at a rate of $115 per hour. In the absence of evidence, or even argument, demonstrating that under the circumstances of this case . . . that $105 per hour is a reasonable rate for filing and "misc. projects," that $110 per hour is a reasonable rate for "document organization," and that $115 per hour is a reasonable rate for "delivery," the court cannot find that the requested fee award is reasonable based upon an analysis of the timesheets. *In re Brooktree Securities Litigation*, 915 F.Supp. 193, 198 (SDCal 1996).
- The Court could not determine why it was necessary to "review documents" for up to ten hours a day, and why attorneys—both partners and associates—were reviewing documents instead of paralegals. *Feuerstein v. Burns*, 569 F.Supp. 268, 273 (DCCal 1983).
- The declaration must also set forth (a) the qualifications, experience and role of each attorney or paralegal for whom fees are sought; (b) the normal rate ordinarily charged for each in the relevant time period; (c) how the rates were comparable to prevailing rates in the community for like-skilled professionals; and (d) proof that "billing judgment" was exercised. On the latter point, the declaration should describe adjustments made to eliminate duplication, excess, associate-turnover expense, and so forth. The declaration must identify the records used to compile the entries and, specifically, state whether and the extent to which the records were contemporaneous versus retroactively prepared. It must state the extent to which any entries include estimates (and what any estimates were based on). Estimates and/or use of retroactively-made records may or may not be allowed, depending on the facts and circumstances. *Z-Rock Communications Corp. v. William A. Exline*, 2004 WL 2496158 (NDCal 2004).

Paralegal Fees: Overstaffing/Excess Time

Outlandish, to be honest about it

- "And I certainly don't mean to impugn Mr. Thompson. I respect him greatly. I simply think that the file was overworked by certain associates [and] paralegals in that firm, and that sixty-some thousand dollars for a two-day court trial is not only unreasonable, I think it's outlandish, to be honest." *Bains v. First American Title*, 2003 WL 1084681 (CalApp 2003) (NOP).

Paralegal took too much time

- The 106.35 hours spent by a paralegal in summarizing 15 deposition transcripts and charging $70.00 per hour is unreasonable. The hours will be reduced to 75 so as to compensate for both the excessive amount of time spent and the relatively high hourly rate for paralegal services. *E.E.O.C. v. Bruno's Restaurant*, 1990 WL 279507 (SDCal 1990).

800 hours for one motion?

- Eight hundred law clerk and paralegal hours to handle a single motion for contempt arising out of employer's non-compliance with consent decree in sex discrimination action was unreasonable. The number of claimed hours would be reduced by one-half. *Bernardi v. Yeutter*, 754 F.Supp. 743 (NDCal 1990).

Extraordinary examples of inflated billing

- On February 13th and 14th, one of the firm's legal assistants expended and billed for 15.5 hours of organizing and filing unidentified documents. For this service, the firm is seeking remuneration in the amount of $992.50. Trial preparation appears to have commenced around March 21st, and lasted through the trial beginning April 8th.

Illustrative of the overstaffing and inflated billing practices for this period of litigation occurred on April 4th, when four attorneys and three legal assistants billed for a total of 66.75 hours for a variety of trial preparation tasks. The amount sought for this single day of legal work is $7,307. It would not be difficult to identify further extraordinary examples of either inflated billing, inefficient practice or lapses in billing judgment. In my opinion, the instances of unreasonably expended hours are too numerous to address specifically. *Real v. Continental Group, Inc.*, 653 F.Supp. 736, 741 (NDCal 1987).

Why were two paralegals in court for the entire trial?

- This Court sees no reason that two attorneys and two paralegals were needed in court for the entire trial; thus, the paralegals' trial times should be subtracted. The Court deducts 90 hours from each paralegal's hours to eliminate the time spent sitting in trial. *Exhibitors' Service, Inc. v. American Multi-Cinema*, 583 F.Supp. 1186, 1193 (DCCal 1984)

9.5 hours of paralegal time for this task is unreasonable

- With respect to the preparation of the fee application, the firm spent 13.8 hours. The firm submits that 13.8 hours is reasonable for this case particularly where 75 percent of the time was spent by a paralegal. The firm's paralegal spent approximately 9.5 hours in preparing the fee application. No information is provided regarding the educational background or experience of the paralegal, but this was a simple fee application consisting of nine pages of narrative, time records totaling forty-eight pages, and ten pages of exhibits. Nine and one-half hours of paralegal time for the preparation of this pleading is unreasonable, particularly in an experienced bankruptcy law firm. *In re Garcia*, 317 B.R. 810 (BkrtcySDCal 2004).

Paralegal fees: other issues

Billing fraud

- The firm's fees included billings by a single attorney for more than 24 hours in a day and for 78 hours over a four-day period. Paralegals and secretaries were sometimes billed as attorneys, at attorney rates. *Center Foundation v. Chicago Ins.*, 227 Cal.App.3d 547, 555, 278 CalRptr 13, 18 (CalApp 1991).

No paralegal fees in a contingency fee case

- Attorneys seeking recovery of costs in a successful securities fraud litigation were not entitled to claim paralegal expenses as a separate cost item; paralegals were legal professionals whose time is recovered through an agreed upon contingency fee for services. "Paralegals should be treated just like associates or other salaried professionals." Their compensation is already included in the percentage fee. *Morganstein v. Esber*, 768 F.Supp. 725, 726 (CDCal 1991).

Paralegal fees and paralegal educational requirements

- If a paralegal fails to meet the educational requirements of California law for paralegals, can the law firm still collect paralegal fees for that paralegal? The trial court noted that compliance with the educational requirements of Business & Professions Code section 6450 is not a prerequisite to recovery of paralegal fees. *Clement v. Keller* 2004 WL 1175265 (CalApp 2004) (NOP).

Paralegal volunteer

- The trial court declined to award plaintiffs compensation for 850 hours of paralegal time because it was of unknown value and was volunteered. In recent years, awards of attorneys' fees for paralegal time have become commonplace. Moreover, it is now clear that the fact that services were volunteered is not a ground for diminishing an award of attorneys' fees. [T]he amount of the award is to be made on the basis of the reasonable market value of the services rendered, and not on the salary paid. Exclusion of paralegal time from the award on the ground that it was volunteered, therefore, was improper. *Sundance v. Municipal Court*, 192 Cal.App.3d 268, 274, 237 CalRptr 269, 273 (CalApp 1987)

Paralegal supervision

Failure to supervise paralegal

- The attorney was "obliged to supervise the work of his paralegal for correctness." *Hawks v. Hawks* 2005 WL 236456 (CalApp 2005) (NOP).
- Attorney discipline upheld. "His health problems provide no excuse for his authorizing a paralegal to sign his name on habeas corpus petitions that [the attorney] did not read." *In re White*, 121 CalApp4th 1453, 1486, 18 CalRptr3d 444, 470 (CalApp 2004).
- The law firm failed to act "competently" in representing bankruptcy debtors, in violation of its responsibilities under California Rules of Professional Conduct, to the extent that law firm allowed paralegals to complete bankruptcy petitions and schedules and to perform other work of a legal character without adequate attorney supervision. This failure of supervision also created a situation

in which paralegals were making final decisions on how important legal aspects of individual bankruptcy filings, such as the claiming of exemptions, should be handled; and this constituted the unauthorized practice of law by those paralegals. *In re Hessinger & Associates*, 192 B.R. 211 (NDCal 1996).

- The attorney in this case conceded that he did not pay proper attention to his personal injury cases and delegated far too many duties to his staff. His paralegal, Kim Burgess-Orlov, apparently handled these duties very well. Yet when Burgess-Orlov was out of the office from October to January, the attorney depended on another employee, who lacked Burgess-Orlov's abilities. Burgess-Orlov testified that when she returned to the office in January, she found that it was in a shambles, that nothing had been done to manage the personal injury cases, that matters were not calendared, that depositions and court dates had been missed, and that cases had been dismissed for failure to attend. *Matter of Sampson*, 1994 WL 454888, 3 Cal. State Bar Ct. Rptr. 119 (CalBarCt 1994).
- Respondent hired Gray to work as a clerk and legal assistant in his personal injury practice. A few months later, respondent heard Gray state to clients that Gray was his partner. Although he told Gray that the statement was improper, he did not protest decisively because he found Gray good for business and wanted to keep Gray's services. *In Matter of Steele*, 1997 WL 438845 (CalBarCt 1997).

Attorney-client privilege and work product

Attorney-client privilege applies to paralegals

- The attorney-client privilege protects communications between a client and its attorney. As a general rule, the privilege does not extend to communications between either the client or its attorney and a third party. There are some well accepted exceptions to this rule. For example, the privilege will protect communications made by the client to the attorney's paralegal. *U.S. v. ChevronTexaco Corp.*, 241 F.Supp.2d 1065, 1070 (NDCal 2002).

Work product rule and paralegals

- The attorney's work product doctrine covers documents created not only by an attorney, but also his agents or employees, including his paralegal. *Rico v. Mitsubishi*, 10 Cal.Rptr.3d 601, 609 (CalApp 2004).

Paralegal notes are not discoverable

- It appears that the trial court inadvertently required production of memorandums and notes of a paralegal in Gallagher's law firm who was present at the briefing of 11 March. Such materials, the work product of Gallagher's law firm, are not discoverable. *Insurance Co. of North America v. Superior Court*, 108 Cal.App.3d 758, 771, 166 Cal.Rptr. 880, 888 (CalApp 1980).

Paralegal mistakes

I meant to say "in favor of" our client

- An attorney's legal assistant mistyped the word "against" instead of the words "in favor of." As a result, the typed document mistakenly offers to settle the matter for a judgment *against* the attorney's client in the amount of $149,999. Not surprisingly, the opposing party jumps at the offer. On appeal, this was held to be an excusable error. The error was a clerical or ministerial mistake that anybody could have made, and the opposing party took unfair advantage of the mistake and suffered no apparent prejudice. *Zamora v. Clayborn*, 28 Cal.4th 249, 47 P.3d 1056 (2002).

Any paralegal should have been able to read the rule correctly

- In this case, the district court did not abuse its discretion in finding excusable neglect for the untimely filing of a notice of appeal due to the failure of the law firm's calendaring system, which resulted when a paralegal misread a clear rule. Therefore the court did not abuse its discretion in granting extension of time to file a notice of appeal. This is so even though "any lawyer or paralegal should have been able to read the rule correctly." In the modern world of legal practice, the delegation of repetitive legal tasks to paralegals has become a necessary fixture. Such delegation has become an integral part of the struggle to keep down the costs of legal representation. Moreover, the delegation of such tasks to specialized, well-educated non-lawyers may well ensure greater accuracy in meeting deadlines than a practice of having each lawyer in a large firm calculate each filing deadline anew. The task of keeping track of necessary deadlines will involve some delegation. The responsibility for the error falls on the attorney regardless of whether the error was made by an attorney or a paralegal. *See* Model Rules of Professional Conduct, Rule 5.5 comment 2 (2002) ("This Rule does not prohibit a lawyer from employing the services of paraprofessionals and delegating functions to them, so long as the lawyer supervises the delegated work and retains responsibility for their work."). We hold that the delegation of the task of ascertaining the deadline was not per se inexcusable neglect. *Pincay v. Andrews*, 389 F.3d 853, 856 (CA9 2004).

Default judgment results from paralegal error

- A default judgment resulted from an error made by a paralegal. The paralegal's mistake is attributable to the attorney responsible for supervising the paralegal. *Hu v. Fang*, 104 Cal.App.4th 61, 63, 127 Cal.Rptr.2d 756, 757 (CalApp 2002).

Failure to find out that the filing fees have been increased

- It is undisputed that the complaint was untimely filed. Appellant's counsel depended upon the erroneous decision of a legal assistant, who did not contact the clerk for up-to-date information on the amount of the required filing fee for a complaint in that county, as to the amount of that fee. *Mirvis v. Crowder*, 32 Cal.App.4th 1684, 1688, 38 Cal.Rptr.2d 644, 646 (CalApp 1995).

Privileged documents inadvertently disclosed

- Inadvertent disclosure during discovery by no stretch of the imagination shows consent to the disclosure. It merely demonstrates that the poor paralegal or junior associate who was lumbered with the tedious job of going through voluminous files and records in preparation for a document production may have missed something. The challenges posed by a large-scale document production are familiar. A two-layer system is often used. First, there is pre-production review in which relatively ministerial determinations are made by employees of the producing party or by clerks, paralegals, or inexperienced associates employed by a law firm. Second, the final decision about what documents should or should not be produced is made by experienced in-house or outside lawyers. Using paralegals instead of attorneys to conduct a privilege review was reasonable only in exigent circumstances and if the paralegals are properly supervised. *U.S. ex rel. Bagley v. TRW, Inc.*, 204 F.R.D. 170 (CDCal 2001) (see also 69 Cal.Rptr.2d 389, 398).

Attorney is not allowed to "foist off" responsibility on a paralegal

- The attorney filed a declaration stating that the requests for extension of time were prepared "on a rush basis" by a paralegal he thought was familiar with the procedures for obtaining a continuance and who he believed had attempted to notify opposing counsel but was unable to do so. In response, the court said, "We reject these evasive explanations. An attorney who himself falsely represents under penalty of perjury that he notified counsel or tried but was unable to do so cannot foist off the responsibility on a paralegal." *Bryan v. Bank of America*, 86 Cal.App.4th 185, 193, 103 Cal.Rptr.2d 148, 153 (CalApp 2001).

Miscellaneous errors

- Paralegal prepares an invalid will in which he (the paralegal) was named executor. *In re Estate of McCune*, 2004 WL 348925 (CalApp 2004) (NOP)
- On appeal, Marroquin argues that, following her deportation order, a paralegal advised her to file an adjustment of status application with the Immigration and Naturalization Service. This advice was incorrect. Once an alien has been placed in deportation proceedings, such motions can only be pursued in the immigration court. *Marroquin v. I.N.S.*, 42 Fed.Appx. 952, 952, 2002 WL 1791530 (CA9 2002) (NSP).

Paralegal involved with crime or fraud

- An investigator testified that in a formal organized fraud ring, there is generally an attorney office, a chiropractic or medical office, a body shop, and a capper. Some fraud rings stage collisions. Organized rings are most prevalent in Southern California. The most common form of fraud is in loosely organized rings. A ring might not always use the same body shop or chiropractic office. When a person goes to a law firm involved in this, he or she usually meets with a legal assistant, not an attorney. Sometimes the capper runs the office and the attorney just provides a law license to facilitate claims. *People v. Hernandez*, 2003 WL 23101085 (CalApp 2003) (NOP).
- Defendant, employed as a paralegal, "stole money by pretending to be an attorney and making other false representations that enabled him to collect "retainer" fees and gain access to victims' bank accounts and credit cards. He was convicted at a bench trial on numerous counts of grand theft by false pretenses, attempted grand theft, and the unauthorized practice of law." *People v. Hylland*, 2002 WL 31839369 (CalApp 2002) (NOP).
- Martinez describes himself as a self-taught paralegal with 25 years' experience at 12 different law firms. While employed as an office assistant at a firm in Santa Ana, California, he was accused of converting $6,000 of client money to his own use. He was charged in a two-count information with grand theft and the fraudulent appropriation of the property of another. He chose to represent himself at trial before a jury. The jury acquitted him on Count 1, grand theft, but convicted him on Count 2, embezzlement. *Martinez v. Court of Appeal*, 120 S.Ct. 684, 687 (US 2000).
- This proceeding concerns serious misconduct by respondent, John M. Rubens, in two successive personal injury practices dominated by paralegals and other non-attorneys. Rubens joined the first practice shortly after his admission to the bar. Nine months later, he left this practice because he

realized his lack of appropriate control over non-attorney staff and because he suspected insurance fraud and the use of cappers, although he had no concrete evidence of such. Within a few months, he joined the second practice, where he again failed to exercise proper control over non-attorney staff. He remained at the second practice for eighteen months, twice as long as he stayed at the first practice, although he not only suspected insurance fraud and the use of cappers, but also knew about forgeries and significant misappropriations. *Matter of Rubens*, 1995 WL 649843 (CalBarCt 1995).

Paralegal assistance to inmates

- If a prison does not provide alternatives, it cannot prevent one inmate from giving legal assistance to another. Otherwise, the inmate in need of help is denied his or her constitutional right of access to the courts. Only reasonable restrictions can be imposed on such assistance. *In re Harrell* 87 Cal.Rptr. 504, 510 (Cal 1970).
- Prison officials typically provide prison law libraries or legal assistants to ensure that prisoners "have a reasonably adequate opportunity to file nonfrivolous legal claims challenging their convictions or conditions of confinement." *Lewis v. Casey*, 116 S.Ct. 2174 (1996). However, the Constitution does not guarantee a prisoner unlimited access to the law library or legal assistants. *Wilder v. Runnels*, 2003 WL 22434102 (NDCal 2003).
- Inmates do not have a First Amendment right to a face-to-face meeting with paralegals. *Easton v. Fallman*, 2001 WL 58976 (NDCal 2001).

Legal document assistant (LDA)

- Hughes sues Gould, referred to as a legal document assistant, who was hired to prepare a trust and related documents. Gould wins on the ground that he did not cause any damages. In the opinion, the court made a number of observations about LDAs. In California, practicing law includes legal advice and counsel and the preparation of instruments and contracts by which legal rights are secured. Thus, generally, preparation of an estate plan would constitute practicing law. Nevertheless, an exception exists for a legal document assistant. Such a person is not practicing law if he or she provides self-help service to a member of the public who is representing him or herself in a legal matter. (Business and Professional Code, § 6400(c).) Self-help service encompasses completing legal documents in a ministerial manner, providing published information that has been written or approved by an attorney, and making published legal documents available. However, a legal document assistant cannot provide any advice, explanation, opinion or recommendation to a consumer about the law. *Hughes v. Gould*, 2002 WL 598534 (CalApp 2002).

Bankruptcy petition preparers (BPP)

- Bankruptcy petition preparers not employed or supervised by any attorney have proliferated across the country. While it is permissible for a petition preparer to provide services solely limited to typing, far too many of them also attempt to provide legal advice and legal services to debtors. These preparers often lack the necessary legal training and ethics regulation to provide such services. *Green v. U.S.*, 1997 WL 16298 (NDCal 1997).
- The bankruptcy petition preparer who prepared the debtor's Chapter 7 petition in this case failed to show that the case presented any special or extraordinary circumstances warranting a fee over the $125 maximum fee allowable under guidelines promulgated by local bankruptcy rules and, thus, was required to disgorge $48 of the $173 fee charged. *In re Agyekum*, 225 B.R. 695 (BAP9 1998).
- The bankruptcy court has jurisdiction and power to disallow excess fees and order the turnover of excess fees paid or payable to bankruptcy petition preparers. *Interpreting 11 U.S.C. 110 Which Governs Conduct of Nonlawyer Bankruptcy Petition Preparers*, 198 B.R. 604 (CDCal 1996).
- The operators of an Internet website that provided bankruptcy preparation services failed to sign bankruptcy petitions that their software generated, failed to provide an identifying number, and intentionally concealed their involvement in the preparation of bankruptcy petitions. The operators thereby engaged in "fraudulent, unfair and deceptive" conduct, of a kind prohibited by bankruptcy statute regulating conduct of bankruptcy petition preparers (BPPs). *In re Reynoso*, 315 B.R. 544 (BAP9 2004).
- The bankruptcy petition preparer did not engage in the unauthorized practice of law simply by providing her client with a document that provided specific advice about the bankruptcy process, where there was no evidence that the petition preparer gave any legal advice herself or pointed out any specific sections of this document in response to questions from client. *In re Leon*, 317 B.R. 131 (BkrtcyCDCal 2004).
- The Bankruptcy Code mandates specific requirements to be followed by bankruptcy petition preparers, making it clear that they may only provide typing services to their customers. *In re Nieves*, 290 B.R. 370 (BkrtcyCDCal 2003).
- By selecting a form that they thought was appropriate for the debtor's purposes, bankruptcy petition preparers assisted the debtor in filing a motion to avoid liens. This was the unauthorized practice of

law under both federal and California law. *In re Powell*, 266 B.R. 450 (BkrtcyNDCal 2001).

- Under California law, a non-lawyer engages in the unauthorized practice of law when he or she determines for a party the kind of legal document necessary to effect the party's purpose. By selecting a form that she thought was appropriate, the non-lawyer was engaged in the unauthorized practice of law. The fact that the form itself may have been prepared by a lawyer does not change the nature of the act. Since the attorney who prepared the form was not supervising the non-lawyer, her use of the attorney's form was unlawful. *In re Boettcher*, 262 B.R. 94, 96 (BkrtcyNDCal 2001).

Unlawful detainer assistants (UDA)

- Appellant pleaded guilty to one count of operating as an unregistered unlawful detainer assistant and one count of conspiring to defraud by false pretenses. *People v. Mousa*, 2003 WL 22884044 (CalApp 2003) (NOP).
- Defendant is charged with violating the Unlawful Detainer Assistants Act. In adopting this act, the Legislature found that "there currently exist numerous unscrupulous individuals . . . who purport to offer protection to tenants from eviction. The[y] . . . represent themselves as legitimate tenants' rights associations, legal consultants, professional - legal assistants, paralegals, attorneys, or typing services . . . . The acts of these unscrupulous individuals . . . are particularly despicable in that they target low-income and non-English-speaking Californians as victims for their fraudulent practices." *Brockey v. Moore*, 107 Cal.App.4th 86, 89, 131 Cal.Rptr.2d 746, 749 (CalApp 2003).

Miscellaneous cases involving paralegals

Paralegal sues California Bar Association and ABA

- Fleming was a paralegal. He believed that the practice of law should not be limited to lawyers. On August 14, 1997, Fleming filed a civil action in the Eastern District of California that named as defendants the State Bar of California and the American Bar Association, among others. In that action, Fleming alleged a number of constitutional and antitrust violations. Judge Coyle was assigned to preside over Fleming's civil case. On a motion by the defendants, Judge Coyle dismissed the case on November 25, 1997, for failure to state a claim for which relief can be granted. *U.S. v. Fleming*, 215 F.3d 930, 933 (CA9 2000).

Praise for paralegal representative

- Plaintiff's representative in this social security case was a legal assistant with a legal services organization and "appears to have been well-versed in the procedures and issues involved in the supplemental hearing." *Hardaway v. Chater*, 1996 WL 663978 (CDCal 1996).

Agency representation by paralegals

- "[A]ccording to the administrative law judge who heard Abdulmeseh's claim [before the Contractor's State License Board], paralegals, advocates, spouses, parents and other non-attorney representatives frequently appear before administrative law judges in licensing cases." *Abdulmeseh v. Glenco*, 2003 WL 150115 (CalApp 2003) (NOP).

Attorney accuses paralegal of intentional infliction of emotional distress—and wins

- Damages of $450,000, awarded to an attorney for intentional infliction of emotional distress by a paralegal. On appeal, the court held that this award was not excessive, where harassment by the paralegal following the attorney's termination of their brief office romance not only caused attorney to suffer depression and weight loss, but also resulted in his loss of partnership and a reduction in his income from nearly $250,000 per year to less than half of that. *Saret-Cook v. Gilbert, Kelly*, 74 Cal.App.4th 1211, 88 Cal.Rptr.2d 732 (CalApp 1999).

Paralegal charged with sexually harassing attorney

- Kimberly Hansen, an attorney, worked in the legal department at an insurance company. Scott Moore was a paralegal at the company and an office manager in the legal department. Hansen alleged that Moore sexually harassed her. A major issue in the case was whether the paralegal was the attorney's supervisor for purposes of the sexual harassment claim (non-supervisory coworkers were not liable under the law being applied in the case). The court found Hansen's lawsuit against Moore was groundless. Among others, the court identified the following factor as relevant to that determination: Moore's status as a paralegal was strongly suggestive that he would not be the supervisor of lawyers. *Hansen v. Moore*, 2002 WL 1019078 (CalApp 2002) (NOP). See also 2002 WL 462489 (NOP).

Litigation paralegal sues her former firm and is accused of improperly taking documents out of the firm upon her termination

- "The instant appeal is only the latest installment in an acrimonious dispute between the law firm of Latham & Watkins and Robyn Devereaux, a one-time litigation paralegal employed by the firm." She brought action against the firm for indemnity for expenses she incurred in connection with her depositions in two actions brought by third parties against the firm. At one of the depositions, she produced certain documents she had removed without permission upon her termination from the law firm. She claimed that she "[blew] the whistle" on the firm for "withholding/destruction of evidence, insurance fraud, and overbilling. *Devereaux v. Latham & Watkins*, 32 Cal.App.4th 1571, 38 Cal.Rptr.2d 849 (CalApp 1995).

A federal judge can't be your paralegal

- Someone representing him or herself (pro se) in court cannot expect the trial judge to give legal advice. "District judges have no obligation to act as counsel or paralegal to pro se litigants." *Pliler v. Ford* 124 S. Ct. 2441, 2446 (US 2004).

Legions of paralegals

- This securities litigation devoured a staggering quantity of productive resources. The record consists of 50 cubic feet of paper and weighs over half a ton. There were 4,500 docket entries below, including almost 400 orders and rulings by the district court. Fifty-seven briefs, consisting of nearly 1800 pages, were filed on appeal, yielding three published opinions. Some 200 attorneys contributed to this imbroglio, supported by legions of paralegals. *Layman v. Combs*, 981 F.2d 1093, 1107 (CA9 1992).

No paralegal laughing in the court!

- "In addition, during the examination of Dr. Martin, the court noted that counsel's legal assistant in the back of the court was 'sharing a laugh' for the second time during the proceedings. The court advised counsel that if further laughing occurred, the assistant would be banned from the courtroom." *Frankel v. Cedars-Sinai Foundation*, 2004 WL 2601543 (CalApp 2004) (NOP).

Paralegal student excluded from jury pool

- A paralegal student was on a jury panel being considered for jury duty. She was dismissed on a peremptory challenge. The trial court found that the paralegal training was a legitimate reason for exercising a peremptory challenge. Her current studies to become a paralegal may cause her to interject her own feelings about the law. *Anderson v. Hickman*, 2004 WL 883403 (NDCal 2004).

The paralegal might not follow the judge's instructions

- It was not error for the prosecutor to reject a paralegal as a juror. The paralegal "had taken classes in criminal law and felt capable of informing people about criminal cases. The prosecutor may have reasonably believed there was a possibility this juror would resist following the court's instructions in favor of his own conception of the law." *People v. Gaines*, 2004 WL 2386748 (CalApp 2004) (NOP).

Juror charged with misconduct for attending paralegal school during trial

- During the final three weeks of this products liability trial, a juror attended night classes in paralegal studies. The subject of one class was the law of products liability. Ford Motor Company argues that the juror's paralegal studies amounted to the improper reception of evidence concerning the subject of the trial, implying that the juror purposely sought out extrajudicial opinion concerning the issues at the trial. The court rejected this argument. The juror's decision to undertake paralegal studies during the trial appears to have been wholly coincidental. The juror inadvertently attended a single class where the subject of an arguably related piece of litigation was mentioned in passing. The juror's actions were not misconduct. *Hasson v. Ford Motor Co.*, 32 Cal.3d 388, 409, 650 P.2d 1171, 1184, 185 Cal.Rptr. 654, 667 (Cal 1982).

Defense paralegal has private meeting with prosecutor

- Defendant's right to be represented by counsel was not violated when his paralegal met with the prosecutor (without defense counsel being present) to inform the prosecutor that the defendant asked the paralegal to make false statements. The meeting was akin to that between opposing counsel; the prosecutor immediately informed defense counsel of the meeting. *U.S. v. Mikaelian*, 168 F.3d 380 (CA9 1999).

D. Something to Check

Go to the online sources that provide free access to state court opinions in California. (See chart in section 5.1). Do a search for any of the following terms: paralegal "legal assistant," "legal document assistant," "unlawful detainer assistant," "bankruptcy petition preparer." Select one of the opinions found by these search terms. How was the term involved in the opinion you selected? Summarize (brief) the opinion.

APPENDIX B

Becoming an Attorney in California with or without Law School

A. Introduction

Some paralegals decide to become attorneys. If you look at the résumés of California attorneys posted on their law firm Web site, you will occasionally see references to their prior employment as paralegals before they attended law school. Some attorneys worked part-time as paralegals while they were in law school. In this section, we explore what is involved in becoming an attorney in California.

In this state, it is possible to become an attorney without going to law school. You need to have a legal education, but it does not have to be through a law school. The requirement is that you study law diligently and in good faith for at least four years through law school *or in a law office in this state and under the personal supervision of a member of the State Bar of California or of a sitting judge.* Obtaining a legal education without attending law school is not common, but the option exists. (See the bar examination statistics in section 3.4.) California is one of a handful of states in the country that allows this alternative.

It is also possible in California to obtain the required legal education through a correspondence school.

B. Summary

Here is a summary of the eligibility requirements to take the California bar examination:

1. Before beginning the study of law, you must have:
   (a) completed at least two years of college, or
   (b) passed certain specified college level equivalency program examinations.
2. You must register with the Committee of Bar Examiners not later than 90 days after beginning the study of law.
3. You must:
   (a) graduate from a law school approved by the American Bar Association, or
   (b) graduate from a law school accredited by the Committee of Bar Examiners of the State Bar of California, or
   (c) complete four years of law study at an unaccredited or correspondence law school registered with the Committee, or
   (d) have studied law in a law office or judge's chambers in accordance with specified rules and guidelines.
4. Those studying law who did not successfully complete their first year of law study at a school approved by the American Bar Association or accredited by the Committee must take the First-Year Law Students' Examination (the "Baby Bar") upon completion of their first year of law study.
5. You must pass:
   (a) the three-day General Bar Examination, consisting of six essay questions, the Multistate Bar Examination (MBE), and two performance tests (PTs).
   (b) the two-hour Multistate Professional Responsibility Examination (MPRE).
6. You must establish current good moral character.
7. You must be in compliance with court ordered child or family support obligations.

C. Requirements for Becoming a California Attorney

The admission of attorneys in California is administered by the Office of Admission of the State Bar Association:

Office of Admission State Bar of California 1149 South Hill Street Los Angeles, CA 90015 213-765-1500	Office of Admission State Bar of California 180 Howard Street San Francisco, CA 94105 415-538-2303

www.calbar.ca.gov/admissions
www.calbar.ca.gov/calbar/pdfs/admissions/feeschedule.pdf
www.calbar.ca.gov/calbar/pdfs/admissions/fee-notice.pdf

Applicants to practice law in California are referred to as "general applicants" if they have not been admitted to practice law in any other state or foreign country. If they are already attorneys in another jurisdiction and are seeking a license to practice in California, they are referred to as "attorney applicants."

The requirements for general applicants to practice law in California fall into seven categories:

1. General Education
2. Registration
3. Legal Education
4. First-Year Law Students' Examination
5. Bar Examination
6. Moral Character
7. Child Support Compliance

(1) General Education

You must have completed at least two years of college before beginning the study of law, or must have passed certain specified College Level Equivalency Program examinations before beginning law study. The college work shall be not less than one-half of the collegiate work acceptable for a bachelor's degree granted upon the basis of a four-year period of study by a college or university approved by the Committee. Rule VII, Section 1. Rules Regulating Admission to Practice Law in California.

(2) Registration

Every general applicant for admission to practice law in California shall register with the Committee not later than 90 days after he or she begins the study of law and shall pay the required fee. Registration required by this Section shall consist of the filing of a form that may inquire into the applicant's age, addresses, general education and legal education. The registration form must be completed under penalty of perjury. Rule V, Section 2. Rules Regulating Admission to Practice Law in California.

Fees:
Registration as a law student: $92
Late registration filing fee: $52

(3) Legal Education

To meet the legal education requirement, an applicant must:

(a) graduate from a law school approved by the American Bar Association or accredited by the Committee; or

(b) study law diligently and in good faith for at least four years in any of the following manners:
  (i) in a law school that is authorized by the State of California to confer professional degrees; is registered with the Committee; and which requires classroom attendance of its students for a minimum of 270 hours a year; or
  (ii) in a law office in this state and under the personal supervision of a member of the State Bar of California who is, and who has been continuously, an active member of the State Bar of California for at least the last past five years; or
  (iii) in the chambers and under the personal supervision of a judge of a court of record of this state; or
  (iv) by instruction in law from a correspondence law school requiring 864 hours of preparation and study per year and which is registered with the Committee; or
  (v) by any combination of these four methods. Rule VII, Section 2. Rules Regulating Admission to Practice Law in California.

Note: As part of the application process of many law schools, you must take the Law School Aptitude Test (LSAT) (*www.lsat.org*).

On the option of obtaining your legal education without attending law school, see More Information at the end of this section.

(4) First-Year Law Students' Examination

Every person who intends to seek admission as a general applicant shall take the First-Year Law Students' Examination (referred to as the "Baby Bar") following completion of one year of law study unless such person is exempt.

An applicant is exempt if he or she has satisfactorily completed the first year course of instruction in a law school:

(a) accredited by the Committee of Bar Examiners; or

(b) approved or provisionally approved by the American Bar Association. . . .

Rule VIII, Section 1. Rules Regulating Admission to Practice Law in California.

The First-Year Law Students' Examination is a one-day, seven-hour essay and multiple-choice examination.

Fees:

Application to take the First Year Law Students' Exam: $488

(5) Bar Examination

The General Bar Examination is a demanding, three-day examination that is administered twice a year. It has three parts: six essay questions, two performance tests (PTs), and the Multistate Bar Examination (MBE).

In addition, the Multistate Professional Responsibility Examination (MPRE) is a separate requirement for admission to practice law in California.

The areas tested on the exam include:

- Civil Procedure
- Community Property
- Constitutional Law
- Contracts
- Business Associations
- Criminal Law and Procedure
- Evidence
- Professional Responsibility (Ethics)
- Real Property
- Remedies
- Torts
- Trusts
- Wills and Succession

Essay Questions

The six essay questions are designed to measure an applicant's ability to identify legal issues, discern material facts from immaterial facts, understand legal principles, apply the law to the given facts, and reason in a logical, lawyer-like manner to a sound conclusion.

Performance Tests (PT)

The PT is a more practice-oriented test. The applicant is given a set of facts along with documents such as a police report; a complaint; a contract; a medical record; a letter from an opposing attorney; and transcript excerpts of a client interview, a deposition, or a court hearing. The exam packet will also include the text of laws such as statutes, regulations, and court opinions. The PT question might take the form of a memo from a senior partner asking a new attorney (the bar applicant) to sort through all this material in order to perform a practical task such as drafting a client letter, preparing a memo identifying alternative strategies, or drafting a section of an appellate brief.

Multistate Bar Examination (MBE)

The MBE is an objective, six-hour examination consisting of 200 multiple-choice questions covering constitutional law, contracts, criminal law and procedure, evidence, real property, and torts.

Multistate Professional Responsibility Examination (MPRE)

The MPRE is a separate exam administered three times a year by the National Conference of Bar Examiners. It is a 60-question, two-hour, multiple-choice examination on professional responsibility (ethics). The test is based primarily on the ABA Model Rules of Professional Conduct.

Fees:
Application to take the General Bar Exam: $529
Application to take the MRPE: $110

(6) Moral Character

An applicant has the burden of establishing his or her current good moral character. This is done through a moral character screening process that begins by filing a moral character application. Recommendations and comments from present and former employers and references supplied by the applicant are considered. Fingerprint cards are sent to the California Department of Justice or the Federal Bureau of Investigations for processing. The Department of Motor Vehicles is contacted. Information provided by the applicant, by law schools, and by other outside sources is verified and studied. If a question arises that cannot be resolved at the staff level, the case is referred to the Subcommittee on Moral Character for determination. The applicant may be asked to meet with a member of this subcommittee.

(7) Child Support Compliance

Applicants who have met all other requirements but who have been certified by the State Department of Social Services as being in non-compliance with court-ordered child or family support will not be certified to the Supreme Court as qualified to practice law in California unless the appropriate release has been obtained.

More Information:

www.calbar.ca.gov/admissions
www.calbar.ca.gov/calbar/pdfs/admissions/feeschedule.pdf

D. California Law Schools

There are four categories of law schools in California:

- those approved by the ABA (ABA);
- those accredited by the Committee of Bar Examiners (CBE);
- correspondence schools (CS); and
- unaccredited law Schools (ULS).

Here is a list of each school in California. The abbreviation after the name indicates the category into which the school fits.

ACTON
Larry H. Layton School of Law (ULS)
www.vanguardnews.com/Layton.htm

ANAHEIM
American College of Law (ULS)
www.aclaw.com

BAKERSFIELD
John William University School of Law (UCL)
johnwilliamuniversity.org

BERKELEY
UC Berkeley Boalt Hall School of Law (ABA)
www.law.berkeley.edu

CERRITOS
Irvine University College of Law (ULS)
www.irvineuniversity.edu/law

CHICO
Cal Northern School of Law (CBE)
www.calnorthern.edu

CLOVIS
San Joaquin College of Law (CBE)
www.sjcl.edu

COSTA MESA
Whittier Law School (ABA)
www.law.whittier.edu

CULVER CITY
California School of Law (CS)
californiaschooloflaw.com

CYPRESS
West Haven University School of Law (CS)
www.westhavenuniv.edu

DAVIS
UC Davis School of Law (ABA)
www.law.ucdavis.edu

DOWNEY
West Coast School of Law (CS)
www.westcsl.com

FRESNO
Oak Brook College of Law (CS)
www.obcl.edu

FULLERTON
Western State University College of Law (ABA)
wsulaw.edu

GLENDALE
Glendale University College of Law (CBE)
www.glendalelaw.edu

INGLEWOOD
University of West Los Angeles School of Law (CBE)
www.uwla.edu

LAKE FOREST
British-American University School of Law (CS)
www.british-american.edu

LONG BEACH
Pacific Coast University School of Law (ULS)
www.pculaw.com

LOS ANGELES
Abraham Lincoln University School of Law (CS)
www.alu.edu
Concord University School of Law (CS)
www.concord.kaplan.edu
Loyola Law School (ABA)
www.lls.edu
People's College of Law (ULS)
www.peoplescollegeoflaw.edu
Southwestern University School of Law (ABA)
www.swlaw.edu
UC Los Angeles School of Law (ABA)
www.law.ucla.edu
University of Southern California Law School (ABA)
www.usc.edu/dept/law
University of West Los Angeles School of Law (CBE)
www.uwla.edu

MALIBU
Pepperdine University School of Law (ABA)
www.law.pepperdine.edu

MODESTO
University of Honolulu School of Law (CS)
www.universityofhonoluluschooloflaw.net

MONTEREY
Monterey College of Law (CBE)
www.montereylaw.edu

NEWPORT BEACH
Newport University School of Law (CS)
www.newport.edu

OAKLAND
East Bay Law School (ULS)
www.eastbaylawschool.org

ONTARIO
University of La Verne College of Law (CBE)
law.ulv.edu

ORANGE
Chapman University School of Law (ABA)
www.chapman.edu/law
Pacific West College of Law (ULS)
www.pacificwestcollege.com

PASADENA
Esquire College (CS)
www.esquirecollege.org

PLEASANT HILL
John F. Kennedy University School of Law (CBE)
www.jfku.edu/law

RIVERSIDE
California Southern Law School (ULS)
www.cslawschool.com

SACRAMENTO
Lincoln Law School of Sacramento (CBE)
www.lincolnlaw.edu
McGeorge School of Law (ABA)
www.mcgeorge.edu
Northwestern California University School of Law (CS)
www.nwculaw.edu

University of Northern California PatiÒo School of Law (ULS)
www.patinolawschool.com

SAN BERNARDINO
Heritage University School of Law (CS)
www.heritageuniv.net

SAN DIEGO
California Western School of Law (ABA)
www.cwsl.edu
Thomas Jefferson School of Law (ABA)
www.tjsl.edu
University of San Diego School of Law (ABA)
www.sandiego.edu/usdlaw
Western Sierra Law School (ULS)
www.wsls.us/tbcm

SAN FRANCISCO
Golden Gate University School of Law (ABA)
www.ggu.edu/schools/law
New College of California School of Law (CBE)
www.newcollege.edu
San Francisco Law School (CBE)
www.sfls.edu
UC Hastings College of Law (ABA)
www.uchastings.edu
University of San Francisco School of Law (ABA)
www.usfca.edu/law

SAN JOSE
Lincoln Law School of San Jose (CBE)
www.lincolnlawsj.edu
Silicon Valley University Law School (ULS)
www.svulaw.com

SAN LUIS OBISPO
Laurel University School of Law (CS)
www.laureluniversity.com

SANTA ANA
Southern California University for Professional Studies College of Law (CS)
www.scups.edu
Trinity Law School (CBE)
www.tls.edu
William Howard Taft University (CS)
www.taftu.edu

SANTA BARBARA
Santa Barbara College of Law (CBE)
www.santabarbaralaw.edu
Southern California Institute of Law (CBE)
www.lawdegree.com

SANTA CLARA
Santa Clara University School of Law (ABA)
www.scu.edu/law

SANTA ROSA
Empire College School of Law (CBE)
www.empcol.edu

STANFORD
Stanford Law School (ABA)
www.law.stanford.edu

STOCKTON
Humphreys College Drivon School of Law (CBE)
www.humphreys.edu

UPLAND
Inland Valley College of Law (ULS)
www.ivucol.org

VENTURA
Southern California Institute of Law (CBE)
www.lawdegree.com
Ventura College of Law (CBE)
www.venturalaw.edu

WOODLAND HILLS
University of West Los Angeles School of Law (CBE)
www.uwla.edu

E. More Information

Should I Go to Law School? 29 Questions to Ask Yourself
www.law.miami.edu/admissions/29questions.html

California Law Schools
stu.findlaw.com/schools/usaschools/california.html
www.alllaw.com/state_resources/california/law_schools
www.loc.gov/law/guide/us-ca.html
calbar.ca.gov/state/calbar/calbar_generic.jsp?cid=10115&id=5128

Legal Education without Law School
www.calbar.ca.gov/calbar/pdfs/admissions/om76.pdf
www.calbar.ca.gov/calbar/pdfs/admissions/om76-8a.pdf
www.calbar.ca.gov/calbar/pdfs/admissions/om76-8b.pdf

The Cost of Law School: Some Examples
www.law.berkeley.edu/students/financial_aid
www.lincolnlawsj.edu/admis_fees.html
www.nwculaw.edu/cgi-bin/nwcu/finances_tuition.html

Financial Aid for Law School
www.lsac.org/LSAC.asp?url=lsac/financial-aid-introduction.asp
studentaid.ed.gov

Maintaining the License to Practice Law
www.calbar.ca.gov/calbar/pdfs/admissions/MCLE_Req.pdf

F. Something to Check

1. To learn more about the requirements for receiving a legal education without attending law school, visit the online sites of the schools listed in section D with the designations CS and ULS.
2. Law School library Web sites often have excellent legal research guides. Select any three law schools listed in section D above. At the Web sites of these law schools, click their law library link. At these law library sites, compare the information provided (including further links) on California legal research. Describe what you are led to. Which law library leads you to the most comprehensive links?

PART 2

Paralegal Employment

A. Introduction

How do new paralegals find their first job? How do experienced paralegals interested in a job change find opportunities that build on their experience? In this section, we present ideas and resources that can be helpful in answering these questions for full-time and part-time work. In addition to general strategies, you will find specific Internet sites that should be checked. Some of the sites cover the entire state, while others focus on specific areas of the state.

Many of the leads will be to traditional employment agencies that match employers with applicants. Staffing agencies are also included. A staffing agency is an employment agency that places temporary workers, often directly paying the workers and handling all of the financial aspects of the placement. A law office will pay the staffing agency, which in turn pays the paralegal's salary for work at the law office. Many employment and staffing agencies do not charge job applicants for their services. (Of course, you should confirm that this is true before using the services of any agency.)

B. General Strategies for Finding Employment

The starting point in your job search should be the school where you received your paralegal education. The program director will be your best guide on what is available. Here are some additional strategies:

- **Paralegal Associations.** Section 1.4 lists every paralegal association in the state. It also gives you related groups such as legal administrator associations. Go to the Web site of every association near the cities or towns where you want to work. Also be sure to check the site of the California Alliance of Paralegal Associations:
  www.caparalegal.org
  (Click "Events and Resources" then "Career Center")
  www.caparalegal.org/capacc.html.
  Find out if any job leads are available on these Web sites. Some associations list current openings that non-members can access. If the newsletter of an association is online, look through recent issues. They may list job openings that are not found elsewhere on the association's Web site. Send an e-mail message to the association asking for leads to employment and staffing agencies in the area. If there is a search box on the site, type in search words such as "employment," "job bank," "paralegal work," and "legal assistant employment."
- **Attorney Job Search Resources.** There are many resources in the state that focus on the search for attorney employment. (Some are listed below.) Don't be reluctant to check out Web sites for attorney employment, since many have pages or links on paralegal employment. If they don't, call or send them an e-mail message, asking for leads on paralegal employment in the area. In the search box on the site, type in search words such as "paralegal" and "legal assistant."
- **Bar Associations.** Bar associations sometimes have employment services for their members, and some of this information might be available to the general public. (The list of bar associations in the state is in section 3.4.) Go to the Web sites of the associations to find out if any leads are available on paralegal employment. Consider sending the bar association an e-mail message asking about paralegal employment and staffing agencies in the area. In the search box on the site, type in search words such as "paralegal" and "legal assistant."
- **General Circulation and Legal Newspapers.** General circulation newspapers often have want ads for paralegals. These newspapers are worth checking, particularly their online editions. Also find out what the legal newspaper is for your area—both hard copy and online. It may have want ads for paralegals. Here are links to California newspapers:
  www.abyznewslinks.com/uniteca.htm
  newslink.org/canews.html
  www.usnpl.com/canews.html
  www.50states.com/news/calif.htm
  www.law.com/jsp/ca (click "Get a Better Job" then "Paralegal" for Job Type)
- **General and Legal Search Engines.** Go to general search engines such as Google (*www.google.com*). Try searches for paralegal employment that include the name of the city where you want to work (e.g., "paralegal employment" "los angeles"). In addition, go to legal search engines such as Findlaw (*www.findlaw.com*) and Lawguru (*www.lawguru.com*), and look for links on their home pages for employment or careers. In the search boxes, type phrases such as "paralegal employment" and "legal assistant employment."
- **Networking.** Many paralegals find employment through the networking contacts they make with attorneys, paralegals, legal secretaries, etc. whom they meet at school, paralegal associations, social clubs, church or synagogue, etc. At these settings, always be ready to ask, "Who do you know who might be looking for paralegals?" There is not a

more powerful question that could be asked of anyone connected with the practice of law.

- **Paralegal Jobs in the Public Sector.** If you are seeking employment in the public sector:
  - see section 2.2 for employment in state government
  - see section 2.3 for employment in federal agencies located in California
  - see section 4.2 for links to employment in California state courts and 4.3 for links to employment in federal courts in the state
  - see section 2.4 for the links to legal aid/legal services offices and other public sector offices in California
  - for directories of public defender offices and associations, check: *www.llrx.com/features/publicdefense.htm*
  - click "Job Postings" at the following site: *www.calegaladvocates.org*
- **Paralegal Jobs in Corporations.** Check the web site of the Association of Corporate Counsel:
  - go to *www.acc.com*
  - click "Career Development" and "Find a Job"
  - click "Advanced Search"
  - for "Locations," select this state
  - type "paralegal" or "legal assistant" in the search box
  - or click "Other" for "Job Level"
- **Direct Contact.** If you already have the name of a law office, go directly to its Web site to find out if it lists any job openings for paralegals. For lists of some California law offices, check:
  www.hg.org/northam-firms.html
  california.lp.findlaw.com
  www.lawresearchservices.com/firms/california-alpha.htm
  www.nalpdirectory.com

C. Specific Resources

Statewide

Adams & Martin Group
www.adamsmartingroup.com/chooseType.aspx

Association of Legal Administrators
www.alanet.org/jobs/current.asp
(for "California," type "paralegal")

CalawJobs
www.calawjobs.com

California Alliance of Paralegal Associations
www.caparalegal.org/capacc.html

Career Builder
www.careerbuilder.com
(type "paralegal" and a California city)

Craigslist
www.craigslist.org
(click "California" and a city; under "Jobs," click "legal/paralegal")

Davidson Legal Staffing
www.davidsonstaffing.com

Detod.com
detod.legalstaff.com

FindLaw Careers—California
careers.findlaw.com

Google Legal Employment Directory
directory.google.com/Top/Society/Law/Employment

HierosGamos—Legal Jobs in California
www.hierosgamos.org/hg/legal_jobs_california.asp
(Select "Paralegal" in the position box)

IntJobs
intjobs.org/law/paralegal.html

JobsNet California
legal.jobs.net/California.htm

Law Crossing
www.lawcrossing.com/lclegalstaff.php
(type "paralegal" as keyword; scroll to "California")

LawGuru
lawguru.legalstaff.com

Legal Assistant Today Job Bank
www.legalassistanttoday.com/jobbank

Legal Resource Center
www.thelccn.com/lrc/shop
(click "Paralegal")

Legal Staff
www.legalstaff.com

Monster—California
jobsearch.monster.com

NALS—The Association for Legal Professionals
nals.legalstaff.com

National Legal Aid & Defender Association
www.nlada.org/Jobs
(select "California")

Nation Job Network
www.nationjob.com/legal

NFPA/Legal Staff
paralegals.legalstaff.com

Robert Half Legal
800-870-8367
roberthalflegal.com

Smart Hunt
smarthunt.com
(type "paralegal" and a California city)

Vault
www.vault.com
(click "Find a Job," "Law Job Board," and then select "California" and "Paralegal")

Selected Cities

Anaheim

Yahoo! Hot Jobs
hotjobs.yahoo.com/jobs/CA/Anaheim/Legal-jobs

Orange County Paralegal Association
www.ocparalegal.org
(Click "Career Center")

Bay Area

Robert Half Legal
415-982-2001; 800-870-8363
roberthalflegal.com

Yahoo! Hot Jobs
hotjobs.yahoo.com/jobs/CA/San-Francisco/Legal-jobs
hotjobs.yahoo.com/jobs/CA/Berkeley/Legal-jobs
hotjobs.yahoo.com/jobs/CA/Fremont/Legal-jobs

Fresno

Yahoo! Hot Jobs
hotjobs.yahoo.com/jobs/CA/Fresno/Legal-jobs

San Joaquin Paralegal Association
www.fresnoparalegal.org
(Click "Job Bank")
www.caparalegal.org/capacc.html

Irvine

Davidson Legal Staffing
www.davidsonstaffing.com

Robert Half Legal
949-752-2334; 800-870-8363
roberthalflegal.com

Los Angeles

Yahoo! Hot Jobs
hotjobs.yahoo.com/jobs/CA/Los-Angeles/Legal-jobs

Los Angeles Paralegal Association/Legal Career Center Network
www.lapa.org (click "Career Center")
www.caparalegal.org/capacc.html

Matrixlegal
www.matrixlegal.com
(click "Career Opportunities")

Robert Half Legal
213-624-8335; 800-870-8363
roberthalflegal.com

Long Beach

Yahoo! Hot Jobs
hotjobs.yahoo.com/jobs/CA/Long-Beach/Legal-jobs

Oakland (see also Bay Area)

Yahoo! Hot Jobs
hotjobs.yahoo.com/jobs/CA/Oakland/Legal-jobs

Robert Half Legal
510-271-0910; 800-870-8363
roberthalflegal.com

Palo Alto (see also Bay Area)

Robert Half Legal
650-812-9790; 800-870-8363
roberthalflegal.com

Riverside

Yahoo! Hot Jobs
hotjobs.yahoo.com/jobs/CA/Riverside/Legal-jobs

Robert Half Legal
951-369-0753; 800-870-8363
roberthalflegal.com

Sacramento

Yahoo! Hot Jobs
hotjobs.yahoo.com/jobs/CA/Sacramento/Legal-jobs

Law Staff
calstaff.com/Lawstaff/index.php

San Diego

Yahoo! Hot Jobs
hotjobs.yahoo.com/jobs/CA/San-Diego/Legal-jobs

Robert Half Legal
619-234-3181; 800-870-8363
roberthalflegal.com

San Fernando

Yahoo! Hot Jobs
hotjobs.yahoo.com/jobs/CA/San-Fernando/Legal-jobs

San Francisco (see also Bay Area)

Robert Half Legal
415-982-2001; 800-870-8363
roberthalflegal.com

San Jose

Yahoo! Hot Jobs
hotjobs.yahoo.com/jobs/CA/San-Jose/Legal-jobs

Santa Ana

Yahoo! Hot Jobs
hotjobs.yahoo.com/jobs/CA/Santa-Ana/Legal-jobs

Santa Barbara

Santa Barbara Paralegal Association
www.sbparalegals.org
(Click "Job Bank")
www.caparalegal.org/capacc.html

Santa Clara

Santa Clara County Paralegal Association
www.caparalegal.org/capacc.html
hotjobs.yahoo.com/jobs/CA/San-Jose/Legal-jobs

Westwood

Robert Half Legal
310-209-6829; 800-870-8363
roberthalflegal.com

D. More Information

U.S. Department of Labor
Paralegals and Legal Assistants
www.bls.gov/oco/ocos114.htm

E. Something to Check

1. List and compare the services of two paralegal employment sites that allow you to submit your resume online.
2. What direct or indirect paralegal employment services are available to you at two paralegal associations and two bar associations closest to your area?
3. What useful information can you obtain at any of the legal secretary association sites in the state?

2.2 Sample Paralegal Job Descriptions in State Government

A. Introduction
B. Legal Assistant
C. Legal Analyst
D. Law Indexer
E. Legal Documents Examiner
F. Examination
G. Court Positions
H. More Information
I. Something to Check

A. Introduction

There are two main job categories for paralegals in state government: legal assistant and legal analyst. Other positions you can check out include law indexer and legal document examiner. These are civil service positions. The State Personnel Board coordinates the hiring of these positions with the specific agencies or departments that have openings for them.

Summary of Steps to Take:

1. Find out if there is an opening (*www.spb.ca.gov/employment*)
2. Read the qualifications for the position
3. Take the examination (see section F below to see what is meant by "examination")
4. Follow the instructions to apply for the position

Not all state employees are included in the state civil service employment process. The following units of government have their own hiring process:

- Governor's office
- State legislature
- University of California and State College campuses
- Court system

You must contact these units directly to inquire about employment opportunities. (See More Information at the end of this section.) They have their own titles, pay scales, and hiring process. An example of a paralegal position in the court system is included below.

B. Legal Assistant

Specification: Legal Assistant
Schematic Code: JY66
Class Code: 1820
Salary: $3,164–$3,846 per month
Definition: Under the immediate direction, control and responsibility of an attorney, performs a wide variety of paralegal duties and other related work.

Distinguishing Characteristics

The class of Legal Assistant is "a paraprofessional class" established to provide full-time employment in a legal program in state service as an assistant to an attorney. The class is designed for permanent employment where incumbents can properly be delegated the more routine paralegal duties by an attorney. It is distinguished from legal clerical classes in that more difficult technical duties and responsibilities are assigned.

Typical Tasks

Under the immediate direction and control of an attorney who shall accept full responsibility for the tasks performed:

- assists in reviewing legal documents;
- assists in reviewing for completeness of information furnished by program staff in matters referred for legal proceedings;
- summarizes, organizes, and indexes prior opinions, testimony, depositions; organizes trial documents and exhibits;

- gathers factual information and performs routine legal research;
- assists in the preparation of pleadings;
- arranges for service of process;
- assists in preparing drafts of petitions, affidavits, orders, etc.;
- prepares documents for opening and closing files;
- prepares correspondence and reports;
- answer inquiries regarding status of cases and departmental procedures by attorneys, parties and the public;
- exchanges legal and factual information with other legal units in the department and other state agencies.

Minimum Qualifications

Education

Successful completion of six semester units of paralegal or undergraduate legal courses, at least three units of which must be in legal research. (Candidates who have completed three semester units of paralegal course work necessary to fulfill the education requirement will be admitted to the examination, but they must submit evidence of completion of the required six units before they can be considered for appointment.)

AND

Experience:

either I or II

I: Two years of experience in the California state service as a Senior Stenographer/Typist, Legal, Range B; Legal Secretary, or other classification with law-related duties, involving the review, preparation, or interpretation of legal documents or involving the conduct of investigations or studies leading to legal actions.

II: Three years of responsible experience as a law clerk or legal secretary in a law office. Academic education above the twelfth grade may be substituted for one year of the required experience on the basis of either (a) one year of general education being equivalent to three months of experience, or (b) two years of education in a recognized attorney assistant program in probate, tax law, labor law, corporate law, litigation or other law-related areas being equivalent to one year of experience.

Knowledge and Abilities

Knowledge of

Basic legal concepts, terminology, principles and procedures; use of legal reference material; legal office management principles.

Ability to

Reason logically; analyze situations accurately and recommend an effective course of action; write effectively; prepare reports and summary sheets that set forth a statement of the facts, applications of the relevant law, and conclusions; read and understand statutes, court decisions, legal documents and similar material; work cooperatively with attorneys, clerical staff, technical staff and the general public; explain the provision of law, procedures, and problems to persons contacted in the work.

Additional Desirable Qualification

Evidence of continuing education, such as additional paralegal or legal coursework.

C. Legal Analyst

Specification: Legal Analyst
Schematic Code: JY62
Class Code: 5237
Salary: $3,589–$4,363 per month
Definition: Under general supervision, provides paralegal and legal analytical support to attorneys; and does other related work.

Distinguishing Characteristics

The class of Legal Analyst is the journey analytical paralegal class established to provide full-time employment in a legal program in state service. Incumbents work as assistants to attorneys. The class is designed for permanent employment where incumbents can be properly delegated difficult and complex paralegal duties which are analytical in nature. *It is distinguished from the class of Legal Assistant in which incumbents perform the less difficult, more routine paralegal duties generally of a processing, monitoring or data gathering nature.* It is distinguished from the class of Senior Legal Analyst in which incumbents, exercising a high degree of independence and only under general direction from attorneys, regularly perform the most difficult paralegal duties in a specialized area of law.

Typical Tasks

Under the general supervision of an attorney who shall accept full responsibility for the tasks performed, the Legal Analyst:

- investigates and analyzes facts and documents in connection with civil litigation;
- assists in criminal trial preparation by coordinating witnesses and processing subpoenas;
- drafts interrogatories and responses to interrogatories;

- interviews witnesses, complainants, and defendants;
- helps draft pleadings and motions;
- assists in the preparation of witness books and exhibit books;
- summarizes deposition transcripts;
- prepares drafts of accusations and statements of issues;
- prepares responses to routine procedural inquiries;
- prepares legislative histories.

Minimum Qualifications

Either I or II

I: *Experience*: Two years of experience in the California state service performing the duties of a Legal Assistant. AND
Education: Successful completion of six semester units of paralegal or undergraduate legal courses, with at least three units of which must be in legal research. (Candidates who have completed three semester units of paralegal course work necessary to fulfill the education requirements will be admitted to the examination, but they must submit evidence of completion of the required six units before they can be considered for appointment.)

II: *Experience*: Two years of experience performing paralegal duties in a private law firm, corporate law office, or governmental legal agency. AND
Education: Twelve semester units in a legal or paralegal curriculum or equivalent to graduation from college.

Knowledge and Abilities

Knowledge of

Basic legal concepts, terminology, principles and procedures; use of legal reference materials; role of a paralegal staff in a legal office.

Ability to

Reason logically and accurately analyze situations; read effectively, prepare reports and summary sheets which set forth the statement of facts, applications of relevant law and conclusions; read and understand statutes; prepare drafts of pleadings; draft litigation discovery documents, such as interrogatories and motions; work cooperatively with attorneys and members of the support staff.

Additional Desirable Qualifications

Evidence of continuing education, such as additional paralegal or legal course work.

D. Law Indexer

Specification: Law Indexer
Schematic Code: CX20
Class Code: 2957
Salary: $2,661–$3,162 per month

This series specification describes a class in the Office of the Legislative Counsel which has major responsibilities in the performance of complex indexing of legislative measures, statutes, resolutions, legal opinions and memoranda.

Definition: Law Indexers are distinguished from other classes by regular performance of complex review, analysis, interpretation, and summarization of legislation, statutes, and legal opinions, to create and edit various legislative and legal publications and research tools, including the California Statutes, the Legislative Index, Table of Sections Affected, California Ballot Pamphlet, California Constitution, Summary digest, Statutory record, and customized legal publications created for various state agencies. These publications are used by the Courts, Legislature, attorneys, governmental agencies, and the public. The Law Indexer is the entry and trainee level for this series. Law Indexers also compile reports for the Legislature and consult with legal staff on conflict of law questions. They perform legal research for legal staff, the Legislature, governmental agencies, and the public.

Minimum Qualifications: Equivalent to graduation from college. Experience in professional indexing may be substituted for the required college education on the basis of one year of experience being equal to one year of education.

Knowledge and Abilities

Knowledge of

Legal terms and concepts used in California law; detailed knowledge of the legislative process, and the structure of, and relationship among legislation, statutes, and codes; legal reference tools and how to use them.

Ability to

Reason logically and creatively; analyze and interpret legislation, statutory law, and legal opinions; abstract relevant data to create legal research tools and publications; translate legal concepts into layperson terms; analyze data and present ideas effectively in writing and orally; prepare reports; work independently as well as a member of a team.

E. Legal Documents Examiner

Specification: Legal Documents Examiner
Schematic Code: CW65
Class Code: 1829

Salary: $3,136–$3,812 per month

Definition: Under general supervision, to review, examine, and make recommendations concerning the legal sufficiency of various legal documents and appeals including those relating to campaign disclosures, conflicts of interest, nomination of candidates election procedures, and property tax assistance; and to do other work as required.

Typical Tasks

- Reviews legal documents to determine whether they comply with the specific code requirements;
- Approves the filing of these documents;
- Answers written and verbal inquiries regarding procedures;
- Gathers factual information and performs routine legal research;
- Prepares case summaries, correspondence, and reports;
- Supervises the work of clerical assistants.

Minimum Qualifications

Experience: Either I or II

I. Two years of experience in the review of legal documents or appeals for compliance with legal requirements; or

II. Three years of responsible experience as a law clerk or legal secretary in a law office. (Experience in California state service applied toward this requirement must include at least one year in a class equivalent in level to that of Senior Legal Stenographer.)

Knowledge and Abilities

Knowledge of

Basic legal terminology, principles, and procedures; use of legal reference material.

Ability to

Reason logically; analyze situations accurately and recommend an effective course of action; write effectively; read and understand statutes, court decisions, legal documents, and similar material; work cooperatively with professional attorneys, clerical staff, technical staff, and the general public; supervise the work of clerical assistants; explain the provisions of law, procedures, and problems to persons contacted in the work.

Additional Desirable Qualifications

Aptitude for and interest in subprofessional legal work; education equivalent to completion of the twelfth grade.

F. Examination

Some civil service positions require applicants to take an examination. This will be indicated on the job bulletin that announces the availability of the position. The exam for most legal positions is *not* a written exam. It might be a "Qualification Appraisal Interview" examination in which the applicant is interviewed to assess the nature of his or her experience and education. There might also be a supplemental exam consisting of a series of questions sent to the applicant covering matters such as experience and education. Applicants are rated based on their answers in these exams.

When an exam is open for testing (accepting applications), the testing department at the agency with the opening will issue an *exam bulletin* (notice of testing) that contains the following information:

- The department conducting the exam, and a telephone number for information
- Where to send your application
- The final file date (the date by which applications must be postmarked), or for file-in-person exams, the date, time, and place to bring your application
- The type of exam to be administered (e.g., written test, oral interview)

For each exam you're interested in, you must fill out a State application (STD-678). You can obtain it online (*www.spb.ca.gov/employment/documents/capp.pdf*), from the State Personnel Board (see address listed under More Information), or from any local California Employment Development Department office.

When your State application is received, you will be notified within 30 days that your application was received and whether you qualify to take the exam. After you pass a State exam, your name will be placed on an employment list which is active for one to four years. During this time, you may be contacted for an interview for a specific job.

G. Court Positions

Positions in the California courts are not coordinated through the state civil service system. The courts have their own titles, job descriptions, and hiring process. Here is one example of a paralegal position in the court system.

Job Title: Paralegal I

Job Requisition: HC-2078

Salary: $3,770–$4,581 per month

Location: San Francisco

The Habeas Corpus Resource Center (HCRC) was established as a judicial branch agency to provide direct legal representation to death row inmates in post-conviction proceedings in state and federal courts.

Applicants are encouraged to carefully read the Minimum Qualifications and apply at a level most appropriate to their qualifications. Starting salary and classification level will be commensurate with the qualifications of the selected individual.

Paralegal I

Under supervision, a Paralegal I:

- assists in performing factual research;
- locating, assembling, analyzing and coding evidence;
- assisting attorneys with development of factual support for claims of relief;
- maintaining case files and scanning documents into a database;
- operating a computerized system for managing documentation;
- gathering and tracking litigant information;
- identifying, contacting, and providing information to expert witnesses.

Working Hours

Monday through Friday from 8:30 a.m. to 5:30 p.m. Paralegals may be required to work overtime and on holidays, evenings, or weekends.

Minimum Qualifications

Equivalent to one year of paralegal experience involving complex litigation; OR one year as a Litigation Support Assistant with the HCRC or one year as a Legal Secretary with the HCRC. A paralegal certificate, JD degree, or directly related college-level education may be substituted for six months of the required experience.

Desirable Qualifications

Fluency in oral and written Spanish; proficient PC skills, preferably in Microsoft Word, Outlook, Excel, and Access.

To Apply

This position requires submission of: (1) official application and (2) response to the supplemental questionnaire.

Selection Procedure

Candidates whose backgrounds best meet the needs of HCRC will be invited to interview with a selection committee.

To apply online, go to:
www.courtinfo.ca.gov/careers
(Click "Tips for Job Applicants")

Supplemental Questionnaire

This supplemental form is intended to provide more detailed information about your work experience, background, and skills. Please answer the questions completely. Your answers will allow us to assess your qualifications in depth. You may use additional pages for your answers if necessary.

1. Why are you interested in working for the Habeas Corpus Resource Center?
2. Please describe your experience in working as a paralegal. Briefly describe your experience in performing paralegal duties involving complex, criminal and/or capital litigation.
3. Please describe your experience in obtaining and reviewing court, social, medical, and legal records.
4. Are you experienced in maintaining case files and database information? If so, briefly describe the scope and depth of your relevant education and experience.
5. If applying for the Senior Paralegal, please describe your experience in providing lead direction or supervising or managing staff. Include your job title, scope of responsibilities, and number and title of employees supervised.
6. These questions refer to your office automation skills. For each computer application, state your level of proficiency as: "Beginner," "Intermediate," "Advanced" or "None."

H. More Information

State Personnel Board
801 Capitol Mall
Sacramento, CA 95814
P.O. Box 944201
Sacramento, CA 94244-2010
916-653-1705
www.spb.ca.gov

Department of Personnel Administration
1515 S Street, North Building, Suite 400
Sacramento, CA 95814
916-324-0455
www.dpa.ca.gov

Pre-Recorded Exam Information
Los Angeles: 213-620-6450 x130
Sacramento: 916-445-0538 x130
San Diego: 619-237-6163 x130
San Francisco: 415-557-7871 x130

General
www.spb.ca.gov/employment
www.spb.ca.gov/employment/other_public_sector_empl.htm
www.spb.ca.gov/employment/gen_info.htm
www.caljobs.ca.gov

Legal Assistant
www.dpa.ca.gov/textdocs/specs/s1/s1820.txt

Legal Analyst
www.dpa.ca.gov/textdocs/specs/s5/s5237.txt

Law Indexer
www.dpa.ca.gov/textdocs/specs/s2/s2957.txt

Legal Document Examiner
www.dpa.ca.gov/textdocs/specs/s1/s1829.txt

Legal Office Administrator
www.dpa.ca.gov/textdocs/specs/s1/s1344.txt

Legal Support Supervisor
www.dpa.ca.gov/textdocs/specs/s1/s1277.txt

Compensation and Benefits
www.spb.ca.gov/employment/benefits.htm#salaries
www.dpa.ca.gov/benefits/employeebenefits.shtm
www.calpers.ca.gov

Court Employment
www.courtinfo.ca.gov/courts/trial/courtlist.htm
(Click your county's Web site to find out if there is an employment link on the court's home page.)
www.courtinfo.ca.gov/careers
www.courtinfo.ca.gov/careers/tips.htm

I. Something to Check

1. Use the links above to find an example of a current job opening for a legal assistant or legal analyst in state government.
2. Go to the Web page of the state courts in your county (*www.courtinfo.ca.gov/courts/trial/courtlist.htm*). Find a current job opening for a paralegal. If there are no job openings, try other counties until you find one.
3. Are there any current job openings for paralegals in any of the federal courts sitting in California? See section 4.3 for a list of sites to check.

2.3 Sample Paralegal Job Description in a Federal Agency Located in California

A. Introduction

The federal government is the largest employer of paralegals in the United States. Its paralegal position is the Paralegal Specialist. This position can be somewhat different from what exists in the private sector. A Paralegal Specialist can be a document examiner, an investigator, or a law clerk, among other descriptions. He or she may work independently in the federal government, and does not always work directly for or under the supervision of an attorney.

In order to make listings of federal job vacancies accessible, an official, centralized web site called USAJobs has been created (*www.usajobs.opm.gov*). It is managed by the Office of Personnel Management (OPM), the agency responsible for federal personnel matters. Vacancies from all federal agencies can be posted at USAJobs.

Using USAJobs
www.usajobs.opm.gov

1. Click "Job Search" and type "paralegal" in the search box.
2. Select "Legal and Claims Examining" in "Job Category Search."

The government identification code for the Paralegal Specialist is GS-950. The positions range from GS-5 to GS-11 on the federal General Schedule (GS) pay scale. (See salary link below.) The pay levels include yearly cost of living increases passed by Congress, as well as locality pay.

In addition to the USAJobs website, some agencies advertise their employment openings in local newspapers and in employment agency publications. Calling local federal agencies directly can also lead to potential employment opportunities, as well as contacting individuals who may be currently employed in a federal agency. Check standard telephone directories for a list of U.S. Government offices in your area.

For more on finding federal employment, see "More Information" below.

Elsewhere in this book you will find additional information on employment:

- in state government agencies (section 2.2)
- in private law firms (section 2.1)
- in corporations (section 2.1)
- in legal service offices (sections 2.1 and 2.4)

B. Sample Job Description

The following job description is for a paralegal position in a federal government agency located in California. It is an example only. The position may no longer be open. We present it here solely to give you an idea of the kinds of positions available in the federal government for California paralegals. Note that the listing also includes the equivalent of interview questions ("Sample Questions Used in Evaluating Applicants"). You should consider preparing answers to such questions when applying for *any* paralegal job.

Title: Paralegal Specialist
Series, Grade: GS-0950-07
Salary Range: $37,041 to $48,152 (For those new to the federal government, pay is typically set at the minimum rate of the appropriate grade. The minimum rate for the GS-7 level is $37,041.)
Promotion Potential: To GS-11
Vacancy Announcement Number: ATR-04-61
Duty Location: Antitrust Division, San Francisco, CA
Number of Vacancies: Two vacancies
Level: This is an entry-level, trainee position.
Appointment: Two-year appointment, which may be renewable up to a total of four years, subject to a one-year trial period in accordance with 5 CFR § 316.304. Full-time, competitive position.
Who May Apply: Open to all qualified persons. Eligible displaced/surplus Department of Justice and federal employees in the local commuting area may apply. This position offers career mobility opportunities.

Duties

This position is located in the San Francisco Field Office of the Antitrust Division. The incumbents perform legal and factual research and closely related duties of a complex nature in support of attorneys engaged in antitrust cases and matters.

Representative duties:

- Performs research using files, library reference materials, corporate records, private and governmental studies, computer databases, and other pertinent sources, to supply needed factual information for inclusion in memoranda, briefs, and similar documents.
- Performs preliminary screening of substantive materials prior to review by attorneys.
- Maintains an accounting system for all materials to be used as exhibits in grand jury proceedings and trials.
- Prepares and organizes charts, graphs, and other material used as exhibits in court.
- Prepares tables of contents, indexes, and tables of authorities for legal briefs, memoranda, and other such documents; reviewing and researching citations, footnotes, textual references, and other entries for accuracy.
- Assists attorneys in conducting interviews with investigative sources and prospective witnesses.
- Travels to the site of trial, grand jury, discovery, etc., and there provides similar paralegal duties as described above.

Qualifications

To qualify for this position, you must satisfy ONE of the requirements described below.

Graduate Education You must have at least one full academic year of graduate level education that demonstrates you possess the knowledge, skills, and abilities necessary to satisfactorily perform the work.

OR

Specialized Experience You must have one year of specialized experience equivalent to at least the GS-5 grade level during which you performed technical assignments that involved developing, authorizing or examining claims or applications that required resolving conflicting data and interpreting a body of laws, rules, regulations and policies; or preparing or reviewing contracts or other legal instruments for legal adequacy and conformance with applicable laws; or selecting and analyzing information to determine the intent of statutes, treaties, and executive orders or legal decisions, opinions, and rulings; or investigating and analyzing evidence of alleged or suspected violations of laws or regulations.

OR

Combination of Graduate Education and Specialized Experience If you have some, but not all, of the graduate education AND specialized experience described above, you may still qualify by combining the amount of creditable education and experience that you do have. To do so, first calculate the percentage of qualifying education you have as a percentage of the education required. Next, calculate the percentage of specialized experience you have as a percentage of the experience required. Then, add the two percentages.

OR

Undergraduate Degree and Superior Academic Achievement You have successfully completed, or will complete a full four-year course of study in any field leading to an undergraduate degree from an accredited college or university, or you possess or expect to possess an undergraduate degree in any field from an accredited college or university, AND you meet one of the following Superior Academic Achievement provisions:

(a) Ranked in the upper third of your college class or major subdivision at the time you apply; or

(b) Earned election to a national scholastic honor society that meets the requirements of the Association of College Honor Societies other than freshman honor societies; or

(c) Earned a grade point average (GPA) of 3.0 or higher on a 4.0 scale based on four years of undergraduate courses, or all undergraduate classes completed during the final two years; or

(d) Earned a GPA of 3.5 or higher on a 4.0 scale based on all completed undergraduate courses in your major, or all undergraduate courses in your major completed during the final two years.

Basis for Rating

Your rating will be based on an evaluation of your experience, education, training, and responses to the Supplemental Qualifications Statement (SQS) items.

Your qualifications will be evaluated on the basis of your competencies in the following areas:

- ability to interpret and analyze material and make well-justified decisions from the analysis;
- skill in writing that reflects organization of subject matter and support for your position and conclusions;
- ability to effectively communicate orally;
- ability to effectively work with others in a team environment; and;
- ability to determine priorities and successfully balance conflicting demands.

How to Apply

Your application will consist of three components. The first component is the occupational questionnaire that you must complete. The second component is your résumé, Optional Application for Federal Employment (OF-612), or Application for Federal Employment (SF-171). The final component of your application consists of "other" application materials. Examples of these other materials include your college transcripts and documentation of veteran status.

Sample Questions Used in Evaluating Applicants

(Note: Your responses are subject to verification through background checks, job interviews, or any other information obtained during the application process.)

- In the past three years how many different paying jobs have you held for more than two weeks?
- On your present or most recent job, how did your supervisor rate you: outstanding; above average; average; below average; not employed; or no rating?
- How many civic or social organizations (which have regular meetings and a defined membership) have you belonged to?
- Have you successfully done work where your primary responsibility was to help others work out their problems?
- Have you successfully done work that constantly required you to work under difficult time constraints?
- Have you successfully planned an event such as a conference, fund-raiser, etc.?
- Have you successfully learned a hobby or leisure activity requiring extensive study or use of complex directions?
- Have you effectively served on a problem-solving, planning, or goal-setting committee or team?
- Have you successfully completed a long-term project outside of work where you were solely responsible for doing the work?
- Have you successfully done work that required extensive on-the-job training?
- Have you worked on several major assignments or projects at the same time with minimal supervision and completed the work on time or ahead of schedule?
- Have you often been asked to proofread or edit the writing of others for content, punctuation, spelling, and grammar?
- Have you suggested or made changes to products or procedures that resulted in better meeting customer needs?
- Have you successfully done work that required you to interact with people at many levels in an organization?
- Have you successfully done work that regularly involved composing letters or writing reports containing several short paragraphs, such as investigation reports, accident reports, performance evaluations, etc.?
- Have you successfully done work that regularly involved answering questions, gathering non-sensitive information, or providing assistance to others, either in person or by telephone?
- Have you successfully done work where you had to coordinate vacation schedules, lunch breaks, etc., with other workers?
- Have you designed or developed something, on your own initiative, to help you or other employees better complete assignments?
- Have you successfully done work that regularly involved being on duty by yourself, or completing nonroutine assignments with minimal or no close supervision?
- Have you taught yourself skills that improved your performance in school or at work (for example, taught yourself typing, computer skills, a foreign language, etc.)?
- Have you successfully completed a complex research project that included collecting and analyzing information, and reporting conclusions or recommendations?
- Have you successfully done work where your supervisor regularly relied on you to make

decisions while he or she was in meetings or out of the office?

- Have you taken the initiative to learn new skills or acquire additional knowledge that improved your performance at work or school, or in leisure activities?
- Have you participated in training classes, workshops, or seminars outside of school that helped you improve your teamwork skills?
- Have you been given additional responsibilities because of your ability to organize and complete your regular work more quickly than expected?

C. More Information

Addresses of Federal Agencies in California
boxer.senate.gov/calLinks/fed.cfm
boxer.senate.gov/calLinks/index.cfm

All Federal Agencies
www.firstgov.gov
(click "A to Z Agency Index")
www.congress.org
(click "Federal Agencies")

Federal Job Search
federaljobsearch.com
(Under "Federal Government Jobs in U.S. by Location," click "California")

Federal Employment Search Sites
www.usajobs.opm.gov
jobsearch.usajobs.opm.gov/a9opm.asp
www.jobsfed.com
hotjobs.yahoo.com/governmentjobs
www.federaljobsearch.com
www.fedworld.gov/jobs/jobsearch.html

Office of Personnel Management Career Opportunities
www.opm.gov/topics.asp

Federal Salaries
www.opm.gov/oca/05tables/index.asp

Qualification Standards for General Schedule (GS) Positions
www.opm.gov/qualifications/SEC-IV/A/gs-admin.asp

D. Something to Check

1. Use the links listed under More Information to find three examples of federal job openings for paralegals in agencies located in California.
2. Go to a list of the Web sites of United States senators (*www.senate.gov*) and United States representatives (*www.house.gov*) in Congress for California. Give examples of information on these sites that might be helpful for someone looking for work as a paralegal in the federal government.

A. Introduction

In this section, you will learn a great deal about working in the public sector as we explore pro bono opportunities for paralegals. Pro bono (or pro bono publico) means for the public good, and refers to work performed without fee or compensation for the benefit of society. Certain kinds of law offices often welcome volunteer or pro bono help. Here are some examples:

- legal aid societies that provide free legal services to the poor
- public interest law offices (e.g., American Civil Liberties Union) that focus on test cases that raise broad issues of social justice
- government offices (e.g., the domestic violence unit of the local district attorney)

Paralegals with full-time jobs might devote one evening or two Saturday afternoons each month to pro bono work. Some employers give their paralegals time off during the work week to do such work.

Paralegals perform a great range of tasks in these settings. They might interview prospective clients to help screen applicants for the services that the office provides. They might do factual research or draft pleadings, particularly in high-volume categories of cases such as divorce or eviction. In addition to substantive tasks such as these, pro bono paralegals might be asked to perform administrative and clerical tasks such as photocopying documents or entering data in a computer database.

Why do paralegals engage in pro bono work? The primary reason is the personal satisfaction derived by working for organizations engaged in socially worthy ventures. Many paralegals feel a professional responsibility to help ensure that disadvantaged individuals have greater access to our justice system. In addition, paralegals can gain practical experience in areas of the law outside their primary expertise. Even if their work is more administrative or clerical than legal, they can gain valuable insights and networking contacts by interacting with the staffs of these offices.

Unemployed paralegals, particularly those just out of school, have an added incentive to do pro bono work. Anything you can say on your résumé about real-world law office experience might help distinguish your résumé from that of someone without such experience.

Of course, all or most of the offices we will be examining also have regular salaried employees. It is not uncommon for a paralegal to be hired by a law office where he or she once did work as a pro bono volunteer.

Before outlining some of the major ways to explore pro bono opportunities in California, two ethical cautions should be covered: confidentiality and conflict of interest.

Everything you learn about a client when working pro bono should be kept confidential. The fact that some of these clients do not pay for their services is irrelevant. A poor person seeking a divorce in a legal aid office has the same right of confidentiality as a Fortune 500 company involved in complex litigation.

As you know from your course in ethics (and as will be examined later in sections 3.2 and 3.3), you need to be aware of the danger that prior client work by an attorney or paralegal could create a conflict of interest for another client in another office. One of the ways this can occur is when the prior work was on behalf of a client who now has an adverse interest with a current client in a different office.

> **Example:** Jim works on behalf of a client named Smith in the case of Smith vs. Jones while Jim is volunteering at the ABC law office. Later, Jim applies for work at the XYZ law office. One of the clients of this firm is Jones who is now suing Smith in a case that is related to, but different from, the case Smith had at the ABC office.

If XYZ hires Jim, there may be a conflict of interest because of Jim's prior work on behalf of Smith. Hiring Jim might eventually disqualify XYZ from continuing to represent Jones.

It is unlikely that pro bono work will create such conflicts of interest, but the cautious paralegal needs to be alert to the possibility. Keep a personal journal in which you note the names of all the parties involved in cases on which you work in any law office. The journal should be private since it contains confidential information. (Client names, for example, are confidential.) Yet when applying for a job, one of the ways an office can determine whether you pose conflict-of-interest risks is to find out what cases you have worked on in the past. It is ethically permissible for you to reveal this information when you are in serious discussions about a new position.

B. Finding Pro Bono Opportunities

To learn about pro bono opportunities for paralegals in your area, start by asking paralegals you know (from school, at the office, at a paralegal association meeting) if they have done any pro bono work, and, if not, whether they know of others who have. Networking with other paralegals in this way can be very productive. Also ask attorneys you know where they or other attorneys do pro bono work. As pointed out later, paralegals often do pro bono work in the same offices where attorneys do such work.

1. Paralegal Associations
Check with the local paralegal associations near you (see the addresses of all state associations in section 1.4). Follow these steps:
   (a) Find out if the association's Web site lists pro bono opportunities or a pro bono coordinator for the association.
   (b) Check the titles of board members and officers of the association to see if anyone on the list covers pro bono matters.
   (c) If the newsletter of the association is online, find out if there are any leads in it on offices that use pro bono help.
   (d) E-mail the president of the association or the association's general information e-mail address to inquire about leads to pro bono work.
   (e) If there is a search box on the site, type in "pro bono."
   (f) Click the e-mail address of any paralegal on the site, introduce yourself, state that you are trying to learn about pro bono opportunities in the area, and ask if this person has any leads. Often all you need to get started is the name of one paralegal doing pro bono work. Such a person will be able to tell you if additional volunteers are needed where he or she does such work or to give you the name of others who would know.

2. Pro Bono Programs Guide for Paralegals
www.probono.net/ca/oppsguide.cfm
(Under "Projects for" click "Paralegals")

3. CASA California
www.californiacasa.org
www.californiacasa.org/htm/volunteer.htm

CASA means "court appointed special advocate." A CASA volunteer (who does not have to be an attorney) is a person who has been selected and trained to help the court define the best interests of a child in juvenile court dependency and wardship proceedings. To fulfill this role, the CASA volunteer becomes a sworn officer of the court.

4. Attorney Pro Bono as a Lead to Paralegal Pro Bono

Very often, a law office that accepts pro bono volunteer work by attorneys also accepts (or would be willing to consider) pro bono volunteer work by paralegals. Hence you need to know what offices in California welcome pro bono work by attorneys. You need to call or e-mail such offices to ask if they accept pro bono work by paralegals. Here is what you could say: "I understand that your office has attorney volunteers. I am a paralegal and am wondering whether the office also uses paralegal volunteers or would consider using them. If not, can you suggest other offices in the area that I might contact?"

Steps to Take to Find out Where Attorneys do Pro Bono Work:

(a) Go to the Web site of the local bar associations in your area (see the addresses in section 3.4). Look for committees, sections, or special programs on pro bono. Type "pro bono" in the association's search box. Send an e-mail to the information office at the association that says, "I'm looking for leads to law offices that accept pro bono work by paralegals and would appreciate any help you can provide."

(b) Go to the state bar association site (*www.calbar.ca.gov*). Type "pro bono" in the search box to obtain possible leads to pro bono opportunities.

(c) Go to the ABA pro bono site:
www.abanet.org/legalservices/probono
Click "Directory of Local Pro Bono Programs." Then click California on the map. These steps should lead you to a site that lists pro bono programs throughout the state:
www.abanet.org/legalservices/probono/directory/california.html

(d) In Google, run a search that contains the name of your city or county, the phrase "pro bono" and the word "~attorney." (The tilde (~) means you want to include synonyms of attorney such as lawyer and counsel.) Here are examples of such queries:
"los angeles" "pro bono" ~attorney
"alameda county" "pro bono" ~attorney

(e) Do the following search in Google or any search engine:
"volunteer lawyers" california

(f) Go to the Web sites of the specialty bar associations that interest you (see section 3.4 for Web sites). Find out if the sites provide information or links to pro bono needs. If not, try to e-mail someone at the association to ask about leads.

(g) Go to site of the Legal Services Corporation, the federal government agency that funds legal service programs (*www.lsc.gov*). Click California on the map or type "California" in the search box. You will be led to a list of all of the legal service programs in the state, many of which welcome pro bono assistance.

(h) Go to Volunteer Match (*www.volunteermatch.org*). Type in your zip code and click "Justice & Legal" in the "Interest Area." You will be led to organizations seeking people who can provide direct or indirect legal help.

5. CALegal Advocates Pro Bono Opportunities
www.calegaladvocates.org
www.calegaladvocates.org/oppsguide.cfm
www.probono.net/ca/oppsguide.cfm

CALegal Advocates will tell you whether paralegals are used in many of the large number of law offices it lists. At the Programs Guide site (*www.probono.net/ca/oppsguide.cfm*), click the "Area of law" pull-down menu and select areas such as the following:

Arts	Health
Civil Rights	HIV/AIDS
Consumer Law	Homeless
Debts/Bankruptcy	Housing
Disability	Immigration
Education	Life Planning
Elder Law	Prisoners
Employment	Public Benefits
Family & Juvenile	Taxes

6. Pro Bono Net California
www.probono.net/ca
(Areas of interest you can explore on pro bono net include Asylum Law, Death Penalty, Health Law, Human Rights, and Prisoners' Rights)

7. Specific Categories of Law Offices That May Need Pro Bono Help

The steps listed above for paralegal and attorney pro bono work will lead you to most of the offices in the state that serve indigent (poor) clients as well as clients in specialty groups. Here are some additional routes to such offices. At the following sites, look for contact links and e-mail addresses where you can inquire about pro bono opportunities for paralegals in your area. If a site does not cover your area of the state, the site will probably be able to tell you (via e-mail) where you might find something closer to you.

Legal Aid and Legal Services Programs in California
www.lsc.gov (click "California" on the map)
www.ptla.org/ptlasite/links.htm

LawHelpCalifornia
www.lawhelpcalifornia.org
(provides extensive referrals to law offices, many of which serve poor and low income clients and hence may welcome pro bono help)

American Civil Liberties Union (northern and southern California)
www.aclunc.org
www.aclu-sc.org

California Lawyers for the Arts
www.calawyersforthearts.org

California Center for Law and the Deaf
www.deaflaw.org

Domestic Violence
www.fvlc.org

Rural Pro Bono Legal Assistance
www.crla.org
www.probono.net/ca/what-about-pro-bono-for-rural-californians.cfm

Immigration Law
www.ilrc.org
www.abanet.org/immigration/probono/probar

AIDS Legal Referral Panel
www.alrp.org

Senior Citizens
www.seniorlegalhotline.org
(click "Other Senior Legal Services")

Disability Rights Education and Defense Fund
dredf.org

Gay Rights
www.balif.org
www.laglc.org
www.aclunc.org
(Click "Issues" then "LGBT")

California Indian Legal Services
www.calindian.org

C. More Information

ABA Pro Bono Sites by State
www.abanet.org/legalservices/probono/directory.html#

Public Interest Clearinghouse
Legal Aid Association of California
www.pic.org
(Click "For Pro Bono")

Corporate Pro Bono
www.corporateprobono.org

National Association of Pro Bono Professionals
www.abanet.org/legalservices/probono/napbpro/home.html

Pro Bono Clinics
www.probono.net/ca/newcases.cfm

Pro Bono Institute
www.probonoinst.org

National Association of Pro Bono Professionals
www.abanet.org/legalservices/probono/napbpro/home.html

Miscellaneous Pro Bono Links
www.ptla.org/ptlasite/probono.htm

Lawyer Referral Services
www.abanet.org/legalservices/lris/directory.html
www.legal-aid.com/lawyer_referral_services.html

Bakersfield
www.gbla.org

Bay Area
www.sfpa.com/a-pbca.htm
www.probono.net/sf

Central California Legal Services
www.centralcallegal.org

Kern County
www.gbla.org

Inland Empire
www.inlandlegal.org

Los Angeles
www.probonola.org
www.kids-alliance.org

Sacramento, San Joaquin, Yolo, El Dorado, Placer
www.vlsp.org

Santa Clara
www.probonoproject.org

D. Something to Check

1. Find any three offices in California that accept pro bono help for adopted children seeking information and possible contact with birth parents.
2. Pick any other area of the law. Find three offices in California that accept pro bono help for those areas of the law.

2.5 Becoming a Notary Public in California

A. Introduction

Very often, law offices work with documents that must be notarized. This is particularly true in offices that do transactional work, e.g., incorporating a company, transferring real estate, probating an estate. A notary public is a public officer who is given authority by the state to attest the genuineness of certain writings, to administer oaths, and to attest to the authenticity of signatures. (47 Cal. Jur. 3d (2007) Notaries Public, § 1)

Paralegals should consider becoming notaries whether or not specifically requested to do so by their employer. Being a notary can be valuable even if this credential is used only occasionally as a backup when others are not readily available inside or outside the office to notarize documents.

Caution, however, is needed when performing notary services. Attorney supervisors have been known to pressure their employees to notarize documents improperly, such as by asking them to notarize a signature that the employee did not personally observe being placed on the document involved. In fact, when paralegals are named as defendants in a suit, the most common reason is false notarization of a signature.

To become a notary public in California and to provide notary services, you must:

1. be a resident of California
2. be at least 18 years of age
3. complete a six-hour course of study
4. pass a written examination
5. be able to read, write, and understand English
6. pass a background check
7. take, subscribe, and file an oath of office
8. file a $15,000 surety bond with the county clerk's office

The cost of becoming a notary in California is approximately $50, not including the cost of the six-hour course (a new requirement added in 2005) nor of obtaining the surety bond.

The notary bond is not an insurance policy for the notary, but rather it provides a limited fund for paying claims against the notary. The notary remains personally liable to the full extent of the damage sustained and may be required to reimburse the bonding company for sums paid by the company because of misconduct or negligence of the notary public.

B. Restrictions and Duties

Unauthorized Practice of Law

California notaries are prohibited from performing any duties that "may be construed as the unlawful practice of law." Among the acts that constitute the practice of law is the preparation, drafting, or selection or determination of the kind of any legal document, or giving advice with relation to any legal documents or matters.

Notarization of Incomplete Documents

A notary public may not notarize a document that is incomplete. If the notary is presented with a document for notarization that he or she knows from experience to be incomplete or is without doubt on its face incomplete, the notary must refuse to notarize the document.

Wills

The California State Bar advises that when a notary public is asked to notarize a document that purports to be a will, the notary public should decline and advise the person requesting the notarization to consult a member of the California State Bar. If an attorney recommends that the document be notarized, a notary may do so.

Notary Seal

Each notary public is required to have and to use a seal, which must *not* be surrendered to an employer upon termination of employment, whether or not the employer paid for the seal. The seal contains (a) the State Seal and the words "Notary Public," (b) the name of the notary public as shown on the commission, (c) the name of the county where the oath of office and notary bond are on file, (d) the expiration date of the notary public commission, and (e) the sequential identification assigned to the notary public.

Improper Use of Notary Seal

Many documents that are acknowledged may later be recorded. A document may not be accepted by the recorder if the notary seal is illegible. Notaries are cautioned to take care that the notary stamp leaves a clear impression. All the elements must be easily discernible. The seal should not be placed over signatures or any printed matter on the document. An illegible or improperly placed seal may result in rejection of the document for recordation and inconveniences and extra expenses for all those involved.

Sequential Journal

A notary public is required to keep one active sequential journal at a time of all acts performed as a notary public. The journal must be kept in a locked and secured area (such as a lock box or locked desk drawer), under the direct and exclusive control of the notary. The journal shall include:

(a) The date, time, and type of each official act (acknowledgment or jurat),

(b) The character of every instrument sworn to, affirmed, acknowledged, or proved before the notary public (e.g., deed of trust);

(c) The signature of each person whose signature is being notarized;

(d) A statement as to whether the identity of a person making an acknowledgment was based on personal knowledge or satisfactory evidence. If identity was established by satisfactory evidence, then the journal shall contain the signature of the credible witness swearing or affirming to the identity of the individual or the type of identifying document, the governmental agency issuing the document, the serial or identifying number of the document, and the date of issue or expiration of the document (e.g., driver's license, Department of Motor Vehicles, #X00000, 00/00/00.);

(e) If the identity of the person making the acknowledgment was established by the oaths or affirmations of two credible witnesses whose identities are proven upon the presentation of satisfactory evidence, the type of identifying documents, the identifying numbers of the documents, and the dates of issuance or expiration of the documents presented by the witnesses to establish their identity (e.g., driver's license, Department of Motor Vehicles, #X00000, 00/00/00.);

(f) The fee charged for the notarial service;

(g) If the document to be notarized is a deed, quitclaim deed, or deed of trust affecting real property, the notary public shall require the party signing the document to place his or her right thumbprint in the journal. If the right thumbprint is not available, then the notary shall have the party use his or her left thumb, or any available finger and shall so indicate in the journal.

Acknowledgement

The form most frequently completed by the notary public is the acknowledgment. In the acknowledgment, the notary public certifies:

(a) that the signer *personally appeared* before the notary public on the date indicated in the county indicated,

(b) to the identity of the signer, and

(c) that the signer acknowledged executing the document.

The notary public sequential journal must contain a statement as to whether the identity of a person making an acknowledgment was based on personal knowledge or satisfactory evidence. If identity was established based on satisfactory evidence then the journal shall contain the signature of the credible witness swearing or affirming to the identity of the individual or the type of identifying document used to establish the person's identity, the governmental agency issuing the document, the serial or identifying number of the document, and the date of issue or expiration of the document. The certificate of acknowledgment must be completely filled out at the time the notary's signature and seal are affixed. The completion of an acknowledgment that contains statements that the notary public knows to be false not only may cause the notary to be liable for civil penalties and administrative action, but is also a *criminal offense.*

Any certificate of acknowledgment taken within this state shall be in substantial conformance with the form in Exhibit 2.5A.

The key wording of an acknowledgment is "personally appeared." It is not acceptable to affix an acknowledgment to a document mailed or otherwise delivered to a notary public when the signer did NOT personally appear before the notary public, even if the signer is known by the notary public. Also, it is not acceptable to affix a notary public seal and signature to a document without the notarial wording.

Exhibit 2.5A **Certificate of Acknowledgment**

State of California
County of ________ }

On______ before me, (here insert name and title of the officer), personally appeared

____

____

______________________________________,

personally known to me (or proved to me on the basis of satisfactory evidence) to be the person(s) whose name(s) is/are subscribed to the within instrument and acknowledged to me that he/she/they executed the same in his/her/their authorized capacity(ies), and that by his/her/their signature(s) on the instrument the person(s), or the entity upon behalf of which the person(s) acted, executed the instrument.
WITNESS my hand and official seal.

NOTARY PUBLIC SIGNATURE NOTARY PUBLIC SEAL

Source: www.ss.ca.gov/business/notary/notary_hdbk.pdf

Jurat

The second form most frequently completed by a notary public is the jurat. The jurat is identified by the wording "Subscribed and sworn to" above the place where the notary public signs his/her name. In the jurat, the notary public certifies:

(a) that the signer *personally appeared* before the notary public on the date indicated and in the county indicated

(b) that the signer signed the document in the presence of the notary public

(c) that the notary public administered the oath

(d) to the identity of the signer.

There is no prescribed wording for the oath, but an acceptable oath would be "Do you swear or affirm that the statements in this document are true?" When administering the oath, the signer and notary traditionally raise their right hands, but this is not a legal requirement. A sample affidavit (written statement made under oath) may be worded as follows: "I certify that I have resided in the State of California for more than five years. /s/ John Doe"

See Exhibit 2.5B for the form of a jurat.

Powers of Attorney

A notary public can certify copies of powers of attorney. A certified copy of a power of attorney that has been certified by a notary public has the same force and effect as the original power of attorney.

Fees

Government Code section 8211 specifies the maximum fees that may be charged for notary public services; however, a notary public may elect to charge no fee or an amount that is less than the maximum

Exhibit 2.5B Jurat

JURAT

State of California

County of ____________________

Subscribed and sworn to (or affirmed) before me on

this_________day of ___________________________,20______,

by ____

personally known to me or proved to me on the basis of satisfactory evidence to be the person(s) who appeared before me.

NOTARY PUBLIC SIGNATURE NOTARY PUBLIC SEAL

Source: www.ss.ca.gov/business/notary/notary_hdbk.pdf

amount prescribed by law. The charging of a fee and the amount of the fee charged is at the discretion of the notary public or the notary public's employer provided it does not exceed the maximum fees. To avoid possible problems, the fees charged (or not charged) should be consistent from customer to customer. The notary public is still required to make an entry in the notary public journal even if no fee was charged, such as "no fee" or "0."

Maximum fees allowable:

(a) For taking an acknowledgment or proof of a deed, or other instrument, to include the seal and the writing of the certificate: $10 for each signature taken.

(b) For administering an oath or affirmation to one person and executing the jurat, including the seal: $10.

(c) For all services rendered in connection with the taking of any deposition: $20 plus $5 for administering the oath to the witness and $5 for the certificate to the deposition.

(d) For every protest for the nonpayment of a promissory note or for the nonpayment or nonacceptance of a bill of exchange, draft, or check: $10.

(e) For serving every notice of nonpayment of a promissory note or of nonpayment or nonacceptance of a bill of exchange, order, draft, or check: $5.

(f) For recording every protest: $5.

(g) For certifying a copy of a power of attorney under Section 4307 of the Probate Code: $10.

(h) No fee shall be charged to notarize signatures on absentee ballot identification envelopes or other voting materials.

(i) No fee may be charged to a United States military veteran for notarization of an application or a claim for a pension, allotment, allowance, compensation, insurance, or any other veteran's benefit.

Notaries Who Are Employees

A private employer, pursuant to an agreement with an employee who is a notary public, may pay the premiums on any bond and the cost of any stamps, seals, or other supplies required in connection with the appointment, commission, or performance of the duties of such notary public. Such agreement may also provide for the remission of fees collected by such notary public to the employer, in which case any fees collected or obtained by such notary public while such agreement is in effect shall be remitted by such notary public to the employer which shall deposit such funds to the credit of the fund from which the compensation of the notary public is paid. The employer may limit, during the employee's ordinary course of employment, the providing of notarial services by the employee solely to transactions directly associated with the business purposes of the employer.

C. More Information

Notary Public Section
Secretary of State
P.O. Box 942877
Sacramento, CA 94277-0001
916-653-3595
www.ss.ca.gov/business/notary/notary.htm

Application
www.ss.ca.gov/business/notary/notary_formsfees.htm

Request for Exam Materials
www.ss.ca.gov/business/notary/notary_cklist_exam_materials.htm

Registering for the Exam
916-263-3520
www.ss.ca.gov/business/notary/notary_cklist_registration.htm

Online Registration
notary.cps.ca.gov

Forms, Fees, and Services
www.ss.ca.gov/business/notary/notary_formsfees.htm

Testing Information
www.cps.ca.gov/TakeATest/notary/howtoreg.asp

Statutes on the California Notary Public
Government Code §§ 8200-8230, 6100 et seq.
Civil Code §§ 1185 et seq.
www.leginfo.ca.gov/calaw.html

Regulations on the California Notary Public
Administrative Code title 2, §§ 20800-20802

Notary Public Handbook
www.ss.ca.gov/business/notary/notary_hdbk.htm

American Notary Exchange
www.americannotaryexchange.com

American Notary Group
www.americannotary.com

American Society of Notaries
www.notaries.org

California Notary Seminars
www.romenotaryseminars.com

National Notary Association
www.nationalnotary.org

North American Notary Association
www.nanotary.com

Notary Access Association
notaryaccess.org

United States Notary Association
www.enotary.org

D. Something to Check

1. Go to the California statutes on notary publics (you'll find the statutes on the Web site listed in More Information; see also section 5.1). When can a notary public's commission be revoked or suspended?
2. On Google (*www.google.com*) or other general search engine, run the following search, "california notary public." Summarize the categories of information found with this search.
3. Find the Web sites of three legal document assistants that offer notary services.

2.6 An Employee or an Independent Contractor?

A. Introduction

Most paralegals are employees of law firms, corporations, or other groups where they work in full-time or part-time positions. There are, however, a fair number of paralegals who have left the security of a regular paycheck in order to open their own business. They have become independent paralegals (sometimes called "freelance paralegals") who offer services to more than one law office, usually charging the office an hourly rate or a per-project flat fee. We are not referring to individuals who offer their services directly to the public without attorney supervision. (See section 1.3 on legal document assistants and unlawful detainer assistants.) Our focus in this section is the independents who can still use the title "paralegal" or "legal assistant" because they work under the supervision of an attorney. However, they are not on the traditional payroll of a single law office. They provide a variety of services to different firms. For example, they might:

- digest the transcript of depositions or other litigation documents
- encode or enter documents into a computer database
- collect and help interpret medical records
- prepare a 706 federal estate tax return
- prepare all the documents needed to probate an estate
- prepare trial exhibits
- conduct an asset search
- compile a chain-of-title report on real property

Such work is performed in the paralegal's office (often in his or her own home) or at the law firms that have retained the paralegal.

The problem is that California and the federal government (particularly the Internal Revenue Service) may conclude that these independent paralegals are not independent enough. They might be considered employees regardless of their title or where they do their work.

For its *employees*, a law office is required to withhold federal and state income taxes, withhold and pay Social Security and Medicare taxes, pay unemployment tax on wages, pay overtime compensation, provide workers' compensation coverage, etc. In general, however, none of this is required for *independent contractors* whom the office hires. In light of this disparity of treatment, offices are occasionally charged with improperly classifying workers as independent contractors in order to avoid their tax withholding and other employee-related obligations.

This raises the basic question: What is an employee? The answer to this question is not always clear.

- The sole test is *not* whether you are on the payroll.
- The sole test is *not* your title.

- The sole test is *not* whether you work full-time or part-time.
- The sole test is *not* whether the law office considers you an independent contractor nor whether you consider yourself to be one.
- The sole test is not whether you have signed an agreement with the law office specifying that you are an independent contractor rather than an employee.

It is quite possible for everyone to consider a worker to be an independent contractor—*except the government*! The California state government and/or the federal government may take the position that the "independent contractor" is in fact an employee in disguise. When such a conclusion is reached, back employment taxes must be paid and penalties are possible. The law office may not be trying to avoid its tax and other responsibilities. It may simply have been mistaken in its definition of an employee. This is not uncommon. Many businesses have been told that workers being paid as independent contractors should have been classified as employees.

Sometimes the issue arises through tort law. For example:

> The ABC law firm hires Mary as an "independent contractor." One of Mary's tasks for the firm is to file pleadings in court. While driving to court one day in her own car, Mary has an accident. The other driver now wants to sue Mary *and* the ABC law firm as her employer.

Whether the driver can also sue ABC depends, in part, on whether Mary is an employee of ABC.

Exhibit 2.6A

Independent Contractor or Employee?

General Guidelines for Determining Who is an Independent Contractor and Who is an Employee

- An individual is an independent contractor if the person for whom the services are performed:
  - has the right to control or direct only the result of the work
  - does not have the right to control or direct the means and methods of accomplishing the result.

- Anyone who performs services for an office is an employee if the office can control what will be done *and* how it will be done through instructions, training, or other means. This is so even when the office gives the worker freedom of action. What matters is that the office has the *right* to control the details of how the services are performed.

- Here is how one court explained the test: "If the alleged employer retains the right to control the manner and means by which the results are to be accomplished, the individual who performs the service is an employee. If only the results are controlled, the individual performing the service is an independent contractor." *National Heritage Enterprises, Inc. v. Division of Employment Sec.* 164 S.W.3d 160, 166 (Mo.App. W.D., 2005)

B. Standards

Under both California and federal law, the key to determining whether someone is an independent contractor is the amount of control that exists over what he or she does and how he or she does it. Related factors are also considered, but control is key. Exhibit 2.6A summarizes the test.

No two independent paralegals operate exactly alike. Different paralegals have different relationships with their attorney clients. Some are given much more independence than others. Hence there is no one answer to the question of whether a particular independent paralegal is an employee or an independent contractor. Each case must be examined separately.

There is California and federal law on when a worker is an employee as opposed to an independent contractor. California applies its own law on state issues such as whether a worker must be covered by workers' compensation. The federal government applies its law when the issue is whether federal income and social security taxes must be withheld. There is substantial similarity between California and federal law on the question. The right of control is central under both laws.

Factors Considered Under California Law

Whether a worker is an employee or an independent contractor depends upon a number of factors, all of which must be considered, and none of which is controlling by itself. California courts apply the "multifactor" or the "economic realities" test adopted by the California Supreme Court in the case of *S. G. Borello & Sons, Inc. v Dept. of Industrial Relations* (1989) 48 Cal.3d 341. In applying this test, the most significant factor to be considered is whether the office for whom the service is rendered has control or the right to control the worker both as to the work done and the manner and means in which it is performed. Related factors that may be considered include:

1. Whether the person performing services is engaged in an occupation or business distinct from that of the person for whom the services are performed;
2. Whether the services provided are part of the regular business of the office receiving the services;
3. Whether the office or the worker supplies the instrumentalities, tools, and the place for the person providing the services;
4. The worker's own investment in the equipment or materials he or she uses in performing the services;
5. Whether the worker hires his or her own helpers in performing the services;
6. Whether the services rendered require a special skill;

7. Whether in the locality the services are usually performed under the direction of the person receiving those services or whether they are usually performed by a specialist without supervision;
8. The worker's opportunity for profit or loss depending on his or her managerial skill;
9. The length of time for which the services are to be performed;
10. The degree of permanence of the working relationship;
11. The method of payment, whether by time or by the job.

Whether the parties believe they are creating an employer-employee relationship may have some bearing on the question, but, like the other factors listed above, this is not determinative. The existence of a written agreement purporting to establish an independent contractor relationship is not determinative and the fact that a worker is issued a 1099 form rather than a W-2 form is also not determinative with respect to independent contractor status.

Even where there is an absence of control over work details, an employer-employee relationship will be found if (1) the office hiring the worker retains pervasive control over the operation as a whole, (2) the worker's duties are an integral part of the operation, and (3) the nature of the work makes detailed control unnecessary.

Presumption under California Labor Code

§ 2750.5. There is a rebuttable presumption affecting the burden of proof that a worker performing services for which a license is required pursuant to Chapter 9 (commencing with Section 7000) of Division 3 of the Business and Professions Code, or who is performing such services for a person who is required to obtain such a license is an employee rather than an independent contractor. Proof of independent contractor status includes satisfactory proof of these factors:

(a) That the individual has the right to control and discretion as to the manner of performance of the contract for services in that the result of the work and not the means by which it is accomplished is the primary factor bargained for.

(b) That the individual is customarily engaged in an independently established business.

(c) That the individual's independent contractor status is bona fide and not a subterfuge to avoid employee status. A bona fide independent contractor status is further evidenced by the presence of cumulative factors such as substantial investment other than personal services in the business, holding out to be in business for oneself, bargaining for a contract to complete a specific project for compensation by project rather than by time, control over the time and place the work is performed, supplying the tools or instrumentalities used in the work other than tools and instrumentalities normally and customarily provided by employees, hiring employees, performing work that is not ordinarily in the course of the principal's work, performing work that requires a particular skill, holding a license pursuant to the Business and Professions Code, the intent by the parties that the work relationship is of an independent contractor status, or that the relationship is not severable or terminable at will by the principal but gives rise to an action for breach of contract.

Factors Considered Under Federal Law

Federal law reaches substantially the same conclusion, but uses different terminology in describing the factors involved. Under federal law, three categories of evidence on control and independence are considered: (1) behavioral control, (2) financial control, and (3) type of relationship. Evidence in these categories are factors to be weighed; they are not absolute guidelines or definitions.

(1) Behavioral Control

Does the office have the right to direct and control *how* the worker does the task for which he or she is hired? Two behavioral facts that help answer this question are the type and degree of instructions received and the training provided.

Instructions the office gives the worker. In general, employees are subject to instructions about when, where, and how to work. Here are examples of the kinds of instructions an office could give on how work should be done:

- when and where to do the work
- what tools or equipment to use
- what other workers to use to assist with the work
- where to purchase supplies and services
- what work must be performed by a specified individual
- what order or sequence to follow

The amount of instruction needed varies among different jobs. Even if no instructions are given, sufficient behavioral control may exist if the office has the *right* to control how the work results are achieved. An office may lack the knowledge to instruct some highly specialized professionals; in other cases, the task may require little or no instruction. The key consideration is whether the office has retained the right to control the details of a worker's performance or has given up this right.

Training the office gives the worker. An employee may be given training on performing the services in a particular manner. Independent contractors, on the other hand, ordinarily use their own methods.

(2) Financial Control

Factors that show whether the office has a right to control the business aspects of the worker's job include:

- The extent to which the worker has unreimbursed business expenses. Independent contractors are more likely to have unreimbursed expenses than are employees. Fixed ongoing costs that are incurred regardless of whether work is currently being performed are especially important. Note, however, that it is possible for employees to incur unreimbursed expenses in connection with the services they perform for their office.
- The extent of the worker's investment. An independent contractor (unlike an employee) often has a significant investment in the facilities he or she uses in performing services for someone else. This is not to say, however, that a significant investment is required for independent contractor status.
- The extent to which the worker makes services available to the relevant market. An independent contractor is generally free to seek out business opportunities. Independent contractors often advertise, maintain a visible business location, and are available to work in the relevant market.
- How the office pays the worker. Assume that a worker is guaranteed a regular wage amount for an hourly, weekly, or other period of time. This usually indicates that he or she is an employee, even when the wage or salary is supplemented by a commission. An independent contractor is usually paid by a flat fee for the job. In some professions, however, such as law, independent contractors are often paid hourly.
- The extent to which the worker can realize a profit or loss. An independent contractor can make a profit or suffer a loss.

(3) Type of Relationship

Facts that show the parties' type of relationship include:

- Written contracts describing the relationship the parties intended to create. Employees often do not have such contracts.
- Whether the office provides the worker with employee-type benefits, such as insurance, a pension plan, vacation pay, or sick pay. Independent contractors are seldom given such benefits.
- The permanency of the relationship. If the office engages a worker with the expectation that the relationship will continue indefinitely, rather than for a specific project or period, this is generally considered evidence that the intent of the office was to create an employer-employee relationship.
- The extent to which services performed by the worker are a key aspect of the regular business of the office. If a worker provides services that are a key aspect of the office's regular business activity, it is more likely that it will have the right to direct and control his or her activities and, therefore, this factor indicates an employer-employee relationship.

Conclusion

When the status of a paralegal is challenged, the various factors under California or federal law will be weighed one by one. The evidence may conflict. Some aspects of what a paralegal does may clearly indicate an independent contractor status, while others may point to an employee-employer relationship. A court will examine the factors to determine where, on balance, a particular worker fits.

C. More Information

Independent Contractor vs. Employee
www.dir.ca.gov/dlse/FAQ_IndependentContractor.htm

IRS Guidance
www.irs.gov/pub/irs-pdf/p15a.pdf
www.irs.gov/businesses/small/article/0,,id=115041,00.html
www.irs.gov/businesses/small/article/0,,id=115045,00.html
www.irs.gov/businesses/small/article/0,,id=99921,00.html

IRS Telephone Help for Employment Questions
800-829-4933

California Chamber of Commerce Help on Personnel Issues
www.hrcalifornia.com

D. Something to Check

1. Using any general search engine (e.g., *www.google.com*) or legal search engine (e.g., *www.findlaw.com*), find and summarize a court opinion from any court in which the issue was whether a worker was an employee or independent contractor.

2. Interview an independent or freelance paralegal with his or her own office in California. Find out how this paralegal typically provides services to law firms. Then apply the three categories of factors (behavioral control, financial control, and type of relationship) to identify evidence of both independent contractor and employee status.

2.7 Overtime Pay under Federal and State Law

A. Introduction

There are two sets of laws that determine whether California paralegals are entitled to overtime compensation (1.5 times regular pay) if they work more than forty hours a week:

- Federal Overtime Law: Fair Labor Standards Act (FLSA)
  www.dol.gov
  www.dol.gov/esa/regs/compliance/whd/fairpay/main.htm
- State Overtime Law: California Labor Code
  www.dir.ca.gov/dlse
  www.dir.ca.gov/dlse/faq%5Fovertime.htm

The standards in both sets of laws must be examined to determine a paralegal's eligibility for overtime compensation. If there is a conflict between federal and state standards, the higher standard will apply—the standard that provides the higher rate of pay. The following discussion assumes that a paralegal at a particular job site is *not* covered by a union contract, which can provide greater wage benefits than either federal or state law.

Under both federal and California law, the focus is on job duties, not job titles. Regardless of what the employee is called, his or her eligibility for overtime compensation will depend on a close analysis of the nature of the actual work performed by the individual employee.

In general, as you will see in the following discussion, many paralegal supervisors are not eligible for overtime compensation, but most line paralegals are. This conclusion applies whether you are applying federal overtime law or state overtime law, even though there are some important differences between the two sets of laws. For most paralegals, the differences do *not* lead to different results.

Nevertheless, you need to know about both sets of laws. It is possible that your particular job qualifies you for overtime compensation under state law, but not under federal law.

If an employee is eligible for overtime, he or she cannot be asked to waive this entitlement as a condition of obtaining or maintaining employment. Some paralegals would prefer *not* to receive overtime compensation even if they are entitled to it. They would rather have their extra work hours rewarded by bonuses and other perks, similar to the way attorneys are rewarded. Yet even these paralegals should know the law in the event that they may one day need to use it, particularly when leaving a position.

B. Federal Overtime Law: Fair Labor Standards Act (FLSA)

Federal overtime law is enforced by the Wage and Hour Division (WHD) of the United States Department of Labor (DOL):

U.S. Department of Labor
Employment Standards Administration
Wage and Hour Division
200 Constitution Avenue, NW
Washington, DC 20210
866-4-USWAGE
www.dol.gov/esa/whd

Under federal law, workers are entitled to overtime compensation if they are paid on a salary basis and earn under $455 a week ($23,660 a year). Most paralegals earn over this amount. Are they also entitled to overtime compensation? In general, the answer is yes, *unless they are exempt.*

There are three main categories of exempt employees under federal law: executive, professional, or administrative (These categories are referred to as the "white collar" exemptions.) Do paralegals fit within any of them? The answer depends on their primary duties, meaning the main or most important tasks they perform. It does not depend on their title, which can vary from employer to employer. Furthermore, because paralegals perform a wide variety of tasks in many different settings, the question of whether they are exempt must be determined on a person-by-person basis—one paralegal at a time. It is possible for a paralegal in an office to be exempt while another paralegal in the same office is nonexempt. (Again, keep in mind that we are talking about federal overtime law; state overtime eligibility will be discussed separately.)

Here is an overview of the three exemptions and how they might apply to paralegals:

Executive Exemption under Federal Law

The employee (1) manages an enterprise such as a department or subdivision that has a permanent status or function in the office; (2) customarily and regularly directs the work of two or more employees; and (3) either has the authority to hire, promote, or fire other employees or can recommend such action and the recommendation is given particular weight.

Many paralegal supervisors meet all three tests of the executive exemption. They often manage the paralegal unit of the firm, supervise more than two employees, and have great influence on who is hired, promoted, or fired in their department. This is not so, however, for line paralegals. Hence they are not exempt under the executive exemption, but many paralegal supervisors would be.

Professional Exemption under Federal Law

The employee performs work that requires advanced knowledge that is customarily acquired by a prolonged course of specialized intellectual instruction. (Advanced knowledge means work that is predominantly intellectual in character, and includes work requiring the consistent exercise of discretion and judgment.) There are two categories of exempt professional employees: learned professionals (whose specialized academic training is a standard prerequisite for entrance into the profession) and creative professionals (who work mainly in the creative arts).

Paralegals do not fit within the professional exemption. They are not "creative professionals" because law is not in the same category as music, theater, or one of the other creative arts. Nor are they "learned professionals," because prolonged specialized instruction is not a standard prerequisite to entering the field. A bachelor's degree, for example, is not a prerequisite to becoming a paralegal.

As we saw in section 1.2, however, there are education requirements that must be met in California before the paralegal title can be used. According to the U.S, Department of Labor, "while some two and four-year colleges offer coursework and certification in paralegal studies, no minimum education or training requirements are established that a person must satisfy before using the occupational title 'paralegal.' This indicates that the occupation lacks a requirement of 'knowledge of an advanced type . . . customarily acquired by a prolonged course of specialized intellectual instruction' as required under 29 C.F.R. § 541.300(a)(2)."

(*www.dol.gov/esa/whd/opinion/FLSA/ 2005/2005_12_16_54_FLSA.htm*)

It is doubtful, however, that the U.S. Department of Labor would consider California's education requirement to be sufficiently "prolonged." Furthermore, someone can perform paralegal tasks in California without meeting these requirements; such individuals would simply not be able to call themselves paralegals.

Administrative Exemption under Federal Law

The employee (1) performs office work that is directly related to the management or general business operations of the employer or of the employer's customers, and (2) exercises discretion and independent judgment with respect to matters of significance.

The question of whether the administrative exemption applies to paralegals is less clear. The first test under the administrative exemption is that the employees perform office work that is "directly related to the management or general business operations of the employer or of the employer's customers." This means "assisting with the running or servicing of the business" such as working on budgets, purchasing equipment, or administering the office's computer database (*www.dol.gov/esa/regs/compliance/whd/fairpay*). Such tasks, however, are not the primary duties of most paralegals, although they may help out in these areas. In the main, paralegals spend most of their time working on individual cases and hence do not meet the first test.

The second test (which also must be met for the administrative exemption to apply) is that the employees exercise "discretion and independent judgment with respect to matters of significance." The phrase "discretion and independent judgment" involves (a) comparing and evaluating possible courses of conduct and (b) acting or making a decision after the various possibilities have been considered. The phrase implies that the employee has authority to make an independent choice, "free from immediate direction or supervision." An employee does *not* exercise discretion and independent judgment if he or she merely uses skills in applying well-established techniques, procedures, or standards described in manuals or other sources.

Do paralegals meet the second test of exercising "discretion and independent judgment with respect to matters of significance"? They certainly work on "matters of significance." Yet it is not clear whether they exercise "discretion and independent judgment." Paralegals are often given some leeway in the performance of their work. Yet if they operate "within closely prescribed limits," they are not exercising discretion and independent judgment. Furthermore, federal officials often take the position that paralegals do not have the kind of independence this exemption requires because of the attorney supervision and approval their work must be given under the rules of ethics. If paralegals make independent choices on client matters, they run the risk of being charged with engaging in the unauthorized practice of law.

According to the U.S., Department of Labor, paralegals usually fit "into that category of employees who apply particular skills and knowledge in preparing assignments. Employees who apply such skills and knowledge generally are not exercising independent judgment, even if they have some leeway in reaching a conclusion. In addition, most jurisdictions have strict prohibitions against the unauthorized practice of law by laypersons. Under the American Bar Association's Code of Professional Responsibility, a delegation of legal tasks to a lay person is proper only if the lawyer maintains a direct relationship with the client, supervises the delegated work, and has complete professional responsibility for the work produced. The implication of such strictures is that the paralegal employees. . . would not have the amount of authority to exercise independent judgments with regard to legal matters necessary to bring them within the administrative exemption." (*www.dol.gov/esa/whd/opinion/FLSA/2005/2005_12_16_54_FLSA.htm*)

To summarize federal overtime law:

- most paralegals are not exempt under the executive exemption (not exempt means overtime pay is required)
- many paralegal supervisors are exempt under the executive exemption (hence no overtime pay for them)
- most paralegals are not exempt under the professional exemption
- most paralegals are probably not exempt under the administrative exemption.

C. State Overtime Law: California Labor Code

State overtime law is enforced by the Division of Labor Standards (DLSE) of the California Department of Industrial Relations (DIR):
Department of Industrial Relations
Division of Labor Standards Enforcement
455 Golden Gate Ave., 9th Floor
San Francisco, CA 94102
415-703-4810; 415-703-4807
www.dir.ca.gov/DLSE/dlse.html
www.dir.ca.gov

California also has three categories of exempt employees to whom overtime compensation does *not* have to be paid: executive, professional, or administrative. Although California uses the same names for the exemptions as federal law, the definitions of the exemptions under California law are not exactly the same as their definitions under federal law. The similarities, however, are substantial.

Before looking more closely at the exemptions under California law, we need to point out that none of the exemptions apply if an employee earns under two times the state minimum wage for full-time employment. This would be approximately $540 a week ($28,080 a year). If you earn less than this amount, you are not exempt and therefore, must be paid overtime under California law. Note that this is a higher threshold than the federal threshold of $455 a week ($23,660 a year). As indicated earlier, if federal and state overtime standards conflict, the standard that would lead to a higher rate of pay controls.

California paralegals who earn less than $28,080 a year must be paid overtime compensation. Those who earn more than $28,080 a year can also receive overtime compensation *unless they are exempt.*

The exemptions are based on the tasks that an employee is "primarily engaged in," which means more than half of his or her work time. Note that this standard is similar but not exactly the same as the federal test of a worker's "primary duty," which means the main or most important tasks they perform.

Executive Exemption under California Law

The employee (1) performs tasks that involve the management of the enterprise or of a customarily recognized department or subdivision thereof; (2) customarily and regularly directs the work of two or more other employees; and (3) has the authority to hire or fire other employees or whose suggestions and recommendations as to the hiring or firing and as to the advancement and promotion or any other change of status of other employees is given particular weight.

In addition, the employee must customarily and regularly exercise discretion and independent judgment in performing the above three tasks. This requirement means engaging in the comparison and evaluation of possible courses of conduct and acting or making a decision after the various possibilities have been considered. The employee must have the authority or power to make an independent choice, free from immediate direction or supervision and with respect to matters of significance. An employee who merely applies his or her memory in following prescribed procedures or determining which required procedure out of the company manual to follow, is not exercising discretion and independent judgment. (*www.dir.ca.gov/dlse/Glossary.asp?Button1=E*)

Professional Exemption under California Law

The employee works in an occupation that is commonly recognized as a learned profession. This means performing work requiring knowledge of an advance type in a field or science or learning customarily acquired by a prolonged course of specialized intellectual instruction and study, as distinguished from a general academic education and from an apprenticeship, and from training in the performance of routine mental, manual, or physical processes, or work that is an essential part of or necessarily incident to any of the above work. The work must be predominantly intellectual and varied in character (as opposed to routine mental, manual, mechanical, or physical work) and is of such character that the output produced or the result accomplished cannot be standardized in relation to a given period of time. Finally, to qualify under the professional exemption, the employee must customarily and regularly exercise discretion and independent judgment in the performance of these duties. (*www.dir.ca. gov/dlse/Glossary.asp?Button1=P*)

Administrative Exemption under California Law

The employee (1) performs work that involves office or non-manual work directly related to management policies or general business operations of his or her employer or his or her employer's customers, and (2) customarily and regularly exercises discretion and independent judgment. The employee must also (a) regularly and directly assist a proprietor or executive, or (b) perform specialized or technical work under only general supervision, or (c) perform special assignments under only general supervision. (*www.dir.ca.gov/dlse/Glossary.asp?Button1=A*)

As you can see by comparing the three exemptions under federal law with those under California law, there are some differences. In general, the tests for the exemptions under state law are stricter than those under federal law, meaning that it is more difficult to be classified as exempt under state law. If a paralegal is exempt under federal law, but not exempt under state law, the latter controls. As mentioned earlier, workers are entitled to be paid under whichever overtime law would lead to the higher rate of pay.

Such paralegals, however, are relatively rare. The different definitions of the exemptions under federal and state law do not appear to be substantial enough to lead to different results. Phrased another way, most paralegals who are not exempt under federal law will probably not be exempt under California law. And if a paralegal supervisor is exempt under federal law, he or she will probably be exempt under state law.

D. Filing a Complaint

To file a *federal* complaint for the failure to receive overtime compensation, contact a district office of the Wage and Hour Division at 866-4-USWAGE:

- Sacramento District Office
- East Los Angeles District Office
- Los Angeles District Office
- San Diego District Office
- Orange Area Office
- San Francisco District Office
- San Jose Area Office

There is a two-year statute of limitations (three years for willful violations). Failure to file a federal claim within this period may mean that the claim is lost.

To file a *state* complaint for the failure to receive overtime compensation, download the complaint form (*www.dir.ca.gov/dlse/Form1.pdf*) and file it at the claim office near you (*www.dir.ca.gov/dlse/Cal-CitiesB.asp*). For state overtime claims, there is a three-year statute of limitations. To avoid losing the claim under California law, it must be filed within three years from the date the claim arose.

E. More Information

Opinion of Wage and Hour Division of the U.S. Department of Labor on Paralegal Entitlement to Overtime Compensation
www.dol.gov/esa/whd/opinion/FLSA/2005/2005_12_16_54_FLSA.htm

Federal Overtime
www.dol.gov/esa/whd
www.dol.gov/esa/regs/compliance/whd/fairpay/complaint.htm

State Overtime
www.dir.ca.gov/dlse/FAQ_Overtime.htm
www.dir.ca.gov/dlse/HowToFileWageClaim.htm
www.dir.ca.gov/dlse/Form1.pdf
www.dir.ca.gov/DLSE/dlse.html

Federal vs State Wage Laws
www.jacksonlewis.com/legalupdates/article.cfm?aid=699
compensation.blr.com
(Click "State/Federal Differences")

F. Something to Check

1. Go to the California Code of Regulations (*ccr.oal.ca.gov*). Find and summarize any three regulations on overtime compensation.
2. Go to the California Labor Code (*www.leginfo.ca.gov/calaw.html*). Find and summarize any three state statutes on overtime compensation.

A. Introduction

It can happen. You're working as a paralegal and suddenly find yourself out of work with no immediate prospects for new employment. One resource to consider while continuing to look for work is unemployment insurance (UI). This program provides weekly unemployment insurance payments ("partial wage replacement") for workers who lose their job through no fault of their own. Even if you are still able to work part-time, you may be eligible for UI benefits.

Eligibility for benefits requires that claimants:

- have received enough wages during the base period to establish a UI claim (this is the "minimum earnings test")
- be totally or partially out of work
- be out of work due to no fault of their own (if fault may have been involved, a telephone interview will be required—see below)
- be physically able to work
- be actively seeking work
- be willing to accept a suitable job.

UI is part of a federal program administered in California by the Employment Development Department (EDD). UI is financed by employers who pay unemployment taxes on up to $7,000 in wages paid to each worker. The actual tax rate varies for each employer, depending in part on the amount of UI benefits paid to former employees. Employers, therefore, can earn a lower tax rate when fewer claims are made on the employer's account by former employees.

The maximum weekly benefit is $450; the minimum is $40. Benefits are based on a claimant's earnings in a 12-month "base period" consisting of four quarters of three months each. In periods of high unemployment in the economy, extended benefits may be available.

For federal tax purposes, UI benefits are considered taxable income and must be reported as such on federal income tax forms. In California, however, they are not considered taxable income.

Minimum Earnings Test

To qualify for benefits in California, a claimant must meet the *minimum earnings test.* He or she must have (1) earned at least $1,300 in the highest quarter of the base period, or (2) have earned at least $900 in the highest quarter and earned total base period earnings of at least 1.25 times the high quarter earnings. For example, if the claimant has $900 earnings in the highest quarter, he or she is also required to have earned a total of $1,125 in the base period ($900 x 1.25 = $1,125).

The maximum amount of a regular UI claim is either 26 times the claimant's weekly benefit amount or one-half of the claimant's base period wages, whichever is less.

When an individual's base period begins depends on when the UI claim is filed. The most recent three to five months before the claim is filed are omitted; therefore, the base period is the 12 months beginning some 15 to 17 months before the claim was filed. For example, all claims filed in April, May, or June would have a base period of 12 months beginning January 1 of the previous year and running through December 31. All claims filed in July, August, or September would have a base period beginning in April of the previous year and ending March 31 of the current year.

B. Filing a UI Claim

There are three ways to file a claim for UI benefits:

- Online (*www.edd.ca.gov/uirep/uiappind.htm*)
- File a paper application; a print version of the application is available online (*www.edd.ca.gov/uirep/uiapp.htm*)
- File by phone (800-300-5616)

You will need to provide the following information:

- Name and social security account number.
- Mailing and residence address, and telephone number.
- Driver's license or ID card number.
- The last date you worked for any employer. If you are now working part-time, the number of hours you work each week.
- Last employer information, including name, address (mailing and physical location), and telephone number. (The agency will be mailing a notice to that employer.)
- Information on all employers during the 18 months prior to filing this claim, including name, period of employment, wages earned, and how you were paid.
- The name of the employer you worked for the longest within the last year and a half; and the number of years you worked for that employer.
- The reason you are no longer working for your last employer, e.g., you quit, were laid off, were fired, or left work because of a trade dispute. (This information will be sent to that employer.)
- Whether you are receiving or expect to receive any payments from a former employer. (Some types of payments may be deducted from your benefits. A few examples of payments that may

be deducted include wages, pension payments, holiday pay, and vacation or sick pay.)

- Whether you are able to work and available to accept work.
- Whether you have a legal right to work in the United States. If applicable, individuals will be asked for their alien registration number.

Terminations Due to Firing or Quitting

If you were fired, quit, or left work because of a trade dispute, you will be scheduled for a future telephone interview. The information the agency obtains during the interview will help it decide if you are eligible to receive benefits. In the case of a discharge or firing, it is the employer's responsibility to prove that you were fired for misconduct connected with work. If you quit, you must show that you had a good reason.

C. Appeals

The EDD will issue its decision in its Notice of Determination/Ruling (DE 1080CT). (*www.edd.ca.gov/uirep/de1080ct.pdf*)

Office of Appeals (Administrative Law Judge)

An employer has the right to appeal EDD's decision to pay a claimant. The Office of Appeals hears the appeal. A claimant has the right to appeal EDD's decision to reduce or deny benefits. An appeal must be submitted within 20 calendar days of the mailing date of the Notice of Determination/Ruling. Mail the appeal to the return address shown on the decision notice.

The Office of Appeals notifies individuals of the time and place of the hearing at least 10 days in advance. An Administrative Law Judge (ALJ) hears the appeal. Testimony is taken under oath. After the hearing, the ALJ mails a decision to all parties.

California Unemployment Insurance Appeals Board

The ALJ's decision includes information about filing an appeal to the California Unemployment Insurance Appeals Board (*www.cuiab.ca.gov*).

The purpose of an appeal to the Appeals Board is to request a review of the ALJ's Decision. An appeal to the Appeals Board must be submitted within 20 calendar days from the date of the ALJ's decision. The Appeals Board will confirm receipt of the appeal and advise interested individuals of the procedural options available to them. Generally, the Appeals Board does not consider new or additional evidence. However, individuals have 10 days from the date of the confirmation letter to ask to present oral or written arguments and new evidence. The acceptance of any additional evidence is at the Board's discretion. The administrative process ends when the Appeals Board issues a written decision.

California Superior Court (Writ of Mandate)

A decision by the Appeals Board completes all administrative remedies. Individuals who disagree with the Appeals Board's decision may file a Writ of Mandate to the Superior Court within six months of the mailing date of the Appeals Board's written decision.

D. More Information

Telephone Assistance
Unemployment Insurance
800-300-5616 (English)
800-326-8937 (Spanish)

Employment Development Office
Unemployment Insurance
P.O. Box 419000
Sacramento, CA 95841-9000
800-300-5616
www.edd.ca.gov

Chief Administrative Law Judge Office
2400 Venture Oaks Way, Suite 200
Sacramento, CA 95833
916-263-6722

California Unemployment Insurance Appeals Board
916-263-6783
www.cuiab.ca.gov

Filing a Claim/Appeal
www.edd.ca.gov/fleclaim.htm
www.edd.ca.gov/uirep/uifc.htm
www.edd.ca.gov/uirep/uifa.htm
www.edd.ca.gov/uirep/uifctx.htm
www.edd.ca.gov/uirep/de8714b.pdf

Application and Other Forms
www.edd.ca.gov/uirep/uiappind.htm
www.edd.ca.gov/uirep/uipub.htm
www.edd.ca.gov/uirep/de1000m.pdf

Unemployment Insurance Statutes (UI Code)
www.leginfo.ca.gov/calaw.html

Unemployment Insurance Regulations (Title 22)
www.cuiab.ca.gov/regulations.shtm
ccr.oal.ca.gov

Unemployment Insurance Administrative Decisions
www.cuiab.ca.gov/precedent_decisions.shtm

Taxation of Unemployment Compensation Benefits
www.irs.gov/taxtopics/tc418.html

E. Something to Check

1. Use the online UI Code to find and summarize a statute on what happens when an applicant for UI benefits was terminated for misconduct.

2. Use the online UI California Code of Regulations to find and summarize a regulation on what happens when an applicant for UI benefits was terminated for misconduct.
3. Use the online UI administrative decisions to find and summarize a decision of the California Unemployment Insurance Appeals Board involving an applicant for UI benefits who was terminated for misconduct.

2.9 Injured Paralegals and Workers' Compensation

A. Introduction
B. Abbreviations
C. Workers' Compensation Benefits
D. The Claims Process
E. Contacts
F. More Information
G. Something to Check

A. Introduction

There are two main reasons California paralegals should know about workers' compensation law in the state: (1) understanding your rights when injured on the job, (2) being aware of one of the state's major agencies in which paralegals are allowed to represent clients at administrative hearings.

What happens if you are injured on your paralegal job? Although paralegal work certainly does not qualify as inherently dangerous work, accidents can occur.

Examples:

- you have an accident while driving to the court clerk's office to file a pleading
- you slip in the hallway on the way back from your supervisor's office
- you drop a laptop on your toe

In addition to physical injuries, workers' compensation covers work-related mental injuries and illnesses, e.g., mental illness caused by sexual harassment of a supervisor or by workplace violence from an unstable client.

The primary system covering on-the-job injuries is workers' compensation. In this section, we provide an overview of your rights and of the practical steps you should take when injured on the job. Workers' compensation is a no-fault system, meaning that injured employees need not prove the injury was someone else's fault in order to receive workers' compensation benefits.

The primary requirement for receiving benefits is that you sustain an injury "arising out of and in the course of" your employment.

There's another reason to learn about workers' compensation in California. You do not have to be an attorney to represent clients before the Workers' Compensation Appeals Board, the main agency responsible for appeals in this area of the law. Clients can be represented by an "attorney or agent." Section 5501 and 5700 of the Labor Code provide as follows:

> § 5501. The application may be filed with the appeals board by any party in interest, his attorney, or other representative authorized in writing. A representative who is not an attorney licensed by the State Bar of this state shall notify the appeals board in writing that he or she is not an attorney licensed by the State Bar of this state.
>
> § 5700. Either party may be present at any hearing, in person, by attorney, or by any other agent, and may present testimony pertinent under the pleadings.
>
> See also Formal Opinion Number 1988-103 in section 3.3 on such representation by paralegals.

Phyllis O'Dea, president of the International Paralegal Management Association (*www.paralegalmanagement.org*) and director of legal assistants at Howard Rice Nemerovsky in San Francisco, points out that paralegals can significantly increase their earning potential when they are able to represent clients at such hearings because of the "extra value to a law firm of having a nonlawyer who can appear at hearings." (Lorelei Laird, "Salaries of Paralegals Reflect Trends in Field," *Los Angeles Daily Journal* 6 (July 21, 2005).)

B. Abbreviations

app: Application for Adjudication of Claim
DOR: Declaration of Readiness to Proceed
DWC: Division of Workers' Compensation
DWC1: Workers' Compensation Claim Form
HCO: Health Care Organization
MPN: medical provider network
PD: permanent disability
PTP: Primary Treating Physician
QME: Qualified Medical Evaluator
SDI: State Disability Insurance
TD: temporary disability
WCAB: Workers' Compensation Appeals Board

C. Workers' Compensation Benefits

There are six basic types of workers' compensation benefits available, depending on the nature, date, and severity of the worker's injury:

1. Medical Care
2. Temporary Disability Benefits

3. Permanent Disability Benefits
4. Vocational Rehabilitation Services
5. Supplemental Job Displacement Benefits
6. Death Benefits

1. Medical Care

Injured workers are entitled to receive all medical care reasonably required to cure or relieve the effects of the injury, with no deductible or co-payments by the injured worker. For dates of injury on or after January 1, 2004, an injured worker is limited to 24 chiropractic and 24 physical therapy visits.

Generally, the employer controls the medical treatment for the first 30 days after the injury is reported, and the employee is then free to select any treating physician or facility. If, however, the employee has notified the employer in writing prior to the injury that he or she has a "personal physician"—a physician or surgeon who has previously treated the employee—the employee may be treated by that physician from the date of injury. Choice of treating physician differs, however, if the employer and employee have opted for a managed care program.

2. Temporary Disability (TD) Benefits

Workers unable to return to work within three days are entitled to temporary disability (TD) benefits to partially replace wages lost as a result of the injury. The benefits are generally designed to replace two-thirds of the lost wages, up to a maximum of $728 per week. Temporary disability benefits are payable every two weeks, on a day designated with the first payment, until the employee is able to return to work or until the employee's condition becomes permanent and stationary.

3. Permanent Disability (PD) Benefits

Workers who are permanently disabled—those who have a permanent labor market handicap—are entitled to receive permanent disability (PD) benefits. A worker who is determined to have a permanent total disability receives the temporary disability benefit—up to $728 per week—for life. A worker determined to have a permanent partial disability receives weekly benefits for a period that increases with the percentage of disability, from four weeks for a one percent permanent disability up to 694.25 weeks for a 99.75 percent disability. Permanent partial disability benefits are also payable at two-thirds of the injured worker's average weekly wages, but are subject to a much lower maximum. As of January 1, 2004, the rates are $220 per week for disabilities less than 69.75 percent and $270 per week for disabilities rated at 70 to 99.75 percent. Those with a permanent partial disability of 70 percent or more also receive a small life pension—a maximum of $257.69 per week—following the final payment of permanent partial disability benefits. The percentage of permanent disability is determined by using the Permanent Disability Rating Schedule and an assessment of the injured worker's permanent impairment and limitations. The assessment is made by either the treating physician or a "Qualified Medical Evaluator" (QME). The medical unit of the Division of Workers' Compensation (DWC) appoints and regulates QMEs.

If there is disagreement with the treating physician's opinion and the worker is *not represented by an attorney*, he or she chooses a physician from a three-member panel obtained from the DWC Medical Unit. If the worker *is represented by an attorney*, the parties must attempt to agree on a physician to perform the evaluation. If they are unable to agree, each side may obtain evaluations from a QME of their choice. If the evaluations are disparate, the amount of permanent disability will be determined by negotiation or, if necessary, litigation.

4. Vocational Rehabilitation Services

Workers injured before January 1, 2004 who are unable to return to their former type of work are entitled to vocational rehabilitation services (up to a maximum cost of $16,000) if these services can reasonably be expected to return the worker to suitable gainful employment. Vocational rehabilitation does *not* apply for to injuries on January 1, 2004 or after.

5. Supplemental Job Displacement Benefit

The Supplemental Job Displacement Benefit is a nontransferable voucher for education-related retraining or skill enhancement, or both, payable to a state-approved or accredited school if the worker is injured on or after January 1, 2004. To qualify for this benefit, the injury must result in a permanent disability, the injured employee does not return to work within 60 days after temporary disability ends, and the employer does not offer modified or alternative work. The maximum voucher amount is $10,000.

6. Death Benefits

In the event a worker is fatally injured, reasonable burial expenses, up to $5,000, are paid. In addition, the worker's dependents may receive support payments for a period of time. These payments are generally payable in the same manner and amount as temporary disability benefits, but the minimum rate of payment is $224 per week. The total aggregate amount of support payments depends on the number of dependents and the extent of their dependency. Generally, the maximum (where three or more total dependents are eligible) is $160,000, though additional benefits are payable if there continues to be any dependent children after the basic death benefit has been paid.

D. The Claims Process

These are the steps an employee must take:

1. Report the injury to the employer immediately. If the employer does not learn of the injury within 30 days, you might lose your right to benefits.
2. It is illegal for the employer to fire or otherwise punish you for having a work injury or illness, for filing a claim, or for testifying in another person's workers' compensation case. (California Labor Code § 132a).
3. Obtain a Workers' Compensation Claim Form (DWC 1). The employer should give you a copy of this form. It is also available online (*www.dir.ca.gov/DWC/forms.html*) and by contacting the district office nearest you (see phone numbers listed under More Information below).
4. Complete only the "Employee" section of the form.
5. Make a copy of the form for your records. Hand-deliver the original or mail it (certified mail, return receipt requested) to your employer.
6. The employer must then complete the "Employer" section of the form. Ask for a copy from your employer.
7. Your employer mails the form to its workers' compensation insurance company.
8. A claims administrator will handle your case for the employer. Claims administrators usually work for the employer's insurance company.
9. The insurance company generally has 14 days to mail you a status letter about your claim. If you do not receive it within this time, call the insurance company.
10. For help in filing the claim, call the Information and Assistance Office in the district office nearest you (see phone numbers listed under More Information).
11. Within one working day after you file a claim form, your employer must authorize treatment for the alleged injury and must continue to provide treatment (up to a maximum cost of $10,000) until the date that liability for the claim is accepted or rejected.
12. A Primary Treating Physician (PTP) will have overall responsibility for your treatment during the first 30 days. In most instances, the employer selects the PTP. If the PTP says you need further care after 30 days, you may be able to switch to a doctor of your choice. (Special rules apply if the employer offers a Health Care Organization (HCO) or has a medical provider network (MPN).) If the employer has not put up a poster describing your rights to workers' compensation (*www.dir.ca.gov/DWC/NoticePoster.pdf*), you may choose your own doctor immediately.
13. If a dispute on your eligibility for benefits cannot be resolved informally with your employer or claims administrator, you can file an Application for Adjudication of Claim (app) (*www.dir.ca.gov/dwc/iwguides/IWGuide10.pdf*) with the Workers' Compensation Appeals Board (WCAB). This opens a case at the WCAB.

    The WCAB consists of 24 local offices throughout the state where disagreements over workers' compensation benefits are initially heard by workers' compensation judges called "referees." The WCAB Reconsideration Unit in San Francisco is a seven-member, judicial body appointed by the governor and confirmed by the Senate that hears appeals of decisions issued by local workers' compensation judges.
14. When you are ready for a hearing, you file a Declaration of Readiness to Proceed (DOR), which requests a hearing before WCAB (*www.dir.ca.gov/DWC/iwguides/IWGuide07.pdf*).
15. At the hearing before a workers' compensation referee, you may be represented "by an attorney or agent" or you may represent yourself.
16. To appeal a decision by a referee, file a Petition for Reconsideration with the Workers' Compensation Appeals Board within 20 days of the date the decision was issued (or 25 days if the decision was mailed to your residence). The Petition for Reconsideration is available online (*www.dir.ca.gov/DWC/iwguides/IWGuide06.pdf*) or at the district office.
17. If you disagree with the final decision of the Workers' Compensation Appeals Board, you can take your case to court.
18. If you are not receiving workers' compensation benefits, you may be able to receive State Disability Insurance (SDI) benefits. To find out if you qualify, call the State Employment Development Department (800-480-3287).

E. Contacts

Division of Workers' Compensation (DWC)
Headquarters
1515 Clay Street
17th Floor
Oakland, CA 94612
510-286-7100; 800-736-7401
www.dir.ca.gov/dwc/DWC_address/Headquarters.html

DWC monitors the administration of workers' compensation claims, and provides administrative and judicial services to assist in resolving disputes that arise in connection with claims for workers' compensation benefits.

Workers' Compensation Appeals Board
Headquarters
P.O. Box 429459
San Francisco, CA 94142
www.dir.ca.gov/wcab/wcab.htm

DWC Information and Assistance Offices & WCAB District Offices

Anaheim
714-738-4038
714-738-4000

Bakersfield
661-395-2514
661-395-2723

Eureka
707-441-5723
707-445-6518

Fresno
559-445-5355
559-445-5051

Goleta
805-968-4158
805-968-0258

Grover Beach
805-481-3380
805-481-4912

Long Beach
562-590-5240
562-590-5001

Los Angeles
213-576-7389
213-576-7335

Oakland
510-622-2861
510-622-2866

Oxnard
805-485-2528
805-485-2533

Pomona
909-623-8568
909-623-4301

Redding
530-225-2047
530-225-2845

Riverside
951-782-4247
951-782-4269

Sacramento
916-263-2741
916-263-2735

Salinas
831-443-3058
831-443-3060

San Bernardino
909-383-4522
909-383-4341

San Diego
619-767-2170
619-767-2083

San Francisco
415-703-5020
415-703-5011

San Jose
408-277-1292
408-277-1246

Santa Ana
714-558-4597
714-558-4121

Santa Monica
310-452-1188
310-452-9114

Santa Rosa
707-576-2452
707-576-2391

Stockton
209-948-7980
209-948-7759

Van Nuys
818-901-5374
818-901-5367

F. More Information

Workers' Compensation Appeals Board Policy and Procedural Manual
www.dir.ca.gov/WCAB
(click "Policy & Procedural Manual")

Workers' Compensation Overview
www.dir.ca.gov/dwc/dwc_home_page.htm
www.dir.ca.gov/dwc/faqs.html

Workers' Compensation Appeals Board Offices
www.dir.ca.gov/dwc/dir2.htm

Information and Assistance
www.dir.ca.gov/DWC/IandA.html

Filing a Claim
www.dir.ca.gov/DWC/iwguides/IWGuide01.pdf

State Compensation Insurance Fund
www.scif.com

Workers' Compensation Regulations
www.dir.ca.gov/samples/search/querydwc.htm

Workers' Compensation Administrative Decisions
www.dir.ca.gov/wcab/wcab_dars.htm

Electronic Access to the State of California Division of Workers' Compensation Database
compdataedex.com

Megalaw: California Workers' Compensation
www.megalaw.com/ca/top/caworkcomp.php

California Applicants Attorneys Association
www.caaa.org

California Attorneys Who Are Workers' Compensation Specialists
www.californiaspecialist.org
(click "Legal Specialty Areas")

California Workers' Compensation Defense Attorneys Association
www.cwcdaa.org

Californians Injured at Work
www.injuredworkerscoalition.com

Injured Workers4Change
www.injuredworkers4change.org/states_links.htm

California Workers' Compensation Institute
www.cwci.org

Workerscompensation.com
www.workerscompensation.com
(click "California")

U.S. Occupational Safety & Health Administration (OSHA)
www.osha.gov

Medical Information and Resources
www.caaa.org/links/default.asp?pageid=18

HR California
hrcalifornia.com

G. Something to Check

1. Use the online workers' compensation regulations to find regulations on any medical injury that you select (*www.dir.ca.gov/samples/search/querydwc.htm*).

What is the definition of that injury in California and what are some of its symptoms?

2. Find three California law firms online that represent clients in workers' compensation cases. Compare their descriptions of the services they offer.
3. Use the online administrative decisions of the WCAB (*www.dir.ca.gov/wcab/wcab_dars.htm*) to find any decision in which a worker was denied workers' compensation benefits. Summarize the decision.
4. Find a legal document assistant online who does workers' compensation work. Describe the services he or she provides.

APPENDIX A

Deductibility of Paralegal Education or Training

A. Introduction
B. Qualifying Work-Related Education (QWRE) that is Deductible
C. More Information
D. Something to Check

A. Introduction

Paralegals can incur education and training expenses (a) before they obtain their first job, (b) while employed, and (c) while looking for a new position after leaving an old one. Are any of these expenses deductible on their federal income tax return as a business expense? In this section, we examine the tax law governing this question.

The cost of obtaining a paralegal education by way of a bachelor's degree, associate degree, or certificate can be significant. In addition, there are the costs of earning the credits required to maintain one's credentials in voluntary certification programs such that of the National Association of Legal Assistants leading to the CLA (Certified Legal Assistant) or CP (Certified Paralegal) credential. Finally, there are the costs of attending continuing legal education (CLE) sessions to comply with California law (see section 1.2) and to keep current in one's field of the law. When paralegals spend their own money for any of these purposes, are they deductible?

B. Qualifying Work-Related Education (QWRE) that is Deductible

You can deduct education costs as a business expense if the education can be classified as *qualifying work-related education* (QWRE). What is QWRE? The following three principles apply:

1. The education must fit within *either* (a) or (b):
   (a) The education is required by your employer or by the law to keep your present salary, status, or job, and this required education serves a bona fide business purpose of the employer.
   (b) The education is used to maintain or improve skills that are needed in your present work.
2. Education that meets the minimum educational requirements of your present trade or business is *not* QWRE.
3. Education that is part of a program of study to qualify you for a new trade or business is *not* QWRE.

Exhibit A summarizes these principles.

Exhibit A

When Does Your Education or Training Constitute Qualified Work-Related Education (QWRE)?

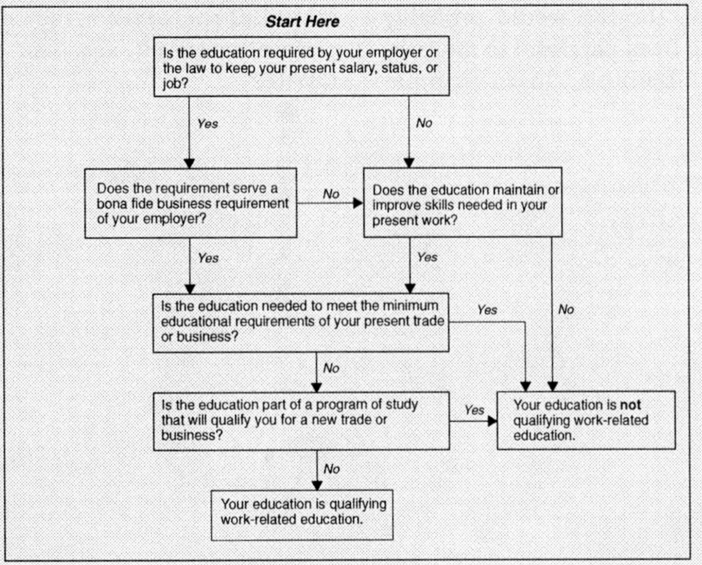

Source: www.irs.gov/pub/irs-pdf/p970.pdf

California law requires all paralegals to have four hours of continuing legal education (CLE) in legal ethics every two years and four hours of general or specialty law every two years. (See a discussion of this requirement in section 1.2. On CLE resources, see also section 1.5.) When you pay for such CLE out of your own pocket, is it deductible as QWRE? The answer is *yes*, since it is required by law to keep your present status, and, as such, it clearly serves a bona fide business purpose of your employer.

Suppose you take *additional* CLE classes—classes not required by law—that you pay for yourself. Or suppose you simply go back to school to take an additional class or two that you pay for on your own. Does such training constitute QWRE? The answer is *yes* if they will help you maintain or improve the paralegal skills you need in your present job.

Of course, your largest education expense will probably be for your initial paralegal training. Can this be QWRE? For most students the answer is *no* because it is a program of study to qualify you for a "new trade or business."

Suppose, however, that you are a legal secretary paying your own way to go to paralegal school part-time or during an extended break from work. Can the cost of this education be QWRE? This is a more difficult question to answer. If as a secretary you were performing some paralegal tasks (even though you were not called a paralegal), an argument can be made that you are not trying to enter a "new trade or business." You are simply expanding (improving) what you already do. It is not clear whether the IRS would accept this argument. If it does, the cost of the paralegal education would be QWRE.

Suppose that you are an experienced paralegal who wants to become an attorney. Can your law school education be QWRE? Since the requirements for being an attorney are substantially different from what is required to be a paralegal, the IRS would probably take the position that going from paralegal to attorney is entering a "new trade of business." In an example provided by the IRS, if an accountant decides to become an attorney, his or her law school education would not be QWRE even if the employer requires the accountant to obtain a law degree. According to the IRS, going from accountant to attorney qualifies the accountant for a "new trade or business."

What about California state income taxes? The information provided on the state's tax planning site (*www.taxes.ca.gov/planning.html*) suggests that the same rules apply:

"Students may deduct qualified education expenses. Qualified education expenses are expenses that are required by the employer or the law for the taxpayer to keep his or her present job. Expenses may also be qualified if the education maintains or improves skills necessary for the taxpayer's work."

C. More Information

Federal Tax Benefits for Education
www.irs.gov/pub/irs-pdf/p970.pdf
www.irs.gov/publications/p970/ch12.html
taxguide.completetax.com/text/Q04_5120.asp
www.unclefed.com/TaxHelpArchives/2002/HTML/p508toc.html

Hope Education Tax Credit
Form 8863
www.irs.gov/pub/irs-pdf/f8863.pdf

Lifetime Earning Credit
www.irs.gov/individuals/article/0,,id=96273,00.html

D. Something to Check

Go to the Internal Revenue Service Web site (*www.irs.gov*). Use its search boxes to try to find material relevant to the following case. Mary is a legal investigator who works for a California law firm. She wants to take an evidence course at a local paralegal school. If she pays for the course herself, under what circumstances, if any, can she deduct the cost as QWRE?

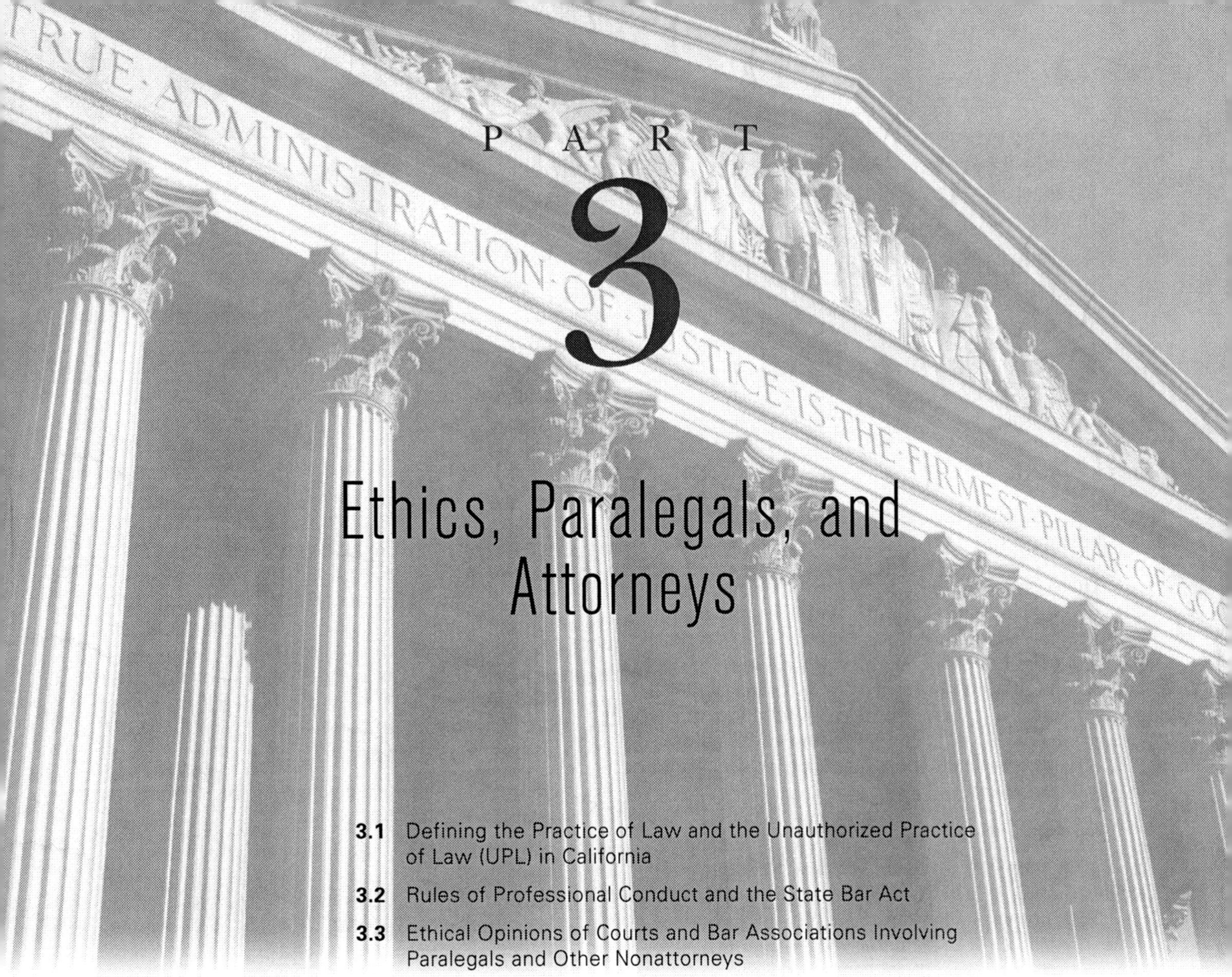

P A R T

3

Ethics, Paralegals, and Attorneys

3.1 Defining the Practice of Law and the Unauthorized Practice of Law (UPL) in California

A. Introduction

There is no statute in California that defines the practice of law, and therefore there is no statutory definition of what constitutes the unauthorized practice of law(UPL). There are, however, statutes that define who is allowed to practice law and what the legal consequences are for engaging in UPL. Most of the definitions of the authorized and unauthorized practice of law come from court opinions, which are our major focus here.

Related topics covered elsewhere in the book:

- Section 1.3: legal document assistants (LDA), unlawful detainer assistants (UDA), immigration consultants (IA), and bankruptcy petition preparers (BPP)
- Section 3.2: the text of the *Rules of Professional Conduct* and the State Bar Act
- Section 3.3: ethics opinions
- Appendix A of Part 3: attorney discipline

B. Themes Covered

Who can practice law
Deciding who can practice law
Criminal penalties for UPL
Civil remedies for UPL
Contempt of court
What is the practice of law
Selling legal forms and kits
Workers' compensation cases
Unemployment compensation cases
Board of Equalization cases (tax)
Small claims court
Special education cases
Attorneys in fact vs attorneys at law
International commercial arbitration
Negotiating agreements
Clearing notes in probate cases
Accountants and UPL
Mother representing her son as UPL
Spouses representing each other as UPL
Examples of attorney discipline
Miscellaneous

C. Applicable Laws

Who can practice law?

- No person shall practice law in California unless the person is an active member of the State Bar. (§ 6125. California Business and Professions Code).

Who decides who can practice law? The courts or the legislature?

- "Courts have "primary and ultimate authority over the attorney admission and discipline process." The legislature must not "impair" the court's "authority over the practice of law." *Obrien v. Jones*, 999 P.2d 95, 97 (Cal 2000). Yet the legislature is allowed "a reasonable degree of regulation and control over the profession and practice of law." While recognizing that the legislature may prescribe reasonable rules and regulations for admission to the bar, such "legislative regulations are, at best, but minimum standards unless the courts themselves are satisfied that such qualifications as are prescribed by legislative enactment are sufficient. . . . In other words, the courts in the exercise of their inherent power may demand more than the Legislature has required." (*Merco Constr. Engineers, Inc. v. Municipal Court*, 581 P.2d 636, 638 (Cal 1978)).

What criminal penalties can be imposed for engaging in the unauthorized practice of law?

- **(a)** Any person advertising or holding himself or herself out as practicing or entitled to practice law or otherwise practicing law who is not an active member of the State Bar, or otherwise authorized pursuant to statute or court rule to practice law in this state at the time of doing so, is guilty of a misdemeanor punishable by up to one year in a county jail or by a fine of up to one thousand dollars ($1,000), or by both that fine and imprisonment. Upon a second or subsequent conviction, the person shall be confined in a county jail for not less than 90 days, except in an unusual case where the interests of justice would be served by imposition of a lesser sentence or a fine. If the court imposes only a fine or a sentence of less than 90 days for a second or subsequent conviction under this subdivision, the court shall state the reasons for its sentencing choice on the record.

  (b) Any person who has been involuntarily enrolled as an inactive member of the State Bar, or has been suspended from membership from the State Bar, or has been disbarred, or has resigned from the State Bar with charges pending, and thereafter practices or attempts to practice law, advertises or holds himself or herself out as practicing or otherwise entitled to practice law, is guilty of a crime punishable by imprisonment in the state prison or county jail. . . . (§ 6126. California Business and Professions Code).

What civil remedies can be used against someone engaged in the unauthorized practice of law?

▸ **(a)** In addition to any remedies and penalties available in any enforcement action brought in the name of the people of the State of California by the Attorney General, a district attorney, or a city attorney, acting as a public prosecutor, the court shall award relief in the enforcement action for any person who obtained services offered or provided in violation of Section 6125 or 6126 or who purchased any goods, services, or real or personal property in connection with services offered or provided in violation of Section 6125 or 6126 against the person who violated Section 6125 or 6126, or who sold goods, services, or property in connection with that violation. The court shall consider the following relief:

(1) Actual damages.
(2) Restitution of all amounts paid.
(3) The amount of penalties and tax liabilities incurred in connection with the sale or transfer of assets to pay for any goods, services, or property.
(4) Reasonable attorney's fees and costs expended to rectify errors made in the unlawful practice of law.
(5) Prejudgment interest at the legal rate from the date of loss to the date of judgment.
(6) Appropriate equitable relief, including the rescission of sales made in connection with a violation of law.

(b) The relief awarded under paragraphs (1) to (6), inclusive, of subdivision (a) shall be distributed to, or on behalf of, the person for whom it was awarded or, if it is impracticable to do so, shall be distributed as may be directed by the court pursuant to its equitable powers.

(c) The court shall also award the Attorney General, district attorney, or city attorney reasonable attorney's fees and costs and, in the court's discretion, exemplary damages as provided in Section 3294 of the Civil Code. . . . (§ 6126.5. California Business and Professions Code).

When can UPL lead to contempt of court?

▸ The following acts or omissions in respect to the practice of law are contempts of the authority of the courts:

(a) Assuming to be an officer or attorney of a court and acting as such, without authority.

(b) Advertising or holding oneself out as practicing or as entitled to practice law or otherwise practicing law in any court, without being an active member of the State Bar. . . . (§ 6127. California Business and Professions Code).

What is the practice of law?

▸ The term "practice law" *in § 6125 of the Business and Professions Code* includes "doing and performing services" in a court of justice in any matter. Also included are "legal advice and legal instrument and contract preparation, whether or not these subjects were rendered in the course of litigation." (*Birbrower, Montalbano, Condon & Frank v. Superior Court*, 949 P.2d 1, 5 (Cal 1998) (citing other cases)).

▸ "As the term is generally understood, the practice of the law is the doing or performing services in a court of justice, in any matter depending therein, throughout its various stages, and in conformity to the adopted rules of procedure. But in a larger sense it includes legal advice and counsel, and the preparation of legal instruments and contracts by which legal rights are secured although such matter may or may not be pending in a court." (*People ex rel. Lawyers Institute of San Diego v. Merchants' Protective Corp.*, 209 P. 363, 365 (Cal 1922) (citing an Indiana case)).

▸ "It must be conceded that ascertaining whether a particular activity falls within [the practice of law] may be a formidable endeavor. . . . In close cases, the courts have determined that the resolution of legal questions for another by advice and action is practicing law" if "difficult or doubtful legal questions are involved which, to safeguard the public, reasonably demand the application of a trained legal mind." Less perplexing is the determination of whether participation on behalf of another in hearings and proceedings before a board or commission constitutes the practice of law. The cases uniformly hold that the character of the act, and not the place where it is performed, is the decisive element, and if the application of legal knowledge and technique is required, the activity constitutes the practice of law, even if conducted before an administrative board or commission." (*Baron v. City of Los Angeles*, 469 P.2d 353, 358 (Cal 1970) (citing other cases)).

Is it possible to have a precise definition of the practice of law?

▸ Any definition of legal practice is, "given the complexity and variability of the subject, incapable of universal application and can provide only a general guide to whether a particular act or activity is the practice of law. To restrict or limit the test in the interest of specificity would also limit its applicability to situations in which the public requires protection. . . . [T]he inherent and necessarily general nature of any definition of legal practice may allow the formulation of hypothetical situations that render the definition unworkable." (*People v. Landlords Professional Services*, 264 Cal. Rptr. 548, 554 (CalApp 1989)).

How do traditional paralegals avoid the unauthorized practice of law?

▸ There are many tasks in a law firm that a nonattorney may appropriately carry out. . . . Paralegals have been used to a great extent in more recent years to do document analysis and control, and a number of other functions that require some training and expertise (but not all of the qualifications of an attorney). In addition, law firms sometimes hire professionals such as economists and accountants to assist in the representation of client interests. This court's decision reflects no disapproval of such conduct. Such work by non-attorneys in a law firm must be preparatory in nature. It may include research, investigation of details, the assemblage of data or other necessary information, and other work that assists the attorney in carrying out the legal representation of a client. The work must be supervised by an attorney. Furthermore, the work must become or be merged into the work of the attorney, so that it becomes the attorney's work product. If the work of the non-attorney employee of a law firm stands on its own, such work constitutes the unauthorized practice of law. (*In re Carlos*, 227 B.R. 535, 539 (BkrtcyCDCal, 1998) (internal cites omitted)).

▸ The line of demarcation as to where [the work of nonlawyers] begins and where it ends cannot always be drawn with absolute distinction or accuracy. Probably as nearly as it can be fixed, and it is sufficient to say that it is work of a preparatory nature, such as research, investigation of details, the assemblage of data and other necessary information, and such other work as will assist the employing attorney in carrying the matter to a completed product, either by his personal examination and approval thereof or by additional effort on his part. The work must be such, however, as loses its separate identity and becomes either the product, or else merged in the product, of the attorney himself. (*Crawford v. State Bar of Cal.*, 355 P.2d 490, 495 (Cal 1960) (citing another case)).

When does the selling of legal forms and kits constitute the practice of law?

▸ Under California law, the sale of legal forms does not amount to the practice of law "as long as the service offered . . . [is] merely clerical, i.e., the service did not engage in the practice of law if it made forms available for the client's use, filled the forms in at the specific direction of the client and filed and served those forms as directed by the client. Likewise, merely giving a client a manual, even a detailed one containing specific advice, for the preparation of [a legal action] would not be the practice of law if the service did not personally advise the client with regard to his specific case." (*People v. Landlords Professional Services*, 264 Cal. Rptr. 548, 553 (CalApp. 1989)).

▸ Under California law, a non-lawyer engages in the unauthorized practice of law when he or she determines for a party the kind of legal document necessary in order to effect the party's purpose. By selecting a form that she thought was appropriate for Boettcher's purposes, Mohr was engaged in the UPL. The fact that the form itself may have been prepared by a lawyer does not change the nature of Mohr's act. Since the attorney who prepared the form was in no way supervising Mohr, her use of the attorney's form was just as unlawful as if Mohr had gone to the courthouse and used a motion to dismiss she found in some file. (*In re Boettcher*, 262 B.R. 94, 96 (BkrtcyNDCal 2001)).

Can paralegals represent workers' compensation claimants?

▸ The Supreme Court of California has "determined that statutes pertaining to workers' compensation provided an exception for lay representatives to practice law without a license and to receive fees." (*99 Cents Only Stores v. Workers' Comp. Appeals Bd.*, 95 Cal. Rptr. 2d 569, 572 (CalApp 2000)).

▸ The application [for the adjudication of a workers' compensation claim] may be filed with the [workers' compensation] appeals board by any party in interest, his attorney, or other representative authorized in writing. A representative who is not an attorney licensed by the State Bar of this state shall notify the appeals board in writing that he or she is not an attorney licensed by the State Bar of this state. Upon the filing of the application, the appeals board shall, where the applicant is represented by an attorney or other representative, serve a conformed copy of the application showing the date of filing and the case number upon applicant's attorney or representative. . . . (§ 5501. California Labor Code).

▸ The hearing on the application may be adjourned from time to time and from place to place in the discretion of the appeals board or the workers' compensation judge holding the hearing. . . . Either party may be present at any hearing, in person, by attorney, or by any other agent, and may present testimony pertinent under the pleadings. (§ 5700. California Labor Code).

Who can represent claimants before the Unemployment Compensation Appeals Board?

▸ Any individual claiming benefits in any proceedings before the appeals board [California Unemployment Insurance Appeals Board] or its authorized representative may be represented by counsel or agent but no such counsel or agent shall charge or receive for such services more than an amount approved by the appeals board. Any person who violates any provision of this section shall for each such violation be fined not less than fifty dollars ($50) nor more than one thousand dollars ($1,000) or be imprisoned not more than six months or both. (§ 1957. Unemployment Insurance Code).

Who can represent taxpayers before the State Board of Equalization?

▸ Representation at hearings.

Taxpayers may be represented at all levels of review by any person of the taxpayer's choosing, including, but not limited to an attorney, appraiser, accountant, bookkeeper, employee, or business associate. (18 California Code of Regulations § 5073(a)).

Can a paralegal (without attorney supervision) give "individual personal" advice to litigants in small claims court cases?

▸ Advice to litigants.

In each county, individual assistance shall be made available to advise small claims litigants and potential litigants without charge. . . . (§ 116.260. California Code of Civil Procedure).

▸ Advisory service; advisors may be paralegals.

(b) Each [small claims] advisory service shall provide the following services: (1) Individual personal advisory services, in person or by telephone, and by any other means reasonably calculated to provide timely and appropriate assistance. . . .

(d) The advisory service shall . . . be administered so as to avoid the existence or appearance of a conflict of interest between the individuals providing the advisory services and any party to a particular small claims action or any judicial officer deciding small claims actions.

(e) Advisors may be volunteers, and shall be members of the State Bar, law students, paralegals, or persons experienced in resolving minor disputes, and shall be familiar with small claims court rules and procedures. Advisors may not appear in court as an advocate for any party. (§ 116.940. California Code of Civil Procedure).

Can paralegals with special knowledge and training accompany and advise individuals at hearings on special education programs?

▸ **(e)** Any party to the hearing [on a special education program] held pursuant to this section shall be afforded the following rights consistent with state and federal statutes and regulations:

(1) The right to be accompanied and advised by counsel and by individuals with special knowledge or training relating to the problems of individuals with exceptional needs. (§ 56505. California Education Code)

▸ The district court ruled that Mr. Foreman was not licensed to practice law and, therefore, was not entitled to collect attorney's fees for his services in the state administrative proceeding. The district court held that Mr. Foreman could only appear at the hearing in a nonlawyer advisor capacity, as allowed under . . . the California Special Education Programs Act. (See California Education Code § 56505(e)(1)) ("The right to be accompanied and advised by counsel and by individuals with special knowledge or training relating to the problems of children and youth with disabilities.") . . . . A person is or is not licensed to practice law in a particular forum. There is no halfway. If not licensed, one cannot practice in that forum, and cannot charge, or receive attorney's fees for such services under penalty of criminal law. Mr. Foreman was not licensed to practice in California, including in state administrative proceedings. While he could appear as a lay advisor, he cannot charge or collect fees for services as an attorney in those proceedings. (*Z.A. v. San Bruno Park School Dist.*, 165 F.3d 1273, 1275–1276 (CA9 (Cal.), 1999)).

Can a nonlawyer who is an attorney in fact (by having a power of attorney) act as an attorney at law?

▸ A power of attorney does not authorize a person to file a petition on behalf of [another]. . . . A power of attorney is a device available to a person to empower another to act on his or her behalf. . . . Despite broad statutory language of the power of attorney with respect to claims and litigation, the attorney in fact may not act as an attorney at law on behalf of his principal . . . . [The law has long] distinguished between an attorney in fact and an attorney at law and emphasized that a power of attorney is not a vehicle which authorizes an attorney in fact to act as an attorney at law. (*In re Marriage of Caballero* 33 Cal. Rptr. 2d 46, 52–53 (CalApp 1994)).

Can a nonlawyer represent clients in international commercial arbitrations?

▸ It is the policy of the State of California to encourage parties to an international commercial agreement or transaction which qualifies for arbitration or conciliation . . . to resolve disputes arising from such agreements or transactions through conciliation. The parties may select or permit an arbitral tribunal or other third party to select one or more persons to serve as the conciliator or conciliators who shall assist the parties in an independent and impartial manner in their attempt to reach an amicable settlement of their dispute. (§ 1297.341. California Code of Civil Procedure). The parties may appear in person or be represented or assisted by any person of their choice. A person assisting or representing a party need not be a member of the legal profession or licensed to practice law in California. (§ 1297.351. California Code of Civil Procedure).

Can a nonlawyer negotiate a reaffirmation agreement?

▸ This case raises the issue of whether a law firm may use a non-attorney to negotiate, on behalf of a creditor client, a reaffirmation agreement with a debtor in a chapter 7 bankruptcy case. The court holds that, where a client hires a law firm to negotiate a contract, the negotiation of the contract constitutes the practice of law that must be performed by an appropriately licensed attorney. Thus, when a law firm uses a non-attorney to negotiate a contract on behalf of a client of the firm, this constitutes the UPL. Such UPL occurs when a non-attorney employee of a law firm negotiates, on behalf of a creditor, the reaffirmation of a debt that may otherwise be dischargeable in a bankruptcy case. (*In re Carlos*, 227 B.R. 535, 536 (BkrtcyCDCal, 1998)).

Can a paralegal in Los Angeles "appear in person" to clear notes in probate cases?

▸ After checking the calendar notes, counsel are encouraged to call the Probate Attorney with any questions counsel may have or explanations that may assist in the clearing of the notes. Counsel may also appear in person to confer with the Probate Attorney to clear notes. . . . Paralegals may call or appear in person to clear notes regarding factual, non-legal matters. (Rule 10.33(b). California Rules, Los Angeles Superior Court).

When does an accountant engage in the practice of law?

▸ An accountant, in preparing income tax returns for others, did not engage in the practice of law. But in preparing taxpayers' applications for a carry-back adjustment of loss sustained by them and resisting an additional assessment proposed by the Treasury Department on the ground that such loss was not a net operating loss within the carry-back provisions of the Internal Revenue Code, the accountant unlawfully engaged in law practice, so as to bar his recovery of compensation from taxpayers for such services. Generally, whenever, as incidental to another transaction or calling, nonlawyers, as part of their regular course of conduct, resolve legal questions for another—at the latter's request and for a consideration—by giving the other advice or by taking action on his or her behalf, the nonlawyers are practicing law if difficult or doubtful legal questions are involved which, to safeguard the public, reasonably demand the application of a trained legal mind. (*Agran v. Shapiro*, 273 P.2d 619, 623, 626 (CalSuperior Court 1954)).

Can a mother represent her son in a paternity action?

▸ We hold that in a paternity action under the Uniform Parentage Act, a non-attorney mother cannot represent her minor son as guardian ad litem in propria persona, even though she cannot afford counsel and her son is a necessary party to the proceeding. We reach this conclusion because in California, as in other jurisdictions, absent specific statutory authorization, a non-attorney who represents another person in court proceedings violates the prohibition against UPL. The result is that the mother in this case, a party in her own right, may represent herself and may serve as guardian ad litem for her minor child, but she may not function as his attorney. (*J.W. v. Superior Court*, 22 Cal. Rptr. 2d 527, 528 (CalApp 1993)).

Can one spouse represent another when they are both parties in litigation?

▸ If a husband and wife are *defendants* in an action, one spouse can assert defenses on behalf of the other spouse even though neither are attorneys ("If a husband and wife are sued together, each may defend for his or her own right, but if one spouse neglects to defend, the other spouse may defend for that spouse's right also." California Code of Civil Procedure § 371). If, however, the spouses are *plaintiffs*, it is the UPL for one of the spouses to represent the other. *Abar v. Rogers*, 177 Cal.Rptr. 655 (Cal App 1981).

Attorneys disciplined in cases involving unauthorized practice of law by paralegals

▸ Attorney placed on 3-year probation. Did not properly supervise a paralegal who, with an associate attorney, participated in a deposition without disclosing he was not an attorney (*calbar.ca.gov/calbar/2cbj/97jul/art04.htm*).

▸ Attorney placed on 4-year probation with 1 year suspension. Attorney's husband worked as a paralegal in her law firm. Former clients mistook the paralegal for an attorney and said he misled them about performing legal services on their behalf. He allegedly tried to renegotiate client leases (*calbar.ca.gov/calbar/2cbj/97jul/art04.htm*).

▸ Attorney placed on 2-year probation with a 90-day suspension. In twelve client matters, the attorney's paralegal entered into settlement negotiations and signed the attorney's name on legal documents without the attorney's knowledge (*calbar.ca.gov/calbar/2cbj/97jul/art04.htm*).

Miscellaneous

▸ A nonattorney who participates in the taking of a deposition is engaged in the unauthorized practice of law. (*Ex parte McCue*, 293 P. 47 (Cal 1930)).

▸ Inactive members of the bar and paralegals. "No member of the State Bar practicing law in this state, or occupying a position in the employ of or rendering any legal service for an active member, occupying a position wherein he or she is called upon to give legal advice or counsel or examine the law or pass upon the legal effect of any act, document or law, shall be enrolled as an inactive member." It has been the State Bar's long-standing interpretation of this language that the services performed by a paralegal fall within this proscription. Therefore, once someone becomes a member of the State Bar of California, its rules require them to be an active member in order to engage in such activities. Further, the foregoing proscription is not limited to clients or the public, but includes the giving of legal advice, examination of the law, etc., without limitation as to the receiver. Therefore, once someone becomes a member of the State Bar of California, they are ineligible to transfer to inactive status even though they are working as a paralegal. (Section 2, Article I, Rules and Regulations of the State Bar of California).

▸ Any attorney or any law firm, partnership, corporation, or association employing an attorney who has resigned, or who is under actual suspension from the practice of law, or is disbarred, shall not permit that attorney to practice law or so advertise or hold himself or herself out as practicing law and shall supervise him or her in any other assigned duties. A willful violation of this section constitutes a cause for discipline. (§ 6133. State Bar Act).

▸ "The State Bar lacks jurisdiction over persons never licensed to practice law or attorneys who have resigned or been disbarred. Nonetheless, in 2003 the State Bar received 262 UPL complaints regarding nonattorneys. Most of those cases were referred to the local district attorney's office for prosecution. During this same period, 41 complaints were received regarding disbarred or resigned attorneys. Many of these also were referred to the local district attorney's office. Violators who come within the purview of the State Bar discipline system are licensed attorneys and attorneys suspended from the practice of law. In 2003, the State Bar received 246 UPL complaints regarding suspended attorneys. These complaints constituted 20 percent of all complaints received via the State Bar intake line in 2003." (Fernando Gaytan, Deborah A. Kelly, "Unauthorized Entry," 27 *Los Angeles Lawyer* 22, 26–27 (November 2004)).

D. More Information

Overview
www.calbar.ca.gov
(click "Ethics"; also, type "practice of law" in the search box)
members.calbar.ca.gov/search/site.aspx?q=paralegal

State Bar Complaint Line Against Attorneys and UPL Information
800-843-9053
415-538-2150

Rules of Professional Conduct Online
www.calbar.ca.gov
(click "Rules of Professional Conduct")

State Bar Act Online
www.leginfo.ca.gov/calaw.html
(click "Business and Professions Code" and then type "state bar act" in the search box)

Legal Advice vs Legal Information
Judicial Council of California
www.courtinfo.ca.gov/programs/access/documents/mayihelpyou.pdf

American Legal Ethics Library
www.law.cornell.edu/ethics
(click "Listing by jurisdiction" then "California")

California Ethics Research Resources
www.ll.georgetown.edu/states/ethics/california.cfm

Legalethics.com
www.legalethics.com/ethics.law
(click "California")

State Ethics Resources
www.ll.georgetown.edu/states/ethics

Research in Legal Ethics
www.abanet.org/cpr/ethicsearch/resource.html

E. Something to Check

1. Run the following search ("unauthorized practice of law california") in any three general search engines (e.g., *www.google.com*, *www.yahoo.com*, *www.search.msn.com*, *www.askjeeves.com*). Prepare a report on the categories of sites to which each search engine leads you. Cluster the same kinds of sites you find into categories (e.g., sites that list cases on UPL in California, sites that list bar associations in California with UPL resources, sites that list attorneys who represent clients suing other attorneys for UPL, etc.). Give a brief description of each category with examples of Web sites in each category. After you finish the report for the three general search engines, comment on which engine was the most productive and why.
2. Pick any three legal search engines (e.g., *www.findlaw.com*, *www.catalaw.com*, *www.washlaw.edu*, *www.lawguru.com*, *www.romingerlegal.com*). How effective is each in leading you to material about the unauthorized practice of law in California? Describe what you are able to find.

3.2 Rules of Professional Conduct and the State Bar Act

A. Introduction

There are three major sources of ethical rules governing attorneys with which paralegals should be familiar. The first is the *Rules of Professional Conduct*, which has been adopted by the state bar and approved by the California Supreme Court. (In this section, the *Rules of Professional Conduct* will be referred to as Rules.) The second is the State Bar Act in the Business and Professions

Code of the state legislature. The third source is the state court opinions that interpret both the Rules and the State Bar Act. Other sources also exist, such as state bar ethics opinions. In this section, we will concentrate on the Rules and the State Bar Act.

For other material on or related to ethics, see also:

- section 1.2 (laws on paralegal status and title)
- section 1.3 (legal document assistants and other independents)
- section 3.1 (on the authorized and unauthorized practice of law)
- section 3.3 (ethics opinions on paralegals)
- section 1.4 (paralegal associations—see references to ethics rules that some of the associations have adopted)
- Part 3, Appendix A (timeline on attorney discipline)

To read the Rules and the State Bar Act online, see the Web addresses listed under More Information at the end of this section.

B. Sections Directly Relevant to Paralegals

While all of the Rules and sections of the State Bar Act are important, the following are of particular relevance to paralegals:

Rules of Professional Conduct:

- Rule 1-130 (unauthorized practice of law)
- Rule 1-310 (forming a partnership with a non-lawyer)
- Rule 1-311 (hiring disbarred or suspended lawyers for paralegal work)
- Rule 1-320 (sharing fees with nonlawyers; payments for referring clients)
- Rule 3-110 (discussion) (lawyer competence includes the duty to supervise non-lawyer employees)

State Bar Act in the Business and Professions Code (B&P):

- § 6013.5 (nonlawyer members of the board of governors of the state bar)
- § 6060(e)(2)(B) (becoming a lawyer without law school)
- § 6077.5 (paralegals working for lawyers engaged in debt collection)
- § 6105 (misuse of a lawyer's name by a nonlawyer)
- § 6125 (who can practice law)
- § 6126 (unauthorized practice of law)
- § 6152 (solicitation by runners or cappers)

C. Index to the Rules and the State Bar Act

(The Rules cites are to the *Rules of Professional Conduct*; the B&P section (§) cites are to the State Bar Act of the Business & Professions Code)

Accounts Rule 4-100
Admission to Practice Rule 1-200; B&P §§ 6060, 6064
Advertising Rule 1-400; B&P §§ 6127, 6157.1
Arbitration B&P § 6200
Bar Association B&P § 6001
Bar Examination B&P § 6060(f)(g)
Business Deals with Clients Rule 3-300
Client Security Fund B&P § 6140.5
Commingling Rule 4-100
Communication with Judge Rule 5-300
Communication with Other Side Rule 2-100
Communication with Witness Rule 5-310
Competence Rule 3-110
Confidentiality Rule 3-100; B&P § 6068(e)
Conflict of Interest Rules 3-300, 3-310, 3-320, 3-600
Contingent Fees B&P § 6146
Continuing Legal Education B&P § 6070
Crime Rules 3-100(B), 3-510(A), 5-110; B&P § 6068(e)(2)
Definitions Rule 1-100(B)
Disbarred Attorney Rule 1-311; §§ B&P 6126(b), 6132, 6133
Discipline Rule 2-400(C); B&P § 6068(i)
Discrimination Rule 2-400
Dividing Fees Rule 2-220(A)
False Statements Rules 1-200(A), 1-400(D); B&P §§ 6068(d), 6157.1
Fees Rule 1-320, 2-200(A), 4-200, 3-700(D); B&P §§ 6146, 6200
Frivolous Claims Rule 3-200(B)
Funds of Clients Rule 4-100; B&P § 6211
Gifts Rules 1-320(B), 2-200(B), 4-400
Harassment Rules 3-200(A), 3-700(B)
Independence Rules 1-600, 3-310(F)
Interest-Bearing Demand Trust Accounts B&P § 6211
Judges Rules 5-200(B), 5-300; B&P § 6068(d)
Juror Contact Rule 5-320
Law Corporations B&P § 6160
Law School B&P § 6060
Lawyer Referral Service Rule 1-600(B)
Liability to Client Rule 3-400
Malice Rule 3-200(A)
Mandatory Withdrawal Rule 3-700(B)
Non-Lawyers Rules 1-310, 1-320, 1-600(A)
Organizations as Clients Rule 3-600
Papers of Clients Rule 3-700(D)
Partnership with Non-Lawyer Rule 1-310
Permissive Withdrawal Rule 3-700(C)
Practice of Law 1-310, Rule 1-600(A); § B&P 6126
Professional Judgment Rule 1-600
Publicity 5-120
Recommending an Attorney Rule 2-200(B)
Referral Fees or Gifts, Rules 1-320(B), 2-200(B)

NOTE: The following contains the text of the California Rules of Professional Conduct and its official discussions on those rules. Any omissions have been indicated by ellipsis dots.

D. Rules of Professional Conduct

Chapter 1. Professional Integrity in General

Rule 1-100. Rules of Professional Conduct, in General

(A) Purpose and Function

Purposes of the Rules

The following rules are intended to regulate professional conduct of members of the State Bar through discipline. They have been adopted by the Board of Governors of the State Bar of California and approved by the Supreme Court of California pursuant to Business and Professions Code sections 6076 and 6077 to protect the public and to promote respect and confidence in the legal profession. These rules together with any standards adopted by the Board of Governors pursuant to these rules shall be binding upon all members of the State Bar.

For a willful breach of any of these rules, the Board of Governors has the power to discipline members as provided by law.

The prohibition of certain conduct in these rules is not exclusive. Members are also bound by applicable law including the State Bar Act (Bus. & Prof. Code, §6000 et seq.) and opinions of California courts. Although not binding, opinions of ethics committees in California should be consulted by members for guidance on proper professional conduct. Ethics opinions and rules and standards promulgated by other jurisdictions and bar associations may also be considered.

These rules are not intended to create new civil causes of action. Nothing in these rules shall be deemed to create, augment, diminish, or eliminate any substantive legal duty of lawyers or the non-disciplinary consequences of violating such a duty.

(B) Definitions

Definitions

(1) "Law Firm" means:
   (a) two or more lawyers whose activities constitute the practice of law, and who share its profits, expenses, and liabilities; or
   (b) a law corporation which employs more than one lawyer; or
   (c) a division, department, office, or group within a business entity, which includes more than one lawyer who performs legal services for the business entity; or (d) a publicly funded entity which employs more than one lawyer to perform legal services.

(2) "Member" means a member of the State Bar of California.

(3) "Lawyer" means a member of the State Bar of California or a person who is admitted in good standing of and eligible to practice before the bar of any United States court or the highest court of the District of Columbia or any state, territory, or insular possession of the United States, or is licensed to practice law in, or is admitted in good standing and eligible to practice before the bar of the highest court of, a foreign country or any political subdivision thereof.

(4) "Associate" means an employee or fellow employee who is employed as a lawyer.

(5) "Shareholder" means a shareholder in a professional corporation pursuant to Business and Professions Code section 6160 et seq.

(C) Purpose of Discussions

Because it is a practical impossibility to convey in black letter form all of the nuances of these disciplinary rules, the comments contained in the Discussions of the rules, while they do not add independent basis for imposing discipline, are intended to provide guidance for interpreting the rules and practicing in compliance with them.

(D) Geographic Scope of Rules

Scope of Rules

(1) As to members: These rules shall govern the activities of members in and outside this state, except as members lawfully practicing outside this state may be specifically required by a jurisdiction in which they are practicing to follow rules of professional conduct different from these rules.

(2) As to lawyers from other jurisdictions who are not members: These rules shall also govern the activities of lawyers while engaged in the performance of lawyer functions in this state; but nothing contained in these rules shall be deemed to authorize the performance of such functions by such persons in this state except as otherwise permitted by law.

(E) These rules may be cited and referred to as "Rules of Professional Conduct of the State Bar of California."

Discussion:

The Rules of Professional Conduct are intended to establish the standards for members for purposes of discipline. The fact that a member has engaged in conduct that may be contrary to these rules does not automatically give rise to a civil cause of action. These rules are not intended to [supersede] existing law relating to members in non-disciplinary contexts. Law firm, as defined by subparagraph (B)(1), is not intended to include an association of lawyers who do not share profits, expenses, and liabilities. The subparagraph is not intended to imply that a law firm may include a person who is not a member in violation of the law governing the unauthorized practice of law.

Rule 1-110. Disciplinary Authority of the State Bar

A member shall comply with conditions attached to public or private reprovals or other discipline administered by the State Bar pursuant to Business and Professions Code sections 6077 and 6078 and rule 956, California Rules of Court.

Rule 1-120. Assisting, Soliciting, or Inducing Violations

A member shall not knowingly assist in, solicit, or induce any violation of these rules or the State Bar Act.

Rule 1-200. False Statement Regarding Admission to the State Bar

False Statements

(A) A member shall not knowingly make a false statement regarding a material fact or knowingly fail to disclose a material fact in connection with an application for admission to the State Bar.

(B) A member shall not further an application for admission to the State Bar of a person whom the member knows to be unqualified in respect to character, education, or other relevant attributes.

(C) This rule shall not prevent a member from serving as counsel of record for an applicant for admission to practice in proceedings related to such admission.

Discussion:

For purposes of rule 1-200 "admission" includes readmission.

Rule 1-300. Unauthorized Practice of Law

Unauthorized Practice of Law

(A) A member shall not aid any person or entity in the unauthorized practice of law.

(B) A member shall not practice law in a jurisdiction where to do so would be in violation of regulations of the profession in that jurisdiction.

Rule 1-310. Forming a Partnership with a Non-lawyer

Partnership with Non-lawyer

A member shall not form a partnership with a person who is not a lawyer if any of the activities of that partnership consist of the practice of law.

Discussion:

Rule 1-310 is not intended to govern members' activities which cannot be considered to constitute the practice of law. It is intended solely to preclude a member from being involved in the practice of law with a person who is not a lawyer.

Rule 1-311. Employment of Disbarred, Suspended, Resigned, or Involuntarily Inactive Member

(A) For purposes of this rule:
- (1) "Employ" means to engage the services of another, including employees, agents, independent contractors and consultants, regardless of whether any compensation is paid;
- (2) "Involuntarily inactive member" means a member who is ineligible to practice law as a result of action taken pursuant to Business and Professions Code sections 6007, 6203(c), or California Rule of Court 958(d); and
- (3) "Resigned member" means a member who has resigned from the State Bar while disciplinary charges are pending.

(B) A member shall not employ, associate professionally with, or aid a person the member knows or reasonably should know is a disbarred, suspended, resigned, or involuntarily inactive member to perform the following on behalf of the member's client:
- (1) Render legal consultation or advice to the client;
- (2) Appear on behalf of a client in any hearing or proceeding or before any judicial officer, arbitrator, mediator, court, public agency, referee, magistrate, commissioner, or hearing officer;
- (3) Appear as a representative of the client at a deposition or other discovery matter;
- (4) Negotiate or transact any matter for or on behalf of the client with third parties;

(5) Receive, disburse or otherwise handle the client's funds; or
(6) Engage in activities which constitute the practice of law.

(C) A member may employ, associate professionally with, or aid a disbarred, suspended, resigned, or involuntarily inactive member to perform research, drafting or clerical activities, including but not limited to:

Hiring Disbarred or Suspended Attorney for Paralegal Work

(1) Legal work of a preparatory nature, such as legal research, the assemblage of data and other necessary information, drafting of pleadings, briefs, and other similar documents;
(2) Direct communication with the client or third parties regarding matters such as scheduling, billing, updates, confirmation of receipt or sending of correspondence and messages; or
(3) Accompanying an active member in attending a deposition or other discovery matter for the limited purpose of providing clerical assistance to the active member who will appear as the representative of the client.

(D) Prior to or at the time of employing a person the member knows or reasonably should know is a disbarred, suspended, resigned, or involuntarily inactive member, the member shall serve upon the State Bar written notice of the employment, including a full description of such person's current bar status. The written notice shall also list the activities prohibited in paragraph (B) and state that the disbarred, suspended, resigned, or involuntarily inactive member will not perform such activities. The member shall serve similar written notice upon each client on whose specific matter such person will work, prior to or at the time of employing such person to work on the client's specific matter. The member shall obtain proof of service of the client's written notice and shall retain such proof and a true and correct copy of the client's written notice for two years following termination of the member's employment with the client.

Required Notice to Bar and to Clients

(E) A member may, without client or State Bar notification, employ a disbarred, suspended, resigned, or involuntarily inactive member whose sole function is to perform office physical plant or equipment maintenance, courier or delivery services, catering, reception, typing or transcription, or other similar support activities.

(F) Upon termination of the disbarred, suspended, resigned, or involuntarily inactive member, the member shall promptly serve upon the State Bar written notice of the termination.

Discussion:

For discussion of the activities that constitute the practice of law, see *Farnham v. State Bar* (1976) 17 Cal. 3d 605 [131 Cal. Rptr. 611]; *Bluestein v. State Bar* (1974) 13 Cal. 3d 162 [118 Cal. Rptr. 175]; *Baron v. City of Los Angeles* (1970) 2 Cal. 3d 535 [86 Cal. Rptr. 673]; *Crawford v. State Bar* (1960) 54 Cal. 2d 659 [7 Cal. Rptr. 746]; *People v. Merchants Protective Corporation* (1922) 189 Cal. 531, 535 [209 P. 363]; *People v. Landlords Professional Services* (1989) 215 Cal. App. 3d 1599 [264 Cal. Rptr. 548]; and *People v. Sipper* (1943) 61 Cal. App. 2d Supp. 844 [142 P.2d 960].)

Cases Defining the Practice of Law

Paragraph (D) is not intended to prevent or discourage a member from fully discussing with the client the activities that will be performed by the disbarred, suspended, resigned, or involuntarily inactive member on the client's matter. If a member's client is an organization, then the written notice required by paragraph (D) shall be served upon the highest authorized officer, employee, or constituent overseeing the particular engagement. (See rule 3-600).

Nothing in rule 1-311 shall be deemed to limit or preclude any activity engaged in pursuant to rules 983, 983.1, 983.2, and 988 of the California Rules of Court, or any local rule of a federal district court concerning admission pro hac vice. (Added by Order of Supreme Court, operative August 1, 1996).

Rule 1-320. Financial Arrangements With Non-lawyers

(A) Neither a member nor a law firm shall directly or indirectly share legal fees with a person who is not a lawyer, except that:

(1) An agreement between a member and a law firm, partner, or associate may provide for the payment of money after the member's death to the member's estate or to one or more specified persons over a reasonable period of time; or

Sharing Fees with Non-lawyers

(2) A member or law firm undertaking to complete unfinished legal business of a deceased member may pay to the estate of the deceased member or other person legally entitled thereto that proportion of the total compensation which fairly represents the services rendered by the deceased member; or
(3) A member or law firm may include non-member employees in a compensation, profit-sharing, or retirement plan even though the plan is based in whole or in part on a profit-sharing arrangement, if such plan does not circumvent these rules or Business and Professions Code section 6000 et seq.; or

Paralegals in Compensation and Retirement Plans

(4) A member may pay a prescribed registration, referral, or participation fee to a lawyer referral service established, sponsored, and operated in accordance with the State Bar of California's Minimum Standards for a Lawyer Referral Service in California.

(B) A member shall not compensate, give, or promise anything of value to any person or entity for the purpose of recommending or securing employment of the member or the member's law firm by a client, or as a reward for having made a recommendation resulting in employment of the member or the member's law firm by a client. A member's offering of or giving a gift or gratuity to any person or entity having made a recommendation resulting in the employment of the member or the member's law firm shall not of itself violate this rule, provided that the gift or gratuity was not offered or given in consideration of any promise, agreement, or understanding that such a gift or gratuity would be forthcoming or that referrals would be made or encouraged in the future.

Referral Fees, Gifts, or Rewards

(C) A member shall not compensate, give, or promise anything of value to any representative of the press, radio, television, or other communication medium in anticipation of or in return for publicity of the member, the law firm, or any other member as such in a news item, but the incidental provision of food or beverage shall not of itself violate this rule.

Discussion:

Rule 1-320(C) is not intended to preclude compensation to the communications media in exchange for advertising the member's or law firm's availability for professional employment.

Rule 1-400. Advertising and Solicitation

(A) For purposes of this rule, "communication" means any message or offer made by or on behalf of a member concerning the availability for professional employment of a member or a law firm directed to any former, present, or prospective client, including but not limited to the following:

(1) Any use of firm name, trade name, fictitious name, or other professional designation of such member or law firm; or

(2) Any stationery, letterhead, business card, sign, brochure, or other comparable written material describing such member, law firm, or lawyers; or

(3) Any advertisement (regardless of medium) of such member or law firm directed to the general public or any substantial portion thereof; or

(4) Any unsolicited correspondence from a member or law firm directed to any person or entity.

(B) For purposes of this rule, a "solicitation" means any communication:

Solicitation Defined

(1) Concerning the availability for professional employment of a member or a law firm in which a significant motive is pecuniary gain; and

(2) Which is

(a) delivered in person or by telephone, or

(b) directed by any means to a person known to the sender to be represented by counsel in a matter which is a subject of the communication.

(C) A solicitation shall not be made by or on behalf of a member or law firm to a prospective client with whom the member or law firm has no family or prior professional relationship, unless the solicitation is protected from abridgment by the Constitution of the United States or by the Constitution of the State of California. A solicitation to a former or present client in the discharge of a member's or law firm's professional duties is not prohibited.

(D) A communication or a solicitation (as defined herein) shall not:

(1) Contain any untrue statement; or

(2) Contain any matter, or present or arrange any matter in a manner or format which is false, deceptive, or which tends to confuse, deceive, or mislead the public; or

False Statements and Deception

(3) Omit to state any fact necessary to make the statements made, in the light of circumstances under which they are made, not misleading to the public; or

(4) Fail to indicate clearly, expressly, or by context, that it is a communication or solicitation, as the case may be; or

(5) Be transmitted in any manner which involves intrusion, coercion, duress, compulsion, intimidation, threats, or vexatious or harassing conduct.

(6) State that a member is a "certified specialist" unless the member holds a current certificate as a specialist issued by the Board of Legal Specialization, or any other entity accredited by the State Bar to designate specialists pursuant to standards adopted by the Board of Governors, and states the complete name of the entity which granted certification.

(E) The Board of Governors of the State Bar shall formulate and adopt standards as to communications which will be presumed to violate this rule 1-400. The standards shall only be used as presumptions affecting the burden of proof in disciplinary proceedings involving alleged violations of these rules. "Presumption affecting the burden of proof" means that presumption defined in Evidence Code sections 605 and 606. Such standards formulated and adopted by the Board, as from time to time amended, shall be effective and binding on all members.

(F) A member shall retain for two years a true and correct copy or recording of any communication made by written or electronic media. Upon written request, the member shall make any such copy or recording available to the State Bar, and, if requested, shall provide to the State Bar evidence to support any factual or objective claim contained in the communication.

Standards:

Pursuant to rule 1-400(E) the Board of Governors of the State Bar has adopted the following standards, . . . as forms of "communication" defined in rule 1-400(A) which are presumed to be in violation of rule 1-400:

Examples of Improper Solicitations

(1) A "communication" which contains guarantees, warranties, or predictions regarding the result of the representation.

(2) A "communication" which contains testimonials about or endorsements of a member unless such communication also contains an express disclaimer such as "this testimonial or endorsement does not constitute a guarantee, warranty, or prediction regarding the outcome of your legal matter."

(3) A "communication" which is delivered to a potential client whom the member knows or should reasonably know is in such a physical, emotional, or mental state that he or she would not be expected to exercise reasonable judgment as to the retention of counsel.

(4) A "communication" which is transmitted at the scene of an accident or at or en route to a hospital, emergency care center, or other health care facility.

Communications Requiring the Word "Advertisement"

(5) A "communication," except professional announcements, seeking professional employment for pecuniary gain, which is transmitted by mail or equivalent means which does not bear the word "Advertisement," "Newsletter" or words of similar import in 12 point print on the first page. If such communication, including firm brochures, newsletters, recent legal development advisories, and similar materials, is transmitted in an envelope, the envelope shall bear the word "Advertisement," "Newsletter," or words of similar import on the outside thereof.

(6) A "communication" in the form of a firm name, trade name, fictitious name, or other professional designation which states or implies a relationship between any member in private practice and a government agency or instrumentality or a public or non-profit legal services organization.

(7) A "communication" in the form of a firm name, trade name, fictitious name, or other professional designation which states or implies that a member has a relationship to any other lawyer or a law firm as a partner or associate, or officer or shareholder pursuant to Business and Professions Code sections 6160–6172 unless such relationship in fact exists.

"Of Counsel"

(8) A "communication" which states or implies that a member or law firm is "of counsel" to another lawyer or a law firm unless the former has a relationship with the latter (other than as a partner or associate, or officer or shareholder pursuant to Business and Professions Code sections 6160–6172) which is close, personal, continuous, and regular.

(9) A "communication" in the form of a firm name, trade name, fictitious name, or other professional designation used by a member or law firm in private practice which differs materially from any other such designation used by such member or law firm at the same time in the same community.

(10) A "communication" which implies that the member or law firm is participating in a lawyer referral service which has been certified by the State Bar of California or as having satisfied the Minimum Standards for Lawyer Referral Services in California, when that is not the case. . . .

Television Ads

(12) A "communication," except professional announcements, in the form of an advertisement primarily directed to seeking professional employment primarily for pecuniary gain transmitted to the general public or any substantial portion thereof by mail or equivalent means or by means of television, radio, newspaper, magazine, or other form of commercial mass media which does not state the name of the member responsible for the communication. When the communication is made on behalf of a law firm, the communication shall state the name of at least one member responsible for it.

(13) A "communication" which contains a dramatization unless such communication contains a disclaimer which states "this is a dramatization" or words of similar import.

Meaning of "No Fee"

(14) A "communication" which states or implies "no fee without recovery" unless such communication also expressly discloses whether or not the client will be liable for costs.

(15) A "communication" which states or implies that a member is able to provide legal services in a language other than English unless the member can actually provide legal services in such language or the communication also states in the language of the communication (a) the employment title of

the person who speaks such language and (b) that the person is not a member of the State Bar of California, if that is the case.

(16) An unsolicited "communication" transmitted to the general public or any substantial portion thereof primarily directed to seeking professional employment primarily for pecuniary gain which sets forth a specific fee or range of fees for a particular service where, in fact, the member charges a greater fee than advertised in such communication within a period of 90 days following dissemination of such communication, unless such communication expressly specifies a shorter period of time regarding the advertised fee. Where the communication is published in the classified or "yellow pages" section of telephone, business or legal directories or in other media not published more frequently than once a year, the member shall conform to the advertised fee for a period of one year from initial publication, unless such communication expressly specifies a shorter period of time regarding the advertised fee. . . .

Yellow Pages Ads

Rule 1-600. Legal Service Programs

(A) A member shall not participate in a nongovernmental program, activity, or organization furnishing, recommending, or paying for legal services, which allows any third person or organization to interfere with the member's independence of professional judgment, or with the client-lawyer relationship, or allows unlicensed persons to practice law, or allows any third person or organization to receive directly or indirectly any part of the consideration paid to the member except as permitted by these rules, or otherwise violates the State Bar Act or these rules.

Nonlawyers Interfering with a Lawyer's Independent Professional Judgment

(B) The Board of Governors of the State Bar shall formulate and adopt Minimum Standards for Lawyer Referral Services, which, as from time to time amended, shall be binding on members.

Discussion:

The participation of a member in a lawyer referral service established, sponsored, supervised, and operated in conformity with the Minimum Standards for a Lawyer Referral Service in California is encouraged and is not, of itself, a violation of these rules.

Rule 1-600 is not intended to override any contractual agreement or relationship between insurers and insureds regarding the provision of legal services.

Rule 1-600 is not intended to apply to the activities of a public agency responsible for providing legal services to a government or to the public.

For purposes of paragraph (A), "a nongovernmental program, activity, or organization" includes, but is not limited to group, prepaid, and voluntary legal service programs, activities, or organizations.

Rule 1-700. Member as Candidate for Judicial Office

(A) A member who is a candidate for judicial office in California shall comply with Canon 5 of the Code of Judicial Ethics. . . .

Chapter 2. Relationship among Members

Rule 2-100. Communication with a Represented Party

(A) While representing a client, a member shall not communicate directly or indirectly about the subject of the representation with a party the member knows to be represented by another lawyer in the matter, unless the member has the consent of the other lawyer.

Communication with the Other Side

(B) For purposes of this rule, a "party" includes:

(1) An officer, director, or managing agent of a corporation or association, and a partner or managing agent of a partnership; or

(2) An association member or an employee of an association, corporation, or partnership, if the subject of the communication is any act or omission of such person in connection with the matter which may be binding upon or imputed to the organization for purposes of civil or criminal liability or whose statement may constitute an admission on the part of the organization.

(C) This rule shall not prohibit:

(1) Communications with a public officer, board, committee, or body; or

(2) Communications initiated by a party seeking advice or representation from an independent lawyer of the party's choice; or

(3) Communications otherwise authorized by law.

Discussion:

Rule 2-100 is intended to control communications between a member and persons the member knows to be represented by counsel unless a statutory scheme or case law will override the rule. There are a number of express statutory schemes which authorize communications between a member and person who would otherwise be subject to this rule. These statutes protect a variety of other rights such as the right of employees to organize and to engage in collective bargaining, employee health and safety, or equal employment opportunity. Other applicable law also includes the authority of government prosecutors and investigators to conduct criminal investigations, as limited by the relevant decisional law.

Rule 2-100 is not intended to prevent the parties themselves from communicating with respect to the subject matter of the representation, and nothing in the rule prevents a member from advising the client that such communication can be made. Moreover, the rule does not prohibit a member who is also a party to a legal matter from directly or indirectly communicating on his or her own behalf with a represented party. Such a member has independent rights as a party which should not be abrogated because of his or her professional status. To prevent any possible abuse in such situations, the counsel for the opposing party may advise that party (1) about the risks and benefits of communications with a lawyer-party, and (2) not to accept or engage in communications with the lawyer-party.

Rule 2-100 also addresses the situation in which member A is contacted by an opposing party who is represented and, because of dissatisfaction with that party's counsel, seeks A's independent advice. Since A is employed by the opposition, the member cannot give independent advice.

As used in paragraph (A), "the subject of the representation," "matter," and "party" are not limited to a litigation context.

Paragraph (B) is intended to apply only to persons employed at the time of the communication. (See *Triple A Machine Shop, Inc. v. State of California* (1989) 213 Cal. App. 3d 131 [261 Cal. Rptr. 493].)

Subparagraph (C)(2) is intended to permit a member to communicate with a party seeking to hire new counsel or to obtain a second opinion. A member contacted by such a party continues to be bound by other Rules of Professional Conduct. (See, e.g., rules 1-400 and 3-310.)

Rule 2-200. Financial Arrangements among Lawyers

Splitting Fees

(A) A member shall not divide a fee for legal services with a lawyer who is not a partner of, associate of, or shareholder with the member unless:

(1) The client has consented in writing thereto after a full disclosure has been made in writing that a division of fees will be made and the terms of such division; and

(2) The total fee charged by all lawyers is not increased solely by reason of the provision for division of fees and is not unconscionable as that term is defined in rule 4-200.

Referral Fees, Gifts, or Rewards

(B) Except as permitted in paragraph (A) of this rule or rule 2-300, a member shall not compensate, give, or promise anything of value to any lawyer for the purpose of recommending or securing employment of the member or the member's law firm by a client, or as a reward for having made a recommendation resulting in employment of the member or the member's law firm by a client. A member's offering of or giving a gift or gratuity to any lawyer who has made a recommendation resulting in the employment of the member or the member's law firm shall not of itself violate this rule, provided that the gift or gratuity was not offered in consideration of any promise, agreement, or understanding that such a gift or gratuity would be forthcoming or that referrals would be made or encouraged in the future.

Rule 2-300. Sale or Purchase of a Law Practice of a Member, Living or Deceased

All or substantially all of the law practice of a member, living or deceased, including goodwill, may be sold to another member or law firm subject to all the following conditions:

(A) Fees charged to clients shall not be increased solely by reason of such sale. . . .

(E) Confidential information shall not be disclosed to a nonmember in connection with a sale under this rule . . . .

Discussion:

Paragraph (A) is intended to prohibit the purchaser from charging the former clients of the seller a higher fee than the purchaser is charging his or her existing clients. . . . Payment of a fee to a non-lawyer broker for arranging the sale or purchase of a law practice is governed by rule 1-320.

Rule 2-400. Prohibited Discriminatory Conduct in a Law Practice

Discrimination Practiced by a Law Firm

(A) For purposes of this rule:

(1) "Law practice" includes sole practices, law partnerships, law corporations, corporate and governmental legal departments, and other entities which employ members to practice law;

(2) "Knowingly permit" means a failure to advocate corrective action where the member knows of a discriminatory policy or practice which results in the unlawful discrimination prohibited in paragraph (B); and

(3) "Unlawfully" and "unlawful" shall be determined by reference to applicable state or federal statutes or decisions making unlawful discrimination in employment and in offering goods and services to the public.

(B) In the management or operation of a law practice, a member shall not unlawfully discriminate or knowingly permit unlawful discrimination on the basis of race, national origin, sex, sexual orientation, religion, age, or disability in:

(1) hiring, promoting, discharging, or otherwise determining the conditions of employment of any person; or

(2) accepting or terminating representation of any client.

(C) No disciplinary investigation or proceeding may be initiated by the State Bar against a member under this rule unless and until a tribunal of competent jurisdiction, other than a disciplinary tribunal, shall have first adjudicated a complaint of alleged discrimination and found that unlawful conduct occurred. Upon such adjudication, the tribunal finding or verdict shall then be admissible evidence of the occurrence or non-occurrence of the alleged discrimination in any disciplinary proceeding initiated under this rule. In order for discipline to be imposed under this rule, however, the finding of unlawfulness must be upheld and final after appeal, the time for filing an appeal must have expired, or the appeal must have been dismissed.

Discussion:

In order for discriminatory conduct to be actionable under this rule, it must first be found to be unlawful by an appropriate civil administrative or judicial tribunal under applicable state or federal law. Until there is a finding of civil unlawfulness, there is no basis for disciplinary action under this rule.

A complaint of misconduct based on this rule may be filed with the State Bar following a finding of unlawfulness in the first instance even though that finding is thereafter appealed. A disciplinary investigation or proceeding for conduct coming within this rule may be initiated and maintained, however, if such conduct warrants discipline under California Business and Professions Code sections 6106 and 6068, the California Supreme Court's inherent authority to impose discipline, or other disciplinary standard.

Chapter 3. Professional Relationship with Clients

Rule 3-100. Confidential Information of a Client

(A) A member shall not reveal information protected from disclosure by Business and Professions Code section 6068, subdivision (e)(1) without the informed consent of the client, or as provided in paragraph (B) of this rule.

(B) A member may, but is not required to, reveal confidential information relating to the representation of a client to the extent that the member reasonably believes the disclosure is necessary to prevent a criminal act that the member reasonably believes is likely to result in death of, or substantial bodily harm to, an individual.

Disclosing Confidential Information

(C) Before revealing confidential information to prevent a criminal act as provided in paragraph (B), a member shall, if reasonable under the circumstances:

Criminal Act by a Client

(1) make a good faith effort to persuade the client: (i) not to commit or to continue the criminal act or (ii) to pursue a course of conduct that will prevent the threatened death or substantial bodily harm; or do both (i) and (ii); and

(2) inform the client, at an appropriate time, of the member's ability or decision to reveal information as provided in paragraph (B).

(D) In revealing confidential information as provided in paragraph (B), the member's disclosure must be no more than is necessary to prevent the criminal act, given the information known to the member at the time of the disclosure.

(E) A member who does not reveal information permitted by paragraph (B) does not violate this rule.

Discussion:

[1] Duty of confidentiality. Paragraph (A) relates to a member's obligations under Business and Professions Code section 6068, subdivision (e)(1), which provides it is a duty of a member: "To maintain inviolate the confidence, and at every peril to himself or herself to preserve the secrets, of his or her client." A member's duty to preserve the confidentiality of client information involves public policies of paramount importance. (*In Re Jordan* (1974) 12 Cal. 3d 575, 580 [116 Cal. Rptr. 371].) Preserving the confidentiality of client information contributes to the trust that is the hallmark of the client-lawyer relationship. The client is thereby encouraged to seek legal assistance and to communicate fully and frankly with the lawyer even as to embarrassing or legally damaging subject matter. The lawyer needs this information to represent the client effectively and, if necessary, to advise the client to refrain from wrongful conduct. Almost without exception, clients come to lawyers in order to determine their rights and what is, in the complex of laws and regulations, deemed to be legal and correct. Based upon experience, lawyers know that almost all clients follow the advice given, and the law is upheld. Paragraph (A) thus recognizes a fundamental principle in the client-lawyer relationship, that, in the absence of the client's informed consent, a member must not reveal information relating to the representation. (See, e.g., *Commercial Standard Title Co. v. Superior Court* (1979) 92 Cal. App. 3d 934, 945 [155 Cal. Rptr. 393].)

Duty of Confidentiality

[2] Client-lawyer confidentiality encompasses the attorney-client privilege, the work-product doctrine

Attorney-Client Privilege

and ethical standards of confidentiality. The principle of client-lawyer confidentiality applies to information relating to the representation, whatever its source, and encompasses matters communicated in confidence by the client, and therefore protected by the attorney-client privilege, matters protected by the work product doctrine, and matters protected under ethical standards of confidentiality, all as established in law, rule and policy. (See *In the Matter of Johnson* (Rev. Dept. 2000) 4 Cal. State Bar Ct. Rptr. 179; *Goldstein v. Lees* (1975) 46 Cal. 3d 614, 621 [120 Cal. Rptr. 253].) The attorney-client privilege and work-product doctrine apply in judicial and other proceedings in which a member may be called as a witness or be otherwise compelled to produce evidence concerning a client. A member's ethical duty of confidentiality is not so limited in its scope of protection for the client-lawyer relationship of trust and prevents a member from revealing the client's confidential information even when not confronted with such compulsion. Thus, a member may not reveal such information except with the consent of the client or as authorized or required by the State Bar Act, these rules, or other law.

Work-Product Rule

[3] Narrow exception to duty of confidentiality under this Rule. Notwithstanding the important public policies promoted by lawyers adhering to the core duty of confidentiality, the overriding value of life permits disclosures otherwise prohibited under Business & Professions Code section 6068(e), subdivision (1). Paragraph (B), which restates Business and Professions Code section 6068, subdivision (e)(2), identifies a narrow confidentiality exception, absent the client's informed consent, when a member reasonably believes that disclosure is necessary to prevent a criminal act that the member reasonably believes is likely to result in the death of, or substantial bodily harm to an individual. Evidence Code section 956.5, which relates to the evidentiary attorney-client privilege, sets forth a similar express exception. Although a member is not permitted to reveal confidential information concerning a client's past, completed criminal acts, the policy favoring the preservation of human life that underlies this exception to the duty of confidentiality and the evidentiary privilege permits disclosure to prevent a future or ongoing criminal act.

[4] Member not subject to discipline for revealing confidential information as permitted under this Rule. Rule 3-100, which restates Business and Professions Code section 6068, subdivision (e)(2), reflects a balancing between the interests of preserving client confidentiality and of preventing a criminal act that a member reasonably believes is likely to result in death or substantial bodily harm to an individual. A member who reveals information as permitted under this rule is not subject to discipline.

[5] No duty to reveal confidential information. Neither Business and Professions Code section 6068, subdivision (e)(2) nor this rule imposes an affirmative obligation on a member to reveal information in order to prevent harm. (See rule 1-100(A).) A member may decide not to reveal confidential information. Whether a member chooses to reveal confidential information as permitted under this rule is a matter for the individual member to decide, based on all the facts and circumstances, such as those discussed in paragraph [6] of this discussion.

No Duty to Reveal to Prevent Harm

[6] Deciding to reveal confidential information as permitted under paragraph (B). Disclosure permitted under paragraph (B) is ordinarily a last resort, when no other available action is reasonably likely to prevent the criminal act. Prior to revealing information as permitted under paragraph (B), the member must, if reasonable under the circumstances, make a good faith effort to persuade the client to take steps to avoid the criminal act or threatened harm. Among the factors to be considered in determining whether to disclose confidential information are the following:

Good Faith Effort to Persuade Client

(1) the amount of time that the member has to make a decision about disclosure;
(2) whether the client or a third party has made similar threats before and whether they have ever acted or attempted to act upon them;
(3) whether the member believes the member's efforts to persuade the client or a third person not to engage in the criminal conduct have or have not been successful;
(4) the extent of adverse effect to the client's rights under the Fifth, Sixth, and Fourteenth Amendments of the United States Constitution and analogous rights and privacy rights under Article 1 of the Constitution of the State of California that may result from disclosure contemplated by the member;
(5) the extent of other adverse effects to the client that may result from disclosure contemplated by the member; and
(6) the nature and extent of information that must be disclosed to prevent the criminal act or threatened harm.

Factors to Consider in Revealing Confidential Information

A member may also consider whether the prospective harm to the victim or victims is imminent in deciding whether to disclose the confidential information. However, the imminence of the harm is not a prerequisite to disclosure and a member may disclose the information without waiting until immediately before the harm is likely to occur.

[7] Counseling client or third person not to commit a criminal act reasonably likely to result in death or substantial bodily harm. Subparagraph (C)(1) provides that before a member may reveal confidential information, the member must, if reasonable under the circumstances, make a good faith effort to persuade the client not to commit or to continue the criminal act, or to persuade the client to otherwise pursue a course of conduct that will prevent the threatened death or substantial bodily harm, or if necessary, do both. The interests protected by such counseling is the client's interest in limiting disclosure of confidential information and in taking responsible action to deal with situations attributable to the client. If a client, whether in response to the member's counseling or otherwise, takes corrective action—such as by ceasing the criminal act before harm is caused—the option for permissive disclosure by the member would cease as the threat posed by the criminal act would no longer be present. When the actor is a nonclient or when the act is deliberate or malicious, the member who contemplates making adverse disclosure of confidential information may reasonably conclude that the compelling interests of the member or others in their own personal safety preclude personal contact with the actor. Before counseling an actor who is a nonclient, the member should, if reasonable under the circumstances, first advise the client of the member's intended course of action. If a client or another person has already acted but the intended harm has not yet occurred, the member should consider, if reasonable under the circumstances, efforts to persuade the client or third person to warn the victim or consider other appropriate action to prevent the harm. Even when the member has concluded that paragraph (B) does not permit the member to reveal confidential information, the member nevertheless is permitted to counsel the client as to why it may be in the client's best interest to consent to the attorney's disclosure of that information.

Safety of the Lawyer

[8] Disclosure of confidential information must be no more than is reasonably necessary to prevent the criminal act. Under paragraph (D), disclosure of confidential information, when made, must be no more extensive than the member reasonably believes necessary to prevent the criminal act. Disclosure should allow access to the confidential information to only those persons who the member reasonably believes can act to prevent the harm. Under some circumstances, a member may determine that the best course to pursue is to make an anonymous disclosure to the potential victim or relevant law-enforcement authorities. What particular measures are reasonable depends on the circumstances known to the member. Relevant circumstances include the time available, whether the victim might be unaware of the threat, the member's prior course of dealings with the client, and the extent of the adverse effect on the client that may result from the disclosure contemplated by the member.

Anonymous Disclosure of Confidential Information

[9] Informing client of member's ability or decision to reveal confidential information under subparagraph (C)(2). A member is required to keep a client reasonably informed about significant developments regarding the employment or representation. Rule 3-500; Business and Professions Code, section 6068, subdivision (m). Paragraph (C)(2), however, recognizes that under certain circumstances, informing a client of the member's ability or decision to reveal confidential information under paragraph (B) would likely increase the risk of death or substantial bodily harm, not only to the originally-intended victims of the criminal act, but also to the client or members of the client's family, or to the member or the member's family or associates. Therefore, paragraph (C)(2) requires a member to inform the client of the member's ability or decision to reveal confidential information as provided in paragraph (B) only if it is reasonable to do so under the circumstances. Paragraph (C)(2) further recognizes that the appropriate time for the member to inform the client may vary depending upon the circumstances. (See paragraph [10] of this discussion.) Among the factors to be considered in determining an appropriate time, if any, to inform a client are:

(1) whether the client is an experienced user of legal services;
(2) the frequency of the member's contact with the client;
(3) the nature and length of the professional relationship with the client;
(4) whether the member and client have discussed the member's duty of confidentiality or any exceptions to that duty;
(5) the likelihood that the client's matter will involve information within paragraph (B);
(6) the member's belief, if applicable, that so informing the client is likely to increase the likelihood that a criminal act likely to result in the death of, or substantial bodily harm to, an individual; and

More Factors to Consider in Revealing Confidential Information

(7) the member's belief, if applicable, that good faith efforts to persuade a client not to act on a threat have failed.

[10] Avoiding a chilling effect on the lawyer-client relationship. The foregoing flexible approach to the member's informing a client of his or her ability or decision to reveal confidential information recognizes the concern that informing a client about limits on confidentiality may have a chilling effect on client communication. (See Discussion paragraph [1].) To avoid that chilling effect, one member may choose to inform the client of the member's ability to reveal information as early as the outset of the representation, while another member may choose to inform a client only at a point when that client has imparted information that may fall under paragraph (B), or even choose not to inform a client until such time as the member attempts to counsel the client as contemplated in Discussion paragraph [7]. In each situation, the member will have discharged properly the requirement under subparagraph (C)(2), and will not be subject to discipline.

[11] Informing client that disclosure has been made; termination of the lawyer-client relationship. When a member has revealed confidential information under paragraph (B), in all but extraordinary cases the relationship between member and client will have deteriorated so as to make the member's representation of the client impossible. Therefore, the member is required to seek to withdraw from the representation (see rule 3-700(B)), unless the member is able to obtain the client's informed consent to the member's continued representation. The member must inform the client of the fact of the member's disclosure unless the member has a compelling interest in not informing the client, such as to protect the member, the member's family or a third person from the risk of death or substantial bodily harm.

Withdrawal after Revealing Confidential Information

[12] Other consequences of the member's disclosure. Depending upon the circumstances of a member's disclosure of confidential information, there may be other important issues that a member must address. For example, if a member will be called as a witness in the client's matter, then rule 5-210 should be considered. Similarly, the member should consider his or her duties of loyalty and competency (rule 3-110).

[13] Other exceptions to confidentiality under California law. Rule 3-100 is not intended to augment, diminish, or preclude reliance upon, any other exceptions to the duty to preserve the confidentiality of client information recognized under California law.

Rule 3-110. Failing to Act Competently

(A) A member shall not intentionally, recklessly, or repeatedly fail to perform legal services with competence.

Competence defined

(B) For purposes of this rule, "competence" in any legal service shall mean to apply the (1) diligence, (2) learning and skill, and (3) mental, emotional, and physical ability reasonably necessary for the performance of such service.

(C) If a member does not have sufficient learning and skill when the legal service is undertaken, the member may nonetheless perform such services competently by (1) associating with or, where appropriate, professionally consulting another lawyer reasonably believed to be competent, or (2) by acquiring sufficient learning and skill before performance is required.

Discussion:

The duties set forth in rule 3-110 include the duty to supervise the work of subordinate attorney and non-attorney employees or agents. (See, e.g., *Waysman v. State Bar* (1986) 41 Cal. 3d 452; *Trousil v. State Bar* (1985) 38 Cal. 3d 337, 342 [211 Cal. Rptr. 525]; *Palomo v. State Bar* (1984) 36 Cal. 3d 785 [205 Cal. Rptr. 834]; *Crane v. State Bar* (1981) 30 Cal. 3d 117, 122; *Black v. State Bar* (1972) 7 Cal. 3d 676, 692 [10 3 Cal. Rptr. 288; 499 P.2d 968]; *Vaughn v. State Bar* (1972) 6 Cal. 3d 847, 857–858 [100 Cal. Rptr. 713; 494 P.2d 1257]; *Moore v. State Bar* (1964) 62 Cal. 2d 74, 81 [41 Cal. Rptr. 161; 396 P.2d577].)

Duty to Supervise Paralegals

In an emergency a lawyer may give advice or assistance in a matter in which the lawyer does not have the skill ordinarily required where referral to or consultation with another lawyer would be impractical. Even in an emergency, however, assistance should be limited to that reasonably necessary in the circumstances.

Rule 3-120. Sexual Relations with Client

(A) For purposes of this rule, "sexual relations" means sexual intercourse or the touching of an intimate part of another person for the purpose of sexual arousal, gratification, or abuse.

Sexual Relationship with Client

(B) A member shall not:

(1) Require or demand sexual relations with a client incident to or as a condition of any professional representation; or

(2) Employ coercion, intimidation, or undue influence in entering into sexual relations with a client; or

(3) Continue representation of a client with whom the member has sexual relations if such sexual relations cause the member to perform legal services incompetently in violation of rule 3-110.

(C) Paragraph (B) shall not apply to sexual relations between members and their spouses or to ongoing consensual sexual relationships which predate the initiation of the lawyer-client relationship.

(D) Where a lawyer in a firm has sexual relations with a client but does not participate in the representation of that client, the lawyers in the firm shall not be subject to discipline under this rule solely because of the occurrence of such sexual relations.

Discussion:

Rule 3-120 is intended to prohibit sexual exploitation by a lawyer in the course of a professional representation. Often, based upon the nature of the underlying representation, a client exhibits great emotional vulnerability and dependence upon the advice and guidance of counsel. Attorneys owe the utmost duty of good faith and fidelity to clients. (See, e.g., *Greenbaum v. State Bar* (1976) 15 Cal. 3d 893, 903 [126 Cal. Rptr. 785]; *Alkow v. State Bar* (1971) 3 Cal. 3d 924, 935 [92 Cal. Rptr. 278]; *Cutler v. State Bar* (1969) 71 Cal. 2d 241, 251 [78 Cal. Rptr 172]; *Clancy v. State Bar* (1969) 71 Cal. 2d 140, 146 [77 Cal. Rptr. 657].) The relationship between an attorney and client is a fiduciary relationship of the very highest character and all dealings between an attorney and client that are beneficial to the attorney will be closely scrutinized with the utmost strictness for unfairness. (See, e.g., *Giovanazzi v. State Bar* (1980) 28 Cal. 3d 465, 472 [169 Cal Rptr. 581]; *Benson v. State Bar* (1975) 13 Cal. 3d 581, 586 [119 Cal. Rptr. 297]; *Lee v. State Bar* (1970) 2 Cal. 3d 927, 939 [88 Cal. Rptr. 361]; *Clancy v. State Bar* (1969) 71 Cal. 2d 140, 146 [77 Cal. Rptr. 657].) Where attorneys exercise undue influence over clients or take unfair advantage of clients, discipline is appropriate. (See, e.g., *Magee v. State Bar* (1962) 58 Cal. 2d 423 [24 Cal. Rptr. 839]; *Lantz v. State Bar* (1931) 212 Cal. 213 [298 P. 497].) In all client matters, a member is advised to keep clients' interests paramount in the course of the member's representation.

Fiduciary Relationship between Lawyer and Client

For purposes of this rule, if the client is an organization, any individual overseeing the representation shall be deemed to be the client. (See rule 3-600.)

Although paragraph (C) excludes representation of certain clients from the scope of rule 3-120, such exclusion is not intended to preclude the applicability of other Rules of Professional Conduct, including rule 3-110.

Rule 3-200. Prohibited Objectives of Employment

A member shall not seek, accept, or continue employment if the member knows or should know that the objective of such employment is:

Harassment

(A) To bring an action, conduct a defense, assert a position in litigation, or take an appeal, without probable cause and for the purpose of harassing or maliciously injuring any person; or

(B) To present a claim or defense in litigation that is not warranted under existing law, unless it can be supported by a good faith argument for an extension, modification, or reversal of such existing law.

Unwarranted Claims or Defenses

Rule 3-210. Advising the Violation of Law

A member shall not advise the violation of any law, rule, or ruling of a tribunal unless the member believes in good faith that such law, rule, or ruling is invalid. A member may take appropriate steps in good faith to test the validity of any law, rule, or ruling of a tribunal.

Advice to Violate the Law

Discussion:

Rule 3-210 is intended to apply not only to the prospective conduct of a client but also to the interaction between the member and client and to the specific legal service sought by the client from the member. An example of the former is the handling of physical evidence of a crime in the possession of the client and offered to the member. (See *People v. Meredith* (1981) 29 Cal. 3d 682 [175 Cal. Rptr. 612].) An example of the latter is a request that the member negotiate the return of stolen property in exchange for the owner's agreement not to report the theft to the police or prosecutorial authorities. (See *People v. Pic'l* (1982) 31 Cal. 3d 731 [183 Cal. Rptr. 685].)

Rule 3-300. Avoiding Interests Adverse to a Client

A member shall not enter into a business transaction with a client; or knowingly acquire an ownership, possessory, security, or other pecuniary interest adverse to a client, unless each of the following requirements has been satisfied:

Entering a Business Deal with a Client

(A) The transaction or acquisition and its terms are fair and reasonable to the client and are fully disclosed and transmitted in writing to the client in a manner which should reasonably have been understood by the client; and

(B) The client is advised in writing that the client may seek the advice of an independent lawyer of the client's choice and is given a reasonable opportunity to seek that advice; and

(C) The client thereafter consents in writing to the terms of the transaction or the terms of the acquisition.

Discussion:

Rule 3-300 is not intended to apply to the agreement by which the member is retained by the client, unless the agreement confers on the member an ownership, possessory, security, or other pecuniary interest adverse to the client. Such an agreement is governed, in part, by rule 4-200.

Rule 3-300 is not intended to apply where the member and client each make an investment on terms offered to the general public or a significant portion thereof. For example, rule 3-300 is not intended to apply where A, a member, invests in a limited partnership syndicated by a third party. B, A's client, makes the same investment. Although A and B are each investing in the same business, A did not enter into the transaction "with" B for the purposes of the rule.

Rule 3-300 is intended to apply where the member wishes to obtain an interest in client's property in order to secure the amount of the member's past due or future fees.

Rule 3-310. Avoiding the Representation of Adverse Interests

Adverse Interests

(A) For purposes of this rule:

(1) "Disclosure" means informing the client or former client of the relevant circumstances and of the actual and reasonably foreseeable adverse consequences to the client or former client;

(2) "Informed written consent" means the client's or former client's written agreement to the representation following written disclosure;

(3) "Written" means any writing as defined in Evidence Code section 250.

(B) A member shall not accept or continue representation of a client without providing written disclosure to the client where:

(1) The member has a legal, business, financial, professional, or personal relationship with a party or witness in the same matter; or

(2) The member knows or reasonably should know that:

(a) the member previously had a legal, business, financial, professional, or personal relationship with a party or witness in the same matter; and

(b) the previous relationship would substantially affect the member's representation; or

(3) The member has or had a legal, business, financial, professional, or personal relationship with another person or entity the member knows or reasonably should know would be affected substantially by resolution of the matter; or

(4) The member has or had a legal, business, financial, or professional interest in the subject matter of the representation.

(C) A member shall not, without the informed written consent of each client:

(1) Accept representation of more than one client in a matter in which the interests of the clients potentially conflict; or

(2) Accept or continue representation of more than one client in a matter in which the interests of the clients actually conflict; or

Conflict of Interest among Clients of the Same Lawyer

(3) Represent a client in a matter and at the same time in a separate matter accept as a client a person or entity whose interest in the first matter is adverse to the client in the first matter.

(D) A member who represents two or more clients shall not enter into an aggregate settlement of the claims of or against the clients without the informed written consent of each client.

Settlement

(E) A member shall not, without the informed written consent of the client or former client, accept employment adverse to the client or former client where, by reason of the representation of the client or former client, the member has obtained confidential information material to the employment.

Prior Client Presenting a Conflict of Interest

(F) A member shall not accept compensation for representing a client from one other than the client unless:

Interfering with a Lawyer's Independent Professional Judgment

(1) There is no interference with the member's independence of professional judgment or with the client-lawyer relationship; and

(2) Information relating to representation of the client is protected as required by Business and Professions Code section 6068, subdivision (e); and

(3) The member obtains the client's informed written consent, provided that no disclosure or consent is required if:

(a) such nondisclosure is otherwise authorized by law; or

(b) the member is rendering legal services on behalf of any public agency which provides legal services to other public agencies or the public.

Discussion:

Rule 3-310 is not intended to prohibit a member from representing parties having antagonistic positions on the same legal question that has arisen in different cases, unless representation of either client would be adversely affected. Other rules and laws may preclude making adequate disclosure under this rule. If such disclosure is precluded, informed written consent is likewise precluded. (See, e.g., Business and Professions Code section 6068, subdivision (e).) Paragraph (B) is not intended to apply to the relationship of a member to another party's lawyer. Such relationships are governed by rule 3-320.

Paragraph (B) is not intended to require either the disclosure of the new engagement to a former client or the consent of the former client to the new engagement. However, both disclosure and consent are required if paragraph (E) applies. While paragraph (B) deals with the issues of adequate disclosure to the present client or clients of the member's present or past relationships to other parties or witnesses or present interest in the subject matter of the representation, paragraph (E) is intended to protect the confidences of another present or former client. These two paragraphs are to apply as complementary provisions.

Paragraph (B) is intended to apply only to a member's own relationships or interests, unless the member knows that a partner or associate in the same firm as the member has or had a relationship with another party or witness or has or had an interest in the subject matter of the representation. Subparagraphs (C)(1) and (C)(2) are intended to apply to all types of legal employment, including the concurrent representation of multiple parties in litigation or in a single transaction or in some other common enterprise or legal relationship. Examples of the latter include the formation of a partnership for several partners or a corporation for several shareholders, the preparation of an ante-nuptial agreement, or joint or reciprocal wills for a husband and wife, or the resolution of an "uncontested" marital dissolution. In such situations, for the sake of convenience or economy, the parties may well prefer to employ a single counsel, but a member must disclose the potential adverse aspects of such multiple representation (e.g., Evid. Code, §962) and must obtain the informed written consent of the clients thereto pursuant to subparagraph (C)(1). Moreover, if the potential adversity should become actual, the member must obtain the further informed written consent of the clients pursuant to subparagraph (C)(2).

Concurrent Representation of Multiple Parties

Subparagraph (C)(3) is intended to apply to representations of clients in both litigation and transactional matters. In *State Farm Mutual Automobile Insurance Company v. Federal Insurance Company* (1999) 72 Cal. App. 4th 1422 [86 Cal. Rptr. 2d 20], the court held that subparagraph (C)(3) was violated when a member, retained by an insurer to defend one suit, and while that suit was still pending, filed a direct action against the same insurer in an unrelated action without securing the insurer's consent. Notwithstanding *State Farm*, subparagraph (C)(3) is not intended to apply with respect to the relationship between an insurer and a member when, in each matter, the insurer's interest is only as an indemnity provider and not as a direct party to the action.

There are some matters in which the conflicts are such that written consent may not suffice for non-disciplinary purposes. (See *Woods v. Superior Court* (1983) 149 Cal. App. 3d 931 [197 Cal. Rptr. 185]; *Klemm v. Superior Court* (1977) 75 Cal. App. 3d 893 [142 Cal. Rptr. 509]; *Ishmael v. Millington* (1966) 241 Cal. App. 2d 520 [50 Cal. Rptr. 592].)

Paragraph (D) is not intended to apply to class action settlements subject to court approval.

Paragraph (F) is not intended to abrogate existing relationships between insurers and insureds whereby the insurer has the contractual right to unilaterally select counsel for the insured, where there is no conflict of interest. (See *San Diego Navy Federal Credit Union v. Cumis Insurance Society* (1984) 162 Cal. App. 3d 358 [208 Cal. Rptr. 494].)

Rule 3-320. Relationship with Other Party's Lawyer

A member shall not represent a client in a matter in which another party's lawyer is a spouse, parent, child, or sibling of the member, lives with the member, is a client of the member, or has an intimate personal relationship with the member, unless the member informs the client in writing of the relationship.

Family or Intimate Relationship between Opposing Lawyers

Discussion:

Rule 3-320 is not intended to apply to circumstances in which a member fails to advise the client of a relationship with another lawyer who is merely a partner or associate in the same law firm as the adverse party's counsel, and who has no direct involvement in the matter.

Rule 3-400. Limiting Liability to Client

A member shall not:

Lawyer Malpractice

(A) Contract with a client prospectively limiting the member's liability to the client for the member's professional malpractice; or

(B) Settle a claim or potential claim for the member's liability to the client for the member's professional malpractice, unless the client is informed in writing that the client may seek the advice of an independent lawyer of the client's choice regarding the settlement and is given a reasonable opportunity to seek that advice.

Discussion:

Rule 3-400 is not intended to apply to customary qualifications and limitations in legal opinions and memoranda, nor is it intended to prevent a member from reasonably limiting the scope of the member's employment or representation.

Rule 3-500. Communication

A member shall keep a client reasonably informed about significant developments relating to the employment or representation, including promptly

Keeping a Client Reasonably Informed

complying with reasonable requests for information and copies of significant documents when necessary to keep the client so informed.

Discussion:

Rule 3-500 is not intended to change a member's duties to his or her clients. It is intended to make clear that, while a client must be informed of significant developments in the matter, a member will not be disciplined for failing to communicate insignificant or irrelevant information. (See Bus. & Prof. Code, §6068, subd. (m).)

A member may contract with the client in their employment agreement that the client assumes responsibility for the cost of copying significant documents. This rule is not intended to prohibit a claim for the recovery of the member's expense in any subsequent legal proceeding.

Work-Product Rule

Rule 3-500 is not intended to create, augment, diminish, or eliminate any application of the work-product rule. The obligation of the member to provide work product to the client shall be governed by relevant statutory and decisional law. Additionally, this rule is not intended to apply to any document or correspondence that is subject to a protective order or nondisclosure agreement, or to override applicable statutory or decisional law requiring that certain information not be provided to criminal defendants who are clients of the member.

Rule 3-510. Communication of Settlement Offer

(A) A member shall promptly communicate to the member's client:

Settlement Offers

(1) All terms and conditions of any offer made to the client in a criminal matter; and

(2) All amounts, terms, and conditions of any written offer of settlement made to the client in all other matters.

(B) As used in this rule, "client" includes a person who possesses the authority to accept an offer of settlement or plea, or, in a class action, all the named representatives of the class.

Discussion:

Rule 3-510 is intended to require that counsel in a criminal matter convey all offers, whether written or oral, to the client, as give and take negotiations are less common in criminal matters, and, even were they to occur, such negotiations should require the participation of the accused.

Any oral offers of settlement made to the client in a civil matter should also be communicated if they are "significant" for the purposes of rule 3-500.

Rule 3-600. Organization as Client

(A) In representing an organization, a member shall conform his or her representation to the concept that the client is the organization itself, acting through its highest authorized officer, employee, body, or constituent overseeing the particular engagement.

Organization as the Client

(B) If a member acting on behalf of an organization knows that an actual or apparent agent of the organization acts or intends or refuses to act in a manner that is or may be a violation of law reasonably imputable to the organization, or in a manner which is likely to result in substantial injury to the organization, the member shall not violate his or her duty of protecting all confidential information as provided in Business and Professions Code section 6068, subdivision (e). Subject to Business and Professions Code section 6068, subdivision (e), the member may take such actions as appear to the member to be in the best lawful interest of the organization. Such actions may include among others:

(1) Urging reconsideration of the matter while explaining its likely consequences to the organization; or

(2) Referring the matter to the next higher authority in the organization, including, if warranted by the seriousness of the matter, referral to the highest internal authority that can act on behalf of the organization.

(C) If, despite the member's actions in accordance with paragraph (B), the highest authority that can act on behalf of the organization insists upon action or a refusal to act that is a violation of law and is likely to result in substantial injury to the organization, the member's response is limited to the member's right, and, where appropriate, duty to resign in accordance with rule 3-700.

Duty to Resign

(D) In dealing with an organization's directors, officers, employees, members, shareholders, or other constituents, a member shall explain the identity of the client for whom the member acts, whenever it is or becomes apparent that the organization's interests are or may become adverse to those of the constituent(s) with whom the member is dealing. The member shall not mislead such a constituent into believing that the constituent may communicate confidential information to the member in a way that will not be used in the organization's interest if that is or becomes adverse to the constituent.

Identity of the Client

(E) A member representing an organization may also represent any of its directors, officers, employees, members, shareholders, or other constituents, subject to the provisions of rule 3-310. If the organization's consent to the dual representation is required by rule 3-310, the consent shall be given by an appropriate constituent of the organization other than the individual or constituent who is to be represented, or by the shareholder(s) or organization members.

Discussion:

Rule 3-600 is not intended to enmesh members in the intricacies of the entity and aggregate theories of partnership.

Rule 3-600 is not intended to prohibit members from representing both an organization and other parties connected with it, as for instance (as simply one example) in establishing employee benefit packages for closely held corporations or professional partnerships.

Rule 3-600 is not intended to create or to validate artificial distinctions between entities and their officers, employees, or members, nor is it the purpose of the rule to deny the existence or importance of such formal distinctions. In dealing with a close corporation or small association, members commonly perform professional engagements for both the organization and its major constituents. When a change in control occurs or is threatened, members are faced with complex decisions involving personal and institutional relationships and loyalties and have frequently had difficulty in perceiving their correct duty. (See *People ex rel Deukmejian v. Brown* (1981) 29 Cal. 3d 150 [172 Cal. Rptr. 478]; *Goldstein v. Lees* (1975) 46 Cal. App. 3d 614 [120 Cal. Rptr. 253]; *Woods v. Superior Court* (1983) 149 Cal. App. 3d 931 [197 Cal. Rptr. 185]; *In re Banks* (1978) 283 Ore. 459 [584 P.2d 284]; 1 A.L.R.4th 1105.) In resolving such multiple relationships, members must rely on case law.

Rule 3-700. Termination of Employment

(A) In General

Withdrawal by Permission

(1) If permission for termination of employment is required by the rules of a tribunal, a member shall not withdraw from employment in a proceeding before that tribunal without its permission.

(2) A member shall not withdraw from employment until the member has taken reasonable steps to avoid reasonably foreseeable prejudice to the rights of the client, including giving due notice to the client, allowing time for employment of other counsel, complying with rule 3-700(D), and complying with applicable laws and rules.

(B) Mandatory Withdrawal

Categories of Withdrawal

A member representing a client before a tribunal shall withdraw from employment with the permission of the tribunal, if required by its rules, and a member representing a client in other matters shall withdraw from employment, if:

Harassment

(1) The member knows or should know that the client is bringing an action, conducting a defense, asserting a position in litigation, or taking an appeal, without probable cause and for the purpose of harassing or maliciously injuring any person; or

(2) The member knows or should know that continued employment will result in violation of these rules or of the State Bar Act; or

(3) The member's mental or physical condition renders it unreasonably difficult to carry out the employment effectively.

(C) Permissive Withdrawal

Factors Justifying Permissive Withdrawal

If rule 3-700(B) is not applicable, a member may not request permission to withdraw in matters pending before a tribunal, and may not withdraw in other matters, unless such request or such withdrawal is because:

(1) The client
   - (a) insists upon presenting a claim or defense that is not warranted under existing law and cannot be supported by good faith argument for an extension, modification, or reversal of existing law, or
   - (b) seeks to pursue an illegal course of conduct, or
   - (c) insists that the member pursue a course of conduct that is illegal or that is prohibited under these rules or the State Bar Act, or
   - (d) by other conduct renders it unreasonably difficult for the member to carry out the employment effectively, or
   - (e) insists, in a matter not pending before a tribunal, that the member engage in conduct that is contrary to the judgment and advice of the member but not prohibited under these rules or the State Bar Act, or
   - **Non-payment of Fees**
   - (f) breaches an agreement or obligation to the member as to expenses or fees.

(2) The continued employment is likely to result in a violation of these rules or of the State Bar Act; or

(3) The inability to work with co-counsel indicates that the best interests of the client likely will be served by withdrawal; or

Lawyer's Mental or Physical Condition

(4) The member's mental or physical condition renders it difficult for the member to carry out the employment effectively; or

(5) The client knowingly and freely assents to termination of the employment; or

(6) The member believes in good faith, in a proceeding pending before a tribunal, that the tribunal will find the existence of other good cause for withdrawal.

(D) Papers, Property, and Fees

Return of Client Papers

A member whose employment has terminated shall:

(1) Subject to any protective order or non-disclosure agreement, promptly release to the client, at the request of the client, all the client papers and property. "Client papers and property" includes correspondence, pleadings, deposition transcripts, exhibits, physical evidence, expert's reports, and other items reasonably necessary to the client's representation, whether the client has paid for them or not; and

(2) Promptly refund any part of a fee paid in advance that has not been earned. This provision is not applicable to a true retainer fee which is paid solely for the purpose of ensuring the availability of the member for the matter.

Discussion:

Subparagraph (A)(2) provides that "a member shall not withdraw from employment until the member has taken reasonable steps to avoid reasonably foreseeable prejudice to the rights of the clients." What such steps would include, of course, will vary according to the circumstances. Absent special circumstances, "reasonable steps" do not include providing additional services to the client once the successor counsel has been employed and rule 3-700(D) has been satisfied.

Paragraph (D) makes clear the member's duties in the recurring situation in which new counsel seeks to obtain client files from a member discharged by the client. It codifies existing case law. (See *Academy of California Optometrists v. Superior Court* (1975) 51 Cal. App. 3d 999 [124 Cal. Rptr. 668]; *Weiss v. Marcus* (1975) 51 Cal. App. 3d 590 [124 Cal. Rptr. 297].)

Paragraph (D) also requires that the member "promptly" return unearned fees paid in advance. If a client disputes the amount to be returned, the member shall comply with rule 4-100(A)(2).

Return of Unearned Fees

Paragraph (D) is not intended to prohibit a member from making, at the member's own expense, and retaining copies of papers released to the client, nor to prohibit a claim for the recovery of the member's expense in any subsequent legal proceeding.

Chapter 4. Financial Relationship with Clients

Rule 4-100. Preserving Identity of Funds and Property of a Client

Client Trust Account

Prohibition of Commingling

(A) All funds received or held for the benefit of clients by a member or law firm, including advances for costs and expenses, shall be deposited in one or more identifiable bank accounts labeled "Trust Account," "Client's Funds Account" or words of similar import, maintained in the State of California, or, with written consent of the client, in any other jurisdiction where there is a substantial relationship between the client or the client's business and the other jurisdiction. No funds belonging to the member or the law firm shall be deposited therein or otherwise commingled therewith except as follows:

(1) Funds reasonably sufficient to pay bank charges.

(2) In the case of funds belonging in part to a client and in part presently or potentially to the member or the law firm, the portion belonging to the member or law firm must be withdrawn at the earliest reasonable time after the member's interest in that portion becomes fixed. However, when the right of the member or law firm to receive a portion of trust funds is disputed by the client, the disputed portion shall not be withdrawn until the dispute is finally resolved.

(B) A member shall:

(1) Promptly notify a client of the receipt of the client's funds, securities, or other properties.

(2) Identify and label securities and properties of a client promptly upon receipt and place them in a safe deposit box or other place of safekeeping as soon as practicable.

(3) Maintain complete records of all funds, securities, and other properties of a client coming into the possession of the member or law firm and render appropriate accounts to the client regarding them; preserve such records for a period of no less than five years after final appropriate distribution of such funds or properties; and comply with any order for an audit of such records issued pursuant to the Rules of Procedure of the State Bar.

Recordkeeping Requirements

(4) Promptly pay or deliver, as requested by the client, any funds, securities, or other properties in the possession of the member which the client is entitled to receive.

(C) The Board of Governors of the State Bar shall have the authority to formulate and adopt standards as to what "records" shall be maintained by members and law firms in accordance with subparagraph (B)(3). The standards formulated and adopted by the Board, as from time to time amended, shall be effective and binding on all members.

Standards:

Records that must be Maintained

Pursuant to rule 4-100(C) the Board of Governors of the State Bar adopted the following standards, effective January 1, 1993, as to what "records" shall be maintained by members and law firms in accordance with subparagraph (B)(3).

(1) A member shall, from the date of receipt of client funds through the period ending five years from the date of appropriate disbursement of such funds, maintain:
  (a) a written ledger for each client on whose behalf funds are held that sets forth:
    (i) the name of such client,
    (ii) the date, amount and source of all funds received on behalf of such client,
    (iii) the date, amount, payee and purpose of each disbursement made on behalf of such client, and
    (iv) the current balance for such client;
  (b) a written journal for each bank account that sets forth:
    (i) the name of such account,
    (ii) the date, amount and client affected by each debit and credit, and
    (iii) the current balance in such account;
  (c) all bank statements and canceled checks for each bank account; and
  (d) each monthly reconciliation (balancing) of (a), (b), and (c).

(2) A member shall, from the date of receipt of all securities and other properties held for the benefit of client through the period ending five years from the date of appropriate disbursement of such securities and other properties, maintain a written journal that specifies:
  (a) each item of security and property held;
  (b) the person on whose behalf the security or property is held;
  (c) the date of receipt of the security or property;
  (d) the date of distribution of the security or property; and
  (e) person to whom the security or property was distributed.

Rule 4-200. Fees for Legal Services

(A) A member shall not enter into an agreement for, charge, or collect an illegal or unconscionable fee.

(B) Unconscionability of a fee shall be determined on the basis of all the facts and circumstances existing at the time the agreement is entered into except where the parties contemplate that the fee will be affected by later events. Among the factors to be considered, where appropriate, in determining the conscionability of a fee are the following:
  (1) The amount of the fee in proportion to the value of the services performed.
  (2) The relative sophistication of the member and the client.
  (3) The novelty and difficulty of the questions involved and the skill requisite to perform the legal service properly.
  (4) The likelihood, if apparent to the client, that the acceptance of the particular employment will preclude other employment by the member.
  (5) The amount involved and the results obtained.
  (6) The time limitations imposed by the client or by the circumstances.
  (7) The nature and length of the professional relationship with the client.
  (8) The experience, reputation, and ability of the member or members performing the services.
  (9) Whether the fee is fixed or contingent.
  (10) The time and labor required.
  (11) The informed consent of the client to the fee.

Rule 4-210. Payment of Personal or Business Expenses Incurred by or for a Client

Lawyer Paying a Client's Expenses

(A) A member shall not directly or indirectly pay or agree to pay, guarantee, represent, or sanction a representation that the member or member's law firm will pay the personal or business expenses of a prospective or existing client, except that this rule shall not prohibit a member:
  (1) With the consent of the client, from paying or agreeing to pay such expenses to third persons from funds collected or to be collected for the client as a result of the representation; or
  (2) After employment, from lending money to the client upon the client's promise in writing to repay such loan; or
  (3) From advancing the costs of prosecuting or defending a claim or action or otherwise protecting or promoting the client's interests, the repayment of which may be contingent on the outcome of the matter. Such costs within the meaning of this subparagraph (3) shall be limited to all reasonable expenses of litigation or reasonable expenses in preparation for litigation or in providing any legal services to the client.

(B) Nothing in rule 4-210 shall be deemed to limit rules 3-300, 3-310, and 4-300. . . .

Rule 4-400. Gifts from Client

Gifts from a Client

A member shall not induce a client to make a substantial gift, including a testamentary gift, to the member or to the member's parent, child, sibling, or spouse, except where the client is related to the member.

Discussion:

A member may accept a gift from a member's client, subject to general standards of fairness and absence of undue influence. The member who participates in the preparation of an instrument memorializing a gift which is otherwise permissible ought not to be subject to professional discipline. On the other hand, where impermissible influence occurred, discipline is appropriate.

(See *Magee v. State Bar* (1962) 58 Cal. 2d 423 [24 Cal. Rptr. 839].)

Chapter 5. Advocacy and Representation

Rule 5-100. Threatening Criminal, Administrative, or Disciplinary Charges

Threats by a Lawyer

(A) A member shall not threaten to present criminal, administrative, or disciplinary charges to obtain an advantage in a civil dispute.

(B) As used in paragraph (A) of this rule, the term "administrative charges" means the filing or lodging of a complaint with a federal, state, or local governmental entity which may order or recommend the loss or suspension of a license, or may impose or recommend the imposition of a fine, pecuniary sanction, or other sanction of a quasi-criminal nature but does not include filing charges with an administrative entity required by law as a condition precedent to maintaining a civil action.

(C) As used in paragraph (A) of this rule, the term "civil dispute" means a controversy or potential controversy over the rights and duties of two or more parties under civil law, whether or not an action has been commenced, and includes an administrative proceeding of a quasi-civil nature pending before a federal, state, or local governmental entity.

Discussion:

Rule 5-100 is not intended to apply to a member's threatening to initiate contempt proceedings against a party for a failure to comply with a court order.

Paragraph (B) is intended to exempt the threat of filing an administrative charge which is a prerequisite to filing a civil complaint on the same transaction or occurrence.

For purposes of paragraph (C), the definition of "civil dispute" makes clear that the rule is applicable prior to the formal filing of a civil action.

Rule 5-110. Performing the Duty of Member in Government Service

A member in government service shall not institute or cause to be instituted criminal charges when the member knows or should know that the charges are not supported by probable cause. If, after the institution of criminal charges, the member in government service having responsibility for prosecuting the charges becomes aware that those charges are not supported by probable cause, the member shall promptly so advise the court in which the criminal matter is pending.

Rule 5-120. Trial Publicity

(A) A member who is participating or has participated in the investigation or litigation of a matter shall not make an extrajudicial statement that a reasonable person would expect to be disseminated by means of public communication if the member knows or reasonably should know that it will have a substantial likelihood of materially prejudicing an adjudicative proceeding in the matter.

Allowable Comments to the Media

(B) Notwithstanding paragraph (A), a member may state:

(1) the claim, offense or defense involved and, except when prohibited by law, the identity of the persons involved;
(2) the information contained in a public record;
(3) that an investigation of the matter is in progress;
(4) the scheduling or result of any step in litigation;
(5) a request for assistance in obtaining evidence and information necessary thereto;
(6) a warning of danger concerning the behavior of a person involved, when there is reason to believe that there exists the likelihood of substantial harm to an individual or the public interest; and
(7) in a criminal case, in addition to subparagraphs (1) through (6):
  (a) the identity, residence, occupation, and family status of the accused;
  (b) if the accused has not been apprehended, the information necessary to aid in apprehension of that person;
  (c) the fact, time, and place of arrest; and
  (d) the identity of investigating and arresting officers or agencies and the length of the investigation.

(C) Notwithstanding paragraph (A), a member may make a statement that a reasonable member would believe is required to protect a client from the substantial undue prejudicial effect of recent publicity not initiated by the member or the member's client. A statement made pursuant to this paragraph shall be limited to such information as is necessary to mitigate the recent adverse publicity.

Discussion:

Rule 5-120 is intended to apply equally to prosecutors and criminal defense counsel. Whether an extrajudicial statement violates rule 5-120 depends on many factors, including: (1) whether the extrajudicial statement presents information clearly inadmissible as evidence in the matter for the purpose of proving or disproving a material fact in issue; (2) whether the extrajudicial statement presents information the member knows is false, deceptive, or the use of which would violate Business and Professions Code section 6068(d); (3) whether the extrajudicial statement violates a lawful "gag" order, or protective order, statute, rule of court, or special rule of confidentiality (for example, in juvenile, domestic, mental disability, and certain criminal proceedings); and (4) the timing of the statement.

Paragraph (A) is intended to apply to statements made by or on behalf of the member.

Subparagraph (B)(6) is not intended to create, augment, diminish, or eliminate any application of the lawyer-client privilege or of Business and Professions Code section 6068(e) regarding the member's duty to maintain client confidence and secrets.

Rule 5-200. Trial Conduct

In presenting a matter to a tribunal, a member:

(A) Shall employ, for the purpose of maintaining the causes confided to the member such means only as are consistent with truth;

(B) Shall not seek to mislead the judge, judicial officer, or jury by an artifice or false statement of fact or law;

False or Misleading Statements

(C) Shall not intentionally misquote to a tribunal the language of a book, statute, or decision;

(D) Shall not, knowing its invalidity, cite as authority a decision that has been overruled or a statute that has been repealed or declared unconstitutional; and

Citing Invalid Law

(E) Shall not assert personal knowledge of the facts at issue, except when testifying as a witness.

Rule 5-210. Member as Witness

A member shall not act as an advocate before a jury which will hear testimony from the member unless:

(A) The testimony relates to an uncontested matter; or

(B) The testimony relates to the nature and value of legal services rendered in the case; or

(C) The member has the informed written consent of the client. If the member represents the People or a governmental entity, the consent shall be obtained from the head of the office or a designee of the head of the office by which the member is employed and shall be consistent with principles of recusal.

Discussion:

Rule 5-210 is intended to apply to situations in which the member knows or should know that he or she ought to be called as a witness in litigation in which there is a jury. This rule is not intended to encompass situations in which the member is representing the client in an adversarial proceeding and is testifying before a judge. In non-adversarial proceedings, as where the member testifies on behalf of the client in a hearing before a legislative body, rule 5-210 is not applicable.

Lawyer as Witness in Jury Cases

Rule 5-210 is not intended to apply to circumstances in which a lawyer in an advocate's firm will be a witness.

Rule 5-220. Suppression of Evidence

A member shall not suppress any evidence that the member or the member's client has a legal obligation to reveal or to produce.

Rule 5-300. Contact with Officials

(A) A member shall not directly or indirectly give or lend anything of value to a judge, official, or employee of a tribunal unless the personal or family relationship between the member and the judge, official, or employee is such that gifts are customarily given and exchanged. Nothing contained in this rule shall prohibit a member from contributing to the campaign fund of a judge running for election or confirmation pursuant to applicable law pertaining to such contributions.

Gifts from a Lawyer

(B) A member shall not directly or indirectly communicate with or argue to a judge or judicial officer upon the merits of a contested matter pending before such judge or judicial officer, except:

Independent Communications with the Court

(1) In open court; or
(2) With the consent of all other counsel in such matter; or
(3) In the presence of all other counsel in such matter; or
(4) In writing with a copy thereof furnished to such other counsel; or
(5) In ex parte matters.

(C) As used in this rule, "judge" and "judicial officer" shall include law clerks, research attorneys, or other court personnel who participate in the decision-making process.

Rule 5-310. Prohibited Contact with Witnesses

A member shall not:

(A) Advise or directly or indirectly cause a person to secrete himself or herself or to leave the jurisdiction of a tribunal for the purpose of making that person unavailable as a witness therein.

Improper Witness Contacts

(B) Directly or indirectly pay, offer to pay, or acquiesce in the payment of compensation to a witness contingent upon the content of the witness's testimony or the outcome of the case. Except where prohibited by law, a member may advance, guarantee, or acquiesce in the payment of:

(1) Expenses reasonably incurred by a witness in attending or testifying.
(2) Reasonable compensation to a witness for loss of time in attending or testifying.
(3) A reasonable fee for the professional services of an expert witness.

Rule 5-320. Contact with Jurors

Improper Juror Contacts

(A) A member connected with a case shall not communicate directly or indirectly with anyone the member knows to be a member of the venire from which the jury will be selected for trial of that case.

(B) During trial a member connected with the case shall not communicate directly or indirectly with any juror.

(C) During trial a member who is not connected with the case shall not communicate directly or indirectly concerning the case with anyone the member knows is a juror in the case.

(D) After discharge of the jury from further consideration of a case a member shall not ask questions of or make comments to a member of that jury that are intended to harass or embarrass the juror or to influence the juror's actions in future jury service.

(E) A member shall not directly or indirectly conduct an out of court investigation of a person who is either a member of a venire or a juror in a manner likely to influence the state of mind of such person in connection with present or future jury service.

(F) All restrictions imposed by this rule also apply to communications with, or investigations of, members of the family of a person who is either a member of a venire or a juror.

(G) A member shall reveal promptly to the court improper conduct by a person who is either a member of a venire or a juror, or by another toward a person who is a either a member of a venire or a juror or a member of his or her family, of which the member has knowledge.

(H) This rule does not prohibit a member from communicating with persons who are members of a venire or jurors as a part of the official proceedings.

(I) For purposes of this rule, "juror" means any empaneled, discharged, or excused juror. . . .

E. State Bar Act

Business and Professions Code

§ 6000. Short Title

This chapter of the Business and Professions Code constitutes the chapter on attorneys. It may be cited as the State Bar Act.

§ 6001. State Bar

State Bar Association

The State Bar of California is a public corporation. It is hereinafter designated as the State Bar. . . .

§ 6010. Board of governors in general

The State Bar is governed by a board known as the board of governors of the State Bar. . . .

§ 6013.5. Public members

Nonlawyer Members of Board of Governors of State Bar

Notwithstanding any other provision of law, six members of the board shall be members of the public who have never been members of the State Bar or admitted to practice before any court in the United States. . . .

§ 6026.5. Public meetings; exceptions

Every meeting of the board shall be open to the public except those meetings, or portions thereof, relating to: . . .

(e) Disciplinary investigations and proceedings, including resignations with disciplinary investigations or proceedings pending, and reinstatement proceedings. . . .

§ 6043.5. Filing knowingly false or malicious report or complaint against attorney

Falsely Accusing a Lawyer of Misconduct

(a) Every person who reports to the State Bar or causes a complaint to be filed with the State Bar that an attorney has engaged in professional misconduct, knowing the report or complaint to be false and malicious, is guilty of a misdemeanor. . . .

§ 6044. Subjects of investigation

The board or any committee appointed by the board, with or without the filing or presentation of any complaint, may initiate and conduct investigations of all matters affecting or relating to . . .

(b) The practice of the law.

(c) The discipline of the members of the State Bar. . . .

§ 6046. Examining committee; powers

The board may establish an examining committee having the power:

Admission to the Practice of Law

(a) To examine all applicants for admission to practice law.

(b) To administer the requirements for admission to practice law.

(c) To certify to the Supreme Court for admission those applicants who fulfill the requirements provided in this chapter. . . .

§ 6053. Examination of mental or physical condition

Lawyer's Mental or Physical Condition

Whenever in an investigation or proceeding provided for or authorized by this chapter, the mental or physical condition of the member of the State Bar is a material issue, the board or the committee having jurisdiction may order the member to be examined by one or more physicians or psychiatrists designated by it. The reports of such persons shall be made available to the member and the State Bar and may be received in evidence in such investigation or proceeding.

§ 6060. Qualifications; examination

Requirements to be a California Lawyer

To be certified to the Supreme Court for admission and a license to practice law, a person who has not been admitted to practice law in a sister state, United States jurisdiction, possession, territory, or dependency or in a foreign country shall:

(a) Be of the age of at least 18 years.

(b) Be of good moral character.

(c) Before beginning the study of law, have done either of the following:
- (1) Completed at least two years of college work, which college work shall be not less than one-half of the collegiate work acceptable for a bachelor's degree granted upon the basis of a four-year period of study by a college or university approved by the examining committee.
- (2) Have attained in apparent intellectual ability the equivalent of at least two years of college work by taking any examinations in subject matters and achieving the scores thereon as are prescribed by the examining committee.

(d) Have registered with the examining committee as a law student within 90 days after beginning the study of law. The examining committee, upon good cause being shown, may permit a later registration.

(e) Have done any of the following:
- (1) Had conferred upon him or her a juris doctor (J.D.) degree or a bachelor of laws (LL.B.) degree by a law school accredited by the examining committee or approved by the American Bar Association.
- (2) Studied law diligently and in good faith for at least four years in any of the following manners:
  - (A) In a law school that is authorized or approved to confer professional degrees and requires classroom attendance of its students for a minimum of 270 hours a year. . . .
  - (B) In a law office in this state and under the personal supervision of a member of the State Bar of California who is, and for at least the last five years continuously has been, engaged in the active practice of law. It is the duty of the supervising attorney to render any periodic reports to the examining committee as the committee may require.

Becoming a Lawyer without Law School

  - (C) In the chambers and under the personal supervision of a judge of a court of record of this state. It is the duty of the supervising judge to render any periodic reports to the examining committee as the committee may require.
  - (D) By instruction in law from a correspondence law school authorized or approved to confer professional degrees by this state, which requires 864 hours of preparation and study per year for four years.
  - (E) By any combination of the methods referred to in this paragraph (2).

Mandatory Ethics Examination and Bar Examination

(f) Have passed any examination in professional responsibility or legal ethics as the examining committee may prescribe.

(g) Have passed the general bar examination given by the examining committee.

(h) (1) Have passed a law students' examination administered by the examining committee after completion of his or her first year of law study. Those who pass the examination within its first three administrations upon becoming eligible to take the examination shall receive credit for all law studies completed to the time the examination is passed. Those who do not pass the examination within its first three administrations upon becoming eligible to take the examination, but who subsequently pass the examination, shall receive credit for one year of legal study only.
- (2) This requirement does not apply to a student who has satisfactorily completed his or her first year of law study at a law school accredited by the examining committee and who has completed at least two years of college work prior to matriculating in the accredited law school, nor shall this requirement apply to an applicant who has passed the bar examination of a sister state or of a country in which the common law of England constitutes the basis of jurisprudence.

The law students' examination shall be administered twice a year at reasonable intervals.

§ 6061. Unaccredited law schools

Unaccredited Law Schools

Any law school that is not accredited by the examining committee of the State Bar shall provide every student with a disclosure statement, subsequent to the payment of any application fee but prior to the payment of any registration fee, containing all of the following information:

(a) The school is not accredited. . . .

(c) The number and percentage of students who have taken and who have passed the first-year law student's examination and the final bar examination in the previous five years. . . .

(d) The number of legal volumes in the library. . . .

§ 6064. Admission

Upon certification by the examining committee that the applicant has fulfilled the requirements for admission to practice law, the Supreme Court may admit such applicant as an attorney at law in all the courts of this State and may direct an order to be entered upon its records to that effect. A certificate of admission thereupon shall be given to the applicant by the clerk of the court.

§ 6064.1. Advocacy of overthrow of government

No person who advocates the overthrow of the Government of the United States or of this State by force, violence, or other unconstitutional means, shall be certified to the Supreme Court for admission and a license to practice law.

§ 6067. Oath

Every person on his admission shall take an oath to support the Constitution of the United States and the Constitution of the State of California, and faithfully to discharge the duties of any attorney at law to the best of his knowledge and ability. A certificate of the oath shall be indorsed upon his license.

§ 6068. Duties of attorney

Duties of Lawyers

It is the duty of an attorney to do all of the following:

(a) To support the Constitution and laws of the United States and of this state.

(b) To maintain the respect due to the courts of justice and judicial officers.

(c) To counsel or maintain those actions, proceedings, or defenses only as appear to him or her legal or just, except the defense of a person charged with a public offense.

Misleading and False Statements

(d) To employ, for the purpose of maintaining the causes confided to him or her those means only as are consistent with truth, and never to seek to mislead the judge or any judicial officer by an artifice or false statement of fact or law.

(e) (1) To maintain inviolate the confidence, and at every peril to himself or herself to preserve the secrets, of his or her client.

Duty of Confidentiality

(2) Notwithstanding paragraph (1), an attorney may, but is not required to, reveal confidential information relating to the representation of a client to the extent that the attorney reasonably believes the disclosure is necessary to prevent a criminal act that the attorney reasonably believes is likely to result in death of, or substantial bodily harm to, an individual.

(f) To advance no fact prejudicial to the honor or reputation of a party or witness, unless required by the justice of the cause with which he or she is charged.

(g) Not to encourage either the commencement or the continuance of an action or proceeding from any corrupt motive of passion or interest.

(h) Never to reject, for any consideration personal to himself or herself, the cause of the defenseless or the oppressed.

Disciplinary Proceedings

(i) To cooperate and participate in any disciplinary investigation or other regulatory or disciplinary proceeding pending against himself or herself. However, this subdivision shall not be construed to deprive an attorney of any privilege guaranteed by the Fifth Amendment to the Constitution of the United States, or any other constitutional or statutory privileges. This subdivision shall not be construed to require an attorney to cooperate with a request that requires him or her to waive any constitutional or statutory privilege or to comply with a request for information or other matters within an unreasonable period of time in light of the time constraints of the attorney's practice. Any exercise by an attorney of any constitutional or statutory privilege shall not be used against the attorney in a regulatory or disciplinary proceeding against him or her.

(j) To comply with the requirements of Section 6002.1 [covering information that must be provided to the state bar].

(k) To comply with all conditions attached to any disciplinary probation, including a probation imposed with the concurrence of the attorney.

(l) To keep all agreements made in lieu of disciplinary prosecution with the agency charged with attorney discipline.

Keeping a Client Reasonably Informed

(m) To respond promptly to reasonable status inquiries of clients and to keep clients reasonably informed of significant developments in matters with regard to which the attorney has agreed to provide legal services.

(n) To provide copies to the client of certain documents under time limits and as prescribed in a rule of professional conduct which the board shall adopt.

(o) To report to the agency charged with attorney discipline, in writing, within 30 days of the time the attorney has knowledge of any of the following:

(1) The filing of three or more lawsuits in a 12-month period against the attorney for malpractice or other wrongful conduct committed in a professional capacity.

Reporting Duties of a Lawyer

(2) The entry of judgment against the attorney in a civil action for fraud, misrepresentation, breach of fiduciary duty, or gross negligence committed in a professional capacity.

(3) The imposition of judicial sanctions against the attorney, except for sanctions for failure to make discovery or monetary sanctions of less than one thousand dollars ($1,000).

(4) The bringing of an indictment or information charging a felony against the attorney.

(5) The conviction of the attorney, including any verdict of guilty, or plea of guilty or no contest, of a felony, or a misdemeanor committed in the course of the practice of law, or in a manner in which a client of the attorney was the victim, or a necessary element of which, as determined by the statutory or common law definition of the misdemeanor, involves improper conduct of an attorney, including dishonesty or other moral turpitude, or an attempt or a conspiracy or solicitation of another to commit a felony or a misdemeanor of that type.

(6) The imposition of discipline against the attorney by a professional or occupational disciplinary agency or licensing board, whether in California or elsewhere.

(7) Reversal of judgment in a proceeding based in whole or in part upon misconduct, grossly incompetent representation, or willful misrepresentation by an attorney.

(8) As used in this subdivision, "against the attorney" includes claims and proceedings against any firm of attorneys for the practice of law in which the attorney was a partner at the time of the conduct complained of and any law corporation in which the attorney was a shareholder at the time of the conduct complained of unless the matter has to the attorney's knowledge already been reported by the law firm or corporation.

(9) The State Bar may develop a prescribed form for the making of reports required by this section, usage of which it may require by rule or regulation.

(10) This subdivision is only intended to provide that the failure to report as required herein may serve as a basis of discipline.

§ 6070. Mandatory Continuing Legal Education

(a) The State Bar shall request the California Supreme Court to adopt a rule of court authorizing the State Bar to establish and administer a mandatory continuing legal education program. The rule that the State Bar requests the Supreme Court to adopt shall require that, within designated 36-month periods, all active members of the State Bar shall complete at least 25 hours of legal education activities approved by the State Bar or offered by a State Bar approved provider, with four of those hours in legal ethics. A member of the State Bar who fails to satisfy the mandatory continuing legal education requirements of the program authorized by the Supreme Court rule shall be enrolled as an inactive member pursuant to rules adopted by the Board of Governors of the State Bar. . . .

Mandatory Continuing Legal Education for Lawyers

(d) The State Bar shall provide and encourage the development of low-cost programs and materials by which members may satisfy their continuing education requirements. Special emphasis shall be placed upon the use of internet capabilities and computer technology in the development and provision of no-cost and low-cost programs and materials. . . .

§ 6076. Rules of professional conduct

With the approval of the Supreme Court, the Board of Governors may formulate and enforce rules of professional conduct for all members of the bar in the State.

§ 6077. Effect of rules; discipline for breach

The rules of professional conduct adopted by the board, when approved by the Supreme Court, are binding upon all members of the State Bar. For a wilful breach of any of these rules, the board has power to discipline members of the State Bar by reproval, public or private, or to recommend to the Supreme Court the suspension from practice for a period not exceeding three years of members of the State Bar.

§ 6077.5. Collection of consumer debt; attorneys and employees

An attorney and his or her employees who are employed primarily to assist in the collection of a consumer debt owed to another . . . shall comply with all of the following . . .

Paralegals Working for Lawyers Engaged in Debt Collection

(b) Any employee of an attorney who is not a member of the State Bar of California, when communicating with a consumer debtor or with any person other than the debtor concerning a consumer debt, shall identify himself or herself, by whom he or she is employed, and his or her title or job capacity.

(c) Without the prior consent of the debtor given directly to the attorney or his or her employee or the express permission of a court of competent jurisdiction, an attorney or his or her employee shall not communicate with a debtor in connection with the collection of any debt at any unusual time or place, or time or place known, or which should be known, to be inconvenient to the debtor. In the absence of knowledge of circumstances to the contrary, an attorney or his or her employee shall assume that the convenient time for communicating with the debtor is after 8 a.m. and before 9 p.m., local time at the consumer's location.

(d) If a debtor notifies an attorney or his or her employee in writing that the debtor refuses to pay a debt or that the debtor wishes the attorney or his or her employee to cease further communications with the debtor, the attorney or his or her employee shall not communicate further with the debtor with respect to such debt, except as follows . . .

(2) To notify the debtor that the attorney or his or her employee or creditor may invoke specific remedies which are ordinarily invoked by such attorney or creditor. . . .

§ 6078. Power to discipline and reinstate

Disbarment

After a hearing for any of the causes set forth in the laws of the State of California warranting disbarment, suspension or other discipline, the board has the power to recommend to the Supreme Court the disbarment or suspension from practice of members or to discipline them by reproval, public or private, without such recommendation. The board may pass upon all petitions for reinstatement.

§ 6079.1. State Bar Court

[For information on the State Bar Court in disciplinary proceedings, see Appendix A of Part 3.]

§ 6105. Permitting misuse of name

Misuse of Lawyer's Name by a Nonlawyer

Lending his name to be used as attorney by another person who is not an attorney constitutes a cause for disbarment or suspension.

§ 6106.8. Sexual involvement between lawyers and clients

(a) The Legislature hereby finds and declares . . . that it is difficult to separate sound judgment from emotion or bias which may result from sexual involvement between a lawyer and his or her client during the period that an attorney-client relationship exists, and that emotional detachment is essential to the lawyer's ability to render competent legal services. Therefore, in order to ensure that a lawyer acts in the best interest of his or her client, a rule of professional conduct governing sexual relations between attorneys and their clients shall be adopted.

(b) With the approval of the Supreme Court, the State Bar shall adopt a rule of professional conduct governing sexual relations between attorneys and their clients in cases involving, but not limited to, probate matters and domestic relations, including dissolution proceedings, child custody cases, and settlement proceedings. . . .

(d) Intentional violation of this rule shall constitute a cause for suspension or disbarment.

§ 6106.9. Sexual relations between attorney and client

Sexual Relationship with Client

(a) It shall constitute cause for the imposition of discipline of an attorney within the meaning of this chapter for an attorney to do any of the following:

(1) Expressly or impliedly condition the performance of legal services for a current or prospective client upon the client's willingness to engage in sexual relations with the attorney.

(2) Employ coercion, intimidation, or undue influence in entering into sexual relations with a client.

(3) Continue representation of a client with whom the attorney has sexual relations if the sexual relations cause the attorney to perform legal services incompetently in violation of Rule 3-100 of the Rules of Professional Conduct of the State Bar of California, or if the sexual relations would, or would be likely to, damage or prejudice the client's case.

(b) Subdivision (a) shall not apply to sexual relations between attorneys and their spouses or persons in an equivalent domestic relationship or to ongoing consensual sexual relationships that predate the initiation of the attorney-client relationship.

(c) Where an attorney in a firm has sexual relations with a client but does not participate in the representation of that client, the attorneys in the firm shall not be subject to discipline under this section solely because of the occurrence of those sexual relations.

(d) For the purposes of this section, "sexual relations" means sexual intercourse or the touching of an intimate part of another person for the purpose of sexual arousal, gratification, or abuse.

(e) Any complaint made to the State Bar alleging a violation of subdivision (a) shall be verified under oath by the person making the complaint.

§ 6125. Necessity of active membership in State Bar

No person shall practice law in California unless the person is an active member of the State Bar.

§ 6126. Unauthorized practice or attempted practice; advertising or holding out; penalties

UPL: Unauthorized Practice of Law

(a) Any person advertising or holding himself or herself out as practicing or entitled to practice law or otherwise practicing law who is not an active member of the State Bar, or otherwise authorized pursuant to statute or court rule to practice law in this state at the time of doing so, is guilty of a misdemeanor punishable by up to one year in a county jail or by a fine of up to one thousand dollars ($1,000), or by both that fine and imprisonment. Upon a second or subsequent conviction, the person shall be confined in a county jail for not less than 90 days, except in an unusual case where the interests of justice would be served by imposition of a lesser sentence or a fine. If the court imposes only a fine or a sentence of less than 90 days for a second or subsequent conviction under this subdivision, the court shall state the reasons for its sentencing choice on the record.

Disbarred and Suspended Attorneys

(b) Any person who has been involuntarily enrolled as an inactive member of the State Bar, or has been suspended from membership from the State Bar, or has been disbarred, or has resigned from the State Bar with charges pending, and thereafter practices or attempts to practice law, advertises or holds himself or herself out as practicing or otherwise entitled to practice law, is guilty of a crime punishable by imprisonment in the state prison or county jail. However, any person who has been involuntarily enrolled as an inactive member of the State Bar pursuant to paragraph (1) of subdivision (e) of Section 6007 and who knowingly thereafter practices or attempts to practice law, or advertises or holds himself or herself out as practicing or otherwise entitled to practice law, is guilty of a crime punishable by imprisonment in the state prison or county jail.

(c) The willful failure of a member of the State Bar, or one who has resigned or been disbarred, to comply with an order of the Supreme Court to comply with Rule 955, constitutes a crime punishable by imprisonment in the state prison or county jail.

(d) The penalties provided in this section are cumulative to each other and to any other remedies or penalties provided by law.

§ 6126.5. Additional remedies and penalties

Remedies for the Unauthorized Practice of Law

(a) In addition to any remedies and penalties available in any enforcement action brought in the name of the people of the State of California by the Attorney General, a district attorney, or a city attorney, acting as a public prosecutor, the court shall award relief in the enforcement action for any person who obtained services offered or provided in violation of Section 6125 or 6126 or who purchased any goods, services, or real or personal property in connection with services offered or provided in violation of Section 6125 or 6126 against the person who violated Section 6125 or 6126, or who sold goods, services, or property in connection with that violation. The court shall consider the following relief:

(1) Actual damages.
(2) Restitution of all amounts paid.
(3) The amount of penalties and tax liabilities incurred in connection with the sale or transfer of assets to pay for any goods, services, or property.
(4) Reasonable attorney's fees and costs expended to rectify errors made in the unlawful practice of law.
(5) Prejudgment interest at the legal rate from the date of loss to the date of judgment.
(6) Appropriate equitable relief, including the rescission of sales made in connection with a violation of law.

(b) The relief awarded under paragraphs (1) to (6), inclusive, of subdivision (a) shall be distributed to, or on behalf of, the person for whom it was awarded or, if it is impracticable to do so, shall be distributed as may be directed by the court pursuant to its equitable powers.

(c) The court shall also award the Attorney General, district attorney, or city attorney reasonable attorney's fees and costs and, in the court's discretion, exemplary damages as provided in Section 3294 of the Civil Code.

(d) This section shall not be construed to create, abrogate, or otherwise affect claims, rights, or remedies, if any, that may be held by a person or entity other than those law enforcement agencies described in subdivision (a). The remedies provided in this section are cumulative to each other and to the remedies and penalties provided under other laws.

§ 6127. Contempt of court

The following acts or omissions in respect to the practice of law are contempts of the authority of the courts:

(a) Assuming to be an officer or attorney of a court and acting as such, without authority.

Advertising

(b) Advertising or holding oneself out as practicing or as entitled to practice law or otherwise practicing law in any court, without being an active member of the State Bar.

Proceedings to adjudge a person in contempt of court under this section are to be taken in accordance with the provisions of Title V of Part III of the Code of Civil Procedure.

§ 6128. Deceit, collusion, delay of suit, and improper receipt of money as misdemeanor

Deceit and Collusion

Every attorney is guilty of a misdemeanor who either:

(a) Is guilty of any deceit or collusion, or consents to any deceit or collusion, with intent to deceive the court or any party.

(b) Willfully delays his client's suit with a view to his own gain.

(c) Willfully receives any money or allowance for or on account of any money which he has not laid out or become answerable for.

Any violation of the provisions of this section is punishable by imprisonment in the county jail not exceeding six months, or by a fine not exceeding two thousand five hundred dollars ($2,500), or by both.

§ 6129. Buying claim as misdemeanor

Buying a Cause of Action

Every attorney who, either directly or indirectly, buys or is interested in buying any evidence of debt or thing in action, with intent to bring suit thereon, is guilty of a misdemeanor.

Any violation of the provisions of this section is punishable by imprisonment in the county jail not exceeding six months, or by a fine not exceeding two thousand five hundred dollars ($2,500), or by both.

§ 6132. Firm names; removal of names of attorneys under discipline

Disbarred and Suspended Attorneys

Any law firm, partnership, corporation, or association which contains the name of an attorney who is disbarred, or who resigned with charges pending, in its business name shall remove the name of that attorney from its business name, and from all signs, advertisements, letterhead, and other materials containing that name, within 60 days of the disbarment or resignation.

§ 6133. Resigned, suspended or disbarred attorneys; supervision of activities by firms

Any attorney or any law firm, partnership, corporation, or association employing an attorney who has resigned, or who is under actual suspension from the practice of law, or is disbarred, shall not permit that attorney to practice law or so advertise or hold himself or herself out as practicing law and shall supervise him or her in any other assigned duties. A willful violation of this section constitutes a cause for discipline.

§ 6140.5. Client Security Fund

Client Security Fund

Dishonest Attorneys

(a) The board shall establish and administer a Client Security Fund to relieve or mitigate pecuniary losses caused by the dishonest conduct of the active members of the State Bar arising from or connected with the practice of law. Any payments from the fund shall be discretionary and shall be subject to regulation and conditions as the board shall prescribe. The board may delegate the administration of the fund to the State Bar Court, or to any board or committee created by the board of governors. . . .

§ 6143.5. Enforcement of child support obligations

Attorney's Failure to Pay Child Support

Any member, active or inactive, failing to pay any child support after it becomes due shall be subject to Section 17520 of the Family Code [on the nonrenewal of licenses for nonpayment of child support].

§ 6146. Contingent fees

Contingent Fees for Medical Malpractice

(a) An attorney shall not contract for or collect a contingency fee for representing any person seeking damages in connection with an action for injury or damage against a health care provider based upon such person's alleged professional negligence in excess of the following limits:

(1) Forty percent of the first fifty thousand dollars ($50,000) recovered.

(2) Thirty-three and one-third percent of the next fifty thousand dollars ($50,000) recovered.

(3) Twenty-five percent of the next five hundred thousand dollars ($500,000) recovered.

(4) Fifteen percent of any amount on which the recovery exceeds six hundred thousand dollars ($600,000).

The limitations shall apply regardless of whether the recovery is by settlement, arbitration, or judgment, or whether the person for whom the recovery is made is a responsible adult, an infant, or a person of unsound mind. . . .

§ 6147. Contingency fee contracts

(a) An attorney who contracts to represent a client on a contingency fee basis shall, at the time the contract is entered into, provide a duplicate copy of the contract, signed by both the attorney and the client, or the client's guardian or representative, to the plaintiff, or to the client's guardian or representative. The contract shall be in writing and shall include, but is not limited to, all of the following:

(1) A statement of the contingency fee rate that the client and attorney have agreed upon.
(2) A statement as to how disbursements and costs incurred in connection with the prosecution or settlement of the claim will affect the contingency fee and the client's recovery.
(3) A statement as to what extent, if any, the client could be required to pay any compensation to the attorney for related matters that arise out of their relationship not covered by their contingency fee contract. This may include any amounts collected for the plaintiff by the attorney.
(4) Unless the claim is subject to the provisions of Section 6146, a statement that the fee is not set by law but is negotiable between attorney and client.
(5) If the claim is subject to the provisions of Section 6146, a statement that the rates set forth in that section are the maximum limits for the contingency fee agreement, and that the attorney and client may negotiate a lower rate.

(b) Failure to comply with any provision of this section renders the agreement voidable at the option of the plaintiff, and the attorney shall thereupon be entitled to collect a reasonable fee.

(c) This section shall not apply to contingency fee contracts for the recovery of workers' compensation benefits. . . .

§ 6147.5. Contingency fee contracts; recovery of claims between merchants

(a) Sections 6147 and 6148 shall not apply to contingency fee contracts for the recovery of claims between merchants . . . arising from the sale or lease of goods or services rendered, or money loaned for use, in the conduct of a business or profession if the merchant contracting for legal services employs 10 or more individuals. . . .

§ 6149. Written fee contract as confidential communication

A written fee contract shall be deemed to be a confidential communication within the meaning of subdivision (e) of Section 6068 and of Section 952 of the Evidence Code.

§ 6151. Definitions

As used in this article:

(a) A runner or capper is any person, firm, association, or corporation acting for consideration in any manner or in any capacity as an agent for an attorney at law or law firm, whether the attorney or any member of the law firm is admitted in California or any other jurisdiction, in the solicitation or procurement of business for the attorney at law or law firm as provided in this article.

(b) An agent is one who represents another in dealings with one or more third persons.

§ 6152. Prohibition of solicitation

Solicitation by Runners or Cappers

(a) It is unlawful for:
(1) Any person, in an individual capacity or in a capacity as a public or private employee, or for any firm, corporation, partnership or association to act as a runner or capper for any attorneys or to solicit any business for any attorneys in and about the state prisons, county jails, city jails, city prisons, or other places of detention of persons, city receiving hospitals, city and county receiving hospitals, county hospitals, superior courts, or in any public institution or in any public place or upon any public street or highway or in and about private hospitals, sanitariums or in and about any private institution or upon private property of any character whatsoever. . . .

(c) Nothing in this section shall be construed to prevent the recommendation of professional employment where that recommendation is not prohibited by the Rules of Professional Conduct of the State Bar of California. . . .

§ 6153. Violations; penalty

Any person, firm, partnership, association, or corporation violating subdivision (a) of Section 6152 is punishable, upon a first conviction, by imprisonment in a county jail for not more than one year or by a fine not exceeding fifteen thousand dollars ($15,000), or by both that imprisonment and fine. . . .

§ 6154. Void contract

(a) Any contract for professional services secured by any attorney at law or law firm in this state through the services of a runner or capper is void. . . .

§ 6155. Referral services

Lawyer Referral Services

(a) An individual, partnership, corporation, association, or any other entity shall not operate for the direct or indirect purpose, in whole or in part, of referring potential clients to attorneys, and no attorney shall accept a referral of such potential clients, unless all of the following requirements are met:
(1) The service is registered with the State Bar of California. . . .
(2) The combined charges to the potential client by the referral service and the attorney to whom the potential client is referred do not exceed

the total cost that the client would normally pay if no referral service were involved. . . .

§ 6157.1. False, misleading, or deceptive statements

No advertisement shall contain any false, misleading, or deceptive statement or omit to state any fact necessary to make the statements made, in light of circumstances under which they are made, not false, misleading, or deceptive.

Advertising

§ 6157.2. Prohibited statements in advertising

No advertisement shall contain or refer to any of the following:

Improper Advertisements

(a) Any guarantee or warranty regarding the outcome of a legal matter as a result of representation by the member.

(b) Statements or symbols stating that the member featured in the advertisement can generally obtain immediate cash or quick settlements.

(c) (1) An impersonation of the name, voice, photograph, or electronic image of any person other than the lawyer, directly or implicitly purporting to be that of a lawyer.

(2) An impersonation of the name, voice, photograph, or electronic image of any person, directly or implicitly purporting to be a client of the member featured in the advertisement, or a dramatization of events, unless disclosure of the impersonation or dramatization is made in the advertisement.

(3) A spokesperson, including a celebrity spokesperson, unless there is disclosure of the spokesperson's title.

(d) A statement that a member offers representation on a contingent basis unless the statement also advises whether a client will be held responsible for any costs advanced by the member when no recovery is obtained on behalf of the client. If the client will not be held responsible for costs, no disclosure is required.

§ 6158. Electronic media advertising

In advertising by electronic media, to comply with Sections 61571.1 and 6157.2, the message as a whole may not be false, misleading, or deceptive, and the message as a whole must be factually substantiated. The message means the effect in combination of the spoken word, sound, background, action, symbols, visual image, or any other technique employed to create the message. Factually substantiated means capable of verification by a credible source.

Media Advertising

§ 6158.1. False, misleading, or deceptive messages

There shall be a rebuttable presumption affecting the burden of producing evidence that the following messages are false, misleading, or deceptive within the meaning of Section 6158:

Examples of Deceptive Advertising

(a) A message as to the ultimate result of a specific case or cases presented out of context without adequately providing information as to the facts or law giving rise to the result.

(b) The depiction of an event through methods such as the use of displays of injuries, accident scenes, or portrayals of other injurious events which may or may not be accompanied by sound effects and which may give rise to a claim for compensation.

(c) A message referring to or implying money received by or for a client in a particular case or cases, or to potential monetary recovery for a prospective client. A reference to money or monetary recovery includes, but is not limited to, a specific dollar amount, characterization of a sum of money, monetary symbols, or the implication of wealth.

§ 6160. Nature, law corporations

Law Corporations

A law corporation is a corporation which is registered with the State Bar of California and has a currently effective certificate of registration from the State Bar pursuant to the Professional Corporation Act, as contained in Part 4 (commencing with Section 13400) of Division 3 of Title 1 of the Corporations Code, and this article. Subject to all applicable statutes, rules and regulations, such law corporation is entitled to practice law. With respect to a law corporation the governmental agency referred to in the Professional Corporation Act is the State Bar.

§ 6161. Application for registration

An applicant for registration as a law corporation shall supply to the State Bar all necessary and pertinent documents and information requested by the State Bar concerning the applicant's plan of operation, including, but not limited to, a copy of its articles of incorporation, certified by the Secretary of State, a copy of its bylaws, certified by the secretary of the corporation, the name and address of the corporation, the names and addresses of its officers, directors, shareholders, members, if any, and employees who will render professional services, the address of each office, and any fictitious name or names which the corporation intends to use. The State Bar may provide forms of application. . . .

§ 6200. Arbitration and mediation of fee disputes

Fee Disputes (Arbitration and Mediation)

(a) The board of governors shall, by rule, establish, maintain, and administer a system and procedure for the arbitration, and may establish, maintain, and administer a system and procedure for mediation of disputes concerning fees, costs, or both, charged for professional services by members of the State Bar or by members of the bar of other jurisdictions. . . .

§ 6210. Funding for free legal services

The Need for Free Legal Services

The Legislature finds that, due to insufficient funding, existing programs providing free legal services in civil matters to indigent persons, especially underserved client groups, such as the elderly, the disabled, juveniles, and non-English-speaking persons, do not adequately meet the needs of these persons. It is the purpose of this article to expand the availability and improve the quality of existing free legal services in civil matters to indigent persons, and to initiate new programs that will provide services to them. The Legislature finds that the use of funds collected by the State Bar pursuant to this article for these purposes is in the public interest, is a proper use of the funds, and is consistent with essential public and governmental purposes in the judicial branch of government. The Legislature further finds that the expansion, improvement, and initiation of legal services to indigent persons will aid in the advancement of the science of jurisprudence and the improvement of the administration of justice.

§ 6211. Establishment by attorney of demand trust account; interest earned to be paid to state bar

Interest-Bearing Demand Trust Accounts

(a) An attorney or law firm, which in the course of the practice of law receives or disburses trust funds, shall establish and maintain an interest bearing demand trust account and shall deposit therein all client deposits that are nominal in amount or are on deposit for a short period of time. All such client funds may be deposited in a single unsegregated account. The interest earned on all such accounts shall be paid to the State Bar of California to be used for the purposes set forth in this article. . . .

§ 6216. Distribution of funds

The State Bar shall distribute all moneys received under the program established by this article for the provision of civil legal services to indigent persons. . . .

§ 6230. Alcohol and drug abuse

Attorneys Impaired by Drug or Alcohol Abuse

It is the intent of the Legislature that the State Bar of California seek ways and means to identify and rehabilitate attorneys with impairment due to abuse of drugs or alcohol, or due to mental illness, affecting competency so that attorneys so afflicted may be treated and returned to the practice of law in a manner that will not endanger the public health and safety.

§ 6231. Attorney Diversion and Assistance Program

(a) The board shall establish and administer an Attorney Diversion and Assistance Program, and shall establish a committee to oversee the operation of the program. . . .

§ 6400. Legal document assistants and unlawful detainer assistants

[For information on legal document assistants and unlawful detainer assistants, see section 1.3.]

§ 6450. Paralegals

[For information on paralegal regulation, see section 1.2.]

F. More Information

Rules of Professional Conduct Online
www.calbar.ca.gov
(click "Rules of Professional Conduct")

State Bar Act Online
www.leginfo.ca.gov/calaw.html
(click "Business and Professions Code" and then type "state bar act" in the search box)

American Legal Ethics Library
www.law.cornell.edu/ethics
(click "Listing by jurisdiction" then "California")

Legalethics.com
www.legalethics.com/ethics.law
(click "California")

California Ethics Research Resources
www.ll.georgetown.edu/states/ethics/california.cfm

Center for Professional Responsibility
www.abanet.org/cpr/links.html
(click the links under "California")

Lexis
www.lexis.com
(CAL library CAETOP file; ETHICS file; CABAR file)

Westlaw
www.westlaw.com
(CAETH-EO database; CAETH-CS database; CA-RULES database)

Professionalism Codes
www.abanet.org/cpr/professionalism/profcodes.html

Beverly Hills Bar Association
Guidelines for Professional Courtesy
www.law.stetson.edu/excellence/litethics/bevhillsbar.htm

Contra Costa County Bar Association
Standards of Professional Courtesy
www.cccba.org/prof/standards.htm

Los Angeles County Bar Association
Litigation Guidelines
www.lacba.org
(type "litigation guidelines" in the search box)

Professionalism Guidelines for Family Law Practitioners
www.law.stetson.edu/excellence/litethics/lacobarfam.htm

Marin County Bar Association
Code of Civility
www.marinbar.org/members/resources/Code_of_Civility.pdf

Orange County Bar Association
Standards for Professionalism and Civility Among Attorneys
www.ocbar.org/conduct.htm

Riverside Bar Association
Guidelines of Professional Courtesy and Civility
www.riversidecountybar.com
(click "Search this Site" then type "professional courtesy" in the search box)

Sacramento Bar Association
Standards of Professional Conduct
www.saccourt.com/geninfo/local_rules/bar.asp

San Diego County Bar Association
Civil Litigation Code of Conduct
www.law.stetson.edu/excellence/litethics/sandiegocobar.htm

Santa Clara County Bar Association
Code of Professionalsim
www.sccsuperiorcourt.org/rules/rules_standingorder.htm

Lawyer Referral Services
www.abanet.org/legalservices/lris/directory
www.legal-aid.com/lawyer_referral_services.html

Research in Legal Ethics
www.abanet.org/cpr/ethicsearch/resource.html

G. Something to Check

Use the free online sites for California court opinions (see section 5.1) to find and summarize one California state court case on solicitation, and another on contingent fees in a medical malpractice case.

3.3 Ethical Opinions of Courts and Bar Associations Involving Paralegals and Other Nonattorneys

A. Introduction

The text of the ethical rules governing attorneys is found in section 3.2. Here we will cover some of the major interpretations of these rules involving paralegals and other nonattorneys. The interpretations are in opinions written by courts and by bar association committees. (Appendix A in Part 1 also presents some summaries of court opinions that raised ethical issues.)

The ethical opinions of bar associations are advisory only. The final authority on ethical matters rests with the California courts and the legislature. Nevertheless, bar ethical opinions are very influential. Courts often adopt the views expressed in the bar opinions.
Table of Cases Included

In re Complex Asbestos Litigation
Formal Opinion Number 1988–103
Formal Opinion Number 1997–148
Formal Opinion Number 1997–150
Formal Opinion Number 1979–50
Formal Opinion Number 1994–138
Ethics Opinion No. 457 (Los Angeles)
Ethics Opinion Number 1983–12 (San Diego)

B. Conflict of Interest and *In re Complex Asbestos Litigation*

One of the most famous ethics cases involving paralegals is *In re Complex Asbestos Litigation.* This case presents the nightmare scenario of a law firm's disqualification from continuing to represent current clients because of a conflict of interest created by its paralegal. Before coming to work for the law firm, the paralegal worked for the opposing counsel on cases handled by his current employer. Hence, at different times, the paralegal worked on both sides of the same litigation.

In re Complex Asbestos Litigation

California Court of Appeals, 1st District

232 Cal. App. 3d 572, 283 Cal. Rptr. 732 (Cal. App. 1st Dist., 1991)

CHIN, Associate Justice

Attorney Jeffrey B. Harrison, his law firm, and their affected clients appeal from an order disqualifying the Harrison firm in nine asbestos-related personal injury actions. The appeal presents the difficult issue of whether a law firm should be disqualified because an employee of the firm possessed attorney-client confidences from previous employment by opposing counsel in pending litigation. We hold that disqualification is appropriate unless there is written consent or the law firm has effectively screened the employee from involvement with the litigation to which the information relates. . . .

Facts

Michael Vogel worked as a paralegal for the law firm of Brobeck, Phleger . . . (Brobeck) from October 28, 1985, to November 30, 1988. Vogel came to Brobeck with experience working for a law firm that represented defendants in asbestos litigation. Brobeck also represented asbestos litigation defendants, including respondents [asbestos manufacturers]. At Brobeck, Vogel worked exclusively on asbestos litigation.

During most of the period Brobeck employed Vogel, he worked on settlement evaluations. He extracted information from medical reports, discovery responses, and plaintiffs' depositions for entry on "Settlement Evaluation and Authority Request" (SEAR) forms. The SEAR forms were brief summaries of the information and issues used by the defense attorneys and their clients to evaluate each plaintiff's case. The SEAR forms were sent to the clients.

Vogel attended many defense attorney meetings where the attorneys discussed the strengths and weaknesses of cases to reach consensus settlement recommendations for each case. The SEAR forms were the primary informational materials the attorneys used at the meetings. Vogel's responsibility at these meetings was to record the amounts agreed on for settlement recommendations to the clients. Vogel sent the settlement authority requests and SEAR forms to the clients. He also attended meetings and telephone conferences where attorneys discussed the recommendations with clients and settlement authority was granted. Vogel recorded on the SEAR forms the amount of settlement authority granted and distributed the information to the defense attorneys.

The SEAR form information was included in Brobeck's computer record on each asbestos case. The SEAR forms contained the plaintiff's name and family information, capsule summaries of medical reports, the plaintiff's work history, asbestos products identified at the plaintiff's work sites, and any special considerations that might affect the jury's response to the plaintiff's case. The SEAR forms also contained information about any prior settlements and settlement authorizations. Information was added to the forms as it was developed during the course of a case. Vogel, like other Brobeck staff working on asbestos cases, had a computer password that allowed access to the information on any asbestos case in Brobeck's computer system.

Vogel also monitored trial events, received daily reports from the attorneys in trial, and relayed trial reports to the clients. Vogel reviewed plaintiffs' interrogatory answers to get SEAR form data and to assess whether the answers were adequate or further responses were needed.

In 1988, Vogel's duties changed when he was assigned to work for a trial team. With that change, Vogel no longer was involved with the settlement evaluation meetings and reports. Instead, he helped prepare specific cases assigned to the team. Vogel did not work on any cases in which the Harrison firm represented the plaintiffs.

During the time Vogel worked on asbestos cases for Brobeck, that firm and two others represented respondents in asbestos litigation filed in Northern California. Brobeck and the other firms were selected for this work by the Asbestos Claims Facility (ACF), a corporation organized by respondents and others to manage the defense of asbestos litigation on their behalf. The ACF dissolved in October 1988, though Brobeck continued to represent most of the respondents through at least the end of the year. Not long after the ACF's dissolution, Brobeck gave Vogel two weeks' notice of his termination, though his termination date was later extended to the end of November.

Vogel contacted a number of firms about employment, and learned that the Harrison firm was looking for paralegals. The Harrison firm recently had opened a Northern California office and filed a number of asbestos cases against respondents. Sometime in the second half of November 1988, Vogel called Harrison to ask him for a job with his firm.

In that first telephone conversation, Harrison learned that Vogel had worked for Brobeck on asbestos litigation settlements. Harrison testified that he did not then offer Vogel a job for two reasons. First, Harrison did not think he would need a new paralegal until February or March of 1989. Second, Harrison was concerned about the appearance of a conflict of interest in his firm's hiring a paralegal from Brobeck. Harrison discussed the conflict problem with other attorneys, and told Vogel that he could be hired only if Vogel got a waiver from the senior asbestos litigation partner at Brobeck.

Vogel testified that he spoke with Stephen Snyder, the Brobeck partner in charge of managing the Northern California asbestos litigation. Vogel claimed he told Snyder of the possible job with the Harrison firm, and that Snyder later told him the clients had approved and that Snyder would provide a written waiver if Vogel wanted. In his testimony, Snyder firmly denied having any such conversations or giving Vogel any conflicts waiver to work for Harrison. The trial court resolved this credibility dispute in favor of Snyder.

While waiting for a job with the Harrison firm, Vogel went to work for Bjork [Bjork, Fleer, Lawrence & Harris], which represented two of the respondents in asbestos litigation in Northern California. Vogel worked for Bjork during December 1988, organizing boxes of materials transferred from Brobeck to Bjork. While there, Vogel again called Harrison to press him for a job. Vogel told Harrison that Brobeck had approved his working for Harrison, and Harrison offered Vogel a job starting after the holidays. During their conversations, Harrison told Vogel the job involved work on complex, nonasbestos civil matters, and later would involve processing release documents and checks for asbestos litigation settlements. Harrison did not contact Brobeck to confirm Vogel's claim that he made a full disclosure and obtained Brobeck's consent. Nor did Harrison tell Vogel that he needed a waiver from Bjork.

Vogel informed Bjork he was quitting to work for the Harrison firm. Vogel told a partner at Bjork that he wanted experience in areas other than asbestos litigation, and that he would work on securities and real estate development litigation at the Harrison firm. Initially, Vogel's work for the Harrison firm was confined to those two areas.

However, at the end of February 1989, Vogel was asked to finish another paralegal's job of contacting asbestos plaintiffs to complete client questionnaires. The questionnaire answers provided information for discovery requests by the defendants. Vogel contacted Bjork and others to request copies of discovery materials for the Harrison firm. Vogel also assisted when the Harrison firm's asbestos trial teams needed extra help. In March 1989, Snyder learned from a Brobeck trial attorney that Vogel was involved in asbestos litigation. In a March 31 letter, Snyder asked Harrison if Vogel's duties included asbestos litigation. Harrison responded to Snyder by letter on April 6. In the letter, Harrison stated Vogel told Snyder his work for the Harrison firm would include periodic work on asbestos cases, and that Harrison assumed there was no conflict of interest. Harrison also asked Snyder to provide details of the basis for any claimed conflict. There were no other communications between Brobeck and the Harrison firm concerning Vogel before the disqualification motion was filed.

In June, a Harrison firm attorney asked Vogel to call respondent Fibreboard Corporation to see if it would accept service of a subpoena for its corporate minutes. Vogel called the company and spoke to a person he knew from working for Brobeck. Vogel asked who should be served with the subpoena in place of the company's retired general counsel. Vogel's call prompted renewed concern among respondents' counsel over Vogel's involvement with asbestos litigation for a plaintiff's firm. On July 31, counsel for three respondents demanded that the Harrison firm disqualify itself from cases against those respondents. Three days later, the motion to disqualify the Harrison firm was filed; it was subsequently joined by all respondents.

The trial court held a total of 21 hearing sessions on the motion, including 16 sessions of testimony. During the hearing, several witnesses testified that Vogel liked to talk, and the record indicates that he would volunteer information in an effort to be helpful.

A critical incident involving Vogel's activities at Brobeck first came to light during the hearing. Brobeck's computer system access log showed that on November 17, 1988, Vogel accessed the computer records for 20 cases filed by the Harrison firm. On the witness stand, Vogel at first flatly denied having looked at these case records, but when confronted with the access log, he admitted reviewing the records "to see what kind of cases [the Harrison firm] had filed." At the time, Vogel had no responsibilities for any Harrison firm cases at Brobeck. The date Vogel reviewed those computer records was very close to the time Vogel and Harrison first spoke. The access log documented that Vogel opened each record long enough to view and print copies of all the information on the case in the computer system. The case information on the computer included the SEAR form data. Many of the 20 cases had been entered on the computer just over a week earlier, though others had been on the computer for weeks or months. The initial computer entries for a case consisted of information taken from the complaint by paralegals trained as part of Brobeck's case intake team. Vogel denied recalling what information for the Harrison firm's cases he saw on the computer, and Brobeck's witness could not tell what specific information was on the computer that day.

Vogel, Harrison, and the other two witnesses from the Harrison firm denied that Vogel ever disclosed any client confidences obtained while he worked for Brobeck. However, Harrison never instructed Vogel not to discuss any confidential information obtained at Brobeck. Vogel did discuss with Harrison firm attorneys his impressions of several Brobeck attorneys. After the disqualification motion was filed, Harrison and his office manager debriefed Vogel, not to obtain any confidences but to discuss his duties at Brobeck in detail and to assess respondents' factual allegations. During the course of the hearing, the Harrison firm terminated Vogel on August 25, 1989.

The trial court found that Vogel's work for Brobeck and the Harrison firm was substantially related, and that there was no express or implied waiver by Brobeck or its clients. The court believed there was a substantial likelihood that the Harrison firm's hiring of Vogel, without first building "an ethical wall" or having a waiver, would affect the outcome in asbestos cases. The court also found that Vogel obtained confidential information when he accessed Brobeck's computer records on the Harrison firm's cases, and that there was a reasonable probability Vogel used that information or disclosed it to other members of the Harrison firm's staff. The court refused to extend the disqualification beyond those cases where there was tangible evidence of interference by Vogel, stating that on the rest of the cases it would require the court to speculate.

The trial court . . . disqualified the Harrison firm in . . . the nine cases pending in San Francisco. The Harrison firm timely noticed an appeal from the disqualification order. . . .

Discussion

A trial court's authority to disqualify an attorney derives from the power inherent in every court, "[t]o control in furtherance of justice, the conduct of its ministerial officers, and of all other persons in any manner connected with a judicial proceeding before it, in every matter pertaining thereto." (Code Civ. Proc., § 128(a)(5); *Comden v. Superior Court (1978) 20 Cal.3d 906, 916, fn. 4; Gregori v. Bank of America* (1989) 207 CalApp.3d 291, 299–300.) . . .

Concerns Raised by Disqualification Motions

Our courts recognize that a motion to disqualify a party's counsel implicates several important interests. These concerns are magnified when, as here, disqualification is sought not just for a single case but for many and, indeed, an entire class of litigation. When faced with disqualifying an attorney for an alleged conflict of interest, courts have considered such interests as the clients' right to counsel of their choice, an attorney's interest in representing a client, the financial burden on the client of replacing disqualified counsel, and any tactical abuse underlying the disqualification proceeding. . . .

An additional concern arises if disqualification rules based on exposure to confidential information are applied broadly and mechanically. In the era of large, multioffice law firms and increased attention to the business aspects of the practice of law, we must consider the ability of attorneys and their employees to change employment for personal reasons or from necessity. . . .

Accordingly, judicial scrutiny of disqualification orders is necessary to prevent literalism from possibly overcoming substantial justice to the parties. . . . However, as the Supreme Court recognized in *Comden,* the issue ultimately involves a conflict between the clients' right to counsel of their choice and the need to maintain ethical standards of professional responsibility. The paramount concern, though, must be the preservation of public trust in the scrupulous administration of justice and the integrity of the bar. The recognized and important right to counsel of one's choosing must yield to considerations of ethics that run to the very integrity of our judicial process.

Confidentiality and the Attorney-Client Relationship

Preserving confidentiality of communications between attorney and client is fundamental to our legal system. The attorney-client privilege is a hallmark of Anglo-American jurisprudence that furthers the public policy of insuring "'the right of every person to freely and fully confer and confide in one having knowledge of the law, and skilled in its practice, in order that the former may have adequate advice and a proper defense.' [Citation.]" (*Mitchell v. Superior Court* (1984) 37 Cal.3d 591, 599.) One of the basic duties of an attorney is "[t]o maintain inviolate the confidence, and at every peril to himself or herself to preserve the secrets, of his or her client." (Bus. & Prof. Code, § 6068(e).) To protect the confidentiality of the attorney-client relationship, the California Rules of Professional Conduct bar an attorney from accepting "employment adverse to a client or former client where, by reason of the representation of the client or former client, the [attorney] has obtained confidential information material to the employment except with the informed written consent of the client or former client." (*Rules Prof. Conduct, rule 3-310(D); Western Continental Operating Co. v. Natural Gas Corp.,* 212 Cal.App.3d 752, 759.)

For these reasons, an attorney will be disqualified from representing a client against a former client when there is a substantial relationship between the two representations. . . . When a substantial relationship exists, the courts presume the attorney possesses confidential information of the former client material to the present representation.

Confidentiality and the Nonlawyer Employee

The courts have discussed extensively the remedies for the ethical problems created by attorneys changing their employment from a law firm representing one party in litigation to a firm representing an adverse party. Considerably less attention has been given to the problems posed by nonlawyer employees of law firms who do the same. The issue this appeal presents is one of first impression for California courts. . . .

The obligation to maintain the client's confidences traditionally and properly has been placed on the attorney representing the client. But nonlawyer employees must handle confidential client information if legal services are to be efficient and cost-effective. Although a law firm has the ability to supervise its employees and assure that they protect client confidences, that ability and assurance are tenuous when the nonlawyer leaves the firm's employment. If the nonlawyer finds employment with opposing counsel, there is a heightened risk that confidences of the former employer's clients will be compromised, whether from base motives, an excess of zeal, or simple inadvertence.

Under such circumstances, the attorney who traditionally has been responsible for protecting the client's confidences—the former employer—has no effective means of doing so. The public policy of protecting the confidentiality of attorney-client communications must depend upon the attorney or law firm that hires an opposing counsel's employee. Certain requirements must be imposed on attorneys who hire their opposing counsel's employees to assure that attorney-client confidences are protected. . . .

Protecting Confidentiality–The Cone of Silence

Hiring a former employee of an opposing counsel is not, in and of itself, sufficient to warrant disqualification of an attorney or law firm. However, when the former employee possesses confidential attorney-client information, materially related to pending litigation, the situation implicates "'. . . considerations of ethics which run to the very integrity of our judicial process.' [Citation.]" (*Comden,* supra, 20 Cal.3d at p. 915, fn. omitted.) Under such circumstances, the hiring attorney must obtain the informed written consent of the former employer, thereby dispelling any basis for disqualification. (Cf. Rules Prof. Conduct, rule 3-310(D); see Civ. Code, § 3515 ("[One] who consents to an act is not wronged by it.") Failing that, the hiring attorney is subject to disqualification unless the attorney can rebut a presumption that the confidential attorney-client information has been used or disclosed in the new employment.

The hiring attorney, and not the prospective employee, must obtain the consent. The prospective employee is unlikely both to know enough about the new job and to have the legal ethics training necessary to obtain informed consent. Also, an individual under economic pressure to get the new job could be tempted to give less attention to candor and honesty than to securing employment. Harrison should not have delegated this sensitive task to a nonlawyer job seeker. Harrison's reliance on Vogel's word alone for the claimed waiver by Brobeck was unreasonable and a serious lapse in judgment.

A law firm that hires a nonlawyer who possesses an adversary's confidences creates a situation, similar to hiring an adversary's attorney, which suggests that confidential information is at risk. We adapt our approach, then, from cases that discuss whether an entire firm is subject to vicarious disqualification because one attorney changed sides. . . . The courts disagree on whether vicarious disqualification should be automatic in attorney conflict of interest cases, or whether a presumption of shared confidences should be rebuttable. An inflexible presumption of shared confidences would not be appropriate for nonlawyers, though, whatever its merits when applied to attorneys. There are obvious differences between lawyers and their nonlawyer employees in training, responsibilities, and acquisition and use of confidential information. These differences satisfy us that a rebuttable presumption of shared confidences provides a just balance between protecting confidentiality and the right to chosen counsel.

The most likely means of rebutting the presumption is to implement a procedure, before the employee is hired, which effectively screens the employee from any involvement with the litigation, a procedure [aptly called a "cone of silence."] Whether a potential employee will require a cone of silence should be determined as a matter of routine during the hiring process. It is reasonable to ask potential employees about the nature of their prior legal work; prudence alone would dictate such inquiries. Here, Harrison's first conversation with Vogel revealed a potential problem—Vogel's work for Brobeck on asbestos litigation settlements.

The leading treatise on legal malpractice also discusses screening procedures and case law. (1 Mallen & Smith, Legal Malpractice (3d ed. 1989) §§ 13.18–13.19, pp. 792–797.) We find several points to be persuasive when adapted to the context of employee conflicts. "Screening is a prophylactic, affirmative measure to avoid both the reality and appearance of impropriety. It is *a* means, but not *the* means, of rebutting the presumption of shared confidences." (Id., § 13.19, at p. 794. . . .) Two objectives must be achieved. First, screening should be implemented before undertaking the challenged representation or hiring the tainted individual. Screening must take place at the outset to prevent any confidences from being disclosed. Second, the tainted individual should be precluded from any involvement in or communication about the challenged representation. To avoid inadvertent disclosures and to establish an evidentiary record, a memorandum should be circulated warning the legal staff to isolate the individual from communications on the matter and to prevent access to the relevant files. (Id., at pp. 795–796.) [A further recommendation by the authors is worth noting. To detect conflicts created by employee hiring, a firm's conflict-checking system should include the identity of adverse counsel to enable a search for those matters where the prospective employee's former employer is or was adverse. (1 Mallen & Smith, Legal Malpractice, supra, § 13.18, at pp. 793–794.)]

The need for such a rule is manifest. We agree with the observations made by the *Williams* court: "[Nonlawyer] personnel are widely used by lawyers to assist in rendering legal services. Paralegals, investigators, and secretaries must have ready access to client confidences in order to assist their attorney employers. If information provided by a client in confidence to an attorney for the purpose of obtaining legal advice could be used against the client because a member of the attorney's [nonlawyer] support staff left the attorney's employment, it would have a devastating effect both on the free flow of information between client and attorney and on the cost and quality of the legal services rendered by an attorney." (*Williams v. Trans World Airlines, Inc.* (W.D. Mo. 1984) 588 F. Supp. 1037, 1044.) Further, no regulatory or ethical rules, comparable to those governing attorneys, restrain all of the many types of nonlawyer employees of attorneys. The restraint on such employees' disclosing confidential attorney-client information must be the employing attorney's admonishment against revealing the information. . . .

The Substantial Relationship Test and Nonlawyer Employees

We decline to adopt the broader rule urged by respondents . . . that disqualification must follow a showing of a "substantial relationship" between the matters worked on by the nonlawyer at the former and present employers' firms. . . . [This would present] unnecessary barriers to employment mobility. Such a rule sweeps more widely than needed to protect client confidences. We share the concerns expressed by the American Bar Association's Standing Committee on Ethics and Professional Responsibility: "It is important that nonlawyer employees have as much mobility in employment opportunity as possible consistent with the protection of clients' interests. To so limit employment opportunities that some nonlawyers trained to work with law firms might be required to leave the careers for which they are trained would disserve clients as well as the legal profession. Accordingly, any restrictions on the nonlawyer's employment should be held to the minimum necessary to protect confidentiality of client information." (Imputed Disqualification Arising from Change in Employment by Nonlawyer Employee, ABA Standing Com. on Ethics & Prof. Responsibility, Informal Opn. No. 88–1526 (1988) p. 3.) Respondents' suggested rule could easily result in nonlawyer employees becoming "Typhoid Marys," unemployable by firms practicing in specialized areas of the law where the employees are most skilled and experienced.

Protecting Confidentiality—The Rule for Disqualification

Absent written consent, the proper rule and its application for disqualification based on nonlawyer employee conflicts of interest should be as follows. The party seeking disqualification must show that its present or past attorney's former employee possesses confidential attorney-client information materially related to the proceedings before the court. [The evidence showing the former employee's possession of such information need not be as dramatic as Vogel's confession in this case. Possession of the information can be shown, for example, by competent evidence of the former employee's job responsibilities or participation in privileged communications. We caution, however, that showing merely potential access to confidences without actual exposure is insufficient. The threat to confidentiality must be real, not hypothetical.]

Once this showing has been made, a rebuttable presumption arises that the information has been used or disclosed in the current employment. The presumption is a rule by necessity because the party seeking disqualification will be at a loss to prove what is known by the adversary's attorneys and legal staff. . . . To rebut the presumption, the challenged attorney has the burden of showing that the practical effect of formal screening has been achieved. The showing must satisfy the trial court that the employee has not had and will not have any involvement with the litigation, or any communication with attorneys or coemployees concerning the litigation, that would support a reasonable inference that the information has been used or disclosed. If the challenged attorney fails to make this showing, then the court may disqualify the attorney and law firm. . . .

There can be no question that Vogel obtained confidential attorney-client information when he accessed the Harrison firm's case files on Brobeck's computer. Respondents need not show the specific confidences Vogel obtained; such a showing would serve only to exacerbate the damage to the confidentiality of the attorney-client relationship. As discussed above, respondents had to show only the nature of the information and its material relationship to the present proceedings. They have done so. . . .

The Harrison firm . . . argues that there was no evidence that Vogel disclosed any confidences to any member of the firm, or that any such information was sought from or volunteered by Vogel. Harrison testified that he never asked Vogel to divulge anything other than impressions about three Brobeck attorneys. Harrison and his office manager also testified that Vogel was not involved in case evaluation or trial tactics discussions at the Harrison firm. However, this evidence is not sufficient to rebut the presumption that Vogel used the confidential material or disclosed it to staff members at the Harrison firm. Moreover, there was substantial evidence to support a reasonable inference that Vogel used or disclosed the confidential information.

Despite Harrison's own concern over an appearance of impropriety, Harrison never told Vogel not to discuss the information Vogel learned at Brobeck and did not consider screening Vogel even after Brobeck first inquired about Vogel's work on asbestos cases. The evidence also amply supports the trial court's observation that Vogel was "a very talkative person, a person who loves to share information." Further, Vogel's willingness to use information acquired at Brobeck, and the Harrison firm's insensitivity to ethical considerations, were demonstrated when Vogel was told to call respondent Fibreboard Corporation and Vogel knew the person to contact there.

The trial court did not apply a presumption of disclosure, which would have been appropriate under the rule we have set forth. The evidence offered by the Harrison firm is manifestly insufficient to rebut the presumption. Beyond that, though, substantial evidence established a reasonable probability that Vogel used or disclosed to the Harrison firm the confidential attorney-client information obtained from Brobeck's computer records. Accordingly, the trial court was well within a sound exercise of discretion in ordering the Harrison firm's disqualification. . . .

Conclusion

We realize the serious consequences of disqualifying attorneys and depriving clients of representation by their chosen counsel. However, we must balance the important right to counsel of one's choice against the competing fundamental interest in preserving confidences of the attorney-client relationship. All attorneys share certain basic obligations of professional conduct, obligations that are essential to the integrity and function of our legal system. Attorneys must respect the confidentiality of attorney-client information and recognize that protecting confidentiality is an imperative to be obeyed in both form and substance. A requisite corollary to these principles is that attorneys must prohibit their employees from violating confidences of former employers as well as confidences of present clients. Until the Legislature or the State Bar choose to disseminate a different standard, attorneys must be held accountable for their employees' conduct, particularly when that conduct poses a clear threat to attorney-client confidentiality and the integrity of our judicial process.

The order of the trial court is affirmed. Each party shall bear its own costs.

C. Supervision of Paralegals Engaged in Administrative Advocacy

Next we examine Formal Opinion 1988–103 of the State Bar of California's Standing Committee on Professional Responsibility and Conduct (COPRAC). The facts of the opinion involve a law firm that wants to allow its paralegals to represent clients at a state administrative agency, the Workers' Compensation Appeals Board (WCAB). Statutes in the Labor Code expressly allow this (see section 3.1). These statutes, however, do not cover potential ethical problems that might arise if a law firm allows its paralegals to provide this representation. Paralegals engaging in such advocacy would be on their own at the agency. There is no attorney present to provide immediate supervision. This raises a number of ethical questions:

- Does paralegal representation at the administrative agency constitute the practice of law?
- When an attorney allows his or her paralegal to represent clients at the agency, what must the attorney do to avoid violating the Rules of Professional Conduct governing attorneys?
- Since the client initially hired the law firm, is the firm obligated to ensure that the quality of paralegal representation at the agency equal that of an attorney?

Read Formal Opinion Number 1988–103 to obtain answers to these questions.

Formal Opinion Number 1988–103

Standing Committee on Professional Responsibility and Conduct (COPRAC). © 2007 The State Bar of California. All Rights Reserved. Reprinted with permission. (The following is the complete text of COPRAC Formal Opinion #1988-103. The text is also printed at *calbar.ca.gov/calbar/html_unclassified/ca88-103.html*). No part of this work, nor of the other State Bar materials presented below, may be reproduced, stored in a retrieval system, or transmitted in any medium without prior written permission of the State Bar of California.

> ISSUE: May a law firm, having advised its client of its intention to do so, delegate authority to a paralegal employee to make appearances at Workers' Compensation Appeals Board hearings and to file petitions, motions or other material?
>
> DIGEST: A law firm may delegate such authority, provided that the paralegal employee is adequately supervised.
>
> AUTHORITIES INTERPRETED: Rules 3-101, 3-103, and 6-101 of the Rules of Professional Conduct of the State Bar of California.
>
> ISSUE: A client has contracted for the services of a law firm for representation in a matter pending before the Workers' Compensation Appeals Board (hereinafter "WCAB"). The law firm employs and intends to utilize the services of the paralegal in connection with the proceedings pending before the WCAB to make appearances, file petitions and present motions. The client has consented to the law firm utilizing the services of the paralegal, after being informed as to the potential consequences of representation by a person of presumably lesser qualification and skills than may be reasonably expected of an attorney. In addition, the status of the

employee as a paralegal rather than an attorney will be fully disclosed at all proceedings at which the paralegal appears and on all documents which the paralegal prepares.

Discussion

It is unlawful for any person to practice law in this state without active membership in the State Bar of California. (Bus. & Prof. Code, sec. 6125.) The practice of law includes the performing of services in any matter pending in a court or administrative proceeding throughout its various stages, as well as the rendering of legal advice and counsel in the preparation of legal instruments and contracts by which legal rights are secured. (cf. *Smallberg v. State Bar* (1931) 212 Cal. 113.)

It has been held that the representation of claimants before the Industrial Accident Commission (predecessor to the WCAB) constitutes the performance of legal services. (Bland v. Reed (1968) 261 Cal.App.2d 445, 448.) However, the representation by a non-attorney of an applicant before the WCAB is expressly authorized by Labor Code sections 5501 and 5700 as follows:

> The application may be filed with the appeals board by any party in interest, his attorney, or other representative authorized in writing . . . Either party may be present at any hearing, in person, by attorney, or by any other agent, and may present testimony pertinent under the pleading.

Thus, the principal issue is whether an attorney may hire a non- attorney to engage in conduct on behalf of the attorney's client which the employee is authorized to perform independently, but which, if performed by the attorney, would constitute the practice of law.

It is the opinion of the Committee that because the client has been informed about, and has consented to the involvement of the paralegal, no violation occurs with respect to dishonesty or deceit. (See Bus. & Prof. Code, secs. 6106, 6128, subd.(a).) In addition, if the status of the employee as a paralegal rather than an attorney is fully disclosed at all proceedings at which the paralegal appears and on all documents which the paralegal prepares, no violation of the prohibition on an attorney lending his or her name to be used as attorney by a person not licensed to practice law will occur. (See Bus. & Prof. Code, sec. 6105.) In addition, because Labor Code sections 5501 and 5700 expressly authorize non-attorneys to represent applicants before the WCAB, the proposed arrangement would not constitute a violation of Rule of Professional Conduct 3-101(A), which provides as follows:

> A member of the State Bar shall not aid any person, association, or corporation in the *unauthorized* practice of law. (Emphasis added.)

Further, there is no indication in the facts presented that the relationship between the paralegal and the law firm would constitute a partnership in violation of Rule of Professional Conduct 3-103, which provides as follows:

> A member of the State Bar shall not form a partnership with a person not licensed to practice law if any of the activities of the partnership consist of the practice of law.

The pivotal consideration is that the client contracted for the services of the law firm, rather than a paralegal, for representation. However, since the safeguards mentioned above have been taken to avoid misleading or deceiving the client or any one else regarding the status of the paralegal, the Committee finds no ethical insufficiency inherent in the participation of the paralegal.

A lawyer or law firm contemplating entering into such an arrangement should remember that an attorney stands in a fiduciary relationship with the client. (*Krusesky v. Baugh* (1982) 138 Cal.App.3d 562, 567.) When acting as a fiduciary, the law imposes upon a member the strictest duty of prudent conduct as well as an obligation to perform his or her duties to the best of the attorney's ability. (*Clark v. State Bar* (1952) 39 Cal.2d 161, 167; and cf. Bus. & Prof. Code, sec. 6067; Rule of Professional Conduct 6-101(A).) However, an attorney does not have to bear the entire burden of attending to every detail of the practice, but may be justified in relying to some extent on non-attorney employees. (*Moore v. State Bar* (1964) 62 Cal.2d 74, 80; *Vaughn v. State Bar* (1972) 6 Cal.3d 847, 857.)

The attorney who delegates responsibilities to his or her employees must keep in mind that he or she, as the attorney, has the duty to adequately supervise the employee. In fact, the attorney will be subject to discipline if the lawyer fails to adequately supervise the employee. (*Chefsky v. State Bar* (1984) 36 Cal.3d 116, 123; *Palomo v. State Bar* (1984) 36 Cal.3d 785, 795; *Gassman v. State Bar* (1976) 18 Cal.3d 125.)

What constitutes adequate supervision will, of course, depend on a number of factors, including, but not limited to, the complexity of the client matter, the level of experience of the paralegal and the facts of the particular case.

It is the opinion of the Committee that, even though the paralegal will be providing substantive legal services to the client, adequate supervision under these unique facts does not require the attorney to ensure that the paralegal performs the services in accordance with the level of competence that would be expected of the attorney under rule 6-101. [The Committee is expressly not addressing the issue of malpractice liability of the attorney which may result from the paralegal providing substantive legal services to the client.]

So long as the paralegal is adequately supervised and the law firm does not mislead the client that the services will be performed in accordance with the attorney level of competence or that an attorney will be handling the matter, the Committee does not believe the attorney would be in violation of the Rules of Professional Conduct.

This opinion is issued by the Standing Committee on Professional Responsibility and Conduct of the State Bar of California. It is advisory only. It is not binding upon the courts, the State Bar of California, its Board of Governors, any persons or tribunals charged with regulatory responsibility or any member of the State Bar.

D. Independent Judgment, Supervision, Fee-splitting, and Solicitation

Formal Opinion Number 1997-148

Standing Committee on Professional Responsibility and Conduct (COPRAC). © 2007 The State Bar of California. All Rights Reserved. (The following is a summary of COPRAC Formal Opinion #1997–148. The summary was prepared by the authors of this book. Selected text is from the Rule 1-320(B) of the Rules of Professional Conduct. For the full text of the opinion, see *www.calbar.ca.gov/calbar/html_unclassified/ca97–148.html*).

In this case, an attorney prepared living trusts for clients recruited by nonattorneys (called marketers by the Committee). The marketers conducted seminars that discussed the advantages of living trusts. Interested audience participants filled out a questionnaire that sought the facts needed to prepare the living trust (e.g., the names of persons the participant wanted as beneficiaries). The marketers then gave the filled-out questionnaire to an attorney who prepared the living trust. The attorney was paid by the marketers for preparing the trusts.

This arrangement was found to be unethical for a number of reasons:

- The attorney's duty includes educating a client on available estate planning options. This was not done here. Only one estate plan was presented—the living trust.
- The attorney permitted essential estate planning tasks, including fact-finding, to be performed by a nonattorneys without exercising independent professional judgment. The marketer decides what information to solicit and to convey to the attorney.
- The nonattorneys are not supervised in collecting facts and in describing the trusts to the audience. They should be as adequately supervised as paralegals would be in a properly run law office.
- An attorney cannot receive payment from participants for legal services and then pay the marketer a share for finding the clients and referring them to the lawyer. Rule 1-320(B) states in part: "A member shall not compensate, give, or promise anything of value to any person or entity for the purpose of recommending or securing employment of the member or the member's law firm by a client, or as a reward for having made a recommendation resulting in employment of the member or the member's law firm by a client. . . ." The attorney should not be able to "sanitize" such impermissible fee-splitting by the simple expedient of having the marketer receive the funds, make the division, and distribute them to the lawyer.
- The arrangement constitutes impermissible in-person solicitation by an attorney through the marketer as his agent.

E. Attorneys in Different Firms Sharing the Same Paralegal

Formal Opinion Number 1997-150

Standing Committee on Professional Responsibility and Conduct (COPRAC). © 2007 The State Bar of California. All Rights Reserved. (The following is a summary of COPRAC Formal Opinion #1997–150. The summary was prepared by the authors of this book. For the full text of the opinion, see *www.calbar.ca.gov/calbar/html_unclassified/ca97–150.html*).

Two attorneys have independent practices, but they would like to share office space, a secretary, and a paralegal. The attorneys have their own clients; they are not engaged in a partnership or corporate practice together. The attorneys want to know what ethical issues might arise as a result of this arrangement.

- Public confusion. Attorneys who have independent practices must not confuse or mislead the public about their professional relationship. The public must not be led to believe that the attorney constitute one law practice or a single firm. Sole practitioners must not use a name or other professional designation that would lead one to believe that they have an associate, partner, or shareholder relationship together.
- Supervision of staff and confidentiality. To maintain competence and preserve confidentiality, staff members must be carefully supervised in the context of adequate office procedures. Whenever attorneys use the same staff or the same space, they must clearly specify how they have maintained separate systems for correspondence, filing, accounting, and client communications so as to preserve the confidentiality of client information.
- Conflict of interest. If the attorneys lead a client to believe that they are a single firm, a partnership by estoppel might be created. This could create conflict of interest issues. Note, however, that in *People v. Pastrano* (1997) 52 Cal. App. 4th 610, the court did not find an actual conflict of interest

when there was a sharing of office space and staff by attorneys with separate practices who represented codefendants in a criminal case.

Hence, attorneys may ethically share space and staff so long as they take reasonable steps under the circumstances to protect against: (1) misleading the public or clients regarding the nature of their relationship; and (2) the disclosure of clients' confidential information to other attorneys or staff in the office.

F. Nonattorney Discloses Confidential Information

Formal Opinion Number 1979–50

Standing Committee on Professional Responsibility and Conduct (COPRAC). © 2007 The State Bar of California. All Rights Reserved. (The following excerpts are from COPRAC Formal Opinion #1979–50. For the full text of the opinion, see *calbar.ca.gov/calbar/html_unclassified/ca79–50.html*)

". . . Attorneys Red and Blue each rent space in a suite owned by Attorney White. A secretary employed by Attorney Blue is frequently used by Attorney Red, who pays Attorney Blue for the secretarial services. In the course of the secretary's special employment, the secretary divulges to Attorney Blue information regarding a competitive bid on property prepared for Attorneys Red and White. It is not clear how harmful the disclosure was but the information was presumably confidential. Apparently there was no plan or effort on the part of Attorney Blue to procure this information; rather, the disclosure could be described as unintended or accidental."

"What preventive steps are any of the attorneys ethically required to take to minimize the risk of such disclosures?" "Is notice to the clients and withdrawal as counsel ethically required?"

"A primary obligation in the attorney-client relationship is the duty to preserve the confidences and secrets of one's client. . . . The hypothetical situation presented indicates that all the attorneys were under an obligation to prevent the stated disclosure by the secretary. A situation where a secretary is shared contains the potential for harm to clients, even though it may be economically necessary or desirable. Accordingly, because of the benefits of this arrangement to all of the attorneys, they each have a duty to preserve the confidences of the respective clients; they act at their peril and should be prepared to withdraw in the event of leaks resulting from this arrangement. Blue, having hired the secretary, should define explicitly what obligations exist with respect to confidentiality and employment by other lawyers. Similarly, attorneys Red and White should have discussed this issue with the secretary and with Blue prior to hiring the secretary to prepare the bid."

"Taking such precautionary steps can be analogized to the circumstances of a lawyer using the services of an outside professional service (e.g., a computerized accounting firm), as part of the rendering of legal services. Particularly when such a firm may handle other law firms or serve clients represented by other attorneys, care must be taken to prevent disclosure of confidences. . . ."

"Assuming a failure to take precautionary steps and the subsequent disclosure about the bid, the attorneys have an obligation to investigate and ascertain the extent of the disclosure. Assuming further that the effect of disclosure was harmful to Red and White's client, all the attorneys were obligated to advise their respective clients of the "leak" but not the details thereof. No ethical obligation exists with respect to notifying the seller of the property, as he is not a client of any of the attorneys."

"In this instance, an apparent violation of rule 6-101 of the Rules of Professional Conduct is present. Further, the attorneys may have acted incompetently by '[n]eglect[ing] a legal matter entrusted to [them].' (ABA Code of Prof. Responsibility, DR 6-101(A)(3).) A member of the State Bar cannot attempt to limit his liability for personal malpractice (rule 6-102, Rules Prof. Conduct), and disclosure is required here, much as it is required when a lawyer negligently permits the statute of limitations to run on his client's cause of action. . . . Despite the fact that Blue's client in fact may be benefited rather than harmed, the appropriate course of action is for all attorneys to disclose the problems to their clients and to withdraw from further employment, pursuant to rule 2-111(A)(2) of the Rules of Professional Conduct."

G. Splitting a Fee with a Paralegal

Formal Opinion Number 1994–138

Standing Committee on Professional Responsibility and Conduct (COPRAC). © 2007 The State Bar of California. All Rights Reserved. (The following is a summary of COPRAC Formal Opinion #1994–138. The summary was prepared by the authors of this book. Selected text from the opinion is in quotation marks. For the full text of the opinion, see *calbar.ca.gov/calbar/html_unclassified/ca94–138.html*).

Attorneys charge clients fees for paralegal work on client cases. When the attorney pays the paralegal a salary, is the attorney splitting a fee with a nonattorney in violation of ethical rules? No, so long as the payments to the paralegal are "not tied to specific legal fees received by the law office." If the paralegal's salary comes from the general law firm account into which all collected fees are deposited, there is no splitting of fees.

H. Bonus Paid to a Paralegal

Ethics Opinion No. 457 (1990)

Los Angeles County Bar Association Professional Responsibility and Ethics Committee (*www.lacba.org/Files/Main%20Folder/Documents/Files/EthicsTOC.pdf*).

An attorney may pay a paralegal a bonus when the bonus is not paid as a percentage of the attorney's fees, it is not bargained for based on the fee the attorney is to receive in a particular case, the paralegal has no expectation of receiving such a bonus, and the bonus is paid as compensation for the paralegal's productivity and performance based on the attorney's subjective assessment. Under such conditions, the bonus does not constitute sharing of legal fees with a nonattorney.

I. Unauthorized Practice of Law

Ethics Opinion 1983–12

Legal Ethics Committee of the San Diego County Bar Association (*www.sdcba.org/ethics/ethicsopinion83-12.html*)

A "divorce center" run by nonattorneys gives advice and assistance in the selection, preparation and filing of various forms in a dissolution of marriage or legal separation matter. This is the unauthorized practice of law. An attorney who associates with such a center to provide legal services would be aiding the unauthorized practice of law by nonattorneys.

While it is difficult to define with specificity the exact nature of what will constitute the practice of law, rendering advice or assistance in the selection, preparation and filing of dissolution documents does fall within the definition set forth in California Business and Professions Code section 6125 and therefore constitutes the unauthorized practice of law. The Rules of Professional Conduct, rules 3-101, 3-102, and 3-103 prohibit a member of the State Bar from aiding in the unauthorized practice of law or from forming a partnership with a person not licensed to practice law. An attorney may not aid a lay person or a nonattorney entity in the unauthorized practice of law and would be prohibited from associating with a nonattorney divorce center which is engaged in such unauthorized practice of law. This opinion does not, of course, prohibit the use of properly supervised paralegals by an attorney in dissolution matters.

J. More Information

Ethics in California

www.law.cornell.edu/ethics/california.html
calbar.ca.gov/state/calbar/calbar_generic.jsp?cid=10128
www.ll.georgetown.edu/states/ethics/california.cfm
www.law.ucla.edu/docs/161959732005guidec5.pdf
www.calbar.ca.gov/state/calbar/calbar_generic.jsp?cid=10158
www.legalethics.com/ethics.law?state=California#opinions

Ethics Opinions in California

calbar.ca.gov/state/calbar/calbar_generic.jsp?cid=10133&id=1129
www.lacba.org/showpage.cfm?pageid=427
www.sdcba.org/ethics/ethicsopinons_toc.html

Lexis

www.lexis.com
(CAL library CAETOP file; ETHICS file; CABAR file)

Westlaw

www.westlaw.com
(CAETH-EO database; CAETH-CS database; CA-RULES database)

Ethics in General

www.abanet.org/cpr/links.html
www.abanet.org/cpr/ethicsearch/resource.html
www.legalethics.com

K. Something to Check

1. Go to the Web site that presents the ethical opinions of the state bar association (*www.calbar.ca.gov/state/calbar/calbar_generic.jsp?cid=10133*). Read the summaries of the opinions printed online. Pick an opinion that interests you. Read it in full.
   (a) What issue(s) were covered in the opinion?
   (b) What authorities did the opinion cite?
   (c) How did the opinion resolve the issue(s)?
2. Shepardize the Asbestos case (232 Cal.App.3d 572). For what purposes has it been cited by other California court opinions?

3.4 California Bar Associations and Related Attorney Organizations

- A. Introduction
- B. Attorneys in California: A Snapshot
- C. State Bar Association
- D. Other Statewide and Regional Associations
- E. Local Bar Associations
- F. More Information
- G. Something to Check

A. Introduction

This section seeks to identify every major attorney organization in the state, particularly the bar associations. Most of the Web sites for these groups have search boxes. To find out what the group has said about paralegals, type "paralegal" or "legal assistant" in the search box. You may be led to news, committee or section activities, or ethical material pertaining to paralegals.

Some of the bar associations listed do not have permanent addresses. Suggestions on how to contact them are included under their names.

For related material on California attorneys, see:

- Part 1, Appendix B (Becoming an Attorney in California)
- Part 3, Appendix A (Disciplinary Proceedings against an Attorney)

Before examining these options, we present an overview of the world of California attorneys.

B. Attorneys in California: A Snapshot

Number of attorneys in California (2007). . . . 210,427
Active . . . 156,910
Inactive . . . 43,565
Judges . . . 1,914
Not entitled to practice . . . 8,037
Average age of active attorneys . . . 47
Average age of newly admitted attorneys . . . 30
Total members of the State Bar of California (2006) . . . 202,000
Total number taking bar exam (2005). . . . 12,863
Number passing . . . 5,882
Percentage passing . . . 46%
Number taking bar exam for the first time . . . 7,190
Percentage of first-time takers who passed . . . 62%
Number of repeat takers . . . 5,673
Percentage of repeat takers who passed . . . 25%
Number taking exam without law school . . . 5
Number in this group who passed . . . 1
Number of attorneys who are white . . . 83%
Number of attorneys who are male . . . 68%
Number of attorneys over 55 who are female . . . 20%
Number of attorneys under 35 who are female . . . almost 50%
Number of attorneys who are minority . . . 17%
Average work week of attorneys in private practice . . . 47.2 hours
Number of attorneys who earn less than $100,000 a year . . . 50%
Number of attorneys who earn between $50,000 and $100,000 a year . . . 34%
Number of attorneys who earn more than $150,000 a year . . . 24%
Number of attorneys who earn more than $300,000 a year . . . 4%

Number of attorneys admitted

1900	126
1910	240
1920	291
1930	656
1940	390
1950	726
1960	1,024
1970	2,612
1980	5,457
1990	6,143
2000	6,221
2005	5,965

Sources:
www.ncbex.org
members.calbar.ca.gov/search/demographics.aspx
www.calbar.ca.gov/calbar/pdfs/whowhat1.pdf
www.metnews.com/articles/2004/barx052504.htm

C. State Bar Association

State Bar of California
180 Howard Street, San Francisco, CA 94105-1639, 415-538-2000
www.calbar.ca.gov
Committees or Sections of Interest to Paralegals

- Law Practice Management and Technology Section
- Standing Committee on Professional Responsibility and Conduct (COPRAC)
- Solo and Small Firm Section
- Standing Committee on Administration of Justice
- Standing Committee on Delivery of Legal Services
- Real Property Law Section

NOTE: The Real Property Section offers associate memberships to non-attorneys. Dues: $50 a year. "With the recent changes in the regulation of paralegals requiring continuing education hours, we think there may be greater interest in the paralegal community in joining the Section. If there is sufficient interest, we are committed to starting a Paralegal Subsection within the Real Property Law Section to serve the paralegal members and give them a voice in Section activities. Please encourage your paralegal friends and colleagues to become associate members of the Section, and please encourage your law firms to pay their dues."

D. Other Statewide and Regional Associations

Academy of California Adoption Lawyers
acal.org

American College of Trial Lawyers
www.actl.com

Armenian Bar Association
www.armenianbar.org

Association of Business Trial Lawyers
(San Joaquin, Los Angeles, Orange County, San Diego)
www.abtl.org/welcome.htm

Association of Defense Counsel of Northern California
www.adcnc.org/links_decisions.htm

Association of Southern California Defense Counsel
www.ascdc.org

Bay Area Lawyers for Individual Freedom
(lesbian, gay, bisexual, transgender rights)
www.balif.org

California Appellate Defense Counsel
www.cadc.net

California Applicants' Attorneys Association
(Workers' Compensation Attorneys)
www.caaa.org

California Association of Black Lawyers
www.calblacklawyers.org

California Association of Certified Family Law Specialists
acfls.org

California Attorneys for Criminal Justice
www.cacj.org

California District Attorneys Association
www.cdaa.org

California Employment Lawyers Association
www.celaweb.org

California Lawyers for the Arts
www.calawyersforthearts.org

California Public Defenders Association
www.cpda.org

California Women Defenders
www.womendefenders.com

California Women Lawyers
www.cwl.org/index.shtml

California Young Lawyers Association
(part of the State Bar Association)
www.calbar.ca.gov/state/calbar/calbar_home.jsp
(type "young lawyers" in the search box)

California Workers' Compensation Defense Attorneys' Association
www.cwcdaa.org

Charles Houston Bar Association
(African-American lawyers)
www.charleshoustonbar.org

Chicano/Latino Bar Association of California
www.larazalawyers.net

Consumer Attorneys of California
caoc.com

Federal Bar Association, California Chapters
(Central Coast, Inland Empire, Los Angeles, Northern District, Orange County, Sacramento, San Diego, San Joaquin)
www.fedbar.org/chapters.html

Hellenic Law Society of Northern California
www.hellenlclaw.org

Iranian American Lawyers Association
my.ialawyers.org/nav/index.pyt

Korean American Bar Association of Northern California
www.kabanc.org

La Raza Lawyers of California
www.larazalawyers.net

Mexican-American Bar Association (Los Angeles)
www.mabalawyers.org

National Association of Railroad Trial Counsel (Pacific Palisades)
www.usnartc.org

South Asian Bar Association of Southern California (Los Angeles)
www.sabasc.org

Southern California Chinese Lawyers Association (Los Angeles)
www.sccla.org

E. Local Bar Associations

ALAMEDA COUNTY
AUBURN
BAKERSFIELD
BEVERLY HILLS
BUTTE COUNTY
CENTURY CITY
CHULA VISTA
CHICO
CONTRA COSTA COUNTY
CORONA DEL MAR
CUPERTINO
DAVIS
EL DORADO
FAIRFIELD
FRESNO
GLENDALE
HEMET
HOLLISTER
INYO COUNTY
IRVINE KERN COUNTY
KINGS COUNTY
LAGUNA HILLS
LA JOLLA
LONG BEACH

LOS ANGELES
MADERA COUNTY
MARIN COUNTY
MARIPOSA COUNTY
MARTINEZ
MERCED
MODESTO
MONTEREY COUNTY
MONO COUNTY
NORWALK
OAKLAND
ORANGE
ORANGE COUNTY
PALO ALTO
PASADENA
PLACER COUNTY
PLACERVILLE
REDWOOD CITY
RIVERSIDE
SACRAMENTO
SAN BENITO COUNTY
SAN BERNADINO
SAN DIEGO
SAN FERNANDO VALLEY
SAN FRANCISCO
SAN JOAQUIN
SAN JOSE
SAN LUIS OBISPO COUNTY
SAN MATEO
SAN RAFAEL
SANTA BARBARA
SANTA CLARA
SANTA CRUZ
SANTA MONICA
SANTA ROSA
SANTA YNEZ VALLEY
SOLANO COUNTY
SONOMA COUNTY
STANISLAUS COUNTY
STOCKTON
SUNNYVALE
TAHOE
TRUCKEE
TULARE COUNTY
VENTURA
VISTA
WEST SACRAMENTO
WOODLAND
WOODLAND HILLS
YOLO COUNTY

ALAMEDA COUNTY
See Oakland

AUBURN
Placer County Bar Association
P.O. Box 4598 Auburn, CA 95604 916-557-9181
www.placerbar.org

BAKERSFIELD
Kern County Bar Association
1675 Chester Avenue, Ste. 220
Bakersfield, CA 93301
661-334-4700
www.kernbar.org

Kern County Women Lawyers Association
www.kernbar.org/lawresources/wla.shtml

BEVERLY HILLS
Beverly Hills Bar Association
300 S. Beverly Drive, Ste. 201
Beverly Hills, CA 90212
310-601-2422
www.bhba.org
(Personnel Referral Service: "The BHBA Personnel Referral Service offers the best legal support staff available . . . if you are looking for employment in a legal office . . . or, if you are an attorney looking for staff.")

BUTTE COUNTY
See Chico

CENTURY CITY
See Los Angeles

CHICO
Butte County Bar Association
530-345-1940
www.buttebar.org

CHULA VISTA
See San Diego

CONTRA COSTA COUNTY
See Martinez

CORONA DEL MAR
Orange County Barristers
www.ocbarristers.net

CUPERTINO
Sunnyvale-Cupertino Bar Association
www.suncupbar.com

DAVIS
See Woodland

EL DORADO COUNTY
See Placerville

FAIRFIELD
Solano County Bar Association
744 Empire Street, Ste 110
Fairfield, CA 94533
707-422-5087
www.solanobar.org

FRESNO
Fresno County Bar Association
1221 Van Ness Ave, Ste. 300
Fresno, CA 93721
559-264-2619
www.fresnocountybar.org

GLENDALE
Glendale Bar Association
818-956-1633
www.glendalebar.com

HEMET
Mt. San Jacinto Bar Association
(At the state bar site [*www.calbar.ca.gov*], type the name of this bar association in the search box.)

HOLLISTER
San Benito County Bar Association
(At the state bar site [*www.calbar.ca.gov*], type the name of this bar association in the search box.)

INYO COUNTY
Inyo County Bar Association
(At the state bar site [*www.calbar.ca.gov*], type the name of this bar association in the search box.)

IRVINE
Orange County Asian American Bar Association
www.ocaaba.org

Orange County Bar Association
PO Box 17777
Irvine, CA 92623-7777
949-440-6700
www.ocbar.org

KERN COUNTY
See Bakersfield

KINGS COUNTY
Kings County Bar Association
(At the state bar site [*www.calbar.ca.gov*], type the name of this bar association in the search box.)

LAGUNA HILLS
Orange County Trial Lawyers Association
www.octla.org

LA JOLLA
See San Diego

LONG BEACH
Long Beach Bar Association
(At the state bar site [*www.calbar.ca.gov*], type the name of this bar association in the search box.)
director@longbeachbar.com
www.cal-bars.com/LBBA

LOS ANGELES
American Academy of Matrimonial Lawyers, Southern California Chapter
www.aamlsocal.com/index.htm

Asian Pacific American Bar Association of Los Angeles County
www.apabala.org

Black Women Lawyers Association of Los Angeles
www.blackwomenlawyersla.org

Century City Bar Association
www.centurycitybar.com

Consumer Attorneys Association of Los Angeles
www.caala.org

Federal Bar Association, Los Angeles Chapter
www.fedbar.org/losangeles.html

Italian-American Lawyers Association
www.iala.lawzone.com

Japanese American Bar Association of Greater Los Angeles
www.jabaonline.org

John M. Langston Bar Association
(African-American Attorneys)
www.langstonbar.org

Korean American Bar Association of Southern California
www.kabasocal.org

Lawyer's Club of Los Angeles County
www.lawyersclub.org

Lesbian and Gay Lawyers Association of Los Angeles
www.lhr.org

Los Angeles County Bar Association
Office Address:
261 S. Figueroa Street, Ste 300
Los Angeles, CA 90012
213-627-2727
www.lacba.org
("The Los Angeles County Bar Association presents job announcements sent to us from various sources . . ." including openings for paralegals.)

Mexican-American Bar Association
www.mabalawyers.org

Norwegian American Bar Association
www.lawzone.com/half-nor

Philippine American Bar Association of Los Angeles
www.philconnect.com/paba

Santa Monica Bar Association
www.smba.net

South Asian Bar Association of Southern California
www.sabasc.org

South Bay Bar Association
www.southbaybar.org

Southern California Chinese Lawyers Association
www.sccla.org

Women Lawyers Association of Los Angeles
www.wlala.org

MADERA COUNTY
Eastern Madera County Bar Association
(At the state bar site [*www.calbar.ca.gov*], type the name of this bar association in the search box.)

MARIN COUNTY
See San Rafael

MARIPOSA COUNTY
Mariposa County Bar Association
(At the state bar site [*www.calbar.ca.gov*], type the name of this bar association in the search box.)

MARTINEZ
Contra Costa County Bar Association
704 Main Street
Martinez, CA 94553
925-686-6900
www.cccba.org

MERCED COUNTY
Merced County Bar Association
(At the state bar site [*www.calbar.ca.gov*], type the name of this bar association in the search box.)

MODESTO
Stanislaus County Bar Association
914 13th St.
Modesto, CA 95354
209-571-5729
stanbar.org

MONO COUNTY
Mono County Bar Association
(At the state bar site [*www.calbar.ca.gov*], type the name of this bar association in the search box.)

MONTEREY COUNTY
Monterey County Bar Association
831-663-6955
www.montereycountybar.org

NORWALK
Southeast District Bar Association
12749 Norwalk Blvd., Ste 107
Norwalk, CA 90650
562-868-6787; 888-861-4LAW
www.sedistrictbarassoc.com

OAKLAND
Alameda County Bar Association
610 16th Street Ste 426
Oakland, CA 94612
510-893-7160
www.acbanet.org

Charles Houston Bar Association
(African-American lawyers)
P.O. Box 1474
Oakland, CA 94604
415-289-7004
www.charleshoustonbar.org

ORANGE
Orange County Women Lawyers Association
www.ocwla.org

ORANGE COUNTY
See Corona del Mar, Irvine, Laguna Hills, Orange

PALO ALTO
Palo Alto Area Bar Association
405 Sherman Ave.
Palo Alto, CA 94306
650-326-8322
www.paaba.org

PASADENA
Pasadena Bar Association
301 E. Colorado Blvd.
Pasadena, CA 91101
626-793-1422
www.pasadenabar.org

PLACER COUNTY
See Auburn

PLACERVILLE
El Dorado County Bar Association
www.edcbarassn.com

REDWOOD CITY
San Mateo County Bar Association
303 Bradford St., Ste B
Redwood City, CA 94063
650-298-4030
www.smcba.org

RIVERSIDE
Riverside County Bar Association
4129 Main St., Ste 100
Riverside, CA 92501
951-682-1015
www.riversidecountybar.com

Inland Empire Latino Lawyers Association
951-369-6211
www.iellaaid.org

Southwest Riverside County Bar Association
www.swrbar.org

SACRAMENTO
La Raza Lawyers of Sacramento
www.larazalawyers.biz/main.htm

Northern California Workers' Compensation Defense Attorneys' Association
www.cwcdaa.org

Sacramento County Bar Association
901 H St., Ste 101
Sacramento, CA 95814
916-448-1087
www.sacbar.org

Sacramento Lawyers for the Equality of Gays and Lesbians
www.geocities.com/WestHollywood/Park/3103

Wiley Manuel Bar Association
Sacramento Association of Black Attorneys
us.geocities.com/wiley_manuel/index.html
wileymanuelbarassociation@webtv.net

Women Lawyers of Sacramento
www.womenlawyers-sacramento.org

SAN BENITO COUNTY
See Hollister

SAN BERNADINO
Inland Empire Latino Lawyers Association
www.iellaaid.org

San Bernardino County Bar Association
555 North Arrowhead
San Bernardino, CA 92401
909-885-1986
www.sbcba.org

Western San Bernardino County Bar Association
www.wsbcba.org

SAN DIEGO
Appellate Defenders
www.adi-sandiego.com

Bar Association of Northern San Diego County (Vista)
www.bansdc.org/public/contact_us.html

Consumer Attorneys of San Diego
www.casd.org

Earl B. Gilliam Bar Association of San Diego
(African-American Attorneys)
www.sdcba.org/lawrelated.html
(Scroll down to this association.)
Foothills Bar Association of San Diego County
www.foothillsbar.org

La Jolla Bar Association
858-454-1839
www.lajollabarassociation.com

Lawyer's Club of San Diego
701 B St.
San Diego, CA 92101
619-595-0650
lawyersclubsandiego.com

North County Bar Association
www.bansdc.org

Pan Asian Lawyers of San Diego
(At the state bar site [*www.calbar.ca.gov*], type the name of this bar association in the search box.)

San Diego Barristers Club
www.sdcba.org/lawrelated.html
(Scroll down to this association.)

San Diego County Bar Association
1333 Seventh Avenue
San Diego, CA 92101
619-231-0781
www.sdcba.org
("Welcome Job Seekers" "Search job listings for attorneys and support staff")

San Diego Defense Lawyers
www.sddl.org

San Diego Intellectual Property Law Association
www.sdipla.org

South Bay Bar Association (Chula Vista)
www.southbaybarassociation.com

Southern California Workers' Compensation Defense Attorneys' Association
www.cwcdaa.org

Tom Homann Law Association
(San Diego's Lesbian, Gay, Bisexual, and Transgender Association)
www.thla.org

SAN FERNANDO VALLEY
See Woodland Hills

SAN FRANCISCO
Asian American Bar Association of the Greater Bay Area
www.aaba-bay.com

Bay Area Lawyers for Individual Freedom
(Lesbians, Gay Men, Bisexuals, Transgender Persons)
415-865-5620
www.balif.org

Bar Association of San Francisco
465 California St., Ste 1100
San Francisco, CA 94104
415-982-1600
www.sfbar.org

Hellenic Law Society of Northern California
www.helleniclaw.org

Korean American Bar Association of Northern California
www.kabanc.org

Lawyer's Club of San Francisco
415-485-1654
www.lawyersclubsf.org

Queen's Bench Bar Association of the San Francisco Bay Area
("Women lawyers frustrated by the resistance of male lawyers")
www.queensbench.org

San Francisco La Raza Lawyers Association
www.larazalawyers.org

San Francisco Trial Lawyers Association
415-956-6401
www.sftla.org/sf

SAN JOAQUIN
See Stockton

SAN JOSE
La Raza Lawyers of California
www.larazalawyers.net

Santa Clara County Bar Association
4 North Second St., Ste 400
San Jose, CA 95113
408-287-2557
www.sccba.com

SAN LUIS OBISPO COUNTY
San Luis Obispo County Bar Association
PO Box 585
San Luis Obispo, CA 93406
805-541-5930
www.slobar.org

SAN MATEO
See Redwood City

SAN RAFAEL
Marin County Bar Association
30 North San Pedro Rd., Ste 140
San Rafael, CA 94903
415-499-1314
www.marinbar.org

SANTA BARBARA
Barristers Club of Santa Barbara
www.sblaw.org/pages/Barristers.html

Santa Barbara County Bar Association
123 West Padre St., Ste E
Santa Barbara, CA 93105
805-569-5511
www.sblaw.org

Santa Barbara Women Lawyers
www.sbwl.org

SANTA CLARA
See Cupertino, Palo Alto, San Jose, Sunnyvale

SANTA CRUZ
Santa Cruz County Bar Association
340 Soquel Ave., Ste 209
Santa Cruz, CA 95062
831-423-5031
www.santacruzbar.org

Women Lawyers of Santa Cruz County
www.wlscc.org
(Membership rates for paralegals: $15)

SANTA MONICA
See Los Angeles

SANTA ROSA
Sonoma County Bar Association
37 Old Courthouse Sq.
Santa Rosa, CA 95404
707-542-1190
www.sonomacountybar.org

SANTA YNEZ VALLEY
Santa Ynez Valley Bar Association
(At the state bar site [*www.calbar.ca.gov*], type the name of this bar association in the search box.)

SOLANO COUNTY
See Fairfield

SONOMA COUNTY
See Santa Rosa

STANISLAUS COUNTY
See Modesto

STOCKTON
San Joaquin County Bar Association
6 S. El Dorado St., Ste 504
Stockton, CA 95202
209-948-0125
www.sjcbar.org

SUNNYVALE
Sunnyvale-Cupertino Bar Association
www.suncupbar.com

TAHOE
See Truckee

TRUCKEE
Tahoe-Truckee Bar Association
PO Box 2614
Truckee, CA 96160
530-584-1134
www.tahoetruckeebar.org

TULARE COUNTY
Tulare County Bar Association
(At the state bar site [*www.calbar.ca.gov*], type the name of this bar association in the search box.)

VENTURA
Ventura County Bar Association
4475 Market St., Ste B
Ventura, CA 93003
805-650-7599
www.vcba.org

Women Lawyers of Ventura County
www.wlvc.org

VISTA
North County Bar Association
PO Box 2381
Vista, CA 92085
760-758-5833
www.bansdc.org

WEST SACRAMENTO
See Woodland

WOODLAND
Yolo County Bar Association
PO Box 1903
Woodland, CA 95776
www.yolobar.com
(Dues for associate member/non-attorneys: $25)

WOODLAND HILLS
San Fernando Valley Bar Association
21300 Oxnard St. Ste 250
Woodland Hills, CA 91367
818-227-0490
www.sfvba.org

YOLO COUNTY
See Woodland

F. More Information

California Bar associations
www.abanet.org/barserv/map/ca2.html
california.lp.findlaw.com/ca03_associations/cabar.html
california.resourcesforattorneys.com/barassociations.html

Lawyer Referral Services
www.abanet.org/legalservices/lris/directory/
www.legal-aid.com/lawyer_referral_services.html

G. Something to Check

1. Which bar sites have the most comprehensive links to California law?
2. Which bar sites have the best information on the area of law in which you work or hope to work?
3. Find an online applications for a bar association or other attorney organization that has a membership category for paralegals or other nonattorneys.

APPENDIX A

Timeline: Disciplinary Proceedings against an Attorney

A. Introduction

In this section, we will outline the steps involved in bringing an ethics complaint against a California attorney for violating one or more of the ethical rules presented earlier in section 3.2. The most recent statistics (2005) on the 151,975 attorneys with active licenses are as follows:

Number of ethics complaints filed: 15,817
Number of these complaints investigated: 5,106
Number of attorneys charged after probable cause determination: 429
Number of private sanctions: 67
Number of public sanctions: 426
Number of disbarments: 57
Number of disbarments on consent: 68
Number of suspensions: 229
Number of probations: 176
Number of calls received by the attorney discipline hotline number (800-843-9053): over 100,000
Staff of disciplinary agency: attorneys (67), paralegals (41), investigators (57)
Average caseload per attorney: 52
Average time from receipt of formal complaint to filing of formal charges: 405 days
Average time from receipt of formal complaint to imposition of public sanction: 621 days

Source: ABA Center for Professional Responsibility, *Survey on Lawyer Discipline Systems* (2005) (*www.abanet.org/cpr/discipline/sold/home.html*).

The main participants in the disciplinary process are the Office of the Chief Trial Council (OCTC) and the State Bar Court (SBC).

Office of the Chief Trial Counsel (OCTC)

The OCTC receives, investigates, and prosecutes allegations of misconduct by California attorneys. There are three main disciplinary units within the OCTC: Intake, Investigations, and Trials.

State Bar of California Off. of Chief Trial Counsel 1149 South Hill St. Los Angeles, CA 90015-2299 800-843-9053 (hotline)	State Bar of California Off. of Chief Trial Counsel 555 Franklin St. San Francisco, CA 94102 800-843-9053

State Bar Court (SBC)

The SBC acts as the administrative arm of the California Supreme Court in the adjudication of disciplinary and regulatory matters involving California attorneys.

Hearing judges hear and make recommendations to the Supreme Court concerning attorney disciplinary cases filed by the State Bar's prosecutor, the Office of the Chief Trial Counsel, against California attorneys alleging violations of the State Bar Act and/or the Rules of Professional Conduct.

Hearing judges also hear and make recommendations to the Supreme Court about regulatory proceedings, such as moral character admissions matters, reinstatement petitions, arbitration enforcement proceedings, etc., that are filed in the State Bar Court.

State Bar Court 1149 South Hill St., 5th Floor Los Angeles, CA 90015 213-765-1400	State Bar Court 180 Howard St., 6th Floor San Francisco, CA 94105 415-538-2050

B. Definitions

Admonition

A written non-disciplinary reprimand issued by the Office of the Chief Trial Counsel or by the State Bar Court.

Complaint

A communication found by the Office of the Chief Trial Counsel to warrant an investigation of alleged misconduct of a State Bar member which, if the allegations are proven, may result in discipline of the member.

Complaint Held

A complaint for which a Statement of the Case (the investigator's report) has been completed, reviewed, and approved and which is being held pending receipt of remaining Statements of the Case on the same respondent.

Complaint Open

A complaint being worked on.

Disbarment

A disciplinary action that prohibits an attorney from practicing law in the state. The attorney's name is stricken from the Roll of California Attorneys.

Dismissal

A proceeding closed by the Office of the Chief Trial Counsel or the State Bar Court for a specific reason, such as no merit or insufficient evidence.

Inquiry

A communication concerning the conduct of a member of the State Bar received by the Office of the Chief Trial Counsel that is designated for evaluation to determine if additional action is warranted.

Involuntary Inactive Enrollment

The transfer of an attorney to inactive status (1) after the attorney is judged to present a substantial threat of harm to clients or the public, or (2) after the attorney is judged to be unable to practice without danger to clients or the public because of a disability, or (3) for other reasons allowed by state law. An attorney on inactive status cannot practice law.

Notice of Discipline Charges

A document filed in State Bar Court containing formal charges against a responder.

Private Reproval

A censure or reprimand issued by the Supreme Court or the State Bar Court that is not a matter of public record unless imposed after the initiation of formal disciplinary proceedings. The reproval may be imposed with duties or conditions.

Probation

A status whereby an attorney retains the legal ability to practice law subject to terms, conditions, and duties for a specified period of time.

Public Reproval

A censure or reprimand issued by the Supreme Court or the State Bar Court that is a matter of public record. The reproval may be imposed with duties or conditions.

Reinstatement

Readmission by the Supreme Court to the practice of law and to membership in the State Bar of a former member who resigned or was disbarred. The former member must demonstrate rehabilitation and present moral qualifications as well as ability and learning in the law.

Request for Further Proceedings

A request from a complaining witness after being advised that the inquiry or complaint has been dismissed or the respondent has been admonished.

Resignation Tendered with Charges Pending

A written relinquishment of the right to practice law and resignation as a member of the State Bar by a member against whom disciplinary charges are pending. Supreme Court acceptance of a resignation is required to make it effective, but as soon as a member submits a resignation in proper form, the member is transferred to inactive status and cannot practice law.

Resource Letter

A letter issued where there is a probable violation or a potential for a future violation of the Rules of Professional Conduct and/or the State Bar Act that is minimal in nature and would not lead to the discipline of the member. The member is referred to various resources that may assist him or her in avoiding future problems and/or the filing of complaints against the member in the future.

Statement of the Case

An investigator's written report of information and evidence submitted to an Office of the Chief Trial Counsel attorney for further action.

Stipulation

An agreement between the respondent and the Office of the Chief Trial Counsel regarding a statement of facts and/or disposition filed by the Office of the Chief Trial Counsel in the State Bar Court.

Suspension

A disciplinary action that prohibits an attorney from practicing law or from holding himself or herself out as a lawyer for a period of time set by the California Supreme Court.

Termination

A proceeding closed due to an external cause, such as death of respondent, disbarment in a separate matter, or resignation with charges pending.

Warning Letter

A letter issued when there is a probable violation of the Rules of Professional Conduct or the State Bar Act that is minimal in nature, does not involve significant harm to the client or the public, and does not involve a misappropriation of client funds.

Source: Glossary of Terms. © 2007 The State Bar of California. All Rights Reserved. (www.calbar.ca.gov/state/calbar/calbar_generic.jsp?cid=10136&id=1649). Reprinted with permission. No part of this work may be reproduced, stored in a retrieval system, or transmitted in any medium without prior written permission of The State Bar of California.

C. Timeline

1. Filing a complaint with Intake Unit

A client—or any consumer—begins the complaint process by filing a complaint with the Intake Unit of the Office of Chief Trial Counsel in Los Angeles. This usually occurs after a call is made to its hotline number (800-843-9053). Attorneys in the Intake Unit make an initial evaluation of whether there has been a violation of the State Bar Act or of the California Rules of Professional Conduct. If an inquiry alleges a serious violation, the inquiry is forwarded to the Investigations Unit.

See Exhibit A for a copy of the complaint form.

2. Investigations Unit investigates

The Investigations Unit investigates matters forwarded from the Intake Unit. The attorney being accused is given the opportunity to respond. The investigator contacts witnesses and examines the relevant documents involved. In less serious cases, the matter may be referred to mandatory mediation or an agreement might be reached with the attorney that he or she meet designated conditions.

3. Notice of Disciplinary Charges filed in State Bar Court

If the case is not dismissed or diverted (e.g., to mediation), a Notice of Disciplinary Charges is filed in State Bar Court and the case is assigned to a hearing judge. To avoid a default judgment, the accused attorney must file an answer. Once disciplinary charges are filed in State Bar Court, the complaint becomes public.

EXHIBIT A Complaint Form Against Attorneys

THE STATE BAR OF CALIFORNIA
CALIFORNIA ATTORNEY COMPLAINT FORM
Read instructions before filling in this form.

Date ____________

(1) Your name and address ____

(2) Telephone number: Home ________________ Work ________________

(3) The name, address and telephone number of the attorney(s) you are complaining about.*(See note below.)*

____

(4) Have you or a member of your family complained about this attorney(s) previously?
Yes ___ No ___ If Yes, please state to whom the previous complaint was made, its approximate date and disposition.

____

(5) Did you employ the attorney? Answer **Yes** or **No** and, if "**Yes**," give the approximate date you employed the attorney(s) and the amount, if any, paid to the attorney(s).

____

(6) If your answer to #5 above is "**No**," what is your connection with the attorney(s)? Explain briefly.

____

(7) Include with this form *(on a separate piece of paper)* a statement of what the attorney(s) did or did not do which is the basis of your complaint. Please state the facts as you understand them. Do not include opinions or arguments. If you employed the attorney(s), state what you employed the attorney(s) to do. Sign and date each separate piece of paper. Additional information may be requested. *(Attach copies of pertinent documents such as a copy of the fee agreement, cancelled checks or receipts and relevant correspondence.)*

(8) If your complaint is about a law suit, answer the following, if known:
a. Name of court *(For example, Superior Court, and name of the county)*

____

b. Title of the suit *(For example, Smith v. Jones).*

____

c. Case number of the suit

____

d. Approximate date the suit was filed

____

e. If you are not a party to this suit, what is your connection with it? Explain briefly.

____

(9) Size of law firm complained about: 1 Attorney ___ 2 – 10 Attorneys ___ 11 + Attorneys ___
Government Attorney ___ Unknown ___

NOTE: *If you are complaining about more than one attorney, include the information requested in items #3 through #8. Use separate sheets if necessary.*

Signature ________

Mail to:

Office of the Chief Trial Counsel/Intake
The State Bar of California
1149 South Hill Street
Los Angeles, California 90015-2299

Source: Complaint Form. © 2007 The State Bar of California. All Rights Reserved (www.calbar.ca.gov/calbar/pdfs/DispComp.pdf). Reprinted with permission. No part of this work may be reproduced, stored in a retrieval system, or transmitted in any medium without prior written permission of The State Bar of California.

Prior to that time, inquiries and investigations by the state bar are confidential.

4. Status Conference

A status conference consists of a meeting of all the parties. It is scheduled by clerks in the State Bar Court. The conference may lead to a settlement conference or a trial date.

5. Trial in State Bar Court

If there is no settlement, the hearing judge at the State Bar Court conducts a trial (either in Los Angeles or San Francisco), leading to a written opinion. In cases involving possible disbarment or suspension, the State Bar Court makes findings of fact, conclusions of law, and a recommendation for discipline that is submitted to the California Supreme Court where the final decision is made.

6. Appeal to State Bar Court's Review Department

The appellate level or department of the State Bar Court is the Review Department, which sits in three-judge panels. Either side can appeal a decision of the State Bar Court to the Review Department. The Department may make its recommendations to the California Supreme Court.

The full text of the published opinions of the Review Department are contained in *The California State Bar Court Reporter.*

7. California Supreme Court Makes Final Decision

The final decision on attorney discipline is made by the California Supreme Court.

D. Client Security Fund

The Client Security Fund can reimburse up to $50,000 for theft (or its equivalent) committed by a California lawyer. It does not cover losses due to attorney incompetence or malpractice. The loss must be caused by dishonesty such as borrowing money from a client with no intention to repay or refusing to refund unearned attorney fees paid in advance to an attorney who performed no services whatever. (For the statute on this fund, see section 3.2, which contains excerpts from § 6140.5 of the Business and Professions Code.)

Client Security Fund
1149 S. Hill Street
Los Angeles, CA 90015-2299
213-765-1140

E. Grading the California Disciplinary System

HALT—An organization of Americans for Legal Reform (*www.halt.org*)—grades the disciplinary system of every state by issuing its Lawyer Discipline Report Card. The 2006 grade it gave California was "D+." (See Exhibit B.) HALT gave California a grade of "C" in 2002.

Here is an explanation of HALT's grading system (the number in brackets after each category is the percent of the overall grade comprised of that category):

Adequacy of Discipline Imposed [35%]

What percentage of grievances does the agency investigate?
A = 90% or more B = 75–89% C = 50–74%
D = 20–49% F = less than 20%
What percentage of investigations result in public sanctions and what percentage leads to private sanctions?
A = 33% or more B = 25–32% C = 15–24%
D = 5–14% F = less than 5%

EXHIBIT B **Grading the California Disciplinary System**

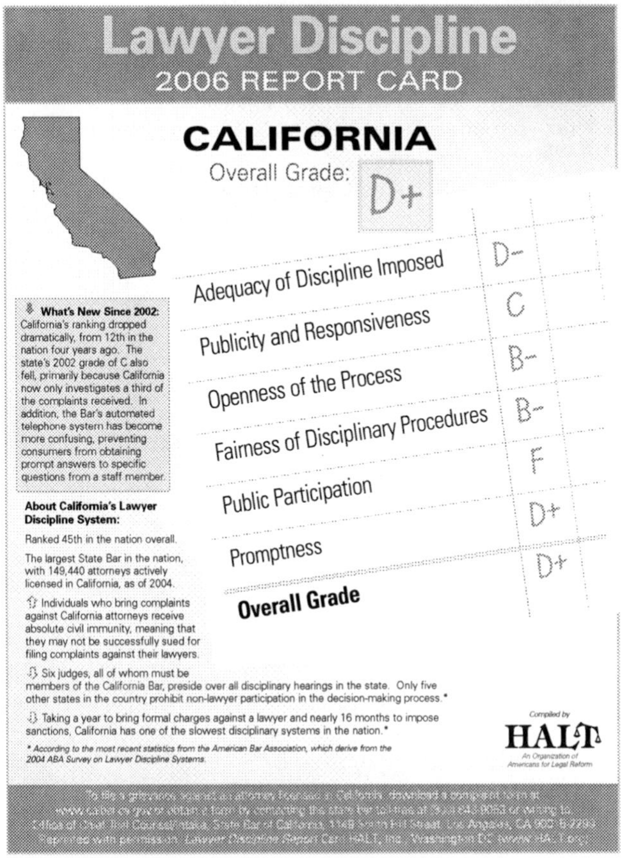
Lawyer Discipline
2006 REPORT CARD

CALIFORNIA
Overall Grade: D+

Adequacy of Discipline Imposed	D-
Publicity and Responsiveness	C
Openness of the Process	B-
Fairness of Disciplinary Procedures	B-
Public Participation	F
Promptness	D+
Overall Grade	D+

What's New Since 2002: California's ranking dropped dramatically, from 12th in the nation four years ago. The state's 2002 grade of C also fell, primarily because California now only investigates a third of the complaints received. In addition, the Bar's automated telephone system has become more confusing, preventing consumers from obtaining prompt answers to specific questions from a staff member.

About California's Lawyer Discipline System:

Ranked 45th in the nation overall.

The largest State Bar in the nation, with 149,440 attorneys actively licensed in California, as of 2004.

Individuals who bring complaints against California attorneys receive absolute civil immunity, meaning that they may not be successfully sued for filing complaints against their lawyers.

Six judges, all of whom must be members of the California Bar, preside over all disciplinary hearings in the state. Only five other states in the country prohibit non-lawyer participation in the decision-making process.*

Taking a year to bring formal charges against a lawyer and nearly 16 months to impose sanctions, California has one of the slowest disciplinary systems in the nation.*

** According to the most recent statistics from the American Bar Association, which derive from the 2004 ABA Survey on Lawyer Discipline Systems.*

Compiled by HALT An Organization of Americans for Legal Reform

Source: www.halt.org/reform_projects/lawyer_accountability/report_card_2006/pdf/CA_LDRC_06.pdf

Publicity and Responsiveness [15%]

Does the disciplinary agency publicize itself sufficiently?
A = advertises in yellow pages, in at least one local newspaper, through flyers in courthouses, and on the Internet
B = 3 of the above C = 2 of the above D = 1 of the above
F = does not advertise its services to the public
Does the agency meet HALT's criteria for a comprehensive, clear, and consumer-friendly Web site and telephone system?
A = at least 95% of criteria
B = 85% C = 75% D = 65% or less
F = no Web site, no telephone system or no brochure

Openness of the Process [15%]

Can a grievant attend hearings?
A = yes C = not unless a witness F = never
Can the general public attend hearings?
A = yes C = only if case reaches public sanctions stage
F = never
Where does the agency publish names of publicly sanctioned lawyers?
A = agency's Web site ***and*** at least one local newspaper
B = agency's Web site ***or*** at least one local newspaper
C = only in publications distributed to lawyers
D = only in the agency's annual report
F = nowhere

Can a consumer find out whether a grievance has ever been filed against her attorney?
A = yes—information about a grievance can be provided
B = no—but information is available once the case reaches the formal charges stage
C = no—but information is available once the case reaches the informal or formal sanctions stage
D = no—but information is available once the case reaches the formal sanctions stage
F = no—information about a disciplinary case may be released

Fairness of Disciplinary Procedures [15%]

Does the state have a "gag rule"?
A = no
C = yes, the agency requests that individuals keep their grievances confidential
F = yes, grievants will be held in contempt of court if they speak about grievance
Are grievants granted civil immunity?
A = yes C = qualified immunity F = no
What is the standard of proof in discipline hearings?
A = "preponderance of the evidence" or its equivalent
C = "clear and convincing evidence" or its equivalent
F = "beyond a reasonable doubt"

Public Participation [15%]

What percentage of nonlawyers serves on hearing panels?
A = majority nonlawyers B = 50% nonlawyers
C = 33–49% nonlawyers D = less than 33% nonlawyers
F = no nonlawyers

Promptness [5%]

On average, how long does it take before the agency brings formal charges against an attorney?
A = less than 3 months B = 3–5 months
C = 6–8 months D = 9 months–1 year
F = more than 1 year
On average, how long does it take before the agency imposes sanctions on an attorney?
A = less than 6 months B = 6 months–1 year
C = 1 year–1-1/2 years D = 1-1/2 years–2 years
F = more than 2 years

F. More Information

Overview
www.calbar.ca.gov/state/calbar/calbar_generic.jsp?cid=10136
www.calbar.ca.gov/calbar/pdfs/whowhat1.pdf
www.calbar.ca.gov/calbar/pdfs/DispComp.pdf

2004 Report on the State Bar of California Discipline System
calbar.ca.gov/calbar/pdfs/reports/2004_Annual-Discipline-Report.pdf

History of Discipline Process
www.calbar.ca.gov/state/calbar/calbar_generic.jsp?cid=10136&id=1648

ABA Survey on Lawyer Disciplinary Systems
www.abanet.org/cpr/discipline/sold/home.html
www.abanet.org/cpr/discipline/sold/toc_2004.html

Client Security Fund
www.calbar.ca.gov/state/calbar/calbar_generic.jsp?cid=10486&id=1379

California Ethics Research Resources
www.ll.georgetown.edu/states/ethics/california.cfm

HALT's Report Card on California's Disciplinary Process
www.halt.org/reform_projects/lawyer_accountability
(click "2006 Report Card" and "CA")

www.halt.org/reform_projects/lawyer_accountability/report_card
(click "California" and "View")

G. Something to Check

Go to the opinions of the State Bar Court and summarize (briefly) one opinion of this court. To read the court's opinions:

- go to *www.calbar.ca.gov*
- click "State Bar Court"
- click "Forms, Opinions and Legal Research"
- click "Published Opinions"

PART

4

Legal System

4.1 Introduction to the State Government of California

A. Introduction

In this section, we present an overview of California state government. More detailed information about the major components of the government can be found in:

- Section 4.2 on state courts
- Section 4.4 on the state legislature
- Section 4.5 on administrative agencies in the executive branch
- Section 4.6 on county and city government

B. Overview

The California Constitution divides the powers of government into three branches: executive, legislative, and judicial. A major exception to this allocation is when the California Senate, which is part of the legislative branch, exerts judicial power by sitting as a court to try statewide-elected officers who have been impeached for misconduct in office.

Exhibit 4.1A presents an overview of the major units of the California state government.

Executive Branch

Governor

The supreme executive power of the state is vested in the governor, whose constitutional mandate is to "see that the law is faithfully executed" (Cal. Const. art. V, § 1). Any citizen of the United States 21 years of age or older, who has been a resident of the state for 5 years or more immediately preceding election is eligible for the office. The governor is elected by popular vote for a term of 4 years.

In addition to strictly executive functions, the governor has an important role in the state's legislative process. He or she submits to the legislature the annual budget and sets forth statements of the state government's anticipated revenues and expenses. The California Constitution defines specific responsibilities for the governor, including:

- duty as commander in chief of the state military establishment
- powers of executive and judicial appointments, and
- power to grant reprieves, commutations of sentence and pardons to those convicted in the courts of California.

All bills enacted by the legislature are subject to the governor's approval before becoming law. The governor has the power to veto bills, and this veto can be set aside only by a two-thirds vote of both the state Assembly and the state Senate. The governor may exercise selective veto powers over appropriation bills to reduce or eliminate any items of appropriation while approving other items covered in the same bill. This is commonly called the "line-item veto."

The cabinet implements the governor's policies. Members of the cabinet include: the secretary of food and agriculture; secretary of business, transportation and housing; secretary of environmental protection; finance director; secretary of health and human services; director of industrial relations; resources secretary; secretary of state and consumer services; secretary of trade and commerce; and the secretary of youth and adult corrections. A complete list will be presented below in Exhibit 4.1B.

By law the governor is responsible for approximately 6,000 appointments, including candidates for the courts.

The governor's office has extensive intergovernmental relations with the state's 58 counties and 775 cities on a wide variety of issues, including state funding for local government, transportation, housing, health, social services, environmental, land use, and employment issues.

EXHIBIT 4.1A Overview of the California State Government

EXECUTIVE BRANCH Statewide Elected Offices	LEGISLATIVE BRANCH	JUDICIAL BRANCH
Governor Lieutenant Governor Attorney General Secretary of State Insurance Commissioner State Treasurer State Controller State Superintendent of Public Instruction State Board of Equalization	State Senate State Assembly Committees, e.g., Senate Judiciary Committee Office of the Legislative Counsel Legislative Analyst's Office	California Supreme Court California Courts of Appeals California Superior Courts

Contacting the Governor

State Capitol Building
Sacramento, CA 95814
916-445-2841
www.governor.ca.gov/state/govsite/gov_homepage.jsp
www.govmail.ca.gov

District Offices

Fresno
559-445-5295

Los Angeles
213-897-0322

Riverside
951-680-6860

San Diego
619-525-4641

San Francisco
415-703-2218

Other Statewide-Elected Offices

Lieutenant Governor
916-445-8994
www.ltg.ca.gov

The lieutenant governor assumes the office of the governor when the governor is absent from the state or unable to perform the duties of the office. As president of the state Senate, the lieutenant governor can preside over the business of the Senate, and in the event of a tie must cast the deciding vote.

Attorney General
800-952-5225
www.ag.ca.gov

The attorney general serves as the chief law officer of the state whose duty is to see that the laws of the state are uniformly and adequately enforced (Cal. Const. art. V, § 13). The attorney general serves as legal counsel to state officers and many state agencies, boards, and commissions.

Secretary of State
916-653-6814
www.ss.ca.gov

The secretary of state serves as the state's chief election officer. He or she charters corporations; commissions notaries public; and oversees the filing of documents such as Uniform Commercial Code financing and tax lien information, certificates of limited partnership, and limited liability companies.

Insurance Commissioner
800-927-4357
www.insurance.ca.gov

The insurance commissioner regulates, investigates, and audits the insurance industry so that companies remain solvent and meet their obligations to insurers.

State Treasurer
916-653-2995
www.treasurer.ca.gov

The state treasurer serves as the state's lead asset manager, banker, and financier. He or she manages the state's pooled money investment account.

State Controller
916-445-2636
www.sco.ca.gov

The state controller serves as the state's chief financial officer, exerting fiscal control over receipts and disbursements of public funds.

State Superintendent of Public Instruction
916-319-0791
www.cde.ca.gov/eo

The state superintendent of public instruction oversees the state public school system.

State Board of Equalization
800-400-7115
www.boe.ca.gov/info/about.htm

The State Board of Equalization ensures equity and uniformity in county property assessments. It also acts as the appellate body for franchise and income tax appeals.

State Agencies, Departments, and Commissions

For a list of the major state agencies, departments, and commissions, see section 4.5 and Exhibit 4.1B.

Legislative Branch

Under the California Constitution, the "legislative power of this State is vested in the California Legislature which consists of the Senate and Assembly, but the people reserve to themselves the powers of initiative and referendum." (Cal. Const. art. IV, § 1). Legislators are elected by district: one senator in each of the forty Senate districts and one member of the Assembly of each of the eighty Assembly districts. (See section 4.4 on how a bill becomes a law.)

Major Units of the Legislature

Assembly
www.assembly.ca.gov/defaulttext.asp

Senate
www.sen.ca.gov

Committees

Assembly
www.assembly.ca.gov/acs/acsframeset8text.asp

Senate
www.senate.ca.gov/~newsen/committees/committees.htp

Office of the Legislative Counsel

www.leginfo.ca.gov/legcnsl.html

The Office of Legislative Counsel (OLC) drafts bills based on the ideas submitted to them by legislators. It also renders legal opinions, provides counsel to the members and committees of the legislature, and represents the legislature in litigation. In addition, it publishes the Legislative Index (which identifies legislative measures) and it compiles and indexes California statutes and codes. The legislative counsel is required by law to make legislative information available to the public on the Internet.

Legislative Analyst's Office

www.lao.ca.gov

The Legislative Analyst's Office (LAO) provides fiscal and policy advice to the legislature and conducts nonpartisan analyses of the state's budget. LAO acts as the "eyes and ears" for the legislature to ensure that the

EXHIBIT 4.1B California State Government: The Executive Branch

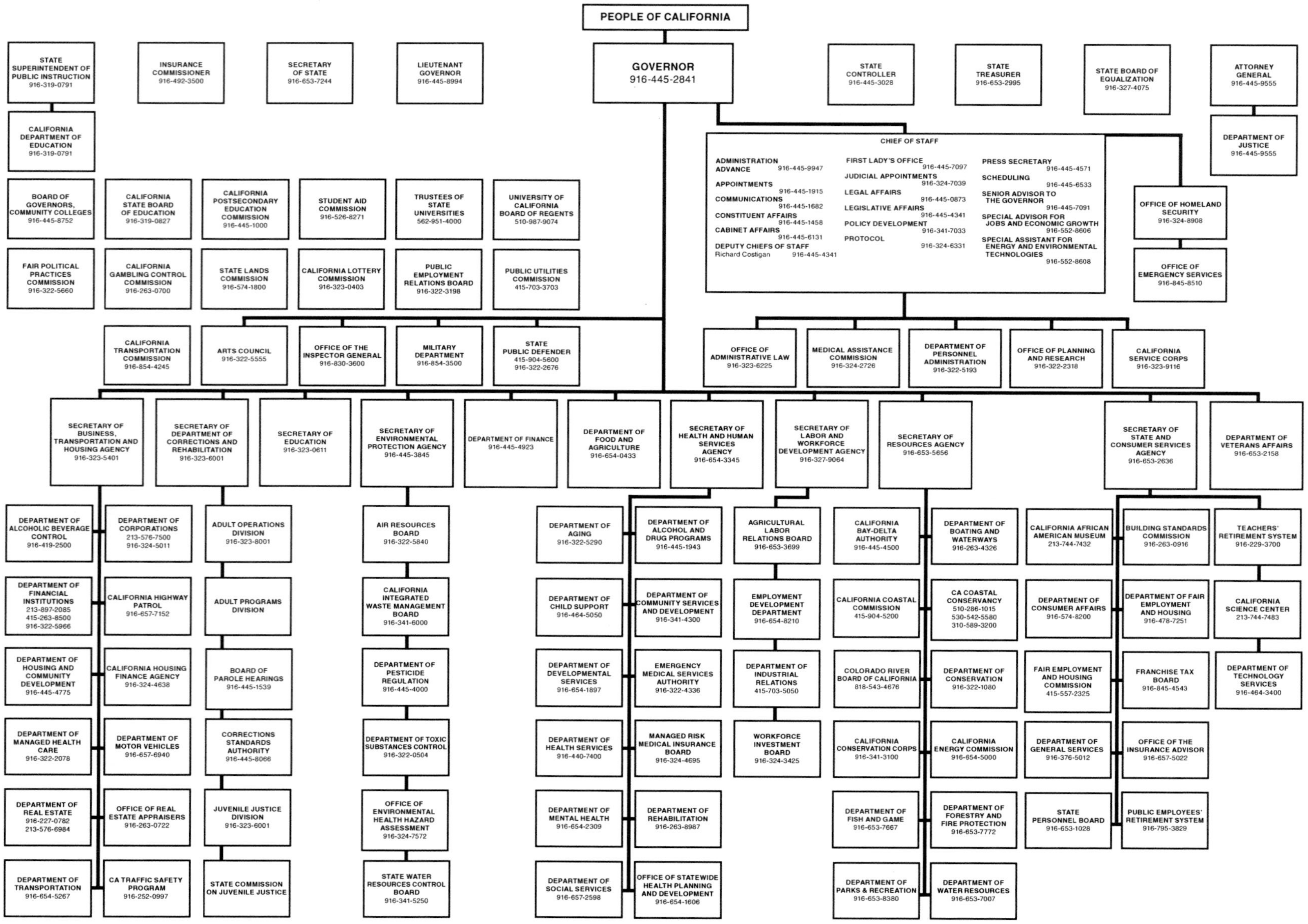

Source: www.cold.ca.gov/Ca_State_Gov_Orgchart.pdf

executive branch is implementing legislative policy in a cost efficient and effective manner. This is done by reviewing and analyzing the operations and finances of state government.

Office of State Publishing

www.osp.dgs.ca.gov/default.htm

The Office of State Publishing prints many of the documents prepared by the legislature in the legislative process.

Judicial Branch

Under the California Constitution, the "judicial power of this State is vested in the Supreme Court, courts of appeal, and superior courts, all of which are courts of record." (Cal. Const. art. VI, § 1).

California Supreme Court

Supreme Court
415-865-7000
www.courtinfo.ca.gov/courts/supreme

California Courts of Appeal

First Appellate District
415-865-7300
www.courtinfo.ca.gov/courts/courtsofappeal/1stDistrict

Second Appellate District
213-830-7000; 805-641-4700
www.courtinfo.ca.gov/courts/courtsofappeal/2ndDistrict

Third Appellate District
916-654-0209
www.courtinfo.ca.gov/courts/courtsofappeal/3rdDistrict

Fourth Appellate District
619-645-2760
www.courtinfo.ca.gov/courts/courtsofappeal/4thDistrictDiv1

Fifth Appellate District
559-445-5491
www.courtinfo.ca.gov/courts/courtsofappeal/5thDistrict

Sixth Appellate District
408-277-1004
www.courtinfo.ca.gov/courts/courtsofappeal/6thDistrict

California Superior Courts

Web sites and phone numbers of all superior courts
www.courtinfo.ca.gov/courts/trial/courtlist.htm

For details on the jurisdiction and lines of appeal among these courts, see section 4.2.

C. More Information

State Government Overview
capitolmuseum.ca.gov
boxer.senate.gov/calLinks/state.cfm

State Government Homepage
www.ca.gov/state/portal/myca_homepage.jsp
(click "Government")

Online State Government Phone Directory
www.cold.ca.gov

Legislative Process
www.leginfo.ca.gov/guide.html#Appendix_A
leginfo.public.ca.gov/pdf/caleg9.pdf

State Constitution
www.leginfo.ca.gov/const.html

State, Local, and Tribal Governments
www.usa.gov
(click links under "By Organization")

D. Something to Check

1. Use the online recourses in this section to determine the current state government deficit in California.
2. Identify any problem that you think exists in your community. Use the online sites in this section to identify government entities or persons in the executive and legislative branches who would probably have the authority to solve or address this problem.

4.2 State Courts in California

A. Introduction

The major California state courts are as follows:

Supreme Court of California
California Courts of Appeal
Superior Courts of California

Exhibit 4.2A summarizes the jurisdiction and lines of appeal among these courts.

EXHIBIT 4.2A California State Court System

Supreme Court of California
(hears appeals as the highest court of review)

- 7 justices (they sit en banc rather than in panels)
- Hears oral arguments in San Francisco, Los Angeles, Sacramento, and in special sessions elsewhere

- Can decide which appeals to hear from the Courts of Appeal (discretionary jurisdiction)
- Must hear all death penalty appeals directly from the Superior Courts (mandatory jurisdiction)
- Also hears:
  - appeals directly from the Public Utilities Commission
  - recommendations from the State Bar on the discipline of attorneys
  - recommendations from the Commission on Judicial Performance on the discipline of judges

- Approximately 9,000 matters are filed each year in the Supreme Court

Courts of Appeal
(hears appeals as the intermediate courts of review)

- 105 justices (cases are decided by three-judge panels)
- 6 Courts of Appeal, one per appellate district:

1st District: San Francisco	4th District: San Diego
2d District: Los Angeles	5th District: Fresno
3d District: Sacramento	6th District: San Jose

- 19 Divisions (each appellate district has one or more divisions for a total of 19)

- The Court of Appeal in each appellate district hears appeals from decisions of the Superior Courts within its district
- A Court of Appeal does *not* hear death penalty decisions from Superior Courts; they go directly to the Supreme Court
- A Court of Appeal also hears appeals (writ proceedings) from decisions of the Workers' Compensation Appeals Board, the Agricultural Relations Appeals Board, and the Public Employment Relations Board

- Approximately 23,000 matters are filed each year in the six Courts of Appeal

Superior Courts
(conducts trials and hears limited appeals)

- 1500 judges; 437 commissioners and referees
- 58 Superior Courts (one in each county, some with multiple locations within a county)

- Superior Courts consist of two types of trial courts and one special appeals court:
  Trial:
  - *Small Claims Court* hears civil cases with claims up to $7,500 (no criminal cases)
  - *Superior Court:*
    - hears all criminal cases involving misdemeanors and felonies
    - hears all limited jurisdiction cases (those involving claims of $25,000 or less)
    - hears all unlimited jurisdiction cases (those involving claims of over $25,000)

  Appeals:
  - *Superior Court Appellate Department* consists of a panel of three Superior Court judges.
    This Department:
    - hears appears of *limited jurisdiction* cases. (*unlimited jurisdiction* cases are appealed directly to one of the six Courts of Appeal)
    - hears appeals of criminal cases involving misdemeanors (felony cases are appealed directly to one of the six Courts of Appeal)
    - A single Superior Court judge hears appeals of Small Claims Court cases

- Approximately 9,000,000 matters are filed each year in the 58 Superior Courts

State Bar Court

In addition, the State Bar Court acts as the administrative arm of the California Supreme Court in the adjudication of disciplinary and regulatory matters involving California attorneys. The State Bar Court is examined in Appendix A of Part 3.

B. California State Courts

Supreme Court of California

There are seven justices on the California Supreme Court, one chief justice and six associate justices. They are appointed by the governor and confirmed by the Commission on Judicial Appointments. The appointments are confirmed by the public at the next general election. At the end of a 12-year term, the voters must decide whether a justice should remain on the court.

Supreme Court of California
350 McAllister Street
San Francisco, CA 94102
415-865-7000

Los Angeles Branch
(213-830-7570)

Sacramento Branch
(916-322-5957)

Supreme Court: Web Site
www.courtinfo.ca.gov/courts/supreme

Supreme Court: Subject Matter Jurisdiction
See Exhibit 4.2A

Supreme Court: Court Rules
www.courtinfo.ca.gov/rules
www.courtinfo.ca.gov/rules/intro

Supreme Court: Biographies of Justices
www.courtinfo.ca.gov/courts/supreme/justices.htm

Supreme Court: Calendar
www.courtinfo.ca.gov/courts/supreme/recent.htm
www.courtinfo.ca.gov/cgi-bin/calendars.cgi
appellatecases.courtinfo.ca.gov

Supreme Court: Practices and Procedures
www.courtinfo.ca.gov/courts/supreme/iopp.htm

Supreme Court: Opinions
(see the research chart in section 5.1)
www.courtinfo.ca.gov/cgi-bin/opinions.cgi
www.courtinfo.ca.gov/opinions
www.findlaw.com/cacases

Supreme Court: Overview
www.courtinfo.ca.gov/courts/supreme/documents/supreme 2003-1.pdf

Supreme Court: Obtaining Copies of Appellate Briefs

Four law libraries in California serve as depositories for appellate briefs filed in the Supreme Court and the Courts of Appeal. You need to contact each library to determine which briefs it has. The libraries are

California State Library (Sacramento)
Witkin State Law Library
www.library.ca.gov
www.library.ca.gov/html/collections.cfm#law
916-654-0185

Bernard E. Witkin Law Library (Oakland)
www.co.alameda.ca.us/law/index.htm
510-208-4800

Los Angeles County Law Library
www.lalaw.lib.ca.us
213-629-3531

San Diego County Public Law Library
www.sdcll.org
619-531-3900

California Courts of Appeal

The middle appeals or intermediate appellate court in California is the Court of Appeal. The state is geographically divided into six appellate districts, each containing a Court of Appeal. There are 105 justices apportioned among the six districts headquartered in San Francisco, Los Angeles, Sacramento, San Diego, Fresno, and San Jose. The rules governing the selection of Supreme Court justices apply to those serving on the Courts of Appeal. Justices are appointed by the governor and confirmed by the Commission on Judicial Appointments. They must then be confirmed by the voters at the next general election.

First Appellate District

California Court of Appeal
First Appellate District
350 McAllister Street
San Francisco, CA 94102
415-865-7300

First Appellate District: Web Site
www.courtinfo.ca.gov/courts/courtsofappeal/1stDistrict

First Appellate District: Subject Matter Jurisdiction
See Exhibit 4.2A

First Appellate District: Court Rules
www.courtinfo.ca.gov/courts/courtsofappeal/1stDistrict/localrules.htm

First Appellate District: Biographies of Justices
www.courtinfo.ca.gov/courts/courtsofappeal/1stDistrict/justices.htm

First Appellate District: Court Calendar and Case Information
appellatecases.courtinfo.ca.gov/calendar.cfm?dist=1
appellatecases.courtinfo.ca.gov/search.cfm?dist=1
www.courtinfo.ca.gov/cgi-bin/calendars.cgi

First Appellate District: Procedures
www.courtinfo.ca.gov/courts/courtsofappeal/1stDistrict/iopp.htm

First Appellate District: Court Forms
www.courtinfo.ca.gov/courts/courtsofappeal/1stDistrict/forms.htm

First Appellate District: Opinions
(see the research chart in section 5.1)
www.courtinfo.ca.gov/cgi-bin/opinions.cgi
www.courtinfo.ca.gov/opinions
www.findlaw.com/cacases

First Appellate District: Obtaining Copies of Appellate Briefs
www.courtinfo.ca.gov/qna/qa24.htm

Second Appellate District

California Court of Appeal Second Appellate District 300 South Spring Street Los Angeles, CA 90013 213-830-7000 (Divisions 1–5 and 7–8)	California Court of Appeal Second Appellate District 200 East Santa Clara Street Ventura, CA 93001 805-641-4700 (Division 6)

Second Appellate District: Web Site
www.courtinfo.ca.gov/courts/courtsofappeal/2ndDistrict

Second Appellate District: Subject Matter Jurisdiction
See Exhibit 4.2A

Second Appellate District: Court Rules
www.courtinfo.ca.gov/courts/courtsofappeal/2ndDistrict/localrules.htm

Second Appellate District: Biographies of Justices
www.courtinfo.ca.gov/courts/courtsofappeal/2ndDistrict/justices.htm

Second Appellate District: Court Calendar and Case Information
appellatecases.courtinfo.ca.gov/calendar.cfm?dist=2
appellatecases.courtinfo.ca.gov/search.cfm?dist=2
www.courtinfo.ca.gov/cgi-bin/calendars.cgi

Second Appellate District: Procedures
www.courtinfo.ca.gov/courts/courtsofappeal/2ndDistrict/iopp.htm

Second Appellate District: Forms
www.courtinfo.ca.gov/courts/courtsofappeal/2ndDistrict/forms.htm

Second Appellate District: Opinions
(see the research chart in section 5.1)
www.courtinfo.ca.gov/cgi-bin/opinions.cgi
www.courtinfo.ca.gov/opinions
www.findlaw.com/cacases

Second Appellate District: Electronic Filing
www.courtinfo.ca.gov/courts/courtsofappeal/2ndDistrict/efile.htm

Second Appellate District: Obtaining Copies of Appellate Briefs
www.courtinfo.ca.gov/qna/qa24.htm

Second Appellate District: Basic Civil Appellate Practice in the Court of Appeal for the Second District
www.lacba.org/showpage.cfm?pageid=2730

Second Appellate District: Civil Appellate Practices and Procedures for the Self-Represented
www.courtinfo.ca.gov/courts/courtsofappeal/2ndDistrict/selfhelp_manual.htm

Third Appellate District

California Court of Appeal
Third Appellate District
900 N Street, Room 400
Sacramento, CA 95814
916-654-0209

Third Appellate District: Web Site
www.courtinfo.ca.gov/courts/courtsofappeal/3rdDistrict

Third Appellate District: Subject Matter Jurisdiction
See Exhibit 4.2A

Third Appellate District: Court Rules
www.courtinfo.ca.gov/courts/courtsofappeal/3rdDistrict/localrules.htm

Third Appellate District: Biographies of Justices
www.courtinfo.ca.gov/courts/courtsofappeal/3rdDistrict/justices.htm

Third Appellate District: Court Calendar and Ca se Information
appellatecases.courtinfo.ca.gov/calendar.cfm?dist=3
appellatecases.courtinfo.ca.gov/search.cfm?dist=3
www.courtinfo.ca.gov/cgi-bin/calendars.cgi

Third Appellate District: Procedures
www.courtinfo.ca.gov/courts/courtsofappeal/3rdDistrict/faq.htm

Third Appellate District: Court Forms
www.courtinfo.ca.gov/courts/courtsofappeal/3rdDistrict/forms.htm

Third Appellate District: Opinions
(see the research chart in section 5.1)
www.courtinfo.ca.gov/cgi-bin/opinions.cgi
www.courtinfo.ca.gov/opinions
www.findlaw.com/cacases
www.courtinfo.ca.gov/courts/courtsofappeal/3rdDistrict/opinions.htm

Third Appellate District: Obtaining Copies of Appellate Briefs
www.courtinfo.ca.gov/qna/qa24.htm

Fourth Appellate District

California Court of Appeal
Fourth Appellate District,
Division 1
750 B Street
San Diego, CA 92101
619-645-2760

California Court of Appeal
Fourth Appellate District,
Division 2
3389 Twelfth Street
Riverside, CA 92501
951-248-0200

California Court of Appeal
Fourth Appellate District,
Division 3
925 N. Spurgeon Street
Santa Ana, CA 92701
714-558-6777

Fourth Appellate District: Web Site
www.courtinfo.ca.gov/courts/courtsofappeal/4thDistrictDiv1
www.courtinfo.ca.gov/courts/courtsofappeal/4thDistrictDiv2
www.courtinfo.ca.gov/courts/courtsofappeal/4thDistrictDiv3

Fourth Appellate District: Subject Matter Jurisdiction
See Exhibit 4.2A

Fourth Appellate District: Court Rules
www.courtinfo.ca.gov/courts/courtsofappeal/4thDistrictDiv1/localrules.htm

Fourth Appellate District: Biographies of Justices
www.courtinfo.ca.gov/courts/courtsofappeal/4thDistrictDiv1/justices.htm

Fourth Appellate District: Case Information and Court Calendar
appellatecases.courtinfo.ca.gov
www.courtinfo.ca.gov/cgi-bin/calendars.cgi
www.courtinfo.ca.gov/courts/courtsofappeal/4thDistrictDiv1/calendars.htm

Fourth Appellate District: Procedures
www.courtinfo.ca.gov/courts/courtsofappeal/4thDistrictDiv1/iopp.htm

Fourth Appellate District: Court Forms
www.courtinfo.ca.gov/courts/courtsofappeal/4thDistrictDiv1/forms.htm

Fourth Appellate District: Opinions
(see the research chart in section 5.1)
www.courtinfo.ca.gov/cgi-bin/opinions.cgi
www.courtinfo.ca.gov/opinions
www.findlaw.com/cacases

Fourth Appellate District: Obtaining Copies of Appellate Briefs
www.courtinfo.ca.gov/qna/qa24.htm

Fifth Appellate District

California Court of Appeal
Fifth Appellate District
2525 Capitol Street
Fresno, CA 93721
559-445-5491

Fifth Appellate District: Web Site
www.courtinfo.ca.gov/courts/courtsofappeal/5thDistrict

Fifth Appellate District: Subject Matter Jurisdiction
See Exhibit 4.2A

Fifth Appellate District: Court Rules
www.courtinfo.ca.gov/courts/courtsofappeal/5thDistrict/localrules.htm

Fifth Appellate District: Biographies of Justices
www.courtinfo.ca.gov/courts/courtsofappeal/5thDistrict/justices.htm

Fifth Appellate District: Court Calendar and Case Information
www.courtinfo.ca.gov/cgi-bin/calendars.cgi?Courts=F
www.courtinfo.ca.gov/cgi-bin/calendars.cgi

Fifth Appellate District: Procedures
www.courtinfo.ca.gov/courts/courtsofappeal/5thDistrict/about.htm

Fifth Appellate District: Court Forms
www.courtinfo.ca.gov/courts/courtsofappeal/5thDistrict/forms.htm

Fifth Appellate District: Opinions
(see the research chart in section 5.1)
www.courtinfo.ca.gov/cgi-bin/opinions.cgi
www.courtinfo.ca.gov/opinions
www.findlaw.com/cacases

Fifth Appellate District: Obtaining Copies of Appellate Briefs
www.courtinfo.ca.gov/qna/qa24.htm

Fifth Appellate District: Self-Help Manual
www.courtinfo.ca.gov/courts/courtsofappeal/5thDistrict/5dca_proper.htm

Sixth Appellate District

California Court of Appeal
Sixth Appellate District
333 West Santa Clara Street
San Jose, CA 95113
408-277-1004

Sixth Appellate District: Web Site
www.courtinfo.ca.gov/courts/courtsofappeal/6thDistrict

Sixth Appellate District: Subject Matter Jurisdiction
See Exhibit 4.2A

Sixth Appellate District: Court Rules
www.courtinfo.ca.gov/courts/courtsofappeal/6thDistrict/localrules.htm

Sixth Appellate District: Biographies of Justices
www.courtinfo.ca.gov/courts/courtsofappeal/6thDistrict/justices.htm

Sixth Appellate District: Case Information
appellatecases.courtinfo.ca.gov

Sixth Appellate District: Procedures
www.courtinfo.ca.gov/courts/courtsofappeal/6thDistrict/iopp.htm

Sixth Appellate District: Court Forms
www.courtinfo.ca.gov/courts/courtsofappeal/6thDistrict/forms.htm

Sixth Appellate District: Opinions
(see the research chart in section 5.1)
www.courtinfo.ca.gov/cgi-bin/opinions.cgi
www.courtinfo.ca.gov/opinions
www.findlaw.com/cacases

Sixth Appellate District: Obtaining Copies of Appellate Briefs
www.courtinfo.ca.gov/qna/qa24.htm

Sixth Appellate District: Appellate Program
www.sdap.org

California Superior Courts

California has fifty-eight trial courts, the Superior Courts, one in each county at some 400 court locations throughout the state. In Superior Courts, trial judges resolve cases by hearing witnesses' testimony, examining physical evidence, and ruling on issues of law.

Appeals in limited civil cases (where $25,000 or less is at issue) and misdemeanors are heard by the Appellate Division of the Superior Court. When a small claims case is appealed, a superior court judge decides the case.

Superior Courts: Web Sites and Postal Addresses
www.courtinfo.ca.gov/courts/trial/courtlist.htm

Superior Courts: Subject Matter Jurisdiction
See Exhibit 4.2A

Superior Court: Court Rules
www.courtinfo.ca.gov/rules
(click "Local Rules")

Superior Court: Biographies of Justices
www.courtinfo.ca.gov/courts/trial
www.courtinfo.ca.gov/courts/trial/courtlist.htm
(click Web site of county court)

Superior Court: Court Forms
www.courtinfo.ca.gov/courts/trial/courtlist.htm
(click "forms")

Small Claims
www.courtinfo.ca.gov/selfhelp/smallclaims

Small Claims: Subject Matter Jurisdiction
See Exhibit 4.2A

Drug Court Project
www.courtinfo.ca.gov/programs/collab/drug.htm

C. More Information

Overview
www.scselfservice.org/home/overview.htm
www.courtinfo.ca.gov/courts/supreme/about.htm
www.courtinfo.ca.gov/courts/courtsofappeal
www.courtinfo.ca.gov/courts/trial

Court Statistics
www.courtinfo.ca.gov/reference/documents/csr2005.pdf

Court Employment
www.courtinfo.ca.gov/courts/trial/courtlist.htm
(click your county's Web site to find out if there is an employment link on the court's home page)
www.courtinfo.ca.gov/careers

D. Something to Check

1. Go to the sites that give you online access to court opinions of the California Supreme Court. Use the search features of the sites to find an opinion on any broad legal topic, e.g., capital punishment, adoption. Summarize what the opinion says about your topic.
2. Go to the Web sites of any three courts mentioned in this section. For the same general kind of litigant filing (e.g., a complaint, an amendment to a prior filing) state the filing fee in each of the three courts.
3. For one of the six Courts of Appeal, go to the biographies of the justices. Pick one justice. Identify a prior job of this justice that might indicate a possible conservative or liberal philosophy of deciding cases. Explain your answer.

4.3 Federal Courts in California

A. Introduction

There are a number of federal courts sitting in California:

United States Court of Appeals for the Ninth Circuit
United States District Courts
United States Bankruptcy Courts
Bankruptcy Appellate Panel
United States Immigration Courts

In this section, we will present an overview of these courts, how they operate, and the major recourses that are available when working with them.

B. Specific Federal Court Details

United States Court of Appeals for the Ninth Circuit

The United States is divided geographically into eleven numbered federal judicial circuits (also called regional circuits). Each circuit has a court of appeals, e.g., the United States Court of Appeals for the First Circuit, the United States Court of Appeals for the Second Circuit, etc. These federal courts of appeals are intermediate appellate courts just below the United States Supreme Court. In addition to the eleven numbered circuits, there are two other circuits: the District of Columbia Circuit and the Federal Circuit, both located in Washington D.C. (The Federal Circuit is a separate and unique court of appeals that has nationwide jurisdiction in specialized cases.)

Each of the fifty states (plus the territories of Guam, Puerto Rico, and the U.S. Virgin Islands) is assigned to one of the eleven numbered circuits. California (along with eight other western and pacific states) is in the ninth circuit. The court of appeals for our circuit is the United States Court of Appeals for the Ninth Circuit, sometimes abbreviated as CA9 or 9th Cir.

The United States Court of Appeals for the Ninth Circuit hears appeals (1) from the United States district courts in California and the other eight states in the circuit, and (2) from the United States Tax Court and from certain federal administrative agencies where the non-governmental parties are from one of the states that make up the Ninth Circuit. The other regional circuits do the same for their circuits. Decisions of the United States courts of appeals are final except as they are subject to review on writ of certiorari by the United States Supreme Court. Judges on the court of appeals have lifetime tenure; they are nominated by the president and confirmed by the U.S. Senate.

Mailing Address
U.S. Court of Appeals, Ninth Circuit
P.O. Box 193939
San Francisco, CA 94119-3939

Street Address (for express/overnight mailings)
U.S. Court of Appeals, Ninth Circuit
95 Seventh Street
San Francisco, CA 94103-1518

Phone
Main Clerk's office: 415-556-9800

Web Site
www.ca9.uscourts.gov
www.ca9.uscourts.gov/ca9/courtinfo.nsf/main/page

Branch Office in California
(authorized to accept limited emergency filings only)
Clerk, U.S. Court of Appeals
125 South Grand Avenue Pasadena, CA 91105-1652
626-229-7250

Opinions
www.ca9.uscourts.gov/ca9/newopinions.nsf/Opinions+by+date
www.findlaw.com/casecode/courts/9th.html
www.law.cornell.edu/federal/opinions.html

Names of Judges
www.ca9.uscourts.gov/ca9/Welcome.nsf/index?OpenPage

PACER Login
pacer.login.uscourts.gov/cgi-bin/login.pl?court_id=09ca
www.ca9.uscourts.gov/ca9/Welcome.nsf/index?OpenPage
800-676-6856

Calendar
www.ca9.uscourts.gov/ca9/Welcome.nsf/index?OpenPage
(click "List of 9th Circuit Judges")

Forms

To obtain court forms, call the clerk's office (415-556-9800). "The majority of the court's forms are also available on the Web site."

Rules
- Federal Rules of Appellate Procedure (FRAP)
- Rules of the United States Court of Appeals for the Ninth Circuit (Circuit Rules); these rules augment the FRAP
- FRAP and Circuit Rules online:
  www.ca9.uscourts.gov/ca9/Welcome.nsf/index?OpenPage
  www.ca9.uscourts.gov/ca9/Documents.nsf/FRAP+and+Circuit+Rules?OpenView
  www.access.gpo.gov/uscode/title28a/28a_3_.html
  judiciary.house.gov/media/pdfs/printers/108th/appel2004.pdf
- Also available by requesting copies from Clerk of Court and on fee-based sites (e.g., *www.westlaw.com*, *www.lexis.com*)

Common Fees
Petition for Review: $250.00
Writ of Mandamus: $250.00
Certification: $9.00
Opinions: $2.00
Attorney Admission: $190.00
Attorney Certificate of Good Standing: $15.00
Oral Argument Tapes: $26.00
General Orders: $5.00
Docket Sheets: $3.00

Briefs

Colors, Page/Word Limitations
- Blue for appellant, red for appellee, grey for reply, green for amicus and intervenor. The covers of the second and third briefs filed according to a cross appeal schedule are red.
- White cover for excerpts of record.
- The length of a principal brief may not exceed 30 pages or a reply brief 15 pages, unless it complies with FRAP 32(a)(7)(B) and (C), which limits the principal brief to 14,000 words of 14 point type, or if monospaced not more than 1,300 lines of text. Reply briefs may not contain more than half of the type volume specified above.

Copies Needed
Briefs: Original + 15 copies (7 copies for pro se parties)
Bill of Cost: Original + 1 copy
CADS: Original + 1 copy
Excerpts of Record: 5 copies
Motions: Original + 4 copies
Petition for Rehearing: Original + 3 copies
Petition for Rehearing En Banc: Original + 50
Petition for Review: Original + 7 copies
Request for Interlocutory Appeal (FRAP 5): Original + 4 copies
Writ of Mandamus: Original + 4 copies

(For a conformed copy, provide an extra copy of the document and a self-addressed stamped envelope.)

"Received" vs "Filed"

Received: A document is received when it arrives.

Filed: Once a document is received, it can be reviewed for appropriateness by the clerk; if all rule requirements have been met, the clerk stamps it "Filed."

Timely
- Only briefs and excerpts are considered timely when served on the due date (FRAP 25(a)(2)(B)).
- All other documents, including motions, petitions for rehearing and cost bills, must be delivered to the court by the due date (FRAP 25(a)(2)(A)).

Pro Se Help
www.ca9.uscourts.gov
(click "Pro Se Brief Info")

Employment Options
www.ca9.uscourts.gov/ca9/joblistings.nsf/employment?openview&expandview
www.uscourts.gov/employment.html

United States District Courts

United States district courts exist within the judicial districts that are part of the regional circuits. In the fifty states, there are eighty-nine district courts. Each state has at least one district court. California has four: Southern District, Central District, Eastern District, and Northern District. In addition to a district court for the District of Columbia, the Commonwealth of Puerto Rico has a district court with jurisdiction corresponding to that of district courts in the various states. Finally district courts also exist in the territories of the Virgin Islands, Guam, and the Northern Mariana Islands for a total of ninety-four district courts in the federal judicial system.

United States district courts are the trial courts of general federal jurisdiction. Within limits set by Congress and the Constitution, they can hear nearly all categories of federal cases, including both civil and criminal matters. Typically, federal courts hear civil cases in which the United States is a party or those involving the United States Constitution, laws enacted by Congress, treaties, and laws relating to navigable waters. Examples include bankruptcy, copyright protection, and violations of maritime law. Another large source of civil cases in district courts are those involving disputes between citizens of different states (diversity of citizenship) if the amount in dispute exceeds $75,000. Federal criminal cases in district courts are filed by the United States attorney who represents the United States. Examples of federal crimes prosecuted in district court include illegal importation of drugs and certain categories of bank fraud.

At present, each district court has from two to twenty-eight federal district judgeships, depending upon the amount of judicial work within its boundaries. Only one judge is usually required to hear and decide a case in a district court, but in limited cases, three judges are called together to comprise the court. Judges of district courts have lifetime tenure; they are nominated by the president and confirmed by the U.S. Senate.

Each district court has one or more magistrate judge and bankruptcy judge, a clerk, a United States attorney, a United States marshal, probation officers, and court reporters. Cases from a district court are reviewable on appeal by the United States court of appeals in the circuit where the district court sits.

As indicated, there are four United States district courts sitting in California:

United States District Court, Southern District
United States District Court, Central District
United States District Court, Eastern District
United States District Court, Northern District

United States District Court, Southern District

Addresses

U.S. District Court
Southern District of CA
940 Front Street
San Diego, CA 92101-8900
619-557-5600

Office of the Clerk
U.S. District Court
Southern District of CA
880 Front Street, Ste 4290
San Diego, CA 92101-8900
619-557-5600

U.S. District Court
Southern District of CA
2003 W. Adams Ave, Ste 220
El Centro, CA 92243
760-353-1271

Web Site
www.casd.uscourts.gov
www.law.cornell.edu/federal/districts.html#circuit

Judges and Staff
www.casd.uscourts.gov/casd/Staff.nsf/Judges?OpenView
www.casd.uscourts.gov/casd/Staff.nsf/Full+List?OpenView

Authorized Judgeships: 8

PACER Login
pacer.casd.uscourts.gov
800-676-6856

Calendar
www.casd.uscourts.gov/casdcalendars

Forms
www.casd.uscourts.gov/casd/filerev.nsf/Forms?OpenView

Local Rules and General Orders
www.casd.uscourts.gov/docs

Federal Rules of Civil Procedure
www.law.cornell.edu/rules/frcp
www.access.gpo.gov/uscode/title28a/28a_4_.html
judiciary.house.gov/media/pdfs/printers/108th/civil2004.pdf

Federal Rules of Criminal Procedure
www.law.cornell.edu/rules/frcrmp
judiciary.house.gov/media/pdfs/printers/108th/civil2004.pdf

Fees
www.casd.uscourts.gov
(click "Filing Procedures" then "General Filing Procedures")

General Filing Procedures Manual
www.casd.uscourts.gov
(click "Filing Procedures" "Reference Documents")

Employment Options
www.casd.uscourts.gov
(click "Human Resources")

United States District Court, Central District

Addresses

U.S. District Court
Central District
Western Division
312 N. Spring Street
Los Angeles, CA 90012
213-894-1565
213-894-2215

U.S. District Court
Central District
Eastern Division
3470 Twelfth Street
Riverside, CA 92501
951-328-4450

U.S. District Court
Central District
Western Division
255 East Temple Street
Los Angeles, CA 90012
213-894-1565
213-894-2215

U.S. District Court
Central District
Southern Division
411 West Fourth Street
Santa Ana, CA 92701
714-338-4750

Web Site
www.cacd.uscourts.gov
www.law.cornell.edu/federal/districts.html#circuit

Judges
www.cacd.uscourts.gov
(click "General Information" then "Directories")

Authorized Judgeships: 27

PACER Login
www.cacd.uscourts.gov
(click "General Information" then "Pacer Access")
800-676-6856

Opinions
www.cacd.uscourts.gov
(click "Recent Opinions")

Calendar
www.cacd.uscourts.gov
(click "General Information" then "PIA Calendar")

Forms
www.cacd.uscourts.gov/cacd/forms.nsf/forms?openview

Local Rules
www.cacd.uscourts.gov/cacd/locrules.nsf/local+rules?openview

Federal Rules of Civil Procedure
www.law.cornell.edu/rules/frcp
www.access.gpo.gov/uscode/title28a/28a_4_.html
judiciary.house.gov/media/pdfs/printers/108th/civil2004.pdf

Federal Rules of Criminal Procedure
www.law.cornell.edu/rules/frcrmp
judiciary.house.gov/media/pdfs/printers/108th/civil2004.pdf

Fees
www.cacd.uscourts.gov
(click "General Information" then "Fee Schedule")

General Orders
www.cacd.uscourts.gov
(click "General Orders")

Employment Options
www.cacd.uscourts.gov
(click "Job Announcements")

United States District Court, Eastern District

Addresses

U.S. District Court
Eastern District
501 I Street
Sacramento, CA 95814
916-930-4000

U.S. District Court
Eastern District
3368 So. Lake Tahoe Blvd.
So. Lake Tahoe, CA 96150
530-246-5416

U.S. District Court
Eastern District
2986 Bechelli Lane
Redding, CA 96002
530-246-5416

U.S. District Court
Eastern District
1130 O Street
Fresno, CA 93721
559-498-7483

U.S. District Court
Eastern District
9004 Castle Cliffs Court
Yosemite, CA 95389
209-372-0320

U.S. District Cour
Eastern District
1300 18th Street
Bakersfield, CA 93301
661-326-6620

Web Site
www.caed.uscourts.gov
www.law.cornell.edu/federal/districts.html#circuit

PACER Login
ecf.caed.uscourts.gov
pacer.caed.uscourts.gov

CM/ECF (electronic filing and service)
www.caed.uscourts.gov
(click "CM/ECF")

Opinions
www.caed.uscourts.gov
(click "Opinions")

Calendar
www.caed.uscourts.gov
(click "Court Calendar")

Forms
www.caed.uscourts.gov
(click "Clerk's Office" then one of the cities)

Local Rules
www.caed.uscourts.gov
(click "local rules")

Federal Rules of Civil Procedure
www.law.cornell.edu/rules/frcp
www.access.gpo.gov/uscode/title28a/28a_4_.html
judiciary.house.gov/media/pdfs/printers/108th/civil2004.pdf

Federal Rules of Criminal Procedure
www.law.cornell.edu/rules/frcrmp
judiciary.house.gov/media/pdfs/printers/108th/civil2004.pdf

Fees
www.caed.uscourts.gov
(click "Clerk's Office" then one of the cities)
(also click "Attorney Info" then "Fee Schedule")

Employment Options
www.uscourts.gov/uscjobvac

United States District Court, Northern District

Addresses

U.S. District Court
Northern District
450 Golden Gate Ave.
San Francisco, CA 94102
415-522-2000

U.S. District Court
Northern District
1301 Clay Street
Oakland, CA 94612
510-637-3530

U.S. District Court
Northern District
280 South 1st Street
San Jose, CA 95113
408-535-5364

Web Site
www.cand.uscourts.gov
www.law.cornell.edu/federal/districts.html#circuit

Judges
www.cand.uscourts.gov
(click "Judges")

Authorized Judgeships: 14

PACER

ecf.cand.uscourts.gov/cand/index.html

Opinions
www.cand.uscourts.gov
(click "opinions")

Calendar
www.cand.uscourts.gov
(click "Calendars")

Forms
www.cand.uscourts.gov
(click "Forms")

Local Rules
www.cand.uscourts.gov
(click "Rules")

Federal Rules of Civil Procedure
www.law.cornell.edu/rules/frcp
www.access.gpo.gov/uscode/title28a/28a_4_.html
judiciary.house.gov/media/pdfs/printers/108th/civil2004.pdf

Federal Rules of Criminal Procedure
www.law.cornell.edu/rules/frcrmp
judiciary.house.gov/media/pdfs/printers/108th/civil2004.pdf

Fees
www.cand.uscourts.gov
(click "Fee Schedule")

Pre Se Help
www.cand.uscourts.gov
(click "Pro Se Handbook")

Employment Options
www.cand.uscourts.gov
(click "Employment")

United States Bankruptcy Courts

Federal courts have exclusive jurisdiction over bankruptcy cases. Such cases cannot be filed in state court. Although United States district courts have jurisdiction over all bankruptcy matters (28 U.S.C. § 1334), they have the authority (28 U.S.C. § 157) to delegate or refer bankruptcy cases to the United States bankruptcy courts. There is a bankruptcy court in each of the ninety-four federal judicial districts. A United States bankruptcy judge is a judicial officer of the United States district court and is appointed for a 14 year term by the majority of judges of the United States court of appeals in the circuit.

The primary purposes of bankruptcy law are: (1) to give an honest debtor a "fresh start" in life by relieving the debtor of most debts and (2) to repay creditors in an orderly manner to the extent that the debtor has property available for payment. The bankruptcy courts are usually in the same physical location as the United States district courts. However, in some areas, based on local space availability, the bankruptcy court may be located in space other than the United States courthouse where the district court is situated.

Kinds of Bankruptcy
www.uscourts.gov/bankruptcycourts/bankruptcybasics.html

Bankruptcy Basics
www.uscourts.gov/bankruptcycourts/bankruptcybasics/process.html
www.uscourts.gov/bankruptcycourts/BB101705final2column.pdf

United States Code: Title 11 (Bankruptcy)
uscode.house.gov/download/title_11.shtml
www.law.cornell.edu/uscode/html/uscode11/usc_sup_01_11.html

United States Bankruptcy Court, Southern District of California

Address

U.S. Bankruptcy Court
Southern District
325 West F Street
San Diego, CA 92101
619-557-5620

Web Site
www.casb.uscourts.gov

Opinions
www.casb.uscourts.gov/html/sitemap.htm
(click "Published Opinions" and "Unpublished Decisions")

Judges
www.casb.uscourts.gov/html/phone_list.htm

PACER
800-676-6856

Calendar
www.casb.uscourts.gov/html/court_calendars2.htm

Forms
www.casb.uscourts.gov/html/latest_forms.htm
www.uscourts.gov/bkforms

Rules
www.casb.uscourts.gov/PDF&Downloads/lrules.pdf

Fees
www.casb.uscourts.gov/html/fee_schedule.htm

United States Bankruptcy Court, Central District of California

Address

U.S. Bankruptcy Court
Central District
255 East Temple Street
Los Angeles, CA 90012
213-894-3118

Also: Riverside (951-774-1000), Santa Ana (714-338-5300), Santa Barbara (805-884-4800), Woodland Hills (818-587-2900)

Web Site
www.cacb.uscourts.gov

Opinions
www.cacb.uscourts.gov
(click "New/Notices/Publications" then "Written Opinions" under "Publications")

PACER
www.cacb.uscourts.gov
(click "general information" then "webPACER")

Forms and Rules
www.cacb.uscourts.gov
(click "Forms/Rules/General Orders")
www.uscourts.gov/bkforms
www.cacb.uscourts.gov
(click "New/Notices/Publications" then "Desk Reference Manual" under "Publications")
www.uscourts.gov/bkforms

Fees
www.cacb.uscourts.gov
(click "general information" then "fee schedule")

Bankruptcy Desk Reference Manual
(click "New/Notices/Publications" then "Desk Reference Manual")

Employment
www.cacb.uscourts.gov
(click "Information" then "Employment Opportunities")

United States Bankruptcy Court, Eastern District of California

Addresses

U.S. Bankruptcy Court
Eastern District
501 I Street
Sacramento, CA 95814
916-930-4400

U.S. Bankruptcy Court
Eastern District
1130 12th Street
Modesto, CA 95354
209-521-5160

U.S. Bankruptcy Court
Eastern District
1130 O Street
Fresno, CA 93721
559-498-7217

Web Site
www.caeb.uscourts.gov

Opinions
www.caeb.uscourts.gov
(click "Opinions")

Judges
www.caeb.uscourts.gov
(click "Court Information" then "Personnel")

PACER
www.caeb.uscourts.gov
(click "Electronic Case Records PACER")

Electronic Filing
www.caeb.uscourts.gov
(click "Electronic Case Filing")

Calendar
www.caeb.uscourts.gov
(click "Court Calendars")

Forms
www.caeb.uscourts.gov
(click "Forms & Publications")
www.uscourts.gov/bkforms

Rules
www.caeb.uscourts.gov
(click "Local Rules")

Fees
www.caeb.uscourts.gov
(click "Filing & Fee Information")

Employment Options
www.caeb.uscourts.gov
(click "Employment Opportunities")

United States Bankruptcy Court, Northern District of California

Addresses

U.S. Bankruptcy Court
Northern District
235 Pine Street
San Francisco, CA 94104
415-268-2300

U.S. Bankruptcy Court
Northern District
99 South E Street
Santa Rosa, CA 95404
707-525-8539

U.S. Bankruptcy Court
Northern District
1300 Clay Street
Oakland, CA 94612
510-879-3600

U.S. Bankruptcy Court
Northern District
280 South First Street
San Jose, CA 95113
408-535-5118

Web Site
www.canb.uscourts.gov

Opinions
www.canb.uscourts.gov
(click "Judges' Decisions")

Judges
www.canb.uscourts.gov
(click "Site Map")

PACER
www.canb.uscourts.gov
(click "PACER")

Calendar
www.canb.uscourts.gov
(click "Calendars")

Forms
www.canb.uscourts.gov
(click "Forms")
(click "Information Manual")
www.uscourts.gov/bkforms

Rules
www.canb.uscourts.gov
(click "Local Rules/General Orders")

Procedures
www.canb.uscourts.gov
(click "Judges' Procedures")
(click "Information Manual")

Fees
www.canb.uscourts.gov
(click "Site Map")

Employment Options
www.canb.uscourts.gov
(click "Job Listings")

Bankruptcy Appellate Panel (BAP)

The Bankruptcy Appellate Panel (BAP) was originally established by the Judicial Council of the Ninth Circuit as an alternative forum to the district courts for hearing bankruptcy appeals. All district courts within the Ninth Circuit have issued general orders providing for the automatic referral of bankruptcy appeals to the BAP for disposition. However, if any party files a timely election to have the appeal heard by a district court, the appeal is administratively transferred. Historically, the BAP handles about sixty percent of the new appeals filed throughout the Ninth Circuit, while 40 percent are heard by the various district courts.

Web Site
www.ce9.uscourts.gov/bap

Where Appeals are Filed
BAP Clerk's Office
Richard H. Chambers United States Court of Appeals Building
125 South Grand Avenue
Pasadena, CA 91105

Information on Appeals from Central District
626-229-7220

United States Immigration Courts

The Executive Office for Immigration Review (EOIR) (*www.usdoj.gov/eoir*) adjudicates matters brought under various immigration statutes to its three administrative tribunals: the Board of Immigration Appeals, the Office of the Chief Immigration Judge, and the Office of the Chief Administrative Hearing Officer.

The Board of Immigration Appeals has nationwide jurisdiction to hear appeals from certain decisions made by immigration judges and by district directors of the Department of Homeland Security (DHS). The Office of the Chief Immigration Judge provides overall direction for more than 200 immigration judges located in fifty-three immigration courts throughout the nation. Immigration judges are responsible for conducting formal administrative proceedings and act independently in their decision-making capacity. Their decisions are administratively final, unless appealed or certified to the Board.

California Immigration Court Locations
www.usdoj.gov/eoir/sibpages/ICadr.htm

Local Operating Rules and Procedures
www.usdoj.gov/eoir/efoia/ocij/locopproc.htm

C. PACER

Public Access to Court Electronic Records (PACER) is an electronic public access service that allows users to obtain case and docket information from federal appellate, district and bankruptcy courts, and from the U.S. Party/Case Index. PACER is a service of the United States judiciary. The PACER Service Center is operated by the Administrative Office of the United States Courts (*pacer.psc.uscourts.gov*).

Currently most courts are available on the Internet. Links to these courts are provided at the PACER site (*pacer.psc.uscourts.gov/cgi-bin/links.pl*). However, a few systems are not available on the Internet and must be dialed directly using communication software (such as ProComm Plus, pcAnywhere, or Hyperterminal) and a modem. Electronic access is available for most courts by registering with the PACER Service Center, the judiciary's centralized registration, billing, and technical support center. You can register online or by phone at (800-676-6856; 210-301-6440).

Each court maintains its own databases with case information. Because PACER database systems are maintained within each court, each jurisdiction will have a different URL or modem number. Accessing and querying information from each service is comparable. The format and content of information provided, however, may differ slightly. Lists of local and toll-free PACER modem numbers are available at the PACER court directory (*pacer.psc.uscourts.gov/cgi-bin/modem.pl*).

D. More Information

Federal Judiciary Overview
www.uscourts.gov
www.firstgov.gov/Agencies/Federal/Judicial.shtml

Guide to the Federal Courts
www.uscourts.gov/journalistguide/welcome.html
www.uscourts.gov/understand02

Federal Court Links
www.uscourts.gov/links.html

Bankruptcy Courts in California
www.caeb.uscourts.gov/data/formpubs/EDC.002-070.pdf

Employment Opportunities in the Federal Courts
www.uscourts.gov/employment/vacancies.html#

Federal Judicial Center
www.fjc.gov

Wikipedia on Federal Courts in California
en.wikipedia.org/wiki/9th_Circuit_Court_of_Appeals

E. Something to Check

1. Go to the sites that give you online access to court opinions of the 9th Circuit. Use the search features of the sites to find an opinion on any broad legal topic, e.g., capital punishment, adoption. Summarize what the opinion says about your topic.
2. For one of the four district courts in California, find the calendar of any judge on the court you select. Name one case on the calendar of that judge.

4.4 State Legislation: How a Bill becomes a California Statute

A. Introduction

In this section, we provide an overview of the legislative process in California, and, more specifically, how a bill becomes a law. For related information, see:

- section 4.1 (introduction to the state government of California, including the major units and offices of the state legislature)
- section 5.1 (doing legal research in California law, including finding state statutes online and on the shelves)

B. How a Bill becomes a California Statute

Introduction

The California State Legislature is made up of two houses:

Senate (*www.sen.ca.gov*)

Assembly (*www.assembly.ca.gov*)

There are forty senators and eighty assembly members who represent the people of the state. The legislative process takes place during sessions, with each session consisting of a 2-year period.

Idea for a Bill

Ideas for bills can come from many sources: individual legislators, the governor, administrative agencies, lobbyists, businesses, community groups, and citizens. The first step is to have a legislator (a senator or assembly member) author the bill.

Author

A legislator sends the idea for the bill to the Office of the Legislative Counsel, where it is drafted into bill form. The draft of the bill is returned to the legislator for introduction. If the author is a senator, the bill is introduced in the Senate. If the author is an assembly member, the bill is introduced in the Assembly.

Office of the Legislative Counsel (*www.leginfo.ca.gov/legcnsl.html*): The OLC drafts bills based on the ideas submitted to it by legislators. It also renders legal opinions, provides counsel to the members and committees of the legislature, and represents the legislature in litigation. In addition, it publishes the Legislative Index (which identifies legislative measures) and it compiles and indexes California statutes and codes. The Legislative Counsel is required by law to make legislative information available to the public on the Internet.

First Reading/Introduction

A bill is introduced (or read) the first time when the bill number, the name of the author, and the descriptive title of the bill are read on the floor of the house. The bill is then sent to the Office of State Publishing. No bill except the Budget Bill may be acted upon until 30 days have passed from the date of its introduction.

Office of State Publishing (*www.osp.dgs.ca.gov/default.htm*): The Office of State Publishing prints many of the documents prepared by the legislature in the legislative process.

Committee Hearings

After introduction, a bill goes to the Rules Committee of the house, where it is assigned to the appropriate policy committee for its first hearing. Bills are assigned to policy committees according to subject area. For example, a Senate bill dealing with health care facilities would first be assigned to the Senate Health and Human Services Committee for policy review. Bills that require the expenditure of funds must also be heard in the fiscal committees, Senate Appropriations and Assembly Appropriations. Each committee is made up of a specified number of senators or assembly members.

Examples of Policy Committees

Assembly Committee on Judiciary
The jurisdiction of this committee includes family law, product liability, tort liability, the Civil Code, and the Evidence Code (excluding criminal procedure) (*www.assembly.ca.gov/acs/newcomframeset.asp?committee=15*)

Senate Standing Committee on Judiciary
The jurisdiction of this committee includes bills pertaining to the Civil Code (except retail credit interest rates), the Code of Civil Procedure, the Evidence Code (except on criminal procedure), the Family Code, and the Probate Code (*www.sen.ca.gov/ftp/sen/committee/STANDING/JUDICIARY/_home1/PROFILE.HTM*)

During the committee hearing, the author presents the bill to the committee, and testimony may be heard in support or opposition to the bill. The committee then votes on whether to pass the bill out of committee, or that it be passed as amended. Bills may be amended several times. It takes a majority vote of the committee membership for a bill to be passed and sent to the next committee or to the floor.

Each house maintains a schedule of legislative committee hearings. Prior to a bill's hearing, a bill analysis is prepared that explains the intended effect of the bill on current law, together with background information. Typically the analysis also lists organizations that support or oppose the bill.

Second and Third Reading

Bills passed by committees are read a second time on the floor in the house of origin and then assigned to a third reading. Bill analyses are also prepared prior to the third reading. When a bill is read the third time, it is explained by the author, discussed by the members, and voted on by a roll-call vote. Bills that require an appropriation, or that take effect immediately, ordinarily require 27 votes in the Senate and 54 votes in the Assembly to be passed. Other bills generally require 21 votes in the Senate and 41 votes in the Assembly. If a bill is defeated, the member may seek reconsideration and another vote.

Repeat Process in Other House

Once the bill has been approved by the house of origin, it proceeds to the other house, where the procedure described above is repeated.

Resolution of Differences

If a bill is amended in the second house, it must go back to the house of origin for concurrence, meaning agreement on those amendments. If the house of origin does not concur in those amendments, the bill is referred to a two-house conference committee to resolve the differences. The committee includes three members from the Senate and three from the Assembly. If a compromise is reached, the bill is returned to both houses for a vote.

EXHIBIT 4.4A The Life Cycle of State Legislation—from Idea into Law

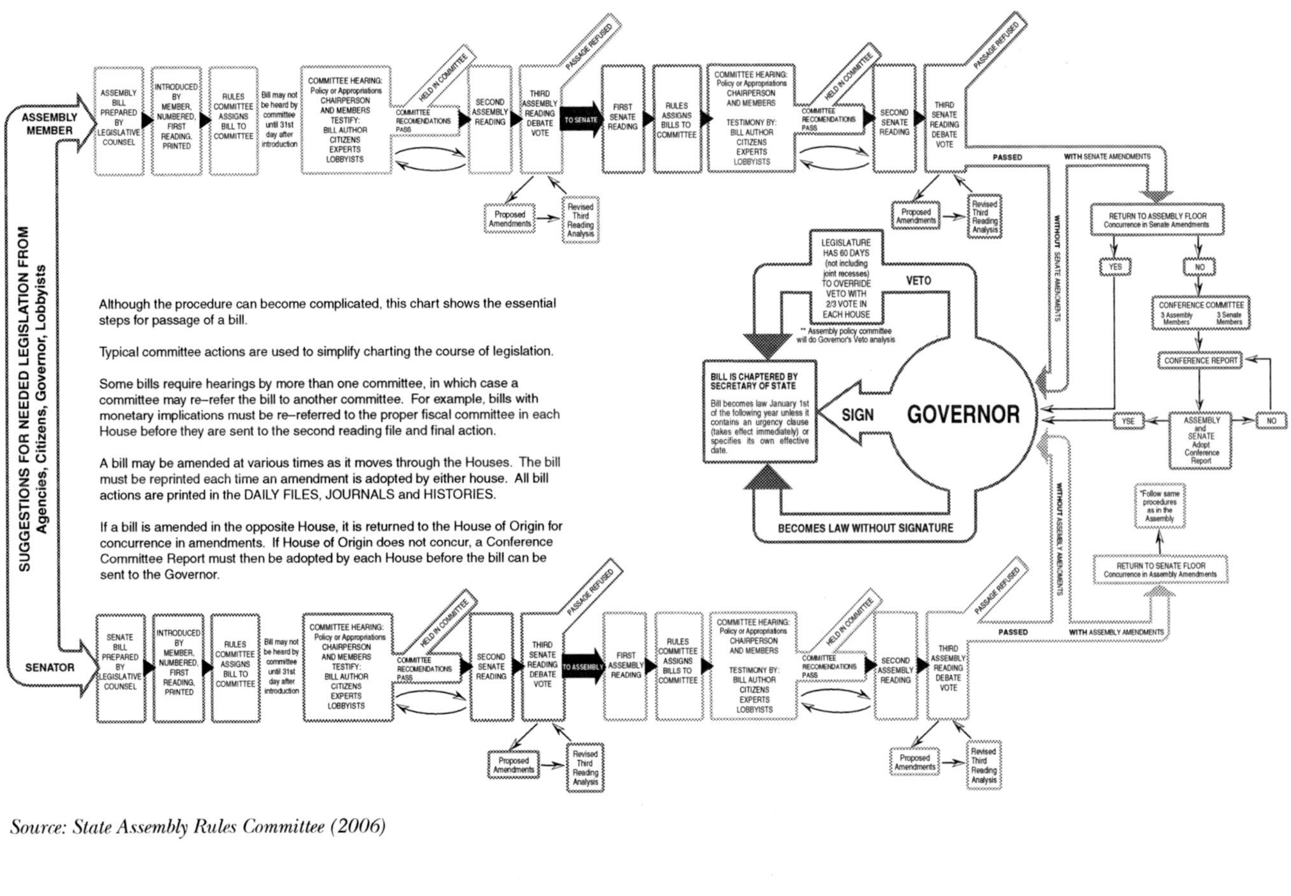

Source: State Assembly Rules Committee (2006)

Governor

If both houses approve a bill, it goes to the governor. The governor has three choices:

(a) sign the bill into law,

(b) allow it to become law without his or her signature, or

(c) veto it.

A governor's veto can be overridden by a two-thirds vote in both houses. Most enacted bills go into effect on the first day of January of the next year. Urgency bills, and certain other measures, take effect immediately after they are enacted into law.

> **Governor** (*www.governor.ca.gov*): For a bill to become law, it must be signed by the governor, unless the legislature overrides the governor's rejection (or veto) of a bill.

Chaptered (Assigned to a Chapter in the California Codes)

Each bill passed by the legislature and approved by the governor is assigned a chapter number by the secretary of state (*www.ss.ca.gov*). These chaptered bills are statutes, and ordinarily become part of the California Codes. The California Codes are a comprehensive collection of laws arranged by subject matter.

> **Secretary of State** (*www.ss.ca.gov*): The Secretary of State assigns a chapter number to every law passed by the California Legislature.

The legislative process described here is outlined in Exhibit 4.4A.

C. More Information

Overview
www.legislature.ca.gov
capitolmuseum.ca.gov/english/citizens/lifecycle/index.html
www.leginfo.ca.gov
www.leginfo.ca.gov/guide.html#Appendix_A

Legislative Publications
www.leginfo.ca.gov/legpubs.html
www.legislature.ca.gov
(click "Publications")

Bill Information
www.leginfo.ca.gov/bilinfo.html
www.legislature.ca.gov
(click "Bill Information")

Legislative Calendar
www.legislature.ca.gov
(click "Calendar and Schedules")

Legislative Research
www.legislature.ca.gov
(click "Legislative Research")

Glossary of Legislative Terms
www.legislature.ca.gov/quicklinks/glossary.html

D. Something to Check

1. Find a bill currently before the legislature on any:
   a. family law topic
   b. criminal law topic
2. Cite one bill or statute that was introduced, authored, or sponsored:
   a. by your state senator
   b. by your assembly member

A. Introduction

This section covers the major state agencies and commissions in California. See also:

- section 4.1 for an overview of state government,
- section 4.2 on the state courts,
- section 4.4 on the state legislature, and
- section 4.6 on county and city governments.

For legal research leads covering issues that pertain to many of these agencies and commissions, see the starter cites in section 5.5.

Main Information Number on California Government

916-322-9900; 916-657-9900

B. Contacts

Administration

(see also Audits, Employment, Governor)

State Government
www.ca.gov
my.ca.gov
www.ca.gov/state/portal/myca_homepage.jsp

Department of General Services
916-376-5000
www.dgs.ca.gov

Little Hoover Commission
916-445-2125
www.lhc.ca.gov/lhc.html

Administrative Law

Office of Administrative Law
916-323-6225
www.oal.ca.gov

State Administrative Manual
916-327-8908
sam.dgs.ca.gov

Office of Administrative Hearings
916-445-4926
www.oah.dgs.ca.gov

Adoption

(see also Social Services)

Department of Social Services Child and Youth Permanency Branch
800 KIDS-4-US; 916-651-7465
www.dss.cahwnet.gov/cdssweb/Adoptions_166.htm

Aerospace Support

Office of Military and Aerospace Support
www.omas.ca.gov

Aging

Department of Aging
916-322-3887; 800-510-2020
www.aging.ca.gov

California Commission on Aging
916-322-5630
www.calaging.org

Bureau of Medi-Cal Fraud and Elder Abuse
800-722-0432
caag.state.ca.us/bmfea/index.htm

Agriculture

(see also Food and Beverage)

Department of Food and Agriculture
916-654-0466
www.cdfa.ca.gov

Agricultural Labor Relations Board
800-449-3699, 916-653-3699
www.alrb.ca.gov

AIDS

Office of AIDS
916-449-5900
www.dhs.ca.gov/ps/ooa/default.htm

Air

(see also Environment)

Air Resources Board
916-322-2990; 800-952-5588
www.arb.ca.gov

Alcohol and Drugs

(see also Food and Beverage, Health, Law Enforcement, Pharmacy)

Alcohol and Drug Programs
916-327-3728, 800-879-2772
www.adp.ca.gov

Department of Alcoholic Beverage Control
916-419-2500
www.abc.ca.gov

Antitrust

(see also Business)

Attorney General Antitrust Section
caag.state.ca.us/antitrust/index.htm

Archives

(see also Library)

State Archives
916-653-2246
www.ss.ca.gov/archives/archives.htm

Arts and Humanities

(see also Tourism)

Arts Council
916-322-6555, 800-201-6201
www.cac.ca.gov

African American Museum
213-744-7432
www.caamuseum.org

California Museum for History, Women and the Arts
www.californiamuseum.org

Council for the Humanities
415-391-1474
www.calhum.org

Assembly

State Assembly
(see also section 4.4)
916-319-2856
www.assembly.ca.gov/defaulttext.asp
www.leginfo.ca.gov

Athletics

Athletics Commission
916-263-2195
www.dca.ca.gov/csac/index.html

Attorney General

(see also Law Enforcement)

Department of Justice

Office of the Attorney General
800-952-5225, 916-322-3360
caag.state.ca.us

Audits

(see also Finance)

Bureau of State Audits
800-952-5665; 916-445-0255
www.bsa.ca.gov/bsa

Automotive Repair

(see also Motor Vehicles)

Bureau of Automotive Repair
800-952-5210
www.smogcheck.ca.gov/stdhome.asp

Banks

(see Finance)

Bar, State

(see also section 3.4)

State Bar of California
888-800-3400; 415-538-2000
800-843-9053 (attorney complaint hotline)
www.calbar.ca.gov

Birth Records

(see Vital Records; see also section 5.7)

Boating

(see also Natural Resources)

Department of Boating and Waterways
888-326-2822; 916-263-1331
www.dbw.ca.gov

Building

(see Construction)

Business

Business, Transportation, and Housing Agency
916-323-5400
www.bth.ca.gov

Secretary of State, Business Portal
916-653-6814
www.ss.ca.gov/business

Department of Corporations
866-275-2677, 866-ASK-CORP
www.corp.ca.gov

Economic Strategy Panel
www.labor.ca.gov/panel

Business Permits
www.calgold.ca.gov

CALTRANS

(see Transportation)

Cemetery

Cemetery and Funeral Bureau
916-322-7737
www.cfb.ca.gov

Child Support Services

(see also Social Services)

Department of Child Support Services
866-249-0773
www.childsup.cahwnet.gov

Office of Child Abuse Prevention
916-651-6960
www.dss.cahwnet.gov/cdssweb/ChildAbuse_188.htm

Civil Rights

(see also Consumer Services, Law Enforcement, Privacy)

Department of Fair Employment and Housing
800-884-1684, 800-233-3212
www.dfeh.ca.gov

Claims against State

Victim Compensation and Government Claims Board
800-955-0045; 800-777-9229
www.boc.ca.gov

Commerce

(see Business)

Complaints Directory

Where to Complain
800-952-5210
www.dca.ca.gov/r_r/cmpltabl/index.html

Conservation

(see also Emergency, Environment, Natural Resources)

Department of Conservation
916-322-1080
www.consrv.ca.gov

Division of Recycling
800-RECYCLE
www.consrv.ca.gov/dor/index.htm

Construction

(see Consumer Services)

Contractors State License Board
800-321-2752
www.cslb.ca.gov

Architects Board
916-445-3394
www.cab.ca.gov

Building Standards Commission
916-263-0916
www.bsc.ca.gov

Consumer Services

(see also Law Enforcement)

State and Consumer Services Agency
916-653-4090
www.scsa.ca.gov

Department of Consumer Affairs
800-952-5210, 916-445-1254
www.dca.ca.gov

Complaint Mediation Program
800-952-5210
www.dca.ca.gov/complainthelp

Consumer Law Section of Department of Justice
caag.state.ca.us/consumers/index.htm

Board of Behavioral Sciences
916-445-4933
www.bbs.ca.gov

Controller

(see also Estate Tax, Finance, Unclaimed Property)

State Controller
916-445-2636
www.sco.ca.gov

Corporations

(see also Business)

Department of Corporations
866-275-2677, 866-ASK-CORP
www.corp.ca.gov

Corrections

(see also Law Enforcement)

Department of Corrections and Rehabilitation
916-323-6001
www.cdcr.ca.gov

Board of Parole Hearings
916-445-1539
www.cya.ca.gov
(click "Board of Parole Hearings")

Division of Juvenile Justice
916-262-1473; 866-466-4292
www.cya.ca.gov
(click "Juvenile Justice")

Office of Inspector General
916-830-3600, 800-700-5972
www.oig.ca.gov

Courts

(see also section 4.2)

California Courts
www.courtinfo.ca.gov
www.courtinfo.ca.gov/courts
www.courtinfo.ca.gov/courts/trial/courtlist.htm

Credit Unions

(see Finance)

Death Records

(see Vital Records; see also section 5.7)

Delta

(see Environment)

Disabilities

(see also Health, Workers' Compensation)

Department of Developmental Services
916-654-1690
www.dds.ca.gov

Department of Rehabilitation
916-263-7365
www.rehab.cahwnet.gov

Dissolution/Divorce Records

(see Vital Records; see also section 5.7)

DMV

(see Motor Vehicles)

Domestic Partnership

Domestic Partnership Registry
916-653-3984
www.ss.ca.gov/dpregistry

Drugs

(see also Health, Law Enforcement, Pharmacy)

Alcohol and Drug Programs
916-327-3728, 800-879-2772
www.adp.ca.gov

Bureau of Narcotic Enforcement
caag.state.ca.us/bne

Earthquakes

(see also Emergency, Environment)

California Earthquake Authority
877-797-4300; 916-325-3800
www.earthquakeauthority.com

Seismic Safety Commission
916-263-5506
www.seismic.ca.gov

Economic Development

(see Business)

Education

Department of Education

Office of State Superintendent
916-319-0800
www.cde.ca.gov

State Board of Education
916-319-0827
www.cde.ca.gov/be

University of California
510-987-0700
www.ucop.edu

State University System
562-951-4000
www.calstate.edu

Community Colleges
916-445-8752
www.cccco.edu

Student Aid Commission
888-CA-GRANT
www.csac.ca.gov

Commission on Teacher Credentialing
888-921-2682
www.ctc.ca.gov

Postsecondary Education Commission
916-445-7933
www.cpec.ca.gov

Elections

Voter Registration
800-345-VOTE
www.ss.ca.gov/elections/elections_vr.htm

Fair Political Practices Commission
866-275-3772 (elections hotline)
www.fppc.ca.gov

Emergency

(see also Environment, Health)

Emergency Medical Services Authority
916-322-4336
www.emsa.ca.gov

Seismic Safety Commission
916-263-5506
www.seismic.ca.gov

Office of Emergency Services
916-845-8911
www.oes.ca.gov

Employment

(see also Labor, Unemployment Insurance, Workers' Compensation)

Employment Development Department
916-653-0707
www.edd.ca.gov

CalJobs
800-758-0398; 916-653-0707
www.caljobs.ca.gov

Labor and Workforce Development Agency
916-327-9064
www.labor.ca.gov

Department of Fair Employment and Housing
800-884-1684 (discrimination)
www.dfeh.ca.gov

Employment Training Panel
916-327-5262
www.etp.cahwnet.gov

California Public Employees' Retirement System
888-225-7377; 916-795-3000
www.calpers.ca.gov

State Teachers' Retirement System
800-228-5453
www.calstrs.com

Public Employment Relations Board
916-322-3198
www.perb.ca.gov

Department of Personnel Administration
916-324-0455
www.dpa.ca.gov

State Personnel Board
916-653-1705
www.spb.ca.gov

Division of Occupational Safety and Health
800-963-9424
www.dir.ca.gov/DOSH/dosh1.html

State Disability Insurance
800-480-3287
www.edd.ca.gov

Conservation Corps
800-952-JOBS
www.ccc.ca.gov

Energy

(see also Environment, Natural Resources)

Energy Commission
800-555-7794; 800-772-3300; 916-654-4000
www.energy.ca.gov

Environment

(see also Emergency, Natural Resources, Water)

Environmental Protection Agency
916-323-2514; 800-CLEANUP
www.calepa.ca.gov

Air Resources Board
916-322-2990; 800-952-5588
www.arb.ca.gov

Department of Toxic Substances Control
800-728-6942; 916-324-1826
www.dtsc.ca.gov

Department of Pesticide Regulation
916-445-4300
www.cdpr.ca.gov

Integrated Waste Management Board
916-341-6000
www.ciwmb.ca.gov

Environmental Resources Evaluation System
916-653-2238
ceres.ca.gov

Delta Protection Commission
916-776-2290
www.delta.ca.gov

Tahoe Conservatory
530-542-5580
www.tahoecons.ca.gov

Spatial Information Library
916-653-1369
gis.ca.gov

Conservation Corps
800-952-JOBS
www.ccc.ca.gov

Equalization

(see Tax)

Estate Tax

(see also Tax)

California Estate Tax
916-445-2636
www.sco.ca.gov/col/taxinfo/estate/index.shtml

Excise Tax

Board of Equalization Excise Tax Division
800-400-7115
www.boe.ca.gov/sptaxprog/spexcise.htm

Families

(see Child Support Services, Domestic Partnership, Health, Social Services)

Fish

(see also Natural Resources)

Department of Fish and Game
800-952-5400; 916-445-0411
www.dfg.ca.gov

Finance

(see also Housing)

Department of Finance
916-445-3878
800-622-0620 (consumer complaints)
www.dof.ca.gov

Department of Financial Institutions
415-263-8500, 800-622-0620
www.dfi.ca.gov

Food and Beverage

Department of Food and Agriculture
916-654-0466
www.cdfa.ca.gov

Department of Alcoholic Beverage Control
916-419-2500
www.abc.ca.gov

Forensic Sciences

(see alsco Law Enforcement)

Bureau of Forensic Sciences
caag.state.ca.us/bfs/index.htm

Forestry

(see also Environment, Natural Resources)

Department of Forestry and Fire Protection
916-653-5121
www.fire.ca.gov

Funeral Services

Cemetery and Funeral Bureau
916-322-7737
www.cfb.ca.gov

Gambling

(see also Law Enforcement)

Division of Gambling Control
916-263-3408
ag.ca.gov/gambling/index.htm

Gambling Control Commission
916-263-0700
www.cgcc.ca.gov

Game

(see also Natural Resources)

Department of Fish and Game
800-952-5400; 916-445-0411
www.dfg.ca.gov

Governor

Office of the Governor
916-445-2841
www.governor.ca.gov

Health

(see also Emergency, Insurance)

Health and Human Services Agency
916-654-3454
www.chhs.ca.gov

Department of Health Services
916-445-1248
www.dhs.ca.gov

Medi-Cal
800-541-5555; 800-786-4346
www.medi-cal.ca.gov

Bureau of Medi-Cal Fraud and Elder Abuse
800-722-0432
caag.state.ca.us/bmfea/index.htm

Department of Managed Health Care
888-HMO-2219
www.dmhc.ca.gov

Medical Board
916-263-2382
www.medbd.ca.gov

Office of AIDS
916-449-5900
www.dhs.ca.gov/ps/ooa/default.htm

Division of Occupational Safety and Health
800-963-9424
www.dir.ca.gov/DOSH/dosh1.html

Department of Developmental Services
916-654-1690
www.dds.ca.gov

Department of Rehabilitation
916-263-7365
www.rehab.cahwnet.gov

Department of Mental Health
800-896-4042, 916-654-3890
www.dmh.cahwnet.gov

Department of Rehabilitation
916-263-7365
www.rehab.cahwnet.gov

Managed Risk Medical Insurance Board
916-324-4695
www.mrmib.ca.gov

Center for Health Statistics

Office of Vital Records
916-445-2684
www.dhs.ca.gov/hisp/chs

Board of Pharmacy
916-445-5014
www.pharmacy.ca.gov

Respiratory Care Board
866-375-0386; 916-323-9983
www.rcb.ca.gov

Board of Registered Nursing
916-322-3350
www.rn.ca.gov

Board of Vocational Nursing and Psychiatric Technicians
916-263-7800
www.bvnpt.ca.gov

Physician Assistant Committee
800-555-8038; 916-561-8780
www.physicianassistant.ca.gov

Rural Health Policy Council
800-237-4492
www.ruralhealth.ca.gov

Office of Statewide Health Planning and Development
916-654-1606
www.oshpd.cahwnet.gov

Office of the Patient Advocate
866-HMO-8900
www.opa.ca.gov

Highway Patrol

(see also Law Enforcement, Motor Vehicles)

California Highway Patrol
800-835-5247; 916-657-7261
www.chp.ca.gov

Horse Racing

Horse Racing Board
916-263-6000
www.chrb.ca.gov

Housing

(see also Real Estate)

Business, Transportation, and Housing Agency
916-323-5400
www.bth.ca.gov
916-323-5400

Housing Finance Agency
916-322-3991, 310-342-1250
www.calhfa.ca.gov

Department of Housing and Community Development
916-445-4782
housing.hcd.ca.gov

Department of Fair Employment and Housing
800-233-3212 (discrimination)
www.dfeh.ca.gov

Identity Theft

(see also Law Enforcement, Privacy)

Identity Theft Registry
888-880-0240
ag.ca.gov/idtheft/index.htm
caag.state.ca.us/idtheft/general.htm

Industrial Relations

(see Business, Labor)

Information on California Government

916-322-9900; 916-657-9900

Insurance

(see also Unemployment Insurance)

Department of Insurance
800-927-HELP
www.insurance.ca.gov

Managed Risk Medical Insurance Board
916-324-4695
www.mrmib.ca.gov

Investigation

(see also Law Enforcement)

Bureau of Investigation
916-319-9070
caag.state.ca.us/cbi

Jobs

(see Employment, Labor)

Justice

(see Attorney General)

Labor

Agricultural Labor Relations Board
800-449-3699, 916-653-3699
www.alrb.ca.gov

Department of Industrial Relations
415-703-5070
www.dir.ca.gov

Labor and Workforce Development Agency
916-327-9064
www.labor.ca.gov
916-327-9064

State Mediation and Conciliation Service
510-873-6465
www.dir.ca.gov/csmcs/smcs.html

Law Enforcement

(see also Corrections, Missing Persons, Public Defender)

Department of Justice

Attorney General
800-952-5225, 916-322-3360
caag.state.ca.us

California Highway Patrol
916-657-7261
www.chp.ca.gov

Bureau of Investigation
916-319-9070
caag.state.ca.us/cbi

Office of Victims' Services
877-433-9069
ag.ca.gov/victimservices

Bureau of Narcotic Enforcement
caag.state.ca.us/bne

Office of Child Abuse Prevention
916-651-6960
www.dss.cahwnet.gov/cdssweb/ChildAbuse_188.htm

Bureau of Medi-Cal Fraud and Elder Abuse
800-722-0432
caag.state.ca.us/bmfea/index.htm

Identity Theft Registry
888-880-0240
ag.ca.gov/idtheft/index.htm
caag.state.ca.us/idtheft/general.htm

Sex Offenders
916-227-4974
www.meganslaw.ca.gov
916-227-4974

Commission on Peace Officer Standards and Training
916-227-3909
www.post.ca.gov

National Guard
916-854-3500
www.calguard.ca.gov

Law Library

(see Library; see also section 5.8)

Legislature

(see also section 4.4)
916-319-2856 (Assembly)
916-651-4171 (Senate)
www.leginfo.ca.gov

Library

(see Archives, Law Library; see also section 5.8)

State Library
916-654-0261
www.library.ca.gov

Witkin State Law Library
916-654-0185
www.co.alameda.ca.us/law/index.htm
www.library.ca.gov/html/collections.cfm#law

Spatial Information Library
gis.ca.gov

Licensing

(see also Business, Consumer Services)

Department of Consumer Affairs
www.dca.ca.gov
(click "License and Complaint History" and "Online Professional Licensing")

Lieutenant Governor

Office of the Lieutenant Governor
916-445-8994
www.ltg.ca.gov

Local Government

(see also section 4.6)

Commission on State Mandates
www.csm.ca.gov

State Association of Counties
www.csac.counties.org

Lobbying

Fair Political Practices Commission
866-275-3772
www.fppc.ca.gov

Lottery

Lottery Commission
800-568-8379, 916-323-7095
www.calottery.com

Marriage Records

(see Vital Records; see also section 5.7)

Mental Health

(see also Health)

Department of Mental Health
800-896-4042, 916-654-3890
www.dmh.cahwnet.gov

Mediation

(see also Labor)

Complaint Mediation Program
800-952-5210
www.dca.ca.gov/complainthelp

Medi-Cal

(see also Health)

Medi-Cal
800-541-5555; 800-786-4346
www.medi-cal.ca.gov

Bureau of Medi-Cal Fraud and Elder Abuse
800-722-0432
caag.state.ca.us/bmfea/index.htm

Military

Office of Military and Aerospace Support
www.omas.ca.gov

Missing Persons

(see also Law Enforcement)

Missing and Unidentified Persons Unit
800-222-3463
ag.ca.gov/missing/index.htm

Motor Vehicles

(see also Automotive Repair, Highway Patrol, Transportation)

Department of Motor Vehicles
800-777-0133
www.dmv.ca.gov

Office of Traffic Safety
916-262-0990
www.ots.ca.gov

National Guard

916-854-3304
www.calguard.ca.gov

Natural Resources

(see also Environment)

Resources Agency
916-653-5656
resources.ca.gov

Energy Commission
800-555-7794; 916-654-4000
www.energy.ca.gov

Department of Conservation
916-322-1080
www.consrv.ca.gov

California Geological Survey
916-445-1923
www.consrv.ca.gov/cgs

Department of Parks and Recreation
800-777-0369, 916-653-6995
www.parks.ca.gov

Department of Water Resources
916-653-5791
www.water.ca.gov

Department of Boating and Waterways
888-326-2822; 916-263-1331
www.dbw.ca.gov

Coastal Commission
415-904-5200
www.coastal.ca.gov

Coastal Conservatory
510-286-1015
www.coastalconservancy.ca.gov

Department of Boating and Waterways
916-263-1331
www.dbw.ca.gov

Department of Fish and Game
916-445-0411
www.dfg.ca.gov

Department of Forestry and Fire Protection
916-653-5121
www.fire.ca.gov

State Lands Commission
800-735-2922
www.slc.ca.gov

Conservation Corps
800-952-JOBS
www.ccc.ca.gov

Nursing

(see Health)

Occupational Safety

(see also Health, Employment)

Division of Occupational Safety and Health
800-963-9424
www.dir.ca.gov/DOSH/dosh1.html

Occupational Safety and Health Appeals Board
916-274-5751
www.dir.ca.gov/oshab/oshab.html

Parks

(see also Environment, Natural Resources)

Department of Parks and Recreation
800-777-0369, 916-653-6995
www.parks.ca.gov

Permits

(see Business)

Personnel

(see Employment)

Pharmacy

(see also Health)

Board of Pharmacy
916-445-5014
www.pharmacy.ca.gov

Prison

(see Corrections)

Privacy

(see also Identity Theft)

Office of Privacy Protection
866-785-9663
www.privacyprotection.ca.gov

Probate

(see also Courts)

Probate Referees
www.sco.ca.gov/eo/probate/index.shtml

Public Assistance

(see Child Support Services, Social Services)

Public Defender

Office of Public Defender
916-322-2676, 415-904-5600
www.ospd.ca.gov

Public Utilities

(see also Natural Resources)

Public Utilities Commission
800-649-7570; 415-703-2782
www.cpuc.ca.gov

Publishing, State

Office of State Publishing
916-445-9110
www.osp.dgs.ca.gov

Real Estate

(see also Housing)

Department of Real Estate
916-227-0864
www.dre.cahwnet.gov

Office of Real Estate Appraisers
916-552-9000
www.orea.ca.gov

Recreation

(see also Environment, Natural Resources)

Department of Parks and Recreation
800-777-0369, 916-653-6995
www.parks.ca.gov

Recycling

(see also Conservation)

Division of Recycling
800-RECYCLE
www.consrv.ca.gov/dor/index.htm

Retirement

(see also Employment)

California Public Employees' Retirement System
888-225-7377; 916-795-3000
www.calpers.ca.gov

Senate

State Senate
(see also section 4.4)
916-651-4171
www.senate.ca.gov
www.leginfo.ca.gov

Secretary of State

Office of Secretary of State
916-653-6814
www.ss.ca.gov

Sex Offenders

(see also Law Enforcement)

Registration
916-227-4974
www.meganslaw.ca.gov

Social Services

(see also Adoption, Child Support, Health)

Department of Social Services
916-445-6951
www.dss.cahwnet.gov

CalWORKs (California Work Opportunity and Responsibility to Kids)
www.dss.cahwnet.gov/cdssweb/california_169.htm

Sports

(see Athletics)

Tahoe

(see Environment)

Tax

(see also Estate Tax)

Tax Information Center
800-400-7115
www.taxes.ca.gov

Franchise Tax Board
800-852-5711
www.ftb.ca.gov

Board of Equalization
800-400-7115
800-401-3661 (Tax Practitioner Hotline)
www.boe.ca.gov

Excise Tax Division
800-400-7115
www.boe.ca.gov/sptaxprog/spexcise.htm

Taxpayers' Rights Advocate
888-324-2798
www.boe.ca.gov/tra/tra.htm

Teachers

(see Education, Employment)

Tobacco Litigation

caag.state.ca.us/tobacco/index.htm

Tourism

(see also Arts)

Division of Tourism
800-862-2543, 916-444-4429
www.visitcalifornia.com

Traffic Safety

(see Law Enforcement, Motor Vehicles, Transportation)

Transportation

(see also Motor Vehicles)

Department of Transportation (CALTRANS)
916-654-5266
www.dot.ca.gov

Business, Transportation, and Housing Agency
916-323-5400
www.bth.ca.gov

Transportation Commission
916-654-4245
www.catc.ca.gov

Treasurer

State Treasurer's Office
916-653-2995
www.treasurer.ca.gov

Unclaimed Property

(see also Controller)

Bureau of Unclaimed Property
800-992-4647; 916-445-2636
www.sco.ca.gov/col/ucp

Unemployment Insurance

(see also section 1.11 and Employment, Insurance, Labor, Workers' Compensation)

Unemployment Insurance Appeals Board
916-263-6722
www.cuiab.ca.gov

Employment Development Department

Unemployment Insurance
800-300-5616
www.edd.ca.gov/fleclaim.htm

Universities, Public

(see Education)

Veterinary Medicine

Veterinary Medical Board
916-263-2610
www.vmb.ca.gov

Victim Services

(see also Law Enforcement)

Office of Victims' Services
877-433-9069
ag.ca.gov/victimservices

Victim Compensation and Government Claims Board
800-777-9229
www.boc.ca.gov

Vital Records

(Birth, death, marriage, dissolution/divorce; see also section 5.7)

Center for Health Statistics

Office of Vital Records
916-445-2684
www.dhs.ca.gov/hisp/chs

Voting

(see Elections)

Water

(see also Environment, Natural Resources)

Department of Water Resources
916-653-5791
www.water.ca.gov

State Water Resources Control Board
916-341-5250
www.swrcb.ca.gov

Department of Boating and Waterways
888-326-2822; 916-263-1331
www.dbw.ca.gov

Welfare

(see Child Support Services, Social Services)

Whistleblowing

Bureau of State Audits
800-952-5665
www.bsa.ca.gov/bsa
www.bsa.ca.gov/hotline

Women

Commission on the Status of Women
916-445-3173
www.statusofwomen.ca.gov

California Museum for History, Women and the Arts
www.californiamuseum.org

Workers' Compensation

(see also Employment, Labor, Unemployment Insurance)

Division of Workers' Compensation
800-736-7401; 510-286-7143
www.dir.ca.gov/dwc
www.dir.ca.gov/DWC/IandA.html

Workers' Compensation Appeals Board
415-703-4600
www.dir.ca.gov/WCAB/wcab.htm

C. More Information

California State Agencies
www.statelocalgov.net/state-ca.cfm
www.pacificsites.com/~lawlib/govern.shtml
govinfo.ucsd.edu/california.html
california.lp.findlaw.com/ca10_california_government
dir.yahoo.com/Regional/u_s__states/california/government
library.humboldt.edu/govdoc/CalAgencyPubs.htm
www.cold.ca.gov (click "agency information")
caag.state.ca.us/resources.htm

Other States
www.statelocalgov.net

D. Something to Check

1. Find the Web sites of three California agencies, offices, or boards that employ paralegals.
2. Identify California agencies, offices, or boards that would have relevant information on (a) abortion, (b) the plight of an insolvent business, and (c) police misconduct.

4.6 Counties and Cities: Some Useful Law-Related Sites

A. Information

This section presents contact information on the following major county and city law-related sites:

- main government site
- courts
- administrative agency list
- district attorney
- public defender
- consumer protection
- child support enforcement
- county/city attorney
- sheriff/police

For similar information about:

- state government, see section 4.1
- state courts, see section 4.2
- public records, see section 5.7
- law libraries, see section 5.8
- federal courts in California, see section 4.3
- bar associations, see section 3.4
- paralegal associations, see section 1.4

B. Sites

Alameda County
Alpine County
Amador County
Anaheim, City of
Bakersfield, City of
Berkeley, City of
Butte County
Calaveras County
Chula Vista, City of
Colusa County
Contra Costa County
Del Norte County
El Dorado County
Fremont, City of
Fresno, City of
Fresno County
Glendale, City of
Glenn County
Humboldt County
Huntington Beach, City of
Imperial County
Inyo County
Kern County
Kings County
Lake County
Lassen County
Long Beach, City of
Los Angeles, City of
Los Angeles County
Madera County
Marin County
Mariposa County
Mendocino County
Merced County
Modesto, City of
Modoc County
Mono County
Monterey County
Napa County
Nevada County
Oakland, City of
Orange County
Oxnard, City of
Placer County
Plumas County
Riverside, City of
Riverside County
Sacramento, City of
Sacramento County
San Benito County
San Bernardino, City of
San Bernardino County
San Diego, City of
San Diego County
San Francisco, City of
San Francisco County
San Jose, City of
San Joaquin County
San Luis Obispo County
San Mateo County
Santa Ana, City of
Santa Barbara County
Santa Clara County
Santa Cruz County
Shasta County
Sierra County
Siskiyou County
Solano County
Sonoma County
Stanislaus County
Stockton, City of
Sutter County
Tehama County
Trinity County
Tulare County
Tuolumne County
Ventura County
Yolo County
Yuba County

Alameda County

(see also Fremont, Oakland)

Alameda: County Government
www.acgov.org/index.htm

Alameda: Courts
www.alameda.courts.ca.gov/courts

Alameda: Administrative Agencies
www.acgov.org/departments.htm

Alameda: District Attorney
510-272-6222
www.acgov.org/da/index.htm

Alameda: Public Defender
510-272-6600
www.acgov.org/defender/index.htm

Alameda: Consumer Protection
510-569-9281
www.co.alameda.ca.us/da/consumer_fraud.htm

Alameda: Child Support Enforcement
800-809-2955
www.acgov.org/css/index.shtml

Alameda: County Counsel
510-272-6700
www.acgov.org/counsel/index.htm

Alameda: Sheriff
510-272-6878
www.alamedacountysheriff.org

Alpine County

Alpine: County Government
530-694-2287
www.alpinecountyca.gov

Alpine: Courts
530-694-2113
www.alpine.courts.ca.gov

Alpine: Administrative Agencies
www.alpinecountyca.gov/departments

Alpine: District Attorney
530-694-2971
www.alpinecountyca.gov
(click "County Officials")

Alpine: Child Support Enforcement
530-694-2235 x234
www.childsup.cahwnet.gov/alpine.asp

Alpine: County Counsel
www.alpinecountyca.gov
(click "County Officials")

Alpine: Sheriff
530-694-2231
www.alpineso.com

Amador County

Amador: County Government
www.co.amador.ca.us

Amador: Courts
209-223-6463
www.amadorcourt.org

Amador: Administrative Agencies
www.co.amador.ca.us/dept_main.htm

Amador: District Attorney
209-223-6444
www.co.amador.ca.us/depts/da/index.htm

Amador: Child Support Enforcement
209-223-6318; 877-466-KIDS
www.co.amador.ca.us/depts/cscsa/index.htm

Amador: County Counsel
209-223-6366
www.co.amador.ca.us/depts/counsel/index.htm

Amador: Sheriff
209-223-6500
www.co.amador.ca.us/depts/sheriff

Anaheim, City of

(see also Orange County)

Anaheim: City Government
www.anaheim.net

Anaheim: Administrative Agencies
www.anaheim.net/article.asp?id=508

Anaheim: City Attorney (Civil)
714-765-5169
www.anaheim.net/section.asp?id=93

Anaheim: City Attorney (Prosecution)
714-870-8200
www.anaheim.net/article.asp?id=444

Anaheim: Police Department
714-765-5100
www.anaheim.net/section.asp?id=124

Bakersfield, City of

(see also Kern County)

Bakersfield: City Government
661-326-3000
www.bakersfieldcity.us

Bakersfield: City Attorney
661-326-3721
www.bakersfieldcity.us
(click "Departments," "City Attorney")

Bakersfield: Police
661-326-3800
www.bakersfieldcity.us/police/index.htm

Berkeley, City of

(see also Alameda County)

Berkeley: City Government
510-981-CITY
www.ci.berkeley.ca.us

Berkeley: Administrative Agencies
www.ci.berkeley.ca.us/departments

Berkeley: City Attorney
510-981-6950
www.ci.berkeley.ca.us/attorney

Berkeley: Police
510-981-5900
www.ci.berkeley.ca.us/police

Butte County

Butte: County Government
www.buttecounty.net

Butte: Courts
530-532-7002
www.buttecourt.ca.gov

Butte: Administrative Agencies
www.buttecounty.net
(click "Departments")

Butte: District Attorney
530-538-7411

Butte: Child Support Enforcement
530-538-7221
dcss.buttecounty.net/default.asp

Butte: County Counsel
530-538-7621

Butte: Sheriff
530-538-7321
www.buttecounty.net/sheriffs

Calaveras County

Calaveras: County Government
209-754-6303
www.co.calaveras.ca.us

Calaveras: Courts
209-754-6311
www.calaveras.courts.ca.gov

Calaveras: Administrative Agencies
www.co.calaveras.ca.us/departments.asp

Calaveras: District Attorney
209-754-6330
www.co.calaveras.ca.us
(click "Departments" "Dist. Attorney")

Calaveras: Public Defender
209-754-4321
www.co.calaveras.ca.us/departments.asp
(click "Public Defender")

Calaveras: Child Support Enforcement
209-754-6780
www.childsup.cahwnet.gov/calaveras.asp

Calaveras: County Counsel
209-754-6314
www.co.calaveras.ca.us
(click "Departments" "Cnty Counsel")

Calaveras: Sheriff
209-754-6500
www.co.calaveras.ca.us
(click "Departments" "Sheriff")

Chula Vista, City of

(see also San Diego County)

Chula Vista: City Government
619-691-5044
www.ci.chula-vista.ca.us

Chula Vista: Administrative Agencies
www.ci.chula-vista.ca.us
(click "City Services")

Chula Vista: Police
619-691-5209
www.chulavistapd.org

Colusa County

Colusa: County Government
530-458-0508
www.colusacountyclerk.com

Colusa: Courts
530-458-5149
www.colusa.courts.ca.gov

Colusa: Administrative Agencies
www.cagenweb.com/colusa/govern.htm

Colusa: District Attorney
530-458-0545

Colusa: Child Support Enforcement
530-458-0555
www.childsup.cahwnet.gov/colusa.asp

Colusa: County Counsel
530-458-8227

Colusa: Sheriff
530-458-0200

Contra Costa County

Contra Costa: County Government
925-335-1086
www.co.contra-costa.ca.us

Contra Costa: Courts
925-646-1542
www.cc-courts.org/admin.htm

Contra Costa: Administrative Agencies
www.co.contra-costa.ca.us
(click "Department List" pull-down menu)

Contra Costa: District Attorney
925-646-2200
www.contracostada.org

Contra Costa: Public Defender
925-335-8000
www.co.contra-costa.ca.us
(click "Public Defender" in the "Department List" pull-down menu)

Contra Costa: Child Support Enforcement
866-244-5382; 925-957-7300
(click "Child Support" in the "Department List" pull-down menu)

Contra Costa: County Counsel
925-335-1800
(click "County Counsel" in the "Department List" pull-down menu)

Contra Costa: Sheriff
925-646-2441

Del Norte County

Del Norte: County Government
707-464-7214
www.co.del-norte.ca.us

Del Norte: Courts
707-464-8115
www.delnorte.courts.ca.gov

Del Norte: Administrative Agencies
www.co.del-norte.ca.us
(click "Agencies & Departments")

Del Norte: District Attorney
707-464-7210
www.co.del-norte.ca.us
(click "Agencies & Departments")

Del Norte: Child Support Enforcement
707-464-7232
www.co.del-norte.ca.us
(click "Agencies & Departments")

Del Norte: County Counsel
707-464-7208
www.co.del-norte.ca.us
(click "Agencies & Departments")

Del Norte: Sheriff
707-464-4191
www.co.del-norte.ca.us
(click "Agencies & Departments")

El Dorado County

El Dorado: County Government
www.co.el-dorado.ca.us

El Dorado: Courts
530-621-6426
eldocourtweb.eldoradocourt.org

El Dorado: Administrative Agencies
www.co.el-dorado.ca.us/edc.html

El Dorado: District Attorney
530-621-6472
www.co.el-dorado.ca.us/eldoda

El Dorado: Public Defender
530-621-6440
www.co.el-dorado.ca.us/public_defend.html

El Dorado: Child Support Enforcement
888-251-4727
www.co.el-dorado.ca.us/childsupport

El Dorado: County Counsel
530-621-5770
www.co.el-dorado.ca.us/counsel.html

El Dorado: Sheriff
530-621-5655
www.co.el-dorado.ca.us/sheriff

Fremont, City of

Fremont: City Government
(see also Alameda County)
510-284-4000
www.ci.fremont.ca.us/CityHall/default.htm

Fremont: Administrative Agencies
www.ci.fremont.ca.us/CityHall/default.htm
(click "Departments")

Fremont: City Attorney
510-284-4030

Fremont: Police
510-790-6800
www.fremontpolice.org

Fresno, City of

(see also Fresno County)

Fresno City: Government
559-621-8000
www.fresno.gov

Fresno City: Administrative Agencies
www.fresno.gov
(click "Government" then "Department Directory")

Fresno City: City Attorney
559-621-7500
www.fresno.gov
(click "Government" then "Department Directory")

Fresno City: Police
559-621-2000
www.fresno.gov
(click "Government" then "Department Directory")

Fresno County

(see also Fresno City)

Fresno County: Government
559-488-3529
www.co.fresno.ca.us

Fresno County: Courts
559-488-2708
www.fresnosuperiorcourt.org

Fresno County: Administrative Agencies
www.co.fresno.ca.us/portal/Departments.asp

Fresno County: District Attorney
559-488-3141
www.co.fresno.ca.us/2860/default.htm

Fresno County: Public Defender
800-742-1011; 559-488-3546
www.co.fresno.ca.us/2880/index.html

Fresno County: Child Support Enforcement
559-494-1111
www.co.fresno.ca.us/2865/default.htm

Fresno County: County Counsel
559-488-3479
www.co.fresno.ca.us/0710/countycounsel.htm

Fresno County: Sheriff
559-488-3939
www.fresnosheriff.org

Glendale, City of

(see also Los Angeles County)

Glendale: City Government
818-548-4844
www.ci.glendale.ca.us

Glendale: Administrative Agencies
www.ci.glendale.ca.us
(click "City Departments")

Glendale: City Attorney
818-548-2080
www.ci.glendale.ca.us
(click "City Departments")

Glendale: Police
818-548-4840
www.ci.glendale.ca.us
(click "City Departments")

Glenn County

Glenn: County Government
www.countyofglenn.net

Glenn: Courts
530-934-6446
www.glenncourt.ca.gov

Glenn: Administrative Agencies
www.countyofglenn.net/common/departments.asp

Glenn: District Attorney
530-934-6525
www.countyofglenn.net
(click "Departments & Agencies")

Glenn: Child Support Enforcement
530-934-6527
www.countyofglenn.net/Family_Support/home_page.asp

Glenn: County Counsel
530-934-6455
www.countyofglenn.net/County_Counsel/home_page.asp

Glenn: Sheriff
530-934-6441
www.countyofglenn.net/Sheriff/home_page.asp

Humboldt County

Humboldt: County Government
www.co.humboldt.ca.us

Humboldt: Courts
707-445-7256
www.courtinfo.ca.gov/courts/trial/humboldt

Humboldt: Administrative Agencies
www.co.humboldt.ca.us/portal/general_info.asp

Humboldt: District Attorney
707-445-7411
www.co.humboldt.ca.us/distatty

Humboldt: Public Defender
707-445-7634
www.co.humboldt.ca.us/pubdefnd

Humboldt: Child Support Enforcement
800-963-8704
www.co.humboldt.ca.us/dcss

Humboldt: County Counsel
707-445-7236
www.co.humboldt.ca.us/cntycsel

Humboldt: Sheriff
707-445-7251
www.co.humboldt.ca.us/sheriff

Huntington Beach, City of

(see also Orange County)

Huntington Beach: City Government
714-536-5202
www.surfcity-hb.org/Government

Huntington Beach: Administrative Agencies
www.surfcity-hb.org/Government/Departments

Huntington Beach: City Attorney
714-536-5555
www.surfcity-hb.org/ElectedOfficials/CityAttorney

Huntington Beach: Police
714-960-8811
www.hbpd.org

Imperial County

Imperial: County Government
760-482-4290
www.co.imperial.ca.us

Imperial: Courts
760-482-4374
www.imperial.courts.ca.gov

Imperial: Administrative Agencies
www.co.imperial.ca.us

Imperial: District Attorney
760-482-4331

Imperial: Public Defender
760-482-4510

Imperial: Child Support Enforcement
760-482-2300
www.childsup.cahwnet.gov/imperial.asp

Imperial: County Counsel
760-482-4400

Imperial: Sheriff
800-452-2051, 760-339-6301
www.icso.org

Inyo County

Inyo: County Government
760-878-0366
www.countyofinyo.org

Inyo: Courts
760-878-0319
www.inyocourt.ca.gov

Inyo: Administrative Agencies
www.countyofinyo.org/county_directory.htm

Inyo: District Attorney
760-878-0282, 760-873-6657

Inyo: Public Defender
760-873-8416

Inyo: Child Support Enforcement
760-873-3659
www.childsup.cahwnet.gov/inyo.asp

Inyo: County Counsel
760-878-0229

Inyo: Sheriff
760-878-0383

Kern County

(see also Bakersfield)

Kern: County Government
661-868-3140
www.co.kern.ca.us

Kern: Courts
661-868-4934
www.kern.courts.ca.gov

Kern: Administrative Agencies
www.co.kern.ca.us/depts

Kern: District Attorney
661-868-2340
www.co.kern.ca.us/da

Kern: Public Defender
661-868-4799
www.co.kern.ca.us/pubdef

Kern: Child Support Enforcement
800-980-2021
www.co.kern.ca.us/childsupport

Kern: County Counsel
661-868-3800
www.co.kern.ca.us/cc

Kern: Sheriff
661-861-3110
www.co.kern.ca.us/sheriff/index.html

Kings County

Kings: County Government
559-582-3211
www.countyofkings.com

Kings: Courts
559-582-1010
www.kings.courts.ca.gov

Kings: Administrative Agencies
www.countyofkings.com (click "Departments")

Kings: District Attorney
559-582-0326
www.countyofkings.com/da/index.htm

Kings: Child Support Enforcement
559-584-1425
www.countyofkings.com/css/Index.htm

Kings: County Counsel
www.countyofkings.com
(click "Departments")

Kings: Sheriff
559-582-3211 x2790
www.countyofkings.com/sheriff/about.htm

Lake County

Lake: County Government
707-263-2580
www.co.lake.ca.us

Lake: Courts
707-263-2374
www.courtinfo.ca.gov/courts/trial/lake

Lake: Administrative Agencies
co.lake.ca.us/countygovernment/departments.asp

Lake: District Attorney
707-263-2251
co.lake.ca.us/countygovernment/da/da.asp

Lake: Public Defender
707-263-2580

Lake: Child Support Enforcement
707-262-4300
dcss.co.lake.ca.us

Lake: County Counsel
707-263-2321

Lake: Sheriff
707-262-4200
www.lakesheriff.com

Lassen County

Lassen: County Government
530-251-8333
www.co.lassen.ca.us

Lassen: Courts
530-251-8205
www.lassencourt.ca.gov

Lassen: Administrative Agencies
www.co.lassen.ca.us/govt

Lassen: District Attorney
530-251-8283
www.co.lassen.ca.us/govt
(open the pull-down menu)

Lassen: Public Defender
530-251-8312
www.co.lassen.ca.us/govt
(open the pull-down menu)

Lassen: Child Support Enforcement
530-251-2630
www.co.lassen.ca.us/govt
(in the pull-down menu click "Department of Child Support")

Lassen: County Counsel
530-251-8334
www.co.lassen.ca.us/govt
(open the pull-down menu)

Lassen: Sheriff
530-251-8013
www.co.lassen.ca.us/govt
(open the pull-down menu)

Long Beach, City of

(see also Los Angeles County)

Long Beach: City Government
562-570-6801
www.longbeach.gov/gov/default.asp

Long Beach: Administrative Agencies
www.longbeach.gov/gov/default.asp

Long Beach: City Attorney
562-570-2200
www.longbeach.gov/attorney

Long Beach: City Prosecutor
562-570-5600
www.longbeach.gov/citypros

Long Beach: Police
562-570-7301
www.longbeach.gov/police/default.asp

Los Angeles, City of

(see also Los Angeles County)

Los Angeles City: Government
213-978-0600
www.lacity.org

Los Angeles City: Administrative Agencies
www.lacity.org
(click "Departments & Bureaus" pull-down menu)

Los Angeles City: City Attorney
213-978-8100
www.lacity.org/atty

Los Angeles City: Police
877-275-5273
www.lapdonline.org

Los Angeles County

(see also Glendale, Long Beach Los Angeles City)

Los Angeles County: Government
213-974-1311
lacounty.info

Los Angeles: Courts
www.lasuperiorcourt.org

Los Angeles: Administrative Agencies
lacounty.info/departments.htm

Los Angeles: District Attorney
213-974-3512
da.co.la.ca.us

Los Angeles: Public Defender
213-974-2811
pd.co.la.ca.us

Los Angeles: Consumer Protection
213-974-1452, 800-593-8222
consumer-affairs.co.la.ca.us

Los Angeles: Child Support Enforcement
800-615-8858; 323-890-9800
childsupport.co.la.ca.us

Los Angeles: County Counsel
213-974-1811
countycounsel.lacounty.info

Los Angeles: Sheriff
323-526-5541
lasd.org

Madera County

Madera: County Government
559-675-7703
www.madera-county.com

Madera: Courts
559-675-7944
madera.courts.ca.gov

Madera: Administrative Agencies
www.madera-county.com
(click "Select a Department")

Madera: District Attorney
559-675-7726
www.madera-county.com/departments/elected.html

Madera: Child Support Enforcement
559-675-7885
www.madera-county.com/childsupportservices

Madera: County Counsel
559-675-7717
www.madera-county.com/countycounsel

Madera: Sheriff
559-675-7770
www.madera-county.com/sheriff

Marin County

Marin: County Government
415-499-7000
www.co.marin.ca.us

Marin: Courts
415-499-6244
www.co.marin.ca.us/depts/MC/main/index.cfm

Marin: Administrative Agencies
www.co.marin.ca.us/nav/OrgIndex.cfm

Marin: District Attorney
415-499-6450
www.co.marin.ca.us/depts/DA/Main/index.cfm

Marin: Public Defender
415-499-6321
www.co.marin.ca.us/depts/PD/Main/index.cfm

Marin: Consumer Protection
415-499-6450
www.co.marin.ca.us/da
(click "Consumer Protection")

Marin: Child Support Enforcement
800-497-7774
www.co.marin.ca.us/depts/FS/Main/index.cfm

Marin: County Counsel
415-499-6117
www.co.marin.ca.us/depts/CL/Main/index.cfm

Marin: Sheriff
415-479-2311
www.co.marin.ca.us/depts/SO/Main/index.cfm

Mariposa County

Mariposa: County Government
209-966-3222
www.mariposacounty.org

Mariposa: Courts
209-966-2005
www.mariposacourts.org

Mariposa: Administrative Agencies
www.mariposacounty.org

Mariposa: District Attorney
209-742-7441
www.mariposacounty.org/districtattorney

Mariposa: Child Support Enforcement
866-636-KIDS
www.mariposacounty.org
(click "Child Support Services")

Mariposa: County Counsel
www.mariposacounty.org/countycounsel

Mariposa: Sheriff
209-966-3615
www.mariposacounty.org/sheriff/index.htm

Mendocino County

Mendocino: County Government
707-463-4441
www.co.mendocino.ca.us

Mendocino: Courts
707-467-6437
www.mendocino.courts.ca.gov

Mendocino: Administrative Agencies
www.co.mendocino.ca.us/ndx.htm

Mendocino: District Attorney
www.co.mendocino.ca.us/da/index.htm

Mendocino: Public Defender
707-463-5433
www.co.mendocino.ca.us/pubdef/index.htm

Mendocino: Child Support Enforcement
800-669-7477; 707-463-4216
www.co.mendocino.ca.us/css

Mendocino: County Counsel
www.co.mendocino.ca.us/coco/index.htm

Mendocino: Sheriff
707-463-4411
www.co.mendocino.ca.us/sheriff

Merced County

Merced: County Government
www.co.merced.ca.us

Merced: Courts
209-725-4100
www.mercedcourt.org

Merced: Administrative Agencies
www.co.merced.ca.us
(click "Departments")

Merced: District Attorney
209-385-7381
www.co.merced.ca.us/da

Merced: Child Support Enforcement
877-521-KIDS
www.merceddcss.com

Merced: County Counsel
209-385-7564
www.co.merced.ca.us/countycounsel

Merced: Sheriff
209-385-7444
www.mercedsheriff.com

Modesto, City of

(see also Stanislaus County)

Modesto: City Government
209-577-5200
www.modestogov.com

Modesto: Administrative Agencies
www.modestogov.com/departments

Modesto: City Attorney
209-577-5284
www.modestogov.com/cao

Modesto: Police
209-572-9500
www.modestopolice.com

Modoc County

Modoc: County Government
530-233-6426
www.modoccounty.us

Modoc: Courts
530-233-6515
www.frontiernet.net/~ldier

Modoc: Administrative Agencies
www.modoccounty.us
www.infopeople.org/modoc/codept.html

Modoc: District Attorney
530-233-6212

Modoc: Child Support Enforcement
530-233-6216
www.modocchildsupport.org

Modoc: County Counsel
530-225-8990

Modoc: Sheriff
530-233-4416

Mono County

Mono: County Government
760-932-5400
www.monocounty.ca.gov
www.monocounty.ca.gov/departments.html

Mono: Courts
760-932-5239
www.monosuperiorcourt.ca.gov

Mono: Administrative Agencies
www.monocounty.ca.gov/departments.html

Mono: District Attorney
760-924-1710
www.monocounty.ca.gov/departments.html

Mono: Child Support Enforcement
760-924-1720
www.childsup.cahwnet.gov/mono.asp

Mono: County Counsel
760-924-1700
www.monocounty.ca.gov/departments.html

Mono: Sheriff
800-447-1912; 760-932-7549
www.monosheriff.org

Monterey County

Monterey: County Government
831-755-5115
www.co.monterey.ca.us

Monterey: Courts
831-775-5400
www.monterey.courts.ca.gov

Monterey: Administrative Agencies
www.co.monterey.ca.us/departments.htm

Monterey: District Attorney
831-647-5070
www.co.monterey.ca.us/da

Monterey: Public Defender
831-755-5058
www.co.monterey.ca.us/pubdef

Monterey: Consumer Protection
831-647-5070
www.co.monterey.ca.us/da

Monterey: Child Support Enforcement
831-755-3200
www.co.monterey.ca.us/mcdcss/Default.asp

Monterey: County Counsel
831-755-5045
www.co.monterey.ca.us/countycounsel

Monterey: Sheriff
831-755-5111
www.co.monterey.ca.us/sheriff

Napa County

Napa: County Government
707-253-4386
www.co.napa.ca.us/gov

Napa: Courts
707-299-1100
www.napa.courts.ca.gov

Napa: Administrative Agencies
www.co.napa.ca.us/gov
(click "Departments")

Napa: District Attorney
707-253-4211
www.co.napa.ca.us
(click "Departments")

Napa: Public Defender
707-253-4442
www.co.napa.ca.us
(click "Departments")

Napa: Child Support Enforcement
888-314-0107; 707-253-4251
www.co.napa.ca.us
(click "Departments")

Napa: County Counsel
707-253-4521
www.co.napa.ca.us
(click "Departments")

Napa: Sheriff
707-253-4517
www.co.napa.ca.us
(click "Departments")

Nevada County

Nevada: County Government
530-265-1480
new.mynevadacounty.com

Nevada: Courts
530-265-1294
court.co.nevada.ca.us

Nevada: Administrative Agencies
new.mynevadacounty.com
(click "Department Sites")

Nevada: District Attorney
530-265-1301
new.mynevadacounty.com/da

Nevada: Public Defender
530-265-1400
new.mynevadacounty.com/publicdefender

Nevada: Child Support Enforcement
888-786-1253
new.mynevadacounty.com/css

Nevada: County Counsel
530-265-1319
new.mynevadacounty.com/ccounsel

Nevada: Sheriff
530-265-1471
new.mynevadacounty.com/sheriff

Oakland, City of

(see also Alameda County)

Oakland: City Government
510-444-2489
www.oaklandnet.com/cityhall.html

Oakland: Administrative Agencies
www.oaklandnet.com/cityhall.html#agencies

Oakland: City Attorney
510-238-3601

Oakland: Police
510-777-3333
www.oaklandpolice.com/index.html

Orange County

(see also Anaheim, Huntington Beach, Santa Ana)

Orange: County Government
714-834-5400
www.oc.ca.gov

Orange: Courts
714-834-2200
www.occourts.org

Orange: Administrative Agencies
www.oc.ca.gov/ocdirectory/ocdirectory.asp

Orange: District Attorney
714-834-3600
www.orangecountyda.com

Orange: Public Defender
714-834-2144
www.pubdef.ocgov.com/index.htm

Orange: Consumer Protection
714-834-3600
www.orangecountyda.com

Orange: Child Support Enforcement
714-541-7600; 888-594-7600
www.css.ocgov.com

Orange: County Counsel
714-834-3300

Orange: Sheriff
714-647-1800
www.ocsd.org

Oxnard, City of

(see also Ventura County)

Oxnard: City Government
805-385-7430
www.ci.oxnard.ca.us

Oxnard: Administrative Agencies
www.ci.oxnard.ca.us/stg_gov.html

Oxnard: City Attorney
805-385-7483
www.ci.oxnard.ca.us/cityattorney/main.html

Oxnard: Police
805-385-7600
www.oxnardpd.org

Placer County

Placer: County Government
530-889-4000
www.placer.ca.gov

Placer: Courts
530-889-6530
www.placercourts.org

Placer: Administrative Agencies
www.placer.ca.gov/depts/depts.htm

Placer: District Attorney
530-889-7000
www.placer.ca.gov/da/da.htm

Placer: Public Defender
530-885-2422
www.placer.ca.gov/defender/defender.htm

Placer: Consumer Protection
530-889-7000
www.placer.ca.gov/da/da.htm

Placer: Child Support Enforcement
877-988-5700
www.placer.ca.gov/ChildSupport.aspx

Placer: County Counsel
530-889-4044
www.placer.ca.gov/counsel/counsel.htm

Placer: Sheriff
530-889-7800
www.placer.ca.gov/sheriff

Plumas County

Plumas: County Government
530-283-6170
www.countyofplumas.com

Plumas: Courts
530-283-6232
www.plumascourt.ca.gov

Plumas: Administrative Agencies
www.countyofplumas.com/depts.htm

Plumas: District Attorney
530-283-6303
www.countyofplumas.com/depts.htm

Plumas: Child Support Enforcement
530-283-6264
www.countyofplumas.com/childsupport/index.htm

Plumas: County Counsel
530-283-6240
www.countyofplumas.com/countycounsel

Plumas: Sheriff
530-283-6375
www.pcso.net

Riverside, City of

(see also Riverside County)

Riverside City: City Government
951-826-5311
www.riversideca.gov

Riverside City: Administrative Agencies
www.riversideca.gov/depts.asp

Riverside City: City Attorney
951-826-5567
www.riversideca.gov/attorney

Riverside City: Police
951-787-7911
www.riversideca.gov/rpd

Riverside County

(see also Riverside City)

Riverside: County Government
951-955-1100
www.co.riverside.ca.us

Riverside: Courts
951-955-1960
www.courts.co.riverside.ca.us

Riverside: Administrative Agencies
www.co.riverside.ca.us/govern.asp

Riverside: District Attorney
951-955-5400
www.riversideda.com

Riverside: Public Defender
951-955-6000
publicdef.co.riverside.ca.us

Riverside: Consumer Protection
951-955-5400
www.riversideda.com

Riverside: Child Support Enforcement
800-521-2778
www.riversidechildsupport.com

Riverside: County Counsel
951-955-6300
www.co.riverside.ca.us/riverside.asp

Riverside: Sheriff
951-955-2400
www.riversidesheriff.org

Sacramento, City of

(see also Sacramento County)

Sacramento City: City Government
www.cityofsacramento.org

Sacramento City: Administrative Agencies
www.cityofsacramento.org/depts.htm

Sacramento City: City Attorney
916-808-5346
www.cityofsacramento.org/cityattorney

Sacramento City: Police
916-264-5471
www.sacpd.org/index.asp

Sacramento County

(see also Sacramento City)

Sacramento: County Government
916-876-6188
www.co.sacramento.ca.us

Sacramento: Courts
916-874-5522
www.saccourt.com

Sacramento: Administrative Agencies
www.co.sacramento.ca.us
(click "Department Index")

Sacramento: District Attorney
916-874-6218
www.da.saccounty.net

Sacramento: Public Defender
916-874-6056
www.publicdefender.saccounty.net

Sacramento: Consumer Protection
916-874-6218
www.da.saccounty.net

Sacramento: Child Support Enforcement
888-271-3906
www.dcss.saccounty.net

Sacramento: County Counsel
916-874-5544
www.saccounty.net/coco/index.html

Sacramento: Sheriff
916-874-5115
www.sacsheriff.com

San Benito County

San Benito: County Government
831-636-4000
www.san-benito.ca.us

San Benito: Courts
831-636-4057
www.sanbenito.courts.ca.gov

San Benito: Administrative Agencies
www.san-benito.ca.us/departments

San Benito: District Attorney
831-636-4126
www.san-benito.ca.us/departments/#da

San Benito: Child Support Enforcement
831-636-4130
www.san-benito.ca.us/departments/#child-supp

San Benito: County Counsel
831-636-4040

San Benito: Sheriff
831-636-4080
www.sbcsheriff.org

San Bernardino, City of

(see also San Bernardino County)

San Bernardino City: Government
909-384-5211
www.ci.san-bernardino.ca.us

San Bernardino City: Administrative Agencies
www.ci.san-bernardino.ca.us
(click "Departments")

San Bernardino City: City Attorney
909-384-5355

San Bernardino City: Police
909-384-5742

San Bernardino County

(see also San Bernardino City)

San Bernardino: County Government
909-387-5417
www.co.san-bernardino.ca.us

San Bernardino: Courts
909-387-6500
www.sbcounty.gov/courts

San Bernardino Administrative Agencies
www.co.san-bernardino.ca.us
(click "Departments")

San Bernardino: District Attorney
909-387-8309
www.co.san-bernardino.ca.us/da

San Bernardino: Public Defender
909-387-8373

San Bernardino: Child Support Enforcement
909-799-1790
hss.co.san-bernardino.ca.us/dcss

San Bernardino: County Counsel
909-387-5455

San Bernardino: Sheriff
909-387-3545
www.co.san-bernardino.ca.us/Sheriff

San Diego, City of

(see also San Diego County)

San Diego City: Government
619-236-6363
www.sandiego.gov

San Diego City: Administrative Agencies
www.sandiego.gov/directories/departments.shtml

San Diego City: City Attorney
619-236-6220

San Diego City: Police
619-531-2000
www.sandiego.gov/police

San Diego County

(see also Chula Vista, San Diego City)

San Diego: County Government
858-694-3900
www.co.san-diego.ca.us

San Diego: Courts
619-531-4420
www.sdcourt.ca.gov

San Diego: Administrative Agencies
www.co.san-diego.ca.us
(click "County Departments")

San Diego: District Attorney
619-531-4040
www.sdcda.org

San Diego: Public Defender
619-338-4700
www.sdcounty.ca.gov/public_defender/index.html

San Diego: Consumer Protection
619-531-3507
www.sdcda.org

San Diego: Child Support Enforcement
619-236-7600
www.sandiegochildsupport.com

San Diego: County Counsel
619-531-4860

San Diego: Sheriff
858-565-5200
www.sdsheriff.net

San Francisco, City of

(see also San Francisco County)

San Francisco City: City Government
415-554-6141
www.ci.sf.ca.us

San Francisco City: City Attorney
415-554-4700
www.sfgov.org/site/cityattorney

San Francisco City: Administrative Agencies
www.ci.sf.ca.us
(click "City Agencies")

San Francisco City: Police
415-553-0123
www.sfgov.org/site/police

San Francisco County

San Francisco County: County Government
415-554-5184
www.sfgov.org/site/bdsupvrs

San Francisco County: Courts
www.sfgov.org/site/courts

San Francisco City: Administrative Agencies
www.sfgov.org/site

San Francisco County: District Attorney
415-553-1752
www.sfgov.org/site/da

San Francisco County: Public Defender
415-553-1671
www.sfgov.org/site/pd

San Francisco County: Consumer Protection
415-553-1752
www.sfgov.org/site/da

San Francisco County: Child Support Enforcement
415-356-2700
www.ci.sf.ca.us/css

San Francisco County: Sheriff
415-554-7225
www.sfgov.org/site/mainpages_index.asp?id=28566

San Jose, City of

(see also Santa Clara County)

San Jose: City Government
408-535-3500
www.sanjoseca.gov

San Jose: Administrative Agencies
www.sanjoseca.gov/depts.html

San Jose: City Attorney
408-535-1900
www.sanjoseca.gov/attorney

San Jose: Police
408-277-8900
www.sjpd.org

San Joaquin County

(see also Stockton)

San Joaquin: County Government
209-468-2429
www.co.san-joaquin.ca.us

San Joaquin: Courts
209-468-2355
www.stocktoncourt.org

San Joaquin: Administrative Agencies
www.co.san-joaquin.ca.us
(click "Departments")

San Joaquin: District Attorney
209-468-2400
www.co.san-joaquin.ca.us/DA

San Joaquin: Public Defender
209-468-2730
www.co.san-joaquin.ca.us/pubdefender

San Joaquin: Child Support Enforcement
209-468-2601
www.sjgov.org/childsupport

San Joaquin: Sheriff
209-468-4400
www.co.san-joaquin.ca.us/sheriff

San Luis Obispo County

San Luis Obispo: County Government
805-781-5000
www.co.slo.ca.us

San Luis Obispo: Courts
805-781-5143; 866-249-9475
www.slocourts.ca.gov

San Luis Obispo: Administrative Agencies
www.co.slo.ca.us
(click "Department Directory")

San Luis Obispo: District Attorney
805-781-5800
www.sloda.com

San Luis Obispo: Child Support Enforcement
805-781-5734
www.co.slo.ca.us/Child_Support

San Luis Obispo: County Counsel
805-781-5400

San Luis Obispo: Sheriff
805-781-4540
www.slosheriff.org

San Mateo County

San Mateo: County Government
650-363-4000
www.co.sanmateo.ca.us

San Mateo: Courts
650-877-5705
www.sanmateocourt.org

San Mateo: Administrative Agencies
www.co.sanmateo.ca.us

San Mateo: District Attorney
650-363-4636
www.co.sanmateo.ca.us

San Mateo: Child Support Enforcement
866-366-8221; 650-366-8221
www.smcdcss.com

San Mateo: County Counsel
650-363-4250
www.co.sanmateo.ca.us

San Mateo: Sheriff
650-599-1664
www.smcsheriff.com

Santa Ana, City of

(see also Orange County)

Santa Ana: City Government
714-647-5400
www.ci.santa-ana.ca.us

Santa Ana: Administrative Agencies
www.ci.santa-ana.ca.us
(click "Departments")

Santa Ana: City Attorney
714-647-5201

Santa Ana: Police
714-245-8665
www.ci.santa-ana.ca.us/pd

Santa Barbara County

Santa Barbara: County Government
805-681-4200
www.countyofsb.org

Santa Barbara: Courts
805-568-2220
www.sbcourts.org/index.asp

Santa Barbara: Administrative Agencies
www.countyofsb.org/locations.asp

Santa Barbara: District Attorney
805-568-2300
www.countyofsb.org/da

Santa Barbara: Public Defender
805-568-3470
www.publicdefendersb.org

Santa Barbara: Consumer Protection
805-568-2300
www.countyofsb.org/da

Santa Barbara: Child Support Enforcement
800-818-1386
www.countyofsb.org/dcss/index.asp

Santa Barbara: County Counsel
805-568-2950
www.countyofsb.org/counsel

Santa Barbara: Sheriff
805-681-4100
www.sbsheriff.org

Santa Clara County

(see also San Jose)

Santa Clara: County Government
408-299-5001
www.sccgov.org

Santa Clara: Courts
408-882-2700
www.sccsuperiorcourt.org

Santa Clara: Administrative Agencies
www.sccgov.org
(click "Agencies & Depts")

Santa Clara: District Attorney
408-299-7400
www.santaclara-da.org

Santa Clara: Public Defender
408-299-7700

Santa Clara: Consumer Protection
408-299-7400
www.santaclara-da.org

Santa Clara: Child Support Enforcement
888-687-7500
www.scc-dcss.org

Santa Clara: County Counsel
408-299-5900

Santa Clara: Sheriff
800-211-2220
www.sccsheriff.org

Santa Cruz County

Santa Cruz: County Government
831-454-2000
www.co.santa-cruz.ca.us

Santa Cruz: Courts
831-454-2020
www.santacruzcourt.org

Santa Cruz: Administrative Agencies
www.co.santa-cruz.ca.us
(click "County Departments and Agencies")

Santa Cruz: District Attorney
831-454-2400
sccounty01.co.santa-cruz.ca.us/DAInternet

Santa Cruz: Child Support Enforcement
831-454-3700
www.santacruzdcss.org

Santa Cruz: County Counsel
831-454-2040

Santa Cruz: Sheriff
831-471-1121
www.scsheriff.com

Shasta County

Shasta: County Government
800-479-8009; 530-225-5561
www.co.shasta.ca.us

Shasta: Courts
530-245-6789
www.shastacourts.com

Shasta: Administrative Agencies
www.co.shasta.ca.us

Shasta: District Attorney
530-245-6300
da.co.shasta.ca.us

Shasta: Child Support Enforcement
800-930-5644; 866-440-4443
www.co.shasta.ca.us

Shasta: County Counsel
530-225-5711

Shasta: Sheriff
530-245-6165
www.co.shasta.ca.us/Departments/Sheriff

Sierra County

Sierra: County Government
530-289-3295
www.sierracounty.ws

Sierra: Courts
530-289-3698
www.sierracourt.org

Sierra: Administrative Agencies
www.sierracounty.ws
(click "Directory")

Sierra: District Attorney
530-289-3269
www.sierracounty.ws

Sierra: Child Support Enforcement
888-823-2845; 530-271-KIDS
new.mynevadacounty.com/css

Sierra: County Counsel
530-289-3212

Sierra: Sheriff
530-289-3700
www.sierracounty.ws

Siskiyou County

Siskiyou: County Government
530-842-8081
www.co.siskiyou.ca.us

Siskiyou: Courts
530-842-8239
www.siskiyou.courts.ca.gov

Siskiyou: Administrative Agencies
www.co.siskiyou.ca.us
(click "County Departments & Services")

Siskiyou: District Attorney
530-842-8125
www.co.siskiyou.ca.us/da/index.htm

Siskiyou: Public Defender
530-842-8105

Siskiyou: Child Support Enforcement
530-841-2950
www.co.siskiyou.ca.us/dcss/index.htm

Siskiyou: County Counsel
530-842-8100

Siskiyou: Sheriff
530-842-8300

Solano County

Solano: County Government
707-421-6100
www.co.solano.ca.us

Solano: Courts
707-421-7827
www.solanocourts.com

Solano: Administrative Agencies
www.co.solano.ca.us/Departments.asp

Solano: District Attorney
707-784-6800
www.co.solano.ca.us/Departments.asp

Solano: Public Defender
707-784-6700
www.co.solano.ca.us/Departments.asp

Solano: Child Support Enforcement
707-784-7210
www.co.solano.ca.us/Departments.asp

Solano: Sheriff
707-421-7000
www.co.solano.ca.us/Departments.asp

Sonoma County

Sonoma: County Government
707-565-2431
www.sonoma-county.org

Sonoma: Courts
707-565-1100
www.sonomasuperiorcourt.com

Sonoma: Administrative Agencies
www.sonoma-county.org/Services

Sonoma: District Attorney
707-565-2311
www.sonoma-county.org/da

Sonoma: Public Defender
707-565-2791
www.sonoma-county.org/pubdef

Sonoma: Child Support Enforcement
888-271-4214; 707-565-4000
www.sonoma-county.org/dcss

Sonoma: County Counsel
707-565-2421
www.sonoma-county.org/counsel

Sonoma: Sheriff
707-565-2511
www.sonomasheriff.org

Stanislaus County

(see also Modesto)

Stanislaus: County Government
209-525-4494
www.co.stanislaus.ca.us

Stanislaus: Courts
209-525-6348
www.stanct.org/courts/index.html

Stanislaus: Administrative Agencies
www.co.stanislaus.ca.us/departments.htm

Stanislaus: District Attorney
209-525-5550
www.stanislaus-da.org

Stanislaus: Public Defender
209-525-4200
www.co.stanislaus.ca.us/pd

Stanislaus: Child Support Enforcement
209-558-3000
www.stancodcss.org

Stanislaus: County Counsel
209-525-6376
www.co.stanislaus.ca.us/Counsel

Stanislaus: Sheriff
209-525-7216
www.stanislaussheriff.com

Stockton, City of

(see also San Joaquin)

Stockton: City Government
209-937-8212
www.stocktongov.com

Stockton: Administrative Agencies
www.stocktongov.com/pages/departments.cfm

Stockton: City Attorney
209-937-8333
www.stocktongov.com/attorney

Stockton: City Police
209-937-8377
www.stocktongov.com/police

Sutter County

Sutter: County Government
530-822-7106
www.co.sutter.ca.us

Sutter: Courts
www.suttercourts.com

Sutter: Administrative Agencies
www.co.sutter.ca.us
(click "County Departments")

Sutter: District Attorney
530-822-7330

Sutter: Public Defender
530-822-7355

Sutter: Child Support Enforcement
530-822-7338

Sutter: County Counsel
530-822-7110

Sutter: Sheriff
530-822-7307
sheriff.co.sutter.ca.us

Tehama County

Tehama: County Government
530-527-4655
www.tehamacountyadmin.org

Tehama: Courts
530-824-4601
www.courtinfo.ca.gov/courts/trial/tehama

Tehama: Administrative Agencies
www.tehamacountyadmin.org/deptroster.cfm

Tehama: District Attorney
530-527-3053
www.tehamada.org

Tehama: Child Support Enforcement
530-527-3110
www.tehamacountyadmin.org/css.cfm

Tehama: County Counsel
530-527-9252

Tehama: Sheriff
530-529-7900
www.tehamaso.org

Trinity County

Trinity: County Government
530-623-1217
www.trinitycounty.org

Trinity: Courts
530-623-1369
www.courtinfo.ca.gov/courts/trial/trinity

Trinity: Administrative Agencies
www.trinitycounty.org
(click "Departments")

Trinity: District Attorney
530-623-1304

Trinity: Child Support Enforcement
530-623-1306

Trinity: County Counsel
530-623-1382

Trinity: Sheriff
530-623-2611

Tulare County

Tulare: County Government
559-733-6531
www.co.tulare.ca.us

Tulare: Courts
559-733-6348
www.tularesuperiorcourt.ca.gov

Tulare: Administrative Agencies
www.co.tulare.ca.us/government/default.asp

Tulare: District Attorney
559-733-6411

Tulare: Public Defender
559-733-6693

Tulare: Child Support Enforcement
559-713-5700

Tulare: County Counsel
559-733-6263

Tulare: Sheriff
559-733-6220

Tuolumne County

Tuolumne: County Government
www.tuolumnecounty.ca.gov

Tuolumne: Courts
209-533-5555
www.tuolumne.courts.ca.gov

Tuolumne: Administrative Agencies
www.tuolumnecounty.ca.gov
(click "Government")

Tuolumne: District Attorney
209-588-5450

Tuolumne: Public Defender
209-532-0430

Tuolumne: Child Support Enforcement
209-533-6400
www.childsup.cahwnet.gov/tuolumne.asp

Tuolumne: County Counsel
209-533-5517

Tuolumne: Sheriff
209-533-5855

Ventura County

(see also Oxnard)

Ventura: County Government
805-654-5000
www.countyofventura.org

Ventura: Courts
805-654-2963
www.ventura.courts.ca.gov

Ventura: Administrative Agencies
www.countyofventura.org/dept.asp

Ventura: District Attorney
805-654-2500
www.ventura.org/vcda

Ventura: Child Support Enforcement
805-654-5200
childsupport.countyofventura.org

Ventura: Sheriff
805-654-2380
www.vcsd.org

Yolo County

Yolo: County Government
530-666-8150
www.yolocounty.org

Yolo: Courts
530-406-6700
www.yolo.courts.ca.gov

Yolo: Administrative Agencies
www.yolocounty.org/org/orgs.htm

Yolo: District Attorney
530-666-8180
www.yoloda.org

Yolo: Public Defender
530-666-8165

Yolo: Consumer Protection
530-666-8180
www.yoloda.org

Yolo: Child Support Enforcement
530-661-2880
www.yolocounty.org/DCSS/Default.htm

Yolo: County Counsel
530-666-8172
www.yolocounty.org/org/counsel

Yolo: Sheriff
530-666-8282
www.yolocountysheriff.com

Yuba County

Yuba: County Government
530-749-7575
www.co.yuba.ca.us

Yuba: Courts
530-749-7600
www.yubacourts.org

Yuba: Administrative Agencies
www.co.yuba.ca.us

Yuba: District Attorney
530-749-7770

Yuba: Public Defender
530-741-2331

Yuba: Child Support Enforcement
530-749-6000

Yuba: County Counsel
530-749-7565

Yuba: Sheriff
530-749-7777
www.co.yuba.ca.us/sheriff/ycso

C. More Information

Assessors
www.boe.ca.gov/proptaxes/assessors.htm

Child Support Agencies
www.childsup.cahwnet.gov/county_locations.asp

Clerks (Recorder-Clerks)
www.co.el-dorado.ca.us/countyclerk/other_rec.html

Consumer Protection
www.calconsumer.org/county.htm
www.dca.ca.gov

County/City Governments
www.csac.counties.org
www.csac.counties.org/default.asp?id=7
www.statelocalgov.net/state-ca.cfm
www.wowworks.com/wowcity/ca.htm
www.cacities.org/index.jsp

County Statistics/Profiles
www.dof.ca.gov/html/fs_data/profiles/pf_home.htm

Courts
www.courtinfo.ca.gov/courts/trial/courtlist.htm
www.dca.ca.gov/publications/small_claims/index.shtml

District Attorneys
en.wikipedia.org/wiki/List_of_California_District_Attorneys
www.cdaa.org/daroster.htm

Domestic Violence Resources
www.aardvarc.org/dv/states/ca.shtml
www.safenetwork.net/directory.cfm

Health Officers, Registrars, and Recorders
www.dhs.ca.gov/hisp/chs/OVR/LocalRegistrar/default.htm

Legal Aid/Legal Service Offices
www.dca.ca.gov/r_r/legalso1.htm
www.crla.org

Public Defenders
www.cpda.org/publicarea/county/countypdwebsites.html
www.cpda.org/PublicArea/HomePublic.html

Vital Records
www.dhs.ca.gov/chs/OVR/default.htm

D. Something to Check

1. Pick one kind of information pertaining to law and government (e.g., enforcement of the dog leash law). Find the Internet address of where this information can be found in any ten California counties or cities.
2. For any county you select, identify the kind of information available online about any aspect of real property in that county.

PART

5

Legal Research and Records Research

A. Introduction

In this section, we will answer the following question:

> Where can you find California primary authority (e.g., cases, statutes) and secondary authority (e.g., legal encyclopedias and treatises) if you need to research an issue of California law?

We will cover both traditional book sources as well as what is available online. For related material, see:

- state courts in California, including links to their opinions (section 4.2)
- federal courts in California, including links to their opinions (section 4.3)
- citing California legal materials (section 5.2)
- research starters for 87 major California topics (section 5.5)
- finding California public records (section 5.7)
- finding law libraries in your area that often have materials on California law (section 5.8)
- finding continuing legal education resources in California (section 1.5)

B. Finding California State Law

Exhibit 5.1A presents an overview of California law found in traditional and online sources.

C. Publishers of Materials on California Law

AccessLaw
www.accesslaw.com

Attorney's BriefCase
www.atybriefcase.com

CaseClerk
www.caseclerk.com

Continuing Education of the Bar-California
ceb.com

CourtForm
www.courtform.com

Daily Journal Corp.
www.dailyjournal.com

Fastcase
www.fastcase.com

JuriSearch
www.jurisearch.com

LawCA
www.lawca.com

Lawdable Press
www.litigationbythenumbers.com

Legal Solutions
www.paralegal.delmar.cengage.com

LexisNexis/Matthew Bender
www.lexisone.com
bender.lexisnexis.com

Loislaw
www.loislaw.com

MacForms
www.macforms.com

Nolo Press
www.nolo.com

TheLaw.net
thelaw.net

VersusLaw
www.versuslaw.com

Delmar, Cengage Learning
www.paralegal.delmar.cengage.com
(type "California" in the search box)

D. More Information

Online Portals to California Legal Research
www.ll.georgetown.edu/states/california.cfm
www.ll.georgetown.edu/states/california-in-depth.cfm
california.lp.findlaw.com
www.publiclawlibrary.org/links.html
www.chesslaw.com/californialaw.htm
www.lawsource.com/also/usa.cgi?ca
lalaw.lib.ca.us
www.nocall.org (click "California Laws")
www.hg.org/usstates.html (click "California")
www.law.cornell.edu/states/california.html
www.aallnet.org/chapter/scall/locating.htm
www.ca.gov/state/portal/myca_homepage.jsp

E. Something to Check

1. Select three of the sources in section C (Publishers of Materials on California Law) that sell the same California materials. Compare what they offer, e.g., description, ease of use, cost.
2. Pick any legal issue (e.g., capital punishment, abortion, community property). Using the free online materials referred to here, find and briefly summarize one case and one statute on your topic.

EXHIBIT 5.1A **California Law on the Shelf and Online**

CATEGORY	WHERE TO FIND IT ON THE SHELF	WHERE TO FIND IT ONLINE FOR A FEE	WHERE TO FIND IT ONLINE FOR FREE (complete, partial, or links)
California Constitution	•*West's Annotated California Code* •*Deering's California Codes, Annotated* (LexisNexis) Note: The constitution is found within these codes.	•Lexis: www.lexis.com CAL library CACNST file •Westlaw: www.westlaw.com CA-ST-ANN database •Others: see addresses below for AccessLaw, FastCase, JuriSearch, Loislaw, TheLawNet, VersusLaw	•www.leginfo.ca.gov/const.html •california.lp.findlaw.com/ca01_ codes •www.legislature.ca.gov
State Statutes (California Codes)	•*Statutes of California* (Office of State Publishing) •*West's Annotated California Code* •*Deering's California Codes, Annotated* (LexisNexis)	•Lexis: www.lexis.com CAL library CODE file •Westlaw: www.westlaw.com CA-ST-ANN database CA-ST database •Others: see addresses below for AccessLaw, FastCase, JuriSearch, Loislaw, TheLawNet, VersusLaw	•www.legislature.ca.gov •www.leginfo.ca.gov/calaw.html •california.lp.findlaw.com/ ca01_codes •www.findlaw.com/casecode (click "California")
State Statutes (session laws & advance services)	•*Statutes and Amendments to the Codes* •*Deering's California Advance Legislative Service* (LexisNexis) •*Deering's California Codes Annotated Advance Code Service* (LexisNexis) •West's California Legislative Service	•Lexis: www.lexis.com CAL library CAALS file •Westlaw: www.westlaw.com CA-LEGIS database	•www.leginfo.ca.gov •www.leginfo.ca.gov/statute.html •www.legislature.ca.gov
Pending Bills		•Lexis: www.lexis.com CAL library CABILL file •Westlaw: www.westlaw.com CA-BILLS database	•www.leginfo.ca.gov/bilinfo.html •www.legislature.ca.gov
Legislative History		•www.legintent.com •www.lrihistory.com •lhclearinghouse.com	•www.leginfo.ca.gov/bilinfo.html •www.legislature.ca.gov (click "Legislative Research") •www.usfca.edu/law_library/calleg.html
State Ballot Propositions			•www.ss.ca.gov (click "Elections & Voter Information") •lalaw.lib.ca.us/ballot.html •www.uchastings.edu/library (click "research databases" then "California ballot")
State Administrative Regulations	•*California Code of Regulations* (Office of Administrative Law/Barclay's/West) •*California Regulatory Notice Register* (Barclay's/West) •*Barclays Regulatory Law Bulletin* (Barclay's/West)	•Lexis: www.lexis.com CAL library CAADMN file •Westlaw: www.westlaw.com CA-ADC database •Others: see addresses below for FastCase, Loislaw, TheLawNet, VersusLaw	•www.calregs.com •ccr.oal.ca.gov •www.ca.gov (click "State Agencies Directory")

State Administrative Law (misc.)	•*State Administrative Manual*		•sam.dgs.ca.gov
State Court Opinions of: **•California Supreme Court** **•California Courts of Appeal** **•Appellate Division of Superior Courts**	•*California Reports* (Cal., Cal.2d, Cal.3d, Cal.4th) •*California Appellate Reports* (Cal.App., Cal.App.2d, Cal.App.3d, Cal.App.4th) •*West's California Reporter* (Cal.Rptr. Cal.Rptr.2d Cal.Rptr.3d) •*Pacific Reporter* (P., P.2d, P.3d)	•Lexis: www.lexis.com CAL library CACTS file •Westlaw: www.westlaw.com CA-CS database •Others: see addresses below for CaseClerk, FastCase, JuriSearch, Loislaw, TheLawNet, VersusLaw	•www.courtinfo.ca.gov/opinions •appellatecases.courtinfo.ca.gov •www.findlaw.com/cacases/index. html •www.findlaw.com/casecode (click "California") •www.lexisone.com
Opinions of the California State Bar Court	•*California State Bar Court Reporter*	•See entries under Ethics below	•calbar.ca.gov/state/calbar/sbc_generic.jsp?cid=13482&id=23383
State Court Rules (Rules of Court)	•*Deering's California Rules of Court* (LexisNexis) •*California Rules of Court* (West)	•Lexis: www.lexis.com CAL library CARULE file •Westlaw: www.westlaw.com CA-RULES database CA-TRIALRULES database •Others: see addresses below for FastCase, JuriSearch, Loislaw, TheLawNet, VersusLaw	•www.courtinfo.ca.gov/rules •www.courtinfo.ca.gov/rules/ localrules.htm •www.llrx.com/courtrules (click "California")
Citators	•*Shepard's California Citations: Part I Cases* •*Shepard's California Citations: Part II Statutes* •*Shepard's California Reporter Citations* •*Shepard's Pacific Reporter Citations*	•Lexis: www.lexis.com CAL Library •KeyCite: www.westlaw.com •Globalcite: Loislaw (see address below)	
Digests of California State Court Opinions	•*California Digest of Official Reports 3d* (West) •*West's California Digest 2d* •*Pacific Digest 2d*	•Westlaw: www.westlaw.com Example of a digest search in the ca-cs database containing all California state cases: di(murder)	
Attorney General Opinions	•*Opinions of the Attorney General of California*	•Lexis: www.lexis.com CAL library CAAG file •Westlaw: www.westlaw.com CA-AG database	•ag.ca.gov/opinions
Jury Instructions	•*California Jury Instructions: Criminal* (7th ed.) (West) (CALJIC) •*California Jury Instructions: Civil* (9th ed.)(West) (BAJI) •*California Forms of Jury Instructions* (Matthew Bender)	•Lexis: www.lexis.com CAL library CJCJUR file •Westlaw: www.westlaw.com CA-JI database	•www.courtinfo.ca.gov/reference/documents/civiljuryinst.pdf •www.courtinfo.ca.gov/jury/criminaljuryinstructions/index.htm
Judicial Forms	•*California Judicial Council Forms Manual* (CEB) •*Judicial Council Forms* (Matthew Bender) •*California Judicial Council Forms Manual* (West)	•Lexis: www.lexis.com CAL library •Westlaw: www.westlaw.com CAJCF database •Others: see addresses below for AccessLaw, JuriSearch, Loislaw, TheLawNet, VersusLaw	•www.courtinfo.ca.gov/forms •california.lp.findlaw.com (click "CA Legal Forms") •california.lp.findlaw.com/ca18_ forms •www.llrx.com/courtrules (click "California") •www.lawca.com

Local Government Laws (charters, codes, ordinances)	Links to local law through county and city sites: •www.csac.counties.org •www.cacities.org (click "all about cities")		•www.bpcnet.com/codes.htm (click "California") •california.lp.findlaw.com/ca01_ codes •municode.com (click "Online Library" then "California") •www.municode.com/resources (click "California") •www.cityattorney.us •www.igs.berkeley.edu/library/calcodes.html
Ethics	•*Rules of Professional Conduct* •*California Compendium on Professional Responsibility* (State Bar) •*California State Bar Court Reporter* •*Ethics Opinions*	•Lexis: www.lexis.com CAL library CAETOP file CAL library ETHICS file CAL library CABAR file •Westlaw: www.westlaw.com CAETH-EO database CAETH-CS database CA-RULES database	•www.calbar.ca.gov (click "ethics")
State Legal Encyclopedia	•*California Jurisprudence 3d* (West) (Cal. Jur. 3d)	•Westlaw: www.westlaw.com CAJUR database	
Legal Treatises on State Law	•*Summary of California Law* (9th ed) (Witkin)(West) •*California Procedure* (4th ed.)(Witkin)West)	•Lexis: www.lexis.com CAL library WITKIN file •Westlaw: www.westlaw.com WITKIN database	
Legal Research Manuals/Guides on California Law	•Dershem, Larry, *California Legal Research Handbook* (Rothman) •Hanft, John, *Legal Research in California* (5th ed.) (West) •Martin, Daniel, *Henke's California Law Guide* (7th ed.) (Lexis/Nexis)		•*Locating the Law*, 4th ed. (www.aallnet.org/chapter/scall/locating.htm) •See "Online Portals to California Legal Research" in More Information at the beginning of this section.
Legal Newspapers	•*Los Angeles Daily Journal* •*San Diego Daily Transcript* •*San Francisco Daily Journal*		•www.dailyjournal.com •www.sddt.com •www.law.com/jsp/ca/index.jsp
Blogs on California Law	•calapp.blogspot.com •calemploymentlaw.blogs.com •legalpad.typepad.com •oc-divorce.typepad.com •sawdaydrake.typepad.com/estate_planning •californiadivorce.blogs.com/blog •sclblog.com •www.calpiblog.com		
Locating California Attorneys	•*Martindale-Hubbell Law Directory* •*Parker Directory of California Attorneys*	•Lexis: www.lexis.com MARHUB library CADIR file •Westlaw: www.westlaw.com WLD-CA database	•www.calbar.ca.gov (click "Attorney Search") •www.martindale.com •lawyers.findlaw.com •lawyers.findlaw.com/lawyer/ state/California

5.2 Citation Examples: Some Comparisons

A. Introduction

There are three major citation systems:

Citation System Explained	Abbreviation Used Here
California Style Manual: A Handbook of Legal Style for California Courts and Lawyers (West Group 4th ed. 2000) (Edward W. Jessen)	Style Manual
The Bluebook: A Uniform System of Citation (Columbia Law Review Ass'n et al. eds., 18th ed. 2005)	Bluebook
ALWD Citation Manual: A Professional System of Citation (2d ed. Aspen Publishers 2003) (Ass'n of Legal Writing Directors & Darby Dickerson)	ALWD

There is considerable similarity in how the three systems cite laws and other categories of materials. Yet there are some important differences you should know about. In this section, we will give examples of citations using all three systems. As you compare the examples, make careful note of large differences (e.g., how words are abbreviated and in what order they are used) as well as seemingly small ones (e.g., the use of spaces and commas).

The examples based on the Style Manual are in parentheses. This is required unless the citation is an integral part of the sentence. A cite is not integral to a sentence if it can be removed without altering the meaning or sense of the sentence.

For a list of abbreviations in citations, see section 5.3.

B. Comparison of Citation Formats

California Constitution

Style Manual: (Cal. Const. art. III, § 8(b)(3).)
Bluebook: Cal. Const. art. III, § 8(b)(3)
ALWD: Cal. Const. art. III, § 8(b)(3)

California Statutes

Style Manual: (Bus. & Prof. Code, § 6400.)
Bluebook: Cal. Bus. & Prof. Code § 6400 (West 2004)
Cal. Bus. & Prof. Code § 6400 (Deering 2004)
ALWD: Cal. Bus. & Prof. Code Ann. § 6400 (West 2004)
Cal. Bus. & Prof. Code Ann. § 6400 (LEXIS 2004)

California Administrative Code

Style Manual: (Cal. Code Regs., tit. 14, § 218.)
Bluebook: Cal. Code Regs. tit. 14, § 218 (2003)
ALWD: Cal. Code Regs. tit. 14, § 218 (2003)

California Court Opinions

California Supreme Court
Style Manual: (*Mejia v. Reed* (2003) 31 Cal.4th 657.)
or:
(*Mejia v. Reed* (2003) 31 Cal.4th 657 [3 Cal.Rptr.3d 390, 74 P.2d 166].)
Bluebook: *Mejia v. Reed,* 74 P.3d 166 (Cal. 2003)
ALWD: *Mejia v. Reed,* 74 P.3d 166 (Cal. 2003)

California Court of Appeals
Style Manual: (*Baldwin v. City of Los Angeles* (1999) 70 Cal.App.4th 819.)
or:
(*Baldwin v. City of Los Angeles* (1999) 70 Cal.App.4th 819 [83 Cal.Rptr.2d 178].)
Bluebook: *Baldwin v. City of Los Angeles,* 83 Cal. Rptr. 2d 178 (Ct. App. 1999)
ALWD: *Baldwin v. City of Los Angeles,* 83 Cal. Rptr. 2d 178 (Ct. App. 2d Dist. 1999)

Federal Court Opinions Applicable in California

United States Supreme Court
Style Manual: (*Sansone v. United States (1965)* 380 U.S. 343 [85 S.Ct. 1004, 13 L.Ed.2d 882.]
Bluebook: *Sansone v. United States,* 380 U.S. 343 (1965)
ALWD: *Sansone v. U.S.,* 380 U.S. 343 (1965)

United States Court of Appeals for the 9th Circuit
Style Manual: (*Lewis v. Sacramento County* (9th Cir. 1996) 98 F.3d 434.)
Bluebook: *Lewis v. Sacramento County,* 98 F.3d 434 (9th Cir. 1996)
ALWD: *Lewis v. Sacramento Co.,* 98 F.3d 434 (9th Cir. 1996)

United States District Court in California
Style Manual: (*Jackson v. East Bay Hosp.* (N.D.Cal. 1997) 980 F.Supp 1341.)
Bluebook: *Jackson v. East Bay Hosp.,* 980 F. Supp 1341 (N.D. Cal. 1997)

ALWD: *Jackson v. East Bay Hosp.*, 980 F. Supp 1341 (N.D. Cal. 1997)

California Attorney General Opinions

Style Manual: (87 Ops.Cal.Atty.Gen. 181 (2004).)
Bluebook: 87 Cal. Att'y Gen. Op. 181 (2004)
ALWD: 87 Op. Cal. Atty. Gen. 181 (2004)

California Rules of Court

Style Manual: (Cal. Rules of Court, rule 200.1.)
Bluebook: Cal. Ct. R. 200.1
ALWD: Cal. Ct. R. 200.1

Law Reviews

Style Manual: (Rhode, *Ethical Perspectives on Legal Practice* (1985) 37 Stan. L.Rev. 589.)
Bluebook: Deborah L. Rhode, *Ethical Perspectives on Legal Practice*, 37 Stan. L. Rev. 589 (1985)
ALWD: Deborah L. Rhode, *Ethical Perspectives on Legal Practice*, 37 Stan. L. Rev. 589 (1985)

Encyclopedias

Style Manual: (61 Cal.Jur.3d (2003) Unfair Competition, § 7.)
Bluebook: 61 Cal. Jur. 3d *Unfair Competition* § 7 (2003)
ALWD: 61 Cal. Jur. 3d *Unfair Competition* § 7 (2003)

Treatises

Style Manual: (4 Witkin & Epstein, Cal. Criminal Law (2d ed.1988) § 13, p. 17.)
Bluebook: 4 Bernard E. Witkin & Norman L. Epstein, *California Criminal Law* § 13, p. 17 (3d ed. 2000)
ALWD: Bernard E. Witkin & Norman L. Epstein, *California Criminal Law* vol. 4, § 13, 17 (3d ed., Witkin Leg. Inst. 2000)

Dictionaries

Style Manual: (Black's Law Dict. (8th ed. 2004) p. 101.)
Bluebook: *Black's Law Dictionary* 101 (8th ed. 2004)
ALWD: *Black's Law Dictionary* 101 (Bryan A. Garner ed., 8th ed., West 2004)

C. More Information

ALWD Citation
www.alwd.org

Bluebook Citation
www.law.cornell.edu/citation
www.lexisnexis.com/shepards/stylecheck

California Style Manual
www.uchastings.edu/?pid=2527
www.dreamsoft.com/shay/Cites.htm
www.courtinfo.ca.gov/courts/courtsofappeal/4thDistrictDiv1/proper/Appendix4.pdf

Comparison Between Bluebook and ALWD
w3.uchastings.edu/lwr_01/CLASSES/alwd-manual.htm
www.uchastings.edu/?pid=2527
www.alwd.org/cm/cmTeachingResources/SecondEdTeaching Rsrc/ALWD2d-BB17ComparisonChart.pdf

Citation in General
www.ualr.edu/cmbarger/Citations.html
www.csulb.edu/library/eref/vref/style.html
freedomlaw.com/LegCitations.html
en.wikipedia.org/wiki/Case_citation

Susan Heinrich-Wells, *Using the California Style Manual and the Bluebook: A Practitioner's Guide* (West Group 2000)

Universal Citation Guide
www.aallnet.org/committee/citation/ucg/appe-index.html

Citation and Style Manuals
www.bgsu.edu/colleges/library/services/govdocs/citing.html
exlibris.memphis.edu/resource/unclesam/citeweb.html

Other Citation Systems
www.bedfordstmartins.com/online/citex.html
www.asu.edu/lib/hayden/govdocs/docscite/docscite.htm

D. Something to Check

According to the *California Style Manual*, what errors in format do you see in the following citations?

(Cal.Const. Art III, sec. 17.)
(Cal. Bus&Prof. Code, § 24.)
(Cal.Code Regs. Tit. 9, § 218.)
(*Davis v. Davis* (1997) 31 Cal. 4th 657.)
(*Hepter v. Jason* (2001) 70 Cal. App. 4th 819.)
(59 Ops. Cal.Atty. Gen. 181 (1989).)
(Calif. Rules of Court, Rule 200.1.)
(David Ray, *Court Injunctions*, 37 Stan. L. Rev. 589 (1979).)
(45 Cal. Jur. 3d (2000) § 7 Abortion.)
(William Stern, *Restraint of Trade*, § 33, p 122 (2d ed. 1988.)

5.3 Abbreviations in Citations

A. Introduction

B. Abbreviation Differences

C. Ninth Circuit

D. More Information

E. Something to Check

A. Introduction

As we saw in section 5.2, there are three major citation systems: The California *Style Manual: A Handbook of Legal Style for California Courts and Lawyers* (California Style Manual); *The Bluebook: A Uniform System of Citation* (Bluebook); and *ALWD Citation Manual: A Professional System of Citation* (ALWD).

One important citation concern is the abbreviation of words and phrases in legal writing. The three citation systems do not always agree on how something should be abbreviated or whether something should be abbreviated at all. In this section, we will compare how the three systems abbreviate important words and phrases. Our focus will be on those abbreviations that *differ* among any one of the three systems, although for major entries we will show the abbreviations even if all three systems agree. Note that often the only difference is whether a space is used between specific letters of the abbreviation.

B. Abbreviation Differences

	California Style Manual	Bluebook	ALWD
affirmed	affd.	aff'd	aff'd
affirmed by memorandum opinion	affd. mem.	aff'd mem.	
affirmed under the name of	affd. sub nom.	aff'd sub nom.	aff'd sub nom.
affirming	affg.	aff'g	aff'g
American Jurisprudence	Am.Jur.	Am. Jur.	Am. Jur.
American Jurisprudence Second	Am.Jur.2d	Am. Jur. 2d	Am. Jur. 2d
American Law Reports Federal	A.L.R.Fed.	A.L.R. Fed.	A.L.R. Fed.
appeal dismissed	app. dism.	appeal dismissed	appeal dismissed
appeal pending	app. pending	appeal pending	
Assistant	Asst.		Asst.
association	assn.	ass'n	assn.
Attorney	Atty.	Att'y	Atty.
building	bldg.	bldg.	bldg.
Bulletin	Bull.	Bull.	Bull.
California App Reports Supplement	Cal.App.Supp.	Cal. App. Supp.	Cal. App. Supp.
California App Reports Supplement Second	Cal.App.2d Supp.	Cal. App. 2d Supp.	Cal. App. 2d Supp.
California App Reports Supplement Third	Cal.App.3d Supp.	Cal. App. 3d Supp.	Cal. App. 3d Supp.
California App Reports Supplement Fourth	Cal.App.4th Supp.	Cal. App. 4th Supp.	Cal. App. 4th Supp.
California Jurisprudence	Cal.Jur.	Cal. Jur.	
California Jurisprudence Second	Cal.Jur.2d	Cal. Jur. 2d	
California Jurisprudence Third	Cal.Jur.3d	Cal. Jur. 3d	
California Law Review	Cal. L.Rev.	Cal. L. Rev.	Cal. L. Rev.
California Appellate Reports	Cal.App.	Cal. App.	Cal. App.
California Appellate Reports Second	Cal. App.2d	Cal. App. 2d	Cal. App. 2d
California Appellate Reports Third	Cal.App.3d	Cal. App. 3d	Cal. App. 3d
California Appellate Reports Fourth	Cal.App.4th	Cal. App. 4th	Cal. App. 4th
California Reporter	Cal.Rptr.	Cal. Rptr.	Cal. Rptr.
California Reporter Second	Cal.Rptr.2d	Cal. Rptr. 2d	Cal. Rptr. 2d

California Reports Second	Cal.2d	Cal. 2d	Cal. 2d
California Reports Third	Cal.3d	Cal. 3d	Cal. 3d
California Reports Fourth	Cal.4th	Cal. 4th	Cal. 4th
California Rules of Court	Cal. Rules of Court, rule	Cal. Ct. R.	
California Uniform Commercial Code	Cal. U. Com. Code	Cal. U.C.C.	Cal. U.C.C.
California Western Law Review	Cal. Western L.Rev.	Cal. W. L. Rev.	Cal. W. L. Rev.
certiorari denied	cert. den.	cert. denied	cert. denied
chapter	ch.	ch.	ch.
comment	com.	cmt.	
comments	coms.	cmts.	
Commission	Com.	Comm'n	Commn.
Committee	Com.	Comm.	Comm.
Court of Appeals	Ct.App.	Ct. App.	App.
Education Code	Ed. Code	Educ. Code	Educ. Code
Federal Supplement	F.Supp.	F. Supp.	F. Supp.
Federal Supplement Second	F.Supp.2d	F. Supp. 2d	F. Supp. 2d
Fish and Game Code	Fish & G. Code	Fish & Game Code	
Florida District Court of Appeals	Fla.Dist.Ct.App.	Fla. Dist. Ct. App.	Fla. Dist. App.
Food and Agriculture Code	Food & Arg. Code	Food & Agric. Code	Food & Agric. Code
footnote	fn.	n.	n.
footnotes	fns.	nn.	nn.
Government Code	Gov. Code	Gov't Code	Govt Code
Harvard Civil Rights-Civil Liberties Law Review	Harv.C.R.-C.L. L.Rev.	Harv. C.R.-C.L. L. Rev.	Harv. Civ. Rights-Civ. Libs. L. Rev.
Harvard Law Review	Harv. L.Rev.	Harv. L. Rev.	Harv. L. Rev.
Hawaii	Hawaii	Haw.	Haw.
Health and Safety Code	Health & Saf. Code	Health & Safety Code	Health & Safety Code
House Bill Number	H.R. No.	H.R.	H.R.
House Committee	House Com.	House Comm.	House Comm.
House Concurrent Resolution Number	H.Con.Res. No.	H.R. Con. Res.	H.R. Con. Res.
House Joint Resolution Number	H.J.Res. No.	H.R.J. Res.	H.R. Jt. Res.
House Report Number	H.R.Rep. No.	H.R. Rep. No.	H.R. Rpt.
House Resolution Number	H.Res. No.	H.R. Res.	H.R. Res.
Internal Revenue Code	Int.Rev. Code	I.R.C.	I.R.C.
Lawyers Edition	L.Ed.	L. Ed.	L. Ed.
Lawyers Edition Second	L. Ed.2d	L. Ed. 2d	L. Ed. 2d
Loyola of Los Angeles Law Review	Loyola L.A. L.Rev.	Loy. L.A. L. Rev.	Loy. L.A. L. Rev.
Michigan Court of Appeals	Mich. App.	Mich. Ct. App.	Mich. App.
modified	mod.	modified	modified
Municipal Court	Mun. Ct.	Mun. Ct.	Mun. Ct.
opinion	opn.	op.	op.
Ohio Court of Appeals	Ohio Ct.App.	Ohio Ct. App.	Ohio App.
Oklahoma Court of Criminal Appeals	Okla.Crim.App.	Okla. Crim. App.	Okla. Crim. App.
Opinion of the Attorney General	Ops.Cal.Atty.Gen.		Cal. Atty. Gen. Op.
Pacific Law Journal	Pacific L.J.	Pac. L.J.	
paragraph	par.	para.	para.
paragraphs	pars.	paras.	paras.
Penal Code	Pen. Code	Penal Code	
Pepperdine Law Review	Pepperdine L.Rev.	Pepp. L. Rev.	Pepp. L. Rev.
petition	petn.	pet.	pet.
probable jurisdiction noted	prob. jur. noted	prob. juris. noted	
Public Contract Code	Pub. Contract Code	Pub. Cont. Code	

Public Resources Code	Pub. Resources Code	Pub. Res. Code	
Railway	Ry.	Ry.	Ry.
rehearing denied	rehg. den.	reh'g denied	
rehearing granted	rehg. granted	reh'g granted	
reporter's transcript	R.T.	R.	Tr. Transcr.
reversed	revd.	rev'd	rev'd
reversed per curiam	revd. per curiam	rev'd per curiam	
reversing	revg.	rev'g	
San Diego Law Review	San Diego L.Rev.	San Diego L. Rev.	San Diego L. Rev.
Santa Clara Law Review	Santa Clara L.Rev.	Santa Clara L. Rev.	Santa Clara L. Rev.
Secretary	Sect.	Sec'y	Sec.
Senate Bill Number	Sen. No.	S.	Sen.
Senate Committee	Sen. Com.	Senate Comm.	Sen. Comm.
Senate Concurrent Resolution Number	Sen.Con.Res. No.	S. Con. Res.	Sen. Con. Res.
Senate Joint Resolution Number	Sen.J.Res. No.	S.J. Res.	Sen. Jt. Res.
Senate Report Number	Sen.Rep. No.	R. Rep. No.	Sen. Rpt.
Senate Resolution Number	Sen.Res. No.	S. Res.	Sen. Res.
Southern California Law Review	So.Cal. L.Rev.	S. Cal. L. Rev.	S. Cal. L. Rev.
Southern Reporter Second	So.2d	So. 2d	So. 2d
Southwestern University Law Review	Sw.U. L.Rev.	Sw. U. L. Rev.	Sw. U. L. Rev.
Stanford Law Review	Stan. L.Rev.	Stan. L. Rev.	Stan. L. Rev.
Streets and Highways Code	Sts. & Hy. Code	Sts. & High. Code	
subdivision	subd.	subdiv.	subdiv.
Supreme Court Reporter	S.Ct.	S. Ct.	S. Ct.
Texas Court of Appeals	Tex.Ct.App.	Tex. Ct. App.	Tex. App.
title	tit.	tit.	tit.
U.C. Davis Law Review	U.C. Davis L.Rev.	U.C. Davis L. Rev.	U. Cal. Davis L. Rev.
U.C.L.A. Law Review	UCLA L.Rev.	UCLA L. Rev.	UCLA L. Rev.
Uniform Commercial Code	U. Com. Code	U.C.C.	U.C.C.
University	U. or Univ.	Univ.	U.
U.S. Bankruptcy Court Central District	Bankr. C.D.Cal.	Bankr. C.D. Cal.	Bankr. C.D. Cal.
U.S. Bankruptcy Court Eastern District	Bankr. E.D.Cal.	Bankr. E.D. Cal.	Bankr. E.D. Cal.
U.S. Bankruptcy Court Northern District	Bankr. N.D.Cal.	Bankr. N.D. Cal.	Bankr. N.D. Cal.
U.S. Bankruptcy Court Southern District	Bankr. S.D.Cal.	Bankr. S.D. Cal.	Bankr. S.D. Cal.
U.S. Court of Appeals (Federal Circuit)	Fed.Cir.	Fed. Cir.	Fed. Cir.
U.S. Court of Federal Claims	Fed.Cl.	Fed. Cl.	Fed. Cl.
U.S. District Court Central District	C.D.Cal.	C.D. Cal.	C.D. Cal.
U.S. District Court Eastern District	E.D.Cal.	E.D. Cal.	E.D. Cal.
U.S. District Court Northern District	N.D.Cal.	N.D. Cal.	N.D. Cal.
U.S. District Court Southern District	S.D.Cal.	S.D. Cal.	S.D. Cal.
Univ. of San Francisco Law Review	U.S.F. L.Rev.	U.S.F. L. Rev.	U.S.F. L. Rev.
Water Code	Wat. Code	Water Code	

C. Ninth Circuit

The United States Court of Appeals for the Ninth Circuit (San Francisco) uses its own abbreviations:

	Key Code	*Case Type*	*Key Code*
Immediate Filing	*	Admin	A
order	o	Bankruptcy	B
order amended	oa	Criminal	C
order amended dissent	oad	Civil v. US	D
order and opinion	oop	Death Penalty	E
second opinion	o2	Federal	F
en banc	eb	Civil by US	G
en banc memorandum	ebm	Habeas	H
en banc order	ebo	Interlocutory	I
concurrence/dissent	cd	Prisoner	J
amended dissent	ad	Judicial Misconduct	K
supplemental opinion	s	Mandamus	M
supplemental dissent	sd	Pacific Territory	P
amended opinion	ao	Civil Rights	R
corrected opinion	co	1292b	T
appendix	app	Diversity	V
		Tax	X

www.ca9.uscourts.gov/ca9/newopinions.nsf/Opinions+by+date

D. More Information

(See also the sources listed under More Information at the end of section 5.2 on citation examples.)

www.llrx.com/columns/reference37.htm
www.aallnet.org/sis/lisp/cite.htm
lib.law.washington.edu/pubs/acron.html
www.ulib.iupui.edu/subjectareas/gov/docs_abbrev.html
www.legalabbrevs.cardiff.ac.uk

E. Something to Check

1. Open any law book, e.g., a school textbook, a court reporter, a statutory code. Find any three abbreviations used in this book that do *not* conform with the California Style Manual, Bluebook, or ALWD. Explain the discrepancies.
2. Use the examples and other material in section 5.2 and 5.3 to determine if there are any improper abbreviations in the following citations according to the California Style Manual:
   (People v. Parks (1971) 4 Calif. 3d 955, 95 Calif.Rpter. 193.)
   (Educ. Code § 244.)
   (35 Harv. Law Re. 226.)
   (25 Calif. Jur 3rd *Felony* § 23 (2002).)

A. Introduction

There are many settings in which paralegals must be able to write quickly. Examples include notetaking while:

- in class
- studying textbooks
- conducting legal research
- receiving instructions from a supervisor
- interviewing a client or witness
- listening to a deposition witness give testimony
- listening to a trial witness give testimony

Using abbreviations in such settings can be helpful. This section presents some commonly used notetaking abbreviations in the law. Some entries have more than one abbreviation, e.g., c/a and coa for cause of action. When a choice is available, pick an abbreviation with which you are comfortable.

These abbreviations are for use in notetaking, *not for use in citations or formal writing.* (For abbreviations in citations, see section 5.3.) The primary purpose of the following abbreviations is to help you take notes that only you will read. Hence feel free to try out, adapt, and add to the following list

B. Notetaking Abbreviations

a answer
a action
aa administrative agency
a/b appellate brief
ABA American Bar Association
a/c appellate court
acct account
acctg accounting
admin administration
admis admission
admr administrator
ADR alternative dispute resolution
aff affirmed (or affidavit)
aka also known as
agt agent
alj administrative law judge
alt alternative (or alternate)
amt amount
ann annotated (or annotation)
ans answer
app appeal
aplt appellant
aple appellee
appnt appellant
appee appellee
apt apartment
ar administrative regulation
a/r assumption of the risk
arb arbitration
asap as soon as possible
assn association
assoc associate
atty attorney
auth authority
b business
b/4 before
ba bar association
bankr bankruptcy
bd board
b/c because
betw/ between
bfp bona fide purchaser
b/k breach of contract
bldg building
b/p burden of proof
BPC Business & Professions Code
bus business
b/w breach of warranty
¢ complaint
© consideration
c. circa [about]
ca court of appeals
CA9 Ninth Circuit
c/a cause of action
CAC California Administrative Code
CAG California Attorney General
CC Civil Code (or Circuit Court)
cc child custody
c/c counterclaim
c-dr creditor
CG California Governor
c/e cross examination
cert certiorari
cf compare
ch chapter (or charter)
CiCt Circuit Court
CJ chief judge
c/l common law
cle continuing legal education
cmmw commonwealth
co company (or county)
coa cause of action
comm committee
commn commission
commr commissioner
compl complaint (or compliance)
conf conference
con law constitutional law
const constitution
consv conservative (or conservation)
cont continued
corp corporation
cp community property
CP Common Pleas
cr criminal (or creditor)
cr-c criminal court
cs child support
CSC California Supreme Court
CSL California State Legislature
csos California secretary of state
ct court
cty county
cv civil
cy calendar year (or county)
cz cause
Δ defendant
d danger (dangerous or defendant)
d. died (or death)
DA district attorney
dba doing business as

DCA District Court of Appeals
d/e direct examination
decrg decreasing
def defendant (or defense)
depo deposition
dept department
df defendant
disc discipline (disciplinary)
dist district
div division
dkt docket
dmg damages
dob date of birth
dod date of death
d-r debtor
dv domestic violence
= equals
e evidence
e/d eminent domain
ee employee
eg example
egs examples
emp employment
en endnote
eng engineer (or engineering)
engr engineer (or engineering)
ent enterprise
eq equity (or equitable)
eqbl equitable
er employer
est estimate (or established or estate)
ev evidence
ex exhibit
exr executor
4cb foreseeable
f fact (or federal)
faq frequently asked questions
FC Family Code
fed federal
fe-st federal statute
fn footnote
fs facts
f-st federal statute
fy fiscal year
g govern
g/r general rule
gt government
gvt government
h husband
hb house bill
hdc holder in due course
HR House of Representatives
hrg hearing
HSC Health & Safety Code
i interest
in interest
inj injunction
ij injury
immig immigration
inj injunction
in interest
incrg increasing
indl individual
indp independent
info information
inj injunction
ins insurance
intl international
i-p in personam
i-r in rem
IRC Internal Revenue Code
IRS Internal Revenue Service
J judge (or justice)
j judgment
JC Juvenile Court
j/d judgment for defendant
jp justice of the peace
j/p judgment for plaintiff
jj judges (or justices)
jt judgment (or joint)
jud judicial
jur jurisdiction
juv juvenile
jxn jurisdiction
k contract
< less than; smaller than
L law
l liable (or liability)
LC Labor Code
lit litigation
ll landlord (or limited liability)
l/l landlord (or limited liability)
llc limited liability company
llp limited liability partnership
LN Lexis-Nexis
lr legal research
ltd limited
Lx Lexis
> more than; greater than
max maximum
mem memorial
mfr manufacturer
mfg manufacturing
mgmt management
mgt management
min minimum
misc miscellaneous
mj major
mkt market
mo majority opinion
mtg mortgage (or meeting)
mtge mortgagee
mtgr mortgagor
mun municipal

number
9C Ninth Circuit
n/a irrelevant (not applicable)
natl national
neg negligence
negl negligence
nt nothing (or note or not)
ntry notary
no number
O owner
o degree
obj object (or objective)
occ occupation
oee offeree
oer offeror
op opinion
ord ordinance
π plaintiff
+ plus
p plaintiff
p. page
PC Penal Code
p/c proximate cause
pee promise
pet petition
petr petitioner
p/f prima facie
pg page
p-j personal judgment
PL public law
pl plaintiff
pol practice of law
por promisor
p/p public policy
p/r personal representative
priv private
pub public
pub-op public opinion
pvt private
pvg privilege
? question
?d questioned
Q equity (or equitable)
® reasonable
r regulation (or record)
re real estate (or regarding)
rec record
recd received
reg regulation
rel-t related to
rep representative (or representation)
resp responsibility
rev reverse
revd reversed
r/o restraining order
roc rules of court
rogs interrogatories
rr railroad
ry railway
rsb reasonable
S statute
$ suppose
s sum
sb Senate Bill
s/b should be
sc supreme court
secy secretary
s/f statute of frauds
Sh Shepard's Citations (or shepardize)
s-h self-help
Sh-z shepardize
s/j summary judgment
s/l strict liability (or statute of limitations)
s/lm statute of limitations
s-mj subject-matter jurisdiction
sn/b should not be
soc society
SOL statute of limitations
sos secretary of state
ss sections
s-st state statute
st statute
stats statistics (or statutes)
std standard
st-st state statute
sub substantial
subj subject (or subjective)
\ therefore
T tort
t testimony
taxn taxation
t/c trial court
tee trustee
test testimony
tp third party
tpr trespasser
tro temporary restraining order
u understanding
U university
ui unemployment compensation (or insurance)
ucc Uniform Commercial Code
upl unauthorized practice of law
usc United States Code
ussc United States Supreme Court
v versus (or against)
VC Vehicle Code
vs versus (or against)
w wife
wc workers' compensation
WIC Welfare & Institutions Code
w/ with
w/i within

WL Westlaw
w/o without
x cross
x/e cross examination
© consideration
¢ complaint
Δ defendant
= equals
< less than; smaller than
> more than; greater than
number
π plaintiff
+ plus
? question
?d questioned
® reasonable
$ suppose
\ therefore

C. More Information

Taking Notes
www.nyls.edu/pages/3083.asp

Abbreviations
lib.law.washington.edu/pubs/acron.html
www.llrx.com/columns/reference37.htm

5.5 Research Starters for 87 Major California Topics

A. Introduction
B. Abbreviations
C. Topics Covered
D. Research Starter Cites
E. More Information
F. Something to Check

A. Introduction

Often in legal research, the first hurdle is finding your first lead. You need a starting point that will guide you into the various categories of case law, statutory law, administrative law, etc. You may also need a lead to a secondary authority, such as a legal treatise or legal encyclopedia, which will provide an overview of an area of the law that may be new to you. In this section, we will provide you with such leads to 87 major topics of California law. They are "starter cites," in the sense that they may lead you to what you need. For more on doing legal research in California law, see section 5.1.

B. Abbreviations

The starter cites use the following abbreviations to the legal materials covered, many of which are found online as well as on the shelves of moderate-sized law libraries:

Codes

The codes are online (*www.leginfo.ca.gov/calaw.html*) or on the shelves in *West's Annotated California Code or Deering's California Codes, Annotated*:

BPC: Business & Professions Code
CC: Civil Code
CCP: Code of Civil Procedure
CCR: California Code of Regulations
ComC: Commercial Code
CorpC: Corporations
EC: Evidence Code
F&A: Food and Agricultural Code
FamC: Family Code
FinC: Financial Code
GC: Government Code
H&SC: Health & Safety Code
IC: Insurance Code
LC: Labor Code
PC: Penal Code
PRC: Public Resources Code
ProbC: Probate Code
RTC: Revenue and Taxation Code
UIC: Unemployment Insurance Code
VC: Vehicle Code
WC: Water Code

Other Sources Cited

CD: California Digest
(The CD will lead you to key numbers within the WestGroup digest system)

CJ: California Jurisprudence 3d
(California is one of the few states that has its own legal encyclopedia)

M-HLD: Martindale-Hubbell Law Digest
(The volume summarizes major laws of every state)

WCP: Witkin, California Procedure

WE: Witkin, California Evidence

WECL: Witkin & Epstein, California Criminal Law

WSCL: Witkin, Summary of California Law
(These four Witkin treatises are standard multivolume treatises that summarize California law)

C. Topics Covered

Topics

Abortion
Administrative Law
Adoption
Affidavits
Agency
Alimony
Annulment
Appeal and Error
Arbitration
Attorney-Client Privilege
Attorneys
Banking
Child Custody
Child Support
Civil Procedure
Commercial Code
Community Property
Constitutional Law
Consumer Protection
Contracts
Corporations
Courts in California
Criminal Law
Damages
Deeds
Discovery
Divorce
Domestic Partnership
Domestic Violence
Employment Discrimination
Enforcement of Judgment
Environment
Equity
Estates
Evidence
Family Law
Fraud
Garnishment
Government
Guardianship
Illegitimacy
Injunctions
Insurance
Intellectual Property
Labor Relations
Landlord and Tenant
Legal Document Assistants and Unlawful Detainer Assistants
Legal Separation
Limited Liability Companies
Marriage
Mediation
Medical Malpractice
Mineral, Water, and Fishing Rights
Minors
Mortgages
Motor Vehicles
Negligence
Notary Public
Paralegals
Partnerships
Pleading
Power of Attorney
Privacy
Privileged Communications
Products Liability
Property Division in Divorce
Real Property
Service of Process
Statute of Frauds
Statute of Limitations
Summary Judgment
Summons
Taxation
Torts
Traffic Laws
Trusts
Unemployment Insurance
Venue
Water Rights
Wills
Workers' Compensation

D. Research Starter Cites

ABORTION

Statutes: BPC §§ 601, 2253; H&SC § 123435; PC § 1108
Regulations: 22 CCR §§ 30302, 75040
Cases: CD: check Abortion and Birth Control, key numbers (🔑) 1ff
Encyclopedia: CJ: check Abortion, Birth Control and Other Reproductive Rights
Summaries:

- M-HLD: go to the vol. for California; under Health, check Abortion
- WSCL: vol. 7, Constitutional Law § 438C; vol. 5 Torts § 355

Internet:
megalaw.com/ca/top/cafamily.php
www.ppacca.org/site/pp.asp?c=kuJYJeO4F&b=139490
www.caral.org

ADMINISTRATIVE LAW

Statutes: GC §§ 11340ff, 11370, 11415.10

Regulations: 1 CCR § 1000 (Administrative Procedure Act)

Cases: CD: check Administrative Law and Procedure, key numbers (🔑) 1ff

Encyclopedia: CJ: check Administrative Law, Public Offices and Employees
Summaries:

- WCP: vol. 9, Administrative Proceedings, §§ 1ff
- WSCL: vol. 7, Constitutional Law, §§ 518ff

Internet:
ccr.oal.ca.gov (California Code of Regulations)
www.oal.ca.gov (Office of Administrative Law)
www.oah.dgs.ca.gov/default.htm (Office of Administrative Law)
sam.dgs.ca.gov/default.htm (State Administrative Manual)

ADOPTION

Statutes: FamC § 8600
Regulations: 22 CCR §§ 35122, 35079
Cases: CD: check Adoption, key numbers (🔑) 1ff
Encyclopedia: CJ: check Family Law §§ 143ff
Summaries:

- M-HLD: go to the vol. for California; under Family, check Adoption
- WSCL: vol. 10, Parent and Child, §§ 342ff

Internet:
www.courtinfo.ca.gov/selfhelp/family/adoption (Self-Help Center)
www.childsworld.ca.gov (Children and Family Services Division)
www.dss.cahwnet.gov/cdssweb/Adoptions_166.htm
megalaw.com/ca/top/cafamily.php

AFFIDAVITS

Statutes: CCP § 2012
Regulations: 22 CCR § 5000 (affidavit defined)
Cases: CD: check Affidavits, key numbers (🔑) 1ff
Encyclopedia: CJ: check Affidavits and Declarations under Penalty of Perjury
Summaries:
- M-HLD: go to the vol. for California; under Documents and Records, check Affidavits
- WE: vol. 1, Introduction §§ 69ff

AGENCY

Statutes: CC § 2296
Cases: CD: check Principal and Agent, key numbers (🔑) 1ff
Encyclopedia: CJ: check Agency
Summaries:
- M-HLD: go to the vol. for California; under Business Organizations, check Agency
- WSCL: vol. 2, Agency and Employment §§ 1ff

ALIMONY (Spousal Support)

Statutes: FamC §§ 142, 155, 3651
Regulations: 22 CCR §§ 110609
Cases: CD: check Divorce, key numbers (🔑) 199ff
Encyclopedia: CJ: check Family Law §§ 1011ff
Summaries:
- M-HLD: go to the vol. for California; under Family, check Alimony
- WSCL: vol. 11, Husband and Wife §§ 206ff

Internet:
megalaw.com/ca/top/cafamily.php
www.cflr.com

ANNULMENT

Statutes: FamC §§ 310, 2000, 2210
Regulations: 2 CCR § 7292.1
Cases: CD: check Marriage, key numbers (🔑) 56ff
Encyclopedia: CJ: check Family Law §§ 85ff (Void and Voidable Marriage)
Summaries:
- M-HLD: go to the vol. for California; under Family, check Marriage (and Annulment under Marriage)
- WSCL: vol. 11, Husband and Wife §§ 58ff

Internet:
www.courtinfo.ca.gov/selfhelp/family/divorce (Self-Help Center)
megalaw.com/ca/top/cafamily.php
www.cflr.com

APPEAL AND ERROR

Statutes: CCP §§ 77, 904.2, 116.770; PC § 1235
Regulations: 1 CCR § 1106
Cases: CD: check Appeal and Error, key numbers (🔑) 1ff
Encyclopedia: CJ: check Appellate Review
Summaries:
- M-HLD: go to the vol. for California; under Civil Actions and Procedure, check Appeal and Error
- WCP: vol. 9, Appeal §§ 1ff

Internet:
www.courtinfo.ca.gov/selfhelp/other/appeals.htm (Self-Help Center)
megalaw.com/ca/top/caapp.php
megalaw.com/ca/top/cacivpro.php

ARBITRATION

Statutes: CCP § 1281
Regulations: 1 CCR § 1232
Cases: CD: check Arbitration, key numbers (🔑) 1ff
Encyclopedia: CJ: check Arbitration and Award; Labor
Summaries:
- M-HLD: go to the vol. for California; under Dispute Resolution, check Arbitration and Award
- WSCL: vol. 11, Equity §§ 36ff
- WCP: vol. 6, Proceedings Without Trial §§484ff

Internet:
megalaw.com/ca/ca.php
www.weblocator.com/attorney/ca/law/b06.html

ATTORNEY-CLIENT PRIVILEGE (see also Attorneys)

Statutes: EC §§ 952, 954
Cases: CD: check Witnesses, key numbers (🔑) 198ff
Encyclopedia: CJ: check Administrative Law §§ 93, 132; Attorneys at Law § 556; Criminal Law: Trial § 698; Wills § 138
Summaries:
- M-HLD: go to the vol. for California; under Civil Actions and Procedure, check Evidence (and Privileged Communications under Evidence)
- WE: vol. 2, Witnesses (Lawyer-Client Privilege) §§ 98ff

ATTORNEYS

Statutes: BPC § 6000 (State Bar Act)
Regulations: 1 CCR §§ 1145, 1222, 1392
Cases: CD: check Attorneys, key numbers (🔑) 1ff
Encyclopedia: CJ: check Attorneys at Law §§ 126ff (Paralegals), 207, 270, 281, 359, 559; Occupations and Trades § 19 (Unlawful Detainer Assistants)
Summaries:
- M-HLD: go to the vol. for California; under Legal Profession, check Attorneys and Counselors
- WCP: vol. 1, Attorneys, §§ 1ff, 128, 177, 311, 397 (Paralegals, Unauthorized Practice of Law), 400B (Legal Document Assistants)
- WSCL: vol. 7, Constitutional Law § 268A (solicitation)

Internet:
www.calbar.ca.gov (California State Bar)
www.courtinfo.ca.gov/selfhelp/lowcost (Self-Help Center)
www.ospd.ca.gov (Office of State Public Defender)
www.weblocator.com/attorney/ca/law/c01.html

BANKING

Statutes: FinC § 102
Regulations: 10 CCR § 10.2
Cases: CD: check Banks and Banking, key numbers (⚷) 1ff
Encyclopedia: CJ: check Banks and Other Financial Institutions
Summaries:
- M-HLD: go to the vol. for California; under Business Regulation and Commerce, check Banks and Banking
- WSCL: vol. 3, Negotiable Instruments §§ 1ff; vol. 9, Taxation §289

Internet:
www.dfi.ca.gov
www.leginfo.ca.gov/calaw.html (Financial Code)

CHILD CUSTODY

Statutes: FamC §§ 3020, 3400
Regulations: 22 CCR § 113300
Cases: CD: check Child Custody, key numbers (⚷) 1ff
Encyclopedia: CJ: check Family Law §§ 888ff
Summaries:
- M-HLD: go to the vol. for California; under Family, check Dissolution of Marriage (and Custody of Children under Dissolution)
- WSCL: vol. 10, Parent and Child §§ 91ff

Internet:
www.courtinfo.ca.gov/selfhelp/family/custody
megalaw.com/ca/top/cafamily.php
www.cflr.com
www.dss.cahwnet.gov/cdssweb (Department of Social Services)

CHILD SUPPORT

Statutes: FamC § 3900
Regulations: 22 CCR §§ 110129, 112100
Cases: CD: check Child Support, key numbers (⚷) 1ff
Encyclopedia: CJ: check Family Law §§ 1069ff
Summaries:
- M-HLD: go to the vol. for California; under Family, check Dissolution of Marriage (and Support of Children under Dissolution) and check Family (see Dissolution of Marriage)
- WSCL: vol. 10, Parent and Child §§ 246ff

Internet:
www.courtinfo.ca.gov/selfhelp/family/support (Self-Help Center)
www.childsup.cahwnet.gov (Department of Child Support Services)
www.childsup.cahwnet.gov/pub/brochures/pub160.pdf
megalaw.com/ca/top/cafamily.php
www.cflr.com

CIVIL PROCEDURE

Statutes: CCP §§ 1ff
Regulations: 1 CCR § 1000 (California Administrative Procedure Act)
Cases: CD: check the vols. for Appeal and Error; Evidence; Pretrial Procedure; Trial; Witnesses, key numbers (⚷) 1ff
Encyclopedia: CJ: check Actions, Appellate Review, Courts, Discovery, Evidence, Trial
Summaries:
- M-HLD: go to the vol. for California; check Civil Actions and Procedure
- WCP: see the index vols. of this set for the topics covered

Internet:
megalaw.com/ca/top/cacivpro.php
www.leginfo.ca.gov/calaw.html (Code of Civil Procedure)

COMMERCIAL CODE

Statutes: ComC § 3101
Regulations: 2 CCR § 22600
Cases: CD: check the vols. for Bills and Notes; Sales, key numbers (⚷) 1ff
Encyclopedia: CJ: check Accord and Satisfaction; Contracts, Documents of Title; Investment Securities; Sales
Summaries:
- M-HLD: go to the vol. for California; under Business Regulation and Commerce, check Commercial Code
- WSCL: vol. 3, Sales § 6; vol. 3, Negotiable Instruments §§ 1ff; vol. 3, Secured Transactions in Personal Property, §§ 1ff

Internet:
www.leginfo.ca.gov/calaw.html (Commercial Code)
caselaw.lp.findlaw.com/cacodes/com.html
www.ss.ca.gov/business/business.htm (California Business Portal)

COMMUNITY PROPERTY

Statutes: FC § 760
Regulations: 18 CCR § 13554 (inheritance tax); 18 CCR § 15301 (gift tax)
Cases: CD: check Husband and Wife, key numbers (⚷) 246ff
Encyclopedia: CJ: check Family Law, §§ 423ff
Summaries:
- M-HLD: go to the vol. for California; under Family, check Husband and Wife (and

Community Property under Husband and Wife)
- WSCL: vol. 11, Community Property §§ 1ff

Internet:
www.leginfo.ca.gov/calaw.html (Family Code)
www.cfli.com/community-property.html

CONSTITUTIONAL LAW, STATE

Cases: CD: check Constitutional Law, key numbers (⚿) 1ff
Encyclopedia: CJ: check Constitutional Law
Summaries:
- WSCL: vol. 7, Constitutional Law §§ 50ff

Internet:
www.leginfo.ca.gov/const.html
www.library.ca.gov/CCRC (Constitution Revision Commission)
megalaw.com/ca/top/caconstitution.php
www.weblocator.com/attorney/ca/law/c04.html

CONSUMER PROTECTION

Statutes: BPC § 300; CC § 1793.22; F&A § 58039
Cases: CD: check Consumer Protection, key numbers (⚿) 1ff
Encyclopedia: CJ: check Consumer and Borrower Protection Laws
Summaries:
- M-HLD: go to the vol. for California; under Business Regulation and Commerce, check Consumer Protection
- WSCL: vol. 3, Sales §§ 51, 293, 297A, 300A

Internet:
www.dca.ca.gov (Department of Consumer Affairs)
www.insurance.ca.gov/docs/FS-Consumer.htm (Consumer Services)
www.privacy.ca.gov (Office of Privacy Protection)
www.consumerfdn.org
www.weblocator.com/attorney/ca/law/c05.html

CONTRACTS

Statutes: B&P § 156; CC §§ 1619ff; ComC § 3101
Cases: CD: check the vols. for Contracts; Sales, key numbers (⚿) 1ff
Encyclopedia: CJ: check Contracts
Summaries:
- M-HLD: go to the vol. for California; check Business Regulation and Commerce
- WSCL: vol. 1, Contracts §§ 1ff; vol. 3, Sales § 33; vol. 3, Negotiable Instruments §§ 1ff; vol. 5, Torts § 642; vol. 11, Equity § 21

Internet:
www.leginfo.ca.gov/calaw.html (Commercial Code)
www.weblocator.com/attorney/ca/law/b02.html

CORPORATIONS

Statutes: CorpC §§ 1ff
Regulations: 10 CCR § 250.9
Cases: CD: check the vols. for Corporations; Securities Regulation key numbers (⚿) 1ff
Encyclopedia: CJ: check Corporations
Summaries:
- M-HLD: go to the vol. for California; under Business Organizations, check Corporations
- WSCL: vol. 9, Corporations §§1ff; vol. 9, Taxation § 290

Internet:
www.corp.ca.gov (Department of Corporations)
www.ss.ca.gov/business/business.htm (California Business Portal)
www.leginfo.ca.gov/calaw.html (Corporations Code)
www.weblocator.com/attorney/ca/law/b19.html

COURTS IN CALIFORNIA

Statutes: Cal Const, Art. VI, §§ 3, 5, 10
Cases: CD: check Courts, key numbers (⚿) 1ff
Encyclopedia: CJ: check Courts
Summaries:
- M-HLD: go to the vol. for California; check Courts and Legislature
- WCP: vol. 2, Courts §§ 1ff

Internet:
www.courtinfo.ca.gov/courts/supreme (Supreme Court)
www.courtinfo.ca.gov/courts/courtsofappeal (Courts of Appeal)
www.courtinfo.ca.gov/courts/trial/courtlist.htm (Superior Courts)
www.courtinfo.ca.gov/selfhelp/smallclaims (Small Claims Court)
www.courtinfo.ca.gov/courtadmin/jc (Judicial Council)
megalaw.com/ca/top/cacivpro.php
www.weblocator.com/attorney/ca/law/c02.html

CRIMINAL LAW

Statutes: PC §§ 1ff
Regulations: 2 CCR § 615.2 (victim compensation); 11 CCR § 900
Cases: CD: check the vols. for Criminal Law; Sentencing and Punishment, key numbers (⚿) 1ff
Encyclopedia: CJ: check Criminal Law
Summaries:
- M-HLD: go to the vol. for California; check Criminal Law
- WSCL: vol. 7, Constitutional Law §§ 415ff
- WECL: see the index vols. of this set for the topics covered

Internet:
www.ag.ca.gov (state attorney general)
www.ospd.ca.gov (Office of State Public Defender)
www.corr.ca.gov (Department of Corrections)
www.ag.ca.gov/cjsc (criminal justice statistics)

www.boc.ca.gov/default.htm (Victim Compensation)
megalaw.com/ca/top/cacriminal.php
www.leginfo.ca.gov/calaw.html (Criminal Code)

DAMAGES

Statutes: CC §§ 41, 1709, 1812.9, 3294, 3345
Cases: CD: check Damages, key numbers (⚿) 1ff
Encyclopedia: CJ: check Damages
Summaries:
- M-HLD: go to the vol. for California; under Civil Actions and Procedure, check Damages
- WSCL: vol. 1, Contracts §§ 813ff; vol. 3, Sales §174; vol. 6, Torts §§ 1316ff, 1477ff

DEEDS (see also Real Property)

Statutes: B&P § 10028; CC § 1054; RTC § 3708
Cases: CD: check the vols. for Deeds; Property key numbers (⚿) 1ff
Encyclopedia: CJ: check Deeds
Summaries:
- M-HLD: go to the vol. for California; under Property, check Deeds
- WSCL: vol. 3, Security Interests in Real Property §§ 1ff; vol. 4, Real Property §135

Internet:
(see Real Property)

DISCOVERY

Statutes: CCP § 2016.010 (Civil Discovery Act)
Regulations: 1 CCR § 1242; 8 CCR § 20237
Cases: CD: check Pretrial Procedure, key numbers (⚿) 11ff
Encyclopedia: CJ: check Discovery and Depositions
Summaries:
- M-HLD: go to the vol. for California; under Civil Actions and Procedure, check Depositions and Discovery
- WE: vol. 2, Discovery §§ 1ff

Internet:
megalaw.com/ca/top/cacivpro.php

DIVORCE (Dissolution of Marriage)

Statutes: FC §§ 310, 2000
Cases: CD: check the vols. for Divorce; Husband and Wife, key numbers (⚿) 1ff
Encyclopedia: CJ: check Family Law, §§ 614ff
Summaries:
- M-HLD: go to the vol. for California; under Family, check Dissolution of Marriage
- WSCL: vol. 11, Community Property §§ 160ff; vol. 11, Husband and Wife §§ 83ff

Internet:
www.courtinfo.ca.gov/selfhelp/family/divorce (Self-Help Center)
www.dhs.ca.gov/hisp/chs/OVR/default.htm (Office of Vital Records)
megalaw.com/ca/top/cafamily.php

DOMESTIC PARTNERSHIP

Statutes: FC § 297
Regulations: 2 CCR § 599.920.5; 2 CCR § 21922; 22 CCR § 1253.12-1
Cases: CD: check Marriage, key numbers (⚿) 17.5ff
Encyclopedia: CJ: check Family Law §§ 107ff, 152, 1014
Summaries:
- M-HLD: go to the vol. for California; under Family, check Domestic Partners
- WSCL: vol. 6, Torts § § 849A, 1209A; vol. 11, Husband and Wife § 36K; vol. 12, Wills and Probate § 238A

Internet:
www.ss.ca.gov/dpregistry (Domestic Partnership Registry)
megalaw.com/ca/top/cafamily.php

DOMESTIC VIOLENCE (see also Criminal Law, Family Law)

Statutes: CC § 1708.6; CCP § 340.15; FC §§ 6203, 6211; PC §§ 264.2, 13700
Regulations: 2 CCR § 654.4 (victim compensation); 22 CCR § 112025 (definition)
Cases: CD: check Criminal Law, key numbers (⚿) 474.4(3)ff
Encyclopedia: CJ: check Family Law §§ 1172ff
Summaries:
- WSCL: vol. 5, Torts § 417E; vol. 11, Husband and Wife § 36A

Internet:
www.courtinfo.ca.gov/selfhelp/protection/dv (Self-Help Center)
megalaw.com/ca/top/cafamily.php
megalaw.com/ca/top/cacriminal.php
ca.rand.org/stats/community/domvio.html

EMPLOYMENT (see Agency, Employment Discrimination, Labor Relations, Workers' Compensation)

EMPLOYMENT DISCRIMINATION

Statutes: GC § 12940; LC § 98.6
Regulations: 2 CCR § 7286.6; 22 CCR § 98413
Cases: CD: check Civil Rights, key numbers (⚿) 1101ff
Encyclopedia: CJ: check Civil Rights § 38; Constitutional Law § 216; Employer and Employee § 97
Summaries:
- M-HLD: go to the vol. for California; under Employment, check Labor Relations (and Fair Employment Practices under Labor Relations)
- WSCL: vol. 7, Constitutional Law § 479

Internet:
www.courtinfo.ca.gov/selfhelp/additionalinfo/links.htm#empdisc (Self-Help Center)
megalaw.com/ca/top/calabor.php
www.dfeh.ca.gov (Department of Fair Employment and Housing)

ENFORCEMENT (EXECUTION) OF JUDGMENT

Statutes: CCP § 680.010 (Enforcement of Judgments Law)
Regulations: 22 CCR § 116130 (Child Support)
Cases: CD: check the vols. for Judgment; Execution key numbers (⚿) 1ff
Encyclopedia: CJ: check Enforcement of Judgments; Judgments
Summaries:
- M-HLD: go to the vol. for California; under Civil Actions and Procedure, check Judgments
- WCP: vol. 8, Enforcement of Judgment §§ 1ff

Internet:
www.courtinfo.ca.gov/selfhelp/smallclaims/collect.htm (Self-Help Center)
www.leginfo.ca.gov/calaw.html (Civil Code; Code of Civil Procedure)

ENVIRONMENT (see also Mineral, Water, and Fishing Rights)

Statutes: PRC § 71110; GC § 12812
Regulations CCR: see title 14 (Natural Resources); title 26 (Toxics); title 27 (Environmental Protection)
Cases: CD: check Environmental Law, key numbers (⚿) 1ff
Encyclopedia: CJ: check Pollution and Conservation Laws
Summaries:
- M-HLD: go to the vol. for California; check Environment
- WSCL: vol. 4, Real Property §§ 56ff

Internet:
www.calepa.ca.gov (California Environmental Protection Agency)
megalaw.com/ca/top/caenvironmental.php
megalaw.com/ca/top/cawater.php
www.leginfo.ca.gov/calaw.html (Public Resources Code)
www.arb.ca.gov/homepage.htm (Air Resources Board)
www.weblocator.com/attorney/ca/law/b23.html

EQUITY

Statutes: CCP §§ 680.190, 871.5; CorpC § 15529
Cases: CD: check Equity, key numbers (⚿) 1ff
Encyclopedia: CJ: check Equity
Summaries:
- WSCL: vol. 11, Equity §§ 1ff

Internet:
megalaw.com/ca/top/cacivpro.php

ESTATES (see also Real Property; Wills)

Statutes: ProbC §§ 1ff
Regulations: 2 CCR § 1138.10 (Estate Tax)
Cases: CD: check the vols. for Estates in Property; Wills, key numbers (⚿) 1ff
Encyclopedia: CJ: check Decedents' Estates; Estates; Trusts; Wills
Summaries:
- M-HLD: go to the vol. for California; check Estates and Trusts
- WSCL: vol. 4, Real Property §§ 231ff; vol. 9, Taxation § 280 (Estate Tax)

Internet:
www.courtinfo.ca.gov/selfhelp/additionalinfo/links.htm#wills (Self-Help Center)
www.leginfo.ca.gov/calaw.html (Probate Code)
www.megalaw.com/ca/top/caprobate.php
megalaw.com/ca/top/caprobate.php

EVIDENCE (see also Civil Procedure)

Statutes: EC §§ 1ff
Regulations: 1 CCR § 1387; 8 CCR § 340.50
Cases: CD: check the vols. for Evidence; Trial; Witnesses, key numbers (⚿) 1ff
Encyclopedia: CJ: check Evidence
Summaries:
- M-HLD: go to the vol. for California; under Civil Actions and Procedure, check Evidence
- WCE: see the index vols. of this set for the topics covered

Internet:
www.leginfo.ca.gov/calaw.html (Evidence Code)
megalaw.com/ca/top/cacivpro.php

FAMILY LAW (see also Child Custody, Child Support)

Statutes: FC §§ 1ff
Regulations: 2 CCR § 7297.0; 17 CCR § 52100; 22 CCR §§ 89231, 112302 (Family Violence)
Cases: CD: check the vols. for Child Custody; Child Support; Divorce; Husband and Wife; Marriage, key numbers (⚿) 1ff
Encyclopedia: CJ: check Family Law
Summaries:
- M-HLD: go to the vol. for California; check Family
- WSCL: vol. 5, Torts §§ 630ff

Internet:
www.courtinfo.ca.gov/selfhelp/family/famlinks.htm (Self-Help Center)
www.courtinfo.ca.gov/selfhelp/family/overview (Self-Help Center)

www.dss.cahwnet.gov/cdssweb (Department of Social Services)
www.childsworld.ca.gov (Children and Family Services Division)
megalaw.com/ca/top/cafamily.php
www.leginfo.ca.gov/calaw.html (Family Code)
www.cflr.com

FRAUD (see also Criminal Law, Torts)

Statutes: BPC § 498; CC §§ 1572, 1623; CorpC § 29536
Regulations: 2 CCR § 22501 (Corporate Fraud); 8 CCR § 150; (Fraudulent Advertising); 10 CCR §§ 260.216, 2698.30 (Insurance Fraud); 18 CCR § 15654 (Taxes)
Cases: CD: check Fraud, key numbers (⚿) 1ff
Encyclopedia: CJ: check Fraud and Deceit
Summaries:
- M-HLD: go to the vol. for California; under Debtor and Creditor, check Fraudulent Sales and Conveyances
- WSCL: vol. 5, Torts §§ 676ff; vol. 12, Wills and Probate § 186

Internet:
www.ss.ca.gov/vcfcf/vcfcf.htm

GARNISHMENT (see also Enforcement of Judgment)

Statutes: CCP § 706.010 (Wage Garnishment Law); Insurance Code § 1064.9; LC § 2929
Regulations: 22 CCR § 1256-35 (Unemployment Compensation)
Cases: CD: check Garnishment, key numbers (⚿) 1ff
Encyclopedia: CJ: check Creditors' Rights and Remedies § 61; Employer and Employee § 78; Family Law § 1354
Summaries:
- M-HLD: go to the vol. for California; under Debtor and Creditor, check Garnishment
- WCP: vol. 8, Enforcement of Judgment §§ 232ff

GOVERNMENT (see also Administrative Law, Courts)

Statutes: GC §§ 1ff
Regulations: title 2 (Administration); title 11 (Law)
Cases: CD: check the vols. for Municipal Corporations; Officers and Public Employees; States, key numbers (⚿) 1ff
Encyclopedia: CJ: check Administrative Law; Government Tort Liability; Municipalities
Summaries:
- M-HLD: go to the vol. for California; check Courts and Legislature; under Introduction, check Government and Legal System
- WSCL: vol. 1, Contracts § 74; vol. 7 Constitutional Law § 50

Internet:
www.leginfo.ca.gov/calaw.html (Government Code)
www.ca.gov/state/portal/myca_homepage.jsp
www.statelocalgov.net/state-ca.cfm

GUARDIANSHIP

Statutes: ProbC § 1400 (Guardianship-Conservatorship Law)
Regulations: 9 CCR § 836.1; 17 CCR § 50510(12)(D); 22 CCR § 7575
Cases: CD: check Guardian and Ward, key numbers (⚿) 1ff
Encyclopedia: CJ: check Guardianship and Conservatorship
Summaries:
- M-HLD: go to the vol. for California; under Family, check Guardian and Ward
- WSCL: vol. 12, Wills and Probate §§ 819ff

Internet:
megalaw.com/ca/top/cafamily.php
www.courtinfo.ca.gov/selfhelp/family/guardianship (Self-Help Center)
www.courtinfo.ca.gov/selfhelp/family/juv (Self-Help Center)

ILLEGITIMACY

Statutes: CC § 7600 (Uniform Parentage Act); ProbC § 6452
Regulations: 22 CCR § 50157(13)(B) (Medi-Cal Eligibility); 22 CCR § 117401 (Paternity)
Cases: CD: check Children Out-of-Wedlock, key numbers (⚿) 1ff
Encyclopedia: CJ: check Family Law §§ 263ff
Summaries:
- M-HLD: go to the vol. for California; under Estates and Trusts, check Descent and Distribution (and Illegitimates under Descent)
- WSCL: vol. 10, Parent and Child § 401

Internet:
www.courtinfo.ca.gov/selfhelp/family/parentage (Self-Help Center)
www.childsup.cahwnet.gov/pub/brochures/pub160.pdf (Paternity)
megalaw.com/ca/top/cafamily.php

INJUNCTIONS

Statutes: CC § 3420; CCP § 525
Cases: CD: check Injunction, key numbers (⚿) 1ff
Encyclopedia: CJ: check Injunctions
Summaries:
- M-HLD: go to the vol. for California; under Civil Actions and Procedure, check Injunctions
- WSCL: vol. 2, Agency §§ 527, 534
- WCP: vol. 6, Provisional Remedies §§ 276ff

INSURANCE

Statutes: IC § 100
Regulations: 10 CCR § 2050
Cases: CD: check Insurance, key numbers (⚿) 1ff
Encyclopedia: CJ: check Insurance Adjusters and Investigations; Insurance Contracts and Coverage; Insurance Companies
Summaries:
- M-HLD: go to the vol. for California; check Insurance
- WSCL: vol. 4, Real Property § 214; vol. 6, Torts §§ 1114ff (Automobile Liability Insurance)

Internet:
www.insurance.ca.gov (Department of Insurance)
megalaw.com/ca/top/cainsurance.php
www.leginfo.ca.gov/calaw.html (Insurance Code)

INTELLECTUAL PROPERTY

Statutes: BPC § 14206; CC § 3426; PRC § 25620.4
Regulations: 18 CCR §§ 24368.1, 13951.12 (Patent, Trademark, Copyright)
Cases: CD: check Copyrights and Intellectual Property, key numbers (⚿) 1ff
Encyclopedia: CJ: check Literary and Artistic Property; Criminal Law Miscellaneous Offenses § 173
Summaries:
- M-HLD: go to the vol. for California; check Intellectual Property
- WSCL: vol. 4, Personal Property § 57

Internet:
www.weblocator.com/attorney/ca/law/b29.html
www.weblocator.com/attorney/ca/law/c10.html
www.ss.ca.gov/business/ts/ts.htm

LABOR RELATIONS (see also Employment Discrimination; Workers' Compensation)

Statutes: LC §§ 1ff
Regulations: 8 CCR § 11701 (Labor Standards Enforcement)
Cases: CD: check Labor and Employment, key numbers (⚿) 1ff
Encyclopedia: CJ: check Employer and Employee; Labor
Summaries:
- M-HLD: go to the vol. for California; under Employment, check Labor Relations
- WSCL: vol. 3, Labor Relations §§ 531ff

Internet:
www.dir.ca.gov/DOSH/dosh1.html (Occupational Safety)
www.labor.ca.gov (Labor and Workforce Development Agency)
www.dfeh.ca.gov (Department of Fair Employment and Housing)
www.leginfo.ca.gov/calaw.html (Labor Code)
www.alrb.ca.gov (Agricultural Labor Relations Board)
megalaw.com/ca/top/calabor.php

LANDLORD AND TENANT

Statutes: CC § 1940.2, CCP § 1161
Regulations: 16 CCR § 3850 (Unlawful Detainer Assistants)
Cases: CD: check Landlord and Tenant, key numbers (⚿) 1ff
Encyclopedia: CJ: check Landlord and Tenant
Summaries:
- M-HLD: go to the vol. for California; under Property, check Landlord and Tenant
- WSCL: vol. 4, Real Property §§ 510ff

Internet:
www.courtinfo.ca.gov/selfhelp/other/landten.htm (Self-Help Center)
megalaw.com/ca/top/calandlord.php

LEGAL DOCUMENT ASSISTANTS and UNLAWFUL DETAINER ASSISTANTS (see also Paralegals)

Statutes: BPC § 6400
Regulations: 16 CCR § 3900; 16 CCR § 3850 (Unlawful Detainer Assistants)
Encyclopedia: CJ: check Attorneys at Law §§ 126ff; Occupations and Trades §§ 19ff
Summaries:
- WCP: vol. 1, Attorneys, §§ 397 (Paralegals, Unauthorized Practice of Law), 400B (Legal Document Assistants)
- WSCL: vol. 4, Real Property § 686A (Unlawful Detainer Assistants)

Internet:
www.calda.org (California Association)
www.caparalegal.org (California Alliance of Paralegal Associations)

LEGAL SEPARATION

Statutes: FC §§ 1840, 2000, 2310, 2333
Cases: CD: check Divorce, key numbers (⚿) 155ff
Encyclopedia: CJ: check Family Law § 639
Summaries:
- M-HLD: go to the vol. for California; under Family, check Dissolution of Marriage (and Legal Separation under Dissolution)
- WSCL: vol. 11, Husband and Wife §§ 171T, 243

Internet:
www.courtinfo.ca.gov/selfhelp/family/divorce (Self-Help Center)
megalaw.com/ca/top/cafamily.php

LIMITED LIABILITY COMPANIES (see also Corporations)

Statutes: CorpC § 17000
Regulations: 3 CCR § 1701.2
Cases: CD: check Limited Liability Companies, key numbers (⚷) 1ff
Encyclopedia: CJ: check Corporations §§ 979ff
Summaries:
- M-HLD: go to the vol. for California; under Business Organizations, check Limited Liability Companies
- WSCL: vol. 9, Corporations § 43A; vol. 9, Partnership § 120

Internet:
www.ss.ca.gov/business/business.htm (California Business Portal)

MARRIAGE (see also Family Law)

Statutes: FC §§ 301ff
Regulations: 2 CCR § 7292.1 (marital status)
Cases: CD: check Marriage, key numbers (⚷) 1ff
Encyclopedia: CJ: check Family Law §§ 18ff
Summaries:
- M-HLD: go to the vol. for California; under Family, check Marriage
- WSCL: vol. 1, Contracts § 598; vol. 11, Husband and Wife §§ 37ff

Internet:
www.courtinfo.ca.gov/selfhelp/family/divorce (Self-Help Center)
www.dhs.ca.gov/hisp/chs/OVR/default.htm (Office of Vital Records)
megalaw.com/ca/top/cafamily.php
www.leginfo.ca.gov/calaw.html (Family Code)

MEDIATION

Statutes: CCP § 1775
Regulations: 1 CCR §§ 1212, 1222
Cases: CD: check Child Custody, key numbers (⚷) 419ff
Encyclopedia: CJ: check Actions § 627; Arbitration and Award §§ 13ff; Building Regulations §§ 106ff; Discovery and Depositions § 23; Family Law § 968; Labor § 258
Summaries:
- M-HLD: go to the vol. for California; under Dispute Resolution, check Mediation
- WCP: vol. 6, Proceedings Without Trial §§ 472ff

Internet:
www.dca.ca.gov/complainthelp (Complaint Mediation)
www.weblocator.com/attorney/ca/law/b06.html
www.scmediation.org

MEDICAL MALPRACTICE

Statutes: CC §§ 56.105; CCP §§ 597.5, 1295; IC §§ 1858.05, 1858.15, 11589
Regulations: 10 CCR § 2644.4 (insurance); 16 CCR § 1354.5 (Disclosure of Judgments)
Cases: CD: check Health, key numbers (⚷) 600ff
Encyclopedia: CJ: check Accord and Satisfaction § 147; Costs § 145; Insurance Contracts § 519; Wrongful Death §§ 23, 81, 85
Summaries:
- WSCL: vol. 6, Torts §§ 774ff

Internet:
www.medbd.ca.gov (Medical Board of California)
www.dbc.ca.gov (Dental Board of California)
physicianassistant.ca.gov (Physician Assistant Committee)

MINERAL, WATER, AND FISHING RIGHTS

Statutes: PRC §§ 1ff; WC §§ 1ff
Regulations: see title 14 (Natural Resources); title 23 (Waters); title 27 (Environmental Protection)
Cases: CD: check Environmental Law; Mines and Minerals; Water and Water Courses, key numbers (⚷) 1ff
Encyclopedia: CJ: check Fish and Game; Mines and Minerals; Water
Summaries:
- M-HLD: go to the vol. for California; check Mineral, Water, and Fishing Rights
- WSCL: vol. 4, Real Property §§ 81(d) 84, 764

Internet:
megalaw.com/ca/top/caenvironmental.php
megalaw.com/ca/top/cawater.php
www.leginfo.ca.gov/calaw.html (Public Resources Code)

MINORS (see also Child Custody, Child Support, Family Law)

Statutes: FC §§ 6502, 6750, 7000
Regulations: 8 CCR § 11706 (dangerous occupations); 17 CCR § 5151 (Consent for Medical Care)
Cases: CD: check Infants, key numbers (⚷) 1ff
Encyclopedia: CJ: check Abortion § 4; Actions § 136; Contracts §§ 17ff; Delinquent and Dependent Children § 196; Family Law §§ 27, 400
Summaries:
- M-HLD: go to the vol. for California; under Family, check Infants
- WSCL: vol. 1, Contracts § 332; vol. 10, Parent and Child §§ 1ff, § 168 (Emancipation); vol. 12, Wills and Probate § 847

Internet:
www.courtinfo.ca.gov/selfhelp/family (Self-Help Center)
www.courtinfo.ca.gov/selfhelp/family/juv (Self-Help Center)
megalaw.com/ca/top/cafamily.php

MORTGAGES (see also Real Property)

Statutes: CC § 2920
Regulations: 10 CCR § 2840.1; 21 CCR § 7113 (Mortgage Banking)

Cases: CD: check Mortgages, key numbers (🔑) 1ff
Encyclopedia: CJ: check Mortages
Summaries:
- M-HLD: go to the vol. for California; check Mortgages
- WSCL: vol. 3, Security Transactions in Real Property § 3

Internet:
www.corp.ca.gov/pub/mb.htm

MOTOR VEHICLES (see also Traffic Law)

Statutes: VC §§ 1ff
Regulations: title 13 (Motor Vehicles)
Cases: CD: check Automobiles, key numbers (🔑) 1ff
Encyclopedia: CJ: check Automobiles; Insurance Contracts § 23;
Summaries:
- M-HLD: go to the vol. for California; under Transportation, check Motor Vehicles
- WSCL: vol. 3, Sales §226

Internet:
www.courtinfo.ca.gov/selfhelp/traffic (Self-Help Center)
www.dmv.ca.gov/pubs/vctop/vc/vc.htm
www.leginfo.ca.gov/calaw.html (Vehicles Code)

NEGLIGENCE (see also Torts)

Statutes: BPC §§ 2727.5, 7707; CC §§ 56.105, 1714, 1785.32, 1840, 3333.2; CCP §§ 597.5; FC § 2124; IC § 533; PC § 20
Regulations: 16 CCR § 1442 (Gross Negligence); 22 CCR §§ 1127-1, 71811 (Nurse Assistants)
Cases: CD: check Negligence; Torts, key numbers (🔑) 1ff
Encyclopedia: CJ: check Negligence; Wrongful Death
Summaries:
- WSCL: vol. 6, Torts § 729ff

Internet:
www.weblocator.com/attorney/ca/law/b32.html

NOTARY PUBLIC

Statutes: GC § 8201
Regulations: 2 CCR § 20800
Cases: CD: check Notaries, key numbers (🔑) 1ff
Encyclopedia: CJ: check Acknowledgments; Notaries Public
Summaries:
- M-HLD: go to the vol. for California; under Documents and Records, check Notaries Public
- WSCL: vol. 4, Real Property § 168
- WCP: vol. 3, Actions § 450(k) (malfeasance)

Internet:
www.ss.ca.gov/business/notary/notary.htm (Regulations)

PARALEGALS (see also Legal Document Assistants)

Statutes: BPC §§ 6450ff
Regulations: 16 CCR § 3900 (Legal Document Assistants); CCR: 16 CCR § 3850 (Unlawful Detainer Assistants); 22 CCR § 7577
Cases: CD: check the vols. for Costs, key number (🔑) 194.18; Prisons, key number (🔑) 4(11)
Encyclopedia: CJ: check Attorneys at Law § 126 (Unlawful Practice by Paralegals); Occupations and Trades § 19 (Legal Document Assistants), §§ 19-23 (Unlawful Detainer Assistants)
Summaries:
- WSCL: vol. 2, Agency and Employment § 12 (Independent Contractors); vol. 12, Wills and Probate § 508(k), 960(c)(3), 964B(6) (fees)
- WCP: vol. 1, Attorneys, § 397 (Paralegals, Unauthorized Practice of Law); vol. 1, Attorneys, § 616 (Disciplinary Proceedings); vol. 1, Attorneys, § 400B (Legal Document Assistants)

Internet:
www.caparalegal.org (California Alliance of Paralegal Associations)

PARTNERSHIPS (see also Corporations; Domestic Partnership)

Statutes: CorpC § 16100 (Uniform Partnership Act)
Regulations: 10 CCR § 260.140.114.2; 18 CCR § 18567
Cases: CD: check Partnership, key numbers (🔑) 1ff
Encyclopedia: CJ: check Partnership
Summaries:
- M-HLD: go to the vol. for California; under Business Organizations, check Partnerships
- WSCL: vol. 9, Partnership §§ 1ff

Internet:
www.ss.ca.gov/business/business.htm (California Business Portal)

PLEADING (see also Civil Procedure)

Statutes: CCP §§ 92, 420
Regulations: 1 CCR § 1014 (Administrative Hearings); 1 CCR § 1350 (Complaint); 8 CCR § 10400 (Workers' Compensation Proceedings)
Cases: CD: check Pleading, key numbers (🔑) 1ff
Encyclopedia: CJ: check Pleading
Summaries:
- M-HLD: go to the vol. for California; under Civil Action and Procedure, check Pleading
- WCP: vol. 4, Pleading §§ 1ff

Internet:
megalaw.com/ca/top/cacivpro.php
www.leginfo.ca.gov/calaw.html (Code of Civil Procedure)

POWER OF ATTORNEY

Statutes: CC §§ 1216, 2400; ProbC § 4124
Regulations: 2 CCR § 1898.6; 8 CCR § 15479; 18 CCR § 5073
Cases: CD: check Principal and Agent, key numbers (🔑) 10ff

Encyclopedia: CJ: check Agency §§ 34, 160.5, 174; Banks § 320
Summaries:
- M-HLD: go to the vol. for California; under Property, check Power of Attorney
- WSCL: vol. 2, Agency and Employment § 246K

Internet:
www.help4srs.org/law/newpahc.htm (Power of Attorney for Health Care)

PRIVACY

Statutes: BPC § 350; CC §§ 1708.8, 1786.52, 1798.73; FC § 1818
Regulations: 5 CCR § 42396 (Universities); 10 CCR § 2689.1 (Insurance); 22 CCR § 70819 (Patients)
Cases: CD: check Constitutional Law, key numbers (⚿) 82.7, 274(5); Torts, key number (⚿) 8.5
Encyclopedia: CJ: check Administrative Law § 195; Assault, §§ 120ff; Constitutional Law § 217; Consumer and Borrower Protection Laws § 544; Criminal Law Miscellaneous Offenses § 139; Criminal Law Trial § 543; Discovery and Depositions § 57; Healing Arts § 286; Schools § 323; Telegraphs and Telephones § 22
Summaries:
- M-HLD: go to the vol. for California; under Business Regulation and Commerce, check Consumer Protection (and Personal Information under Business Regulation)
- WSCL: vol. 5, Torts §§ 577; vol. 7, Constitutional Law §§ 454ff

Internet:
www.privacy.ca.gov (Office of Privacy Protection)

PRIVILEGED COMMUNICATIONS (see also Evidence, Privacy)

Statutes: BPC § 6094; CC § 3426.11; EC § 950; PC § 629.80
Regulations: 17 CCR § 1540; 22 CCR § 41670
Cases: CD: check Witnesses, key numbers (⚿) 184ff
Encyclopedia: CJ: check Evidence § 473
Summaries:
- M-HLD: go to the vol. for California; under Civil Actions and Procedure, check Evidence (and Privileged Communications under Evidence)
- WCE: vol. 2, Witnesses §§ 59ff; § 98 (attorney and client); §§ 169, 187 (Husband and Wife); §196 (Physician and Patient); § 211 (Psychotherapist); § 238 (Clergy and Penitent)

PRODUCTS LIABILITY

Statutes: CC § 1714.45
Cases: CD: check the vols. for Negligence; Products Liability; Torts, key numbers (⚿) 1ff
Encyclopedia: CJ: check Products Liability
Summaries:
- WSCL: vol. 6, Torts §§ 948ff, 1241ff

Internet:
www.weblocator.com/attorney/ca/law/b32.html

PROPERTY DIVISION IN DIVORCE (see also Divorce)

Statutes: FC § 2100
Cases: CD: check Divorce, key numbers (⚿) 248ff
Encyclopedia: CJ: check Family Law §§ 756, 1526
Summaries:
- M-HLD: go to the vol. for California; under Family, check Dissolution of Marriage (and Division of Property under Dissolution)
- WSCL: vol. 11, Husband and Wife §§ 294ff

Internet:
www.courtinfo.ca.gov/selfhelp/family/divorce (Self-Help Center)
megalaw.com/ca/top/cafamily.php

REAL PROPERTY (see also Landlord Tenant)

Statutes: BPC § 10000 (Real Estate Law); CC §§ 1054ff
Regulations: see title 10, chapter 6 (Commissioner of Real Estate)
Cases: CD: check the vols. for Estates in Property; Property, key numbers (⚿) 1ff
Encyclopedia: CJ: check Property §§ 18, Real Estate
Summaries:
- M-HLD: go to the vol. for California; under Property, check Real Property
- WSCL: vol. 3, Security Interests in Real Property §§ 1ff; vol. 4, Real Property §§ 1ff; vol. 9, Taxation §§ 126ff; vol. 11, Community Property §§ 1ff

Internet:
www.dre.cahwnet.gov (Department of Real Estate)
www.hcd.ca.gov (Housing and Human Development)
www.dfeh.ca.gov (Department of Fair Employment and Housing)
www.orea.ca.gov (Office of Real Estate Appraisers)
www.weblocator.com/attorney/ca/law/c22.html

SERVICE OF PROCESS

Statutes: CC § 1788.15; CCP § 414.10; CorpC § 8210
Regulations: 10 CCR § 280.152 (consent to service)
Cases: CD: check Process, key numbers (⚿) 48ff
Encyclopedia: CJ: check Process, Notices, and Subpoenas
Summaries:
- M-HLD: go to the vol. for California; under Civil Actions and Procedure, check Process
- WCP: vol. 3, Actions §§ 874ff

Internet:
megalaw.com/ca/top/cacivpro.php

STATUTE OF FRAUDS

Statutes: CC §§ 1624
Cases: CD: check Frauds, Statute of, key numbers (🔑) 1ff
Encyclopedia: CJ: check Frauds, Statute of
Summaries:
- M-HLD: go to the vol. for California; under Business Regulation and Commerce, check Frauds, Statute of
- WSCL: vol. 1, Contracts § 261; vol. 3, Sales § 31

STATUTE OF LIMITATIONS

Statutes: CC § 1369.550; CCP §§ 360.5, 458, 597.5; ComC § 2725, 3118
Cases: CD: check Limitation of Actions, key numbers (🔑) 1ff
Encyclopedia: CJ: check Limitation of Actions
Summaries:
- M-HLD: go to the vol. for California; under Civil Actions and Procedure, check Limitation of Actions
- WSCL: vol. 3, Sales § 206; vol. 12, Wills § 609

Internet:
megalaw.com/ca/top/cacivpro.php

SUMMARY JUDGMENT (see also Civil Procedure)

Statutes: CCP § 437c
Regulations: 1 CCR § 1386 (Arbitration); 8 CCR § 10490 (Workers' Compensation)
Cases: CD: check Judgment, key numbers (🔑) 178ff
Encyclopedia: CJ: check Accord and Satisfaction § 48; Appellate Review § 72; Declaratory Relief § 106; Judgments §§ 36ff
Summaries:
- M-HLD: go to the vol. for California; under Civil Actions and Procedure, check Judgments (and Summary Judgments under Judgment)
- WCP: vol. 6, Proceedings Without Trial § 178

Internet:
megalaw.com/ca/top/cacivpro.php

SUMMONS (see also Civil Procedure)

Statutes: CCP § 412.20
Regulations: 1 CCR § 1305 (Administrative Hearings)
Cases: CD: check Process, key numbers (🔑) 10ff
Encyclopedia: CJ: check Process, Notices, and Subpoenas
Summaries:
- M-HLD: go to the vol. for California; under Civil Actions and Procedure, check Process
- WCP: vol. 3, Actions §§ 875, 896ff

TAXATION

Statutes: RTC §§ 1ff
Regulations: see title 18 (Public Revenues)
Cases: CD: check Taxation, key numbers (🔑) 1ff
Encyclopedia: CJ: check Death and Transfer Taxes; Family Law § 1481; Franchise and In Lieu Taxes § 2; Income Taxes; Municipalities § 171; Property Taxes; Sales and Use Taxes; Taxpayers' Actions
Summaries:
- M-HLD: go to the vol. for California; check Taxation
- WSCL: vol. 9, Taxation §§ 1ff

Internet:
www.courtinfo.ca.gov/selfhelp/additionalinfo/links.htm#taxes (Self-Help Center)
www.ftb.ca.gov (Franchise Tax Board)
www.boe.ca.gov (Board of Equalization)
www.ss.ca.gov/business/tax.htm

TORTS (see also Medical Malpractice, Negligence)

Statutes: CC §§ 1365.9, 1708.6, 3333; CCP § 1038; GC § 815.3; ProbC § 18002
Cases: CD: check the vols. for Negligence; Products Liability; Torts, key numbers (🔑) 1ff
Encyclopedia: CJ: check Assault and Other Wilful Torts; Damages; Negligence; Nuisances; Trespass to Realty; Wrongful Death
Summaries:
- WSCL: vol. 2, Agency and Employment §§ 113, 135; vol. 2, Workers' Compensation § 36; vol. 5, Torts §§ 1ff; vol. 11, Equity §§ 82ff

Internet:
www.dir.ca.gov/DOSH/dosh1.html (Occupational Safety)
www.weblocator.com/attorney/ca/law/b32.html

TRAFFIC LAWS

Statutes: VC §§ 1ff
Regulations: see title 13 (Motor Vehicles)
Cases: CD: check Automobiles, key numbers (🔑) 5ff
Encyclopedia: CJ: check Criminal Law Crimes Against Administration of Justice §§ 296ff
Summaries:
- M-HLD: go to the vol. for California; under Transportation, check Traffic Regulation
- WECL: vol. 2, Crimes §§ 197ff, 253ff

Internet:
www.courtinfo.ca.gov/selfhelp/traffic (Self-Help Center)
www.dmv.ca.gov (Department of Motor Vehicles)
www.chp.ca.gov (California Highway Patrol)
www.ots.ca.gov (Office of Traffic Safety)
www.leginfo.ca.gov/calaw.html (Vehicle Code)
www.ncsconline.org/wc/CourTopics/statelinks.asp?id=41&topic=IntCts

TRUSTS

Statutes: CCP §§ 366.3, 709.010; ProbC §§ 80, 104, 15000 (The Trust Law), 15407
Regulations: 10 CCR § 10.178 (Trust Company)
Cases: CD: check Trusts, key numbers (🔑) 1ff

Encyclopedia: CJ: check Trusts
Summaries:
- M-HLD: go to the vol. for California; check Estates and Trusts
- WSCL: vol. 11, Trusts §§ 1ff

Internet:
megalaw.com/ca/top/caprobate.php
www.courtinfo.ca.gov/selfhelp/additionalinfo/links.htm#wills (Self-Help Center)

UNEMPLOYMENT INSURANCE

Statutes: UIC §§ 1ff
Regulations: see title 22, division 1
Cases: CD: check Social Security and Public Welfare, key numbers (⚿) 251ff
Encyclopedia: CJ: check Unemployment Compensation
Summaries:
- M-HLD: go to the vol. for California; under Employment, check Labor Relations (and Unemployment under Labor Relations)
- WSCL: vol. 2, Agency and Employment § 347

Internet:
www.cuiab.ca.gov (Unemployment Insurance Appeals Board)
www.leginfo.ca.gov/calaw.html (Unemployment Insurance Code)

VENUE (see also Civil Procedure)

Statutes: CC § 1812.10; CCP § 392.
Regulations: 8 CCR § 10410 (Workers' Compensation Case)
Cases: CD: check Venue, key numbers (⚿) 1ff
Encyclopedia: CJ: check Venue
Summaries:
- M-HLD: go to the vol. for California; under Civil Actions and Procedure, check Venue
- WCP: vol. 3, Actions §§ 701ff

Internet:
megalaw.com/ca/top/cacivpro.php

WATER RIGHTS

Statutes: WC §§ 1ff
Regulations: see title 23 (Waters)
Cases: CD: check Waters and Water Courses, key numbers (⚿) 1ff
Encyclopedia: CJ: check Water
Summaries:
- M-HLD: go to the vol. for California; check Mineral, Water, and Fishing Rights
- WSCL: vol. 4, Real Property §§ 754ff

Internet:
wwwdwr.water.ca.gov (Department of Water Resources)
megalaw.com/ca/top/caenvironmental.php
megalaw.com/ca/top/cawater.php
www.leginfo.ca.gov/calaw.html (Water Code)
www.dbw.ca.gov (Department of Boating and Waterways)

WILLS (see also Estates)

Statutes: ProbC § 6100
Cases: CD: check Wills, key numbers (⚿) 1ff
Encyclopedia: CJ: check Wills
Summaries:
- M-HLD: go to the vol. for California; under Estates and Trusts, check Wills
- WSCL: vol. 12, Wills and Probate §§ 1ff

Internet:
www.courtinfo.ca.gov/selfhelp/additionalinfo/links.htm#wills (Self-Help Center)
megalaw.com/ca/top/caprobate.php

WORKERS' COMPENSATION

Statutes: LC §§ 60, 3200
Regulations: see title 8, division 1
Cases: CD: check Workers' Compensation, key numbers (⚿) 1ff
Encyclopedia: CJ: check Work Injury Compensation
Summaries:
- M-HLD: go to the vol. for California; under Employment, check Workers' Compensation
- WSCL: vol. 2, Workers' Compensation §§ 1ff

Internet:
www.dir.ca.gov/wcab/wcab.htm (Workers' Compensation Appeals Board)
www.dir.ca.gov/dwc/dwc_home_page.htm (Division of Workers' Compensation)
www.courtinfo.ca.gov/selfhelp/additionalinfo/links.htm#workcomp (Self-Help Center)
megalaw.com/ca/top/caworkcomp.php

E. More Information

(See also section 5.1 on California legal research.)
www.leginfo.ca.gov/calaw.html
california.lp.findlaw.com
california.lp.findlaw.com/ca01_codes
megalaw.com/ca/ca.php

F. Something to Check

One of the ways that law firms try to attract clients is to provide law summaries and overviews on their Web sites. Pick any two topics covered in this section (e.g., adoption, limited liability companies). For each topic, find three California law firm Web sites that provide summaries or overviews of California law on the topic. Compare the quality and quantity of what you learn about the law at each site. To locate the law firms, go to any search engine (e.g., www.google.com) and type in "California", "law", or "lawyer", and your topic, e.g., "California law adoption" or "California lawyer adoption".

5.6 Self-Help Resources in California

A. Introduction

B. Resources

C. More Information

D. Something to Check

A. Introduction

Where do California citizens go when they are representing themselves but would still like some assistance? Such individuals are sometimes said to be engaged in "self-help." They are proceeding pro se, acting on their own behalf. (Another meaning of self-help is to take steps to obtain redress outside the legal system.) It is useful to know about self-help resources for two main reasons. First, a law office will sometimes refer citizens to self-help materials when the office cannot provide representation. Second, self-help resources often provide excellent overviews of the law that everyone should know about. Even if persons have attorney representation, they may sometimes consult self-help materials in order to be able to communicate with their attorneys more intelligently.

For related sections, see:

- 2.4 Pro Bono Help
- 4.2 State Courts in California
- 5.1 California State Legal Research
- 5.5 Research Starters
- 5.7 Public Records Research
- 6.1 Timeline: Civil Case
- 6.4 Timeline: Criminal Case

The number of self-help litigants in the state is extensive. According to the Administrative Office of the Courts in California:

- Most of the six million annual traffic filings involve self-represented litigants;
- All of the nearly 400,000 annual small claims filings involve self-represented litigants;
- Of the estimated 94,500 child custody mediation cases handled by California courts each year, at least half involve one or more self-represented parents;
- Fewer than 16 percent of child support cases involve parents who both are represented by attorneys, and in more than 63 percent of child support cases, neither parent has representation;
- Ninety-seven percent of proceedings processed through the local child support agencies involve at least one self-represented parent; and
- A significant number of self-represented litigants are native Spanish speakers.

Many of the self-help resources in this section involve small claims and family law matters. The links in the sites, however, often lead to resources for other kinds of cases as well.

B. Resources

1. General
2. Self-Help in Specific Legal Subjects
3. Self-Help in Specific Counties

1. General

California Courts Self-Help Center
www.courtinfo.ca.gov/selfhelp
www.courtinfo.ca.gov/selfhelp/additionalinfo/links.htm

This excellent resource provides legal definitions, overviews of court procedure, and links to legal forms.

County-by-County Self-Help Resources
www.courtinfo.ca.gov/selfhelp/lowcost/helpcourt.htm

Fact Sheet: Programs for Self-Represented Litigants
www.courtinfo.ca.gov/selfhelp/pressroom/documents/summary.pdf

Ask a Legal Research Question of a Law Librarian
www.247ref.org/portal/access_law3.cfm

The "Ask a Librarian" program allows anyone to direct research questions (via e-mail) to librarians at major public law libraries across the state.

Family Law Facilitators
www.courtinfo.ca.gov/selfhelp/lowcost/flf.htm
www.courtinfo.ca.gov/selfhelp/lowcost/helpcourt.htm

Each county has a family law facilitator who works for the superior court. He or she is a licensed attorney working out of a court-based office to help citizens with cases involving family law. This service is free. Facilitators do not represent individual clients. Rather, their role is to guide litigants through procedures related to child support, maintenance of health insurance, and spousal support. They assist with cases involving the local child support agency, many of which are public assistance reimbursement cases. In addition, many courts enlist volunteer attorneys or provide funding that enables facilitators to assist self-represented litigants in other family law areas, including divorce, custody, and visitation. Family law facilitators can assist parties with forms, court procedures, and support calculations, and they provide workshops and referrals to community agencies that assist parents and families. Statewide, facilitators help more than 30,000 self-represented litigants each month.

Small Claims Court Advisor
www.lasuperiorcourt.org/smallclaims

Some counties provide free counseling for small claims litigants. Here, for example, is a description of the program for one county: "The Los Angeles County Department of Consumer Affairs' Small Claims Court Advisor Program provides information and counseling to litigants and potential litigants concerning all aspects of the Small Claims Court process, including case preparation, collection, venue, appeals and more. Call (213) 974-9759 for 24-hour recorded information or to speak with an advisor between the hours of 8:30 A.M. and 4:30 P.M."

Small Claims Self-Help
www.courtinfo.ca.gov/selfhelp/smallclaims
secure.icandocs.org/newweb/modules.html#sc

Online Forms and Instructions
www.courtinfo.ca.gov/cgi-bin/forms.cgi
www.courtinfo.ca.gov/forms
www.courtinfo.ca.gov/selfhelp/forms

EZLegalFile
www.ezlegalfile.org
www.ezlegalfile.org/index.jsp

This interactive program will help you fill out the forms necessary to request or respond to papers on a variety of legal matters.

I-Can Legal Modules
www.icandocs.org
secure.icandocs.org/newweb
secure.icandocs.org/newweb/locations.html

These modules create properly formatted pleadings, provide court tours, and educate users on the law and the steps needed to pursue their matter.

Self-Help Center Links
www.publiclawlibrary.org/help.html
www.courtinfo.ca.gov/selfhelp/lowcost/libraries.htm

California Association of Legal Document Assistants
www.calda.org
www.calda.org/products.asp

2. Self-Help in Specific Subject Matters

Adoption	Guardianship
Criminal Law	Immigration Law
Domestic Violence	Landlord-Tenant
Eviction	Tax Law
Family Law	Unlawful Detainer

Adoption Self-Help Resources
www.courtinfo.ca.gov/selfhelp/family/adoption

Criminal Law Self-Help Resources
www.courtinfo.ca.gov/selfhelp/other/crimlaw.htm

Domestic Violence Self-Help Resources
www.ezlegalfile.org
secure.icandocs.org/newweb/modules.html#dv

Eviction Self-Help Resources
www.courtinfo.ca.gov/selfhelp/other/landten.htm
www.ezlegalfile.org
secure.icandocs.org/newweb/modules.html#ud

Family Law Self-Help Resources
www.courtinfo.ca.gov/selfhelp/family/overview
www.courtinfo.ca.gov/selfhelp/lowcost/flf.htm
www.ezlegalfile.org
secure.icandocs.org/newweb/modules.html#disso
www.calbar.ca.gov/state/calbar/calbar_generic.jsp?cid=10180&id=1398

Guardianship Self-Help Resources
www.ezlegalfile.org

Immigration Law Self-Help Resources
www.courtinfo.ca.gov/selfhelp/other (click "Immigration Law")

Landlord-Tenant Self-Help Resources
www.courtinfo.ca.gov/selfhelp/other/landten.htm
www.ezlegalfile.org
secure.icandocs.org/newweb/modules.html#ud

Tax Law Self-Help Resources
www.courtinfo.ca.gov/selfhelp/additionalinfo/links.htm#taxes

Unlawful Detainer Self-Help Resources
www.courtinfo.ca.gov/selfhelp/other/landten.htm
www.ezlegalfile.org
secure.icandocs.org/newweb/modules.html#ud

3. Self-Help in Specific Counties

- Alameda County
- Amador County
- Butte County
- Calaveras County
- Colusa County
- Contra Costa County
- El Dorado County
- Fresno County
- Glenn County
- Humboldt County
- Inyo County
- Kern County
- Kings County
- Los Angeles County
- Madera County
- Marin County
- Mariposa County
- Mendocino County
- Mono County
- Monterey County
- Napa County
- Nevada County
- Orange County
- Placer County
- Plumas County
- Riverside County
- Sacramento County
- San Benito County
- San Bernardino County
- San Diego County
- San Francisco County
- San Joaquin County
- San Luis Obispo County
- San Mateo County
- Santa Barbara County
- Santa Clara County
- Santa Cruz County
- Shasta County
- Sierra County
- Siskiyou County
- Solano County
- Sonoma County
- Stanislaus County
- Sutter County
- Tehama County
- Trinity County
- Tulare County
- Tuolumne County
- Ventura County
- Yolo County
- Yuba County

Alameda County Self-Help Resources
www.alameda.courts.ca.gov/selfhelp
www.alameda.courts.ca.gov/courts/divs/small/index.shtml
www.alameda.courts.ca.gov/courts/divs/family/familylaw.shtml

Amador County Self-Help Resources
www.amadorcourt.org/self/self.html
www.amadorcourt.org/smallclaims/smallclaims.html
www.courtinfo.ca.gov/selfhelp/lowcost/flfcounty.htm#amador

Butte County Self-Help Resources
www.courtinfo.ca.gov/selfhelp/lowcost/butte.htm
www.buttecourt.ca.gov/departments/self_help/default.htm
www.buttecourt.ca.gov/departments/family_law/default.htm

Calaveras County Self-Help Resources
www.courtinfo.ca.gov/selfhelp/lowcost/calaveras.htm
www.calaveras.courts.ca.gov (click "Self Help and Representation Information")

Colusa County Self-Help Resources
www.colusa.courts.ca.gov (click "Self-help")

Contra Costa County Self-Help Resources
www.cc-courthelp.org
cc-courts.org/smallcl.htm
www.cc-courts.org/famlaw.htm

El Dorado County Self-Help Resources
eldocourtweb.eldoradocourt.org/small-claims.html

Fresno County Self-Help Resources
www.fresnosuperiorcourt.org/family/sshc.php
www.courtinfo.ca.gov/selfhelp/smallclaims/fresno.htm
www.fresnosuperiorcourt.org/family/facilitators_office.php

Glenn County Self-Help Resources
www.courtinfo.ca.gov/selfhelp/lowcost/glenn.htm
www.glenncourt.ca.gov/court_info/claims.html
www.glenncourt.ca.gov/court_info/facilitator.html

Humboldt County Self-Help Resources
www.courtinfo.ca.gov/courts/trial/humboldt/smallclaims.htm

Inyo County Self-Help Resources
www.inyocourt.ca.gov/small%20claims.htm
www.inyocourt.ca.gov/family%20law.htm#Family%20Law%20Facilitator

Kern County Self-Help Resources
www.kern.courts.ca.gov/smallclaims.asp
www.kern.courts.ca.gov/flf.asp

Kings County Self-Help Resources
www.courtinfo.ca.gov/selfhelp/lowcost/flfcounty.htm#kings

Los Angeles County Self-Help Resources
www.lasuperiorcourt.org
www.courtinfo.ca.gov/selfhelp/lowcost/losangeles.htm
www.lasuperiorcourt.org/smallclaims
www.lasuperiorcourt.org/familylaw/sup-facilitator.htm

Madera County Self-Help Resources
madera.courts.ca.gov/MaderaSelfHelp.htm
madera.courts.ca.gov/MaderaProceduresSmallClaimsLaw.htm
www.courtinfo.ca.gov/selfhelp/lowcost/flfcounty.htm#madera

Marin County Self-Help Resources
www.co.marin.ca.us/depts/MC/main/smallclaims.cfm
www.courtinfo.ca.gov/selfhelp/lowcost/marin.htm
www.co.marin.ca.us/depts/MC/main/facilitator-general.cfm

Mariposa County Self-Help Resources
www.mariposacourts.org/MariposaSelfHelp.htm
www.mariposacourts.org/Dept_SmallClaims.htm
www.courtinfo.ca.gov/selfhelp/lowcost/flfcounty.htm#mariposa

Mendocino County Self-Help Resources
www.mendocino.courts.ca.gov/selfhelp.html
www.mendocino.courts.ca.gov/small.html#4
www.mendocino.courts.ca.gov/famfacil.html

Mono County Self-Help Resources
www.monosuperiorcourt.ca.gov/small_claims.htm
www.courtinfo.ca.gov/selfhelp/lowcost/flfcounty.htm#mono

Monterey County Self-Help Resources
www.monterey.courts.ca.gov/small_claims.html
www.courtinfo.ca.gov/selfhelp/lowcost/flfcounty.htm#monterey

Napa County Self-Help Resources
www.mynapa.info/LIVING/Living.asp?LID=168
www.napa.courts.ca.gov/Family/family_facilitator.htm

Nevada County Self-Help Resources
court.co.nevada.ca.us/services/self_help/index.htm
court.co.nevada.ca.us/services/small_claims/advisor.htm

Orange County Self-Help Resources
www.occourts.org/civil/smclaims.asp
www.occourts.org/family/flfacil.asp

Placer County Self-Help Resources
www.placercourts.org/d_fcc.htm
www.courtinfo.ca.gov/selfhelp/lowcost/flfcounty.htm#placer

Plumas County Self-Help Resources
www.courtinfo.ca.gov/selfhelp/smallclaims/plumas.htm
www.courtinfo.ca.gov/selfhelp/lowcost/flfcounty.htm#plumas

Riverside County Self-Help Resources
www.courts.co.riverside.ca.us/kiosks/kiosk.htm
www.courts.co.riverside.ca.us/selfhelp.htm
www.courts.co.riverside.ca.us/kiosks/familylaw.htm

Sacramento County Self-Help Resources
www.saccourt.com/family/self_help_center/center.asp
www.saccourt.com/index/smallclaims.asp

San Benito County Self-Help Resources
www.sanbenito.courts.ca.gov/family_law_facilitator.htm

San Bernardino County Self-Help Resources
www.courtinfo.ca.gov/selfhelp/smallclaims/sanbernardino.htm

San Diego County Self-Help Resources
www.sdcourt.ca.gov (click "Small Claims")
www.sdcourt.ca.gov (click "Family & Children")

San Francisco County Self-Help Resources
www.courtinfo.ca.gov/selfhelp/lowcost/sanfrancisco.htm
sfgov.org/site/courts_page.asp?id=3743
sfgov.org/site/courts_page.asp?id=3666

San Joaquin County Self-Help Resources
www.stocktoncourt.org/courts/selfhelp.htm
www.stocktoncourt.org/courts/smclaims8.htm
www.stocktoncourt.org/courts/selfhelp1.htm

San Luis Obispo County Self-Help Resources
www.slocourts.ca.gov/civil/family/facsch.cfm

San Mateo County Self-Help Resources
www.sanmateocourt.org (click "Online Help Center")
www.sanmateocourt.org/director.php?filename=./famlaw/faminfo.html

Santa Barbara County Self-Help Resources
www.sbcourts.org/srl
www.sbcourts.org/general_info/case_types/small_claims.htm
www.sbcourts.org/special_programs/fam_law_fac.htm

Santa Clara County Self-Help Resources
www.scselfservice.org/default.htm
www.scselfservice.org/small/smallresources.htm#sca
www.scselfservice.org/fam/clinic.htm

Santa Cruz County Self-Help Resources
www.courtinfo.ca.gov/selfhelp/smallclaims/santacruz.htm
www.santacruzcourt.org/Family%20Law/family_law_facilitator.htm

Shasta County Self-Help Resources
www.shastacourts.com/page.php?page=burney#SCAdvisor
www.courtinfo.ca.gov/selfhelp/lowcost/flfcounty.htm#shasta

Sierra County Self-Help Resources
www.sierracourt.org/mediator.html

Siskiyou County Self-Help Resources
www.courtinfo.ca.gov/selfhelp/lowcost/flfcounty.htm#siskiyou
www.siskiyou.courts.ca.gov (click "California Courts Self-Help Center")

Solano County Self-Help Resources
www.solanocourts.com/general/court/small.htm
www.solanocourts.com/pdf/crt_family_dwn2.pdf

Sonoma County Self-Help Resources
sonomasuperiorcourt.com/index.php?v=svcs_resources#Self
www.sonomasuperiorcourt.com/index.php?v=civil_smcl_div
www.sonomasuperiorcourt.com/index.php?v=fam_law_div

Stanislaus County Self-Help Resources
www.stanct.org/courts/smallclaims/index.html
www.stanct.org/courts/familylaw/index.html

Sutter County Self-Help Resources
www.courtinfo.ca.gov/selfhelp/lowcost/sutter.htm
www.courtinfo.ca.gov/selfhelp/smallclaims/sutter.htm
www.suttercourts.com/index.asp?webfile=familycontact

Tehama County Self-Help Resources
www.courtinfo.ca.gov/selfhelp/lowcost/tehama.htm
www.courtinfo.ca.gov/selfhelp/lowcost/flfcounty.htm#tehama

Trinity County Self-Help Resources
www.courtinfo.ca.gov/courts/trial/trinity/smallclaims.htm
www.courtinfo.ca.gov/selfhelp/lowcost/flfcounty.htm#trinity

Tulare County Self-Help Resources
www.tularesuperiorcourt.ca.gov/new/html/small_claims.htm
www.courtinfo.ca.gov/selfhelp/lowcost/flfcounty.htm#tulare

Tuolumne County Self-Help Resources
www.tuolumne.courts.ca.gov/family.htm
www.courtinfo.ca.gov/selfhelp/smallclaims/tuolumne.htm
www.courtinfo.ca.gov/selfhelp/lowcost/flfcounty.htm#tuolumne

Ventura County Self-Help Resources
www.ventura.courts.ca.gov (click "legal self help")
www.courtinfo.ca.gov/selfhelp/lowcost/ventura.htm

Yolo County Self-Help Resources
www.yolocourts.com/faq_smallclaims.html
www.yolocourts.com/family_law_fac.html

Yuba County Self-Help Resources
www.yubacourts.org/Forms.htm

C. More Information

Public Law Libraries
www.publiclawlibrary.org

SelfHelpSupport.Org
www.selfhelpsupport.org
www.selfhelpsupport.org/resourcesforselfrepresent378.cfm

ABA Legal Information Resources
www.abalawinfo.org
www.abanet.org/legalservices/findlegalhelp/main.cfm?id=CA

LawHelp.Org
www.lawhelp.org

Nolo Press Self-Help Law Center
www.nolo.com

Yahoo Self-Help Resources
dir.yahoo.com/Government/Law/Self_Help

Pro Se Law Center
www.pro-selaw.org/pro-selaw/index.asp

Legal Information Law Institute
www.law.cornell.edu/index.html

FindForms
www.findforms.com
(type "california" in the search box)

City Legal Guide
www.citylegalguide.com
(click "California" on the map)

Protecting Your Rights
www.atlanet.org/pressroom/Links.aspx

Kids and the Law
www.calbar.ca.gov/state/calbar/calbar_generic.jsp?cid=10180&id=1398

Teenagers and the Law
www.calbar.ca.gov/state/calbar/calbar_generic.jsp?cid=10180&id=17523

Seniors and the Law
www.calbar.ca.gov/state/calbar/calbar_generic.jsp?cid=10180&id=7970

D. Something to Check

1. Find online self-help information on collecting child support in California.
2. Find online self-help information on suing your neighbor in California for damage done to a common fence.

5.7 Public Records Research

- A. Introduction
- B. California Public Records Act (PRA)
- C. Search Resources
- D. More Information
- E. Something to Check

A. Introduction

There are a large variety of public records that a law firm may seek to obtain. For example:

Business Records

Corporations	Sales Tax Registrations
Fictitious Names	Tax Liens
Limited Liability Companies	Trademarks and Service Marks
Partnerships	UCC Filings
Real Estate	

Individual Records

Accident Reports	Marriage
Bankruptcies	Occupational Licenses
Birth	Vehicle Ownership
Court Judgments	Workers' Compensation Claims
Criminal Records	
Death	
Divorce	

Access to these records varies. Some are available to the general public, while others are subject to substantial restrictions.

This section will provide starting points in finding out what is available. Some of the Internet sites and phone numbers in this section will lead you to complete access to the records involved. Others will simply help you make inquiries about what might be available.

B. California Public Records Act (PRA)

caselaw.lp.findlaw.com/cacodes/gov/6250-270.html
www.foiadvocates.com/records.html

The PRA is similar to the federal Freedom of Information Act. The purpose of both acts is to give private citizens greater access to government information. With some exceptions, the PRA considers all records maintained by most state agencies to be public records, but also recognizes the right to individual privacy. (Government Code §§ 6250-6270)

§ 6250. In enacting this chapter, the Legislature, mindful of the right of individuals to privacy, finds and declares that access to information concerning the conduct of the people's business is a fundamental and necessary right of every person in this state.

6253(c). Each agency, upon a request for a copy of records, shall, within 10 days from receipt of the request, determine whether the request, in whole or in part, seeks copies of disclosable public records in the possession of the agency and shall promptly notify the person making the request of the determination and the reasons therefor.

California Public Records Act Information
www.parks.ca.gov/?page_id=1084
www.thefirstamendment.org/publicrecordsact.pdf
caag.state.ca.us/publications/summary_public_records_act.pdf

C. Search Resources

Accident Reports

Department of Motor Vehicles
Accident Reports
800-777-0133
www.dmv.ca.gov
Request copy of SR-1 accident report:
www.dmv.ca.gov/forms/sr/sr19c.htm

California Highway Patrol (local offices):
www.chp.ca.gov/offices/offices.html
Accident Incident Information
cad.chp.ca.gov

Accountants (license records)

California Board of Accountancy
916-263-3680
www.dca.ca.gov/cba

Acupuncturists (license records)

California Acupuncture Board
916-445-3021
www.acupuncture.ca.gov

Alcohol Beverage Control (license records)

916-419-2500
www.abc.ca.gov
www.abc.ca.gov/datport/LQSMenu.html

Appliance Repair Businesses (license records)

(see Electronics)

Architects (license records)

California Architects Board
916-445-3394
www.cab.ca.gov
www.cab.ca.gov/licensee-main.htm

Assessor Records (property ownership and valuation)

www.boe.ca.gov/proptaxes/assessors.htm
www.calassessor.org
homepage.mac.com/researchventures

Attorney General

(see Criminal Records)

Attorneys (license records)

State Bar of California
415-538-2577; 800-843-9053
members.calbar.ca.gov/search/member.aspx

Automotive Repair Businesses (license records)

Bureau of Automotive Repair
800-952-5210
www.smogcheck.ca.gov/StdHome.asp

Banks

(see Financial Institutions)

Barbers (license records)

Board of Barbering and Cosmetology
800-952-5210
www.barbercosmo.ca.gov/index.html

Birth Records

Office of Vital Records
916-445-2684
www.dhs.ca.gov/chs/OVR/default.htm
www.dhs.ca.gov/chs/OVR/OrderCert.htm
www.dhs.ca.gov/chs/OVR/BirthOrderCert.htm

["Before birth and death records are registered in our office (state database) and available for purchase, they're registered (County Health Department) and recorded (County Recorder's Office) at the local level in the county where the event took place."]

County Registrars/Recorders
www.dhs.ca.gov/chs/OVR/LocalRegistrar/default.htm
www.co.el-dorado.ca.us/countyclerk/other_rec.html

National Center for Health Statistics: California
www.cdc.gov/nchs/howto/w2w/californ.htm

Brokers

(see Real Estate Brokers)

Business Filings

(see also Corporations Records, UCC Transactions)
916-657-5448
kepler.ss.ca.gov/list.html

Campaigns

(see Elections)

Cemeteries (license records)

Cemetery and Funeral Bureau
916-322-7737; 800-952-5210
www.cfb.ca.gov

Contractors (license records)

Contractors State License Board
800-321-2752
www.cslb.ca.gov

Corporations Records

Secretary of State
916-657-5448
kepler.ss.ca.gov/list.html
www.ss.ca.gov/business/corp/corp_naav.htm

Cosmologists (license records)

Board of Barbering and Cosmetology
800-952-5210
www.barbercosmo.ca.gov/index.html

County Government Records

(see also section 4.6 for sites to all county governments)
County Government sites
www.csac.counties.org

Court Opinions

(see also sections 4.2 and 5.1 on finding California court opinions)
www.courtinfo.ca.gov/opinions

Court Records

(check the sites of individual California courts)
Supreme Court
www.courtinfo.ca.gov/courts/supreme
Courts of Appeals
www.courtinfo.ca.gov/courts/courtsofappeal
Superior Courts
www.courtinfo.ca.gov/courts/trial
www.courtinfo.ca.gov/courts/trial/courtlist.htm
www.sccba.com/courtresource/caltrial.cfm

Court Reporters (license records)

Court Reporters Board of California
916-263-3660
www.courtreportersboard.ca.gov

Credit Unions

(see Financial Institutions)

Criminal Records

(see also Inmate Locator, Sex Offenders)

Find criminal records at the county level. For example:
www.lasuperiorcourt.org/Criminal
(click "Index of Defendants")

California Department of Justice
caag.state.ca.us/consumers/general/pra.php
www.caag.state.ca.us
(type "records" in search box)
ag.ca.gov/consumers/general/pra.htm

"Requesting Your Record"
www.las-elc.org/lcriminalrecords.pdf

Criminal Records and Background Checks
www.privacyrights.org/fs/fs16a-califbck.htm

Death Records

Office of Vital Records
Department of Health Services
916-445-2684
www.dhs.ca.gov/chs/OVR/default.htm
www.dhs.ca.gov/chs/OVR/OrderCert.htm
www.dhs.ca.gov/hisp/chs/ovr/deathordercert.htm

["Before birth and death records are registered in our office (state database) and available for purchase, they're registered (County Health Department) and recorded (County Recorder's Office) at the local level in the county where the event took place."]

County Registrars/Recorders
www.dhs.ca.gov/chs/OVR/LocalRegistrar/default.htm
www.co.el-dorado.ca.us/countyclerk/other_rec.html

National Center for Health Statistics: California
www.cdc.gov/nchs/howto/w2w/californ.htm

Dentists (license records)

Dental Board of California
916-263-2300
www.dbc.ca.gov

Dental Hygienists/Assistants (license records)

Committee on Dental Auxiliaries
916-263-2595
www.comda.ca.gov

Divorce/Dissolution of Marriage Records

Office of Vital Records
916-445-2684
www.dhs.ca.gov/hisp/chs/OVR/MarriageDissolutionOrderCert.htm

("This office issues a Certificate of Record for divorces that occurred only between 1962 and June 1984. A Certificate of Record includes the names of the parties to the divorce, the county where the divorce was filed, and the court case number. A Certificate of Record is not a certified copy of the divorce decree. If you need a certified copy of the actual divorce decree, you'll need to contact the Superior Court in the county where the divorce was filed.")

Superior Court Web Sites
www.courtinfo.ca.gov/courts/trial
www.courtinfo.ca.gov/courts/trial/courtlist.htm

National Center for Health Statistics: California
www.cdc.gov/nchs/howto/w2w/californ.htm

Doctors

(see Dentists, Physicians)

Elections, Campaigns, Lobbying Records, Major Donors, Ballot Measures

Cal-Access
916-657-2166
cal-access.ss.ca.gov/Campaign
www.ss.ca.gov/elections/elections.htm

Electronics and Appliance Repair Businesses (license records)

Bureau of Electronic and Appliance Repair
916-574-2069; 800-952-5210
www.bear.ca.gov

Engineers (license records)

Board for Professional Engineers and Land Surveyors
916-263-2222
www.dca.ca.gov/pels

Fictitious Names

Fictitious business names are not filed with the Secretary of State's office. There is no central registry at the state level. Fictitious Business Name Statements are filed with the county where the principal place of business is located. For example:
www.lavote.net/CLERK/Business_Name.cfm

County Registrars/Recorders
www.dhs.ca.gov/chs/OVR/LocalRegistrar/default.htm
www.co.el-dorado.ca.us/countyclerk/other_rec.html

Financial Institutions

(Banks, Credit Unions, Savings & Loan Associations, Trust Companies)
Department of Financial Institutions
800-622-0620; 415-263-8500

415-263-8513 (Legal Division)
www.dfi.ca.gov/directry

Financial Services (license records)

(financial planners, investment advisers, securities brokers)
Department of Corporations
Financial Services Division
866-275-2677; 800-347-6995
www.corp.ca.gov/fsd/lic

Funeral Trade (license records)

(see Cemeteries)

Health Statistics

Center for Health Statistics
www.dhs.ca.gov/chs/OVR/LocalRegistrar/default.htm

Insurance Brokers and Companies (license records)

California Department of Insurance
800-927-4357
www.insurance.ca.gov/docs/index.html
www.insurance.ca.gov/docs/FS-Licensestatus.htm

Inmate Locator

California Department of Corrections
916-445-6713
www.vinelink.com/index.jsp
www.publicrecordfinder.com/criminal.html

Investment Advisors

(see Financial Services)

Licenses

(see Occupational Licenses)

Limited Liability Companies Records

Secretary of State
916-657-5448
kepler.ss.ca.gov/list.html
www.ss.ca.gov/business/llc/llc_naav.htm

Limited Partnerships Records

Secretary of State
916-657-5448
www.ss.ca.gov/business/lp/lp_naav.htm

Lobbying Records

(see Elections)

Marriage Records

www.dhs.ca.gov/chs/OVR/Marriage/Default.htm
The county clerk issues public and confidential marriage licenses and maintains a permanent index of all confidential marriages registered. The marriage officiant, e.g., a clergyperson, performs the marriage ceremony, completes the marriage license, and returns it to the county recorder's office. For confidential marriages, the marriage license is returned to the county clerk's office for registration. The county recorder is the local registrar of public marriages under the direction of the state registrar.

County Registrars/Recorders/Clerks
www.dhs.ca.gov/chs/OVR/LocalRegistrar/default.htm
www.co.el-dorado.ca.us/countyclerk/other_rec.html
www.calelections.org
National Center for Health Statistics: California
www.cdc.gov/nchs/howto/w2w/californ.htm

Motor Vehicles

(see Vehicle Records)

Nurses (license records)

Board of Registered Nursing
916-322-3350
www.rn.ca.gov

Occupational License Records

Department of Consumer Affairs
800-952-5210
www2.dca.ca.gov/pls/wllpub/wllquery$.startup
www.dca.ca.gov
(click "Licensee Information")

Optometrists (license records)

Board of Optometry
800-547-4576; 916-323-8720
www.optometry.ca.gov

Partnership Records

Secretary of State
916-657-5448
kepler.ss.ca.gov/list.html

Pharmacists (license records)

Board of Pharmacy
916-445-5014
www.pharmacy.ca.gov

Physical Therapists (license records)

Physical Therapy Board
916-561-8200
www.ptb.ca.gov

Physician Assistants (license records)

Physician Assistant Committee
800-555-8030; 916-561-8780
physicianassistant.ca.gov

Physicians (license records)

Medical Board of California
916-263-2382
www.medbd.ca.gov
www.medbd.ca.gov/Order_Documents.htm

Real Estate Brokers (license records)

Department of Real Estate
916-227-0864
www.dre.ca.gov/licstats.htm

Sales and Use Tax Registrations

Board of Equalization
800-400-7115
www.boe.ca.gov/info/reg.htm

Savings & Loan Associations

(see Financial Institutions)

School

(see Teacher, Public School)

Securities

(see also Financial Services)
Department of Corporations
Investment and Financing Authority
866-275-2677
www.corp.ca.gov/srd/security.htm

Sex Offender Registration Records

(see also Criminal Records)
www.meganslaw.ca.gov
meganslaw.ca.gov/sexreg.htm

Teacher, Public School (credential records)

California Commission on Teacher Credentialing
888-921-2682
www.ctc.ca.gov
teachercred.ctc.ca.gov/teachers/PublicSearchProxy

Therapists (license records)

Board of Behavioral Sciences
916-445-4933
www.bbs.ca.gov

Trademarks and Service Mark Registration Records

Secretary of State
916-653-4984
www.ss.ca.gov/business/ts/ts.htm

Trust Companies

(see Financial Institutions)

UCC Transactions

Secretary of State
916-653-3516
www.ss.ca.gov/business/ucc/ucc.htm
www.ss.ca.gov/business/ucc/ra_9_overview.htm
www.ss.ca.gov/business/ucc/ucc_fees.pdf

Unclaimed Property Records

Bureau of Unclaimed Property
800-992-4647
www.sco.ca.gov/col/ucp

Uniform Commercial Code Filings

(see UCC Transactions)

Vehicle Records

Department of Motor Vehicles
www.dmv.ca.gov/dl/authority.htm

Veterinarians (license records)

Veterinary Medical Board
916-263-2610
www.vmb.ca.gov
www.vmb.ca.gov/lic1list.htm

Workers' Compensation

800-736-7401
www.dir.ca.gov/dwc/dwc_home_page.htm

D. More Information

State Archives
These archives provide access to the historic records of state government and some local governments. Records include older constitutions, legislative records, election records, case files and administrative records of the courts, etc.
916-653-7715
www.ss.ca.gov/archives/archives.htm

Guidelines for Access to California Department of Justice Public Records
caag.state.ca.us/consumers/general/pra.php

General Information and Links

www.publicrecordfinder.com/states/california.html
www.searchsystems.net
www.searchsystems.net/list.php?nid=17
www.searchsystems.net
www.virtualchase.com/topics/introduction_public_records.shtml
www.oatis.com/publicrecords.htm
www.publicrecordfinder.com/states/california.html
www.probusresearch.com
www.brbpub.com
proagency.tripod.com/skp-ca.html
www.50states.com/publicrecords/california.htm
www.casebreakers.com
www.pretrieve.com
www.vitalchek.com

Westlaw

www.westlaw.com

Examples of public records databases: People Finder-Person Tracker, Name Tracker, Telephone Tracker, Address Alert, Skip Tracer, Social Security Number Alert, Death Records, Professional Licenses; People Finder Plus Assets Library-Combined Asset Locator, Aircraft Registration Records, Watercraft Registration Records, Stock Locater Records, Motor Vehicle Registration Records, Real Property Assessor Records, Real Property Transactions; People Finder, Assets Plus Adverse Filings Library—Combined Adverse Filings, Bankruptcy Records, UCC, Liens/Civil Judgment Filings, Uniform Commercial Code Filings, Liens/Civil Judgment Filings; Public Records Library—U.S. Business Finder Records, Corporate and Limited Partnership Records, "Doing Business As" Records, Litigation Preparation Records, Executive Affiliation Records, Name Availability Records.

Lexis

www.lexis.com
www.lexisnexis.com

Examples of public records databases: Bankruptcy Filings, Business Locators, Corporate Filings (Business and Corporate Information, Limited Partnership Information, Fictitious Business Name Information, Franchise Index), Civil and Criminal Court Filings, Judgments and Liens (Including UCC and State Tax Liens), Jury Verdicts and Settlements, Professional Licenses Information, Person Locators (Military Locator, Voter Registration Record Information from 26 states, Social Security Death Records from 1962, Inmate Records from six states, Criminal History Records from 37 states), Personal Property Records (including Aircraft Registrations, Boat Registrations, Motor Vehicle Registrations from 20 states), Real Property Records (Deed Transfers, Tax Assessor Records, Mortgage Records).

E. Something to Check

1. In the Yellow Pages, select three people or businesses in three different service categories that probably require a license in California (e.g., contractor, funeral home). Go to the Web site for each service.
   a. What kinds of information are available about that service?
   b. What information can you find about the three people or businesses you selected? For example, were you able to verify that the person or business has a current valid license?
2. Go to a search site that allows you to find public records on individuals (e.g., *www.pretrieve.com*). Type in someone's name (e.g., your own) to find out what public records are available online.

5.8 Finding Law Libraries in Your Area

A. Introduction

Elsewhere in this handbook we cover the extensive online availability of California law (see section 5.1). Suppose, however, that you would like to go to a bricks-and-mortar law library to use its resources? You're looking for a facility where you can take books off the shelf. What options are available to you?

There are three major kinds of law libraries in California to which you have full or partial access:

County Law Libraries (CLL)

Federal Depository Libraries (FDL)

State Document Depository Libraries (SDDL)

The list below will tell you which libraries fall into these three categories. Some libraries fall into more than one category. After each entry, you will find the designations "CLL," "FDL," and "SDDL." This will indicate the kind of library it is or the kind of legal materials it offers—and to which you are entitled free access.

Before you visit any of the libraries on this list, you should phone the library or check its Web site to determine its location, hours, and any restrictions on using its materials.

County Law Libraries (CLL)

County law libraries exist in every county in the state. They are the best free law libraries available in the state and among the best in the country. Ninety percent of the budget of a county law library comes from court filing fees that parties pay to the courts. Most of these libraries have a complete collection of state and federal laws as well as treatises and formbooks.

Federal Depository Libraries (FDL)

A federal depository library is a public or private library that receives free federal government publications, to which it must allow access by the general public. The publications include federal statutes, federal regulations, and federal court opinions. If the library is private, e.g., a private university library, the public right of free access may be limited to those publications which the library receives from the federal government under the federal depository program. A private library has the right to prevent the public from using the rest of its collection.

State Document Depository Libraries (SDDL)

A state document depository is a public or private library that receives free state government publications, to which it must allow access by the general public. The state documents include state agency reports, legislative proceedings and hearings, directories, etc. If the library is private, it can restrict the public from using the rest of its collection.

B. Abbreviations

CA California

CLL County Law Libraries

FDL Federal Depository Libraries

Lib Library

SDDL State Document Depository Libraries

Univ University

C. Law Library Listings by City and County

Alameda
Alameda County
Alhambra
Alhambra County
Alpine County
Alturas
Amador County
Arcadia
Arcata
Auburn
Bakersfield
Berkeley
Butte County
Calaveras County
Carson
Calexico
Chico
Chula Vista
Claremont
Colusa
Contra Costa County
Corona
Costa Mesa
Crescent City
Culver City
Davis
Del Norte County
Downey
Downieville
El Centro
El Dorado County
Escondido
Eureka
Fairfield
Fremont
Fresno
Fresno County
Fullerton
Garden Grove
Glenn County
Hanford
Hayward
Hollister
Humboldt County
Imperial County
Independence
Indio
Inglewood
Inyo County
Irvine
Jackson
Kern County
Kings County
La Jolla
Lake County
Lakeport
Lakewood
Lancaster
Lassen County
Long Beach
Los Angeles County
Los Angeles
Madera
Madera County
Malibu
Mammoth Lakes
Marin County
Mariposa
Mariposa County
Markleeville
Martinez
Marysville
Mendocino County
Menlo Park
Merced
Merced County
Modesto
Modoc County
Mono County
Montebello
Monterey
Monterey County
Monterey Park
Napa
Napa County
Nevada County
Nevada City
Newbury Park
Northridge
Norwalk
Oakland
Oceanside
Ontario
Orange County
Oroville
Palm Springs

Palo Alto
Pasadena
Pleasant Hill
Placer County
Placerville
Plumas County
Pomona
Quincy
Red Bluff
Redding
Redlands
Redwood City
Rohnert Park
Riverside
Riverside County
Rosemead
Sacramento
Sacramento County
Salinas
San Andreas
San Benito
San Bernardino
San Bernardino County
San Diego
San Diego County
San Francisco
San Francisco County
San Joaquin County
San Jose
San Luis Obispo
San Luis Obispo County
San Mateo County
San Rafael
Santa Ana
Santa Barbara
Santa Barbara County
Santa Clara County
Santa Cruz
Santa Cruz County
Santa Rosa
Shasta County
Red Bluff
Redding
Richmond
Sierra County
San Bernardino
San Bernardino County
San Joaquin County
San Jose
San Leandro
San Luis Obispo
San Luis Obispo County
San Marcos
San Mateo
San Mateo County
San Rafael
Santa Ana
Santa Clara
Santa Clara County
Santa Cruz
Santa Cruz County
Santa Maria
Santa Monica
Santa Rosa
Sierra County
Siskiyou County
Solano County
Sonoma County
Sonora
Stanford
Stanislaus County
Stockton
Susanville
Sutter County
Tehama County
Torrance
Trinity County
Tulare County
Tuolumne County
Turlock
Ukiah
Valencia
Vallejo
Ventura
Ventura County
Visalia
Vista
Weaverville
West Covina
Whittier
Willows
Woodland
Yolo County
Yreka
Yuba City
Yuba County

AAA

Alameda

Alameda Free Lib (SDDL)
510-747-7713
www.ci.alameda.ca.us/library

Alameda County

See Alameda, Berkeley, Fremont, Hayward, Oakland, San Leandro

Alhambra

Alhambra Public Lib (SDDL)
626-570-5005
www.alhambralibrary.org

Alhambra County

See Alhambra

Alpine County

See Markleeville

Alturas

Modoc County Law Lib (CLL)
530-223-6515

Amador County

See Jackson

Arcadia

Arcadia Public Lib (FDL)
626-821-5569; 626-574-5400
www.ci.arcadia.ca.us/home/index.asp?page=823

Arcata

Humboldt State Univ Lib (FDL) (SDDL)
707-826-3441; 707-826-3419
library.humboldt.edu/govdoc/index.html

Auburn

Placer County Law Lib (CLL)
530-823-2573
cchristm@vfr.net

Placer County Lib (SDDL)
530-886-4500
www.placer.ca.gov/library

BBB

Bakersfield

CA State Univ, Bakersfield (FDL) (SDDL)
661-654-3172
www.csub.edu/library/govinfo.shtml

Beale Memorial Lib (FDL)
661-868-0770
www.kerncountylibrary.org/beale.html

Kern County Law Lib (CLL) (SDDL)
661-868-5320
www.kerncountylawlibrary.org

Kern County Lib (SDDL)
661-868-0770
www.kerncountylibrary.org

Berkeley

Berkeley Public Lib (SDDL)
510-981-6148; 510-981-6100
www.berkeleypubliclibrary.org

Univ of CA, Berkeley
510-642-6657 (Doe Library) (FDL)
510-642-2569 (Moffitt Lib) (SDDL)
www.lib.berkeley.edu/doemoff/gov_info.html
510-642-0900 (Law Library) (FDL) (SDDL)
www.law.berkeley.edu/library/collections/govDocs.html

Butte County

See Chico, Oroville

CCC

Calexico

San Diego State Univ (FDL)
760-768-5633; 760-768-5585 (Imperial Valley)
www.ivcampus.sdsu.edu/library

Calaveras County

See San Andreas

Carson

CA State Univ, Dominguez Hills (FDL) (SDDL)
310-243-3715
library.csudh.edu/govdocs.htm

Carson Regional Lib (FDL) (SDDL)
310-830-0901
www.colapublib.org/services/govsvcs/internet.html

Chico

CA State Univ, Chico (FDL) (SDDL)
530-898-5710
www.csuchico.edu/library/gov/govindex.html

Chula Vista

Chula Vista Public Lib (SDDL)
619-691-5069
www.chulavista.lib.ca.us

Claremont

Claremont Univ Consortium (FDL) (SDDL)
909-607-3959
libraries.claremont.edu/govdocs

Colusa

Colusa County Law Lib (CLL)
530-458-0430

Contra Costa County

See Martinez, Pleasant Hill, Richmond

Corona

Corona Public Lib (SDDL)
951-736-2387
www.coronapubliclibrary.org

Costa Mesa

Whittier Law School Lib (FDL) (SDDL)
714-444-4141 x482
www.law.whittier.edu/library/about.asp

Crescent City

Del Norte County Law Lib (CLL)
707-464-8115 x126; 707-464-7217
pataba@earthlink.net

Culver City

County of Los Angeles Public Lib (FDL) (SDDL)
310-559-1676 (Culver City)
www.colapublib.org/services/govsvcs

DDD

Davis

Univ of CA, Davis
530-752-3330 (Law Library) (FDL) (SDDL)
lawlibrary.ucdavis.edu
530-752-1624 (Shields) (FDL) (SDDL)
old.lib.ucdavis.edu/govdoc

Del Norte County

See Crescent City

Downey

Downey City Lib (FDL)
562-904-7360
www.downeylibrary.org/services/#publications

Downieville

Sierra County Law Lib (CLL)
530-289-3269

EEE

El Centro

Imperial County Law Lib (CLL)
760-482-4374

El Dorado County

See Placerville

Escondido

Escondido Public Lib (SDDL)
760-839-4839
www.ci.escondido.ca.us/library

Eureka

Humboldt County Law Lib (CLL)
707-269-1270

Humboldt County Lib (SDDL)
707-269-1900; 707-269-1905
www.co.humboldt.ca.us/library

FFF

Fairfield

Solano County Law Lib (CLL)
707-421-6520
cerowan@solanocounty.com

Fremont

Fremont Main Lib (SDDL)
510-745-1444
www.aclibrary.org/branches/frm/fremonthome.asp

Fresno

CA State Univ, Fresno (FDL) (SDDL)
559-278-2335; 559-278-2596
www.lib.csufresno.edu/subjectresources

Fresno County Public Law Lib (CLL)
559-237-2227
www.co.fresno.ca.us/9899/index.htm

Fresno County Public Lib (FDL) (SDDL)
559-488-3195
www.fresnolibrary.org/ref/govdoc.html

Fresno County

See Fresno

Fullerton

CA State Univ, Fullerton (FDL) (SDDL)
714-278-3449
guides.library.fullerton.edu/docslinks

Fullerton Public Lib (SDDL)
714-738-6333
www.ci.fullerton.ca.us/library

GGG

Garden Grove

Orange County Public Lib (FDL) (SDDL)
714-530-0711
www.ocpl.org/index.asp

Glenn County

See Willows

HHH

Hanford

Kings County Law Lib (CLL)
559-582-3211 x4430

Hayward

Alameda County Law Lib (CLL)
South County Branch
510-670-5230
www.co.alameda.ca.us/law/index.htm

CA State Univ, East Bay Lib (FDL) (SDDL)
510-885-3765; 510-885-3000
www.library.csuhayward.edu/staff/govdocs

Hayward Public Lib (SDDL)
510-293-8685
www.library.ci.hayward.ca.us

Hollister

San Benito County Law Lib (CLL)
831-636-9525

Humboldt County

See Arcata, Eureka

III

Independence

Inyo County Law Lib (CLL)
760-878-0260

Imperial County

See El Centro

Indio

Riverside County Law Lib (CLL)
Desert Branch
760-863-8316
www.lawlibrary.co.riverside.ca.us

Ingelwood

Inglewood Public Lib (FDL) (SDDL)
310-412-5380
www.cityofinglewood.org/depts/library

Inyo County

See Independence

Irvine

Univ of CA, Irvine (FDL) (SDDL)
949-824-7234; 949-824-4976
www.lib.uci.edu/libraries/collections/govinfo/gimain.html

JJJ

Jackson

Amador County Law Lib (CLL)
209-223-2144

KKK

Kern County

See Bakersfield

Kings County

See Hanford

LLL

La Jolla

Univ of CA, San Diego Lib (FDL) (SDDL)
858-534-3336
govinfo.ucsd.edu

Lake County

See Lakeport

Lakeport

Lake County Law Lib (CLL)
707-263-2205

Lakewood

Angelo M. Iacoboni Public Lib (FDL) (SDDL)
562-866-1777
www.colapublib.org/services/govsvcs/internet.html

Lancaster

Lancaster Public Lib (FDL) (SDDL)
661-948-5029
www.colapublib.org/services/govsvcs/internet.html

Lassen County

See Susanville

Long Beach

CA State Univ, Long Beach Lib (FDL) (SDDL)
562-985-4027
www.csulb.edu/library/guide/governmentdocuments.html

Long Beach Public Lib (FDL) (SDDL)
562-570-5655
www.lbpl.org

Los Angeles

CA State Univ, Los Angeles Lib (FDL) (SDDL)
323-343-4927
www.calstatela.edu/library/guides/govpubs.htm

Los Angeles County Law Lib (FDL) (SDDL)
213-629-3531
lalaw.lib.ca.us/GPOhome.html

Los Angeles Public Lib Central (FDL) (SDDL)
213-228-7000
www.lapl.org
www.lapl.org/resources/guides/findgovdoc.html

Loyola Law School Law Lib (FDL) (SDDL)
213-736-1177
library.lls.edu/govdocs/index.html

Southwestern Univ Law Lib (FDL) (SDDL)
213-738-6725
www.swlaw.edu/library

Univ of CA, Los Angeles
310-825-1323 (Young Library) (FDL) (SDDL)
www.library.ucla.edu/yrl/reference/govinfo/index.htm
310-825-6414 (Law Library) (FDL) (SDDL)
www1.law.ucla.edu/~library

Univ of Southern CA
213-740-6482 (Law Lib) (FDL) (SDDL)
lawweb.usc.edu/library
213-740-1769 (Von KleinSmid Lib) (FDL) (SDDL)
www.usc.edu/isd/libraries

Los Angeles County

See Arcadia, Carson, Claremont, Culver City, Downey, Inglewood, Lakewood, Lancaster, Los Angeles, Long Beach, Malibu, Montebello, Monterey Park, Northridge, Norwalk, Pasadena, Pomona, Rosemead, Santa Monica, Torrance, Valencia, West Covina, Whittier.

MMM

Madera

Madera County Law Lib (CLL)
559-673-0378
maderalawlibrary@sbcglobal.net

Madera County

See Madera

Malibu

Pepperdine Univ Payson Lib (FDL)
310-506-4238
library.pepperdine.edu
library.pepperdine.edu/information/government

Mammoth Lakes

Mono County Law Lib (CLL)
760-934-4777

Marin County

See San Rafael

Mariposa

Mariposa County Law Lib (CLL)
209-966-2005; 209-966-3222

Mariposa County

See Mariposa

Markleeville

Alpine County Law Lib (CLL)
530-694-2113
lisacobourn@alpine.courts.ca.gov

Martinez

Contra Costa County Public Law Lib (CLL)
925-646-2783
www.cccpllib.org

Marysville

Yuba County Law Lib (CLL)
530-749-7380
dgzzz@hotmail.com

Mendocino County

See Ukiah

Menlo Park

U.S. Department of the Interior Geological Survey Lib (FDL)
650-329-5027
library.usgs.gov

Merced

Merced County Law Lib (CLL)
209-385-7332
www.co.merced.ca.us/lawlibrary

Merced County

See Merced

Modesto

Stanislaus County Law Lib (CLL)
209-558-7759
www.stanislauslawlibrary.arrival.net

Stanislaus County Free Lib (SDDL)
209-558-7814
www.stanislauslibrary.org/index1.html

Modoc County

See Alturas

Mono County

See Mammoth Lakes

Montebello

Montebello Regional Lib (FDL) (SDDL)
323-722-6551
www.colapublib.org/services/govsvcs/internet.html

Monterey

U.S. Naval Postgraduate School Knox Lib (FDL)
831-656-2485
www.nps.edu/Library

Monterey County

See Monterey, Salinas

Monterey Park

Bruggemeyer Memorial Lib (FDL)
626-307-1368; 626-307-1458
ci.monterey-park.ca.us/home/index.asp?page=180

NNN

Napa

Napa City-County Lib (SDDL)
707-253-4235; 800-248-8402
www.co.napa.ca.us/library

Napa County Law Lib (CLL)
707-299-1201

Napa County

See Napa

Nevada City

Nevada County Law Lib (CLL)
530-265-2918
new.mynevadacounty.com/lawlibrary

Nevada County

See Nevada City

Newbury Park

Thousand Oaks Lib (SDDL)
805-498-2139
www.toaks.org/library

Northridge

CA State Univ, Northridge Lib (FDL) (SDDL)
818-677-2285
library.csun.edu/Find_Resources/Government_Publications

Norwalk

County of Los Angeles Public Lib (FDL) (SDDL)
562-868-0775
www.colapublib.org/services/govsvcs/internet.html

OOO

Oakland

Bernard E. Witkin Alameda County Law Lib (CLL) (SDDL)
510-208-4800
www.co.alameda.ca.us/law/index.htm

Mills College Lib (SDDL)
510-430-2385
www.mills.edu/academics/library/index.php

Oakland Public Lib (FDL) (SDDL)
510-238-3138
www.oaklandlibrary.org/links/sbssgovlinks.html

Oceanside

Oceanside Public Lib (SDDL)
760-435-5580
www.library.ci.oceanside.ca.us

Ontario

Ontario City Lib (FDL) (SDDL)
909-395-2004
www.ci.ontario.ca.us/index.cfm/6728

Univ of La Verne Law Lib (FDL) (SDDL)
909-460-2070
law.ulv.edu/%7Elawlib/govdocs.html

Orange County

See Costa Mesa, Fullerton, Garden Grove, Irvine, Santa Ana

Oroville

Butte County Law Lib (CLL)
530-538-7122
www.quiknet.com/~buttelaw

Butte County Lib (SDDL)
530-538-7525
www.buttecounty.net/BCLibrary

PPP

Palm Springs

Palm Springs Public Lib (FDL)
760-323-8294
www.palmspringslibrary.org

Palo Alto

Santa Clara County Law Lib (CLL)
North County Branch
650-324-6529

Pasadena

CA Institute of Technology Lib (FDL) (SDDL)
626-395-6419
library.caltech.edu/collections/government/default.htm

Pasadena Public Lib (FDL) (SDDL)
626-744-4066
www.ci.pasadena.ca.us/library

Placer County

See Auburn

Placerville

El Dorado County Law Lib (CLL)
530-621-6423
www.co.el-dorado.ca.us/lawlibrary.html

El Dorado County Lib (SDDL)
530-621-5540
www.eldoradolibrary.org/homepage.html

Pleasant Hill

Contra Costa County Lib (FDL) (SDDL)
925-646-6434
www.ccclib.org/government/pubs.html

Plumas County

See Quincy

Pomona

CA State Pomona Univ Lib (SDDL)
909-869-3084
www.csupomona.edu/~library

QQQ

Quincy

Plumas County Law Lib (CLL)
530-283-6325 (closed 10/1/03)
www.countyofplumas.com/lawlibrary

Plumas County Lib (SDDL)
530-283-6310
www.psln.com/PCLibQ

RRR

Red Bluff

Tahama County Law Lib (CLL)
530-529-5033

Redding

Shasta County Lib (FDL) (SDDL)
530-225-5769
www.shastacountylibrary.org

Shasta County Public Law Lib (CLL)
530-245-6243; 530-245-6243

Redlands

Univ of Redlands Lib (FDL)
909-335-4021
redlandsapps.redlands.edu//library/govdocs.htm

A.K. Smiley Public Lib (SDDL)
909-798-7565
www.akspl.org

Redwood City

Redwood City Public Lib (FDL) (SDDL)
650-780-7026
www.rcpl.info/services/governmentinfo.html

San Mateo County Law Lib (CLL) (SDDL)
650-363-4913
www.smcll.org

Rohnert Park

Sonoma State Univ Information Center (SDDL)
707-664-2161
libweb.sonoma.edu

Richmond

Richmond Public Lib (FDL) (SDDL)
510-620-6561
www.ci.richmond.ca.us/index.asp?NID=105

Riverside

Riverside County Law Lib (CLL) (SDDL)
951-955-6390
www.lawlibrary.co.riverside.ca.us

Riverside Public Lib (FDL) (SDDL)
951-826-5201
www.riversideca.gov/library

Univ of CA, Riverside Lib (FDL) (SDDL)
951-827-3226
library.ucr.edu/?view=collections/govpub

Riverside County

See Corona, Indio, Palm Springs, Riverside

Rosemead

Rosemead Lib (SDDL)
626-573-5220
www.colapublib.org/services/govsvcs/internet.html

SSS

Sacramento

CA State Archives (SDDL)
916-653-2246
www.ss.ca.gov/archives/archives_e.htm

CA State Lib (FDL) (SDDL)
916-654-0069
www.library.ca.gov/html/gps.cfm

CA State Univ, Sacramento Lib (FDL) (SDDL)
916-278-5673
library.csus.edu/default.asp

McGeorge School of Law Lib (FDL) (SDDL)
916-739-7164
www.mcgeorge.edu/campus_resources/library

Sacramento County Public Law Lib (FDL) (CLL) (SDDL)
916-874-6011
www.saclaw.org

Sacramento Public Lib Central (FDL) (SDDL)
916-264-2920
www.saclibrary.org

Sacramento County

See Sacramento

Salinas

Monterey County Law Lib (CLL)
831-755-5046
fp.redshift.com/mcolawlib

Monterey County Library (SDDL)
831-755-5838
www.co.monterey.ca.us/library/default.htm

San Andreas

Calaveras County Law Lib (CLL)
209-754-6314
mibold@aol.ca.gov

San Benito County

See Hollister

San Bernardino

CA State Univ, San Bernardino Lib (FDL) (SDDL)
909-880-5091
www.lib.csusb.edu/gov/govdoc.cfm

Law Lib for San Bernardino County (FDL) (CLL) (SDDL)
909-885-3020
www.sblawlibrary.org

San Bernardino Public Lib (SDDL)
909-381-8221
www.sbpl.org

San Bernardino Valley College Lib (SDDL)
909-384-4448
lr.valley.sbccd.cc.ca.us/libhome.htm

San Bernardino County

See Ontario, Redlands, San Bernardino

San Diego

CA Western School of Law Lib (SDDL)
619-525-1419
www.cwsl.edu/main/home.asp

San Diego County Public Law Lib (FDL) (CLL) (SDDL)
619-685-6552
www.sdcll.org

San Diego Public Lib Central (FDL) (SDDL)
619-236-5813
www.sannet.gov/public-library

San Diego State Univ Lib (FDL)
619-594-6724
infodome.sdsu.edu/research/guides/gov/unitedstates.shtml

Univ of San Diego Research Center (FDL) (SDDL)
619-260-4612
www.sandiego.edu/lrc

San Diego County

See Calexico, Chula Vista, Escondido, La Jolla, Oceanside, San Diego, San Marcos, Vista

San Francisco

CA Supreme Court Lib (FDL)
415-865-7178
www.sandiego.edu/lrc

Golden Gate Univ Law Lib (FDL) (SDDL)
415-442-6680
www.ggu.edu/lawlibrary/specialcollections/govdocs

San Francisco Law Lib (CLL)
415-554-6821
www.sfgov.org/site/sfll_index.asp

San Francisco Public Lib (FDL) (SDDL)
415-557-4500
sfpl4.sfpl.org/librarylocations/main/gic/gic.htm

San Francisco State Univ Lib (FDL) (SDDL)
415-338-1557
www.library.sfsu.edu

Univ of CA Hastings Law Lib (FDL) (SDDL)
415-565-4751
traynor.uchastings.edu/library

Univ of San Francisco Law Lib (FDL) (SDDL)
415-422-6679
www.usfca.edu/library/govdocs

San Francisco County

See San Francisco

San Joaquin County

See Stockton

San Jose

Santa Clara County Law Lib (CLL) (SDDL)
408-299-3568
sccll.org

San Jose State Univ Lib (FDL) (SDDL)
408-808-2100
www.sjlibrary.org/research/databases

San Leandro

San Leandro Public Lib (FDL)
510-577-3971
www.ci.san-leandro.ca.us/sllibrary.html

San Luis Obispo

CA Polytechnic State Univ Lib (FDL) (SDDL)
805-756-2649
discover.lib.calpoly.edu/datagenie

San Luis Obispo County Law Lib (CLL) (SDDL)
805-781-5855
www.rain.org/~slolawli

San Luis Obispo City County Lib (SDDL)
805-781-5989
www.slolibrary.org

San Luis Obispo County

See San Luis Obispo

San Marcos

CA State Univ, San Marcos Lib (FDL) (SDDL)
760-750-4348
library.csusm.edu/finding/government_documents

San Mateo

College of San Mateo Lib (FDL)
650-574-6100
www.smccd.net/accounts/csmlibrary/govdoc.html

San Mateo Public Lib (SDDL)
650-522-7818
www.cityofsanmateo.org/dept/library/index.html

San Mateo County

See Menlo Park, San Mateo, Redwood City

San Rafael

Marin County Free Lib (FDL)
415-499-6058
co.marin.ca.us/library

Marin County Law Lib (CLL)
415-499-6356

Santa Ana

Orange County Public Law Lib (FDL) (CLL) (SDDL)
714-834-3397
www.oc.ca.gov/lawlib
www.oc.ca.gov/lawlib/govdocs.htm

Santa Barbara

Santa Barbara County Law Lib (CLL) (SDDL)
805-568-2296
www.countylawlibrary.org

Santa Barbara Public Lib (SDDL)
855-564-5604
www.sbplibrary.org

Univ of CA, Santa Barbara Lib (FDL)
805-893-3133
www.library.ucsb.edu/subjects/gov/govt-fed.html

Santa Barbara County

See Santa Barbara, Santa Maria

Santa Clara

Santa Clara Univ Lib (FDL) (SDDL)
408-554-5385
www.scu.edu/library/services/govdocs

Santa Clara County

See Palo Alto, San Jose, Santa Clara, Stanford

Santa Cruz

Santa Cruz County Law Lib (CLL) (SDDL)
831-457-2525
www.lawlibrary.org

Santa Cruz Public Lib (SDDL)
831-420-5730
www.santacruzpl.org

Univ of CA, Santa Cruz Lib (FDL) (SDDL)
831-459-2347
library.ucsc.edu/gov

Santa Cruz County

See Santa Cruz

Santa Maria

Santa Maria Public Lib (SDDL)
805-925-0994
www.ci.santa-maria.ca.us/210.html

Santa Monica

Santa Monica Public Lib (SDDL)
310-451-8859
www.smpl.org

Santa Rosa

Sonoma County Law Lib (CLL) (SDDL)
707-565-2668
www.sonomacountylawlibrary.org

Sonoma County Public Lib (FDL) (SDDL)
707-545-0831
www.sonoma.lib.ca.us/ref/usdocs.html

Shasta County

See Redding

Sierra County

See Downieville

Siskiyou County

See Yreka

Solano County

See Fairfield, Vallejo

Sonoma County

See Rohnert Park, Santa Rosa

Sonora

Tuolumne County Law Lib (CLL)
209-536-0308
lawlib@mlode.com

Stanford

Stanford Univ
650-723-9372 (Green Library) (SDDL)
www-sul.stanford.edu/depts/green/index.html

650-725-1064 (Jonsson Library) (FDL)
library.stanford.edu/depts/jonsson/index.html
650-25-800: (Law Library) (FDL) (SDDL)
www.law.stanford.edu/library

Stanislaus County

See Modesto, Turlock

Stockton

San Joaquin County Law Lib (CLL) (SDDL)
209-468-3920
www.sjclawlib.org

Public Lib of Stockton and San Joaquin County (FDL) (SDDL)
209-937-8221
www.stockton.lib.ca.us

Univ of the Pacific Lib (SDDL)
209-946-2433
library.uop.edu

Susanville

Lassen County Law Lib (CLL)
530-251-8189
nholsey@lassencourt.ca.gov

Sutter County

See Yuba City

TTT

Tehama County

See Red Bluff

Torrance

Torrance Public Lib (FDL) (SDDL)
310-618-5959
www.torrnet.com/Library/5465.htm

Trinity County

See Weaverville

Tulare County

See Visalia

Tuolumne County

See Sonora

Turlock

CA State Univ, Stanislaus Lib (FDL) (SDDL)
209-667-3233
www.library.csustan.edu/special_collections/index.htm

UUU

Ukiah

Mendocino County Law Lib (CLL)
707-463-4201
www.pacificsites.com/~lawlib

VVV

Valencia

County of Los Angeles Public Lib (FDL) (SDDL)
661-259-8942
www.colapublib.org/services/govsvcs/internet.html

Vallejo

Solano County Lib System (SDDL)
707-553-5568
www.solanolibrary.com

Ventura

Ventura County Law Lib (CLL) (SDDL)
805-642-8982
www.infopeople.org/ventura/vclaw

Ventura County

See Newbury Park, Ventura

Visalia

Tulare County Public Law Lib (CLL)
559-733-6395
www.co.tulare.ca.us/government/law/default.asp

Tulare County Free Lib (SDDL)
559-733-6954
tularecountylibrary.org/index.html

Vista

San Diego County Lib (SDDL)
North County Branch
760-940-4386
www.sdcll.org/location.htm

WWW

Weaverville

Trinity County Law Lib (CLL)
101 Court Street
530-623-1201

West Covina

County of Los Angeles Public Lib (FDL) (SDDL)
626-962-3541
www.colapublib.org/services/govsvcs/internet.html

Whittier

Whittier College Lib (FDL) (SDDL)
562-907-4247
web.whittier.edu/academic/library

Whittier Public Lib (SDDL)
562-464-3450
www.whittierpl.org

Willows

Glenn County Law Lib (CLL)
530-934-6415
www.quiknet.com/~buttelaw/glennres.html

Woodland

Yolo County Law Lib (CLL)
530-666-8918
www.yolocounty.org/org/library/law.htm

XYZ

Yolo County

See Davis, Woodland

Yreka

Siskiyou County Law Lib (CLL)
530-842-8390

Yuba City

Sutter County Law Lib (CLL)
530-822-7388

Yuba County

See Marysville

D. More Information

County Law Libraries
www.publiclawlibrary.org/find.html
www.library.ca.gov/assets/acrobat/CACountyLaw.pdf

Federal Depository Libraries
www.library.ca.gov/html/gps05a.cfm
www.access.gpo.gov/cgi-bin/modalldep.cgi?cmd+CA
www.gpoaccess.gov/libraries.html
www.library.ca.gov/html/gps02.cfm

State Document Depository Libraries
www.library.ca.gov/html/gps_cal3.cfm
www.library.ca.gov/html/gps_cal1.cfm

Northern California Association of Law Libraries
www.nocall.org

Southern California Association of Law Libraries
www.aallnet.org/chapter/scall

E. Something to Check

1. Contact the closest county law libraries (CLL) to you. Does it have the current paper edition of the *Martindale-Hubbell Law Directory*? Does it have Witkin, *Summary of California Law*?
2. Call a federal depository library (FDL) near you that is a private institution, e.g., a private university. Assume that you wanted to go to this library to use the Code of Federal Regulations (CFR) volumes on the shelves of this library. (You want to look at a "hard copy" of the CFR rather than examine it online.) Ask someone at the library how you would do this. Do you need a special pass? In short, how do you gain admission to use the materials (like the CFR) that this private library receives under the federal depositary program?

5.9 Hotline Resources and Complaint Directories

A. Introduction

On the job, you sometimes need quick access to the phone number or Web site of commonly used resources. This section provides many of them. See also section 4.5 on state agencies for similar leads.

B. Hotline Resources

AARP Hotline (American Association of Retired Persons)

888-687-2277
www.aarp.org

Abortion

800-230-PLAN
www.plannedparenthood.org
(enter "California" in drop down state box)

Adoption and Foster Care Hotline

800-KIDS-4-US
www.childsworld.ca.gov

Adult Abuse Hotlines (by county)

(see Elder Abuse)

Agencies of State Government

(see also section 4.5)
www.ca.gov (click "State Agencies Directory")
www.cold.ca.gov

AIDS Hotline

800-342-2437; 800-367-AIDS
www.aidshotline.org/crm/asp/refer

Air Resources Board

(see also Environmental Protection)
800-242-4450; 800-952-5588
www.arb.ca.gov

Air Travel Complaints

800-255-1111 (safety); 866-289-9673 (security); 202-366-2220 (service)
airconsumer.ost.dot.gov
contact.tsa.dhs.gov/default.aspx

Alcohol and Drug Abuse

(see also Substance Abuse)
800-729-6686
ncadi.samhsa.gov

Alzheimer's Helpline

800-272-3900
www.alz.org

Attorney Complaint Hotline

(see also section Appendix A of Part 3)
800-843-9053
www.calbar.ca.gov (click "Ethics")

Attorney General (California)

800-952-5225
www.ag.ca.gov

Auditor, State

800-952-5665
www.bsa.ca.gov/bsa

Automobile Complaints

800-952-5210
www.smogcheck.ca.gov/stdhome.asp
www.ftc.gov/ftc/consumer.htm

Banks (consumer complaints)

800-622-0620
www.dfi.ca.gov/consumer
www.dfi.ca.gov/contact
www.dfi.ca.gov/consumer/consumercomplaint.asp

Bar (State Bar Association)

(see also section 3.4)
888-800-3400
www.calbar.ca.gov

Battered Women

(see Domestic Violence)

Birth Records

(see also section 5.7)
916-445-2684
www.dhs.ca.gov/hisp/chs/OVR/ordercert.htm

Continuing Education of the Bar (CEB)

800-232-3444
www.ceb.com

California Government

916-657-9900
www.ca.gov

Cancer Hotline

800-4-CANCER
www.cancer.gov/newscenter

CEB

(see Continuing Education of the Bar)

Cellular Phone Complaints

888-CALL-FCC
www.fcc.gov/cgb/complaints.html

Child Abuse Hotline

800-792-5200; 800-422-4453
www.childhelpusa.org
www.safestate.org/index.cfm?navID=6
www.childwelfare.gov/pubs/reslist/tollfree.cfm

Child Protective Service Hotlines (by county)

www.childsworld.ca.gov/res/pdf/EmergencyR_315.pdf

Children, Missing

(see Missing Children)

Child Support Services

866-249-0773
www.childsup.cahwnet.gov
Citizenship
800-375-5283
www.uscis.gov

City Governments

(see also section 4.6)
www.ca.gov/Government.html
www.ca.gov/state/portal/myca_homepage.jsp
(click "City" under "Government")

Civil Rights

(see also Discrimination; Fair Housing and Employment; Gay and Lesbian Rights)
United States Civil Rights Commission
800-552-6843
www.usccr.gov

Coast Guard

800-368-5647
www.uscg.mil/USCG.shtm

Complaints Directory (where to complain)

800-952-5210
www.dca.ca.gov/r_r/cmpltabl/index.html
(click: accountants, airlines, ambulances, attorneys, automobiles, banks, businesses, cable TV, chiropractors, contractors, credit, dentists, discrimination, doctors, employment, finance companies, food, funeral services, grocery stores, hospitals, hotels, housing, insurance, investments, landlords, loan companies, medicare, mortgages, moving companies, notaries, nurses, nursing homes, pharmacies, personnel agencies, physicians, plumbers, psychologists, real estate, recycling, restaurants, roofers, sales, savings and loan, schools, sports, taxes, teachers, telephones, television, title companies, toys, transportation, travel, trucking, utilities, veterinarians, vocational training, warranties, water, etc.)

Congress

www.congress.org
202-224-3121
www.house.gov
202-225-3121
www.senate.gov
202-225-3121

Consumer Affairs (complaints)

800-952-5210
www.dca.ca.gov

Consumer Product Safety Complaints Hotline

800-638-2772
www.cpsc.gov

Contractors (inquiries or complaints)

800-321-2752
www.cslb.ca.gov

Corporation Information

866-ASK-CORP
www.corp.ca.gov/contactus/contact.htm

Corrections (Prison)

Inspector General Hotline
916-830-3600
www.oig.ca.gov

County Governments

(see also section 4.6)
www.ca.gov/Government.html
www.ca.gov/state/portal/myca_homepage.jsp
(click "County under Government")

Courts, Federal (California)

www.uscourts.gov/courtlinks/index.cfm
(click the map of California)
www.ca9.uscourts.gov

Courts, State

www.courtinfo.ca.gov
(click "courts")
Credit Bureaus
Equifax
800-685-1111
www.equifax.com
Experian
888-397-3742
www.experian.com
TransUnion
800-916-8800; 800-888-4213
www.transunion.com

Crime Statistics (statewide)

caag.state.ca.us/cjsc
ag.ca.gov/cjsc/content/cjscinfo.htm

Crime Statistics (by county)

caag.state.ca.us/cjsc/statisticsdatatabs/CrimeCo.htm

Death Records

(see also section 5.7)
916-445-2684
www.dhs.ca.gov/hisp/chs/OVR/ordercert.htm

Department of Motor Vehicles

(see DMV)
Disability Rights and Services
(see also Civil Rights)
800-514-0301
www.ada.gov

Discrimination

(see also Civil Rights, Fair Housing and Employment)
Equal Employment Opportunity Commission
800-669-4000
www.eeoc.gov

Disability (State Disability Insurance)

800-480-3287
www.edd.ca.gov

Disease Control Hotline

800-CDC-INFO
www.bt.cdc.gov

Divorce/Dissolution Records

(see also section 5.7)
916-445-2684
www.dhs.ca.gov/hisp/chs/OVR/ordercert.htm

Doctors

(see also Health, Medical, Physicians)

DMV

800-777-0133
www.dmv.ca.gov

Domestic Violence Hotline

800-799-SAFE
www.ndvh.org

Drug and Alcohol Abuse

(see also Substance Abuse)
800-729-6686
ncadi.samhsa.gov

Education (school directory)

www.cde.ca.gov/re/sd

Elder Abuse

916-322-5295; 888-436-3600; 800-822-6222
www.safestate.org/index.cfm?navID=195
www.ag.ca.gov/bmfea/elder.htm
ag.ca.gov/bmfea/reporting.htm
www.elderabusecenter.org

Elder Abuse: County Hotlines

www.dss.cahwnet.gov/pdf/apscolist.pdf

Elections Hotline

866-275-3772
www.fppc.ca.gov
Emergencies
916-845-8911 (state)
www.oes.ca.gov
800-621-FEMA (federal)
www.fema.gov

Employment (CalJobs)

(matching employers and seekers)
800-758-0398
www.caljobs.ca.gov

Employment Discrimination

800-884-1684
www.dfeh.ca.gov

Employment in Government

www.ca.gov/state/portal/myca_homepage.jsp
(click "Find a Job" under "Working in CA")

Energy Hotline

California Energy Commission
800-772-3300
www.energy.ca.gov

Environmental Protection

(see also section 4.5)
800-CLEANUP; 916-323-2514 (state)
www.calepa.ca.gov
www.earth911.org/master.asp
800-621-8431; 800-424-8802 (federal)
www.epa.gov
Equal Employment Opportunity Commission
800-669-4000
www.eeoc.gov

Ethics Hotline

800-2ETHICS; 800-238-4427
www.calbar.ca.gov
(click "Ethics Hotline")

Fair Housing and Employment

(see also Civil Rights, Discrimination)
800-233-3212; 800-884-1684
www.dfeh.ca.gov
800-669-9777
www.hud.gov/offices/fheo

Fair Political Practices Hotline

(see Elections Hotline)

Federal Government

800-FED-INFO; 800-333-4636
www.firstgov.gov

Federal Trade Commission

202-326-2222; 877-FTC-HELP
www.ftc.gov

Fish and Game Hotline

800-952-5400
www.dfg.ca.gov

Food Safety

916-654-0466 (state)
www.cdfa.ca.gov
888-INFO-FDA; 800-535-4555 (federal)
www.fda.gov
www.fsis.usda.gov/oa/topics/foodsec_cons.htm

Forms, Judicial Council

www.courtinfo.ca.gov/forms

Franchise Tax Board

800-852-5711
www.ftb.ca.gov

Fraud Hotline

(see also Insurance Fraud, Internet Crime, MediCal Fraud, Postal Fraud)
California Department of Social Services
800-344-TIPS
Gay and Lesbian Rights
(see also Civil Rights)
415-621-2493; 619-232-2121; 213-977-9500
ACLU (California)
www.aclu.org/lgbt
(click "Your Local ACLU)

Government

(see also Agencies, California, City, County, Federal, Governor, Legislature; sections 4.1 through 4.6)
Government: California
916-322-9900; 916-657-9900 (information)
www.ca.gov/Government.html
Online State Government Phone Directory
www.cold.ca.gov/contactus.html
Government: Federal
800-FED-INFO; 800-333-4636
www.firstgov.gov
www.consumeraction.gov/selected.shtml

Government Employment

www.ca.gov/state/portal/myca_homepage.jsp
(click "Find a Job" under "Working in CA")

Governor

916-445-2841
www.governor.ca.gov

Hate Crimes

800-884-1684
www.dfeh.ca.gov/Contact/FileCase.asp
www.safestate.org/index.cfm?navID=13

Health (HMO rights, patient advocate)

(see also Medical, mediCal, Medicare)
866-HMO-8900
www.opa.ca.gov

Health Advocates, California (Medicare)

(see also Medical, mediCal, Medicare)
www.cahealthadvocates.org

Highway Patrol

800-835-5247; 916-657-7261
www.chp.ca.gov
www.chp.ca.gov/offices/offices.html

HMO Help Center

888-HMO-2219
www.hmohelp.ca.gov

HMO Rights

866-HMO-8900
www.opa.ca.gov

Housing (Fair Employment and Housing)

800-233-3212
www.dfeh.ca.gov

Identity Theft

877-ID-THEFT
www.consumer.gov/idtheft
www.idtheftcenter.org/index.shtml
www.csac.ca.gov/doc.asp?id=1133
www.ftc.gov
(click "File a Complaint" then "Identity Theft Complaint Form")
Immigration Services
800-375-5283
www.uscis.gov
Insurance Consumer Hotline
800-927-4357
www.insurance.ca.gov

Insurance Fraud Hotline

800-927-4357
www.insurance.ca.gov

Internet Crime

(see also Fraud)
www.ic3.gov

IRS

(see Tax)

Judicial Council Forms

www.courtinfo.ca.gov/forms

Landlord-Tenant Rights

www.dca.ca.gov/legal
(see links under "Tenant-Landlord")
Legislature (Assembly & Senate)
www.leginfo.ca.gov/yourleg.html
www.leginfo.ca.gov/guide.html

Legislature (bill information)

www.leginfo.ca.gov
www.leginfo.ca.gov/guide.html

Legislature (State Code)

www.leginfo.ca.gov/calaw.html
www.leginfo.ca.gov/guide.html

LexisNexis/Matthew Bender

800-223-1940; 800-356-6548
www.lexisone.com

Licenses

www.ca.gov/state/portal/myca_homepage.jsp
(click "Licenses")
commerce.ca.gov
(click "Permits and Licenses")
www.calgold.ca.gov
("Business permits made simple")
www.dfg.ca.gov/mrd/permits.html
(click fish and game link)

Local Government

(see Government)

Marriage Records

(see also section 5.7)
www.dhs.ca.gov/hisp/chs/OVR/ordercert.htm

Medical Board Complaint Unit

(see also Health)
800-633-2322; 916-263-2382
www.medbd.ca.gov

MediCal Ombudsman

(see also Health)
800-896-4042
www.dmh.cahwnet.gov/Ombud/default.asp

MediCAL Fraud

(see also Health)
800-822-6222
ag.ca.gov/bmfea/reporting.htm

Medicare (CalMedicare)

(see also Health)
800-434-0222; 800-633-4227
www.calmedicare.org

Mental Health Information Hotline

National Alliance for the Mentally Ill
800-950-6264
www.nami.org

Missing Children Hotline

800-843-5678; 800-222-3463
www.missingkids.com
www.childwelfare.gov/pubs/reslist/tollfree.cfm

Ninth Circuit

(see Courts, Federal)

Nolo Press

800-728-3555
www.nolo.com

Nursing Home (state certification)

800-236-9747
www.dhs.ca.gov/lnc/NHAP/default.htm

Occupational Safety and Health (Cal/OSHA)

800-963-9424; 510-286-7000
www.dir.ca.gov/occupational_safety.html

Parks and Recreation

800-777-0369, 916-653-6995
www.parks.ca.gov

Patient Advocate (HMO rights)

866-HMO-8900
www.opa.ca.gov

Permits and Licenses

(see Licenses)

Physicians (local medical societies)

(see also Health, Medical)
new.cmanet.org/PUBLICDOC.cfm/63

Physicians (Medical Board Complaint Unit)

800-633-2322; 916-263-2382
www.medbd.ca.gov

Poison Control Hotline

800-222-1222; 800-876-4766
www.poison.org

Police Departments

(see also Highway Patrol)
www.post.ca.gov/library/other/agency_page.asp
www.cops.cc

Pollution

(see also Environmental Protection)
800-952-5588
www.arb.ca.gov

Postal Fraud

800-372-8347
www.usps.com/postalinspectors

Pregnancy

Planned Parenthood Hotline
800-230-PLAN
www.plannedparenthood.org

Prison

(see Corrections)

Privacy Protection

(see also Identity Theft)
866-785-9663
www.privacy.ca.gov/cover/links.htm

Public Defender (state)

916-322-2676, 415-904-5600
www.ospd.ca.gov

Public Utilities Commission (complaints)

800-649-7570
www.cpuc.ca.gov

Rape Hotline

800-656-HOPE; 818-793-3385
www.rainn.org

Real Estate, Department of (enforcement/complaints)

916-227-0864
www.dre.ca.gov

Recycling

800-732-5293
www.consrv.ca.gov

Red Cross

800-435-7669
www.redcross.org

Runaway Hotline

(see also Youth Crisis Hotline)
800-RUNAWAY
www.nrscrisisline.org

Secretary of State

916-653-6814
www.ss.ca.gov

Self-Help Resources

(see also section 5.6)
www.courtinfo.ca.gov/selfhelp

Senate

(see Legislature)

Sex Offender Information

(Megan's Law)
916-227-4974
caag.state.ca.us/megan/index.htm

Sheriff Offices (by county)

www.calsheriffs.org
www.cops.cc
www.bdcorr.ca.gov/links/link_pages/web_other.htm

Social Security Information Hotline

800-772-1213
www.ssa.gov

STD Hotline

800-227-8922
www.ashastd.org
Student Financial Aid Hotline
800-4-FED-AID
studentaid.ed.gov

Substance Abuse Information Hotline

(see also Drug and Alcohol Abuse)
800-662-HELP; 800-66-AYUDA

Suicide Prevention Hotline

800-273-TALK
www.suicidepreventionlifeline.org

Tax, Federal Income

800-829-1040 (individuals); 800-829-4933 (businesses)
www.irs.gov

Tax, State Income

800-338-0505; 800-852-5711
www.ftb.ca.gov
www.taxes.ca.gov

Tax Evasion Hotline (state)

888-334-3300
www.ftb.ca.gov

Taxpayers' Rights Advocate

Board of Equalization
888-324-2798
www.boe.ca.gov/info/contra.htm

Tax Practitioner Hotline

Board of Equalization
800-401-3661
www.boe.ca.gov/info/contact.htm

Tenant-Landlord Rights

(see Landlord-Tenant Rights)

Tourism in California

800-862-2543
gocalif.ca.gov

Unclaimed Property

800-992-4647
www.sco.ca.gov/col/ucp/index.shtml

Unemployment Insurance Claims

800-300-5616
www.edd.ca.gov/uirep/uiloc.htm

Vital Records

www.dhs.ca.gov/hisp/chs/OVR/ordercert.htm

Victim Compensation

800-777-9229
www.boc.ca.gov
www.boc.ca.gov/Victims.htm

Victim Resources (crime)

800-851-3420
www.ojp.usdoj.gov/ovc

Delmar Group/Westlaw

800-328-4880; 800-WESTLAW
www.paralegal.delmar.cengage.com

Whistleblowing (Bureau of State Audits)

800-952-5665
www.bsa.ca.gov/bsa

Whistleblowing (Attorney General)

800-952-5225; 916-322-3360
caag.state.ca.us

White House

202-456-1414
www.whitehouse.gov

Witkin Law Institute

800-537-2707
www.witkin.com

Workers' Compensation

800-736-7401; 510-286-7100
www.dir.ca.gov/DWC/dir2.htm

Youth Crisis Hotline (California)

(see also Runaway Hotline)
800-843-5200
www.calyouth.org

C. More Information

www.ca.gov/state/portal/myca_homepage.jsp
www.focusas.com/California.html
california.lp.findlaw.com/ca17_calif_law_web_sites
govinfo.ucsd.edu/calagen.html

D. Something to Check

What hotline resources might help a client concerned about the following circumstances?

1. Stalking
2. Insolvency
3. Credit discrimination

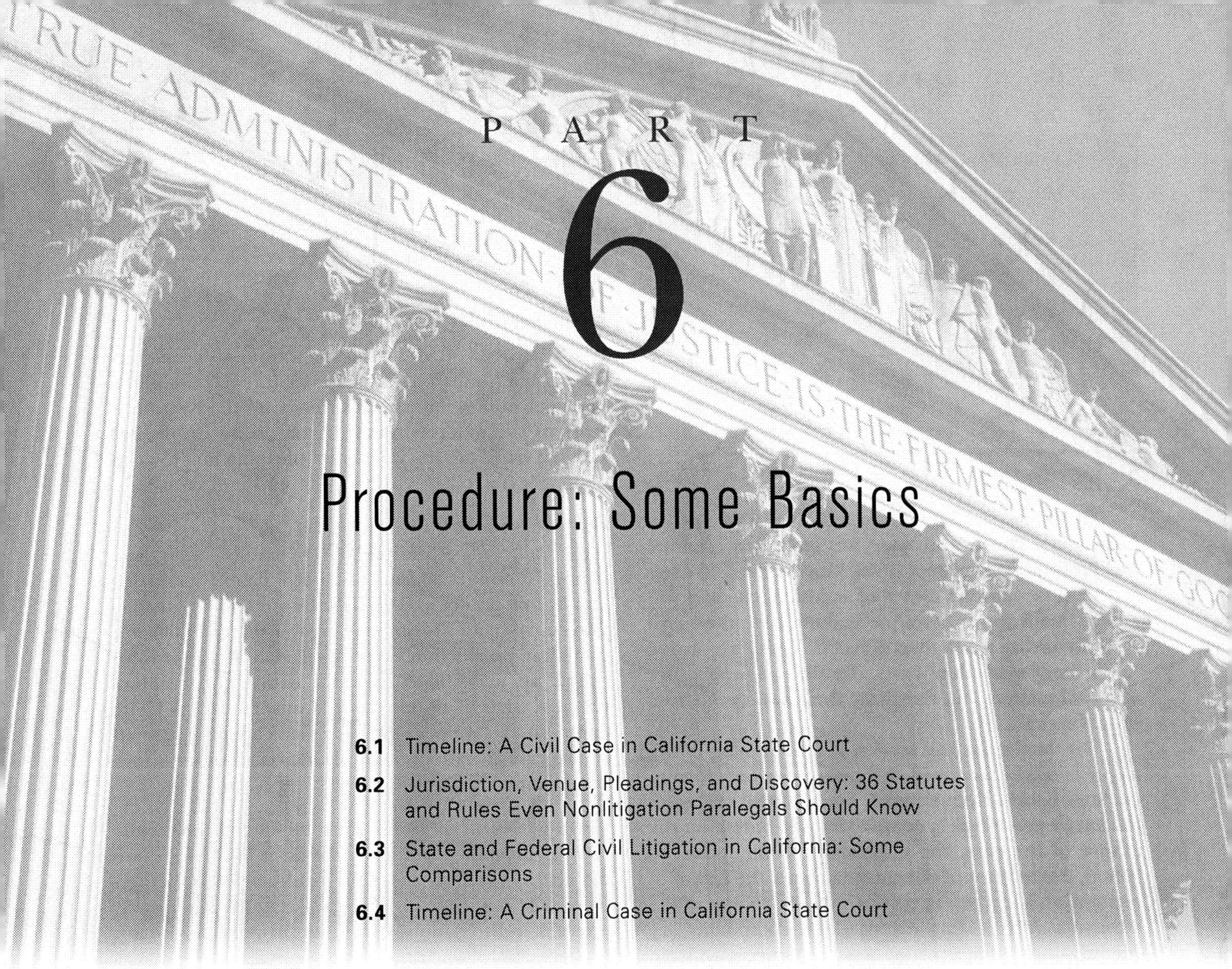

PART

6

Procedure: Some Basics

6.1 Timeline: A Civil Case in California State Court

A. Introduction

There are over 1.5 million civil cases filed in California state courts each year, not including criminal and juvenile delinquency cases. Most of the civil cases raise tort or contract causes of action. Such cases will be our main focus here, particularly unlimited civil cases involving more than $25,000. These are called "unlimited jurisdiction" cases. (Family and probate are also civil matters, but they have their own specialized procedures.)

The timeline in this section describes many of the major events in contested civil cases commonly filed in our state courts. Keep in mind, however, that civil cases can vary a great deal in complexity, depending on the nature of the case, the magnitude of the issues involved, the amount of potential damages, the extent of contention between the parties, and the caliber of the attorneys. Also adding diversity and complexity are the local rules that apply only to the court in which a case is being litigated. Our timeline primarily covers rules of statewide applicability.

See also the following related sections:

- overview of California state courts (section 4.2)
- jurisdiction, venue, pleading, and discovery (section 6.2)
- example of a civil complaint (section 7.1)
- self-help resources (section 5.6)
- overview of federal courts sitting in California (section 4.3)
- some comparisons between state and federal civil procedure (section 6.3)

Abbreviations

BAJI: Book of Approved Jury Instructions
CALJIC: California Jury Instructions, Civil
CRC: California Rules of Court
CCP: California Code of Civil Procedure
Govt: California Government Code

B. Overview of a Civil Case

Exhibit 6.1A presents an overview of many of the major events involved in the litigation of unlimited jurisdiction cases in California state courts.

Preliminary Considerations

Statute of limitations The statute of limitations places time limits on filing a lawsuit. For example, a personal injury claim must usually be filed within 2 years of the date of injury. If you do not bring suit within 2 years, the suit is "barred" meaning that you can no longer sue. (CCP § 312)

Subject-matter jurisdiction Our state trial court is the California Superior Court. There is one in each county. It conducts trials of all civil cases. Claims for money that do not exceed $25,000 are limited jurisdiction cases. Claims for money greater than $25,000 are unlimited jurisdiction cases. Small claims cases involve claims up to $5,000. (Superior courts also conduct criminal trials of all felonies and misdemeanors.) The *Superior Court Appellate Division* hears appeals of small claims cases, limited civil jurisdiction cases, and misdemeanor cases.

Venue Most civil claims must be filed in the county where a defendant resides or conducts business, where the claim arose, or where the contract was to be performed. Claims involving real estate are generally brought in the county where the property is located. (CCP §§ 392, 395)

Arbitration and mediation Throughout the case, efforts to resolve the dispute without litigation are often made. This can include arbitration, mediation, and other methods of alternative dispute resolution (ADR). See the discussion of alternative dispute resolution below.

Commencement of the Case; Pleadings & Motions

Complaint The civil case begins with the filing of the complaint with the Superior Court. (In some kinds of cases this pleading is called the petition.) The complaint shall contain (a) a statement of the facts constituting the cause of action, in ordinary and concise language, and (b) a demand for judgment for the relief to which the pleader claims to be entitled. If the recovery of money or damages is demanded, the amount demanded shall be stated. (CCP § 425.10)

Summons The plaintiff must complete the summons and present it to the court clerk when filing a complaint. The summons notifies the defendants of the action ("Notice! You have been sued.") and lists the parties and the time within which the defendants must

EXHIBIT 6.1A **Bringing and Defending a Civil Case in California State Courts**

(The following overview covers many of the major events in a typical unlimited jurisdiction case filed in a California Superior Court; variations will depend on factors such as the complexity of the case and the applicability of local rules.)

PRELIMINARY CONSIDERATIONS	COMMENCEMENT OF THE CASE; PLEADINGS & MOTIONS	DISCOVERY	SUMMARY JUDGMENT	CASE MANAGEMENT	ALTERNATIVE DISPUTE RESOLUTION (ADR)	TRIAL	APPEAL
• Statute of limitations • Subject-matter jurisdiction • Venue • Arbitration and mediation	• Complaint • Summons • Civil Case Cover Sheet • Personal service on defendant • Proof of service • Substituted service • Answer • Cross-complaint • Demurrer • Motion to strike • Amending the complaint • Request for statement of damages • Default judgment • Motion to set aside default judgment	• Interrogatories • Depositions • Requests for admissions • Inspection and production • Physical or mental examinations (IME) • Motion to compel response • Motion for a protective order • Meet and confer	• Motion for summary judgment	• Case management conference • Mandatory settlement conference (MSC) • § 998 offers to compromise	• Arbitration • Trial de novo • Mediation • Neutral evaluation • Other ADR methods	• Time • Pretrial conference • Motion in limine • Voir dire • Opening statements • Examination of witnesses • Exhibits • Motion for a judgment of nonsuit • Motion for a directed verdict • Closing arguments • Instructions to the jury • Verdict • Notice of entry of judgment • Motion for recovery of costs • Motion for judgment notwithstanding the verdict • Motion for new trial	• Appellate courts • Posting bond • Notice of appeal • Notice of cross-appeal • Civil case information statement • Appellate briefs • Reporter's transcript • Notice of designation/ clerk's transcript • Oral argument • Court of Appeal decision • Request for review by the California Supreme Court • Supreme Court decision

file a response (30 days) to the complaint. The clerk signs the summons, places the seal of the court on it, and returns it to the person filing the complaint. (The original is returned to the clerk after all the defendants are served.) (CCP § 412.20)

Civil Case Cover Sheet With the first paper filed in the action (usually the complaint), the plaintiff must also file a Civil Case Cover Cheet. This form will indicate the kind of case being filed (e.g., contract, auto tort, medical malpractice, or other personal injury) including whether it is limited civil case (amount demanded is $25,000 or less) or an unlimited civil case (amount demanded exceeds $25,000). (Judicial Council Form 982.2(b)(1)); (CRC 3.220)

Personal service on defendant When you sue someone, you must provide formal notice that you have started the legal process. This is called "service." When serving the other side, you provide copies of the papers you filed in court to commence the action. For a civil case, the summons and complaint must be served on each defendant named in the complaint. For personal service, the server personally delivers the summons and complaint to the defendant or someone qualified to accept service for the defendant. The server must be over 18 and not be a party to the case. Servers can be friends, relatives, the sheriff, or a licensed process server. (CCP § 414.10)

Proof of service The person serving the summons and complaint must complete and sign a proof of service form. After the defendants are served, the proof of service together with the original summons is filed with the court. The proof of service states that a copy of the summons and complaint was served on each defendant. The signed original proof of service and a copy of it are taken to the court clerk. On the copy, the clerk will stamp "Filed" and return it to you. (CCP § 417.10)

Substituted service If a copy of the summons and complaint cannot with reasonable diligence be personally delivered to the person to be served, a summons may be served by leaving a copy of the summons and complaint at the person's dwelling house, usual place of abode, usual place of business, or usual mailing address (other than a post office box), in the presence of a competent member of the household or a person apparently in charge of his or her office, place of business, or usual mailing address (other than a post office box), at least 18 years of age, who shall be informed of the contents thereof, and by thereafter mailing a copy of the summons and of the complaint by first-class mail, postage prepaid to the person to be served at the place where a copy of the summons and complaint were left. Service of a summons in this manner is deemed complete on the 10th day after the mailing. (CCP § 415.20(b))

Answer The defendant has 30 calendar days from the date the defendant was personally served to file an answer or other response (e.g., a demurrer) with the clerk of the court. (CCP § 412.20) The failure to respond within the required time period can result in a default judgment. The answer to a complaint shall contain: (1) The general or specific denial of the material allegations of the complaint controverted by the defendant. (2) A statement of any new matter constituting a defense. (CCP § 431.30) Affirmative relief may not be claimed in the answer.

Cross-complaint In addition to filing an answer, the defendant can file a cross-complaint against the plaintiff or against another defendant. This pleading asserts an independent action and is treated like a complaint, e.g., it must be properly served and the side against whom it is filed has 30 days from the date of service in which to respond at the risk of receiving a default judgment. (CCP § 428.10)

Demurrer A demurrer is a motion brought by a defendant to challenge a defective complaint. The demurrer says that even if everything the plaintiff alleges is true, he or she cannot recover. The demurrer might be brought when the defendant does not believe the plaintiff has stated sufficient facts to support the cause of action or when the defendant asserts that the court lacks subject matter jurisdiction. A demurrer can be brought as to the entire complaint, or as to one or more causes of action. (CCP §§ 430.10, 430.30) The defendant must file the demurrer within 30 days after service of the complaint. (CCP § 430.40(a))

Motion to strike A motion to strike is usually brought to request that the court delete an improper allegation or statement from a complaint. Sometimes a motion to strike is directed to one word or phrase, sometimes it is directed to an entire cause of action. A motion to strike can be filed with a demurrer. (CCP § 435)

Amending the complaint Instead of filing an opposition to the motion to strike, the plaintiff can amend the complaint. This can be done without first obtaining the court's permission if no defendant has filed an answer. Once an answer is filed, the plaintiff can amend the complaint (a) with the consent of the opposing sides, usually obtained by way of stipulation, or (b) upon an order from the court permitting the filing of an amended complaint. (CCP § 472)

Request for statement of damages When a complaint is filed in an action to recover damages for personal injury or wrongful death, the defendant may at any time request a statement setting forth the nature and amount of damages being sought. The request shall be served upon the plaintiff, who shall serve a responsive statement as to the damages within 15 days. (CCP § 425.11)

Default judgment If any defendant has failed to file a response within the time period provided by law, the plaintiff can request that a default be entered against the defendant who failed to respond.

Motion to set aside default judgment Once a default is entered against a defendant, that defendant cannot file a response to the complaint or appear in the action unless the court sets aside the default, which may be done at the court's discretion, upon a motion brought by the defendant, showing good cause for failing to respond to the complaint on time. (CCP § 473.5)

Discovery

Interrogatories Interrogatories are written questions posed to a party, requiring a written response. A defendant may propound interrogatories to a party to the action without leave of court at any time. A plaintiff may propound interrogatories to a party without leave of court at any time that is 10 days after the service of the summons on that party, whichever occurs first. (CCP § 2030.020) Within 30 days after service of interrogatories, the party to whom the interrogatories are propounded shall serve the original of the response to them on the propounding party. (CCP § 2030.260)

Depositions An oral deposition is a questioning of a witness under oath in the presence of a court reporter, who takes down the testimony in written form. Any party may take the oral deposition of any person, including any party to the action. (CCP § 2025.010) The defendant may serve a deposition notice without leave of court at any time after that defendant has been served or has appeared in the action, whichever occurs first. The plaintiff may serve a deposition notice without leave of court on any date that is 20 days after the service of the summons on, or appearance by, any defendant. (CCP § 2025.210)

Requests for admissions Requests for admissions are written requests from a party that any other party to the action admit the genuineness of specified documents, or the truth of specified matters of fact, opinion relating to fact, or application of law to fact. A request for admission may relate to a matter that is in controversy between the parties. (CCP § 2033.010) A defendant may make requests for admission by a party without leave of court at any time. A plaintiff may make requests for admission by a party without leave of court at any time that is 10 days after the service of the summons on, or appearance by, that party, whichever occurs first. (CCP § 2033.020) Within 30 days after service of requests for admission, the party to whom the requests are directed shall serve the original of the response to them on the requesting party, and a copy of the response on all other parties who have appeared, unless on motion of the requesting party the court has shortened the time for response, or unless on motion of the responding party the court has extended the time for response. (CCP § 2033.250)

Inspection and production Any party may obtain discovery by inspecting documents, tangible things, and land or other property that are in the possession, custody, or control of any other party to the action. A party can demand that the other party produce and permit inspection and copying of a document; produce and permit inspection, photographing, testing, or sampling a tangible thing; and allow entry on any land or other property that is in the possession, custody, or control of the party on whom the demand is made, and to inspect, measure, survey, photograph, test, or sample the land or other property, or any designated object or operation on it. (CCP §§ 2031.010) A defendant may make a demand for inspection without leave of court at any time. A plaintiff may make a demand for inspection without leave of court at any time that is 10 days after the service of the summons on, or appearance by, the party to whom the demand is directed, whichever occurs first. (CCP § 2031.020) Within 30 days after service of an inspection demand, the party to whom the demand is directed shall serve the original of the response to it on the party making the demand, and a copy of the response on all other parties who have appeared in the action. (CCP § 2031.060)

Physical or mental examination (IME: independent medical examination) Any party may obtain discovery by means of a physical or mental examination of (1) a party to the action, (2) an agent of any party, or (3) a natural person in the custody or under the legal control of a party, in any action in which the mental or physical condition (including the blood group) of that party or other person is in controversy in the action. (CCP § 2032.020) If the plaintiff is seeking recovery for personal injuries, the physical examination shall be scheduled for a date that is at least 30 days after service of the demand. (CCP § 2032.220)

Motion to compel response If the parties disagree on what constitutes proper discovery, or if a party fails to respond to a proper discovery request, a motion may be brought to compel a response. (CRC Rule 335; CCP § 2025.480)

Motion for a protective order If a party is abusing the discovery process to harass the other side, or is demanding information that is privileged or otherwise protected from disclosure by law, the responding party may bring a motion for a protective order. (CCP § 2017.020)

Meet and confer Before either side files a motion to compel or for a protective order, the parties may be required to "meet and confer" to try to resolve their dispute. Failure to first meet and confer can result in the court imposing monetary fines, called sanctions. Sanctions can also be imposed for discovery abuses. (CCP § 2016.040)

Summary Judgment

Motion for summary judgment A summary judgment is a resolution of the legal issues when the material facts are not in dispute. Any party may move for summary judgment if it is contended that the action has no merit or that there is no defense to the action or proceeding. The motion may be made at any time after 60 days have elapsed since the general appearance in the action or proceeding of each party against whom the motion is directed or at any earlier time after the general appearance that the court, with or without notice and upon good cause shown, may direct. Notice of the motion and supporting papers shall be served on all other parties to the action at least 75 days before the time appointed for hearing. The motion shall be supported by affidavits, declarations, admissions, answers to interrogatories, depositions, and matters of which judicial notice shall or may be taken. The supporting papers shall include a separate statement setting forth plainly and concisely all material facts which the moving party contends are undisputed. The motion for summary judgment shall be granted if all the papers submitted show that there is no triable issue as to any material fact and that the moving party is entitled to a judgment as a matter of law. (CCP § 437c)

Case Management

Case management conference A case management conference is scheduled within a designated number of days after the complaint is filed (e.g., 180 days in Los Angeles). Notice of the date of the conference must be given to all parties no later than 45 days before the conference. No later than 30 calendar days before the date set for the case management conference, the parties must meet and confer, in person or by telephone, to consider each of the topics to be covered at the conference. No later than 15 calendar days before the date set for the case management conference, each party must file a case management statement in which the party indicates a willingness to participate in mediation or other methods of alternate dispute resolution (ADR), states the status of discovery, and provides other information about the case to date. At the conference, the case management judge can set the case for trial or assign the case to an ADR process. (CRC Rule 212)

Mandatory settlement conference (MSC) On the court's own motion or at the request of any party, the court may set a MSC. Trial counsel and parties must personally attend the conference, unless excused by the court for good cause. No later than 5 court days before the date set for the settlement conference, each party must submit to the court and serve on each party a MSC statement containing a good faith settlement demand and an itemization of economic and non-economic damages by each plaintiff and a good faith offer of settlement by each defendant. The statement must set forth and discuss in detail all facts and law pertinent to the issues of liability and damages involved in the case as to that party and comply with any additional requirement imposed by local rule. (CRC Rule 222)

§ 998 offers to compromise Section 998 of the California Code of Civil Procedure provides a procedure for making a formal settlement offer (not less than 10 days prior to commencement of trial), which if accepted ends the case, and if rejected, may entitle the party making the offer to recover certain costs associated with the lawsuit. If the party who rejects the offer fails to obtain a more favorable result after trial, he or she may be obligated to pay the expert witness fees incurred by the party making the offer. (CCP § 998)

Alternative Dispute Resolution (ADR)

Arbitration A neutral person (the arbitrator) reviews evidence, hears arguments, and makes a decision (award) to resolve the dispute after an informal hearing. There are two kinds of arbitration in California: (1) Private arbitration, by agreement of the parties involved in the dispute, takes place outside of the courts and is normally binding. In most cases "binding" means that the arbitrator's decision (award) is final and there will not be a trial or an appeal of that decision. (2) "Judicial arbitration" takes place within the court process and is not binding unless the parties agree at the outset to be bound. A party to this kind of arbitration who does not like a judicial arbitration award may file a request for trial with the court within a specified time (see trial de novo below). However, if that party does not do better in the trial than in arbitration, he or she may have to pay a penalty. (CCP § 1141.11) (CRC Rule 1605)

Trial de novo Within 30 days after a judicial arbitration award is filed with the clerk of the court, a party may request a trial by filing with the clerk a request for trial, with proof of service of a copy upon all other parties appearing in the case. The case must be restored to the civil active list for prompt disposition, in the same position on the list it would have had if there had been no arbitration in the case, unless the court orders otherwise for good cause. The case must be tried as though no arbitration proceedings had occurred. No reference may be made during the trial to the arbitration award, to the fact that there had been arbitration proceedings, to the evidence adduced at the arbitration hearing, or to any other aspect of the arbitration proceedings, and none of the foregoing may be used as affirmative evidence, or by way of impeachment, or for any other purpose at the trial. (CRC Rule 1616)

Mediation A neutral person (the mediator) assists the parties in reaching a mutually acceptable resolution of their dispute. Unlike lawsuits and some other types of ADR, the mediator does not decide how the dispute is to be resolved; the parties do. (CRC Rules 1580(c))

Neutral evaluation A neutral person (the evaluator) gives an opinion on the strengths and weaknesses of each party's evidence and arguments and makes an evaluation of the case. Each party gets a chance to present his or her side and hear the other side. This may lead to a settlement or at least help the parties prepare to resolve the dispute later on. If the neutral evaluation does not resolve the dispute, the parties may go to court or try another form of ADR.

Other ADR methods There are several other types of ADR besides mediation, arbitration, and neutral evaluation. Some of these are conciliation, settlement conferences, fact-finding, mini-trials, and summary jury trials. Sometimes parties will try a combination of ADR methods.

Trial

Time Trials are generally scheduled 300 to 330 days after filing the complaint. Fast track rules require that most cases be completed within a year from the filing of the complaint. Even if the other side agrees to a continuance of the trial, the court is unlikely to grant a request for a continuance unless good cause can be shown. (Govt §§ 68603 et seq.)

Pretrial conference Local rules establish when a pretrial conference is held. At this conference, the parties give the judge an overview and update of the case and the judge makes rulings on matters that need to be addressed before formal trial proceedings begin. Witness lists and proposed jury instructions are often presented at the pretrial conference. Decisions of the judge may be embodied in a pretrial conference order, which is subject to amendment. (CCP §§ 576, 576)

Motion in limine One of the matters that can be covered in the pretrial conference is the motion in limine. This motion seeks a court ruling on what evidence will be admissible at trial. If one side does not want certain evidence brought to the attention of the jury, it will bring a motion in limine to have the evidence excluded before the jury sees or hears it. The court will consider the motion and rule on whether the evidence may be introduced at the trial before it is brought to the attention of the jury.

Voir dire Prospective jurors are examined in a process called voir dire. The judge and the attorneys ask them questions to determine if they are free of bias (prejudice) or whether there is any other reason why any of them cannot be fair and impartial. After the questions, each side may challenge potential jurors either because of cause (meaning the juror would likely be biased) or by exercising a limited number of peremptory challenges that each side has. Reasons do not have to be stated for exercising a peremptory challenge. (Sometimes a challenge is made against an entire pool of prospective jurors on the ground that there has been a systematic exclusion of a specified group that is underrepresented in the pool.) After voir dire is concluded, the jury will be empanelled to hear the evidence in the case. (CCP § 226)

Opening statements The court will give each side an opportunity to make an opening statement. The defense can make an opening statement immediately after the plaintiff's case, or can wait until the conclusion of plaintiff's case. An opening statement tells the jury what the side expects the evidence to show. After the plaintiff's opening statement, the defendant can make a motion for judgment of nonsuit. See the discussion of this motion below.

Examination of witnesses The plaintiff presents its case first, since the plaintiff has the burden of proof. After each witness has testified under direct examination, the other side may cross-examine the witness regarding the testimony already given. After cross-examination, the party that called the witness may conduct a redirect examination, followed by a possible recross-examination by the other side. After all the plaintiff's witnesses have testified, the plaintiff will "rest." Then it is the defendant's turn to present its version of the case.

Exhibits Exhibits to be introduced into evidence are usually pre-marked before the start of the trial. The courtroom clerk labels each exhibit with a number or letter. (Numbers might be used for plaintiff exhibits and letters for defendant exhibits.) When introducing evidence, it is generally necessary to establish a legal basis for considering the evidence through the witness who will be testifying about the exhibit. Establishing a legal basis for considering evidence is called "laying an evidentiary foundation." Before accepting an item into evidence, the judge will ask the opposing side if there is any objection to admitting the exhibit into evidence.

Motion for a judgment of nonsuit After the plaintiff has presented its evidence (or after the plaintiff's opening statement), the defense sometimes brings a motion for a nonsuit, whereby the defense asks the court to dismiss the lawsuit because plaintiff failed to prove its case. (CCP § 581c)

Motion for a directed verdict Either side can also request a directed verdict. If granted, the court essentially instructs the jury that there is no issue of fact for them to resolve, and as a matter of law, the result of the case must be decided a certain way. If the motion is granted, the jury does not deliberate on the issue involved.

Closing arguments At the end of the defendant's case, plaintiff's attorney will be asked to make a closing argument, followed by the defendant attorney's closing argument. The plaintiff is entitled to a final rebuttal after the defendant's closing argument. The closing argument is a party's final summary of the case and argument for a favorable verdict.

Instructions to the jury Either before or after the closing arguments by the attorneys, the judge will explain to the jury the law that applies to the case. This is the judge's instruction (charge), which the jury must follow in arriving at a verdict. Prior to this time, each side is given the opportunity to propose instructions it would like the judge to give the jury. (CALJIC; BAJI)

Verdict After the judge's instruction, the jury is sent to a private room to deliberate on the verdict. The jury selects a foreperson whose duty is to see that discussion takes place in a free and orderly manner and that every juror is given an opportunity to participate. The jury will reach a general verdict (which simply states which side wins) or a special verdict (which is the jury's answers to specific questions put to it by the court). If a jury cannot arrive at a verdict within a reasonable time and indicates to the judge that there is no possibility that it can reach a verdict, the judge, in his or her discretion, may dismiss the jury and declare a mistrial, sometimes referred to as a "hung jury."

Notice of entry of judgment If the jury reaches a verdict, the judge signs the verdict. It is then filed with the clerk and recorded in the judgment book, which is a record of all judgments by courts in the jurisdiction. A copy of the recorded judgment is attached to a notice of entry of judgment, which states that an order or judgment has been entered. (CCP § 664.5)

Motion for recovery of costs The prevailing party can file a motion to recover its reasonable litigation costs and expenses, e.g., filing fees. (CCP § 1033.5)

Motion for judgment notwithstanding the verdict (JNOV) After a jury returns a verdict, the losing side may bring a motion for judgment notwithstanding the verdict. This motion asks the court to disregard the jury's verdict if it is not supported by the evidence or otherwise contrary to the law and to replace it with a different verdict. (CCP § 629)

Motion for a new trial At the conclusion of a case, the losing side may make a motion for a new trial if it can be shown that newly discovered material evidence exists, which could not, with reasonable diligence, have been discovered and produced at the trial. Other grounds for a new trial include jury misconduct, excessive or inadequate damages, and irregularity in the proceedings. (CCP § 657)

Appeal

(See also Exhibit 6.4B (Appeal Process) in section 6.4.)

Appellate courts Appeals of unlimited jurisdiction cases (unlimited civil cases), in which the amount of money at issue exceeds $25,000, are to a California Court of Appeal. The party appealing is the appellant. The party against whom the appeal is filed is the respondent. Appeals of limited jurisdiction cases (limited civil cases), in which the amount of money at issue is $25,000 or less, are to the appellate division of the superior court. (CCP § 902) The following sequence of events applies primarily to the appeal of unlimited civil cases.

Posting bond A losing party (the judgment debtor) wishing to stay the execution of a money judgment must post a bond ("undertaking") that covers 150% of the judgment amount if a surety company is used or 200% if the bond is posted in cash. (CCP § 917.1)

Notice of appeal A notice of appeal of a judgment in an unlimited civil case is filed by the appellant with the clerk in the superior court that rendered the judgment. The clerk informs all the parties and the appellate court that the notice of appeal has been filed. (CRC Rule 1) The notice of appeal must be filed on or before the earliest of: (1) 60 days after the superior court clerk mails the party filing the notice of appeal a document entitled "Notice of Entry" of judgment or a file-stamped copy of the judgment, showing the date either was mailed; (2) 60 days after the party filing the notice of appeal serves or is served by a party with a document entitled "Notice of Entry" of judgment or a file-stamped copy of the judgment, accompanied by proof of service; or (3) 180 days after entry of judgment. (CRC Rule 2(a))

Notice of cross-appeal A respondent who also wishes to appeal the judgment files a cross-appeal and notice of cross-appeal within 20 days after the court clerk mails the notification of the first appeal. (CRC Rule 3(e))

Civil case information statement The appellant files a civil case information statement with the appellate court. The statement provides basic appeal information, e.g., the names of the parties and the kind of judgment being appealed. A copy of the judgment being appealed (showing the date it was entered) must be attached to the statement. (CRC Rule 1(f))

Appellate briefs An appellate brief is a party's written description of the facts in the case, the relevant law, and the party's argument on why the trial court's decision should be affirmed or reversed. After filing the notice of appeal, the appellant files an appellate brief with the appellate court. The brief states reasons why the judgment appealed from was in error. In response, the respondent files an opposing brief. Finally, in response to this opposing brief, the appellant can file a reply brief. (CRC Rule 15)

Reporter's transcript Within 10 days after filing the notice of appeal, an appellant must serve and file in superior court either a notice designating a reporter's transcript (a transcription of the oral statements made in the trial) or a notice of intent to proceed without a reporter's transcript, unless the appellant proceeds by agreed or settled statement under rule 6 or 7. (CRC Rule 4)

Notice of designation/clerk's transcript Within 10 days after filing the notice of appeal, an appellant must serve and file a notice in superior court designating the documents to be included in the clerk's transcript (files and exhibits in the trial), unless the appeal proceeds by allowed alternatives (e.g., under Rules 5.1 or 5.2) instead of a clerk's transcript. (CRC Rule 5(1))

Oral argument The case is not retried on appeal. Rather, the parties are allowed to present oral arguments before one or more appellate court judges on why the trial court's decision should be affirmed or reversed. The Court of Appeal clerk must send a notice of the time and place of oral argument to all parties at least 20 days before the argument date. The presiding judge may shorten the notice period for good cause; in that event, the clerk must immediately notify the parties by telephone or other expeditious method. Each side is allowed 30 minutes for argument. (CRC Rule 23)

Court of Appeal decision The Court of Appeal can affirm, reverse, or modify the judgment below, or it can send the case back (remand it) for further proceedings. In general a Court of Appeal decision is final 30 days after filing. (CRC Rule 24(b))

Request for review by the California Supreme Court After the decision by the Court of Appeal, a party can file a request (or petition) for review with the California Supreme Court. The petition for review must be served and filed within 10 days after the Court of Appeal decision is final. (CRC Rule 28(e)) Review is discretionary with the Supreme Court. With very few exceptions (e.g., death penalty cases) the Supreme Court can refuse the request. The refusal means that the decision below stands.

Supreme Court decision If the Supreme Court grants the request, appellate briefs are filed and oral argument is scheduled. The California Supreme Court can affirm, reverse, or modify the judgment below, or it can send the case back (remand it) for further proceedings.

C. More Information

Web Sites of California Trial Courts
www.courtinfo.ca.gov/courts/trial/courtlist.htm

ADR (Alternate Dispute Resolution) in California
www.courtinfo.ca.gov/reference/4_3adr.htm

California Code of Civil Procedure
www.leginfo.ca.gov/calaw.html

Jury Trials
www.courtinfo.ca.gov/jury/process.htm

California Court Rules
www.courtinfo.ca.gov/rules
www.courtinfo.ca.gov/rules/titleone

California Civil Jury Instructions
www.courtinfo.ca.gov/jury/civiljuryinstructions/index.htm

Judicial Council Forms
www.courtinfo.ca.gov/forms

Statistics on California Courts
www.courtinfo.ca.gov/reference/documents/csr2004.pdf

Overview of Appeals in California Courts
www.lacba.org/showpage.cfm?pageid=2730
www.courtinfo.ca.gov/courts/courtsofappeal/5thDistrict/5dca_proper.htm
www.courtinfo.ca.gov/courts/courtsofappeal/4thDistrictDiv1/iopp.htm
www.courtinfo.ca.gov/courts/courtsofappeal/2ndDistrict/selfhelp_manual.htm

D. Something to Check

Go to the Web site of the superior court in your county (*www.courtinfo.ca.gov/courts/trial/courtlist.htm*) and to the court of appeal to which decisions of that superior court are appealed (see section 4.2).

1. What assistance is available on these sites for trials and appeals of civil cases in those courts?
2. Go to the online local rules of the superior court. For unlimited jurisdiction cases, find any three rules that supplement the rules provided in this section.

6.2 Jurisdiction, Venue, Pleadings, and Discovery: 36 Statutes and Rules Even Nonlitigation Paralegals Should Know

A. Introduction
B. Abbreviations
C. The Rules
D. More Information
E. Something to Check

A. Introduction

Even if you do not work in litigation now, at some time in your career there is a good chance that you will. A majority of the paralegals you will meet at paralegal association gatherings work in some phase of litigation, either on the front lines or in indirect capacities. Attorneys and paralegals in *transaction* practices often have litigation on their mind—from the perspective of how to avoid it! In short, litigation dominates a large portion of the legal world. Knowing some of the essential rules of civil litigation in the California courts will help you communicate intelligently with (and perhaps be better prepared one day to join) attorneys and paralegals in the world of litigation.

In this section, we introduce excerpts from thirty-six of the most important litigation rules in California in two areas where paralegals have their most prominent roles: pleadings and discovery. Because the rules are excerpted rather than presented in full, you of course will need to go to the codes or rules themselves to obtain the full text whenever working on an a client's case.

Consider this recommendation: read through the excerpts at least once or twice a year. Each time you do, you will increase your "litigation literacy," and gain a richer context for many of the nonlitigation tasks you perform.

See also the following related sections:

- overview of California state courts (section 4.2)
- timeline of a civil case in California state courts (section 6.1)
- example of a civil complaint (section 7.1)
- some comparisons between state and federal civil procedure (section 6.3)
- overview of federal courts sitting in California (section 4.3)

B. Abbreviations

CCP: Code of Civil Procedure

CRC: California Rules of Court

C. The Rules

Table of Contents

SUBJECT-MATTER JURISDICTION

§ 86. Jurisdiction (CCP)

Limited Civil Cases

(a) The following civil cases and proceedings are limited civil cases:

(1) Cases at law in which the demand, exclusive of interest, or the value of the property in controversy amounts to twenty-five thousand dollars ($25,000) or less. . . .

(3) Actions to cancel or rescind a contract when the relief is sought in connection with an action to recover money not exceeding twenty-five thousand dollars ($25,000) or property of a value not exceeding twenty-five thousand dollars ($25,000). . . .

§ 88. Unlimited civil case (CCP)

Unlimited Civil Cases

A civil action or proceeding other than a limited civil case may be referred to as an unlimited civil case.

VENUE (Place of Trial)

§ 392(a). Venue, proper court (real property actions) (CCP)

(a) Subject to the power of the court to transfer actions and proceedings as provided in this title, the superior court in the county where the real property that is the subject of the action, or some part thereof, is situated, is the proper court for the trial of the following actions:

Venue in Land Cases

(1) For the recovery of real property, or of an estate or interest therein, . . . and for injuries to real property.

(2) For the foreclosure of all liens and mortgages on real property. . . .

§ 395(a). Venue, proper court (negligence, dissolution of marriage, child support, breach of contract) (CCP)

Except as otherwise provided by law and subject to the power of the court to transfer actions or proceedings as provided in this title, the superior court in the county where the defendants or some of them reside at the commencement of the action is the proper court for the trial of the action.

Venue in Negligence, Dissolution, Child Support, and Contract Cases

- If the action is for injury to person or personal property or for death from wrongful act or negligence, the superior court in either the county where the injury occurs or the injury causing death occurs or the county where the defendants, or some of them reside at the commencement of the action, is a proper court for the trial of the action.
- In a proceeding for dissolution of marriage, the superior court in the county where either the petitioner or respondent has been a resident for three months next preceding the commencement of the proceeding is the proper court for the trial of the proceeding.
- In a proceeding to enforce an obligation of support under Section 3900 of the Family Code, the superior court in the county where the child resides is the proper court for the trial of the action. . . .
- . . . [I]f a defendant has contracted to perform an obligation in a particular county, the superior court in the county where the obligation is to be performed, where the contract in fact was entered into, or where the defendant or any defendant resides at the commencement of the action is a proper court for the trial of an action founded on that obligation, and the county where the obligation is incurred is the county where it is to be performed, unless there is a special contract in writing to the contrary. . . .

§ 395.5. Venue, proper court (actions against corporations) (CCP)

A corporation or association may be sued in the county where the contract is made or is to be performed, or where the obligation or liability arises, or the breach occurs; or in the county where the principal place of business of such corporation is situated, subject to the power of the court to change the place of trial as in other cases.

Venue When Suing Corporations

§ 397. Venue, change of place of trial, grounds

The court may, on motion, change the place of trial in the following cases:

Change of Venue

(a) When the court designated in the complaint is not the proper court.

(b) When there is reason to believe that an impartial trial cannot be had therein.

(c) When the convenience of witnesses and the ends of justice would be promoted by the change. . . .

§ 402(a). Venue, place of trial, local rules

(a) Except as otherwise provided by law:

(1) A superior court may specify by local rule the locations where certain types of actions or proceedings are to be filed. . . .

(3) A superior court may not dismiss a case, and the clerk may not reject a case for filing, because it is filed, or a person seeks to file it, in a court location other than the location specified by local rule. However, the court may transfer the case on its own motion to the proper court location. . . .

PLEADINGS: GENERAL

§ 92. Pleadings; answer; motions (CCP)

(a) The pleadings allowed are complaints, answers, cross-complaints, answers to cross-complaints and general demurrers.

Pleadings that are Allowed

(b) The answer need not be verified, even if the complaint or cross-complaint is verified.

(c) Special demurrers are not allowed.

(d) Motions to strike are allowed only on the ground that the damages or relief sought are not supported by the allegations of the complaint.

(e) Except as limited by this section, all other motions are permitted.

PLEADINGS: FORMAT REQUIRED

Rule 201. Pleadings: Form of papers presented for filing (CRC)

(a) As used in this rule: (1) "Papers" includes all documents, except exhibits or copies of documents, that are offered for filing in any case; but it does not include Judicial Council and local court forms, records on appeal in limited civil cases, or briefs filed in appellate divisions. (2) "Recycled" as applied to paper means "recycled paper product" as defined by section 42202 of the Public Resources Code.

Papers Defined

(b) (1) The use of recycled paper is required for . . . [a]ll original papers filed with the court and all copies of papers, documents, and exhibits, whether filed with the court or served on other parties. . . .

(c) (1) All papers must be typewritten or printed or be prepared by a photocopying or other duplication process that will produce clear and permanent copies equally as legible as printing in type not smaller than 12 points, on opaque, unglazed paper, white or unbleached, of standard quality not less than 20-pound weight, 8 1/2 by 11 inches.

Type Size and Font

(2) The typeface must be essentially equivalent to Courier, Times Roman, or Helvetica.

(3) The color of print must be blue-black or black.

(d) (1) Only one side of the paper may be used, and the lines on each page must be one and one-half spaced or double spaced and numbered consecutively.

(2) Descriptions of real property may be single spaced and footnotes, quotations, and printed forms of corporate surety bonds and undertakings may be single spaced and have unnumbered lines. . . .

(3) The left margin must be at least one inch from the left edge of the paper and the right margin at least 1/2 inch from the right edge of the paper.

Required Margins

(4) Line numbers must be placed at the left margin and separated from the text of the paper by a vertical column of space at least 1/5 inch wide or a single or double vertical line. Each line number must be aligned with a line of type or the line numbers must be evenly spaced vertically on the page. Line numbers must be consecutively numbered beginning with the number 1 on each page. There must be at least three line numbers for every vertical inch on the page.

(e) [Page numbering and hole punching]

(1) Each page must be numbered consecutively at the bottom.

(2) Each paper must consist entirely of original pages without riders, and must be firmly bound together at the top.

(3) Exhibits may be fastened to pages of the specified size and, when prepared by a machine copying process, must be equal to typewritten material in legibility and permanency of image.

(4) Each paper presented for filing must contain two pre-punched normal-sized holes, centered 2 1/2 inches apart, and 5/8 inch from the top of the paper.

(f) The first page of each paper must be in the following form:

The First Page of Each Paper

(1) In the space commencing 1 inch from the top of the page with line 1, to the left of the center of the page, the name, office address or, if none, residence address, telephone number, fax number and e-mail address (if provided), and State Bar membership number of the attorney for the party in whose behalf the paper is presented, or of the party if he or she is appearing in person; but the name, office address, telephone number, and State Bar membership number of the attorney printed on the page is sufficient. Inclusion of a fax number or e-mail address on any document is optional, and its inclusion does not constitute consent to service by fax or e-mail unless otherwise provided by law.

(2) In the first 2 inches of space between lines 1 and 7 to the right of the center of the page, a blank space for the use of the clerk.

(3) On line 8, at or below 3 1/3 inches from the top of the paper, the title of the court.

(4) Below the title of the court, in the space to the left of the center of the page, the title of the case. In the title of the case on each initial complaint or cross-complaint, the name of each party must commence on a separate line beginning at the left margin of the page. On any subsequent pleading or paper, it is sufficient in the title of the case to (1) state the name of the first party on each side, with appropriate indication of other parties, and (2) state that a cross-action or cross-actions are involved, if applicable.

(5) To the right of and opposite the title, the number of the case.

(6) Below the number of the case, the nature of the paper and, on all complaints and petitions,

the character of the action or proceeding. In a case having multiple parties, any answer, response, or opposition must specifically identify the complaining, propounding, or moving party and the complaint, motion, or other matter being answered or opposed.

(7) Below the nature of the paper or the character of the action or proceeding, the name of the judge and department, if any, to which the case is assigned.

(8) Below the nature of the paper or the character of the action or proceeding, the word "Referee:" followed by the name of the referee, on any paper filed in a case pending before a referee appointed pursuant to Code of Civil Procedure section 638 or 639.

(9) On the complaint, petition, or application filed in a limited civil case, below the character of the action or proceeding, the amount demanded in the complaint, petition, or application, stated as follows: "Amount demanded exceeds $10,000" or "Amount demanded does not exceed $10,000," as required by Government Code section 72055.

(10) In the caption of every pleading and every other paper filed in a limited civil case, the words: "Limited Civil Case," as required by Code of Civil Procedure section 422.30(b).

(11) If a case is reclassified by an amended complaint, cross-complaint, amended cross-complaint, or other pleading under Code of Civil Procedure section 403.020 or 403.030, the caption must indicate that the action or proceeding is reclassified by this pleading . . . The caption or title must state that the case is a limited civil case reclassified as an unlimited civil case, or an unlimited civil case reclassified as a limited civil case, or other words to that effect.

(g) [Footer] Except for exhibits, each paper filed with the court must bear a footer in the bottom margin of each page, placed below the page number and divided from the rest of the document page by a printed line. The footer must contain the title of the paper (examples: "Complaint," "XYZ Corp.'s Motion for Summary Judgment") or some clear and concise abbreviation. The title of the paper must be in at least 10-point type.

Required Footers

(h) Additions, deletions, or interlineations must be initialed by the clerk or judge at the time of filing. All copies served must conform to the original filed, including the numbering of lines, pagination, additions, deletions, and interlineations.

(i) Each separately stated cause of action, count, or defense must be separately numbered.

(j) [Acceptance for filing] The clerk of the court must not accept for filing or file any papers that do not comply with this rule, except:

(1) The clerk must not reject a paper for filing solely on the ground that it is handwritten or handprinted or that the handwriting or handprinting is in a color other than blue-black or black.

(2) For good cause shown, the court may permit the filing of papers that do not comply with this rule.

PLEADINGS: COMPLAINT (Statement of Facts)

§ 425.10. Statement of facts; demand for judgment (CCP)

(a) A complaint or cross-complaint shall contain both of the following:

Statement of Facts

(1) A statement of the facts constituting the cause of action, in ordinary and concise language.

(2) A demand for judgment for the relief to which the pleader claims to be entitled. If the recovery of money or damages is demanded, the amount demanded shall be stated.

(b) Notwithstanding subdivision (a), where an action is brought to recover actual or punitive damages for personal injury or wrongful death, the amount demanded shall not be stated, but the complaint shall comply with Section 422.30 and, in a limited civil case, with subdivision (b) of Section 70613 of the Government Code.

PLEADINGS: SUBSCRIPTION AND VERIFICATION OF PLEADINGS

§ 446(a). Subscription of pleadings; necessity of verification (CCP)

Every pleading shall be subscribed by the party or his or her attorney. When the state [or unit thereof] . . . is plaintiff, the answer shall be verified, unless an admission of the truth of the complaint might subject the party to a criminal prosecution, or, unless a county thereof, city, school district, district, public agency, or public corporation, or an officer of the state, or of any county, city, school district, district, public agency, or public corporation, in his or her official capacity, is defendant. When the complaint is verified, the answer shall be verified.

Subscription of Pleadings

In all cases of a verification of a pleading, the affidavit of the party shall state that the same is true of his own knowledge, except as to the matters which are therein stated on his or her information

Verification of Pleadings

or belief, and as to those matters that he or she believes it to be true; and where a pleading is verified, it shall be by the affidavit of a party, unless the parties are absent from the county where the attorney has his or her office, or from some cause unable to verify it, or the facts are within the knowledge of his or her attorney or other person verifying the same. When the pleading is verified by the attorney, or any other person except one of the parties, he or she shall set forth in the affidavit the reasons why it is not made by one of the parties.

When a corporation is a party, the verification may be made by any officer thereof. . . .

PLEADINGS: QUESTIONNAIRES SERVED WITH COMPLAINT

§ 93. Questionnaires served with complaint (CCP)

Case Questionnaires

(a) The plaintiff has the option to serve case questionnaires with the complaint, using forms approved by the Judicial Council. The questionnaires served shall include a completed copy of the plaintiff's completed case questionnaire, and a blank copy of the defendant's case questionnaire.

(b) Any defendant upon whom a case questionnaire is served shall serve a completed defendant's case questionnaire upon the requesting plaintiff with the answer.

(c) The case questionnaire shall be designed to elicit fundamental information about each party's case, including names and addresses of all witnesses with knowledge of any relevant facts, a list of all documents relevant to the case, a statement of the nature and amount of damages, and information covering insurance coverages, injuries and treating physicians. The Judicial Council shall design and develop forms for case questionnaires. . . .

PLEADINGS: ANSWER

431.30. Answer; contents; information and belief (CCP)

Answers to Complaints

(b) The answer to a complaint shall contain:

(1) The general or specific denial of the material allegations of the complaint controverted by the defendant.

(2) A statement of any new matter constituting a defense.

(c) Affirmative relief may not be claimed in the answer. . . .

(e) If the defendant has no information or belief upon the subject sufficient to enable him or her to answer an allegation of the complaint, he or she may so state in his or her answer and place his or her denial on that ground.

Information or Belief

(f) The denials of the allegations controverted may be stated by reference to specific paragraphs or parts of the complaint; or by express admission of certain allegations of the complaint with a general denial of all of the allegations not so admitted; or by denial of certain allegations upon information and belief, or for lack of sufficient information or belief, with a general denial of all allegations not so denied or expressly admitted.

Statement of Defenses

(g) The defenses shall be separately stated, and the several defenses shall refer to the causes of action which they are intended to answer, in a manner by which they may be intelligibly distinguished.

STATUTE OF LIMITATIONS

§ 335. Periods of limitation prescribed (CCP)

Statutes of Limitations

The periods prescribed for the commencement of actions other than for the recovery of real property, are as follows:

- Within two years: An action for assault, battery, or injury to, or for the death of, an individual caused by the wrongful act or neglect of another. (CCP § 335.1)
- Within four years: An action upon any contract, obligation or liability founded upon an instrument in writing, except as provided in § 336a of this code. . . . (CCP § 337)

SUMMONS

412.20. Summons; formalities; contents (CCP)

Summons

(a) Except as otherwise required by statute, a summons shall be directed to the defendant, signed by the clerk and issued under the seal of the court in which the action is pending, and it shall contain:

(1) The title of the court in which the action is pending.

(2) The names of the parties to the action.

(3) A direction that the defendant file with the court a written pleading in response to the complaint within 30 days after summons is served on him or her.

Default Judgment

(4) A notice that, unless the defendant so responds, his or her default will be entered upon application by the plaintiff, and the plaintiff may apply to the court for the relief demanded in the complaint, which could result in garnishment of wages, taking of money or property, or other relief.

(5) The following statement in boldface type: "You may seek the advice of an attorney in any matter connected with the complaint or this summons. Such attorney should be consulted promptly so that your pleading may be filed or entered within the time required by this summons."

(6) The following introductory legend at the top of the summons above all other matter, in boldface type, in English and Spanish: "Notice! You have been sued. The court may decide against you without your being heard unless you respond within 30 days. Read information below."...

SERVICE OF PROCESS

§ 414.10. Service of process: authorized persons (CCP)

A summons may be served by any person who is at least 18 years of age and not a party to the action.

Service of Process

§ 415.20(a). Service of process: leaving copy of summons and complaint; mailing (CCP)

In lieu of personal delivery of a copy of the summons and complaint to the person to be served . . . , a summons may be served by leaving a copy of the summons and complaint during usual office hours in his or her office or, if no physical address is known, at his or her usual mailing address, other than a United States Postal Service post office box, with the person who is apparently in charge thereof, and by thereafter mailing a copy of the summons and complaint by first-class mail, postage prepaid to the person to be served at the place where a copy of the summons and complaint were left. When service is effected by leaving a copy of the summons and complaint at a mailing address, it shall be left with a person at least 18 years of age, who shall be informed of the contents thereof. Service of a summons in this manner is deemed complete on the 10th day after the mailing. . . .

Substituted Service

DISCOVERY: SCOPE OF DISCOVERY

§ 2017.010. Persons entitled to discovery; matters discoverable (CCP)

Unless otherwise limited by order of the court in accordance with this title, any party may obtain discovery regarding any matter, not privileged, that is relevant to the subject matter involved in the pending action or to the determination of any motion made in that action, if the matter either is itself admissible in evidence or appears reasonably calculated to lead to the discovery of admissible evidence. Discovery may relate to the claim or defense of the party seeking discovery or of any other party to the action. Discovery may be obtained of the identity and location of persons having knowledge of any discoverable matter, as well as of the existence, description, nature, custody, condition, and location of any document, tangible thing, or land or other property.

What Is Discoverable

DISCOVERY: ELECTRONIC MEANS

§ 2017.710. Technology defined (CCP)

Subject to the . . . purpose of permitting and encouraging cost-effective and efficient discovery, "technology," as used in this chapter, includes, but is not limited to, telephone, e-mail, CD-ROM, Internet Web sites, electronic documents, electronic document depositories, Internet depositions and storage, videoconferencing, and other electronic technology that may be used to improve communication and the discovery process.

Internet Depositions and Other Use of Technology

§ 2017.710(d). Technology defined (CCP)

Pursuant to an order authorizing the use of technology in conducting discovery, discovery may be conducted and maintained in electronic media and by electronic communication. The court may enter orders prescribing procedures relating to the use of electronic technology in conducting discovery, including orders for service of discovery requests and responses, service and presentation of motions, conduct of discovery in electronic media, and production, storage, and access to information in electronic form.

DISCOVERY: WORK-PRODUCT RULE

§ 2018.020. Policy of the state (CCP)

It is the policy of the state to do both of the following:

(a) Preserve the rights of attorneys to prepare cases for trial with that degree of privacy necessary to encourage them to prepare their cases thoroughly and to investigate not only the favorable but the unfavorable aspects of those cases.

Attorney Work Product

(b) Prevent attorneys from taking undue advantage of their adversary's industry and efforts.

§ 2018.030. Writings and written documentation (CCP)

(a) A writing that reflects an attorney's impressions, conclusions, opinions, or legal research or theories is not discoverable under any circumstances.

(b) The work product of an attorney, other than a writing described in subdivision (a), is not discoverable unless the court determines that denial of discovery will unfairly prejudice the party seeking discovery in preparing that party's claim or defense or will result in an injustice.

DISCOVERY: METHODS

§ 2019.010. Approved methods of discovery (CCP)

Methods of Discovery

Any party may obtain discovery by one or more of the following methods:

(a) Oral and written depositions.

(b) Interrogatories to a party.

(c) Inspections of documents, things, and places.

(d) Physical and mental examinations.

(e) Requests for admissions.

(f) Simultaneous exchanges of expert trial witness information.

DISCOVERY: DEPOSITION

§ 2025.010. Persons and entities within the state subject to deposition (CCP)

Oral Depositions

Any party may obtain discovery . . . by taking in California the oral deposition of any person, including any party to the action. The person deposed may be a natural person, an organization such as a public or private corporation, a partnership, an association, or a governmental agency.

§ 2028.010. Procedures applicable (CCP)

Depositions by Written Questions

Any party may obtain discovery by taking a deposition by written questions instead of by oral examination. Except as modified in this chapter, the procedures for taking oral depositions . . . apply to written depositions.

DISCOVERY: INTERROGATORIES

§ 2030.010. Scope of discovery; restrictions (CCP)

Interrogatories

(a) Any party may obtain discovery . . . by propounding to any other party to the action written interrogatories to be answered under oath.

(b) An interrogatory may relate to whether another party is making a certain contention, or to the facts, witnesses, and writings on which a contention is based. An interrogatory is not objectionable because an answer to it involves an opinion or contention that relates to fact or the application of law to fact, or would be based on information obtained or legal theories developed in anticipation of litigation or in preparation for trial.

§ 2030.220. Answers in response (CCP)

(a) Each answer in a response to interrogatories shall be as complete and straightforward as the information reasonably available to the responding party permits.

(b) If an interrogatory cannot be answered completely, it shall be answered to the extent possible.

(c) If the responding party does not have personal knowledge sufficient to respond fully to an interrogatory, that party shall so state, but shall make a reasonable and good faith effort to obtain the information by inquiry to other natural persons or organizations, except where the information is equally available to the propounding party.

DISCOVERY: INSPECTION, COPYING, AND TESTING

§ 2031.010. Persons subject to demand (CCP)

Inspection, Copying, and Testing

(a) Any party may obtain discovery . . . by inspecting documents, tangible things, and land or other property that are in the possession, custody, or control of any other party to the action.

(b) A party may demand that any other party produce and permit the party making the demand, or someone acting on that party's behalf, to inspect and to copy a document that is in the possession, custody, or control of the party on whom the demand is made.

(c) A party may demand that any other party produce and permit the party making the demand, or someone acting on that party's behalf, to inspect and to photograph, test, or sample any tangible things that are in the possession, custody, or control of the party on whom the demand is made.

(d) A party may demand that any other party allow the party making the demand, or someone acting on that party's behalf, to enter on any land or other property that is in the possession, custody, or control of the party on whom the demand is made, and to inspect and to measure, survey, photograph, test, or sample the land or other property, or any designated object or operation on it.

DISCOVERY: PHYSICAL OR MENTAL EXAMINATION

§ 2032.020. Persons subject to discovery (CCP)

Physical or Mental Examination

(a) Any party may obtain discovery . . . by means of a physical or mental examination of (1) a party to the action, (2) an agent of any party, or (3) a natural person in the custody or under the legal control of a party, in any action in which the mental or physical condition (including the blood group) of that party or other person is in controversy in the action.

(b) A physical examination conducted under this chapter shall be performed only by a licensed physician or other appropriate licensed health care practitioner.

(c) A mental examination conducted under this chapter shall be performed only by a licensed physician, or by a licensed clinical psychologist who holds a doctoral degree in psychology and has had at least five years of postgraduate experience in the diagnosis of emotional and mental disorders.

§ 2032.510. Attendance at examination (CCP)

(a) The attorney for the examinee or . . . that attorney's representative, shall be permitted to attend and observe any physical examination conducted for discovery purposes, and to record stenographically or by audiotape any words spoken to or by the examinee during any phase of the examination. . . .

Observing the Physical Examination

(c) If an attorney's representative is to serve as the observer, the representative shall be authorized to so act by a writing subscribed by the attorney which identifies the representative.

(d) If in the judgment of the observer the examiner becomes abusive to the examinee or undertakes to engage in unauthorized diagnostic tests and procedures, the observer may suspend it to enable the party being examined or producing the examinee to make a motion for a protective order. . . .

DISCOVERY: REQUESTS FOR ADMISSIONS

§ 2033.010. Persons subject to admission requests (CCP)

Any party may obtain discovery . . . by a written request that any other party to the action admit the genuineness of specified documents, or the truth of specified matters of fact, opinion relating to fact, or application of law to fact. A request for admission may relate to a matter that is in controversy between the parties.

Requests for Admission

§ 2033.220. Scope of response (CCP)

(a) Each answer in a response to requests for admission shall be as complete and straightforward as the information reasonably available to the responding party permits.

(b) Each answer shall:

(1) Admit so much of the matter involved in the request as is true, either as expressed in the request itself or as reasonably and clearly qualified by the responding party.

(2) Deny so much of the matter involved in the request as is untrue. . . .

(c) If a responding party gives lack of information or knowledge as a reason for a failure to admit all or part of a request for admission, that party shall state in the answer that a reasonable inquiry concerning the matter in the particular request has been made, and that the information known or readily obtainable is insufficient to enable that party to admit the matter.

DISCOVERY: SIMULTANEOUS EXCHANGE OF INFORMATION

§ 2034.210. Simultaneous exchange of information (CCP)

After the setting of the initial trial date for the action, any party may obtain discovery by demanding that all parties simultaneously exchange information concerning each other's expert trial witnesses to the following extent:

Simultaneous Exchange of Information

(a) Any party may demand a mutual and simultaneous exchange by all parties of a list containing the name and address of any natural person, including one who is a party, whose oral or deposition testimony in the form of an expert opinion any party expects to offer in evidence at the trial.

(b) If any expert designated by a party under subdivision (a) is a party or an employee of a party, or has been retained by a party for the purpose of forming and expressing an opinion in anticipation of the litigation or in preparation for the trial of the action, the designation of that witness shall include or be accompanied by an expert witness declaration under Section 2034.260.

(c) Any party may also include a demand for the mutual and simultaneous production for inspection and copying of all discoverable reports and writings, if any, made by any expert described in subdivision (b) in the course of preparing that expert's opinion.

DISCOVERY: PROTECTIVE ORDERS AND SANCTIONS

§ 2017.020. Judicial limits upon discovery (CCP)

(a) The court shall limit the scope of discovery if it determines that the burden, expense, or intrusiveness of that discovery clearly outweighs the likelihood that the information sought will lead to the discovery of admissible evidence. The court may make this determination pursuant to a motion for protective order by a party or other affected person. . . .

Protective Order

(b) The court shall impose a monetary sanction . . . against any party, person, or attorney who unsuccessfully makes or opposes a motion for a protective order, unless it finds that the one subject to the sanction acted with substantial justification or that other circumstances make the imposition of the sanction unjust.

§ 2023.101. Conduct subject to sanctions

Sanctions

Misuses of the discovery process include, but are not limited to, the following:

(a) Persisting, over objection and without substantial justification, in an attempt to obtain information or materials that are outside the scope of permissible discovery.

(b) Using a discovery method in a manner that does not comply with its specified procedures.

(c) Employing a discovery method in a manner or to an extent that causes unwarranted annoyance, embarrassment, or oppression, or undue burden and expense.

(d) Failing to respond or to submit to an authorized method of discovery.

(e) Making, without substantial justification, an unmeritorious objection to discovery.

(f) Making an evasive response to discovery.

(g) Disobeying a court order to provide discovery.

(h) Making or opposing, unsuccessfully and without substantial justification, a motion to compel or to limit discovery.

(i) Failing to confer in person, by telephone, or by letter with an opposing party or attorney in a reasonable and good faith attempt to resolve informally any dispute concerning discovery, if the section governing a particular discovery motion requires the filing of a declaration stating facts showing that an attempt at informal resolution has been made.

SUMMARY JUDGMENT

§ 437c. Grounds for and effect of summary judgment

(a) Any party may move for summary judgment in any action or proceeding if it is contended that the action has no merit or that there is no defense to the action or proceeding. The motion may be made at any time after 60 days have elapsed since the general appearance in the action or proceeding of each party against whom the motion is directed or at any earlier time after the general appearance that the court, with or without notice and upon good cause shown, may direct. Notice of the motion and supporting papers shall be served on all other parties to the action at least 75 days before the time appointed for hearing. However, if the notice is served by mail, the required 75-day period of notice shall be increased by five days if the place of address is within the State of California, 10 days if the place of address is outside the State of California but within the United States, and 20 days if the place of address is outside the United States, and if the notice is served by facsimile transmission, Express Mail, or another method of delivery providing for overnight delivery, the required 75-day period of notice shall be increased by two court days. The motion shall be heard no later than 30 days before the date of trial, unless the court for good cause orders otherwise. The filing of the motion shall not extend the time within which a party must otherwise file a responsive pleading.

D. More Information

California Code of Civil Procedure
www.leginfo.ca.gov/calaw.html

California Court Rules
www.courtinfo.ca.gov/rules
www.courtinfo.ca.gov/rules/titleone

Judicial Council Forms
www.courtinfo.ca.gov/forms

General
www.courtinfo.ca.gov/selfhelp
www.scselfservice.org/civ/general/plaintiff.htm
www.placercourts.org/ftp/handout/HandoutCivil.pdf
www.glenncourt.ca.gov/court_info/self_help.html

E. Something to Check

1. Go to the site that gives you access to Judicial Council forms (*www.courtinfo.ca.gov/forms*). Maker a list of the forms that are relevant to the statutes and rules excerpted in this section.
2. Go to the site that contains the Code of Civil Procedure (*www.leginfo.ca.gov/calaw.html*). Do a search for any three topics covered in the statutes excerpted in this section. Look for *additional* statutes on these topics. Summarize what you find.

6.3 State and Federal Civil Litigation in California: Some Comparisons

A. Introduction

Overviews of state court jurisdiction and civil litigation are presented in sections 4.2, 6.1, and 6.2. Federal courts sitting in California are discussed in section 4.3. In this section, we will briefly outline some comparisons between litigating civil cases in California courts and in the federal courts. Criminal cases are covered in sections 6.4 and 7.6.

Abbreviations

EC: California Evidence Code

FRCP: Federal Rules of Civil Procedure

CCP: California Code of Civil Procedure

USC: United States Code

B. Comparisons

Some comparisons between state and federal civil litigation are presented in Exhibit 6.3A.

EXHIBIT 6.3A State and Federal Civil Litigation: Some Points of Comparison

State Litigation	Federal Litigation
Major courts California Supreme Court California Court of Appeal California Superior Court Superior Court Appellate Division Small Claims Court	Major courts Supreme Court of the United States United States Courts of Appeals United States District Courts United States Immigration Courts United States Court of Int'l Trade United States Court of Federal Claims United States Court of Appeals for the Armed Services United States Tax Court United States Court of Appeals for Veterans Claims Judicial Panel on Multidistrict Litigation
Subject-matter jurisdiction Limited civil cases ($25,000 or less) Unlimited civil cases (over $25,000) (CCP §§ 85, 88)	Subject-matter jurisdiction Federal questions Diversity cases (over $75,000) (28 USC §§ 1331; 1332)
Venue Local actions (e.g., foreclosure action in the county where the land is located; dissolution of marriage action in the county of the petitioner's residence) Transitory actions (e.g., contract action in the county where the contract was entered or is to be performed) (CCP §§ 392, 395)	Venue Examples: District where a substantial part of the events or omissions giving rise to the claim occurred or where the property in dispute is located Any district if the defendant is an alien (28 USC § 1391)
Forum non conveniens When a court upon motion of a party or its own motion finds that in the interest of substantial justice an action should be heard in a forum outside this state, the court shall stay or dismiss the action in whole or in part on any conditions that may be just. CCP § 410.30(a)	Forum non conveniens For the convenience of parties and witnesses, in the interest of justice, a district court may transfer any civil action to any other district or division where it might have been brought. (28 USC § 1404(a))
Joinder of parties Compulsory (e.g., CCP § 389) Permissive (e.g., CCP § 378)	Joinder of parties Compulsory (FRCP 19) Permissive (FRCP 20)

State Litigation	Federal Litigation
Complaint Fact Pleading. A complaint shall contain (1) A statement of the facts constituting the cause of action, in ordinary and concise language. (2) A demand for judgment for the relief to which the pleader claims to be entitled. If the recovery of money or damages is demanded, the amount demanded shall be stated. (CCP § 425.10)	Complaint Notice Pleading. A pleading which sets forth a claim for relief shall contain a "short and plain statement" of the claim showing that the pleader is entitled to relief, and a demand for judgment for the relief the pleader seeks. Relief in the alternative or of several different types may be demanded. (FRCP 8(a)) "Each averment of a pleading shall be simple, concise, and direct. No technical forms of pleading or motions are required." (FRCP (8)(e)(1))
Caption (a) Every pleading shall contain a caption setting forth: (1) The name of the court and county in which the action is brought. (2) The title of the action. (b) In a limited civil case, the caption shall state that the case is a limited civil case, and the clerk shall classify the case accordingly. (CCP § 422.30) In the complaint, the title of the action shall include the names of all the parties; but, except as otherwise provided by statute or rule of the Judicial Council, in other pleadings it is sufficient to state the name of the first party on each side with an appropriate indication of other parties. (CCP. § 422.40)	Caption Every pleading shall contain a caption setting forth the name of the court, the title of the action, the file number, and a designation as in Rule 7(a). In the complaint the title of the action shall include the names of all the parties, but in other pleadings it is sufficient to state the name of the first party on each side with an appropriate indication of other parties. (FRCP 10(a))
Statement of damages Where an action is brought to recover actual or punitive damages for personal injury or wrongful death, the amount demanded shall not be stated. (CCP § 425.10)	Statement of damages When items of special damage are claimed, they shall be specifically stated. (FRCP 9(g))
Subscription Every pleading shall be subscribed by the party or his or her attorney. (CCP § 446)	Subscription Every pleading, written motion, and other paper shall be signed by at least one attorney of record in the attorney's individual name, or, if the party is not represented by an attorney, shall be signed by the party. (FRCP 11)
Time limit for service Local rules may provide that the action will be dismissed if the summons and complaint are not served on the defendant within a specified time, e.g., 60 or 90 days after filing the complaint.	Time limit for service If service of the summons and complaint is not made upon a defendant within 120 days after the filing of the complaint, the court, upon motion or on its own initiative after notice to the plaintiff, shall dismiss the action without prejudice as to that defendant or direct that service be effected within a specified time. (FRCP 4(m))
Answer The answer to a complaint shall contain: (1) The general or specific denial of the material allegations of the complaint controverted by the defendant. (2) A statement of any new matter constituting a defense. Affirmative relief may not be claimed in the answer. (CCP § 431.30(b)(c))	Answer A party shall state in short and plain terms the party's defenses to each claim asserted and shall admit or deny the averments upon which the adverse party relies. (FRCP 8(b)) Each averment of a pleading shall be simple, concise, and direct. No technical forms of pleading or motions are required." (FRCP (8)(e)(1))
Time limit for answer Except as otherwise required by statute, a summons shall contain a direction that the defendant file with the court a written pleading in response to the complaint within 30 days after summons is served on him or her. (CCP § 412.20(a))	Time limit for answer Unless a different time is prescribed in a statute of the United States, a defendant shall serve an answer within 20 days after being served with the summons and complaint. (FRCP 12(a)(1))
Amendments to pleadings Any pleading may be amended once by the party of course, and without costs, at any time before the answer or demurrer is filed, or after demurrer and before the trial of the issue of law thereon, by filing the same as amended and serving a copy on the adverse party, and the time in which the adverse party must respond thereto shall be computed from the date of notice of the amendment. (CCP § 472)	Amendments to pleadings A party may amend the party's pleading once as a matter of course at any time before a responsive pleading is served or, if the pleading is one to which no responsive pleading is permitted and the action has not been placed upon the trial calendar, the party may so amend it at any time within 20 days after it is served. (FRCP 15(a))
What is discoverable: scope of discovery Any party may obtain discovery regarding any matter, not privileged,	What is discoverable: scope of discovery Parties may obtain discovery regarding any matter, not privileged, that is

State Litigation	Federal Litigation
that is relevant to the subject matter involved in the pending action or to the determination of any motion made in that action, if the matter either is itself admissible in evidence or appears reasonably calculated to lead to the discovery of admissible evidence. Discovery may be obtained of the identity and location of persons having knowledge of any discoverable matter, as well as of the existence, description, nature, custody, condition, and location of any document, tangible thing, or land or other property. (CCP § 2017.010)	relevant to the claim or defense of any party, including the existence, description, nature, custody, condition, and location of any books, documents, or other tangible things and the identity and location of persons having knowledge of any discoverable matter. For good cause, the court may order discovery of any matter relevant to the subject matter involved in the action. Relevant information need not be admissible at the trial if the discovery appears reasonably calculated to lead to the discovery of admissible evidence. (FRCP Rule 26(b))
Work-product rule (a) A writing that reflects an attorney's impressions, conclusions, opinions, or legal research or theories is not discoverable under any circumstances. (b) The work product of an attorney, other than a writing described in subdivision (a), is not discoverable unless the court determines that denial of discovery will unfairly prejudice the party seeking discovery in preparing that party's claim or defense or will result in an injustice. (CCP 2018.030)	Work-product rule A party may obtain discovery of documents and tangible things prepared in anticipation of litigation or for trial by or for another party only upon a showing that the party seeking discovery has substantial need of the materials in the preparation of the party's case and that the party is unable without undue hardship to obtain the substantial equivalent of the materials by other means. (FRCP 26(b)(3))
Attorney-client privilege A client has a privilege to refuse to disclose, and to prevent another from disclosing, a confidential communication between client and lawyer if the privilege is claimed by the holder of the privilege or the person who was the lawyer at the time of the confidential communication. (EC § 954)	Attorney-client privilege Under the doctrine of attorney-client privilege, confidential communications between a client and an attorney for the purpose of obtaining legal advice are privileged. A court cannot compel revelation of these communications through discovery or testimony in civil or criminal matters. *Denius v. Dunlap* 209 F.3d 944, 952 (7th Cir. 2000)
Methods of discovery Interrogatories (CCP § 2030.020) Deposition (CCP § 2025.010) Requests for admissions (CCP § 2033.010) Inspection of documents, tangible things, and land or other property (CCP § 2031.010) Physical or mental examination (CCP § 2032.020)	Methods of discovery Interrogatories (FRCP 33) Deposition (FRCP 30) Requests for admissions (FRCP 36) Production of documents and things and entry on land for inspection and other purposes (FRCP 34) Physical or mental examination (FRCP 35)
Summary judgment Any party may move for summary judgment if it is contended that the action has no merit or that there is no defense to the action or proceeding. The motion may be made at any time after 60 days have elapsed since the general appearance in the action or proceeding of each party against whom the motion is directed. The motion for summary judgment shall be granted if all the papers submitted show that there is no triable issue as to any material fact and that the moving party is entitled to a judgment as a matter of law. (CCP § 437c(a)(c))	Summary judgment A party may, at any time after the expiration of 20 days from the commencement of the action move for a summary judgment. The judgment sought shall be rendered forthwith if the pleadings, depositions, answers to interrogatories, and admissions on file, together with the affidavits, if any, show that there is no genuine issue as to any material fact and that the moving party is entitled to a judgment as a matter of law. A summary judgment may be rendered on the issue of liability alone although there is a genuine issue as to the amount of damages. (FRCP 56(a)(c))
Formal planning procedures Case management conference (CRC Rule 212) Mandatory settlement conference (CRC Rule 222)	Pretrial planning procedures Pretrial conferences (FRCP 16(a-c)) Final pretrial conferences (FRCP 16(d))
Alternate dispute resolution Alternative dispute resolution process or ADR process means a process, other than formal litigation, in which a neutral person or persons resolve a dispute or assist parties in resolving their dispute. Arbitration Mediation Neutral evaluation Conciliation Settlement conference Fact-finding Minitrials Summary jury trials (CRC Rules 1580ff) (CCP § 1141.11)	Alternate dispute resolution An alternative dispute resolution process includes any process or procedure, other than an adjudication by a presiding judge, in which a neutral third party participates to assist in the resolution of issues in controversy, through processes such as early neutral evaluation, mediation, minitrial, and arbitration. Each United States district court shall authorize, by local rule the use of alternative dispute resolution processes in all civil actions. Each United States district court shall devise and implement its own alternative dispute resolution program to encourage and promote the use of alternative dispute resolution in its district. (28 USC § 651)

C. More Information

Federal Rules of Civil Procedure
www.law.cornell.edu/rules/frcp/?
www.lectlaw.com/tcrf.htm

California Code of Civil Procedure
www.leginfo.ca.gov/calaw.html

California Court Rules
www.courtinfo.ca.gov/rules

Federal Courts Overview
www.uscourts.gov/journalistguide/welcome.html

Miscellaneous
www.west.net/~smith/smjuris.htm

D. Something to Check

Using the online sites that give the text of state and federal statutes (see the sites under More Information), compare the state and federal rules on:

1. Interrogatories
2. Sanctions for failure to comply with discovery requests

6.4 Timeline: A Criminal Case in California State Court

A. Introduction

There are over seven million criminal filings in the California state courts each year consisting of felonies, misdemeanors, and infractions:

Total: 7,189,583
Felonies: 261,832
Nontraffic misdemeanors: 532,556
Nontraffic infractions: 290,261
Traffic misdemeanors: 725,585
Traffic infractions: 5,379,198

Source: Judicial Council of California, *2005 Court Statistics Report,* Table 7a, "Total Criminal Filings . . ." (2005) (*www.courtinfo.ca.gov/reference/documents/csr2005.pdf*)

In this section, we will focus on the relatively serious criminal case, in which a felony or misdemeanor is involved. Such cases can vary a great deal in complexity depending on the nature of the charge, the extent of contention between the state and the accused, and the caliber of attorneys representing both sides. With this qualification in mind, the overview presented here will apply to many serious criminal cases brought in the California state courts. See also the following related sections:

- overview of California state courts (section 4.2)
- example of a criminal complaint (section 7.5)
- overview of federal courts sitting in California (section 4.3)

B. Overview of a Criminal Case

The criminal case begins when a prosecutor files formal charges, a suspect is arrested, or a grand jury issues an indictment. Exhibit 6.4A presents an overview of a typical criminal case in the California state courts.

Crime Alleged

There are three major categories of crimes that can be committed in California: felonies, misdemeanors, and infractions.

Felony A crime punishable by a year or more in prison or by the death penalty.

Misdemeanor A crime punishable by up to a year in county jail.

Infraction A minor violation, such as many traffic violations, for which the maximum sentence is a fine. An infraction is neither a felony nor a misdemeanor.

Police

Investigation The police investigate reported crimes by collecting physical evidence and by interviewing the victim, witnesses, and suspects.

Arrest An officer may arrest a suspect without an arrest warrant if a crime is committed in the officer's presence or if he or she has probable cause to believe any felony or certain misdemeanors have been committed outside his or her presence.

Charging/warrant request The officer submits a charging/warrant request to the district attorney's office, asking that charges be authorized.

District Attorney

In most cases, the prosecutor first becomes involved in a case when he or she receives the warrant request from the police. If, however, a search warrant had been sought earlier, the prosecutor may have reviewed it.

Evaluation of warrant request The prosecutor must evaluate the warrant request to determine whether the accused should be formally charged with a crime and, if so, with what crime or crimes. The test for whether the prosecutor will file a charge is whether he or she reasonably believes that probable cause exists that the suspect committed the offense, and reasonably believes the charge can be proven beyond a reasonable doubt at trial, based on what is known about the case at the present time.

Further investigation If not enough information is available in the reports, witness statements, and whatever else the police provides, the prosecutor can send the case back to the police to request further specific investigation.

If the decision is to go forward and the suspect is not already in custody, the police may arrest him or her.

Arraignment

The arraignment is the first court appearance for anyone charged with a misdemeanor or felony. If the accused is in custody, he or she has the right to an arraignment within 48 hours of being arrested.

Complaint At the arraignment, the defendant is told what crime he or she is charged with, and is advised of the constitutional rights to a jury or court trial, appointed attorney, presumption of innocence, etc. The charging document is called a complaint. (For an example, see section 7.5.)

Bail Bail is property (e.g., money) temporarily given to ensure that an accused who is released from custody will return for future court proceedings. The court sets the amount and the conditions of bail. One condition might be that there is no contact with the victim. In some cases, release is without bail. This is known as "OR," meaning release on one's "own recognizance."

Property bond When defendants do not have enough money to post bail, the court may allow them to post a property bond. This is a pledge of real property to the court to guarantee appearance in all court proceedings. If the defendant does not come to court when he or she is supposed to, the court will take the posted property as if it were cash bail. Before the court accepts a property bond, a hearing is held to determine who the legal owner of the property is, and how much it is worth.

Counsel If a defendant charged with a felony or a misdemeanor cannot afford to hire an attorney, the court will appoint one from the public defender's office. No such appointments are made in infraction cases since they do not result in jail or prison terms.

Plea The court will ask the defendant to plead to the charges against him or her: guilty, not guilty, or, in

EXHIBIT 6.4A The Prosecution of a Criminal Case in California State Courts

CRIME ALLEGED	POLICE	DISTRICT ATTORNEY	ARRAIGNMENT	DISCOVERY	PRELIMINARY HEARING	SECOND ARRAIGNMENT	PRETRIAL HEARINGS	TRIAL	APPEAL
• Felony • Misdemeanor • Infraction	• Investigation • Arrest • Charging/warrant request	• Evaluation of warrant request • Further investigation	• Complaint • Bail • Property bond • Counsel • Plea • Guilty plea • Not guilty plea • Grand jury indictment	• Informal • Mandatory disclosures	• Burden on the state • "Bound over"	• Information • Plea	• Motions • Ground rules	• Jury selection • Opening statements • State's case • Defense's case • Rebuttal • Closing statements • Jury instructions • Verdict • Probation report • Sentencing	• Notice of appeal • Appellate briefs • Oral arguments • Further appeals

some cases, nolo contendere. In a plea of nolo contendere, the defendant does not contest the charges, which has the same legal effect as a guilty plea. If the defendant "stands mute" or remains silent when asked to plead, the court will treat the response as a plea of not guilty.

Guilty plea At the arraignment, if the defendant pleads guilty, the judge can impose a sentence immediately, or postpone sentencing until a sentencing recommendation is made in a probation report. The defendant must be represented by an attorney in felony cases (unless waived in a noncapital case).

Not guilty plea (a) If at the arraignment the defendant pleads not guilty to a misdemeanor, the judge will set a date for trial. (Preliminary hearings are not held for misdemeanor offenses or infractions.) The trial will be held within 30 days if the defendant is in custody or within 45 days if the defendant is not in custody, unless the defendant waives the right to a speedy trial. (b) If at the arraignment the defendant pleads not guilty to a felony, a preliminary hearing is held.

Grand jury indictment An alternative in felony cases is a grand jury indictment. California allows a prosecution to be initiated by either a criminal grand jury indictment or a preliminary hearing in court. Criminal grand juries are not often used. The most common cases for which they are used involve public officials, police officers, white collar crimes, and any other case deemed appropriate by the district attorney. If a criminal grand jury investigates allegations of a felony and indicts a defendant, a preliminary hearing is not required. Grand jury proceedings are closed to the public and may not be discussed outside the grand jury room. Once an indictment occurs, the case is referred directly to superior court for trial.

Discovery

Before trial, the parties can engage in discovery to obtain the disclosure of facts needed to prepare for trial. Under the constitution, there are certain facts (particularly exculpatory facts) that the state must discloser to the defendant.

Informal Immediately after arrest, informal discovery requests can be made. Before a party may seek court enforcement of any of the disclosures required by statute, a party must make an informal request of opposing counsel for the desired materials and information.

Mandatory disclosures Mandatory disclosures (those required by law) shall be made at least 30 days prior to the trial, unless good cause is shown why a disclosure should be denied, restricted, or deferred. If the material and information becomes known to, or comes into the possession of, a party within 30 days of trial, disclosure shall be made immediately, unless good cause is shown why a disclosure should be denied, restricted, or deferred. "Good cause" is limited to threats or possible danger to the safety of a victim or witness, possible loss or destruction of evidence, or possible compromise of other investigations by law enforcement.

Preliminary Hearing

Probable cause At the preliminary hearing, the district attorney must convince the judge that there is probable cause to believe that a crime was committed and that the defendant committed the crime. This step (or the alternative, a grand jury indictment) is necessary to make sure that only defendants against whom there is significant evidence will undergo a felony trial. (This standard of probable cause is much lower than the standard that will later be applied at the trial: proof beyond a reasonable doubt.) At the preliminary hearing, the defendant has an attorney, can cross-examine the state's witnesses, and can present his or her own evidence. If the district attorney fails to show probable cause, the judge can dismiss the case and allow the defendant to go free, or drop the charge to a misdemeanor and set the case for a trial on the reduced charge.

"Bound over" If enough evidence is presented to show probable cause that the defendant committed a felony, he or she will be "bound over" (held over) for trial, with the next step being another arraignment.

Second Arraignment

Information After the case is "bound over" for a felony trial, the defendant is again arraigned (given formal notice of the charges against him or her). The charging document is called an "information."

Plea The defendant is advised of his or her constitutional rights and enters a plea to the charge: guilty, not guilty, or stand mute.

Pretrial Hearings

Motions After arraignment, the parties may file motions requesting rulings on evidentiary matters. For example, defense counsel may file a motion to suppress evidence allegedly obtained by an illegal search and seizure.

Ground rules Case discussions may occur involving the judge, prosecutor, and defense attorney. Hearings are held on motions. All of this activity sets the parameters or ground rules for the full trial ahead. Simultaneously, efforts continue to try to resolve the case without a trial (e.g., through a plea bargain).

Trial

Criminal trials are relatively rare. Over 90 percent of the cases are disposed of by defendants' pleas of guilty. When a trial is held, the steps are often as follows:

Jury selection Twelve citizens are selected for the jury, plus alternate jurors if the trial is not expected to be brief. Sometimes, both sides agree to let the trial judge decide the case without a jury; this is called a "court trial." In a jury trial, the jury is the "trier of fact"; in a court trial, the judge is.

Opening statements The prosecutor gives an opening statement to the jury. The statement outlines what the state expects to prove. Defense counsel can then give its opening statement or can decide to give it later in the trial.

State's case The prosecutor presents its case by calling witnesses and presenting evidence. The defense can cross-examine the state's witnesses. The prosecution then rests.

Defense's case The defense presents its case by calling witnesses and presenting evidence. The prosecutor can cross-examine the defense's witnesses. The defense then rests.

Rebuttals After both sides have presented their evidence, each has a chance to present rebuttal (opposing) evidence.

Closing statements Each side then presents to the jury its closing argument, in which the attorney analyzes and interprets the evidence that was presented.

Jury instructions Finally, the judge gives the jury detailed legal instructions about the crime and explains the deliberation process they should follow in reaching a verdict.

Verdict The jury then goes to the jury room to deliberate and reach a verdict. All twelve jurors must agree on a guilty verdict.

Probation report If the jury reaches a guilty verdict in a felony case, the judge will order a probation report and schedule a sentencing hearing for 20 days later. The probation department prepares a report for the judge that summarizes the crime and gives the defendant's personal and criminal backgrounds. Generally, the victim is contacted for a recommendation of sentence. The probation officer concludes the report with a recommended sentence. A defendant found guilty of a misdemeanor can be sentenced immediately without a probation report.

Sentencing The maximum sentence for an infraction is a fine; for a misdemeanor it is up to 1 year in a county jail; and for a felony it is time in a state prison or, for some murders, death. In lieu of institutionalization, the court can release the defendant on probation under designated supervision and conditions. Some counties offer "diversion" programs that allow a judge to order a defendant to obtain medical treatment or counseling or to do community service work. The diversion program may take the place of a fine or jail sentence in certain types of misdemeanor and felony cases. The court can also order restitution to the victim.

Appeal

The defendant may appeal infraction, misdemeanor, or felony convictions. In some circumstances the state may file an appeal. Appeals of death penalty convictions are automatic. The party filing an appeal is called the appellant. The party against whom an appeal is filed is the respondent. The appeal is made to the California Court of Appeal. A further appeal may be possible to the California Supreme Court. Exhibit 6.4B outlines the process.

EXHIBIT 6.4B Appeal Process

How an Appeal Is Processed

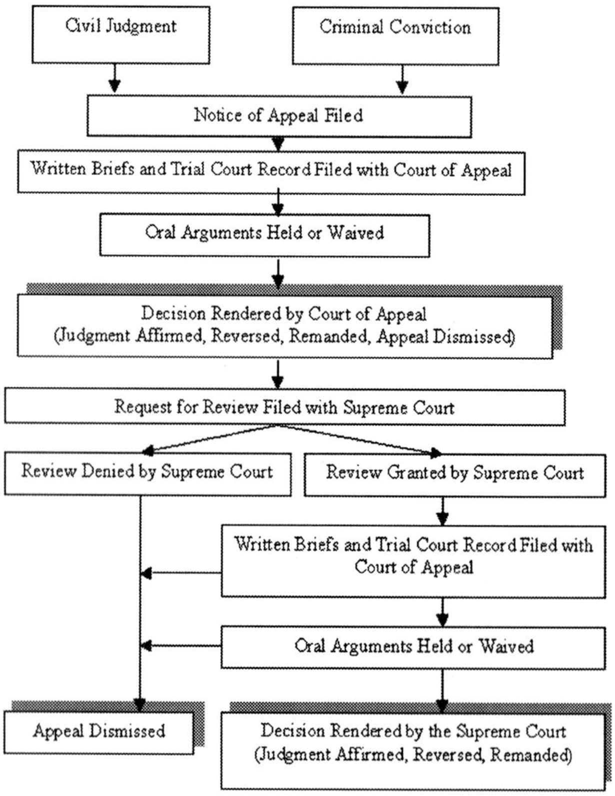

Source: www.scselfservice.org/home/overview.htm

Notice of appeal The first step in an appeal is filing the written Notice of Appeal. This notice tells the other parties in the case and the court that a party is appealing a decision of the trial court.

Appellate briefs An appellate brief is a party's written description of the facts in the case, the relevant law, and the party's argument on why the trial court's decision should be affirmed or reversed.

Oral Arguments The case is not retried on appeal. Rather, the parties are allowed to present oral arguments before one or more appellate court judges on why the trial court's decision should be affirmed or reversed. The parties, however, can waive their right to present oral arguments and rely entirely on the arguments made in their appellate briefs.

Further appeals The Court of Appeal can affirm, reverse, remand the case for further proceedings, or dismiss the appeal. After its decision, a party can file a request for review with the California Supreme Court. If granted, appellate briefs are filed and oral argument is scheduled. The court can affirm, reverse, or remand the case for further proceedings.

C. More Information

General

caag.state.ca.us
www.lasuperiorcourt.org/Criminal
www.da.saccounty.net/info/anatomy.htm
scselfservice.org/home/overview.htm
www.ocgov.com/da/text/prosecution.htm
caag.state.ca.us/publications/victimshandbk/cvhcrt.htm
www.courtinfo.ca.gov/reference/4_13crim.htm

California Penal Code

www.leginfo.ca.gov/calaw.html
(click "Penal Code")

D. Something to Check

1. Go to the Web site for the state courts in your county (see sections 4.2 and 4.6). What information or assistance does it provide for defendants, witnesses, or jurors in criminal cases?
2. Select any three general search engines (e.g., *www.google.com*) and any three legal search engines or portals (e.g., *www.findlaw.com*). Run this search: "california criminal cases". What are the different categories of results you find? Compare the six sites you used for this search.

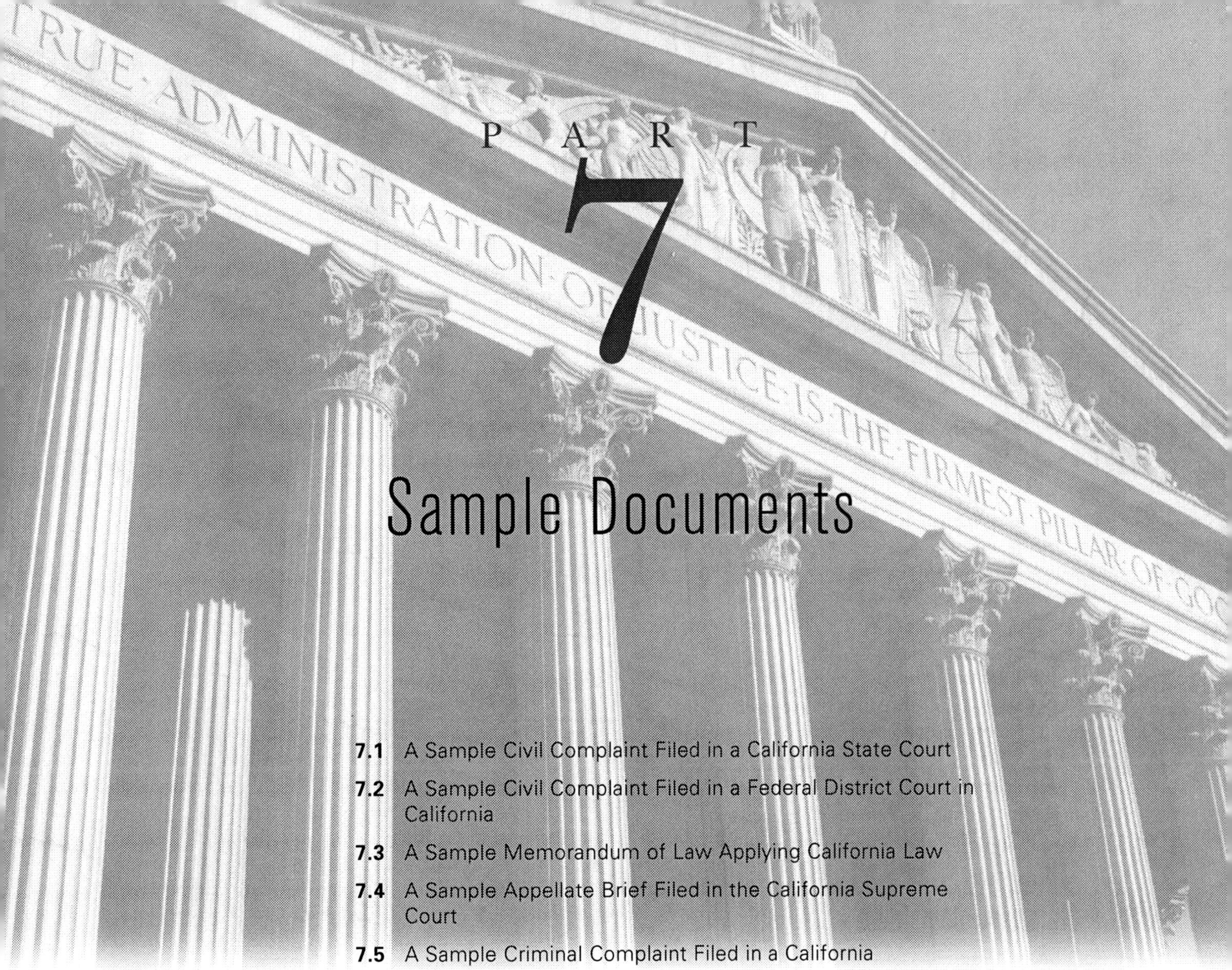

PART

7

Sample Documents

7.1 A Sample Civil Complaint Filed in a California State Court

A. Introduction

This section presents an example of a civil complaint filed in a California state superior court. The complaint is brought by Google, the search engine, for breach of contract and related tort causes of action. Compare this complaint to the sample *federal* civil complaint printed in section 7.2. See also the following related sections:

- 4.2 (overview of California state courts)
- 6.3 (some of the distinctions between state and federal civil procedure)
- 6.2 (some of the major statutes and rules covering pretrial procedures, including the drafting of complaints and other pleadings)
- 7.5 (containing a state criminal complaint)

B. A State Civil Complaint

Exhibit 7.1A contains a sample complaint filed in a state California court.

C. More Information

For more information on complaints filed in California state courts, see:

California Court Forms
www.courtinfo.ca.gov/selfhelp/forms
www.courtinfo.ca.gov/selfhelp/forms/tips.htm

Superior Court Drafting and Filing Procedures
www.courtinfo.ca.gov/courts/trial/courtlist.htm
(click the "Web Site" for your county and then look for links to forms, rules, procedures, and self-help)

D. Something to Check

1. What different kinds of complaint forms are made available by the Judicial Council of California or by any individual California court?
2. The beginning of the Google complaint tells you what attorney and law firm represented Google. Go to that law firm's Web site. Describe the kind of practice that this law firm engages in. Where did this attorney go to law school and what other kinds of cases has he worked on at the firm? (Be sure to do a search for "google" on the firm's site.)
3. Use any search engine to find information about the litigation begun by the complaint in this section. In the search engine you select, insert various combinations of party names, e.g., google "auctions expert". What happened in the case?

7.2 A Sample Civil Complaint Filed in a Federal District Court in California

A. Introduction

In this section, we look at the essential components of a civil complaint filed in a United States district court sitting in California. The complaint challenges the constitutionality of the partial-birth abortion statute. Compare this complaint to the sample civil complaint in section 7.1 filed in a state court. See also section 6.3 covering some of the distinctions between state and federal civil procedure.

For more on federal courts in California, see section 4.3.

B. A Federal Civil Complaint

Exhibit 7.2A contains a sample complaint filed in a federal court sitting in California.

C. More Information

For more information on federal complaints, see:

United States District Court Central District of California
www.cacd.uscourts.gov
(click "Filing Procedures")
(click "Forms" at top of screen, then "Civil Forms")

United States District Court Eastern District of California
www.caed.uscourts.gov/caed/staticOther/page_455.htm
(click "Local Rules", download them, and run a search for "complaint")

EXHIBIT 7.1A Sample Civil Complaint Filed in a California State Court

DAVID H. KRAMER, Esq. (State Bar No. 168452)
WILSON SONSINI GOODRICH & ROSATI
650 Page Mill Road
Palo Alto, California 94304-1050
650-493-9300

Attorneys for Plaintiff
GOOGLE INC.

SUPERIOR COURT OF THE STATE OF CALIFORNIA

SANTA CLARA COUNTY

GOOGLE INC., a Delaware corporation Plaintiff, v. AUCTIONS EXPERT INTERNATIONAL, L.L.C., a Texas Limited Liability Company, Sergio Morfin, an individual, and Alexei Leonov, an individual, and Does 1-50 Defendants	)))))))))))	Case No. 104CV030560 Complaint for Breach of Contract; Breach of Duty of Good Faith and Fair Dealing; Tortious Interference with Contract; Concealment and Fraud

November 15, 2004.

Demand for Jury Trial

Plaintiff Google Inc. ("Google") alleges on personal knowledge as to its own acts and on information and belief as to the actions of others, as follows:

THE PARTIES

1. Plaintiff Google is a Delaware corporation with its principal place of business in Mountain View, California, within Santa Clara County.

2. Defendant Auctions Expert International, L.L.C. ("Auctions Expert") is a Texas limited liability company with its principal place of business in Houston, Texas. Auctions Expert engaged in the misconduct that is the subject of this action and caused injury within Santa Clara County, California.

3. Defendant Sergio Morfin is an individual residing in Houston, Texas and is the managing member of Auctions Expert. He participated personally in the misconduct that is the subject of this action and caused injury within Santa Clara County, California.

EXHIBIT 7.1A

4. Defendant Alexei Leonov is an individual residing in Houston, Texas and is the founder and President of Auctions Expert. He participated personally in the misconduct that is the subject of this action and caused injury within Santa Clara County, California.

5. There has existed and still exists such unity of interest and ownership among and between Defendants Auctions Expert, Sergio Morfin and Alexei Leonov that the separate personalities of the company and the individuals have ceased to exist.

6. Google does not know the true identities of the defendants sued as Does 1- 50 and therefore sued them under fictitious names. Google will amend this complaint to alleged their true identities when those identities become known.

JURISDICTION AND VENUE

7. Jurisdiction in this Court is proper because each of the causes of action arises under California law and because the total amount of damages is within the jurisdiction of the Superior Court.

8. Venue in this judicial district is proper under Cal. Civ. Proc. Code § 395 because this is a judicial district in which a substantial part of the events giving rise to the claims occurred.

BACKGROUND FACTS

Google

9. Google's mission is to organize the world's information and make it universally accessible and useful. As part of that mission, Google operates a web site where users can search through publicly accessible web pages, digital images, news stories, product listings and discussion groups. Its award winning web search service responds to over 200 million queries a day at no cost to users. Google supports this endeavor through various advertising programs including AdSense Online which is the focus of this action.

Google AdSense Online

10. AdSense Online is a program through which Google and web site authors share in revenues derived from the display of unobtrusive and context-sensitive advertising appearing in connection with the authors' own web sites.

11. AdSense Online helps overcome two limitations of web site authors' ability to derive advertising value for their sites' content. Internet advertising has been beyond the reach of most small web site authors because of the cost and complexity of developing a network of advertisers and the associated billing and other customer service costs of servicing those advertisers over time. AdSense Online removes that barrier by allowing web authors to use Google's extensive advertising network with minimal extra effort and no extra expenditure.

EXHIBIT 7.1A Sample Civil Complaint Filed in a California State Court

12. Even authors who have managed to obtain advertising for their sites have realized limited revenue because such advertising is often not well targeted to the interests of visitors to their sites. For example, a web page describing travels to Italy may display an advertisement for computer hard drives. Because poorly targeted advertising is unlikely to be of interest to users, its value is low, as are payments for displaying it. Adsense Online helps authors derive more advertising revenue by providing advertisements that are targeted to the contents of a web page.

13. With Adsense Online, Google provides ads relevant to an author's page from Google's own network of advertisers. The advertiser pays Google for the user's click and Google, in turn, pays the majority of the money it receives back to the web site author.

14. For web site authors, using AdSense Online is a straightforward process. A potential web site author signs up using Google's online form. The author can then leverage Google's advertising network, its billing and customer service infrastructure, and its advanced search technology which aids in determining which ads are relevant to an individual web page.

15. Because advertisers pay Google for each click on their advertisements, Google strives to ensure that each click is generated by a user legitimately interested in accessing the site being advertised. Google strictly prohibits all web site authors participating in AdSense Online from artificially and/or fraudulently generating clicks in any manner.

<u>Defendants' Misconduct</u>

16. This case arises from Defendants' breach of the AdSense Online Agreement and abuse of the AdSense Online service.

17. In August 2003, Auctions Expert became a Google AdSense Online participant and agreed to Google's AdSense Online Terms and Conditions. Defendants then proceeded to flagrantly abuse the AdSense Online service by artificially and/or fraudulently generating ad clicks. These clicks were worthless to advertisers but generated significant and unjust revenue for Defendants who were paid by Google as if the clicks were legitimate.

18. Once Google discovered Defendants' misconduct, Google terminated their AdSense Online participation and credited advertisers for every click generated by an ad displayed on the Auctions Expert web site. Google now seeks damages and restitution from Defendants who still retain the payments Google made to them.

<u>FIRST CAUSE OF ACTION</u>

<u>Breach of Contract (Against All Defendants)</u>

19. Google realleges each and every allegation set forth in Paragraphs 1 through 18 inclusive, and incorporates them by reference herein.

EXHIBIT 7.1A

20. In August 2003, Google and Auctions Expert entered into an agreement that included Google's Standard Terms and Conditions for participation in AdSense Online (the "Agreement"), a copy of which is attached as Exhibit A.

21. Under the Agreement, Auctions Expert was to be paid a percentage of the Google advertising revenue based on the number of legitimate clicks generated from Google advertisements appearing on the Auctions Expert web site.

22. Under the Agreement, Auctions Expert was prohibited from generating artificial and/or fraudulent clicks on any Google advertisements it hosted. In addition, Auctions Expert was prohibited from authorizing or encouraging any third party to engage in such activity.

23. Google performed all conditions, covenants and promises required to be performed by Google in accordance with the terms of the Agreement, except those that Google was prevented or legally excused from performing and those as to which its performance was waived.

24. Defendants breached the Agreement by generating artificial and/or fraudulent clicks on the Google advertisements appearing on their site.

25. Defendants' breach of the Agreement has unjustly enriched Defendants and proximately caused Google damage in an amount to be proven at trial. Wherefore, Google prays for relief as set forth below.

<u>SECOND CAUSE OF ACTION</u>

Breach of Implied Covenant of Good Faith and Fair Dealing (Against All Defendants)

26. Google realleges each and every allegation set forth in Paragraphs 1 through 25, inclusive, and incorporates them by reference herein.

27. The Agreement contained an implied covenant of good faith and fair dealing, providing that neither party would act to deprive the other of the benefits of the Agreement between them.

28. The principal benefit for which Google contracted was the referral of individuals legitimately interested in a particular advertisement to an advertiser who, in turn, pays Google based on the number of legitimate clicks it receives.

29. The implied covenant obligated Defendants to refrain from generating illegitimate clicks so as to increase their revenues at Google's expense. In doing so, Defendants breached the implied covenant of good faith and fair dealing.

30. Defendants' bad faith conduct has unjustly enriched them and caused Google damage in an amount to be proven at trial. Wherefore, Google prays for relief as set forth below.

<u>THIRD CAUSE OF ACTION</u>

Fraud - Intentional Misrepresentation (Against All Defendants)

31. Google realleges each and every allegation set forth in Paragraphs 1 through 30, inclusive, and incorporates them by reference herein.

32. Defendants were well aware of the manner in which Google calculated clicks on advertisements from its affiliated sites. Specifically, they knew that when a user clicked on an advertisement on Defendants' site, the user's computer would make a request to Google's computers to access the site being advertised, and inform Google's computers that the request was generated from Defendants' site. Defendants knew further that Google's computers would record that request as an expression of the user's legitimate interest in accessing the advertised site.

33. By artificially manufacturing clicks on advertisements on their site, and causing requests to be sent to Google's computers, Defendants represented to Google that each of those clicks was legitimate and that the individual clicking desired to access the site being advertised.

34. Defendants knew that such representations were false. Defendants' clicks were not legitimate, and the individual clicking had no desire to access the site that was advertised.

35. Defendants' misrepresentations to Google through its generation of artificial clicks were intentional and made with scienter in an effort to induce Google to pay Defendants for clicks that were not legitimate.

36. Google did, in fact, rely on Defendants' misrepresentations as to the legitimacy of the clicks that Defendants caused to be sent by paying Defendants for those clicks.

37. As a direct result of Defendants' fraudulent conduct, Defendants have been unjustly enriched, and Google has been damaged in an amount to be proven at trial. Wherefore, Google prays for relief as set forth below.

<u>PRAYER FOR RELIEF</u>

WHEREFORE, Google prays for judgment as follows:

(i) For an award of compensatory damages in an amount to be proven at trial arising from Defendants' breach of contract, breach of the implied covenant of good faith and fair dealing, tortious interference with contract, fraudulent concealment and fraudulent misrepresentation, along with applicable interest;

(ii) For punitive damages sufficient to punish Defendants for their malicious and fraudulent behavior and to deter similar misconduct by Defendants in an amount to be proven at trial;

(iii) For an accounting, disgorgement and restitution by Defendants to Google of all amounts paid to Defendants under the Google Online AdSense Program;

(iv) For an award of Google's costs of suit; and

(v) For such other, further, and different relief as the Court deems proper under the circumstances.

<u>JURY TRIAL DEMAND</u>

Plaintiff Google Inc. demands trial by jury on all claims so triable.

DATED: November 15, 2004

Respectfully submitted,

WILSON SONSINI GOODRICH & ROSATI

By: ____________________

David H. Kramer

Attorneys for Plaintiff,
GOOGLE INC.

EXHIBIT 7.2A Sample Federal Complaint Filed in a Federal Court in California

BINGHAM MCCUTCHEN LLP
BETH H. PARKER (SBN 104773)
TERESA FEDERER (SBN 221454)
GISELLE FAHIMIAN (SBN 225572)
Three Embarcadero Center
San Francisco, CA 94111-4067
Telephone: 415.393.2000
Facsimile: 415.393.2286

PLANNED PARENTHOOD FEDERATION OF AMERICA
EVE C. GARTNER*
HELENE T. KRASNOFF*
ROGER K. EVANS*
434 W. 33rd Street
New York, New York 10001
Telephone: 212.541.7800
Facsimile: 212.247.6811

Attorney for Plaintiffs

* *Pro hac vice* motion pending

UNITED STATES DISTRICT COURT
NORTHERN DISTRICT OF CALIFORNIA
SAN FRANCISCO DIVISION

PLANNED PARENTHOOD FEDERATION OF AMERICA, INC. and PLANNED PARENTHOOD GOLDEN GATE Plaintiffs v. JOHN ASHCROFT, Attorney General of the United States, in his official capacity Defendant	Civil Action No. **03 CV 4872** COMPLAINT

Plaintiffs, by and through their attorneys, bring this complaint against the above-named Defendant, his employees, agents, and successors in office, and in support thereof state the following:

I. INTRODUCTORY STATEMENT

1. This is a constitutional challenge to S.3, the "Partial-Birth Abortion Ban Act of 2003" (to be codified at 18 U.S.C. § 1531) [hereinafter "the Act"]. The Act passed the House and

EXHIBIT 7.2A

the Senate and was sent to the President for signature. It will take effect at 12:01 a.m. on the day after it is signed. President Bush has repeatedly made clear his intention to sign this bill into law. A copy of the Act is attached as Exhibit A.

2. Plaintiffs seek declaratory and injunctive relief against the Act, which bans what the Act calls "partial-birth abortion." Those physicians who provide banned abortions risk criminal penalties and civil liability. The Act must be enjoined and declared unconstitutional because it suffers from the identical two constitutional flaws as the Nebraska statute banning so-called "partial-birth abortion" that was struck down by the United States Supreme Court in *Stenberg v. Carhart*, 530 U.S. 914 (2000).

3. First, in contravention of the Supreme Court's clear holding, the Act bans abortion procedures without providing any exception for when such procedures are necessary or appropriate for the pregnant woman's health and without providing an adequate exception to protect women's lives. The Act thus deprives physicians of the discretion they need to make appropriate medical judgments regarding which abortion procedure to use, and requires physicians to use methods of abortion that impose unnecessary health risks upon patients.

4. Second, the term "partial-birth abortion," which is not a recognized medical term, is defined so broadly in the Act as to chill physicians from providing the safest and most common methods of abortion used in the second trimester of pregnancy prior to viability. The Act thus imposes an "undue burden" on the right to obtain previability abortions. Alternatively, the Act is so vague that it fails to give physicians fair warning of which abortion procedures are prohibited.

5. For these reasons, the Act violates the rights of Plaintiffs, their employees, their agents, and their patients to privacy and due process guaranteed under the Fifth Amendment of the United States Constitution. II.

II. JURISDICTION AND VENUE

6. Jurisdiction is conferred on this Court by 28 U.S.C. § 1331.

7. Plaintiffs' claim for declaratory and injunctive relief is authorized by 28 U.S.C. §§ 2201 and 2202, by Rules 57 and 65 of the Federal Rules of Civil Procedure, and by the general legal and equitable powers of this Court.

8. Venue is appropriate under 28 U.S.C. § 1391(e) because administrative offices and healthcare facilities of Plaintiffs Planned Parenthood Golden Gate (PPGG) are located in this district, and PPGG provides abortions that may be banned under the Act in this district. Plaintiff Planned Parenthood Federation of America (PPFA) has a national office located in this district. Therefore, a substantial part of the events or omissions giving rise to the Plaintiffs' claims occur in this district.

EXHIBIT 7.2A Sample Federal Complaint Filed in a Federal Court in California

III. PARTIES

A. Plaintiffs

9. Plaintiff PPFA is a not-for-profit corporation organized under the laws of New York. One of PPFA's national offices is located in San Francisco, California. PPFA is the leading national voluntary health organization in the field of reproductive health care. Some Planned Parenthood member-affiliates provide second-trimester abortions that fall within the proscriptions of the Act, including dilation and evacuation (D&E) abortions, which are the most common method for performing abortions in the second-trimester of pregnancy. These Planned Parenthood member-affiliates reasonably fear that if they continue to provide second-trimester abortions, they and their employees and agents will risk criminal prosecution and civil liability under the Act.

10. PPGG sues on its own behalf, on behalf of its current and future physicians, medical residents and their faculty supervisors, and all PPGG employees, staff, servants, officers, and agents who perform, participate or assist in the performance of, supervise, and/or train in the provision of, second-trimester abortion services at PPGG facilities and/or on PPGG patients, and who are at risk of criminal prosecution and civil lawsuits under the Act, and on behalf of its patients.

B. Defendant

11. Defendant John Ashcroft is the Attorney General of the United States and heads the United States Department of Justice, which is the agency of the United States government responsible for enforcement of federal laws, including the Act. Defendant Ashcroft is sued in his official capacity, as are his successors.

IV. THE STATUTORY FRAMEWORK

12. The Act makes it a crime for any physician, "in or affecting interstate or foreign commerce," to "knowingly perform[ ] a partial-birth abortion." 18 U.S.C. § 1531(a). A "partial-birth abortion" is defined as:

> an abortion in which the person performing the abortion –
> (A) deliberately and intentionally vaginally delivers a living fetus until, in the case of a head-first presentation, the entire fetal head is outside the body of the mother, or, in the case of breech presentation, any part of the fetal trunk past the navel is outside the body of the mother, for the purpose of performing an overt act that the person knows will kill the partially delivered living fetus; and
> (B) performs the overt act, other than completion of delivery, that kills the partially delivered living fetus. . . .

18 U.S.C. § 1531(b)(1). This prohibition applies throughout pregnancy, regardless of fetal viability.

EXHIBIT 7.2A

13. The Act contains a single limited exception. Only where a so-called partial-birth abortion "is necessary to save the life of a mother whose life is endangered by a physical disorder, physical illness, or physical injury" is the Act inapplicable. 18 U.S.C. § 1531(a). The exception does not appear to apply to the Act's civil penalties.

14. Violation of the Act is punishable by up to two years imprisonment or a fine, or both. 18 U.S.C. § 1531(a).

15. In addition to criminal penalties, the Act provides for civil lawsuits. It allows the woman's husband, if she is married, or her parents, if she is under 18 years of age, to bring a civil action against any physician who allegedly performs a so-called "partial-birth abortion." 18 U.S.C. § 1531(c)(1).

V. THE EFFECTS OF THE ACT

A. Effect on Women's Health

16. Women seek abortions for a variety of deeply personal reasons, including the inability or hardship of raising a child, the fact that the pregnancy results from rape or incest, because continuing the pregnancy threatens their lives and/or health, or because they are carrying a fetus with congenital anomalies. For all these women, the inability to obtain an abortion due to the Act would be devastating.

17. The effect of the Act on women seeking later abortions would be particularly tragic. Although only about 12% of abortions performed nationwide occur in the second trimester of pregnancy, women seeking these abortions are frequently in difficult life circumstances. For example, women carrying fetuses with serious abnormalities such as anencephaly (absence of a brain) or trisomies 13 and 18 (chromosomal abnormalities that cause multiple disabilities and mental retardation) are forced to seek abortions in the second trimester because the diagnosis of the abnormalities is not possible, or much more difficult, until then. In addition, women may be seeking abortions to avert a risk to their health, which may not have arisen or become apparent until the second trimester.

18. The sole exception to the Act's ban is ineffective to protect women's life and health. The exception permits a physician to perform a so-called "partial-birth abortion" only when it "is necessary to save the life of a mother whose life is endangered by a physical disorder, physical illness, or physical injury." 18 U.S.C. § 1531(a). The flaws in this exception are several. First, the Act fails to allow a banned abortion when the woman's health is endangered by the pregnancy but the physician cannot certify that her life is threatened.

19. Second, the Act does not permit a banned procedure where, regardless of the woman's health status, in the best medical judgment of the physician, that procedure would be the safest or most medically appropriate for a particular patient. It may, therefore, force women to undergo riskier procedures. It thus fails to protect the health of women seeking abortions.

20. Even if the Act bans only D&E abortions in which the fetus remains intact or largely intact when it is extracted from the uterus (sometimes referred to as intact D&E or dilation and extraction ["D&X"] abortions), an adequate life and health exception is necessary. This is because such abortions may be the safest for some women in some circumstances.

B. Effect on Women's Access to Abortion and other Medical Services

21. The actions that the Act defines as constituting a "partial-birth abortion" could occur in any D&E abortion, including but not limited to intact D&E abortions, as well as in any induction abortion. This is because:

(a) in all D&E or induction abortions, the person performing the abortion "deliberately and intentionally vaginally delivers a . . . fetus," 18 U.S.C. §1531(b)(1)(A), and in many instances, the fetus is "living" when that occurs;

(b) in any D&E or induction abortion, the fetus, while still "living," may emerge until "in the case of a head-first presentation, the entire fetal head is outside the body of the mother, or, in the case of breech presentation, any part of the fetal trunk past the navel is outside the body of the mother," id.

22. While not all D&E or induction abortions will proceed in a manner that violates the Act, physicians cannot know or predict in advance which abortions will so proceed. Accordingly, performing any D&E or induction abortion places doctors at risk of violating the Act.

23. Together, D&E and induction abortions account for more than 95% of previability abortions performed in the second trimester of pregnancy.

24. If neither D&E nor induction abortions were available, the only remaining abortion option for women in the second trimester of pregnancy would be hysterotomy or hysterectomy, both of which involve many times the risk of either D&E or induction procedures, and must be performed in a hospital. Moreover, hysterectomy precludes future childbearing. For those reasons, they have been virtually abandoned as methods of abortion.

25. The Act's definition of "partial-birth abortion" fails to give Plaintiffs fair warning as to what conduct is prohibited. The Act thus forces physicians to guess—under threat of criminal prosecution and civil liability—whether performing an accepted medical procedure falls within the Act's proscription.

26. If the Act is allowed to take effect, access to abortions in the second trimester of pregnancy—with the exception of hysterotomy and hysterectomy—would be severely curtailed in the United States because Plaintiffs and other abortion providers would be chilled from performing D&E and induction abortion procedures in the safest manner because doing so could result in a procedure that is banned by the Act.

VI. INJUNCTIVE RELIEF

27. Plaintiffs have no adequate remedy at law and will suffer irreparable harm for continued violations of their and their patients' constitutional rights if the Act goes into effect.

28. By prohibiting health care facilities and physicians, at any stage of pregnancy, from performing so-called "partial-birth abortions" where necessary to preserve the woman's health or where that procedure would be the most medically appropriate for the woman, and by limiting the circumstances under which a physician can perform a so-called "partial-birth abortion" to preserve the woman's life, the Act violates the right of women to privacy, life, and liberty guaranteed by the Due Process Clause of the Fifth Amendment.

WHEREFORE, Plaintiffs ask this Court:

A. To issue a temporary restraining order, a preliminary injunction, and a permanent injunction restraining Defendant, his employees, agents, and successors from enforcing the challenged Act;

B. To enter judgment declaring the challenged Act to be in violation of the United States Constitution;

C. To grant such other and further relief as this Court should find just and proper, including attorneys' fees and costs.

DATED: October 31, 2003

BINGHAM McCUTCHEN LLP

PLANNED PARENTHOOD FEDERATION OF AMERICA

By:________________________,

Beth H. Parker
Attorneys for Plaintiffs Planned Parenthood Federation of America, Inc. and Planned Parenthood Golden Gate

United States District Court Northern District of California
www.cand.uscourts.gov
(click "Pro Se Handbook") (see chapter 3 "What Is Included in a Complaint")
www.cand.uscourts.gov
(click "Rules - Procedures and Guidelines")
(click "Forms - Civil")

United States District Court Southern District of California
www.casd.uscourts.gov
(click "Filing Procedures - General Filing Procedures")
(click "Filing Procedures - Forms" see "Complaint" links)

D. Something to Check

1. What different kinds of complaint forms are made available on the Web sites of the four United States district courts in California?
2. The beginning of the Planned Parenthood complaint in this section tells you which attorneys in California and New York represented the plaintiffs. Use google (*www.google.com*) or other general search engines to find basic biographical information about each attorney.
3. Use any search engine to find information about the litigation begun by the complaint in this section. In the search engine you select, insert various combinations of party names and the case number. What happened in the case?

7.3 A Sample Memorandum of Law Applying California Law

A. Introduction

This section presents a sample memorandum of law that analyzes California law. It is an internal memo in the sense that it will not be filed with the court nor shown to anyone outside the office. It is designed for discussion and analysis solely for members of the firm working on the case of a client. Hence the memo is *not* an advocacy document; it is not designed to convince a court or an opponent to take a particular position. Consequently, the memo does not hide or downplay the weaknesses in the client's position. It presents the strengths and weaknesses of the client's case.

All law firms do not use the same format for a memorandum of law. Most firms, however, have the same basic five components: facts, issues or questions, brief answer, analysis or discussion, and conclusion. Firms may package these components in different ways (and may add others), but all of the five basic components are often present.

The format selected for the sample memorandum of law has five parts presented in the following order:

I. Statement of Facts
II. Questions Presented
III. Brief Answer
IV. Discussion
V. Conclusion

B. Sample Memorandum of Law

MEMORANDUM

To: H. Robinson

From: R. Davis

RE: Fox v. Ethicon, Inc.; #01-3442-4

Statute of Limitations for an amended complaint that adds a product's liability claim against a new defendant

Date: October 1, 2001

I. Statement of Facts

On April 10, 1999, our client, Brandi Fox, underwent gastric bypass surgery performed by Dr. Herbert Gladen. During this surgery, Fox was unconscious as the result of general anesthesia and, thus, did not observe the procedures or equipment used. After the surgery, Fox went home. She returned, however, to the hospital a few days after the surgery because she did not feel well. Her condition deteriorated, and she was taken to the operating room for exploratory surgery on May 13, 1999. Dr. Gladen found a perforation or leak at the staple closure of the small intestine, which caused fluid to leak into Fox's abdominal cavity. He attempted to close it. In his report he did not state the cause for the perforation ("[N]o reason could be identified for the perforation." *Operative Report*, 3, May 20, 1999.) Subsequently, Fox remained hospitalized until March 4, 2000, and required additional surgeries.

After Fox retained our firm, we filed a medical malpractice action on June 28, 2000 against her surgeon, Dr. Gladen, the hospital, and Does 1 to 100, asserting that "Defendants lacked the necessary knowledge and skill to properly care for Fox's condition and were negligent and unskillful in the diagnosis, treatment and prescription procedures utilized in treating her condition. The negligence claimed is for negligently performing presurgical, surgical, and postsurgical care so as to cause injuries and damages to Fox."

We deposed Dr. Gladen on August 13, 2001. During the deposition, Dr. Gladen testified that when he performed a postsurgery exploration of Fox's abdomen he found a leak at the staple closure of the small intestine. Dr. Gladen further testified that the bowel had been stapled using an Ethicon GIA-type stapler, that the stapler had been furnished by the hospital, and that he had found on previous occasions that such a stapler had caused postsurgery leaks.

We are preparing an amended complaint that will add the manufacturer of the stapler (Ethicon, Inc.) as a named defendant, asserting products liability claims that Fox was injured by an "Ethicon GIA-type stapler" on or about April 10, 1999. The counts against Ethicon will be strict liability relating to the design, manufacture, and assembly of the stapler, negligence, and breach of implied warranty. The amended complaint will add the following allegation:

> "Fox did not discover, nor suspect, nor was there any means through which her reasonable diligence would have revealed, or through which she would have suspected the Ethicon GIA-type Stapler as a cause of her injury until the deposition of Dr. Gladen was taken on August 13, 2001."

At the earliest, however, the amended complaint will be filed 31 months after the initial surgery. We anticipate that Ethicon will raise (via demurrer) the defense that the cause of action against it was time barred by the 1-year statute of limitations. (Code Civ. Proc. § 340(3).) The California legislature has changed this to 2 years (Code Civ. § 335.1), but this extended period is not retroactive to cover our action.

II. Issue Presented

For purposes of the statute of limitations, is the accrual of a cause of action for products liability delayed until the injured party has reason to believe that such a cause of action exists even though the party has already filed a medical malpractice action against another wrongdoer?

III. Brief Answer

Yes. If a party can establish that reasonable diligence would not have led to a suspicion that the injury was caused by a specific product, a products liability cause of action does not accrue until such a suspicion manifested. The statute of limitations starts to run at that time.

IV. Discussion

The statute of limitations begins to run once the cause of action accrues. ("Civil actions, without exception, can only be commenced within the periods prescribed in this title, after the cause of action shall have accrued." Code Civ. Proc., § 312.) A cause of action accrues at "the time when the cause of action is complete with all of its elements." (*Norgart v. Upjohn Co.*, (1999) 21 Cal.4th 383, 397 [87 Cal.Rptr.2d 453, 981 P.2d 79].) An important exception to the general rule of accrual is the "discovery rule," which postpones accrual of a cause of action until the plaintiff discovers, or has reason to discover, the cause of action. (*Norgart, supra*, 21 Cal.4th at p. 397.) Fox's position will be that she did not discover the Ethicon cause of action until the deposition on August 13, 2001 when Dr. Gladen told us about the prior problems with the Ethicon stapler.

Ethicon will argue that once Fox discovered the basis of her cause of action against the doctor for medical malpractice, there was an imputed simultaneous discovery of every other related cause of action, including the one against Ethicon. The strongest case in Ethicon's favor is the Court of Appeals decision of *Bristol-Myers Squibb Co. v. Superior Court* (1995) 32 Cal.App.4th 959, 966 [38 Cal.Rptr.2d 298]. In *Bristol-Myers Squibb*, the plaintiff's silicone breast implant was ruptured in 1982. Two years later, the plaintiff learned that the implant had ruptured, that silicone was migrating down her arm, and that the silicone was a cause of physical injury in the form of ulcerations. The plaintiff argued that because she had been told that silicone was an inert and harmless substance, she did not actually suspect the manufacturer of the implant of wrongdoing until after reading a newspaper article in late 1990. The Court of Appeal held that the statute of limitations on the plaintiff's products liability cause of action against the manufacturers of her silicone breast implants began to run when the statute of limitations on her medical malpractice action commenced. "When a plaintiff has cause to sue based on knowledge or suspicion of negligence the statute starts to run as to all potential defendants," regardless of whether those defendants are alleged as wrongdoers in a separate but related cause of action. (*Bristol-Myers Squibb, supra,* at p. 966 [38 Cal.Rptr.2d 298].) This is the essence of imputed simultaneous discovery of causes of action.

There is, however, a delayed discovery rule, which the California Supreme Court discussed in *Norgart v. Upjohn Co., supra.* Under the discovery rule, the accrual of the cause of action is postponed "until the plaintiff discovers, *or has reason to discover,* the cause of action." (*Norgart, supra,* 21 Cal.4th at p. 397) (emphasis added). A reason to discover the cause of action exists when the plaintiff "has reason at least to suspect a factual basis for its elements." (*Id.* at p. 398.) Ethicon will argue that the principle of imputed simultaneous discovery is still applicable. Its position will be that when a plaintiff sues based on knowledge *or suspicion* of negligence, including medical malpractice, the statute of limitations begins to run as to all defendants, including manufacturers possibly liable under products liability theories. This rule announced by the Court of Appeals in *Bristol-Myers Squibb* was not rejected by the Supreme Court in *Norgart.*

In *Norgart,* parents sued the manufacturer of the prescription drug Halcion for the wrongful death of their daughter 6 years after the daughter's suicide was allegedly caused by the drug's side effects. At the time of the daughter's death in 1985, the father suspected some outside agent had caused her to commit suicide. Prior to the death, the parents were aware of their daughter's depression and prior suicide attempts. Soon after her death, the father had reason to learn of a connection between her suicide and Halcion because the connection was disclosed by the package insert Upjohn Co. prepared. The insert cautioned about the possibility the drug could intensify depression and mentioned suicide and intentional overdoses. Under these circumstances, the Supreme Court found as a matter of law that the parents had reason to suspect wrongdoing by Upjohn Co. in manufacturing and distributing Halcion soon after their daughter's suicide. (*Norgart, supra,* 21 Cal.4th at pp. 406–407.)

The *Norgart* court expressly declined to rule on the principle of imputed simultaneous discovery announced in *Bristol-Myers Squibb* because in *Norgart* the "reason to suspect wrongdoing" by the manufacturer existed soon after the daughter's death. Hence the California Supreme Court has not adopted the bright-line rule of *Bristol-Myers Squibb.*

In arguing against this bright-line rule, we need to point out that the Court of Appeals in *Bristol-Myers Squibb* failed to distinguish between a plaintiff's ignorance of the identity of the person who committed a suspected wrong and ignorance of the existence of a cause of action. The Supreme Court has said that ignorance of the identity of the defendant does not delay accrual of a cause of action, but that ignorance of a generic element of the cause of action does. Such a distinction certainly exists in the context of a products liability action. Although the identity of the manufacturer-wrongdoer is not an essential element of a products liability cause of action, and therefore ignorance of its identity will not delay the running of the statute of limitations (*Bernson v. Browning-Ferris Industries* (1994) 7 Cal.4th 926, 932 [30 Cal.Rptr.2d 440, 873 P.2d 613]), a plaintiff's ignorance of wrongdoing involving a product's defect will usually delay accrual because such wrongdoing is essential to that cause of action. (*Clark v. Baxter Healthcare Corp.* (2000) 83 Cal.App.4th 1048, 1060 [100 Cal.Rptr.2d 223].)

Consequently, we can argue that if a plaintiff's reasonable and diligent investigation discloses only one kind of wrongdoing (medical malpractice of a doctor) when the injury was actually caused by tortious conduct of a wholly different sort (defective product of Ethicon), the discovery rule postpones accrual of the statute of limitations on the newly discovered claim. Fox had no reason to suspect the identity of Ethicon as a wrongdoer nor the very existence of products liability causes of action.

Fox is prepared to testify (and state in deposition) that (1) she was never told during the course of her care and treatment subsequent to the gastric bypass surgery that the stapler had malfunctioned in any way or was responsible for the postsurgery problems she suffered; (2) she did not believe she was told that a stapler type instrument was to be used on her during the gastric bypass surgery; and (3) she first became aware of a possible stapler malfunction when her attorneys told her about the doctor's testimony after his deposition.

V. Conclusion

Fox has a strong argument that the cause of action against Ethicon did not accrue until August 13, 2001, which is within the statute of limitations period. She can use the delayed discovery rule by pleading facts that show her inability to have discovered the necessary information about the products liability claim earlier despite reasonable diligence. The likelihood is that the Supreme Court, faced with the issue for the first time, will not accept the bright-line rule of imputed simultaneous discovery.

C. More Information

www.ualr.edu/cmbarger
(click "Format Guidelines")
users.ipfw.edu/vetterw/a339-research-sample-memo.htm

D. Something to Check

Find a memorandum of law online on any legal issue in any state. Compare its format or structure to the sample memorandum presented here in the products liability case involving the surgery stapler.

A. Introduction

An appellate brief is a document submitted by a party to an appellate court and served on the opposing party, in which arguments are presented on why the appellate court should affirm (approve), reverse, or otherwise modify what a lower court has done. There are a number of roles that paralegals perform in this area of appellate practice. They might be asked to go through the transcript of the trial record to find references that the attorney wants to use in the brief. Or they might be asked to cite check the brief by making sure that:

- all quotations are accurate
- all citations are in the format required by court rules
- the brief itself is in the format required by court rules
- all laws cited are still valid

The last role is performed by Shepardizing or KeyCiting each case, statute, or other law to make sure that it has not been overruled or changed since the time it was cited in the brief. Occasionally, an experienced paralegal will be asked to draft a portion of an appellate brief.

The main state courts in which appellate briefs are filed are the California Supreme Court and the California courts of appeal. In this section we concentrate on those filed in the California Supreme Court, specifically the Opening Brief on the Merits.

B. Rule 14 on Contents and Form

Before examining a sample brief, review these excerpts from Rule 14 on the content and form of appellate briefs.

California Rules of Court

Rule 14. Contents and form of briefs

(a) Contents

(1) Each brief must:
(A) begin with a table of contents and a table of authorities separately listing cases, constitutions, statutes, court rules, and other authorities cited;
(B) state each point under a separate heading or subheading summarizing the point, and support each point by argument and, if possible, by citation of authority; and
(C) support any reference to a matter in the record by a citation to the record.
(2) An appellant's opening brief must:
(A) state the nature of the action, the relief sought in the trial court, and the judgment or order appealed from;
(B) state that the judgment appealed from is final, or explain why the order appealed from is appealable; and
(C) provide a summary of the significant facts limited to matters in the record.

(b) Form

(1) A brief may be reproduced by any process that produces a clear, black image of letter quality. The paper must be white or unbleached, recycled, 8 1/2 by 11 inches, and of at least 20-pound weight.
(2) Any conventional typeface may be used. The typeface may be either proportionally spaced or monospaced.
(3) The type style must be roman; but for emphasis, italics or boldface may be used, or the text may be underscored. Case names must be italicized or underscored. Headings may be in uppercase letters.
(4) Except as provided in (11), the type size, including footnotes, must not be smaller than 13-point, and both sides of the paper may be used.
(5) The lines of text must be unnumbered and at least one-and-a-half-spaced. Headings and footnotes may be single-spaced. Quotations may be block-indented and single-spaced. Single-spaced means six lines to a vertical inch.
(6) The margins must be at least 1 1/2 inches on the left and right and 1 inch on the top and bottom.
(7) The pages must be consecutively numbered. The tables and the body of the brief may have different numbering systems.
(8) The brief must be bound on the left margin. If the brief is stapled, the bound edge and staples must be covered with tape.
(9) The brief need not be signed.

(10) The cover, preferably of recycled stock, must be in the color prescribed by rule 44(c) and must state:
(A) the title of the brief;
(B) the title, trial court number, and Court of Appeal number of the case;
(C) the names of the trial court and each participating trial judge;
(D) the name, address, telephone number, and California State Bar number of each attorney filing or joining in the brief, but the cover need not state the bar number of any supervisor of the attorney responsible for the brief; and
(E) the name of the party that each attorney on the brief represents.
(11) If the brief is produced on a typewriter:
(A) A typewritten original and carbon copies may be filed only with the presiding justice's permission, which will ordinarily be given only to unrepresented parties proceeding in forma pauperis. All other typewritten briefs must be filed as photocopies.
(B) Both sides of the paper may be used if a photocopy is filed; only one side may be used if a typewritten original and carbon copies are filed.
(C) The type size, including footnotes, must not be smaller than standard pica, 10 characters per inch. Unrepresented incarcerated litigants may use elite type, 12 characters per inch, if they lack access to a typewriter with larger characters.

(c) Length

(1) A brief produced on a computer must not exceed 14,000 words, including footnotes. Such a brief must include a certificate by appellate counsel or an unrepresented party stating the number of words in the brief. The person certifying may rely on the word count of the computer program used to prepare the brief.
(2) A brief produced on a typewriter must not exceed 50 pages.
(3) The tables, a certificate under (1), and any attachment under (d) are excluded from the limits stated in (1) or (2).
(4) A combined brief in an appeal governed by rule 16 must not exceed double the limits stated in (1) or (2).
(5) On application, the presiding justice may permit a longer brief for good cause.

(d) Attachment to briefs

A party filing a brief may attach copies of exhibits or other materials in the appellate record. The attachment must not exceed a total of 10 pages, but on application the presiding justice may permit a longer attachment for good cause.

(e) Noncomplying briefs

If a brief does not comply with this rule:
(1) the reviewing court clerk may decline to file it, but must mark it "received but not filed" and return it to the party; or
(2) if the brief is filed, the reviewing court may, on its own or a party's motion, with or without notice:
(A) order the brief returned for corrections and refiling within a specified time;
(B) strike the brief with leave to file a new brief within a specified time; or
(C) disregard the noncompliance.

C. Sample Appellate Brief Filed in California Supreme Court: Opening Brief on the Merits

Case No. SI 19750

IN THE SUPREME COURT
OF THE STATE OF CALIFORNIA

CHARLES E. MORRIS, IV
Plaintiff and Appellant

vs.

SILVINO DE LA TORRE dba VICTORIA'S MEXICAN FOOD
Defendant and Respondent

OPENING BRIEF ON THE MERITS

Fourth District Court of Appeal No. DO 040278
San Diego County Superior Court Case No. GIS 004607
Honorable Luis R. Vargas

Daniels, Fine, Israel & Schonbuch, LLP
Mark R. Israel, State Bar No. 125199
1801 Century Park East, 9th Floor
Los Angeles, California 90067
(310) 556-7900

Clements & Knock
Thomas V. Clements, State Bar No. 110356
7850 El Cajon Boulevard, Suite 500
La Mesa, California, 92041
(619) 680-6900

Attorneys for Defendant and Respondent SILVINO DE LA TORRE dba
VICTORIA'S MEXICAN FOOD

TABLE OF CONTENTS

Case No. SI 19750

TABLE OF AUTHORITIES

CASES

Alvarez v. Jacmar Pacific Pizza Corporation (2002)
100 Cal.App.4th 1190 . . . . 10, 11, 18

Andrews v. Wells (1988)
204 Cal.App.3d 533 . . . . 20, 21, 23

Ann M. v. Pacific Plaza Shopping Center (1993)
6 Cal.4th 666 . . . . 7, 8, 9, 10, 11, 24

Breaux v. Gino's, Inc. (1984)
153 Cal.App.3d 379 . . . . 18, 19

Clarke v. Hoek (1985)
74, Cal.App.3d 208 19

Forrand v. Foodmaker, Inc. (1986)
182 Cal.App.3d 196 . . . . 14, 15, 22, 23

Gregorian v. National Convenience Stores, Inc. (1985)
174 Cal.App.3d 944 16

Hansra v. Superior Court (Magana) (1992)
7 Cal.App.4th 630 23

Hassoon v. Shamieh (2001)
89 Cal.App.4th 1191 . . . . 9, 10, 11, 12, 15

Helms v. Church's Fried Chicken, Inc. (1986)
81 N.C.App. 427 17

Kentucky Fried Chicken of California, Inc. v. Superior Court (Brown) (1997)
14 Cal.4th 814 16

Knighlen v. Sam's Parking Valet (1988)
206 Cal.App.3d 69 18

Mala v. Mala (2003)
105 Cal.App.4th 1121 . . . . 18, 23

Morris v. De La Torre (2003)
111 Cal.App.4th 1047 6

Sharon P. v. Arman, Ltd. (1999)
21 Cal.4th 1181 . . . . 8, 9, 10, 11, 12, 13

Vandermost v. Alpha Beta Co. (1985)
164 Cal.App.3d 771 16

Vega v. Tree House Sports Bar (2003)
Cal.App. Unpub. LEXIS 9284 10

Young v. Desert View Management Corporation (1969)
275 Cal.App.2d 294 . . . . 13, 14, 16

Zelig v. County of Los Angeles (2002)
27 Cal.4th 1112 . . . . 19, 20, 22, 23, 24

STATUTES

California Rules of Court
14(c)(1) 26

28(e)(6) 26

I.

QUESTION PRESENTED FOR REVIEW

1. Is a business owner liable for the criminal conduct of a third party in the absence of "prior similar incidents" of such conduct?

2. Does a business owner have a duty to respond to unforeseeable third party criminal conduct by summoning aid for the victim of such conduct?

II.

INTRODUCTION

Charles Morris was repeatedly stabbed by Richard Allen Cuevas near a taco shop operated by Silvino De La Torre known as Victoria's Mexican Food. The Court of Appeal held that, although the vicious criminal attack by Cuevas was unforeseeable, De La Torre nevertheless had a duty to summon aid in response to the third party's "dangerous conduct." The Court of Appeal concluded that foreseeability "is of no moment" in evaluating the duty of employees to respond once they are aware of "contemporaneous criminal conduct occurring at the business" and that requiring employees to "summon aid in response to such dangerous conduct occurring at the business premises is a minimal safety measure that imposes no undue hardship on a business owner." In fact, the decision of the Court of Appeal is inconsistent with existing precedent, significantly expands the scope of business owner liability for third party criminal conduct, and imposes an unfair and unreasonable burden on California businesses and their employees.

. . . .

For the foregoing reasons, defendant urges this Court to reaffirm that a business owner is not legally responsible for the unforeseen criminal act of a third party. Foreseeability as established through "prior similar incidents" is the appropriate measure of liability. This standard imposes a uniform and predictable standard for business owner liability and permits response to third party criminal conduct in a reflective, reasoned and cost-effective manner.

III

FACTUAL BACKGROUND

Victoria's Mexican Food is a taco shop in a shopping center located in the City of San Diego. De La Torre leases the premises from owners Richard and Ruth Karlson. On July 31, 2000, Edwin

-2-

Gallegos drove Charles Morris and three other friends to Victoria's. All intended to purchase food, except Morris who was complaining of a stomach ache. When they arrived, two of the party went into the taco shop; Morris remained in the parking lot sitting on the hood of the car. (Clerk's Transcript ["C.T."] 25.)

Two Hispanic males pulled into the parking lot at the same time or shortly after Morris arrived. One, subsequently identified as Richard Cuevas, was shirtless, and had "Nestor" tattooed across his stomach. Cuevas immediately told Morris that he was in his "hood" and was "not supposed to be here." Cuevas punched Morris and a fight broke out. (Id.)

Cuevas ran into the taco shop and yelled for a "filero" (Spanish slang for a knife). The taco shop employees did not respond because they were terrified. Cuevas then broke through a door separating the counter area from the kitchen and stole a 15 inch butcher knife. (C.T. 26, 63.) Cuevas ran into the parking lot and stabbed Morris twice in the lower back. (Id.) Two of Morris's friends ran across the street to a pay phone and called 911. Meanwhile, Cuevas slashed three tires on the Gallegos vehicle. (C.T. 26, 64.) After slashing the tires, Cuevas chased Morris eastbound on Coronado Boulevard. Cuevas caught Morris and stabbed him repeatedly. Cuevas then fled to his vehicle with his friend and sped off. (Id.)

Morris filed an amended complaint against Silvino De La Torre and Richard and Ruth Karlson alleging causes of action for negligence, premises liability and battery. (C.T. 6.)

On August 10, 2001, De La Torre moved from summary judgment on Morris's amended complaint. De La Torre asserted that he owed no duty of care to Morris as a matter of law based upon the lack of foreseeability of the criminal acts of Cuevas; the lack of prior similar incidents before the attack; the lack of a "special relationship" between De La Torre and Morris because Morris was not a customer at the time of the attack; and because Morris was not attacked on premises controlled by De La Torre, but rather in the parking lot of the shopping center, property owned and controlled by the Karlsons, and down the street, away from the shopping center. (C.T. 18–50.)

On December 17, 2001, the Honorable Luis R. Vargas granted the motion for summary judgment. The trial court concluded that although Morris offered evidence of prior incidents of criminal activity on or near the subject premises, these incidents were not similar to the criminal activity which caused the injury to Morris. Further, plaintiff offered no admissible evidence that any activity by defendant or his employees created or enhanced the peril to Morris. As such, the court found no duty as a matter of law. (C.T. 157–158.)

-3-

On December 21, 2001, Morris moved for reconsideration of the summary judgment as to De La Torre. (C.T. 161–209.) On March 1, 2002, the trial court granted plaintiff's motion for reconsideration. Upon reconsideration, the court affirmed its prior ruling granting summary judgment to De La Torre. The court found no "special relationship" between Morris and De La Torre because the undisputed evidence established that Morris was not a customer of the taco shop at the time of the attack. (C.T. 211.)

On or about May 22, 2002, plaintiff filed his notice of appeal from the judgment in favor of De La Torre. (C.T. 228–231.) On September 3, 2003, Division One of the Fourth Appellate District issued its opinion reversing the summary judgment in favor of De La Torre. (Appendix A.) The decision was published as *Morris v. De La Torre* (2003) 111 Cal.App.4th 1047. The Court of Appeal held that De La Torre had no duty to take protective measures such as hiring security personnel or issuing warnings *before* the violent assault by Cuevas due to a lack of prior similar incidents. The court noted that Morris, who was a regular customer, "did not realize there was a gang problem at the taco shop." Further, "despite evidence of prior fights and gang harassment at the premises, there was no indication that there had been any serious assaultive conduct." (Appendix at p. 17.) Nevertheless, although the Court of Appeal "agreed" that the acts which caused the injury to Morris were not foreseeable under the circumstances, "this conclusion does not end our inquiry." The Court of Appeals states: "Whether such conduct was foreseeable is of no moment in evaluating the duty of employees to respond once they are aware of contemporaneous criminal conduct occurring at the business." (Id. at p. 20.) The Court of Appeal held that the employees of the taco shop had a legal duty to summon aid once they became aware of the altercation between Cuevas and Morris. The Court of Appeal premised this legal duty to act upon a "special relationship" between Morris and the taco shop based upon the factual conclusions that Morris had been "frequently" a customer at the taco shop; Morris was with friends who entered to the taco shop to purchase food; the gang violence was directed at Morris and his friends; and Cuevas used the taco shop's premises to effectuate the assault by entering it and retrieving a knife. (Id. at pp. 23–24.)

On October 14, 2003, De La Torre timely filed his petition for review by this Court. On December 10, 2003, the petition for review was granted.

-4-

IV

<u>LEGAL DISCUSSION</u>

A. The Concept of Foreseeability should Govern Imposition of a Duty Upon a Business Owner to Respond to Third Party Criminal Conduct

In the landmark case of Ann *M. v. Pacific Plaza Shopping Center* (1993) 6 Cal.4th 666, this Court discussed the scope of a commercial landlord's duty of care in the context of a third party attack upon an employee of a shopping center. *Ann M.* noted that landowners must maintain their premises in a reasonably safe condition and that in the case of a landlord, the general duty of maintenance includes "the duty to take reasonable steps to secure common areas against *foreseeable* criminal acts of third parties that are likely to occur in the absence of such precautionary measures." (*Id.* at p. 674.) Emphasizing foreseeability as a "crucial factor" in determining the existence of a duty, the Court held that "a duty to take affirmative action to control the wrongful acts of a third party will be imposed *only* where such conduct can be reasonably anticipated." (*Id.* at p. 676.) (Emphasis added.) *Ann M.* concluded that in light of the significant monetary and social costs on landowners, "a high degree of foreseeability" is required to impose a duty to hire security guards, and that the requisite degree of foreseeability "rarely, if ever, can be proven in the absence of prior similar incidents of violent crime on the landlord's premises." To hold otherwise "would be to impose an unfair burden upon landlords and, in effect, would force landlords to become the insurers of public safety, contrary to well-established policy in this state." (Id. at p. 679.)

. . . .

B. The California Courts Generally Decline to Impose Liability Upon a Business Owner Based Upon the Response of Employees to Contemporaneous Criminal Activity

The California courts, recognizing the difficulty in imposing liability upon a business owner for the response of his or her employees to exigent circumstances, have generally declined to impose liability upon the owner for "contemporaneous" criminal conduct, even where the response of the employee worsens the position of the injured customer or invitee.

In *Young v. Desert View Management Corporation* (1969) 275 Cal.App.2d 294, the court affirmed a judgment following non-suit in favor of the defendant in an action for personal injuries sustained by a patron of a restaurant bar who was shot by a robber. In this case, Young had dinner in defendant's

-5-

restaurant and thereafter went into the bar. While he was there, a man entered the coffee shop, laid a pistol on the cash register and demanded money from the assistant manager-cashier. The robber grabbed the cashier and starting walking towards the coffee shop. The cashier broke away from the robber, ran through the kitchen and into the bar where she said to fellow employees "Help, I have been robbed." A cocktail waitress heard her and said to Young "a man robbed—just robbed Helen. Help. Let's get a license number." Young went outside to get the number where he was shot in the back by the robber.

. . . .

C. Existing Case Law does not Justify Finding a "Special Relationship" Between De La Torre and Morris

The holding of the Court of Appeal that defendant's employees had a duty to summon aid in response to the criminal conduct of Cuevas is based upon the conclusion that a "special relationship" existed between Morris and De La Torre. This conclusion is not supportable under existing California case law.

In *Clark v. Hoek* (1985) 174 Cal.App.3d 208, the court explained the "special relationship" doctrine as follows:

> [T]he rule that conduct is negligent where some unreasonable risk of danger to others would have been foreseen by a reasonable person is applicable only to cases of misfeasance. Absent a special relationship giving rise to a duty to act, a person is under no duty to take affirmative action to assist or protect another, no matter how great the danger in which the other is placed, or how easily he could be rescued. (Citations omitted.) A corollary to this principle is that an individual is under no duty to control the conduct of third parties unless a special relationship exists between the individual and either the third parties or the persons affected by their conduct. (Id. at p. 215.)

For example, these general rules bar recovery when plaintiffs, having suffered injury inflicted by third parties who are engaged in criminal activities, claim that their injuries could have been prevented by timely assistance from a law enforcement officer.

. . . .

D. The Decision of the Trial Court should be Affirmed and Judgment Entered in Favor of Defendant

This Court has repeatedly held that a legal duty to take measures to protect against third party criminal conduct is imposed where such conduct is "foreseeable," which in turn "rarely, if

-6-

ever, can be proven in the absence of prior similar incidents of violent crimes on the landowner's premises." (*Ann M., supra*, 6 Cal.4th at p. 679.) This standard is based upon the realization that moral blame for a criminal attack rests with the attacker, and to impose liability in the absence of notice through prior similar incidents would unfairly force landlords to become insurers of public safety. (*Ibid.*)

. . . .

V.

CONCLUSION

For all of the foregoing reasons, defendant and respondent Silvino De La Torre respectfully requests that this Court reverse the judgment of the Court of Appeal and remand with directions to enter judgment in favor of defendant.

Date: February 9, 2004

Respectfully Submitted,
DANIELS, FINE, ISRAEL &
SCHONBUCH, LLP
by________________
Mark R. Israel
Attorneys for Defendant and
Respondent
SILVINO DE LA TORRE dba
VICTORIA'S
MEXICAN FOOD

APPENDIX

CERTIFICATE OF COMPLIANCE WITH CALIFORNIA RULES OF COURT 14 AND 28

I, Mark R. Israel, an attorney, hereby certify that there are 7,505 words in the foregoing Petition for Review in compliance with Cal. Rules of Court 14(c)(1) and does not exceed 30 pages in compliance with Cal. Rules of Court 28(e)(6). I have relied upon the word count of Microsoft Word 2000 in preparing this Certificate.

____
Mark R. Israel

-7-

D. More Information

Four law libraries in California serve as depositories for appellate briefs. Their collection holdings vary. Each library's Web site provides information about location, hours of service, and telephone numbers:

California State Library
Bernard E. Witkin State Law Library
916-654-0185
www.library.ca.gov

Bernard E. Witkin Alameda County Law Library
510-208-4800
www.acgov.org/law/collection.htm
www.co.alameda.ca.us/law/index.htm

Los Angeles County Law Library
213-629-3531
www.lalaw.lib.ca.us

San Diego County Public Law Library
619-531-4449
www.sdcll.org

Other Resources on Appellate Briefs to Check:
www.courtinfo.ca.gov/qna/qa24.htm
www.legaline.com/freebriefslinks.html
www.lawsource.com/also/usa.cgi?usb
www.llrx.com/columns/reference43.htm
www.westlaw.com
www.lexis.com

E. Something to Check

1. Assume that you have been asked to cite check the appellate brief in the Morris case. Pick any five quotes from cases in the brief. Check the accuracy of the quotes by comparing them to the texts of the opinions themselves.
2. Using the online leads presented in More Information, find an appellate brief submitted to any California state court or to any federal court sitting in California.

7.5 A Sample Criminal Complaint Filed in a California State Court

A. Introduction
B. A State Criminal Complaint
C. More Information
D. Something to Check

A. Introduction

This section presents an example of a criminal complaint filed in a California state superior court. The complaint involves the Scott Peterson murder trial, a case of international notoriety. Peterson was eventually convicted of murdering his pregnant wife, Laci Peterson, and "Baby Conner Peterson, a fetus." See also section 4.2 on the state court system and section 6.4 for a timeline on the prosecution of a criminal case.

B. A State Criminal Complaint

Exhibit 7.5A contains the original complaint and arrest warrant.
(*news.findlaw.com/hdocs/docs/peterson/captrson42103cmp.pdf*)
(*courttv.aol.com/trials/peterson/docs/complaint.html?page=1*)
(*courttv.aol.com/trials/peterson/docs/warrant.html*)

C. More Information

For more information on criminal complaints (indictments) filed in California state courts, see:

California Criminal Law Resources
www.megalaw.com/ca/top/cacriminal.php

Cases in the Criminal Division
www.lasuperiorcourt.org/Criminal

Reports on California Criminal Law
www.courtinfo.ca.gov/reference/4_13crim.htm

California Drug Courts
www.courtinfo.ca.gov/reference/documents/cadrugct.pdf

Criminal Law Directory: California
www.criminal-lawyers-ca.com

California Penal Code
www.leginfo.ca.gov/calaw.html
(check "Penal Code")

California State Attorney General
caag.state.ca.us

Crime Statistics in California
caag.state.ca.us/cjsc/index.htm

Michael Jackson Indictment
news.findlaw.com/cnn/docs/jacko/camj43004ind.html

D. Something to Check

1. On the Internet, find the current status of the criminal case against Scott Peterson.
2. In the California Penal Code (*www.leginfo.ca.gov/calaw.html*), quote from any sentence in one of the statutes mentioned in the Peterson criminal complaint.
3. Find online information about paralegals who work in criminal law offices in California.

EXHIBIT 7.5A Complaint and Arrest Warrant in a State Criminal Case

PROVIDED BY FindLaw WWW.FINDLAW.COM

STANISLAUS COUNTY SUPERIOR COURT
STATE OF CALIFORNIA

THE PEOPLE OF THE STATE OF CALIFORNIA,

vs.

SCOTT LEE PETERSON
(DOB: 10/24/1972)
(IN CUSTODY)

DEFENDANT(S)

No. 1056770

FILED
03 APR 21 AM 10:05
THE SUPERIOR COURT
COUNTY OF STANISLAUS
BY ______________ DEPUTY

COMPLAINT -- CRIMINAL

State of California)
County of Stanislaus) ss.

MPD 02-142591
Booking #558289

On April 21, 2003, K. VELLA, STANISLAUS COUNTY DISTRICT ATTORNEY'S OFFICE, complains and alleges, upon information and belief, that said defendant(s) did commit the following crime(s) in the County of Stanislaus, State of California.

COUNT I: On or about and between December 23, 2002 and December 24, 2002, defendant did commit a felony, MURDER, violation of Section 187 of the California Penal Code, in that the defendant did willfully, unlawfully, and feloniously and with malice aforethought murder Laci Denise Peterson, a human being.

SPECIAL ALLEGATION: It is further alleged as to Count I, MURDER, that the defendant acted intentionally, deliberately and with premeditation.

ENHANCEMENT: TERMINATION OF PREGNANCY. During the commission of the murder of Laci Denise Peterson, the defendant, with the knowledge that Laci Denise Peterson was pregnant, did inflict injury on Laci Denise Peterson resulting in the termination of her pregnancy, a violation of Section 12022.9(a) of the California Penal Code.

COUNT II: On or about and between December 23, 2002 and December 24, 2002, defendant did commit a felony, MURDER, violation of Section 187 of the California Penal Code, in that the defendant did willfully, unlawfully, and feloniously and with malice aforethought murder Baby Conner Peterson, a fetus.

EXHIBIT 7.5A

PROVIDED BY FindLaw WWW.FINDLAW.COM

SPECIAL ALLEGATION: It is further alleged as to Count II, MURDER, that the defendant acted intentionally, deliberately and with premeditation.

THE FOLLOWING SPECIAL ALLEGATION APPLIES TO BOTH COUNTS:

SPECIAL ALLEGATION: It is further alleged as to Counts I & II, MURDER, the defendant committed more than one murder in the 1st or 2nd degree in this proceeding, and is a special circumstance within the meaning of Penal Code section 190.2(a)(3).

RD:kv
(Disk 83)

All of which is contrary to law in such cases made and provided, and against the peace and dignity of the People of the State of California.

Said Complaint therefore prays that a warrant be issued for the arrest of said defendant(s) and that said defendant(s) be dealt with according to law.

I certify under penalty of perjury, at Modesto, California, that the foregoing is true and correct.

Dated: 21 april 03 ______________ K. Vella ______________
Complainant

EXHIBIT 7.5A

MODESTO POLICE DEPARTMENT
STANISLAUS COUNTY JAIL
PRE-BOOKING / PROBABLE CAUSE DECLARATION

SUPERVISOR APPROVAL | CLASS CODE MISD ☐ FEL ☒ | COMPLETE REPORT ☐ FACE PAGE ☐ P.C. ONLY ☒ | PAGE 1 OF 1 | FILE NUMBERS 02-142591 | PLT Z | BEAT 99 | RD 99

D | Name (Last, First, Middle) PETERSON, SCOTT LEE | AKA | BOOKING NUMBER 558289

ADDRESS 523 COVENA AVE, | CITY MODESTO CA. | PHONE [redacted] | SOLD NUMBER 242127

OCCUPATION — | BUSINESS ADDRESS REFUSED — | EMPLOYER

DOB 10/24/72 | AGE 30 | RACE W | SEX M | HGT. 6-0 | WGT. 200 | HAIR BLN | EYES BRN | BUILD MED | COMP. LHT | [redacted]

CLOTHING BLUE SWEATER, WHT POLO SHIRT, WHT SHORTS, NIKE T-SHOES | SIGNATURE OF ARRESTING CITIZEN

Code | Name (Last, First, Middle) | Residence Address | Residence Phone
Occupation | Race | Sex | Age | Date of Birth | Business/School Address | Business Phone
Code | Name (Last, First, Middle) | Residence Address | Residence Phone
Occupation | Race | Sex | Age | Date of Birth | Business/School Address | Business Phone

Date & Time of Offense 12/23/02 / 12/24/02 | Location of Offense 523 COVENA AVE, MODESTO | LOCATION OF VEHICLE ☐ NONE ☐ TOWED BY

Date & Time of Arrest 04/18/03 - 1110 | Location of Arrest CALLAS / TORREY PINES RD SAN DIEGO | ☐ LEFT at SCENE ☒ REL. TO JOE PETERSON

48 HRS. EXPIRES - DATE/TIME 04/22/03 - 1110 | DATE/TIME REC'D. AT JAIL | VEHICLE DESC./LIC.

OFFICER CRAIG GROGAN | COMPUTER NO. M682 | AGENCY P.D. MODESTO | CASE NO. 02-142591 | ARREST NO.

☐ ON VIEW ☐ 11&B ☐ CITZS. ☒ WARR. ☒ FEL. ☐ MISD.
CHARGE 187 PC (2 COUNTS) PROBABLE CAUSE WARRANT OF ARREST

☐ ON VIEW ☐ 11&B ☐ CITZS. ☐ WARR. ☐ FEL. ☐ MISD.
CHARGE

☐ ON VIEW ☐ 11&B ☐ CITZS. ☐ WARR. ☐ FEL. ☐ MISD.
CHARGE

NARRATIVE / FACTS ESTABLISHING PROBABLE CAUSE FOR ARREST:

ON FRIDAY 04/18/03 AT 1110 HRS, DOJ SPECIAL AGENT SUPERVISOR ERNIE LIMON, SPECIAL AGENT PETER SHEAR AND OFFICER CLAUDE JUBRAN COMPLETED A FELONY TRAFFIC STOP AND ARREST AT MY REQUEST. SCOTT LEE PETERSON WAS ARRESTED FOR AN OUTSTANDING PROBABLE CAUSE WARRANT IN SAN. DIEGO CO. CA. PETERSON WAIVED BOOKING IN THAT JURISDICTION AND WAS TRANSPORTED TO STANISLAUS COUNTY JAIL FOR BOOKING

COPIES TO:

I declare under penalty of perjury that the foregoing is true and correct to the best of my information and belief.

Executed on 4/18/03 at Stanislaus County, CA. BY: [signature] IBM# 10259

ON THE BASIS OF ☒ the foregoing declaration, ☐ telephone declaration, I HEREBY DETERMINE THAT: ☒ there IS ☐ there is NOT probable cause to believe this arrestee has committed a crime.

Date: 4/19/03 Time: 1450 Magistrate: [signature]

EXHIBIT 7.5A

```
B O O K I N G   R E G I S T E R
STANISLAUS COUNTY JAIL
MODESTO CALIFORNIA 95353
BOOKING DATE 04/19/2003 00:09                       BOOKING..: 558289
ARREST DATE  04/18/2003 11:10                       FILE NO..: 02-142591
----------------------------------------------------------------------
PETERSON, SCOTT LEE                                 ID NUMBER: SC242127
523 COVENA AVE           MODESTO, CA  95354         (209) [redacted]
----------------------------------------------------------------------
RACE....... W    SEX........ M    AGE........ 30    D.O.B.. 10/24/1972
HEIGHT..... 6 00 WEIGHT..... 180  HAIR....... BRN   EYES.... BRN
BIRTHPLACE.. CA  CITIZEN.... US   MARITAL STATUS.... SINGLE
SOC SEC NO.. [redacted]           DRIVERS LICENSE.. [redacted] CA
OCCUPATION.. SALES                EMPLOYER.. TRADE CORP/MODESTO
----------------------------------------------------------------------
*     EMERGENCY NOTIFICATION INFORMATION        RELATION [redacted]
PETERSON, LEE                                   FATHER

ILLNESS/INJURY: REFER TO MEDICAL PRE-SCREEN/CLRD. BY MEDICAL / INTAKE
----------------------------------------------------------------------
*  BOOKING CHARGE(S)               HOW
*  --------CODE-------- CTS F/M ARR --BAIL-- --FINE-- ----WARRANT----
01 187 PC                 2  F  RAM  NO BAIL            RAMEY
    MURDER                                  COURT: STAN.SUPERIOR

            TOTAL FINE $      0      TOTAL BAIL $ NO BAIL
----------------------------------------------------------------------
ARREST LOCATION : CALLAS / TORREY PINES RD   SAN DIEGO, CA  92121
VEHICLE LOCATION: REL TO JOE PETERSON        SAN DIEGO, CA  92121
----------------------------------------------------------------------
**      LAW ENFORCEMENT PERSONS                          NO.   AGENCY
ACCOMPANYING OFFICER..
ARRESTING OFFICER.....GROGAN, CRAIG DETECTIVE MPD        M682  MPD
BOOKING OFFICER.......PORTER, ROSANNE LEGAL CLK III      SA02


PETERSON, SCOTT LEE                               ID NUMBER: SC242127
CHARGE(S): 187 PC                        FINE:        0 BAIL: NO BAIL
P R O P E R T Y            CASH:      0.00     BOOKING..:  558289
----------------------------------------------------------------------
 BRN BELT, BRN SUNGLASSES, MISC.PAPER, VISA CARD..NOPT
 WHT SHIRT, KHAKI SHORTS, blu sweater (RP)
 BLU/GRY TENNIS SHOES..NOCT
----------------------------------------------------------------------
I CERTIFY THAT THE ABOVE IS A CORRECT ITEM LIST OF MY PERSONAL PROPERTY.
                    SIGNATURE X________
RD ______ CLASS _____ IBM# ______   * * * * END OF BOOKING REGISTER * * * *
```

EXHIBIT 7.5A

PEOPLE OF THE STATE OF CALIFORNIA)
)
Plaintiff,)
vs.)
Scott Lee PETERSON Defendant)
)

PROBABLE CAUSE WARRANT OF ARREST*

(P.C. §814 and §1427;
Peo. V. Ramey, 16 Cal.3d 263;
Peo. V. Sesslin, 68 Cal.2d 418.)

FILED
03 APR 21 AM 6: 5
... OF THE SUPERIOR COURT
COUNTY OF STANISLAUS
BY ________ 4289
DEPUTY

COUNTY OF STANISLAUS:
THE PEOPLE OF THE STATE OF CALIFORNIA:

To any Peace Officer of said State:

Complaint upon oath having been this day made before me by Detective Craig Grogan, I find that there is probable cause to believe that two counts of the crime of: 187 PC, homicide committed on or about Monday December 23 , 2002 or Tuesday December 24, 2002, in the County of Stanislaus by **Scott Lee Peterson**, date of birth, 10/24/72.

YOU ARE THEREFORE COMMANDED forthwith to arrest the above-named Defendant and bring him/her before any magistrate in Stanislaus County pursuant to Penal Code Sections 187.

The within named defendant may be admitted to bail in the sum of:

NO BAIL ~~Dollars:~~

WITNESS, my hand this 17th day of April 2003.

[signature]
Judge of the Superior Court
County of Stanislaus, State of California

IDENTIFICATION INFORMATION

AKA* ________ Address ________ Phon[redacted]

N/A ________ Business: Trade Corp

Name: Scott Lee Peterson

Address 523 Covena Ave

Phon[redacted]

DOB 10/24/72 HT 6'-0" WT 200 Hair: brown Eyes: brown

DDL#[redacted] CII# ________

FBI# ________ SS# ________

Local Agency # 02-142591

Other Information None

*An arrest under this warrant does not initiate a criminal proceeding. After arrest, submit all reports and copies of this warrant and affidavit to the District Attorney who will review for a complaint. Retain original of this warrant and affidavit as evidence.

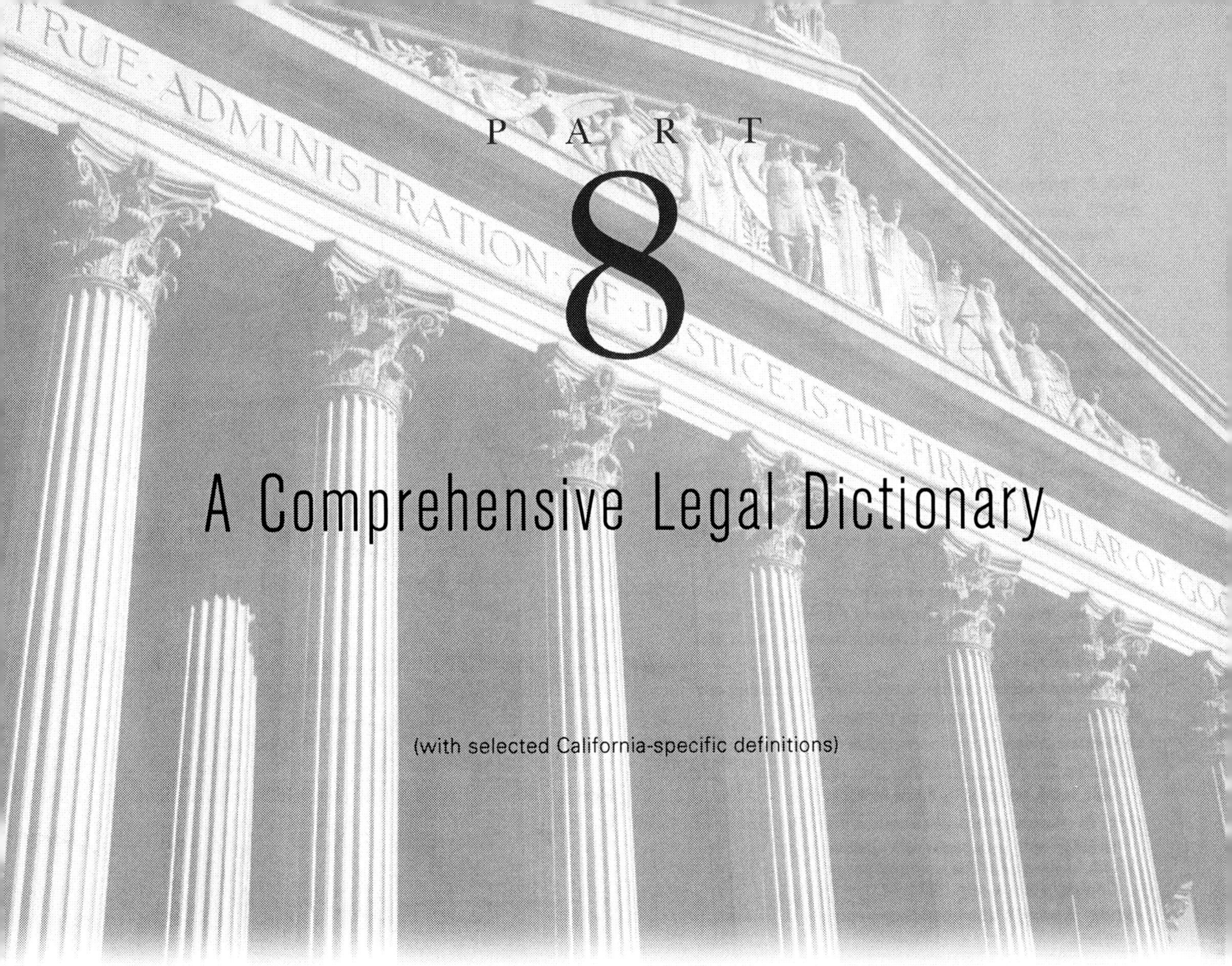

PART 8

A Comprehensive Legal Dictionary

(with selected California-specific definitions)

A

AAA American Arbitration Association (*www.adr.org*).

AAfPE American Association for Paralegal Education (*www.aafpe.org*).

AALS Association of American Law Schools (*www.aals.org*).

a aver et tener To have and to hold. See habendem clause.

ABA American Bar Association (*www.abanet.org*).

abaction Stealing animals, often by driving them off.

abandonee The person to whom something is abandoned or relinquished.

abandonment A total surrender of property, persons, or rights.

A voluntary relinquishment of a right or property without vesting ownership in another. *Cerro de Alcala*, 216 Cal.Rptr. 84 (Cal.Super., 1985)

abatable nuisance A nuisance that can be diminished or eliminated.

abatement 1. Termination or nullification. 2. A suspension of proceedings. 3. A reduction of testamentary legacies because estate assets are insufficient to pay debts and other legacies.

abatement of action A complete ending or quashing of a suit.

abator Someone who abates a nuisance.

abdication A voluntary renunciation of a privilege or office.

abduction The unlawful taking away of someone (e.g., child, wife, ward, servant) by force or trickery.

abet To encourage or assist another, often in criminal activity.

To aid or assist perpetrator with requisite mental state, that is, with knowledge of his wrongful purpose. *People v. Ott*, 148 Cal.Rptr. 479 (Cal.App., 1978)

abettor A person who encourages another to commit a crime.

abeyance Suspension; not finally settled or vested.

ability The power or capacity to perform.

ab initio From the beginning.

abjuration Renunciation under oath, formally giving up rights.

abnormally dangerous Extrahazardous (ultrahazardous) even if reasonable care is used.

It is impossible to define abnormally dangerous activities. "The essential question is whether the risk created is so unusual, . . . as to justify the imposition of strict liability, . . . even though it is carried on with all reasonable care." *Travelers Indemnity*, 34 Cal.Rptr.2d 337, 344 (Cal.App., 1994)

abode Dwelling place; residence.

abogado An advocate or lawyer (Spanish).

abolish To eliminate or cancel.

aboriginal Pertaining to inhabitants from earliest times.

abortifacient Causing abortion.

abortion 1. An induced termination of a pregnancy. 2. A miscarriage.

above 1. With a superior status. 2. Earlier or before.

abridge 1. To diminish. 2. To condense or shorten.

abrogate To annul, cancel, or destroy.

abscond To flee in order to avoid arrest or legal process.

absentee landlord A lessor who does not live on the leased premises.

absolute Unconditional; final.

absolute deed A deed that transfers land without encumbrances.

absolute law An immutable law of nature.

absolute liability See strict liability.

absolute nuisance A nuisance for which one is liable without regard to whether it occurred through negligence or other fault.

absolution Release from an obligation or penalty.

absolutism A political system in which one person has total power.

absorption The assimilation of one entity or right into another.

abstain To refrain from; to refuse to use the jurisdiction that a court has.

abstention doctrine If a matter can be tried in federal or state court, a federal court can decline its jurisdiction to avoid unnecessary interference with the state.

abstract A summary or abridgment.

abstraction Taking something, often wrongfully, with intent to defraud.

abstract of record Abbreviated history of court proceedings to date.

abstract of title A condensed history or summary of conveyances, interests, and encumbrances that affect title to land.

abuse 1. Improper use. 2. Physical or mental mistreatment.

abuse of discretion A decision that is manifestly unreasonable, depriving someone of a substantive right.

Exercising discretion in an arbitrary, capricious or patently absurd manner resulting in a manifest miscarriage of justice. *People v. Shaw*, 74 Cal.Rptr.2d 915 (Cal.App., 1998)

abuse of process A tort consisting of (a) the use of a civil or criminal process, (b) for a purpose for which the process is not designed, (c) resulting in actual damage.

A willful misuse of process; a showing of malice, whether express or implied, is required. *Slaughter*, 209 Cal.Rptr. 189 (Cal.App., 1984)

abut To be next to or touch; to share a common border.

abutters Owners of property joined at a common border.

accede 1. To agree. 2. To attain an office.

accelerated depreciation Taking more depreciation deductions during the early years of the life of an asset.

acceleration Causing something to occur sooner, e.g., to pay an obligation, to enjoy a benefit.

acceleration clause A clause in a contract or instrument stating what will trigger an earlier payment schedule.

acceptance 1. Agreement (express or implied) with the terms of an offer. 2. The act of receiving a thing with the intention of retaining it. 3. The commitment to honor a draft or bill of exchange.

"Acceptance" is a manifestation of assent by the offeree in the manner invited or required by the offer. *In re First Capital*, 40 Cal.Rptr.2d 816 (Cal.App., 1995)

access Opportunity to enter, visit with, or be intimate with.

access easement See easement.

accession 1. An increase through addition. 2. A country's acceptance of a treaty. 3. The right to own what is added to land by improvements or natural growth.

accessory 1. One who, without being present, helps another commit or conceal a crime. 2. A subordinate part.

Accessories are persons who, after a felony has been committed, harbor, conceal or aid a principal in the felony with the intent that the principal avoid criminal liability therefor and knowing that the principal has committed the felony or been charged with or convicted thereof. *People v. Coffman*, 17 Cal.Rptr.3d 710 (Cal., 2004)

accessory after the fact One who knows a crime has been committed (although not present at the time) and who helps the offender escape.

accessory before the fact One who assists or encourages another to commit a crime, although not present at the time it is committed.

accident An unexpected misfortune whether or not caused by negligence or other fault.

accommodated party See accommodation party.

accommodation 1. A favor, e.g., making a loan, acting as a cosigner. 2. An adjustment or settlement. 3. Lodging.

accommodation indorser See accommodation party.

accommodation paper A promissory note or bill of exchange that is cosigned by a person (who does not receive payment or other consideration) in order to help someone else secure credit or a loan. The person signing is the accommodation party.

accommodation party Someone who signs a promissory note or other negotiable instrument in any capacity, e.g., as indorser, without receiving payment or other consideration, in order to act as surety for another party (called the accommodated party).

accomplice A person who participates with another in an offense before, during, or after its commission.

One who knowingly, voluntarily, and with common intent with the principal offender unites in the commission of the crime. *People v. Verlinde*, 123 Cal.Rptr.2d 322 (Cal.App., 2002)

accord 1. An agreement or contract to settle a dispute. 2. An agreement for the future discharge of an existing debt by a substituted performance. Also called executory accord. Once the debt is discharged, the arrangement is called an accord and satisfaction.

accord and satisfaction See accord (2).

Accord and satisfaction" is the substitution of a new agreement for and in satisfaction of preexisting agreement between same parties, often to settle a claim at a lesser amount. *In re Marriage of Thompson*, 48 Cal.Rptr.2d 882 (Cal.App., 1996)

account 1. A financial record of debts, credits, transactions, etc. 2. An action or suit to force the defendant to explain his or her handling of a fund in which the plaintiff has an interest. Also called accounting.

accountable Responsible; liable.

accountant A person skilled in keeping financial records and accounts.

account debtor The person who has obligations on an account.

accounting 1. A bookkeeping system for recording financial transactions. 2. A settling of an account with a determination of what is owed. 3. See account (2).

accounting period The period of time, e.g., a year, used by a taxpayer for the determination of tax liability.

account payable A regular business debt not yet paid.

account receivable A regular business debt not yet collected.

account stated An agreement on the accuracy of an account, stating the balance due.

An express or implied agreement between debtor and creditor that a certain sum shall be accepted in discharge of the debtor's obligation. *West*, 67 Cal.Rptr. 831 (Cal.App., 1968)

accredit 1. To acknowledge or recognize officially. 2. To accept the credentials of a foreign envoy.

accredited investor An investor who is financially sophisticated.

accretion Growth in size by gradual accumulation. An increase of land by natural forces, e.g., soil added to a shore.

accrual basis A method of accounting in which revenues are recorded when earned or due, even though not collected, and expenditures are recorded when liabilities are incurred, whether paid or not.

accrue To come into existence as a right; to vest.

accrued dividend A declared dividend yet to be paid.

accumulated earnings tax A penalty tax on a corporation that retains its earnings beyond the reasonable needs of the business.

accumulation trust A trust in which the trustee must invest trust income rather than pay it out to beneficiaries.

accumulative sentence See consecutive sentences.

accusation A charge that one has committed a crime or other wrong.

accusatory instrument A document charging someone with a crime, e.g., an indictment.

accused The person accused or formally charged with a crime.

acknowledgment 1. An affirmation that something is genuine. 2. A formal statement of a person executing an instrument that he or she is doing so as a free act. 3. An acceptance of responsibility.

acknowledgment of paternity A formal admission by a father that a child is his.

ACLU American Civil Liberties Union (*www.aclu.com*).

acquaintance rape Rape by someone the victim knows.

acquest Property acquired by a means other than inheritance.

acquiesce To consent passively; to comply without protest.

acquire To obtain; to gain ownership of.

acquit 1. To release someone from an obligation. 2. To declare that the accused is innocent of the crime.

acquittal 1. A discharge or release from an obligation. 2. A formal declaration of innocence of a crime.

Instead of meaning that certain acts did not happen, an acquittal means they were not proved beyond a reasonable doubt. *People v. Santamaria*, 35 Cal.Rptr.2d 624 (Cal., 1994)

acquittance A written discharge from an obligation.

ACRS Accelerated cost-recovery system.

act 1. Something done voluntarily; an external manifestation of the will. 2. A law passed by the legislature.

acting Temporarily functioning as or substituting for.

actio A right or claim.

action 1. A civil or criminal court proceeding. 2. Conduct.

An "action" is a lawsuit brought in a court; a formal complaint within the jurisdiction of a court of law. *Gil*, 17 Cal.Rptr.3d 420 (Cal.App., 2004)

actionable Pertaining to that which can become the basis of a lawsuit.

actionable per se Pertaining to words that on their face and without the aid of extrinsic proof are defamatory. They are called actionable words.

actionable words See actionable per se.

action at law An action in a court of law, not in a court of equity.

An "action at law" is one for which a jury trial was permitted at common law as it existed at the time the state Constitution was first adopted in 1850. *Nwosu*, 19 Cal.Rptr.3d 416 (Cal.App., 2004)

action on the case An action to recover for damages caused indirectly rather than directly or immediately. Also called trespass on the case.

active trust See special trust.

act of bankruptcy Debtor's conduct that could trigger involuntary bankruptcy.

act of God A force of nature; an unusual force of nature.

The generally accepted definition of "act of God" only includes acts occasioned exclusively by violence of nature without the intervention of any human agency. *Korean American*, 28 Cal.Rptr.2d 530 (Cal.App., 1994)

act of state doctrine Courts of one country should not judge the validity of an act of another country that occurs within the latter.

actual Real; existing in fact.

actual authority The authority a principal intentionally confers on an agent or permits the agent to believe has been conferred.

actual cash value 1. Fair market value. 2. Replacement cost less depreciation.

actual damages Damages that compensate for an actual or proven loss.

Actual damages is synonymous with compensatory damages. *Saunders*, 50 Cal.Rptr.2d 395 (Cal.App., 1996)

actual fraud See positive fraud.

actual loss Amounts paid or payable as a result of a substantial loss.

actual malice 1. Conscious wrongdoing; intent to injure. Also called malice in fact. 2. Knowledge of the falsity of a defamatory statement or a reckless disregard as to truth or falsity.

Recklessly disregard the truth or know the statement is false. *Rosenaur*, 105 Cal.Rptr.2d 674 (Cal.App., 2001)

actual notice Notice given to a person directly and personally. Also called express notice.

Genuine (not imputed) knowledge. *Rosenthal*, 191 Cal.Rptr. 300 (Cal.App., 1983)

actual value Fair market value.

actuary One skilled in statistics for risk and premium calculations.

actus reus The physical deed or act that is wrongful.

ADA Americans with Disabilities Act (*www.eeoc.gov/ada*).

ad damnum clause A clause stating the damages claimed.

addict A habitual user of something, e.g., a drug.

additur A practice by which a judge offers a defendant the choice between a new trial and accepting a damage award higher than what the jury awarded.

adduce To present or introduce.

ADEA Age Discrimination in Employment Act (*www.eeoc.gov/policy/adea.html*).

adeem To take away; to revoke a bequest.

ademption The extinction of a specific bequest or devise because of the disappearance of or disposition of the subject matter of the gift from the estate of the testator in his or her lifetime.

The extinction or withdrawal of gift by some act of testator clearly indicating intent to revoke the gift. *In re Newsome*, 56 Cal.Rptr. 874 (Cal.App. 1967)

adequate consideration Fair and reasonable consideration.

adequate remedy at law A legal remedy, e.g., damages, that is complete, practical, and efficient.

adhesion contract A standard contract offered on a take-it-or-leave-it basis to a consumer who has no meaningful choice as to its terms.

A standardized contract, which, imposed and drafted by the party of superior bargaining strength, relegates to subscribing party only the opportunity to adhere to or reject the contract. *Allan*, 59 Cal.Rptr.2d 813 (Cal.App., 1996)

ad hoc For this special purpose only.

ad hominem Appealing to emotions or personal matters, not to reason.

ad idem On the same matter.

ad interim Temporarily.

adjacent Lying near or close by; next to.

adjective law Procedural law, rules of practice.

The rules according to which substantive law is administered. *Alkus*, 80 Cal.App.2d 1 (Cal.App., 1947)

adjoining Touching; contiguous.

adjourn To postpone or suspend until another time.

adjournment Postponing a session until another time.

adjudge To decide judicially.

adjudicate To judge; to resolve a dispute judicially.

adjudication A determination or judgment by a court of law.

adjudicative facts Facts concerning the who, what, when, where, and how pertaining to a particular case.

adjunction Adding or attaching one thing to another.

adjure To request solemnly.

adjust 1. To assess and determine what will be paid under an insurance policy. 2. To set a new payment plan for debts.

adjustable-rate mortgage (ARM) A mortgage with a fluctuating interest rate tied to a market index. Also called variable-rate mortgage (VRM).

adjusted basis The cost or other original basis of an asset reduced by deductions for depreciation and increased by capital improvements.

adjusted gross income (AGI) Gross income less allowable deductions.

adjuster One who determines (or settles) the amount of a claim.

An agent hired by a principal, the insurer, to investigate a claim. *Sanchez*, 84 Cal.Rptr.2d 799 (Cal.App., 1999)

ad litem For the suit, for purposes of this litigation.

administration 1. The persons or entities managing an estate, a government agency, or other organization. 2. The management and settlement of the estate of a decedent.

administrative agency See agency (2).

administrative discretion An administrative agency's power to use judgment in choosing among available alternatives.

administrative law The laws governing and created by administrative agencies.

Administrative Law Judge (ALJ) A hearing officer within an administrative agency. Also called hearing examiner.

All hearings of state agencies required to be conducted under this chapter shall be conducted by administrative law judges. Cal. Government Code § 11502

Administrative Procedure Act (APA) A federal or state statute on rulemaking and hearing procedures before administrative agencies.

An "agency may conduct an adjudicative proceeding under the administrative adjudication provisions of the Administrative Procedure Act." Cal. Government Code § 11415.10

administrative remedy Relief granted by an administrative agency.

administrator 1. A manager. 2. A person appointed by the court to manage the estate of someone who dies without a will (i.e., intestate) or who dies with a will that does not name a functioning executor.

administrator ad litem An administrator appointed by the court to represent an estate of a decedent in a court proceeding.

administrator cum testamento annexo (CTA) See cum testamento annexo.

administrator de bonis non (DBN) See de bonis non.

administratrix A woman who administers the estate of the deceased.

admiralty The law that applies to maritime disputes or offenses involving ships and navigation. Also called maritime law.

admissible Allowed into court to determine its truth or believability.

admission 1. An assertion of the truth of a fact. 2. An official acknowledgement of someone's right to practice law.

An extrajudicial recital of facts by the defendant that tends to establish his guilt. *People v. Brackett*, 280 Cal.Rptr. 305 (Cal.App., 1991)

admission against interest A statement by a party that is harmful to a position he or she is taking in the litigation.

admit To accept as true or valid.

admonition 1. A reprimand. 2. A warning from a judge to a jury.

adopt To go through a formal process of establishing a relationship of parent and child between persons.

adoptee The person adopted.

ADR See alternative dispute resolution.

ad testificandum To or for testifying.

adult A person who has reached the age of majority (e.g., 21, 18).

adulterate To contaminate by adding something inferior.

adultery Sexual relations between a married person and someone other than his or her spouse.

ad valorem tax A tax based on a percentage of the value of property.

advance 1. To lend. 2. To pay or supply something before it is due.

advance directive A statement of one's wishes regarding medical treatment upon becoming incompetent. Also called living will or healthcare proxy.

advancement A gift in advance, usually by a parent to a child. The amount or value of the gift is deducted from what the recipient eventually receives when the giver dies intestate (i.e., without a valid will).

advance sheet A pamphlet containing laws (e.g., court opinions) that comes out before a later volume of the same set.

adventure 1. A risky business venture, e.g., a shipment of goods at sea.

adversary An opponent.

adversary proceeding A hearing in which the opponents are present.

adversary system A method of resolving a legal dispute whereby the parties argue their conflicting claims before a neutral decision-maker.

adverse Having opposite interests, against.

adverse interest Goals or claims of one person that are different from or opposed to those of another.

adverse parties Parties in a suit with conflicting interests.

"Adverse party" includes every party who will be adversely affected by granting the motion. *Mundt*, 35 Cal.Rptr. 848 (Cal.App., 1963)

adverse possession A method of obtaining title to the land of another by using the land under a claim of right in a way that is open, exclusive, hostile to the current owner, and continuous.

To establish title by "adverse possession," claimant's possession must be by actual occupation that gives reasonable notice to owner and hostile to owner's title, claimant must claim property as his own either under color of title or claim of right, his possession must be continuous and uninterrupted for five years, and he must pay all taxes against property during such period. *Bell*, 318 P.2d 110 (Cal.App., 1958)

adverse witness See hostile witness.

advice 1. An opinion offered as guidance. 2. Notice that a draft has been drawn.

advice and consent The U.S. Senate's approval power on treaties and major presidential appointments. U.S. Const. art. II, § 2.

advisement Careful consideration.

advisory jury A jury whose verdict is not binding on the court.

advisory opinion An opinion of a court that is not binding.

advocacy Arguing for or against something; pleading.

advocate One who argues or pleads for another.

AFDC See Aid to Families with Dependent Children.

aff'd Affirmed.

affect To act on (upon); to influence.

affected class 1. Persons who suffered job discrimination. 2. Persons who constitute a class for bringing a class action.

affecting commerce Involving commerce or trade.

aff'g Affirming.

affiant Someone who makes an affidavit.

affidavit A written or printed statement of facts made under oath before a person with authority to administer the oath.

A written statement verified by oath or affirmation. Cal. Code of Civil Procedure § 2003; *Donnellan*, 103 Cal.Rptr.2d 882 (Cal.App., 2001)

affidavit of service A sworn statement that a document (e.g., summons) has been delivered (served) to a designated person.

affiliate A subsidiary; one corporation controlled by another.

affiliation order An order determining paternity.

affinity Relationship by marriage, not by blood.

affirm 1. To declare that a judgment is valid. 2. To assert formally, but not under oath. The noun is affirmance.

affirmance See affirm.

affirmation A solemn declaration, often a substitute for an oath.

affirmative action Steps designed to eliminate existing and continuing discrimination, to remedy the effects of past discrimination, and to create systems to prevent future discrimination.

affirmative charge An instruction that removes an issue from the jury.

affirmative defense A defense raising new facts that will defeat the plaintiff's claim even if the plaintiff's fact allegations are proven.

New matter that defendants are required to plead and prove. *Marich*, 7 Cal.Rptr.3d 60 (Cal.App., 2003)

affirmative easement An easement that forces the landowner to allow the easement holder to do specific acts on the land.

affirmative relief Relief (e.g., damages) a defendant could have sought in his or her own suit, but instead is sought in a counterclaim or cross-claim.

Relief that operates not as a defense but affirmatively and positively to defeat the plaintiff's cause of action. *Martha P.*, 12 Cal.Rptr.3d 142 (Cal.App., 2004)

affirmative warranty An insurance warranty that asserts the existence of a fact at the time the policy is entered into.

affix To attach; to add to permanently.

affray Fighting in a public place so as to cause terror in the public.

affreightment A contract to transport goods by ship.

aforementioned See aforesaid.

aforesaid Mentioned earlier in the document.

aforethought Thought of beforehand; premeditated.

a fortiori With greater force; all the more so.

after-acquired property Property acquired after a particular event, e.g., after making a will, after giving a security interest.

after-acquired title rule When a seller does not obtain title to an asset until after attempting to sell it, title automatically vests in the buyer the moment the seller obtained it.

after-born child A child born after the execution of a will.

age discrimination Discrimination on the basis of one's age.

agency 1. A relationship in which one person acts for and can bind another. 2. A governmental body, other than a court or legislature, that carries out the law.

Agency is the bilateral relationship which results from the manifestation of consent by one person to another that the other shall act on his behalf and subject to his control. *Van't Rood*, 6 Cal.Rptr.3d 746 (Cal.App., 2003)

agency shop A business or other entity that collects union dues from all employees, even those who decided not to join the union.

agent 1. A person authorized to act for another. 2. A power or force that produces an effect.

age of consent The age at which one can marry without parental consent or have sexual intercourse without the partner committing statutory rape.

age of majority The age at which a person has the right to vote, enter a contract that cannot be disaffirmed, make a will, etc. Also called full age.

age of reason The age at which a child is deemed capable of making reasoned judgments and, therefore, can commit a crime or tort.

aggravated assault A more serious crime of assault for reasons such as the defendant's intent to cause serious bodily harm.

aggravation Circumstances that increase the enormity of a crime or tort, e.g., using a weapon.

aggregate Combined into a whole.

aggregation The unpatentability of an invention because its parts lack a composite integrated mechanism.

aggregation doctrine To reach the jurisdictional amount in a federal diversity case, the total of all the claims cannot be added.

aggrieved party One whose legal rights have been invaded.

Aggrieved party with standing to appeal is one who has an immediate, pecuniary, and substantial interest which is injured by the judgment. *Schmidt*, 44 Cal.Rptr.2d 297 (Cal.App., 1995)

AGI See adjusted gross income.

agio Money paid to convert one kind of money into another.

agreed case Facts agreed upon by the parties, allowing a court to limit itself to deciding the questions of law on those facts. Also called case agreed, case stated.

agreement Mutual assent by the parties; a meeting of the minds.

An agreement is a manifestation of mutual assent by two or more persons to one another and has a wider meaning than contract, bargain, or promise. *Stevens*, 168 P.2d 492 (Cal.App., 1946)

aid and abet Assist or encourage someone to commit a crime.

To instigate, encourage, promote, or aid with guilty knowledge of the wrongful purpose of the perpetrator. *People v. Camarillo*, 72 Cal.Rptr. 296 (Cal.App., 1968)

aider by verdict A jury verdict cures technical pleading defects.

Aid to Families with Dependent Children (AFDC) Federal public assistance replaced by TANF (Temporary Assistance for Needy Families).

airbill A bill of lading used in a shipment of goods by air.

air rights The right of a landowner to use all or part of the airspace above his or her land.

air piracy Using force or threats to seize or hijack an aircraft.

aka Also known as.

alderman A member of the local legislative body.

aleatory Depending on uncertain circumstances or contingencies.

aleatory contract A contract in which performance depends on uncertain events, e.g., an insurance contract.

ALI See American Law Institute (*www.ali.org*).

***Alford* plea** A defendant pleads guilty, but does not admit guilt. *NC v. Alford*, 96 S. Ct. 160 (1970).

alias Otherwise known as; an assumed name.

alias summons; alias writ A new summons or writ given when the original one was issued without effect.

alibi A defense alleging absence from the scene of the crime.

alien One who is not a citizen of the country where he or she resides.

alienable Legally transferable to the ownership of another.

alienage The condition or status of an alien.

alienate To transfer; to transfer title.

alienation clause A clause in an insurance policy that voids the policy if the property being insured is sold or transferred.

alienation of affections The tort of causing a diminishment of the marital relationship between the plaintiff and his or her spouse.

alienee A person to whom property is conveyed or transferred.

alieni juris Under another's power.

alienor A person who transfers or conveys property.

alimony A court-ordered payment of money or other property by one spouse to another for support after divorce or separation. Also called spousal support.

An allowance for support and maintenance pending or subsequent to divorce. *Wilson*, 189 P.2d 266 (CA 1948)

alimony in gross Alimony in the form of a single definite sum that cannot be modified. Also called lump-sum alimony.

alimony pendente lite See temporary alimony.

aliquot An exact division or fractional part.

aliunde rule Jury deliberations may not be scrutinized, unless there is evidence from a source other than a juror to impeach the jury verdict.

ALJ See administrative law judge.

allegation A statement of fact that one expects to prove.

alleged Asserted as true, but not yet proven.

allegiance Loyalty owed to a government.

***Allen* charge** A supplementary instruction given to a deadlocked jury to encourage it to reach a verdict. Also called dynamite charge. *Allen v. U.S.*, 17 S. Ct. 154 (1896).

The charge did not direct jurors to decide case but reminded them of duty to attempt to reach an accommodation and said it was their duty to deliberate with goal of arriving at verdict if they could do so without violence to their individual judgments. *People v. Moore*, 117 Cal.Rptr.2d 715 (Cal.App., 2002)

all faults A sale of goods "as is," in their present condition.

all fours See on all fours.

allocation A setting aside or designation for a purpose.

allocatur It is allowed. In Pennsylvania, the permission to appeal.

allocution 1. The judge asks a convicted defendant if he or she has anything to say before sentence is imposed. 2. The defendant's right to make such a statement.

A formal inquiry by judge of defendant as to whether he has any cause to show why sentence should not be pronounced. *People v. Cross*, 28 Cal.Rptr. 918 (Cal.App., 1963)

allodial Owned absolutely, free and clear.

allograph A writing or signature made by one person for another.

allonge A slip of paper attached to a negotiable instrument to provide space for more indorsements.

A paper so attached to instrument as in effect to become part of it. *Lopez*, 49 Cal.Rptr. 122 (Cal.App., 1966)

allotment A share, e.g., the land awarded to an individual American Indian.

allotment certificate A document stating the number of shares of a security to be purchased, payment terms, etc.

allowance 1. Portion assigned or bestowed. 2. Deduction or discount.

alluvion The washing up of sand or soil so as to form firm ground.

alteration Making something different, e.g., modifying real property, changing the language or meaning of a document.

alter ego rule Personal liability can be imposed on shareholders who use the corporation for personal business.

When the corporate form is used to perpetrate a fraud or accomplish some other wrongful or inequitable purpose, the courts will ignore the corporate entity, and deem the corporation's acts to be those of the persons actually controlling the corporation. *Sonora*, 99 Cal.Rptr.2d 824 (Cal.App., 2000)

alternate valuation The value of assets 6 months after death.

alternative contract A contract that gives options for performance.

alternative dispute resolution (ADR) Arbitration, mediation, and similar methods of resolving a dispute without litigation.

alternative minimum tax (AMT) A tax imposed to assure that enough income tax is paid by persons with large deductions, credits, or exclusions.

alternative pleading Alleging facts or claims in a complaint or other pleading that are not necessarily consistent.

alternative relief Inconsistent relief sought on the same claim.

alternative writ A writ requiring a person to do a specified thing or to show cause why he or she should not be compelled to do it.

amalgamation Consolidation, e.g., two corporations into a new one.

ambassador An officer of high diplomatic rank representing a country.

ambit Boundary; the limits of a power.

ambulance chasing Soliciting injury victims by or for an attorney.

Business & Professions Code, § 6152(a)(1) [unlawful for person to act as a "runner or capper" or to solicit business for an attorney]; *Estate of Wright*, 108 Cal.Rptr.2d 572 (Cal.App., 2001)

ambulatory 1. Revocable. 2. Able to walk.

ameliorating waste Waste by a tenant that in fact improves the land.

amenable Subject to answer to the law; legally accountable.

amendment A formal change (e.g., addition, subtraction, correction) made in the text of a document (e.g., statute, legislative bill, pleading, contract).

amercement A fine or punishment imposed (e.g., on a public official) at the court's discretion.

American Law Institute (ALI) An organization of scholars that writes model acts and restatements of the law (*www.ali.org*).

American Association for Paralegal Education (AAfPE) A national association of paralegal schools (*www.aafpe.org*).

American Bar Association (ABA) A national voluntary association of attorneys (*www.abanet.org*).

American rule Each side in litigation pays its own attorney fees and court costs unless a statute provides otherwise. Under the English rule, also called loser-pays, the losing party may be required to pay the attorney fees and court costs incurred by the winning side.

California has adopted the American rule, under which each party bears its own attorney fees in litigation. Cal. Code of Civil Procedure § 1021. *Pacific*, 94 Cal.Rptr.2d 756 (Cal.App., 2000)

amicable action An action brought by mutual consent of the parties to seek a ruling on facts they do not dispute.

amicus curiae Friend of the court. A nonparty who obtains court permission to file a brief with its views on the case.

amnesty A pardon for crimes, often granted to a group.

amortization 1. The gradual elimination of a debt, often by making regular payments toward principal along with interest payments. 2. Writing off the cost of an intangible asset over its useful life.

amotion Removing or turning someone out.

amount in controversy The amount sued for. The amount needed (over $75,000) to establish diversity jurisdiction in federal court. Also called jurisdictional amount (28 U.S.C. § 1332(a)).

analogous 1. Sufficiently similar to lend support. 2. Involving facts and rules that are similar to those now under consideration.

anarchist One who believes government should not exist.

anarchy The absence of political authority or order.

ancestor A person from whom one is descended; a forebear.

ancient documents Deeds and other writings 20 or more years old that are presumed to be genuine if kept in proper custody.

Authenticity of ancient document. Cal. Evidence Code § 643

ancient lights rule Windows with outside light for a period of time (e.g., 20 years) cannot be blocked off by an adjoining landowner.

ancillary Supplementary; subsidiary.

ancillary administration An administrator appointed by the court for property or the decedent located in a different jurisdiction.

ancillary jurisdiction Authority of a court to hear claims that otherwise would not be within its jurisdiction if these claims are sufficiently related to the case properly before the court.

and his heirs Words giving transferee a fee simple absolute.

animo With the intention.

animus 1. Intention, e.g., animus furandi (intent to steal), animun testandi (intent to make a will). 2. Animosity; ill will.

annexation 1. Merging or attaching one thing to another. 2. The formal takeover or appropriation of something (e.g., territory).

annotated statutes A collection of statutes that include research references such as case summaries interpreting the statutes.

annotation A remark or note on a law, e.g., a summary of a case.

annual exclusion The amount one can give away each year gift-tax free.

annual percentage rate (APR) The true cost of borrowing money expressed as an annual interest rate.

annual report A corporation's annual financial report to stockholders.

annuitant A beneficiary of an annuity.

annuity A fixed sum payable periodically to a person for life or a specific period of time.

A periodic payment made unconditionally without any contingency. *In re Luckel's Estate*, 312 P.2d 24 (Cal.App., 1957)

annuity certain An annuity that continues paying for a set period even if the annuitant dies within the period.

annuity due An annuity payable at the start of each pay period.

annul To obliterate or nullify.

annulment 1. A nullification or voiding. 2. A declaration that a valid marriage never existed or that an attempted marriage is invalid.

A divorce terminates a legal status, whereas an annulment establishes that a marital status never existed. *Whealton*, 63 Cal.Rptr. 291 (Cal., 1967)

answer 1. The first pleading of the defendant that responds to the plaintiff's claims. 2. To assume someone else's liability.

ante Before, prior to.

ante litem motam Before the suit began or arose.

antecedent Preexisting.

antecedent debt A debt that preexists an event, e.g., filing for bankruptcy. A prior debt may be consideration for a new promise to pay.

antedate 1. To backdate; to place a date on a document that is earlier than the date the document was written. 2. To precede.

antenuptial Occurring before marriage. See premarital agreement.

antichresis An agreement giving the creditor the income from and possession of the property pledged, instead of interest.

anticipation 1. Doing something before its scheduled time. 2. Prior disclosure or use of an invention, jeopardizing its patentability.

anticipatory breach A repudiation of a contract duty before the time fixed in the contract for the performance of that duty.

A total breach occurring when the promisor without justification and before he has committed a breach makes a positive statement to promisee indicating he will not or cannot perform his contractual duties. *Daum*, 39 Cal.Rptr. 443 (Cal.App., 1964)

anticipatory search warrant A search warrant usable only on a future date, not upon issuance.

antidumping law A law against selling imported goods at less than their fair price if the imports hurt comparable domestic products.

antilapse A gift in a will goes to the heirs of the beneficiary to prevent the gift from failing because the beneficiary predeceases the testator.

antinomy A contradiction between two laws or propositions.

anti-racketeering See RICO.

antitrust law Laws against price fixing, monopolies, and other anticompetitive practices and restraints of trade.

APA See Administrative Procedure Act.

apostille A certificate authenticating foreign documents.

apparent 1. Capable of being seen; visible. 2. Seeming.

apparent authority An agent's authority the principal reasonably leads another to believe the agent had. Also called ostensible authority.

Authority created (and its scope defined) by the acts of the principal in placing the agent in such a position that he appears to have the authority which he claims or exercises. *Blanton*, 212 Cal.Rptr. 151, 157 (CA 1985)

apparent defects Defects observable upon reasonable inspection. Also called patent defects.

apparent heir An heir who will inherit unless he or she predeceases the ancestor or is disinherited by will. Also called heir apparent.

app. Appellate; appeal.

appeal Asking a higher tribunal to review or reconsider the decision of an inferior tribunal.

appealable Sufficiently final so that it can be appealed.

appeal bond A bond of a party filing an appeal to cover the opponent's costs if the appeal is later deemed to have been not genuine.

appearance Formally coming before a tribunal as a party or as a representative of a party.

appellant The person or party who brings the appeal.

appellate Concerning appeals or an appellate court.

appellate brief See brief (1).

appellate jurisdiction The power of an appellate court to review and correct the decisions of a lower tribunal.

appellee The person against whom an appeal is brought. Respondent.

append To attach.

appoint To give someone a power or authority.

appointee The person selected.

apportionment 1. A proportional division. 2. The process of allocating legislators among several political subdivisions.

The process employed by the Workers' Compensation Appeals Board to allocate legal responsibility. *Marsh*, 30 Cal.Rptr.3d 598 (Cal.App., 2005)

appraisal Estimation of value or worth.

appraisal remedy A shareholder's right to have its shares bought back by the corporation due to dissent with an extraordinary corporate decision.

appraiser Someone who impartially evaluates (appraises) property.

appreciation Increase in property value, often due to inflation.

apprehension 1. Knowledge. 2. Fear. 3. Seizure or arrest.

appropriation 1. Taking control or possession. 2. An invasion-of-privacy tort committed by the use of a person's name, likeness, or personality for commercial gain without authorization. 3. The legislature's setting aside of money for a specific purpose.

approval sale See sale on approval.

appurtenance A thing or right belonging or attached to something else.

Things belonging to another thing as principal and pass as incident to the principal thing. *Von Rohr*, 173 P.2d 828 (Cal.App., 1946)

appurtenant Belonging to; incident to the principal property.

appurtenant easement See easement appurtenant.

APR See annual percentage rate.

a priori Deductively; derived from logic or self-evident propositions, without reference to observed experience.

arbiter A referee or judge, someone who can resolve a dispute.

arbitrage Simultaneous matched purchase and sale of identical or equivalent securities in order to profit from price discrepancies.

arbitrament 1. The decision of an arbitrator. 2. The act of deciding.

arbitrary Capricious, subjective. Biased individual preferences.

Action is arbitrary not only when it is capricious, but when facts do not reasonably justify conclusion. *Hollon*, 64 Cal.Rptr. 808 (Cal.App., 1967)

arbitration The submission of a dispute to an impartial third person for a binding decision as an alternative to litigation.

arbitration clause A contract clause providing for compulsory arbitration of disputes under the contract.

arbitrator The person rendering the decision in arbitration.

arguendo In arguing; for the sake of argument.

argument A presentation of reasons for a legal position.

argumentative Containing conclusions as well as facts; contentious.

Jury instruction is argumentative when it invites the jury to draw inferences favorable to one of the parties. *People v. Lewis*, 110 Cal.Rptr.2d 272 (CA 2001)

arise 1. To stem from or originate. 2. To come into notice.

aristocracy A government ruled by a superior or privileged class.

ARM See adjustable-rate mortgage.

armed robbery Robbery committed while armed with a dangerous weapon.

arm's length As between two strangers who are looking out for their own self-interests.

arraignment A court proceeding in which the accused is formally charged with a crime and enters a plea of guilty, not guilty, etc. The verb is arraign.

arrangement with creditors A plan whereby the debtor settles with his or her creditors or obtains more time to repay debts.

array A group of persons summoned to be considered for jury duty.

arrearages, arrears Unpaid debts; overdue debts.

arrest Taking someone into custody to answer a criminal charge.

Taking into physical custody, minimal body searching, booking and incarceration or release on bail. *People v. Monroe*, 16 Cal.Rptr.2d 267 (Cal.App., 1993)

arrest of judgment A court's staying of a judgment because of errors.

arrest record 1. A form filled out when the police arrest someone. 2. A list of a person's prior arrests.

arrest warrant A written order of a judge or magistrate that a person be arrested and brought before the court.

arrogation Claiming or seizing something without authority or right.

arson The willful and malicious burning of property.

At common law, arson was the willful and malicious burning of the dwelling house of another, but it has been extended by statute to include many acts of burning not involving special danger to the person. *Ex parte Bramble*, 187 P.2d 411 (CA 1947)

art 1. Applying knowledge and skill to produce a desired result. 2. A process or method to produce a useful result. 3. See terms of act.

art. Article.

artful pleading An attempt to phrase a federal claim as a state claim.

article A part or subdivision of a law or document.

Article I court A federal court created by legislation. Also called legislative courts.

Article III court A federal court created by the United States Constitution in article III. Also called constitutional court.

articled clerk In England, one apprenticed to a solicitor.

Articles of Confederation The governing document for the thirteen original states.

articles of impeachment Formal accusations against a public official asserted as grounds for removing him or her from office.

articles of incorporation The document that establishes (incorporates) a corporation and identifies its basic functions and rules.

artifice Contrivance, trick, or fraud.

artificial person A legal person. An entity, such as a corporation, created under the laws of the state and treated in some respects as a human being. Also called fictitious person, juristic person.

artisan's lien See mechanic's lien.

ascendant An ancestor, e.g., grandparent.

as is In its present condition; no warranty given.

asportation Carrying away for purposes of larceny.

To satisfy the asportation requirement for robbery, no great movement is required, and it is not necessary that the property be taken out of the physical presence of the victim; slight movement is enough. *People v. Hill*, 72 Cal.Rptr.2d 656 (CA 1998)

assailant One who attacks or assaults another.

assault 1. As a tort, assault is an act intended to cause harmful or offensive contact with another or an imminent apprehension of such contact and the other is thereby placed in such imminent apprehension. 2. As a crime, assault may require an intent to cause physical harm and actual contact with the victim.

assault and battery The crime of battery.

assay An examination to test the quality and quantity of metals.

assembly 1. A gathering of people for a common goal. 2. One of the houses of the legislature in many states.

assent Agreement, approval.

assert To declare; to state as true.

assessable stock Stock that subjects the holder to an additional assessment or contribution.

assessment 1. A determination of the value of something, often for purposes of taxation. 2. A determination of the share that is due from someone; an amount assessed. 3. The requirement of an additional payment to a business.

The process of ascertaining and adjusting shares respectively to be contributed by several persons toward common beneficial object according to benefit received. *Dare*, 91 Cal.Rptr. 124 (Cal.App., 1970)

assessed ratio The ratio of assessed value to fair market value.

assessment work Labor on a mining claim each year to maintain the claim.

assessor A technical expert or adviser, e.g., on making assessments.

asset Anything of value; tangible or intangible property.

asset depreciation range IRS's range of depreciable lives of assets.

asseveration A solemn declaration.

assign 1. To transfer or convey property or rights. 2. To point out or specify, e.g., errors. 3. See assigns.

assigned counsel A court-appointed attorney for a poor person.

assigned risk A person an insurance company is required to insure.

assignee The person to whom property or rights are transferred.

assignment The transfer of ownership or rights.

A manifestation by the owner of a right indicating his intention to transfer the right to another. *O'Donnell*, 67 Cal.Rptr. 274 (Cal.App., 1968)

assignment for benefit of creditors A transfer of the debtor's property to a trustee, with authority to liquidate the debtor's affairs and distribute the proceeds equitably to creditors.

assignment of errors A party's list of errors claimed to have been made by a trial court submitted to an appellate court on appeal.

assignor The person who transfers property or rights.

assigns Assignees; persons to whom property or rights are transferred.

assise; assize An old English court, law, or writ.

assistance of counsel. See effective assistance of counsel.

associate An attorney employee who hopes one day to be promoted to partner.

associate justice An appellate court judge who is not the chief justice.

association 1. An organization of people joined for a common purpose. 2. An unincorporated company or other organization.

assume 1. To take upon oneself. 2. To suppose without proof.

assumpsit 1. A promise. 2. An action for breach of contract.

assumption 1. The act of taking something upon oneself. 2. Something taken for granted without proof.

assumption of mortgage A property buyer's agreement to be personally liable for payment of an already existing mortgage.

assumption of the risk The knowing and voluntary acceptance of the risk of being harmed by someone's negligence or other conduct.

Assumption of risk refers to (a) primary assumption of risk in which the issue is whether defendant owed plaintiff a duty of care, and (b) secondary assumption of risk, in which defendant had breached a duty of care but issue was whether plaintiff had chosen to face the risk of harm presented by defendant's breach. *Vine*, 13 Cal.Rptr.3d 370 (Cal.App., 2004)

assurance 1. A statement tending to inspire confidence. 2. Insurance. 3. A pledge or guarantee. 4. The act (and the document) that conveys real property.

assured A person who has been insured.

asylum 1. A sanctuary or hiding place. 2. A government's protection given to a political refugee from another country. Also called political asylum.

at bar Currently before the court.

at issue In dispute.

at large 1. Free. 2. An entire area rather than one of its districts.

at law Pertaining to a court of law as opposed to a court of equity.

at risk Pertaining to an investment that could lead to actual loss.

attaché A person in a diplomatic office with a specific specialty.

attachment The act or process of taking, apprehending, or seizing persons or property, by virtue of writ, summons, or other judicial order, and bringing same into custody of the law.

A remedy by which a plaintiff with a contractual claim to money may have defendant's property seized before judgment and held by a levying officer for execution after judgment. *Waffer*, 82 Cal.Rptr.2d 241 (Cal.App., 1999)

attachment bond A bond given by one whose property has been attached in order to reclaim it and provide protection to the party who attached it.

attainder The loss of civil rights upon receiving a death sentence or being designated as an outlaw.

attaint 1. To disgrace or condemn to attainder. 2. To accuse a jury of giving a false verdict.

attempt An overt act or conduct (beyond mere preparation) performed with the intent to commit a crime that was not completed.

An attempt to commit any crime requires a specific intent to commit that particular offense. *People v. Montes*, 5 Cal.Rptr.3d 800 (Cal.App., 2003)

attendant circumstances Relevant facts surrounding an event.

attenuation Illegally obtained evidence might be admissible if the link between the illegal conduct and the evidence is so attenuated as to dissipate the taint.

attest To affirm to be true or genuine; to bear witness.

attestation clause A clause stating that you saw (witnessed) someone sign a document or perform other tasks related to the validity of the document.

attorn 1. To transfer something to another. 2 To acknowledge being the tenant of a new landlord.

attorney 1. One licensed to practice law. A lawyer. Also called attorney at law. 2. One authorized to act in place of or for another. Also called attorney-in-fact.

Attorney-in-fact is simply an agent acting under written grant of authority. *Delos*, 155 Cal.Rptr. 843 (Cal.App., 1979)

attorney at law See attorney (1).

attorney-client privilege A client and an attorney can refuse to disclose communications between them if their purpose was to facilitate the provision of legal services to the client.

attorney general The chief attorney for the government.

attorney in fact See attorney (2).

attorney of record The attorney noted in the court files as the attorney representing a particular party.

attorney's lien The right of an attorney to retain possession of money or property of a client until his or her proper fees have been paid.

The equitable right to have fees and costs due to attorney for services in suit secured to him out of judgment or recovery. *Isrin*, 45 Cal.Rptr. 320 (CA 1965)

attorney work product See work product rule.

attornment See attorn.

attractive nuisance doctrine A duty of reasonable care is owed to prevent injury to a trespassing child unable to appreciate the danger from an artificial condition or activity on land to which the child can be expected to be attracted. Also called turntable doctrine.

attribution Assigning one taxpayer's ownership interest to another.

at-will employee An employee with no contract protection. An employee who can quit or be terminated at any time and for any reason.

auction A public sale of assets to the highest bidder.

audit An examination of records to verify financial or other data.

auditor Someone who performs audits, often an accountant.

augmented estate A decedent's estate with adjustments keyed to the length of marriage and gifts decedent made shortly before death.

authentication Evidence that a writing or other physical item is genuine and is what it purports to be.

Authentication simply requires a party to establish the genuineness and authenticity of the writing. Cal. Evidence Code, §§ 1400. *Interinsurance*, 118 Cal.Rptr. 596 (Cal.App., 1975)

author An originator of a work in various media (e.g., print, film) plus other participants with copyright protection, e.g., translators.

authority 1. The power or right to act. 2. A source relied upon.

authorize To give power or permission; to approve.

authorized stock See capital stock (1).

automobile guest statute See guest statute.

autopsy An examination of a cadaver to identify the cause of death. Also called postmortem.

autoptic evidence See demonstrative evidence.

autrefois acquit A plea that one has already been acquitted of the offense.

autre vie Another's life.

aver To assert or allege.

average 1. Usual, ordinary, norm. 2. Mean, median. 3. Partial loss or damage.

averment A positive allegation or assertion of fact.

avoid 1. To annul or cancel. 2. To escape.

avoidable consequences See mitigation of damages.

Under avoidable consequences doctrine, person injured by another's wrongful conduct will not be compensated for damages that injured person could have avoided by reasonable effort or expenditure. *State Dept. of Health*, 6 Cal.Rptr.3d 441 (CA 2003)

avoidance Escaping; invalidating. See also confession and avoidance.

avowal 1. An offer to prove. 2. An acknowledgement.

avulsion The sudden loss or addition to land caused by flood or by a shift in the bed or course of a stream.

award What a court or other tribunal gives or grants via its decision.

axiom An established or self-evident principle.

AWOL Absent without leave or permission. See also desertion.

B

baby act A minor's defense of infancy in a breach of contract action.

BAC See blood alcohol concentration.

bachelor of laws See LL.B.

back To assume financial responsibility for; to indorse.

bad 1. Defective. 2. Void or invalid.

bad check A check dishonored for insufficient funds.

bad debt An uncollectible debt.

bad faith 1. Dishonest purpose. Also called mala fides. 2. The absence of a reasonable basis to delay or deny an insurance claim.

Bad faith implies dishonesty, fraud and concealment. *Davy*, 5 Cal.Rptr. 488 (Cal.App., 1960)

badge of fraud Factors from which an inference of fraud can be drawn.

bad law 1. A court opinion that fails to follow precedent or statutes. 2. A court opinion whose broader implications are unfortunate even though probably accurate for the narrow facts before the court.

bad title Title that is so defective as to be unmarketable.

bail 1. Money or other property deposited with the court as security to ensure that the defendant will reappear at designated times. Failure to appear forfeits the security. 2. Release of the defendant upon posting this security. 3. The one providing this security.

Bail is the person in whose custody the defendant is placed when released from jail and who acts as surety. *People v. Ranger*, 1 Cal.Rptr.3d 875 (Cal.App., 2003)

bailable offense An offense for which an accused is eligible for bail.

bail bond A surety contract under which the surety will pay the state the amount of the bond if the accused fails to appear in court.

A bail bond is in the nature of a contract between the government and the surety; the surety acts as a guarantor of the defendant's appearance under risk of forfeiture of the bond. *Overland*, 23 Cal.Rptr.3d 676 (Cal.App., 2005)

bailee One to whom property is entrusted under a contract of bailment.

bailiff A court officer with duties in court, e.g., keep order.

bail jumping See jump bail.

bailment A delivery of personal property by one person to another under an express or implied contract whereby the property will be redelivered when the purpose of the contract is completed.

bailment for hire A bailment under which the bailee is paid.

bailor One who delivers property to another under a contract of bailment.

bailout 1. Financial help to one in need of rescue. 2. Seeking alternative tax treatment of income.

bait and switch Using a low-priced item to lure a customer to a merchant who then pressures the customer to buy another item at a higher price.

balance 1. To calculate the difference between what has been paid and what is due. 2. To check to ensure that debits and credits are equal. 3. The equality of debits and credits. 4. See balancing test.

balance sheet A dated statement showing assets, liabilities, and owners' investment.

balancing test Weighing competing interests or values in order to resolve a legal issue.

balloon note A note on a loan calling for a large final payment and smaller intervening periodic payments.

ballot A paper or other media on which to vote; a list of candidates.

ban 1. To prohibit. 2. An announcement.

banc Bench. See also en banc.

banish See exile.

bank A financial institution that receives money on deposit, exchanges money, makes loans, and performs similar functions.

The term "bank" means the slope or elevation of land that bounds the bed of the stream in a permanent or longstanding way. *People v. Osborn*, 11 Cal.Rptr.3d 14 (Cal.App., 2004)

bank bill See bank note.

bank credit Money a bank allows a customer to borrow.

bank draft A check that one bank writes on its account with another bank.

banker's lien The right of a bank to seize property of a depositor in the bank's possession to satisfy a customer's debt to the bank.

bank note A promissory note issued by a bank payable to bearer on demand and usable as cash. Also called bank bill.

bankrupt 1. Unable to pay debts as they are due. 2. A debtor undergoing a bankruptcy proceeding.

bankruptcy 1. The federal process by which a bankruptcy court gives a debtor relief by liquidating some or all of the unsecured debts or by otherwise rearranging debts and payment schedules. 2. Insolvency.

bankruptcy estate Assets of a debtor when bankruptcy is filed.

bankruptcy trustee See trustee in bankruptcy.

bar 1. The court or court system. 2. The courtroom partition behind which spectators sit. 3. All the attorneys licensed to practice in a jurisdiction. 4. The examination taken by attorneys to become licensed to practice law. 5. An impediment or barrier to bringing or doing something.

An integrated bar conditions the practice of law in a particular state upon membership and mandatory dues payments. *Keller*, 255 Cal.Rptr. 542 (CA 1989)

bar association An association of members of the legal profession.

bar examination See bar (4).

bare licensee One who enters the land for his or her own purposes, but with the express or implied consent of the occupier. Also called naked licensee.

bareboat charter A document under which one who charters or leases a boat becomes for the period of the charter the owner for all practical purposes. Also called demise charter.

bargain 1. To negotiate the terms of a contract. 2. An agreement establishing the obligations of the parties.

bargain and sale deed A deed of conveyance without covenants.

bargaining agent A union bargaining on behalf of its members.

bargaining unit A group of employees allowed to conduct collective bargaining for other employees.

barratry 1. Persistently instigating or stirring up lawsuits. 2. Fraud or other misconduct by a captain or crew that harms the ship owner.

Common barratry is the practice of exciting groundless judicial proceedings. Cal. Penal Code § 158

barrister An attorney in England and other Commonwealth countries who is allowed to try cases in specific courts.

barter To exchange goods or services without the use of money.

basis 1. The foundation; the underlying principle. 2. The cost or other amount assigned to an asset for income tax purposes.

bastard A child born before its parents were married or born from those who never married. An illegitimate child.

bastardy proceeding See paternity suit.

battered child syndrome A diagnosis that a child's injury or injuries are not accidental and are presumed to have been caused by someone of mature strength, such as an adult caregiver.

A medical diagnosis based on probability—as is the case with the battered child syndrome diagnosis—is admissible; the lack of scientific certainty does not deprive the medical opinion of its evidentiary value. *People v. Cegers*, 9 Cal.Rptr.2d 297 (Cal.App., 1992)

battered woman syndrome Psychological helplessness because of a woman's financial dependence, loneliness, guilt, shame, and fear of reprisal from her husband or boyfriend who has repeatedly battered her in the past.

battery An intentional touching of the person of another that is harmful or offensive. Battery can be a tort and a crime.

Any intentional, unlawful and harmful contact by one person with the person of another. *Piedra*, 21 Cal.Rptr.3d 36 (Cal.App., 2004)

bear 1. To produce or yield. 2. To carry.

bearer One who holds or possesses a negotiable instrument that is payable to bearer or to cash.

bearer paper Commercial paper payable to one who holds or possesses it.

belief The mind's acceptance that something is probably true or certain.

belief-action There are no unconstitutional beliefs, but a person's actions can violate constitutional rights.

belligerent A country at war or in armed conflict.

below 1. Pertaining to a lower court in the judicial system. 2. Later in the document.

bench The court, the judge's seat, or the judiciary.

bench conference A meeting at the judge's bench between the judge and the attorneys out of the hearing of the jury. Also called a sidebar conference.

bench memo A memorandum of law by a party's attorney for a trial judge or by a law clerk for a judge.

bench trial A trial without a jury. Also called nonjury trial.

bench warrant A judge's direct order for the arrest of a person.

A process issued by court itself, or from the bench, for attachment of a person to compel his attendance before court. Cal. Code of Civil Procedure §§ 1211. *Silvagni*, 321 P.2d 15 (Cal.App., 1958)

beneficial Tending to the benefit of a person.

beneficial interest A right to a benefit from property or an estate as opposed to the legal ownership of that property or estate.

Beneficial interest (on the issue of standing) means some special interest to be served or some particular right to be preserved or protected over and above the interest held in common with the public at large. *Chen*, 13 Cal.Rptr.3d 248 (Cal.App., 2004)

beneficial owner See equitable owner.

beneficial use A right to the benefits of property when legal title to the property may be held by others.

beneficiary 1. A person whom a trust was created to benefit. 2. A person entitled to insurance benefits. 3. One who receives a benefit.

benefit Assistance, advantage, profit, or privilege; payment or gift.

benefit of clergy 1. A former right of clerics not to be tried in secular courts. 2. The approval or blessing given by a religious rite.

benefit of the bargain rule 1. In a fraud action, the damages should be the value as represented less the value actually received. 2. In a contract action, the damages should be what would place the victim in the position he or she would have been in if the contract had not been breached. Also called loss of bargain rule.

bequeath To give property (sometimes only personal property) by will.

bequest Property (sometimes only personal property) given in a will.

A demonstrative legacy is a testamentary term frequently used interchangeably with the term "bequest" in describing gifts of personal property in general. *Estate of Lindner,* 149 Cal.Rptr. 331 (Cal.App., 1978)

best efforts Diligence more exacting than the duty of good faith.

best evidence rule When a factual dispute arises about a writing, painting, photograph, or recording, the original should be produced unless it is unavailable. Also called original document rule.

The Best Evidence Rule is repealed and replaced with the Secondary Evidence Rule. Cal. Evidence Code § 1521

bestiality Sexual relations between a human and an animal.

bestow To give or convey.

best use See highest and best use.

betterment A property improvement beyond mere repairs.

beyond a reasonable doubt See reasonable doubt.

BFOQ See bona fide occupational qualification.

BFP See bona fide purchaser.

BIA Bureau of Indian Affairs (*www.doi.gov/bureau-indian-affairs.html*).

biannual 1. Twice a year. 2. Every 2 years.

bias A tendency or inclination to think and to act in a certain way. A danger of prejudgment. Prejudice.

Actual bias defined as a state of mind that would prevent that person from acting impartially. *People v. Hillhouse,* Cal.Rptr.2d 45 (CA 2002)

bicameral Having two chambers or houses in the legislature.

bid 1. An offer to perform a contract for a designated price. 2. An offer to pay a designated price for property, e.g., auction bid.

bid and asked Price ranges quoted for securities in an over-the-counter market.

bid bond A bond to protect the government if a bidder fails to enter the contract according to its bid.

bid in A bid on property by its owner to set a floor auction price.

bid shopping A general contractor's use of a low subcontractor's bid as a tool to negotiate lower bids from other subcontractors.

biennial 1. Occurring every 2 years. 2. Lasting 2 years.

biennium A 2-year period.

bifurcated trial A case in which certain issues are tried separately (e.g., guilt and punishment; liability and damages).

bigamy Marrying while still in a valid marriage with someone else.

bilateral contract A contract of mutual promises between the parties.

A contract in which each party is both a promisor and a promisee. *Smith,* 18 Cal.Rptr. 833 (Cal.App., 1962)

bilateral mistake See mutual mistake.

bill 1. A proposed statute. Legislation under consideration for enactment by the legislature. 2. The statute that has been enacted. 3. A statement of money owed. 4. Paper money. 5. A pleading that states a claim in equity. Also called bill in equity. 6. A list of specifics or particulars. 7. A draft. See bill of exchange.

billable Pertaining to tasks for which an attorney, paralegal, or other timekeeper can charge a client fees.

bill in equity See bill (5).

bill of attainder An act of the legislature that imposes punishment (e.g., death) on a specific person or group without a trial.

A legislative act that inflicts punishment without a judicial trial. *California State Employees' Assn.,* 108 Cal.Rptr. 251 (Cal.App., 1973)

bill of exchange See draft (1).

bill of health A certificate on the health of a ship's cargo and crew.

bill of indictment A document asking the grand jury to determine whether enough evidence exists to bring a formal criminal charge against the accused.

bill of lading A document from a carrier that lists (and acknowledges receipt of) the goods to be transported and the terms of their delivery.

A document evidencing the receipt of goods for shipment issued by a person engaged in the business of transporting or forwarding goods, and that, by its terms, evidences the intention of the issuer that the person entitled under the document has the right to receive, hold, and dispose of the document and the goods it covers. Bill of lading includes an airbill. Cal. Commercial Code § 1201(6)

bill of pains and penalties An act of the legislature that imposes punishment (other than death) on a specific person or group without a trial.

bill of particulars A more detailed statement of the civil claims or criminal charges brought against another.

bill of review A request that a court of equity revise a decree.

bill of rights A list of fundamental rights, e.g., the first ten amendments to the U.S. Constitution.

bill of sale A document that conveys title to personal property from seller to buyer.

bind To place under a legal duty.

binder 1. A contract giving temporary protection to the insured until a formal policy is issued. 2. A statement (and often a deposit) to secure the right to purchase property.

A binder is a temporary contract of insurance. *Adams,* 132 Cal.Rptr.2d 24 (Cal.App., 2003)

binding instruction See mandatory instruction.

bind over 1. To hold or transfer for further court proceedings. 2. To place under an obligation.

blackacre A fictitious name for a parcel of land. Also, whiteacre.

black code Laws of southern states regulating slavery.

black letter law A statement of a fundamental or basic principle of law. Also called hornbook law.

blackmail Unlawful demand of money or property under threat of bodily harm, property damage, accusation of crime, or exposure. Extortion.

black market Illegal avenues for buying and selling.

blanket bond 1. A bond protecting against loss from employee dishonesty. 2. A bond covering a group rather than named persons.

blank indorsement An indorsement without naming a person to whom the instrument is to be paid.

When indorsed in blank, an instrument becomes payable to bearer and may be negotiated by transfer of possession alone until specially indorsed. Cal. Commercial Code § 3205(b)

blasphemy Language or acts showing contempt for God or sacred matters.

blind trust A trust with a trustee who acts without control or influence by the owner or settlor to avoid a conflict of interest.

blockage rule A tax rule allowing a lower value for a large block of shares than the sum of their individual values.

blockbusting Persuading homeowners to sell by asserting that minority newcomers will lower property values.

blood alcohol concentration (BAC) The percentage of alcohol in a person's blood.

blotter A book recording daily events, e.g., arrests.

bluebook 1. Popular name of *A Uniform System of Citation*, a citation guidebook. 2. A directory of government offices and employees.

blue chip Pertaining to a high-quality investment stock.

blue flu Police officers call in sick as a labor protest.

blue laws Laws regulating Sunday commerce.

blue ribbon jury A jury with members having special skills.

blue sky laws State securities laws to prevent fraud.

California's blue sky law (Corporations Code, § 25000 et seq.) makes it unlawful to offer or sell in this state any security in an issuer transaction unless such sale has been qualified. *People ex rel. Bender*, 269 Cal.Rptr. 106 (Cal.App., 1990)

board 1. A group of persons with authority to manage or advise. 2. Regular meals.

boarder One to whom meals are supplied, often with a room.

board of aldermen A local legislative body, e.g., city council.

board of directors Individuals elected by shareholders to hire officers and set policy.

board of education A government body that manages local public schools.

board of equalization A government agency with responsibility for ensuring that the tax burden is distributed fairly in a particular state or district.

The board of equalization was created to equalize property values by adjusting individual assessments. *International Medication*, 67 Cal.Rptr.2d 394 (Cal.App., 1997)

board of pardons A government agency with the power to issue pardons.

board of parole See parole board.

board of supervisors The body that governs a county.

board of trade 1. An organization of businesses that promote common business interests. 2. The governing body of a commodities exchange.

bodily harm Physical damage to the body, including injury, illness, and pain.

bodily heir See heir of the body.

bodily injury Physical harm or damage to the body. Also called physical injury.

body 1. A collection or laws. 2. The main section(s) of a document. 3. A person, group, or entity.

body corporate Another term for corporation.

body execution Taking a person into custody by order of the court.

body of the crime See corpus delicti.

body politic The people of a nation or state as a political group.

bogus Counterfeit, sham.

boilerplate Standard language commonly used in some documents.

boiler room sale A high-pressure phone sale of goods and services, e.g., securities.

bona fide In good faith; sincere.

bona fide occupational qualification (BFOQ) Sex or other discrimination that is reasonably necessary for the operation of a particular business.

bona fide purchaser (BFP) One who has purchased property for value without notice of defects in the title of seller or of any claims in the property by others. Also called good faith purchaser, innocent purchaser.

One who has purchased property for value without any notice of any defects in the title of the seller. *Walters*, 102 Cal.Rptr. 89 (Cal.App. 1972)

bona immobilia Immovable property such as land.

bond 1. A certificate that is evidence of a debt in which the entity that issues the bond (a company or a governmental body) promises (a) to pay the bondholders a specified amount of interest for a specified amount of time and (b) to repay the loan on the expiration date. 2. An obligation to perform an act (e.g., payment of a sum of money) upon the occurrence or nonoccurrence of a designated condition. 3. A promise or binding agreement.

A surety bond is a written instrument executed by the principal and surety in which the surety agrees to answer for the debt, default, or miscarriage of the principal. *American Contractors*, 9 Cal.Rptr.3d 835 (Cal.App., 2004)

bond discount An amount that is lower than the face value of the bond.

bonded Placed under or secured by a bond.

bonded debt A debt that has the added backing or security of a bond.

bonded warehouse A private warehouse that stores imported goods subject to special taxes or custom duties.

bondholder One who holds a government, corporate, or commercial bond.

bond issue Bonds offered for sale at the same time.

bond premium An amount that is higher than the face value of the bond.

bondsman A surety; a person or business that guarantees a bond.

bonification A forgiveness of taxes, usually on exports.

bonus Extra; a consideration paid in addition to what is strictly due.

Something given in addition to employee's agreed compensation. *J. C. Peacock*, 16 Cal.Rptr. 518 (Cal.App., 1961)

book 1. To enter charges against someone on a police register. The process is called booking. 2. To engage the services of someone. 3. Books: original financial or accounting records. Also called books of account. See also shop-book rule.

book entry 1. A note in a financial ledger or book. 2. A statement acknowledging ownership of securities.

booking See book (1).

bookkeeper One who records financial accounts and transactions.

bookmaking Taking or placing or offering to take or place a bet for another.

The making of a betting book, including the taking of bets. Cal. Penal Code, § 337a. *People v. Thompson*, 24 Cal.Rptr. 101 (Cal.App., 1962)

bookie One engaged in bookmaking.

books; books of account See book (3).

book value 1. The value at which an asset is carried on a balance sheet. 2. Net worth.

Boolean search A computer search that allows words to be included or excluded by using operatives such as AND, OR, and NOT in the query.

boot 1. The taxable component in a transaction that is otherwise not taxable. 2. An additional payment or consideration.

bootlegger One who deals in (e.g., copies, sells) products illegally.

bootstrap sale Using the future earnings of a business to acquire that business.

border search A search upon entering the country, usually at the border.

borough A political subdivision of a state with self-governing powers.

borrowed servant rule See loaned servant doctrine.

bottomry A contract by which the owner of a ship borrows money for a voyage, giving the ship as security for the loan.

bought and sold notes Written confirmations of a sale from a broker to the buyer and seller.

bound 1. To identify the boundary. 2. Obligated. See also bind.

bound over See bind over.

bounty 1. A reward. 2. Generosity.

boycott A concerted refusal to work or do business with a particular person or business in order to obtain concessions or to express displeasure with certain practices of the person or business.

Civil Code, § 51.5 specifies that business establishments may not "discriminate against, boycott or blacklist, or refuse to buy from, contract with, sell to, or trade with any person in this state." *Alch*, 19 Cal.Rptr.3d 29 (Cal.App., 2004)

***Brady* material** Evidence known by the prosecution to be favorable to the defense must be disclosed to the defendant. *Brady v. Maryland*, 83 S. Ct. 1194 (1963).

brain death Irreversible cessation of circulatory and respiratory functions, or irreversible cessation of all functions of the entire brain, including the brain stem. Also called legal death.

branch A subdivision, member, or department.

Brandeis brief An appellate brief in which economic and social studies are included along with legal principles.

breach The breaking or violation of a legal duty or law.

breach of contract The failure to perform a contract obligation.

breach of promise to marry Breaking an engagement (promise) to marry.

breach of the peace A violation or disturbance of the public tranquility and order. Disorderly conduct.

Breach of the peace as used in misdemeanor statute means a disruption of public order by acts which are themselves violent or which tend to incite others to violence. Cal. Penal Code, § 415. *In re Bushman*, 83 Cal.Rptr. 375 (CA 1970)

breach of trust Violation of a fiduciary obligation by a trustee.

breach of warranty Breaking an express or implied warranty.

breaking a close Trespassing on land.

breaking and entering See burglary.

breaking bulk Unlawfully opening by a bailee of a container entrusted to his or her care and stealing the contents.

breathalyzer A device to measure blood alcohol concentration.

breve A writ.

bribe An offer, acceptance, or solicitation of an unlawful payment with the understanding that it will corruptly affect the official action of the recipient.

bridge loan A short-term loan given until other funding is arranged.

brief 1. Shorthand for appellate brief, which is a document submitted by a party to an appellate court in which arguments are presented on why the appellate court should affirm (approve), reverse, or otherwise modify what a lower court has done. 2. A document submitted to a trial court in support of a particular position. 3. A summary of the main or essential parts of a court opinion. 4. Shorthand for a trial brief, which is an attorney's personal notes on how to conduct a trial.

bright-line rule A clear-cut (but sometimes overly simple) legal principle that resolves a dispute.

bring an action To sue someone.

broad interpretation See liberal construction.

broker An agent who arranges or negotiates contracts for others.

A person whose business it is to bring a buyer and seller together. *Rhode*, 210 P.2d 768 (Cal.App., 1949)

brokerage 1. The business or occupation of a broker. 2. The wages or commissions of a broker.

broker-dealer A firm that buys and sells securities as an agent for others and as a principal, buying or selling in its own name.

brutum fulmen 1. An empty threat. 2. An invalid judgment.

bubble An extravagant commercial project based on deception.

bucket shop A fraudulent business that pretends to be engaged in securities transactions.

buggery Sodomy or bestiality.

building code Laws that provide standards for constructing buildings.

building line Distances from the ends and sides of the lot beyond which construction may not extend.

bulk goods Goods not divided into parts or packaged in separate units.

bulk sale or transfer The sale of all or a large part of a seller's inventory, not in the ordinary course of the seller's business.

bulletin An ongoing or periodic publication.

bull market A stock market climate of persistent rising prices.

bumping 1. Depriving someone of a reserved seat due to overbooking. 2. Replacing a worker with someone more senior.

burden 1. A duty or responsibility. 2. A limitation or hindrance.

burden of going forward The obligation to produce some evidence tending to prove (not necessarily conclusive evidence) one's case. Also called burden of producing evidence, burden of production.

A party's obligation to introduce evidence sufficient to establish a prima facie case, or, in other words, sufficient to avoid nonsuit. *Fisher*, 209 Cal.Rptr. 682 (Cal., 1984)

burden of persuasion The obligation to convince the trier of fact (judge or jury) that the party has introduced enough evidence on the truth of its version of the facts to meet the standard of proof, e.g., preponderance of the evidence. Also called risk of nonpersuasion.

Burden of production entails only the presentation of evidence, while a burden of persuasion entails the establishment through such evidence of a requisite degree of belief. Cal. Evidence Code §§ 110, 115. *Aguilar*, 107 Cal.Rptr.2d 841 (CA 2001)

burden of producing evidence See burden of going forward.

burden of production See burden of going forward.

burden of proof The obligation of proving the facts of one's claim. This obligation is met by meeting the burden of going forward and the burden of persuasion.

***Burford* abstention** To avoid unnecessary federal-state friction, a federal court can refuse to review a state court's decision involving complex state regulations or sensitive state policies. *Burford v. Sun Oil Co.*, 63 S. Ct. 1098 (1943).

burglary 1. Entering a building of another with the intent to commit a felony therein. 2. Breaking and entering the dwelling house of another in the nighttime with the intent to commit a felony therein.

The entry of any of a number of enumerated private spaces, with intent to commit grand or petit larceny or any felony. Cal. Penal Code § 459. *In re Ryan N.*, 112 Cal.Rptr.2d 620 (Cal.App., 2001)

burgle To commit burglary; to burglarize.

bursar Someone in charge of funds, especially at a college.

business agent 1. One selected by union members to represent them. 2. A manager of another's business affairs.

business compulsion Exerting improper economic coercion on a business in a weak or vulnerable position. Also called economic duress.

business entry rule An exception to the hearsay rule allowing the introduction into evidence of entries (records) made in the ordinary course of business. Also called the business records exception.

business expense An amount paid for goods or services used in operating a taxpayer's business or trade.

business invitee Someone who has been expressly or impliedly invited to be present or to remain on the premises, primarily for a purpose directly or indirectly connected with business dealings between them. Also called business guest, business visitor.

business judgment rule Courts will defer to good-faith decisions made by boards of directors in business dealings and presume the decisions were made in the best interests of the company.

A presumption that directors' decisions are based on sound business judgment; courts will not interfere in business decisions made by directors in good faith and in absence of conflict of interest. *Lee*, 57 Cal.Rptr.2d 798 (Cal.App., 1996)

business records exception See business entry rule.

business trust An unincorporated business in which a trustee manages its property for the benefit and use of the trust beneficiaries. Also called common law trust, Massachusetts trust.

business visitor See business invitee.

but-for test A test for causation: an event (e.g., injury) would not have happened without the act or omission of the defendant.

"But for" or "sine qua non" test for establishing cause in fact asks whether injury would not have occurred but for defendant's conduct. *Maupin*, 237 Cal.Rptr. 521 (Cal.App., 1987)

buy and sell agreement An arrangement under which there is a right or duty of one or more owners of an entity to buy another owner's interest upon the occurrence of certain events, e.g., an owner dies or withdraws.

buyer in the ordinary course of business One who buys goods in good faith, without knowledge that the sale violates the rights of another person in the goods, and in the ordinary course from a person (other than a pawnbroker) in the business of selling goods of that kind. UCC 1-201(b)(9).

by-bidding Planting someone to make fictitious auction bids. Also called puffing.

bylaws Rules governing internal affairs of an organization.

by operation of law See operation of law.

bypass trust A trust designed to take full advantage of the unified credit against estate taxes by reducing the surviving spouse's estate.

by the entirety See tenancy by the entirety.

C

CA Court of Appeals.

cabinet An advisory board or council of a chief executive.

caduary Subject to forfeiture.

c.a.f. See cost and freight.

calendar A list of cases awaiting court action or bills awaiting legislative action.

calendar call A hearing to determine the status of, and establish court dates for, cases on the court calendar.

call 1. A demand for payment. 2. A demand to present bonds or other securities for redemption before maturity. 3. A property boundary landmark. 4. See call option.

callable Subject to be called and paid for before maturity.

callable bonds See redeemable bond.

call option The right to buy something at a fixed price.

call premium The added charge paid to redeem a bond prior to maturity.

calumny A false and malicious accusation.

camera See in camera.

cancellation 1. Striking or crossing out. 2. Invalidation, termination.

Cancellation implies the termination prior to expiration of the term. *Farmers*, 56 Cal.Rptr. 775 (Cal.App., 1967)

c&f See cost and freight.

cannabis The plant from which marijuana is prepared.

canon A rule, law, or principle.

canonical disability An impediment justifying a church annulment.

canon law Ecclesiastical law; Roman church jurisprudence.

canons of construction Rules for interpreting statutes and contracts.

Canons of construction are not dispositive in construing statutes, but are guides to help courts determine likely legislative intent. *Burris*, 22 Cal.Rptr.3d 876 (CA 2005)

canvass 1. To examine carefully, e.g., the votes cast. 2. To solicit votes, contributions, opinions, etc.

capacity 1. Legal qualification or competency to do something. 2. The ability to understand the nature of one's acts. 3. Occupation, function, or role.

capias A writ requiring that someone be taken into custody.

capias ad respondendum A writ commanding the sheriff to bring the defendant to court to answer the claims of the plaintiff.

capias ad satisfaciendum A writ commanding the sheriff to hold a judgment debtor until the latter satisfies its judgment debt.

capias pro fine A writ commanding the sheriff to arrest someone who has not paid a fine.

capita Head, person. See also per capita.

capital 1. Assets available for generating more wealth. 2. Assets less liabilities; net worth. 3. Relating to the death penalty.

capital asset See fixed assets.

capital budget Projected spending to buy long-term or fixed assets.

capital gains tax A tax on the sale or exchange of a capital asset.

capital goods Assets (e.g., tools) used to produce goods and services.

capitalization 1. The total value of stocks and other securities used for long-term financing. 2. See capitalize.

capitalize 1. To treat an asset as capital; to classify an expenditure as a long-term investment. 2. To provide with investment funds. 3. To determine current value of cash flow.

capital loss Loss realized on the sale or exchange of a capital asset.

capital market The market for long-term securities.

capital punishment A death sentence.

capital stock 1. All of the stock a corporation is authorized to issue. Also called authorized stock. 2. The total par value of stock a corporation is authorized to issue.

The capital stock of corporation represents the amount of money or property contributed by shareholders to be used as financial foundation from which business of corporation is to be carried on. *In re Talbot's Estate*, 74 Cal.Rptr. 920 (Cal.App., 1969)

capital surplus Surplus other than retained earnings. Funds owners pay over par value.

capitation tax See poll tax.

capitulary A collection or code of laws.

capricious Impulsive; not based on evidence, law, or reason.

caption 1. The heading or introductory part of a pleading, court opinion, memo, or other document that identifies what it is, the names of the parties, the court involved, etc. 2. Arresting someone.

care 1. Caution in avoiding harm. 2. Heed. 3. Supervision or comfort.

career criminal See habitual criminal.

careless Absence of reasonable care; negligent.

carjacking Using violence or threats to take a vehicle from the driver.

carnal knowledge Sexual intercourse.

carrier 1. A person or company engaged in transporting passengers or goods for hire. See also common carrier. 2. An insurance company.

carrier's lien The legal right of a carrier to hold cargo until its owner pays the agreed shipping costs.

carry 1. To transport. 2. To bear the burden of. 3. To have in stock. 4. To list on one's accounts as a debt.

For robbery, carrying away which requires some slight movement of the property. *People v. Duran*, 106 Cal.Rptr.2d 812 (Cal.App., 2001)

carryback Applying a loss or deduction from one year to a prior year.

carrying charge 1. Charges of a creditor, in addition to interest, for providing credit. 2. Costs involved in owning land, e.g., taxes.

carryover Applying a loss or deduction from one year to a later year.

carryover basis When property is transferred in a certain way (e.g., by gift) the basis of the property in the transferee is the same as (is carried over from) the transferor's basis.

cartel 1. An association of producers or sellers of any product joined together to control the production, sale, or price of the product. 2. An agreement between enemies while at war.

Cartels—agreements among producers to set prices above the competitive level by lowering production, *Fisher*, 209 Cal.Rptr. 682 (CA 1984)

carve out To separate income from the property that generates it.

CASA Court appointed special advocate (*www.nationalcasa.org*).

case 1. A court's written explanation of how it applied the law to the facts to resolve a legal dispute. See also opinion. 2. A pending matter on a court calendar. 3. A client matter handled by a law office. 4. A statement of arguments and evidence. See also action on the case.

case agreed See agreed case.

casebook A law school textbook containing many edited court opinions.

caselaw (case law) The law found within court opinions. See also common law.

case method Learning law by studying court opinions.

case-in-chief The presentation of evidence by one side, not including the evidence it introduces to counter the evidence of the other side.

case of first impression See first impression.

case or controversy For a federal court to hear a case, the plaintiff must have suffered a definite and concrete injury.

case reports See reporter (3).

case stated See agreed case.

cash basis Reporting or recognizing revenue only when actually received and expenses only when actually paid out.

cash dividend A dividend paid by a corporation in money.

cash flow 1. Cash from income-producing property. 2. Income less expenses over a designated period of time.

cashier's check A check drawn by a bank on its own funds, signed by a bank officer, and payable to a third party named by a customer.

A draft with respect to which the drawer and drawee are the same bank or branches of the same bank. Cal. Commercial Code § 3104(g). *Spencer*, 74 Cal.Rptr.2d 576 (Cal.App., 1998)

cash out To receive cash for one's total ownership interest.

cash price A lower price if paid in cash rather than with credit.

cash sale A sale in which the buyer and seller exchange goods and full payment in cash at same time.

cash surrender value Cash available upon surrender of an insurance policy before it becomes payable in the normal course (e.g., at death). Also called surrender value.

cash value See fair market value.

castle doctrine See retreat rule.

casual 1. Unexpected. 2. Occasional. 3. Without formality.

casual ejector A fictitious defendant who casually enters the land to eject the person lawfully in possession of it.

casualty 1. A serious accident. 2. A person injured or killed.

casualty insurance Insurance against loss from accident. (Covers many different kinds of insurance.)

Most property/casualty insurance companies are multiline. In other words, these companies do not limit their underwritings to one particular line of insurance. *Radian*, 26 Cal.Rptr.3d 464 (Cal.App., 2005)

casualty loss Damage to property due to an event that is sudden, unexpected, and unusual in nature.

catching bargain An unconscionable purchase from one who has an estate in reversion or expectancy.

caucus A meeting of the members of a particular group, e.g., a political party.

causa A cause; what produces an effect.

causa causans The predominating effective cause.

causa mortis In contemplation of approaching death. Also phrased mortis causa.

causa proxima The immediate cause.

causa sine qua non "But-for" cause. Without (but-for) the act or omission, the event in question would not have occurred.

causation Bringing something about. Producing an effect.

cause 1. Bringing something about. Producing an effect. 2. A reason, justification, or ground. 3. A lawsuit.

Cause of injury, damage, loss, or harm is something that is a substantial factor in bringing it about. *Espinosa*, 37 Cal.Rptr.2d 541 (Cal.App., 1995)

cause of action The facts that give a person a right to judicial relief. A legally acceptable reason for suing.

The right to relief in court. *Franchise Tax Board*, 151 Cal.Rptr. 460 (Cal.App., 1978)

cautionary instruction A judge's caution or warning to the jury to avoid outside contact about the case, to ignore certain evidence, or to consider the evidence for a limited purpose.

caveat 1. A warning or admonition. 2. A party's notice filed in court asking that the case be stopped.

caveat actor Let the doer (the actor) beware.

caveatee The person being challenged by someone who files a caveat. The latter is the caveator.

caveat emptor Let the buyer beware. A buyer should examine and judge the product on his or her own.

The ancient doctrine of *caveat emptor* has lingered on to a very large extent in judicial consideration of the responsibility of a vendor of land. (Prosser & Keeton) *Lewis*, 14 Cal.Rptr.3d 636 (Cal.App., 2004)

CC Circuit Court; County Court; Civil Code.

C corporation A corporation whose income is taxed at the corporate level; it has not chosen S corporation status. Also called subchapter C corporation.

CD Certificate of deposit.

cease and desist order A court or agency order prohibiting the continuation of a course of conduct.

cede 1. To surrender or yield. 2. To assign or transfer.

cedent A person who transfers something. One who cedes.

censor A person who examines material in order to identify and remove what is objectionable.

censure 1. An official reprimand. 2. To express formal disapproval.

census An official counting of a population.

center of gravity doctrine In conflict-of-law cases, courts apply the law of the place that has the most significant contacts or relationship with the matter in dispute.

ceremonial marriage A marriage entered in compliance with statutory requirements, e.g., obtaining a marriage license.

cert. See certiorari.

certificated Having met the qualifications for certification from a school or training program.

certificate A document that asserts the truth of something or that something has been done, e.g., that requirements have been met.

A written testimony to the truth of any fact. *Donnellan*, 103 Cal.Rptr.2d 882 (Cal.App., 2001)

certificate of acknowledgement The confirmation that the signature on a document was made by a person who is who he or she claimed to be.

certificate of convenience and necessity An authorization from a regulatory agency that a company can operate a public utility.

certificate of deposit (CD) A document from a bank confirming that a named person has a designated amount of money in the bank, usually for a fixed term earning a fixed rate of interest. A time deposit.

certificate of incorporation A document issued by the state to a company that grants its status as a corporation.

certificate of occupancy A document confirming that the premises comply with building codes regulations.

certificate of title A document confirming who owns designated property, including who holds encumbrances such as liens.

certification 1. The act of affirming the truth or authenticity of something. 2. A request by a federal court that a state court resolve a state issue relevant to a case in the federal court. 3. The process by which a nongovernmental organization grants recognition to a person who has met the qualifications established by that organization.

certification mark Any word, name, symbol, or device used to certify some aspect of goods or services, e.g., their origin.

certified Having complied with the qualifications for certification.

certified check A check drawn on funds in a depositor's account whose payment is guaranteed by the bank on which it is drawn.

certified copy A duplicate of an original document, certified as an exact reproduction. Also called exemplified copy.

Certified Legal Assistant (CLA) The credential bestowed by the National Association of Legal Assistants (NALA) (*www.nala.org*) for meeting its criteria such as passing a national, entry-level certification exam.

Certified Public Accountant (CPA) An accountant who has met the requirements to be certified as a public accountant (*www.aicpa.org*).

certiorari (cert.) An order (or writ) by a higher court that a lower court send up the record of a case because the higher court has decided to use its discretion to review that case.

cession A surrender or yielding up.

cestui ("he who") One who benefits, a beneficiary.

cestui que trust Beneficiary of a trust. See also trust.

cf. Compare.

CFI Cost, freight, and insurance.

CFR See Code of Federal Regulations (*www.gpoaccess.gov/cfr*).

Ch. Chancellor; chancery; chapter.

chain of causation The sequence of actions and omissions that led to or resulted in the harm or other event in question.

chain of custody A list of places an item of physical evidence has been in and the name of anyone who has possessed it over a period of time.

chain of title The history of ownership of land. From the original title holder to the present holder.

Conveyance outside the chain of title failed to afford him constructive notice. *Van't Rood*, 6 Cal.Rptr.3d 746 (Cal.App., 2003)

challenge 1. A formal objection to the selection of a particular prospective juror. 2. A protest or calling into question.

challenge for cause An objection to selecting a prospective juror because of specified causes or reasons, e.g., bias.

challenge to the array A formal protest to the manner in which the entire pool or panel of prospective jurors has been selected.

chamber 1. A room, e.g., a judge's office. 2. A legislative body.

A room adjacent to a courtroom in which a judge performs duties of his office. *People v. Valenzuela*, 66 Cal.Rptr. 825 (Cal.App., 1968)

champerty Conduct by an individual (called the champertor) who promotes or supports someone else's litigation, often by helping to finance the litigation in exchange for a share in the recovery.

chancellor 1. Judge in a court of equity. 2. An officer of high rank.

chancery 1. Equity jurisprudence. 2. A court of equity.

change of venue The transfer of a suit begin in one court to another court in the same judicial system.

Removing the proceedings to another county. *Gray*, 196 Cal.Rptr. 808 (Cal.App., 1983)

chapter 1. A subdivision of a code. 2. A division of an organization.

Chapter 11 A category of bankruptcy (found in chapter 11 of the bankruptcy act) in which the debtor is allowed to postpone payment of debts in order to reorganize the capital structure of his or her business.

character evidence Evidence of a person's habits, personality traits, and moral qualities.

charge 1. To instruct a jury, particularly on the law pertaining to the verdict it must reach. 2. A jury instruction. 3. To accuse someone of a crime. 4. To impose a burden or obligation; to assign a duty. 5. To defer payment. 6. A person (e.g., a child) entrusted to the care of another. 7. Price.

chargé d'affaires A diplomatic officer of a lower rank.

charge off To treat or report as a loss.

charitable Having the character or purpose of the public good; philanthropic, eleemosynary.

Charitable uses are those of religious, educational, political or general social interest to mankind, or as those for the relief of poverty or beneficial to the community generally. *In re Thomason's Estate*, 54 Cal.Rptr. 229 (Cal.App., 1966)

charitable contribution A gift of money or other property to a charitable organization.

charitable deduction An income tax deduction taken for gifts to a qualified tax-exempt charitable organization.

charitable remainder annuity trust A trust that pays designated amounts to beneficiaries for a period of time after which the trust property goes to a charity.

charitable trust A trust established to serve a purpose that is beneficial to a community. Also called public trust.

charter 1. The fundamental law governing a municipality or other local unit of government, authorizing it to perform designated functions. 2. A document creating an organization that states its fundamental purposes and powers. 3. The legal authorization to conduct business 4. To rent for temporary use.

chattel Personal property.

chattel mortgage A mortgage or lien on personal property as security for a debt.

chattel paper A document that is evidence of both a monetary obligation and a security interest in specific goods.

check 1. A written order instructing a bank to pay on demand a certain amount of money from the check writer's account to the person named on the check (the payee). See also negotiable instrument. 2. To control; to hold within bounds. 3. To examine for accuracy; to investigate. 4. To deposit for safekeeping.

check kiting A form of bank fraud in which the kiter opens accounts at two or more banks, writes checks on insufficient funds on one account, and then, taking advantage of bank processing delays, covers the overdraft by depositing a check on insufficient funds from the other account. Also called kiting.

checkoff An employer's deduction of union dues from employee wages and turning the dues over to the union.

checks and balances An allocation of powers among the three branches of government (legislative, executive, and judicial) whereby one branch can block, check, or review what another branch wants to do (or has done) in order to maintain a balance of power among the branches.

chief justice The presiding judge (called a justice) in a higher court. In a lower court, he or she is often called the chief judge.

child 1. A son or daughter. 2. A person under the age of majority.

Child (in the intestacy laws) is a human being born alive, not an unborn child or fetus. Cal. Probate Code §§ 6402(a). *Cheyanna*, 78 Cal.Rptr.2d 335 (Cal.App., 1998)

child abuse Physically or emotionally harming a child, intentionally or by neglect.

child abuse report law A law that requires designated individuals (e.g., teachers) to report suspected child abuse to the state.

child molestation Subjecting a child to sexual advances, contact, or activity.

child neglect The failure to provide a child with support, medical care, education, moral example, discipline, and other necessaries.

Neglect means the negligent treatment or the maltreatment of a child by a person responsible for the child's welfare under circumstances indicating harm or threatened harm to the child's health or welfare. Cal. Penal Code § 11165.2

child pornography Visual portrayal of a person under 18 engaged in sexual activity, actual or simulated.

child support The obligation of a parent to pay a child's basic living expenses.

chilling effect Being hindered or inhibited from exercising a constitutional right, e.g., free speech.

Chinese wall Steps taken in an office to prevent a tainted employee from having any contact with a particular case in order to avoid a disqualification of the office from the case. The employee is tainted because he or she has a conflict of interest in that case.

We prefer to use the term "ethical wall" rather than the more common, and often criticized term, "Chinese Wall." *Henriksen*, 14 Cal.Rptr.2d 184 (Cal.App., 1992)

chit 1. A voucher for food and drinks. 2. A short letter or note.

choate Complete; perfected or ripened.

choate lien A perfected lien, enforceable without further steps.

choice of evils Acts otherwise criminal may be justifiable if performed under extraordinary circumstances out of some immediate necessity to prevent a greater harm from occurring. Also called necessity.

choice of law Deciding which jurisdiction's law should govern when an event involves the law of more than one jurisdiction.

chose Chattel; a thing.

chose in action 1. A right to recover something in a lawsuit, e.g., money. 2. The thing itself that embodies the right to sue. Also called thing in action.

churning A broker's excess trading in a customer's account to benefit the broker (via commissions), not the client.

CIF See cost, insurance, and freight.

circuit 1. One of the 13 appellate subdivisions in the federal judicial system. 2. Pertaining to a court that has jurisdiction in several counties or areas. 3. A district traveled by a judge.

circular note See letter of credit.

circumstantial evidence Evidence of a fact that is not based on personal knowledge or observation from which another fact might be inferred. Also called indirect evidence.

Evidence from which the principal fact is inferred. Cal. Code of Civil Procedure §§ 1831, 1832. *People v. Goldstein*, 293 P.2d 495 (Cal.App., 1956)

citation; cite 1. A reference to any legal authority printed on paper or stored in a computer database. 2. An order to appear in court to answer a charge. 3. An official notice of a violation.

citator A book, CD-ROM, or online service with lists of citations that can help assess the current validity of an opinion, statute, or other authority and give leads to additional relevant material.

cite checking Examining citations in a document to assess whether the format of the citation is correct, whether quoted material is accurate, and whether the law cited is still valid.

citizen A person born or naturalized in a country to which he or she owes allegiance and who is entitled to full civil rights.

citizen's arrest A private person making an arrest for a crime that is a breach of the peace committed in his or her presence or for reasonably believing the person arrested has committed a felony.

civil Pertaining to (a) private rights, (b) noncriminal cases, (c) the state or citizenship, (d) public order and peace, and (e) legal systems of Western Europe other than England.

civil action A lawsuit to enforce private rights.

civil arrest The arrest of the defendant until he or she satisfies the judgment.

An auxiliary remedy designed to keep defendant within reach of court's final process. *Carradine*, 171 P.2d 911 (Cal.App., 1946)

civil assault The tort of assault.

civil code 1. A collection of statutes governing noncriminal matters. 2. The code containing the civil law of France, from which the civil code of Louisiana is derived.

civil commitment Noncriminal confinement of those who because of incompetence or addiction cannot care for themselves or who pose a danger to themselves or to society. Also called involuntary commitment.

civil conspiracy A combination of two or more persons acting in concert to commit an unlawful act and an overt act that results in damages.

Civil conspiracy is a theory of joint liability (not a tort) so that all who cooperate in another's wrong may be held liable. *Thompson*, 270 Cal.Rptr. 90 (Cal.App., 1990)

civil contempt The refusal of the party to comply with a court order, resulting in punishment that can be avoided by compliance.

A means of enforcing a contractual right as judicially determined in an order or judgment. Cal. Code of Civil Procedure § 1209. *Share*, 263 Cal.Rptr. 753 (Cal.App., 1989)

civil court A court that hears noncriminal cases.

civil damage law See Dram Shop Act.

civil death The status of a person who has lost civil rights (e.g., to vote) because of a conviction of certain crimes. Also called legal death.

civil disabilities Civil rights that are lost when a person is convicted of a serious crime (e.g., to drive a car).

Civil disabilities flowing from the conviction. *Boyll*, 194 Cal.Rptr. 717 (Cal.App., 1983)

civil disobedience Breaking the law (without using violence) to show the injustice or unfairness of the law.

civilian One who is not a police officer or in the military.

civil law 1. The law governing civil disputes. Any law other than criminal law. 2. The statutory or code law applicable in Louisiana and many Western European countries other than England.

civil liability Damages or other noncriminal responsibility.

civil liberties Basic individual rights that should not be unduly restricted by the state (e.g., freedom of speech).

civil penalty A fine or assessment for violating a statute or administrative regulation.

civil procedure Laws governing the mechanics of resolving a civil (noncriminal) dispute in a court or administrative agency.

civil rights Basic individual rights (e.g., to vote) guaranteed by the United States Constitution and special statutes.

Decisions of the United States Supreme Court defining fundamental civil rights are persuasive authority, but are to be followed by California courts only when they provide no less individual protection than is guaranteed by California law. *American Academy*, 263 Cal.Rptr. 46 (Cal.App., 1989)

civil service Nonmilitary government employment, often obtained through merit and competitive exams.

civil union A same-sex relationship with the same *state* benefits and responsibilities the state grants spouses in a marriage.

CLA See Certified Legal Assistant (*www.nala.org*).

Claflin trust A trust that cannot be terminated by a beneficiary. Also called indestructible trust.

claim 1. A right to sue. 2. To demand as one's own or as one's right. 3. To assert something.

claim and delivery A suit to recover personal property that was wrongfully taken or kept.

A remedy by which a party with a superior right to a specific item of personal property may recover possession of that specific property before judgment. Cal. Code of Civil Procedure § 511.010; *Waffer*, 82 Cal.Rptr.2d 241 (Cal.App., 1999)

claimant One who makes a demand or asserts a right or claim.

claim jumping Asserting a mining claim that infringes on the claim of another.

claim of right 1. A good-faith assertion that one was entitled to do something. 2. If a taxpayer receives income (without restrictions) that he or she claimed the right to have, it must be reported in the year received even if it may have to be returned in a later year.

Under the claim-of-right defense, a defendant's good faith belief, even if mistakenly held, that he has a right or claim to property he takes from another can negate the felonious intent necessary for conviction of theft. Cal. Penal Code §§ 211, 484. *People v. Tufunga*, 90 Cal.Rptr.2d 143 (CA 1999)

claim preclusion See res judicata.

claims court A court in which a party seeks to resolve claims against the government, e.g., United States Court of Federal Claims.

claims-made policy Insurance that covers only claims actually filed (i.e., made) during the period in which the policy is in effect.

The insurance carrier agrees to assume liability for any errors, including those made prior to inception of policy, as long as claim is made during the policy period. *Homestead*, 52 Cal.Rptr.2d 268 (Cal.App., 1996)

class A group with common characteristics, e.g., persons injured by the same product.

class action A lawsuit in which one or more members of a class sue (or are sued) as representative parties on behalf of everyone in the class, all of whom do not have to be joined in the lawsuit. Also called representative action.

class gift A gift to a group containing an unknown number of persons at the time the gift is made.

clause A subdivision of a sentence in a law or other document.

Clayton Act A federal antitrust statute prohibiting price discrimination and other monopolistic practices. 15 USC § 12.

CLE See Continuing Legal Education.

clean bill A proposed statute (bill) that has been substantially revised and introduced to the legislature as a new bill.

clean bill of lading A bill of lading without qualifications.

clean hands doctrine A party may not be allowed to assert an equitable claim or defense if his or her conduct has been unfair or in bad faith. Also called unclean hands doctrine.

When a party seeking some remedy has violated conscience, good faith, or other equitable principle in his prior conduct, the court will refuse to award him any remedy. *Crittenden*, 234 P.2d 642 (Cal.App., 1951)

clear 1. Free from encumbrance. 2. To vindicate or acquit. 3. To pay a check according to the instructions of the maker. 4. To pass through a clearinghouse. 5. Obvious, unambiguous.

clearance card A letter from an employer given to a departing employee stating facts such as the duration of the latter's employment.

clear and convincing evidence Evidence demonstrating that the existence of a disputed fact is much more probable than its nonexistence. This standard is stronger than preponderance of the evidence but not as strong as beyond a reasonable doubt.

Proof by clear and convincing evidence requires a finding of high probability, or evidence so clear as to leave no substantial doubt. Cal. Evidence Code § 115. *In re Michael G.*, 74 Cal.Rptr.2d 642 (Cal.App., 1998)

clear and present danger Imminent risk of severe harm, the test used to help determine whether the state can restrict First Amendment freedoms.

clearing 1. The process by which checks are exchanged and pass through the banking system. 2. A ship leaving port in compliance with laws.

clearinghouse A place where banks exchange checks and drafts drawn on each other and reconcile accounts.

clearly erroneous The definite and firm conviction of an appellate court that a mistake has been made by a lower court.

clear title 1. Title that is free of reasonable doubt as to its validity. Marketable title. 2. Title that is clear of encumbrances.

clemency Leniency from the president or a governor to a criminal, e.g., a pardon or reduction in sentence. Also called executive clemency.

clergy-penitent privilege A privilege preventing spiritual advisors from disclosing confessions or religious confidences made to them. Also called priest-penitent privilege.

clerical error A copying error or other minor mistake.

Those errors, mistakes, or omissions that are not the result of the judicial function [i.e., judicial reasoning]. *Smith*, 251 P.2d 720 (Cal.App., 1952)

clerk 1. An official who manages records and files and performs other administrative duties, e.g., a court clerk. 2. A law student or recent law school graduate who works for a law office or judge, usually for a short period of time. 3. One who performs general office duties.

clerkship Employment as a clerk in a legal office. See clerk (2).

client One who hires or receives services from a professional, e.g., an attorney.

client security fund A fund (often run by the bar association) used to compensate victims of attorney misconduct.

client trust account An attorney's bank account that contains client funds that may not be used for office operating expenses. Also called trust account.

It is unethical to commingle client funds with the attorney's own funds in his client trust account. Rule 4-100(A); *In re Gadda*, 2002 WL 31012596 (Cal.Bar Ct., 2002)

Clifford trust A fixed-term trust in which the principal is returned to the grantor after a period of time.

close 1. Land that is enclosed. 2. To bring to completion.

close corporation; closed corporation; closely held corporation A corporation whose shares are held by a small group, e.g., a family.

closed-end mortgage A mortgage loan whose principal cannot be increased during the life of the loan and cannot be prepaid.

closed shop A business whose employees must be members of a union as a condition of employment.

An establishment in which the employer by agreement hires and retains in employment only union members in good standing. *Chavez*, 339 P.2d 801 (CA 1959)

closing The meeting in which a transaction is finalized. Also called settlement.

closing argument The final statements by opposing trial attorneys to the jury (or to the trial judge if there is no jury) summarizing the evidence and requesting a favorable decision. Also called final argument, summation, summing up.

closing costs Expenses incurred in the sale of real estate in addition to the purchase price.

cloture A legislative procedure to end debate and allow a vote.

cloud on title A claim or encumbrance on land, which, if valid, would affect or impair the title rights of the owner.

cluster zoning Modifications in zoning restrictions in exchange for other land being set aside for public needs, e.g., a park.

coaching Telling a witness how to give testimony on the stand.

COBRA See Consolidated Omnibus Budget Reconciliation Act.

coconspirator One who engages in a conspiracy with another. Under the conspirator exception to the hearsay rule, statements of one coconspirator can be admitted against another coconspirator if made in furtherance of the conspiracy.

If only two persons are involved and one is government agent or informer, then the other cannot be convicted of conspiracy; a government agent by definition cannot be a coconspirator. *People v. Liu*, 54 Cal.Rptr.2d 578 (Cal.App., 1996)

COD Collect on delivery.

code A systematic collection of laws, rules, or guidelines, usually organized by subject matter.

code civil The code containing the civil law of France. Also called the Code Napoléon.

codefendant One of two or more defendants sued in the same civil case or prosecuted in the same criminal case.

Code Napoléon See code civil.

code pleading See fact pleading.

codicil A supplement that adds to or changes a will.

codification Collecting and systematically arranging laws or rules by subject matter.

coercion Compelling something by force or threats. Overpowering another's free will by force or undue influence.

cognizable 1. Pertaining to what can be heard and resolved by a court. 2. Capable of being known.

A cognizable group exists, for purposes of determining whether prosecutor has exercised peremptory challenges to exclude such group from jury, if its members share a common perspective. *People v. Cervantes*, 284 Cal.Rptr. 410 (Cal.App., 1991)

cognizance 1. The power of a court to hear and resolve a particular dispute. 2. Judicial notice. 3. Awareness or recognition.

cognovit A written statement that acknowledges liability or the validity of a debt. The statement confesses judgment.

A cognovit note (also called judgment note) is a promissory note containing a cognovit.

cohabitation Living together as a couple or in a sexual relationship.

coheir One of several persons to whom an inheritance passes or descends. A joint heir.

coif A ceremonial cap or other headpiece. See also Order of the Coif.

coinsurance A sharing of the risks between two or more insurers or between the insurer and the insured.

COLA Cost of living adjustment.

cold blood Premeditated killing.

collapsible corporation A corporation set up to be sold or liquidated before it earns substantial income.

collateral 1. Property pledged as security for the satisfaction of a debt. 2. Not in the direct line of descent. 3. Not directly relevant. 4. Accompanying but of secondary importance.

collateral attack A challenge or attack against the validity of a judgment that is not raised in a direct appeal from the court that rendered the judgment.

An attempt to avoid the effect of a judgment or order or dismissal with prejudice made in some other proceeding. *Wouldridge*, 71 Cal.Rptr. 394 (Cal.App., 1968)

collateral estoppel When parties have litigated and resolved an issue in one case, they cannot relitigate the issue in another case against each other even if the two cases raise different claims or causes of action. Also called direct estoppel, estoppel by judgment, estoppel by record, issue preclusion.

It prohibits the same parties from retrying an issue of ultimate fact identical to an issue actually and necessarily decided in a prior proceeding that resulted in a final judgment on the merits. *In re Cruz*, 129 Cal.Rptr.2d 31 (Cal.App., 2003)

collateral fraud Deception by one party that does not pertain to the actual issues that were resolved in a trial but which prevented the other party from presenting its case fairly. Also called extrinsic fraud.

Extrinsic or collateral fraud, justifying equity court in setting aside final judgment, must be of such character as to prevent trial of issues presented to court for determination. *Estate of Standing*, 222 P.2d 465 (Cal.App., 1950)

collateral heir One who is not of the direct line of the deceased, but comes from a collateral line, as a brother, aunt, or a cousin of the deceased. Also called heir collateral.

collateral order doctrine An appeal of a nonfinal order will be allowed if the order conclusively determines the disputed question, resolves an important issue that is completely separate from the merits of the dispute, and is effectively unreviewable on appeal from a final judgment.

collateral source rule The amount of damages caused by the tortfeasor shall not be reduced by any injury-related funds received by the plaintiff from sources independent of the tortfeasor such as a health insurance policy of the plaintiff.

collateral warranty A warranty of title given by someone other than the seller.

collation 1. A comparison of a copy with the original to determine the correctness of the copy. 2. Taking into account property already given to some heirs as an advancement.

collecting bank A bank handling a check for collection other than the payor bank.

collective bargaining Negotiations between an employer and representatives of its employees on working conditions.

collective mark A mark used by members of an organization (e.g., a union) to indicate membership or to identify what it offers.

colloquium Extrinsic facts showing that a defamatory statement was of and concerning the plaintiff. A complaint alleging such facts.

The plaintiff must sustain the burden of proof, by way of colloquium, that the defamatory meaning attached to him. *Carlisle*, 20 Cal.Rptr. 405 (Cal.App., 1962)

colloquy A formal discussion, e.g., between the judge and the defendant to determine if the defendant's plea is informed.

collusion 1. An agreement to commit fraud. 2. An agreement between a husband and wife that one or both will lie to the court to facilitate the obtaining of their divorce.

colorable 1. Plausible. Having at least some factual or legal support. 2. Deceptively appearing to be valid.

color of law 1. Acting or pretending to act in an official, governmental capacity. 2. The pretense of law.

color of office Asserted official or governmental authority.

color of title A false appearance of having title to property.

Color of title, as regards adverse possession, merely means a semblance of title as distinguished from paramount or actual title. *Yuba*, 177 P.2d 642 (Cal.App., 1947)

comaker See cosigner.

combination The union or association of two or more persons or entities to achieve a common end. See also conspiracy, restraint of trade.

combination in restraint of trade An agreement among businesses to create a monopoly or otherwise stifle competition.

combination patent A combination of known elements which, when combined, accomplish a patentable function or result.

coming and going rule See going and coming rule.

comity Giving effect to the laws of another state, not as a requirement, but rather out of deference or respect.

California courts may, but are not required to, execute the judgment of a foreign nation as a matter of comity. *In re Stephanie M*, 27 Cal.Rptr.2d 595, (CA 1994)

commerce Buying, selling, or exchanging goods or services.

Commerce Clause The clause in the U.S. Constitution (art. I, § 8, cl. 3) giving Congress the power to regulate commerce among the states, with foreign nations, and with Indian tribes.

commercial bank A bank with a variety of services such as providing loans, checking accounts, and safety deposit boxes.

commercial bribery The advantage secured over a competitor by corrupt dealings with agents of prospective purchasers.

commercial frustration An excuse not to perform a contract due to an unforeseen event not under the control of either party.

commercial impracticability See impracticability.

commercial law The law governing commercial transactions such as the sale and financing of goods and services.

commercial paper 1. A negotiable instrument (e.g., a draft, a promissory note) used in commerce. 2. A short-term, unsecured negotiable note, often sold to meet immediate cash needs.

commercial speech Expression related solely to the economic interests of the speaker and its audience.

Speech that does no more than propose a commercial transaction Cal. Const. Art. 1, § 2(a). *Baba,* 21 Cal.Rptr.3d 428 (Cal.App., 2004)

commercial unit Goods considered a single whole for purposes of sale, the value of which would be materially impaired if divided into parts.

commingling Mixing what should be kept separate, e.g., depositing client funds in a single account with general law firm funds or an attorney's personal funds.

Commingling is committed when a client's money is intermingled with that of his attorney and its separate identity lost so that it may be used for the attorney's personal expenses or subjected to claims of his creditors. *Black,* 18 Cal.Rptr. 518 (CA 1962)

commission 1. The granting of powers to carry out a task. 2. A government body granted power to carry out a task. 3. Compensation, often a percentage of the value of the transaction. 4. The act of committing something, usually a crime.

commitment 1. An agreement or pledge to do something. 2. The act of institutionalizing someone as to a prison or mental hospital.

commitment fee A fee paid by a loan applicant for a lender's promise to lend money at a defined rate on a specified date.

committee 1. A group appointed to perform a function on behalf of a larger group. 2. A special guardian appointed to protect the interests of an incompetent person.

committee of the whole A special committee consisting of the entire membership of a deliberative body.

commodity Something useful; an article of commerce.

common 1. The legal right to use another's land or waters. 2. Land set apart for use by the general public. 3. Shared.

common carrier A company that holds itself out to the general public as engaged in transporting people or goods for a fee.

One who offers to the general public to carry goods or persons and is bound to accept anyone who tenders the price of carriage. Cal. Civil Code § 2168. *Webster,* 4 Cal.Rptr.2d 714 (Cal.App., 1992)

common disaster An event causing the death of two or more persons with shared interests, without clear evidence of who died first.

common enemy doctrine Landowners can fend off surface waters (e.g., rain) as needed, without liability to other landowners.

common law 1. Judge-made law in the absence of controlling statutory law or other higher law. Law derived from court opinions. 2. Law based on the legal system of England.

The common law is all the statutory and case law background of England and the American colonies before the American revolution. *People v. Rehman,* 61 Cal.Rptr. 65 (Cal.App., 1967)

common law action An action based on the common law. See also action at law.

common law copyright The author's proprietary interest in his or her creation before it has been made available to the pubic.

common law marriage A marriage entered without license or ceremony by persons who have agreed to marry, have lived together as husband and wife, and have held themselves out as such.

common law trust See business trust.

common nuisance See public nuisance.

Common Pleas The name of the trial court in some states and an intermediate appellate court in others.

common situs picketing Picketing an entire construction project even though the labor grievance is with only one subcontractor.

common stock Stock in a corporation with voting rights and the right to dividends after preferred stockholders have been paid.

commonwealth 1. A nation or state as a political entity. (In the United States, four states are officially designated commonwealths: KY, MA, PA, and VA.) 2. A political unit that is voluntarily united with the United States but is self-governing, e.g., Northern Mariana Islands.

community 1. A section or neighborhood in a city or town. 2. A group of people with common interests. 3. The marital entity that shares or owns community property.

community notification law See Megan's law.

community property Property in which each spouse has a one-half interest because it was acquired during the marriage (by a method other than gift or inheritance to one spouse only) regardless of who earned it.

Property acquired during marriage by either spouse, other than by gift or inheritance. Cal. Family Code § 760. *In re Marriage of Weaver,* 26 Cal.Rptr.3d 121 (Cal.App., 2005)

community trust An entity that operates a charitable trust.

commutation 1. A change of punishment to one that is less severe. 2. An exchange or substitution.

commutative contract A contract in which what each party promises or exchanges is considered equal in value.

commutative justice A system of justice in which the goal is fundamental fairness in transactions among the parties.

commuted value The present value of a future interest or payment.

compact An agreement, often between states or nations.

company An association of persons who are engaged in a business.

company union An employer-controlled union of employees in a single company.

comparable worth Jobs requiring the same levels of skill should receive equal pay whether performed by men or women.

comparative negligence In a negligence action, the plaintiff's damages will be reduced in proportion to the plaintiff's negligence in causing his or her own injury.

In any action for personal injury, property damage, or wrongful death, based upon principles of comparative fault, . . . [e]ach defendant shall be liable only for the amount of non-economic damages allocated to that defendant in direct proportion to that defendant's percentage of fault. Cal. Civil Code § 1431.2(a)

comparative rectitude When both spouses have grounds for a divorce, it will be granted to the spouse least at fault.

compelling state interest A substantial need for the state to act that justifies the resulting restriction on the constitutional right claimed by the person challenging the state's action.

compensating balance The minimum balance a bank requires one of its borrowers to have on deposit.

compensation 1. Payment of wages or benefits for services rendered. 2. Payment for a loss incurred. Indemnification.

compensatory damages Money to restore an injured party to his or her position prior to the injury or wrong. Actual damages.

Actual damages in Cal. Government Code § 12987 means compensatory damages; the latter include nonquantifiable general damages for emotional distress and pecuniarily measurable special damages for out-of-pocket losses. *Walnut*, 284 Cal.Rptr. 718 (CA 1991)

competency proceeding A hearing to determine if someone has the mental capacity to do something, e.g., to stand trial.

competent 1. Having the knowledge and skill reasonably necessary to represent a particular client. 2. Having sufficient understanding to be allowed to give testimony as a witness. 3. Having the ability to understand the criminal proceedings, to consult with one's attorney, and to assist in one's own defense. 4. Having the capacity to manage one's own affairs.

competent evidence Evidence that is relevant and admissible.

compilation 1. A collection of laws, usually statutes. 2. An original work formed by the collection and assembling of preexisting works.

complainant One who files a complaint to initiate a civil lawsuit or who alleges that someone has committed a crime.

complaint 1. A plaintiff's first pleading, stating a claim against the defendant. Also called petition. 2. A formal criminal charge.

completion bond A bond given as insurance to guarantee that a contract will be completed within the agreed-upon time. Also called performance bond, surety bond.

complex trust See discretionary trust.

composition An agreement between a debtor and two or more creditors on what will be accepted as full payment.

compos mentis Of sound mind; competent.

compound 1. To adjust or settle a debt or other claim by paying a lesser amount. 2. To accept an illegal payment in exchange for not prosecuting a crime. 3. To calculate interest on both the principal and on interest already accrued. 4. A mixture of parts.

compound interest See compound (3).

compounding a crime Receiving something of value in exchange for an agreement to interfere with a prosecution or not to prosecute.

compromise To settle a dispute through mutual concessions.

An adjustment of conflicting claims. *Isaacson*, 69 Cal.Rptr. 379 (Cal.App., 1968)

compromise verdict A verdict that results when jurors resolve their inability to reach unanimity by conceding some issues to entice agreement on others.

comptroller A fiscal officer of an organization appointed to examine accounts, issue financial reports, and perform other accounting duties. Also spelled controller.

compulsion 1. Forcing someone to do or refrain from doing something. 2. An irresistible impulse.

Compulsion or coercion is some actual or threatened exercise of power possessed, or supposed to be possessed. *Southern Service*, 97 P.2d 963 (CA 1940)

compulsory arbitration Arbitration that parties are required to undergo to resolve their dispute.

compulsory counterclaim A claim that arises out of the same subject matter as the opposing party's claim.

compulsory joinder Someone who must be joined as a party if his or her absence means that complete relief is not possible for the parties already in the lawsuit or that one or more of the parties may be subject to inconsistent or multiple liability.

compulsory process A summons or writ that compels a witness to appear in court, usually by subpoena or arrest.

compurgator Someone called to give testimony for the defendant.

computer crime The use of a computer to commit an illegal act, e.g., accessing or damaging computer data without authorization.

concealed weapon A weapon carried on a person in such a manner as to conceal it from the ordinary sight of another.

Weapon carried in defendant's pocket was a concealed weapon though the officer was able to see it as he looked down through opening of pocket. *People v. May*, 109 Cal.Rptr. 396 (Cal.App., 1973)

concerted Planned or accomplished together. Concerted activity is the conduct of employees who have joined together to achieve common goals on conditions of employment.

concert of action 1. A person cannot be prosecuted for both a substantive offense and a conspiracy to commit that offense where an agreement between two or more persons is a necessary element of the substantive offense. Also called Wharton's rule. 2. Concerted action (conduct planned by persons) results in liability for each other's acts.

conciliation 1. Conduct taken to restore trust in an effort to resolve a dispute. 2. Settlement of a conflict without undue pressure or coercion.

conclusion of fact An inference of fact drawn from evidence of another fact. See also finding of fact.

conclusion of law The result of applying the law to the facts. See also holding.

conclusive 1. Decisive. 2. Supported by substantial evidence.

conclusive presumption An inference of fact that the fact finder must find despite any evidence to the contrary. Also called irrebuttable presumption.

A presumption that requires the fact finder to find an ultimate fact upon proof of the existence of certain predicate facts regardless of whether there is other evidence to disprove the ultimate fact. *In re Heather B*, 11 Cal.Rptr.2d 891 (Cal.App., 1992)

conclusory Pertaining to an argument that states a conclusion without providing the underlying facts to support the conclusion.

concur 1. To agree. 2. To accept a conclusion but for different reasons. See also concurring opinion.

concurrent 1. At the same time. 2. With the same authority.

concurrent cause A cause that acts together (simultaneously) with another cause to produce an injury or other result.

concurrent condition A condition that one party must fulfill at the same time that another party must fulfill a mutual condition.

Concurrent conditions are conditions precedent that are mutually dependent. *Pittman*, 3 Cal.Rptr.2d 340 (Cal.App., 1992)

concurrent covenants Two covenants that must be performed or ready to be performed simultaneously.

concurrent jurisdiction The power of two or more courts to resolve the same dispute. Also called coordinate jurisdiction.

concurrent negligence Negligence by two or more persons who, though not working in concert, combine to produce a single injury.

concurrent power A legislative power that can be exercised by the federal or state government, or by both.

concurrent resolution A measure adopted by both houses of the legislature but does not have the force of law.

concurrent sentence A sentence served simultaneously, in whole or in part, with another sentence.

Concurrent sentences run together during the time that the periods of such sentences overlap. Cal Penal Code, § 669. *Ex parte Roberts*, 255 P.2d 782 (CA 1953)

concurring opinion A court opinion in which a judge agrees with the result of the majority opinion but for different reasons.

condemn 1. To set apart or expropriate (take) property for public use in exercise of the power of eminent domain. 2. To judge someone to be guilty. 3. To declare to be unfit.

condemnee A person whose property is taken for public use.

condition 1. An uncertain future event upon which a legal result (e.g., a duty to pay) is dependant. 2. A prerequisite.

An event that must occur or be excused before performance on the contract becomes due. *In re Marriage of Hasso*, 280 Cal.Rptr. 919 (Cal.App., 1991)

conditional Depending on or containing a condition.

conditional bequest A gift in a will that will be effective only if a specific event (condition) occurs or fails to occur.

conditional contract An executory (i.e., unperformed) contract whose existence and performance depends on a contingency.

conditional fee 1. See contingent fee. 2. See fee simple conditional.

conditional privilege A right to do or say something that can be lost if done or said with malice. Also called a qualified privilege.

A privilege that will not protect a defendant who has acted maliciously. *Hassan*, 3 Cal.Rptr.3d 623 (CA 2003)

conditional sale A sale in which the buyer does not receive title until making full payment.

conditional use Permitted land use upon compliance with specified conditions. Also called special exception, special use.

A conditional use may be permitted if it is shown that its use is essential or desirable to the public convenience. *Tustin*, 339 P.2d 914 (Cal.App., 1959)

condition of employment A job requirement.

condition precedent An act or event (other than a lapse of time) that must occur before performance becomes due.

condition subsequent An act or event that will, if it occurs, render an obligation invalid.

condominium A real estate interest that combines two forms of ownership: exclusive ownership of an individual unit of a multi-unit project and common ownership of the common project areas.

Condominium means joint dominion or co-ownership. *Nahrstedt*, 33 Cal.Rptr.2d 63 (CA 1994)

condonation Overlooking or forgiving, e.g., one spouse's express or implied forgiveness of the marital fault of the other.

conference committee A committee consisting of members of both houses of the legislature that seeks to reach a compromise on two versions of the same bill the houses passed.

confession A statement acknowledging guilt.

A declaration by a person that he is guilty of the crime with which he is charged. *People v. Wright*, 78 Cal.Rptr. 75 (Cal.App., 1969)

confession and avoidance A plea that admits some facts but avoids their legal effect by alleging new facts.

confession of judgment See cognovit.

confidence game Obtaining money or other property by gaining a victim's trust through deception.

confidential communication An exchange of information that is privileged—the exchange cannot be disclosed against the will of the parties involved.

confidential relationship 1. See fiduciary relationship. 2. A relationship that requires non-disclosure of certain facts.

A confidential relationship may be founded on a moral, social, domestic, or merely personal relationship as well as on a legal relationship, and may exist where there is no fiduciary relation. *Persson*, 23 Cal.Rptr.3d 335 (Cal.App., 2005)

confirmation 1. Giving formal approval. 2. Corroboration. 3. Rendering enforceable something that is voidable.

confiscation Seizing private property under a claim of authority.

conflict of interest Divided loyalty that actually or potentially harms someone who is owed undivided loyalty.

Conflicts of interest embrace all situations in which defense counsel's loyalty to the defendant is threatened by his responsibilities to another client or to third person or by his own interests. *People v. Hardy*, 5 Cal.Rptr.2d 796 (CA 1992)

conflict of laws Differences in the laws of two coequal legal systems (e.g., two states) involved in a legal dispute. The choice of which law to apply in such disputes.

conformed copy An exact copy of a document with notations of what could not be copied.

conforming In compliance with the contract or the law.

conforming use A use of land that complies with zoning laws.

confrontation Being present when others give evidence against you and having the opportunity to question them.

confusion of goods The mixing of like things belonging to different owners so that sorting out what each originally owned is no longer possible. Also called intermixture of goods.

conglomerate A corporation that has diversified its operations, usually by acquiring enterprises in widely different industries.

Congress 1. The national legislature of the United States. 2. A formal meeting of representatives of different groups (congress).

Congressional Record (Cong. Rec.) The official record of the day-to-day proceedings of Congress.

conjoint Joined together; having a joint interest.

conjugal Pertaining to marriage or spouses, e.g., the rights that one spouse has in the other's companionship, services, support, and sexual relations.

connecting-up Evidence demonstrating the relevance of prior evidence.

connivance A willingness or a consent by one spouse that a marital wrong be committed by the other spouse.

consanguinity Relationship by blood or a common ancestor.

conscience of the court The court's power to apply equitable principles.

conscientious objector A person who for religious or moral reasons is sincerely opposed to war in any form.

conscious parallelism A process, not in itself unlawful, by which firms in a concentrated market might share monopoly power.

consecutive sentences Sentences that are served one after the other—in sequence. Also called accumulative sentences, cumulative sentences.

consensus ad idem A meeting of the minds; agreement.

consent Voluntary agreement or permission, express or implied.

consent decree A court decree agreed upon by the parties.

consent judgment An agreement by the parties (embodied in a court order) settling their dispute.

A judgment entered by a court under the authority of, and in accordance with, the contractual agreement of the parties. *Norgart*, 87 Cal.Rptr.2d 453 (CA 1999)

consent search A search consented to by the person affected who has the authority to give the consent.

consequential damages Losses or injuries that do not flow directly from a party's action, but only from some of the consequences or results of such action.

conservator A person appointed by the court to manage the affairs of someone, usually an incompetent. A guardian.

consideration A bargained-for promise, act, or forbearance. Something of value exchanged between the parties.

The act or return promise, bargained for and given in exchange for a promise giving benefit to the promisor or imposing a detriment on the promisee. Cal. Civil Code, § 1605. *Peterson*, 18 Cal.Rptr. 800 (Cal.App., 1962)

consignment Transferring goods to someone, usually for sale by the latter. The one transferring the goods is the consignor; the person receiving them is the consignee.

Consignment sale is one in which a merchant takes possession of goods and holds them for sale with obligation to pay owner from proceeds of the sale. *Bank of California*, 62 Cal.Rptr.2d 90 (Cal.App., 1997)

consignee, consignor See consignment.

consolidated appeal An appeal from two or more parties who file a joint notice of appeal and proceed as a single appellant.

Consolidated Omnibus Budget Reconciliation Act (COBRA). A federal statute that gives workers limited rights to keep their health insurance policy when they leave a job.

consolidation 1. A joining together or merger. 2. Combining two or more corporations that dissolve into a new corporate entity. 3. Uniting the trial of several actions into one court action.

consolidation loan A new loan that pays the balances owed on previous loans that are then extinguished.

consortium 1. The benefits that one spouse is entitled to receive from the other, e.g., companionship, cooperation, services, affection, and sexual relations. 2. The companionship and affection a parent is entitled to receive from a child and that a child is entitled to receive from a parent. 3. An association or coalition of businesses or other organizations.

conspiracy An agreement between two or more persons to commit a criminal or other unlawful act or to perform a lawful act by unlawful means. Also called criminal conspiracy.

Conspiracy exists when one or more persons have the specific intent to agree or conspire to commit an offense together with proof of the commission of an overt act by one or more of the parties to such agreement in furtherance of the conspiracy. Cal. Penal Code § 184. *People v. Herrera*, 98 Cal.Rptr.2d 911 (Cal.App., 2000)

constable A peace officer whose duties (e.g., serving writs) are similar to (but not as extensive as) those of a sheriff.

constitution The fundamental law that creates the branches of government, allocates power among them, and defines some basic rights of individuals.

constitutional Pertaining to or consistent with the constitution.

constitutional court See Article III court.

constitutional fact A fact whose determination is decisive of constitutional rights.

constitutional law The body of law found in and interpreting the constitution.

constitutional right A right guaranteed by a constitution.

construction An interpretation of a law or other document. The verb is construe.

constructive True legally even if not factually.

constructive bailment An obligation imposed by law on a person holding chattels to deliver them to another.

constructive contempt See indirect contempt.

constructive contract See implied in law contract.

constructive delivery Acts that are the equivalent of the actual delivery of something.

constructive desertion The misconduct of the spouse who stayed home that justified the other spouse's departure from the home.

constructive discharge Acts by an employer that make working conditions so intolerable that an employee quits.

For a constructive discharge, an employer must create or permit working conditions so intolerable or aggravated that a reasonable person in the employee's position would feel compelled to resign. *Cloud*, 90 Cal.Rptr.2d 757 (Cal.App., 1999)

constructive eviction A landlord's causing or allowing premises to become so uninhabitable that a tenant leaves.

constructive fraud A breach of a duty that violates a fiduciary relationship. Also called legal fraud.

Any act, omission, or concealment involving a breach of legal or equitable duty, trust or confidence that results in damage to another even though the conduct is not otherwise fraudulent. *Assilzadeh*, 98 Cal.Rptr.2d 176 (Cal.App., 2000)

constructive knowledge What one does not actually know, but should know or has reason to know and, therefore, is treated as knowing.

constructive notice Information the law assumes one has because he or she could have discovered it by proper diligence and had a duty to inquire into it.

constructive possession Control or dominion one rightfully has over property that he or she does not actually possess.

constructive receipt of income Having control over income without substantial restriction even though not actually received.

constructive service See substituted service.

constructive trust A trust implied as an equitable remedy to prevent unjust enrichment by one who has obtained the legal right to property by wrongdoing. Also called implied trust, involuntary trust, trust de son tort, trust ex delicto, trust ex maleficio.

An equitable remedy to prevent unjust enrichment and enforce restitution, under which one who wrongfully acquires property of another holds it involuntarily as constructive trustee. *Coppinger*, 185 Cal.Rptr. 24 (Cal.App., 1982)

construe See construction.

consul An official in a foreign country who promotes the commercial and other interests of his or her own country.

consumer A buyer of goods and services for personal use rather than for resale or manufacturing.

consumer credit Credit to buy goods or services for personal use.

consumer goods Products used or bought for personal, family, or household use.

consumer lease A lease of personal property for personal, family, or household use.

consumer price index (CPI) A measurement by the Bureau of Labor Statistics of average monthly changes in prices of basic goods and services bought by consumers (*www.bls.gov/cpi*).

consummate 1. To complete or bring to fruition. 2. To engage in the first act of sexual intercourse after marriage.

contemner (contemnor) One who commits contempt.

contemplation of death The thought of death as a primary motive for making a transfer of property.

contemporaneous Existing or occurring in the same period of time.

contempt Disobedience of or disrespect for the authority of a court or legislature.

Willful failure to comply with an order of the court constitutes contempt. Cal. Code of Civil Procedure § 1209(a). *In re Rubin*, 108 Cal.Rptr.2d 593 (CA 2001)

contest To challenge; to raise a defense against a claim.

contested Challenged; litigated.

contingency 1. A possible event. 2. Uncertainty. 3. A contingent fee.

contingent 1. Uncertain; pertaining to what may or may not happen. 2. Dependent; conditional.

Liable but not certain to occur. *Cametal*, 11 Cal.Rptr. 280 (Cal.Super., 1961)

contingent annuity An annuity whose commencement or exact terms of payment depend on an uncertain future event.

contingent beneficiary A person who receives a gift or insurance proceeds if a condition occurs.

contingent estate An estate that will become a present or vested estate if an event occurs or condition is met.

contingent fee A fee that a paid only if the case is successfully resolved by litigation or settlement. Also called conditional fee.

contingent interest An interest whose enjoyment is dependent on an uncertain event.

contingent liability Liability that depends on an uncertain event.

contingent remainder A remainder that is limited to take effect either to an uncertain person or upon an uncertain event. Also called executory remainder.

continuance An adjournment or postponement of a session.

continuing jurisdiction A court's power (by retaining jurisdiction) to modify its orders after entering judgment.

continuing legal education (CLE) Training in the law (often short term) received after completing one's formal legal training.

continuing offense An offense involving a prolonged course of conduct.

Continuing offense, for ex post facto purposes, ordinarily is marked by continuing duty in defendant to do an act which he fails to do. *Wright*, 63 Cal.Rptr.2d 322 (CA 1997)

continuing trespass Allowing a structure or other permanent invasion on another's land.

contra Against; in opposition to.

contraband Property that is unlawful to possess, import, export, or trade.

Goods or merchandise whose importation, exportation, or possession is forbidden. *People v. Lamonte*, 61 Cal.Rptr.2d 810 (Cal.App., 1997)

contract A legally enforceable agreement. A promise that, if breached, will entitle the aggrieved to a remedy.

An agreement to do or not to do a certain thing and it gives rise to an obligation or legal duty that is enforceable in an action at law. *Schaefer*, 19 Cal.Rptr.2d 212 (Cal.App., 1993)

contract carrier A private company that transports passengers or property under individual contracts, not for the general public.

Contract Clause A clause in the U.S. Constitution (art. I, § 10, cl. 1) providing that no state shall pass a law impairing the obligation of contracts.

contract for deed An agreement to sell property in which the seller retains title or possession until full payment has been made. Also called land sales contract.

contract implied in fact See implied in fact contract.

contract implied in law See implied in law contract.

contract of adhesion See adhesion contract.

contract under seal A signed contract that has the waxed seal of the signer attached. Consideration was not needed. Also called special contract, specialty.

contractor A person or company that enters contracts to supply materials or labor to perform a job.

contributing to the delinquency of a minor Conduct by an adult that is likely to lead to illegal or immoral behavior by a minor.

contribution 1. The right of one tortfeasor who has paid a judgment to be proportionately reimbursed by other tortfeasors who have not paid their share of the damages caused by all the tortfeasors. 2. The right of one debtor who has paid a common debt to be proportionately reimbursed by the other debtors.

Contribution distributes loss equally among all tortfeasors, each bearing his pro rata share. Cal. Code of Civil Procedure §§ 875, 876. *Herrero*, 38 Cal.Rptr. 490 (Cal.App., 1964)

contributory 1. Helping to bring something about. 2 Pertaining to one who pays into a common fund or benefit plan.

contributory negligence Unreasonableness by the plaintiff that helps cause his or her own injury or loss.

Conduct on part of the plaintiff that falls below the standard to which he should conform for his own protection, and that is a legally contributing cause, with the negligence of defendant, in bringing about plaintiff's harm. *Fonseca*, 104 Cal.Rptr. 566 (Cal.App., 1972)

controlled substance A drug whose possession or use is prohibited or otherwise strictly regulated.

controller See comptroller.

controlling interest Ownership of enough of the stock of a company to be able to control it.

controversy A dispute that a court can resolve; a justiciable dispute. An actual rather than a hypothetical dispute.

contumacy Refusal to obey a court order. Contempt.

convenience and necessity See certificate of convenience and necessity.

convention 1. An agreement or treaty. 2. A special assembly.

conventional 1. Customary. 2. Based on agreement rather than law.

conventional mortgage A mortgage that is not government insured.

conversation See criminal conversation.

conversion 1. An intentional interference with personal property that is serious enough to force the wrongdoer to pay its full value. An action for conversion is called trover. 2. Changing the nature of property.

Substantial interference or an exertion of wrongful dominion over the personal property of another. *Heaps*, 21 Cal.Rptr.3d 239 (Cal.App., 2004)

convertible security One kind of security (e.g., bond) that can be exchanged for another kind (e.g., stock).

conveyance A transfer of an interest in land. A transfer of title.

conveyancer One skilled in transferring interests in land.

convict 1. To find a person guilty of a crime. 2. A prisoner.

conviction 1. A finding of guilty of a crime. 2. A firm belief.

cooling off period 1. A period of time during which neither side can take any further action. 2. The time given to a buyer to cancel the purchase.

cooperative 1. A business owned by customers that use its goods and services. 2. A multiunit building owned by a corporation that leases units to individual shareholders of the corporation.

A limited-equity housing cooperative is a corporation which meets the criteria of Section 11003.2 and which also meets the criteria of Section 33007.5 of the Cal. Health and Safety Code. Cal. Business & Professions Code § 11003.4

coordinate jurisdiction See concurrent jurisdiction.

coparcenary An estate that arises when several persons inherit property from the same ancestor to share equally as if they were one person or one heir. Also called estate in coparcenary, parcenary.

coparcener A concurrent or joint heir through coparcenary. Also called parcener.

copyhold Tenure as laid out in a copy of the court roll (an old form of land tenure).

copyright (©) The exclusive right for a fixed number of years to print, copy, sell, or perform original works. 17 U.S.C. § 101.

coram nobis ("before us") An old remedy allowing a trial judge (via a writ of error) to vacate its own judgment because of factual errors. If the request to vacate is made to an appellate court, the remedy was called coram vobis ("before you").

A limited remedy to correct errors of fact, not errors of law. *People v. Crawford*, 1 Cal.Rptr. 811 (Cal.App., 1959)

coram vobis See coram nobis.

core proceeding A proceeding that invokes a substantive bankruptcy right. 28 U.S.C.A. § 157(b).

corespondent 1. The person who allegedly had sexual intercourse with a defendant charged with adultery. 2. A joint respondent.

corner Dominance over the supply of a particular commodity.

coroner A public official who inquires into suspicious deaths.

corporal punishment Punishment inflicted on the physical body.

The Cal. Education Code (§ 49001) provides: "(a) For the purposes of this section corporal punishment means the willful infliction of, or willfully causing the infliction of, physical pain on a pupil.

corporate-opportunity doctrine Corporate directors and officers must not take personal advantage of business opportunities they learn about in their corporate role if the corporation itself could pursue those opportunities.

corporate veil Legitimate corporate actions are not treated as shareholder actions. See piercing the corporate veil.

corporation An organization that is an artificial person or legal entity that has limited liability and can have an indefinite existence separate from its shareholders.

An artificial being, invisible, intangible, and existing only in contemplation of law; it possesses only those properties which the charter of its creation confers upon it. *State Farm*, 8 Cal.Rptr.3d 56 (Cal.App., 2003)

corporation counsel A city's salaried attorney.

corporeal Tangible; pertaining to the body.

corporeal hereditament Anything tangible that can be inherited, e.g., land.

Corporeal hereditament generally refers to tangible realty. *Gerhard*, 69 Cal.Rptr. 612 (CA 1968)

corpus 1. Assets in a trust. Also called res, trust estate, trust fund. 2. Principal as opposed to interest or income. 3. A collection of writings. 4. The main part of a body (anatomy).

corpus delicti ("body of the crime") The fact that a loss or injury has occurred as a result of the criminal conduct of someone.

Corpus delicti of a crime consists of two elements: fact of injury or loss or harm, and existence of criminal agency as its cause. *People v. Martinez*, 59 Cal.Rptr.2d 54 (Cal.App., 1996)

corpus juris A collection or body of laws.

correction 1. The system of imposing punishment and treatment on offenders. 2. Removing an error. 3. A market adjustment.

correspondent An intermediary for an organization that needs access to a particular market.

corroborating evidence Supplemental or supporting evidence.

corruption of blood Punishment by taking away the right to inherit or transfer property to blood relatives.

corrupt practices act A statute regulating campaign contributions, spending, and disclosure.

cosigner One who signs a document along with another, often to help the latter secure a loan. The cosigner can have repayment obligations upon default of the other. Also called comaker.

cost and freight (c&f)(c.a.f.) The price includes the cost of the goods and of transporting them.

cost basis The acquisition costs of purchasing property.

cost, insurance, and freight (CIF) The price includes the cost of purchasing, insuring, and transporting the goods.

cost-of-living clause A clause providing an automatic wage or benefit increase tied to cost-of-living rises as measured by indicators such as the Consumer Price Index.

costs Court-imposed charges or fees directly related to litigation in that court, e.g., filing fees. (Usually does not include attorney fees.) Also called court costs.

Costs of a civil action consist of the expenses of litigation, usually excluding attorney fees. *Baker-Hoey*, 3 Cal.Rptr.3d 593 (Cal.App., 2003)

costs to abide event Court costs that will be awarded to the prevailing party at the conclusion of the case.

cotenancy An interest in property whereby two or more owners have an undivided right to possession.

cotrustees Two or more persons who administer a trust together.

council An assembly or body that meets to advise or to legislate.

counsel 1. An attorney. A client's lawyer. Also called counselor, counselor at law. 2. Advice. 3. To give advice, to advise.

counselor See counsel (1).

count In pleading, a separate claim (cause of action) or charge.

counterclaim An independent claim by one side in a case filed in response to a claim asserted by an opponent.

Counterclaim merely need tend to diminish or defeat plaintiff's recovery. Cal. Code of Civil Procedure §§ 438, 442. *Holtzendorff*, 58 Cal.Rptr. 886 (Cal.App., 1967)

counterfeit To copy without authority in order to deceive by passing off the copy as genuine; fraudulent imitation, forgery.

countermand To change or revoke instructions previously given.

counteroffer A response by someone to whom an offer is made that constitutes a new offer, thereby rejecting the other's offer.

counterpart A corresponding part or a duplicate of a document.

countersign To sign in addition to the signature of another in order to verify the identity of the other signer.

county The largest territorial and governmental division within most states.

The state subdivision exercising within its boundaries the sovereignty of the state. Cal. Welfare & Institutions Code § 17000. *Union*, 196 Cal.Rptr. 602 (Cal.App., 1983)

county commissioners Officers who manage county government.

coupon An interest or dividend certificate attached to a bond or other instrument that can be detached and presented for payment.

course of business What is usually and normally done in a business. Also called ordinary or regular course of business.

course of dealing A pattern of prior conduct between the parties.

course of employment Conduct of an employee that fulfills his or her employment duties.

For an injury to occur in course of employment, employee must be engaged in work he has been hired to perform or some expectable personal act incidental thereto. *Department of Water*, 60 Cal.Rptr. 829 (Cal.App., 1967)

course of performance Repeated occasions for performing a contract in the past by either party with knowledge of the nature of the performance and opportunities for objection to it.

court 1. A unit of the judicial branch of government that applies the law to disputes and administers justice. 2. A judge or group of judges on the same tribunal.

court costs See costs.

court en banc See en banc.

court-martial A military court for trying members of the armed services for offenses violating military law.

court of appeals The middle appeals court in most judicial systems and the highest appellate court in a few.

court of chancery See chancery (2), equity (1).

court of claims A court that hears claims against the government for which sovereign immunity has been waived.

court of common pleas (C.P.) A trial court in several states, e.g., Ohio, Pennsylvania. 2. An appellate court in some states.

court of equity See court of law, equity (1).

court of law 1. A court that applied the common law as opposed to a court of equity that applied equitable principles.

court reporter See reporter.

covenant A promise or contract, e.g., a promise made in a deed or other legal instrument.

covenantee One to whom a promise by covenant is made.

covenant for quiet enjoyment A grantor's promise that the grantee's possession will not be disturbed by any other claimant with a superior lawful title.

Under California law, covenant of quiet enjoyment insulates tenant against any act or omission on the part of landlord, or anyone claiming under him, which interferes with tenant's right to use and enjoy premises for purposes contemplated by the tenancy. *Brucia*, 307 F.Supp.2d 1079 (N.D.Cal., 2003)

covenant marriage A form of marriage that requires proof of premarital counseling, a promise to seek marital counseling when needed during the marriage, and proof of marital fault to dissolve.

covenant not to compete A promise in an employment contract or contract for the sale of a business not to engage in competitive activities, usually within a specified geographic area and for limited time. Also called restrictive covenant.

covenant of seisin An assurance that the grantor has the very estate in quantity and quality that he or she purports to convey to the grantee. Also called right-to-convey covenant.

covenant of warranty An assurance that the grantee has been given good title and a promise to provide compensation if the title is attacked.

covenantor One who makes a promise by covenant to another.

covenant running with the land A covenant whose benefits or duties bind all later purchasers of the land.

cover The right of a buyer, after breach by the seller, to purchase goods in substitution for those due from the seller.

Cover is a mechanism available to avoid lost profits because of the buyers' inability to resell or otherwise commercially use property of which the sellers' breach deprived them. *Bishop*, 52 Cal.Rptr.2d 134 (Cal.App., 1996)

coverage The amount and extent of risk included in insurance.

coverture The legal status of a married woman whereby her civil existence for many purposes merged with that of her husband.

craft union A labor union whose members do the same kind of work (e.g., plumbing) across different industries. Also called horizontal union.

credibility Believability; the extent to which something is worthy of belief.

credit 1. The ability to acquire goods or services before payment. 2. Funds loaned. 3. An accounting entry for a sum received. 4. A deduction from the amount owed.

credit bureau A business that collects financial information on the creditworthiness of potential customers of businesses.

credit insurance Insurance against the risk of a debtor's nonpayment due to insolvency or other cause.

credit line See line of credit.

creditor One to whom a debt is owed.

One in whose favor an obligation exists, by reason of which he is or may become entitled to payment of money. *Downey*, 227 P.2d 484 (Cal.App., 1951)

creditor beneficiary A third person who is to receive the benefit of the performance of a contract (of which he or she is not a direct party) in satisfaction of a legal duty owed to him or her by one of the parties of that contract.

One cannot be a creditor beneficiary, and thus have right to enforce a contract in which he is not a party, unless promissor's performance of contract will discharge some form of legal duty owed to beneficiary from promisee. *New Hampshire*, 192 Cal.Rptr. 548 (Cal.App., 1983)

creditor's bill An equitable proceeding brought by a judgment creditor to enforce the judgment out of the judgment debtor's property that cannot be reached by ordinary legal process.

credit rating An assessment of one's ability to repay debts.

crime Conduct defined as criminal by the government.

crime against humanity Conduct prohibited by international law that is knowingly committed as part of a widespread or systematic attack against any civilian population.

crime against nature See sodomy.

crimen falsi A crime involving false statements, e.g., perjury.

crime of passion A crime committed in the heat of an emotionally charged moment.

criminal 1. One who has committed or been convicted of a crime. 2. Pertaining to crimes.

criminal action A prosecution for a crime.

criminal assault See assault.

criminal attempt See attempt.

criminal conspiracy See conspiracy.

criminal contempt An act directed against the authority of the court that obstructs the administration of justice and tends to bring the court into disrepute.

criminal conversation (crim. con.) A tort that is committed when the defendant has sexual relations with the plaintiff's spouse.

Sexual intercourse of an outsider with a husband or wife. *Hirschy*, 253 P.2d 93 (Cal.App., 1953)

criminal forfeiture An action against a defendant convicted of a crime to seize his or her property as part of the punishment.

criminalize To declare that specific conduct will constitute a crime.

criminal law Laws defining crimes, punishments, and procedures for investigation and prosecution. Also called penal law.

criminal mischief See malicious mischief.

criminal negligence Conduct that is such a gross deviation from the standard of reasonable care that it is punishable as a crime.

Aggravated, culpable, gross, or reckless conduct that is such a departure from what would be the conduct of an ordinarily prudent or careful person under the same circumstances as to be incompatible with a proper regard for human life. Cal. Penal Code § 20. *People v. Valdez*, 118 Cal.Rptr.2d 3 (CA 2002)

criminal procedure The law governing the investigation and prosecution of crimes, including sentencing and appeal.

criminal syndicalism Advocacy of crime or other unlawful methods of achieving industrial or political change.

criminal trespass Knowingly entering or remaining on land with notice that this is forbidden.

criminology The study of the causes, punishment, and prevention of crime.

critical legal studies (CLS) The theory that law is not neutral but exists to perpetuate the interests of those who are rich and powerful. *Critical race theory* emphasizes the disadvantages imposed on racial minorities under this theory.

critical stage A step in a criminal investigation or proceeding that holds significant consequences for the accused, at which time the right to counsel applies.

cross action 1. A claim brought by the defendant against the plaintiff in the same action. Sometimes called a counterclaim. 2. A claim brought by one defendant against another defendant or by one plaintiff against another plaintiff in the same action. Also called a cross-claim.

cross appeal An appeal by the appellee in the case that the appellant has appealed.

cross bill An equitable claim brought by the defendant against the plaintiff or another defendant in the same suit.

cross-claim See cross action (2).

cross collateral 1. Pooling collateral among participants. 2. Collateral used to secure additional loans or accounts.

cross-complaint 1. A claim by the defendant against another party in the same case. 2. A claim by the defendant against someone not now a party in the case that is related to the claim already filed against the defendant.

Cross-complaint is a separate pleading, based on an independent cause of action. *Wilson*, 83 Cal.Rptr.2d 192 (Cal.App., 1999)

cross-examination Questioning a witness by an opponent after the other side called and questioned that witness.

crown cases A criminal case brought in England.

cruel and unusual punishment Degrading or disproportionate punishment, shocking the conscience and offending human dignity.

Punishment that is so disproportionate to the crime committed that it shocks the conscience and offends fundamental notions of human dignity. *People v. Rhodes*, 24 Cal.Rptr.3d 834 (Cal.App., 2005)

cruelty The intentional or malicious infliction of serious mental or physical suffering on another.

CTA See cum testamento annexo.

culpable At fault; blameworthy.

cum Together with, along with.

cum testamento annexo (CTA) Concerning administration of an estate where no executor is named in the will, or where one is named but is unable to serve. Administration with the will annexed.

cumulative That which repeats earlier material and consolidates it with new material. Added and combined into one unit.

cumulative dividend A dividend that, if not paid in one period, is added to dividends to be paid in the next period.

cumulative evidence Additional evidence tending to prove the same point as other evidence already given.

Evidence is cumulative if it is repetitive of evidence already before jury. *People v. Evers*, 12 Cal.Rptr.2d 637 (Cal.App., 1992)

cumulative legacy An additional gift of personal property in the same will (or its codicil) to the same person.

cumulative sentences See consecutive sentences.

cumulative voting A type of voting in which a voter is given as many votes are there are positions to fill and can use the votes for one candidate or spread them among several candidates.

curative Tending to correct or cure a mistake or error.

curator A guardian or custodian of another's affairs.

cure 1. To remove a legal defect or error. 2. The seller's right, after delivering defective goods, to redeliver conforming goods.

current asset Property that can readily be converted into cash.

current liabilities A debt that is likely to be paid within the current business cycle, usually a year.

curtesy A husband's right to lifetime use of land his deceased wife owned during the marriage if a child was born alive to them.

curtilage The land (often enclosed) immediately surrounding and associated with a dwelling house.

custodial interrogation Questioning by law enforcement officers after a person is taken into custody or otherwise deprived of his or her freedom in any significant way.

Interrogation of prison inmate, conducted under circumstances where no restraint is placed upon the inmate over and above that associated with his prisoner status, is not a custodial interrogation within scope of Miranda. *People v. Fradiue*, 95 Cal.Rptr.2d 1 (Cal.App., 2000)

custodian One with responsibility for the care and custody of property, a person, papers, etc.

custody The protective care and control of a thing or person.

custom 1. An established practice that has acquired the force of law. 2. A tax (duty) on the importation and exportation of goods.

cy-pres As near as possible. The intention of the author of an instrument (e.g., will, trust) will be carried out as closely as possible if carrying it out literally is impossible.

Where compliance with the literal terms of a charitable trust became impossible, the funds would be put to the next best use, in accord with the dominant charitable purposes of the donor. *In re Vitamin*, 132 Cal.Rptr.2d 425 (Cal.App., 2003)

D

DA 1. District Attorney. 2. Deposit account.

dactylography The study of identification through fingerprints.

damage An injury or loss to person, property, or rights.

damages Monetary compensation a court can award for wrongful injury or loss to person or property.

Damages describes a payment made to compensate a party for injuries suffered. *Inline*, 23 Cal.Rptr.3d 216 (Cal.App., 2005)

damnum absque injuria A loss that cannot be the basis of a lawsuit because it was not caused by a wrongful act.

dangerous instrumentality An object or condition that in its normal operation is an implement of destruction or involves grave danger.

date of issue The date fixed or agreed upon as the beginning or effective date of a security or document in a series (e.g., bonds).

date rape Rape committed by the victim's social escort.

Date rape, often called acquaintance rape, is an issue that has emerged recently as a widespread phenomenon. *People v. Salazar*, 193 Cal.Rptr. 1 (Cal.App., 1983)

day in court The right to assert your claim or defense in court.

daybook A book on which daily business transactions are recorded.

dba (d/b/a) Doing business as. A trade name; an assumed name.

dbn See de bonus non.

DC District Court; District of Columbia.

dead freight The amount paid for the portion of a ship's cargo space that is contracted for but not used.

deadlock 1. A standstill due to a refusal of the parties to compromise. 2. The threatened destruction of a business that results when contending shareholders owning an equal number of shares cannot agree.

deadly force Force that is likely or intended to cause death or great bodily harm.

deadly weapon A weapon or other instrument intended to be used or likely to be used to cause death or great bodily harm. Also called lethal weapon.

dead man's statute A rule making some statements of a dead person inadmissible when offered to support claims against the estate of the dead person.

dealer 1. One who buys goods for resale to others. 2. One who buys and sells securities on his or her own account rather than as an agent.

death Permanent cessation of all vital functions and signs.

The cessation of life, ceasing to exist, total stoppage of circulation of blood and consequent cessation of animal and vital functions. *Thomas*, 215 P.2d 478 (Cal.App., 1950)

deathbed declaration See dying declaration.

death certificate An official record of someone's death, often including vital information such as the date and cause of death.

death knell exception A nonfinal order is appealable if delaying the appeal will cause a party to lose substantial rights.

death penalty Capital punishment; a death sentence.

death qualified rule In a death penalty case, prospective jurors who oppose the death penalty should not be selected.

death tax See estate tax, inheritance tax.

death warrant A court order to carry out a death sentence.

debar To prohibit someone from possessing or doing something.

de bene esse Conditionally allowed for now.

debenture A bond or other debt backed by the general credit of a corporation and not secured by a lien on any specific property.

Serial obligations or notes representing indebtedness but are not ordinarily secured by any specific mortgage, lien or pledge of security, rather, they are issued on a corporation's credit. *Kessler*, 155 Cal.Rptr. 94 (Cal.App., 1979)

de bonis non (dbn) Of the goods not administered. An administrator de bonis non is an administrator appointed (in place of a former administrator or executor) to administer the remainder of an estate.

debit A sum owed; an entry made on the left side of an account.

debt An amount of money that is due; an enforceable obligation.

debt capital Money raised by issuing bonds rather than stock.

debtor One who owes a debt, usually money.

Guarantor is a debtor within the meaning of Article 9 of Cal. Commercial Code §§ 9504, 9504(3). *American National*, 246 Cal.Rptr. 381 (Cal.App., 1988)

debtor in possession A debtor in bankruptcy while still running its business.

debt service Payments to be made to a lender, including interest, principal, and fees.

deceased A dead person.

decedent A dead person.

decedent's estate Property (real and personal) in which a person has an interest at the time of his or her death.

deceit Willfully or recklessly misrepresenting or suppressing material facts with the intent to mislead someone.

decertify 1. To withdraw or revoke certification. 2. To declare that a union can no linger represent a group of employees.

decision A determination of a court or administrative agency applying the law to the facts to resolve a conflict.

decisional law Case law; the law found in court opinions.

declarant A person who makes a declaration or statement.

declaration 1. A formal or explicit statement. 2. An unsworn statement. 3. The first pleading of the plaintiff in an action at law.

declaration against interest A statement made by a nonparty that is against his or her own interest. The statement can be admitted as an exception to the hearsay rule if it was made by someone with personal knowledge who is now not available as a witness.

Evidence of a statement by a declarant having sufficient knowledge of the subject is not made inadmissible by the hearsay rule if the declarant is unavailable as a witness and the statement, when made, was so far contrary to the declarant's pecuniary or proprietary interest . . . that a reasonable man in his position would not have made the statement unless he believed it to be true. Cal. Evidence Code § 1230

declaration of trust The establishment of a trust by one who declares that he or she holds the legal title to property in trust for another.

declaratory judgment A binding judgment that declares rights, status, or other legal relationships without ordering anything to be done.

A speculative eventuality does not present an actual controversy that can be resolved by means of a declaratory judgment. *Cardellini*, 226 Cal.Rptr. 659 (Cal.App., 1986)

declaratory statute A statute passed to remove doubt about the meaning of an earlier statute. Also called expository statute.

decree 1. A court order. 2. The decision of a court of equity.

decree nisi A decree that will become absolute unless a party convinces the court that it should not be. Also called order nisi, rule nisi.

decretal Pertaining to a decree.

decriminalization A law making legal what was once criminal.

dedication A gift of private land (or an easement) for public use.

deductible 1. What can be taken away or subtracted. 2. The amount of a loss the insured must bear before insurance payments begin.

deduction The part taken away, e.g., an amount that can be subtracted from gross income when calculating adjusted gross income.

deed 1. A document transferring (conveying) an interest in land. 2. An act; something that is done or carried out.

deed of trust A security instrument (similar to a mortgage) in which title to real property is given to a trustee as security until the debt is paid. Also called trust deed, trust indenture.

Trust deed or deed of trust as used in this part includes mortgage. Cal. Business & Professions Code § 10028. Each deed of trust and evidence of debt executed in connection with a shared appreciation loan shall contain . . . Cal. Civil Code § 1917.074.

deem To treat as if; to regard something as true or present even if this is not actually so.

deep pocket An individual, business, or other organization with resources to pay a potential judgment. The opposite of *shallow pocket*.

The Fair Responsibility Act, known as the Deep Pocket Initiative, was adopted to change the long standing common law rule of joint and several liability of multiple tortfeasors. Cal. Civil Code § 1431.2. *Kesmodel*, 15 Cal.Rptr.3d 118 (Cal.App., 2004)

Deep Rock doctrine A controlling shareholder's loan to its own company that is undercapitalized may, in fairness, be subordinated in bankruptcy to other loan claims.

deface To mar or destroy the physical appearance of something.

de facto 1. In fact. 2. Functioning or existing even if not formally or officially encouraged or authorized.

de facto corporation An enterprise that attempts to exercise corporate powers even though it was not properly incorporated in a state where it could have incorporated and where it made a good faith effort to do so.

de facto government A government that has assumed the exercise of sovereignty over a nation, often by illegal or extralegal means.

de facto segregation Segregation caused by social, economic, or other factors rather than by state action or active government assistance.

defalcation 1. A fiduciary's failure to account for funds entrusted to it. Misappropriation; embezzlement. 2. The failure to comply with an obligation.

defamation The publication of a written (or gestured) defamatory statement (libel) or an oral one (slander) of and concerning the plaintiff that harms the plaintiff's reputation.

default 1. The failure to carry out a duty. 2. The failure to appear.

default judgment A judgment against a party for failure to file a required pleading or otherwise respond to the opponent's claim.

defeasance 1. The act of rendering something null and void. 2. An instrument that defeats the force or operation of an estate or deed upon the fulfillment of a condition.

There are two types of defeasible estates: a fee simple determinable and a fee simple subject to a condition subsequent. *City of Palm Springs*, 82 Cal.Rptr.2d 859 (Cal.App., 1999)

defeasible Subject to being revoked or avoided.

defeasible fee See fee simple defeasible.

defeat To prevent, frustrate, or circumvent; to render void.

defect A shortcoming; the lack of something required.

defective Lacking in some particular that is essential to completeness, safety, or legal sufficiency.

defend 1. To protect or represent someone. 2. To contest or oppose.

defendant One against whom a civil action or criminal prosecution is brought.

defender 1. One who raises defenses. 2. One who represents another.

defense 1. An allegation of fact or a legal theory offered to offset or defeat a claim or demand. 2. The defendant and his or her attorney.

A defense is that which is offered as a reason in law or fact why the plaintiff should not recover or establish what he seeks. *Gil*, 17 Cal.Rptr.3d 420 (Cal.App., 2004)

deferred annuity An annuity that begins payment at a future date.

deferred compensation Work income set aside for payment in the future.

deferred income Income to be received in the future, after it was earned.

deficiency 1. A shortage or insufficiency. 2. The amount still owed.

deficiency judgment A judgment for an unpaid balance after the creditor has taken the secured property of the debtor.

A personal judgment against a debtor for a recovery of the secured debt measured by the difference between the debt and the net proceeds received from the foreclosure sale of the real property securing the debt. *Dreyfuss*, 101 Cal.Rptr.2d 29 (CA 2000)

deficit 1. An excess of outlays over revenues. 2. An insufficiency.

defined benefit plan A pension plan where the amount of the benefit is fixed but the amount of the contribution is not.

defined contribution plan A pension plan where the amount of the contribution is generally fixed but the amount of the benefit is not.

definite failure of issue See failure of issue.

definite sentence See determinate sentence.

definitive Complete; settling the matter.

defraud To use deception to obtain something or harm someone.

degree 1. The measure or scope of the seriousness of something; a grade or level of wrongdoing. 2. One of the steps in a process. 3. A step in the line of descent.

degree of care The standard of care that is required.

degree of proof The level of believability or persuasiveness that one's evidence must meet.

dehors Beyond the scope, outside of.

de jure Sanctioned by law; in compliance with the law.

de jure segregation Segregation allowed or mandated by the law.

A racially discriminatory purpose or a current condition of segregation resulting from intentional state action. *Tinsley*, 197 Cal.Rptr. 643 (Cal.App., 1983)

del credere agent A business agent or factor who guarantees the solvency and performance of the purchaser.

delectus personae The right of a partner to exercise his or her preference on the admission of new partners.

delegable duty A responsibility that one can ask another to perform.

delegate 1. To appoint a representative. 2. A representative.

delegation 1. The granting of authority to act for another. 2. The persons authorized to act as representatives.

deliberate 1. To weigh or examine carefully. 2. Intentional.

deliberative process privilege The government can maintain secrecy when needed to ensure the free exchange of ideas in the making of policy.

delict, delictum A tort or offense; a violation of the law.

delinquency 1. A violation of duty. 2. The failure to pay a debt. 3. Misconduct, unruly, or immoral behavior by a minor.

delinquent 1. Pertaining to that which is still due; in arrears. 2. Failing to abide by the law or to conform to moral standards. 3. A minor who has committed an offense or other serious misconduct.

delisting Removing a security from the list of what can be traded on an exchange.

delivery 1. The act by which something is placed in the possession or control of another. 2. That which is delivered.

Delivery is a term of art in the law of sales denoting the point at which ownership is transferred. Cal. Commercial Code § 2401. *Satco*, 192 Cal.Rptr. 449 (Cal.App., 1983)

demand 1. To claim as one's due or right. 2. The assertion of a right.

demand deposit Any bank deposit that the depositor may withdraw (demand) at any time without notice.

demand loan A loan without a set maturity date that the lender can demand payment of at any time. A call loan.

demand note A note that must be paid whenever the lender requests (demands) payment.

demeanor Outward or physical appearance or behavior; deportment.

demesne 1. Domain. 2. Land a person holds in his or her own right.

de minimis Very small; not significant enough to change the result.

demise 1. A lease. A conveyance of land to another for a term. 2. The document that creates a lease. 3. To convey or create an estate or lease. 4. To transfer property by descent or by will. 5. Death.

demise charter See bareboat charter.

democracy A system of government controlled by the people directly or through elected representatives.

demonstrative bequest; demonstrative legacy A gift by will payable out of a specific fund.

demonstrative evidence Evidence (other than testimony) addressed to the senses. Physical evidence offered for illumination and explanation, but otherwise unrelated to the case. Also called autopic evidence.

Demonstrative evidence is admissible for the purpose of illustrating and clarifying a witness' testimony so long as a proper foundation is laid. *People v. Roldan*, 27 Cal.Rptr.3d 360 (CA 2005)

demur 1. To state a demurrer. 2. To take exception.

demurrer A pleading that admits, for the sale of argument, the allegations of fact made by the other party in order to show that even if they are true, they are do not entitle this party to relief.

A pleading used to challenge the legal sufficiency of an opponent's pleading based on defects that appear either on the face of the pleading under attack or from matters outside the pleading that are judicially noticeable. *County of Fresno*, 78 Cal.Rptr.2d 272 (Cal.App., 1998)

denial 1. A declaration that something the other side alleges is not true. 2. Rejection; refusing to do something.

de novo Anew; as if for the first time. See trial de novo.

depecage Under conflicts of law principles, a court can apply the laws of different jurisdictions to different disputes in the same case.

dependency 1. A geographically separate territory under the jurisdiction of another country or sovereign. 2. A relationship in which one person relies on another for society or a standard of living.

dependent 1. One who derives his or her main support from another. 2. A person who can be claimed as a personal exemption by a taxpayer.

dependent covenant A party's agreement or promise whose performance is conditioned on and subject to prior performance by the other party.

dependent relative revocation The revocation of an earlier will was intended to give effect to a later will, so if the later will is inoperative, the earlier will shall take effect.

This doctrine is designed to carry out the probable intention of the testator when there is no reason to suppose that he intended to revoke his earlier will if the later will became inoperative. *Estate of Anderson*, 65 Cal.Rptr.2d 307 (Cal.App., 1997)

depletion An exhausting or reduction during the taxable year of oil, gas, or other mineral deposits and reserves.

deponent One who gives testimony at a deposition.

deport To banish or exile someone to a foreign country.

depose 1. To question a witness in a deposition. 2. To give testimony. 3. To remove from office or power.

deposit 1. To place for safekeeping. 2. An asset placed for safekeeping. 3. Money given as security or earnest money for the performance of a contract. Also called security deposit.

depositary A person or institution (e.g., bank) that receives an asset for safekeeping.

depositary bank The first bank to which checks or other deposits are taken for collection.

deposition A method of discovery by which parties or their prospective witnesses are questioned outside the courtroom before trial.

The officer for a deposition seeking discovery only of business records for copying . . . shall be a professional photocopier registered under Chapter 20 . . . or a person exempted from the registration requirements. . . . Ann.Cal.C.C.P. § 2020.420

deposition de bene esse A deposition of a witness who will not be able to testify at trial, taken in order to preserve his or her testimony.

depository The place where an asset is placed and kept for safekeeping.

depreciable life The period over which an asset may reasonably be expected to be useful in a trade or business. Also called useful life.

depreciation A gradual decline in the value of property caused by use, deterioration, time, or obsolescence.

deputy One duly authorized to act on behalf of another.

deregulate To lessen government control over an industry or business.

derelict 1. Abandoned property. 2. Delinquent in a duty.

dereliction 1. A wrongful or shameful neglect or abandonment of one's duty. 2. The gaining of land from the water as a result of a shrinking back of the sea or river below the usual watermark.

derivative 1. Coming from another; secondary. 2. A financial instrument whose value is dependent on another asset or investment.

Liability in this case is derivative, i.e., liability is imposed on one person for the direct acts of another. *Richard B*, 32 Cal.Rptr.3d 244 (Cal.App., 2005)

derivative action 1. A suit by a shareholder to enforce a corporate cause of action. Also called a derivative suit, representative action. 2. An action to recover for a loss that is dependent on an underlying tort or wrong committed against someone else.

derivative evidence Evidence that is inadmissible because it is derived or spawned from other evidence that was illegally obtained.

derivative suit See derivative action (1).

derivative work A translation or other transformation of a preexisting work.

derogation 1. A partial repeal or abolishing of a law, as by a subsequent act that limits its scope or force. 2. Disparaging or belittling, or undermining something or someone.

descend To be transferred to persons entitled to receive a deceased's assets by intestate succession. To pass by inheritance.

descendant Offspring; persons in the bloodline of an ancestor.

Descendants are children, grandchildren, and their children to the remotest degree. Cal. Probate Code, § 41. *In re Gilbert's Estate*, 307 P.2d 395 (Cal.App., 1957)

descent A transfer to persons entitled to receive a deceased's assets by intestate succession. Passing by inheritance.

descent and distribution 1. See intestate succession. 2. The passing of a decedent's assets by intestacy or will.

desecrate To violate something that is sacred; to defile.

desegregation The elimination of policies and laws that led to racial segregation.

desertion 1. The voluntary, unjustified leaving of one's spouse for an uninterrupted period of time with the intent not to return to resume marital cohabitation. 2. The willful failure to fulfill a support obligation. 3. Remaining absent (without authority) from one's military place of duty with the intent to remain away permanently.

design defect A flaw rendering a product unreasonably dangerous because of the way in which it was designed or conceived.

The product failed to perform as safely as an ordinary consumer would expect when used in an intended or reasonably foreseeable manner; the risk of danger inherent in the design outweighs the benefits of such design. *Baker*, 143 Cal.Rptr. 225 (CA 1978)

designer drug A synthetic substitute for an existing controlled substance or drug, often made to avoid anti-drug laws.

destination contract A contract in which the risk of loss passes to the buyer when the seller tenders the goods at the destination.

destructibility of contingent remainders A contingent remainder must vest before or at the end of the preceding estate, or it fails (is destroyed).

desuetude 1. Discontinuation of use. 2. The equivalent of a repeal of a law by reason of its long and continued nonuse.

detainer 1. Withholding possession of land or goods from another. Keeping someone or something in your custody. See also unlawful detainer. 2. A request or writ that an institution continue keeping someone in custody.

detention Holding in custody; confinement.

determinable 1. Capable of coming to an end (terminable) upon the occurrence of a contingency. 2. Susceptible of being determined, ascertained, or settled.

determinable fee See fee simple determinable.

determinate sentence A sentence to confinement for a fixed period. Also called definite sentence.

A sentence consisting of a specific number of months or years in prison. *People v. Smithson*, 94 Cal.Rptr.2d 170 (Cal.App., 2000)

determination 1. The final decision of a court or administrative agency. 2. The ending of an estate or property interest.

detinue An action for the recovery of personal property held (detained) wrongfully by another.

detraction Transferring property to another state upon a transfer of the title to it by will or inheritance.

detriment 1. Any loss or harm to person or property. 2. A legal right that a promisee gives up. Also called legal detriment.

detrimental reliance A loss, disadvantage, or change in one's position for the worse because of one's reliance on another's promise.

Detrimental reliance on the promise is regarded as a substitute for consideration. *Toscano*, 21 Cal.Rptr.3d 732 (Cal.App., 2004)

devaluation A reduction in the value of a currency in relation to other currencies.

devastavit An act of omission, negligence, or misconduct of an administrator or other legal representative of an estate.

devest See divest.

deviation Departure from established or usual conduct or ideology.

deviation doctrine A variation in the terms of a will or trust will be allowed to avoid defeating the purposes of the document.

"Deviation" from the terms of private trusts is analogous to the cy pres doctrine applicable to charitable trusts. *Estate of Mabury*, 127 Cal.Rptr. 233 (Cal.App., 1976)

device 1. A mechanical or electronic invention or gadget. 2. A scheme.

devise The gift of property (sometimes only real property) by a will.

devisee The person to whom property is devised or given in a will.

devisor The person who devises or gives property in a will.

devolution The transfer or transition of a right, title, estate, or office to another or to a lower level. The verb is devolve.

devolve See devolution.

dicta See dictum, which is the singular form of dicta.

dictum 1. An observation made by a judge in an opinion that is not essential to resolve the issues before the court; comments that go beyond the facts before the court. Also called obiter dictum. 2. An authoritative, formal statement or announcement.

Dicta consists of observations and statements unnecessary to the appellate court's resolution of the case. *Garfield*, 80 Cal.Rptr.2d 527 (Cal.App., 1998)

dies A day; days, e.g., dies non juridicus: A day on which courts are not open for business.

diet The name of the legislature in some countries.

digest An organized summary or abridgment. A set of volumes that contain brief summaries of court opinions, arranged by subject matter and by court or jurisdiction.

dilatory plea A plea raising a procedural matter, not on the merits.

diligence 1. Persistent activity. 2. Prudence, carefulness.

dilution Diminishing the strength or value of something, e.g., voting strength by increasing the number of shares issued, uniqueness of a trademark by using it on too many different products.

diminished capacity or responsibility A mental disorder not amounting to insanity that impairs or negates the defendant's ability to form the culpable mental state to commit the crime. Also called partial insanity.

Diminished capacity is used to refer to lack of capacity to achieve state of mind requisite for commission of crime. *McGuire*, 79 Cal.Rptr. 155 (Cal.App., 1969)

diminution in value As a measure of damages, the difference between the fair market value of the property with and without the damage.

diplomatic immunity A diplomat's exemption from most laws of the host country.

direct 1. To command, regulate, or manage. 2. To aim or cause to move in a certain direction. 3. Without interruption; immediate. 4. In a straight line of descent, as opposed to a collateral line.

direct attack An attempt to have a judgment changed in the same case or proceeding that rendered the judgment, e.g., an appeal.

direct cause See proximate cause.

direct contempt A contempt committed in the presence of the court or so near the court as to interrupt its proceedings.

direct damages See general damages.

directed verdict A judge's decision not to allow the jury to deliberate because only one verdict is reasonable. In federal court, the verdict has been replaced by a *judgment as a matter of law* (see this phrase).

direct estoppel See collateral estoppel.

direct evidence Evidence that, if believed, proves a fact without using inferences or presumptions; evidence based on what one personally saw, heard, or touched. Also called positive evidence.

Evidence that is applied to the fact to be proved, immediately and directly, and without the aid of any intervening fact or process. *People v. Rivera*, 135 Cal.Rptr.2d 682 (Cal.App., 2003)

direct examination The first questioning of a witness by the party who has called the witness. Also called examination in chief.

direct line A line of descent traced through those persons who are related to each other directly as descendants or ascendants.

director 1. One who directs or guides a department, organization, or activity. 2. A member of the board that oversees and controls the managers or officers of an entity such as a corporation.

directory Nonmandatory. Pertaining to a clause or provision in a statute or contract that is advisory rather than involving the essence of the statute or contract.

A requirement is directory if the failure to comply with a procedural step will not have effect of invalidating the governmental action to which procedural requirement relates. *California Correctional Peace Officers Assn.*, 43 Cal.Rptr.2d 693 (CA 1995)

directory trust A trust whose details will by filled out by later instructions.

direct tax A tax imposed directly on property rather than on the transfer of property or on some other right connected with property.

disability 1. Legal incapacity to perform an act. 2. A physical or mental condition that limits one's ability to participate in a major life activity such as employment. Also called incapacity.

disaffirm To repudiate; to cancel or revoke consent.

disallow To refuse to allow; to deny or reject.

disavow To repudiate; to disclaim knowledge of or responsibility for.

disbar To expel an attorney or revoke his or her license to practice law.

disbursement Paying out money; an out-of-pocket expenditure.

discharge 1. To relieve of an obligation. 2. To fulfill an obligation. 3. To release or let go. 4. To cancel a court order. 5. To shoot. 6. To release from employment or service.

discharge in bankruptcy The release of a bankrupt from all nonexcepted debts in a bankruptcy proceeding.

disciplinary rule (DR) A rule stating the minimum conduct below which no attorney should fall without being subject to discipline.

disclaimer The repudiation of a one's own or another's claim, right, or obligation.

A renunciation of all claims. *Axe*, 220 P.2d 781 (Cal.App., 1950)

disclosure 1. The act of revealing that which is secret or not known. 2. Complying with a legal duty to provide specified information.

discontinuance 1. The plaintiff's withdrawal or termination of his or her suit. 3. In zoning, the abandonment of a use.

discount 1. An allowance or deduction from the original price or debt. 2. The amount by which interest is reduced from the face value of a note or other financial instrument at the outset of the loan. 3. The amount by which the price paid for a security is less than its face value.

A discount as used in Insurance Code sections and related statutes prohibiting rebates is a method of computing rate. Cal. Insurance Code, §§ 750, 751, 11738. *State Compensation*, 294 P.2d 440 (CA 1956)

discounting Converting future cash flows into a present value.

discount rate 1. A percentage of the face amount of commercial paper (e.g., note) that an issuer pays when transferring the paper to a financial institution. 2. The interest rate charged by the Federal Reserve to member banks.

discoverable Pertaining to information or other materials an opponent can obtain through a deposition or other discovery device.

discovered peril doctrine See last clear chance doctrine.

discovery Compulsory exchanges of information between parties in litigation. Pretrial devices (e.g., interrogatories) to obtain information about a suit from the other side.

Under the discovery rule, the statute of limitations does not begin to run until plaintiff either actually discovers the injury and its cause or could have discovered it through exercise of reasonable diligence. *Angeles*, 51 Cal.Rptr.2d 594 (Cal.App., 1996)

discredit To cast doubt on the credibility of a person, an idea, or evidence.

discretion 1. The power or right to act by the dictates of one's own judgment and conscience. 2. The freedom to decide among options. 3. Good judgment; prudence.

discretionary review An appeal that an appellate court agrees to hear when it has the option of refusing to hear it.

discretionary trust A trust giving the trustee discretion to decide when a beneficiary will receive income or principal and how much. Also called complex trust.

discrimination 1. Differential imposition of burdens or granting of benefits. 2. Unreasonably granting or denying privileges on the basis of sex, age, race, nationality, religion, or handicap.

Discrimination for purposes of commerce clause analysis simply means different treatment of in-state and out-of-state economic interests that benefits former and burdens latter. *Pacific Merchant*, 48 Cal.Rptr.2d 582 (CA 1995)

disenfranchise To deprive someone of a right or privilege, e.g., the right to vote. Also called disfranchise.

disfranchise See disenfranchise.

disgorge To surrender unwillingly.

dishonor To refuse to accept or pay a draft or other negotiable instrument when duly presented.

disinheritance Taking steps to prevent someone from inheriting property.

disinterested Objective; without bias; having nothing to gain or lose.

disintermediation The withdrawal by depositors of funds from low-yielding bank accounts for use in higher-yielding investments.

disjunctive allegations Assertions pleaded in the alternative, e.g., he stole the car or caused it to be stolen.

dismissal 1. An order that ends an action or motion without additional court proceedings. 2. A discharge; an order to go away.

A dismissal is the withdrawal of an application for judicial relief by the party seeking such relief or the removal of the application by a court. *English*, 114 Cal.Rptr.2d 93 (Cal.App., 2001)

dismissal without prejudice Termination of the action that is not on the merits, meaning that the party can return later with the same claim.

dismissal with prejudice Termination of the action that is the equivalent of an adjudication on the merits, meaning that the party is barred from returning later with the same claim.

disorderly conduct Behavior that tends to disturb the peace, endanger the health of the community, or shock the public sense of morality.

disorderly house A dwelling where acts are performed that tend to corrupt morals, promote breaches of the peace, or create a nuisance.

disparagement The intentional and false discrediting of the plaintiff's product or business (sometimes called trade libel when written, or slander of goods when spoken) or the plaintiff's title to property (sometimes called slander of title) resulting in specific monetary loss.

Disparagement of title occurs when one, without privilege to do so, publishes a false statement that disparages title to property and causes pecuniary loss. *Truck Ins.*, 61 Cal.Rptr.2d 497 (Cal.App., 1997)

disparate impact Conduct that appears neutral on its face but that disproportionately and negatively impacts members of one race, sex, age, disability, or other protected group.

disparate treatment Intentionally treating some people less favorably than others because of sex, age, race, nationality, religion, or disability.

Intentional discrimination against one or more persons on prohibited grounds. *Carter*, 19 Cal.Rptr.3d 519 (Cal.App., 2004)

dispensation An exemption from a duty, burden, penalty, or law.

disposition 1. The act of distributing or transferring assets. 2. The final ruling or decision of a tribunal. 3. An arrangement or settlement. 4. Temperament or characteristics.

dispossess To evict from land; to deprive of possession.

disputable presumption See rebuttable presumption.

dispute 1. A controversy. 2. The conflict leading to litigation.

disqualification That which renders something ineligible or unfit.

disseisin Wrongful dispossession of another from property.

dissent 1. A judge's vote against the result reached by the judges in the majority on a case. 2. A dissenting opinion.

dissipation 1. Wasting, squandering, or destroying. 2. The use of marital property by a spouse for a personal purpose.

The dissipation by husband of community assets by means of unauthorized gifts is a conversion of the property of the wife. *Fields*, 205 P.2d 402 (Cal.App., 1949)

dissolution 1. Cancellation. 2. The act or process of terminating a legal relationship or organization. 3. A divorce.

dist. ct. District court.

distinguish To point out an essential difference; to demonstrate that a particular court opinion is inapplicable to the current legal dispute.

distrain To take and hold the personal property of another until the latter performs an obligation.

distrainee A person who is distrained.

distrainer or distrainor One who seizes property under a distress.

distraint Property seized to enforce an obligation.

distress Seizing property to enforce an obligation, e.g., a landlord seizes a tenant's property to secure payment of delinquent rent.

distress sale 1. A foreclosure sale; a forced sale to pay a debt. 2. A sale at below market rates because of a pressure to sell.

distributee One who shares in the distribution of an estate. An heir.

distribution 1. The apportionment and division of something. 2. The transfer of property under the law of intestate succession after estate taxes and other debts are paid.

distributive finding A jury's finding in part for the plaintiff and in part for the defendant.

distributive justice A system of justice where the goal is the fair allocation of available goods, services, and burdens.

district A geographic division for judicial, political, electoral, or administrative purposes.

district attorney A prosecutor representing the government in criminal cases in an area or district. Also called prosecuting attorney or state attorney.

district court A trial court in the federal and some state judicial systems.

disturbance of the peace See breach of the peace.

divers Various, several.

diversion 1. Turning aside or altering the natural course or route of a thing. 2. An alternative to criminal prosecution leading to the dismissal of the charges if the accused completes a program of rehabilitation. Also called diversion program, pretrial diversion, or pretrial intervention.

diversity of citizenship The disputing parties are citizens of different states. This fact gives jurisdiction (called diversity jurisdiction) to a United States District Court when the amount in controversy exceeds $75,000.

divest To dispose of or be deprived of rights, duties, or possessions. Also spelled devest.

divestiture 1. The selling, spinning off, or surrender of business assets. 2. The requirement that specific property, securities, or other assets be disposed of, often to avoid a restraint of trade.

Divestiture of powers. The district may divest itself of any power provided in § 61600. Cal. Government Code § 61602

divided custody A custody arrangement in which the parents alternate having full custody (legal and physical) of a child.

dividend A share of corporate profits given pro rata to stockholders.

divisible Capable of being divided.

divisible contract A contract with parts that can be enforced separately so that the failure to perform one part does not bar recovery for performance of another.

A contract in which two or more separate partial performances on each side are agreed to be exchanged for partial performances on the other side, so that the failure to perform one part does not bar recovery for performance of another. *Filet*, 94 Cal.Rptr.2d 438 (Cal.App., 2000)

divisible divorce A divorce decree that dissolves the marriage in one proceeding but that resolves other marital issues such as property division and child custody in a separate proceeding.

divorce A declaration by a court that a validly entered marriage is dissolved.

divorce a mensa et thoro See legal separation.

divorce a vinculo matrimonii An absolute divorce that terminates the marital relationship.

DNA fingerprinting The process of identifying the genetic makeup of an individual based on the uniqueness of his or her DNA pattern. Deoxyribonucleic acid (DNA) is the carrier of genetic information in living organisms.

DNR Do not resuscitate (a notice concerning terminally ill persons).

dock 1. The space in a criminal court where prisoners stand when brought in for trial. 2. A landing place for boats.

docket 1. A list of pending court cases. 2. A record containing brief notations on the proceedings that have occurred in a court case.

docket number A consecutive number assigned to a case by the court and used on all documents filed with the court during the litigation of that case.

doctor of jurisprudence See juris doctor.

doctor-patient privilege A patient and doctor can refuse to disclose communications between them concerning diagnosis or treatment. Also called physician-patient privilege.

[A] patient, whether or not a party, has a privilege to refuse to disclose, and to prevent another from disclosing, a confidential communication between patient and physician. Cal. Evidence Code § 994

doctrine A rule or legal principle.

document 1. Any physical or electronic embodiment of words or ideas (e.g., letter, X-ray plate). 2. To support with documentary evidence or with authorities. 3. To create a written record.

documentary evidence Evidence in the form of something written.

document of title A document giving its holder the right to receive and dispose of goods covered by the document (e.g., a bill of lading).

doing business Carrying on or conducting a business.

doli capax Capable of having the intent to commit a crime.

dolus Fraud; deceitfulness.

domain 1. Land that is owned; an estate in land. 2. Absolute ownership and control. 3. The territory governed by a ruler.

***Dombrowski* doctrine** To protect First Amendment rights, a federal court can enjoin state criminal proceedings based on a vague statute. *Dombrowski v. Pfister*, 85 S. Ct. 1116 (1965).

domestic Concerning one's own country, state, jurisdiction, or family.

domestic corporation A corporation established in a particular state.

domestic partners Persons in a same-sex (or unmarried opposite-sex) relationship who are emotionally and financially interdependent and who register with the government to receive marriage-like benefits.

Domestic partners are two adults who have chosen to share one another's lives in an intimate and committed relationship of mutual caring. Cal. Family Code § 297

domestic relations Family law (e.g., the law on adoption and divorce).

domestic violence Actual or threatened physical injury or abuse by one member of a family or household on another member. Cal. Penal Code § 13700

domicile 1. The place where someone has physically been present with the intention to make that place a permanent home; the place to which one would intend to return when away. 2. The place where a business has its headquarters or principal place of business. 3. The legal residence of a person or business. (Residence and domicile are sometimes used interchangeably.)

For purpose of establishing residence necessary to dissolve marriage, residency is synonymous with domicile, and means both active residence and intention to remain. *In re Marriage of Dick*, 18 Cal.Rptr.2d 743 (Cal.App., 1993)

domiciliary Someone who has established a domicile in a place.

domiciliary administration The administration of an estate in the state where the decedent was domiciled at the time of death.

dominant estate The parcel of land that is benefited from an easement. Also called dominant tenement.

dominant tenement See dominant estate.

dominion Ownership or sovereignty; control over something.

donated surplus Assets contributed by shareholders to a corporation.

donatio A gift or donation.

donative intent The donor's intent that title and control of the subject matter of the gift be irrevocably and presently transferred.

donee One to whom a gift or power of appointment is given.

donee beneficiary A nonparty to a contract who receives the benefit of the contract as a gift.

A person is a donee beneficiary of contract made by other parties only if the promisee's contractual intent is either to make a gift to him or to confer on him a right against promisor. *Dateline Builders*, 194 Cal.Rptr. 258 (Cal.App., 1983)

donor One who makes a gift, confers a power, or creates a trust.

dormant In abeyance, suspended; temporarily inactive.

dormant judgment An unsatisfied judgment that has remained unexecuted for so long that it needs to be revived before it can be executed.

dormant partner A partner who receives financial benefits from a business, but does not run it and may be unknown to the public. Also called a silent partner, sleeping partner.

double hearsay A hearsay statement contained within another hearsay statement.

double indemnity Twice the benefit for losses from specified causes.

double insurance Overlapping insurance whereby an insured has two or more policies on the same subject and against same the risks.

double jeopardy A second prosecution for the same offense after acquittal or conviction; multiple punishments for the same offense.

Double jeopardy bars successive trials for the same offense. *In re Cruz*, 129 Cal.Rptr.2d 31 (Cal.App., 2003)

double taxation Taxing the same thing twice for the same purpose by the same taxing authority during identical taxing periods.

double will See mutual wills (1).

doubt Uncertainty of mind. See also reasonable doubt.

doubtful title Title that raises serious doubts as to its validity.

dower A wife's right to a life estate in one-third of the land her deceased husband owned in fee at any time during the marriage.

down payment An amount of money paid by the buyer to the seller at the time of sale, which represents only a part of the total cost.

dowry Property that a woman brings to her husband upon marriage.

DR See disciplinary rule.

draft 1. An unconditional written order (e.g., a check) by the first party (called the drawer) instructing a second party (called the drawee or payor, e.g., a bank) to pay a specified sum on demand or at a specified time to a third party (called the payee) or to bearer. Also called bill of exchange. 2. A preliminary version of a plan, drawing, memo, or other writing. 3. Compulsory selection; conscription.

Draft is an order to pay a sum certain in money, signed by a drawer, payable on demand or at a definite time, and to order or bearer. Cal. Commercial Code, §§ 3102(1)(b) *People v. Norwood*, 103 Cal.Rptr. 7 (Cal.App., 1972)

Dram Shop Act A law imposing civil liability on a seller of liquor to one whose intoxication causes injury to a third person. Also called civil damage law.

draw 1. To prepare a legal document. 2. To withdraw money. 3. To make and sign (e.g., draw a check to pay the bill). 4. To pick a jury. 5. An advance against profits or amounts owed.

drawee The bank or other entity ordered to pay the amount on a draft.

drawer One who makes and signs a draft for the payment of money.

Dred Scott case The U.S. Supreme Court case holding that slaves and former slaves were not citizens even if they lived in states where slavery was not legal. *Scott v. Sanford*, 60 U.S. 393 (1867).

driving under the influence (DUI); driving while intoxicated (DWI) The offense of operating a motor vehicle while impaired due to alcohol or drugs. States may treat DWI as more serious than or the same as DUI.

It is unlawful for any person who is under the influence of any alcoholic beverage or drug, or under the combined influence of any alcoholic beverage and drug, to drive a vehicle. Cal. Vehicle Code § 23152(a)

droit A legal right; a body of law.

drug-free zone Geographic areas (e.g., near schools) where conviction of a drug offense will lead to increased punishment.

dry 1. Without duties. 2. Prohibiting the sale or use of liquor.

dry trust See passive trust.

dual capacity doctrine An employer may be liable in tort to its employee if it occupies, in addition to its capacity as employer, a second capacity that confers on it obligations independent of those imposed on an employer.

dual citizenship The status of a person who is a citizen of the United States and of another country at the same time.

dual contract Two contracts by the same parties for the same matter or transaction, something entered to mislead others.

dual-purpose doctrine An employee injured on a trip serving both business and personal purposes is covered under workers' compensation if the trip would have been made for the employer even if there was no personal purpose.

Where employee is combining his or her own business with that of employer or is attending to both at substantially same time, in which case the employer will be held responsible, unless it clearly appears that the employee could not have been directly or indirectly serving employer. *Gipson*, 30 Cal.Rptr. 253 (Cal.App., 1963)

dubitante Having doubt.

duces tecum Bring with you. See also subpoena duces tecum.

due 1. Payable now or on demand; owing. 2. Proper, reasonable.

due-bill An acknowledgement of indebtedness; an IOU.

due care See reasonable care.

due course See holder in due course.

due diligence Reasonable prudence and effort in carrying out an obligation.

Due diligence connotes persevering application, untiring efforts in good earnest, efforts of a substantial character. *People v. Mendoza*, 2004 WL 2601202 (Cal.App., 2004)

due notice Notice likely to reach its target; legally prescribed notice.

due process of law Fundamental fairness in having a dispute resolved according to established procedures and rules, e.g., notice, hearing.

DUI See driving under the influence.

duly In due and proper form or manner.

dummy 1. One who buys property and holds the legal title for someone else, usually to conceal the identity of the real owner. 2. Sham.

dummy corporation A corporation formed to avoid personal liability or conceal the owner's identity, not to conduct a legitimate business.

dumping 1. Selling in quantity at a very low price. 2. Selling goods abroad at less than their fair market price at home. 3. Shifting a nonpaying patient onto another health care provider.

dun To make a demand for payment.

duplicate A copy or replacement of the original.

duplicity 1. Deception. 2. Improperly uniting two or more causes of action in one count or two or more grounds of defense in one plea. 3. Improperly charging two or more offenses in a single count of an indictment.

duress 1. Coercion; the unlawful use of force or threat of force. 2. Wrongful confinement or imprisonment.

The defense of duress requires that threat or menace be accompanied by direct or implied demand that defendant commit the criminal act charged. *People v. Steele*, 253 Cal.Rptr. 773 (Cal.App., 1988)

duress of goods A tort of seizing or detaining another's personal property and wrongfully requiring some act before it is returned.

***Durham* rule** See insanity (3).

duty 1. A legal or moral obligation that another has a right to have performed. 2. The obligation to conform to a standard of conduct prescribed by law or by contract. Also called legal duty. 3. A function or task expected to be performed in one's calling. 4. A tax on imports or exports.

Duty is simply an expression of the sum total of those considerations of policy that lead the law to say that the particular plaintiff is entitled to protection. *Coldwell*, 11 Cal.Rptr.3d 564 (Cal.App., 2004)

duty of tonnage See tonnage (2).

dwelling house The building that is one's residence or abode.

DWI See driving while intoxicated.

dying declaration A statement of fact by one conscious of imminent death about the cause or circumstances of his or her death. An exception to the hearsay rule. Also called deathbed declaration.

dynamite instruction See *Allen* charge.

E

E&O See errors and omissions insurance.

earmarking To set aside or reserve for a designated purpose.

earned income Income (e.g., wages) derived from labor and services.

earned income credit A refundable tax credit on earned income for low income workers who have dependent children and who maintain a household.

earned premium The portion of an insurance premium that has been used thus far during the term of a policy.

earned surplus The surplus a corporation accumulates from profits after dividends are paid. Also called retained earnings.

earnest money Part of the purchase price paid by a buyer when entering a contract to show the intent and ability to carry out the contract.

earnings report A company report showing revenues, expenses, and losses over a given period and the net result. Also called an income statement, profit-and-loss statement.

easement A property interest in another's land that authorizes limited use of the land, e.g., a right-of-way across private property.

A nonpossessory interest in the land of another that gives its owner the right to use the land of another or to prevent the property owner from using his land. *Beyer*, 29 Cal.Rptr.3d 561 (Cal.App., 2005)

easement appurtenant An easement interest that attaches to the land and passes with it when conveyed.

easement by implication See implied easement.

easement by prescription See prescriptive easement.

easement in gross A personal right to use the land of another that usually ends with the death of the person possessing this right. An easement that does not benefit a particular piece of land.

eavesdrop To listen to another's private conversation without consent.

Interception of communications by the use of equipment not connected to any transmission line. Cal. Penal Code §§ 631(a), 632(a). *People v. Ratekin*, 261 Cal.Rptr. 143 (Cal.App., 1989)

easement of access The right to travel over the land of another to reach a road or other location.

ecclesiastical Pertaining to the church. See also canon law.

economic duress See business compulsion.

economic realities test The totality of commercial circumstances that a court will examine to determine the nature of a relationship.

economic strike A strike over wages, hours, working conditions, or other conditions of employment, not over an unfair labor practice.

edict A formal decree, command, law, or proclamation.

EEOC Equal Employment Opportunity Commission (*www.eeoc.gov*).

effect 1. That which is produced. 2. To bring about or cause.

effective assistance of counsel Representation provided by an attorney using the skill, knowledge, time, and resources of a reasonably competent attorney in criminal cases.

effective date The date a law, treaty, or contract goes into effect and becomes binding or enforceable.

effective tax rate The percentage of total income actually paid for taxes.

effects Personal property; goods.

efficient cause See proximate cause.

efficient intervening cause See intervening cause.

efficient market A market in which material information on a company is widely available and accurately reflected in the value of the stock.

eggshell skull An unusually high vulnerability to injury.

egress The means or right to leave a place. The act of leaving.

ejectment An action for the recovery of the possession of land and for damages for the wrongful dispossession.

ejusdem generis Where general words follow a list of particular words, the general words will be interpreted as applying only to things of the same class or category as the particular words in the list.

A general term or category is restricted to those things that are similar to those which are enumerated specifically. *Eller*, 133 Cal.Rptr.2d 324 (Cal.App., 2003)

election A selection among available persons, conduct, rights, etc.

election by spouse The right of a widow or widower to choose between what a deceased spouse gives the surviving spouse by will or the share of the decedent's estate designated by statute.

election of remedies A choice by a party between two inconsistent remedies for the same wrong.

elective share The statutory share a surviving spouse chooses over what the will of his or her deceased spouse provides.

elector 1. A voter. 2. A member of the electoral college.

electoral college A body of electors chosen to elect the president and vice-president based on the popular vote in each individual state.

eleemosynary Having to do with charity.

element 1. A constituent part of something. 2. A portion of a rule that is a precondition of the applicability of the entire rule.

elisor A person appointed by the court to perform duties of a disqualified sheriff or coroner.

eloign To remove something in order to conceal it from the court.

emancipation 1. Setting free. 2. The express or implied consent of a parent to relinquish his or her control and authority over a child.

Emancipation of a child is the relinquishment by a parent of control and authority over the child, conferring on the child the right to his or her earnings and terminating the parent's legal duty to support the child. *Perkins*, 295 P.2d 972 (Cal.App., 1956)

embargo A government prohibition of ships into or out of its waters or of the exchange of goods and services to or from a particular country.

embezzlement Fraudulently taking personal property of another, which was initially acquired lawfully because of a position of trust.

The appropriation to one's own use of property delivered for devotion to a particular purpose other than one's own enjoyment of it. Cal. Penal Code, §§ 484, 487. *People v. Kagan*, 70 Cal.Rptr. 732 (Cal.App., 1968)

emblements The crops produced by the labor of a tenant.

embracery The crime of corruptly trying to influence a jury by promises, entertainments, etc. Also called jury tampering.

emend To correct or revise.

emergency doctrine 1. One will not be liable for ordinary negligence when confronted with an emergency situation he or she did not aid in creating. Also called imminent peril doctrine, sudden emergency doctrine. 2. A warrantless search is allowed if the police have an objectively reasonable belief that an emergency has occurred and that someone within the residence is in need of immediate assistance. 3. In an emergency, consent to medical treatment for a child or unconscious adult will be implied if no one is available to give express consent.

One who without negligence is suddenly and unexpectedly confronted with peril arising from either the actual presence, or the appearance, of imminent danger to himself or to others, is not required to use the same judgment and prudence required in the exercise of ordinary care in calmer and more deliberate moments. *Leo*, 264 P.2d 1 (CA 1953)

eminent domain The power of government to take private property for public use upon the payment of just compensation. The exercise of eminent domain is called *condemnation.*

emolument Payment or other benefit for an occupation or office.

emotional distress Mental or emotional suffering or pain, e.g., depression, shame, worry. Also called mental anguish, mental distress, mental suffering.

empanel See impanel.

employee One hired by another who has the right to control the employee in the material details of how the work is performed.

Employee Retirement Income Security Act (ERISA) A federal statute creating the Pension Benefit Guarantee Corporation to regulate private pension plans (29 USC § 1001) (*www.pbgc.gov*).

employee stock ownership plan (ESOP) An employee benefits plan that primarily invests in the shares of stock of the employer creating the plan.

employers' liability See workers' compensation.

employment at will See at-will employee.

emptor A buyer or purchaser. See also caveat emptor.

enabling statute The statute that allows (enables) an administrative agency to carry out specified delegated powers.

enact To make into a law, particularly by a legislative body.

enacting clause A clause in a statute (often in the preamble) that states the authority by which it is made (e.g., "Be it enacted . . .").

enactment 1. The method or process by which a bill in a legislature becomes a law. 2. A statute.

Enactment means a constitutional provision, statute, charter, provision, ordinance or regulation. Cal. Government Code § 810.6; *Dateline*, 194 Cal.Rptr. 258 (Cal.App., 1983)

en banc or in banc By the full membership of a court as opposed to one of its smaller groupings or panels. Also called by the full bench or full court.

encroach To trespass, interfere with, or infringe on another's property or rights. Also spelled incroach.

encumbrance Every right to, interest in, or claim on land that diminishes the value of land, e.g., a mortgage or easement. Also spelled incumbrance.

Any right to, or interest in, land that may subsist in another to the diminution of its value, but consistent with passing of the fee. *1119 Delaware*, 20 Cal.Rptr.2d 438 (Cal.App., 1993)

encumbrancer Someone who holds an encumbrance (e.g., a lien) against land.

endorsee See indorsee.

endorsement 1. See indorsement. 2. A modification to an insurance policy. An insurance policy rider.

endorser See indorser.

endowment 1. A special gift or fund for an institution. 2. An endowment insurance policy will pay the insured a stated sum at the end of a definite period, or, if the insured dies before such period, to pay the amount to the person designated as beneficiary.

enfeoff To invest someone with a freehold estate. See also feoffment.

enforcement Forcing someone to comply with a law or other obligation.

enfranchisement 1. Giving a right or franchise, e.g., the right to vote. 2. Freeing someone from bondage.

engage 1. To hire or employ. 2. To participate.

English rule See American rule.

engrossment 1. Copying or drafting a document (e.g., a bill) for its final execution or passage. 2. Preparing a deed for execution. 3. Buying up or securing enough of a commodity in order to obtain a monopoly.

engrossed bill The version of a bill passed by one of the chambers of the legislature after incorporating amendments or other changes.

enjoin 1. To require a person to perform or to abstain from some act. 2. To issue an injunction.

enjoyment 1. The ability to exercise a right or privilege. 2. Deriving benefit from possession.

enlarge To make or become bigger. To allow more time.

Enoch Arden doctrine The presumption that a spouse is dead after being missing without explanation for a designated number of years.

enroll To register or record officially.

enrolled agent An attorney or nonattorney authorized to represent taxpayers at the Internal Revenue Service.

enrolled bill A bill that is ready to be sent to the chief executive after both chambers of the legislature have passed it.

entail To impose a limitation on who can inherit real property; it does not pass to all the heirs of the owner.

enter 1. To place anything before a court or on the court record. 2. To go into or onto. 3. To become part of or party to.

enterprise 1. A venture or undertaking, often involving a financial commitment. 2. Any individual, partnership, corporation, association, or other legal entity, and any union or group of individuals associated in fact although not a legal entity. 18 USC § 1961(4). See also RICO.

Limited partnership may be an enterprise within meaning of federal Racketeer Influenced and Corrupt Organizations Act (RICO). *Gervase*, 37 Cal.Rptr.2d 875 (Cal.App., 1995)

enterprise liability theory Liability for harm caused by a product is spread over the entire industry or enterprise that made the product.

enticement 1. The tort of wrongfully (a) encouraging a wife to leave or stay away from her husband or (b) forcing or encouraging a child to leave or stay away from his or her parent. 2. The crime of luring a child to an area for sexual contact.

Entice means to lure, induce, tempt, incite, or persuade a person to do a thing. *Berger*, 43 P.2d 610 (Cal.App., 1935)

entire Whole, without division; indivisible.

entirety The undivided whole; the entire amount or extent. See also tenancy by the entirety.

entitlement 1. The right to benefits, income, or other property. 2. The right to receive a government benefit that cannot be abridged without due process.

entity An organization that has a legally independent existence that is separate from its members.

entrapment Conduct by a government official that instigates or induces the commission of a crime by someone not ready and willing to commit it in order to prosecute him or her for that crime.

Police conduct that offers suspect an opportunity to commit a crime is not entrapment; however, appeal by police that would induce such person to commit the act because of friendship or sympathy, instead of desire for personal gain, is entrapment. *People v. Lee*, 268 Cal.Rptr. 595 (Cal.App., 1990)

entry 1. The act of making a notation or record; the notation or record itself. 2. The act of presenting something before the court for or on the record. 3. The right or act of going into or onto real property. 4. Entering a building with one's whole body, a part of the body, or a physical object under one's control (for purposes of burglary).

enumerated Specifically or expressly listed or mentioned (e.g., the enumerated powers of Congress in the Constitution).

enure See inure.

en ventre sa mere In its mother's womb; an unborn child. Also spelled in ventre sa mere.

environmental impact statement (EIS) A detailed report on the potential positive and negative environmental effects of a proposed project or law.

envoy A diplomat of the rank of minister or ambassador.

EO See executive order.

eo die On that day.

eo instanti At that instant.

eo nomine By that name.

Equal Employment Opportunity Commission (EEOC) The federal regulatory agency that enforces antidiscrimination laws (*www.eeoc.gov*).

equality The status of being equal in rights, privileges, immunities, opportunities, and duties.

equalization 1. The act or process of making equal; bringing about uniformity or conformity to a common standard. 2. Adjusting tax assessments to achieve fairness.

Adjustment of ad valorem tax assessment levels of various categories of property to uniform percentage of full value is called equalization. *American Airlines*, 51 Cal.Rptr.2d 251 (CA 996)

equal protection of the law A constitutional guarantee that the government will not deny a person or class of persons the same treatment it gives other persons or other classes under like circumstances. 14th Amendment, U.S. Constitution.

Equal Rights Amendment A proposed amendment to the U.S. Constitution that did not pass. ("Equality of rights under the law shall not be denied or abridged by the United States or by any State on account of sex.")

equipment Implements needed for designated purposes or activities, including goods that do not qualify as consumer goods, farm products, or inventory.

equitable 1. Just; conformable to the principles of what is right. 2. Available or sustainable in equity or under the principles of equity.

equitable adoption A child will be considered the adopted child of a person who agreed to adopt the child but failed to go through the formal adoption procedures.

Equitable adoption allows a person who was accepted and treated as a natural or adopted child, and as to whom adoption typically was promised or contemplated but never performed, to share in inheritance of the foster parents' property. *In re Estate of Ford*, 8 Cal.Rptr.3d 541 (CA 2004)

equitable abstention doctrine Where an order of a state agency predominantly affects local matters, a federal court should refuse to exercise its equity powers to restrain enforcement of the order if adequate state judicial relief is available to the aggrieved party.

equitable action An action seeking equitable remedy relief (e.g., an injunction) rather than damages.

equitable assignment An assignment that, though invalid at law, will be enforced in equity.

equitable defense A defense (e.g., unclean hands, laches) that was once recognized only by courts of equity but is now recognized by all courts.

equitable distribution The fair, but not necessarily equal, division of all marital property upon divorce in a common law property state.

equitable election An obligation to choose between two inconsistent or alternative rights or claims (e.g., a party cannot accept the benefits of a will and also refuse to recognize the validity of the will in other respects).

equitable estate An estate recognized by courts of equity.

equitable estoppel The voluntary conduct of a person will preclude him or her from asserting rights against another who justifiably relied on the conduct and who would suffer damage or injury if the person is now allowed to repudiate the conduct. Also called estoppel in pais.

A person may not deny existence of a state of facts if he or she intentionally led another to believe a particular circumstance to be true and to rely upon such belief to his or her detriment. *Wells Fargo*, 61 Cal.Rptr.2d 826 (Cal.App., 1997)

equitable lien A restitution right enforceable in equity to have a fund or specific property, or its proceeds, applied in whole or part to the payment of a particular debt or class of debts.

The right to subject property, not in possession of the lienor, to the payment of a debt as a charge against that property. *Farmers Ins.*, 61 Cal.Rptr.2d 707 (Cal.App., 1997)

equitable mortgage Any agreement to post certain property as security before the security agreement is formulized.

equitable owner The person who is recognized in equity as the owner of the property even though bare legal title to the property is in someone else. Also called beneficial owner.

equitable recoupment Using a claim barred by the statute of limitations as a defense to offset or diminish another party's related claim.

equitable relief An equitable remedy (e.g., injunction, specific performance) that is available when remedies at law (e.g., damages) are not adequate.

equitable restraint doctrine A federal court will not intervene to enjoin a pending state criminal prosecution without a strong showing of bad faith and irreparable injury. Also called *Younger* abstention. *Younger v. Harris*, 91 S. Ct. 746 (1971)

equitable servitude See restrictive covenant (1).

equitable title 1. The right (enforceable against the trustee) to the beneficial enjoyment of the trust property or corpus under the terms of the trust. 2. The right of the person holding equitable title to have legal title transferred to him or her upon the performance of specified conditions.

equitable tolling A litigant may sue after the statute of limitations has expired if, despite due diligence, he or she was prevented from suing due to inequitable circumstances, e.g., wrongful concealment of vital information by the other party.

Equitable tolling doctrine relieves plaintiff from bar of limitations statute when, possessing several legal remedies he or she, reasonably and in good faith, pursues one designed to lessen extent of his or her injuries or damage. *Kolani*, 75 Cal.Rptr.2d 257 (Cal.App., 1998)

equity 1. Justice administered according to fairness in a particular case, as contrasted with strictly formalized rules once followed by common-law courts. 2. Fairness, justice, and impartiality. 3. The monetary value of property in excess of what is owed on it. Net worth. 4. Shares of stock in a corporation.

Equity is the value of the property or enterprise above the indebtedness against it. *Kline*, 11 Cal.Rptr.3d 581 (Cal.App., 2004)

equity capital The investment of owners in exchange for stock.

equity court A court with the power to apply equitable principles.

equity financing Raising capital by issuing stock, as opposed to bonds.

equity loan A loan to a homeowner that is secured by the amount of equity in the home at the time of the loan. A home equity loan.

equity of redemption Before foreclosure is finalized, the defaulting debtor-mortgagor can recover (redeem) the property upon payment of the debt plus interest and costs. Also called right of redemption.

equivalent 1. Equal in value or effect; essentially equal. 2. Under the doctrine of equivalents, an accused patent infringer cannot avoid liability for infringement by changing only minor or insubstantial details of the claimed invention while retaining the invention's essential identity.

ERA See Equal Rights Amendment.

erase 1. To wipe out or obliterate written words or marks. 2. To seal from public access.

ergo Therefore; consequently.

***Erie* doctrine** Federal courts in diversity cases will apply the substantive law of the state in which the federal court is situated, except as to matters governed by the U.S. Constitution and acts of Congress. *Erie v. Tompkins*, 58 S. Ct. 817 (1938).

ERISA See Employee Retirement Income Security Act.

erroneous Involving error, although not necessarily illegal.

error A mistaken judgment or incorrect belief as to the existence or the consequences of a fact; a false application of the law.

errors and omissions insurance (E&O) Insurance against liability for negligence, omissions, and errors in the practice of a particular profession or business. A form of malpractice insurance for nonintentional wrongdoing.

escalator clause A clause in a contract or lease providing that a payment obligation will increase or decrease depending on a measurable standard such as changing income or the cost-of-living index. Also called fluctuating clause.

escape clause A provision in a contract or other document allowing a party to avoid liability or performance under defined conditions.

Escape clause is one that provides for avoidance of liability by insurer when there is other valid insurance. *Underground Constr.*, 122 Cal.Rptr. 330 (Cal.App., 1975)

escheat A reversion of property to the state upon the death of the owner when no one is available to claim it by will or inheritance.

***Escobedo* rule** Statements of a suspect in custody who is the focus of a police investigation are inadmissible if not told of his or her right to counsel and to remain silent. *Escobedo v. Illinois*, 84 S. Ct. 1758 (1964).

escrow Property (e.g., money, a deed) delivered to a neutral person (e.g., bank, escrow agent) to be held until a specified condition occurs, at which time it is to delivered to a designated person.

An escrow involves the deposit of documents and/or money with a third party to be delivered on the occurrence of some condition. *Summit*, 117 Cal.Rptr.2d 541 (CA 2002)

ESOP See employee stock ownership plan.

espionage Spying to obtain secret information about the activities or plans of a foreign government or rival company.

Esq. See esquire.

Esquire (esq.) A courtesy title given to an attorney.

essence 1. The gist or substance of something. 2. That which is indispensable. See also time is of the essence.

establish 1. To make or institute. 2. To prove. 3. To make secure.

establishment 1. A business or institution. 2. The act of creating, building or establishing. 3. Providing governmental sponsorship, aid, or preference. 4. The people or institutions that dominate a society.

Establishment Clause Government cannot establish an official religion, become excessively entangled with religion, nor endorse one form of religion over another. First Amendment, U.S. Constitution.

estate 1. An interest in real or personal property. 2. The extent and nature of one's interest in real or personal property. 3. All of the assets and liabilities of a decedent after he or she dies. 4. All of the property of whatever kind owned by a person. 5. Land.

Estate encompasses totality of assets and liabilities of decedent, including all manner of property, real and personal, choate or inchoate, corporeal or incorporeal. *Estate of Adams*, 306 P.2d 623 (Cal.App., 1957)

estate at sufferance The interest that someone has in land he or she continues to possess after the permission or right to possess it has ended. Also called holdover tenancy, tenancy at sufferance.

estate at will See tenancy at will.

estate by the entirety See tenancy by the entirety.

estate for years An estate whose duration is known at the time it begins. A tenancy for a term.

estate from year to year See periodic tenancy.

estate in common See tenancy in common.

estate in expectancy See future interest.

estate of inheritance An estate that may be inherited.

estate per autre vie See life estate pur autre vie.

estate planning Presenting proposals on how a person can have assets distributed at death in a way that will achieve his or her goals while taking maximum advantage of tax and other laws.

estate tail See fee tail.

estate tax A tax on the transfer property at death; the tax is based on the value of what passes by will or intestacy. Also called death tax.

Estate tax is levied on right to transmit property, while inheritance tax is levied on right to receive property. Cal. Revenue & Taxation Code, § 14101. *Allen*, 103 Cal.Rptr. 275 (Cal.App., 1972)

estimated tax The current year's anticipated tax that is paid quarterly on income not subject to withholding.

estop To stop or prevent something by estoppel.

estoppel 1. Stopping a party from denying something he or she previously said or did, especially if the denial would harm someone who reasonably relied on it. 2. Stopping a party from relitigating an issue.

Estoppel is applicable where the conduct of one side has induced the other to take such a position that it would be injured if the first should be permitted to repudiate its acts. *Leasequip*, 126 Cal.Rptr.2d 782 (Cal.App., 2002)

estoppel by deed A party to a deed will be stopped from denying the truth of a fact stated in a deed (e.g., that the party owns the land being transferred) as against someone induced to rely on the deed.

estoppel by judgment See collateral estoppel.

estoppel by laches Denial of relief to a litigant who unreasonably delayed enforcing his or her claim.

estoppel by record See collateral estoppel.

estoppel by silence Estoppel against a person who had a duty to speak, but refrained from doing so and thereby misled another.

estoppel certificate A signed statement certifying that certain facts are correct (e.g., that mortgage payments are current) as of the date of the statement and can be relied upon by third parties.

estoppel in pais See equitable estoppel

estover 1. The right to use, during a lease, any timber on the leased premises to promote good resource management. 2. Support or alimony.

et. al. And others.

ethical 1. Conforming to minimum standards of professional conduct. 2. Pertaining to moral principles or obligations.

ethics 1. Rules that embody the minimum standards of behavior to which members of an organization are expected to conform. 2. Standards of professional conduct.

et seq. And following. When used after a page or section number, the reference is to several pages or sections after the one mentioned.

et ux. And wife.

et vir. And husband.

Euclidian zoning Comprehensive zoning in which every square foot of the community is within some fixed zone and is subject to the predetermined set of land use restrictions applicable to that zone. Zoning by district.

eurodollar A U.S. dollar on deposit in a bank outside the United States, especially in Europe.

euthanasia The act of painlessly putting to death those persons who are suffering from incurable diseases or conditions. Also called mercy killing.

One who commits euthanasia bears no ill will toward his victim and believes his act is morally justified, but he nonetheless acts with malice if he is able to comprehend that society prohibits his act regardless of his personal belief. Cal. Penal Code, § 187. *People v. Conley*, 49 Cal.Rptr. 815 (CA 1966)

evasion 1. The act of avoiding something, usually by artifice. 2. The illegal reduction of tax liability, e.g., by underreporting income.

evasive answer An answer that neither admits nor denies a matter.

evergreen agreement A contract that automatically renews itself.

eviction 1. The use of legal process to dispossess a land occupier. 2. Depriving one of land or rental property he or she has held or leased.

evidence Anything that could be offered to prove or disprove an alleged fact. Examples: testimony, documents, fingerprints.

Evidence is matter that makes clear truth of fact, persuades court of existence of fact, or produces just conviction of truth. *In re Eugene M.*, 127 Cal.Rptr. 851 (Cal.App. 1976)

evidence aliunde See extrinsic evidence.

evidentiary fact 1. A subsidiary fact required to prove an ultimate fact. 2. A fact that is evidence of another fact.

evidentiary harpoon Deliberately introducing inadmissible evidence in order to prejudice the jury against the accused.

ex; Ex. without, from, example; Exchequer.

ex aequo et bono According to dictates of equity and what is good.

examination 1. Questioning someone under oath. 2. An inspection.

examination in chief See direct examination.

examined copy A copy of a record or other document that has been compared with the original and often sworn to be a true copy.

examiner One authorized to conduct an examination; one appointed by the court to take testimony of witnesses.

except 1. To leave out. 2. Other than.

exception 1. An objection to an order or ruling of a hearing officer or judge. 2. The act of excluding or separating something out (e.g., a judge excludes something from an order; a grantor retains an interest in property transferred). 3. That which is excluded.

excess Pertaining to an act, amount, or degree that is beyond what is usual, proper, or necessary.

excess insurance Supplemental insurance coverage available once the policy limits of the other insurance policies are exhausted.

excessive Greater than what is usual, proper, or necessary.

Surpassing the usual, the proper, or a normal measure of proportion. *County of San Diego*, 2005 WL 1532223 (Cal.App., 2005)

excessive bail A sum that is disproportionate to the offense charged and beyond what is reasonably needed to deter evasion by flight.

excess of jurisdiction Action taken by a court or other tribunal that is not within its authority or powers.

excessive verdict A verdict that is clearly exorbitant and shocking.

exchange 1. A transaction (not using money) in which one piece of property is given in return for another piece of property. 2. Swapping things of value. 3. The conversion of the money of one country for that of another. The price of doing so is the rate of exchange. 4. Payment using a bill of exchange or credits. 5. An organization bringing together buyers and sellers of securities or commodities, e.g., New York Stock Exchange.

Exchequer The treasury department in England.

excise A tax that is not directly imposed on persons or property but rather on performing an act (e.g., manufacturing, selling, using), on engaging in an occupation, or on the enjoyment of a privilege.

excited utterance A statement relating to a startling event or condition, made while under the stress of excitement caused by the event or condition. An exception to the hearsay rule.

Evidence of a statement is not made inadmissible by the hearsay rule if the statement was made spontaneously while the declarant was under the stress of excitement caused by such perception. Cal. Evidence Code § 1240(b)

exclusion 1. Denial of entry, admittance, or admission. 2. A person, event, condition, or loss not covered by an insurance policy. 3. Income that does not need to be included in gross income.

exclusionary rule Evidence obtained in violation of the constitution (e.g., an illegal search and seizure), will be inadmissible.

exclusive Not allowing others to participate; restricted; belonging to one person or group.

exclusive agency An agreement in which the owner grants a broker the right to sell property to the exclusion of other brokers, but allows the owner to sell the property through his or her own efforts.

exclusive jurisdiction The power of a court to hear a particular kind of case to the exclusion of all other courts.

exclusive listing An agreement giving only one broker the right sell the owner's property for a defined period. Also called exclusive agency listing.

An exclusive agency listing agreement is one prohibiting owner from selling property through agency of another broker during listing period. *Carlsen*, 67 Cal.Rptr. 747 (Cal.App., 1968)

ex contractu Arising from or out of a contract.

exculpate To free from guilt or blame.

exculpatory clause A clause in a lease or other contract relieving a party from liability for injury or damages he or she may wrongfully cause.

exculpatory evidence Any evidence tending to show excuse or innocence.

exculpatory-no doctrine An individual who merely supplies a negative and exculpatory response to an investigator's questions cannot be prosecuted for making a false statement to a government agency even if the response is false. The doctrine preserves the individual's self-incrimination protection.

ex curia Out of or away from court.

excusable neglect The failure to take the proper step (e.g., to file an answer) at the proper time that will be excused (forgiven) because the failure was not due to carelessness, inattention, or recklessness but rather was due to (a) an unexpected or unavoidable hindrance or accident, (b) reliance on the care and vigilance of one's attorney, or (c) reliance on promises made by an adverse party.

Neglect that might have been the act or omission of a reasonably prudent person under the same or similar circumstances. Cal. Government Code § 946.6(c)(1). *Department of Water*, 99 Cal.Rptr.2d 173 (Cal.App., 2000)

excuse A reason one should be relieved of a duty or not be convicted.

ex delicto Arising from a tort, fault, crime, or malfeasance.

ex dividend (x)(xd) Without dividend. Upon purchase of shares ex dividend, the seller, not the buyer, receives the next dividend.

execute 1. To complete, perform, or carry into effect. 2. To sign and do whatever else is needed to finalize a contract or other instrument to make it legal. 3. To enforce a judgment. 4. To put to death.

executed contract 1. A contract that has been carried out according to its terms. 2. See execute (2).

An executed contract is one, the object of which is fully performed. All others are executory. Cal. Civil Code § 1661

executed trust A trust in which nothing remains to be done for it to be carried out.

execution 1. Carrying out or performing some act to its completion. 2. Signing and doing whatever else is needed to finalize a document and make it legal. 3. The process of carrying into effect the decisions in a judgment. A command (via a writ) to a court officer (e.g., sheriff) to seize and sell the property of the losing litigant in order to satisfy the judgment debt. Also called general execution, writ of execution. 4. Implementing a death sentence.

"Execution of judgment of conviction" is process of carrying judgment into effect. *People v. Karaman*, 14 Cal.Rptr.2d 801 (CA 1992)

execution sale See forced sale.

executive 1. Pertaining to that branch of government that is charged with carrying out or enforcing the laws. 2. A managing official.

Managing representative or managing employee who has general discretionary powers of direction and control. *Jordan*, 130 Cal.Rptr. 446 (Cal.App., 1976)

executive agreement An agreement between the United States and another country that does not require the approval of the Senate.

executive clemency See clemency.

executive order (EO) An order issued by the chief executive pursuant to specific statutory authority or to the executive's inherent authority to direct the operation of government agencies and officials.

executive privilege The privilege, based on the separation of powers, that exempts the executive branch from disclosing information in order to protect national security and also to protect confidential advisory and deliberative communications among government officials.

executive session A meeting of a board or governmental unit that is closed to the general public.

executor A person appointed by someone writing a will (a testator) to carry out the provisions of the will.

executory Yet to be executed or performed; remaining to be carried into operation or effect; dependent on a future performance or event.

executory contract A contract that is wholly unperformed or in which substantial duties remain to be performed by both sides.

An executory contract is one in which some act remains to be done, while an executed contract is one in which everything is completed. *Linville*, 283 P.2d 34 (Cal.App., 1955)

executory interest A future interest created in one other than the grantor, which is not a remainder and vests upon the happening of a condition or event and in derogation of a vested freehold interest.

executory trust A trust that cannot be carried out until a further conveyance is made. Also called imperfect trust.

executrix A woman appointed by a will to carry it out. A female executor.

exemplar 1. Nontestimonial identification evidence, e.g., fingerprints, blood sample. 2. A typical example; a model.

exemplary damages See punitive damages.

exemplification An official copy of a public record, ready for use as evidence.

A exemplification of record is a certificate by a County Clerk attesting that the 14 attached pages constitute the original warrant, affidavit, and return. *Evans*, 2003 WL 22847098 (Cal.App., 2003)

exemplified copy See certified copy.

exempt Relieved of a duty others still owe.

exemption 1. Release or freedom from a duty, liability, service, or tax. 2. A right of a debtor to retain a portion of his or her property free from the claims of creditors. 3. A deduction from adjusted gross income.

exercise 1. To make use of. 2. To fulfill or perform; to execute.

ex facie On its face; apparently.

ex gratia As a matter of grace; as a favor rather than as required.

exhaustion of remedies Using available dispute-solving avenues (remedies) in an administrative agency before asking a court to review what the agency did.

The statute allowing suit for retaliatory conduct did not relieve employee from exhausting administrative remedies. *Campbell*, 25 Cal.Rptr.3d 320 (CA 2005)

exhibit 1. A document, chart, or other object offered or introduced into evidence. 2. An attachment to a pleading, instrument, or other document.

exigency (exigence) An urgent need, requiring an immediate response.

exigent circumstances 1. An emergency justifying the bypassing of normal procedures. 2. An emergency requiring swift action to prevent imminent threat to life or property, escape, or destruction of evidence.

An exception to the warrant requirement exists when exigent circumstances make necessary the conduct of a warrantless search, which means an emergency situation requiring swift action. *People v. Panah*, 25 Cal.Rptr.3d 672 (CA 2005)

exile 1. Banishment from the country. 2. A person banished.

ex officio Because of or by virtue of one's position or office.

exonerate To free or release from guilt or blame; responsibility or duty.

exoneration 1. Releasing one from a burden, charge, blame, responsibility, or duty. 2. The right to be reimbursed by reason of having paid what another should be compelled to pay. 3. A surety's right, after the principal's debt has matured, to compel the principal to honor its obligation to the creditor.

ex parte With only one side present; involving one party only.

On one side only; by or for one party; done for, in behalf of, or on the application of, one party only. *Heller*, 32 Cal.Rptr.2d 200 (CA 1994)

ex parte order A court order requested by one party and issued without notice to the other party.

expatriation 1. The abandonment of one's country and becoming a citizen or subject of another. 2. Sending someone into exile.

expectancy 1. The bare hope (but more than wishful thinking) of receiving a property interest of another, such as may be entertained by an heir apparent. 2. A reversion or remainder.

expectation damages The cost of restoring the non-breaching party to the position in which it would have been if the contract not been breached. Also called expectancy damages.

expectation of privacy The belief that one's activities and property would be private and free from government intrusion.

expenditure 1. The act of spending or paying out money. 2. An amount spent. An expense.

expense 1. What is spent for goods and services. 2. To treat (write off) as an expense for tax and accounting purposes.

experience rating A method of determining insurance rates by using the loss record (experience) of the insured over a period of time.

expert One who is knowledgeable, through experience or education, in a specialized field.

expert witness A person qualified by scientific, technical, or other specialized knowledge or experience to give an expert opinion relevant to a fact in dispute.

If a witness is testifying as an expert, his testimony in the form of an opinion is limited to such an opinion as is [r]elated to a subject that is sufficiently beyond common experience. Cal. Evidence Code § 801

export 1. To carry or send abroad. 2. A commodity that is exported.

expository statute See declaratory statute.

ex post facto After the fact; operating retroactively.

ex post facto law A law that punishes as a crime an act that was innocent when done, that makes punishment more burdensome after its commission, or that deprives one of a defense that was available when the act was committed.

exposure The financial or legal risk one has assumed or could assume.

express Definite; unambiguous and not left to inference. Direct.

express agency The actual agency created when words of the principal specifically authorize the agent to take certain actions.

express authority Authority that the principal explicitly grants the agent to act in the principal's name.

express condition A condition agreed to by the parties themselves rather than imposed by law.

express contract An oral or written agreement whose terms were stated by the parties rather than implied or imposed by law.

expressio unius est exclusio alterius A canon of interpretation that when an author (e.g., the legislature) expressly mentions one thing, we can assume it intended to exclude what it does not mention.

express malice 1. Ill will, the intent to harm. Actual malice; malice in fact. 2. Harming someone with a deliberate mind or formed design.

Express malice for purposes of murder conviction does not require more than intent to kill. *People v. Saille*, 2 Cal.Rptr.2d 364 (CA 1991)

express notice See actual notice.

express power A power that is specifically listed or mentioned.

express repeal An overt statement in a statute that it repeals an earlier statute.

express trust A trust created or declared in explicit terms for specific purposes, usually in writing.

Express trust arises from intention of parties to set aside property under stewardship of trustee for benefit of a beneficiary. *Del Costello*, 185 Cal.Rptr. 582 (Cal.App., 1982)

express waiver Oral or written statements intentionally and voluntarily relinquishing a known right or privilege.

express warranty A seller's affirmation of fact, description, or specific promise concerning a product that becomes part of the basis of the transaction or bargain.

Principal elements of an express warranty are an affirmation of fact or promise by the seller and reliance thereon by the buyer. *Burr*, 268 P.2d 1041 (CA 1954)

expropriation The government's taking of private property for public purposes. See also eminent domain.

expulsion A putting or driving out; a permanent cutting off from the privileges of an institution or society.

expunge To erase or eliminate.

expungement of record The process by which the record of a criminal conviction, an arrest, or an adjudication of delinquency is destroyed or sealed after the expiration of a designated period of time.

The eradication of a record of conviction or adjudication upon the fulfillment of prescribed conditions. *People v. Frawley*, 98 Cal.Rptr.2d 555 (Cal.App., 2000)

ex rel. (ex relatione) Upon relation or information. A suit ex rel. is brought by the government in the name of the real party in interest (called the realtor).

ex rights (x)(xr) Without certain rights, e.g., to buy additional securities.

extension 1. An increase in the length of time allowed. 2. An addition or enlargement to a structure.

extenuating circumstances See mitigating circumstances.

exterritoriality An exemption from a foreign country's local laws, enjoyed by diplomats when living in that country.

extinguishment The destruction or cancellation of a right, power, contract, or estate.

extort To compel or coerce; to obtain by force, threats, or other wrongful methods.

extortion 1. Obtaining property from another through the wrongful use of actual or threatened force, violence, or fear. 2. The use of an actual or apparent official right (i.e., color of office) to obtain a benefit to which one is not entitled. See also blackmail.

Extortion requires specific intent of inducing victim to consent to part with his or her property. Cal. Penal Code §§ 211, 518. *People v. Torres*, 39 Cal.Rptr.2d 103 (Cal.App., 1995)

extra 1. Additional. 2. Beyond or outside of.

extradition The surrender by one state (or country) to another of an individual who has been accused or convicted of an offense in the state (or country) demanding the surrender.

extrajudicial Outside of court and litigation. Done or given outside the course of regular judicial proceedings.

extralegal Not governed, regulated, or sanctioned by law.

extraneous evidence See extrinsic evidence.

extraordinary remedy A remedy (e.g., habeas corpus, writ of mandamus) allowed by a court when more traditional remedies are not adequate.

Extraordinary remedy refers to writs of mandamus, quo warranto, habeas corpus, and other similar actions. *Gales*, 55 Cal.Rptr.2d 460 (Cal.App., 1996)

extraordinary session A session of the legislature called to address a matter that cannot wait till the next regular session. Also called special session.

extraordinary writ A special writ (e.g., habeas corpus) using a court's discretionary or unusual power. Also called prerogative writ.

extraterritoriality The application of a country's jurisdiction and laws to occurrences outside that country's borders.

It embodies a principal of comity that mandates that one state not expand its regulatory powers in a manner that encroaches upon the sovereignty of its fellow states. *Hatch*, 94 Cal.Rptr.2d 453 (Cal.App., 2000)

extrinsic evidence External evidence; evidence that is not contained in the body of an agreement or other document; evidence outside of the writing. Also called extraneous evidence, evidence aliunde.

extrinsic fraud See collateral fraud.

ex warrants (x)(xw) Without warrants. See also warrant (3).

eyewitness A person who saw or experienced the act, fact, or transaction about which he or she is giving testimony.

F

fabricated evidence Evidence that is manufactured or made up with the intent to mislead.

face 1. That which is apparent to a spectator; outward appearance. 2. The front of a document.

face amount 1. The amount of coverage on an insurance policy. 2. See par value.

face value See par value.

facial Pertaining to what is apparent in a document—the words themselves—as opposed to their interpretation.

A facial challenge to the constitutional validity of a statute or ordinance considers only the text of the measure itself, not its application. *Ocean Park*, 8 Cal.Rptr.3d 421 (Cal.App., 2004)

facilitation Aiding; making it easier for another to commit a crime.

facility of payment clause A provision in an insurance policy permitting the insurer to pay the death benefits to a third person on behalf of the beneficiary.

facsimile 1. An exact copy of the original. 2. Transmitting printed text or pictures by electronic means. Fax.

fact A real occurrence. An event, thing, or state of mind that actually exists or that is alleged to exist, as opposed to its legal consequences.

fact-finder The person or body with the duty of determining the facts. If there is a jury, it is the fact-finder; if not, it is the judge or hearing officer. Also called trier of fact.

fact-finding The determination of the facts relevant to a dispute by examining evidence.

factor 1. One of the circumstances or considerations that will be weighed in making a decision, no one of which is usually conclusive. 2. A circumstance or influence that brings about or contributes to a result. 3. An agent who is given possession or control of property of the principal and who sells it for a commission. 4. A purchaser of accounts receivable at a discount.

Used car dealer is a factor when automobile owner puts automobile in dealer's possession to be sold, and, as such, dealer has ostensible authority to deal in the property of his principal as his own. *Pacific Finance*, 285 P.2d 632 (CA 1955)

factoring The purchase of accounts receivable at a discounted price.

factor's act A statute that protects good-faith buyers of goods from factors or agents who did not have authority to sell.

fact pleading Pleading those alleged facts that fit within the scope of a legally recognized cause of action. Also called code pleading.

fact question See issue of fact.

factual impossibility Facts unknown by or beyond the control of the actor that prevent the consummation of the crime he or she intends to commit.

factum 1. A fact, deed, or act, e.g., the execution of a will. 2. A statement of facts.

factum probandum The fact to be proved.

factum probans The evidence on the fact to be proved; an evidentiary fact.

failure 1. The lack of success. 2. An omission or neglect of something expected or required. Deficiency.

failure of consideration Failure of performance. The neglect, refusal or failure of one of the contracting parties to perform or furnish the agreed upon consideration.

Failure of consideration is failure to execute a promise the performance of which has been exchanged for performance by other party. *Taliaferro*, 31 Cal.Rptr. 64 (Cal.App., 1963)

failure of issue Dying without children or other descendants who can inherit. Also called definite failure of issue.

failure to prosecute A litigant's lack of due diligence (e.g., failure to appear) in pursuing a case in court. Want of prosecution.

faint pleader Pleading in a misleading or collusive way.

fair Free from prejudice and favoritism, evenhanded; equitable.

fair comment The honest expression of opinion on a matter of legitimate public interest.

fair hearing A hearing that is conducted according to fundamental principles of procedural justice (due process), including the rights to an impartial decision maker, to present evidence, and to have the decision based on the evidence presented.

fair market value The amount at which property would change hands between a willing buyer and a willing seller, neither being under any compulsion to buy or sell and both having reasonable knowledge of the relevant facts. Also called cash value, market value, true value.

The highest price that would be agreed to by a seller, being willing to sell but under no obligation or urgent necessity to do so, and a buyer, being ready and able to buy but under no particular necessity to do so. *In re Marriage of Cream*, 16 Cal.Rptr.2d 575 (Cal.App., 1993)

fairness doctrine A former rule of the Federal Communications Commission that a broadcaster must provide coverage of issues of public importance that is adequate and that fairly reflects differing viewpoints. Replaced by the equal-time doctrine.

fair preponderance of the evidence See preponderance of the evidence.

fair trade laws Statutes that permitted manufacturers or distributors of brand goods to fix minimum retail prices.

fair trial A trial in which the accused's legal rights are safeguarded, e.g., the procedures are impartial.

fair use The privilege of limited use of copyrighted material without permission of the copyright holder.

fair warning A due process requirement that a criminal statute be sufficiently definite to notify persons of reasonable intelligence that their planned conduct is criminal.

faith 1. Confidence. 2. Reliance or trust in a person, idea, or thing.

false 1. Knowingly, negligently, or innocently untrue. 2. Not genuine.

false advertising A misdescription or deceptive representation of the specific characteristics of products being advertised.

false arrest An arrest made without privilege or legal authority.

False imprisonment consists of the unlawful violation of the personal liberty of another person, while a false arrest is merely one way in which a false imprisonment may be accomplished; the two are not separate torts. *Hagberg*, 7 Cal.Rptr.3d 803 (CA 2004)

false impersonation See false personation.

false imprisonment The intentional confinement of someone within fixed boundaries set by the defendant where the victim was conscious of the confinement or was harmed by it.

false light An invasion-of-privacy tort committed by unreasonably offensive publicity that places another in a false light.

false personation The crime of falsely representing yourself as someone else for purposes of fraud or deception. Also called false impersonation.

false pretenses Obtaining money or other property by using knowingly false statements of fact with the intent to defraud.

Obtaining property by false pretenses is the fraudulent or deceitful acquisition of both title and possession. *People v. Traster*, 4 Cal.Rptr.3d 680 (Cal.App., 2003)

false representation See misrepresentation.

false return 1. A false statement filed by a process server, e.g., falsely stating that he or she served process. 2. An incorrect tax return. A tax return that is knowingly incorrect.

false statement 1. A falsehood. 2. Knowingly stating what is not true. Covering up or concealing a fact.

false swearing See perjury.

false verdict A verdict that is substantially unjust or incorrect.

falsi crimen See crimen falsi.

falsify To forge or alter something in order to deceive. To counterfeit.

family 1. A group of people related by blood, adoption, marriage, or domestic partnership. 2. A group of persons who live in one house and under one head or management.

family car See family purpose.

family court A special court with subject matter jurisdiction over family law matters such as adoption, paternity, and divorce.

Family court refers to activities of one or more superior court judicial officers who handle litigation arising under the Cal. Family Code; it is not separate court with special jurisdiction, but is instead superior court performing one of its general duties. *In re Chantal S.*, 51 Cal.Rptr.2d 866 (CA 1996)

family farmer A farmer whose farm has income and debts that qualify it for Chapter 12 bankruptcy relief. 11 USA § 101(18).

family law The body of law that defines relationships, rights, and duties in the formation, existence, and dissolution of marriage and other family units.

family purpose (automobile/car) doctrine The owner of a car who makes it available for family use will be liable for injuries that result from negligent operation of the car by a family member.

Fannie Mae Federal National Mortgage Association (FNMA) (*www.fanniemae.com*).

FAS See free alongside ship.

fascism A system of government characterized by nationalism, totalitarianism, central control, and often, racism.

fatal Pertaining to or causing death or invalidity.

fatal error See prejudicial error.

fatal variance A variance between the indictment and the evidence at trial that deprives the defendant of the due process guarantee of notice of the charges or exposes him or her to double jeopardy.

***Fatico* hearing** A proceeding to hear arguments on a proposed sentence for the defendant. *Fatico v. U.S.*, 603 F.2d 1053 (2d Cir. 1979).

fault An error or defect in someone's judgment or conduct to which blame and culpability attaches. The wrongful breach of a duty.

Fault connotes some form of active participation in creating the injuries for which the plaintiff seeks to recover. *Kitzig*, 97 Cal.Rptr.2d 762 (Cal.App., 2000)

favored beneficiary A beneficiary in a will who is suspected of exerting undue influence on the decedent in view of the relative size of what this beneficiary receives under the will.

FBI Federal Bureau of Investigation (*www.fbi.gov*).

FCC Federal Communications Commission (*www.fcc.gov*).

FDA Food and Drug Administration (*www.fda.gov*).

FDIC Federal Deposit Insurance Corporation (*www.fdic.gov*).

fealty Allegiance of a feudal tenant (vassal) to a lord.

feasance The performance of an act or duty.

featherbedding Requiring a company to hire more workers than needed.

A practice, whether created by law or agreement, that requires a business to employ persons in excess of the number of employees reasonably required to perform actual services. *Burlington*, Cal.Rptr.3d 503 (Cal.App., 2003)

Fed 1. Federal. 2. Federal Reserve System (*www.federalreserve.gov*).

federal United States; pertaining to the national government of the United States.

Federal Circuit Court of Appeals for the Federal Circuit (*www.fedcir.gov*), one of the thirteen federal courts of appeal.

federal common law Judge-made law created by federal courts when resolving federal questions.

federal courts Courts with federal jurisdiction created by the U.S. Constitution under Article III or by Congress under Article I. The main federal courts are the U.S. district courts (trial courts), the U.S. courts of appeals, and the United States Supreme Court.

federalism The division of powers between the United States (federal) government and the state governments.

It is a well-settled part of "Our Federalism" that "the National Government will fare best if the States and their institutions are left free to perform their separate functions in their separate ways." (Younger v. Harris) *People v. McKay*, 117 Cal.Rptr.2d 236 (CA 2002)

federal magistrate See magistrate.

federal preemption See preemption.

federal question A legal issue based on the U.S. Constitution, a statute of Congress, a treaty, or a federal administrative law.

Federal Register (Fed. Reg.) The official daily publication for rules, proposed rules, and notices of federal agencies and organizations, as well as executive orders and other presidential documents (*www.gpoaccess.gov/fr*).

federal rules Rules of procedure that apply in federal courts (*www.uscourts.gov/rules/newrules4.html*).

Federal Torts Claims Act (FTCA) The federal statute that specifies the torts for which the federal government can be sued because it waives sovereign immunity for those torts (28 USC §§ 1346, 2671).

federation An association or joining together of states, nations, or organizations into a league.

fee 1. Payment for labor or a service. 2. An estate in land that can be passed on by inheritance.

fee simple An estate over which the owner's power of disposition is without condition or limitation, until he or she dies without heirs. Also called fee simple absolute.

fee simple absolute See fee simple.

fee simple conditional A fee that is limited or restrained to particular heirs, exclusive of others. Also called conditional fee.

fee simple defeasible A fee that is subject to termination upon the happening of an event or condition.

There were two types of defeasible estates: a fee simple determinable, the reversionary interest of which was the possibility of reverter; and a fee simple subject to a condition subsequent, the reversionary interest of which was the right of reentry. *City of Palm Springs*, 82 Cal.Rptr.2d 859 (Cal.App., 1999)

fee simple determinable A fee subject to the limitation that the property automatically reverts to the grantor upon the occurrence of a specified event.

A determinable fee in real property is one subject to a contingency upon the happening of which the fee terminates ipso facto and title to the property reverts to the grantor. *People By and Through*, 26 Cal.Rptr. 853 (Cal.App., 1963)

fee splitting A single bill to a client covering the fee of two or more attorneys who are not in the same law firm.

fee tail An estate that can be inherited by the lineal heirs, e.g., children (not the collateral heirs) of the first holder of the fee tail. Also called estate tail. If the estate is limited to female lineal heirs, it is a fee tail female; if it is limited to male lineal heirs, it is a fee tail male.

fee tail female; fee tail male See fee tail.

fellow servant rule An employer will not be liable for injuries to an employee caused by the negligence of another employee (a fellow servant). This rule has been changed by workers' compensation law.

felon Someone convicted of a felony.

felonious 1. Malicious. Done with the intent to commit a serious crime. 2. Concerning a felony.

felonious assault A criminal assault that amounts to a felony.

felonious homicide Killing another without justification or excuse.

felony Any offense punishable by death or imprisonment for a term exceeding a year; a crime more serious than a misdemeanor.

felony murder rule An unintended death resulting from the commission or attempted commission of certain felonies is murder.

Felony-murder rule eliminates the need to establish malice, an element of murder charge, as to person who perpetrates certain felonies. *People v. Smith*, 72 Cal.Rptr.2d 918 (Cal.App., 1998)

feme covert A married woman.

feme sole An unmarried woman.

fence 1. A receiver of stolen property. 2. To sell stolen property to a fence. 3. An enclosure or boundary about a field or other space.

feoffee One to whom a feoffment is conveyed. A feoffor conveys it.

feoffment The grant of land as a fee simple (i.e., full ownership of an estate). The grant of a freehold estate.

ferae naturae Of a wild nature; untamed, undomesticated.

***Feres* doctrine** The federal government is not liable under the Federal Tort Claims Act for injuries to members of the armed services where the injuries arise incident to military service. *Feres v. U.S.*, 71 S. Ct. 153 (1950).

fertile octogenarian rule A person is conclusively presumed to be able to have children (and therefore heirs) at any age.

feudalism A social and political system in medieval Europe in which laborers (serfs) were bound to and granted the use of land in return for services provided to their lords.

FHA Federal Housing Administration (*www.hud.gov/offices/hsg/fhahistory.cfm*).

fiat 1. An authoritative order or decree. 2. An arbitrary command.

FICA Federal Insurance Contributions Act (a statute on social security payroll taxes).

fiction of law See legal fiction.

fictitious 1. Based on a legal fiction. 2. False; imaginary.

fictitious name 1. The name to be used by a business. A d/b/a (doing business as) name. 2. An alias.

fictitious payee A payee on a check named by the drawer or maker without intending this payee to have any right to its proceeds.

An instrument is drawn to order of fictitious payee if it is not intended that the person named on its face have any interest in it. *Security-First*, 137 P.2d 452 (CA 1943)

fictitious person See artificial person.

fidelity bond or **insurance** A contract whereby the insurer agrees to indemnify the insured against loss resulting from the dishonesty of an employee or other person holding a position of trust.

fides Faith, honesty, veracity.

fiduciary One whose duty is to act in the interests of another with a high standard of care. Someone in whom another has a right to place great trust and to expect great loyalty.

fiduciary bond A bond that a court requires of fiduciaries (e.g., trustees, executors) to guarantee the performance of their duties.

fiduciary duty A duty to act with the highest standard of care and loyalty for another's benefit, always subordinating one's own personal interests.

fiduciary relationship A relationship in which one owes a fiduciary duty (see this phrase) to another, e.g., attorney-client relationship. Also called confidential relationship.

A fiduciary relationship is any relation existing between parties to a transaction wherein one of the parties is duty bound to act with the utmost good faith for the benefit of the other party. *Hydro-Mill*, 10 Cal.Rptr.3d 582 (Cal.App., 2004)

fiduciary shield doctrine A person's business in a state solely as a corporate officer does not create personal jurisdiction over that person.

field warehousing Financing by pledging inventory under the control of the lender or a warehouser working on behalf of the lender.

fieri facias (fi. fa.) A writ or order to a sheriff to seize and sell the debtor's property to enforce (satisfy) a judgment.

fi. fa. See fieri facias.

FIFO First in, first out. An inventory flow assumption by which the first goods purchased are assumed to be the first goods used or sold.

Fifth Amendment The amendment to the U.S. Constitution that provides rights pertaining to grand juries, double jeopardy, self-incrimination, due process of law, and just compensation for the taking of private property.

fighting words Words likely to provoke a violent reaction when heard by an ordinary citizen and consequently may not have free-speech protection.

For purposes of First Amendment, fighting words are those which by their very utterance inflict injury or tend to incite immediate breach of peace. *In re Alejandro*, 43 Cal.Rptr.2d 471 (Cal.App., 1995)

file 1. To deliver a document to a court officer so that it can become part of the official collection of documents in a case. To deliver a document to a government agency. 2. To commence a lawsuit. 3. A law firm's collection of documents for a current or closed case.

file wrapper The entire record of the proceedings on an application in the U.S. Patent and Trademark Office. Also called prosecution history.

file wrapper estoppel One cannot recapture in an infringement action the breadth of a patent previously surrendered in the patent office.

filiation 1. The relationship between parent and child. 2. A court determination of paternity.

filiation proceeding A judicial proceeding to establish paternity.

filibuster A tactic to delay or obstruct proposed legislation, e.g., engaging in prolonged speeches on the floor of the legislature.

filing A document delivered to a court or government agency.

filius nullius ("son of nobody") An illegitimate child.

final 1. Not requiring further judicial or official action. 2. Conclusive. 3. Last.

final argument See closing argument.

final judgment; final decree A judgment or decree that resolves all issues in a case, leaving nothing for future determination other than the execution or enforcement of the judgment.

The one final judgment rule is a fundamental principle of appellate practice that prohibits review of intermediate rulings by appeal until final resolution of the case. *Fontani*, 28 Cal.Rptr.3d 833 (Cal.App., 2005)

final submission Completing the presentation (including arguments) of everything a litigating party has to offer on the facts and law.

finance 1. To supply with funds; to provide with capital or loan money to. 2. The management of money, credit, investments, etc.

finance charge The extra cost (e.g., interest) imposed for the privilege of deferring payment of the purchase price.

finance company A company engaged in the business of making loans.

financial institution A bank, trust company, credit union, savings and loan association, or similar institution engaged in financial transactions with the public such as receiving, holding, investing, or lending money.

Financial institution means a state or national bank, state or federal savings and loan association or credit union, or like organization. Cal Probate Code § 40

financial responsibility law A law requiring owners of motor vehicles to prove (through personal assets or insurance) that they can satisfy judgments against them involving the operation of the vehicles.

financial statement A report summarizing the financial condition of an organization or individual on or for a certain date or period.

financing statement A document filed as a public record to notify third parties, e.g., prospective buyers or lenders, that there may be an enforceable security interest in specific property.

find To make a determination of what the facts are.

finder Someone who finds or locates something for another. An intermediary who brings parties together (e.g., someone who secures mortgage financing for a borrower).

A finder is a person whose employment is limited to bringing the parties together so that they may negotiate their own contract. *Tyrone*, 106 Cal.Rptr. 761 (CA 1973)

finder of fact See fact-finder.

finder's fee A fee paid to someone for finding something or for bringing parties together for a business transaction.

finding of fact The determination of a fact. A conclusion, after considering evidence, on the existence or nonexistence of a fact.

fine 1. To order someone to pay a sum of money to the state as a criminal or civil penalty. 2. The money so paid.

A civil penalty, by virtue of its partially punitive purpose, is a fine for purposes of the constitutional protection under the excessive fines clauses of the State Constitution. Cal. Const. Art. 1, § 17. *City and County of San Francisco*, 92 Cal.Rptr.2d 418 (Cal.App., 2000)

fine print The part of an agreement or other document containing exceptions, disclaimers, or other details, often difficult to read.

fingerprint The unique pattern of lines on a person's fingertip that can be made into an impression, often for purposes of identification.

firefighter's rule Negligence in causing a fire or other dangerous situation furnishes no basis for liability to a firefighter, police officer, or other professional who is injured while responding to the danger.

firm 1. A business or professional entity. 2. Fixed, binding.

firm offer An offer that remains open and binding (irrevocable) for a period of time until accepted or rejected.

First Amendment The amendment to the U.S. Constitution that provides rights pertaining to the establishment and free exercise of religion, freedom of speech and press, peaceful assembly, and petitioning the government.

first degree The most serious level of an offense.

first-degree murder Killing another with premeditation, with extreme cruelty or atrocity, or while committing another designated felony.

Killing that was willful, deliberate and premeditated and by method designed to produce pain and suffering sufficient to constitute torture was murder of first degree. Cal. Penal Code, § 189. *People v. Wattie*, 61 Cal.Rptr. 147 (Cal.App., 1967)

first impression Concerning an issue being addressed for the first time.

first in, first out See FIFO.

first lien; first mortgage A lien or mortgage with priority that must be satisfied before other liens or mortgages on the same property.

first offender A person convicted of a crime for the first time and, therefore, may be entitled to more lenient sentencing or treatment.

first refusal See right of first refusal.

fiscal Pertaining to financial matters, e.g., revenue, debt, expenses.

fiscal year Any 12 consecutive months chosen by a business as its accounting period (e.g., 7/01/08 to 6/30/09).

fishing expedition Unfocused questioning or investigation. Improper discovery undertaken with the purpose of finding an issue.

The evidentiary hearing should not be used as a fishing expedition to search for possible misconduct. *People v. Schmeck*, 2005 WL 2036176 (CA 2005). The documents have been requested with adequate specificity to preclude the possibility that defendant is engaging in a fishing expedition. *Pitchess*, 113 Cal.Rptr. 897 (CA 1974)

fitness for a particular purpose See warranty of fitness for a particular purpose.

fix 1. To determine or establish something, e.g., price, rate. 2. To prearrange something dishonestly. 3. To fasten or repair. 4. An injection or dose of heroin or other illegal drug.

fixed asset An asset (e.g., machinery, land) held long-term and used to produce goods and services. Also called capital assets.

fixed capital Fixed assets. Money invested in fixed assets.

fixed charges Expenses or costs that must be paid regardless of the condition of the business (e.g., tax payments, overhead).

fixed income Income that does not fluctuate (e.g., interest on a bond).

fixed liability 1. A debt that is certain as to obligation and amount. 2. A debt that will not mature soon; a long-term debt.

fixed rate An interest rate that does not vary for the term of the loan.

fixture Something that is so attached to land as to be deemed a part of it. An item of personal property that is now so connected to the land that it cannot be removed without substantial injury to itself or the land.

A thing is deemed to be affixed to land when it is attached to it by roots, as in the case of trees . . . or permanently attached to what is thus permanent, as by means of cement, plaster, nails, bolts, or screws. Cal. Civil Code § 660

flagrante delicto See in flagrante delicto.

flat rate A fixed payment regardless of how much of a service is used.

flight Fleeing to avoid arrest or detention.

float 1. The time between the writing of a check and the withdrawal of the funds that will cover it. 2. The total amount representing checks in the process of collection. 3. To allow a given currency to freely establish its own value as against other currencies in response to supply and demand.

floater policy An insurance policy that is issued to cover items that have no fixed location (e.g., jewelry that is worn).

floating capital Funds available for current needs; capital in circulation.

floating debt Short-term debt for current needs.

floating interest rate A rate of interest that is not fixed; the rate may fluctuate by market conditions or be pegged to an index.

floating lien A lien on present and after-acquired assets of the debtor during the period of the loan.

floating zone A special detailed use district of undetermined location; it "floats" over the area where it may be established.

floor 1. The minimum or lowest limit. 2. Where legislators sit and cast their votes. 3. The right of someone to address the assembly.

floor plan financing A loan secured by the items for sale and paid off as the items are sold.

flotsam Goods that float on the sea when cast overboard or abandoned.

FLSA Fair Labor Standards Act (29 USC § 201) (*www.dol.gov/esa/whd/flsa*).

FNC See forum non conveniens.

FOB See free on board.

FOIA See Freedom of Information Act.

follow 1. To accept as authority. 2. To go or come after.

forbearance Deciding not to take action, e.g., to collect a debt.

Forbearance is an agreement to extend time for payment of an obligation due, either before or after the obligation's due date. *DCM Partners*, 278 Cal.Rptr. 778 (Cal.App.Dist., 1991)

for cause For a reason relevant to one's ability and fitness to perform a duty as a juror, employee, fiduciary, etc.

force Strength or pressure directed to an end; physical coercion.

Terms violence and force are synonymous when used in relation to assault and include any application of force even though it entails no pain or bodily harm and leaves no mark. Cal. Penal Code, § 240. *People v. Flummerfelt*, 313 P.2d 912 (Cal.App., 1957)

forced heir A person who by law must receive a portion of a testator's estate even if the latter tries to disinherit that person.

forced sale 1. A court-ordered sale of property to satisfy a judgment. Also called execution sale. 2. A sale one is pressured to make.

force majeure An unexpected event; an irresistible and superior force that could not have been foreseen or avoided.

Acts beyond anybody's control (force majeure). *Truck Ins.*, 72 Cal.Rptr.2d 851 (Cal.App., 1998)

forcible detainer 1. Unlawfully (and often by force) keeping possession of land to which one is no longer entitled. 2. See forcible entry and detainer.

forcible entry Taking possession of land with force or threats of violence. Using physical force to enter land or gain entry into a building.

forcible entry and detainer 1. A summary, speedy, and adequate remedy to obtain the return of possession of land to which one is entitled. Also called forcible detainer. 2. Using physical force or threats of violence to obtain and keep possession of land unlawfully.

foreclosure The procedure to terminate the rights of a defaulting mortgagor in property that secured the mortgagor's debt. The lender-mortgagee can then sell the property to satisfy the remaining debt.

Foreclosure. A mortgagee may foreclose the right of redemption of the mortgagor in the manner prescribed by the Code of Civil Procedure. Cal. Civil Code § 2931

foreign Pertaining to another country or to one of the 50 states of the United States other than the state you are in.

foreign administrator A person appointed in another state or jurisdiction to manage the estate of the deceased.

foreign commerce Trade involving more than one nation.

foreign corporation A corporation chartered or incorporated in one state or country but doing business in another state or country.

foreign exchange 1. The currency of another country. 2. Buying, selling, or converting one country's currency for that of another.

foreman 1. The presiding member and spokesperson of a jury. 2. A superintendent or supervisor of other workers. Also called foreperson.

forensic 1. Belonging to or suitable in courts of law. 2. Pertaining to the use of scientific techniques to discover and examine evidence. 3. Concerning argumentation. 4. Forensics: ballistics or firearms evidence.

forensic medicine The science of applying medical knowledge and techniques in court proceedings to discover and interpret evidence.

foreperson See foreman.

foreseeability The extent to which something can be known in advance; reasonable anticipation of something.

forestalling the market Buying products on their way to market in order to resell them at a higher price.

forfeiture The loss of property, rights, or privileges because of penalty, breach of duty, or the failure to make a timely claim of them.

Whereas forfeiture is the failure to make the timely assertion of a right, waiver is the intentional relinquishment or abandonment of a known right. *People v. Dickerson*, 19 Cal.Rptr.3d 545 (Cal.App., 2004)

forgery 1. Making a false document or altering a real one with the intent to commit a fraud. 2. The document or thing that is forged.

form 1. Technical matters of style, structure, and format not involving the merits or substance of something. 2. A document, usually preprinted as a model, to be filled in and adapted to one's needs. 3. See forms of action.

formal 1. Following accepted procedures or customs. 2. Pertaining to matters of form as opposed to content or substance. 3. Ceremonial.

formal contract 1. A contract under seal or other contract that complies with prescribed formalities. 2. A contract in writing.

forma pauperis See in forma pauperis.

former adjudication See collateral estoppel and res judicata on when a former adjudication (prior judgment) on the merits will prevent relitigating issues and claims.

former jeopardy, defense of A person cannot be tried or prosecuted for the same offense more than once. See also double jeopardy.

forms of action The procedural devices or actions (e.g., trespass on the case) that are used to take advantage of common-law theories of liability.

fornication Sexual relations between unmarried persons or between married persons who are not married to each other.

forswear 1. To give up something completely. To renounce something under oath. 2. To swear falsely; to commit perjury.

forthwith Without delay; immediately.

fortiori See a fortiori.

fortuitous Happening by chance or accident rather than by design.

A fortuitous event . . . is an event which *so far as the parties to the contract are aware,* is dependent on chance. It may be beyond the power of any human being to bring the event to pass; it may be within the control of third persons; it may even be a past event, such as the loss of a vessel, *provided that the fact is unknown to the parties.* (Restatement of Contracts) *Great Southwest Fire Ins.*, 280 Cal.Rptr. 249 (Cal.App., 1991)

forum 1. The court; the court where the litigation is brought. 2. A setting or place for public discussion.

forum domicilii The court in the jurisdiction where a party is domiciled.

forum non conveniens (FNC) The discretionary power of a court to decline the exercise of the jurisdiction it has when the convenience of the parties and the ends of justice would be better served if the action were brought and tried in another forum that also has jurisdiction.

When a court upon motion of a party or its own motion finds that in the interest of substantial justice an action should be heard in a forum outside this state, the court shall stay or dismiss the action in whole or in part on any conditions that may be just. Cal. Code of Civil Procedure § 410.30(a)

forum rei The court in the jurisdiction where the defendant is domiciled or the subject matter of the case is located.

forum selection clause A contract clause stating that any future litigation between the parties will be conducted in a specified forum (jurisdiction).

forum shopping Choosing a court or jurisdiction where you are most likely to win.

forward contract An agreement to buy or sell goods at a specified time in the future at a price established when the contract is entered. The agreement is not traded on an exchange.

foster home A home that provides shelter and substitute family care temporarily or for extended periods when a child's own family cannot properly care for him or her, often due to neglect or delinquency.

foundation 1. A fund for charitable, educational, religious, or other benevolent purpose. 2. The underlying basis or support for something. Evidence that shows the relevance of other evidence.

To support the motion for discovery of information in a police officer's personnel file, defendant must show plausible factual foundation for the discovery requested. *Warrick*, 29 Cal.Rptr.3d 2 (CA 2005)

founder One who establishes something, e.g., an institution or trust fund.

founding father A leader in establishing a country or organization.

four corners The contents of a written document; what is written on the surface or face of a document.

four corner's rule 1. The intention of the parties to a contract or other instrument is to be ascertained from the document as a whole and not from isolated parts thereof. 2. If a contract is clear on its face, no evidence outside the contract may be considered to contradict its terms.

frame 1. To formulate or draft. 2. To produce false evidence that causes an innocent person to appear guilty.

franchise 1. The right to vote. 2. A contract that allows a business (the franchisee) the sole right to use the intellectual property and brand identity, marketing experience, and operational methods of another business (the franchisor) in a certain area. 3. A government authorization to engage in a specified commercial endeavor or to incorporate.

Franchise means a contract or agreement, either expressed or implied, whether oral or written, between two or more persons by which: (1) A franchisee is granted the right to engage in the business of offering, selling or distributing goods or services under a marketing plan or system prescribed in substantial part by a franchisor; and. . . . Cal Corporations Code § 31005

franchisee The person or entity granted a franchise.

franchise tax A tax on the privilege of engaging in a business.

franchisor The person or entity that grants a franchise.

franking privilege The privilege of sending certain matter through the mail without paying postage. Also called frank.

fraternal benefit association or **society** A nonprofit association of persons of similar calling or background who aid and assist one another and promote worthy causes.

fratricide The killing of a brother or sister.

fraud A false statement of material fact made with the intent to mislead by having the victim rely on the statement. A tort is committed if the victim suffers actual damage due to justifiable reliance on the statement.

Fraud and dishonesty are closely synonymous; fraud may consist in misrepresentation or concealment of material facts or statement of fact made with consciousness of its falsity. *Fort*, 185 Cal.Rptr. 836 (Cal.App., 1982)

fraud in fact See positive fraud.

fraud in law Constructive or presumed fraud.

fraud in the factum A misrepresentation about the essential nature or existence of the document itself.

fraud in the inducement Misrepresentation as to the terms other aspects of a contractual relation, venture, or other transaction that leads (induces) a person to agree to enter into the transaction with a false impression or understanding of the risks or obligations he or she has undertaken.

fraud on the market theory When false information artificially inflates the value of a stock, it is presumed that purchasers on the open market relied on that information to their detriment.

frauds, statute of See statute of frauds.

fraudulent Involving fraud.

fraudulent concealment 1. Taking affirmative steps to hide or suppress a material fact that one is legally or morally bound to disclose. 2. An equitable doctrine that estops a defendant who concealed his or her wrongful conduct from asserting the statute of limitations.

fraudulent conveyance Transferring property without fair consideration in order to place the property beyond the reach of creditors.

A fraudulent conveyance under the Uniform Fraudulent Transfer Act (UFTA), involves a transfer by the debtor of property to a third person undertaken with the intent to prevent a creditor from reaching that interest to satisfy its claim. Cal Civil Code § 3439. *Filip*, 28 Cal.Rptr.3d 884 (Cal.App., 2005)

FRCP Federal Rules of Civil Procedure. See federal rules.

free 1. Not subject to the legal constraint of another. 2. Not subject to a burden. 3. Having political rights. 4. To liberate. 5. Without cost.

free alongside ship (FAS) The quoted price includes the cost of delivering the goods to a designated point alongside of the ship. The risk of loss is with the seller up to this point.

Unless otherwise agreed the term F.A.S. vessel (which means "free alongside") at a named port, even though used only in connection with the stated price, is a delivery term under which the seller must (a) At his own expense and risk deliver the goods alongside the vessel in the manner usual in that port or on a dock designated and provided by the buyer; and.. . . . Cal. Commercial Code § 2319(2)

free and clear Not subject to liens or other encumbrances.

freedom of association The right protected in the First Amendment to join with others for lawful purposes.

freedom of contract The right of parties to enter a bargain of their choice subject to reasonable government regulation in the interest of public health, safety, and morals.

freedom of expression The rights protected in the First Amendment concerning freedom of speech, press, and religion.

Freedom of Information Act (FOIA) A federal statute making information held by federal agencies available to the public unless the information is exempt from public disclosure (5 USC § 552). Many states have equivalent statutes for state agencies.

freedom of religion The right protected in the First Amendment to believe and practice one's form of religion or to believe in no religion. In addition, the right to be free of governmental promotion of religion or interference with one's practice of religion.

freedom of speech The right protected in the First Amendment to express one's ideas without government restrictions subject to the right of the government to protect public safety and to provide a remedy for defamation.

Publicizing of facts of labor dispute in peaceful manner is within freedom of speech guaranteed by Fourteenth Amendment. *Di Giorgio*, 30 Cal.Rptr. 350 (Cal.App., 1963)

freedom of the press The First Amendment prohibition against government restrictions that abridge the freedom of the press, such as imposing prior restraint or censorship.

freedom of the seas The right of ships to travel without restriction in the sea beyond the territorial waters of any nation.

free exercise clause The clause in the First Amendment stating that "Congress shall make no law . . . prohibiting the free exercise" of religion.

freehold An estate in land for life, in fee simple, or in fee tail. An estate in real property of uncertain or unlimited duration, unlike a leasehold, which is for a definite period of time.

Freehold estates are distinguishable from other forms of estates in that they are of indeterminate duration and carry with them title to land. Cal. Civ. Code §§ 762, 765. *Pacific*, 2 Cal.Rptr.2d 536 (CA 1991)

freelance paralegal See independent paralegal.

free on board (FOB) In a sales price quotation, the seller assumes all responsibilities and costs up to the point of delivery on board.

Unless otherwise agreed the term F.O.B. (which means "free on board") at a named place, even though used only in connection with the stated price, is a delivery term under which (a) When the term is F.O.B. the place of shipment, the seller must at that place ship the goods in the manner provided in this division (Section 2504) and bear the expense and risk of putting them into the possession of the carrier; or. . . . Cal. Commercial Code § 2319(1)

freeze To hold something (e.g., wages, prices) at a fixed level; to immobilize or maintain the status quo.

freeze-out Action by major shareholders or a board of directors to eliminate minority shareholders or to marginalize their power.

fresh Prompt; without material interval.

fresh complaint rule A victim's complaint of sexual assault made to another person soon after the event is admissible.

Common-law fresh complaint doctrine, providing that victim's extrajudicial report of sex offense is admissible to prove that such complaint was made, no longer provides sound basis for admitting such evidence, as the premise underlying doctrine, that true victims will report such offenses to someone, has been discredited. *People v. Brown*, 35 Cal.Rptr.2d 407 (CA 1994)

fresh pursuit 1. A police officer, engaged in a continuous and uninterrupted pursuit, can cross geographic or jurisdictional lines to arrest a felon even if the officer does not have a warrant. 2. A victim of property theft can use reasonable force to obtain it back just after it is taken. Also called hot pursuit.

friendly Pertaining to someone who is favorably disposed; not hostile.

friendly suit A suit brought by agreement between the parties to obtain the opinion of the court on their dispute.

friend of the court See amicus curiae.

friendly takeover The acquisition of one company by another that is approved by the boards of directors of both companies.

fringe benefits Benefits provided by an employer that are in addition to the employee's regular compensation (e.g., vacation).

frisk To conduct a pat-down search of a suspect in order to find concealed weapons.

frivolous 1. Involving a legal position that cannot be supported by a good-faith argument based on existing law or on the need for a change in the law. 2. Clearly insufficient on its face.

frivolous appeal An appeal that is devoid of merit or one that has no reasonable chance of succeeding.

Appeal is frivolous only when it is prosecuted for improper motive—to harass the respondent or delay the effect of an adverse judgment—or when it indisputably has no merit. *Millennium*, 23 Cal.Rptr.3d 500 (Cal.App., 2005)

frolic Employee conduct outside the scope of employment because it is personal rather than primarily for the employer's business.

front A person or organization acting as a cover for illegal activities or to disguise the identity of the real owner or principal.

frontage The land between a building and the street; the front part of property.

front-end load A sales fee or commission (the load) levied at the time of making a stock or mutual fund purchase.

frozen assets Nonliquid assets. Assets that cannot be easily converted into cash.

fructus The fruit or produce of land.

fruit 1. The effect, consequence, or product of something. 2. Evidence resulting from an activity.

fruit and tree doctrine One cannot avoid taxation on income simply by assigning it to someone else.

fruit of the poisonous tree doctrine Evidence derived directly or indirectly from illegal governmental activity (e.g., an illegal search and seizure), is inadmissible as trial evidence.

An exclusionary rule that prohibits the introduction of evidence that is causally connected to an unlawful search and is designed to deter police misconduct. *People v. Navarro*, 32 Cal.Rptr.3d 706 (Cal.App., 2005)

fruits of crime Stolen goods or other products of criminal conduct.

frustration Preventing something from occurring. Rendering something ineffectual.

frustration of contract or **purpose** See commercial frustration.

FTC Federal Trade Commission (*www.ftc.gov*).

fugitive One who flees in order to avoid arrest, prosecution, prison, service of process, or subpoena to testify (18 USC § 1073).

full age See age of majority.

full bench; full court See en banc.

full coverage Insurance with no exclusions or deductibles.

full faith and credit A state must recognize and enforce (give full faith and credit to) the legislative acts, public records, and judicial decisions of sister states. U.S. Constitution, art. IV, § 1.

full settlement An adjustment of all pending matters and the mutual release of all prior obligations existing between the parties.

full warranty A warranty that covers labor and parts for all defects.

functus officio Without further official authority once the authorized task is complete.

fund 1. Money or other resources available for a specific purpose. 2. A group or organization that administers or manages money. 3. To convert into fixed-interest, long-term debt.

fundamental Serving as an essential component; basic.

fundamental error See plain error.

fundamental law Constitutional law; the law establishing basic rights and governing principles.

fundamental right A basic right that is either explicitly or implicitly guaranteed by the constitution.

Fundamental right means a fundamental constitutional right. Cal.Const. Art. 1, § 7. *Bernardo*, 9 Cal.Rptr.3d 197 (Cal.App., 2004)

funded debt 1. A debt that has resources earmarked for the payment of interest and principal as they become due. 2. Long-term debt that has replaced short-term debt.

fungible Commercially interchangeable; substitutable; able to be replaced by other assets of the same kind. Examples: grain, sugar, oil.

future advances Funds advanced by a lender after creation of, but still secured by, the mortgage or other security agreement.

future damages Sums awarded for future pain and suffering, impairment of earning capacity, future medical expenses, and other future losses.

future earnings Income that a party is no longer able to earn because of injury or loss of employment.

future estate See future interest.

future interest An interest in real or personal property in which possession, use, or other enjoyment is future rather than present. Also called estate in expectancy, future estate.

A future interest in property is an interest that is not, but may become, a present interest. *Estate of Sigourney*, 113 Cal.Rptr.2d 274 (Cal.App., 2001)

futures Commodities or securities sold or bought for delivery in the future.

futures contract A contract for the sale or purchase of a commodity or security at a specified price and quantity for future delivery.

FY Fiscal year.

G

GAAP Generally Accepted Accounting Principles

gag order 1. A court order to stop attorneys, witnesses, or media from discussing a current case. 2. An order by the court to bind and gag a disruptive defendant during his or her trial.

gain 1. Profit; excess of receipts over costs. 2. Increments of value.

gainful employment Available work for pay.

gambling Risking money or other property for the possibility—chance—of a reward. Also called gaming.

game laws Laws regulating the hunting of wild animals and birds.

gaming See gambling.

GAO General Accountability Office (*www.gao.gov*).

gaol A place of detention for temporary or short-term confinement; jail.

garnishee; garnishnor (garnisher) A garnishee is the person or entity in possession of a debtor's property that is being reached or attached (via garnishment) by a creditor of the debtor. The creditor is the garnishor (garnisher).

garnishment A court proceeding by a creditor to force a third party in possession of the debtor's property (e.g., wages) to turn the property over to the creditor to satisfy the debt.

Garnishment is a sub-category of attachment and refers to seizure or attachment of property belonging to or owing to debtor but which is presently in possession of a third party. *Randone*, 96 Cal.Rptr. 709 (CA 1971)

gavelkind A feudal system under which all sons shared land equally upon the death of their father.

gender discrimination Discrimination based on one's sex or gender.

GBMI Guilty but mentally ill. See also insanity.

general administrator A person given a grant of authority to administer the entire estate of a decedent who dies without a will.

general agent An agent authorized to conduct all of the principal's business affairs, usually involving a continuity of service.

general appearance Acts of a party from which it can reasonably be inferred that the party submits (consents) to the full jurisdiction of the court.

A general appearance in an action, which is one in which the defendant participates in the action in a manner that recognizes the court's jurisdiction. *Factor Health*, 2005 WL 1793569 (Cal.App., 2005)

general assembly A legislative body in some states.

general assignment A transfer of a debtor's property for the benefit of all creditors. See also assignment for benefit of creditors.

general average contribution rule When one engaged in a maritime venture voluntarily incurs a loss (e.g., discards part of the cargo) to avert a larger loss of ship or cargo, the loss incurred is shared by all who participated in the venture.

general bequest A gift in a will payable out of the general assets of the estate. A gift in a will of a designated quantity or value of property.

Whether bequests of stock were general or specific depended on whether testator intended to give a specific thing and that alone, or to give a bequest which, in any event, should be paid out of his general estate. *In re Buck's Estate*, 196 P.2d 769 (CA 1948)

general contractor One who contracts to construct an entire building or project rather than a portion of it; a prime contractor who hires subcontractors, coordinates the work, etc. Also called original contractor, prime contractor.

general counsel The chief attorney or law firm that represents a company or other organization in most of its legal matters.

General Court The name of the legislature in Massachusetts and in New Hampshire.

general creditor See unsecured creditor.

general court marshal A military trial court consisting of five members and one military judge, which can impose any punishment.

general damages Damages that naturally, directly, and frequently result from a wrong. The law implies general damages to exist; they do not have to be specifically alleged. Also called direct damages.

General damages are ordinarily confined to those which would naturally arise from breach of contract, or which might have been reasonably contemplated or foreseen by both parties, at the time they made contract, as probable result of breach of contract by defendant. *Mendoyoma*, 87 Cal.Rptr. 740 (Cal.App., 1970)

general demurrer A demurrer challenging whether an opponent has stated a cause of action or attacking a petition in its entirety. See also demurrer.

The sole issue raised by a general demurrer is whether the facts pleaded state a valid cause of action, not whether they are true. *Kerivan*, 195 Cal.Rptr. 53 (Cal.App., 1983)

general denial A response by a party that controverts all of the allegations in the preceding pleading, usually the complaint.

general deposit Placing money in a bank to be repaid upon demand or to be drawn upon from time to time in the usual course of banking business.

Money deposited with a bank for a particular purpose but with depositor's consent commingled with other funds is a general deposit. *Bank of America*, 208 P.2d 772 (Cal.App., 1949)

general devise A gift in a will to be satisfied out of testator's estate generally; it is not charged upon any specific property or fund.

general election A regularly scheduled election.

general execution See execution (3).

general finding A finding in favor of one party and against the other.

general jurisdiction The power of a court to hear any kind of case, with limited exceptions.

Jurisdiction is general when it will encompass any cause of action against the defendant. *Dunne*, 8 Cal.Rptr.2d 483 (Cal.App., 1992)

general intent The state of mind in which a person is conscious of the act he or she is committing without necessarily understanding or desiring the consequences of that action.

When the definition of a crime consists of only the description of a particular act, without reference to intent to do a further act or achieve a future consequence, intention is deemed to be a general intent. *People v. Alvarado*, 23 Cal.Rptr.3d 391 (Cal.App., 2005)

general law A law that applies to everyone within the class regulated by the law.

A law is general when it applies equally to all persons embraced in a class founded on some natural, intrinsic, or constitutional distinction. *Beamon*, 4 Cal.Rptr. 396 (Cal.App., 1960)

general legacy A gift of personal property in a will that may be satisfied out of the general assets of the testator's estate.

general lien A lien that attaches to all the goods of the debtor, not just the goods that causes the debt.

general partner A business co-owner who can participate in the management of the business and is personally liable for its debts.

general partnership A partnership in which all the partners are general partners, have no restrictions on running the business, and have unlimited liability for the debts of the business. An association of two or more persons to carry on as co-owners of a business for profit.

general power of appointment A power of appointment exercisable in favor of any person that the donee (i.e., the person given the power) may select, including the donee him or herself.

A general power of appointment is one which may be exercised in favor of anyone, including the donee, and is equivalent to a grant of absolute ownership. *Estate of Thorndike*, 153 Cal.Rptr. 487 (Cal.App., 1979)

general power of attorney A grant of broad powers by a principal to an agent.

general statute A statute that operates equally upon all persons and things within the scope of the statute. A statute that applies to persons or things as a class. A statute that affects the general public.

general strike Cessation of work by employees throughout an entire industry or country.

general verdict A verdict for one party or the other, as opposed to a verdict that answers specific questions.

When a jury is asked to pronounce generally in favor of the plaintiff or defendant on all or any of the issues, they render a general verdict. Cal. Code of Civil Procedure § 624. *Shaw*, 100 Cal.Rptr.2d 446 (Cal.App., 2000)

general warrant A blanket warrant that does not specify the items to be searched for or the persons to be arrested.

general warranty deed See warranty deed.

General Welfare Clause The clause in the federal constitution giving Congress the power to impose taxes and spend for defense and the general welfare. U.S. Constitution, art. I, § 8, cl. 1.

generation-skipping transfer A transfer of assets to a family member who is more than one generation below the transferor, e.g., from grandparent to grandchild.

generation-skipping trust Any trust having younger generation beneficiaries of more than one generation in the same trust. A trust that makes a generation-skipping transfer.

generic 1. Relating to or characteristic of an entire group or class. 2. Not having a brand name. Identified by its nonproprietary name.

Generic name means a short title descriptive of the policy being illustrated such as whole life, "term life" or "flexible premium adjustable life." Cal. Insurance Code § 10509.953(e)

generic drug A drug not protected by trademark that is the same as a brand name drug in safety, strength, quality, intended use, etc.

genetic markers Separate genes or complexes of genes identified as a result of genetic tests. In paternity cases, such tests may exclude a man as the biological father, or may show how probable it is that he is the father.

Geneva Conventions International agreements on the conduct of nations at war, e.g., protection of civilians, treatment of prisoners of war.

genocide Acts committed with intent to destroy, in whole or in part, a national, ethnic, racial, or religious group, e.g., killing members of the group, causing them serious mental harm, or imposing measures designed to prevent births within the group.

gentleman's agreement An agreement, usually unwritten, based on trust and honor. It is not an enforceable contract.

genuine Authentic; being what it purports to be; having what it says it has.

germane Relevant; on point.

gerrymander Dividing a geographic area into voting districts in order to provide an unfair advantage to one political party or group by diluting the voting strength of another party or group.

County officials gerrymandered the configuration of the proposed water district in a manner that would exclude those property owners with water wells on their parcels. *Not About Water Committee*, 116 Cal.Rptr.2d 526 (Cal.App., 2002)

gestational surrogacy The sperm and egg of a couple are fertilized in vitro in a laboratory; the resulting embryo is then implanted in a surrogate mother who gives birth to a child with whom she has no genetic relationship.

gift A transfer of property to another without payment or consideration. To be irrevocable, (a) there must be a delivery of the property; (b) the transfer must be voluntary; (c) the donor must have legal capacity to make a gift; (d) the donor must intend to divest him or herself of title and control of what is given; (e) the donor must intend that the gift take effect immediately; (f) there must be no consideration (e.g., payment) from the donee; (g) the donee must accept the gift.

Essentials of valid completed gift of personalty are competency of donor to contract, voluntary intent to make gift, actual or symbolic delivery, actual or imputed acceptance, complete divestment of all control by donor, and lack of consideration for gift. *Bank of America*, 20 Cal.Rptr. 126 (Cal.App., 1962)

gift causa mortis A gift made in contemplation of imminent death subject to the implied condition that if the donor recovers or the donee dies first, the gift shall be void.

gift in contemplation of death See gift causa mortis.

gift inter vivos See inter vivos gift.

gift over A gift of property that takes effect when a preceding estate in the property ends or fails.

gifts to minors act The Uniform Transfers to Minors Act covering adult management of gifts to minors, custodial accounts for minors, etc.

gift tax A tax on the transfer of property by gift, usually paid by the donor, although a few states tax the donee.

gilt-edged 1. Of the highest quality. 2. Pertaining to a very safe investment.

Ginnie Mae (GNMA) Government National Mortgage Association (*www.ginniemae.gov*).

gist The central idea or foundation of a legal action or matter.

give To make a gratuitous transfer of property. See also gift.

giveback A reduction in wages or other benefits agreed to by a union during labor bargaining.

gloss A brief explanatory note. An interpretation of a text.

GNP See gross national product.

go bare To engage in an occupation or profession without malpractice insurance.

go forward 1. To proceed with one's case. 2. To introduce evidence.

going and coming rule The scope of employment usually does not include the time when an employee is going to or coming from work. Respondeat superior during such times does not apply.

An employee is generally not considered to be acting within scope of employment when going to or coming from place of work, for purposes of employer's potential liability for employee's torts under respondeat superior. *Depew*, 73 Cal.Rptr.2d 673 (Cal.App., 1998)

going concern An existing solvent business operating in its ordinary and regular manner with no plans to go out of business.

going-concern value What a willing purchaser, in an arm's length transaction, would offer for a company as an operating business as opposed to as one contemplating liquidation.

going private Delisting equity securities from a securities exchange. Going from a publicly owned corporation to a close corporation.

going public Issuing stock for public purchase for the first time; becoming a public corporation.

golden parachute Very high payments and other economic benefits made to an employee upon his or her termination.

golden rule 1. A guideline of statutory interpretation in which we presume that the legislature did not intend an interpretation that would lead to absurd or ridiculous consequences. 2. Urging jurors to place themselves in the position of the injured party or victim.

The golden rule argument, in which plaintiff's counsel asks jurors to put themselves in the plaintiff's shoes and ask what compensation they would personally expect for pain and suffering, is impermissible. *Cassim*, 16 Cal.Rptr.3d 374 (CA 2004)

good 1. Sufficient in law; enforceable. 2. Valid. 3. Reliable.

good behavior Law-abiding. Following the rules. A standard used to grant inmates early release.

good cause A cause that affords a legal excuse; a legally sufficient ground or reason. Also called just cause, sufficient cause.

Good cause for termination in the context of implied employment contracts means fair and honest reasons, regulated by good faith that are not trivial, arbitrary or capricious. *Cotran*, 69 Cal.Rptr.2d 900 (CA 1998)

good consideration Consideration based on blood relationship or natural love and affection. Also called moral consideration.

good faith A state of mind indicating honesty and lawfulness of purpose; the absence of an intent to seek an undue advantage; a belief that known circumstances do not require further investigation.

good faith bargaining Going to the bargaining table with an open mind and a sincere desire to reach agreement.

good faith exception Evidence is admissible (in an exception to the exclusionary rule) if the police reasonably rely on a warrant that is later invalidated because of the lack of probable cause.

Evidence obtained in objectively reasonable reliance on defective search warrant is admissible. *People v. Smith*, 37 Cal.Rptr.2d 524 (Cal.App., 1995)

good faith purchaser See bona fide purchaser.

goods 1. Movable things other than money or intangible rights. 2. Any personal property.

Good Samaritan Someone who comes to the assistance of another without a legal obligation to do so. Under good-samaritan laws of most states, a person aiding another in an emergency will not be liable for ordinary negligence in providing this aid.

goods and chattels 1. Personal property. 2. Tangible personal property.

good time Credit for an inmate's good conduct that reduces prison time.

good title A valid title; a title that a reasonably prudent purchaser would accept. Marketable title.

goodwill The reputation of a business that causes it to generate additional customers. The advantages a business has over its competitors due to its name, location, and owner's reputation.

Goodwill value is a transferable property right which is generally defined as the amount a willing buyer would pay for a going concern above the book value of the assets. *Redevelopment Agency*, 27 Cal.Rptr.3d 126 (Cal.App., 2005)

govern 1. To direct or control by authority; to rule. 2. To be a precedent or controlling law.

government 1. The process of governing. 2. The framework of political institutions by which the executive, legislative, and judicial functions of the state are carried on. 3. The sovereign power of a state.

governmental function 1. An activity of government authorized by law for the general public good. 2. A function that can be performed adequately only by the government. An essential function of government.

governmental immunity See sovereign immunity.

government contract A contract in which at least one of the parties is a government agency or branch.

government corporation A government-owned corporation that is a mixture of a corporation and a government agency created to serve a predominantly business function in the public interest.

government security A security (e.g., a treasury bill) issued by the government or a government entity.

governor A chief executive official of a state of the United States.

grace period Extra time past a due date given to avoid a penalty (e.g., cancellation) that would otherwise apply to the missed date.

graded offense A crime that can be committed in different categories or classes of severity, resulting in different punishments.

graduated lease A lease for which the rent will vary depending on factors such as the amount of gross income produced.

graduated payment mortgage (GPM) A mortgage that begins with lower payments and that increase over the term of the loan.

graduated tax See progressive tax.

graft Money or personal gain unlawfully received because of one's position of public trust.

grandfather clause A special exemption for those already doing what will now be prohibited or otherwise restricted for others.

Grandfather clauses have allowed persons licensed as drugless practitioners prior to abolition of the classification to continue practicing and to renew their licenses annually. *Tain*, 30 Cal.Rptr.3d 330 (Cal.App., 2005)

grand jury A jury of inquiry that receives accusations in criminal cases, hears the evidence of the prosecutor, and issues indictments when satisfied that a trial should be held.

grand larceny Unlawfully taking and carrying away another's personal property valued in excess of a statutorily set amount (e.g., $100).

grant 1. To give property or a right to another with or without compensation. 2. To transfer real property by deed or other instrument. 3. Something given or transferred.

Use of the word "grant" in conveyance impliedly covenants that the grantor has not conveyed the same estate to others. Cal. Civil Code, § 1113. *Babb*, 37 Cal.Rptr. 533 (Cal.App., 1964)

grantee The person to whom a grant is made or property is conveyed.

grant-in-aid Funds given by the government to a person or institution for a specific purpose, e.g., education or research.

granting clause That portion of a deed or instrument of conveyance that contains the words of transfer of an interest.

grantor The person who makes the grant or conveys property.

grantor-grantee index A master index by grantor name to all recorded instruments (e.g., deeds, mortgages) allowing you to trace the names of sellers and buyers of land up to the present owner.

grantor trust A trust in which the grantor is taxed on its income because of his or her control over the income or corpus.

gratis Without reward or consideration. Free.

gratuitous 1. Given or granted free, without consideration. 2. Unwarranted; unjustified.

An involuntary deposit is gratuitous, the depositary being entitled to no reward. Cal. Civil Code § 1845

gratuitous bailment A bailment in which the care and custody of the bailor's property by the bailee is without charge or expectation of payment.

gratuitous promise A promise made by one who has received no consideration for it.

gravamen The essence of a grievance; the gist of a charge.

gray market A market where goods are legally sold at lower prices than the manufacturer would want or that are imported bearing a valid United States trademark, but without consent of the trademark holder.

Gray market activities involve removal of visible and secret manufacturer's serial numbers from products, replacing those numbers with numbers of their own, and thereafter selling materials to retailers at price below that charged by manufacturers and/or their authorized affiliates. *People v. Superior Court*, 26 Cal.Rptr.2d 173 (Cal.App., 1993)

great bodily injury A significant or substantial injury or damage; a serious physical impairment. Also called serious bodily harm.

great care The amount of care used by reasonable persons when involved in very important matters. Also called utmost care.

Great Charter See Magna Carta.

Great Writ See habeas corpus.

green card The government-issued registration card indicating the permanent resident status of an alien.

greenmail Inflated payments to buy back the stock of a shareholder (a raider) who has threatened a corporate takeover.

Green River ordinance An ordinance that prohibits door-to-door commercial solicitations without prior consent.

grievance 1. An injury or wrong that can be the basis for an action or complaint. 2. A charge or complaint. 3. A complaint about working conditions or about a violation of a union agreement.

grievance procedure Formal steps established to resolve disputes arising under a collective bargaining agreement.

gross 1. Glaring, obvious. 2. Reprehensible. 3. Total; before or without diminution or deduction.

gross estate The total assets of a person at his or her death before deductions are taken.

gross income All income from whatever source before exemptions, deductions, credits, or other adjustments.

gross lease A lease in which the tenant pays only rent; the landlord pays everything else, e.g., taxes, utilities, insurance, etc.

gross national product (GNP) The total value of all goods and services produced in a given period.

gross negligence 1. The intentional failure to perform a manifest duty in reckless disregard of the consequences to the life or property of another. 2. The failure to use even slight care and diligence. Also called willful negligence.

Gross negligence is the want of even scant care or an extreme departure from the ordinary standard of conduct. Cal. Government Code § 831.7(c)(5). *Wood*, 4 Cal.Rptr.3d 340 (Cal.App., 2003)

gross receipts The total amount of money (and any other consideration) received from selling goods or services.

ground 1. Foundation; points relied on. 2. A reason that is legally sufficient to obtain a remedy or other result.

ground rent 1. Rent paid to the owner for the use of undeveloped land, usually to construct a building on it. 2. A perpetual rent reserved to the grantor (and his or her heirs) from land conveyed in fee simple.

group annuity A policy that provides annuities to a group of people under a single master contract.

group boycott Agreements among competitors within the same market tier not to deal with other competitors or market participants.

Group boycotts, or concerted refusals by traders to deal with other traders, have long been held to be in the forbidden category. *Peters*, 58 Cal.Rptr.2d 690 (Cal.App., 1996)

group insurance A single insurance policy covering a group of individuals, e.g., employees of a particular company.

group legal services A form of legal insurance in which members of a group make a periodic payment for future legal services.

growth stock The stock in a company that is expected to have higher than average growth, particularly in the value of the stock.

GSA General Services Administration (*www.gsa.gov*).

guarantee 1. An assurance that a particular outcome will occur, e.g., a product will perform as stated or will be repaired at no cost. Also called guaranty. 2. A promise to fulfill the obligation of another if the latter fails to do so. 3. To give security. 4. Security given.

guaranteed stock The stock of one corporation whose dividends are guaranteed by another corporation, e.g., by a parent corporation.

guarantor One who makes a guaranty; one who becomes secondarily liable for another's debt or performance.

guaranty 1. A promise to fulfill the obligation of another if the latter fails to do so. 2. See guarantee (1).

Guaranty is simply additional security for obligor's debt. *Hodges*, 56 Cal.Rptr.2d 700 (Cal.App., 1996)

guardian A person who lawfully has the power and duty to care for the person, property, or rights of another who is incapable of managing his or her affairs (e.g., a minor, an insane person).

guardian ad litem (GAL) A special guardian appointed by the court to represent the interests of another (e.g., a minor) in court. See also ad litem.

guardianship 1. The office, duty, or authority of a guardian. 2. The fiduciary relationship that exists between guardian and ward.

guest 1. A passenger in a motor vehicle who is offered a ride by someone who receives no benefits from the passenger other than hospitality, goodwill, and the like. 2. One who pays for the services of a restaurant or place of lodging. 3. A recipient of one's hospitality, especially at home.

guest statute A statute providing that drivers of motor vehicles will not be liable for injuries caused by their ordinary negligence to nonpaying guest passengers.

If one is to be a guest in a vehicle and accept a ride therein, within guest statute, there must be a host who can extend an invitation for the ride. Cal. Vehicle Code, § 17158. *Whitehill*, 64 Cal.Rptr. 584 (Cal.App., 1967)

guilty 1. A defendant's plea that accepts (or does not contest) the criminal charge against him or her. 2. A determination by a jury or court that the defendant has committed the crime charged. 3. Responsible for criminal or civil wrongdoing.

H

habeas corpus ("you have the body") A writ designed to bring a party before a court in order to test the legality of his or her detention or imprisonment. Also called the Great Writ.

The function of the writ of habeas corpus is to determine the legality of one's detention. *Ex parte Connor*, 108 P.2d 10 (CA 1940)

habeas corpus ad faciendum et recipiendum A writ to move a civil case (and the body of the defendant) from a lower to a higher court.

habeas corpus ad prosequendum A writ issued for the purpose of indicting, prosecuting, and sentencing a defendant already confined within another jurisdiction.

habeas corpus ad testificandum A writ used to bring in a prisoner detained in a jail or prison to give evidence before the court.

habendum clause The portion of a deed (often using the words, "to have and to hold") that describes the ownership rights being transferred (i.e., the estate or interest being granted).

The ordinary use of the habendum is to define or limit the quality of interest, or the estate which the grantee is to have in the property granted. *Boyer*, 259 P. 38 (CA 1927)

habitability The condition of a building that allows it to be enjoyed because it is free from substantial defects that endanger health or safety.

habitable Suitable or fit for living.

habitation 1. Place of abode; one's dwelling or residence. 2. Occupancy.

habitual Customary, usual, regular.

habitual criminal A repeat offender. Also called career criminal, recidivist.

half blood (half brother, half sister) The relationship between persons who have the same father or the same mother, but not both.

halfway house A house in the community that helps individuals make the adjustment from prison or other institutionalization to normal life.

hand down To announce or file an opinion by a court.

handicap A physical or mental impairment or disability that substantially limits one or more of a person's major life activities.

harassment Intrusive or unwanted acts, words, or gestures (often persistent and continuing) that have a substantial adverse effect on the safety, security, or privacy of another and that serve no legitimate purpose.

Term "harasses" as used in stalking statute prohibits a course of conduct directed at a specific person that a reasonable person would consider as seriously alarming, seriously annoying, or seriously tormenting to reasonable person. Cal. Penal Code § 646.9(a, e). *People v. Ewing*, 90 Cal.Rptr.2d 177 (Cal.App., 1999)

harbor To shelter or protect, often clandestinely and illegally.

hard cases Cases in which a court sometimes overlooks fixed legal principles when they are opposed to persuasive equities.

hard labor Forced physical labor required of an inmate.

harm 1. Loss or detriment to a person. 2. To injure.

harmless Not causing any damage.

harmless error An error that did not prejudice the substantial rights of the party alleging it. Also called technical error.

To find error harmless the Court of Appeal must find beyond a reasonable doubt that it was unimportant in relation to everything else the jury considered on the issue in question. *People v. Song*, 22 Cal.Rptr.3d 118 (Cal.App., 2004)

Hatch Act A federal statute that prohibits federal employees from engaging in certain types of political activities (5 USC § 1501).

hate crime A crime motivated by hatred, bias, or prejudice, based on race, color, religion, national origin, ethnicity, gender, or sexual orientation of another individual or group of individuals.

have and hold See habendum clause.

hazard 1. A risk or danger of harm or loss. The chance of suffering a loss. 2. Danger, peril.

hazardous Exposed to or involving danger. Risky.

Arising out of that hazardous recreational activity broadly encompasses the objectively foreseeable risks of participating in a hazardous recreational activity. Cal. Government Code § 831.7(a). *Wood*, 4 Cal.Rptr.3d 340 (Cal.App. 3d Dist., 2003)

H.B. House Bill. A proposed statute considered by the House of Representatives.

headnote A short-paragraph summary of a portion of a court opinion printed before the opinion begins. Also called syllabus.

head of household 1. The primary income earner in a household. 2. An unmarried taxpayer (or married if living and filing separately) who maintains a home that for more than one-half of the taxable year is the principal place of abode of certain dependents, such as an unmarried child.

head tax See poll tax.

healthcare proxy See advance directive.

health maintenance organization (HMO) A prepaid health insurance plan consisting of a network of doctors and healthcare institutions that provide medical services to subscribers.

hearing 1. A proceeding designed to resolve issues of fact or law. Usually, an impartial officer presides, evidence is presented, etc. The hearing is *ex parte* if only one party is present; it is *adversarial* if both parties are present. 2. A meeting of a legislative committee to consider proposed legislation or other legislative matters. 3. A meeting in which one is allowed to argue a position.

hearing officer; hearing examiner See administrative law judge.

hearsay 1. What one learns from another rather than from first-hand knowledge. 2. An out-of-court statement offered to prove the truth of the matter asserted in the statement. A "statement, other than one made by the declarant while testifying at the trial or hearing, offered in evidence to prove the truth of the matter asserted." Federal Rule of Evidence 801(c).

Hearsay evidence is evidence of a statement that was made other than by a witness while testifying at the hearing and that is offered to prove the truth of the matter stated. Cal. Evidence Code § 1200(a)

heart balm statute A law abolishing heart balm actions, which are actions based on a broken heart or loss of love (e.g., breach of promise to marry, alienation of affections, criminal conversation).

heat of passion Fear, rage, or resentment in which a person loses self-control due to provocation. Also called hot blood, sudden heat of passion.

Heat of passion that would justify giving of voluntary manslaughter instruction is such a passion as would naturally be aroused in mind of ordinarily reasonable person under the given facts and circumstances. *People v. Williams*, 46 Cal.Rptr.2d 730 (Cal.App., 1995)

hedge To safeguard oneself from loss on a bet, bargain, or speculation by making compensatory arrangements on the other side. To reduce risk by entering a transaction that will offset an existing position.

hedge fund A special investment fund that uses aggressive (higher risk) strategies such as short selling and using derivatives.

hedonic damages Damages that cover the victim's loss of pleasure or enjoyment of life.

heinous Shockingly odious or evil.

heir 1. One designated by state law to receive all or part of the estate of a person who dies without leaving a valid will (intestate). Also called heir at law, legal heir. 2. One who inherits (or is in line to inherit) by intestacy or by will.

Heir refers to those individuals who may inherit by intestate succession under California law. Cal. Code of Civil Procedure § 377.60; Cal. Probate Code §§ 6401, 6402. *Rosales*, 7 Cal.Rptr.3d 13 (Cal.App., 2003)

heir apparent See apparent heir.

heir at law See heir (1).

heir collateral See collateral heir.

heir of the blood One who inherits because of a blood relationship with the decedent in the ascending or descending line.

heir of the body A blood relative in the direct line of descent, e.g., children, grandchildren (excluding adopted children).

heir presumptive See presumptive heir.

heirs and assigns Words used to convey a fee simple estate.

held Decided. See also hold.

henceforth From this (or that) time on.

hereafter 1. From now on. 2. At some time in the future.

hereditament 1. Property, rights, or anything that can be inherited. 2. Real property.

hereditary Capable of being inherited. Pertaining to inheritance.

hereditary succession See intestate succession.

herein In this section; in the document you are now reading.

hereto To this (document or matter).

heretofore Before now; up to now.

hereunder 1. By the terms of or in accordance with this document. 2. Later in the document.

herewith With this or in this document.

heritable Capable of being inherited.

hermeneutics The science or art of interpreting documents.

hidden asset Property of a company that is either not stated on its books or is stated at an undervalued price.

hidden defect A deficiency in property that could not be discovered by reasonable and customary observation or inspection and for which a lessor or seller is generally liable if such defect causes harm. Also called inherent defect, latent defect.

high crime A major offense that is a serious abuse of governmental power. Can be the basis of impeachment and removal from office.

highest and best use The use of property that will most likely produce the highest market value, greatest financial return, or the most profit.

high-low agreement A compromise agreement under which the parties set a minimum (floor) and maximum (ceiling) for damages. The defendant will pay at least the floor (if the jury awards less than this amount) but no more than the ceiling (if the jury awards over that amount).

high seas That portion of the ocean or seas that is beyond the territorial jurisdiction of any country.

high-water line or **mark** The line on the shore to which high tide rises under normal weather conditions.

High water mark is mark made by fixed plane of high tide where it touches land, and, as land along body of water gradually builds up or erodes, ordinary high water mark necessarily moves, and thus mark or line of mean high tide, i.e., the legal boundary, also moves. Cal. Civil Code §§ 670, 830. *Lechuza*, 70 Cal.Rptr.2d 399 (Cal.App., 1997)

hijack To seize possession of a vehicle from another; to seize a vehicle and force it to go in another direction.

Hijacking means an unauthorized person causing, or attempting to cause, by violence or threat of violence, a public conveyance to go to an unauthorized destination. Cal. Penal Code § 1547

HIPAA Health Insurance Portability and Accountability Act. A federal statute providing protections such as maintaining the privacy of personal health information. (*www.hhs.gov/ocr/hipaa*).

hire 1. To purchase the temporary use of a thing. 2. To engage the services of another for a fee.

hiring hall An agency or office operated by a union (or by both union and management) to place applicants for work.

hit and run The crime of leaving the scene of an accident without being identified.

HMO See health maintenance organization.

hoard To accumulate assets beyond one's reasonable needs, often anticipating an increase in their market price.

Hobbs Act A federal anti-racketeering act that makes it illegal to obstruct, delay, or affect interstate commerce or attempt to conspire to do so by robbery, physical violence, or extortion (18 USC § 1951).

hobby losses A nondeductible loss suffered when engaged in an activity that is not pursued for profit.

hodgepodge See hotchpot.

hold 1. To possess something by virtue of lawful authority or title. 2. To reach a legal conclusion; to resolve a legal dispute. 3. To restrain or control; to keep in custody. 4. To preside at.

holder 1. One who has possession of something, e.g., a check, bond, document of title. 2. One who has legally acquired possession of a negotiable instrument (e.g., a check, a promissory note) and who is entitled to receive payment on the instrument.

holder for value Someone who has given something of value for a promissory note or other negotiable instrument.

holder in due course (HDC; HIDC) One who gives value for a negotiable instrument in good faith, without any apparent defects, and without notice that it is overdue, has been dishonored, or is subject to any claim or defense.

One who has taken a negotiable instrument from the original payee for value without notice of any infirmities in the instrument or defect in the title of the person negotiating it. *Seaboard*, 227 P.2d 892 (Cal.App., 1951)

hold harmless To assume any liability in a transaction thereby relieving another from responsibility or loss. Also called save harmless.

holding 1. A court's answer to or resolution of a legal issue before it. 2. A court ruling. 3. Property owned by someone.

holding company A company that owns stock in and supervises the management of other companies.

holding period The length of time a taxpayer owns a capital asset, which determines whether a gain or loss will be short-term or long-term.

holdover tenancy See estate at sufferance.

holdover tenant A tenant who retains possession of the premises after the expiration of a lease or after a tenancy at will has been ended.

holograph A handwritten document.

holographic will A will written entirely by the testator in his or her own handwriting, often without witnesses.

A holographic will must be written, dated and signed entirely by the hand of testator and it must be executed with testamentary intent. *In re Bloch's Estate*, 248 P.2d 21 (CA 1952)

home equity conversion mortgage A first mortgage that provides for future payments to a homeowner based on accumulated equity.

homeowner's policy A multiperil insurance policy covering damage to a residence and liability claims based on home ownership.

homeowner's warranty (HOW) A warranty and insurance protection program offered by many home builders, providing protection for 10 years against major structural defects. A construction warranty.

home port doctrine A vessel engaged in interstate and foreign commerce is taxable only at its home port (e.g., where it is registered).

home rule A designated amount of self-government granted to local cities and towns.

The principle of home rule refers to a local government's power to control and finance its own local affairs. *County of Sonoma*, 101 Cal.Rptr.2d 784 (Cal.App., 2000)

homestead The dwelling house and adjoining land where the owner or his or her family lives.

homestead exemption laws Laws that allow a householder or head of a family to designate a residence and adjoining land as his or her homestead that, in whole or part, is exempt from execution or attachment for designated general debts.

homicide The killing of one human being by another. Whether the killing is a crime depends on factors such as intent.

Homicide simply connotes death of individual at hands of another. *Barber*, 195 Cal.Rptr. 484 (Cal.App., 1983)

homologate To approve; to confirm officially.

Hon. Honorable.

honor To accept or pay a check or other negotiable instrument when presented for acceptance or payment.

honorable discharge A declaration by the government that a member of the military left the service in good standing.

honorarium A fee for services when no fee was required.

honorary trust A trust that may not be enforceable because it has no beneficiary to enforce it. Example: a trust for the care of a pet.

horizontal agreement An agreement between companies that directly compete at the same level of distribution, often in restraint of trade.

horizontal merger The acquisition of one company by another company producing the same or a similar product and selling it in the same geographic market. A merger of corporate competitors.

horizontal price fixing An agreement by competitors at the same market level to fix or control prices they will charge for their goods or services.

horizontal privity The relationship between a supplier and a nonpurchasing party who is affected by the product, such as a relative of the buyer or a bystander.

horizontal property acts A statute on condominiums or cooperatives.

horizontal restraint See horizontal agreement.

Distributors cannot lawfully agree to divide territories or customers; such conduct is sometimes called a horizontal restraint. *Guild*, 162 Cal.Rptr. 87 (Cal.App., 1980)

horizontal union See craft union.

hornbook A book summarizing the basics or fundamentals of a topic.

hornbook law See black letter law.

hostile environment sexual harassment A work setting in which severe and pervasive conduct of a sexual nature creates a hostile or offensive working environment.

Hostile work environment when harassment is sufficiently pervasive so as to alter conditions of employment and create abusive work environment. Cal. Government Code § 12940(h)(1). *Beyda*, 76 Cal.Rptr.2d 547 (Cal.App., 1998)

hostile fire 1. A fire that breaks out or spreads to an unexpected area. 2. Gunfire from an enemy.

hostile possession Possession asserted to be superior to or incompatible with anyone else's claim to possession.

hostile witness A witness who manifests bias or prejudice, who appears aligned with the other side, or who refuses to answer questions. Also called adverse witness.

hot blood See heat of passion.

hot cargo 1. Goods produced or handled by an employer with whom a union has a dispute. 2. Stolen goods.

hotchpot Mixing or blending all property, however acquired, in order to divide it more equally. Also called hodgepodge.

hot pursuit See fresh pursuit.

house 1. Living quarters; a home. 2. One of the chambers of a legislature (e.g., U.S. House of Representatives, Md. House of Delegates).

house bill (H.B.)(H.) Proposed legislation considered by the House of Representatives.

housebreaking Breaking and entering a dwelling-house with the intent to commit any felony therein. Also called burglary.

house counsel An attorney who is an employee of a business or organization, usually on salary. Also called in-house counsel.

household 1. Belonging or pertaining to the house and family. 2. A group of persons living together.

Household may be broadly defined as collection of persons, whether related or not, who lived together as group or unit of permanent or domestic character, with one head, under one roof or within common curtilage, who direct their attention toward common goal consisting of their mutual interest. *Jacobs*, 278 Cal.Rptr. 52 (Cal.App., 1991)

House of Representatives (H.R.) See house (2).

H.R. See House of Representatives.

H. Res. House resolution. See also concurrent resolution.

H.R. 10 plan See Keogh plan.

humanitarian doctrine See last clear chance doctrine.

hung jury A jury so irreconcilably divided in opinion that a verdict cannot be agreed upon.

husband-wife immunity See interspousal immunity.

husband-wife privilege See marital communications privilege.

hybrid security A security that combines the features of a debt instrument and an equity instrument.

hypothecate To pledge property as security or collateral for a debt without transferring title or possession.

hypothesis An assumption or theory to be proven or disproven.

hypothetical 1. Based on conjecture; not actual or real, but presented for purposes of discussion and analysis. 2. A set of assumed facts presented for the sake or argument and illustration.

hypothetical question A question in which the person being interviewed (e.g., an expert witness) is asked to give an opinion on a set of facts that are assumed to be true for purposes of the question.

A party calling an expert witness and proposing to ask a hypothetical question need not prepare and submit in advance a written statement of such question, unless the court otherwise directs. Los Angeles County Superior Court Rules, Rule 8.85

I

ibid. In the same place; in the work previously cited or mentioned.

ICJ See International Court of Justice (*www.icj-cij.org*).

id. The same. (Id. refers to the case or other authority cited immediately above or before in the text or footnotes.)

idem sonans Sounding the same. A misspelled signature can be effective if the misspelled name sounds the same as the correct spelling.

identify 1. To establish the identity of someone or something. 2. To associate or be associated with. 3. To specify the subject of a contract.

identity of interests Two persons being so closely related that suing one acts as notice to the other. Being only nominally separate.

identity of parties Two persons being so closely related that a judgment against one will bar (via res judicata) a later suit against the other.

Identity of parties means not only that parties must be identical in person, but that capacity in which they appear must be same. *Holman*, 205 P.2d 767 (Cal.App., 1949)

identity theft Knowingly transferring or using a means of identification of another person with the intent to commit any unlawful activity.

i.e. That is; in other words.

IFP See in forma pauperis.

ignoramus We do not know. (A notation by a grand jury indicating a rejection of the indictment.)

ignorance The absence of knowledge.

ignorantia juris non excusat Ignorance of the law excuses no one.

illegal Against the law; prohibited by law.

illegal entry 1. Unauthorized entry with intent to commit a crime. 2. Entry into a country by an alien at the wrong time or place or by fraud; or eluding immigration officers when here.

Burglary is defined as illegal entry with the intent to commit theft or any felony. *People v. Lagunas*, Cal.Rptr.2d 67 (CA 1994)

illegality That which is contrary to law.

illegally obtained evidence Evidence collected in violation of a suspect's statutory or constitutional rights.

illegitimate 1. Born out of wedlock. 2. Contrary to law.

illicit Not permitted, illegal; improper.

illicit cohabitation Two unmarried persons living together as man and wife.

Illinois Land Trust See land trust.

illusory Deceptive, based on false appearances; not real.

illusory contract An agreement in which one party's consideration is so insignificant that a contract obligation cannot be imposed.

illusory promise An apparent promise that leaves the promisor's performance entirely within the discretion of the promisor.

imbecility Severe mental retardation or cognitive disfunction.

imitation Substantial duplication; resembling something enough to cause confusion with the genuine article.

immaterial Not material. Tending to prove something not in issue.

Evidence that does not relate to matter in issue is immaterial. Cal. Evidence Code §§ 210. *People v. Torrez*, 37 Cal.Rptr.2d 712 (Cal.App., 1995)

immaterial variance A discrepancy between the pleading and the proof that is so slight that it misleads no one.

immediate annuity An annuity bought with a lump sum that starts making payments soon after its purchase.

immediate cause The last of a series or chain of events that produced the occurrence or result; a cause immediate in time to what occurred.

Immediate cause of the loss means that which is immediate in time to the occurrence of the damage. Cal. Insurance Code, §§ 530, 532. *Sabella*, Cal.Rptr. 689 (CA 1963)

immemorial Beyond human memory. Exceptionally old.

immigrant A foreigner who comes into a country with the intention to live there permanently.

imminent Near at hand; about to occur.

imminent peril doctrine See emergency doctrine.

immoral Contrary to good morals; inimical to public welfare according to the standards of a given community.

immovables Land and those things so firmly attached to it as to be regarded as part of it; property that cannot be moved.

immunity 1. Exemption or freedom from a duty, penalty, or liability. 2. A complete defense to a tort claim whether or not the defendant committed the tort. 3. The right not to be subjected to civil or criminal prosecution.

immunize To grant immunity to; to render immune.

impact rule A party may recover emotional distress damages in a negligence action only if he or she suffered accompanying physical injury or contact.

impair To cause something to lose some or all of its quality or value.

impair the obligation of contracts To nullify or materially change existing contract obligations. See also Contract Clause.

impanel To enlist or enroll. To enroll or swear in (a list of jurors) for a particular case. Also spelled empanel.

imparl 1. To delay a case in an attempt to settle. 2. To seek a continuance for more time to answer and pursue settlement options.

impartial Favoring neither side; unbiased.

impasse A deadlock in negotiations. The absence of hope of agreement.

impeach To attack; to accuse of wrongdoing; to challenge the credibility of.

impeachment 1. An attack or challenge because of impropriety, bias, or lack of veracity. 2. A procedure against a public officer before a quasi-political court (e.g., a legislative body), instituted by written accusations called articles of impeachment that seek his or her removal from office.

Calling into question a witness' veracity. Cal. Code of Civil Procedure §§ 2037.5. *Gallo,* 211 Cal.Rptr. 27 (Cal.App., 1985)

impediment A legal obstacle that prevents the formation of a valid marriage or other contract.

imperfect Missing an essential legal requirement. Unenforceable.

imperfect trust See executory trust.

impersonation Pretending or representing oneself to be another.

impertinent Irrelevant or not responsive to the issues in the case.

implead To bring a new party into the lawsuit on the ground that the new party may be liable for all or part of the current claim. The procedure is called impleader or third-party practice.

implied Expressed by implication; suggested by the circumstances.

implied acquittal A guilty verdict on a lesser included offense is an implied acquittal of the greater offense about which the jury was silent.

implied agency An actual agency established through circumstantial evidence.

implied authority Authority that is necessary, usual, and proper to perform the express authority delegated to the agent by the principal.

implied consent Consent inferred from the surrounding circumstances.

implied consent law A law providing that a person who drives a motor vehicle in the state is deemed to have given consent to a test that determines the alcoholic or drug content of that person's blood.

implied contract An implied in fact contract or an implied in law contract (see these terms.)

implied in fact Inferred from the facts and circumstances.

implied in fact contract An actual contract whose existence and the parties' intentions are inferred from facts rather than by express agreement.

A contract implied in fact is one not expressed by the parties but implied from facts showing a mutual intention to contract. *Gold,* 3 Cal.Rptr. 117 (Cal.App., 1960)

implied in law Imposed by law; arising by operation of law.

implied in law contract An obligation created by the law to avoid unjust enrichment. Also called constructive contract, quasi contract.

implied easement An easement created by law when land is conveyed that does not contain an express easement, but one is implied as an intended part of the transaction. Also called easement by implication, way of necessity.

implied malice Malice that is inferred from conduct, e.g., reckless disregard for human life. Also called legal malice, malice in law.

implied notice Knowledge implied from surrounding facts so that the law will treat one as knowing what could have been discovered by ordinary care.

implied powers Powers presumed to have been granted because they are necessary to carry into effect expressly granted powers.

implied promise A fictional promise created by law to impose a contract liability, and thereby avoid fraud or unjust enrichment.

implied trust See constructive trust, resulting trust.

implied warranty A warranty imposed by operation of law regardless of the parties'intent. See also warranty of fitness for a particular purpose, warranty of habitability, warranty of merchantability.

imply 1. To suggest; to state something indirectly. 2. To impose or declare something by law.

import To bring goods into a country from a foreign country.

impossibility That which no person in the course of nature or the law can do or perform; that which cannot exist.

impossibility of performance doctrine A defense to a breach of contract when performance becomes objectively impossible, not due to anyone's fault.

The equitable maxim that the law never requires impossibility means not only strict impossibility but also impracticability because of extreme and unreasonable difficulty, expense, injury, or loss involved. Cal. Civil Code § 3531. *Board of Supervisors v. McMahon,* 268 Cal.Rptr. 219 (Cal.App., 1990)

imposts A duty that is levied. An import tax.

impotence The inability to perform the act of sexual intercourse.

imposter One who deceives by pretending to be someone else.

impound To seize and take into custody of the law.

impoundment 1. Seizing and taking something into custody of the law. 2. Refusing to spend money appropriated by the legislature.

impracticability 1. A defense to breach of contract when performance can be undertaken only at an excessive and unreasonable cost. 2. Difficulty or inconvenience of joining all parties because of their large number.

Impracticability or futility of bringing civil action to trial within statutory five-year period is unreasonable difficulty or expense of bringing case to trial due to circumstances not caused by plaintiff. Cal. Code of Civil Procedure §§ 583.130, 583.340, 583.340(c). *Bank of America v. Superior Court,* 246 Cal.Rptr. 521 (Cal.App., 1988)

impracticable Excessively burdensome to perform.

impress 1. To force someone into public service, e.g., military service. 2. To impose a constructive trust. The noun is impressment.

impression See first impression.

imprimatur ("let it be printed") Official approval to publish a book.

imprison To put in prison; to place in confinement.

improper 1. Not in accord with proper procedure or taste. 2. Wrongful.

improved land Land that has been developed, e.g., by adding roads.

improvement An addition to or betterment of land (usually permanent) that enhances its capital value. Something beyond mere repairs.

Improvements means buildings or structures attached to the real property. Cal. Civil Code § 2955.5

improvident Lacking in care and foresight. Ill-considered.

impulse A sudden urge or thrusting force within a person.

impunity Exemption or protection from penalty or punishment.

impute To credit or assign to; to ascribe. To attribute to another or to make another responsible because of a relationship that exists.

imputed disqualification If one attorney or employee in a firm has a conflict of interest with a client, the entire firm is ineligible to represent that client. Also called vicarious disqualification.

imputed income A monetary value assigned to certain property, transactions, or situations for tax purposes (e.g., the value of a home provided by an employer for an employee).

imputed knowledge Information that a person does not actually know, but should know or has reason to know and, therefore, is deemed to know.

imputed negligence Negligence of one person that is attributed to another solely because of a special relationship between them.

in absentia In the absence of.

inadequate remedy at law An ineffective legal remedy, e.g., damages, justifying a request for an equitable remedy, e.g., injunction.

inadmissible Cannot be received and considered.

inadvertence An oversight; a consequence of carelessness, not planning.

inalienable Incapable of being bought, sold, transferred, or assigned. Also called unalienable.

in banc See en banc.

in being In existence; existing in life.

in blank Not identifying a particular indorsee. Not filled in.

Inc. Incorporated.

in camera In private with the judge; in chambers; without spectators.

incapacity 1. The existence of a legal impediment preventing action or completion. 2. Physical or mental inability. 3. See disability (2).

Incapacity is legal disability, such as minority or incompetency, which deprives party of right to represent his or her own interests in court. *American Alternative Energy,* 49 Cal.Rptr.2d 686 (Cal.App., 1996)

incarcerate To imprison or confine in jail.

incendiary 1. A bomb or other device designed to cause fire. 2. One who maliciously and willfully sets fire to property.

incest Sexual intercourse between a man and woman who are related to each other within prohibited degrees (e.g., brother and sister).

in chief 1. Main or principal. 2. See case-in-chief.

inchoate Begun but not completed; partial.

inchoate crime A crime in its early stage, constituting another crime. The inchoate crimes are attempt, conspiracy, and solicitation.

inchoate dower A wife's interest in the land of her husband during his life; a possibility of acquiring dower.

inchoate lien A lien in which the amount, exact identity of the lienor, and time of attachment must await future determination.

incident 1. Connected with, inherent in, or arising out of something else. 2. A dependent or subordinate part. 3. An occurrence.

incidental Depending upon and secondary to something else.

incidental beneficiary One who will be benefited by performance of a promise but who is neither a promisee nor an intended beneficiary.

A person is an incidental beneficiary if neither the facts showing a person to be a donee beneficiary or a creditor beneficiary exists. Cal. Civil Code, § 1559. *Southern California Gas,* 22 Cal.Rptr. 540 (Cal.App., 1962)

incidental damages 1. The additional expenses reasonably incurred because of a breach of contract. 2. In class actions, those damages that flow directly from liability to the class as a whole on claims forming the basis of the injunctive or declaratory relief.

incident of ownership An ownership right retained in an insurance policy, e.g., the right to change beneficiaries.

incite To urge, persuade, stir up, or provoke another.

included offense See lesser included offense.

income Money or other financial gain derived from one's business, labor, investments, and other sources.

income in respect of a decedent (IRD) The right to income earned by a decedent at death that was not included in his or her final income tax return.

income splitting Seeking a lower total tax by allocating income from persons in higher tax brackets to those in lower tax brackets.

income statement See earnings report.

income tax A tax on the net income of an individual or entity.

in common Shared together equally.

incompatibility Such discord between a husband and wife that it is impossible for them to live together in a normal marital relationship

incompetent 1. Failing to meet legal requirements; unqualified. 2. Not having the skills needed. Physically or mentally impaired.

Defendants are incompetent to stand trial when they suffer a mental disorder or developmental disability rendering them unable to understand the nature of the criminal proceedings or to assist counsel in the conduct of a defense in a rational manner. *People v. Avila*, 11 Cal.Rptr.3d 894 (Cal.App., 2004)

incompetent evidence Evidence that is not admissible.

inconsistent Not compatible. Mutually repugnant; the acceptance of one fact, position, or claim implies the abandonment of the other.

in contemplation of death With a view toward death. See contemplation of death.

incontestability clause An insurance policy clause providing that after a period of time (e.g., 2 years), the insurer cannot contest it on the basis of fraud, mistake, or statements made in the application.

inconvenient forum See forum non conveniens.

incorporate 1. To form a corporation. 2. To combine or include within.

The word incorporate as used in statute pertaining to holographic wills means formed or combined into one body or unit; intimately united, joined or blended or to unite with or introduce into something already existent. Cal. Probate Code, § 53. *Estate of Nielson*, 165 Cal.Rptr. 319 (Cal.App., 1980)

incorporation by reference Making one document a part of another document by stating that the former shall be considered part of the latter.

incorporation doctrine See selective incorporation.

incorporator A person who is one of the original founders (formers) of a corporation.

incorporeal Not having a physical nature; intangible.

incorporeal hereditament An intangible land right that is inheritable.

An inheritable right stemming from corporeal property but which is not itself corporeal. *Howard*, 269 Cal.Rptr. 807 (Cal.App., 1990)

incorrigible incapable of being corrected or reformed. Unmanageable.

increment An increase or addition in amount or quality.

incriminate 1. To charge with a crime; to accuse someone. 2. To show involvement in the possibility of crime or other wrongdoing.

incriminating Tending to demonstrate criminal conduct.

incriminating statement A statement that tends to establish a person's guilt.

incriminatory Charging or showing involvement with a crime.

incroach See encroach.

inculpatory Tending to show involvement with crime.

incumbent 1. One presently holding an office. 2. Obligatory.

incumbrance See encumbrance.

incur To become liable or subject to; to bring down upon oneself.

indebitatus assumpsit An action based on undertaking a debt.

indecent Sexually vulgar, but not necessarily obscene.

indecent assault Unconsented sexual contact with another.

indecent exposure Displaying one's self in public (especially one's genitals) in such manner as to be offensive to common decency.

indecent speech Vulgar or offensive (but not necessarily obscene) speech concerning sexual or excretory activities and organs.

indefeasible Not capable of being defeated, revoked, or made void.

indefinite Not definite or fixed; lacking fixed boundaries.

indefinite failure of issue A failure of issue (dying without descendants who can inherit) whenever it occurs.

indefinite sentence See indeterminate sentence.

indemnify To compensate or promise to compensate someone for a specified loss or liability that has resulted or that might result.

indemnitee A person who is indemnified by another.

indemnitor A person who indemnifies another.

indemnity 1. The duty of one person to pay for another's loss, damage, or liability. 2. A right to receive compensation to make one person whole from a loss that has already been sustained but which in justice ought to be sustained by the person from whom indemnity is sought.

A right that inures to a person who has been compelled by reason of some legal obligation to pay money due to the initial negligence of another. *Fremont*, 17 Cal.Rptr.3d 80 (Cal.App., 2004)

indemnity insurance Insurance covering losses to the insured's person or to his or her own property. Also called first-party insurance.

indenture 1. A deed with the top of the parchment having an irregular (indented) edge. 2. A written agreement under which bonds and debentures are issued; the agreement sets forth terms such as the maturity date and the interest rate. 3. An apprenticeship agreement.

independent 1. Not subject to control or limitation from an outside source. 2. Not affiliated; autonomous.

independent agency A government board, commission, or other agency that is not subject to the policy supervision of the chief executive.

independent contractor One who operates his or her own business and contracts to do work for others who do not control the method or administrative details of how the work is performed.

A person who is employed by another to perform work; who pursues an independent employment or occupation in performing it; and who follows the employer's desires only as to the results of the work, and not as to the means whereby it is to be accomplished. *Wilson*, 111 Cal.Rptr.2d 173 (Cal.App., 2001)

independent counsel 1. An outside attorney hired to conduct an investigation or perform other special tasks. 2. Counsel chosen by an insured or with the approval of the insured, but paid by the insurer.

independent covenant An obligation that is not conditioned on performance by the other party.

independent paralegal An independent contractor (a) who sells his or her paralegal services to, and works under the supervision of, one or more attorneys or (b) who sells his or her paralegal services directly to the public without attorney supervision. Also called freelance paralegal or legal technician. Note, however, that in some states (e.g., California) the paralegal and legal assistant titles are limited to those who work under attorney supervision.

independent source rule Illegally obtained evidence will be admitted if the government shows that it is also obtained through sources wholly independent of the illegal search or other constitutional violation.

indestructible trust See Claflin trust.

indeterminate Not designated with particularity; not definite.

indeterminate sentence A prison sentence that is not fixed by the court but is left to the determination of penal authorities within minimum and maximum time limits set by the court. Also called indefinite sentence.

A sentence of some number of years to life is an indeterminate sentence. Cal. Penal Code § 1170. *People v. Felix*, 94 Cal.Rptr.2d 54 (CA 2000)

index fund A mutual fund that seeks to match the results of a stock market index, e.g., the S&P 500.

indexing 1. Adjusting wages or other payments to account for inflation. 2. Tracking investments to an index, e.g., the S&P 500.

Indian reservation Land set apart for tribal use of Native Americans (American Indians).

indicia Signs or indications of something; identifying marks.

indict To bring or issue an indictment.

indictable Subject or liable to being indicted.

indictable offense A crime that must be prosecuted by indictment.

indictment A formal accusation of crime made by a grand jury.

indigent 1. Impoverished. 2. Without funds to hire a private attorney.

Indigent person means either a person whose income is 125 percent or less of the current poverty threshold established by the OMB of the United States, a disabled person whose income after meeting medical and other disability-related special expenses is 125 percent or less of that current poverty threshold, or a person who receives or is eligible to receive supplemental security income. Cal. Business & Professions Code § 8030.4(f)

indignity Humiliating, degrading treatment of another.

indirect contempt Behavior outside the presence of the judge that defies the authority or dignity of the court. Also called constructive contempt.

indirect evidence See circumstantial evidence.

indirect tax A tax upon some right, privilege, or franchise.

indispensable evidence Evidence essential to prove a particular fact.

indispensable party A party so essential to a suit that no final decision can be rendered without his or her joinder. The case cannot be decided on its merits without prejudicing the rights of such a party.

individual retirement account (IRA) A special account in which qualified persons can set aside a certain amount of tax-deferred income each year for savings or investment. The amount is subject to income tax upon withdrawal at the appropriate time.

indorse To place a signature on a check or other negotiable instrument to make it payable to someone other than the payee or to accept responsibility for paying it. Also spelled endorse.

indorsee The person to whom a check or other negotiable instrument is transferred by indorsement. Also spelled endorsee.

indorsement 1. Signing a check or other negotiable instrument to transfer or guarantee the instrument or to acknowledge payment. 2. The signature itself. Also spelled endorsement.

Indorsement means a signature, other than that of a signer as maker, drawer, or acceptor, that alone or accompanied by other words is made on an instrument for the purpose of (1) negotiating the instrument, (2) restricting payment of the instrument, or (3) incurring indorser's liability on the instrument. . . . Cal. Commercial Code § 3204

indorser One who transfers a check or other negotiable instrument by indorsement.

inducement 1. The benefit or advantage that motivates a promisor to enter a contract. 2. An introductory statement in a pleading, e.g., alleging extrinsic facts that show a defamatory meaning in a libel or slander case. 3. Persuading or influencing someone to do something.

industrial relations The relationship between employer and employees on matters such as collective bargaining and job safety.

industrial union A labor union with members in the same industry (e.g., textiles) irrespective of their skills or craft. Also called vertical union.

industry An occupation or business that is a distinct branch of manufacture and trade, e.g., the steel industry.

inebriated Intoxicated; drunk.

ineffective assistance of counsel See effective assistance of counsel.

in equity Pertaining to (or in a court applying) equitable principles.

inescapable Being helpless to avoid a result by oneself; inevitable.

in esse In being, actually existing.

in evidence Before the court, having been declared admissible.

inevitable accident See unavoidable accident.

inevitable discovery doctrine Illegally obtained evidence is admissible if it inevitably would have been discovered by lawful means.

infamous 1. Having a notorious reputation; shameful. 2. Denied certain civil rights due to conviction of a crime.

infamous crime A crime punishable by imprisonment or the loss of some civil rights.

A crime involving moral corruption and dishonesty thereby branding perpetrator a threat to integrity of the elective process. Cal.Const. art. 2, § 1. *Otsuka*, 51 Cal.Rptr. 284 (CA 1966)

infancy 1. See minority (1). 2. Childhood at its earliest stage.

infanticide The murder or killing of an infant soon after its birth.

inference 1. A process of reasoning by which a fact to be established is deduced from other facts. Reaching logical conclusions from evidence. 2. A deduction or conclusion reached by this process.

inferior court Any court that is subordinate to the highest court within its judicial system. Also called lower court.

infeudation Granting legal possession of land in feudal times.

infirm Lacking health; weak or feeble.

infirmative Tending to weaken a criminal charge.

infirmity Physical or mental weakness; frailty due to old age.

in flagrante delicto In the act of committing an offense.

infliction of emotional distress See intentional infliction of emotional distress.

in force In effect; legally operative.

informal Not following formal or normal procedures or forms.

Informal means that no formal discovery shall be conducted, no formal rules of evidence shall be applied, and no court reporter shall be used for the proceedings. Cal. Insurance Code § 10082.3

informal contract 1. An oral contract. 2. A binding contract that is not under seal.

informal proceedings Proceedings that are less formal (particularly in applying the rules of evidence) than a court trial.

informant See informer.

in forma pauperis (IFP) With permission (as a poor person) to proceed without paying filing fees or other court costs.

information A formal accusation of a criminal offense from the prosecutor rather than from a grand jury indictment.

information and belief Good faith belief as to the truth of an allegation, not based on firsthand knowledge.

informed consent Agreement to let something happen based on having a reasonable understanding of the benefits and risks involved.

Under the informed consent doctrine, the patient must have the capacity to reason and make judgments, the decision must be made voluntarily and without coercion, and the patient must have a clear understanding of the risks and benefits of the proposed treatment alternatives or nontreatment, along with a full understanding of the nature of the disease and the prognosis. *Conte*, 132 Cal.Rptr.2d 855 (Cal.App., 2003)

informed intermediary A skilled and knowledgeable individual (e.g., a doctor) in the chain of distribution between the manufacturer of a product and the ultimate consumer. Also called learned intermediary.

informer A person who informs against another; one who brings an accusation against another on the basis of a suspicion that the latter has committed a crime. Also called informant.

informer's privilege The government's limited privilege to withhold the identity of persons who provide information of possible violations of law.

infra Below; later in the text.

infraction A violation (often minor) of a law, agreement, or duty.

Parking violations qualified as infractions, within meaning of Vehicle Code provision authorizing imposition of fine on every person convicted of infraction. Cal. Vehicle Code § 42001. *People v. Levinson*, 19 Cal.Rptr.2d 229 (Cal.Super., 1993)

infringement An invasion of a right; a violation of a law or duty.

infringement of copyright The unauthorized use of copyrighted material (17 USC § 106).

infringement of patent An unauthorized making, using, offering for sale, selling, or importing an invention protected by patent (35 USC § 271(a)).

infringement of trademark The unauthorized use or imitation of a registered trademark on goods of a similar class likely to confuse or deceive (15 USC § 1114).

in futuro At a future time.

ingress The act or right of entering.

in gross In a large sum or quantity; undivided.

in haec verba In these words; verbatim.

inherent Existing as a permanent or essential component.

inherently dangerous Being susceptible to harm or injury in the nature of the product, service, or activity itself. Requiring great caution.

inherent defect See hidden defect.

inherent power A power that must necessarily exist in the nature of the organization or person, even if not explicitly granted.

inherent right A fundamental, nontransferable right that is basic to the existence of a person or organization. An inalienable right.

inherit 1. To take by inheritance. 2. To take by will.

inheritance 1. Property received by an heir when an ancestor dies without leaving a valid will (i.e., intestate). 2. Property received through the will of a decedent.

inheritance tax A tax on the right to receive property by descent (intestate succession) or by will. Also called death tax, succession tax.

The California inheritance tax is not a property tax but is a succession tax, imposed by reason of the beneficial succession to property on the death of the owner. Cal. Revenue & Taxation Code, § 13301. *Kirkwood*, 273 P.2d 532 (CA 1954)

in hoc In this regard.

in-house counsel See house counsel.

in invitum Against an unwilling party.

initial appearance The first criminal court appearance by the accused during which the court informs him or her of the charges, makes a decision on bail, and determines the date of the next proceeding.

initiative The electorate's power to propose and directly enact a statute or change in the constitution or to force the legislature to vote on the proposal.

injunction A court order requiring a person or organization to do or to refrain from doing something.

injuria absque damno A legal wrong, from which no loss or damage results, will not sustain a lawsuit for damages.

injurious falsehood 1. The publication of a false statement that causes special damages. 2. The publication of a false statement that is derogatory to plaintiff's business of a kind calculated to prevent others from dealing with the business or otherwise to interfere with its relations with others, to its detriment. Sometimes called disparagement.

Injurious falsehood or disparagement may consist of the publication of matter derogatory to the plaintiff's title to his property, or its quality, or to his business in general. *Atlantic Mutual*, 123 Cal.Rptr.2d 256 (Cal.App., 2002)

injury 1. Any harm or damage to another or oneself. 2. An invasion of a legally protected interest of another.

in kind 1. Of the same species or category. 2. In goods or services rather than money.

in lieu of In place of.

in limine At the outset. Preliminarily. See also motion in limine.

in loco parentis In the place of a parent; assuming the duties of a parent without adoption.

inmate A person confined in a prison, hospital, or other institution.

innocence 1. The absence of guilt. 2. The lack of cunning or deceit.

innocent Free from guilt; untainted by wrongdoing.

Innocent landowner means a person who owns a site, did not cause or contribute to a release or threatened release at the site. . . . Cal. Health & Safety Code § 25395.75

innocent agent One who engages in illegal conduct on behalf of the principal wrongdoer without knowing of its illegality.

innocent construction rule If words can be interpreted as harmless or defamatory, the harmless interpretation will be adopted.

innocent party 1. One who has not knowingly or negligently participated in wrongdoing. 2. One without actual or constructive knowledge of any limitations or defects.

innocent purchaser See bona fide purchaser.

innocent spouse A spouse who did not know or have reason to know that the other spouse understated the taxes due on their joint tax return.

innocent trespasser One who enters the land of another under the mistaken belief that it is permissible to do so.

inn of court An association or society of the main trial attorneys (called barristers) in England that has a large role in their legal training and admission to practice.

innominate Belonging to no specific class.

innuendo 1. The portion of a complaint that explains a statement's defamatory meaning when this is not clear on its face. 2. An indirect derogatory comment or suggestion.

inoperative No longer in force or effective.

in pais Done informally or without legal proceedings.

in pari delicto In equal fault; equally culpable.

in pari materia Upon or involving the same matter or subject. Statutes in pari materia are to be interpreted together to try to resolve any ambiguity or inconsistency in them.

in perpetuity Forever.

in personam Against the person. See also personal judgment.

in personam jurisdiction See personal jurisdiction.

in posse Capable of being; not yet in actual being or existence.

in praesenti At the present time; now

in propria persona (in pro per) In one's own person. See pro se.

inquest An inquiry by a coroner or medical examiner to determine the cause of death of a person who appears to have died suddenly or by violence.

Holding of inquest in coroner's discretion or upon request. Cal. Government Code § 27491.6

inquiry 1. A careful examination or investigation. 2. A question.

inquiry notice Knowledge of facts that would lead a reasonably cautious person to inquire further.

inquisitorial system The fact-finding system in some civil law countries in which the judge has a more active role in questioning the witnesses and in conducting the trial than in an adversary system.

in re In the matter of. A way of designating a court case in which there are no adversary parties in the traditional sense.

in rem (against the res or thing) Pertaining to a proceeding or action binding the whole world in which the court resolves the status of a specific property or thing. The action is not against a person.

An in rem action or proceeding is one that seeks to affect the interests of all persons in a particular property or thing. *People ex rel. Gwinn*, 100 Cal.Rptr.2d 29 (Cal.App., 2000)

in rem jurisdiction The court's power over a particular res, which is a thing within the territory over which the court has authority.

INS Immigration and Naturalization Service (*www.uscis.gov*).

insane delusion An irrational, persistent belief in nonexistent facts.

insanity 1. That degree of mental illness that negates an individual's legal responsibility or capacity to perform certain legal actions. Also called lunacy. 2. Model Penal Code test: As a result of a mental disease or defect, the accused lacks substantial capacity to appreciate the criminality of his or her conduct or to conform the conduct to the law. Also called substantial capacity test. 3. *Durham* test: The unlawful act was the product of mental disease or mental defect. 4. *M'Naghten* test: Laboring under such a defect of reason, from disease of the mind, as not to know the nature and quality of the act the accused was doing, or if the accused did know it, he or she did not know that it was wrong. Also spelled *McNaghten.* Also called right-and-wrong test. 5. Irresistible impulse test: An urge to commit an act induced by a mental disease so that the person is unable to resist the impulse to commit the act even if he or she knows that the act was wrong.

Insanity, under California law, means that at the time the offense was committed, the defendant was incapable of knowing or understanding the nature of his act or of distinguishing right from wrong. Cal. Penal Code § 1026(a). *People v. Ferris,* 30 Cal.Rptr.3d 426 (Cal.App., 2005)

inscription Entering, enrolling, or registering a fact or name on a list or record.

in se In and of itself. See malum in se.

insecurity clause A clause stating that a party may accelerate payment or performance or require collateral (or additional collateral) when he or she feels insecure because of a danger of default.

insider 1. One with knowledge of facts not available to the general public. 2. An officer or director of a corporation or anyone who owns more than 10 percent of its shares.

insider trading Conduct by corporate employees (or others who owe a fiduciary duty to the corporation) who trade in their company's stock based on material, nonpublic information, or who tip others about confidential corporate information. Trading in securities based on material, nonpublic information acquired in violation of a duty of confidence owed to the source of the information.

insolvency The condition of being unable to pay one's debts as they mature or fall due in the usual course of one's trade and business.

Insolvency under the Uniform Fraudulent Conveyance Act means insufficiency of entire property and assets of individual to pay his or her debts. Cal. Civil Code, § 3439.02(a). *T W M Homes,* 29 Cal.Rptr. 887 (Cal.App., 1963)

in specie In kind; in the same or like form.

inspection An examination of the quality or fitness of something.

installment A part of a debt payable in stages or successive periods.

installment contract A contract that requires or authorizes the delivery of goods in separate lots to be separately accepted or paid for. UCC 2–612.

installment credit A commercial arrangement in which the buyer pays for goods or services in more than one payment (often at regular intervals), for which a finance charge may be imposed.

installment loan A loan to be repaid in specified (often equal) amounts over a designated period.

installment note See serial note.

installment sale A commercial arrangement in which a buyer makes an initial down payment and agrees to pay the balance in installments over a period of time. The seller may keep title or take a security interest in the goods sold until full payment is made.

instance 1. Bringing of a law suit. 2. Occurrence. 3. Urgent insistance.

instant 1. Now under consideration. 2. The present.

instanter At once.

in statu quo In the same condition in which it was.

instigate To stimulate or goad someone to act; to incite.

in stirpes See per stirpes.

institute 1. To inaugurate or begin. 2. An organization that studies or promotes a particular area. 3. Legal treatise or textbooks.

institution 1. The commencement of something. 2. An enduring or established organization. 3. A place for the treatment of those with special needs. 4. A basic practice or custom, e.g., marriage.

instruction See charge (1).

instrument 1. A formal written document that gives expression to or embodies a legal act or agreement, e.g., contract, will. 2. See negotiable instrument. 3. A means by which something is achieved.

instrumentality A means or agency by which something is done.

insubordination Intentional disregard of instructions. Disobedience.

Insubordination can be rightfully predicated only upon refusal to obey some order which a superior officer is entitled to give and entitled to have obeyed and such order must be reasonably related to duties of subordinate officer or employee. *Forstner,* 52 Cal.Rptr. 621 (Cal.App., 1966)

insufficient evidence Evidence that cannot support a finding of fact.

insurable Capable of being insured against loss.

insurable interest Any actual, legal, and substantial economic interest in the safety or preservation of the subject of the insurance.

insurance A contract to provide compensation for loss or liability that may occur by or to a specified subject by specified risks.

Statute defining insurance requires two elements: (1) shifting one party's risk of loss to another party, and (2) distribution of that risk among similarly situated persons. Cal. Insurance Code § 22. *Automotive Funding,* 7 Cal.Rptr.3d 912 (Cal.App., 2003)

insurance adjuster A person who investigates, values, and tries to settle insurance claims.

insurance broker An intermediary or middleman between the public and an insurer on insurance matters such as the sale of an insurance policy. A broker is not tied to a particular insurance company.

insurance policy An instrument in writing by which one party (insurer) engages for the consideration of a premium to indemnify another (insured) against a contingent loss by providing compensation if a designated event occurs, resulting in the loss.

insurance trust A trust containing insurance policies and proceeds for distribution under the terms of the trust.

insure 1. To obtain insurance. 2. To issue a policy of insurance.

insured The person covered or protected by insurance.

insurer The underwriter or insurance company that issues insurance.

insurgent One in revolt against government or political authority.

insurrection A rising of citizens or subjects in revolt against civil authority. Using violence to overthrow a government.

intangible 1. Without physical form. 2. Property or an asset that is a "right" (e.g., copyright, option) rather than a physical object even though the right may be evidenced by something physical such as a written contract.

intangible asset; intangible property See intangible (2).

integrated bar A bar association to which all lawyers must belong if they want to practice law. Also called unified bar.

Integrated bar is a compulsory association of attorneys which conditions the practice of law in a particular state upon membership and mandatory dues payments. *Keller*, 255 Cal.Rptr. 542 (CA 1989)

integrated contract A contract that represents the complete and final understanding of the parties' agreement.

integration 1. Bringing together different groups, e.g., different races. 2. Making something whole or entire. Combining into one.

integration clause A contract clause stating that the writing is meant to represent the parties' entire and final agreement. Also called merger clause.

intellectual property Intangible property rights that can have commercial value (e.g., patents, copyrights, trademarks, trade names, trade secrets) derived from creative or original activity of the mind or intellect.

intend 1. To have in mind as a goal; to plan. 2. To mean or signify. See also intent.

intended use doctrine Manufacturers must design their products so that they are reasonably safe for their intended users.

intendment The true meaning or intention of something.

intent 1. One's state of mind while performing an act. 2. The design or purpose of a person in acting. The desire to cause the consequences of one's acts or the knowledge with substantial certainty that the consequences will follow from what one does.

For tort law purposes, intent means state of mind about consequences of act, not about act itself; intent is broader than desire or purpose to bring about physical results, and extends not only to those consequences which are desired, but also to those which actor believes are substantially certain to follow from what actor does. *Willard*, 48 Cal.Rptr.2d 607 (Cal.App., 1995)

intention 1. The purpose or design with which an act is done. Goal. See also intent. 2. Determination or willingness to do something.

intentional Deliberately done; desiring the consequences of an act or knowing with substantial certainty that they will result.

intentional infliction of emotional distress (IIED) The tort of intentionally or recklessly causing severe emotional distress by an act of extreme or outrageous conduct. Also called outrage.

inter alia Among other things.

intercept 1. To seize benefits owed to a parent to cover delinquent child support obligations. 2. To covertly acquire the contents of a communication via an electronic or other device. To wiretap.

interdict 1. To forbid, prevent, restrict. 2. To intercept and seize. 3. An injunction or prohibition. 4. One incapacitated by an infirmity.

interest 1. A right, claim, title, or legal share in something; a right to have the advantage accruing from something. 2. A charge that is paid to borrow money or for a delay in its return when due.

interested Involved, nonobjective; having a stake in the outcome.

Interest on Lawyers' Trust Accounts (IOLTA) A program in which designated client funds held by an attorney are deposited in a bank account, the interest from which can be used (often through a foundation) to help finance legal services for low-income persons.

Programs, such as that authorized by Business & Professions Code § 6211(a) authorizing pooling nominal, short-term client deposits to generate interest income for indigent service funding are generally referred to by the acronym IOLTA. *Carroll*, 213 Cal.Rptr. 305, (Cal.App., 1985)

interference 1. Hindering or obstructing something. 2. Meddling. 3. A patent proceeding to determine who has priority in an invention.

interference with prospective advantage The tort of intentionally interfering with a reasonable expectation of an economic advantage, usually a commercial or business advantage.

interim 1. Intervening time; meantime. 2. Temporary.

interim order A temporary order that applies until another order is issued.

interlineation Writing between the lines of an existing document.

interlocking director A member of the board of directors of more than one corporation at the same time.

interlocutory Not final; interim.

interlocutory appeal An appeal before the trial court reaches its final judgment.

interlocutory decree An intermediate decree or judgment that resolves a preliminary matter or issue.

An interlocutory decree is distinguished from a final decree in that it is not a final and conclusive determination of the rights of the parties. Cal. Code of Civil Procedure § 662. *Solorza*, 211 P.2d 891 (Cal.App., 1949)

interlocutory injunction See preliminary injunction.

interlocutory order An order made before final judgment on an incidental or ancillary matter. Also called intermediate order.

interloper One who meddles in the affairs of others.

intermeddler See officious intermeddler.

intermediary A go-between or mediator who tries to resolve conflicts.

intermediary bank Any bank (other than a depositary or payor bank) to which an item is transferred in the course of collection.

intermediate In the middle position.

intermediate court An appellate court below the court of last resort.

intermediate order See interlocutory order.

intermittent easement An easement that is used only occasionally.

intermixture of goods See confusion of goods.

intern 1. To restrict or confine a person or group. 2. A student obtaining practical experience and training outside the classroom.

An intern is an indoor or resident physician, surgeon, or similar officer in hospital and specifically one serving in hospital as preparation for independent practice after completing required course of study. *Garfield*, 221 P.2d 705 (Cal.App., 1950)

internal law The law within a state or country; local law.

internal revenue Tax revenue from internal (not foreign) sources.

Internal Revenue Code (IRC) The federal statute in title 26 of the U.S. Code that codifies federal tax laws.

Internal Revenue Service (IRS) The federal agency responsible for enforcing most federal tax laws (*www.irs.gov*).

internal security Laws and government activity to counter threats from subversive activities.

international agreements Contracts (e.g., treaties) among countries.

International Court of Justice (ICJ) The judicial arm of the United Nations that renders advisory opinions and resolves disputes submitted to it by nations (*www.icj-cij.org*).

international law The legal principles and laws governing relations between nations. Also called law of nations, public international law.

International Paralegal Management Association (IPMA) An association of paralegal managers at law firms and corporations (*www.paralegalmanagement.org*).

internment The confinement of persons suspected of disloyalty.

interplead 1. To file an interpleader. 2. To assert your claim or position on an issue in a case already before the court.

interpleader A remedy or suit to determine a right to property held by a disinterested third party (called the stakeholder) who is in doubt about ownership and who, therefore, deposits the property with the trial court to permit interested parties to litigate ownership.

The following civil cases and proceedings are limited civil cases: . . . actions of interpleader where the amount of money or the value of the property involved does not exceed twenty-five thousand dollars ($25,000). Cal. Code of Civil Procedure § 86(a)

Interpol International Criminal Police Organization; a coordinating group for international law enforcement (*www.interpol.int*).

interpolation Inserting words in a document to change or clarify it.

interpose To submit or introduce something, especially a defense.

interpret To explain the meaning of language or conduct. To construe.

interpretive rule The rule of an administrative agency that explains or clarifies the meaning of existing statutes and regulations.

interrogation A methodical questioning of someone, e.g., a suspect.

Interrogation includes express questioning as well as police words or action likely to elicit an incriminating response. *People v. Wojtkowski*, 213 Cal.Rptr. 846 (Cal.App., 1985)

interrogatories A discovery device consisting of written questions about a lawsuit submitted by one party to another.

in terrorem clause A clause with a threat, e.g., a clause in a will stating that a gift to a beneficiary will be forfeited if he or she contests the validity of the will. Also called a no-contest clause.

inter se; inter sese Among or between themselves.

interspousal Relating to or between husband and wife.

interspousal immunity Spouses cannot sue each other for personal torts, e.g., battery. Also called husband-wife immunity.

interstate Involving two or more states.

interstate commerce The exchange of goods or services (commerce) between two or more states of the United States (including a U.S. territory or the District of Columbia).

interstate compact An agreement between two or more states (and approved by Congress) that is designed to meet common problems.

interval ownership See time-sharing.

intervening Coming or occurring between two times or events.

intervening cause A new and independent force that breaks the causal connection between the original wrong and the injury; a later cause that so interrupts the chain of events as to become the proximate cause of the injury. Also called efficient intervening cause.

An intervening force is one that actively operates to produce harm after the defendant's negligent act or omission has been committed. *Arreola*, 122 Cal.Rptr.2d 38 (Cal.App., 2002)

intervenor A person with an interest in real or personal property who applies to be made a party to an existing lawsuit involving that property.

intervention The procedure by which a third person, not originally a party but claiming an interest in the subject matter of the suit, is allowed to come into the case to protect his or her own interests.

inter vivos Between or pertaining to the living.

inter vivos gift A gift that takes effect when the donor is living.

inter vivos trust A trust that takes effect when its creator (the settler) is living. Also called living trust.

intestacy Dying without a valid will.

intestate 1. Without making a valid will. 2. The person who dies without making a valid will.

intestate succession The transfer of property to the relatives of a decedent who dies without leaving a valid will. Also called descent and distribution, hereditary succession.

in testimonium In witness; in evidence whereof.

in the matter of See in re.

intimidate To coerce unlawfully.

in toto In total; completely.

intoxication A significantly lessened physical or mental ability to function normally, caused by alcohol or drugs.

A person is intoxicated within meaning of automobile guest statute, if intoxicating liquor has so far affected his nervous system, brain or muscles as to impair appreciably his ability to operate automobile as an ordinarily prudent and cautious man, in full possession of his faculties and using reasonable care, would operate or drive similar vehicle under like conditions. Cal. Vehicle Code, § 17158. *DeArmond*, 297 P.2d 57 (Cal.App., 1956)

intra Within.

intrastate commerce Commerce that occurs exclusively within one state.

intra vires Within the power; within the scope of lawful authority.

intrinsic Pertaining to the essential nature of a thing.

intrinsic evidence The evidence found within the writing or document itself.

intrinsic fraud Fraud that goes to the existence of a cause of action or an issue in the case, e.g., perjured testimony.

intrinsic value The true, inherent, and essential value of a thing, not depending on externals, but the same everywhere and to everyone.

intrusion 1. Wrongfully entering upon or taking something. 2. See invasion of privacy (1)(c).

inure 1. To take effect. 2. To habituate. Also spelled enure.

in utero In the uterus.

invalid 1. Having no legal effect. 2. A disabled person.

invasion 1. An encroachment on the rights of others. 2. Making payments from the principal of a trust rather than from its income.

invasion of privacy 1. Four separate torts. (a) Appropriation: The use of a person's name, likeness, or personality for commercial gain without authorization. (b) False light: Unreasonably offensive publicity that places another in a false light. (c) Intrusion: An unreasonably offensive encroachment or invasion into someone's private affairs or concerns. (d) Public disclosure of a private fact: Unreasonably offensive publicity concerning the private life of a person. 2. A constitutional prohibition of unreasonable governmental interferences with one's private affairs or effects.

Nothing in this chapter shall in any way affect the right of any consumer to maintain an action against an investigative consumer reporting agency for invasion of privacy. Cal. Civil Code § 1786.52

invention The creation of a potentially patentable process or device through independent effort. The discovery of a new process or product.

inventory 1. A detailed list of property or assets. 2. Goods in stock held for sale or lease or under contracts of service, raw materials, works in process, or materials used or consumed in a business.

in ventre sa mere See en ventre sa mere.

inverse condemnation A cause of action for the taking of private property for public use without proper condemnation proceedings.

An inverse condemnation action is an eminent domain action initiated by one whose property was taken for public use. Cal.Const. Art. 1, § 19. *Barham*, 88 Cal.Rptr.2d 424 (Cal.App., 1999)

inverse order of alienation doctrine One seeking to collect on a lien or mortgage on land sold off in successive parcels must collect first from any land still with the original owner; if this land is insufficient to satisfy the debt, he or she must resort to the parcel last sold, and then to the next to the last, and so on until the debt is satisfied.

invest 1. To use money to acquire assets in order to produce revenue. 2. To give power or authority to. 3. To devote to a task; to commit.

investment advisor One who, for compensation, engages in the business of advising others (directly or through publications) on the value of securities or the advisability of investing in, purchasing, or selling securities, or who, as a part of a regular business, publishes reports about securities.

investment bank A financial institution engaged in underwriting, selling securities, raising capital, and giving advice on mergers and acquisitions.

investment company A company in the business of investing, reinvesting, or trading in securities (15 USC § 80a-3). A company that sells shares and invests in securities of other companies. Also called an investment trust.

investment contract A contract in which money is invested in a common enterprise with profits to come solely from the efforts of others.

An investment contract is one which contemplates the entrusting of money or other capital to another with the expectation of deriving a profit or income therefrom to be created through the efforts of other persons. Cal. Corporations Code, § 25008(a). *Oil Lease Service*, 327 P.2d 628 (Cal.App., 1958)

investment income Income from investment capital rather than income resulting from labor. Also called unearned income.

investment securities Instruments such as stocks, bonds, and options used for investment.

investment trust See investment company.

investment tax credit A credit against taxes, consisting of a percentage of the purchase price of capital goods and equipment.

invidious discrimination An arbitrary classification that is not reasonably related to a legitimate purpose. Offensively unequal treatment.

invited error rule On appeal, a party cannot complain about an error for which he or she is responsible, such as an erroneous ruling that he or she prompted or invited the trial court to make.

invitee One who enters land upon the express or implied invitation of the occupier of the land to use the land for the purpose for which it is held open to the public or to pursue the business of the occupier.

An invitee is one who by express or implied invitation is brought or comes on the premises for the land possessor's advantage, or their mutual benefit or common interest. *Beauchamp*, 77 Cal.Rptr. 914 (Cal.App., 1969)

invocation 1. Calling upon for assistance or authority. 2. The enforcement of something. The verb is invoke.

invoice A document giving the price and other details of a sale of goods or services.

involuntary 1. Not under the control of the will. 2. Compulsory.

involuntary bailment A bailment arising by an accidental, nonnegligent leaving of personal property in the possession of another.

involuntary bankruptcy Bankruptcy forced on a debtor by creditors.

involuntary commitment See civil commitment.

involuntary confession A confession obtained by threats, improper promises, or other unlawful pressure from someone in law enforcement.

Defendant's statement is involuntary, and must be suppressed, only if a threat actually induced defendant to make the statement. *People v. Lucas*, 48 Cal.Rptr.2d 525 (CA 1995)

involuntary conversion The loss or destruction of property through theft, casualty, or condemnation.

involuntary dismissal A dismissal of an action for failure to prosecute the action or to comply with a court rule or order.

involuntary dissolution The forced termination of the existence of a corporation or other legal entity.

involuntary intoxication Intoxication resulting when one does not knowingly and willingly ingest an intoxicating substance.

involuntary manslaughter The unintentional killing of another without malice while engaged in an unlawful activity that is not a felony and does not naturally tend to cause death or great bodily harm or while engaged in a lawful activity with a reckless disregard for the safety of others.

Killing in the commission of an unlawful act, not amounting to felony; or in the commission of a lawful act which might produce death, in an unlawful manner, or without due caution and circumspection. Cal. Penal Code § 192

involuntary nonsuit The dismissal of an action when the plaintiff fails to appear, gives no evidence on which a jury could find a verdict, or receives an adverse ruling that precludes recovery.

involuntary servitude The condition of being compelled to labor for another (with or without compensation) by force or imprisonment.

involuntary trust See constructive trust.

IOLTA See Interest on Lawyers' Trust Accounts.

IPMA See International Paralegal Management Association (*www.paralegalmanagement.org*).

ipse dixit An unproven or unsupported assertion made by a person.

ipso facto By that very fact; in and of itself.

ipso jure By the law itself; by the mere operation of law.

IRA See individual retirement account.

IRC See Internal Revenue Code.

irrational Illogical, not guided by a fair assessment of the facts.

irrebuttable presumption See conclusive presumption.

irreconcilable differences A no-fault ground of divorce that exists when persistent, unresolvable disagreements between the spouses lead to an irremediable breakdown of the marriage.

Dissolution of the marriage or legal separation of the parties may be based on irreconcilable differences, which have caused the irremediable breakdown of the marriage. Cal. Family Code § 2310

irrecusable Cannot be challenged or rejected.

irregular Not according to rule, proper procedure, or the norm.

irrelevant Not tending to prove or disprove any issue in the case.

Evidence is irrelevant if it leads only to speculative inferences. Cal. Evidence Code § 210. *People v. Morrison*, 21 Cal.Rptr.3d 682 (CA 2004)

irremediable breakdown See irretrievable breakdown.

irreparable Not capable of being repaired or restored.

irreparable injury Harm that cannot be adequately redressed by an award of monetary damages. An injunction, therefore, is possible.

irresistible impulse See insanity (5).

irretrievable breakdown A no-fault ground of divorce that exists when there is such discord and incompatibility between the spouses that the legitimate objects of matrimony have been destroyed and there is no reasonable possibility of resolution. Also called irremediable breakdown.

irrevocable Not capable of being revoked or recalled.

irrevocable trust A trust that cannot be terminated by its creator.

IRS See Internal Revenue Service (*www.irs.gov*).

issuable 1. Open to debate or litigation. 2. Allowed or authorized for issue or sale. 3. Possible.

issue 1. To send forth, announce, or promulgate. 2. A legal question. A point or matter in controversy or dispute. 3. Offspring; lineal descendants, e.g., child, grandchild. 4. A group or class of securities offered for sale in a block or at the same time. Also called stock issue. 5. The first delivery of a negotiable instrument.

issue of fact A dispute over the existence or nonexistence of an alleged fact. The controversy that exists when one party asserts a fact that is disputed by the other side. Also called question of fact or fact question.

Issue of fact is one where the evidence introduced will support a decision on either side, that is to say, reasonable minds could fairly differ as to the answer to the question posed. *Pan Asia Venture*, 88 Cal.Rptr.2d 118 (Cal.App., 1999)

issue of law A question of what the law is, what the law means, or how the law applies to a set of established, assumed, or agreed-upon facts. Also called legal question, question of law.

A question of what the law is, what the law means, or how the law applies to a set of established, assumed, or agreed-upon facts. *Pan Asia Venture*, 88 Cal.Rptr.2d 118 (Cal.App., 1999)

issue preclusion See collateral estoppel.

item 1. An instrument or a promise or order to pay money handled by a bank for collection or payment. 2. An entry on an account. 3. A part of something.

itemized deduction A payment that is allowed as a deduction from adjusted gross income on a tax return.

J

J Judge; justice.

jactitation False boasting; false claims causing harm.

JAG See Judge Advocate General.

jail A place of confinement, usually for persons awaiting trial or serving sentences for misdemeanors or minor crimes.

jailhouse lawyer An inmate who is allowed to give legal assistance and advice to other prisoners if the institution provides no alternatives.

Jane Doe; Jane Roe A fictitious name for a female party in legal proceedings if the real name is unknown or is being kept confidential.

***Jason* clause** A clause in a bill of lading requiring a general average contribution (see this phrase). *The Jason,* 32 S. Ct. 560 (1912).

jaywalking Failure to use crosswalks or to comply with other regulations for crossing the street.

J.D. See Juris Doctor.

***Jencks* rule** After a witness called by the federal prosecutor has testified on direct examination, the court shall, on motion of the defendant, order the prosecution to produce any statement of the witness in the possession of the prosecution that relates to the subject matter of the testimony to aid the defendant in the cross-examination of this witness. 18 USC § 3500(b); *Jencks v. U.S.,* 77 S. Ct. 1007 (1957).

jeopardy The risk of conviction and punishment once a criminal defendant has been placed on trial. Legal jeopardy.

Jeopardy attaches when a defendant is placed on trial in a court of competent jurisdiction, on a valid accusatory pleading, before a jury duly empaneled and sworn, and a discharge of that jury without a verdict bars a retrial unless the defendant consented thereto or legal necessity required it. Calif.Const. art. 1, § 13; *People v. Boyd,* 99 Cal.Rptr. 553 (Cal.App., 1972)

jeopardy assessment If the collection of a tax appears to be in question, the IRS may assess and collect the tax immediately without going through the usual formalities.

jetsam Goods that the owner voluntarily throws overboard in an emergency in order to lighten the ship.

jettison To discard or throw overboard in order to lighten the load of a ship in danger. Goods thrown overboard for this purpose.

Jim Crow law A law that intentionally discriminates against blacks.

JJ Judges; justices.

JNOV See judgment notwithstanding the verdict.

jobber 1. One who buys goods from manufacturers and sells them to retailers. A wholesaler. 2. One who does odd jobs or piecework.

John Doe; Richard Roe A fictitious name for a male party in legal proceedings if the real name is unknown or is being kept confidential.

joinder Uniting two or more parties as plaintiffs, two or more parties as defendants, or two or more claims into a single lawsuit.

Joinder. All persons may join in one action as plaintiffs if: (1) They assert any right to relief jointly, severally, or in the alternative, in respect of or arising out of the same transaction, occurrence, or series of transactions or occurrences and if any question of law or fact common to all these persons will arise in the action. . . . Cal. Code of Civil Procedure § 378(a)

joinder of issue The assertion of a fact by a party in a pleading and its denial by the opposing party. The point in litigation when opponents take opposite positions on a matter of law or fact.

joint 1. Shared by or between two or more. 2. United or coupled together in interest or liability.

joint account An account of two or more persons containing assets that each can withdraw in full, and, upon the death of one of them, is payable to the others rather than to the heirs or beneficiaries of the decedent.

joint adventure See joint venture.

joint and mutual will A single will executed by two or more persons disposing of property owned individually or together that shows that the devises or dispositions were made in consideration of one another.

One instrument executed jointly by two or more persons, the provisions of which are reciprocal. *Estate of Mulholland,* 97 Cal.Rptr. 617 (Cal.App., 1971)

joint and several Together as well as individually or separately.

joint and several liability Legally responsible together and individually. Each wrongdoer is individually responsible for the *entire* judgment; the plaintiff can choose to collect from one wrongdoer or from all of them until the judgment is satisfied.

joint and survivor annuity An annuity with two beneficiaries (e.g., husband and wife) that continues to make payments until both beneficiaries die.

joint annuity An annuity with two beneficiaries that stops making payments when either dies.

joint bank account See joint account.

joint committee A legislative committee whose membership is from both houses of the legislature.

joint custody This phrase can mean (a) joint legal custody in which both parents share the right to make the major decisions on raising their child, who may reside primarily with one parent, (b) joint physical custody in which the child resides with each parent individually for alternating, although not necessarily equal, periods of time, or (c) both joint legal custody and joint physical custody.

Joint custody means joint physical custody and joint legal custody. Cal. Family Code § 3002

joint enterprise See joint venture.

joint estate A form of joint ownership, e.g., joint tenancy, tenancy in common, tenancy by the entirety.

joint legal custody See joint custody.

joint liability Two or more parties together have an obligation or liability to a third party. Liability that is owed to a third party by two or more parties together.

If two or more judgment debtors are jointly liable on a money judgment: (a) A judgment debtor who has satisfied more than his or her due proportion of the judgment, whether voluntarily or through enforcement procedures, may compel contribution from another judgment debtor who has satisfied less than his or her due proportion of the judgment. Cal. Code of Civil Procedure § 882

joint lives The duration of an estate lasting until either one of two named persons dies.

joint obligation An obligation incurred by two or more debtors to a single performance to one creditor.

joint ownership Two or more persons who jointly hold title to, or have an interest in, property.

joint physical custody See joint custody.

joint resolution A resolution passed by both houses of a legislative body.

joint return A federal, state, or local tax return filed by a husband and wife together regardless of who earned the income.

joint stock company An unincorporated association of individuals who hold shares of the common capital they contribute. Also called stock association.

joint tenancy Property that is owned equally by two or more persons (called joint tenants) with the right of survivorship. Joint tenants have one and the same interest; accruing by one and the same conveyance, instrument, or act; commencing at one and the same time; with one and the same undivided possession.

An estate owned jointly in undivided equal shares by two or more persons, and the principal characteristic of the joint tenancy property ownership is the right of survivorship which accrues to the surviving joint tenant. Cal. Civil Code, § 683; *Estate of Gebert*, 157 Cal.Rptr. 46 (Cal.App., 1979)

joint tortfeasors Two or more persons who together commit a tort. One or more persons jointly or severally liable in tort for the same loss to person or property.

jointure A widow's freehold estate in lands (in lieu of dower) to take effect on the death of her husband and to continue during her life.

joint venture An association of persons who jointly undertake some commercial enterprise in which they share profits. An agreement among members of a group to carry out a common purpose, in which each has an equal voice in the control and direction of the enterprise. Also called joint adventure, joint enterprise.

joint will A single testamentary instrument (will) executed by more than one person. It can dispose of property owned individually and jointly.

joint work A work prepared by two or more authors with the intention that their contributions be merged into inseparable or interdependent parts of a unitary whole (17 USC § 101).

Jones Act The federal statute that provides a remedy to seamen injured in the course of employment due to negligence (46 App. USC § 688).

journal 1. A book in which entries are made, often on a regular basis. 2. A periodical or magazine.

journalist's privilege 1. The privilege of a journalist not to disclose information obtained while gathering news, including the identity of sources. Also called reporter's privilege. 2. The qualified privilege of the media (asserted in defamation actions) to make fair comment about public figures on matters of public concern.

journeyman A person who has progressed through an apprenticeship in a craft or trade and is now qualified to work for another.

joyriding Driving an automobile without authorization but without the intent to steal it.

Any person who shall, without the permission of the owner thereof, take any vessel for the purpose of temporarily using or operating the same, is guilty of a misdemeanor. Cal. Penal Code § 499b

J.P. See justice of the peace.

J.S.D. Doctor of Juridical Science.

judge 1. A public officer appointed or elected to preside over and to administer the law in a court of justice or similar tribunal. 2. To resolve a dispute authoritatively.

Referees of Workers' Compensation Appeals Board are officers of judicial system performing judicial functions and are "judges" for purposes of Code of Judicial Conduct. *Fremont Indemnity*, 200 Cal.Rptr. 762 (Cal.App., 1984)

judge advocate A legal officer or adviser in the military. A legal officer on the staff of the Judge Advocate General.

Judge Advocate General (JAG) The senior legal officer in the army, navy, or air force (see e.g., *www.jag.navy.mil*).

judge-made law 1. Law created by judges in court opinions. Law derived from judicial precedents rather than from statutes. 2. A court decision that fails to apply the intent of the legislature. Also called judicial legislation.

judgment The final conclusion of a court that resolves a legal dispute or that specifies what further proceedings are needed to resolve it.

judgment as a matter of law A judgment on an issue in a federal jury trial (and in some state jury trials) ordered by the judge against a party because there is no legally sufficient evidentiary basis for a reasonable jury to find for that party on that issue. The judgment may be rendered before or after the verdict. In some state courts, the judgment is called a *directed verdict* if it is rendered before the jury reaches a verdict and a *judgment notwithstanding the verdict* (JNOV or judgment n.o.v.) if it is rendered after the jury reaches a verdict.

judgment by default See default judgment.

judgment book The book or docket in which the clerk enters the judgments that are rendered.

judgment creditor A person in whose favor a money judgment (damages) is entered or who becomes entitled to enforce it.

judgment debtor A person ordered to pay a money judgment (damages) rendered against him or her.

judgment in personam See personal judgment.

judgment in rem A judgment concerning the status or condition of property. The judgment is against or on the property, not a person. See also in rem.

A judgment in personam can result only from personal obligation following person wherever he may be and enforceable wherever he may be found, whereas "judgment in rem" is one which may be pronounced upon status of some particular subject-matter. *Perry*, 259 P.2d 953 (Cal.App., 1953)

judgment lien A lien on property of a judgment debtor giving the judgment creditor the right to levy on it to satisfy the judgment.

judgment nisi ("a judgment unless") A judgment that will stand unless the party affected by it appears and shows cause against it.

judgment non obstante veredicto See judgment notwithstanding the verdict.

judgment note See cognovit.

judgment notwithstanding the verdict (JNOV) A court judgment that is opposite to the verdict reached by the jury. Also called judgment non obstante veredicto or judgment n.o.v. In federal court, it is called a *judgment as a matter of law* (see this phrase).

judgment n.o.v. See judgment notwithstanding the verdict.

judgment on the merits A judgment, rendered after evidentiary inquiry and argument, determining which party is in the right, as opposed to a judgment based solely on a technical point or procedural error.

judgment on the pleadings A judgment based solely on the facts alleged in the complaint, answer, and other pleadings.

judgment proof A person without assets to satisfy a judgment.

judgment quasi in rem A judgment determining a particular person's interest in specific property within the court's jurisdiction. See also quasi in rem.

judicature 1. The judiciary. 2. The administration of justice. 3. The jurisdiction or authority of a judge.

judicial Pertaining to the courts, the office of a judge, or judgments.

judicial act A decision or other exercise of power by a court.

judicial activism Writing court decisions that invalidate arguably valid statutes, fail to follow precedent, or that inject the court's political or social philosophy. Sometimes called judicial legislation.

judicial admission A deliberate, clear statement of a party on a concrete fact within the party's peculiar knowledge that is conclusive upon the party making it, thereby relieving the opposing party from presenting any evidence on it.

A judicial admission may be an allegation of a pleading or an attorney's concession or stipulation to facts; it is not merely evidence of a fact, but is a conclusive concession of truth of matter which has effect of removing it from issues. *Smith*, 147 Cal.Rptr. 1 (Cal.App., 1978)

judicial bonds Generic term for bonds required by a court for appeals, costs, attachment, injunction, etc.

judicial discretion The ability or power of a court (when it is not bound to decide an issue one way or another) to choose between two or more courses of action. Also called legal discretion.

judicial economy Efficiency in the use of the courts' resources.

judicial immunity The exemption of judges from civil liability arising out of the discharge of judicial functions.

judicial legislation 1. Statutes creating or involving the courts. 2. See judge-made law (2), judicial activism.

judicial lien A lien that arises by judgment, sequestration, or other legal or equitable process or proceeding (11 USC § 101).

judicial notice A court's acceptance of a well-known fact without requiring proof of that fact.

The recognition and acceptance by the court, for use by the trier of fact or by the court, of the existence of a matter of law or fact that is relevant to an issue in the action without requiring formal proof of the matter. *Lockley*, 110 Cal.Rptr.2d 877 (Cal.App., 2001)

judicial power The power of the court to decide and pronounce a judgment and carry it into effect between parties in the case.

judicial question A question that is proper for the courts to resolve.

judicial restraint Courts should resolve issues before them without reaching other issues that do not have to be resolved, follow precedent closely without injecting personal views and philosophies, and defer to the right of the legislature to make policy.

judicial review 1. The power of a court to interpret statutes and administrative laws to determine their constitutionality. 2. The power of a court to examine the legal and factual conclusions of a lower court or administrative agency to determine whether errors were made.

judicial sale A sale based on a court decree ordering the sale.

judicial separation See legal separation.

judiciary The branch of government vested with the judicial power; the system of courts in a country; the body of judges; the bench.

jump bail To fail to appear at the next scheduled court appearance after having been released on bail.

junior Subordinate; lower in rank or priority.

junior bond A bond that has a lower payment priority than other bonds.

junior lien A lien that has a lower priority than other liens on the same property.

junk science Unreliable, potentially misleading scientific evidence.

jura Rights; laws.

jural Pertaining to law, justice, rights, and legal obligations.

jurat A certificate of a person before whom a writing was sworn. A certification by a notary public that the person signing the writing (e.g., an affidavit) appeared before the notary and swore that the assertions in the writing were true.

When executing a jurat, a notary shall administer an oath or affirmation to the affiant and shall determine, from personal knowledge or satisfactory evidence as described in Section 1185 of the Civil Code, that the affiant is the person executing the document. Cal. Government Code § 8202

jure By the law; by right.

juridical Relating to the law or the administration of justice.

juris Of law; of right.

jurisdiction 1. The power of a court to decide a matter in controversy. 2. The geographic area over which a particular court has authority. 3. The scope of power or authority that a person or entity can exercise. See also personal jurisdiction, in rem jurisdiction, quasi in rem jurisdiction, and subject-matter jurisdiction.

Jurisdiction to adjudicate matters in marital case involves three requirements: (1) that court has authority to adjudicate specific matter raised by pleadings (subject matter jurisdiction); (2) that court has in rem jurisdiction over marital "res" to terminate marital status (in rem jurisdiction); and (3) that court has jurisdiction over parties to adjudicate personal rights and obligations (personal jurisdiction). Cal. Family Code § 2010. *In re Marriage of Jensen*, 7 Cal.Rptr.3d 701 (Cal.App., 2003)

jurisdictional amount See amount in controversy.

jurisdictional dispute Competing claims by different unions that their members are entitled to perform certain work.

jurisdictional facts Those facts that must exist before the court can properly take jurisdiction of the particular case.

jurisdiction in personam See personal jurisdiction.

jurisdiction in rem See in rem jurisdiction.

jurisdiction of the subject matter See subject-matter jurisdiction.

jurisdiction quasi in rem See quasi in rem jurisdiction.

Juris Doctor (J.D.) Doctor of law. The standard degree received upon completion of law school. Also called doctor of jurisprudence.

jurisprudence The philosophy of law; a science that ascertains the principles on which legal rules are based. The system of laws.

jurist A legal scholar; a judge.

juristic person See artificial person.

juror A member of a jury.

jury A group of persons selected to resolve disputes of fact and to return a verdict based on the evidence presented to them.

The official group of persons actually sworn to act at trial, usually 12 in number, and never more than 12. Calif.Const. art. 1, §§ 7; Cal. Code of Civil Procedure § 193. *Turlock*, 50 Cal.Rptr. 70 (Cal.App., 1966)

jury box The courtroom location where the jury observes the trial.

jury charge See charge (1).

jury commissioner An official in charge of prospective jurors.

jury instructions See charge (1).

jury list A list of citizens who could be called for jury duty.

jury nullification A jury's refusal to apply a law perceived to be unjust or unpopular by acquitting a defendant in spite of proof of guilt.

jury panel A list or group of prospective jurors. Also called venire.

jury tampering See embracery.

jury trial The trial of a matter before a judge and jury as opposed to a trial solely before a judge. The jury decides the factual issues.

jury wheel A system for the storage and random selection of the names or identifying numbers of prospective jurors.

jus (jura plural) Law; system of law; right; power; principle.

jus accrescendi The right of survivorship or accrual.

jus cogens A rule or legal principle that the parties cannot change.

jus gentium The law of nations; international law.

jus publicum 1. Public law. 2. State ownership of land.

just Conforming to what is legal or equitable.

Honorable and fair, consistent with moral right and valid within the law, and legitimate, as well as in conformity with what is morally right or good, merited, deserved, and conforming to what is lawful. Cal. Code of Civil Procedure §§ 1176(a). *Selma Auto*, 52 Cal.Rptr.2d 599 (Cal.App., 1996)

just cause See good cause.

just compensation Compensation that is fair to both the owner and the public when the owner's property is taken for public use through eminent domain.

jus tertii The right of a third person or party.

justice 1. A judge, usually of a higher court. 2. The proper administration of the law; the fair resolution of legal disputes.

justice court A lower court (e.g., a justice of the peace court) that can hear minor civil or criminal matters.

justice of the peace (J.P.) A judicial magistrate of inferior rank with limited jurisdiction over minor civil or criminal cases.

justiciable Appropriate for court resolution.

justifiable Warranted or sanctioned by law. Defensible.

justifiable homicide Killing another when permitted by law (e.g., in self-defense).

Killing is not justifiable if it did not constitute lawful defense of self, others, or property, prevention of a felony, or preservation of the peace. Cal. Penal Code § 195. *People v. Orr*, 27 Cal.Rptr.2d 553 (Cal.App., 1994)

justification A just or lawful reason to act or to fail to act.

juvenile One under 18 (or other age designated by law) and, therefore, not subject to be treated as an adult for purposes of the criminal law.

juvenile court A special court with jurisdiction over minors alleged to be neglected or juvenile delinquents.

juvenile delinquent A minor (e.g., someone under 18) who has committed an act that would be a crime if committed by an adult. Also called youthful offender.

K

k Contract.

kangaroo court A sham legal proceeding in which a person's rights are disregarded and the result is a foregone conclusion due to bias.

K.B. See King's Bench.

keeper A person or entity that has the custody or management of something or someone.

Keogh plan A retirement plan for self-employed taxpayers, the contributions to which are tax deductible. Also called H.R. 10 plan.

KeyCite The citator on Westlaw that allows online checking of the subsequent history of cases, statutes, and other laws.

key number A number assigned to a topic by West Group in its indexing or classification system of case law.

key man insurance Life insurance on employees who are crucial to a company. The company pays for the insurance and is the beneficiary.

kickback A payment made by a seller of a portion of the purchase price to the buyer or to a public official in order to induce the purchase or to influence future business transactions.

kiddie tax A popular term used for the tax paid by parents at their rate for the investment (unearned) income of their children.

kidnapping Taking and carrying away a human being by force, fraud, or threats against the victim's will and without lawful authority.

Kidnapping for ransom. Any person who seizes, confines, inveigles, entices, decoys, abducts, conceals, kidnaps or carries away another person by any means whatsoever with intent to hold or detain, or who holds or detains, that person for ransom, reward or to commit extortion or to exact from another person any money or valuable thing, or any person who aids or abets any such act, is guilty of a felony, . . . Cal. Penal Code § 209(a)

kin One's relatives; family, kindred.

kind Generic class; type. See also in kind.

kindred Family, relatives.

King's Bench (K.B.) One of the superior courts of common law in England. If the monarch is a queen, the court is called Queen's Bench.

kiting See check kiting.

knock-and-announce rule Police must announce their presence before forcibly entering premises to be searched. An exception (called the useless-gesture exception) exists if the occupants already know why the police are there.

knock down Final acceptance of a bid by an auctioneer.

knowingly With awareness or understanding; conscious or deliberate; intentionally.

knowledge Acquaintance with fact or truth. Understanding obtained by experience or study. Awareness.

For purposes of criminal law, knowledge is not identical with intent; it is, nevertheless, a mental state. *People v. Valenzuela*, 112 Cal.Rptr.2d 209 (Cal.App., 2001)

L

labor Mental or physical exertion or work, usually for a wage.

Labor includes labor, work, or service whether rendered or performed under contract, subcontract, partnership, station plan, or other agreement if the labor to be paid for is performed personally by the person demanding payment. Cal. Labor Code § 200(b)

labor contract A collective bargaining agreement between a union and an employer covering wages, conditions of labor, and related matters.

laborer's lien A lien on property of someone responsible for paying for the work of a laborer on that property.

Labor-Management Relations Act The federal statute that covers procedures to settle strikes involving national emergencies, protects employees who do not want to join the union, and imposes other restrictions on unions (29 USC § 141). Also called Taft-Hartley Act.

labor organization A union.

labor union See union.

laches A party's unreasonable delay in asserting a legal or equitable right and another's detrimental good-faith change in position because of the delay.

An unreasonable delay in asserting an equitable right, causing prejudice to an adverse party such as to render the granting of relief to the other party inequitable. *Nicolopulos*, 130 Cal.Rptr.2d 626 (Cal.App., 2003)

lading See bill of lading.

LAMA See International Paralegal Management Association (*www.paralegalmanagement.org*).

lame duck 1. An elected official still in office who has not been or cannot be reelected. 2. A member of a stock exchange who has overbought and cannot meet his or her obligations.

lame duck session A legislative session conducted after the election of new members but before they are installed.

land 1. The surface of the earth, anything growing or permanently attached to it, the airspace above the earth, and what exists beneath the surface. 2. An interest in real property.

land bank A federally created bank under the Federal Farm Loan Act organized to make loans on farm land at low interest rates.

land grant A gift or donation of public land by the government to an individual, corporation, or other government.

landlord The owner who leases land, buildings, or apartments to another. Also called lessor.

landlord's lien The right of a landlord to levy upon goods of a tenant in satisfaction of unpaid rents or property damage.

landmark 1. A monument or other marker set up on the boundary line of two adjoining estates to fix such boundary. 2. Historically important. A landmark case establishes new and significant legal principles.

land sales contract See contract for deed.

land trust A trust that gives legal and equitable title of real property to a trustee but management and control of the property to the trust beneficiary. Also called Illinois Land Trust.

land use planning The use of zoning laws, environmental impact studies, and coordination efforts to develop the interrelated aspects of a community's physical environment and its social and economic activities.

lapping Theft of cash receipts from a customer that is covered up by crediting someone else's receipts to that customer.

lapse 1. To end because of a failure to use or a failure to fulfill a condition. 2. To fail to vest because of the death of the prospective beneficiary before the death of the donor. 3. A slip, mistake, or error. 4. A period of time.

lapsed Expired; no longer effective.

larcenous Having the character of or contemplating larceny.

larceny The wrongful taking and carrying away of another's personal property with the intention to deprive the possessor of it permanently.

Chapter 5. Larceny [Theft] Theft defined. Every person who shall feloniously steal, take, carry, lead, or drive away the personal property of another. . . . Cal. Penal Code § 484(a)

larceny by trick Larceny by using fraud or false pretenses to induce the victim to give up possession (but not title) to personal property.

lascivious Tending to incite lust; obscene.

last antecedent rule Qualifying words will be applied only to the word or phrase immediately preceding unless the qualifying words were clearly intended to apply to other language in the document as well.

last clear chance doctrine A plaintiff who has been contributorily negligent in placing himself or herself in peril can still recover if the negligent defendant had the last opportunity (clear chance) to avoid the accident and failed to exercise reasonable care to do so. Also called discovered peril doctrine, humanitarian doctrine, supervening negligence.

(1) The plaintiff by his own negligence has put himself in a helpless position; (2) the defendant knew that plaintiff was in a position of helpless peril; and (3) the defendant thereafter had a last clear chance to avoid the accident, not a mere possible chance. *Gillingham*, 69 Cal.Rptr. 728 (Cal.App., 1968)

last in, first out (LIFO) An accounting assumption that the last goods purchased are the first ones sold or used.

last resort The end of the appeal process, referring to a court from which there is no further appeal.

last will The testator's most recent will before dying.

latent Concealed; dormant or not active.

latent ambiguity A lack of clarity in otherwise clear language that arises when some extrinsic evidence creates a necessity for interpretation.

Ambiguity in document is a latent ambiguity if resorting to extrinsic evidence reveals that what appears to be perfectly clear language is in fact susceptible of more than one reasonable interpretation. *Los Angeles City Employees Union,* 220 Cal.Rptr. 411 (Cal.App., 1985)

latent defect See hidden defect.

lateral support right The right to have land in its natural state supported by adjoining land.

laundering Concealing or disguising the source or origin of something (e.g., money) that was obtained illegally.

law 1. A rule of action or conduct prescribed by a controlling authority and having binding force. 2. The aggregate body of rules governing society. 3. The legal profession.

law clerk 1. An attorney's employee who is in law school studying to be an attorney or is waiting to pass the bar examination. 2. One who provides research and writing assistance to a judge.

law day 1. The date on which a mortgagor can avoid foreclosure by paying the debt on the mortgaged property. 2. May 1st, the date each year set aside to honor our legal system.

law enforcement officer Someone empowered by law to investigate crime, make arrests for violations of the criminal law, and preserve the peace.

lawful Legal, authorized by law.

law journal A legal periodical of a law school or bar association. See also law review.

law list A list or directory of attorneys containing brief information relevant to their practice.

law merchant The practices and customs of those engaged in commerce that developed into what is known today as commercial law.

law of nations See international law.

law of nature See natural law.

law of the case doctrine An appellate court's determination of a legal issue binds both the trial court and the court on appeal in any subsequent appeal involving the same case and substantially the same facts.

The decision of an appellate court, stating a rule of law necessary to the decision of the case, conclusively establishes that rule and makes it determinative of the rights of the same parties in any subsequent retrial or appeal in the same case. *Bell,* 9 Cal.Rptr.3d 544 (Cal.App., 2004)

law of the land 1. The law that applies in a country, state or region. 2. Due process of law and related constitutional protections.

law of the road Traffic laws.

law reports, law reporters See reporter (3), report (2).

law review (L. Rev.) A legal periodical (usually student-edited) published by a law school. Also called law journal.

Law School Admission Test (LSAT) A standardized aptitude test used by many law schools in making decisions on admission.

lawsuit A court proceeding that asserts a legal claim or dispute. Also called a suit.

lawyer See attorney (1).

lay 1. Nonprofessional; not having expertise. 2. Nonecclesiastical; not belonging to the clergy. 3. To state or allege in a pleading.

layaway A seller's agreement with a consumer to hold goods for sale at a later date at a specified price.

layoff A temporary or permanent termination of employment at the will of the employer.

lay witness A person giving only fact or lay (not expert) opinion testimony.

LBO See leveraged buyout.

lead counsel The attorney managing the case of a client with several attorneys. The primary attorney in a class action.

leading case An opinion that has had an important influence in the development of the law on a particular point.

leading question A question to someone being interviewed or examined that suggests the answer within the question.

A leading question is a question that suggests to the witness the answer that the examining party desires. Cal. Evidence Code § 764

learned intermediary See informed intermediary.

lease 1. A contract for the use or possession of real or personal property for a designated rent or other consideration. Ownership of the property is not transferred. 2. To let or rent.

leaseback The sale of property to a buyer who gives the seller the right to lease the property from the buyer. Also called sale and leaseback.

leasehold An estate in real property held by a tenant/lessee under a lease; property held by a lease.

Leasehold is an estate in land and an interest in real property and lease is primarily a conveyance in that it transfers an estate to lessee. *Evans,* 42 Cal.Rptr. 133 (Cal.App., 1965)

leave 1. To give in a will; to bequeath. 2. To withdraw or depart. 3. Permission to do something, e.g., to be absent from work or military service.

ledger A book used to record business transactions.

legacy 1. Any gift in a will. 2. A gift of personal property in a will. 3. Something handed down from an ancestor.

legal 1. Authorized, required, permitted, or involving the law. 2. Pertaining to law rather than to equity.

legal age See age of consent, age of majority, age of reason.

legal aid A system (often government-funded) of providing legal services to people who cannot afford counsel.

legal assistant See paralegal.

legal cap Long ruled paper in tablet form.

legal capital The par or stated value of outstanding stock. Also called stated capital.

legal cause See proximate cause.

Legal cause exists if the actor's conduct is a substantial factor in bringing about the harm and there is no rule of law relieving the actor from liability. *Anaya,* 93 Cal.Rptr.2d 228 (Cal.App., 2000)

legal certainty test A court will find federal diversity jurisdiction on the basis of the plaintiff's complaint unless it appears to a legal certainty that the claim is for less than the jurisdictional amount.

legal conclusion A statement of legal consequences, often without including the facts from which the consequences arise. See also conclusion of law.

legal consideration See valuable consideration.

legal custody 1. The right and duty to make decisions about raising a child. 2. The detention of someone by the government.

legal death See brain death, civil death.

legal description A description of real property by various methods (e.g., by metes and bounds), including a description of portions subject to any easements or other restrictions.

legal detriment See detriment.

legal discretion See judicial discretion.

legal duty See duty (2).

legal entity An artificial person (e.g., a corporation) that functions in some ways as a natural person (e.g., it can sue and be sued).

legalese Technical language or jargon used by attorneys.

legal ethics Rules that embody the minimum standards of behavior to which members of the legal profession are expected to conform.

[T]he fundamental rule of [legal] ethics—that of common honesty—without which the profession is worse than valueless. . . . *In re Davis*, 2003 WL 21904732 (Cal.Bar, 2003)

legal fiction An assumption of fact made by a court in order to dispose of a matter with justice even though the fact may not be true.

legal fraud See constructive fraud.

legal heir See heir (1).

legal holiday A day designated as a holiday by the legislature. A day on which court proceedings and service of process cannot occur.

legal impossibility A defense asserting that the defendant's intended acts, even if completed, would not amount to a crime.

The defense of impossibility means a legal impossibility. *People v. Fratianno*, 282 P.2d 1002 (Cal.App., 1955)

legal injury An invasion of a person's legally protected interest.

legal interest 1. A legally protected right or claim. A legal share of something. 2. A rate of interest authorized by law.

legal investments Those investments, sometimes called legal lists, in which banks and other financial institutions may invest.

legal issue A legal question. See also issue of law.

legality 1. Lawfulness; the state of being in accordance with law. 2. A technical legal requirement.

legalize To declare or make legal that which was once illegal.

legal list See legal investments.

legal malice 1. Pertaining to wrongful conduct committed or continued with a willful or reckless disregard for another's rights. 2. Malice that is inferred. Also called implied malice.

legal malpractice The failure of an attorney to use such skill, prudence, and diligence as reasonable attorneys of ordinary skill and capacity commonly possess and exercise under the same circumstances. Professional misconduct or wrongdoing by attorneys.

Elements of cause of action for legal malpractice are: lawyer's duty to use such skill, prudence and diligence as members of the profession commonly possess, breach of that duty, proximate causal connection between the breach and resulting injury, and actual loss or damage. *Younan*, 59 Cal.Rptr.2d 103 (Cal.App., 1996)

legal name The designation of a person or entity recognized by the law.

legal notice Notification of something in a manner prescribed by law.

legal opinion An attorney's interpretation (often in writing) of how the law applies to facts in a client's case.

legal positivism The legal theory that the validity of laws is based, not on natural law or morality, but on being duly enacted or decreed by the three branches of government and accepted by society.

legal proceedings Formal actions in court or administrative tribunals to establish legal rights or resolve legal disputes.

legal question See issue of law.

legal realism The legal theory that the development of law in court opinions is based on public policy and social science considerations rather than on a pure or rigid legal analysis of rules.

legal representative One who represents the legal interests of another, e.g., one who is incapacitated.

legal reserve Assets that a business (e.g., insurance company, bank) must set aside to be available to meet the demands of its customers.

legal residence The residence required by law for legal purposes, e.g., receipt of process. See also domicile (3).

legal separation A court order allowing spouses to live separately and establishing their rights and duties while separated, but still married. Also called divorce a mensa et thoro, judicial separation, limited divorce.

legal technician See independent paralegal.

legal tender Coins and currencies that can be used to pay debts.

legal title 1. A title that is recognizable and enforceable in a court of law. 2. A title that provides the right of ownership but no beneficial interest in the property. See also beneficial interest.

legatee The person to whom personal property (and sometimes real property) is given by will.

legation A diplomatic mission; the staff and premises of such a mission.

legislate To enact laws through legislation. To make or pass a law.

legislation 1. The enactment of laws by a legislative body. 2. Law or laws passed by a legislature. 3. A statute; a body of statutes.

Legislation means a bill, resolution, or constitutional amendment. Cal. Government Code § 87102.5

legislative Pertaining to the enactment of laws by a legislative body.

legislative council A body that plans legislative strategy, primarily between sessions of the legislature.

legislative counsel The person or office that assists legislators by conducting research and drafting proposed legislation.

legislative court See Article I court.

legislative history Hearings, debates, reports, and all other events that occur in the legislature before a bill is enacted into a statute.

legislative immunity An immunity from civil suit enjoyed by a member of the legislature while engaged in legislative functions.

legislative intent The design, aim, end, or plan of the legislature in passing a particular statute.

legislative rule A rule of an administrative agency based on its quasi-legislative power. An administrative rule that creates rights or assigns duties rather than merely interprets a governing statute. Also called substantive rule.

legislative veto A legislative method of rejecting administrative action. The agency's action (e.g., a rule) would be valid unless nullified by resolutions of the legislature. On the unconstitutionality of such vetoes, see *INS v. Chadha*, 103 S. Ct. 2764 (1983).

legislator A member of a legislative body.

legislature The assembly or body of persons that makes statutory laws for a state or nation.

Legislature includes any Member of the Legislature, any legislative officer, any standing, joint, or select committee or subcommittee of the Senate and Assembly, and any other agency or employee of the Legislature. Cal. Government Code § 9072

legitimacy 1. The condition of being born within a marriage or acquiring this condition through steps provided by law. 2. The condition of being in compliance with the law or with established standards.

legitimate 1. Lawful, valid, or genuine. 2. Born to married parents or to parents who have legitimated the child.

legitimation 1. Making legitimate or lawful. 2. The procedure of legalizing (legitimating) the status of an illegitimate child.

legitime A portion of decedent's estate that must be reserved for a forced heir such as a child. See also forced heir.

lemon law A law giving a buyer of a new car with major defects the right to a refund or to have it replaced.

lend 1. To provide money to another for a period of time, often for an interest charge. 2. To give something of value to another for a fixed or indefinite time, with or without compensation, with the expectation that it will be returned.

lese majesty A crime against the sovereign, e.g., treason. Also spelled leze majesty.

lessee A person who rents or leases property from another. A tenant.

lesser included offense A crime composed solely of some but not all of the elements of a greater crime so that it would be impossible to commit the greater offense without committing the lesser. Also called included offense.

An offense is a lesser included offense if either the statutory elements of the greater offense, or the facts actually alleged in the accusatory pleading, include all the elements of the lesser offense, such that the greater cannot be committed without also committing the lesser. *People v. Medina*, 31 Cal.Rptr.3d 772 (Cal.App., 2005)

lessor A person who rents or leases property to another. A landlord.

let 1. To allow. 2. To lease or rent. 3. To award a contract to one of the bidders.

lethal weapon See deadly weapon.

letter A writing that grants a power, authority, or right.

letter of attornment A letter to a tenant stating that the premises have been sold and that rent should be paid to the new owner.

letter of credit (LOC) An engagement by a bank or other issuer (made at the request of a customer) to honor demands for payment by a third party upon compliance with conditions stated in the letter. Also called circular note.

A documentary letter of credit is a method of payment whereby the promise of a stable financial source, usually a bank, is substituted for the promise of a credit applicant, usually a purchaser of goods. *DBJJJ, Inc.*, 19 Cal.Rptr.3d 904 (Cal.App., 2004)

letter of intent (LOI) A nonbinding writing that states preliminary understandings of one or both parties to a possible future contract.

letter rogatory A court's request to a court in a foreign jurisdiction for assistance in a pending case, e.g., to take the testimony of a witness in the other jurisdiction.

Whenever any mandate, writ, letters rogatory, letter of request, or commission is issued out of any court of record in any other state, territory, or district of the United States, or in a foreign nation, or whenever, on notice or agreement, it is required to take the oral or written deposition of a natural person in California, the deponent may be compelled to appear and testify, and to produce documents and things, in the same manner, and by the same process as may be employed for the purpose of taking testimony in actions pending in California. Cal. Code of Civil Procedure § 2029.010

letter ruling A written statement issued to a taxpayer by the IRS that interprets and applies the tax laws to a specific set of facts.

letters of administration The court document that authorizes a person to manage the estate of someone who has died without a valid will.

letters of marque A government authorization to a private citizen to seize assets of a foreign country.

letters patent A public document issued by the government that grants a right, e.g., a right to the sole use of an invention.

letters testamentary A formal document issued by a court that empowers a person to act as an executor of a will.

letter stock See restricted security.

levari facias A writ of execution to satisfy a party's judgment debt out of his or her profits and other assets.

leverage 1. The use of credit or debt to increase profits and purchasing power. The use of a smaller investment to generate a larger rate of return through borrowing. 2. Added power or influence.

leveraged buyout (LBO) Taking over a company by using borrowed funds for a substantial part of the purchase. The sale of a corporation in which at least part of the purchase price is obtained through debt assumed by the corporation.

levy 1. To assess or impose a tax, charge, or fine. 2. To seize assets in order to satisfy a claim. 3. To conscript into the military. 4. To wage or carry on. 5. A tax, charge, or fine.

Levy has various meanings and must be determined in its context. *Alpha Beta Acme Markets*, 68 Cal.Rptr. 327 (Cal.App., 1968). Levy, in context of execution on real property, is merely the act by which property to be taken and sold is designated or set aside. *Grothe*, 15 Cal.Rptr.2d 38 (Cal.App., 1992)

lewd Indecent, obscene; inciting to lustful desire.

lex Law or a collection of laws.

lex fori The law of the forum where the suit is brought.

LexisNexis A fee-based legal research computer service.

lex loci contractus The law of the place where the contract was formed or will be performed.

lex loci delicti The law of the place where the wrong (e.g., the tort) took place.

leze majesty See lese majesty.

liability 1. The condition of being legally responsible for a loss, penalty, debt, or other obligation. 2. The obligation owed.

liability insurance Insurance in which an insurer pays covered damages the insured is obligated to pay a third person.

liability without fault See strict liability.

liable Obligated in law; legally responsible.

libel 1. A defamatory statement expressed in writing or other graphic or visual form such as by pictures or signs. See also defamation. 2. A plaintiff's pleading in an admiralty or ecclesiastical court.

Two forms of defamation are slander or libel; slander requires an oral utterance while libel requires a publication. Cal. Civil Code §§ 44–46. *Joel*, 80 Cal.Rptr.2d 247 (Cal.App., 1998)

libelant The complainant in an admiralty or ecclesiastical court.

libelee The defendant in an admiralty or ecclesiastical court.

libelous Defamatory; constituting or involving libel.

libel per quod A writing that requires extrinsic facts to understand its defamatory meaning. Libel that requires proof of special damages.

libel per se A written defamatory statement that is actionable without proof that the plaintiff suffered special damages. Libel that is defamatory on its face.

If a defamatory meaning appears from the language itself without the necessity of explanation or the pleading of extrinsic facts, there is libel per se. *Palm Springs Tennis Club*, 86 Cal.Rptr.2d 73 (Cal.App., 1999)

liberal construction An expansive or broad interpretation of the meaning of a statute or other law to include facts or cases that are within the spirit and reason of the law.

liberty 1. Freedom from excessive or oppressive restrictions imposed by the state or other authority. 2. A basic right or privilege.

license 1. Permission to do what would otherwise be illegal or a tort. 2. The document that evidences this permission.

licensee 1. One who enters land for his or her own purposes or benefit, but with the express or implied consent of the owner or occupier of the land. 2. One who has a license.

A licensee is a person who is privileged to enter upon land by virtue of possessor's consent or permission, usually for purposes of his own, having no relation to business of owner or occupant. *Hardin*, 42 Cal.Rptr. 748 (Cal.App., 1965)

licensor One who gives or grants a license.

licentious Without moral restraint. Disregarding sexual morality.

licit Permitted by law, legal.

lie 1. A deliberately or intentionally false statement. 2. To make a false statement intentionally. 3. To be sustainable in law.

lie detector See polygraph.

lien A charge, security, or encumbrance on property; a creditor's claim or charge on property for the payment of a debt.

lien creditor One whose claim is secured by a lien on particular property of the debtor.

lienee One whose property is subject to a lien.

lienholder; lienor One who has a lien on the property of another.

life annuity An annuity that guarantees payments for the life of the annuitant.

life-care contract A contract (often with a nursing care facility) to provide designated health services and living care for the remainder of a person's life in exchange for an up-front payment.

life estate An estate in property whose duration is limited to the life of an individual. Also called estate for life, life tenancy.

A life estate is an estate whose duration is limited to life of person holding it or some other person. *In re Smythe's Estate*, 282 P.2d 141 (Cal.App., 1955)

life estate pur autre vie A life estate whose duration is measured by the life of someone other than the possessor of the estate. Also called estate pur autre vie.

life expectancy The number of years a person of a given age and sex is expected to live according to statistics.

life in being The remaining length of time in the life of a person who is in existence at the time that a future interest is created.

life insurance A contract for the payment of a specified amount to a designated beneficiary upon the death of the person insured.

Life insurance means insurance upon the lives of persons or appertaining thereto. Cal. Insurance Code § 10509.953

life interest An interest in property whose duration is limited to the life of the party holding the interest or of some other person.

life tenant One who possesses a life estate. A tenant for life.

LIFO See last in, first out.

lift To rescind or stop.

like-kind exchange The exchange of property held for productive use in a trade or business or for investment on which no gain or loss shall be recognized if such property is exchanged solely for property of like kind or character that is to be held either for productive use in a trade or business or for investment (26 USC § 1031).

limine See in limine, motion in limine.

limitation 1. Restriction. 2. The time allowed by statute for bringing an action at the risk of losing it. See also statute of limitations.

limited (Ltd.) 1. Restricted in duration or scope. 2. A designation indicating that a business is a company with limited liability.

limited admissibility Allowing evidence to be considered for isolated or restricted purposes.

limited divorce See legal separation.

limited jurisdiction The power of a court to hear only certain kinds of cases. Also called special jurisdiction.

limited liability Restricted liability; liability that can be satisfied out of business assets, not out of personal assets.

limited-liability company (L.L.C.) A hybrid business entity with features of a corporation and a partnership. The company has a legal existence separate from its members/owners who can participate in the management of the company and have limited liability.

A limited liability company is a hybrid business entity formed under the Corporations Code and consisting of at least two members who own membership interests. *Denevi*, 18 Cal.Rptr.3d 276 (Cal.App., 2004). Cal. Corporations Code § 17001

limited-liability partnership (L.L.P.) A type of partnership in which a partner has unlimited liability for his or her wrongdoing but not for the wrongdoing of other partners.

limited partner A partner who takes no part in running the business and who incurs no liability for partnership obligations beyond the contribution he or she invested in the partnership.

limited partnership (L.P.) A type of partnership consisting of one or more general partners who manage the business and who are personally liable for partnership debts, and one or more limited partners who take no part in running the business and who incur no liability for partnership obligations beyond the contribution they invested in the partnership.

"Limited partnership" means a partnership formed by two or more persons having as members one or more general partners and one or more limited partners. Cal. Business & Professions Code § 19805(w)

limited power of appointment A power of appointment that restricts who can receive property under the power or under what conditions anyone can receive it. Also called special power of appointment.

limited publication The distribution of a work to a selected group for a limited purpose, and without the right of reproduction, distribution, or sale.

limited purpose public figure See public figure.

limited warranty A warranty that does not cover all defects or does not cover the full cost of repair.

lineage Line of descent from a common ancestor.

lineal Proceeding in a direct or unbroken line; from a common ancestor.

lineal heir One who inherits in a line either ascending or descending from a common source, as distinguished from a collateral heir.

line item veto The chief executive's rejection of part of a bill passed by the legislature, allowing the rest to become law with his or her signature.

line of credit The maximum amount of money that can be borrowed or goods that can be purchased on credit. Also called credit line.

lineup A group of people, including the suspect, shown at one time to a witness, who is asked if he or she can identify the person who committed the crime. The procedure is called a showup if the witness is shown only one person.

Lineup is a relatively formalized procedure wherein a suspect, who is generally already in custody, is placed among a group of other persons whose general appearance resembles the suspect; the result is essentially a test of the reliability of the victim's identification and the requirement of counsel's presence encourages the police to adopt regulations ensuring the fairness of such procedures. *People v. Dampier*, 205 Cal.Rptr. 728 (Cal.App., 1984)

link-in-chain principle The privilege against self-incrimination covers questions that could indirectly connect (link) someone to a crime.

liquid Consisting of cash or what can easily be converted into cash.

liquidate 1. To pay and settle a debt. 2. To wind up the affairs of a business or estate by identifying assets, converting them into cash, and paying off liabilities.

liquidated claim A claim as to which the parties have already agreed what the damages will be or what method will be used to calculate the damages that will be paid.

liquidated damages An amount the parties agree will be the damages if a breach of contract occurs. Also called stipulated damages.

Liquidated damages are a sum that the contracting parties agree will be forfeited upon a breach. *ABI, Inc.*, 200 Cal.Rptr. 563 (Cal.App., 1984)

liquidity The condition of being readily convertible into cash.

lis pendens 1. A pending lawsuit. 2. A recorded notice that an action has been filed affecting the title to or right to possession of the real property described in the notice. Also called notice of pendency. 3. Jurisdiction or control that courts acquire over property involved in a pending lawsuit.

list 1. A court's case docket. 2. A series or registry of names. 3. See listing.

listed security A security that is bought or sold on an exchange.

listing 1. A contract between an owner of real property and a real estate agent authorizing the latter to find a buyer or tenant in return for a fee or commission. 2. A contract between a firm and a stock exchange, covering the trading of that firm's securities on the stock exchange. 3. Making a schedule or inventory.

A listing is at most an offer to use services of broker that can be accepted by rendering the services impliedly requested. *Hooper*, 251 P.2d 330 (Cal.App., 1952)

list price The published or advertised retail price of goods.

literal construction See strict construction.

literary property 1. The corporal or physical embodiment (e.g., a book) of an intellectual production. 2. The exclusive right of an owner to possess, use, and dispose of his or her intellectual productions.

literary works Under copyright law, works, "expressed in words, numbers, or other verbal or numerical symbols or indicia, regardless of the nature of the material objects, such as books, periodicals, manuscripts, phonorecords, film, tapes, disks, or cards, in which they are embodied." Audiovisual works are not included. (17 USC § 101).

litigant A party in litigation.

litigate To resolve a dispute or seek relief in a court of law.

litigation 1. The formal process of resolving a legal dispute through the courts. 2. A lawsuit.

litigious Prone to engage in disputes and litigation.

littoral Concerning or belonging to the shore or coast.

A littoral right is a right attaching to land abutting a natural lake or pond, and accords that land the same status as a riparian right. *Tusher*, 80 Cal.Rptr.2d 126 (Cal.App., 1998)

livery of seisin A ceremony to transfer legal title of land (e.g., deliver a twig, as a symbol of the whole land).

living apart As a ground for divorce, the spouses live separately for a designated period of consecutive time with no present intention of resuming marital relations.

living trust See inter vivos trust.

living will A formal document that expresses a person's desire not to be kept alive through artificial or extraordinary means if in the future he or she suffers from a terminal condition.

LL.B.; LL.M.; LL.D. Law degrees: bachelor of laws (LL.B.), master of laws (LL.M.), doctor of laws (LL.D.). See also Juris Doctor.

LKA Last known address.

L.L.C. See limited-liability company.

L.L.P. See limited-liability partnership.

load The charge added to the cost of insurance or securities to cover commissions and administrative expenses. See also no-load.

loan 1. Anything furnished for temporary use. 2. The act of lending.

A loan is delivery of sum of money to another under contract to return at some future time an equivalent amount with or without additional sum agreed upon for its use. *Golden State Lanes*, 42 Cal.Rptr. 568 (Cal.App., 1965)

loan commitment An enforceable promise to make a loan for a specified amount on specified terms.

loaned servant doctrine When an employer lends its employee to another employer for some special service, the employee becomes (for purposes of respondeat superior liability) the employee of the party to whom he or she has been loaned with respect to that service.

loan for consumption A contract in which a lender delivers to a borrower goods that are consumed by use, with the understanding that the borrower will return to the lender goods of the same kind, quantity, and quality.

loan for use A loan of personal property for normal use and then returned.

loan ratio The ratio, expressed as a percentage, of the amount of a loan to the value of the real property that is security for the loan.

loansharking Lending money at excessive rates with the threat or actual use of force to obtain repayment.

loan value The maximum amount one is allowed to borrow on a life insurance policy or other property.

lobbying Attempts to influence the policy decisions of a public official, particularly a legislator.

lobbyist One in the business of lobbying.

local action An action that must be brought in a particular state or county, e.g., where the land in dispute is located.

local agent A person who takes care of a company's business in a particular area or district.

local assessment A tax upon property in a limited area for improvements (e.g., sidewalk repair) that will benefit property within that area.

local law 1. A law that is limited to a specific geographic region of the state. 2. The law of one jurisdiction, usually referring to a jurisdiction other than the one where a case is in litigation.

local option The right of a city or other local government to accept or reject a particular policy, e.g., Sunday liquor sales.

local union A unit or branch of a larger labor union.

lockdown The confinement of inmates to their cells or dorms, usually as a security measure.

lockout Withholding work from employees or temporarily closing a business due to a labor dispute.

lockup A place of detention in a police station, court, or other facility while awaiting further official action. A holding cell.

loco parentis See in loco parentis.

locus A locality. The place where a thing occurs or exists.

locus contractus The place where the last act is performed that makes an agreement a binding contract.

locus delicti The place of the wrong. The place where the last event occurred that was necessary to make the party liable.

The statutory, not constitutional, concept of a right to be tried in the county in which the crime was committed. Cal. Penal Code § 777. *People v. Sering*, 283 Cal.Rptr. 507 (Cal.App., 1991)

locus in quo The place or scene of the occurrence or event.

locus poenitentiae The last opportunity to reconsider and withdraw before legal consequences (civil or criminal) occur.

locus sigilli (L.S.) The place where a document's seal is placed.

lodestar A method of calculating an award of attorney fees authorized by statute. The number of reasonable hours spent on a case is multiplied by a reasonable hourly rate. Sometimes considered above the lodestar are the quality of representation and the risk that there would be no fee.

Lodestar is the basic fee for comparable legal services in the community; it may be adjusted by the court based on factors including: (1) the novelty and difficulty of the questions involved; (2) the skill displayed in presenting them; (3) the extent to which the nature of the litigation precluded other employment by the attorneys; and (4) the contingent nature of the fee award. *Ketchum*, 104 Cal.Rptr.2d 377 (CA 2001)

lodger One who uses a dwelling without acquiring exclusive possession or a property interest, e.g., one who lives in a spare room of a house.

logrolling Trading political votes or favors.

LOI See letter of intent.

loitering Remaining idle in essentially one place. Walking about aimlessly.

Loitering proscribed by statute making it unlawful to loiter or wander upon streets or from place to place without apparent reason or business connotes lingering in designated places for purpose of committing crime as opportunity may be discovered and excludes notion of waiting for lawful purpose. Cal. Penal Code, § 647(e). *People v. Caylor*, 85 Cal.Rptr. 497 (Cal.App., 1970)

long Holding securities or commodities in the hope that prices will rise.

long-arm statute A statutory method of obtaining personal jurisdiction by substituted service of process over a nonresident defendant who has sufficient purposeful contact with a state.

long-term capital gain The gain (profit) realized on the sale or exchange of a capital asset held for the required period of time.

lookout 1. Keeping careful watch. 2. One who keeps careful watch.

Lord Campbell's Act A statute giving certain relatives of a decedent a wrongful-death claim for a tort that caused the death of the decedent.

Lord Mansfield's rule Testimony of either spouse is inadmissible on whether the husband had access to the wife at the time of conception if such evidence would tend to declare the child to be illegitimate.

loser-pays See American rule.

loss 1. Damage, detriment, or disadvantage to person or property. 2. The amount by which expenses exceed revenues. 3. The amount by which the basis of property exceeds what is received for it.

loss leader An item sold by a merchant at a low price (e.g., below cost) in order to entice people to come into the store.

loss of bargain rule See benefit of the bargain rule.

loss of consortium Interference with the companionship, services, affection, and sexual relations one spouse receives from another.

The loss of certain rights and privileges inhering in the marital relationship, including companionship, emotional support, love, and sexual relations. *Zwicker*, 118 Cal.Rptr.2d 912 (Cal.App., 2002)

loss payable clause An insurance clause designating someone other than the insured to receive insurance proceeds.

loss ratio The ratio between claims paid out and premiums received by an insurance company.

lost property Property that the owner has parted with through neglect or inadvertence and the whereabouts of which is unknown to the owner.

lost-volume seller A seller who, upon a buyer's breach, resells the goods to a second buyer who would have bought the same kind of goods from the seller even if the first buyer had not breached.

lost will A decedent's executed will that cannot be located.

lot 1. One of several parcels into which real property is divided. 2. A number of associated persons or things taken collectively. 3. A number of units of something offered for sale or traded as one item. 4. The shares purchased in one transaction.

lottery A scheme for the distribution of prizes by chance for which a participant pays something of value to enter.

Lottery is defined by three elements: a prize, distribution by chance, and consideration; "consideration" is the fee that a participant pays the operator for entrance; "chance" means that winning and losing depend on luck and fortune rather than or at least more than, judgment and skill; and "prize" encompasses property that the operator offers to distribute to one or more winning participants and not to keep for himself. *Hotel Employees and Restaurant Employees Intern. Union*, 88 Cal.Rptr.2d 56 (CA 1999)

lower court See inferior court.

L. Rev. See law review.

L.P. See Limited partnership.

LSAT See Law School Admission Test.

Ltd. See limited.

lucid interval A temporary restoration to sanity, during which an insane person has sufficient intelligence to enter a contract.

lucrative title Title acquired without giving consideration.

lucri causa The intent to derive profit. For the sake of gain.

lump-sum alimony See alimony in gross.

lump-sum payment A single amount paid at one time.

lunacy See insanity (1).

luxury tax An excise tax on expensive, nonessential goods.

lying in wait Waiting and watching for an opportune time to inflict bodily harm on another by surprise.

To constitute lying in wait within statute declaring murder perpetrated by lying in wait first degree murder, elements of waiting, watching and concealment must be present. Cal. Penal Code, § 189. *People v. Merkouris*, 297 P.2d 999 (CA 1956)

lynch law Seizing persons suspected of crimes and summarily punishing them without legal trial or authority.

M

MACRS See Modified Accelerated Cost Recovery System.

magistrate 1. A judicial officer who has some but not all the powers of a judge. Also called referee. In federal court, the duties of a United States Magistrate were once performed by a United States Commissioner. 2. A public civic officer with executive power.

Authority of a magistrate is purely statutory; a magistrate is not a judge. *People v. Miskiewicz*, 204 Cal.Rptr. 873 (Cal.App., 1984)

magistrate court An inferior court with limited jurisdiction over minor civil or criminal matters. Also called police court.

Magna Carta The Great Charter of 1215, considered the foundation of constitutional liberty in England.

mail box rule 1. The proper and timely mailing of a document raises a rebuttable presumption that the document has been received by the addressee in the usual time. 2. A prisoner's court papers are deemed filed when given to the proper prison authorities. 3. A contract is formed upon the act of mailing where the use of the mail is authorized by both parties.

mail fraud The use of the U.S. Postal Service to obtain money by false pretenses or to commit other acts of fraud (18 USC § 1341).

mail-order divorce Obtaining a divorce from a state or country with no jurisdiction to award it, because, for example, neither spouse was domiciled there.

maim The infliction of a serious (and often disabling) bodily injury.

main purpose rule Under the statute of frauds, contracts to answer for the debt of another must be in writing *unless* the main purpose of the promisor's undertaking is his or her own benefit or protection.

This exception to the statute of frauds, concerning a benefit to the defendant himself, upon having promised to answer to the debt of another, has been called the main purpose rule. *Seneca Communications*, 163 Cal.Rptr. 176 (Cal.App., 1980)

maintain 1. To make repairs or perform upkeep tasks. 2. To bear the expenses for the support of. 3. To declare or affirm. 4. To continue or carry forward. 5. To involve oneself or meddle in another's lawsuit.

maintenance 1. Support or assistance. See also separate maintenance. 2. Keeping something in working order. 3. Becoming involved or meddling in someone else's lawsuit.

major dispute A dispute under the Railway Labor Act that relates to the formation or alteration of a collective bargaining agreement (45 USC § 155).

major federal action Projects that require an environmental impact statement because of their significant environmental effects.

majority 1. The age at which a person is entitled to the management of his or her own affairs and to the enjoyment of adult civil rights. 2. Greater than half of any total.

majority opinion The opinion in which more than half of the voting judges on the court joined.

make To formalize the creation of an instrument; to execute.

make law 1. To enact a law. To legislate. 2. To establish or expand upon a prior legal principle or rule in a court opinion.

maker One who signs a promissory note or other negotiable instrument.

make-whole rule An insurer cannot enforce subrogation rights against settlement funds until the insured is fully compensated (made whole). An insured who settles with a third-party tortfeasor is liable to the insurer-subrogee only for any excess received over the total amount of the insured's loss.

mala fides See bad faith (1).

mala in se See malum in se.

mala prohibita See malum prohibitum.

malefactor One who is guilty of a crime or offense. A wrongdoer.

malfeasance Wrongdoing, usually by a public official.

malice 1. The intentional doing of a wrongful act without just cause or excuse. 2. The intent to inflict injury; ill will. 3. Reckless or wanton disregard.

Malice giving rise to liability for punitive damages refers both to evil motive and to conduct evincing conscious disregard for probability that actor's conduct will result in injury to others. Cal. Civil Code §§ 3294. *Siva*, 194 Cal.Rptr. 51 (Cal.App., 1983)

malice aforethought 1. A fixed purpose or design to do some physical harm to another. 2. In a murder charge, the intention to kill, actual or implied, under circumstances that do not constitute excuse (e.g., insanity) or justification (e.g., self-defense) or mitigate the degree of the offense to manslaughter.

malice in fact See actual malice (1).

malice in law See implied malice.

malicious 1. Doing a wrongful act intentionally and without just cause or excuse. 2. Pertaining to conduct that is certain or almost certain to cause harm.

malicious mischief Intentional, wanton, or reckless damage or destruction of another's property. Also called criminal mischief.

malicious prosecution A tort with the following elements: (a) To initiate or procure the initiation of civil or criminal legal proceedings; (b) without probable cause; (c) with malice or an improper purpose; (d) the proceedings terminate in favor of the person against whom the proceedings were brought.

malpractice 1. The failure of a professional to exercise the degree of skill commonly applied under the circumstances by an ordinary, prudent, and reputable member of the profession in good standing. 2. Professional misconduct.

Malpractice (professional, nonmedical) Standard Of Care. A [insert type of professional] is negligent if [he/she] fails to use the skill and care that a reasonably careful [insert type of professional] would have used in similar circumstances. This level of skill, knowledge, and care is sometimes referred to as "the standard of care." California Civil Jury Instructions 600

malum in se A wrong in itself; an act that is inherently and essentially evil and immoral in its nature (plural: mala in se).

malum prohibitum An act that is wrong because laws prohibit it; the act is not wrong in itself (plural: mala prohibita).

manager One who administers an organization or project.

managing agent A person given general powers to exercise judgment and discretion in dealing with matters entrusted to him or her.

mandamus A court order or writ to a public official to compel the performance of a ministerial act or a mandatory duty.

A writ of mandate may be issued by any court to any inferior tribunal, corporation, board, or person, to compel the performance of an act which the law specially enjoins, as a duty resulting from an office, trust, or station, or to compel the admission of a party to the use and enjoyment of a right or office to which the party is entitled, and from which the party is unlawfully precluded by such inferior tribunal, corporation, board, or person. Cal. Code of Civil Procedure § 1085(a)

mandate 1. A court order, especially to a lower court. 2. To require. 3. An authorization to act.

mandatory Compulsory, obligatory.

mandatory injunction An injunction that requires an affirmative act or course of conduct.

mandatory instruction An instruction to the jury that if it finds that a certain set of facts (laid out by the judge) exists, then it must reach a verdict for one party and against the other. Also called binding instruction.

mandatory sentence A sentence of incarceration that, by statute, must be served; the judge has no discretion to order alternatives.

manifest 1. Evident to the senses, especially to sight. 2. A list of a vehicle's cargo or passengers.

manifest necessity Extraordinary circumstances requiring a mistrial; a retrial can occur without violating principles of double jeopardy.

manifesto A formal, public statement declaring policies or intentions.

manifest weight of the evidence, against the As a standard of review, an opposite finding is clearly called for; the verdict is unreasonable, arbitrary, or not based on the evidence.

manipulation Activity designed to deceive investors by controlling or artificially affecting the price of securities, e.g., creating a misleading appearance of active trading. Also called stock manipulation.

Mann Act A federal statute making it a crime to transport someone in interstate or foreign commerce for prostitution or other sexually immoral purpose (18 US. § 2421).

manslaughter The unlawful killing of another without malice.

Manslaughter is the unlawful killing of a human being without malice. It is of three kinds: (a) Voluntary—upon a sudden quarrel or heat of passion. (b) Involuntary—in the commission of an unlawful act, not amounting to felony; or in the commission of a lawful act which might produce death, in an unlawful manner, or without due caution and circumspection. This subdivision shall not apply to acts committed in the driving of a vehicle. (c) Vehicular. . . . Cal. Penal Code § 192

manual 1. Made or performed with the hands. 2. A book with basic practical information or procedures.

manumission The act of liberating a slave from bondage.

***Mapp* hearing** A hearing in a criminal case to determine whether seized evidence is admissible. *Mapp v. Ohio*, 81 S. Ct. 1684 (1961).

Marbury v. Madison The United States Supreme Court case that ruled that the courts can determine whether an act of Congress is constitutional. 5 U.S. 137 (1803).

margin 1. The edge or border. 2. An amount available beyond what is needed. 3. The difference between the cost and the selling price of a security. 4. An amount a buyer on credit must give to a securities broker to cover the broker's risk of loss. 5. The difference between the value of collateral securing a loan and the amount of the loan.

margin account An account allowing a client to borrow money from a securities broker in order to buy more stock, using the stock as collateral.

margin call A demand by a broker that a customer deposit additional collateral to cover broker-financed purchases of securities.

marijuana or **marihuana** A drug prepared from cannabis plant leaves.

marine insurance Insurance that covers hazards encountered in maritime transportation, including risks of river and inland navigation.

marital agreement 1. A contract between spouses. See also postnuptial agreement, separation agreement. 2. See premarital agreement.

marital communications privilege A spouse has a privilege to refuse to disclose and to prevent others from disclosing private or confidential communications between the spouses during the marriage. Also called husband-wife privilege, spousal privilege.

Confidential marital communication privilege. Subject to Section 912 and except as otherwise provided in this article, a spouse . . . whether or not a party, has a privilege during the marital relationship and afterwards to refuse to disclose, and to prevent another from disclosing, a communication if he claims the privilege and the communication was made in confidence between him and the other spouse while they were husband and wife. Cal. Evidence Code § 980

marital deduction The amount of the federal estate and gift tax deduction allowed for transfers of property from one spouse to another (26 USC § 2056).

marital portion The part of a deceased spouse's estate that must be received by a surviving spouse.

marital property Property acquired by either spouse during the marriage that does not constitute separate property, plus any appreciation of separate property that occurs during the marriage. See also separate property.

maritime Pertaining to the sea, navigable waters, and commerce thereon.

maritime contract A contract on ships, commerce or navigation on navigable waters, transportation by sea, or maritime employment.

maritime law See admiralty.

mark 1. Language or symbols used to identify or distinguish one's service. Short for servicemark and trademark. 2. A substitute for the signature.

market 1. The place or geographic area where goods and services are bought and sold. 2. An exchange where securities or commodities are traded. 3. The geographical or economic extent of commercial demand.

marketable Capable of attracting buyers; fit to offer for sale.

marketable title A title that a reasonably prudent buyer, knowing all the facts, would be willing to accept.

A marketable title means one which a reasonable purchaser, well informed as to the facts and their legal bearings, willing and anxious to perform his contract, would, in exercise of prudence ordinarily exercised by businessmen, be willing and ought to accept. *Wilson*, 235 P.2d 431 (Cal.App., 1951)

market-maker Any "dealer who, with respect to a security, holds himself out (by entering quotations in an inter-dealer communications system or otherwise) as being willing to buy and sell such security for his own account on a regular or continuous basis." 15 USC § 78c(a)(38).

market order An order to buy or sell securities at the best price currently obtainable.

market price The prevailing price in a given market. The last reported price.

market share The percentage of total industry sales made by a particular company.

market value See fair market value.

Market value, the price for which an informed buyer and an informed seller would transfer the property, provides the measure of value for property tax assessment purposes. Cal. Const. Art. 13, § 1; Cal. Revenue & Taxation Code § 110.5. *Bontrager*, 118 Cal.Rptr.2d 182 (Cal.App., 2001)

mark up 1. The process by which a legislative committee puts a bill in its final form. 2. An increase in price, usually to derive profit.

marriage 1. The legal union of one man and one woman as husband and wife. 2. The status of being a married couple.

marriage certificate The document filed by the person performing a marriage ceremony containing evidence that the ceremony took place.

marriage license The document (issued by the government) giving a couple authorization to be married.

marriage settlement See premarital agreement, separation agreement.

marshal 1. A federal judicial officer (U.S. Marshal) who executes court orders, helps maintain security, and performs other duties for the court. 2. A local police or fire department official.

marshaling 1. Arranging, ranking by priority, or disposing in order. 2. An equitable principle compelling a senior creditor to attempt to collect its claim first from another source that is unavailable to a junior creditor.

martial law Rule (or rules) imposed by military authorities over civilian matters.

Martindale-Hubbell Law Directory A set of books that contain a state-by-state list of attorneys and a digest of state and foreign laws.

***Mary Carter* agreement** A contract in which one or more defendants (a) agree to remain in the case, (b) guarantee the plaintiff a certain minimum monetary recovery regardless of the outcome of the lawsuit, and (c) have their liability reduced in direct proportion to the increase in the liability of the nonagreeing defendants. *Booth v. Mary Carter Paint Co.*, 202 So. 2d 8 (Fla.Dist.Ct.App., 1967).

mass picketing Picketing in large numbers, usually obstructing the ingress and egress of the target's employees, customers, or suppliers.

Massachusetts trust See business trust.

master 1. An employer. A principal who hires others and who controls or has the right to control their physical conduct in the performance of their service. 2. An officer appointed by the court to assist it in specific judicial duties (e.g., take testimony). Also called special master. 3. One who has reached the summit of his or her trade, and who has the right to hire apprentices and journeymen. 4. Main or central.

master agreement A labor agreement at one company that becomes the pattern for agreements in an entire industry.

master and servant An employer-employee relationship in which the employer reserves the right to control the manner or means of doing the work.

Relationship of master and servant or "employer and employee" exists whenever employer retains right to direct how work shall be done as well as result to be accomplished, but right to exercise complete or authoritative control, rather than mere suggestion as to detail, must be shown. *Burlingham*, 137 P.2d 9 (CA 1943)

master deed The major condominium document that will govern individual condominium units within a condominium complex.

master in chancery An officer in a court of equity who acts as an assistant to the judge in tasks such as taking testimony.

master limited partnership A limited partnership whose ownership interest is publicly traded.

master of laws (LL.M.) An advanced law degree earned after obtaining a Juris Doctor (J.D.) degree.

master plan A comprehensive land-use plan for the development of an area.

master policy An insurance policy that covers a group of persons, e.g. health or life insurance written as group insurance.

material 1. Essential, important, or relevant; having influence or effect. 2. Pertaining to concrete, physical matter.

Evidence is material under the Brady standard if there is a reasonable probability that, had the evidence been disclosed to the defense, the result of the proceeding would have been different. *City of Los Angeles*, 124 Cal.Rptr.2d 202 (CA 2002)

material allegation An allegation that is essential to a claim or defense.

material alteration A change in a document or instrument that alters its meaning or effect.

A material alteration is one that works a change in the meaning or legal effect of the contract. *Verdugo*, 240 Cal.App.2d 527 (Cal.App., 1966)

material breach A failure to perform a substantial part of a contract, justifying rescission or other remedy.

material evidence Relevant evidence a reasonable mind might accept.

material fact An influential fact; a fact that will affect the result.

material issue An important issue the parties need to resolve.

materialman One who furnishes materials (supplies) for construction or repair work.

material witness A witness who can give testimony on a fact affecting the merits of the case.

When an informer is a material witness on the issue of guilt, the People must disclose his identity or incur a dismissal. (see Cal. Evidence Code, §§ 1041, 1042.) *Eleazer*, 1 Cal.3d 847 (CA 1970)

maternal Pertaining to, belonging to, or coming from the mother.

matricide The killing of one's mother.

matrimonial action A divorce proceeding or other action pertaining to the status of a marriage.

matter 1. A case or dispute; the subject for which representation is sought. 2. Something that a tribunal can examine or establish.

matter in controversy 1. The subject of litigation. 2. The amount of damages sought.

matter of See in re.

matter of fact A subject involving the truth or falsity of a fact.

matter of law A subject involving the interpretation or application of the law. See also judgment as a matter of law.

matter of record Pertaining to a subject that is part of or within an official record.

mature Due or ripe for payment, owing; developed, complete.

maxim A principle; a general statement of a rule or a truth.

mayhem The crime of depriving another of a limb or of disabling, disfiguring, or rendering it useless, especially for self-defense.

The crime is mayhem if the blow results in putting out the eye even if the person who unlawfully strikes another does not have the specific intent to commit the offense. Cal. Penal Code §§ 203. *People v. Villegas*, 113 Cal.Rptr.2d 1 (Cal.App., 2001)

MBE Multistate bar examination.

***McNabb-Mallory* rule** Confessions or incriminating statements can be excluded from evidence if obtained during a period of unnecessary delay in taking the accused before a magistrate. *McNabb*, 63 S. Ct. 608 (1943); *Mallory*, 77 S. Ct. 1356 (1957).

***McNaghten* rule** See insanity (4).

M.D. 1. Middle District. 2. Doctor of medicine.

MDL See multidistrict litigation.

MDP See multidisciplinary practice.

mean high tide The average height of all the high waters (tides) over a complete or regular tidal cycle of 18.6 years.

means 1. That which is used to attain an end. A cause. 2. Assets or available resources.

means test The determination of eligibility for a public benefit based on one's financial resources.

mechanic's lien A right or interest in real or personal property (in the nature of an encumbrance) that secures payment for the performance of labor or the supply of materials to maintain or improve the property. Also called artisan's lien.

mediation A method of alternate dispute resolution (ADR) in which the parties submit a dispute to a neutral third person (the mediator) who helps the parties resolve their dispute; he or she does not render a decision resolving it for them.

Although mediation takes many forms and has been defined in many ways, it is essentially a process where a neutral third party who has no authoritative decision-making power intervenes in a dispute to help the disputants voluntarily reach their own mutually acceptable agreement. Cal. Evidence Code §§ 1115. *Travelers Cas.*, 24 Cal.Rptr.3d 751 (Cal.App., 2005)

mediator See mediation.

Medicaid A federal-state public assistance program that furnishes health care to people who cannot afford it.

medical examiner A public officer who conducts autopsies and otherwise helps in the investigation and prosecution of death cases.

Medicare A federal program of medical insurance for the elderly.

meeting of creditors A bankruptcy hearing or meeting in which creditors can examine the debtor.

meeting of the minds Mutual agreement and assent of the parties to the substance and terms of their contract.

Megan's law A state law (named in honor of a victim) requiring the registration of sex offenders and a method of notifying the community when they move into an area. Also called community notification law.

memorandum 1. A written statement or note that is often brief and informal. 2. A brief record of a transaction or occurrence. 3. A written analysis of how the law applies to a given set of facts.

memorandum decision (mem.) The decision of a court with few or no supporting reasons, often because it follows established principles. Also called memorandum opinion.

Memorandum opinions. The Courts of Appeal should dispose of causes that raise no substantial issues of law or fact by memorandum or other abbreviated form of opinion. Judicial Council, Standards of Judicial Administration, § 6.

memorandum of points and authorities A document submitted to a trial court that makes arguments with supporting authorities for something a party wishes to do, e.g., have a motion granted.

memorial 1. A statement of facts in a petition or demand to the legislature or to the executive. 2. A summary or abstract of a record.

mensa et thoro Bed and board. See also legal separation.

mens rea A guilty mind that produces the act. The unlawful intent or recklessness that must be proved for crimes that are not strict liability offenses.

Mens rea means that there must be a joint operation and intent to constitute the commission of a criminal offense. *People v. Hernandez*, 39 Cal.Rptr. 361 (CA 1964). "In every crime or public offense there must exist a union, or joint operation of act and intent, or criminal negligence." Cal. Penal Code § 20.

mental anguish See emotional distress.

mental cruelty Conduct causing distress that endangers the mental and physical health of a spouse (a fault ground for divorce).

mental defect or disease See insanity (2) and (3).

mental distress; mental suffering See emotional distress.

mercantile Commercial; involving the business of merchants.

merchant A person in the business of purchasing and selling goods.

merchantable Fit for the ordinary purposes for which the goods are used. The noun is merchantability.

mercy killing See euthanasia.

meretricious Involving vulgarity, unlawful sexual relations, or insincerity.

merger 1. The fusion or absorption of one duty, right, claim, offense, estate, or property into another. 2. The absorption of one company by another. The absorbed company ceases to exist as a separate entity.

Merger of corporation is absorption of one corporation by another which survives, retains its name and corporate identity together with added capital, franchises and powers of merged corporation and continues combined business. *Phillips*, 264 Cal.Rptr. 311 (Cal.App., 1989)

merger clause See integration clause.

meritorious Legally plausible. Having merit; not frivolous.

merits See on the merits.

mesne Intermediate; occurring between two periods or ranks.

mesne process Any writ or process issued between commencement of the action and execution of the judgment.

mesne profits Profits accruing between two periods while held by one in wrongful possession.

messuage A dwelling house, its outbuildings, and surrounding land.

metes and bounds A system of describing the boundary lines of land with their terminal points and angles on the natural landscape.

metropolitan Pertaining to a city and its suburbs.

Mexican divorce A divorce granted by a court in Mexico by mail order or when neither spouse was domiciled there.

migratory divorce A divorce obtained in a state to which one or both spouses briefly traveled before returning to their original state.

military commission A military court for violations of martial law.

military government A government in which civil or political power is under the control of the military.

military jurisdiction Jurisdiction of the military in the areas of military law, military government, and martial law.

military law A system of laws governing the armed forces.

military will; military testament A will that may be valid even if it does not comply with required formalities when made by someone in military service. Also called sailor's will, seaman's will, soldier's will.

militia A citizen military force not part of the regular military.

mill One-tenth of one cent.

mineral A lifeless substance formed or deposited through natural processes and found either in or upon the soil or in the rocks beneath the soil.

mineral lease A contract or other form of authorization to explore, develop, or remove deposits of oil, gas, or other minerals. A mining lease allows such activity in a mine or mining claim.

mineral right The right to explore for and remove minerals, with or without ownership of the surface of the land.

miner's inch A unit for measuring water flow through a hole one-inch square in a miner's box (about 9 gallons a minute).

minimal diversity A plaintiff is a citizen of one state and at least one of the defendants is a citizen of another state.

minimum contacts Purposely availing oneself of the privilege of conducting activities within a state, thus invoking the benefits and protections of its laws. (Basis of personal jurisdiction over a nonresident.)

For determining personal jurisdiction over a nonresident defendant under due process, minimum contacts with the forum state exist where the defendant's conduct in the forum state is such that he should reasonably anticipate being subject to suit there, and it is reasonable and fair to force him to do so. *F. Hoffman-La Roche*, 30 Cal.Rptr.3d 407 (Cal.App., 2005)

minimum-fee schedule A bar association list of the lowest fees an attorney can charge for designated legal services. Such lists violate antitrust law.

minimum wage The lowest allowable wage certain employers may pay.

mining lease See mineral lease.

minister 1. An agent; one acting on behalf of another. 2. An administrator in charge of a government department. 3. A diplomatic representative or officer.

ministerial Involving a duty that is to be performed in a prescribed manner without the exercise of judgment or discretion.

A ministerial duty is an act that a public officer is obligated to perform in a prescribed manner required by law when a given state of facts exists. *Jackson*, 130 Cal.Rptr.2d 72 (Cal.App., 2003)

ministry The duties or functions of a religious minister.

minitrial An abbreviated presentation of each side's case that the parties agree to make to each other and to a private, neutral third party, followed by discussions that seek a negotiated settlement. An example of alternate dispute resolution.

minor A person under the legal age, often 18. One who has not reached the age of majority.

minority 1. The status of being below the minimum age to enter a desired relationship (e.g., marriage) or perform a particular task. Also called infancy, nonage. 2. The smaller number. 3. A group of persons of the same race, gender, or other trait that differs from the dominant or majority group in society and that is often the victim of discrimination.

minority opinion An opinion of one or more justices that disagrees with the majority opinion. It is often a dissenting opinion.

minority shareholder Any shareholder who does not own or control more than 50 percent of the voting shares of a corporation.

minute book The book maintained by the court clerk containing a record (the minutes) of court proceedings.

minutes A record of what occurred at a meeting.

***Miranda* warnings** Prior to any custodial interrogation, a person must be warned that: (a) he or she has a right to remain silent, (b) any statement made can be used as evidence against him or her, (c) he or she has the right to his or her own attorney or one provided at government expense. *Miranda v. Arizona*, 86 S. Ct. 1602 (1966).

Mirandize To give a suspect the *Miranda* warnings.

misadventure An accident or misfortune (e.g., killing), often occurring while performing a lawful act.

Misfortune when applied to a criminal act is analogous with the word "misadventure" and bears the connotation of accident while doing a lawful act. *People v. Gorgol*, 265 P.2d 69 (Cal.App., 1953).

misapplication The wrongful use of legally possessed assets.

misappropriate To take wrongfully; to use someone else's property to one's own advantage without permission. See also appropriation (2).

misbranding The use of a label that is false or misleading.

miscarriage of justice A fundamentally unfair result.

A miscarriage of justice occurs when it is reasonably probable that a result more favorable to the appealing party would have been reached in the absence of the error. Cal. Const. Art. 6, §§ 13; Cal. Code of Civil Procedure §§ 475. *Lundy*, 104 Cal.Rptr.2d 545 (Cal.App., 2001)

miscegenation Marriage between persons of different races.

mischarge An erroneous charge to a jury.

mischief 1. Conduct that causes discomfort, hardship, or harm. 2. The evil or danger that a statute is intended to cure or avoid.

misconduct Wrongdoing; a breach of one's duty.

misdelivery Delivery of mail or goods to someone other than the specified or authorized recipient.

misdemeanant A person convicted of a misdemeanor.

misdemeanor A crime, not as serious as a felony, punishable by fine or by detention in an institution other than a prison or penitentiary.

misdemeanor-manslaughter The unintentional killing of a human being while committing a misdemeanor.

misfeasance Improper performance of an otherwise lawful act.

Misfeasance is improper performance of act that is otherwise proper, and nonfeasance is nonperformance of act that should be performed. *Jacoves*, 11 Cal.Rptr.2d 468 (Cal.App., 1992)

misjoinder Improper joining of parties, causes of action, or offenses.

mislay To forget where you placed something you intended to retrieve.

misleading Leading one astray or into error, often intentionally.

misprision 1. Nonperformance of a duty by a public official. 2. A nonparticipant's concealment or failure to disclose a crime. Misprision of felony occurs when the crime involved is a felony.

misrepresentation 1. Any untrue statement of fact. 2. A false statement of fact made with the intent to deceive. Also called false representation. See also fraud.

Misrepresentation must be material and knowingly false representation of fact. *Orient Handel*, 237 Cal.Rptr. 667 (Cal.App., 1987)

mistake An unintentional act, omission, or error arising from ignorance, surprise, imposition, or misplaced confidence.

mistake of fact 1. An unconscious ignorance or forgetfulness of the existence or nonexistence of a material fact, past or present. 2. An honest and reasonable belief in the existence of circumstances, which, if true, would make the act for which the person is indicted an innocent act.

Mistake of fact is a mistake, not caused by the neglect of a legal duty on the part of the person making the mistake, and consisting in: 1. An unconscious ignorance or forgetfulness of a fact past or present, material to the contract; or, 2. Belief in the present existence of a thing material to the contract, which does not exist, or in the past existence of such a thing, which has not existed. Cal. Civil Code § 1577

mistake of law A misunderstanding about legal requirements or consequences.

mistrial A trial terminated before its normal conclusion because of unusual circumstances, misconduct, procedural error, or jury deadlock.

mitigate To render less painful or severe.

mitigating circumstances Facts that can be considered as reducing the severity or degree of moral culpability of an act, but do not excuse or justify it. Also called extenuating circumstances.

Mitigating circumstances, which defendant may prove in slander action, are those which tend to show that defendant acted in good faith, with honesty of purpose, and not maliciously. Cal. Code of Civil Procedure § 461. *Clay*, 299 P.2d 1025 (Cal.App., 1956)

mitigation-of-damages rule An injured party has a duty to use reasonable diligence to try to minimize his or her damages after the wrong has been inflicted. Also called avoidable consequences.

mittimus 1. An order commanding that a person be detailed or conveyed to a prison. 2. An order for the transfer of records between courts.

mixed nuisance A nuisance that injures the public at large and also does some special damage to an individual or class of individuals.

mixed question of law and fact An issue involving the application of the law to the facts when the facts and the legal standards are not in dispute.

For appellate review, mixed questions of law and fact are those where the facts are established, the law is undisputed, and the issue is whether the law as applied to the established facts is violated. *People v. Kennedy*, 31 Cal.Rptr.3d 160 (CA 2005)

***M'Naghten* rule** See insanity (4).

MO See modus operandi

model act A statute proposed to all state legislatures for adoption.

Model Penal Code A proposed criminal law code proposed by the American Law Institute. For its test for insanity, see insanity (2).

Model Rules of Professional Conduct The current ethical rules for attorneys recommended to the states by the American Bar Association.

modification An alteration or change; a new qualification.

Modified Accelerated Cost Recovery System (MACRS) A method to calculate the depreciation tax deduction over a shorter period.

modus Manner or method.

modus operandi (MO) A method of doing things, e.g., a criminal's MO.

moiety 1. One-half. 2. A portion or part.

molest 1. To abuse sexually. 2. To disturb or harass.

Annoy and "molest" ordinarily relate to offenses against children, with connotation of abnormal sexual motivation; forbidden annoyance or molestation is not concerned with child's state of mind, but rather refers to defendant's objectionable acts that constitute the offense. Cal. Penal Code § 647.6(a). *People v. Lopez*, 79 Cal.Rptr.2d 195 (CA 1998)

money 1. Coins and paper currency or other legal medium of exchange. 2. Assets that are readily convertible into cash.

money demand A claim for a specific dollar amount.

money had and received An action to prevent unjust enrichment when one person obtains money that in good conscience belongs to another.

money judgment The part of a judgment that requires paying money (damages).

money laundering See laundering.

money market The financial market for dealing in short-term financial obligations such as commercial paper and treasury bills.

money order A type of negotiable draft purchased from an organization such as the Postal Service and used as a substitute for a check.

money supply The total amount of money circulating and on deposit in the economy.

monition 1. A summons to appear in an admiralty case. 2. A warning.

monopoly A market where there is a concentration of a product or service in the hands of a few, thereby controlling prices or limiting competition. A power to control prices or exclude competition.

month to month tenancy A lease without a fixed duration that can be terminated on short notice, e.g., a month. See also periodic tenancy.

monument Natural or artificial boundary markers or objects on land.

moot 1. Pertaining to a nonexistent controversy where the issues have ceased to exist from a practical point of view. 2. Subject to debate.

A question may be deemed moot when, although it initially presented an existing controversy, passage of time or acts of parties or a court decision have deprived the controversy of its life. *Boccato*, 204 Cal.Rptr. 727 (Cal.App., 1984)

moot case A case that seeks to resolve an abstract question that does not rest upon existing facts.

moot court A simulated court where law students argue a hypothetical case for purposes of learning and competition.

moral 1. Pertaining to conscience or to general principles of right conduct. 2. Pertaining to a duty binding in conscience but not in law. 3. Demonstrating correct character or behavior.

moral certainty A very high degree of probability although not demonstrable to an absolute certainty. Beyond a reasonable doubt.

moral consideration See good consideration.

moral evidence Evidence based on belief or the general observations of people rather than on what is absolutely demonstrable.

moral hazard The risk or probability that an insured will destroy the insured property or permit it to be destroyed to collect on the insurance.

moral right A right of integrity enjoyed by the creator of a work even if someone else now owns the copyright. Examples include the right to be acknowledged as the creator and to insist that the work not be distorted.

Art Preservation Act recognizes that an artist has personal rights in his or her work that are retained even after work has been sold. This bundle of rights is known by French term "*droit moral*" or "moral rights". Cal. Civil Code § 987. *Lubner*, 53 Cal.Rptr.2d 24 (Cal.App., 1996)

moral turpitude Conduct that is dishonest or contrary to moral rules.

moratorium Temporary suspension. A period of delay.

more or less An approximation; slightly larger or smaller.

morgue A place where dead persons are kept for identification or until burial arrangements are made.

mortality tables A guide used to predict life expectancy based on factors such as a person's age and sex.

mortgage An interest in property created by a written instrument providing security for the performance of a duty or the payment of a debt. A lien or claim against property given by the buyer to the lender as security for the money borrowed.

A mortgage is a security for the performance of an agreement. *Workmon Const.*, 36 Cal.Rptr. 17 (Cal.App., 1963)

mortgage bond A bond for which real estate or personal property is pledged as security that the bond will be paid as stated in its terms.

mortgage certificate Document evidencing one's ownership share in a mortgage.

mortgage commitment A written notice from a lending institution that it will advance mortgage funds for the purchase of specified property.

mortgage company A company that makes mortgage loans, which it then sells to investors.

mortgagee A lender to whom property is mortgaged.

mortgage market The existing supply and demand for mortgages, including their resale. Rates and terms being offered by competing mortgagees.

mortgagor The debtor who mortgages his or her property; one who gives legal title or a lien to the mortgagee to secure the mortgage loan.

mortis causa See causa mortis.

mortmain statute A statute that restricts one's right to transfer property to institutions such as churches that would hold it forever.

most favored nation clause (MFN) A treaty promise that each side will grant to the other the broadest rights that it gives any other nation.

motion An application for an order or ruling from a court or other decision-making body.

A motion is an application for an order. Cal. Code of Civil Procedure § 1003. *Schoenberg*, 59 Cal.Rptr. 359 (Cal.App., 1967)

motion for a more definite statement A request that the court order the other side to make its pleading more definite, since it is so vague or ambiguous that one cannot frame a responsive pleading.

motion in limine A request for a ruling on the admissibility of evidence prior to or during trial but before the evidence has been offered.

motion to dismiss A request, usually made before the trial begins, that the judge dismiss the case because of lack of jurisdiction, insufficiency of the pleadings, or the reaching of a settlement.

motion to strike A request that the court remove specific statements, claims, or evidence from the pleadings or the record.

motion to suppress A request that the court eliminate from a criminal trial any illegally secured evidence.

motive A cause or reason that moves the will and induces action or inaction.

Motive describes the reason a person chooses to commit a crime; it is not synonymous with "intent." CALJIC 2.51. *People v. Petznick*, 7 Cal.Rptr.3d 726 (Cal.App., 2003)

movables Things that can be carried from one place to another. Personal property.

movant One who makes a motion or applies for a ruling or order.

move To make an application or request for an order or ruling.

moving papers Papers or documents submitted in support of a motion.

mug 1. To criminally assault someone, often with the intent to rob. 2. A human face. A mug shot is a photograph of a suspect's face.

mulct 1. A penalty or punishment such as a fine. 2. To defraud a person of something.

mulier 1. A woman; a wife. 2. A son who is legitimate.

multidisciplinary practice (MDP) A partnership of attorneys and nonattorney professionals that offers legal and nonlegal services.

multidistrict litigation (MDL) Civil actions with common questions of fact pending in different federal district courts that are transferred to one district solely for consolidated pretrial proceedings under a single judge before returning to their original district courts.

multifarious 1. Improperly joined claims, instructions, or parties. 2. Diverse.

multilateral agreement An agreement among three or more parties.

multiple access The defense in a paternity case that more than one lover had access to the mother during the time of conception.

multiple listing An arrangement among real estate agents whereby any member agent can sell property listed by another agent. The latter shares the fee or commission with the broker who made the sale.

A multiple listing service is a facility of cooperation of agents and appraisers, operating through an intermediary which does not itself act as an agent or appraiser, through which agents establish express or implied legal relationships with respect to listed properties, or which may be used by agents and appraisers, pursuant to the rules of the service, to prepare market evaluations and appraisals of real property. Cal. Civil Code § 1087

multiplicity 1. A large number or variety of matters or particulars. 2. The improper charging of a single offense in several counts.

multiplicity of actions Several attempts to litigate the same right or issue against the same defendant.

municipal 1. Pertaining to a city, town, or other local unit of government. 2. Pertaining to a state or nation.

municipal bond A bond or other debt instrument issued by a state or local unit of government to fund public projects. Also called municipal security.

municipal corporation A city, county, village, town or other local governmental body established to run all or part of local government. Also called municipality.

Municipal corporation means a city and county or incorporated city. Cal. Public Utilities Code § 2904

municipal court An inferior court with jurisdiction over relatively small claims or offenses arising within the local area where it sits.

municipal ordinance See ordinance.

municipality 1. The body of officials elected or appointed to administer a local government. 2. See municipal corporation.

municipal securities See municipal bond.

muniments Documents used to defend one's title or other claim.

murder The unlawful, premeditated killing of a human being.

(a) Murder is the unlawful killing of a human being, or a fetus, with malice aforethought. (b) This section shall not apply to any person who commits an act that results in the death of a fetus if any of the following apply: (1) The act complied with the Therapeutic Abortion Act . . . (3) The act was solicited, aided, abetted, or consented to by the mother of the fetus. Cal. Penal Code § 187

mutatis mutandis With the necessary changes in any of the details.

mutilate 1. To maim, to dismember, to disfigure someone. 2. To alter or deface a document by cutting, tearing, burning, or erasing, without totally destroying it.

mutiny An insurrection or uprising of seamen or soldiers against the authority of their commanders.

mutual Reciprocal, common to both parties. In the same relationship to each other.

mutual company A company owned by its clients or customers.

mutual fund An investment company with a pool of assets, consisting primarily of portfolio securities, and belonging to the individual investors holding shares in the fund.

mutual insurance company An insurance company that has no capital stock and in which the policyholders are the owners.

mutuality An action by each of two parties; reciprocation; both sides being bound.

mutuality of contract; mutuality of obligation 1. Liability or obligation imposed on both parties under the terms of the agreement. 2. Unless both sides are bound, neither is bound.

mutual mistake A mistake common to both parties wherein each labors under a misconception respecting the terms of the agreement. Both contracting parties misunderstand the fundamental subject matter or term of the contract. Mistake of both parties on the same fact. Also called bilateral mistake.

Mutual mistake for which reformation will lie must involve a misconception shared by both parties. *Renshaw*, 250 P.2d 612 (Cal.App., 1952)

mutual wills 1. Separate wills made by two persons, which are reciprocal in their provisions and by which each testator makes testamentary disposition in favor of the other. Also called double will, reciprocal will. 2. Wills executed pursuant to an agreement between testators to dispose of their property in a particular manner, each in consideration of the other.

N

naked licensee See bare licensee.

naked power A mere authority to act, not accompanied by any interest of the holder of the power in the subject-matter of the power.

naked trust See passive trust.

NALA See National Association of Legal Assistants (*www.nala.org*).

NALS See National Association of Legal Secretaries, now called NALS the Association for Legal Professionals (*www.nals.org*).

named insured The person specifically mentioned in an insurance policy as the one protected by the insurance.

Napoleonic Code See code civil.

narcotic Any addictive drug that dulls the senses or induces sleep.

Narcotic drug means any of the following, whether produced directly or indirectly by extraction from substances of vegetable origin, or independently by means of chemical synthesis, or by a combination of extraction and chemical synthesis: (a) *Opium and opiate, and . . . Cal. Health & Safety Code § 11019*

National Association of Legal Assistants (NALA) A national association of paralegals (*www.nala.org*).

National Association of Legal Secretaries A national association of legal secretaries and paralegals, now called NALS the Association for Legal Professionals (*www.nals.org*).

national bank A bank incorporated under federal law.

National Federation of Paralegal Associations (NFPA) A national association of paralegals (*www.paralegals.org*).

nationality The status that arises as a result of a person's belonging to a nation because of birth or naturalization.

nationalization The acquisition and control of privately owned businesses by the government.

Native American A member of the indigenous peoples of North, South, and Central America.

natural affection The affection that naturally exists between parent and child and among other close relatives.

natural death Death not caused by accidental or intentional injury.

natural heirs Next of kin by blood (consanguinity) as distinguished from collateral heirs or those related by adoption.

naturalization The process by which a person acquires citizenship after birth.

Naturalization is the process by which person acquires nationality after birth and becomes entitled to privileges of US citizenship. *People v. Gontiz*, 68 Cal.Rptr.2d 786 (Cal.App., 1997)

natural law A system of rules and principles (not created by human authority) discoverable by our rational intelligence as growing out of and conforming to human nature.

natural monument Boundary markers or objects on land that are not artificial.

natural object of bounty Descendants, surviving spouse, and other close relatives who are assumed to become recipients of the estate of a decedent.

natural person A human being. See also artificial person.

natural right A right based on natural law.

Natural rights are those which grow out of the nature of humans and depend upon their personality and are distinguished from those created by positive laws enacted by a duly constituted government to create an orderly civilized society. *In re Gogabashvele's Estate*, 16 Cal.Rptr. 77 (Cal.App., 1961)

navigable water A body of water over which commerce can be carried on.

navigation The art, science, or business of traveling the sea or other navigable waters in ships or vessels.

N.B. (nota bene) Note well, take notice, attention.

necessaries 1. The basic items needed by family members to maintain a standard of living. 2. Food, medicine, clothing, shelter, or personal services usually considered reasonably essential for preservation and enjoyment of life. 3. Goods or services reasonably needed in a ship's business for a vessel's continued operation.

necessary 1. Essential. 2. Logically true.

Necessary (for purposes of determining if a municipal power is implied) means convenient, useful, appropriate, or suitable, and not indispensable. *Zack*, 13 Cal.Rptr.3d 323 (Cal.App., 2004)

Necessary and Proper Clause The clause in the U.S. Constitution (art. I, § 8, cl. 18) giving Congress the power to enact laws that are needed to carry out its enumerated powers.

necessary party A party with a legal or beneficial interest in the subject matter of the lawsuit and who should be joined if feasible.

necessity 1. A privilege to make reasonable use of someone's property to prevent immediate harm or damage to person or property. 2. See choice of evils. 3. Something necessary or indispensable.

ne exeat A writ that forbids a person from leaving the country, state, or jurisdiction of the court.

negative act Not acting when a duty to act exists.

negative averment An allegation of a fact that must be proved by the alleging party even though the allegation is phrased in the negative.

negative covenant A promise not to do or perform some act.

negative easement An easement that precludes the owner of land subject to the easement (the servient estate) from doing an act which would otherwise be lawful.

negative evidence Testimony or other evidence about what did not happen or does not exist.

negative pregnant A negative statement that also implies an affirmative statement or admission (e.g., "I deny that I owe $500" may be an admission that at least some amount is owed).

A mere denial of the literal truth of the total statement, but not of its substance. *Vogel*, Cal.Rptr.3d 350 (Cal.App., 2005)

neglect 1. The failure to perform an act one has a duty to perform. 2. Carelessness. See also child neglect.

negligence Harm or damage caused by not doing what a reasonably prudent person would have done under like circumstances. A tort with the following elements: (a) a duty of reasonable care, (b) a breach of this duty, (c) proximate cause, (d) actual damages.

The failure to exercise the care a person of ordinary prudence would exercise under the circumstances. *Delaney*, 82 Cal.Rptr.2d 610 (CA 1999)

negligence per se Negligence as a matter of law when violating a statute that defines the standard of care.

negligent Unreasonably careless. See also neglect, negligence.

negligent entrustment Creating an unreasonable risk of harm by carelessly allowing someone to use a dangerous object, e.g., a car.

negligent homicide Death due to the failure to perceive a substantial and unjustifiable risk that one's conduct will cause the death of another person.

negligent infliction of emotional distress (NIED) Carelessly causing someone to suffer substantial emotional distress.

negotiability words Words that make an instrument negotiable, e.g., "to the order of."

negotiable 1. Legally capable of being transferred by indorsement or delivery. See also negotiation (1). 2. Open to compromise.

negotiable bill of lading A bill of lading that requires delivery of goods to the bearer of the bill or, if to the order of a named person, to that person.

A negotiable bill of lading, in effect, requires delivery to the bearer of the bill or, if to the order of a named person, to that person, while a nonnegotiable bill of lading is one in which the consignee is specified. *BII Finance*, 115 Cal.Rptr.2d 312 (Cal.App., 2002)

negotiable instrument Any writing (a) signed by the maker or drawer; (b) containing an unconditional promise or order to pay a sum certain in money; (c) is payable on demand or at a definite time; and (d) is payable to order or to bearer. UCC § 3-104(a).

negotiate 1. To bargain with another concerning a sale, settlement, or matter in contention. 2. To transfer by delivery or indorsement. See also negotiation (1).

negotiated plea See plea bargaining.

negotiation 1. The transfer of an instrument through delivery (if the instrument is payable to bearer), or through indorsement and delivery (if it is payable to order) in such form that the transferee becomes a holder. 2. The process of submitting and considering offers.

nemo est supra leges No one is above the law.

nepotism Granting privileges or patronage to one's relatives.

net The amount that remains after all allowable deductions.

net assets See net worth.

net asset value (NAV) The per share value of a company or mutual fund measured by its assets less debts divided by the number of shares.

net estate The portion of a probate estate remaining after all allowable deductions and adjustments.

net income Income subject to taxation after allowable deductions and exemptions have been subtracted from gross or total income.

net lease A lease in which the tenant pays not only rent, but also items such as taxes, insurance, and maintenance charges.

Net lease is type of agreement often used in commercial leases of entire buildings, defining characteristic of which is virtually complete transfer of incidents of ownership from landlord to tenant. *Hadian*, 35 Cal.Rptr.2d 589 (CA 1994)

net listing A listing in which the amount of real estate commission is the difference between the selling price of the property and a minimum price set by the seller.

net operating loss (NOL) The excess of allowable deductions over gross income.

net premium 1. The amount of an insurance premium less expenses such as commission. 2. The amount required by an insurer to cover the expected cost of paying benefits.

net weight The weight of an article after deducting the weight of the box or other wrapping.

net worth The total assets of a person or business less the total liabilities. Also called net assets.

The sum of the following: (a) Issued and outstanding capital stock. (b) Issued and outstanding capital certificates. (c) Paid-in surplus. (d) Retained earnings. (e) Pledged savings accounts of a mutual association with the approval of the commissioner. (f) General reserves and other amounts as the commissioner prescribes. Cal. Financial Code § 5120

net worth method To reconstruct the income of a taxpayer, the IRS compares his or her net worth at the beginning and end of the tax year and makes adjustments for personal expenses and allowable deductions.

neutral Not taking an active part with either of the contending sides; disinterested, unbiased.

neutrality laws Acts of Congress that forbid military assistance to either of two belligerent powers with which we are at peace.

ne varietur It must not be altered (a notary's inscription).

new and useful For an invention to be patented, it must be novel and provide some practical benefit.

newly discovered evidence Evidence discovered after the trial and not discoverable before the trial by the exercise of due diligence.

new matter A fact not previously alleged by either party in the pleadings.

newsman's privilege See journalist's privilege.

new trial Another trial of all or some of the same issues that were resolved by judgment in a prior trial.

new value Newly given money or money's worth in goods, services, new credit, or release by a transferee of property previously transferred (11 USC § 547(a)(2)).

next friend Someone specially appointed by the court to look after the interests of a person who cannot act on his or her own (e.g., a minor). Also called prochein ami.

next of kin 1. The nearest blood relatives of the decedent. 2. Those who would inherit from the decedent if he or she died intestate.

Surviving next of kin in the following order: 1. Husband or wife, 2. Children, 3. Father and mother, 4. Grandchildren, 5. Brothers and sisters, 6. Nieces and nephews. Cal. Government Code § 9359.9

nexus A causal or other connection or link.

NFPA See National Federation of Paralegal Associations (*www.paralegals.org*).

NGO Nongovernmental organization.

NGRI Not guilty by reason of insanity.

nighttime 1. The period between sunset and sunrise when there is not enough daylight to discern a person's face. 2. Thirty minutes after sunset to 30 minutes before sunrise.

Nighttime means between the hours of 10 p.m. and 7 a.m. Cal. Civil Code § 3482.1. Daytime is the period of time between sunrise and sunset. Nighttime is the period of time between sunset and sunrise. Cal. Government Code § 6807

nihil dicit ("he says nothing") The name of the judgment against a defendant who omits to plead or answer the plaintiff.

nihil est ("there is nothing") A form of return made by a sheriff when he or she has been unable to serve a writ.

nil (nihil) Nothing.

nisi Unless. Refers to the rule that something will remain or be valid unless an opponent comes forward to demonstrate otherwise.

nisi prius (n.p.) ("unless before") A civil trial court with a jury (in New York and Oklahoma).

NLRB National Labor Relations Board (*www.nlrb.gov*).

no action letter A letter from a government agency that no action will be taken against a person based on the facts before the agency.

no bill A grand jury statement that the evidence is insufficient to justify a formal charge or indictment. Also called not found.

no contest 1. See nolo contendere. 2. See in terrorem clause.

no evidence A challenge to the legal sufficiency of the evidence to support a particular fact finding.

no eyewitness rule If there is no direct evidence (e.g., eyewitness testimony) of what decedent did or failed to do immediately before an injury, the trier of facts may infer that decedent was using ordinary care for his or her own safety.

no fault Pertaining to legal consequences (e.g., granting a divorce, paying insurance benefits) that will occur regardless of who was at fault or to blame.

no-knock search warrant A warrant that authorizes the police to enter the premises without first announcing themselves.

nolle prosequi (nol-pros) A formal notice by the government that a criminal prosecution will not be pursued.

no-load Sold without a commission.

nolo contendere ("I will not contest it") A plea in a criminal case in which the defendant does not admit or deny the charges. The effect of the plea, however, is similar to a plea of guilty in that the defendant can be sentenced to prison, fined, etc. Also called no contest, non vult contendere.

For the suspension or revocation of licenses, any plea of nolo contendere is deemed a conviction. Cal. Vehicle Code § 13375

nol-pros See nolle prosequi.

nominal 1. In name only; not real or substantial. 2. Trifling.

nominal consideration Consideration so small as to bear no relation to the real value of what is received.

nominal damages A trifling sum (e.g., $1) awarded to the plaintiff because there was no significant loss or injury suffered, although a technical invasion of rights did occur.

Nominal damages describes two types of award: a trifling or token allowance for mere technical invasion of a right, without actual damage, and the very different allowance made when actual damages are substantial, but their extent and amount is difficult of precise proof. *Kluge*, 38 Cal.Rptr. 607 (Cal.App., 1964)

nominal party A party who has no interest in the result of the suit or no actual interest or control over the subject matter of the litigation but is present to satisfy a technical rule of practice.

nominal trust See passive trust.

nominee 1. One who has been nominated or proposed for an office or appointment. 2. One designated to act for another. An agent.

nominee trust 1. A trust in which the trustee lacks power to deal with the trust property except as directed by the trust beneficiaries. 2. A trust in which property is held for undisclosed beneficiaries.

nonaccess A paternity defense in which the alleged father asserts the absence of opportunities for sexual intercourse with the mother.

nonage See minority (1).

non assumpsit A plea in an assumpsit action that the undertaking was not made as alleged.

non compos mentis Not sound of mind. Mentally incompetent.

nonconforming use A use of land that is permitted because the use was lawful prior to a change in the zoning law even though the new law would make the use illegal.

noncore proceeding A nonbankruptcy proceeding related to the debtor's estate that, in the absence of a petition in bankruptcy, could have been brought in a state court.

nondelegable duty An affirmative duty that cannot be escaped by entrusting it to a third party such as an independent contractor.

nonexclusive listing See open listing.

nonfeasance The failure to perform a legal duty.

Nonfeasance is nonperformance of act that should be performed. Misfeasance is improper performance of act that is otherwise proper. *Jacoves*, 11 Cal.Rptr.2d 468 (Cal.App., 1992)

nonintervention will A will providing that the executor shall not be required to account to any court or person.

nonjoinder The failure to join a necessary person to a suit.

nonjury trial See bench trial.

nonjusticiable Inappropriate or improper for judicial resolution.

nonmailable Pertaining to what cannot be transported by U.S. mail because of size, obscene content, etc.

nonnegotiable 1. Not capable of transfer by indorsement or delivery. 2. Fixed; pertaining to what will not be bargained.

non obstante veredicto Notwithstanding the verdict. See judgment notwithstanding the verdict.

nonperformance The failure or refusal to perform an obligation.

nonprofit corporation A corporation whose purpose is not to make a profit. Also called not-for-profit corporation.

non prosequitur ("he does not prosecute") A judgment against a plaintiff who fails to pursue his or her action.

nonrecourse creditor A creditor who can look only to its collateral for satisfaction of its debt, not to the debtor's other assets.

nonresident alien One who is neither a citizen nor a resident of the country he or she is presently in.

nonstock corporation A corporation whose ownership is not determined by shares of stock.

nonsuit A termination or dismissal of an action by a plaintiff who is unable to prove his or her case, defaults, fails to prosecute, etc.

If the defendant's motion for a judgment of nonsuit is granted, the judgment of nonsuit operates as an adjudication upon the merits. Cal. Code of Civil Procedure § 581c

nonsupport The failure to provide food, clothing, and other support needed for living to someone to whom an obligation of support is owed.

nonuse The failure to exercise a right or claim.

non vult contendere He will not contest. See also nolo contendere.

no par stock Stock issued without a value stated on the stock certificate.

noscitur a sociis ("it is known by its associates") A word with multiple meanings is often best interpreted with regard to the words surrounding it.

A restrictive meaning of a listed item in a statute if acceptance of a more expansive meaning would make other items in the list unnecessary or redundant, or would otherwise make the item markedly dissimilar to the other items in the list. *English*, 114 Cal.Rptr.2d 93 (Cal.App., 2001)

no-strike clause A commitment by a labor union not to strike during the period covered by the collective bargaining agreement.

nota bene (N.B.) Note well; attention.

notarial Performed or taken by a notary public.

notarize To certify or attest, e.g., the authenticity of a signature.

notary public One authorized to perform notarial acts such as administering oaths, taking proof of execution and acknowledgment of instruments, and attesting the authenticity of signatures.

note See promissory note.

not-for-profit corporation See nonprofit corporation.

not found See no bill.

not guilty 1. A jury verdict acquitting the accused. 2. A plea entered by the accused that denies guilt for a criminal charge.

not guilty by reason of insanity (NGRI) A verdict of not guilty because of a finding of insanity. See also insanity.

notice 1. Information or knowledge about something. 2. Formal notification. 3. Knowledge of facts that would naturally lead an honest and prudent person to make inquiry.

The term "notice" imports that information given thereby comes from authentic source and is directed to someone who is to act or refrain from acting in consequence of information contained in notice. *Bird*, 31 Cal.Rptr. 386 (Cal.App., 1963)

notice by publication Notice given through a broad medium such as a general circulation newspaper.

notice of appeal Notice given to a court (through filing) and to the opposing party (through service) of an intention to appeal.

notice of appearance A formal notification to a court by an attorney that he or she is representing a party in the litigation.

notice of pendency See lis pendens (2).

notice pleading Pleading by giving a short and plain statement of a claim that shows the pleader is entitled to relief.

notice to quit A landlord's written notice to a tenant that the landlord wishes to repossess the leased premises and end the tenancy.

notorious 1. Well-known for something undesirable. 2. Conspicuous.

notorious possession Occupation or possession of property that is conspicuous or generally known. Also called open possession.

NOV See judgment notwithstanding the verdict.

novation The substitution by mutual agreement of one debtor for another or of one creditor for another, whereby the old debt is extinguished, or the substitution of a new debt or obligation for an existing one.

The substitution of a new contractual obligation for an existing one; essential to a novation is that it clearly appear that the parties intended to extinguish rather than merely modify the original agreement. Cal. Civil Code § 1530. *Howard*, 269 Cal.Rptr. 807 (Cal.App., Dist., 1990)

novelty That which has not been known or used before. Innovation.

NOW account An interest-bearing savings account on which checks can be written. NOW means negotiable order of withdrawal.

nude Lacking something essential.

nudum pactum ("a bare agreement") A promise or undertaking made without any consideration.

nugatory Without force; invalid.

nuisance A substantial interference with the reasonable use and enjoyment of private land (private nuisance); an unreasonable interference with a right that is common to the general public (public nuisance).

nuisance per se An act, occurrence, or structure that is a nuisance at all times and under all circumstances.

Nuisance per se arises when a legislative body, in the exercise of the police power, expressly declares a particular object or substance, activity, or circumstance to be a nuisance. *Jones*, 94 Cal.Rptr.2d 661 (Cal.App., 2000)

null; null and void Having no legal effect; binding no one.

nulla bona "No goods" on which a writ of execution can be levied.

nullification 1. The state or condition of being void or without legal effect. 2. The process of rendering something void.

nullify To invalidate; to render void.

nullity Having absolutely no legal effect. Something that is void.

nullius filius ("the son of no one") An illegitimate child.

nul tiel record ("no such" record) A plea asserting that the record relied upon in the opponent's claim does not exist.

nunc pro tunc ("now for then") With retroactive effect. As if it were done as of the time that it should have been done.

nuncupative will An oral will declared or dictated in anticipation of imminent death.

NYSE New York Stock Exchange (*www.nyse.com*).

O

oath 1. A solemn declaration. 2. A formal pledge to be truthful.

obiter dictum See dictum (1).

object 1. To express disapproval; to consider something improper or illegal and ask the court to take action accordingly. 2. The end aimed at; the thing sought to be accomplished.

objection 1. A formal disagreement or statement of opposition. 2. The act of objecting.

An objection to all evidence is essentially the same as a general demurrer or motion for judgment on the pleadings. *Edwards*, 61 Cal.Rptr.2d 518 (Cal.App., 1997)

objective 1. Real in the external world; existing outside one's subjective mind. 2. Unbiased. 3. Goal.

obligation 1. Any duty imposed by law, contract, or morals. 2. A binding agreement to do something, e.g., to pay a certain sum.

obligee The person to whom an obligation is owed; a promisee or creditor.

obligor The person under an obligation; a promisor or debtor.

obliterate To destroy; to erase or wipe out.

obloquy Abusive language; disgrace due to defamatory criticism.

obscene Material that enjoys no free-speech protection if: (a) the average person, applying contemporary community standards, finds that the work, taken as a whole, appeals to the prurient interest in sex; (b) the work depicts or describes, in a patently offensive way, sexual conduct specifically defined by the applicable state law; and (c) the work, taken as a whole, lacks serious literary, artistic, political, or scientific value.

Obscene matter means matter, taken as a whole, that to the average person, applying contemporary statewide standards, appeals to the prurient interest, that, taken as a whole, depicts or describes sexual conduct in a patently offensive way, and that, taken as a whole, lacks serious literary, artistic, political, or scientific value. Cal. Penal Code § 311

obscenity 1. See obscene. 2. Conduct tending to corrupt the public morals by its indecency or lewdness.

obsolescence Diminution in value caused by changes in taste or new technology, rendering the property less desirable on the market; the condition or process of falling into disuse.

obstruction of justice Conduct that impedes or interferes with the administration of justice (e.g., hindering a witness from appearing).

obvious Easily discovered or readily apparent.

occupancy 1. Obtaining possession of real property for dwelling or lodging purposes. 2. The period during which one is in actual possession of land.

occupation 1. Conduct in which one is engaged. 2. One's regular employment or source of livelihood. 3. Conquest or seizure of land.

occupational disease A disease resulting from exposure during employment to conditions or substances detrimental to health.

Occupational Safety and Health Administration (OSHA) A federal agency that develops workplace health and safety standards, and conducts investigations to enforce compliance (*www.osha.gov*).

occupation tax A tax imposed for the privilege of carrying on a business or occupation.

A business or occupation tax is usually defined as a revenue-raising levy upon the privilege of doing business within the taxing jurisdiction. *Weekes*, 146 Cal.Rptr. 558 (CA 1978)

occupying the field A form of preemption (see this word) where a federal rule is so pervasive that no room is left for states to supplement it.

occurrence policy Insurance that covers all losses from events that occur during the period the policy is in effect, even if the claim is not actually filed until after the policy expires.

odd lot An irregular or nonstandard amount for a trade, e.g., less than 100.

odd lot doctrine For workers' compensation, permanent total disability may be found in the case of workers who, while not altogether incapacitated for work, are so handicapped that they will not be employed regularly in any well-known branch of the labor market.

odium Contempt or intense dislike. Held in disgrace.

of age See adult, majority (1).

of counsel 1. An attorney who is semiretired or has some other special status in the law firm other than regular member or employee. 2. An attorney who assists the principal attorney in a case.

offender One who has committed a crime or offense.

offense A crime or violation of law for which a penalty can be imposed.

offensive 1. Disagreeable, objectionable, displeasing. 2. Offending the personal dignity of an ordinary person who is not unduly sensitive.

To be offensive, the contact must be of a character that would offend a person of ordinary sensitivity, and be unwarranted by the social usages prevalent at the time and place at which the contact is made. Civil Jury Instruction (CA BAJI) 7.51

offer 1. A proposal presented for acceptance or rejection. 2. To request that the court admit an exhibit into evidence.

offeree The person to whom an offer is made.

offering The sale or offer for sale of an issue of securities.

offer of compromise An offer to settle a case.

offer of proof Telling the court what evidence a party proposes to present after the judge has ruled it inadmissible so that a record will be made for a later appeal of this ruling.

offeror The party who makes an offer.

office 1. A position of trust and authority. 2. A place where everyday administrative business is conducted. 3. A unit or subdivision of government.

officer A person holding a position of trust, command, or authority in organizations.

officer of the court A person who has a responsibility in carrying out or assisting in the administration of justice in the courts, such as judges, bailiffs, court clerks, and attorneys.

official 1. An elected or appointed holder of a public office. An officer. 2. Concerning that which is authorized. 3. Proceeding from, sanctioned by, or pertaining to an officer.

Official Gazette Publication of the U.S. Patent and Trademark Office.

official immunity The immunity of government employees from personal liability for torts they commit while performing discretionary acts within the scope of their employment.

Except as otherwise provided by statute, a public employee is not liable for an injury resulting from his act or omission where the act or omission was the result of the exercise of the discretion vested in him, whether or not such discretion be abused. Cal. Government Code § 820.2

official notice The equivalent of judicial notice when taken by an administrative law judge or examiner.

official report or **official reporter** A collection of court opinions whose printing is authorized by the government.

officious intermeddler One who interferes in the affairs of another without justification (or invitation) and is generally not entitled to restitution for any benefit he or she confers. Also called intermeddler.

offset A deduction; that which compensates for or counters something else. See also setoff.

An offset may be defined as a claim that serves to counterbalance or to compensate for another claim. *Steinmeyer*, 116 Cal.Rptr. 57 (Cal.App., 1974)

Old Age, Survivors, and Disability Insurance A federal program providing financial benefits for retirement and disability. Also called Social Security.

oligarchy Government power in the hands of a few persons.

oligopoly A market structure in which a few sellers dominate sales of a product, resulting in high prices.

ombudsman One who investigates and helps resolve grievances that people have within or against an organization, often employed by the organization.

omission 1. The intentional or unintentional failure to act. 2. Something left out or neglected.

omnibus bill 1. A legislative bill that includes different subjects in one measure. 2. A legislative bill covering many aspects of one subject.

omnibus clause 1. A clause in an instrument (e.g., a will) that covers all property not specifically mentioned or known at the time. 2. A clause extending liability insurance coverage to persons using the car with the permission of the named insured.

on all fours Pertaining to facts that are exactly the same, or almost so; being a very close precedent.

on demand Upon request; when demanded.

onerous Unreasonably burdensome or one-sided.

on information and belief See information and belief.

on its face Whatever is readily observable, e.g., the language of a document. See also face.

In equal protection context, a statute that establishes a classification "on its face" classifies persons for different treatment by its own terms. Cal.Const. Art. 1, § 7(a). *People v. Superior Court,* 89 Cal.Rptr.2d 326 (Cal.App., 1999)

on or about Approximately.

one man (person), one vote The equal protection requirement that each qualified voter be given an equal opportunity to participate in an election.

on point 1. Germane, relevant. 2. Covering or raising the same issue (in a case, law review article, etc.) as the one before you.

on the brief Helped to research or write the appellate brief.

on the merits Pertaining to a court decision that is based on the facts and on the substance of the claim, rather than on a procedural ground.

on the pleadings Pertaining to a ruling based on the allegations in the pleadings rather than on evidence presented in a hearing.

on the record Noted or recorded in the official record of the proceeding.

open 1. Visible, apparent, exposed. 2. Still available or active. 3. Not restricted. 4. Not resolved or settled.

open account 1. A type of credit from a seller that permits a buyer to make purchases on an ongoing basis without security. 2. An unpaid account.

An open account is one that is continuous or current, uninterrupted or unclosed by settlement or otherwise, consisting of a series of transactions; also one in which some item in the contract is left open and undetermined by the parties. *Fresno Credit,* 227 P.2d 851 (Cal.App., 1951)

open and notorious Conspicuous, generally recognized, or commonly known.

open court A court in session to which the general public may or may not be invited.

open end 1. Without a defined time or monetary limit. 2. Allowing further additions or other changes.

open-end mortgage A mortgage that allows the debtor to borrow additional funds without providing additional collateral.

open field doctrine No violation of one's constitutional right to privacy occurs when the police search an open field without a warrant.

opening statement An attorney's statement to the jury made before presenting evidence that summarizes the case he or she intends to try to establish during the trial.

open listing A listing available to more than one agent in which the owner agrees to pay a commission to any agent who produces a ready, willing, and able purchaser. Also called nonexclusive listing.

open market An unrestricted competitive market in which any buyer and purchaser is free to participate.

An open market transaction is one where sale price is negotiated between buyer and seller, as distinguished from a sale resulting from submission of bids where seller sells to highest bidder or buyer buys from lowest bidder. Cal. Revenue & Taxation Code, §§ 110, 401. *Guild,* 124 Cal.Rptr. 96 (Cal.App., 1975)

open order An order placed with a broker that remains viable (open) until filled or the client cancels the order.

open policy See unvalued policy.

open possession See notorious possession.

open price The amount to be paid has yet to be determined or settled.

open shop A business in which union membership is not a condition of employment.

operating lease A short-term lease that expires before the end of the useful life of the leased property.

operating loss See net operating loss.

operation of law The means by which legal consequences are imposed by law, regardless of the intent of the parties involved.

The phrase "operation of law" expresses the manner in which rights, and sometimes liabilities, devolve upon a person by the mere application to the particular transaction of the established rules of law, without the act or co-operation of the party himself. *Smith,* 116 Cal.Rptr.2d 728 (Cal.App., 2002)

opinion 1. A court's written explanation of how it applied the law to the facts to resolve a legal dispute. 2. A belief or conclusion expressing a value judgment that is not objectively verifiable.

opinion evidence Beliefs or inferences concerning facts in issue.

opinion of the attorney general Formal legal advice from the chief law officer of the government to another government official or agency.

opportunity cost Benefits a business foregoes by choosing one course of action (e.g., an investment) over another.

opportunity to be heard A due process requirement of being allowed to present objections to proposed government action that would deprive one of a right.

oppression 1. An act of cruelty; conduct intended to frighten or harm. 2. Excessive and unjust use of authority. 3. Substantial inequality of bargaining power of the parties to the contract and an absence of real negotiation or a meaningful choice on the part of the weaker party.

option 1. An agreement that gives the person to whom the option is granted (the optionee) the right within a limited time to accept an offer. The right to buy or sell a stated quantity of securities or other goods at a set price within a defined time. 2. An opportunity to choose.

Option is a continuing, irrevocable offer to sell property to an optionee within the time constraints of the option contract and at the price set forth therein. *Erich*, 167 Cal.Rptr. 538 (Cal.App., 1980)

option contract A unilateral agreement to hold an offer open. See option (1).

optionee The person to whom an option is granted.

OR Own recognizance. See also personal recognizance.

oral Spoken, not written.

oral argument A spoken presentation to the court on a legal issue, e.g., telling an appellate court why the rulings of a lower tribunal were valid or were in error.

oral contract See parol contract.

oral trust A trust established by its creator (the settler) by spoken words rather than in writing.

oral will See nuncupative will.

ordeal An ancient form of trial in which the innocence of an accused person was determined by his or her ability to come away from an endurance test (e.g., hold a red-hot iron in the hand) unharmed.

order 1. A command or instruction from a judge or other official. 2. An instruction to buy or sell something. 3. The language on a check (or other draft) directing or ordering the payment or delivery of money or other property to a designated person.

An order is a document which is either entered in the court's permanent minutes or signed by the judge and stamped filed. *Michael*, 106 Cal.Rptr.2d 240 (Cal.App., 2001)

order bill of lading A negotiable instrument, issued by a carrier to a shipper at the time goods are loaded aboard ship, that serves as a receipt that the carrier has received the goods for shipment, as a contract of carriage for those goods, and as documentary evidence of title to those goods.

ordered liberty The constitutional balance between respect for the liberty of the individual and the demands of organized society.

order nisi See decree nisi.

Order of the Coif An honorary organization of law students whose membership is based on excellence.

order paper A negotiable instrument payable to a specific person or to his or her designee (it is payable to order, not to bearer).

order to show cause See show cause order.

ordinance 1. A law passed by the local legislative branch of government (e.g., city council) that declares, commands, or prohibits something. Also called municipal ordinance. 2. A law or decree.

ordinary Usual; regularly occurring.

ordinary care Reasonable care under the circumstances.

Ordinary care requires the avoidance of unreasonable risk and therefore turns upon basic question of whether foreseeable risk of danger outweighs utility of act or manner in which it is done. *Chaplis*, 158 Cal.Rptr. 395 (Cal.App., 1979)

ordinary course of business See course of business.

ordinary income Wages, dividends, commissions, interest earned on savings, and similar kinds of income; income other than capital gains.

ordinary life insurance See whole life insurance.

ordinary negligence The failure to use reasonable care (often involving inadvertence) that does not constitute gross negligence or recklessness. Sometimes called simple negligence.

ordinary prudent person See reasonable man (person).

organic Inherent, integral, or basic.

organic law The fundamental law or constitution of a state or nation; laws that establish and define the organization of government.

organization A society or group of persons joined in a common purpose.

organize To induce persons to join an organization, e.g., a union.

organized crime A continuing conspiracy among highly organized and disciplined groups to engage in supplying illegal goods and services.

Organized crime means crime that is of a conspiratorial nature and that is either of an organized nature and seeks to supply illegal goods and services such as narcotics, prostitution, loan sharking, gambling, and pornography, or that, through planning and coordination of individual efforts, seeks to conduct the illegal activities of arson for profit, hijacking, insurance fraud, . . . Cal. Penal Code § 186.2(d)

organized labor Employees in labor unions.

original 1. The first form, from which copies are made. 2. New and unusual.

original contractor See general contractor.

original document rule See best evidence rule.

original intent The meaning understood by the framers or drafters of the U.S. Constitution, a statute, a contract, or other document.

original jurisdiction The power of a court to be the first to hear and resolve a case before it is reviewed by another court.

original package doctrine Goods imported into a state cannot be taxed by that state if they are in their original packaging when shipped.

original promise A promise, made for the benefit of the promisor, to pay or guarantee the debt of another.

original writ The first process or initial step in bringing or prosecuting a suit.

origination fee A fee charged by the lender for preparing the loan documents and processing the loan.

orphan's Court See probate court.

OSHA See Occupational Safety and Health Administration (*www.osha.gov*).

ostensible Apparent; appearing to be accurate or true.

ostensible agency An agency that arises when the principal's conduct allows others to believe that the agent possesses authority, which in fact does not exist.

ostensible authority The authority a principal intentionally or by lack of ordinary care allows a third person to believe the agent possesses. See also apparent authority.

Ostensible authority is such as a principal, intentionally or by want of ordinary care, causes or allows a third person to believe the agent to possess. Cal. Civil Code § 2317. *People v. Surety Ins.*, 186 Cal.Rptr. 385 (Cal.App., 1982)

OTC See over-the-counter.

our federalism Federal courts must refrain from hearing constitutional challenges to state action when federal action is regarded as an improper intrusion on the right of a state to enforce its own laws in its own courts.

oust To remove; to deprive of possession or of a right.

ouster Turning out (or keeping excluded) someone entitled to possession of property. Wrongful dispossession.

outlaw 1. To prohibit or make illegal. 2. A person excluded from the benefits and protection of the law. 3. A fugitive.

out-of-court Not part of a court proceeding.

out-of-court settlement The resolution or settlement of a legal dispute without the participation of the court.

out-of-pocket expenses Expenditures made out of one's own funds.

out-of-pocket rule The damages awarded will be the difference between the purchase price and the real or actual value of the property received.

Out-of-pocket damages on a fraud claim restores plaintiff to financial position he enjoyed prior to fraudulent transaction, awarding difference in actual value between what plaintiff gave and what he received. *Fragale*, 1 Cal.Rptr.3d 616 (Cal.App., 2003)

output contract A contract in which one party agrees to sell its entire output, which the other party agrees to buy during a designated period.

outrage See intentional infliction of emotional distress.

outrageous Shocking; beyond the bounds of human decency.

outside director A member of a board of directors who is not an officer or employee of the corporation.

outstanding 1. Uncollected, unpaid. 2. Publicly issued and sold.

over Passing or taking effect after a prior estate or interest ends or is terminated.

overbreadth doctrine A law is invalid, though designed to prohibit legitimately regulated conduct, if it is so broad that it includes within its prohibitions constitutionally protected freedoms.

A governmental purpose to control or prevent activities constitutionally subject to state regulation may not be achieved by means that sweep unnecessarily broadly and thereby invade the area of protected freedoms. *In re Englebrecht*, 79 Cal.Rptr.2d 89 (Cal.App., 1998)

overdraft 1. A check written on an account with less funds than the amount of the check. 2. The act of overdrawing a bank account.

overhead The operating expenses of a business (e.g., rent, utilities) for which customers or clients are not charged a separate fee.

overissue To issue shares in an excessive or unauthorized quantity.

overreaching Taking unfair advantage of another's naiveté or other vulnerability, especially by deceptive means.

override 1. To set aside, supersede, or nullify. 2. A commission paid to managers on sales made by subordinates. 3. A commission paid to a real estate agent when a landowner makes a sale on his or her own (after the listing agreement expires) to a purchaser who was found by the agent.

overrule 1. To decide against or deny. 2. To reject or cancel an earlier opinion as precedent by rendering an opposite decision on the same question of law.

overt act 1. An act that reasonably appears to be about to inflict great bodily harm, justifying the use of self-defense. 2. An outward act from which criminality may be implied. 3. An outward objective action performed by one of the members of a conspiracy.

Overt act, as element of conspiracy, means any step taken or act committed by one or more of the conspirators that goes beyond mere planning or agreement to accomplish conspiracy's objective. *People v. Profit*, 229 Cal.Rptr. 148 (Cal.App., 1986)

over-the-counter (OTC) 1. Sold or transferred independent of a securities exchange. 2. Sold without the need of a prescription.

owelty Money paid to equalize a disproportionate division of property.

ownership The right to possess, control, and use property, and to convey it to others. Having rightful title to property.

oyer Reading a document aloud in court or a petition to have such a reading.

oyer and terminer A special court with jurisdiction to hear treason and other criminal cases. A judge's commission to hear such cases.

oyez Hear ye; a call announcing the beginning of a court proceeding or a proclamation.

P

P.A. See professional association.

PAC See political action committee.

PACE See Paralegal Advanced Competency Exam (*www.paralegals.org*).

PACER See Public Access to Court Electronic Records (*pacer.psc.uscourts.gov*).

pack 1. To assemble with an improper purpose. 2. To fill or arrange.

pact 1. A bargain. 2. An agreement between two or more nations or states.

pactum An agreement. See also nudum pactum.

paid-in capital Money or property paid to a corporation by its owners for its capital stock.

paid-in surplus That portion of the surplus of a corporation not generated by profits but contributed by the stockholders. Surplus accumulated by the sale of stock at more than par value.

In addition to the minimum capital required, the commissioner may require that the consideration for the issuance of capital stock shall be sufficient to create a paid-in surplus in an amount satisfactory to the commissioner. Cal. Financial Code § 5602

pain Physical discomfort and distress.

pain and suffering Physical discomfort or emotional distress; a disagreeable mental or emotional experience.

pains and penalties See bill of pains and penalties.

pais See in pais.

palimony Support payments ordered after the end of a nonmarital relationship if the party seeking support was induced to sustain or initiate the relationship by a promise of support or if support is otherwise equitable.

palming off Misrepresenting one's own goods or services as those of another. Also called passing off.

***Palsgraf* rule** Negligence liability is limited to reasonably foreseeable harm. *Palsgraf v. Long Island R. Co.*, 162 N.E. 99 (NY 1928).

pander To engage in pandering. A panderer is one who panders.

pandering The recruitment of prostitutes. Acting as a go-between to cater to the lust or base desires of another.

Pandering. A person who does any of the following is guilty of pandering: (1) Procures another person for the purpose of prostitution. . . . Cal. Penal Code § 266i

panel 1. A group of judges, usually three, who decide a case in a court with a larger number of judges. 2. A list of persons summoned to be examined for jury duty or to serve on a particular jury. 3. A group of attorneys available in a group legal services plan.

paper A written or printed document that is evidence of a debt. Commercial paper; a negotiable instrument.

paper loss; paper profit An unrealized loss or gain on a security or other investment that is still held. Loss or profit that will not become actual until the asset is sold or closed out.

papers Pleadings, motions, and other litigation documents filed in court.

paper title The title listed or described on public records after the deed is recorded. Also called record title.

par 1. An acceptable average or standard. 2. See par value.

paralegal A person with legal skills who works under the supervision of an attorney or who is otherwise authorized by law to use his or her skills; this person performs substantive tasks that do not require all the skills of an attorney and that most secretaries are not trained to perform. Also called legal assistant.

Paralegal means a person who holds himself or herself out to be a paralegal, who is qualified by education, training, or work experience, who either contracts with or is employed by an attorney, law firm, corporation, governmental agency, or other entity, and who performs substantial legal work under the direction and supervision of an active member of the State Bar of California . . . Cal. Business & Professions Code § 6450(a)

Paralegal Advanced Competency Exam (PACE) The certification exam of the National Federation of Paralegal Associations for experienced paralegals (*www.paralegals.org*).

parallel citation A citation to an additional reporter where you can read the same court opinion.

paramount title Superior title as among competing claims to title.

paraphernalia 1. Property kept by a married woman on her husband's death in addition to her dower. 2. Equipment used for an activity.

parcel 1. To divide into portions and distribute. 2. A small package or wrapped bundle. 3. A part or portion of land.

parcenary See coparcenary.

parcener See coparcener.

pardon An act of government exempting an individual from punishment for crime and from any resulting civil disabilities.

parens patriae The state's power to protect and act as guardian of persons who suffer disabilities (e.g., minors, insane persons).

The traditional role and obligation of the state to act as guardian of children and other incompetents. *Quigley*, 76 Cal.Rptr.2d 792 (Cal.App. 4 Dist., 1998)

parent A biological or adoptive mother or father of another.

parental kidnapping A parent's taking and removing his or her child from the custody of a person with legal custody without the latter's consent with the intent of defeating the custody jurisdiction of the court that currently has such jurisdiction.

parental liability law A law that makes parents liable (up to a limited dollar amount) for torts committed by their minor children.

parental rights The rights of a parent to raise his or her children, receive their services, and control their income and property.

parent corporation A corporation that controls another corporation (called the subsidiary corporation) through stock ownership.

pari delicto See in pari delicto.

pari materia See in pari materia.

parish 1. A territorial government division in Louisiana. 2. An ecclesiastical division of a city or town administered by a pastor.

parity Equality in amount, status, or value.

parliament A legislative body of a country, e.g., England.

parliamentarian An expert who provides advice on parliamentary law.

parliamentary Pertaining to the parliament or to its rules.

parliamentary law Rules of procedure to be followed by legislatures and other formal organizations.

parol 1. Spoken rather than in writing. 2. An oral statement.

parol contract A contract that is not in writing. Also called oral contract.

parole Allowing a prisoner to leave confinement before the end of his or her sentence.

parole board A government agency that decides if and under what conditions inmates can be released before completing their sentences.

parolee An ex-prisoner who has been placed on parole.

parol evidence rule Prior or contemporaneous oral statements cannot be used to vary or contradict a written contract the parties intended to be final.

Extrinsic evidence is not admissible to contradict express terms in a written contract or to explain what the agreement was. *Cerritos*, 97 Cal.Rptr.2d 432 (Cal.App., 2000)

parole officer A government official who supervises persons on parole.

partial average See particular average.

partial breach A nonmaterial breach of contract that entitles a party to a remedy but not the right to consider the contract terminated.

partial disability A worker's inability to perform jobs he or she could perform before a work injury, even though still able to perform other gainful jobs subject to the disability.

Permanent total disability means a permanent disability with a rating of 100 percent permanent disability only. Permanent partial disability means a permanent disability with a rating of less than 100 percent permanent disability. Cal. Labor Code § 4452.5(a)(b)

partial insanity See diminished capacity.

partial verdict A verdict that is not the same on all the counts charged or on all the defendants in the trial.

particeps criminis A participant in a crime; an accomplice or accessory.

participation loan A loan issued or owned by more than one lender.

particular average An accidental partial loss of goods at sea by one who must bear the loss alone. Also called partial average.

particular estate An estate less than a fee simple, e.g., life estate.

particular lien A right to hold property as security for labor or funds expended on that specific property. Also called special lien.

particulars The details. See also bill of particulars.

partition The dividing of land held by co-owners into distinct portions, resulting in individual ownership.

partner 1. One who has united with others to form a partnership. 2. Two or more persons engaged in a jointly owned business.

partnership A voluntary association of two or more persons to place their resources in a jointly owned business or enterprise, with a proportional sharing of profits and losses.

Partnership connotes co-ownership in partnership property with a sharing in the profits and losses of a continuing business. *Vogel*, 245 P.2d 1069 (Cal.App., 1952)

partnership association A hybrid type of business with characteristics of a close corporation and a limited partnership.

part performance rule When an oral agreement fails to meet the requirements of the statute of frauds, the agreement may sometimes still be enforced when a relying party has partly performed the agreement.

party 1. One who brings a lawsuit or against whom a lawsuit is brought. 2. One who is concerned with, has an interest in, or takes part in the performance of an act. 3. A formal political association.

party aggrieved See aggrieved party.

party in interest See real party in interest.

party to be charged One against whom another seeks to enforce a contract.

par value An amount stated in a security, policy, or other instrument as its value. Also called face amount, face value, par, stated value.

pass 1. To utter or pronounce. 2. To transfer. 3. To enact into law by a legislative body. 4. To approve. 5. To forego.

passage Enactment into law by a legislative body.

passbook A bank document that records a customer's account activities.

passenger Any occupant of a motor vehicle other than the operator.

passim Here and there; in various places throughout.

passing off See palming off.

passion Any strong emotion that often interferes with cool reflection of the mind. See also heat of passion.

passive 1. Submitting without active involvement. 2. Inactive.

passive negligence The unreasonable failure to do something; carelessly permitting defects to exist.

Passive negligence is found in mere nonfeasance, such as failure to discover dangerous condition or to perform duty imposed by law. *Herman*, 132 Cal.Rptr. 86 (Cal.App., 1976)

passive trust A trust whose trustee has no active duties. Also called dry trust, naked trust, nominal trust, simple trust.

passport A document that identifies a citizen, constitutes permission to travel to foreign countries, and acts as a request to foreign powers that the citizen be allowed to pass freely and safely.

past consideration An earlier benefit or detriment that was not exchanged for a new promise.

past recollection recorded A written record of a matter about which a witness now has insufficient memory. The record may be read into evidence if it was made or adopted by the witness when the matter was fresh in his or her memory. Fed. R. Evid. 803(5). An exception to the hearsay rule. Also called recorded recollection.

Past recollection recorded. The statement concerns a matter as to which the witness has insufficient present recollection to enable him to testify fully and accurately, and the statement is contained in a writing which: (1) Was made at a time when the fact recorded in the writing actually occurred or was fresh in the witness' memory; (2) Was made at a time when the fact recorded in the writing actually occurred or was fresh in the witness' memory. . . . Cal. Evidence Code § 1237(a)

patent 1. A grant of a privilege or authority by the government. 2. A grant made by the government to an inventor for the exclusive right to make, use, and sell an invention for a term of years.

patentable Suitable to be patented because the device or process is novel, useful, and nonobvious.

patent defect See apparent defects.

patentee A person to whom a patent is granted; the holder of a patent.

patent infringement See infringement of patent.

patent medicine Packaged medicines or drugs sold over the counter under a trademark or other trade symbol.

paternity The state or condition of being a father.

paternity suit A court action to determine whether a person is the father of a child for whom support is owed. Also called bastardy proceeding.

patient-physician privilege See doctor-patient privilege.

pat. pend. Patent (application is) pending.

patricide 1. Killing one's father. 2. One who has killed his or her father.

patrimony 1. Heritage from one's ancestors. 2. That which is inherited from a father. 3. The total value of a person's rights and obligations.

patronage 1. The power to offer political jobs or other privileges. 2. Assistance received from a patron. 3. The customers of a business.

pattern 1. A reliable sample of observable features. 2. A model.

pauper A person so poor that he or she needs public assistance.

pawn To deliver personal property to another as security for a loan.

pawnbroker A person in the business of lending money upon the deposit of personal property as security.

Every person engaged in the business of receiving goods, including motor vehicles, in pledge as security for a loan is a pawnbroker within the meaning of this division. Cal. Financial Code § 21000

payable 1. Able to be paid. 2. Money or a balance owed.

payable to bearer Payable to whoever possesses the instrument.

payable to order Payable to a named person, the payee.

payee One to whom or to whose order a check or other negotiable instrument is made payable. One who receives money.

payer or payor One who makes or should make payment, particularly on a check or other negotiable instrument.

payment 1. The partial or full performance of an obligation by tendering money or other consideration. 2. An amount paid.

payment bond A guarantee from a surety that laborers and material suppliers will be paid if the general contractor defaults.

Payment bond means a bond with good and sufficient sureties that is conditioned for the payment in full of the claims of all claimants and that also by its terms is made to inure to the benefit of all claimants so as to give these persons a right of action to recover upon this bond in any suit brought to foreclose the liens provided for in this title or in a separate suit brought on the bond. An owner, original contractor, or a subcontractor may be the principal upon any payment bond. Cal. Civil Code § 3096

payment in due course Payment made in good faith at or after maturity to the holder without notice that his or her title is defective.

payment into court Property deposited into court for eventual distribution by court order.

payor See payer.

payroll tax 1. A tax on employees based on their wages. 2. A tax on employers as a percentage of wages paid to employees.

P.C. See professional corporation.

PCR See postconviction relief.

P.D. 1. See public defender. 2. Police department.

peace Orderly behavior in the community. Public tranquility.

peaceable 1. Without force or violence. 2. Gentle, calm.

peaceable possession 1. Possession that is continuous and not interrupted by adverse claims or attempts to dispossess. 2. Peaceful enjoyment.

peace bond A bond required of one who threatens to breach the peace.

peace officers A person designated by public authority to keep the peace and to arrest persons suspected of crime.

"County peace officers" includes: (a) All sheriffs, undersheriffs, chief deputy sheriffs, jailers, turnkeys, deputy sheriffs, bailiffs, process servers, constables, deputy constables, motorcycle officers, its heads and assistant heads of all divisions of the sheriff's office, and all their regularly appointed deputies. Cal. Government Code § 31904

peculation Misappropriation of money or goods. Embezzlement.

pecuniary Relating to money.

pecuniary interest A financial interest, e.g., the opportunity, directly or indirectly, to share in the profit (or loss) derived from a transaction.

pederasty Sexual relations (oral or anal) between a man and boy.

penal Concerning or containing a penalty.

penal action 1. A civil action based on a statute that subjects a wrongdoer to liability in favor of the person wronged as a punishment for the wrongful act. 2. A criminal prosecution.

penal bond A bond obligating the payment of a specified penalty (called the penal sum) upon nonperformance of a condition.

penal code A compilation of statutes on criminal law.

penal institution See penitentiary.

penal law See criminal law.

penal statute A statute that defines a crime and its punishment.

penal sum See penal bond.

penalty 1. Punishment for a criminal or civil wrong. 2. An extra charge imposed if a stated condition (e.g., late payment) occurs.

For limitations purposes, penalty includes any law compelling defendant to pay plaintiff other than what is necessary to compensate him for legal damage done him by former. Cal. Code of Civil Procedure § 340. *People ex rel. Dept. of Conservation*, 55 Cal.Rptr.2d 610 (Cal.App., 1996)

penalty clause A contract clause imposing a stated penalty (rather than actual damages) for nonperformance.

pendency While waiting; while still undecided.

pendent Undecided; pending.

pendente lite During the progress of the suit; pending the litigation.

pendent jurisdiction The power of a court to hear a claim over which it has no independent subject-matter jurisdiction if the facts of the claim are closely enough related on the facts of a main claim over which it does have such jurisdiction.

pending Under consideration; begun but not yet completed.

penetration An intrusion, however slight, of any object or any part of the defendant's body into the genital or anal openings of the victim's body.

penitentiary A place of confinement for persons convicted of crime, usually serious crimes. Also called penal institution, prison.

***Pennoyer* rule** A personal judgment requires personal jurisdiction. *Pennoyer v. Neff*, 95 U.S. 714 (1877).

penny stocks High-risk equity securities, often selling at less than $1 a share and usually not traded on an approved securities exchange.

penology The study of prisons and the rehabilitation of criminals.

pen register A device that records the numbers dialed on a telephone but not the conversations themselves.

pension Regularly paid funds as a retirement or other benefit.

Pension means payments for life derived from contributions made from employer controlled funds. Cal. Government Code § 20054

pension plan A plan of an employer, primarily to pay determinable retirement benefits to its employees or their beneficiaries.

penumbra doctrine Implied constitutional rights, e.g., the right of privacy, exist on the periphery of explicit constitutional rights.

peonage Illegally compelling one to perform labor to pay off a debt.

people The prosecution in a criminal case representing the citizenry.

peppercorn A small amount; nominal consideration.

per By; for each.

per annum Annually.

per autre vie See pur autre vie.

per capita 1. For each person. 2. Divided equally among each person.

Per stirpes means by root or stock or by representation, while per capita, the antithetical term, means by heads or polls, according to number of individuals, or share and share alike. *Lombardi*, 40 Cal.Rptr. 899 (Cal.App., 1965)

percentage depletion A method of taking a depletion deduction based on a percentage of gross income from an oil or gas well.

percentage lease A lease in which the rent is a percentage of gross or net sales, often with a minimum required payment.

per curiam opinion (an opinion "by the court" as a whole). A court opinion, usually a short one, that does not name the judge who wrote it.

per diem By the day; an allowance or amount of so much per day.

peremptory 1. Conclusive; final. 2. Without need for explanation.

peremptory challenge The right to challenge and remove a prospective juror without giving any reasons. Such challenges, however, cannot be used to discriminate against a protected minority.

A party may not use a peremptory challenge to remove a prospective juror on the basis of an assumption that the prospective juror is biased merely because of his or her race, color, religion, sex, national origin, sexual orientation, or similar grounds. Cal. Code of Civil Procedure § 231.5

peremptory instruction An instruction by the judge to the jury that it must obey. (The equivalent of a directed verdict.)

perfect 1. Complete, executed. 2. To follow all procedures needed to complete or put in final form so that it is legally enforceable.

perfected Completed, executed; legally enforceable.

perfect tender rule Exact (perfect) performance by the seller of its obligations can be a condition of the enforceability of the contract.

performance The fulfillment of an obligation according to its terms.

performance bond See completion bond.

peril That which may cause damage or injury; exposure to danger.

peril of the sea A peril peculiar to the sea that cannot be guarded against by ordinary human skill and prudence.

periodic Happening at fixed intervals; recurring now and then.

periodic alimony Alimony paid indefinitely at scheduled intervals. Also called permanent alimony.

periodic tenancy A tenancy that continues indefinitely for successive periods (e.g., month to month, year to year) unless terminated by the parties.

perjury Making a false statement under oath concerning a material matter with the intent to provide false testimony. Also called false swearing.

Every person who, having taken an oath that he or she will testify, declare, depose, or certify truly in any of the cases in which the oath may be administered, willfully and contrary to the oath, states as true any material matter which he or she knows to be false is guilty of perjury. Cal. Penal Code § 118(a)

perks See perquisites.

permanent Continuing indefinitely.

permanent alimony See periodic alimony.

permanent injunction An injunction issued after a court hearing on the merits of the underling issues. Also called perpetual injunction.

permissive 1. Allowable; optional. 2. Lenient.

permissive counterclaim A counterclaim that does not arise out of the same transaction or occurrence that is basis of the plaintiff's claim.

permissive joinder The joinder of a party that is allowed (but not required) if the claims involved arise out of the same occurrence and there are questions of law or fact that will be common to all the parties.

permissive presumption A presumption that allows (but does not require) the fact finder to infer the presumed fact.

Permissive presumption allows, but does not require, the trier of fact to infer the elemental fact from proof by the prosecutor of the basic one. Cal. Evidence Code §§ 600(a). *People v. McCall*, 8 Cal.Rptr.3d 337 (CA 2004)

permissive use A use expressly or impliedly within the scope of permission.

permissive waste A tenant's failure to use ordinary care to preserve and protect the property, such as allowing deterioration for lack of repair.

permit 1. To expressly agree to the doing of an act. 2. A formal document granting the right to do something. A license.

perp (slang) Perpetrator of a crime.

perpetrate To commit or carry out an act, often criminal in nature.

perpetrator A person who commits a crime or other serious wrong.

perpetual injunction See permanent injunction.

perpetual lease A lease of land with no termination date.

perpetual succession The uninterrupted (perpetual) existence of a corporation even though its owners (shareholders) change.

perpetuation of testimony Procedures to ensure that the testimony of a deposition witness will be available for trial.

perpetuity 1. Continuing forever. 2. A future interest that will not vest within the period prescribed by law.

perquisites (perks) Incidental benefits in addition to salary.

per quod Needing additional facts or proof of special damages.

per se In itself; inherently. Without needing additional facts.

persecution The offensive infliction of suffering or harm upon those who differ in race, religion, sexual orientation, or beliefs.

person A natural person, plus legal entities such as corporations that the law endows with some of the rights and duties of natural persons.

Person means any individual, firm, company, association, organization, partnership, limited liability company, or corporation. Cal. Business & Professions Code § 7590.1(a)

personal Pertaining to a person or to personal property.

personal bond A bail bond with no sureties.

personal chattel Tangible or intangible personal property.

personal effects Articles intimately or closely associated with the person (e.g., clothing, jewelry, wallet).

Personal effects constitute tangible things, chattels and subject of personal use. *In re Townsend's Estate*, 34 Cal.Rptr. 275 (Cal.App., 1963)

personal exemption A deduction from adjusted gross income for an individual and qualified dependents.

personal injury (PI) Injury, damage, or invasion of one's body or personal rights. Harm to personal (as opposed to property) interests.

personality The legal status of being a person.

personal judgment A judgment against the person (over whom the court had personal jurisdiction) that may be satisfied out of any property of that person. Also called judgment in personam.

personal jurisdiction A court's power over a person to adjudicate his or her personal rights. Also called *in personam jurisdiction.* More limited kinds of jurisdiction include the court's power over a person's interest in specific property (*quasi in rem jurisdiction*) or over the property itself (*in rem jurisdiction*).

personal knowledge Firsthand knowledge rather than what others say.

A present recollection of an impression derived from the exercise of the witness's own senses. Cal. Evidence § 702(a). *Alvarez*, 95 Cal.Rptr.2d 719 (Cal.App., 1999)

personal liability An obligation that one can be forced to pay or satisfy out of personal (not just business) assets.

personal notice Information communicated directly to a person.

personal property Everything, other than real property, that can be owned, e.g., a car, a stock option.

personal recognizance Pretrial release of a defendant in a criminal case without posting a bond, based solely on a promise to appear. Release on own recognizance (ROR).

personal representative A person appointed to administer the estate and legal affairs of someone who has died or who is incapacitated.

personal right A right that inheres in the status of an individual as opposed to his or her property rights.

personal service Handing a copy of a notice or summons to the defendant.

The actual delivery of the papers to the defendant in person. *Sternbeck*, 307 P.2d 970 (Cal.App., 1957)

personalty Personal property.

personam See in personam, personal judgment.

per stirpes Taking the share a deceased ancestor would have been entitled to (had he or she lived) rather than taking as individuals in their own right. Taking by right of representation. Also called in stirpes.

persuasive authority Any source a court relies on in reaching its decision that it is not required to rely on.

pertinent Relevant to an issue.

petit Lesser, minor.

petition 1. A formal written request. 2. A complaint.

petitioner One who presents a petition or complaint to a tribunal.

petit jury An ordinary jury called and sworn in (impaneled) to try a particular civil or criminal case. Also called petty jury, trial jury. See also grand jury.

petition in bankruptcy A formal application from a debtor to a bankruptcy court to file for bankruptcy.

pettifogger 1. One who quibbles over trivia. 2. An incompetent, ill-prepared attorney who sometimes engages in questionable practices.

petty Of less importance or merit.

petty jury See petit jury.

petty larceny The larceny or stealing of personal property with a value below a statutorily set amount (e.g., $200).

petty offense A minor violation of the law, e.g., a traffic violation.

Party charged with civil contempt is charged with a petty offense and is, therefore, not entitled to a jury trial. Cal. Code of Civil Procedure §§ 1209–1222. *Pacific Tel*, 72 Cal.Rptr. 177 (Cal.App., 1968)

p.h.v. See pro hac vice.

physical Pertaining to the body or other material (nonmental) things.

physical evidence See real evidence (1).

physical fact A thing or action that can be perceived by the senses.

physical-fact rule The testimony of a witness that is positively contradicted by physical facts can be disregarded.

physical injury See bodily injury.

physician-patient privilege See doctor-patient privilege.

PI See personal injury.

picket To patrol or demonstrate outside a business or other organization in order to protest something it is doing or proposing and thereby pressure it to change.

Picket describes conduct of one who patrols an area or stations himself at a place bearing some insignia or sign designed to persuade or protest. Cal. Penal Code, § 171f. *Simpson*, 92 Cal.Rptr. 417 (Cal.App., 1971)

pickpocket One who secretly steals something from another's person.

piecework Work for which one is paid by the number of units produced.

piercing the corporate veil A process by which a court disregards the limited liability normally afforded corporations and instead imposes personal liability on officers, directors, and shareholders.

pilferage Stealing; petty larceny.

pillage Using force or violence to rob someone, often in times of war.

pimp One who solicits customers for prostitutes.

pioneer patent A patent concerning a function or advance never before performed or one of major novelty and importance.

piracy 1. Robbery or seizure of a ship at sea or airplane in motion. See also hijack. 2. Copying in violation of intellectual property laws.

P.J. Presiding judge.

P.L. See public law.

place of abode One's residence or domicile.

placer claim A mining claim to loose minerals in sand or gravel.

plagiarism Using another's original ideas or expressions as one's own.

plain error An obvious, prejudicial error an appellate court will hear even if it was not raised at trial. Also called fundamental error.

plain meaning The usual and ordinary meaning given to words by reasonable persons at the time and place of their use.

The plain meaning of insurance policy language is the meaning a layperson would ordinarily attach to it. *Garamendi*, 31 Cal.Rptr.3d 395 (Cal.App., 2005)

plaintiff The person who initiates a civil action in court.

plaintiff in error The appellant; the party bringing the appeal.

plain view doctrine An officer can seize objects without a warrant if they can plainly be seen, there is probable cause they are connected to a crime, and the officer is lawfully present.

planned unit development (PUD) Development of land areas where standard zoning rules are suspended to achieve mixed-use flexibility.

plant patent A patent granted to someone who invents or discovers and asexually reproduces any distinct and new variety of plant.

plat 1. A map showing streets, easements, etc. 2. A small land area.

plea 1. The first pleading of the defendant in a civil case. 2. The defendant's formal response to a criminal charge, e.g., not guilty.

plea bargaining Negotiations whereby an accused pleads guilty to a lesser included offense or to one of multiple charges in exchange for the prosecution's agreement to support a dismissal of some charges or a lighter sentence. Also called negotiated plea.

A method of disposing of criminal prosecutions through a guilty plea by the defendant in return for a reciprocal benefit, generally consisting of a less severe punishment than that which could result if he were convicted of all offenses charged. *People v. Renfro*, 22 Cal.Rptr.3d 680 (Cal.App., 2004)

plead To file a pleading, enter a plea, or argue a case in court.

pleadings Formal litigation documents (e.g., a complaint, answer) filed by parties that state or respond to claims or defenses of other parties.

plea in abatement A plea objecting to the timing or other defect in the plaintiff's claim without challenging its merits.

plea in bar A plea that seeks a total rejection of a claim or charge.

plebiscite A vote of the people on a proposed law or policy.

pledge 1. Delivering personal property as security for the payment of a debt or other obligation. A bailment for this purpose. 2. A solemn promise or agreement to do or forbear something.

Pledge is bailment for security and is effected by delivery of possession of pledged property, although title remains in pledgor. *Hartford*, 270 Cal.Rptr. 12 (CA 1990)

pledgee The person to whom something is delivered in pledge.

pledgor The person who pledges; the one who delivers goods in pledge.

plenary 1. Complete, unlimited. 2. Involving all members.

plenary jurisdiction A court's unlimited judicial power over the parties and subject matter of a legal dispute.

plenipotentiary Someone (e.g., a diplomat) with full powers to act.

PLI Practicing Law Institute (*www.pli.edu*).

plottage The additional value of adjacent, undeveloped lots when combined into a single tract.

PLS See professional legal secretary (*www.nals.org*).

plurality The largest number of votes received even though this number is not more than half of all votes cast or that could have been cast.

plurality opinion The controlling opinion that is joined by the largest number of judges on the bench short of a majority.

pluries Process (e.g., a writ) that issues in the third (or later) instance after earlier ones been ineffectual.

PMI See private mortgage insurance.

pocket part A pamphlet inserted into a small pocket built into the inside back (and occasionally front) cover of a book. The pamphlet contains text that supplements or updates the material in the book.

pocket veto The president's "silent" or indirect rejection of a bill by not acting on it within 10 weekdays of receiving it if the legislature adjourns during this period.

POD account Pay-on-death account. An account payable to the owner during his or her life, and upon death, to a designated beneficiary.

point 1. A distinct legal position or issue. 2. A fee or service charge equal to one percent of the principal amount of the loan. 3. A unit for measuring the price or value of stocks or other securities.

point of error A lower court error asserted as a ground for appeal.

point reserved An issue on which the trial judge will rule later in the trial, allowing the case to proceed. Also called reserved point.

points and authorities See memorandum of points and authorities.

poisonous tree doctrine See fruit of the poisonous tree doctrine.

poison pill Steps by a corporation to discourage a hostile takeover, e.g., issuing new shares that would increase the takeover costs.

police A unit of the government charged with maintaining public order primarily through the prevention and investigation of crime.

police court See magistrate court.

police power The power of the state to enact laws, within constitutional limits, to promote public safety, health, morals, and convenience.

The power of sovereignty or power to govern, the inherent reserved power of the state to subject individual rights to reasonable regulation for the general welfare. *Massingill,* 125 Cal.Rptr.2d 561 (Cal.App., 2002)

policy 1. The principles by which an organization is managed. 2. An insurance contract. 3. A lottery-type numbers game.

policyholder An owner of an insurance policy, usually the insured.

political action committee (PAC) An organization (other than a political party or candidate committee) that uses fundraising or contributions to advocate the election or defeat of a clearly identified candidate for office or the victory or defeat of a public question.

political asylum See asylum (2).

political offense Crimes against a state or political order, e.g., treason.

political question A question that a court should not resolve because it concerns policy choices that are constitutionally committed for resolution to the legislative or executive branches or because of the absence of judicially discoverable and manageable standards for resolving it.

Political question rule compels dismissal of a lawsuit when complete deference to role of the legislative or executive branch is required and there is nothing upon which a court can adjudicate without impermissibly intruding upon authority of another branch of government. *Schabarum,* 70 Cal. Rptr.2d 745 (Cal.App., 1998)

poll the jury To ask each juror how he or she voted on the verdict.

poll tax A tax imposed on each individual regardless of income. Also called capitation tax, head tax.

polyandry Having more than one husband at the same time.

polygamy Having more than one spouse at the same time.

polygraph An instrument to record physiological processes, e.g., blood pressure, to detect lying. Also called lie detector.

Ponzi scheme A fraudulent investment scheme whereby returns to investors are financed, not through the success of an underlying business venture, but from the funds of newly attracted investors.

pool 1. To combine for a common purpose. 2. A combination or agreement by persons or companies to carry out a joint purpose. 3. A sum of money made up of stakes contributed by bettors in a game of chance.

Pool selling is the selling or distribution of shares or chances in a wagering pool. *People v. Coppla,* 224 P.2d 828 (Cal.App., 1950)

popular Pertaining to the general public.

pornography The portrayal of erotic behavior designed to cause sexual excitement. The portrayal is protected unless it is obscene.

port authority A government agency that plans and regulates traffic through a port by sea vessels, airplanes, public transportation, etc.

portfolio All the investments held by one person or institution.

port of entry The port where goods and travelers from abroad may enter the country. The port containing a station for customs officials.

positive evidence See direct evidence.

positive fraud Fraud that is actual or intentional rather than implied or constructive. Also called actual fraud, fraud in fact.

positive law Law actually and specifically enacted by a proper authority, usually a legislative body.

positivism See legal positivism.

posse See in posse.

posse comitatus ("the power or force of the county") Citizens called by the sheriff for special purposes, e.g., to help keep the peace.

possession 1. The actual custody or control of something. 2. That which one holds, occupies, or controls. 3. That which one owns.

Defendant has possession of a weapon when it is under his dominion and control. *People v. Pena,* 88 Cal.Rptr.2d 656 (Cal.App., 1999)

possession is nine-tenths of the law A false adage that nevertheless reflects the truth that the law does not always make it easy for a rightful property owner to oust someone in wrongful possession.

possessor One who has possession or custody of property.

possessory Relating to, founded on, or claiming possession.

possessory action An action to assert the right to keep or maintain possession of property.

possessory interest The right to exert control over specific property to the exclusion of others whether or not the right is based on title.

possibility of reverter The interest remaining in a grantor who conveys a fee simple determinable or a fee simple conditional. Any reversionary interest that is subject to a condition precedent. Also called reverter.

A possibility of reverter is created when the duration of an estate is limited by a measure of its life additional to that inherent in the estate itself and is created by a conveyance of a fee simple which is to last "until" a named event or "during" a period limited by such an event or "as long as" a certain state of facts continues and any expression conveying the same idea is sufficient. *Alamo School,* 6 Cal.Rptr. 272 (Cal.App., 1960)

post To send by mail. See also posting.

post-conviction relief (PCR) A remedy sought by a prisoner to challenge the legality of his or her conviction or sentence. A prisoner's collateral attack of his or her final judgment.

postdate To insert a date that is later than the actual date.

posterity 1. All descendants of a person. 2. Future generations.

posthumous Referring to events occurring after the death of a person.

posting 1. A form of substituted service of process by placing process in a prominent place (e.g., the front door of the defendant's residence). 2. The transfer of an original entry of debits or credits to a ledger. 3. The steps followed by a bank in paying a check. 4. Making something available on the Internet. 5. Making payment.

postmortem 1. Pertaining to what occurs after death. 2. See autopsy.

postnuptial agreement An agreement between spouses on the division of their property in the event of death or divorce.

postpone 1. To put off. 2. To subordinate or give a lower priority.

post-trial discovery Discovery procedures (e.g., deposition) conducted after judgment to help enforce (e.g., collect) a judgment.

pourover trust A trust that receives property from a will.

pourover will A will that transfers property to a trust.

poverty affidavit A written declaration of one's finances for purposes of qualifying for free legal services or other public benefit.

power 1. The right, ability, or authority to do something. 2. The right of a person to produce a change in a given legal relation by doing or not doing a given act. 3. Control over another.

power coupled with an interest A right or power to do some act, together with an interest in the subject matter on which the power is to be executed.

power of acceptance The right of an offeree to create a contract by accepting the terms of the offer.

power of appointment A power created when one person (the donor) grants another (the donee) authority to designate beneficiaries of the donor's property.

Power of appointment is a delegation by donor, in disposition of his property, to donee who does not become the owner and holds only as trustee. *Estate of Sevegney*, 118 Cal.Rptr. 728 (Cal.App., 1975)

power of attorney A document that authorizes another to act as one's agent or attorney-in-fact.

power of sale The right to sell property, e.g., the right of a trustee or mortgagee to sell the real property mortgaged in the event of a default.

pp. Pages.

PPO Preferred provider organization, a group of health care providers.

practice 1. A repeated or customary action; habitual performance. 2. The rules, forms, and methods used in a court or administrative tribunal. 3. The exercise of a profession or occupation.

practice of law Using legal skills to assist a specific person resolve his or her specific legal problem. The work of a lawyer in counseling and representing clients on legal matters.

The practice of law includes legal advice and counsel, and the preparation of legal instruments and contracts by which legal rights are secured although such matter may or may not be pending in a court. Rules of Professional Conduct, Rule 3, Cal. Business & Professions Code § 6076. *Bluestein*, 118 Cal.Rptr. 175 (CA 1974)

praecipe 1. A formal request that a court take some action. 2. A writ ordering an action or a statement of why it should not be taken.

praedial See predial.

praesenti See in praesenti.

prayer for relief The portion of a complaint or other pleading that sets forth the requested relief (e.g., damages) sought from the court.

preamble A clause at the beginning of a law (e.g., statute) or instrument (e.g., contract) setting out its objectives.

precarious Uncertain; at the whim or discretion of someone.

precatory Embodying a recommendation, hope, or advice rather than a positive command or direction; pertaining to a wish.

precedent A prior decision that can be used as a standard or guide in a later similar case.

precept 1. A rule imposing a standard of conduct or action. 2. A warrant, writ, or order.

precinct A subdivision or other geographical unit of local government.

preclusion order An order preventing a party from introducing specific evidence, usually because of a violation of discovery rules.

precognition A pretrial questioning of a potential witness.

precontract A contract designed to prevent a person from entering another contract of the same nature with someone else.

predatory pricing A company's artificially low prices designed to drive out competition so that it can reap monopoly profits at a later time.

A single firm, having a dominant share of the relevant market, cuts its prices in order to force competitors out of the market, or perhaps to deter potential entrants from coming in. Cal. Business & Professions Code §§ 17043, 17049, 17071. *Fisherman's Wharf*, 7 Cal.Rptr.3d 628 (Cal.App., 2003)

predecessor One who goes or who has gone before. A prior holder.

predial Pertaining or attached to land. Also spelled praedial.

predisposition A defendant's tendency or inclination to engage in certain conduct, e.g., illegal activity.

preemption 1. Under the Supremacy Clause, federal laws take precedence over (preempts) state laws when Congress (a) expressly mandates the preemption, (b) regulates an area so pervasively that an intent to preempt the entire field may be inferred, or (c) enacts a law that directly conflicts with state law. 2. The right of first purchase.

Express preemption of local law requires an express statement by the Legislature that it intends a state law to fully occupy the area. *Valley Vista*, 13 Cal.Rptr.3d 433 (Cal.App., 2004)

preemptive right The right of a stockholder to maintain a proportionate share of ownership by purchasing a proportionate share of any new stock issues. Also called subscription right.

pre-existing duty rule When a contracting party does or promises something that it is already legally obligated to do, there is no adequate consideration because the party has not incurred a detriment.

prefer 1. To submit for consideration; to file or prosecute. 2. To give advantage, priority, or privilege.

preference 1. Making a payment or a transfer by an insolvent debtor to one of the creditors, to the detriment of the other creditors. 2. The choice of one over another; the choice made.

preferential shop A job site in which union members are given priority or advantage over non-union members in hiring, promotion, etc.

preferred dividend A dividend payable to preferred shareholders, which has priority over dividends payable to common shareholders.

preferred risk An insurance classification of people who statistically have fewer accidents or have better health records and who, therefore, are often eligible for a reduced rate.

preferred stock Stock in a corporation that has a claim to income (dividends) or liquidation assets ahead of holders of common stock.

prejudice 1. Bias. A leaning toward or against one side of a cause for a reason other than merit. 2. Detriment or harm to one's legal rights.

prejudicial error An error justifying a reversal because it probably affected the outcome and was harmful to the substantial rights of the party objecting to the error. Also called fatal error, reversible error.

Error is prejudicial error when it is probable that the party against whom it was made would have achieved a better result but for the error. Cal. Code of Civil Procedure § 475. *Sargent Fletcher*, 3 Cal.Rptr.3d 279 (Cal.App., 2003)

preliminary Introductory; prior to the main body or theme.

preliminary examination See preliminary hearing.

preliminary hearing A pretrial hearing on whether probable cause exists that the defendant committed a crime. Also called preliminary examination, probable cause hearing.

preliminary injunction A temporary order to preserve the status quo and prevent irreparable loss of rights prior to a trial on the merits. Also called interlocutory injunction, temporary injunction.

premarital agreement A contract made by two persons about to be married that covers spousal support, property division, and related matters in the event of the separation of the parties, the death of one of them, or the dissolution of the marriage by divorce or annulment. Also called antenuptial agreement, marriage settlement, prenuptial agreement.

Premarital agreement means an agreement between prospective spouses made in contemplation of marriage and to be effective upon marriage. Cal. Family Code § 1610(a)

premeditated Considered, deliberated, or planned beforehand.

premise A statement that is a basis of an inference or conclusion.

premises 1. Land, its buildings, and surrounding grounds. 2. The part of a deed describing the interest transferred and related information, e.g., why the deed is being made. 3. The foregoing statements.

premium 1. An extra payment or bonus. 2. The payment to an insurance company to keep the policy. 3. The amount by which the market value of a bond or other security exceeds its par or face value.

prenuptial agreement See premarital agreement.

prepackaged bankruptcy (prepack) A plan negotiated between debtor and creditors prior to filing for bankruptcy.

prepaid legal services A plan by which a person pays premiums to cover future legal services. Also called legal plan, group legal services.

prepayment penalty An extra payment imposed when a promissory note or other loan is paid in full before it is due.

preponderance of evidence The burden of proof that is met when the evidence establishes that it is more likely than not that the facts are as alleged. Also called fair preponderance of the evidence.

Preponderance of evidence means such evidence as, when weighed with that opposed to it, has more convincing force, and from which it results that greater probability of truth lies therein. *In re Corey*, 41 Cal.Rptr. 379 (Cal.App., 1964)

prerogative An exclusive right or privilege of a person or office.

prerogative writ See extraordinary writ.

prescription 1. A method of acquiring ownership or title to property or rights by reason of continuous usage over a designated period of time. 2. An order for drugs issued by a licensed health professional. 3. A direction; a practice or course or action that is ordered. 4. The laying down or establishing of rules or directions.

prescriptive easement An easement created by an open, adverse, continuous use of another's land under claim of right over a designated period of time.

presence 1. Being physically present. 2. Being in physical proximity to or with something, including a sensory awareness of it.

present 1. Currently happening. 2. In attendance. 3. Under examination.

present danger See clear and present danger.

presentence report A probation report on the background of a convicted offender to assist the judge in imposing a sentence.

present estate An interest in property that can be possessed and enjoyed now, not just in the future. Also called present interest.

presenting bank Any bank presenting an item except a payor bank.

present interest See present estate.

present memory refreshed See present recollection refreshed.

presentment 1. A grand jury's accusation of crime that is not based on a prosecutor's request for an indictment. 2. Producing a check or other negotiable instrument for acceptance or payment.

present recollection refreshed A use by witnesses of writings or other objects to refresh their memory so that testimony can be given about past events from present recollection. Also called present memory refreshed, present recollection revived, refreshing memory or recollection.

presents This document being considered; the present instrument.

present sense impression A statement describing or explaining an event or condition made while perceiving it or immediately thereafter.

present value The amount of money you would have to be given now in order to produce or generate, with compound interest, a certain amount of money in a designated period of time. Also called present worth.

Present value of a gross award of future damages is that sum of money prudently invested at the time of judgment which will return, over the period the future damages are incurred, the gross amount of the award. *Holt,* 86 Cal.Rptr.2d 752 (Cal.App., 1999)

preside To be the person in authority; to direct the proceedings.

president The chief executive officer of an organization or country.

presidential elector See electoral college.

president judge The presiding or chief judge on some courts.

presume To take for granted as true before establishing it as such.

presumption An assumption or inference that a certain fact is true once another fact is established.

A presumption is a species of evidence which, unless controverted, is sufficient proof of the existence of the fact to which it relates. *People v. Theodore,* 262 P.2d 630 (Cal.App., 1953)

presumption of death A presumption that a person is no longer alive after being missing without explanation for a set period of time.

presumption of fact An inference; a logical inference or conclusion that the trier of the facts is at liberty to draw or refuse to draw.

presumption of innocence An accused cannot be convicted of a crime unless the government proves guilt beyond a reasonable doubt. The accused does not have the burden of proving his or her innocence.

presumption of law A particular conclusion the court must reach in absence of evidence to the contrary.

presumption of paternity; presumption of legitimacy A man is presumed to be the natural father of a child if he and the child's natural mother are married to each other and the child is conceived or born during the marriage. The presumption also applies if he receives the child into his home and holds the child out as his natural child.

presumption of survivorship In a common disaster involving multiple victims, a younger, healthier victim is presumed to have died after the others in the absence of evidence to the contrary.

presumptive 1. Providing a logical basis to believe; probable. 2. Created by or arising out of a presumption.

presumptive evidence Evidence sufficient to establish a given fact and which, if not rebutted or contradicted, will remain sufficient.

presumptive heir A person who can inherit if a closer relative is not born before the ancestor dies. Also called heir presumptive.

presumptive trust See resulting trust.

pretermit To pass by, omit, or disregard.

pretermitted heir A child or spouse omitted in a will by a testator.

Where will left all of testator's property to his surviving son and daughter-in-law, without mentioning surviving son of testator's deceased son or indicating that such omission was intentional, no settlement was made on such grandson, and he was not given any part of testator's estate by testator before his death, grandson was pretermitted heir. *In re Brainard's Estate,* 174 P.2d 702 (Cal.App., 1946)

pretext arrest A valid arrest for an improper reason, e.g., to investigate a different offense for which an arrest is not valid.

pretrial conference A meeting of the attorneys and the judge (or magistrate) before the trial to attempt to narrow the issues, to secure stipulations, and to make a final effort to settle the case without a trial.

pretrial detention Keeping someone in custody before trial.

pretrial discovery Devices parties can use to uncover facts that will help them prepare for trial (e.g., depositions, interrogatories).

pretrial diversion; pretrial intervention See diversion (2).

pretrial order A judge's order before a trial stating the issues to be tried and any stipulations of the parties.

prevail 1. To be in general use or practice. 2. To succeed.

prevailing party The party winning the judgment.

Parties may be considered prevailing parties for attorney fees purposes if they succeed on any significant issue in litigation that achieves some of the benefit the parties sought in bringing suit. *Bowman,* 31 Cal.Rptr.3d 447 (Cal.App., 2005)

preventive detention Detaining someone before trial to prevent fleeing, future antisocial behavior, or self-inflicted harm.

preventive justice Restraining orders, peace bonds, and other remedies designed to keep the peace and prevent future wrongdoing.

price discrimination A difference in price a seller charges different customers for the same product or one of like quality.

price fixing An agreement on prices that otherwise would be set by market forces. Any means calculated to eliminate competition and manipulate price.

price supports Devices (e.g., government subsidies) to keep prices from falling below a set level.

priest-penitent privilege See clergy-penitent privilege.

prima facie 1. On the face of it, at first sight. 2. Sufficient.

prima facie case A case as presented that will prevail until contradicted and overcome by contrary evidence.

The words prima facie mean at first view, and a prima facie case is one that is received or continues until contrary is shown and can be overthrown only by rebutting evidence adduced on other side. *Maganini,* 221 P.2d 241 (Cal.App., 1950)

prima facie evidence Sufficient evidence of a fact unless rebutted.

prima facie tort The intentional infliction of harm without justification, resulting in special damages.

primary activity A strike, picketing, or other action directed against an employer with whom a union has a labor dispute.

primary authority Any law (e.g., case, statute) that a court could rely on in reaching a decision.

primary boycott Action by a union to urge its members and the public not to patronize a firm with which the union has a labor dispute.

primary election An election by a party's voters to select (nominate) candidates to run in a general election.

primary evidence The best or highest quality evidence available.

primary jurisdiction doctrine Although a case is properly before a court, if there are issues requiring administrative expertise, the court can refrain from acting until the administrative agency acts.

The doctrine requires that the suit be stayed until the agency resolves the issue, whereupon the lawsuit resumes if the agency's resolution, assuming it survives review by whatever court has jurisdiction to review the agency's decisions, has not resolved the entire controversy. *Wise*, 34 Cal.Rptr.3d 222 (Cal.App., 2005)

primary liability Liability for which one is directly responsible, rather than secondarily after someone else fails to pay or perform.

primary market 1. The market where new issues of securities are first sold. 2. The main target of an initial offering of goods and services.

prime contractor See general contractor.

prime rate The lowest rate of interest charged by a bank to its best (most creditworthy) customers for short-term loans.

primogeniture 1. The status of being the first-born of siblings. 2. The right of the oldest son to inherit the entire estate.

principal 1. The amount of debt not including interest. 2. The initial sum invested. 3. A perpetrator of a crime. 4. One who permits an agent to act on his or her behalf. 5. One with prime responsibility for an obligation. 6. See corpus (2).

prior 1. Before in time or preference. 2. An earlier conviction.

prior art Any relevant knowledge, acts, and descriptions that pertain to, but predate, the invention in question.

prior consistent statement An earlier statement made by a witness that supports what he or she is now saying at the trial.

prior inconsistent statement An earlier statement made by a witness that conflicts what he or she is now saying at the trial.

priority A legal preference or precedence, e.g., the right to be paid first.

prior lien A lien with rights superior to other liens.

prior restraint A judicial or other government restriction on a publication before it is published.

Pior restraint is an administrative or judicial order that forbids certain speech in advance of the time the communication is to occur. *San Jose Mercury News*, 18 Cal.Rptr.3d 645 (Cal.App., 2004)

prison See penitentiary.

prisoner A person in police custody serving a prison sentence.

privacy The absence of unwanted attention into one's private concerns or affairs. Being left alone. See also invasion of privacy.

The right of privacy is the right to live one's life in seclusion, without being subjected to unwarranted and undesired publicity, in short, it is the right to be let alone. *Kerby*, 127 P.2d 577 (Cal.App., 1942)

private 1. Pertaining to individual or personal matters as opposed to public or official ones. 2. Restricted in use to designated persons or groups. 3. Confidential. 4. Not sold or offered to the general public.

private act See private law (2).

private bill A proposal for a private law. See private law (2).

private corporation A corporation established by private individuals for a nongovernmental or nonpublic purpose.

private foundation A charitable organization whose main source of funds is not the general public.

privateer A privately owned ship authorized by the government to attack enemy ships.

private international law Conflict of laws involving different states or countries. See also international law.

private investigator Someone other than a police officer who is licensed to do detective work or to conduct investigations.

private law 1. The law governing private persons and their interelationships. 2. A law that applies to specifically named persons or groups and has little or no permanence or general interest. A special law.

private mortgage insurance (PMI) Insurance to protect the lender if the debtor dies or defaults.

private necessity A privilege to make reasonable use of another's property to prevent an immediate threat of harm or damage to one's private property.

private nuisance A substantial interference with the reasonable use and enjoyment of private land.

Unlike public nuisance, which is an interference with the rights of the community at large, private nuisance is a civil wrong based on disturbance of rights in land. *Oliver*, 90 Cal.Rptr.2d 491 (Cal.App., 1999)

private offering A sale of an issue of securities to a limited number of persons. Also called private placement.

private person One who is not a public official, public figure, or member of the military.

private placement 1. The placement of a child for adoption by the parents or their intermediaries rather than by a state agency. 2. See private offering.

private sale A sale that was not open to the public through advertising, auction, or real estate agents.

private statute See private law (2).

privatize Convert from government control or ownership to the private sector.

privies See privy.

privilege 1. A special legal benefit, right, immunity, or protection. 2. A defense that authorizes conduct that would otherwise be wrongful.

privilege against self-incrimination 1. A criminal defendant cannot be compelled to testify. 2. The right not to answer incriminating questions by the government that could directly or indirectly connect oneself to the commission of a crime.

privileged Protected by a privilege, e.g., does not have to be disclosed.

privileged communication A communication that does not have to be disclosed. A statement protected by privilege.

Conversation between incarcerated defendant and a visitor at jail was not a privileged communication. *People v. Apodaca*, 60 Cal.Rptr. 782 (Cal.App., 1967)

Privileges and Immunities Clause The clause in the U.S. Constitution (art. IV, § 2) that "citizens of each state shall be entitled to all Privileges and Immunities of citizens" in every other state. A state cannot discriminate within its borders against citizens of other states.

privity A relationship that persons share in property, a transaction, or a right. Mutuality of interest.

privity of contract The relationship that exists between persons who enter a contract with each other.

privity of estate A mutual or successive relationship to the same rights in property.

privy A person who is in privity with another; someone so connected with another as to be identified with him or her in interest (plural: privies).

prize 1. A reward given to a winner. 2. A vessel seized during war.

pro For.

probable cause 1. A reasonable belief that a specific crime has been committed and that the defendant committed the crime. Also called sufficient cause. 2. A reasonable belief that evidence of a crime will be found in a particular place. 3. A reasonable ground for a belief in the existence of supporting facts.

Probable cause or reasonable cause sufficient to justify an arrest is a state of facts that would lead a person of ordinary care and prudence to believe and conscientiously entertain an honest and strong suspicion that person is guilty of a crime. *People v. Knight*, 18 Cal.Rptr.3d 384 (Cal.App., 2004)

probable cause hearing See preliminary hearing.

probate 1. A court procedure to establish the validity of a will and to oversee the administration of the estate. 2. To establish the validity of a will.

probate court A court for probating wills, supervising the administration of estates, and handling related family law issues. Also called orphan's court, surrogate's court.

probate estate Assets owned by the decedent at death plus assets later acquired by the decedent's estate.

probation 1. The conditional release of a person convicted of a crime in lieu of a prison sentence. Conditions can include attending drug counseling and remedial training. 2. A trial or test period for a new employee to determine competence and suitability for the job.

probationer A convicted offender on probation.

probation officer A government employee who supervises probationers.

probative Furnishing proof; tending to prove or disprove.

probative evidence Evidence that contributes toward proof.

probative fact A fact from which an ultimate or decisive fact may be inferred or proven.

probative value The extent to which evidence tends to establish whatever it is offered to prove.

Probative value, within provision of Evidence Code vesting trial court with discretion to exclude evidence if its probative value is outweighed by probability that its submission would create substantial danger of undue prejudice, means that trial court, in weighing probative value, necessarily considers, among other things, credibility of witnesses who testify to proffered evidence. Cal. Evidence Code, § 352. *People v. Chapman*, 123 Cal.Rptr. 862 (Cal.App., 1975)

pro bono Concerning or involving legal services that are provided for the public good (pro bono publico) without fee or compensation. Sometimes also applied to services given at a reduced rate. Shortened to pro bono.

procedendo A writ ordering a lower court to proceed to judgment.

procedural due process Minimum requirements of procedure (e.g., notice and the opportunity to be heard) that are constitutionally mandated before the government deprives a person of life, liberty, or property.

procedural law A law that governs the steps or mechanics of resolving a dispute in a court or administrative agency.

procedure A method or process by which something is done, e.g., to resolve a legal dispute in court or in an administrative agency.

proceeding 1. A part or step in a lawsuit, e.g., a hearing. 2. A sequence of events. 3. Going forward or conducting something.

proceeds Money derived from some possession, sale, or other transaction. The yield.

process 1. A summons, writ, or court order, e.g., to appear in court. 2. Procedures or proceedings in an action or prosecution.

Process is action taken pursuant to judicial authority. *Adams*, 3 Cal.Rptr.2d 49 (Cal.App., 1992)

process server Someone with the authority to serve or deliver process.

prochein ami See next friend.

proclamation An official and public declaration.

pro confesso As having accepted responsibility or confessed.

proctor One who manages the affairs of another. A supervisor.

procuration The appointment of an agent. A power of attorney.

procurement 1. Obtaining or acquiring something. 2. The persuasion of another to engage in improper sexual conduct.

procurement contract A government contract to acquire goods or services.

procuring cause 1. See proximate cause. 2. The chief means by which a sale of property was effected, entitling the broker to a commission.

Procuring cause means the cause originating a series of events that, without break in their continuity, resulted in accomplishment of the prime object of employment. *Rose*, 317 P.2d 1027 (Cal.App., 1957)

prodition Treason.

produce 1. To bring forth or yield. 2. Products of agriculture.

producing cause See proximate cause.

product Something produced by physical labor, intellectual effort, or natural processes. A commercial item that is used or consumed.

production of documents See request for production.

products liability A general term that covers different causes of action (e.g., negligence, strict liability in tort, and breach of warranty) based on defective products that cause harm.

profert The document relied on in the pleading is produced in court.

professional association (P.A.) 1. Two or more professionals (e.g., doctors) who practice together. 2. A group of professionals organized for a common purpose, e.g., continuing education, lobbying.

professional conduct See Model Rules of Professional Conduct.

professional corporation (P.C.) A corporation of persons performing services that require a professional license, e.g., attorneys.

A corporation organized under the General Corporation Law or pursuant to subdivision (b) of Section 13406 that is engaged in rendering professional services in a single profession. Cal. Corporations Code § 13401(b)

professional legal secretary (PLS) A certification credential of NALS, the Association for Legal Professionals (*www.nals.org*).

professional responsibility Ethical conduct of professionals.

proffer To tender or offer.

profiling Targeting, suspecting, or selecting out individuals based on group characteristics, e.g., race.

profit The gross proceeds of a business transaction less the costs of the transaction; excess of revenue over expenses. Gain.

profit-and-loss (P&L) statement See earnings report.

profit à prendre The right to enter another's land and remove something of value from the soil or the products of the soil. Also called right of common.

profiteering Making excessive profits through unfair advantage.

profit sharing A company plan in which employees can share profits.

pro forma 1. Perfunctorily; as a formality. 2. Provided in advance for purposes of description or projection.

progressive tax A type of graduated tax that applies higher tax rates as one's income range increases. Also called graduated tax.

pro hac vice (p.h.v.) ("for this particular occasion") Pertaining to permission given to an out-of-state attorney to practice law in the jurisdiction for this case only.

prohibited degree A relationship too close to be allowed to marry.

prohibition 1. Suppression or interdiction; an order forbidding something. 2. A law preventing the manufacture, sale, or transportation of intoxicating liquors. 3. See writ of prohibition.

prohibitory injunction. A court order that a person refrain from doing a specific act. An injunction that maintains the status quo.

An injunction that preserves the subject of litigation in statu quo and leaves parties in same position as they were prior to entry of judgment. *Dosch*, 13 Cal.Rptr. 765 (Cal.App., 1961)

prolixity Superfluous statements of fact in a pleading or as evidence.

promise 1. A manifestation of an intention to act or to refrain from acting in a specified way so as to justify the promisee in understanding that a commitment has been made. 2. To make a commitment.

promisee The person to whom a promise has been made.

promisor The person who makes a promise.

promissory estoppel The rule that a promise (not supported by consideration) will be binding if (a) the promisor makes a promise he or she should reasonably expect will induce action or forbearance by the promisee, (b) the promise does induce such action or forbearance, and (c) injustice can be avoided only by enforcement of the promise.

The theory of recovery that is allowed where injustice can be avoided only by enforcement of the promise and usually occurs where plaintiff has made a complete and substantial change of position in reliance upon the promise. *Hilltop*, 43 Cal.Rptr. 605 (Cal.App., 1965)

promissory note A written promise to pay. An unconditional promise in writing made by one person to another, signed by the maker, engaging to pay on demand, or at a fixed or determinable future time, a certain sum of money, to order or to bearer. Also called note.

promissory warranty A commitment by the insured that certain facts will continue or remain true after the insurance policy takes effect.

promoter 1. One who promotes or furthers some venture. 2. One who takes preliminary steps in the organization of a corporation or business.

promulgate 1. To announce officially. 2. To put into effect.

pronounce To declare formally.

proof 1. The effect of being persuaded by evidence that a fact has been established or refuted. 2. Evidence that establishes something.

proof beyond a reasonable doubt See reasonable doubt.

proof of claim A written statement a creditor files with the bankruptcy court showing the amount and character of the debt owed to the creditor.

proof of loss Providing an insurer with the information and evidence needed to determine its liability under an insurance policy.

proof of service Evidence that a summons or other process has been served on a party in an action. Also called certificate of service, return of service.

proof to a moral certainty See moral certainty.

pro per See in propria persona, pro se.

proper lookout The duty of a driver to see what is clearly visible or what in the exercise of due care would be visible.

proper party A person whose interest may be affected by the action and, therefore, may be joined, but whose presence is not essential for the court to adjudicate the rights of others.

property 1. That which one can possess, enjoy, or own. 2. The right of ownership. 3. The quality or characteristic of a thing.

Property means an interest, present or future, legal or equitable, vested or contingent, in real or personal property, including income and earnings. Cal. Family Code § 1610(b)

property settlement An agreement dividing marital property between spouses upon separation or divorce. A court judgment on this division.

property tax A tax on real or personal property that one owns, the amount often dependent on the value of the property.

prophylactic Acting to prevent something.

proponent An advocate; one who presents or offers an argument, proposal, or instrument.

proposal An offer or plan.

propound To offer or propose for analysis or acceptance.

proprietary 1. Owned by a private person or company. 2. Pertaining to ownership.

proprietary drug A drug that has the protection of a patent.

proprietary function A function of a municipality that (a) traditionally or principally has been performed by private enterprise, or (b) is conducted primarily to produce a profit or benefit for the government rather than for the public at large.

proprietary interest One's right or share based on property ownership.

Proprietary interest means any membership, coownership, stock ownership, legal or beneficial interest, profit-sharing arrangement, or other proprietary interest, designated arranged or held, directly or indirectly in any form. Cal. Business & Professions Code § 18630

proprietary lease A lease in a cooperative apartment between the owner-cooperative and a tenant-stockholder.

proprietor The owner of property, e.g., a business. See also sole proprietorship.

pro rata Proportionately; according to a certain rate or factor.

pro rata clause A clause in an insurance policy that the insurer will be liable only for the proportion of the loss represented by the ratio between its policy limits and the total limits of all available insurance.

prorate To divide, calculate, or distribute proportionally.

proscription A prohibition or restriction.

pro se (on one's own behalf) Appearing for or representing oneself. Also called in propria persona, pro per.

prosecute To initiate and pursue a civil case or a criminal case.

prosecuting attorney See district attorney, prosecutor (1).

prosecuting witness The person (often the victim) who instigates a criminal charge and gives evidence.

The phrase "prosecuting witness" is ordinarily used in two connections. It most often denotes the victim who is a witness. However, it is also employed more generally to refer to witnesses for the prosecution who are neither the victim nor the complainant. Cal. Penal Code § 868. *Ortega*, 185 Cal.Rptr. 297 (Cal.App., 1982)

prosecution 1. Court proceedings to determine the guilt or innocence of a person accused of a crime. 2. The prosecuting attorney or the government in a criminal case. 3. Pursuing a lawsuit.

prosecution history See file wrapper.

prosecutor 1. The representative of the government in a criminal case. 2. One who instigates a prosecution or files a complaint.

prosecutorial discretion The right of prosecutors to decide whether to charge someone for a crime, whether to plea bargain, and whether to ask for a particular sentence.

prosecutory Involving or relating to a prosecution.

prospective Pertaining to or applicable in the future; expected.

prospective law A law applicable to cases or events arising after its enactment.

prospectus A document containing facts on a company designed to help a prospective investor decide whether to invest in the company.

prostitution Engaging in sexual activities for hire.

Any lewd act between persons for money or other consideration, requiring sexual contact between the prostitute and the customer. Cal. Penal Code § 647(b). *Wooten*, 113 Cal.Rptr.2d 195 (Cal.App., 2001)

pro tanto For so much; to the extent of.

protected class A group of people (e.g., members of a minority race) given special statutory protection against discrimination.

protection Defending or shielding from harm; coverage.

protection order See restraining order.

protective custody Being held under force of law for one's own protection or that of the public.

protective order 1. A court order designed to protect a person from harassment during litigation. 2. See restraining order.

An order that includes any of the following restraining orders: enjoining specific acts of abuse and excluding a person from a dwelling. Cal. Family Code § 6218

protective trust A trust designed to protect trust assets from the spendthrift tendencies of the beneficiary.

pro tem (pro tempore) For the time being; temporarily.

protest 1. A formal declaration of dissent or disapproval. 2. A written declaration (often by a notary public) that a check or other negotiable instrument was presented but not paid or accepted. 3. A disagreement that a debt is owed but paying it while disputing it.

prothonotary A chief clerk of court.

protocol 1. The etiquette of diplomacy. 2. A brief summary of a document, e.g., a treaty. 3. The first copy or draft of a treaty; an amendment of a treaty. 4. The formal record or minutes of a meeting.

prove To establish a fact or position by sufficient evidence.

province 1. A division of the state or country. 2. A sphere of expertise or authority.

provision 1. A section or part of a legal document. 2. A stipulation.

provisional remedy A temporary remedy, pending final court action.

proviso A condition, exception, or stipulation in a law or document.

provocation Inciting another to do a particular deed.

proximate Nearest or closest; close in causal connection.

proximate cause The legally sufficient cause of an event when (a) the defendant is the cause in fact of the event, (b) the event was the foreseeable consequence of the original risk created by the defendant, and (c) there is no policy reason why the defendant should not be liable for what he or she caused in fact. Also called direct cause, efficient cause, legal cause, procuring cause, producing cause.

That cause which, in natural and continuous sequence and unbroken by any efficient intervening cause, produced the injury or damage complained of and without which such result would not have occurred; "proximate cause" is legal cause. Cal. Government Code, § 815.6. *Whitcombe*, 141 Cal.Rptr. 189 (Cal.App., 1977)

proxy 1. An agent; one authorized to act for another. 2. The authorization to act for another.

proxy marriage The performance of a valid marriage ceremony through agents because one or both of the prospective spouses are absent.

proxy statement A document mailed to shareholders giving information on matters for which the company is seeking proxy votes.

prudent Cautious; careful in adapting means to ends.

prudent investor rule A trustee must use such diligence and prudence in managing and investing a trust fund as a reasonable person would use.

prurient Pertaining to a shameful or morbid interest in sex.

P.S.; p.s. 1. Public Statute (P.S.). See public law (1). 2. Postscript (p.s.).

psychotherapist-patient privilege A patient can refuse to disclose, and can prevent others from disclosing, confidential communications between patient and psychotherapist involving the patient's diagnosis or treatment.

The patient has a privilege to refuse to disclose, and to prevent another from disclosing, a confidential communication between patient and psychotherapist. Cal. Evidence Code § 1014

public 1. The community at large. 2. Open for use by everyone. 3. Traded on the open market.

Public Access to Court Electronic Records (PACER) An electronic public access service that allows subscribers to obtain case and docket information from federal courts via the Internet (*pacer.psc.uscourts.gov*).

public accommodation A business or place that is open to, accepts, or solicits the patronage of the general public.

public act See public law (1).

public administrator Someone appointed by the court to administer an intestate estate when relatives or associates of the decedent are not available to do so.

publication 1. Making something known to people. 2. Communication of a statement to someone other than the plaintiff.

public bill A legislative proposal for a public law.

public contract A contract (often with a private person or business) in which a government buys goods or services for a public need.

public convenience and necessity Reasonably meeting the needs of the public, justifying the grant of public funds or a license for a project or service.

public corporation 1. A company whose shares are traded on the open market. Also called publicly held corporation. 2. A corporation owned by the government and managed under special laws in the public interest.

Public corporation means any county, city and county, city, town, municipal corporation, district of any kind or class, authority, redevelopment agency or political subdivision of this state. Cal. Government Code § 67510

public defender (P.D.) An attorney appointed by a court and paid by the government to represent indigent defendants in criminal cases.

public domain 1. Work product or other property that is not protected by copyright or patent. A status that allows access to anyone without fee. 2. Government-owned land.

public duty doctrine The government is not liable for a public official's negligent conduct unless it is shown that the official breached a duty owed to the injured person as an individual as opposed the breach of an obligation owed to the public in general.

public easement An easement for the benefit of the general public.

public figure A person who has assumed special prominence in the affairs of society. A public figure for a limited purpose is a person who has voluntarily become involved in a controversy of interest to the general public.

public forum Settings or places traditionally available for public expression and debate, such as public streets and the radio.

public hearing A hearing open to the general public.

Notice of a public hearing means a notice that includes the date, time, and place of a public hearing and a general explanation of the matter to be considered. Cal. Government Code § 65094

publici juris ("of public right") Being owned by the public and subject to use by anyone.

public interest 1. A matter of health or welfare that concerns the general public. 2. The well-being of the public.

public interest law Law involving broad societal issues.

public international law See international law.

public land Government-owned land.

public law (P.L.; Pub. L.) 1. A statute that applies to the general public or to a segment of the public and has permanence or general interest. Also called public act, public statute. 2. Laws governing the operation of government or relationships between government and private persons. The major examples are constitutional law, administrative law, and criminal law.

publicly held corporation See public corporation (1).

public necessity The privilege to make a reasonable use of someone's property to prevent an immediate threat of harm or damage to the public.

public nuisance Unreasonably interfering with a right of the general public. An act that adversely affects the safety, health, morals, or convenience of the public. Also called common nuisance.

A public nuisance is one which affects at the same time an entire community or neighborhood, or any considerable number of persons, although the extent of the annoyance or damage inflicted upon individuals may be unequal. Cal. Civil Code § 3480

public offering A sale of stock to the public on the open market.

public office A position created by law by which an individual is given power to perform a public function for a given period.

public official An elected or appointed holder of a public office.

public policy Principles inherent in customs and societal values that are embodied in a law.

public property Government-owned property.

public purpose Benefit to or welfare of the public as a goal of government action.

public record A record the government must keep that may or may not be open to the public.

Public record for purposes of Public Record Act is broad and intended to cover every conceivable kind of record that is involved in the governmental process. Cal. Government Code § 6252(e). *Coronado Police Officers*, 131 Cal.Rptr.2d 553 (Cal.App., 2003)

public records exception Some written statements that would normally be excluded as hearsay may be admitted into evidence if they qualify as public records and reports (Federal Rules of Evidence Rule 803(8)).

public sale A sale in which members of the public are invited to become buyers.

public security Bonds, notes, certificates of indebtedness, and other instruments evidencing government debt.

public service commission A government commission that supervises or regulates public utilities.

public statute (P.S.) See public law (1).

public trial A trial that the general public can observe.

public trust See charitable trust.

public use 1. A use that confers some benefit or advantage to the public. A use affecting the public generally, or any number thereof, as distinguished from particular individuals. 2. A use of an invention by one under no restriction or obligation of secrecy to the inventor.

public utility A company or business that regularly supplies the public with some commodity or service that is of public consequence and need (e.g., electricity).

public works Construction, demolition, installation, or repair work on roads, dams, and similar structures done under contract with public funds.

public wrong An offense against the state or the general community, e.g., a crime, public nuisance, or breach of a public contract.

publish To make known, to make public; to distribute or disseminate.

puffing 1. A seller's opinion consisting of an exaggeration of quality or overstatement of value. 2. See by-bidding.

puisne Subordinate in rank.

***Pullman* abstention** Federal courts can refrain or postpone the exercise of federal jurisdiction when a federal constitutional issue might be mooted or presented in a different posture by a state court determination of pertinent state law. *Railroad Comm'n v. Pullman*, 61 S. Ct. 643 (1941).

punishment Any fine, penalty, confinement, or other sanction imposed by law for a crime, offense, or breach of a duty.

punitive damages Damages that are added to actual or compensatory damages in order to punish outrageous or egregious conduct and to deter similar conduct in the future. Also called exemplary damages, smart money, vindictive damages.

Punitive damages are damages other than compensatory damages which may be awarded against person to punish him for outrageous conduct. *Wetherbee*, 95 Cal.Rptr. 678 (Cal.App., 1971)

pur autre vie For or during the life of another. Also spelled per autre vie.

purchase Acquisition by buying; receiving title to property by a means other than descent, inheritance, or gift.

purchase money mortgage A mortgage taken back when purchasing property to secure payment of the balance of the purchase price.

purchase money resulting trust A trust imposed when title to property is transferred to one person, but the entire purchase price is paid by another.

purchase money security interest (PMSI) A security interest taken or retained by a seller to secure all or part of the price of the collateral, or a security interest taken by one who gives value that is used by the debtor to acquire the collateral.

"Purchase money security interest" means "purchase money security interest" as defined in Section 9103 of the Commercial Code. Cal. Code of Civil Procedure § 697.590

purchaser One who acquires property by buying it for a consideration.

pure accident See unavoidable accident.

pure plea A plea stating matters not in the bill to defeat the claim.

pure race statute See race statute.

purge To clear or exonerate from a charge or of guilt.

purloin To steal.

purport 1. To appear to be; to claim or seem to be. 2. Meaning.

purpose Goal or objective.

purposely Intentionally; with a specific purpose.

purpresture An encroachment on public rights or the appropriation to private use of that which belongs to the public.

Building of a landfill beyond low water mark by littoral owner without permit constitutes a "purpresture" which belongs to the state. *Woods*, 50 Cal.Rptr. 515 (Cal.App., 1966)

pursuant to In accordance with; under.

pursuit of happiness The phrase in the Declaration of Independence interpreted to mean the right to be free in the enjoyment of our faculties, subject to restraints that are necessary for the common welfare.

purview The body, scope, or extent of a something, e.g., a statute or other law.

putative Generally regarded or reputed, believed.

putative father A man reputed or alleged to be the biological father of a child born out of wedlock.

putative marriage A marriage that has been solemnized in proper form and celebrated in good faith by one or both parties, but which, by reason of some legal infirmity, is either void or voidable.

Putative marriage is matrimonial union solemnized in due form and in good faith, but which is void or voidable due to some legal infirmity; its basis is belief that marriage is valid. *In re Long's Estate*, 18 Cal.Rptr. 105 (Cal.App., 1961)

put option The right to sell a specified security or commodity at a specified price. See also call option.

pyramid scheme A sales device or plan in which participants are recruited to pay the person who recruited them, hoping to receive payments from the persons they recruit. A pyramid scheme rewards participants for inducing other people to join the program, whereas a Ponzi scheme operates strictly by paying earlier investors with money tendered by later investors.

pyramiding Speculating on stocks or commodities by using unrealized (paper) profits as margin for more purchases.

Q

Q.B. Queen's Bench. See King's Bench.

QDRO See qualified domestic relations order.

QTIP Qualified terminable interest property.

qua As; in the character or capacity of.

quaere Ask, question; a query.

qualification 1. A quality or circumstance that is legally or inherently necessary to perform a function. 2. A restriction or modification in a document or transaction.

qualified 1. Eligible; possessing legal power or capacity. 2. Restricted or imperfect.

qualified acceptance A counteroffer; an acceptance that modifies the offer.

qualified disclaimer An irrevocable and unqualified refusal by a person to accept an interest in property (26 USC § 2518).

qualified domestic relations order (QDRO) A court order that allows a nonemployee to reach retirement benefits of an employee or former employee in order to satisfy a support or other marital obligation to the nonemployee.

A domestic relations order is qualified if it creates or recognizes the existence of an *alternate payee's* right to, or assigns to an *alternate payee* the right to, receive all or a portion of the benefits payable with respect to a participant under a plan. *In re Marriage of Shelstead*, 78 Cal.Rptr.2d 365 (Cal.App., 1998)

qualified immunity A government official's immunity from liability for civil damages when performing discretionary functions if his or her conduct does not violate clearly established statutory or constitutional rights of which a reasonable person would have known.

qualified indorsement An indorsement that limits the liability of the indorser of a negotiable instrument.

qualified privilege See conditional privilege.

qualify 1. To make oneself fit or prepared. 2. To limit or restrict.

quantum meruit ("as much as he deserves") 1. An equitable theory of recovery based upon an implied agreement to pay for benefits or goods received. 2. The measure of damages imposed when a party prevails on the equitable claim of unjust enrichment.

Quantum meruit refers to the well-established principle that the law implies a promise to pay for services performed under circumstances disclosing that they were not gratuitously rendered. *Huskinson*, 9 Cal.Rptr.3d 693 (CA 2004)

quantum valebant An action seeking payment for goods sold and delivered based on an implied promise to pay as much as the goods are reasonably worth.

quarantine Isolation of persons, animals, goods, or vehicles suspected of carrying a contagious disease.

quare clausum fregit See trespass quare clausum fregit.

quash To vacate or annul; to suppress completely.

quasi Somewhat the same, but different; resembling.

quasi contract See implied in law contract.

quasi corporation A body or entity (often part of the government) that has some of the characteristics of a corporation but is not a corporation in the full sense.

quasi estoppel A party should be precluded from asserting, to another's disadvantage, a right or claim that is inconsistent with a position previously taken by the party.

quasi in rem jurisdiction A court's power over a person, but restricted to his or her specific interest in property within the territory over which the court has authority.

A quasi in rem proceeding is not purely in rem, but is brought against someone personally although the real objective is to deal with particular property. *People v. Pollard*, 109 Cal.Rptr.2d 207 (Cal.App., 2001)

quasi judicial Pertaining to the power of an administrative agency (or official in the executive branch) to hear and determine controversies between the public and individuals in a manner that resembles a judicial trial.

quasi legislative Pertaining to the power of an administrative agency (or official in the executive branch) to write rules and regulations in a manner that resembles the legislature.

An administrative agency acts in its quasi-legislative capacity when it adopts rules or regulations to fill in the details of the statutes enacted by the Legislature. *Megrabian*, 30 Cal.Rptr.3d 262 (Cal.App., 2005)

quasi-suspect classification A classification such as one based on gender or illegitimacy that will receive intermediate scrutiny by the court to determine its constitutionality.

Queen's Bench (Q.B.) See King's Bench.

question 1. An issue to be resolved. 2. Something asked; a query.

question of fact; question of law See issue of fact; issue of law.

quia emptores A 1290 English statute that had the effect of facilitating the alienation of fee-simple tenants.

quia timet An equitable remedy to be protected from anticipated future injury where it cannot be avoided by a present action at law.

quick assets Cash and assets readily convertible into cash (other than inventory).

quid pro quo Something for something; giving one thing for another. Quid pro quo sexual harassment exists when an employer conditions an employment benefit upon sexual favors from an employee.

quiet 1. Free from interference or adverse claims. 2. To make secure.

quiet enjoyment Possession of land that is not disturbed by superior ownership rights asserted by a third person.

Covenant of quiet enjoyment is not broken until there has been an actual or constructive eviction. *Petroleum*, 122 Cal.Rptr. 114 (Cal.App., 1975)

quiet title action An action to resolve conflicting claims to land. An action asserting an interest in land and calling on others to set forth their claims.

quit 1. To surrender possession. 2. To cease.

qui tam action An action in which a private plaintiff is allowed to sue under a statute that awards part of any penalty recovered to the plaintiff and the remainder to the government.

Qui tam plaintiffs sue as informers under a statute on behalf of themselves and the State of California; qui tam plaintiffs may recover damages and penalties on behalf of public entities for themselves and the entities. Cal. Government Code § 12650. *Campbell*, 25 Cal.Rptr.3d 320 (CA 2005)

quitclaim 1. To transfer the extent of one's interest. 2. To surrender a claim.

quitclaim deed A deed that transfers any interest or claim the grantor may have, without warranting that the title is valid.

quittance A release from debt.

quod vide (q.v.) A reference directing the reader elsewhere in the text for more information.

quorum The minimum number of members who must be present in a deliberative body before business may be transacted.

quota 1. An assigned goal; the minimum sought. 2. A proportional part or allotment.

quotation 1. A word-for-word reproduction of text from another source. 2. A statement of current price.

quotient verdict A verdict on damages reached when the jurors agree to average the figures each juror states as his or her individual verdict.

Quotient verdicts are statutorily prohibited; it is one in which jurors agree to be bound by average of their views, each juror writes amount on slip of paper, sums are added and divided by 12. Cal. Code of Civil Procedure § 657. *Fredrics*, 35 Cal.Rptr.2d 246 (Cal.App., 1994)

quo warranto A court inquiry (by writ) to determine whether someone exercising government power is legally entitled to do so.

q.v. See quod vide.

R

® The symbol indicating registration of a trademark or service mark with the U.S. Patent and Trademark Office.

race The historical division of humanity by physical characteristics. A grouping based on ancestry or ethnic characteristics.

race notice statute A recording law giving priority to the first party to record, unless this person had notice of an unrecorded prior claim.

Brown should prevail over Davis using a straightforward race/notice analysis, because he took without notice of Davis' claim, gave value (in the form of a note), and duly recorded his deed. *Lewis*, 37 Cal.Rptr.2d 63 (Cal.App., 1994)

race statute A recording law giving priority to the first party to record, even if this person had notice of another's unrecorded prior claim. Also called pure race statute.

racial discrimination Discrimination based on one's race.

racketeer One who commits racketeering.

Racketeer Influenced and Corrupt Organizations Act (RICO) A federal statute imposing civil and criminal penalties for racketeering offenses such as engaging in a pattern of fraud, bribery, extortion, and other acts enumerated in the statute (18 USC § 1961). Some states have enacted similar statutes.

racketeering Crime engaged in as a business or organized enterprise, often involving illegal activity such as extortion, bribery, gambling, prostitution, and drug sales.

raid 1. An effort to entice personnel or customers away from a competitor. 2. A hostile attempt to take over a corporation by share purchases. 3. A sudden attack or forcible entry by law enforcement.

railroad To rush someone through without due care or due process.

rainmaker An attorney who brings fee-generating cases into the office due to his or her contacts or reputation.

raise 1. To increase. 2. To invoke or put forward. 3. To gather or collect. 4. To create or establish.

raise a check To increase the face amount of a check fraudulently.

rake-off A share of profits, often taken as a payoff or bribe.

RAM See reverse annuity mortgage.

ransom Money or other payment sought for the return of illegally detained persons or property.

rape Nonconsensual sexual intercourse.

Rape is an act of sexual intercourse accomplished with a person not the spouse of the perpetrator (1) Where a person is incapable of giving legal consent, (2) Where it is accomplished against a person's will, . . . Cal. Penal Code § 261(a)

rape shield law A law imposing limits on defendant's use of evidence of the prior sexual experiences of an alleged rape victim.

rap sheet The arrest and conviction record of someone.

rasure Erasing part of a document by scraping.

ratable 1. Able to be evaluated or apportioned. 2. Taxable. 3. Proportionate.

rate 1. Relative value. A measure or degree in relationship to another measure. 2. Cost or price.

rate base The fair value of the property of a utility (or other entity) upon which a reasonable return is allowed.

rate of exchange See exchange (3).

rate of return Earnings or profit as a percentage of an investment.

ratification 1. An adoption or confirmation of a prior act or transaction, making one bound by it. 2. Formal approval.

Ratification of its agent's acts by a corporation is the confirmation and acceptance of a previous act. *Cruz*, 99 Cal.Rptr.2d 435 (Cal.App., 2000)

ratio decidendi The ground, reason, principle, or rule of law that is the basis of a court's decision.

rational basis test A law will be upheld as constitutional if it rationally furthers a legitimate government objective.

ravish 1. To rape. 2. To seize and carry away by force.

re In the matter of; concerning or regarding.

reacquired stock See treasury securities (1).

ready, willing, and able Having sufficient funds, capacity, and desire to complete the transaction.

reaffirmation 1. A confirmation or approval of something already agreed to. 2. An agreement by a debtor to pay an otherwise dischargeable debt.

real 1. Pertaining to stationary or fixed property such as land. 2. True or genuine.

real chattel A personal property interest that is less than a freehold or fee interest. An example is a lease of land.

real defense A defense such as duress and fraud in the factum that is good against everyone, including a holder in due course.

real estate See real property.

real estate broker An agent or intermediary who negotiates or arranges agreements pertaining to the sale and lease of real property.

A person acts as a real estate broker only if he or she is acting (1) for compensation and (2) on behalf of someone else. Cal. Business & Professions Code § 10131. *Horning*, 29 Cal.Rptr.3d 717 (Cal.App., 2005)

real estate investment trust (REIT) A business that invests in real estate on behalf of its shareholders.

Real Estate Settlement Procedures Act (RESPA) A federal law on disclosure of settlement costs in the sale of residential property financed by a federally insured lender (12 USC § 2601).

real evidence 1. Evidence that was actually involved in the incident being considered by the court. Also called physical evidence. 2. Evidence produced for inspection at trial.

realization 1. Conversion of an asset into cash. 2. The receipt by a taxpayer of actual economic gain or loss from the disposition of property.

realized gain or loss The difference between the amount realized on the disposition of property and the adjusted basis of the property.

real party in interest The person who benefits from or is harmed by the outcome of the case and who by substantive law has the legal right to enforce the claim in question. Also called party in interest.

real property Land and anything permanently attached or affixed to the land such as buildings, fences, and trees. Also called real estate, realty.

realtor A real estate broker or agent, often a member of the National Association of Realtors (*www.realtor.org*).

realty See real property.

reapportionment Redrawing boundaries of a political subdivision to reflect population changes, leading to a reallocation of legislative seats. Also called redistricting.

reargument Another presentation of arguments before the same court.

reason 1. An inducement, motive, or ground for action. 2. The faculty of the mind to form judgments based on logic.

reasonable Sensible and proper under the circumstances. Fair.

reasonable care The degree of care a person of ordinary prudence and intelligence would use under the same or similar circumstances to avoid injury or damage. Also called due care, ordinary care.

Care that a reasonably careful and prudent person, having in view dangers to be avoided and likelihood of injury therefrom, would exercise under the circumstances. *Irelan-Yuba*, 116 P.2d 611 (CA 1941)

reasonable diligence The care and persistence of an ordinarily prudent person under the same or similar circumstances.

reasonable doubt Doubt that would cause prudent people to hesitate before acting in matters of importance to themselves. The standard of proof needed to convict someone of a crime is proof beyond a reasonable doubt.

Reasonable doubt is defined as follows: It is not a mere possible doubt; because everything relating to human affairs is open to some possible imaginary doubt. It is that state of the case which, after the entire comparison and consideration of all the evidence, leaves the minds of the jurors in that condition that they cannot say they feel an abiding conviction of the truth of the charge. Cal. Jury Instructions—Criminal, 2.90

reasonable force Force that an average person of ordinary intelligence in like circumstances would deem necessary.

reasonable man (person) A person who uses ordinary prudence under the circumstances to avoid injury or damage. (A legal guide or standard.) Also called ordinary prudent person.

reasonable suspicion A particularized and objective reason based on specific and articulable facts for suspecting someone of criminal activity.

reasonable time As much time as is needed, under the particular circumstances involved, to do what a contract or duty requires to be done.

reasonable use A use of one's property that is consistent with zoning rules and does not interfere with the lawful use of surrounding property.

reasonable woman test A female plaintiff states a prima facie case of hostile environment sexual harassment when she alleges conduct that a reasonable woman would consider sufficiently severe or pervasive to alter the conditions of employment and create an abusive working environment.

rebate A reduction or return of part to the price.

rebellion Organized and open resistance, by force and arms, to a government or ruler committed by a subject.

rebut To refute, oppose, or repel.

rebuttable presumption An inference of fact that can be overcome by sufficient contrary evidence. Also called disputable presumption.

A preliminary assumption in the absence of contrary evidence. Cal. Evidence Code § 604. *Fisher*, 209 Cal.Rptr. 682 (CA 1984)

rebuttal Arguments or evidence given in reply to explain or counter an opponent.

recall 1. Removing a public official from office before the end of his or her term by a vote of the people. 2. A request by the manufacturer to return a defective product. 3. Revocation of a judgment.

recant To repudiate or retract something formally.

recapitalization A change or adjustment in the capital structure (stock, bonds, or other securities) of a corporation.

recaption Retaking chattels once in your possession or custody.

recapture 1. To retake or recover. 2. The recalculation of tax liability in order to remove improperly taken deductions or credits.

receipt 1. Written acknowledgment of receiving something. 2. Taking physical possession of something. 3. Receipts: income, money received.

receivable 1. Awaiting collection. 2. The amount still owed.

receiver A person appointed by the court to manage property in litigation or in the process of bankruptcy.

receivership The condition of a company or individual over whom a receiver has been appointed. See receiver.

receiving stolen property Receiving or controlling stolen movable property of another, knowing that it has been stolen.

A crime that is completed upon taking possession of property with knowledge that it is stolen. Cal. Penal Code, § 496. *Williams*, 146 Cal.Rptr. 311 (Cal.App., 1978)

recess An interval when business is suspended without adjourning.

recidivism The tendency to return to a life of crime.

recidivist Repeat offender; habitual criminal.

reciprocal 1. Given or owed to each other. 2. Done in return.

reciprocal negative easement When an owner sells a portion of land with a restrictive covenant that benefits the land retained by the owner, the restriction becomes mutual.

reciprocal wills See mutual wills (1).

reciprocity A mutual exchange of the same benefits or treatment.

recision See rescission.

recital The formal setting forth of facts or reasons.

reckless Consciously failing to exercise due care but without intending the consequences; wantonly disregarding risks.

Reckless conduct rises to the level of a conscious choice of a course of action with knowledge of the serious danger to others involved in it. *Intrieri*, 12 Cal.Rptr.3d 97 (Cal.App., 2004)

reckless disregard Conscious indifference to consequences.

reckless endangerment Creating a substantial risk of major injury or death.

recklessness Knowing but disregarding a substantial risk that an injury or wrongful act may occur.

reclamation 1. Converting unusable land into land that is usable. 2. A seller's right to recover possession of goods from an insolvent buyer.

recognition 1. A formal acknowledgment or confirmation. 2. The point at which a tax on gain or loss is accounted for.

recognizance An obligation recorded in court to do some act required by law, e.g., to appear at all court proceedings.

recollection The act of recalling or remembering.

reconciliation 1. The voluntary resumption of full marital relations. 2. The bringing of financial accounts into consistency or agreement.

reconduction 1. Renewing a lease. 2. The forcible return of illegal aliens.

reconsideration A review or reevaluation of a matter.

reconstruction 1. Rebuilding. 2. Re-creating an event.

reconveyance A transfer back. The return of something, e.g., title.

record 1. To make an official note of; to enter in a document. 2. A formal account of some act or event, e.g., a trial. 3. The facts that have been inscribed or stored.

Records, as used in statute providing for criminal punishment of person who eavesdrops upon or records a confidential communication, prohibits "real time" interception of a communication (listening as it occurs) and mechanical recording of a communication for later play back. Cal. Penal Code §§ 630, 632(a). *People v. Drennan*, 101 Cal.Rptr.2d 584 (Cal.App., 2000)

recordation The formal recording of an instrument (e.g., a deed) with a county clerk or other public registry.

record date A date by which a shareholder must officially own shares in order to be entitled to a dividend or to vote.

recorded recollection See past recollection recorded.

recorder 1. An officer appointed to maintain public records, e.g., recorder of deeds. 2. A magistrate or judge with limited jurisdiction in some states.

recorder's court A court with limited criminal jurisdiction.

recording act; recording statute A law on recording deeds and other property instruments in order to establish priority among claims.

record owner Anyone recorded in a public registry as the owner.

record title See paper title.

recoupment 1. The defendant's right to a deduction from the plaintiff's damages due to plaintiff's breach of duty arising from the same contract. 2. An equitable remedy that permits the offset of mutual debts based on the same transaction or occurrence. 3. A reimbursement or recovery.

recourse 1. Turning or appealing for help; a way to enforce a right. 2. The right of a holder of a negotiable instrument to recover against an indorser or other party who is secondarily liable. 3. The right to reach other assets of the debtor if the collateral is insufficient.

Endorsement of conditional sale contract with recourse pledges that endorser guarantees payment of contract obligations. *Ranchers Bank*, 97 Cal.Rptr. 78 (Cal.App., 1971)

recover 1. To obtain by court judgment or legal process. 2. To have restored; to regain possession.

recovery 1. That which is awarded by court judgment or legal process. 2. Restoration.

recrimination 1. A charge by the accused against the accuser. 2. An accusation that the party seeking the divorce has committed a serious marital wrong that in itself is a ground for divorce.

recross-examination Another cross-examination of a witness after redirect examination.

recusal A judge's (or other decision maker's) removal of him or herself from a matter because of a conflict of interest. Also called recusation. The verb is recuse.

redaction Revising or editing a text. Removing confidential or inappropriate parts of a text.

reddendum A provision in a deed in which the grantor reserves something out of what had been granted (e.g., rent).

redeemable bond A bond that the issuer may call back for payment before its maturity date. Also called callable bond.

redemption 1. Buying back; reclaiming or regaining possession by paying a specific price. Recovering what was mortgaged. 2. The repurchase of a security by the issuing corporation. 3. Converting shares into cash.

Redemption amount means the total amount which would be necessary to redeem tax-defaulted property at the time an election is made to pay delinquent taxes in installments under this article. Cal. Revenue & Taxation Code § 4216(a)

red herring 1. A diversion from the main issue; an irrelevant issue. 2. A preliminary prospectus.

redhibition Avoiding a sale due to a major defect in the thing sold.

redirect examination Another direct examination of a witness after he or she was cross-examined.

rediscount rate The rate the Federal Reserve System charges a member bank on a loan secured by paper the bank has already resold.

redistricting See reapportionment.

redlining 1. The discriminatory practice of denying credit or insurance to geographic areas due to the income, race, or ethnicity of its residents. 2. Showing the portions of an earlier draft of a text that have been stricken out.

redraft A second note or bill drafted by the original drawer after the first draft has been dishonored.

redress Damages, equitable relief, or other remedy.

reductio ad absurdum Disproving an argument by showing that it leads to an absurd consequence or conclusion.

reduction to practice The point in time at which an invention is sufficiently tested to demonstrate it will work for its intended purpose.

redundancy Needless repetition; superfluous matter in a pleading.

reentry Retaking possession of land.

reexchange The expenses incurred due to a dishonor of a bill of exchange in a foreign country.

refer To send for further consideration or action.

referee A person to whom a judge refers a case for specific tasks, e.g., to take testimony and to file a report with the court.

A person appointed to exercise judicial powers, to take testimony, to hear parties, and report his or her findings. *Department of Motor Vehicles*, 76 Cal.Rptr. 804 (Cal.App., 1969)

referee in bankruptcy A court-appointed officer who performs administrative and judicial functions in bankruptcy cases.

reference 1. The act of referring or sending a case for further consideration or action. 2. A source of information. 3. A citation in a document.

referendum The electorate's power to give final approval to an existing provision of the constitution or statute of the legislature.

The means by which the electorate is entitled, as a power reserved by it under the state Constitution, to approve or reject measures passed by a legislative body. Cal. Const. Art. 4, § 1. *Wal-Mart*, 33 Cal.Rptr.3d 817 (Cal.App., 2005)

refinance To replace one loan for another on different terms.

reformation An equitable remedy to correct a writing so that it embodies the actual intent of the parties.

reformatory A correctional institution for youthful offenders.

refreshing memory or **recollection** See present recollection refreshed.

refugee One seeking refuge in one country after being unwilling or unable to return to another.

refund 1. The return of an overpayment. 2. The return of the price paid for the returned product. 3. To finance again; to refinance.

refunding Refinancing a debt. Replacing a bond with a new bond issue.

reg. See regulation.

regent 1. A member of the governing board of a school. 2. A governor or ruler.

regime 1. A system of rules. 2. The current government.

register 1. To record formally. 2. To enroll. 3. A book containing official facts. 4. One who keeps official records. 5. A probate judge.

Register means to issue a certificate showing the ownership of a certificated security or, in the case of an uncertificated security, to initiate or transfer an account showing ownership of securities. Cal. Probate Code § 5501(b)

registered bond See registered security.

registered check A check guaranteed by a bank for a customer who provides funds for its payment.

registered mail Mail that is numbered and tracked by the U.S. Postal Service to monitor a safe delivery.

registered representative A representative who meets the requirements of the Securities and Exchange Commission to sell securities to the public.

registered security 1. A stock, bond, or other security whose owner is recorded (registered) by the issuer. 2. A security for sale for which a registration statement has been filed.

register of ships A customs list containing data on vessels, e.g., their owner and country of registration.

registrar The official in charge of keeping records.

registration Inserting something in an official record; formally applying or enrolling. The process by which persons or institutions list their names on an official roster.

registration statement A statement disclosing relevant financial and management data to potential investors in the securities of a company.

registry 1. A book or list kept for recording or registering documents or facts, e.g., a deed, the nationality of a ship. 2. A probate judge.

regressive tax A tax whose rate decreases as the tax base increases.

regs. See regulation.

regular course of business See course of business.

regular session One of the meetings scheduled at fixed times.

regulate To adjust or control by rule, method, or principle.

regulation (reg.) 1. A rule governing conduct; the management of conduct by rules. 2. An administrative agency's rule or order that carries out statutes or executive orders that govern the agency.

A regulation subject to the Administrative Procedure Act (APA) has two principal identifying characteristics: first, the agency must intend its rule to apply generally rather than in a specific case, and second, the rule must implement, interpret, or make specific the law enforced or administered by the agency, or govern the agency's procedure. Cal. Government Code § 11342.600. *California Advocates*, 130 Cal.Rptr.2d 823 (Cal.App., 2003)

Regulation D A regulation of the Securities and Exchange Commission governing the limited offer and sale of unregistered securities.

regulatory agency A government agency that regulates an area of public concern and that can implement statutes by issuing regulations.

regulatory offense 1. A crime created by statute. 2. A minor offense.

regulatory taking Government regulation that deprives a private owner of all or substantially all practical uses of his or her property.

A form of eminent domain that occurs when a government agency, in exercise of its police power, adopts or enforces regulation that goes too far, either by failing to substantially advance legitimate state interest or by denying the owner all economically beneficial or productive use of his or her land. *Healing*, 27 Cal.Rptr.2d 758 (Cal.App., 1994)

rehabilitation 1. Restoration of credibility to an impeached witness. 2. Improving the character of an offender to prevent recidivism. 3. A reorganizing of debts in bankruptcy.

rehearing An additional hearing to correct an error or oversight.

reimburse 1. To pay back. 2. To indemnify.

reinstate To restore; to place again in a former condition or office.

reinsurance A contract by which one insurer (called the reinsurer) insures all or part of the risks of another insurer; insurance for insurers.

REIT See real estate investment trust.

rejection A refusal to accept something, e.g., an offer, performance.

rejoinder Defendant's response to a plaintiff's reply or replication.

relation back The rule that an act done at one time is considered by a fiction of the law to have been done at a prior time.

The relation back doctrine focuses on factual similarity rather than rights or obligations arising from the facts, and permits added causes of action to relate back to the initial complaint so long as they arise factually from the same injury. *Dudley*, 108 Cal.Rptr.2d 739 (Cal.App., 2001)

relative A person related by blood or marriage.

relator 1. See ex rel. 2. An informer. 3. One who applies for a writ.

release 1. To set free from custody. 2. To discharge or relinquish a claim against another. 3. To allow something to be communicated or published. 4. The giving up of a right, claim, interest, or privilege.

release on own recognizance (ROR) See personal recognizance.

relevance Logically connected to the matter at hand. Being relevant.

relevant Logically tending to establish or disprove a fact. Pertinent. Relevant evidence is evidence having any tendency to make the existence of a fact more probable or less probable than it would be without the evidence.

reliance Faith or trust felt by someone; dependence on someone.

relict A widow or widower.

reliction The gradual alteration of land by withdrawing water.

relief 1. Redress sought from a court. 2. Assistance to the poor.

religion A belief system of faith and worship, often involving a supernatural being or power.

rem See in rem.

remainder 1. A future estate or interest arising in someone other than the grantor or transferor (or the heirs of either) that will take effect upon the natural termination of a prior estate. 2. That which is left over; the remaining portions not otherwise disposed of.

remainderman One who holds or is entitled to a remainder.

Remainderman as used in this chapter means the person ultimately entitled to the principal, whether named or designated by the terms of the transaction by which the principal was established or determined by operation of law. Cal. Civil Code § 731.03

remand 1. To send back for further action. 2. To return to custody.

remediable Capable of being remedied.

remedial 1. Intended to correct wrongs and abuses. 2. Providing an avenue of redress.

remedial action 1. Action to solve long-term environmental damage. 2. Action to redress an individual wrong.

remedial statute 1. A statute that provides a remedy or means to enforce a right. 2. A statute designed to correct an existing law.

remedy 1. The means by which a right is enforced or the violation of a right is prevented or redressed. 2. To correct.

remise To give up or release.

remission 1. Canceling or relinquishing a debt or claim. 2. Pardon or forgiveness.

remit 1. To send or forward. 2. To transmit (money). 3. To refer for further action. 4. To cancel or excuse; to pardon. 5. To mitigate.

remittance Money sent (or the sending of money) as payment.

remitter 1. A person who purchases an instrument from its issuer if the instrument is payable to an identified person other than the purchaser. 2. The relation back of a later defective title to an earlier valid one. 3. Sending a case back to a lower court. 4. One who sends payment to another.

remittitur The power of the court to order a new trial unless a party agrees to reduce the jury verdict in its favor by a stated amount.

Remittitur transfers jurisdiction back to the inferior court so that it may act upon the case again, consistent with the judgment of the reviewing court. *People v. Tulare County*, 28 Cal.Rptr.3d 276 (Cal.App., 2005)

remonstrance A statement of grievances or reasons against something.

remote 1. Removed in relation, space, or time. 2. Minor or slight.

remote cause 1. A cause too removed in time from the event. 2. A cause that some independent force took advantage of to produce what was not the probable or natural effect of the original act.

removal The transfer of a person or thing from one place to another, e.g., transfer of a case from one court to another.

render To pronounce or deliver. To report formally.

rendition 1. Returning a fugitive to a state where he or she is wanted. 2. Making or delivering a formal decision.

renewal A reestablishment of a legal duty or relationship.

renounce To repudiate or abandon.

rent Cash or other consideration (often paid at intervals) for the use of property.

Rent is the consideration paid by the tenant to the landlord for the use, enjoyment and possession of the leased premises, and it is the means by which landlords make a profit on their property. *Action Apartment*, 114 Cal.Rptr.2d 412 (Cal.App., 2001)

rent-a-judging A method of alternate dispute resolution in which the parties hire a private person (e.g., a retired judge) to resolve their dispute.

rental 1. Something rented. 2. Rent to be paid.

rent strike An organized effort by tenants to withhold rent until grievances are resolved, e.g., repair of defective conditions.

renunciation The abandonment or waiver of a right or venture.

renvoi The doctrine under which the court of the forum, in resorting to a foreign law, adopts the rules of the foreign law as to conflict of laws, which rules may in turn refer the court back to the law of the forum.

reopen To allow new evidence to be introduced in a trial that was completed. To review a closed case.

reorganization A financial restructuring of a corporation for purposes of achieving bankruptcy protection, tax benefits, or efficiency.

reorganization plan A corporation's proposal to a bankruptcy court for restructuring under Chapter 11.

rep. See report, reporter, representative, republic.

reparable injury An injury for which money compensation is adequate.

reparation Compensation for an injury or wrong. Expiation.

repeal The express or implied abrogation of a law by a legislative body. Rescind.

repeat offender Someone convicted of a crime more than once.

replacement cost The current cost of creating a substantially equivalent structure or other asset.

replevin An action to recover possession of personal property wrongfully held or detained and damages incidental to the detention.

replevin bond A bond posted by the plaintiff when seeking replevin.

replevy To regain possession of personal property through replevin.

replication A plaintiff's response to the defendant's plea or answer.

Replication transaction means a derivative transaction or combination of derivative transactions effected in order to replicate the investment characteristic of another authorized transaction. Cal. Insurance Code § 1211

reply A plaintiff's response to the defendant's counterclaim, plea, or answer.

reply brief The appellate brief filed by the appellant in response to the appellee's brief. A brief responding to an opponent's brief.

repo 1. An agreement to buy back a security. 2. See repossession.

report (rep.) 1. A written account of a court decision. 2. A volume (or set of volumes) of court opinions. Also called reports. 3. A volume (or set of volumes) of administrative decisions. 4. A formal account or descriptive statement.

reporter (rep.) 1. The person in charge of reporting the decisions of a court. 2. The person who takes down and transcribes proceedings. 3. A volume (or set of volumes) of court opinions. Also called case reports.

reporter's privilege See journalist's privilege (1).

reports See report (2).

repose See statute of repose.

repossession (repo) The taking back of property, e.g., a creditor's seizure of property bought on credit by a debtor in default.

representation 1. The act of representing or acting on behalf of another. 2. A statement of fact expressed by words or conduct, often made to induce another's conduct. 3. See also per stirps.

Inadequate representation by counsel is representation that reduces proceedings to a farce or sham. *People v. Aikens*, 74 Cal.Rptr. 882 (CA 1969)

representative (rep.) 1. One who acts on behalf of another. 2. A legislator. 3. Serving as an example.

representative action See derivative action; class action.

reprieve A stay or postponement in carrying out a sentence.

reprimand An official declaration that an attorney's conduct was unethical. The declaration does not affect the attorney's right to practice law. A *private reprimand* is not disclosed to the public; a *public reprimand* is.

reprisal Action taken in retaliation.

reproductive rights Rights pertaining to one's reproductive and sexual life, e.g., using contraceptives, access to abortion.

republic Government in which supreme authority lies with the voters who act through elected representatives. A republican form of government.

republication 1. Repetition of a statement already published or communicated once. 2. Steps that reestablish a revoked will, e.g., adding a codicil to it.

repudiation 1. Denial or rejection. 2. Declaring a refusal to perform.

repugnant Incompatible; irreconcilably inconsistent.

reputation The views or esteem others have of a person.

request for admission A method of pretrial discovery in which one party asks another to admit or deny the substance of a statement, e.g., a statement of fact.

A written request that any other party to the action admit the genuineness of specified documents, or the truth of specified matters of fact, opinion relating to fact, or application of law to fact. Cal. Code of Civil Procedure § 2033.010

request for instructions A party's request that the trial judge provide the jury with the instructions stated in the request.

request for production A method of pretrial discovery consisting of a demand that the other side make available documents and other tangible things for inspection, copying, and testing.

requirements contract A contract in which the buyer agrees to buy all of its goods and services from a seller, which agrees to fill these needs during the period of the contract.

An agreement by a tenant to rent all office space in landlords' building which tenant required for its operations was a requirements contract. *Fisher*, 29 Cal.Rptr. 210 (Cal.App., 1963)

requisition 1. A formal request or demand. 2. The seizure of property by the state.

res 1. The subject matter of a trust or will. 2. A thing or object, a status.

res adjudicata See res judicata.

resale A sale of goods after another buyer of those goods breaches its contract to buy them.

resale price maintenance A form of vertical price-fixing by which a manufacturer sets the price at which its buyers resell to others.

rescind 1. To annul or repeal. 2. To cancel a contract.

rescission A party's cancellation of a contract because of a material breach by the other party or by mutual agreement. Also spelled recision.

Restoration by the plaintiff of any benefits received under the contract, coupled with restitution to the plaintiff of the consideration which he or she gave. *Denevi*, 18 Cal.Rptr.3d 276 (Cal.App., 2004)

rescript 1. A direction from a court to a clerk on how to dispose of a case. 2. The decision of the appellate court sent to the trial court.

rescue doctrine An injured rescuer can recover from the original tortfeasor who negligently caused the event that precipitated the rescue.

reservation 1. A right or interest created for the grantor in land granted to the grantee. 2. A tract of land to which a Native American tribe retains the original title or which is set aside for its use. 3. A condition through a limitation, qualification, or exception.

reserve 1. To keep back or retain. 2. A fund set aside to cover future expenses, losses, or claims.

reserve banks Member banks of the Federal Reserve System.

reserve clause A contract clause giving club owners a continuing and exclusive right to the services of a professional athlete.

reserved point See point reserved.

reserved powers Powers not delegated to the federal government by the U.S. Constitution nor prohibited by it to the states and hence are reserved to the states or to the people. (U.S. Const. amend. X.)

reserve price The minimum auction price a seller will accept.

res gestae declarations Spontaneous or unfiltered statements made in the surrounding circumstances of an event (e.g., excited utterances) are sometimes admissible as exceptions to the hearsay rule.

Where a declaration is made under the immediate influence of the occurrence to which it relates and so near the time of that occurrence as to negative any probability of fabrication, declaration is admissible as res gestae. *White*, 167 P.2d 530 (Cal.App., 1946)

residence 1. Living or remaining in a particular locality for more than a transitory period but without the intent to stay there indefinitely. If this intent existed, the place would be a domicile. Sometimes, however, residence and domicile are treated as synonyms. 2. A fixed abode or house.

residency The place where one has a residence.

resident One who occupies a dwelling and has an ongoing physical presence therein. This person may or may not be a domiciliary.

resident agent One authorized to accept service of process for another.

resident alien A noncitizen who legally establishes a long-term residence or domicile in this country.

residual 1. Pertaining to that which is left over or what lingers. 2. Payment for reuse of a protected work.

residuary What is left over. See also residuary estate.

residuary bequest A bequest of the residuary estate.

residuary clause A clause in a will disposing of the residuary estate.

A clause in a will by which that part of property is disposed of which remains after satisfying bequests and devises. *In re Lefranc's Estate*, 239 P.2d 617 (CA 1952)

residuary devise A devise of the residuary estate.

residuary estate The remainder of an estate after all debts and claims are paid and after all specific bequests (gifts) are satisfied. Also called residuary, residue, residuum.

residuary legacy A legacy of the residuary estate.

residuary legatee The person who receives the residuary estate.

residue What is left over. See also residuary estate.

residuum What is left over. See also residuary estate.

res inter alios acta ("a thing done among others") A person cannot be affected by the words or acts of others with whom he or she is in no way connected, and for whose words or acts he or she is not legally responsible.

res ipsa loquitur ("the thing speaks for itself") An inference of the defendant's negligence arises when the event producing the harm (a) was of a kind that ordinarily does not occur in the absence of someone's negligence, (b) was caused by an agency or instrumentality within the defendant's exclusive control, and (c) was not due to any voluntary action or contribution on the part of the plaintiff.

For the presumption of negligence to arise under doctrine of res ipsa loquitur, it must be shown that accident was of kind that ordinarily does not occur absent someone's negligence, that cause or instrumentality was within defendant's exclusive control, and that it was not due to plaintiff's voluntary action or contribution; when these prerequisites are met, trier of fact is allowed to assume existence of presumed fact unless defendant introduces evidence to contrary. Cal. Evidence Code § 646(b). *Blackwell*, 54 Cal.Rptr.2d 209 (Cal.App., 1996)

resisting arrest Intentionally preventing a peace officer from effecting a lawful arrest.

res judicata ("a thing adjudicated") A final judgment on the merits will preclude the same parties from later relitigating the same claim and any other claim based on the same facts or transaction that could have been raised in the first suit but was not. Also called claim preclusion.

res nova A question the courts have not yet addressed.

resolution. 1. An expression of the opinion or will of an assembly or group. 2. A decision or authorization. The verb is to resolve.

resort A place or destination to obtain redress or assistance.

RESPA See Real Estate Settlement Procedures Act.

respite A delay, e.g., a temporary suspension of the execution of a sentence, additional time to pay a debt.

respondeat superior ("let the master answer") An employer or principal is responsible (liable) for the wrongs committed by an employee or agent within the scope of employment or agency.

Employers are responsible for torts of their employees if committed in course and scope of employment. Cal. Civil Code § 2338. *Avila*, 213 Cal.Rptr. 314 (Cal.App., 1985)

respondent 1. The party against whom a claim, petition, or bill is filed. 2. The party against whom an appeal is brought; the appellee.

responsibility 1. Being accountable, liable, or at fault. 2. A duty.

responsible bidder An experienced, solvent, available contract bidder.

responsive Constituting an answer or response; nonevasive.

responsive pleading A pleading that replies to a prior pleading of an opponent.

rest To indicate to the court that a party has presented all of the evidence he or she intends to submit at this time.

Restatements Treatises of the American Law Institute (e.g., *Restatement (Second) of Torts*) that state the law and indicate changes in the law that the Institute would like to see implemented (*www.ali.org*).

restitution 1. Making good or giving an equivalent value for any loss, damage, or injury. 2. An equitable remedy to prevent unjust enrichment.

restraining order A court order not to do a threatened act, e.g., to harass someone, to transfer assets. Also called protection order, protective order.

restraint Restriction, prohibition; confinement.

A prior restraint is an administrative or judicial order that forbids certain speech in advance of the time the communication is to occur. *San Jose Mercury News*, 18 Cal.Rptr.3d 645 (Cal.App., 2004)

restraint of marriage An inducement or obligation not to marry that results from a condition attached to a gift.

restraint of trade Contracts or combinations that tend to or are designed to eliminate competition, artificially set prices, or otherwise hamper a free market in commerce.

restraint on alienation A provision in an instrument (e.g., a deed) that prohibits or restricts transfers of the property by the grantee.

restricted security Stock whose sale to the public is restricted. The stock is not registered with the Securities and Exchange Commission. Also called letter stock.

restrictive covenant 1. A restriction created by covenant or agreement (e.g., in a deed) on the use of land. Also called equitable servitude. 2. See covenant not to compete.

restrictive indorsement An indorsement that limits or conditions the further negotiability of the instrument.

resulting trust A remedy used when a person makes a disposition of property under circumstances that raise the inference that he or she did not intend to transfer a beneficial interest to the person taking or holding the property. Also called implied trust, presumptive trust.

Payment of purchase price of automobile by one other than the one designated as transferee thereof on the registration and title papers created a resulting trust, and the transferee held legal title as trustee for the person furnishing consideration as the owner of beneficial interest. *Henry*, 200 P.2d 785 (CA 1948)

resulting use An implied use remaining with the grantor in a conveyance without consideration.

retailer A business that sells goods to the ultimate consumer.

retain 1. To engage the services of or employ. 2. To hold.

retainage A portion of the contract price withheld to assure that the contractor will satisfy its obligations and complete the project.

retained earnings See earned surplus.

retainer 1. The act of hiring or engaging the services of someone, usually a professional. 2. An amount of money (or other property) a client pays a professional as a deposit or advance against future fees, costs, and expenses of providing services.

A sum of money paid by a client to secure an attorney's availability over a given period of time and such a fee is earned by attorney when paid since the attorney is entitled to the money regardless of whether he or she actually performs any services for the client. *Baranowski*, 154 Cal.Rptr. 752 (CA 1979)

retaliatory eviction An eviction because the tenant has complained about the leased premises.

retirement 1. Voluntarily withdrawing from one's occupation or career. 2. Taking out of circulation.

retirement plans Pension or other benefit plans for retirement.

retraction Withdrawing a declaration, accusation, or promise. Recanting.

retraxit Voluntary withdrawal of a lawsuit that cannot be rebrought.

retreat rule Before using deadly force in self-defense against a deadly attack, there is a duty to withdraw or retreat if this is a safe alternative, unless (under the castle doctrine) the attack occurs in one's home or business.

retrial A new trial of a previously tried case.

retribution Punishment that is deserved.

retroactive Applying or extending to a time prior to enactment or issuance. Also called retrospective.

A statute is retrospective or retroactive, if it affects rights, obligations, acts, transactions, and conditions which are performed or exist prior to the adoption of the statute. *Bullard*, 28 Cal.Rptr.3d 225 (Cal.App., 2005)

retrocession Ceding back something, e.g., title, jurisdiction.

retrospective See retroactive.

return 1. A report of a court officer on what he or she did with a writ or other court instrument. 2. Profit. 3. See tax return.

return day The day on which a litigation event must occur, e.g., file an answer, appear in court.

return of service See proof of service.

rev'd See reversed.

revenue Gross income; total receipts.

revenue bond A government bond payable by public funds.

Revenue Procedure The position of the Internal Revenue Service on procedural requirements for matters before it.

Revenue Ruling (Rev. Rul.) The opinion of the Internal Revenue Service of how the tax law applies to a specific transaction.

revenue stamp A stamp used to certify that a tax has been paid.

reversal An appellate court's setting aside of a lower court decision.

reverse annuity mortgage (RAM) A mortgage on a residence in which the borrower receives periodic income and the loan is repaid when the property is sold or the borrower dies. Also called reverse mortgage.

reversed (rev'd) Overturned on appeal.

reverse discrimination Discrimination against members of a majority group, usually because of affirmative action for a minority group.

reverse mortgage See reverse annuity mortgage.

reverse stock split Calling in all outstanding shares and reissuing fewer shares with greater value.

reversible error See prejudicial error.

reversion The undisposed portion of an estate remaining in a grantor when he or she conveys less than his or her whole estate and, therefore, retains a portion of the title. The residue of the estate left with the grantor.

A reversion can exist only when the estate conveyed is less than a fee simple, that is, is a particular estate, the classic example being a reversion arising from the granting of a life estate. Cal. Civil Code, § 768. *Alamo School*, 6 Cal.Rptr. 272 (Cal.App., 1960)

reversionary interest The interest that a person has in the reversion of property. See reversion. Any future interest left in a transferor.

reversioner A person who is entitled to an estate in reversion.

revert To turn back; to return to.

reverter See possibility of reverter.

revest To vest again with a power or interest.

rev'g Reversing.

review 1. To examine or go over a matter again. 2. The power of a court to examine the correctness of what a lower tribunal has done. Short for judicial review (see this phrase).

Revised Statutes (R.S.; Rev. Stat.) A collection of statutes that have been revised, rearranged, or reenacted as a whole.

revival Renewing the legal force or effectiveness of something.

revocable Susceptible of being withdrawn, canceled, or invalidated.

revocable trust A trust that the maker (settlor) can cancel or revoke.

revocation Canceling, voiding, recalling, or destroying something.

revolving credit An extension of credit to customers who may use it as desired up to a specified dollar limit.

A revolving account means an account established by an agreement pursuant to which the buyer promises to pay, in installments, to a retail seller, his outstanding balance incurred in retail installment sales and which provides for a finance charge. Cal. Civil Code § 1802.7

Rev. Rul. See Revenue Ruling.

Rev. Stat. See Revised Statutes.

RFP Request for production; request for proposals.

Richard Roe See John Doe.

RICO See Racketeer Influenced and Corrupt Organizations Act.

rider An amendment or addition attached to a legislative bill, insurance policy, or other document.

right 1. Morally, ethically, or legally proper. 2. A legal power, privilege, immunity, or protected interest one can claim.

right-and-wrong test See insanity (4).

right of action The right to bring a suit. A right that can be enforced.

right of common See profit à pendre.

right of election See election by spouse.

right of first refusal A right to equal the terms of another offer.

A right of first refusal is a preemptive right to purchase property on the terms and conditions of an offer to purchase by a third person. *Pellandini*, 7 Cal.Rptr.3d 413 (Cal.App., 2003)

right of privacy See invasion of privacy.

right of redemption 1. A mortgagor's right to redeem property after it has been foreclosed. 2. See equity of redemption.

right of re-entry The estate that the grantor may acquire again upon breach of a condition under which it was granted.

right of survivorship A joint tenant's right to receive the entire estate upon the death of the other joint tenant.

right of way 1. The right to pass over the land of another. 2. The right in traffic to pass or proceed first.

A right of way is primarily a privilege to pass over another's land. Cal. Civil Code § 801. *Beyer*, 29 Cal.Rptr.3d 561 (Cal.App., 2005)

right to bear arms The Second Amendment right "to keep and bear arms."

right-to-convey covenant See covenant of seisin.

right to counsel A constitutional right to an appointed attorney in some criminal and juvenile delinquency cases when the accused cannot afford private counsel.

right to die A right of a competent, terminally ill adult to refuse medical treatment.

right to travel A constitutional right to travel freely between states.

right-to-work law A state law declaring that employees are not required to join a union as a condition of receiving or retaining a job.

rigor mortis Muscular rigidity or stiffening shortly after death.

riot Three or more persons assembled together for a common purpose and disturbing the peace by acting in a violent or tumultuous manner.

riparian right The right of owners of land adjoining a waterway to make reasonable use of the water, e.g., for ingress, egress, and fishing.

ripeness doctrine A court will decline to address a claim unless the case presents definite and concrete issues, a real and substantial controversy exists, and there is a present need for adjudication. See also justiciable.

The ripeness requirement precludes courts from issuing purely advisory opinions, for instance, in cases in which parties seek a judicial declaration on a question of law, though no actual dispute or controversy ever existed between them requiring the declaration for its determination. *Rolfe*, 127 Cal.Rptr.2d 871 (Cal.App., 2002)

risk The danger or hazard of a loss or injury occurring.

risk capital An investment of money or property in a business, often a new venture involving high risk. See also venture capital.

risk of loss Responsibility for loss, particularly during transfer of goods. The danger of bearing this responsibility.

risk of nonpersuasion See burden of persuasion.

robbery Unlawfully taking property from the person of another (or in his or her presence) by the use of violence or threats.

Robert's Rules of Order Rules for conducting meetings. A parliamentary manual.

rogatory letters See letter rogatory.

roll 1. The record of official proceedings. 2. An official list.

rollover 1. Refinancing or renewing a short-term loan. 2. Reinvesting funds in a plan that qualifies for the same tax treatment.

Roman Law The legal system and laws of ancient Rome that is the foundation of civil law in some European countries.

root of title The recorded conveyance that begins a chain-of-title search on specific real property.

ROR Release on own recognizance. See personal recognizance.

ROTH IRA An individual retirement account with nondeductible contributions but tax-free distributions after age 59½.

round lot The unit of trading securities, e.g., 100 shares.

royalty 1. Payment for each use of a work protected by copyright or patent. 2. Payment for the right to extract natural resources.

R.S. See Revised Statutes.

rubric 1. The title of a statute. 2. A rule. 3. A category. 4. A preface.

rule 1. An established standard, guide, or regulation. 2. A court procedure. 3. The controlling authority. 4. To decide a point of law.

rule against accumulations Limits on a trust's accumulation of income.

rule against perpetuities No interest is valid unless it must vest, if at all, within 21 years (plus a period of gestation) after the death of some life or lives in being (i.e., alive) at the time the interest was created.

The rule against perpetuities, or more accurately the rule against remoteness of vesting, requires that within a fixed period the absolute interest must vest. *In re Sahlender's Estate*, 201 P.2d 69 (Cal.App., 1948)

rule in Shelley's case When in the deed or other instrument an estate of freehold is given to a person and a remainder to his or her heirs in fee or in tail, that person takes the entire estate—a fee simple absolute.

rule in Wild's case If X devises land to Y and Y's children, the devise is a fee tail (if Y has no children at the time of the devise) but a joint tenancy (if Y has children at that time).

rulemaking The process and power of an administrative agency to make rules and regulations.

rule nisi See decree nisi.

rule of completeness A party may introduce the whole of a statement if any part is introduced by the opposing party.

rule of four The United States Supreme Court will accept a case on certiorari if at least four justices vote to do so.

rule of law 1. A legal principle or ruling. 2. Supremacy of law.

rule of lenity When there is ambiguity in a criminal statute, particularly as to punishment, doubts are resolved in favor of the defendant.

Language in a penal statute that truly is susceptible of more than one reasonable construction in meaning or application ordinarily is construed in the manner that is more favorable to the defendant. *People v. Hagedorn*, 25 Cal.Rptr.3d 879 (Cal.App., 2005)

rule of reason 1. In antitrust cases, the issue is whether the restraint's anticompetitive effects substantially outweigh the procompetitive effects for which the restraint is reasonably necessary. 2. A requirement to consider pertinent evidence and reasonable alternatives in decision making.

rules committee A legislative committee establishing agendas and procedures for considering proposed legislation.

rules of professional conduct See Model Rules of Professional Conduct.

ruling A judicial or administrative decision.

run 1. To apply or be effective. 2. To expire because of elapsed time. 3. To accompany or go with a conveyance.

runaway shop An employer who relocates or transfers work for antiunion reasons.

runner 1. One who solicits business, especially accident cases. 2. An employee who delivers and files papers.

Except as otherwise allowed by law, the employment of runners, cappers, steerers, or other persons to procure patients constitutes unprofessional conduct. Cal. Business & Professions Code § 1003(a)

running account A continuous record kept to show all the transactions (charges and payments) between a debtor and creditor.

running with the land See covenant running with the land.

S

sabotage Willful destruction of property or interference with normal operations of a government or employer.

safe harbor Protection from liability if acting in good faith.

said Before mentioned; aforementioned.

sailor's will See military will.

salable Fit to be offered for sale. Merchantable.

salary Compensation for services paid at regular intervals.

A fixed compensation; the equivalent of compensation. *Treu*, 268 P.2d 482 (CA 1954)

sale The transfer of title to property for a consideration or price. A contract for this transfer.

sale and leaseback See leaseback.

sale by sample A sale of goods in quantity or bulk with the understanding that they will conform in quality with a sample.

sale in gross A sale of land in which the boundaries are identified but the quantity of land is unspecified or deemed to be immaterial.

sale on approval A conditional sale that is absolute only if the buyer is satisfied with the goods, whether or not they are defective.

sale or return A sale to a merchant buyer who can return any unsold goods (even if not defective) if they were received for resale.

sales tax A tax on the sale of goods and services, computed as a percentage of the purchase price.

salvage 1. Property saved or remaining after a casualty. 2. Rescue of assets from loss. 3. Payment for saving a ship or its cargo.

Salvage means the controlled removal of metallic discards from the solid waste stream at a permitted solid waste facility for the express purpose of recycling or reuse. Cal. Public Resources Code § 42162

salvage value An asset's value after its useful life for the owner has ended.

same evidence test When the same acts violate two distinct statutory provisions, the double-jeopardy test of whether there are two offenses or one is whether each provision requires proof of a fact the other does not.

sanction 1. A penalty for a violation. 2. Approval or authorization.

S&L See savings and loan association.

sane Of sound mind; able to distinguish right from wrong.

sanitary Pertaining to health and hygiene.

sanity The condition of having a sound mind.

sanity hearing A hearing to determine fitness to stand trial or whether institutionalization is needed.

satisfaction The discharge or performance of a legal obligation.

satisfaction contract A contract in which the stated standard of performance is the satisfaction of one of the parties (e.g., a contract giving an employer sole discretion to decide if an employee should be terminated for unacceptable work).

A contract involving matters of fancy, taste, or judgment and, in such a contract, the promisor is the sole judge of his or her satisfaction. *Pugh*, 250 Cal.Rptr. 195 (Cal.App., 1988)

satisfaction of judgment 1. Full payment or compliance with a judgment. 2. A document so stating.

satisfaction piece A statement by the parties that the obligation between them has been paid or satisfied.

save harmless See hold harmless.

saving clause 1. A clause in a statute that preserves certain rights, remedies, privileges, or claims. 2. See severability clause. 3. See saving-to-suitors clause.

savings and loan association (S&L) A financial institution that specializes in making mortgage loans for private homes.

Savings association includes a savings association, a savings and loan association, and a savings bank. Cal. Financial Code § 143

saving-to-suitors clause A statutory clause allowing certain admiralty claims to be brought in nonadmiralty courts (28 USC § 1333). Also called saving clause.

savings bank trust See Totten trust.

savings bond A United States government bond that cannot be traded.

S.B. See senate bill.

scab A worker who crosses a picket line to work or otherwise acts in disregard of positions or demands of a union. Also called strikebreaker.

scalper One who resells something at an inflated price for a quick profit.

scandalous matter Irrelevant matter in a pleading that casts a derogatory light on someone's moral character or uses repulsive language.

scènes à faire General themes that cannot be copyrighted.

schedule A written list or plan. An inventory.

scheduled property A list of properties with their values.

scheme A plan of action, often involving deception.

scienter 1. Intent to deceive or mislead. 2. Knowingly done.

Fraudulent representations require scienter, an intentional, conscious misrepresentation. *Hale*, 121 Cal.Rptr. 144 (Cal.App., 1975)

sci. fa. See scire facias.

scintilla A minute amount; a trace.

scire facias (sci. fa.) 1. A writ ordering one to appear on a matter of record and show cause why another should not be able to take advantage of that record. 2. The procedure by which a lienholder prosecutes a lien to judgment.

scope of authority An agent's express or implied authorization to act for the principal.

scope of employment That which is foreseeably done by an employee for an employer under the latter's specific or general control.

Employees act within scope of employment when they are engaged in work they were employed to perform or when their acts are incident to their duty and were performed for the benefit of their employers and not to serve their own purpose. Cal. Government Code §§ 911.2, 950.2. *Fowler*, 50 Cal.Rptr.2d 484 (Cal.App., 1996)

S corporation A corporation whose shareholders are taxed on the income of the corporation. Also called subchapter S corporation.

scrip 1. A substitute for money. 2. A document entitling one to a benefit. 3. A document representing a fraction of a share.

scrip dividend A dividend in the form of the right to receive future issues of stock.

script 1. Handwriting. 2. The original document.

scrivener One who prepares documents. A professional copyist or drafter.

seal An impression or sign to attest the execution of an instrument or to authenticate the document.

sealed bid A bid that is not revealed until all bids are submitted.

sealed records Publicly filed documents that are kept confidential.

sealed verdict A jury verdict not yet officially given to the court.

seaman's will See military will

search An examination by police of private areas (e.g., one's person, premises, or vehicle) in an attempt to discover evidence of a crime.

A governmental intrusion upon or invasion of a citizen's personal security in an area in which he or she has a reasonable expectation of privacy. *In re Cody S*, 16 Cal.Rptr.3d 653 (Cal.App., 2004)

search and seizure See unreasonable search.

search warrant A court order allowing a law enforcement officer to search designated areas and to seize evidence of crime found there.

seasonable Within the agreed-upon time; timely; at a reasonable time.

seaworthy Properly constructed and equipped for a sea voyage.

secession The act of withdrawing.

secondary Subordinate; inferior.

secondary authority Any nonlaw a court can rely on in its decision. Writings that describe or explain, but do not constitute, the law.

secondary boycott A boycott of customers or suppliers with whom the union has no labor dispute to induce them to stop dealing with a business with whom the union does have a labor dispute. The boycott can include picketing.

secondary easement An incident to an easement that allows those things necessary to the full enjoyment of the easement.

secondary evidence Evidence that is not the stronger or best evidence.

secondary liability Liability that applies only if the wronged party cannot obtain satisfaction from the person with primary liability.

secondary market A market for previously available goods or services.

secondary meaning Public awareness that a common or descriptive name or symbol identifies the source of a particular product or service.

Business name incorporating the name of a person acquires secondary meaning when the name and the business become synonymous in the public mind and the primary meaning of the name as a word identifying the person is submerged in favor of its meaning as a word identifying the business. Cal. Civil Code, § 3369. *Visser*, 29 Cal.Rptr. 367 (Cal.App., 1963)

secondary picketing See secondary boycott.

second-degree murder The unlawful taking of human life without premeditation or other facts that make the crime first-degree murder.

second-look See wait and see.

second mortgage A mortgage with a ranking in priority that is immediately below a first mortgage on the same property.

secretary The corporate officer in charge of keeping official records.

secret partner A partner whose identity is not known by the public.

secta 1. Followers. 2. A lawsuit.

section 1. A subdivision of a law or document. 2. A square mile area.

secundum 1. Second. 2. According to.

secured Backed by collateral, a mortgage, or other security.

secured creditor; secured party A creditor who can reach collateral of the debtor if the latter fails to pay the debt.

secured transaction A contract in which the seller or lender is a secured creditor.

securities See also security (2).

securities broker One in the business of buying and selling securities for others.

securitize To convert an asset into a security offered for sale.

security 1. Collateral that guarantees a debt or other obligation. 2. A financial instrument that is evidence of a debt interest (e.g., a bond), an ownership/equity interest, (e.g., a stock) or other specially defined rights (e.g., a futures contract). 3. Surety. 4. The state of being secure.

security agreement An agreement that creates or provides for a security interest.

security deposit See deposit (3).

security interest A property interest that secures a payment or the performance of an obligation.

An interest in personal property or fixtures that secures payment or performance of an obligation. Cal. Commercial Code § 1201(36)(a)

sedition Communicating, agreeing to, or advocating lawlessness, treason, commotions, or revolt against legitimate authority.

seditious libel Libelous statements designed to incite sedition.

seduction Wrongfully inducing another, without the use of force, to engage in sexual relations.

segregation The unconstitutional separation of people based on categories such as race, religion, or nationality.

seise To hold in fee simple.

seisin or **seizin** Possession of land under a claim of freehold estate.

seize To take possession forcibly.

seizure Taking possession of person or property.

select committee A committee set up for a limited or special task.

selective enforcement Enforcing the law primarily against a member of certain groups or classes of people, often arbitrarily.

selective incorporation The process of making only some of the Bill of Rights applicable to the states through the Fourteenth Amendment. Total incorporation makes all of them applicable.

Selective Service System A federal agency in charge of military registration and, if needed, a draft (*www.sss.gov*).

selectman An elected municipal officer in some towns.

self-authenticating Not needing extrinsic proof of authenticity.

self-dealing Acting to benefit oneself when one should be acting in the interest of another to whom a fiduciary duty is owed.

self-defense The use of force to repel threatened danger to one's person or property.

For self-defense, the jury must conclude that defendant was actually in fear of his or her life or serious bodily injury and that the conduct of the other party was such as to produce that state of mind in a reasonable person. *People v. Wilson*, 132 Cal.Rptr. 813 (Cal.App., 1976)

self-employment tax Social security tax on the self-employed.

self-executing Immediately or automatically having legal effect.

self-help Acting to redress a wrong without using the courts.

self-incrimination Acts or declarations by which one implicates oneself in a crime; exposing oneself to criminal prosecution.

self-insurance Funds set aside by a business to cover any loss.

self-proving Not requiring proof outside of the documents themselves.

self-serving declaration An out-of-court statement benefiting the person making it.

sell To transfer an asset by sale.

seller One who sells enters a contract to sell.

Seller means a person who has entered into a consumer contract with a consumer. Cal. Civil Code § 1799.201(h)

semble It would appear.

senate The upper chamber of a two-house (bicameral) legislature.

senate bill (S.B.; S.) A bill pending or before passage in the senate.

senior Higher in age, rank, preference, or priority.

senior interest An interest that is higher in precedence or priority.

seniority Greater rights than others based on length of service.

senior judge A judge with the longest tenure or who is semi-retired.

senior lien A lien on property that has priority over other liens.

senior mortgage A mortgage that has priority over other mortgages.

sentence Punishment imposed by the court on one convicted of a crime.

A sentence is a judgment in a criminal action; it is a declaration to defendant of his or her disposition or punishment once criminal guilt has been ascertained. *People v. Rodriquez*, 34 Cal.Rptr. 907 (Cal.App., 1963)

SEP See simplified employee pension plan.

separability clause See severability clause.

separable Capable of being separated.

separable controversy A dispute that is part of the entire controversy, yet by its nature is independent and can be severed from the whole.

separate Distinct, not joined.

separate but equal Segregated with equal opportunities and facilities.

separate maintenance Support by one spouse to another while separated.

separate property Property acquired by one spouse alone (a) before marriage, (b) during marriage by gift, will, or intestate succession, or (c) during marriage but after separating from the other spouse.

Everything acquired by wife after marriage as a gift is her separate property. *In re Claussenius' Estate*, 216 P.2d 485 (Cal.App., 1950)

separate trial An individual (separate) trial of one of the defendants jointly accused of a crime or of one of the issues in any case.

separation Living separately while still married.

separation agreement A contract between spouses who have separated or who are about to separate in which the terms of their separation (e.g., child custody, property division) are spelled out.

separation of powers The division of government into judicial, legislative, and executive branches with the requirement that each branch refrain from encroaching on the authority of the other two.

sequester 1. To separate or isolate a jury or witness. 2. To seize or take and hold funds or other property. Sometimes called sequestrate.

sequestrate See sequester.

sequestrator One who carries out an order or writ of sequestration.

sergeant at arms An officer who keeps order in a court or legislature.

serial bonds A number of bonds issued at the same time but with different maturity dates.

serial note A promissory note payable in regular installments. Also called installment note.

seriatim One by one in a series; one following after another.

series bonds Groups of bonds usually issued at different times and with different maturity dates but under the same indenture.

serious bodily harm See great bodily injury.

servant One employed to perform service, whose performance is controlled by or subject to the control of the master or employer.

Relationship of servant and master does not exist unless employer retains right to direct mode and manner in which the work shall be done. *Skelton*, 261 P.2d 339 (Cal.App., 1953)

serve To deliver a legal notice or process.

service 1. Delivery of a legal notice or process. 2. Tasks performed for others. 3. To pay interest on.

service by publication Publishing a notice in a newspaper or other media as service of process upon an absent or nonresident defendant.

service charge An added cost or fee for administration or handling.

servicemark (SM) See mark (1).

service of process A formal delivery of notice to a defendant that a suit has been initiated to which he or she must respond.

servient estate; servient tenement The track of land on which an easement is imposed or burdened. Also called servient tenement.

servitude 1. An easement or similar right to use another's land. 2. The condition of forced labor or slavery.

session 1. A continuous sitting of a court, legislature, council, etc. 2. Any time in the day during which such a body sits.

session laws (S.L.; sess.) Uncodified statutes enacted by a legislature during a session, printed chronologically.

set aside 1. To vacate a judgment, order, etc. 2. Set-aside: Something reserved for a special reason.

setback The distance that buildings are set back from property lines.

setoff 1. A defendant's claim against the plaintiff that is independent of the plaintiff's claim. 2. A debtor's right to reduce a debt by what the creditor owes the debtor.

Setoff is founded on the equitable principle that either party to a transaction involving mutual debts and credits can strike a balance, holding him or herself owing or entitled to the net difference. *Keith G*, 72 Cal.Rptr.2d 525 (Cal.App., 1998)

settlement 1. An agreement resolving a dispute without full litigation. 2. Payment or satisfactory adjustment of an account. 3. Distributing the assets and paying the debts of an estate. 4. See closing.

settlement option Choices available to pay life insurance benefits.

settlor One who makes a settlement of property (e.g., one who creates a trust). Also called trustor.

severability clause A clause in a statute or contract providing that if parts of it are declared invalid, the remaining parts shall continue to be effective. Also called saving clause, separability clause.

several 1. A few. 2. Distinct or separate, e.g., a person's several liability is distinct from (and can be enforced independently of) someone else's liability.

Where parties to a contract promise separate performances to be rendered respectively by each of them, or where each of them makes only a separate promise that the same performance shall be rendered, the obligation is several as distinguished from joint. *Douglas*, 210 P.2d 727 (Cal.App., 1949)

severally Apart from others, separately.

severalty The condition of being separate or distinct.

severance 1. Separating claims or parties. 2. Removing; cutting off.

severance tax A tax on natural resources removed from the land.

sewer service Falsely claiming to have served process.

sex discrimination Discrimination that is gender-based.

sexual abuse; sexual assault Rape or other unlawful sexual contact with another.

sexual harassment Unwelcome conduct of a sexual nature on the job.

Sexual harassment, within meaning of California Fair Employment and Housing Act (CFEHA), is defined as verbal, physical, or sexual behavior directed at individual because of her, or his, gender, and includes, but is not limited to, conduct which is verbal (such as epithets, derogatory comments or slurs) as well as physical and visual insults. Cal. Government Code § 12940(h). *Flait*, 4 Cal.Rptr.2d 522 (Cal.App., 1992)

sexual predator A person with a propensity to commit sexual assault.

shadow jurors Persons hired by one side to observe a trial as members of the general audience and, as the trial progresses, to give feedback to a jury consultant hired by the attorney of one of the parties, who will use the feedback to assess strategy for the remainder of the trial.

shall 1. Is required to, must. 2. Should. 3. May.

sham Counterfeit, a hoax; frivolous, without substance.

sham transaction Conduct with no business purpose other than tax avoidance.

share 1. The part or portion that you contribute or own. 2. An ownership interest in a corporation. A unit of stock.

share and share alike To divide equally.

shareholder One who owns a share in a corporation. Also called stockholder.

shareholder's derivative action See derivative action (1).

shelf registration Registration with the Securities and Exchange Commission involving a delayed stock sale.

shell corporation A corporation with no assets or active business.

Shelley's Case See rule in Shelley's case.

shelter An investment or other device to reduce or defer taxes.

shepardize To use *Shepard's Citations* to find data on the history and currentness of cases, statutes, and other legal materials. See also citator.

sheriff's deed A deed given a buyer at a sheriff's sale.

sheriff's sale A forced sale based on a court order.

When the sheriff sells real estate, under and by virtue of an execution or order of court, he or his successors in office shall execute and deliver to the purchaser or purchasers all such deeds and conveyances as are required by law and necessary for the purpose. Cal. Code of Civil Procedure § 262.4

shield law 1. A law to protect journalists from being required to divulge confidential sources. 2. See rape shield law.

shifting income Transferring income to someone in a lower tax bracket.

shifting the burden Transferring the burden of proof (or the burden to produce evidence) from one party to another during a trial.

shipment contract A sale in which the risk of loss passes to the buyer when the seller duly delivers the goods to the carrier.

shop A place of business or employment.

shop-book rule A rule allowing regularly kept original business records into evidence as an exception to the hearsay rule.

shoplifting The theft of goods displayed for sale.

A merchant may detain a person for a reasonable time for the purpose of conducting an investigation whenever the merchant has probable cause to believe the person to be detained is attempting to unlawfully take or has unlawfully taken merchandise from the merchant's premises. Cal. Penal Code § 490.5(f)(1)

shop steward A union official who helps enforce the union contract.

short sale A sale of a security the seller does not own that is made by the delivery of a security borrowed by, or for the account of, the seller.

short summons A summons with a shorter-than-usual response time.

short-swing profit Profit earned on stock by a corporate insider within 6 months of purchase or sale.

short-term capital gain Gain from the sale or exchange of a capital asset held for less than a year or other designated short term.

show To establish or prove.

show cause order A court order to appear and explain why the court should not take a proposed action to provide relief.

shower One who takes the jury to a scene involved in the case.

showup See lineup.

shut-in royalty A payment by a lessee to continue holding a functioning well that is not being currently utilized due to a weak oil or gas market.

shyster Slang for an unscrupulous attorney.

sic A signal alerting the reader that you are quoting exactly, including the error in the quote.

sidebar conference See bench conference.

sight draft A draft payable on demand when shown.

sign 1. To affix one's signature (or mark substitute). 2. To indicate agreement.

signatory The person or nation signing a document.

signature One's name written by oneself. A word, mark, or symbol indicating identity or intended to authenticate a document.

Signature means (1) A handwritten or mechanical signature, or a copy thereof; or (2) Any representation of a person's name, including, but not limited to, a printed or typewritten representation, that serves the same purpose as a handwritten or mechanical signature. Cal. Civil Code § 3344.5(d)

signing statement An announcement by the president upon signing a bill into law that states the president's objections, interpretation, or intention in implementing the law.

silent partner See dormant partner.

silent witness theory Evidence such as photographs may be admitted without testimony of a witness if there is sufficient proof of the reliability of the process that produced the evidence.

silver platter doctrine The former rule that evidence obtained illegally by state police is admissible in federal court if no federal officer participated in the violation of the defendant's rights.

simple 1. Not aggravated. 2. Uncomplicated. 3. Not under seal.

simple assault; simple battery An assault or battery not accompanied by aggravating circumstances.

simple interest Interest on the principal only, not on any interest earned on the principal.

Simple-interest basis means the determination of a finance charge, other than an administrative finance charge, by applying a constant rate to the unpaid balance as it changes from time to time, . . . Cal. Civil Code § 1802.20

simple negligence See ordinary negligence.

simple trust 1. A trust requiring the distribution of all trust income to the beneficiaries. 2. See passive trust.

simpliciter Simply; unconditionally.

simplified employee pension plan (SEP) An employee benefit plan consisting of an annuity or an individual retirement account.

simulated sale A sham sale in which no consideration was exchanged.

Simultaneous Death Act A statute providing that when two people die together but without evidence of who died first, the property of each may be disposed of as if each survived the other.

sine die ("without day") With no day being designated.

sine prole (s.p.) Without issue.

sine qua non An essential condition.

single-juror charge A jury instruction stating that if a single juror is not reasonably satisfied with the plaintiff's evidence, the jury cannot find for the plaintiff.

single-publication rule Only one defamation cause of action exists for the same communication, even if it was heard or read by many.

sinking fund Regular deposits and interest accrued thereon set aside to pay long-term debts.

SIPC Securities Investor Protection Corporation (*www.sipc.org*).

sister corporations Corporations controlled by the same shareholders.

sistren Sisters. Female colleagues.

sit 1. To hold a session. 2. To occupy an office.

sit-down strike Employees' refusal to work while at the work site.

sitting In session.

situs Position. The place where a thing happened or is located.

S.J.D. Doctor of Juridical Science.

skip person A recipient of assets in a generation-skipping transfer.

skiptracing Efforts to locate persons (e.g., debtors) or assets.

S.L. See session laws.

slander Defamation that is oral or gestured.

Two forms of defamation are slander or libel; slander requires an oral utterance while libel requires a publication. Cal. Civil Code §§ 44–46. *Joel*, 80 Cal.Rptr.2d 247 (Cal.App., 1998)

slander of goods; slander of title See disparagement.

slander per se Slander that accuses a person of unchastity or sexual misconduct, of committing a crime of moral turpitude, of engaging in business or professional misconduct, or of having a loathsome disease.

SLAPP See Strategic Lawsuit Against Public Participation.

slavery A status or system of enforced labor and bondage.

sleeping partner See dormant partner.

slight care More than the absence of care but less than ordinary care.

slight negligence The failure to exercise great care.

slip law One act of the legislature printed in a single pamphlet.

slip opinion The first printing of a single court opinion.

slowdown Causing production to decrease as a union or labor protest.

SM Servicemark. See mark (1)

small-claims court A court that uses more informal procedures to resolve smaller claims — those under a designated amount.

small loan acts Laws on interest-rate limits for small consumer loans.

smart money 1. See punitive damages. 2. Funds of a shrewd investor.

smuggle To import or export goods illegally without paying duties.

social guest One invited to enter or remain on another's property to enjoy private hospitality, not for a business purpose.

Employee's guest at employer's party for employees was a guest at the party, and thus, as to the guest, employer was a social host within social host immunity statute. Cal. Civil Code § 1714(b, c). *DeBolt*, 227 Cal.Rptr. 258 (Cal.App., 1986)

society 1. An association of persons united for a common purpose. 2. Companionship and love among family members.

sodomy Oral sex or anal intercourse between humans, or between humans and animals. Also called unnatural offense.

soil bank A federal program paying farmers not to grow certain crops.

soldier's will See military will.

sole actor doctrine The knowledge of an agent is treated as the knowledge of his or her principal.

sole custody Only one parent makes all child-rearing decisions.

sole proprietorship A form of business that does not have a separate legal identity apart from the one person who owns all assets and assumes all debts and liabilities.

solicitation 1. A request for something. 2. Enticing or urging someone to commit a crime. 3. An appeal or request for clients or business.

Solicitation is offer or invitation to another to commit crime, but is not, by itself, an attempt. *People v. Sanchez*, 71 Cal.Rptr.2d 309 (Cal.App., 1998)

solicitor 1. One who solicits. 2. A lawyer for a city or government agency. 3. A British lawyer who prepares documents and gives clients legal advice but (unlike a barrister) does not do extensive trial work.

solicitor general A high-ranking government litigator.

solvent Able to meet one's financial obligations.

Son of Sam law A law against criminals earning income by selling the story of their crime to the media.

sound 1. Healthy; able. 2. Marketable. 3. Well-founded. 4. To be actionable.

source of law The authority for court opinions or statutes, e.g., constitutions, other court opinions and statutes, and custom.

sovereign 1. Having supreme power. 2. The ruler or head of state.

sovereign immunity The sovereign (i.e., the state) cannot be sued in its courts without its consent. Also called governmental immunity.

sovereignty Supreme political authority.

s.p. 1. Same principle. 2. See sine prole.

speaker The chairperson or presiding officer of an assembly.

speaking demurrer A demurrer that alleges facts that are not in the pleadings. See also demurrer.

speaking motion Saying more than called for by the motion or pleading.

special act See private law (2).

special administrator An estate administrator with limited duties.

The special administrator has the power to do all of the following without further order of the court: (1) Take possession of all of the real and personal property of the estate of the decedent and preserve it from damage, waste, and injury. (2) Collect all claims, rents, and other income belonging to the estate. . . . Cal. Probate Code § 8544

special agent An agent delegated to do a specific act.

special appearance Appearing solely to challenge the court's jurisdiction.

special assessment An additional tax on land that benefits from a public improvement.

special contract 1. An express contract with explicit terms. 2. See contract under seal.

special counsel An attorney hired by the government for a particular matter.

special court-martial An intermediate level of court-martial.

special damages Actual and provable economic losses, e.g., lost wages.

Unlike general damages for breach of contract, special damages are those losses that do not arise directly and inevitably from any similar breach of any similar agreement; instead, they are secondary or derivative losses arising from circumstances that are particular to the contract or to the parties. *Lewis*, 22 Cal.Rptr.3d 340 (CA 2004)

special demurrer A challenge to the form of a pleading.

special deposit A deposit in a bank made for safekeeping or for some special application or purpose.

special exception 1. A challenge to the form of a claim. 2. See conditional use.

special-facts rule A duty of disclosure exists when special circumstances make it inequitable for a corporate director or officer to withhold information from a stockholder.

special finding A finding of essential facts to support a judgment.

special grand jury A grand jury called for a limited or special task.

special guaranty A guarantee enforceable only by designated persons.

special indorsement An indorsement that specifies the person to whom the instrument is payable or to whom the goods are to be delivered.

If an indorsement is made by the holder of an instrument, whether payable to an identified person or payable to bearer, and the indorsement identifies a person to whom it makes the instrument payable, it is a special indorsement. Cal. Commercial Code § 3205(a)

special interrogatory A separate question a jury is asked to answer.

specialist One possessing special expertise, often certified as such.

special jurisdiction See limited jurisdiction.

special jury A jury chosen for its special expertise or for a case of special importance. Also called struck jury.

special law See private law (2).

special lien See particular lien.

special master See master (2).

special meeting A nonregular meeting called for a special purpose.

special power of appointment See limited power of appointment.

special power of attorney A power of attorney with limited authority.

special prosecutor An attorney appointed to conduct a criminal investigation of a matter.

special session See extraordinary session.

special trust A trust whose trustee has management duties other than merely giving trust assets to beneficiaries. Also called active trust.

specialty See contract under seal.

special use See conditional use.

special use valuation Real property valued on its actual current use rather than on its best possible use.

special verdict A jury's fact findings on fact questions given to it by the judge, who then states the legal consequences of the findings.

A special verdict is that by which the jury find the facts only, leaving the judgment to the Court. The special verdict must present the conclusions of fact as established by the evidence, and not the evidence to prove them; and those conclusions of fact must be so presented as that nothing shall remain to the Court but to draw from them conclusions of law. Cal. Code of Civil Procedure § 624

special warranty deed 1. A deed in which the grantor warrants title only against those claiming by or under the grantor. 2. A quitclaim deed.

specie 1. See in specie. 2. Coined money.

specification 1. A list of contract requirements or details. 2. A statement of charges. 3. Invention details in a patent application.

specific bequest A gift of specific or unique property in a will.

specific denial A denial of particular allegations in a claim.

specific devise A devise of a specific property.

specific intent Desiring (intending) the precise criminal consequences that follow one's act.

specific legacy A gift of specific or unique property in a will.

specific performance An equitable remedy directing the performance of a contract according to the precise terms agreed upon by the parties.

Specific performance cannot be enforced in favor of a party who has not fully and fairly performed all the conditions precedent on his part to the obligation of the other party, except where his failure to perform is only partial, and either entirely immaterial, or capable of being fully compensated. Cal. Civil Code § 3392

spectograph A machine used for voiceprint analysis.

speculation 1. Seeking profits through investments that can be risky. 2. Theorizing in the absence of sufficient evidence and knowledge.

speculative damages Damages that are not reasonably certain; damages that are too conjectural to be awarded.

speech Spoken communication.

Speech or Debate Clause The clause in the U.S. Constitution (art. I, § 6, cl. 1) giving members of Congress immunity for what they say during their legislative work.

speedy trial A trial that begins after reasonable preparation by the prosecution and is conducted with reasonable dispatch.

spendthrift One who spends money irresponsibly.

spendthrift trust A trust whose assets are protected against the beneficiary's improvidence and are beyond the reach of his or her creditors.

A spendthrift trust is created when the trust instrument provides that the beneficiary may not assign his interest and the trust is not subject to the claims of creditors. *Ventura*, 11 Cal.Rptr.3d 489 (Cal.App., 2004)

spin-off A new and independent corporation that was once part of another corporation whose shareholders will own the new corporation.

spirit of the law The underlying meaning or purpose of the law.

split See stock split.

split gift A gift from a spouse to a nonspouse that is treated as having been given one-half by each spouse.

split-off A new corporation formed by an existing corporation, giving shares of the new corporation to the existing corporation's stockholders in exchange for some of their shares in the existing corporation.

split sentence A sentence served in part in an institution and suspended in part or served on probation for the remainder.

splitting a cause of action Suing on only part of a cause of action now and on another part later.

split-up Dividing a corporation into two or more new corporations.

spoliation Intentionally destroying, altering, or concealing evidence.

sponsor 1. One who makes a promise or gives security for another. 2. A legislator who proposes a bill.

spontaneous declaration An out-of-court statement or utterance (made with little time to reflect or fabricate) about a perceived event. An exception to the hearsay rule.

Spontaneous statement. Evidence of a statement is not made inadmissible by the hearsay rule if the statement: (a) Purports to narrate, describe, or explain an act, condition, or event perceived by the declarant; and (b) Was made spontaneously while the declarant was under the stress of excitement caused by such perception. Cal. Evidence Code § 1240

spot zoning Singling out a lot or small area for different zoning treatment than similar surrounding land.

spousal abuse Physical, sexual, or emotional abuse of one's spouse.

spousal privilege See marital communications privilege.

spousal support See alimony.

spread The difference between two amounts, e.g., the buyer's bid price and the seller's asked price for a security.

springing use A use that is dependent or contingent on a future event.

sprinkling trust A trust that spreads income among different beneficiaries at the discretion of the trustee.

spurious Counterfeit or synthetic; false.

squatter One who settles on land without legal title or authority.

squeeze-out An attempt to eliminate or weaken the interest of an owner, e.g., a minority shareholder.

ss. 1. Sections. 2. Sometimes used to abbreviate scilicet, meaning to wit.

SSI See Supplemental Security Income.

stake 1. A deposit to be held until its ownership is resolved. 2. A land boundary marker. 3. A bet. 4. An interest in a business.

stakeholder See interpleader.

stale No longer effective due to the passage of time.

stalking Repeatedly following or harassing someone, who is thereby placed in reasonable fear of harm.

stamp tax The cost of stamps affixed to legal documents such as deeds.

stand See witness stand.

standard 1. A yardstick or criterion. 2. Customary.

Standard means a specification of design, performance, and procedure, or of the instrumentation, equipment, surrounding conditions, and skills required during the conduct of a procedure. Cal. Public Resources Code § 25600(e)

standard deduction A fixed deduction from adjusted gross income, used by taxpayers who do not itemize their deductions.

standard mortgage clause An mortgage clause stating that the interest of the mortgagee will not be invalidated by specified acts of the mortgagor.

standard of care The degree of care the law requires in a particular case, e.g., reasonable care in a negligence case.

standard of need A level of need qualifying one for public benefits.

standard of proof The degree to which the evidence of something must be convincing before a fact finder can accept it as true.

standing A person's right to seek relief from a court.

Standing refers to the requisite interest to support an action or the right to relief. *Windham*, 135 Cal.Rptr.2d 834 (Cal.App., 2003)

standing committee An ongoing committee.

standing mute A defendant refusing to answer or plead to the charge.

standing orders Rules adopted by a court governing practice before it.

Star Chamber 1. An early English court known for arbitrariness. 2. A term used to describe an arbitrary or secret tribunal or proceeding.

stare decisis ("stand by things decided") Courts should decide similar cases in the same way. Precedent should be followed.

stat. Statute.

state 1. A sovereign government. 2. A body of people in a defined territory organized under one government.

state action 1. Conduct of a government. 2. Court proceedings made available to protect or enforce conduct of a private person or entity.

state bank A bank chartered by a state.

stated account See account stated.

stated capital See legal capital.

stated value See par value.

statement 1. An assertion of fact or opinion. 2. An organized recitation of facts.

statement of affairs A list of assets and debts.

state of mind 1. One's reasons and motives for acting or failing to act. 2. See mens rea. 3. The condition or capacity of a mind.

state-of-mind exception An out-of-court declaration of an existing motive or reason is admissible as an exception to the hearsay rule.

A statement of state of mind is one that (1) reflects the declarant's mental state, and (2) is offered, among other purposes, to prove the declarant's conduct, including the declarant's future conduct in accordance with his or her expressed intent, unless the statement was made under circumstances indicating lack of trustworthiness. Cal. Evidence Code §§ 1250, 1252. *People v. Griffin*, 15 Cal.Rptr.3d 743 (CA 2004)

state's attorney The prosecutor or district attorney.

state secrets Government information that would threaten national security or compromise diplomacy if disclosed to the public.

state's evidence Testimony of one criminal defendant against another.

states' rights 1. The political philosophy that favors increased powers for state governments as opposed to expanding the powers of the federal government. 2. Powers not granted to the federal government and not forbidden to the states "are reserved to the states" and the people. U.S. Const. amend. X.

status crime; status offense 1. A crime that consists of having a certain personal status, condition, or character. Example: vagrancy. 2. Conduct by a minor that, if engaged in by an adult, would not be legally prohibited.

status quo The existing state of things.

statute 1. A law passed by the state or federal legislature that declares, commands, or prohibits something. 2. A law passed by any legislative body.

statute of frauds A law requiring some contracts (e.g., one that cannot be performed within a year of its making) to be in writing and signed by the party to be charged by the contract.

statute of limitations A law stating that civil or criminal actions are barred if not brought within a specified period of time.

Statute of limitations is the collective term applied to acts or parts of acts that prescribe the periods beyond which a plaintiff may not bring a cause of action. *Fox*, 27 Cal.Rptr.3d 661 (CA 2005)

statute of repose A law barring actions unless brought within a designated time after an act of the defendant. The law extinguishes the cause of action after a fixed period of time, regardless of when the cause of action accrued.

statute of uses An old English statute that converted certain equitable titles into legal ones.

Statutes at Large The United States Statutes at Large is the official chronological collection of the acts and resolutions of a session of Congress.

statutory Pertaining to or required by a statute.

statutory construction The interpretation of statutes.

statutory employer An employer of a worker covered by workers' compensation.

statutory foreclosure A nonjudicial foreclosure of a mortgage.

statutory lien A lien created by statute.

Statutory lien means a lien arising solely by force of a statute on specified circumstances or conditions. Cal. Code of Civil Procedure § 1800(a)(9)

statutory rape Sexual intercourse with a person under a designated age (e.g., 16) even if the latter consents.

stay The suspension of a judgment or proceeding.

stealing Unlawfully taking and keeping the property of another.

stenographic record The transcript of a trial or deposition.

step-up basis The tax basis of inherited property, which is its value on the date the donor died or on the alternate valuation date.

step transaction doctrine For tax purposes, a series of formally separate steps are treated as a single transaction.

stet ("let it stand") 1. Leave the text unchanged (usually meaning undo the last correction). 2. A stay.

steward See shop steward.

sting An undercover operation to catch criminals.

stipulated damages See liquidated damages.

stipulation 1. An agreement between parties on a matter, often so that it need not be argued or proven at trial. 2. A requirement or condition.

A stipulation is an agreement between opposing counsel ordinarily entered into for the purpose of avoiding delay, trouble, or expense in the conduct of the action, and serves to obviate need for proof or to narrow the range of litigable issues. *Mileikowsky*, 26 Cal.Rptr.3d 831 (Cal.App., 2005)

stirpes See per stirpes.

stock 1. An ownership interest or share in a corporation. 2. The capital raised by a corporation, e.g., through the sale of shares. 3. Goods to be sold by a merchant.

stock association See joint stock company.

stockbroker One who buys or sells stock on behalf of others.

stock certificate Documentary evidence of title to shares of stock.

stock corporation A corporation whose capital is divided into shares.

stock dividend A dividend paid in additional shares of stock.

stock exchange The place at which shares of stock are bought and sold.

stockholder See shareholder.

stockholder's derivative action See derivative action (1).

stock in trade 1. Inventory for sale. 2. Equipment used in business.

stock issue See issue (4).

stock manipulation See manipulation.

stock market See market (2).

stock option A right to buy or sell stock at a set price within a specified period of time.

stock right A shareholder's right to purchase new stock issues before the public can make such purchases.

stock split Each individual share is split into a larger number of shares without changing the total number of shareholders.

Stock split means the pro rata division, otherwise than by a share dividend, of all the outstanding shares of a class into a greater number of shares of the same class by an amendment to the articles stating the effect on outstanding shares. Cal. Corporations Code § 188

stock warrant See warrant (3).

stolen property Property taken by theft or embezzlement.

stop and frisk Temporary detention, questioning, and "patting down" of a person whom the police reasonably believe has committed or is about to commit a crime and may have a weapon. Also called Terry stop.

stop-loss order An order to buy or sell securities when they reach a particular price. Also called stop order.

stop order 1. An instruction of a customer who has written a check that his or her bank should not honor it. A stop-payment order. 2. See stop-loss order.

stoppage in transit (in transitu) A seller's right to repossess goods from a carrier before they reach the buyer when payment by the later is in doubt.

stop-payment order See stop order (1).

straddle The option to purchase or sell the same asset.

straight bill of lading A bill of lading that names a specific person to whom the goods are to be delivered.

straight life insurance See whole life insurance.

straight-line depreciation Depreciation computed by dividing the purchase price of an asset (less its salvage value) by its estimated useful life.

stranger Someone not a participant or party to a transaction.

Strategic Lawsuit Against Public Participation (SLAPP) A meritless suit brought primarily to chill the free speech of the defendant.

Anti-SLAPP actions. The Legislature finds and declares that there has been a disturbing increase in lawsuits brought primarily to chill the valid exercise of the constitutional rights of freedom of speech and petition for the redress of grievances. Cal. Code of Civil Procedure § 425.16(a)

straw man 1. A cover or front. 2. A fictitious person or argument.

street name A broker's name on a security, not that of its owner.

strict construction A narrow construction; nothing is taken as intended that is not clearly expressed in the literal language of the law or document. Also called literal construction.

strict foreclosure A transfer of title (to the mortgaged property) to the mortgagee without a foreclosure sale upon the mortgagor's default.

stricti juris According to a strict or narrow construction of the law.

strict liability Legal responsibility even if one used reasonable care and did not intend harm. Also called absolute liability, liability without fault.

A strict liability crime is one that dispenses with a mens rea, scienter, or wrongful intent element. *People v. Sargent*, 81 Cal.Rptr.2d 835 (CA 1999)

strict scrutiny The standard requiring a government to show its law is the least restrictive way to further a compelling state interest.

strike 1. An organized work stoppage or slowdown by workers in order to press demands. 2. To remove something.

strikebreaker See scab.

strike suit A shareholder derivative action that is baseless.

striking a jury Selecting a jury for a particular or special case.

struck jury 1. A jury chosen by a process that allows the parties to take turns striking names from a large panel of prospective jurors until a sufficient number exists for a jury. 2. See special jury.

style The title or name of a case.

suable Capable of being sued.

sua sponte On one's own motion; voluntarily.

sub Under; secondary.

subagent Someone used by an agent to perform a duty for the principal.

subchapter C corporation See C corporation.

subchapter S corporation See S corporation.

subcontract A contract that performs all or part of another contract.

subcontractor One who performs under a subcontract.

subdivision 1. The division of something into smaller parts. 2. A portion of land within a development.

subinfeudation A feudal system of vassals creating vassals of their own.

subjacent support The support of land by land that lies beneath it.

subject 1. A citizen or resident under another; one governed by the laws of a sovereign. 2. A theme or topic acted upon.

subject-matter jurisdiction The power of the court to resolve a particular category of dispute.

Subject matter jurisdiction is the court's power to hear and resolve a particular dispute or cause of action, while personal jurisdiction relates to the power to bind a particular party. *Donaldson*, 25 Cal.Rptr.3d 584 (CA 2005)

sub judice Under judicial consideration; before a court.

sublease A lease of leased premises. A lease (called a sublease, subtenancy, or underlease) granted by an existing lessee (called a sublessor) to another (called a sublessee, subtenant, or undertenant) of all or part of the leased premises for a portion of the sublessor's original term.

sublessee; sublessor See sublease.

subletting The granting of a sublease.

submission 1. Yielding to authority. 2. An argument to be considered.

sub modo Within limits; subject to qualifications.

sub nominee (sub nom.) Under the name or title.

subordinate 1. One who works under another's authority. 2. To place in a lower priority or rank.

subordination agreement An agreement to accept a lower priority than would otherwise be due.

Subordination is act or process by which person's rights or claims are ranked below those of others. *Miscione*, 61 Cal.Rptr.2d 280 (Cal.App., 1997)

suborn To induce another to commit an illegal act, e.g., perjury.

subornation of perjury Instigating another to commit perjury.

subpoena A command to appear in a court, agency, or other tribunal.

subpoena ad testificandum A command to appear to give testimony.

subpoena duces tecum A command to appear and bring specified things, e.g., records.

subrogation The substitution of one party (called the subrogee) in place of another party (called the subrogor), along with any claim, demand, or right the latter party had.

Subrogation is defined as the substitution of another person in place of the creditor or claimant to whose rights he or she succeeds in relation to the debt or claim. *Hartford*, 20 Cal.Rptr.3d 128 (Cal.App., 2004)

subrogee; subrogor See subrogation.

subscription 1. A signature; the act of writing one's name on a document. 2. An agreement to purchase new securities of a corporation.

subscription right See preemptive right.

subsequent Occurring or coming later.

subsidiary 1. Under another's control. 2. A branch or affiliate.

subsidiary corporation A corporation owned or controlled by another corporation.

sub silentio Under silence; without specific reference or notice.

substance 1. The material or essential part of a thing. 2. A drug.

substantial 1. Not imaginary. 2. Considerable in amount or degree.

substantial capacity test See insanity (2).

substantial compliance Compliance with the essential requirements.

substantial evidence Relevant evidence a reasonable mind might accept as adequate to support a conclusion.

Substantial evidence means evidence consisting of adequate and well-controlled investigations, including clinical investigations, by experts qualified by scientific training and experience to evaluate the effectiveness of the drug or device involved. Cal. Health & Safety Code § 110025(a)

substantial justice A fair proceeding or trial even if minor procedural errors are made.

substantial performance Performance of the essential terms.

substantiate To establish by supporting evidence. To support with proof.

substantive due process The constitutional requirement (based on the 5th and 14th Amendments) that legislation be rationally related to a legitimate government purpose.

substantive evidence Evidence offered to support a fact in issue.

substantive law Nonprocedural laws that define or govern rights and duties.

substantive rule See legislative rule.

substituted basis The basis of property in the hands of the transferor becomes the transferee's basis of that property.

substituted service Service by an authorized method (e.g., by mail) other than personal service. Also called constructive service.

substitution Taking the place of another.

subtenancy; subtenant See sublease.

subversive Pertaining to the overthrow or undermining of a government.

succession 1. Obtaining property or interests by inheritance rather than by deed or contract. The acquisition of rights upon the death of another. 2. Taking over or continuing the rights of another entity.

Although succession is defined in statute as the acquisition of title to the property of one who dies without disposing of it by will, the word frequently possesses the somewhat broader meaning of the acquisition of rights upon the death of another. Cal. Probate Code, § 200. *Estate of Russell*, 95 Cal.Rptr. 88 (Cal.App., 1971)

succession tax See inheritance tax.

successor A person or entity that takes the place of or follows another.

successor in interest One who follows another in ownership or control of property.

sudden emergency doctrine See emergency doctrine (1).

sudden heat of passion See heat of passion.

sue To commence a lawsuit.

sue out To ask a court for an order.

suffer 1. To feel physical or emotional pain. 2. To allow or admit.

sufferance The absence of rejection; passive consent.

sufficient Adequate for the legal purpose involved.

sufficient cause See good cause, probable cause (1).

sufficient consideration Consideration that creates a binding contract.

suffrage The right to vote.

suicide The voluntary termination of one's life.

sui generis ("of its own kind") Unique.

sui juris ("of one's own right") Possessing full civil rights.

suit See lawsuit.

suitor A plaintiff, one who sues.

sum certain An exact amount.

summary 1. Not following usual procedures. 2. Done quickly. 3. Short or concise.

summary court-martial The lowest-level court-martial.

summary judgment A judgment on a claim or defense rendered without a full trial because of the absence of genuine conflict on any of the material facts involved.

The motion for summary judgment shall be granted if all the papers submitted show that there is no triable issue as to any material fact and that the moving party is entitled to a judgment as a matter of law. Cal. Code of Civil Procedure § 437c(c)

summary jury trial A nonbinding trial argued before a mock jury as a case evaluation technique and an incentive to settle.

summary proceeding A nonjury proceeding that seeks to achieve a relatively prompt resolution.

summary process A special procedure that provides an expeditious remedy.

summation; summing up See closing argument.

summons 1. A notice directing the defendant to appear in court and answer the plaintiff's complaint or face a default judgment. 2. A notice directing a witness or juror to appear in court.

A summons shall contain a notice that, unless the defendant so responds, his or her default will be entered upon application by the plaintiff. Cal. Code of Civil Procedure § 412.20(a)

sumptuary Regulating personal expenditures; restricting immorality.

Sunday closing laws See blue laws.

sunset law A law that automatically terminates a program unless it is affirmatively renewed.

sunshine law A law requiring increased public access to government meetings and records.

suo nomine In his own name.

Superfund A government fund for hazardous-waste cleanup.

superior Having a higher rank, authority, or interest.

superior court A trial court in most states.

supermajority Two-thirds, 60 percent, or any other voting requirement of greater than half plus one.

supersede To supplant; to annul by replacing.

supersedeas A writ or bond to stay the enforcement of a judgment.

superseding cause An intervening cause that is beyond the foreseeable risk originally created by the defendant's unreasonable acts or omissions and thereby cuts off the defendant's liability.

An independent event that intervenes in the chain of causation, producing harm of a kind and degree so far beyond the risk the original wrongdoer should have foreseen that the law deems it unfair to hold him or her responsible. *People v. Brady*, 29 Cal.Rptr.3d 286 (Cal.App., 2005)

supervening cause A superseding cause.

supervening negligence See last clear chance doctrine.

supplemental jurisdiction Jurisdiction over a claim that is part of the same controversy over which the court already has jurisdiction.

supplemental pleading A pleading that adds facts to or corrects an earlier pleading.

The plaintiff and defendant, respectively, may be allowed, on motion, to make a supplemental complaint or answer, alleging facts material to the case occurring after the former complaint or answer. Cal. Code of Civil Procedure § 464(a)

Supplemental Security Income (SSI) A government income benefit program (part of social security) for the aged, blind, or disabled.

supplementary proceeding A new proceeding that supplements another, e.g., to help collect a judgment.

support 1. Provide a standard of living. 2. Maintenance with necessities. 3. Foundation.

suppress To stop or prevent.

suppression hearing A pretrial criminal hearing to decide if evidence was seized illegally and should be inadmissible (i.e., suppressed).

suppression of evidence 1. A prosecutor's failure to disclose exculpatory evidence to the defense. 2. Evidence held inadmissible at a suppression hearing.

supra Above; mentioned earlier in the document.

supremacy Being in a higher or the highest position of power.

Supremacy Clause The clause in the U.S. Constitution (art. VI, cl. 2) that has been interpreted to mean that when valid federal law and state law conflict, federal law controls.

supreme court 1. The highest court in the federal and in most state judicial systems. 2. In New York, it is a trial court with some appellate jurisdiction. 3. The Supreme Court of Appeals is the highest state court in West Virginia. 4. The Supreme Judicial Court is the highest state court in Maine and Massachusetts.

surcharge 1. An added charge or tax. 2. A charge imposed on a fiduciary for misconduct.

surety One who becomes liable for the payment of another's debt or the performance of another's contractual obligation. The surety generally becomes primarily and jointly liable with the other, the principal.

A surety or guarantor is one who promises to answer for the debt, default or miscarriage of another. Cal. Civil Code, § 2787. *Superior Wholesale*, 70 Cal.Rptr. 636 (Cal.App., 1968)

surety bond See completion bond.

suretyship The contractual relation whereby one person (the surety) agrees to answer for the debt, default, or miscarriage of another (the principal), with the surety generally being primarily and jointly liable with the principal.

surplus What is left over. The amount remaining after the purpose of a fund or venture has been accomplished.

surplusage Extraneous matter or words in a statute, pleading, or instrument that do not add meaning.

surprise Something unexpected, often unfairly so.

surrebuttal A rebuttal to a rebuttal.

surrejoinder An answer of the defendant to a rejoinder.

surrender 1. To return a power, claim, or estate. 2. To release.

surrender value See cash surrender value.

surrogacy The status or act of being a substitute for another.

surrogate 1. A substitute for another. 2. A probate judge.

Surrogate means an adult, other than a patient's agent or conservator, authorized under this division to make a health care decision for the patient. Cal. Probate Code § 4643

surrogate mother A woman who gestates an embryo and bears a child for another person. The surrogate relinquishes her parental rights.

surrogate's court See probate court.

surtax 1. An additional tax added to something already taxed. 2. A tax levied on a tax.

surveillance Close and continual observation of a person or place.

survey 1. A map that measures boundaries, elevations, and structures on land. 2. A study or poll.

survival action An action brought on behalf of a decedent to recover damages the decedent suffered up to the time of his or her death. The action seeks what the decedent would have sought if he or she had not died.

survivorship See right of survivorship.

survivorship annuity An annuity that continues paying benefits to the survivor of the annuitant after the latter's death.

suspect classification A classification in a statute whose constitutional validity (under the Equal Protection Clause) will be measured by the standard of strict scrutiny. An example would be a preference in a statute on the basis of on race, alienage, or national origin.

suspended sentence A sentence that is imposed but postponed, allowing the defendant to avoid prison if he or she meets specified conditions.

suspension A temporary delay or interruption, e.g., the removal of the right to practice law for a specified period.

suspicion A belief that someone has or may have committed wrongdoing but without proof.

sustain 1. To uphold or agree with. 2. To support or encourage. 3. To endure, withstand, or suffer.

swear 1. To take or administer an oath. 2. To talk obscenely.

sweating Questioning an accused through harassment or threats.

sweetheart deal An arrangement providing beneficial treatment that is illegal or ethically questionable.

syllabus 1. A brief summary or outline. 2. See headnote.

symbolic delivery The constructive delivery of property by delivering something that represents the property, e.g., a key to a building.

symbolic speech Nonverbal activity or conduct that expresses a message or thought, e.g., the hood worn by the KKK; expressive conduct.

Symbolic speech, i.e., message implied by conduct, is protected by First Amendment if speaker intends to convey particularized message through his or her conduct and if likelihood is great that message would be understood by those who view it. *In re Alcala*, 271 Cal.Rptr. 674 (Cal.App., 1990)

sympathy strike A strike against an employer with whom the workers do not have a labor dispute in order to show support for other workers on strike.

synallagmatic Reciprocal, bilateral.

syndicalism A movement advocating control of industry by labor unions. Criminal syndicalism is an act or plan intended to accomplish change in industrial ownership or government by means of unlawful force, violence, or terrorism.

syndicate A group formed to promote a common interest.

synopsis A brief summary.

T

tacit Understood without being openly stated; implied by silence.

tacking 1. One claiming adverse possession adds its period of possession to that of a previous possessor to meet the statutory period. 2. Gaining priority for a lien by joining it to a superior lien.

tail Limitation in the right of inheritance. See fee tail.

tail female Limitation to female heirs. See fee tail.

tail male Limitation to male heirs. See fee tail.

taint 1. A defect or contamination. 2. A felony conviction.

tainted evidence Illegally obtained evidence.

take 1. To seize or obtain possession. 2. To acquire by eminent domain.

takeover Obtaining control, management, or ownership.

taking See take.

talesman A prospective juror. A bystander called to serve on a jury.

tamper To meddle or change something without authorization.

Tamper means to rearrange, injure, alter, interfere with, or otherwise to prevent from performing normal or customary function. Cal. Civil Code § 1882

TANF See Temporary Assistance to Needy Families.

tangible Having physical form. Capable of being touched or seen.

target corporation A corporation that someone wants to take over.

tariff 1. A tax paid on categories of imported or exported goods. 2. A list of rates or fees charged for services.

tax Compulsory monetary payments to support the government.

taxable Subject to taxation.

taxable estate A decedent's gross estate less allowable deductions.

taxable gift See gift tax.

taxable income Gross income less deductions and exemptions.

taxable year; tax year A calendar year or a taxpayer's fiscal year.

The calendar year or the fiscal year upon the basis of which the taxable income is computed. If no fiscal year has been established, taxable year means the calendar year. Cal. Revenue & Taxation Code § 17010

tax avoidance Using lawful tax-reducing steps and strategies.

tax benefit rule When already deducted losses and expenses are recovered in a later year, the recovery is listed as income in the later year.

tax bracket The range of income to which the same tax rate is applied.

tax certificate An instrument issued to the buyer of property at a tax sale entitling him or her to the property after the redemption period.

tax court A court that hears appeals involving tax disputes.

tax credit A subtraction from the tax owed rather than from income.

tax deduction A subtraction from income to arrive at taxable income.

tax deed A deed given to the purchaser by the government to property purchased at a tax sale.

tax deferred Not taxable until later.

tax evasion; tax fraud See evasion (2).

tax exempt; tax free Not subject to taxation.

tax home One's principal place of employment or business.

taxing power A government's power to impose taxes.

tax lien A government's lien on property for nonpayment of taxes.

tax preference items Regular deductions that must be factored back in when calculating the alternative minimum tax.

tax rate The percentage used to calculate one's tax.

tax refund An overpayment of taxes that can be returned or credited.

tax return The form used to report income and other tax information.

Tax return means a return, declaration, statement, refund claim, or other document required to be made or to be filed in connection with state or federal income taxes or state bank and corporation franchise taxes. Cal. Civil Code § 1799.1a

tax roll A government list of taxable assets and taxpayers.

tax sale The forced sale of property for nonpayment of taxes.

tax shelter An investment or other device to reduce or defer taxes.

tax title The title obtained by a buyer of property at a tax sale.

technical error See harmless error.

teller 1. A bank employee who receives and pays out money. 2. A vote counter at an election.

temporary Lasting for a limited time; transitory.

temporary alimony An interim order of spousal support pending the final outcome of the action for divorce or legal separation. Also called alimony pendente lite.

Temporary Assistance to Needy Families (TANF) The welfare program that replaced Aid to Families with Dependent Children (AFDC).

temporary injunction See preliminary injunction.

temporary restraining order (TRO) An order maintaining the status quo pending a hearing on the application for a permanent injunction.

A TRO may prohibit the defendant from (a) Transferring any interest in the property. (b) Concealing or otherwise removing the property. (c) Impairing the value of the property. Cal. Civil Code § 1861.17

tenancy 1. The possession or holding of real or personal property by right or title. 2. Possession or occupancy of land under a lease.

tenancy at sufferance See estate at sufferance.

tenancy at will A lease with no fixed term or duration. Also called estate at will.

tenancy by the entirety A form of joint tenancy for a married couple. Co-ownership of property by spouses with a right of survivorship. Also called estate by the entirety.

For the purpose of division of property on dissolution of marriage . . . property acquired by the parties during marriage in joint form, including tenancy by the entirety is presumed to be community property. Cal. Family Code § 2581

tenancy for years A tenancy for any predetermined time period, not just for years. Also called tenancy for a term.

tenancy from year to year See periodic tenancy.

tenancy in common Ownership of property by two or more persons in shares that may or may not be equal, each person having an equal right to possess the whole property but without the right of survivorship. Also called estate in common.

tenant 1. One who pays rent to possess another's land or apartment for a temporary period. 2. One who holds a tenancy.

tenantable Habitable, fit for occupancy.

A dwelling shall be deemed untenantable if it substantially lacks effective waterproofing plumbing or gas facilities. Cal. Civil Code § 1941.1

tenant for life One who holds a life estate.

tender 1. To offer payment or other performance. 2. An offer.

tender of delivery An offer of conforming goods by the seller.

tender offer An offer to purchase shares at a fixed price in an attempt to obtain a controlling interest in a company.

tender years doctrine In custody disputes, very young children should go to the mother unless she is unfit.

tenement 1. An apartment or other residence. 2. An estate of land.

ten-K (10-K) A company's annual financial report filed with the SEC.

tentative trust See Totten trust.

tenure 1. The right to permanent employment subject to termination for cause in compliance with procedural safeguards. 2. The right to hold land subordinate to a superior.

term 1. A fixed period. 2. A word or phrase. 3. A contract provision.

terminable interest An interest that ends upon a given time or condition.

It is the intent of the Legislature to abolish any remaining application of the terminable interest doctrine in California relating to the division of public retirement benefits of a member in the event of dissolution of marriage or death if the division is made under this chapter. Cal. Education Code § 22666

termination 1. The end of something. 2. Discontinuation.

term life insurance Life insurance for a specified or limited time.

term loan A loan that must be paid within a specified date.

terms of art Words or phrases with a special or technical meaning. Also called words of art.

territorial Pertaining to a particular area or land.

territorial court A court in a United States territory, e.g., Guam.

territorial waters Inland and surrounding bodies of water controlled by a nation, including water extending three miles offshore.

territory 1. A geographical area. 2. A part of the United States with its own branches of government but not part of or within any state.

terrorem clause A condition in a will that voids gifts to any beneficiary who contests the will. Also called no-contest clause.

An in terrorem or no contest clause in a will or trust instrument creates a condition upon gifts and dispositions provided, in essence, conditioning a beneficiary's right to take the share provided to that beneficiary under such an instrument upon the beneficiary's agreement to acquiesce to the terms of the instrument. *In re Estate of Davies*, 26 Cal.Rptr.3d 239 (Cal.App., 2005)

terrorism Politically motivated violence against noncombatants. Using or threatening violence to intimidate for political or ideological goals.

***Terry* stop** See stop and frisk.

testament A will.

testamentary Pertaining to a will.

testamentary capacity Sufficient mental ability to make a will. Knowing the nature of a will, the extent of one's property, and the natural objects of one's bounty.

testamentary class A group of beneficiaries under a will whose number is not known when the will is made.

testamentary disposition A transfer of assets to another by will.

testamentary gift A gift made in a will.

testamentary intent The intent to make a revocable disposition of property that takes effect after the testator's death.

Testamentary intent does not refer to testator's intentions regarding particular dispositions of property, but rather, means testator's general intent to make revocable disposition of his or her property, effective on testator's death. *Estate of Smith*, 71 Cal.Rptr.2d 424 (Cal.App., 1998)

testamentary trust A trust created in a will and effective on the death of the creator.

testate 1. Having died leaving a valid will. 2. See testator.

testate succession Acquiring assets by will.

testator One who has died leaving a valid will. Also called testate.

testatrix A female testator.

test case Litigation brought to create a new legal principle or right.

teste The clause in a document that names the witness.

testify To give evidence as a witness. To submit testimony under oath.

testimonium clause A clause in the instrument giving the date on which the instrument was executed and by whom.

testimony Evidence given by a witness under oath.

test oath An oath of allegiance and fidelity to the government.

theft Taking personal property with the intent to deprive the owner of it permanently. Larceny.

theory of the case The application of the law to the facts to support the judgment you are seeking.

***Thibodaux* abstention** A federal court can abstain from exercising its federal jurisdiction when facing difficult and unresolved state law issues involving policy. *Louisiana Power v. Thibodaux*, 79 S. Ct. 1070 (1959).

thief One who commits larceny or theft.

thing in action See chose in action.

third degree Overly aggressive or abusive interrogation techniques.

third party A nonparty or nonparticipant who is involved in a transaction in some way.

third-party beneficiary One for whose benefit a contract is made but who is not a party to the contract.

A third party beneficiary contract must either satisfy an obligation of the promisee to pay money to the beneficiary, or the circumstances indicate the promisee intends to give the beneficiary the benefit of the promised performance. *Medical Staff*, 33 Cal.Rptr.3d 853 (Cal.App., 2005)

third-party complaint A defendant's complaint against someone who is not now a party on the basis that the latter may be liable for all or part of what the plaintiff might recover from the defendant.

third-party plaintiff A defendant who files a third-party complaint.

third-party practice See implead.

threat An expression of an intent to inflict pain or damage.

three-judge court A panel of three judges hearing a case.

three-strikes law A statute imposing harsher sentences for persons convicted of their third felony.

The people of the State of California do hereby find and declare that Proposition 184 (the "Three Strikes" law) was overwhelmingly approved in 1994 with the intent of protecting law-abiding citizens by enhancing the sentences of repeat offenders who commit serious and/or violent felonies. Cal. Penal Code § 289

through bill of lading A contract covering the transport of cargo from origin to destination, including the use of additional carriers.

ticket 1. A paper giving the holder a right. 2. A traffic citation.

tideland Land covered and uncovered each day by the action of tides.

tie-in See tying arrangement.

time-barred Pertaining to a claim barred by a statute of limitations.

time bill See time draft.

time deposit A bank deposit that remains in the account for a specified time and is not payable on demand before that time without penalty.

time draft A draft payable on a specified date. Also called time bill.

time immemorial Time beyond the reach of memory or records.

time is of the essence The failure to do what is required by the time specified will be considered a breach of the contract.

timely Within the time set by contract or law.

time note A note payable only at a definite time.

time, place, or manner restriction The government can restrict the time, place, or manner of speech and assembly, but not their content.

time-sharing Joint ownership of property that is used or occupied for limited alternating time periods. Also called interval ownership.

Time-share plan means any arrangement whereby a purchaser, in exchange for consideration, receives ownership rights in or the right to use accommodations for a period of time less than a full year during any given year, on a recurring basis for more than one year, but not necessarily for consecutive years. Cal. Business & Professions Code § 11212

tippee One who receives material inside information about a company. See also insider trading.

title The legal right to control, possess, and dispose of property. All ownership rights in property.

title company A company that issues title insurance.

title insurance Insurance for losses incurred due to defects in the title to real property.

title search A determination of whether defects in the title to real property exist by examining relevant public records.

title state See title theory.

title theory The theory that a mortgagee has title to land until the mortgage debt is paid. States that so provide are called title states.

TM See trademark.

to have and to hold See habendum clause.

toll 1. Payment for the use of something. 2. To stop the running of.

tombstone ad An advertisement (sometimes printed in a black-border box) for a public securities offering.

tonnage 1. The weight carrying capacity of ships. 2. A duty on ships.

tontine A financial arrangement among a group in which the last survivor receives the entire fund.

Torrens title system A system for land registration under which a court issues a binding certificate of title.

tort A civil wrong (other than a breach of contract) for which the courts will provide a remedy such as damages.

A tort is a wrong" for which society provides a remedy, with the term "wrong" implying some fault on part of wrongdoer. *Barrett*, 272 Cal.Rptr. 304 (Cal.App., 1990)

tortfeasor A person who has committed a tort.

tortious Pertaining to conduct that can lead to tort liability.

tortious interference with prospective advantage See interference with prospective advantage.

total breach A breach that so substantially impairs the value of the contract to the injured party at the time of the breach that it is just in the circumstances to allow recovery of damages based on all the injured party's remaining rights to performance.

total disability Inability to engage in any gainful occupation.

total incorporation See selective incorporation.

total loss Damage beyond physical repair; complete destruction.

Totten trust A trust created by a deposit of funds in a bank account in trust for a beneficiary. The trustee is the depositor, who retains the power to revoke the trust. Also called savings bank trust, tentative trust.

An account in the name of one or more parties as trustee for one or more beneficiaries where the relationship is established by the form of the account and the deposit agreement with the financial institution and there is no subject of the trust other than the sums on deposit in the account. Cal. Probate Code § 80

to wit That is to say, namely.

township 1. A political subdivision, usually part of a county. 2. A square tract that is six miles on each side.

tract index A publicly kept index of parcels (tracts) of land.

trade Commerce. Buying, selling, or bartering goods or services.

trade acceptance A bill of exchange drawn by a seller on the buyer of goods for the amount of the purchase, and accepted for payment by the buyer at a set time.

trade association An organization of businesses in an industry that promotes the interests of the inductry.

trade dress The total image or overall appearance of a product.

trade fixture Personal property affixed to the realty by a tenant who uses it in its business and has the right to remove it.

trade libel See disparagement.

trademark (TM) A distinctive word, mark, or emblem that serves to identify a product with a specific producer and to distinguish it from others. See also infringement.

trade name A name or symbol that identifies and distinguishes a business.

trade secret A business formula, pattern, device, or compilation of information known only by certain individuals in the business and used for competitive advantage.

The test for a trade secret is whether matter sought to be protected is information (1) that is valuable because it is unknown to others and (2) that the owner has attempted to keep secret. *DVD Copy Control,* 10 Cal.Rptr.3d 185 (Cal.App., 2004)

trade union A union or workers in the same trade or craft.

trade usage A practice or method of dealing having such regularity of observance in a place, vocation, or trade as to justify an expectation that it will be observed in the transaction in question.

traffic 1. Commerce or trade. 2. Transportation of people or things.

tranche A slice or portion of a bond offering or other investment.

transact To have dealings; to carry on.

transaction 1. The act of conducting something. 2. A business deal.

transactional immunity Immunity from prosecution for any matter about which a witness testifies.

Transactional immunity protects him against later prosecution related to matters about which he testified, whereas use immunity protects a witness only against the actual use of his compelled testimony and its fruits. *Fuller,* 104 Cal.Rptr.2d 525 (Cal.App., 2001)

transcript A word-for-word account. A written copy of oral testimony.

transfer To deliver or convey an interest. To place with another.

transfer agent An agent appointed by a corporation to keep records on registered shareholders, handle transfers of shares, etc.

transferee One to whom an interest is conveyed.

transfer payments Payments made by the government to individuals for which no services or goods are rendered in return.

transferred-intent rule The defendant may be held responsible for a wrong committed against the plaintiff even if the defendant intended a different wrong against a different person.

If A shoots at B with malice aforethought, but kills C, who is standing nearby, A is deemed liable for murder notwithstanding lack of intent to kill C. *People v. Sanchez,* 111 Cal.Rptr.2d 129 (CA 2001)

transfer tax A tax imposed on the transfer of property by will, inheritance, or gift.

transitory action An action that can be tried wherever the defendant can be personally served.

transmit To send or transfer something (e.g., an interest, a message) to another person or place.

transmutation The voluntary change of separate property into marital property or vice versa.

traveler's check A cashier's check that requires the purchaser's signature when purchased and countersigned when cashed.

traverse A formal denial of material facts stated in an opponent's pleading.

treason An attempt by overt acts to overthrow the government of the state to which one owes allegiance or to give aid and comfort to its foreign enemies.

treasurer An officer with responsibility over the receipt, custody, and disbursement of moneys or funds. The chief financial officer.

treasure trove Valuable property found hidden in a private place and whose owner is unknown.

treasury 1. The funds of an organization. 2. The place where such funds are stored.

Treasury bill (T-bill) A short-term debt security of the U.S. government that matures in a year or less.

Treasury bond (T-bond) A long-term debt security of the U.S. government that matures in more than 10 years.

treasury certificate An obligation of the U.S. government with a 1 year maturity and interest paid by coupon.

Treasury note (T-note) An intermediate-term debt security of the U.S. government that matures in more than 1 year but not more than 10 years.

treasury securities 1. A corporation's stock that it reacquires. Also called treasury stock. 2. Debt instruments of the U.S. government.

treatise A book that gives an overview of a topic.

treaty A formal agreement between two or more nations. Senate approval is required for U.S. treaties.

treble damages Three times the amount of damages found to be owed.

trespass A wrongful interference with another's person or property.

Trespass is an unlawful interference with possession of property. *Staples,* 235 Cal.Rptr. 165 (Cal.App., 1987)

trespass de bonis asportatis Wrongfully taking and carrying away the goods of another.

trespasser A wrongdoer who commits a trespass.

trespass on the case See action on the case.

trespass quare clausum fregit Wrongfully entering the enclosed land of another.

trespass to chattels An intentional interference with another's personal property, resulting in dispossession or intermeddling.

trespass to land A wrongful entry on another's land.

trespass vi et armis A wrongful interference with another's person or property through force.

trial A judicial proceeding that applies the law to evidence in order to resolve conflicting legal claims.

Trial, for purposes of motion to voluntarily dismiss action prior to commencement of trial, is not restricted to jury or court trials on the merits, but includes other procedures that effectively dispose of the case. Cal. Code of Civil Procedure § 581(b)(1),(c). *Mary Morgan,* 57 Cal.Rptr.2d 4 (Cal.App., 1996)

trial brief 1. An attorney's presentation to a trial court of the legal issues and positions of his or her client. 2. An attorney's strategy notes for trial. Also called trial book, trial manual.

trial by ordeal See ordeal.

trial court The first court that provides a complete forum to hear evidence and arguments on a legal claim. A court of original jurisdiction. Also called court of first instance.

trial de novo A new trial as if a prior one had not taken place.

trial jury See petit jury.

tribal land Reservation land held by a tribe for its community.

tribunal A court or other body that adjudicates disputes.

trier of fact See fact-finder.

TRO See temporary restraining order.

trover See conversion (1).

true bill A grand jury's notation on a bill of indictment that there is enough evidence for a criminal trial. A grand jury indictment.

true value See fair market value.

trust A device or arrangement by which its creator (the settlor or trustor) transfers property (the corpus) to a person (the trustee) who holds legal title for the benefit of another (the beneficiary or cestui que trust).

A trust is a personal relationship between the trustee and the beneficiary. It does not create an interest in the trust res per se. *Farmers Ins.*, 61 Cal.Rptr.2d 707 (Cal.App., 1997)

trust account See client trust account.

trust company A company or bank that serves as a trustee for trusts. A trust officer is the employee in charge of a trust.

Trust company means a corporation, industrial bank, or a commercial bank that is authorized to engage in the trust business. Cal. Financial Code § 107

trust deed 1. The document setting up a trust. 2. See deed of trust.

trust de son tort See constructive trust.

trustee The person or company holding legal title to property for the benefit of another.

trustee in bankruptcy A person appointed or elected to administer the estate of a debtor in bankruptcy.

trust estate See corpus (1).

trust ex delicto See constructive trust.

trust ex maleficio See constructive trust.

trust fund See corpus (1).

trust fund doctrine An insolvent corporation's assets are held in trust for its creditors.

trust indenture 1. The document specifying the terms of a trust. 2. See deed of trust.

trust instrument The document setting up a trust.

trust officer See trust company.

trustor See settlor.

trust receipt A document stating that a dealer/borrower is holding goods in trust for the benefit of the lender.

Trust receipts are a method of securing a debt and not of creating a debt. *Klett*, 242 P.2d 873 (CA 1952)

trust territory A territory placed under the administration of a country by the United Nations.

trusty A trusted prisoner given special privileges and duties.

truth-in-lending Required disclosure of credit terms.

try 1. To litigate. 2. To decide a legal dispute in court.

turnkey contract A contract in which the builder agrees to complete the work of building and installation to the point of readiness for occupancy.

turnover order A court order that the losing litigant transfer property to the winning litigant.

turntable doctrine See attractive nuisance doctrine.

turpitude Depravity.

Turpitude, with reference to disciplinary proceedings against attorney, means anything done contrary to justice, honesty, modesty or good morals. *Herron*, 147 P.2d 543 (CA 1944)

twisting Deception to induce an insured to switch insurance policies.

two-dismissal rule A voluntary dismissal of a second action operates as a dismissal on the merits if the plaintiff has previously dismissed an action involving the same claim.

two-issue rule A jury verdict involving two or more issues will not be set aside if the verdict is supported as to at least one of the issues.

two-witness rule In a perjury or treason case, proof of falsity of the testimony cannot be established by the uncorroborated testimony of a single witness.

tying arrangement A seller conditions the sale of one product or service on the buyer's purchase of a separate product or service.

U

uberrima fides Highest degree of good faith.

ubi Where.

UCC See Uniform Commercial Code.

UCCC Uniform Consumer Credit Code.

UCMJ Uniform Code of Military Justice.

UFTA Uniform Fraudulent Transfer Act.

ukase An official decree or proclamation.

ultimate facts Facts essential to a cause of action or a defense.

ultrahazardous See abnormally dangerous.

ultra vires Beyond the scope of corporate powers; unauthorized.

An act which is beyond the powers conferred upon a corporation by its charter or by the laws of the state of incorporation. *Marsili*, 124 Cal.Rptr. 313 (Cal.App., 1975)

umbrella policy An insurance policy that covers risks not covered by homeowners, automobile, or other standard liability policies.

umpire A neutral person asked to resolve or help resolve a dispute.

unalienable See inalienable.

unanimous opinion An opinion in which all judges or justices are in full agreement.

unauthorized practice of law (UPL) Engaging in acts that require either a license to practice law or other special authorization by a person who does not have the license or special authorization.

It is unlawful for any person engaged in the business or acting in the capacity of a legal document assistant or unlawful detainer assistant to do any of the following: (e) Engage in the unauthorized practice of law, including, but not limited to, giving any kind of advice, explanation, opinion, or recommendation to a consumer about possible legal rights, remedies, defenses, options, selection of forms, or strategies. Cal. Business & Professions Code § 6411

unavoidable accident An accident that could not have been prevented by ordinary care. Also called inevitable accident, pure accident.

uncertificated security A security not represented by an instrument, the transfer of which is registered on the issuer's books.

unclean hands doctrine See clean hands doctrine.

unconditional Without contingencies or conditions.

unconscionable So one-sided as to be oppressive and grossly unfair.

unconstitutional Contrary to or inconsistent with the constitution.

uncontested Unopposed; without opposition.

An action or proceeding is "uncontested" when no answer or opposition is filed. *E.N.W.*, 198 Cal.Rptr. 355 (Cal.App., 1983)

uncontrollable impulse An impulse or urge that cannot be resisted.

undercapitalized Insufficient capital to run a profitable business.

under color of law See color of law.

underlease See sublease.

under protest Waiving no rights; to be challenged later, but paid now.

undersigned The person signing at the end of the document or page.

understanding 1. A meeting of the minds; agreement. 2. Interpretation.

undertaking 1. A promise or guaranty. 2. A bail bond. 3. A task.

undertenant See sublease.

under the influence See driving under the influence.

underwriting 1. Assuming a risk by insuring it. The process of deciding whether to insure a risk. 2. An agreement to buy the shares of a new issue of securities not purchased by the public.

undisclosed principal A principal whose existence and identity are not revealed by the agent to a third party.

undivided interest; undivided right; undivided title The interest of each individual in the entire or whole property rather than in a particular part of it.

undivided profits Accrued profit a corporation has not distributed.

undue influence Improper persuasion, coercion, force, or deception that substitutes the will of one person for the free will of another.

Undue influence is that kind of influence or supremacy of one mind over another by which the latter is prevented from acting according to his or her own wish or judgment. Cal. Civil Code, § 2235. *In re Estate of De Mont*, 282 P.2d 963 (Cal.App., 1955)

unearned income 1. Income that has been received but not yet earned, e.g., prepaid rent. 2. See investment income.

unemployment compensation Temporary income from the government to persons who have lost their jobs (for reasons other than misconduct) and are looking for work.

unethical In violation of standards of practice or an ethical code.

unfair competition Passing off one's goods or services as those of another. Trade practices that unfairly undermine competition.

To show a business practice is unfair under state deceptive business practices statute, the plaintiff must show the conduct threatens an incipient violation of an antitrust law, or violates the policy or spirit of one of those laws because its effects are comparable to or the same as a violation of the law, or otherwise significantly threatens or harms competition. Cal. Business & Professions Code § 17200. *Byars*, 135 Cal.Rptr.2d 796 (Cal.App., 2003)

unfair labor practice Acts by workers, employers, or unions that are illegal under laws on labor-management relations.

unicameral Having one house or chamber in the legislature.

unified bar See integrated bar.

unified transfer tax A single or unified federal tax on property transfers during one's life and at death.

uniform Without change or variation; the same in all cases.

Uniform Code of Military Justice (UCMJ) The rules governing discipline in the armed forces.

Uniform Commercial Code (UCC) A law adopted in all states (with some variations) on commercial transactions (e.g., sale of goods, negotiable instruments).

uniform laws Laws proposed by the National Conference of Commissioners on Uniform State Laws to state legislatures, which may adopt, modify, or reject them (*www.nccusl.org*).

unilateral Affecting only one side; obligating only one side.

unilateral contract A contract in which only one party makes a promise and the other party completes the contract by rendering performance.

A unilateral contract is one in which no promisor receives a promise as consideration for his or her promise. *Smith*, 18 Cal.Rptr. 833 (Cal.App., 1962)

unilateral mistake A mistake by only one of the parties to a contract.

unincorporated association A group of persons formed (but not incorporated) to promote a common enterprise or objective.

uninsured motorist coverage Insurance protection when injured by motorists without liability insurance.

union An association that negotiates with employers on labor issues.

union certification A government declaration that a particular union is the bargaining representative of a group of workers.

union shop A business where all workers must join the union.

United States (U.S.) The federal government.

United States Attorney An attorney who represents the federal government.

United States Code (USC) An official codification of permanent and public federal statutes organized by subject matter.

United States Commissioner See magistrate (1).

United States courts The federal courts (*www.uscourts.gov*).

United States Marshal See marshal (1).

United States Magistrate See magistrate (1).

United States Reports (U.S.) The official collection of opinions of the U.S. Supreme Court.

United States Statutes at Large See Statutes at Large.

unit investment trust A trust investing in a portfolio of securities.

Unit investment trusts. A unit investment trust that has previously qualified the sale of its securities pursuant to. . . . Cal. Corporations Code § 25111

unit rule Valuing shares by multiplying the sale price of one share on a stock exchange by the total number of shares.

unity The four elements of a joint tenancy: 1) unity of interest (the interests of all the joint tenants have the same nature, extent, and duration); 2) unity of title (all the joint tenants had their estate created by the same instrument); 3) unity of time (the interests of all the joint tenants vested at the same time); and 4) unity of possession (all the joint tenants have the right to possess the whole property).

universal agent An agent with full powers to act for the principal.

unjust enrichment Receiving a benefit that in justice and in equity belongs to another.

One person should not be permitted unjustly to enrich him or herself at the expense of another, but should be required to make restitution of or for property or benefits received, retained, or appropriated, where it is just and equitable that such restitution be made, and where such action involves no violation or frustration of law or opposition to public policy, either directly or indirectly. *California Emergency*, 4 Cal.Rptr.3d 583 (Cal.App., 2003)

unlawful Contrary to the law; illegal.

unlawful arrest An arrest without a warrant or probable cause.

unlawful assembly Three or more persons who meet to do an unlawful act or a lawful act in a violent, boisterous, or tumultuous manner.

unlawful detainer Remaining in possession of real property unlawfully by one whose original possession was lawful.

Unlawful detainer occurs when person remains in possession of property after expiration of term for which it is let to him or her. *Chan*, 250 Cal.Rptr. 851 (Cal.Super., 1988)

unlawful entry 1. A trespass on real property. 2. Entering a country illegally.

unlawful force The wrongful use of force against another.

unliquidated Not determined or specified; not ascertained in amount.

unlisted security A security not registered with a stock exchange.

unmarketable title A title an ordinary prudent buyer would not accept.

unnatural offense See sodomy.

unnecessary hardship Ground for a variance from a zoning regulation based on the unreasonableness of its application.

unprofessional conduct Conduct that violates the ethical code.

unrealized Pertaining to a gain or loss on paper. See realization (2).

unreasonable Irrational; arbitrary or capricious.

Falling below the standard of care; evincing indifference to reality or appropriate conduct; foolish, irrational or unwise; exceeding reasonable limits. *Smith*, 2003 WL 21419592 (Cal.App., 2003)

unreasonable restraint of trade A restraint of trade whose anticompetitive effects outweigh its procompetitive effects.

unreasonable search A search conducted without probable cause or consent, or that is otherwise illegal.

unrelated business income Income of a non-profit organization that is taxable because it is not substantially related to the organization's main purpose.

unrelated offenses Crimes that are separate and independent.

unresponsive Not answering the question or charge; irrelevant.

unreviewable Not ripe or suitable for review by a court or other body.

unsecured creditor A creditor unprotected by a lien or other security in any property of the debtor. Also called general creditor.

unsound 1. Unhealthy 2. Not based on sufficient evidence or analysis.

unsworn Not given under oath.

untenantable Unfit for the purpose leased.

untimely Too soon or too late.

unvalued policy An insurance policy in which the value of the thing insured is not agreed upon and stated in the policy. Also called open policy.

unwritten law Law derived from custom. Law not formally promulgated but collected from court opinions and learned treatises.

UPA Uniform Partnership Act.

UPC Uniform Probate Code.

UPL See unauthorized practice of law.

upset price The lowest action price a seller will accept.

U.S. See United States.

usage A custom or practice that is widely known or established.

Trade usage is a uniform practice or course of conduct followed in certain lines of business or professions, or in some procedure or phase of business or profession. *Hayter*, 22 Cal.Rptr.2d 229 (Cal.App., 1993)

USC See United States Code.

USCA United States Code Annotated.

U.S.D.C. United States District Court.

use 1. Taking, employing, or applying something. 2. The value of something. 3. The profit or benefit of land. 4. A purpose.

useful Having practical utility.

useful life See depreciable life.

use immunity Compelled statements cannot be used in a later criminal trial.

Use immunity protects a witness only against the actual use of the witness's compelled testimony, as well as the use of evidence derived therefrom. *People v. Kennedy*, 31 Cal.Rptr.3d 160 (CA 2005)

useless-gesture exception See knock-and-announce rule.

use tax A tax on goods bought outside the state.

usufruct A right to use another's property without damaging it.

usurious Pertaining to usury.

usury Lending money at an interest rate above what is authorized by law.

utility 1. Usefulness, providing a benefit. 2. See public utility.

UTMA Uniform Transfers to Minors Act.

utmost care See great care.

utter 1. To place or send into circulation. 2. To say or publish. See also excited utterance.

ux. (uxor) Wife.

V

v. Versus; volume.

VA Veterans Administration, now the Department of Veterans Affairs (*www.va.gov*).

vacant succession Succession when no one claims it, when all the heirs are unknown, or when all the known heirs to it have renounced it.

vacate 1. To cancel or set aside. 2. To surrender possession.

vacation 1. Cancellation or setting aside. 2. A period of time between sessions or terms.

vacatur ("it is annulled") Setting aside.

vagrancy Wandering without a home or lawful means of support.

vague Unclear or imprecise.

vagueness Not giving fair warning of what is commanded or prohibited.

valid Having the force of law; legally sufficient. Meritorious.

valuable consideration A benefit to the promisor or detriment to the promisee. Any valid consideration. Also called legal consideration.

Valuable consideration is not limited to payment of money or other material exchange, but may be based on promise, consist of cancellation of debt, or arise out of waiver of right. *In re Bishop's Estate*, 25 Cal.Rptr. 763 (Cal.App., 1962)

valuation 1. Determining the value of something. 2. The appraised price.

value 1. Monetary worth. 2. Usefulness; desirability. 3. Consideration.

value-added tax (VAT) A tax on whatever additional value is added at the various stages of production.

valued policy An insurance policy in which the value of the thing insured is agreed upon and stated in the policy as the amount to be paid in the event of a loss.

vandalism Willful or malicious destruction of property.

variable annuity An annuity in which benefit payments fluctuate with the performance of the fund's earnings.

variable-rate mortgage (VRM) See adjustable-rate mortgage.

variance 1. Permission not to follow a zoning requirement. 2. An inconsistency between two allegations, positions, or provisions.

A variance is an exception to fixed standards of a basic and specific zoning ordinance. *Matthews*, 21 Cal.Rptr. 914 (Cal.App., 1962)

VAT See value-added tax.

vehicular homicide Killing while operating a motor vehicle illegally, particularly with gross negligence.

vel non Or not; or without it.

vendee A buyer.

vendor A seller.

vendor's lien A seller's lien securing the unpaid purchase price.

venire See jury panel.

venire facias A writ requiring the sheriff to summon a jury.

venireman, veniremember, venireperson A prospective member of a jury.

venture A business enterprise or other undertaking that often has an element of risk and speculation.

venture capital An investment in a business, often involving potentially high risks and gains. Also called risk capital.

venue The proper county or geographical area in which a court with jurisdiction may hear a case. The place of the trial.

Venue is the county or other territory in which a case may be heard, or the place from which the jury will be selected. *Alexander*, 8 Cal.Rptr.3d 111 (Cal.App., 2003)

veracity Accuracy, truthfulness.

verbal Concerned with words; expressed orally.

verbal act An utterance to which the law attaches duties and liabilities.

verdict The jury's decision on the fact questions it was asked to resolve.

verification 1. Confirmation of correctness. 2. A declaration (often sworn) of the authenticity or truth of something.

Verification is an affidavit of the truth of the matter stated and the object of verification is to assure good faith in averments or statements of a party. Gov.Code, § 53052; Cal. Code of Civil Procedure. §§ 446, 2009. *Sheeley*, 30 Cal.Rptr. 121 (Cal.App., 1963)

versus (vs.)(v.) Against (e.g., Smith vs. Jones).

vertical integration The performance within one business of two or more steps in the chain of production and distribution.

vertical merger A merger between two businesses with a buyer-seller relationship with each other.

vertical price fixing An attempt by someone in the chain of distribution to set prices that someone lower on that chain will charge. An attempt by a supplier to fix the prices charged by those who resell its products.

vertical union See industrial union.

vest To give an immediate, fixed right of present or future enjoyment. To confer ownership or title.

vested Fixed; absolute, not subject to be defeated by a condition.

The term vested in the sense of "fundamental vested right" to determine scope of judicial review of administrative action refers to preexisting right which may not be abridged except by judicial action, while term "vested" as used in "vested rights" doctrine regarding land use whereby right may not be precluded by change in laws is merely right which government is estopped to deny. *Whaler's Village*, 220 Cal.Rptr. 2 (Cal.App., 1985)

vested estate; vested interest An estate or interest in which there is a present fixed right either of present or of future enjoyment.

vested remainder An estate in land that presently exists unconditionally in a definite or ascertained person, but the actual enjoyment of it is deferred until the termination of a previous estate.

vested right A right that cannot be infringed upon or taken away.

veto A chief executive's rejection of a bill passed by the legislature.

vexatious Without reasonable or just cause; annoying.

viable 1. Able to live outside the womb. 2. Practicable.

viatical settlement A contract of a terminally ill person to sell his or her life insurance policy, allowing the buyer to collect the death benefits.

vicarious Experienced, endured, or substituting for another.

vicarious disqualification See imputed disqualification.

vicarious liability Liability imposed on one party for the conduct of another, based solely upon the status of the relationship between the two.

Vicarious liability is based on the concept that one person's wrongful act will be imputed to another despite the fact the latter is free from fault. *Wise*, 100 Cal.Rptr.2d 437 (Cal.App., 2000)

vice 1. In substitution for; in place of. 2. Immoral; illegal; defect.

vicinage Vicinity; the area or locale where the crime was committed from which prospective jurors will be drawn.

Vicinage is the Sixth Amendment right to have the jury drawn from the district wherein the crime was committed. *People v. Sering*, 283 Cal.Rptr. 507 (Cal.App., 1991)

victim impact statement Comments made during sentencing by a victim on the impact of the crime on his or her life.

victimless crime A crime with a consenting victim or without a direct victim, e.g., drug use or possession.

victualer One who serves food prepared for eating on the premises.

videlicet See viz.

vi et armis With force and arms.

vinculo matrimonii Marriage bond. See divorce a vinculo matrimonii.

vindictive damages See punitive damages.

violation 1. Breaching a law or rule. 2. Rape or sexual assault.

violent Involving great or extreme physical or emotional force.

vir 1. A man. 2. A husband.

virtual representation doctrine A person may be bound by a judgment even though not a party if one of actual parties in the suit is so closely aligned with that person's interests as to be his or her virtual representative.

vis (power) Force; disturbance.

visa An authorization on a passport giving the holder permission to enter or leave a country.

visitation Time allowed someone without custody to spend with a child.

vis major An irresistible force or natural disaster; a loss caused by nature that was not preventable by reasonable care.

Force majeure or vis major is not necessarily limited to the equivalent of an act of God, but the test is whether under the particular circumstances there is such an insuperable interference occurring without the party's intervention as could not have been prevented by prudence, diligence and care. *Pacific*, 174 P.2d 441 (CA 1946)

vital statistics Public records on births, deaths, marriages, diseases, etc.

vitiate To impair or destroy the legal efficacy of something.

viva voce By word of mouth, orally.

viz (abbreviation for videlicet) Namely, in other words.

void 1. Having no legal force or binding effect. 2. To invalidate.

void ab initio Invalid from its inception or beginning.

voidable Valid but subject to being annulled or declared void.

voidable preference A debtor's transfer of assets to a creditor (before filing for bankruptcy) that constitutes an advantage over other bankruptcy creditors.

void for vagueness A law that is so obscure that a reasonable person could not determine what the law purports to command or prohibit.

Criminal responsibility should not attach where one could not reasonably understand that his contemplated conduct is proscribed. *People v. Hodges*, 83 Cal.Rptr.2d 619 (Cal.App., 1999)

voir dire ("to speak the truth") A preliminary examination of (a) prospective jurors for the purpose of selecting persons qualified to sit on a jury or (b) prospective witnesses to determine their competence to testify.

volenti non fit injuria ("to a willing person it is not wrong") There is no cause of action for injury or harm to which one consented.

voluntary 1. By choice; proceeding from a free and unconstrained will. 2. Intentional. 3. Without consideration; gratuitous.

voluntary bankruptcy A petition for bankruptcy filed by the debtor.

voluntary bar A bar association attorneys are not required to join.

voluntary commitment Civil commitment or institutionalization with the consent of the person committed or institutionalized.

voluntary dismissal A dismissal of a suit at the plaintiff's request.

voluntary manslaughter The intentional, unlawful killing of someone without malice or premeditation. Murder reduced to manslaughter.

voluntary trust 1. A trust created by express agreement. 2. A trust created as a gift.

A voluntary trust within California statute providing that every voluntary trust shall be revocable by trustor unless expressly made irrevocable. *Gaylord*, 153 F.2d 408 (C.A.9 1946)

voluntary waste Harm to real property committed by a tenant intentionally or negligently.

volunteer 1. One who voluntarily performs an act (e.g., pays someone's debt) without a duty to do so. 2. One who acts without coercion.

vote A formal expression of one's choice for a candidate or position.

voter One who votes or who has the qualifications to vote.

voting stock Stock entitling a holder to vote, e.g., for directors.

voting trust An agreement between stockholders and a trustee whereby the rights to vote the stock are transferred to the trustee.

vouch To give a personal assurance or to serve as a guarantee.

voucher 1. A receipt for payment. 2. An authorization to pay.

vouching-in A mechanism whereby a defendant in a proceeding may notify a non-party, the vouchee, that a suit is pending against the defendant and that, if liability is found, the defendant will look to the vouchee for indemnity and hold it to the findings in that suit.

VRM See adjustable-rate mortgage.

vs. See versus.

W

***Wade* hearing** A pretrial hearing on the admissibility of lineup or other identification evidence. *United States v. Wade*, 87 S. Ct. 1926 (1967).

wage Payments made to a hired person for his or her labor or services.

Compensation given to a hired person for his or her services, remuneration payable for a given period, or compensation paid a person hired to do work or business. *People v. Rogers*, 271 P.2d 231 (Cal.Super., 1954)

wage and hour laws Statutes on minimum wages and maximum work hours.

wage assignment 1. A court order to withhold someone's wages in order to satisfy a debt. An attachment by a creditor of a debtor's wages. 2. A contract transferring the right to receive wages.

wage earner's plan A new payment schedule or plan for the payment of all or a portion of a debtor's debts in a Chapter 13 bankruptcy when the debtor still has regular income.

wager policy An insurance policy to one with no insurable interest in the risks covered by the policy.

wait and see Basing the rule against perpetuities on vesting that actually occurs rather than what might occur. Also called second look.

waiting period The time that must elapse before the next legal step can occur or a right can be exercised.

waiver The express or implied voluntary relinquishment of a right, claim, or benefit.

The intentional relinquishment of a known right. *West*, 116 Cal.Rptr.2d 849 (Cal.App., 2002)

walkout A labor strike or departure in protest.

want of consideration A total lack of consideration for a contract.

wanton A conscious disregard of consequences. Malicious.

war Armed conflict between nations, states, or groups.

war crimes Conduct in violation of international laws governing wars.

ward 1. A person (e.g., minor) placed by the court under the care or protection of a guardian. 2. A division of a city or town.

warden A superintendent or person in charge.

warehouseman; warehouser Someone in the business of offering storage facilities.

warehouseman's lien A lien of a warehouseman in goods it is storing that provides security for unpaid storage charges.

warehouse receipt A receipt issued by a person engaged in the business of storing goods for hire. The receipt is a document of title.

warrant 1. A court order commanding or authorizing a specific act, e.g., to arrest someone, to search an area. 2. A document providing authorization, e.g., to receive goods or make payment. 3. A long-term option to purchase stock at a given price. Also called stock warrant. 4. To guarantee or provide a warranty.

Warrant is simply an option to purchase the shares of a corporation at a specified price and for a specified period of time; it differs from an option in that it is issued in the form of a security. *Robert Half*, 78 Cal.Rptr.2d 453 (Cal.App., 1998)

warrantless arrest An arrest made without a warrant. The arrest is proper if a misdemeanor is committed in the officer's presence or if the officer has probable cause to believe that a felony has been committed.

warranty 1. A commitment imposed by contract or law that a product or service will meet a specified standard. 2. A guarantee in a deed that assures the conveyance of a good and clear title.

warranty deed A deed in which the grantor promises to convey a specified title to property that is free and clear of all encumbrances. Also called general warranty deed.

warranty of fitness for a particular purpose An implied warranty that goods will meet a buyer's special need when the seller knows the buyer is relying on the seller's expertise for such need.

A warranty implied by law when a seller has reason to know that a buyer wishes goods for a particular purpose and is relying on the seller's skill and judgment to furnish those goods. *Martinez*, 6 Cal.Rptr.3d 494 (Cal.App., 2003)

warranty of habitability An implied promise by a landlord that the premises are free of serious defects that endanger health or safety.

warranty of merchantability An implied promise that the goods are fit for the ordinary purposes for which they are used.

warranty of title A seller's warranty that he or she owns what is being sold and that there are no undisclosed encumbrances on it.

wash sale A deceptive transaction involving the sale and purchase of securities that does not change beneficial ownership.

waste 1. Serious harm done to real property that affects the rights of holders of future interests in the property. 2. Refuse.

Injury to the inheritance, defined as waste, occurs if market value of property is substantially or permanently diminished or depreciated. *Dieterich*, 5 Cal.Rptr.2d 388 (Cal.App., 1992)

wasting asset An asset with a limited life or subject to depletion.

wasting trust A trust, the res of which consists of property that is gradually being depleted by payments to the beneficiaries.

watered stock 1. Stock issued at less than par value. 2. Stock issued at an inflated price.

water rights Rights to use water in its natural state, e.g., a lake.

waybill The non-negotiable document containing details of a carrier's contract for the transport of goods and acknowledging their receipt.

way of necessity See implied easement.

ways and means Methods and sources for raising government revenue.

weapon An instrument used for combat or to inflict great bodily harm.

weight of the evidence The inclination of the evidence to support one side over another; the persuasiveness of the evidence presented.

welfare 1. The well-being and the common blessings of life. 2. Public assistance; government aid to those in need.

well-pleaded complaint rule Federal-question jurisdiction exists only when a federal issue is presented on the face of the plaintiff's complaint.

Westlaw (WL) West Group's system of computer-assisted legal research.

Wharton rule See concert of action.

whereas 1. That being the case; since. 2. Although.

whereby By means of which; through which.

whiplash Injury to the cervical spine (neck) due to a sudden jerking of the head.

Injuries of the whiplash variety, i.e., those caused by a sudden movement of head and neck, was sudden stopping of automobile in which plaintiff was riding, or subsequent collision with defendant's following automobile. *Bankston*, 20 Cal.Rptr. 874 (Cal.App., 1962)

whistleblower One who discloses wrongdoing. A worker who reports employer wrongdoing to a public body.

whiteacre See blackacre.

white-collar crime A nonviolent crime, often involving a business.

white knight One who helps prevent a hostile takeover of a target corporation.

white slavery Forced prostitution.

whole law All the law in a jurisdiction, including choice of law rules.

whole life insurance Insurance covering the insured's entire life, not just for a term. Also called ordinary life insurance, straight life insurance.

wholesale Selling goods to one who is in the business of reselling them.

widow's (or **widower's**) **allowance** Part of a decedent's estate set aside by law for the surviving spouse, which most creditors cannot reach.

widow's (or **widower's**) **election** See election by spouse.

wildcat strike A strike called without authorization from the union.

Wild's case See rule in Wild's case.

will 1. An instrument that a person makes to dispose of his or her property upon his or her death. 2. Desire or choice.

A will is a disposition of property to take effect at death of testator. *In re Smilie's Estate*, 222 P.2d 692 (Cal.App., 1950)

will contest A challenge to the validity of a will.

willful Voluntary, intentional, deliberate.

willful negligence See gross negligence.

will substitute An alternative method or device (e.g., life insurance) that is used to achieve all or part of what a decedent's will is designed to accomplish.

wind up To settle the accounts and liquidate the assets of a business about to be dissolved.

wire fraud A scheme to defraud using interstate electronic communication.

wiretapping Using mechanical devices to conversations. Electronic eavesdropping.

Wiretapping is intercepting communications by an unauthorized connection to the transmission line whereas eavesdropping is interception of communications by the use of equipment that is not connected to any transmission line. Cal. Penal Code §§ 631(a), 632(a). *People v. Ratekin*, 261 Cal.Rptr. 143 (Cal.App., 1989)

with all faults As is; no warranty given.

withdraw 1. To remove, take back, or retract. 2. To take (funds) out of.

withholding tax Income taxes taken from one's salary or other income.

without prejudice With no loss or waiver of rights or privileges.

without recourse Disclaiming liability to subsequent holders in the event of non-payment.

Indorsement of note "without recourse" is a qualified indorsement, and indorser warrants that he or she has no knowledge of any fact that will render note valueless, but does not warrant that obligor will pay. Cal. Civil Code, § 3119. *Fleming*, 11 Cal.Rptr. 737 (Cal.App., 1961)

with prejudice Ending all further rights; ending the controversy.

witness 1. To see, hear, or experience something. 2. A person who gives testimony, often under oath.

witness stand The place in court where a witness gives testimony.

wobbler An offense that could be charged as a felony or a misdemeanor.

words actionable in themselves Words that constitute libel per se or slander per se.

words of art See terms of art.

words of limitation In a conveyance or will, words that describe the duration or quality of an estate being transferred.

words of negotiability See negotiability words.

words of purchase Words designating the recipients of a grant.

work The physical or mental exertion of oneself for a purpose. Labor.

workers' compensation A no-fault system of benefits for workers injured on the job. Also called employers' liability.

work for hire An employee-authored work whose copyright is owned by the employer.

workhouse A jail for persons convicted of lesser offenses.

working capital Current assets of a business less its current liabilities.

working papers A permit certifying one's right to work.

workout A restructuring of the payment and other terms of a debt.

work product rule Material prepared by or for an attorney in anticipation of litigation is not discoverable, absent a showing of substantial need.

Privilege of attorney work product doctrine applies to product of attorney's effort, research, and thought in preparation of his client's case, and includes results of his own work and that of his employees in investigating both the favorable and unfavorable aspects of the case, legal theories and strategy as reflected in interviews, statements, memoranda, correspondence, briefs, and any other writings reflecting attorney's impressions, conclusions, opinions, research, or theories. *2,022 Ranch*, 7 Cal.Rptr.3d 197 (Cal.App., 2003)

work release program A program allowing inmates to leave the institution for employment during part of the day.

work stoppage A cessation of work, often due to a labor dispute.

work-to-rule A slowdown due to excessive compliance with work rules.

World Court The International Court of Justice (*www.icj-cij.org*).

worth 1. The monetary or emotional value of something. 2. Wealth.

worthier title doctrine A person who receives by will what he or she would have inherited as an heir by intestacy, takes as an heir.

wraparound mortgage A second mortgage in which the lender of additional funds assumes the payments on the first mortgage.

A note and deed of trust with essentially the same terms and conditions as the existing mortgage, except that the amount of indebtedness includes a debt owed by the trustor on another obligation secured by the same property. *Mead*, 2004 WL 1304409 (Cal.App., 2004)

wreck The cast-aside wreckage of a ship or its cargo.

writ A written court order to do or refrain from doing an act.

write-down; write-up A reduction (write-down) or an increase (write-up) in the value of an asset as noted in an accounting record.

write-off Removing a worthless asset from the books of account.

writ of assistance A writ to transfer possession of land after a court has determined the validity of its title.

writ of capias See capias.

writ of certiorari See certiorari.

writ of coram nobis See coram nobis.

writ of error An appellate court's writ that the record of a lower court proceeding be delivered for review.

writ of error coram nobis See coram nobis.

writ of execution See execution (3).

writ of habeas corpus See habeas corpus.

writ of mandamus See mandamus.

writ of ne exeat See ne exeat.

writ of possession A writ to repossess real property.

writ of prohibition A writ to correct or prevent judicial proceedings that lack jurisdiction.

writ of quo warranto See quo warranto.

writ of right A writ issued as a matter of course or right.

writ of supersedeas See supersedeas.

wrong A violation of the right of another. A breach of duty.

Tort is a wrong for which society provides remedy, with the term "wrong" implying some fault on part of wrongdoer. *Barrett*, 272 Cal.Rptr. 304 (Cal.App., 1990)

wrongdoer One who does what is illegal.

wrongful birth action An action by parents of an unwanted impaired child for negligence in failing to warn them of the risks that the child would be born with birth defects. The parents seek their own damages.

wrongful conception See wrongful pregnancy action.

wrongful death action An action by a decedent's next of kin for their damages resulting from a wrongful injury that killed the decedent.

wrongful discharge Terminating employment for a reason that violates a contract, the law, or public policy.

wrongful life An action by or on behalf of an unwanted impaired child for negligence that precluded an informed parental decision to avoid the child's conception or birth. The child seeks its own damages.

Wrongful life is cause of action brought by an infant alleging that, due to negligence of defendant, birth occurred. *Gami*, 22 Cal.Rptr.2d 819 (Cal.App., 1993)

wrongful pregnancy action An action by parents of an unwanted healthy child for negligence in performing a sterilization procedure. Also called wrongful conception.

X

x 1. The mark used as the signature of someone who is illiterate. 2. See ex dividend. 3. See ex rights. 4. See ex warrants.

Y

year-and-a-day rule Death occurring more than one year and a day after the alleged criminal act cannot be a homicide, e.g., murder, manslaughter.

yellow-dog contract A contract forbidding union membership.

Statutes prohibiting such management tactics as yellow dog contracts (e.g., Cal. Labor Code § 922) (Any person . . . who coerces or compels . . . any person . . . not to join or become a member of any labor organization . . . is guilty of a misdemeanor.) *Service Employees*, 197 Cal.Rptr. 316 (Cal.App., 1983)

yield 1. To relinquish or surrender. 2. Profit stated as an annual rate of return on an investment.

***Younger* abstention** See equitable restraint doctrine.

youthful offender See juvenile delinquent.

Z

z-bond A bond payable upon satisfaction of all prior bond classes.

zealous witness A witness overly eager or anxious to help one side.

zero coupon bond A bond that does not pay interest.

zipper clause A contract clause that closes out bargaining during the contract term, making the written contract the exclusive statement of the parties' rights and obligations.

zone An area set aside or that has distinctive characteristics.

zone of danger test To recover for negligent infliction of emotional distress, the plaintiff must have been frightened due to actual personal physical danger caused by defendant's negligence.

zone of employment The place of employment and the area thereabout, including the means of ingress and egress under control of the employer.

zone of privacy Activities and areas of a person given constitutional protection against unreasonable intrusion or interference.

zoning Geographic divisions within which regulations impose land use requirements covering permissible uses for buildings, lot size limitations, etc.

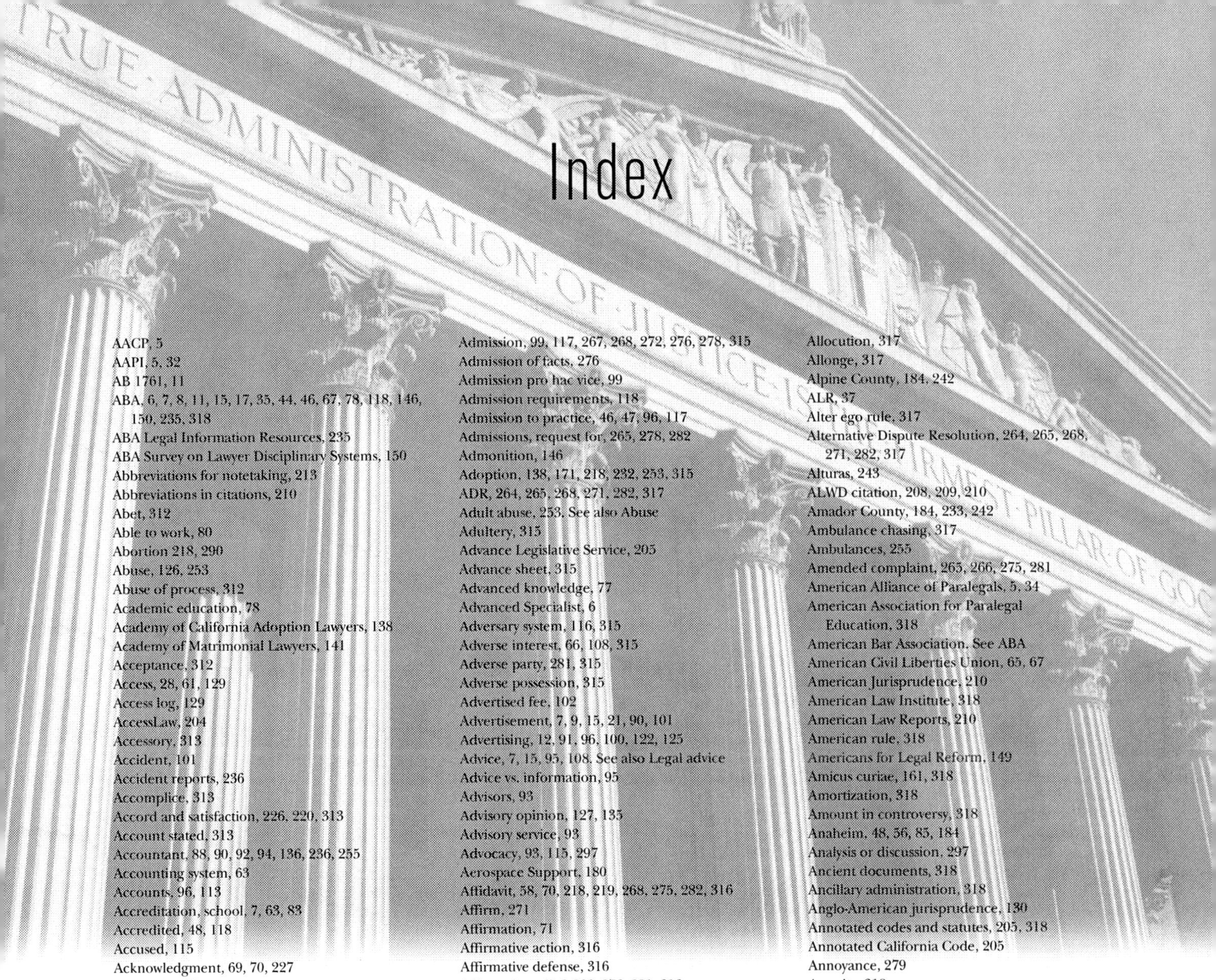

Index